European Union Law

The European Union has existed for over half a century; and European law has come to influence almost all fields of national law, including administrative law, constitutional law, contract law, criminal law and even tort law.

But what is the European Union? How does it work, and how does it produce European law? Written with exceptional clarity, *European Union Law* offers a classic textbook for students and practitioners of European law alike. Using a clear framework, it guides readers through all the core constitutional and substantive topics of EU law. Extracts from classic case law are complemented with extensive and critical discussion of the theoretical and practical aspects of the European Union and its law. Chapters are enriched with almost 150 colour figures and tables, which clarify complex topics and illustrate relationships and processes. Suggestions for further reading direct students to significant pieces of the academic literature for deeper self-study, and a companion website with full 'Lisbonised' versions of the cases cited in the text completes the learning package.

New to this Second Edition:
- A Brexit chapter covers the negotiation process and the possible future relationship between the United Kingdom and the European Union.
- A new section on EU private international law and EU criminal law has been added.
- The sections on delegated legislation, human rights and the free movement of persons have been significantly extended.
- The discussions of the case law have been increased, with all chapters aiming to reflect the judicial and legislative practice as at 31 December 2017.

Robert Schütze is Professor of European Law at Durham University and Visiting Professor at the College of Europe (Bruges) as well as LUISS (Rome).

European Union Law

Second Edition

ROBERT SCHÜTZE

CAMBRIDGE
UNIVERSITY PRESS

CAMBRIDGE
UNIVERSITY PRESS

University Printing House, Cambridge CB2 8BS, United Kingdom

One Liberty Plaza, 20th Floor, New York, NY 10006, USA

477 Williamstown Road, Port Melbourne, VIC 3207, Australia

314–321, 3rd Floor, Plot 3, Splendor Forum, Jasola District Centre, New Delhi – 110025, India

79 Anson Road, #06–04/06, Singapore 079906

Cambridge University Press is part of the University of Cambridge.

It furthers the University's mission by disseminating knowledge in the pursuit of
education, learning, and research at the highest international levels of excellence.

www.cambridge.org
Information on this title: www.cambridge.org/9781108470094
DOI: 10.1017/9781108555913

First published 2015
Reprinted 2017
Second Edition 2018
Reprinted 2019

Printed and bound in Great Britain by Clays Ltd, Elcograf S.p.A.

A catalogue record for this publication is available from the British Library.

Library of Congress Cataloging-in-Publication Data
Names: Schütze, Robert, author.
Title: European Union law / Robert Schütze.
Description: New York : Cambridge University Press, 2018. | Includes
  bibliographical references and index.
Identifiers: LCCN 2017061574 | ISBN 9781108470094 (alk. paper)
Subjects: LCSH: Law – European Union countries.
Classification: LCC KJE947 .S3837 2018 | DDC 341.242/2–dc23
LC record available at https://lccn.loc.gov/2017061574

ISBN 978-1-108-47009-4 Hardback
ISBN 978-1-108-45520-6 Paperback

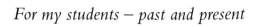

For my students – past and present

Summary Contents

Preface

European Union law is a complex subject, whose constant change and expansion makes it hard to pin down. This is my personal attempt to do so. Most existing European Union law books still suffer – I believe – from three defects: two with regard to their form, and one with regard to their substance.

First, in the face of significant changes in the structural and normative set up of the Union, why do most traditional textbooks still adhere to a syllabus arrangement that was formed in the 1970s and 1980s? This is particularly striking for the constitutional part, where – even in the best of textbooks – I find no clear rationale behind the particular order of chapters.

Second, almost all British textbooks appear to be written as if the European Treaties – the primary sources of all Union law – hardly existed. There is no guidance on how to read the Treaties, and it often seems that a Treaty provision only 'comes into existence' when the European Courts refer to it in a case. (Legal realism, yes, but legal reality must surely extend to the Treaties and Union legislation?) So strong is the Court-centricity of many a common law author that they seem to forget that the Treaties and all Union legislation offer a text and a structure with its own logic (and faults), and that the Court will primarily address them as an interpreter – not as 'the' creator of European law.

Third, and with regard to substance, why do most EU law textbooks still not contain a discussion of what the Union is? And how can a European Union law textbook not deal – at least briefly – with the common agricultural policy or regional policy? Together both represent almost three-quarters of the Union budget and play a particular role in the social and legal 'reality' of EU citizens. What would we say of a contract law textbook that did not say what a contract is and did not deal with sales contracts?

A textbook should be a compass through the most important theories and realities of the law; and this book tries to be such a compass for EU law. It has arranged the mass of EU legislation and jurisprudence in three parts. Part I deals with the 'Constitutional Foundations' of the Union legal order. Part II analyses how the Union adopts and enforces secondary Union law, while Part III explores the internal market as well as some of the most important substantive Union policies.

This second edition of *European Union Law* comes at a time of deep uncertainty – especially with regard to the United Kingdom's decision to withdraw from the European Union. A special chapter at the end of the book tries to explain the past, present and future of the British exit ('Brexit') decision (see Chapter 19). Yet nothing is certain here, especially with regard to the future

EU–UK relationship; and only a later edition may retrospectively offer more clarity on this point. A third edition is planned for early 2020 and will therefore come at a time when the United Kingdom will (probably) already have left the European Union.

Detailed Contents

Illustrations

Tables

Table of Cases

Contents

1. Court of Justice of the European Union

(a) European Court of Justice: Cases (numerical)

8/55, Fédération Charbonnière de Belgique *v.* High Authority of the ECSC, [1955] ECR (English Special Edition) 245 231, 360

9/56, Meroni & Co., Industrie Metallurgische, SpA *v.* High Authority of the European Coal and Steel Community, [1958] ECR 133 333–4

1/58, Stork & Cie *v.* High Authority of the European Coal and Steel Community, [1958] ECR (English Special Edition) 17 448

20/59, Italy *v.* High Authority, [1960] ECR 325 380

30/59, De Gezamenlijke Steenkolenmijnen in Limburg *v.* High Authority of the European Coal and Steel Community, [1961] ECR 1, 239

36/59, 37/59, 38/59 and 40/59, Geitling Ruhrkohlen-Verkaufsgesellschaft mbH, Mausegatt Ruhrkohlen-Verkaufsgesellschaft mbH and I. Nold KG *v.* High Authority of the European Coal and Steel Community, [1959] ECR (English Special Edition) 423 449

6/60, Humblet *v.* Belgium, [1960] ECR (English Special Edition) 559 422

10/61, Commission *v.* Italy, [1962] ECR 1 125

2/62 and 3/62, Commission *v.* Luxembourg and Belgium, [1962] ECR 425 507

16/62 and 17/62, Confédération nationale des producteurs de fruits et légumes and others *v.* Council, [1962] ECR 471 89, 363

25/62, Plaumann *v.* Commission, [1963] ECR 95 365–6, 369–71, 375

26/62, Van Gend en Loos *v.* Netherlands Inland Revenue Administration, [1963] ECR (English Special Edition) 1 78, 82–4, 87, 97, 206, 212, 403

(b) European Court of Justice: Cases (alphabetical)

(c) European Court of Justice: Opinions (numerical)

(d) General Court: Cases (numerical)

2. Other jurisdictions

(a) European Court of Human Rights: Cases (chronological)

(b) European Free Trade Association (EFTA): Cases (chronological)

(c) German Constitutional Court: Cases (chronological)

(d) United Kingdom Cases (Chronological)

(e) United States Supreme Court: Cases (chronological)

Table of Union Secondary Law

Contents

1. EU Regulations (numerical)

EEC Council: Regulation No. 17: First Regulation implementing Articles 85 and 86 of the Treaty, [1959–1962] OJ English Special Edition 87 680

Regulation 19/65/EEC of the Council of 2 March 1965 on application of Article 85 (3) of the Treaty to certain categories of agreements and concerted practices, [1965–1966] English Special Edition 35 734

Regulation (EEC) No. 120/67 of the Council of 13 June 1967 on the common organisation of the market in cereals, [1967] OJ English Special Edition 33 583

Regulation (EEC) No. 1612/68 of the Council of 15 October 1968 on freedom of movement for workers within the Community, [1968] OJ English Special Edition 475 232, 599–600

Regulation (EEC) No. 1408/71 of the Council of 14 June 1971 on the application of social security schemes to employed persons and their families moving within the Community, [1971] OJ English Special Edition 416 607, 668

Regulation (EEC) No. 2821/71 of the Council of 20 December 1971 on application of Article 85(3) of the Treaty to categories of agreements, decisions and concerted practices, [1971] OJ L 285/46 734

Council Regulation (EEC) No. 797/85 of 12 March 1985 on improving the efficiency of agricultural structures, [1985] OJ L 93/1 92

Council Regulation (EEC) No. 2137/85 of 25 July 1985 on the European Economic Interest Grouping (EEIG), [1985] OJ L 199/1 637

Council Regulation (EEC) No. 4064/89 of 21 December 1989 on the control of concentrations between undertakings, [1989] OJ L 395/1 757, 761, 765

Council Regulation (EEC) No. 2328/91 of 15 July 1991 on improving the efficiency of agricultural structures, [1991] OJ L 218/1 92

Council Regulation (EEC) No. 1768/92 of 18 June 1992 concerning the creation of a supplementary protection certificate for medicinal products, [1992] OJ L 182/1 567

Council Regulation No. 259/93 on the supervision and control of shipments of waste within, into and out of the European Community, [1993] OJ L 30/1 143

2. EU Directives (numerical)

3. EU Decisions (numerical)

4. International Agreements (alphabetical)

Table of Equivalents

TREATY ON THE FUNCTIONING OF THE EUROPEAN UNION

Lisbon Treaty numbers and their Amsterdam and Pre-Amsterdam equivalents (Amsterdam and Pre-Amsterdam is TEC unless specified otherwise)

Lisbon	Amsterdam	Pre-Amsterdam	Lisbon	Amsterdam	Pre-Amsterdam
1			43	37	43
2			44	38	46
3			45	39	48
4			46	40	49
5			47	41	50
6			48	42	51
7	3TEU	CTEU	49	43	52
8	3(2)	3(2)	50	44	54
9			51	45	55
10			52	46	56
11	6	3c	53	47	57
12	153(2)	129a	54	48	58
13			55	264	221
14	16	7d	56	49	59
15	255	191a	57	50	60
16	286	213b	58	51	61
17			59	52	63
18	12	6	60	53	64
19	13	6a	61	54	65
20	17	8	62	55	66
21	18	8a	63	56	73b
22	19	8b	64	57	73c
23	20	8c	65	58	73d
24	21	8d	66	59	73f
25	22	8e	67	61	73i
26	14	7a		29TEU	K.1TEU
27	15	7c	68		
28	23	9	69		
29	24	10	70		
30	25	12	71	36TEU	K.8TEU
31	26	28	72	64(1)	73l(1)
32	27	29		33TEU	K.4TEU
33	135	116	73		
34	28	30	74		
35	29	34	75	60	73g
36	30	36	76		
37	31	37	77	62	73j
38	32	38	78	63(1),(2),64(2)	73k(1),(2),73l(2)
39	33	39	79	63(3),(4)	73k(3),(4)
40	34	40	80		
41	35	41	81	65	73m
42	36	42	82	31TEU	K.3TEU

Lisbon	Amsterdam	Pre-Amsterdam	Lisbon	Amsterdam	Pre-Amsterdam
83	31TEU	K.3TEU	125	103	104b
84			126	104	104c
85	31TEU	K.3TEU	127	105	105
86			128	106	105a
87	30TEU	K.2TEU	129	107	106
88	30TEU	K.2TEU	130	108	107
89	32TFEU	K.4TEU	131	109	108
90	70	74	132	110	108a
91	71	75	133		
92	72	76	134	114	109c
93	73	77	135	115	109d
94	74	78	136		
95	75	79	137		
96	76	80	138	111(4)	109(4)
97	77	81	139		
98	78	82	140	121(1),122(2),123(5)	109j,109k,109l
99	79	83	141	123(3),117(2)	109l(3),109f(2)
100	80	84	142	124(1)	109m(1)
101	81	85	143	119	109h
102	82	86	144	120	109i
103	83	87	145	125	109n
104	84	88	146	126	109o
105	85	89	147	127	109p
106	86	90	148	128	109q
107	87	92	149	129	109r
108	88	93	150	130	109s
109	89	94	151	136	117
110	90	95	152		
111	91	96	153	137	118
112	92	98	154	138	118a
113	93	99	155	139	118b
114	95	100a	156	140	118c
115	96	101	157	141	119
116	96	101	158	142	119a
117	97	102	159	143	120
118			160	144	121
119	4	3a	161	145	122
120	98	102a	162	146	123
121	99	103	163	147	124
122	100	103a	164	148	125
123	101	104	165	149	126
124	102	104a	166	150	127

Lisbon	Amsterdam	Pre-Amsterdam	Lisbon	Amsterdam	Pre-Amsterdam
167	151	128	209	179	130w
168	152	129	210	180	130x
169	153(1),(3),(4),(5)	129a	211	181	130y
170	154	129b	212	181a	130y
171	155	129c	213		
172	156	129d	214		
173	157	130	215		
174	158	130a	216		
175	159	130b	217	310	238
176	160	130c	218		
177	161	130d	219	111(1),(3),(5)	109(1),(3),(5)
178	162	130e	220	302,303,304	229,230,231
179	163	130f	221		
180	164	130g	222		
181	165	130h	223	190(4),(5)	138(3)
182	166	130i	224	191(2)	138(3)
183	167	130j	225	192(2)	138b
184	168	130k	226	193	138c
185	169	130l	227	194	138d
186	170	130m	228	195	138e
187	171	130n	229	196	139
188	172	130o	230	197(2)–(4)	140
189			231	198	141
190	173	130p	232	199	142
191	174	130r	233	200	143
192	175	130s	234	201	144
193	176	130t	235		
194			236		
195			237	204	147
196			238	205(1),(3)	148(1),(3)
197			239	206	150
198	182	131	240	207	151
199	183	132	241	208	152
200	184	133	242	209	153
201	185	134	243	210	154
202	186	135	244		
203	187	136	245	213	157
204	188	136a	246	215	159
205			247	216	160
206	131	110	248	217(2)	161
207	133	113	249	218(2)	162(2)
208	177/178	130u/130v	250	219	163

Lisbon	Amsterdam	Pre-Amsterdam	Lisbon	Amsterdam	Pre-Amsterdam
251	221(2),(3)	165	293	250	189a
252	222	166	294	251	189b
253	223	167	295		
254	224	168	296	253	190
255			297	254	191
256	225	168a	298		
257	225a	168a	299	256	192
258	226	169	300	257/258/263	193/194/198a
259	227	170	301	258(1),(2),(4)	194(1),(2),(4)
260	228	171	302	259	195
261	229	172	303	260	196
262	229a	172	304	262	198
263	230	173	305	263(2),(3),(4)	198a(2),(3),(4)
264	231	174	306	264	198b
265	232	175	307	265	198c
266	233	176	308	266	198d
267	234	177	309	267	198e
268	235	178	310	268/270	199/201a
269			311	269	200
270	236	179	312		
271	237	180	313	272(1)	203
272	238	181	314	272(2–10)	203
273	239	182	315	273	204
274	240	183	316	271	202
275			317	274	205
276			318	275	205a
277	241	184	319	276	206
278	242	185	320	277	207
279	243	186	321	278	208
280	244	187	322	279	209
281	245	188	323		
282	8	4a	324		
283	112	109a	325	280	210
284	113	109b	326		
285	246	188a	327		
286	247	188b	328		
287	248	188c	329		
288	249	189	330		
289			331		
290	202	145	332		
291	202	145	333		
292			334		

Lisbon	Amsterdam	Pre-Amsterdam	Lisbon	Amsterdam	Pre-Amsterdam
335	282	211	347	297	224
336	283	212	348	298	225
337	284	213	349	299(2)–(4)	227
338	285	213a	350	306	233
339	287	214	351	307	234
340	288	215	352	308	235
341	289	216	353		
342	290	217	354	309	236
343	291	218	355	299(2)–(6)	227
344	292	219	356	312	240
345	295	222	357	313	247
346	296	223	358		

Abbreviations

AFSJ	Area of Freedom, Security and Justice
AJIL	*American Journal of International Law*
BYIL	*British Yearbook of International Law*
CAP	Common Agricultural Policy
CCP	Common Commercial Policy
CDE	*Cahiers de droit européen*
CEE	charges having equivalent effect
CFSP	Common Foreign and Security Policy
CML Rev.	*Common Market Law Review*
CMO	Common Market Organisation
CoA	Court of Auditors
Coreper	Committee of Permanent Representatives
COSI	Standing Committee on Internal Security
CPR	Common Provisions Regulation
CSDP	Common Security and Defence Policy
CSF	Common Strategic Framework
CST	Civil Service Tribunal
CT	Constitutional Treaty
CYELS	*Cambridge Yearbook of European Legal Studies*
DCI	Development Cooperation Instrument
DG	Directorate-General
EBA	Everything but Arms
EC	European Community [Treaty]
ECB	European Central Bank
ECHR	European Convention on Human Rights
ECJ	European Court of Justice
ECLR	*European Competition Law Review*
ECN	European Competition Network
ECOFIN	Council of Ministers for Economics and Finance
ECOWAS	Economic Community of West African States
ECR	European Court Reports
ECSC	European Coal and Steel Community
ECtHR	European Court of Human Rights
EDC	European Defence Community
EEA	European Economic Area
EEAS	European External Action Service
EEC	European Economic Community [Treaty]
EFC	Economic and Financial Committee
EFSM	European Financial Stability Mechanism

EFTA	European Free Trade Association
EHRR	European Human Rights Report
EJIL	*European Journal of International Law*
ELJ	*European Law Journal*
EL Rev.	*European Law Review*
EMU	European Monetary Union
ENP	European Neighbourhood Policy
EPA	Economic Partnership Agreement
EPC	European Political Cooperation
ERDF	European Regional and Development Fund
ESCB	European System of Central Banks
ESM	European Stability Mechanism
EU (old)	European Union (Maastricht) Treaty
EUMR	EU Merger Regulation
EuR	*Europarecht*
Euratom	European Atomic Energy Community
FYRM	Former Yugoslav Republic of Macedonia
GATS	General Agreement on Trade in Services
GATT	General Agreement on Tariffs and Trade
GBER	General Block Exemption Regulation
GC	General Court
GDP	Gross Domestic Product
GSP	Generalised System of Preferences
HA	Humanitarian Aid
ICJ	International Court of Justice
ICLQ	*International and Comparative Law Quarterly*
IGC	Intergovernmental Conference
ILO	International Labour Organization
JHA	Justice and Home Affairs
LDCs	least developed countries
MEEQRs	measures having an equivalent effect to quantitative restrictions
MEP	Member of the European Parliament
MFN	most favoured nation
MLR	*Modern Law Review*
MoU	memorandum of understanding
NATO	North Atlantic Treaty Organization
NCA	national competition authority
NCB	National Central Bank
OCT	Overseas Countries and Territories
OECD	Organisation for Economic Co-operation and Development
OEEC	Organisation for European Economic Co-operation
OJ	*Official Journal of the European Union*
OMC	Open Method of Coordination
PJCC	Police and Judicial Cooperation in Criminal Matters
PSC	Political and Security Committee

QMV	qualified majority voting
RTDE	*Revue trimestrielle de droit européen*
SEA	Single European Act
SGEI	Services of General Economic Interest
SGP	Stability and Growth Pact
TA	Treaty of Amsterdam
TC	Technical Cooperation
TEC	Treaty establishing the European Community
TEU	Treaty on European Union (post Lisbon)
TFEU	Treaty on the Functioning of the European Union
TN	Treaty of Nice
TRIPS	Agreement on Trade-Related Aspects of Intellectual Property Rights
TSCG	Treaty on Stability, Coordination and Governance in the Economic and Monetary Union
UN	United Nations
US	United States
VAT	value added tax
WEU	Western European Union
WTO	World Trade Organization
Yale LJ	*Yale Law Journal*
YEL	*Yearbook of European Law*

Acknowledgements

Thankful acknowledgements are made to Hart Publishing, Kluwer Law International, Oxford University Press, Sweet & Maxwell, as well as Wiley for their kind permission to incorporate sections from previously published material. Chapter 2 represents a shortened and amended version of a chapter published in *From Dual to Cooperative Federalism: The Changing Structure of European Law* (Oxford University Press, 2009). The online chapter 18B is a shortened version of a chapter from my *Foreign Affairs and the EU Constitution: Selected Essays* (Cambridge University Press, 2014). For illustrations 1.1, 5.2, 5.3, 6.1, 6.2, 6.7, 7.5, 10.4, 18.4, 18.5, 18.6, 19.2, 19.3 and 19.4 acknowledgements go – respectively – to the BBC, Wikipedia and the European Union's website(s).

I would like to thank again everyone who has helped in a myriad of professional and private ways in the past and present, and especially to Roberta Bassi, Vilmos Budovari, David Held, Gleider Hernández, Roger Masterman, Maria Perez-Crespo, Dieter and Isolde Schütze, and most particularly my students at Durham, Bruges and Rome. On the editorial side, I wish to thank Caitlin Lisle for shepherding this edition, but special thanks must again go to Sinéad Moloney and Valerie Appleby, whose flexibility, brilliance and efficiency helped me lay the foundations of the first edition of this textbook.

Part I Constitutional Foundations

The European Union has existed for over half a century; and since 1952, it has significantly grown – both geographically and thematically. Having started with only six European States, today's European Union has 28 Member States and acts in almost all areas of modern life. Its constitutional and institutional structures have also dramatically changed in the past six decades.

The Union's remarkable historical evolution is discussed in Chapter 1. What type of legal 'animal' is the European Union? Chapter 2 analyses this question from a comparative constitutional perspective. We shall see that the Union is not a State, but a 'Federation of *States*'. Standing in between international and national law, the Union's federal character thereby expresses itself in a number of normative and institutional ways. Chapters 3 and 4 explore the two key normative qualities of European Union law, namely its 'direct effect' and its 'supremacy'. Chapters 5 and 6 then look at the institutional structure of the European Union. Each Union institution will here be analysed as regards its internal composition, internal powers and internal procedures. The interplay *between* the various institutions in the exercise of the Union's governmental functions will be discussed in Part II.

1

Constitutional History
From Paris to Lisbon

Contents

Introduction

The idea of European integration is as old as the European idea of the sovereign State.[1] Yet the spectacular rise of the latter overshadowed the idea of European union for centuries. Within the twentieth century, two ruinous world wars and the social forces of globalisation have however increasingly discredited the idea

---

[1] R. H. Foerster, *Die Idee Europa 1300–1946, Quellen zur Geschichte der politischen Einigung* (Deutscher Taschenbuchverlag, 1963).

of the *sovereign* State. The decline of the nation State has found expression in the spread of inter-State cooperation;[2] and the rise of international cooperation has itself caused a fundamental transformation in the substance and structure of international law.[3]

The various efforts at European cooperation after the Second World War formed part of this general transition from an international law of coexistence to an international law of cooperation.[4] 'Europe was beginning to get organised.'[5] This development began with three international organisations. First: the Organisation for European Economic Cooperation (1948), which had been created after the Second World War by 16 European States to administer the international aid offered by the United States for European reconstruction.[6] Second, the Western European Union (1948, 1954) that established a security alliance to prevent another war in Europe.[7] Third, the Council of Europe (1949), which had *inter alia* been founded to protect human rights and fundamental freedoms in Europe.[8] None of these grand international organisations was to lead to the European Union. The birth of the latter was to take place in a much humbler sector: coal and steel.

The 1951 Treaty of Paris set up the European Coal and Steel Community (ECSC).[9] Its original members were six European States: Belgium, France, Germany, Italy, Luxembourg and the Netherlands. This first Community had been created to *integrate* one industrial sector; and the very concept of *integration*

---

[2] G. Schwarzenberger, *The Frontiers of International Law* (Stevens, 1962).

[3] C. de Visscher, *Theory and Reality in Public International Law* (Princeton University Press, 1968).

[4] W. G. Friedmann, *The Changing Structure of International Law* (Stevens, 1964).

[5] A. H. Robertson, *European Institutions: Co-operation, Integration, Unification* (Stevens & Sons, 1973), 17.

[6] The 'European Recovery Programme', also known as the 'Marshall Plan', was named after the (then) Secretary of State of the United States, George C. Marshall. Art. 1 of the OEEC Treaty stated: 'The Contracting Parties agree to work in close cooperation in their economic relations with one another. As their immediate task, they will undertake the elaboration and execution of a joint recovery programme.' In 1960, the Organisation for European Economic Co-operation (OEEC) was transformed into the thematically broader Organisation for Economic Co-operation and Development (OECD) with the United States and Canada becoming full members of that organisation.

[7] Art. IV of the 1948 Brussels Treaty stated: 'If any of the High Contracting Parties should be the object of an armed attack in Europe, the other High Contracting Parties will, in accordance with the provisions of Article 51 of the Charter of the United Nations, afford the party so attacked all the military and other aid and assistance in their power.'

[8] The most important achievement of the Council of Europe was the development of a common standard of human rights in the form of the European Convention on Human Rights (ECHR). The Convention was signed in 1950 and entered into force in 1953. The Convention established the European Court of Human Rights (ECtHR) in Strasbourg (1959).

[9] For a detailed discussion of the negotiations leading up to the signature of the ECSC Treaty, see H. Mosler, 'Der Vertrag über die Europäische Gemeinschaft für Kohle und Stahl' (1951–2) 14 *Zeitschrift für ausländisches öffentliches Recht und Völkerrecht* 1.

indicated the wish of the contracting States 'to break with the ordinary forms of international treaties and organisations'.[10]

The Treaty of Paris led to the 1957 Treaties of Rome, which created two additional Communities: the European Atomic Energy Community and the European (Economic) Community. The 'three Communities' were partly 'merged' in 1967,[11] but continued to exist in relative independence. A major organisational leap was taken in 1993, when the three Communities were themselves integrated into the European Union. For a decade, this European Union was under constant constitutional construction. And, in an attempt to prepare the Union for the twenty-first century, a European Convention was charged to draft a Constitutional Treaty in 2001. The latter failed; and it took almost another decade to rescue the reform as the 2007 Reform (Lisbon) Treaty. This Lisbon Treaty has replaced the 'old' European Union with the 'new' European Union.

This chapter surveys the historical evolution of the European Union in four sections. Section 1 starts with the humble origins of the Union: the European Coal and Steel Community (ECSC). While limited in its scope, the ECSC introduced a supranational formula that was to become the trademark of the European Economic Community (EEC). The EEC will be analysed in section 2, while section 3 investigates the development of the (old) European Union founded through the Treaty of Maastricht. Section 4 reviews the reform efforts of the last decade, and analyses the structure of the – substantively – new European Union as established by the Treaty of Lisbon. Concentrating on the constitutional evolution of the European Union,[12] this chapter will *not* present its geographic development.[13]

1. From Paris to Rome: The European Coal and Steel Community

The initiative to integrate the coal and steel sector came – after an American suggestion – from France.[14] The French Foreign Minister, Robert Schuman,

---

[10] *Ibid.*, 24 (translated: R. Schütze).

[11] This was achieved through the 1965 'Merger Treaty' (see Treaty establishing a Single Council and a Single Commission of the European Communities).

[12] For an overview of the Union's constitutional amendments, see Appendix, section 1.

[13] For an overview of the Union's geographic development, see (online) Chapter 18B, section 4(d).

[14] This is how the (then) US Secretary of State, Dean Acheson, wrote to the French Foreign Minister, Robert Schuman: 'Whether Germany will in the future be a benefit or a curse to the free world will be determined, not only by Germany, but by the occupying powers. No country has a greater stake than France in the answer. Our own stake and responsibility is also great. Now is the time for French initiative and leadership of the type required to integrate the German Federal Republic promptly and decisively into Western Europe … We here in America, with all the will in the world to help and support, cannot give the lead. That, if we are to succeed in this joint endeavour, must come from France' (US Department of State, *Foreign Relations of the United States*, III (1949) (Government Printing Office, 1974), 623 and 625).

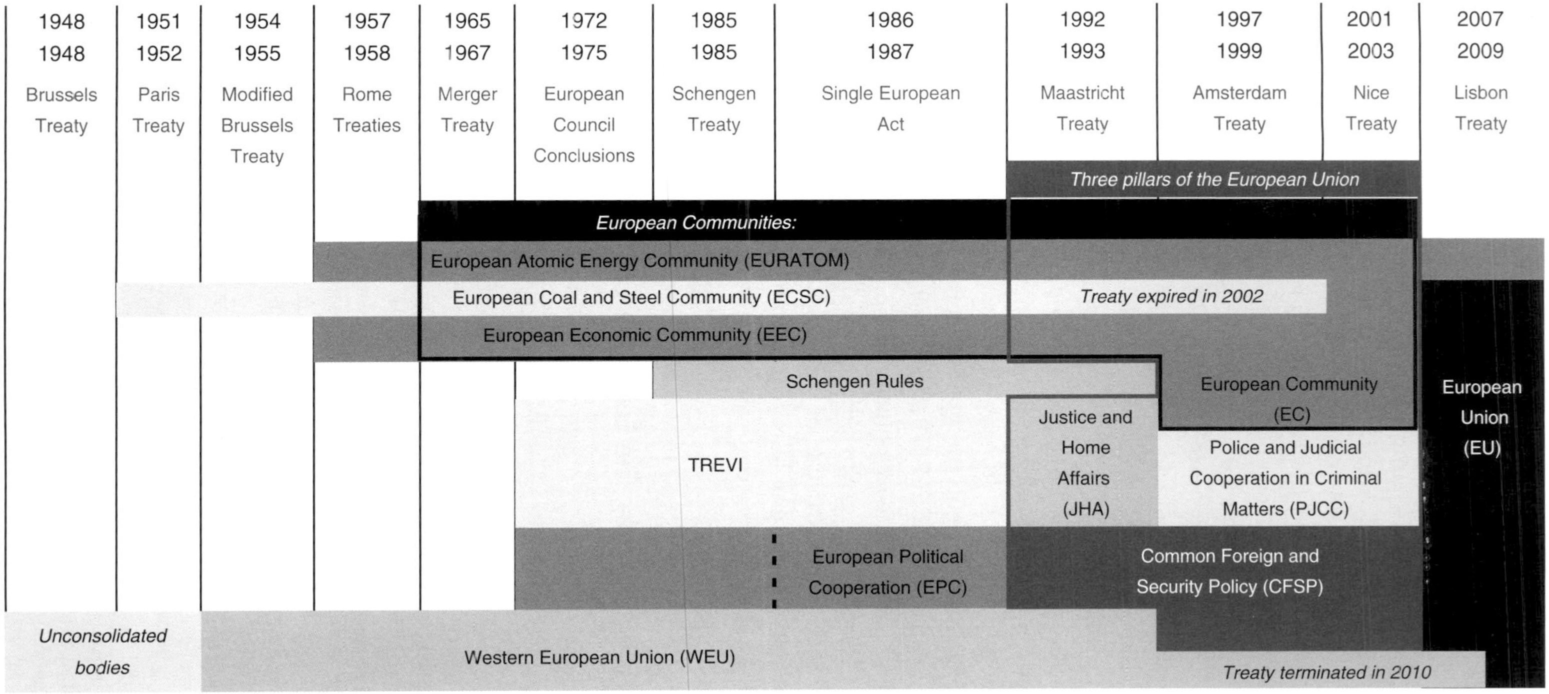

1948	1951	1954	1957	1965	1972	1985	1986	1992	1997	2001	2007
1948	1952	1955	1958	1967	1975	1985	1987	1993	1999	2003	2009
Brussels Treaty	Paris Treaty	Modified Brussels Treaty	Rome Treaties	Merger Treaty	European Council Conclusions	Schengen Treaty	Single European Act	Maastricht Treaty	Amsterdam Treaty	Nice Treaty	Lisbon Treaty

Three pillars of the European Union

European Communities:

European Atomic Energy Community (EURATOM)

European Coal and Steel Community (ECSC)

Treaty expired in 2002

European Economic Community (EEC)

European Community (EC)

Schengen Rules

Justice and Home Affairs (JHA)

Police and Judicial Cooperation in Criminal Matters (PJCC)

TREVI

European Political Cooperation (EPC)

Common Foreign and Security Policy (CFSP)

European Union (EU)

Western European Union (WEU)

Treaty terminated in 2010

Unconsolidated bodies

Figure 1.1 Historical Evolution of the Union

revealed the plan to build a European Community for Coal and Steel on 9 May 1950:

> Europe will not be made all at once, nor according to a single, general plan. It will be formed by taking measures which work primarily to bring about real solidarity. The gathering of the European nations requires the elimination of the age-old opposition of France and Germany. The action to be taken must first of all concern these two countries. With this aim in view, the French Government proposes to take immediate action on one limited but decisive point. The French Government proposes that Franco-German production of coal and steel be placed under a common [Commission], within an organisation open to the participation of the other European nations. *The pooling of coal and steel production will immediately ensure the establishment of common bases for economic development as a first step in the federation of Europe, and will change the destinies of those regions which have long been devoted to the manufacture of arms, to which they themselves were the constant victims.*[15]

The 'Schuman Plan' was behind the Treaty of Paris (1951) establishing the European Coal and Steel Community. Six European States would create this Community for a period of 50 years.[16] The Treaty of Paris was no grand international peace treaty. It was designed to 'remove the main obstacle to an economic partnership'.[17] This small but decisive first step towards a federal or *supranational* Europe will be discussed first. The 'supranational' idea would soon be exported into wider fields. However, the attempt to establish a supranational European Defence Community, and with it a European Political Community, would fail. Until the 1957 Rome Treaties, the European Coal and Steel Community would thus remain the sole supranational Community in Europe.

a. The (Supranational) Structure of the ECSC

The structure of the ECSC differed from that of ordinary intergovernmental organisations. It was endowed with a 'Commission',[18] a Parliament,[19] a 'Council'

---

[15] Schuman Declaration (Paris, 9 May 1950), reproduced in A. G. Harryvan and J. van der Harst (eds.), *Documents on European Union* (St Martin's Press, 1997), 61 (emphasis added).

[16] Art. 97 ECSC: 'This Treaty is concluded for a period of fifty years from its entry into force.' The Paris Treaty entered into force on 23 July 1952 and expired 50 years later.

[17] J. Gillingham, *Coal, Steel, and the Rebirth of Europe, 1945–1955: The Germans and French from Ruhr Conflict to Economic Community* (Cambridge University Press, 1991), 298.

[18] The original name in the ECSC Treaty was 'High Authority'. In the wake of the 1965 'Merger Treaty' this name was changed to 'Commission' (*ibid.*, Art. 9).

[19] Originally, the ECSC Treaty used the name 'Assembly'. However, in order to simplify the terminology and to allow for horizontal comparisons between the various Communities, I have chosen to refer to the 'Assembly' throughout as 'Parliament'. Early on, the Assembly renamed itself 'Parliament', a change that was only formally recognised by the 1986 SEA.

and a 'Court'.[20] The ECSC Treaty had placed the Commission at its centre. It was its duty to ensure that the objectives of the Community would be attained.[21] To carry out this task, the Commission would adopt decisions, recommendations and opinions.[22] The Commission would thereby be composed in the following way:

> The [Commission] shall consist of nine members appointed for six years and chosen on the grounds of their general competence ... The members of the [Commission] shall, in the general interest of the Community, be completely independent in the performance of these duties, they shall neither seek nor take instructions from any Government or from any other body. They shall refrain from any action incompatible with the *supranational character of their duties*. Each Member State undertakes to respect this *supranational character* and not to seek to influence the members of the [Commission] in the performance of their tasks.[23]

The Commission constituted the supranational heart of the new Community. The three remaining institutions were indeed peripheral to its functioning. The Parliament, consisting of delegates who would 'be designated by the respective Parliaments from among their members',[24] had purely advisory functions.[25] The Council,[26] composed of representatives of the national governments,[27] was charged to 'harmonise the action of the [Commission] and that of the Governments, which are responsible for the general economic policies of their countries'.[28] Finally, a Court – formed by seven independent judges – was to 'ensure that in the interpretation and application of this Treaty, and of rules laid down for the implementation thereof, the law is observed'.[29]

---

[20] Art. 7 ECSC. 21   [21] *Ibid.*, Art. 8.

[22] *Ibid.*, Art. 14. Community acts were thus considered to be acts of the Commission, even if other Community organs had been involved in the decision-making process.

[23] *Ibid.*, Art. 9 (emphasis added).

[24] *Ibid.*, Art. 21.

[25] *Ibid.*, Art. 22. The Parliament's powers were defined in Art. 24 ECSC and consisted of discussing the general report submitted by the Commission, and a motion of censure on the activities of the Commission.

[26] During the drafting of the ECSC Treaty, the Council had been – reluctantly – added by Jean Monnet to please the Netherlands. The Netherlands had argued that coal and steel issues could not be separated from broader economic issues (see D. Dinan, *Europe Recast: A History of European Union* (Palgrave, 2004), 51). Under the Paris Treaty, the Council's task was primarily that of 'harmonising the action of the [Commission] and that of the governments, which are responsible for the general economic policy of their countries' (Art. 26 ECSC). It was seen as a 'political safeguard' to coordinate activities that fell into the scope of the ECSC with those economic sectors that had not been brought into the Community sphere, see Mosler, 'Der Vertrag über die Europäische Gemeinschaft für Kohle und Stahl' (n. 9 above), 41.

[27] Art. 27 ECSC.   [28] *Ibid.*, Art. 26.   [29] *Ibid.*, Art. 31.

In what ways was the European Coal and Steel Community a 'supranational' organisation?[30] The Community could carry out its tasks through the adoption of 'decisions', which would be 'binding in their entirety'.[31] And the directly applicable nature of ECSC law led early commentators to presume an 'inherent supremacy of Community law'.[32] The novel character of the Community – its 'break' with the ordinary forms of international organisations – thus lay in the normative quality of its secondary law. The transfer of decision-making powers to the Community represented a transfer of 'sovereign' powers.[33] While the Community still lacked *physical* powers,[34] it was its *normative* powers that would become identified with its 'supranational' character.[35]

However, this was only one dimension of the Community's 'supranationalism'. Under the Treaty of Paris, the organ endowed with supranational powers was itself 'supranational', that is: independent of the will of the Member States. As the Commission was composed of independent 'bureaucrats', it could act by a majority of its members.[36] (While the Commission was admittedly not the only organ of the European Coal and Steel Community, it was its *central* decision-maker.) This ability of the Community to bind Member States against their will here departed from the 'international' ideal of sovereign equality of States. And, indeed, it was *this* decisional dimension that had inspired the very notion of supranationalism. Early analysis consequently linked the concept of supranationality to the decision-making mode of the Community.[37]

But the legal formula behind the European Coal and Steel Community was dual: the absence of a normative veto in the national legal orders was complemented by the absence of a decisional veto in the Community legal order.[38] This

---

[30] On the birth of the term 'supranational', see in particular: P. Reuter, 'Le Plan Schuman' (1952) 81 *Recueil des Cours de l'Académie de la Haye* 519.

[31] Art. 14(2) ECSC.

[32] See G. Bebr, 'The Relation of the European Coal and Steel Community Law to the Law of the Member States: A Peculiar Legal Symbiosis' (1958) 58 *Columbia Law Review* 767, 788 (emphasis added): '*The fact that Community law can be enforced directly demonstrates the inherent supremacy of the Community law better than any analogy to traditional international treaties which do not penetrate so deeply into national legal systems.*'

[33] Reuter, 'Le Plan Schuman' (n. 30 above), 543.

[34] According to Art. 86 ECSC, it was the Member States 'to take all appropriate measures, whether general or particular, to ensure fulfilment of the obligations resulting from decisions or recommendations of the institutions of the Community and to facilitate the performance of the Community's tasks'.

[35] See A. H. Robertson, 'Legal Problems of European Integration' (1957) 91 *Recueil des Cours de l'Académie de la Haye* 105 at 143–5.

[36] Art. 13 ECSC (repealed by the Merger Treaty and replaced by Art. 17 ECSC).

[37] G. Bebr, 'The European Coal and Steel Community: A Political and Legal Innovation' (1953–4) 63 *Yale LJ* 1 at 20–4 defining 'supranational powers' as those 'exercised by the [Commission]' alone, 'limited supranational powers' as those acts for which 'the [Commission] needs the concurrence of the Council of Ministers' – qualified or unanimous.

[38] See H. L. Mason, *The European Coal and Steel Community: Experiment in Supranationalism* (Martinus Nijhoff, 1955), 34–5.

dual nature of supranationalism was to become the trademark of the European Union and attempts were soon made to export it into wider fields.

b. The (Failed) European Defence Community

The European Coal and Steel Community had only been 'a first step in the federation of Europe';[39] and the six Member States soon tried to expand the supranational sphere to the area of defence. The idea came from the (then) French Prime Minister, René Pleven. The 'Pleven Plan' suggested 'the creation, for our common defence, of a European army under the political institutions of a united Europe'.[40] For that '[a] minister of defence would be nominated by the participating governments and would be responsible, under conditions to be determined, to those appointing him and to a European [Parliament]'.[41] The plan was translated into a second Treaty signed in Paris that was to establish a second European Community: the European Defence Community (EDC).

The 1952 Paris Treaty was to 'ensure the security of the Member States against aggression' through 'the *integration* of the defence forces of the Member States'.[42] The Treaty thus envisaged the creation of a European army under the command of a supranational institution.[43] Due to disagreement between the Member States, the exact nature of the supranational *political* institution to command the European army had, however, been deliberately left open. The Treaty postponed the problem until six months *after* its coming into force by charging the future Parliament of the EDC to produce an institutional solution. In the words of the EDC Treaty:

> Within the period provided for in Section 2 of this Article, the [Parliament] shall study:
> (a) the creation of a [Parliament] of the European Defence Community elected on a democratic basis;
> (b) the powers which might be granted to such [a Parliament]; and
> (c) the modifications which should be made in the provisions of the present Treaty relating to other institutions of the Community, particularly with a view to safe-guarding an appropriate representation of the States.
> In its work, the [Parliament] will particularly bear in mind the following principles:

---

[39] See 'Schuman Declaration' (n. 15 above).

[40] For the 'Pleven Plan', see Harryvan and van der Harst (eds.), *Documents on European Union* (n. 15 above), 67.

[41] *Ibid.*   [42] Art. 2(2) EDC.

[43] *Ibid.*, Art. 9 states: 'The Armed Forces of the Community, hereinafter called "European Defence Forces" shall be composed of contingents placed at the disposal of the Community by the Member States with a view to their fusion under the conditions provided for in the present Treaty. No Member State shall recruit or maintain national armed forces aside from those provided for in Article 10 below.' On the history and structure of the European Defence Community (EDC), see G. Bebr, 'The European Defence Community and the Western European Union: An Agonizing Dilemma' (1954–5) 7 *Stanford Law Review* 169.

> The definitive organisation which will take the place of the present transitional organisation should be conceived so as to be capable of constituting one of the elements of an ultimately federal or confederal structure, based upon the principle of the separation of powers and including, particularly, a bicameral representative system.
>
> The [Parliament] shall also study the problems to which the coexistence of different organisations for European cooperation, now in being or to be created in the future, give rise, in order to ensure that these organisations are coordinated within the framework of the federal or confederal structure.[44]

The problem with this postponement strategy was that it did not work. The exact nature of the political authority behind a European army came soon to be seen as part and parcel of the EDC. And, in order to obtain French ratification of the EDC Treaty, the Council of the European Coal and Steel Community decided to create an ad hoc Parliament that would anticipate the work of the future Parliament of the EDC.[45]

The fruit of this anticipatory effort was a proposal for a European Political Community.[46] The Draft Treaty establishing the European Political Community suggested the establishment of a 'European Community of a supranational character', which was to be 'founded upon a union of peoples and States'.[47] The European Political Community aimed at merging the European Coal and Steel Community and the EDC into a new overall institutional structure.[48] Its central institution was a 'Parliament' that would have consisted of two Houses – the House of the Peoples and the Senate. This bicameral parliament would have been the principal lawmaking organ of the European (Political) Community.[49] The novel constitutional structure thus promised to establish a democratic and responsible political authority behind the EDC. Yet despite all efforts and assurances,

---

[44] Art. 38 EDC.

[45] G. Clemens et al., *Geschichte der europäischen Integration* (UTB, 2008), 114.

[46] Draft Treaty embodying the Statute of the European Community (Secretariat of the Constitutional Committee, 1953).

[47] Art. 1 Draft Treaty.

[48] *Ibid.*, Art. 5: 'The Community, together with the European Coal and Steel Community, and the European Defence Community, shall constitute a single legal entity, within which certain organs may retain such administrative and financial autonomy as is necessary to the accomplishment of the tasks assigned by the treaties instituting the European Coal and Steel Community and the European Defence Community.' See also Art. 56 Draft Treaty: 'The Community shall, with due regard to the provisions of Article 5, exercise the powers and competence of the European Coal and Steel Community and those of the European Defence Community.'

[49] *Ibid.*, Art. 10: 'Parliament shall enact legislation and make recommendations and proposals. It shall also approve the budget and pass a bill approving the accounts of the Community. It shall exercise such powers of supervision as are conferred upon it by the present Statute.' For an analysis of the European Political Community, see A. H. Robertson, 'The European Political Community' (1952) 29 *BYIL* 383.

the EDC – and with it the European Political Community – was a failure. The French Parliament rejected the ratification of the second Paris Treaty in 1954.

The failure of the EDC discredited the idea of *political* integration for decades. And European integration consequently returned to the philosophy of *economic* integration.[50] A first suggestion for a 'European revival' concerned the integration of an economic sector adjacent to coal: nuclear energy. This French proposal for further sectoral integration met the criticism of those Member States favouring the creation of a common market for *all* economic sectors.[51] In the end, a compromise solution was chosen that proposed the creation of *two* additional European Communities: the European Atomic Energy Community and the European Economic Community. Each Community was based on a separate international treaty signed in Rome in 1957.

Thanks to its non-sectoral approach, the second Rome Treaty would become the foundation and yardstick for all future European projects.[52] By establishing a common market, the European Economic Community was to 'lay the foundations of *an ever closer union* among the peoples of Europe'.[53]

2. From Rome to Maastricht: The European (Economic) Community

The idea of a European Economic Community had first been discussed in 1955 in the Italian city of Messina. The Messina Conference had charged Paul-Henry Spaak with producing a report on the advantages of a common market. On the basis of the 'Spaak Report', the 1957 Rome Treaty establishing the European Economic Community decided to create a common market – both in industrial and agricultural products.

The inner core of the European common market was the creation of a customs union. A customs union is an economic union with *no* internal customs duties and *one* external customs tariff.[54] But the idea behind the EEC Treaty went

---

[50] In the words of Paul H. Spaak: 'After the [EDC] venture it was not reasonable to repeat exactly the same experiment a few months later. A means must be found of reaching the same goal – that distant goal of an integrated Europe – by other methods and through other channels. We then considered that, having failed on the political plane, we should take up the question on the economic plane and use the so-called functional method, availing ourselves to some extent – although, of course, without drawing any strict parallels – of the admittedly successful experiment already made with the European Coal and Steel Community.' See Address to the Parliament, 21 October 1955 – quoted in Robertson, *European Institutions* (n. 5 above), at 26.

[51] Clemens et al., *Geschichte der europäischen Integration* (n. 45 above), 126.

[52] According to Dinan, *Europe Recast* (n. 26 above), 76: 'most member states regarded Euratom as irrelevant'.

[53] Art. 2 EEC (emphasis added).

[54] The existence of a single external custom distinguishes a customs union from a free trade area. Within the 'European' context, such a free trade area exists in the European Free Trade Association (EFTA) established in 1960. EFTA had originally been suggested by the United Kingdom to create a counterweight to the EEC's common market project. The original seven EFTA members were: Austria, Denmark, Norway, Portugal, Sweden, Switzerland and the United Kingdom.

beyond a customs union. It aimed at the establishment of a common market in goods as well as 'the abolition, as between Member States, of obstacles to freedom of movement for persons, services and capital'.[55] The European Economic Community was equally charged with, *inter alia*, the adoption of a common transport policy and 'the institution of a system ensuring that competition in the common market is not distorted'.[56]

The Rome Treaty was thus – much more than the Treaty of Paris – a framework treaty. It provided a basic constitutional framework and charged the European institutions with adopting legislation to fulfil the objectives of the Treaty. What would this mean for the character of the European Economic Community?

a. Normative Supranationalism: The Nature of European Law

Like the ECSC, the European Economic Community would enjoy autonomous powers. The EEC Treaty indeed acknowledged two 'supranational' instruments in Article 189 EEC. The Community could directly act upon individuals through legislative 'regulations' or executive 'decisions'. These acts were designed to be directly applicable within the national legal orders. But the Court soon showed its eagerness to go beyond the drafter's design by declaring that, since 'the Community constitutes a new legal order of international law', individuals' rights 'arise not only where they are expressly granted by the Treaty, but also by reason of obligations which the Treaty imposes in a clearly defined way upon individuals as well as upon the Member States'.[57] The direct application of Community law – its ability to be applied by national courts – would indeed become the 'ordinary' state of European law.[58]

This normative quality of European law contrasted with the 'ordinary' state of international law:

> By contrast with ordinary international treaties, the EEC Treaty has created its own legal system which, on the entry into force of the Treaty, became an integral part of the legal systems of the Member States and which their courts are bound to apply … The integration into the laws of each Member State of provisions which derive from the Community, and more generally the terms and the spirit of the Treaty, make it impossible for the States, as a corollary, to accord precedence to a unilateral and subsequent measure over a legal system accepted by them on a basis of reciprocity. Such a measure cannot therefore be inconsistent with that legal system. The executive force of Community law cannot vary from one State to another in deference to subsequent domestic laws, without jeopardizing the attainment of the objectives of the Treaty[.][59]

---

[55] Art. 3(c) EEC.   [56] *Ibid.*, Art. 3(e) and (f).
[57] Case 26/62, *Van Gend en Loos* [1963] ECR 1 at 12.
[58] On this point, see Chapter 3.
[59] Case 6/64, *Costa* v. *ENEL* [1964] ECR 585 at 593–4.

This famous passage announced the supremacy of Community law over national law. Where two equally applicable norms of European and national law would come into conflict, the former would prevail over the latter. The law stemming from the EEC Treaty was 'an independent source of law' that 'could not, because of its special and original nature, be overridden by domestic legal provisions, however framed, without being deprived of its character as Community law and without the legal basis of the Community itself being called into question'.[60] European law would thus not only enjoy direct application it would also be a supreme law in the Member States. The Court here confirmed and developed the supranational quality of European law anticipated by the European Coal and Steel Community.

b. Decisional Supranationalism: The Governmental Structure

The Rome Treaty had established a number of institutions, which were modelled on those of the Paris Treaty.[61] Yet underneath formal similarities, the institutional balance within the European Economic Community differed significantly from that of the European Coal and Steel Community. Indeed, the EEC Treaty carefully avoided all references to the concept of 'supranationalism'.[62]

Early doubts about the supranational nature of the EEC were not confined to semantics. The enormously enlarged scope for European integration had required a price: the return to a more international format of decision-making. Emblematically, the EEC Treaty now charged the Council – not the Commission – with the task '[t]o ensure that the objectives set out in this Treaty are attained'.[63] Instead of the 'supranational' Commission, it was the 'international' Council that operated as the central decision-maker.[64] The Council was composed of 'representatives of the Member States';[65] and it would, when deciding by unanimous agreement, follow traditional international law logic.[66] However, the Rome Treaty avoided a purely international solution by insisting on the prerogative of the (supranational) Commission to initiate Community bills.

---

[60] *Ibid.*, at 594.

[61] Art. 4 EEC. The Rome Treaty had been drafted on the understanding that the Parliament and the Court of the European Coal and Steel Community would be the same for the European Economic Community. However, the executive organs of both Communities still differed. This institutional 'separatism' changed with the 1965 Merger Treaty that 'merged' the executive organs of all three Communities.

[62] R. Efron and A. S. Nanes, 'The Common Market and Euratom Treaties: Supranationality and the Integration of Europe' (1957) 6 ICLQ 670 at 682.

[63] Art. 145 EEC.

[64] See Robertson, 'Legal Problems of European Integration' (n. 35 above), 159–60: 'Indeed, it was the reluctance of governments in subsequent years to accept anything in the nature of the supranational which produced the result that the powers of the Commission of the EEC were less extensive than those of the [ECSC Commission].'

[65] Art. 146 EEC.

[66] Efron and Nanes, 'The Common Market and Euratom Treaties' (n. 62 above), 675.

Decisional supranationalism could moreover be seen at work once the Council acted by (qualified) majority. Following a transitional period,[67] the Rome Treaty indeed envisaged a range of legal bases allowing for qualified majority voting in the Council. Yet famously, the supranational machinery received – early on – an intergovernmental spanner. The political interruption stemmed from France. But this time it was not the French Parliament which rocked the European boat. Behind the first constitutional crisis of the young EEC stood the (then) French President, General Charles de Gaulle.

What was the General's problem? The Community was about to start using qualified majority voting when it passed into the third transitional phase on 1 January 1966.[68] In March 1965, the Commission had made a – daring – proposal for the financing of the Community budget. The Council stormily discussed the proposal in June of that year; and after an inconclusive debate, the French Foreign Minister declared the discussions to have failed. The Commission made a new proposal, but the French government boycotted the Council. This boycott became famous as France's 'empty chair' policy. France would not take its chair within the Council unless a 'compromise' was found that balanced the (imminent) move to majority voting with France's national interests. To solve this constitutional conflict, the Community organised two extraordinary Council sessions in Luxembourg (as Brussels was the place of the – supranational – devil). The compromise between the supranational interests of the Community and the national interests of its Member States became known as the 'Luxembourg Compromise'.[69] The latter declared:

> Where, in the case of decisions which may be taken by majority vote on a proposal of the Commission, very important interests of one or more partners are at stake, the Members of the Council will endeavour, within a reasonable time, to reach solutions which can be adopted by all the Members of the Council while respecting their mutual interests and those of the Community, in accordance with Article 2 of the Treaty. With regard to the preceding paragraph, the French delegation considers that where very important interests are at stake, the discussion must be continued

[67] The Rome Treaty had established a transitional period of 12 years, divided into three stages of four years. The procedure for this transitional period was set out in Art. 8 EEC. During the first two stages of the transitional period unanimous decisions would remain the rule; e.g. Art. 43(2) EEC: 'The Council shall, on a proposal from the Commission and after consulting the [Parliament], acting unanimously during the first two stages and by a qualified majority thereafter, make regulations, issue directives, or take decisions, without prejudice to any recommendations it may also make.'

[68] While Art. 8 EEC had envisaged a political decision to pass from the first to the second stage (para. 3), the passage from the second to the third stage was to be automatic. France would thus not have been able to block the transition by 'legal' means established in the EEC Treaty.

[69] 'Final Communiqué of the Extraordinary Session of the Council' [1966] 3 *Bulletin of the European Communities* 5.

until unanimous agreement is reached. The six delegations note that there is a divergence of views on what should be done in the event of a failure to reach complete agreement. The six delegations nevertheless consider that this divergence does not prevent the Community's work being resumed in accordance with the normal procedure.[70]

The formal status of the Luxembourg Compromise, as well as its substantive content, was ambiguous. Textually, its wording did not grant each Member State a constitutional right to veto Community decisions. Nonetheless, decision-making in the Council would henceforth take place under the 'shadow of the veto'.[71] The Damoclean sword of the Luxembourg Compromise led to consensual decision-making within the Council even for legal bases that allowed for (qualified) majority voting.[72] This 'constitutional convention' would influence the decisional practice of the Community for almost two decades.[73]

But the young European Economic Community (partly) balanced this decline of decisional supranationalism *in the Council* by a rise of decisional supranationalism in two other Community institutions. A small but significant step towards decisional supranationalism was achieved in the European Parliament, when the Community chose to replace the financial contributions of the Member States with its own resources.[74] To compensate for this decline of *national* parliamentary control over State contributions, it was felt necessary to increase the *supranational* controlling powers of the European Parliament.[75] And to increase the democratic credentials of that Parliament, the latter was 'transformed' from an

---

[70] *Ibid*.

[71] For this nice metaphor, see J. Weiler, 'The Transformation of Europe' (1990–1) 100 *Yale LJ* 2403 at 2450.

[72] There is not yet much historical evidence on the politico-constitutional impact of the Luxembourg Compromise. Suffice to say here that the 1974 Paris Communiqué (n. 94 below), para. 6, noted that the Heads of State 'consider that it is necessary to renounce the practice which consists of making agreement on all questions conditional on the unanimous consent of the Member States, whatever their respective position may be regarding the conclusions reached in Luxembourg on 28 January 1966'.

[73] On the gradual decline of the Luxembourg Compromise, see L. Van Middelaar, 'Spanning the River: The Constitutional Crisis of 1965–1966 as the Genesis of Europe's Political Order' (2008) 4 *European Constitutional Law Review* 98 at 119–23.

[74] See 'First Budget Treaty' ('Treaty amending Certain Budgetary Provisions', 1970), [1971] OJ L 2/1 and 'Second Budget Treaty' ('Treaty amending Certain Financial Provisions', 1975), [1977] OJ L 359/1.

[75] The First Budget Treaty distinguished between compulsory and non-compulsory expenditure and gave Parliament the power to control the latter (see Art. 4 of the 1970 Budget Treaty). The 1975 Treaty increased the budgetary power of Parliament to reject the Community budget as a whole (see Art. 12 of the 1975 Budget Treaty), and would create the Court of Auditors (see Art. 15 of the 1975 Budget Treaty).

'assembly' of national parliamentarians into a directly elected Parliament.[76] Sadly, this rise in the Parliament's democratic credentials was not immediately matched by a rise in its powers beyond the budgetary process. Parliamentary involvement in the exercise of the Community's legislative powers would have to wait until the Single European Act.[77]

Until this time, it was a third institution that came to rescue the 'deficient Community legislator' – the Court of Justice.[78] In the late 1970s, the Court decided to take decision-making into its own hands. Instead of waiting for *positive* integration through European legislation, the Court chose to integrate the common market *negatively*. This strategy of 'negative integration' would not depend on political agreement within the Council.[79] It pressed for market integration by judicial means.

The famous illustration of this shift *within* decisional supranationalism from positive integration to negative integration is *Cassis de Dijon*.[80] The case concerned a sales prohibition of a French fruit liqueur in Germany. The importer had applied for a marketing authorisation, which had been refused by the German authorities on the grounds that, in the absence of European harmonisation, the national rules on consumer protection applied. Despite a proposal for the harmonisation of the relevant national rules,[81] no action had been forthcoming as a result of the decisional blockage in the Council. This would originally have been the end of the story. But after a decade of judicial patience, the Court was having none of it. It declared that – even in the absence of positive harmonisation – the Member States could not impose their national legislation on imports, unless this was justified by *European* mandatory requirements of public interest.[82] The judgment elevated the principle of mutual recognition to a general constitutional principle of the common market. The constitutional

---

[76] This transformation had been envisaged, from the very beginning, by Art. 138(3) EEC: 'The [Parliament] shall draw up proposals for elections by direct universal suffrage in accordance with a uniform procedure in all Member States. The Council shall, acting unanimously, lay down the appropriate provisions, which it shall recommend to Member States for adoption in accordance with their respective constitutional requirements.' The Council decision was taken on 20 September 1976 and the Member States ratified it in 1977. On 8 April 1978, the Council decided to hold the Parliament's first elections on 7–10 June 1979.

[77] Beyond its budgetary powers, Parliament remained primarily an 'advisory' institution – even if its advice was to be a compulsory procedural requirement. See Case 138/79, *Roquette Frères* v. *Council (Isoglucose)* [1980] ECR 3333.

[78] P. Pescatore, 'La Carence du législateur communautaire et le devoir du juge', in G. Lüke, G. Ress and M. R. Will (eds.), *Rechtsvergleichung, Europarecht und Staatenintegration: Gedächtnisschrift für Léontin-Jean Constantinesco* (Heymanns, 1983), 559.

[79] The distinction between 'positive' and 'negative' integration is said to stem from J. Pinder, 'Positive Integration and Negative Integration: Some Problems of Economic Union in the EEC' (1968) 24 *World Today* 88.

[80] Case 120/78, *Rewe-Zentral* v. *Bundesmonopolverwaltung für Branntwein* (*Cassis de Dijon*) [1979] ECR 649.

[81] *Ibid.*, para. 8.   [82] *Ibid.*

idea behind *Cassis de Dijon* was that the decline of decisional supranationalism in the Council would, if need be, be compensated for by the rise of judicial supranationalism.

c. Intergovernmental Developments outside the EEC

The analysis of the second period in the evolution of the European Union would be incomplete if we concentrated solely on the supranational developments *within* the European Economic Community. There were important developments *outside* the Community, which would – with time – shape the structure and content of the future European Union. These intergovernmental developments began when the transitional period of the EEC came to a close by the end of the 1960s. Far from constituting the 'dark ages' of the Community, this period saw '[t]he revival of ambition'.[83] The search for a 'Europe of the second generation' began in 1969 with the Hague Summit.[84] Its Final Communiqué called *inter alia* for the promotion of 'economic and monetary union', and 'progress in the matter of political unification'.[85]

The possibility of economic and monetary union was explored in the Werner Report.[86] The report called for the realisation of monetary union 'to ensure growth and stability within the Community and reinforce the contribution it can make to economic and monetary equilibrium in the world and make it a pillar of stability'.[87] However, disagreement existed on how to achieve this aim. Should economic union precede monetary union; or should monetary union precede and precipitate economic union?[88] The dispute was never resolved; but a compromise would – after years of debate and delay – lead to the establishment of the European Monetary System in 1979.

The possibility of political union was explored in the Davignon Report, which laid the foundations for a 'European Political Cooperation'. The report linked political unification with cooperation in the field of foreign policy. This cooperation was to 'ensure greater mutual understanding with respect to the major issues of international politics, by exchanging information and consulting regularly' and to 'increase their solidarity by working for a harmonisation of

---

[83] This is the title of ch. 11 of D. Urwin, *The Community of Europe: A History of European Integration since 1945* (Longman, 1994).

[84] See R. Bieber (ed.), *Das Europa der Zweiten Generation: Gedächtnisschrift für Christoph Sasse* (Engel, 1981).

[85] 'Final Communiqué of the Meeting of the Heads of State or Government of the EEC (The Hague, 1969)', in Harryvan and van der Harst (eds.), *Documents on European Union* (n. 15 above), 168–9, paras. 8 and 15.

[86] For the Werner Report, see also *ibid.*, 169.   [87] *Ibid.*, 170.

[88] The former option was advocated by Germany and is known as the 'coronation theory', and its advocates were referred to as the 'economists'. The second option was argued by France and is known as the 'locomotive theory', and its advocates were known as the 'monetarists'.

views, concertation of attitudes and joint action when it appears feasible and desirable'.[89]

To achieve these objectives, the Member States decided to have their foreign Ministers regularly meet at the initiative of the President-in-office of the Council. But importantly, this was not the creation of a supranational foreign policy: European Political Cooperation was a strictly international mechanism outside the European Communities. In this way, old French wounds from the (failed) European Defence and Political Communities would not be reopened.[90]

A third international development concerned the area of justice and home affairs. Following discussions on European Political Cooperation, the Member States decided to set up the 'TREVI' mechanism.[91] Originally designed as a political instrument to fight international terrorism, its scope was subsequently enlarged to the coordination of police and judicial efforts to combat organised crime. In light of this development, some Member States were increasingly willing to abolish border controls; and an international treaty between five Member States was signed in 1985 near Schengen.[92] The Schengen Agreement and its implementing convention aimed at establishing an area without border controls, with common rules on visas, and police and judicial cooperation.[93] This 'Schengen Area' would constitute an independent intergovernmental regime outside the European Communities until it was integrated into the European Union structure a decade later.

Finally, there is a fourth intergovernmental development that emerges in this period of European integration: the birth of the 'European Council'. The 1969 Hague Summit had shown the potential for impulse that the Heads of State or Government could give to the evolution of the European Communities. And when the Community traversed the global recession in the 1970s, the Heads of State or Government decided to realise this potential and began to meet regularly. The Final Communiqué of the 1974 Paris Summit thus 'institutionalised' these summit meetings in the following terms:

---

[89]   Harryvan and van der Harst (eds.), *Documents on European Union* (n. 15 above), 173 at 174.
[90]   Urwin, *Community of Europe* (n. 83 above), 147.
[91]   The mechanism was established following the Rome European Council of 1 December 1975. In French, the acronym 'TREVI' came to stand for 'terrorism', 'radicalism', 'extremism' and 'international violence'. However, 'Trevi' is also the name of a famous fountain in Rome.
[92]   Agreement between the Governments of the States of the Benelux Economic Union, the Federal Republic of Germany and the French Republic on the gradual abolition of checks at their common borders ('Schengen Agreement') [2000] OJ L 239, 13–18. The original 'Schengen States' were: Belgium, France, Germany, Luxembourg and the Netherlands. These Member States signed the 1990 Convention implementing the Schengen Agreements [2000] OJ L 239/19–62.
[93]   The Schengen Agreement and the Schengen Convention contained provisions dealing with police cooperation, see Arts. 39–47 of the Schengen Convention. For an early analysis of 'Schengen', see J. Schutte, 'Schengen: Its Meaning for the Free Movement of Persons in Europe' (1991) 28 *CML Rev.* 549.

> Recognizing the need for an overall approach to the internal problems involved in achieving European unity and the external problems facing Europe, the Heads of Government consider it essential to ensure progress and overall consistency in the activities of the Communities and in the work on political cooperation. The Heads of Government have therefore decided to meet, accompanied by the Ministers of Foreign Affairs, three times a year and whenever necessary, in the Council of the Communities in the context of political cooperation. The administrative secretariat will be provided for in an appropriate manner with due regard to existing practices and procedures. In order to ensure consistency in Community activities and continuity of work, the Ministers of Foreign Affairs, meeting in the Council of the Community, will act as initiators and coordinators. They may hold political cooperation meetings at the same time.[94]

The establishment of the European Council as a semi-permanent 'government' of the European Communities was a momentous development.[95] While formally created 'outside' the Rome Treaty, it would evolve into a powerful political motor of European integration and thereby complement the task of the supranational engine of the Commission.

d. Supranational and Intergovernmental Reforms through the Single European Act

Despite important supranational and intergovernmental developments within and without the European Communities over 30 years, the first major Treaty reform would only take place in 1986 through the Single European Act (SEA). The Act received its name from the fact that it combined two reforms in a *single* document. On the one hand, the SEA represented a constitutional reform of the European Economic Community.[96] On the other hand, it reformed the European Political Cooperation as an

---

[94] Communiqué of the Meeting of the Heads of State or Government (Paris, 1974) reproduced in Harryvan and van der Harst (eds.), *Documents on European Union* (n. 15 above), 181.

[95] This was confirmed in the Solemn Declaration on European Union (Stuttgart, 1983), reproduced in Harryvan and van der Harst (eds.), *Documents on European Union* (n. 15 above), 214 at 215 (para. 2.1.2): 'In the perspective of the European Union, the European Council provides a general political impetus to the construction of Europe; defines approaches to further the construction of Europe and issues general political guidelines for the European Communities and European Political Cooperation; deliberates upon matters concerning European Union in its different aspects with due regard to consistency among them; initiates cooperation in new areas of activity; solemnly expresses the common position in questions of external relations.'

[96] Title II of the SEA deals with 'Provisions amending the Treaties establishing the European Communities'.

intergovernmental mechanism outside the formal structure of the European Communities.[97]

The core of the constitutional reform within the European Communities lay in the idea of completing the internal market by '1992'.[98] The project had been devised in the 1985 White Paper 'Completing the Internal Market',[99] which would become the centrepiece of the newly invested Delors Commission. Leaving the legislative failures of the past behind, it sought to revamp the idea of positive integration. A fresh term – the internal market – reflected the desire to break with the past and to realise this fundamental aim of the original Rome Treaty.

In order to achieve this aim, the SEA not only expanded the Community's competences significantly, but it equally reformed its institutional structure in three ways. First, the Single European Act expanded supranational decision-making in the Council by adding legal bases allowing for (qualified) majority voting.[100] Second, the legislative powers of the European Parliament were significantly enhanced by means of a new lawmaking procedure: the cooperation procedure.[101] Third, the Court of Justice would be assisted by another court. Due to its jurisdiction 'to hear and determine at first instance', the Court would become known as the 'Court of First Instance'.[102]

The constitutional reforms of the Single European Act however also left important aspects outside the supranational structure of the European Communities. Indeed, all four intergovernmental developments discussed in the previous section continued to be outside the European Treaties. Indeed, the Single European Act did *not* bring the 'European Monetary System' under a supranational roof.[103] The SEA did *not* integrate foreign affairs – even if it placed the EPC on a more formal legal footing. The SEA did *not* bring justice and home affairs within the scope of the European Treaties. And, while formally recognising the European

---

[97] *Ibid.*, Art. 1: 'Political Cooperation shall be governed by Title III. The provisions of that Title shall confirm and supplement the procedures agreed in the reports of Luxembourg (1970), Copenhagen (1973), London (1981), the Solemn Declaration on European Union (1983) and the practices gradually established among the Member States.'

[98] *Ibid.*, Art. 13 was to introduce the following provision into the EEC Treaty: 'The Community shall adopt measures with the aims of progressively establishing the internal market over a period expiring on 31 December 1992 ... The internal market shall comprise an area without internal frontiers in which the free movement of goods, persons, services and capital is ensured in accordance with the provisions of this Treaty.'

[99] 'Completing the Internal Market: White Paper from the Commission to the European Council', COM (85) 310.

[100] The most famous additional legal basis to put this constitutional mandate into effect was – what is today – Art. 114 TFEU allowing the Community to adopt harmonisation measures by qualified majority.

[101] See Arts. 6 and 7 SEA.   [102] *Ibid.*, Art. 11.

[103] However, in order to ensure the convergence of economic and monetary policies, Art. 20 SEA imposed a duty on the Member States to 'take account of the experience acquired in cooperation within the framework of the European Monetary System (EMS) and in developing the ECU'.

Council,[104] the SEA had *not* elevated it to the status of a Community institution. It would take two more decades before all four issues were finally resolved.

These future developments took place in a third historical period. They will be discussed in the next section.

3. From Maastricht to Nice: The (Old) European Union

Thanks to its thematic proximity to the internal market, economic and monetary union soon came to be seen as the next stage in the process of European integration. Following the Delors Report,[105] the 1989 European Council decided to push the matter by calling for an Intergovernmental Conference.[106] The decision provoked an inspired response from the European Parliament, which argued that it was 'increasingly necessary rapidly to transform the European Community into a European Union of [the] federal type'.[107] Pointing to the Single European Act,[108] Parliament insisted: 'the agenda of the Intergovernmental Conference must be enlarged beyond economic and monetary union'.[109] Having received eminent support,[110] this request for a link between *monetary* and *political* union was heard by the European Council.[111] The European Council thus called for *two* parallel intergovernmental conferences. They would result in the Treaty on European Union signed in Maastricht in 1992, which entered into force a year later.[112]

---

[104] Art. 2 SEA.

[105] European Communities, 'Report of the Committee for the Study of Economic and Monetary Union' (1989) 4 *Bulletin of the European Communities* 8. For an early analysis of the report, see N. Thygesen, 'The Delors Report and European Economic and Monetary Union' (1989) 65 *International Affairs* 637.

[106] European Council (Madrid, 26 and 27 June 1989), 'Conclusions of the Presidency' (1989) 6 *Bulletin of the European Communities* 8 at 11.

[107] European Parliament, Resolution of 14 March 1990 on the Intergovernmental Conference in the context of Parliament's strategy for European Union ([1990] OJ C 96/114), preamble B.

[108] The commitment to review the procedures on European Political Cooperation had been made in Art. 30(12) SEA: 'Five years after the entry into force of this Act the High Contracting Parties shall examine whether any revision of Title III is required.'

[109] European Parliament (n. 107 above), para. 1.

[110] See the letter by the German Chancellor Kohl and the French President Mitterrand to the Irish Presidency (19 April 1990), in Harryvan and van der Harst (eds.), *Documents on European Union* (n. 15 above), 252: 'In the light of far-reaching changes in Europe and in view of the completion of the single market and the realisation of economic and monetary union, we consider it necessary to accelerate the political construction of the Europe of the Twelve.'

[111] European Council (Rome, 14 and 15 December 1990), 'Presidency Conclusions' (1990) 12 *Bulletin of the European Communities* 7.

[112] The Treaty on European Union was, at first, rejected by Denmark. It was eventually ratified after concessions made to Denmark by the Edinburgh European Council (see 'Denmark and the Treaty on European Union' [1992] OJ C 348/1). The German Constitutional Court posed a second ratification challenge. On the famous 'Maastricht Decision' of the German Constitutional Court, see Chapter 2, section 4(b).

The Treaty on European Union represented 'a new stage in the process of European integration'.[113] Yet it was a constitutional compromise: the Member States had been unable to agree on placing all new policies into the supranational structure of the European Communities. From the four Single European Act 'leftovers', solely economic and monetary union would become a supranational policy – and that at the price of differential integration.[114] By contrast, the European Council as well as the two remaining intergovernmental policies – Foreign and Security Policy and Justice and Home Affairs – would retain their international character. However, it was agreed to strengthen their institutional links with the Community system. This was achieved by placing the European Council, the two intergovernmental policies *as well as the European Communities* under a common legal roof: the European Union. The overall constitutional structure of the Union was thereby defined by the first article of the (old) Treaty on European Union:

> By this Treaty, the High Contracting Parties establish among themselves a European Union, hereinafter called 'the Union'. This Treaty marks a new stage in the process of creating an ever closer union among the peoples of Europe, in which decisions are taken as closely as possible to the citizens. The Union shall be founded on the European Communities, supplemented by the policies and forms of cooperation established by this Treaty. Its task shall be to organise, in a manner demonstrating consistency and solidarity, relations between the Member States and between their peoples.[115]

The provision established a separate international organisation – the European Union – that was different from the European Communities. What was the relationship between the two organisations? Due to the textual structure of the Maastricht Treaty, the relationship came to be compared – somewhat misleadingly – to a Greek temple. This temple architecture became the defining characteristic of the 'old' (Maastricht) European Union and will be discussed first. Subsequent treaty amendments within this third period kept the Union's pillar structure intact, but strengthened and widened the supranational elements of the First Pillar significantly.

---

[113] Preamble of the TEU.

[114] 'Differential integration' means that not all Member States take part in the integration project. The decision to establish a differential constitutional regime for economic and monetary union had been taken early on in the negotiations of the Maastricht Treaty. Only those States fulfilling the 'convergence criteria' would be allowed to participate. In addition, the Member States agreed to allow for opt-outs to those Member States that, while entitled to participate, would not wish to do so. For a closer analysis of differential integration within EMU, see Chapter 18, section 1(b).

[115] Art. A EU (old).

a. The Temple Structure: The Three Pillars of the (Maastricht) Union

The legal structure of the Maastricht *Treaty* led the European Union to be identified with a Greek temple. The 'common provisions' would form the roof of the Union 'temple'. They laid down common objectives,[116] and established that the Union was to 'be served by a single institutional framework'.[117] Underneath this common roof were the three pillars of the Union: the European Communities (First Pillar), the Common Foreign and Security Policy (Second Pillar) and Justice and Home Affairs (Third Pillar). The base of the temple was formed by a second set of provisions common to all three pillars: the 'final provisions' of the Maastricht Treaty. These final provisions not only determined the relationship between the pillars,[118] but also contained common rules for their amendment.[119] Importantly, apart from the common and final provisions, each of the three pillars was subject to its own rules. The constitutional fragmentation caused by the Maastricht Treaty was consequently criticised as having created a 'Europe of bits and pieces'.[120]

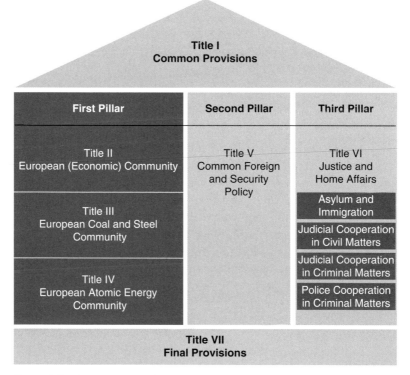

Figure 1.2 Pillar Structure of the 'Old' (Maastricht) Union

---

[116]   Art. B EU (old).
[117]   Art. C EU (old). Remarkably, no common legal personality was established for the Union.
[118]   Art. M EU (old).   [119] Art. N EU (old).
[120]   D. Curtin, 'The Constitutional Structure of the Union: A Europe of Bits and Pieces' (1993) 30 *CML Rev.* 17.

aa. The First Pillar: The European Communities

At the heart of the Maastricht Treaty lay a fundamental reform of the European Communities and, in particular: the European Economic Community. And due to its substantially enlarged scope, the latter would henceforth be renamed the European Community.[121]

The Maastricht Treaty significantly enlarged the competences of the European Community. Most importantly, it introduced a supranational monetary policy and thereby established the European System of Central Banks (ESCB) and the European Central Bank (ECB).[122] The primary objective of the latter was to maintain price stability and its basic tasks would include 'to define and implement the monetary policy of the Community' and 'to conduct foreign exchange operations'.[123] The ECB would eventually have the exclusive right to authorise the issue of bank notes ('euros') within the Community.[124] The process leading to monetary union was thereby divided into three stages. Participation in the third stage would depend on the fulfilment of certain economic criteria.[125] Member States were obliged to avoid excessive government deficits and the Commission would be entitled to monitor budgetary discipline.[126] For two Member States, this was too much supranationalism and they decided to 'opt out' of economic and monetary union.[127]

What institutional changes were brought by the Maastricht reform? With regard to political union, the Maastricht Treaty created a number of important innovations. First, it introduced the political status of a 'citizenship of the Union'.[128] Apart from free movement rights, Union citizens would henceforth

---

[121] Art. G(A)(1) EU (old). 'The term "European Economic Community" shall be replaced by the term "European Community".'

[122] Art. G(B)(7) EU (old).

[123] Art. G(D)(25) EU (old).

[124] *Ibid.* The timetable was set by what was to become the future Art. 100j EC. The Council was called to decide 'not later than 31 December 1996 whether it is appropriate for the Community to enter the third stage; and if so, set the date for the beginning of the third stage' (*ibid.*, para. 3). And, if that had not been done by the end of 1997, it was provided that 'the third stage shall start on 1 January 1999' (*ibid.*, para. 4).

[125] Art. G(D)(25) EU (old) – inserting Art. 109j EC. The convergence criteria were further defined in the Protocol on the Convergence Criteria referred to in Art. 109j of the TEU that was attached to the Maastricht Treaty.

[126] Art. G(D)(25) EU (old) – inserting Art. 104c EC. The details of the excessive deficit procedure referred to in Art. 104c EC Treaty were spelled out in the Protocol on the excessive deficit procedure attached to the Maastricht Treaty. For a closer analysis of the EMU provisions, see Chapter 18, section 1.

[127] See Protocol on Certain Provisions relating to the United Kingdom, which recognised 'that the United Kingdom shall not be obliged or committed to move to the third stage of Economic and Monetary Union without a separate decision to do so by its government and Parliament' (recital 1). For the similar position of Denmark, see Protocol on Certain Provisions relating to Denmark.

[128] Art. G(C) EU (old) – introducing Art. 8(1) EC: 'Citizenship of the Union is hereby established. Every person holding the nationality of a Member State shall be a citizen of the Union.'

enjoy a number of political rights. These would include 'the right to vote and to
stand as a candidate at municipal elections' in another Member State, 'the right
to vote and to stand as a candidate in elections to the European Parliament' in
another Member State, as well as the right to protection by the diplomatic or
consular authorities of any Member State.[129] Second, the constitutional prerogatives of the European Parliament were significantly expanded.[130] The most
striking aspect of the rising *democratic* supranationalism within the Union was the
introduction of a new legislative procedure: the co-decision procedure. Going
beyond the cooperation procedure of the Single European Act, the co-decision
procedure would allow the European Parliament to 'co-decide' European legislation on a par with the Council.[131] Finally, the Maastricht Treaty continued the
expansion of qualified majority voting in the Council.

bb. The Second Pillar: Common Foreign and Security Policy

Under the Single European Act, the cooperation of national foreign affairs
within the 'European Political Cooperation' had still been conducted *outside*
the European Treaties. This changed with the Maastricht Treaty which brought
foreign and security affairs *inside* the European Union. A Common Foreign
and Security Policy (CFSP) would henceforth constitute the Union's Second
Pillar.[132] The latter could potentially cover the area of defence;[133] yet the exact
legal relationship between a future Common Security and Defence Policy
(CSDP) and the 'Western European Union' was left for another day.[134]

Importantly, the integration of foreign and security policy into the Union
did not mean that it had become a supranational policy. On the contrary, the
Maastricht compromise determined that the CFSP could retain its international
character. The dominant Union actors were thus the European Council and
the Council – two intergovernmental institutions. The role of the supranational

---

[129] Art. G(C) EU (old) – introducing Arts. 8a to 8c EC.
[130] Art. G(D) (53) EU (old) – amending Art. 173 EC that now allowed for actions by the European Parliament for the purpose of protecting its prerogatives.
[131] For a discussion of this procedure, see Chapter 7, section 3(a).
[132] Art. J EU (old): 'A common foreign and security policy is hereby established[.]'
[133] Art. J.4(1) EU (old): 'The common foreign and security policy shall include all questions relating to the security of the Union, including the eventual framing of a common defence policy, which might in time lead to a common defence.'
[134] Art. J.4(6) EU (old): 'With a view to furthering the objective of this Treaty and having in view the date of 1998 in the context of Article XII of the Brussels Treaty, the provisions of this Article may be revised as provided for in Article N(2) on the basis of a report to be presented in 1996 by the Council to the European Council, which shall include an evaluation of the progress made and the experience gained until then.' The relationship between the EU and the Western European Union (WEU) was further clarified by a Declaration relating to Western European Union. This declared that the 'WEU will be developed as the defence component of the European Union and as a means to strengthen the European pillar of the Atlantic Alliance' (para. 2). And according to para. 3: 'The objective is to build up WEU in stages as the defence component of the European Union. To this end, WEU is prepared, at the request of the European Union, to elaborate and implement decisions and actions of the Union which have defence implications.'

institutions was, by contrast, minimalist. The Parliament only enjoyed the right to be consulted and to make recommendations,[135] while the Commission was only entitled to be 'fully associated' with the CFSP.[136] The decisional intergovernmentalism within the CFSP was matched by its normative intergovernmentalism. Indeed, the objectives of the CFSP were not to be pursued by the Community's ordinary legal acts – such as regulations and decisions. On the contrary, the Second Pillar had established a number of specific instruments such as 'common positions' and 'joint actions'.[137] And since the Court of Justice was not to have any jurisdiction within this area,[138] the direct effect and supremacy of these instruments was in serious doubt.

cc. The Third Pillar: Justice and Home Affairs

The Third Pillar expanded the competences of the European Union into the field of 'Justice and Home Affairs' so as to better achieve the free movement of persons. For this purpose, it was given the power to act, *inter alia*, in the areas of asylum, immigration, judicial cooperation in civil and criminal matters, and police cooperation.[139] The 'Justice and Home Affairs' pillar would thus incorporate and replace the TREVI mechanism. However, the Union would not (yet) integrate the 'Schengen Area' and its *acquis*.

The nature of the Third Pillar was as international as that of the Second Pillar. Its decision-making processes as well as the normative quality of its law lacked a supranational character.[140]

b. A Decade of 'Constitutional Bricolage': Amsterdam and Nice

The decade following the Maastricht Treaty was an accelerated decade: treaty amendment followed treaty amendment. The increased demand for constitutional change was partly caused by a changed geopolitical context. With the fall of the Berlin Wall in 1989, Eastern Europe wished to join Western Europe under the legal roof of the European Union. Eastern enlargement however posed formidable constitutional problems. How could an institutional system that worked for 12 States be made to work for twice that number? But *widening* was only one aspect of the demand for constitutional change. The Union equally wished to *deepen* its evolution towards political union by establishing more democratic and transparent institutions.

The search for institutional solutions to these questions began with the 1997 Treaty of Amsterdam and continued with the 2001 Treaty of Nice. While both treaties introduced *minor* changes, none succeeded in offering the

---

[135] Art. J.7 EU (old).   [136] Art. J.9 EU (old).

[137] Arts. J.1(3) as well as J.2 and J.3 EU (old).

[138] Art. L EU (old).   [139] Art. K.1 EU (old).

[140] This was – partly – qualified by the Court of Justice in Case C-105/03, *Pupino* [2005] ECR I-5285. For a discussion of this case, see S. Peers, 'Salvation outside the Church: Judicial Protection in the Third Pillar after the "Pupino" and "Segi" Judgments' (2007) 44 *CML Rev.* 883.

much-needed *major* constitutional reform of the Union. Both reforms indeed represented a constitutional 'bricolage' of pragmatic and temporary political compromises.[141]

aa. The Amsterdam Treaty: Dividing the Third Pillar

What will the Treaty of Amsterdam be remembered for?[142] In addition to minor changes within the First and Second Pillar,[143] its central reform lay in the changes brought to the Third Pillar – that is: Justice and Home Affairs.

The Amsterdam Treaty 'split asunder' what the Maastricht Treaty had joined together.[144] Indeed, from the subject areas originally falling within the Third Pillar, only those dealing with criminal law survived into the 'new' Third Pillar. The remainder, dealing essentially with asylum and immigration as well as judicial cooperation in civil matters, was transferred to the First Pillar, as a more supranational approach for these matters had become favourable. The breaking up of the (old) 'Justice and Home' pillar left the new Third Pillar with a radically limited scope. The latter now only covered 'common actions among the Member States in the field of police and judicial cooperation in criminal matters and preventing and combating racism and xenophobia'.[145] After the Amsterdam amputation, the 'new' Third Pillar therefore came to be known as the Police and Judicial Cooperation in Criminal Matters (PJCC) pillar. This shortened pillar remained an intergovernmental pillar – even if there were some minor supranational additions.[146]

---

[141]   P. Pescatore, 'Nice: Aftermath' (2001) 38 *CML Rev.* 265.

[142]   Until 2009, European lawyers might have been tempted to mention the renumbering of the Treaties affected by the Amsterdam Treaty. However, this – dubious – achievement has now been lost, as the Lisbon Treaty has changed the numbering for the second time.

[143]   Within the First Pillar, the Amsterdam Treaty extends and reforms the co-decision procedure (L. Gormley, 'Reflections on the Architecture of the European Union after the Treaty of Amsterdam', in P. Twomey and D. O'Keeffe (eds.), *Legal Issues of the Amsterdam Treaty* (Hart, 1999), 57). The notable change in the Second Pillar was the creation of the new post of 'High Representative for the Common Foreign and Security Policy' (see Art. 1(10) TA – inserting new Art. J.16 EU (old)). Moreover, the Amsterdam Treaty brought the WEU closer to the EU in Part I, Art. 1(10) TA – inserting new Art. J.7 EU (old): 'The Western European Union (WEU) is an integral part of the development of the Union providing the Union with access to an operational capability notably in the context of paragraph 2. It supports the Union in framing the defence aspects of the common foreign and security policy as set out in this Article. The Union shall accordingly foster closer institutional relations with the WEU with a view to the possibility of the integration of the WEU into the Union, should the European Council so decide. It shall in that case recommend to the Member States the adoption of such a decision in accordance with their respective constitutional requirements.'

[144]   S. Peers, 'Justice and Home Affairs: Decision-making after Amsterdam' (2000) 25 *EL Rev.* 183.

[145]   Art. 1(11) TA – Art. K.1 EU (old).

[146]   On this point, see the excellent analysis by J. Monar, 'Justice and Home Affairs in the Treaty of Amsterdam: Reform at the Price of Fragmentation' (1998) 23 *EL Rev.* 320.

What happened to the 'amputated' part of the (old) Third Pillar? The Amsterdam Treaty inserted it into the First Pillar, and thus transformed this *Union* policy to a *Community* policy. The new title introduced into the EC Treaty thus granted the Community powers in the area of 'visa, asylum, immigration and other policies related to free movement of persons'.[147] This was a supranational policy, albeit with intergovernmental traits.[148]

But this was not all. The Member States finally agreed to 'incorporate' the Schengen Agreement and its legal offspring into the European Union.[149] The incorporation of the Schengen *acquis* under the roof of the European Union was legally complex for three reasons. First, not all Member States were parties to the international agreements and a legal solution had to be found for the non-participants.[150] Second, some *non*-Member States of the Union had been associated with the Schengen Agreement and would thus wish to be associated with the incorporation and future development of the Schengen *acquis*.[151] Third, since the old Third Pillar had been split into two parts – one supranational and one intergovernmental – the Schengen *acquis* could not be incorporated in one piece. It would also need to be divided according to whether the subject matter fell into the (new) First or the (new) Third Pillar. For that reason, the Schengen Protocol left it to the Council to determine 'in conformity with the relevant provisions of the Treaties, the legal basis for each of the provisions or decisions which constitute the Schengen acquis'.[152] But as long as the Council had not taken any implementing measures, 'the provisions or decisions which constitute the Schengen acquis [would] be regarded as acts based on Title VI of the Treaty on European Union', that is: acts of the Third Pillar.[153]

---

[147] See Art. 1(15) TA – introducing the (new) Title III(a) into Part III of the EC Treaty. The price for this 'supranationalisation' was differential integration. Indeed, the United Kingdom and Ireland opted out of this new title (see Protocol on the Position of the United Kingdom and Ireland). And according to the Protocol on the Application of certain aspects of Art. 7a establishing the European Community to the United Kingdom and to Ireland, border controls for persons travelling into these two states would continue to be legal (*ibid.*, Art. 1), and this would also hold true with regard to border controls for persons coming from these two States (*ibid.*, Art. 3). On the complex position of Denmark, see Protocol on the Position of Denmark.

[148] On this point, see K. Hailbronner, 'European Immigration and Asylum Law under the Amsterdam Treaty' (1998) 35 *CML Rev.* 1047 at 1053ff.

[149] See Protocol Integrating the Schengen acquis into the framework of the European Union – preamble 2. The Annex to the Protocol identifies the 'Schengen Acquis' with the Schengen Agreement, the Schengen Convention, the Accession Protocols and Agreements, and the decisions and declarations adopted by the (Schengen) Executive Committee or bodies established under it.

[150] Arts. 3 and 4 of the Schengen Protocol.

[151] The two non-Member States are the Republic of Iceland and the Kingdom of Norway, whose legal status is determined by Art. 6 of the Schengen Protocol.

[152] *Ibid.*, Art. 2(1) – second indent; and see also *ibid.*, Art. 5.

[153] *Ibid.*, Art. 2(1) – fourth indent.

bb. *The Nice Treaty: Limited Institutional Reform*

Despite the political prospect of Eastern enlargement, the Amsterdam Treaty had postponed a 'comprehensive review of the provisions of the Treaties on the composition and functioning of the institutions'.[154] In light of these 'Amsterdam leftovers',[155] the principal aim of the Nice Treaty was the – overdue – institutional reform of the European Union. Past amendments had not changed the *structural* composition of its institutions. Each enlargement had simply increased their membership. This 'policy of pulling up chairs' would reach a limit with Eastern enlargement.[156]

High expectations were therefore brought to the next amending Treaty. These heightened expectations, the Nice Treaty did *not* fulfil. The aim of a 'comprehensive review' of the institutional structure and decision-making system was not met. This substantial failure was soon seen as the result of the formal method of negotiation. The Nice Treaty had shown the procedural shortcomings of inter-governmental conferences for *major* Treaty reforms.[157]

What were the institutional changes nonetheless affected by the Nice Treaty? The Nice Treaty chiefly addressed the Amsterdam leftovers in a Protocol on the Enlargement of the European Union. This contained provisions for the composition of the European Parliament,[158] the Council[159] and the Commission.[160]

---

[154] See Art. 2 of the Protocol on the Institutions with the Prospect of Enlargement of the European Union. The provision reads as follows: 'At least one year before the membership of the European Union exceeds twenty, a conference of representatives of the governments of the Member States shall be convened in order to carry out a comprehensive review of the provisions of the Treaties on the composition and functioning of the institutions.' The Protocol thereby envisaged that 'the Commission shall comprise one national of each of the Member States, provided that, by that date, the weighting of the votes in the Council has been modified, whether by re-weighting of the votes or by dual majority, in a manner acceptable to all Member States, taking into account all relevant elements, notably compensating those Member States which give up the possibility of nominating a second member of the Commission' (*ibid.*, Art. 1).

[155] European Council (Helsinki, 10–11 December 1999), 'Presidency Conclusions' (1999) 12 *Bulletin of the European Communities* 1 at para. 16: 'Following the Cologne Conclusions and in the light of the Presidency's report, the Conference will examine the size and composition of the Commission, the weighting of votes in the Council and the possible extension of qualified majority voting in the Council, as well as other necessary amendments to the Treaties arising as regards the European institutions in connection with the above issues and in implementing the Treaty of Amsterdam.'

[156] R. Barents, 'Some Observations on the Treaty of Nice' (2001) 8 *Maastricht Journal of European and Comparative Law* 121 at 122.

[157] Famously, after the prolonged and aggravated Nice Treaty negotiations, Tony Blair (former UK Prime Minister) is reported to have exclaimed: 'We cannot go on working like this!'

[158] Art. 2 Enlargement Protocol.

[159] *Ibid.*, Art. 3. The heart of this provision was the definition of what constitutes a qualified majority in the Council, and involved a reweighing of the votes of the Member States.

[160] *Ibid.*, Art. 4. The core of the provision was formed by two rules. Para. 1 reduced the number of Commissioners to 'one national of each of the Member States'. However, para. 2 qualified this, when the Union would reach 27 Member States: 'The number of Members of the Commission shall be less than the number of Member States. The Members of the Commission shall be chosen according to a rotation system based on the principle

With regard to the Court of Justice, the Nice Treaty also effected some changes in the EC Treaty as well as in the Protocol on the Statute of the European Court of Justice. But, importantly, the Court's jurisdiction would not be widened significantly. Finally, while a 'Charter of Fundamental Rights of the European Union' had been proclaimed at Nice,[161] its status would remain that of a *non-*binding instrument *outside* the European Union.

The Nice Treaty was self-conscious about its minor achievements. While they opened the way for Eastern enlargement, the 'comprehensive review' mandate had not been fulfilled. For that reason, the Member States added the Nice 'Declaration on the Future of the Union' that called for 'a deeper and wider debate about the future of the European Union'. Setting itself the deadline of its 2001 Laeken meeting, the European Council committed itself to 'a declaration containing appropriate initiatives for the continuation of this process'.[162] This process should address the following questions:

> – how to establish and monitor a more precise delimitation of powers between the European Union and the Member States, reflecting the principle of subsidiarity;
> – the status of the Charter of Fundamental Rights of the European Union, proclaimed in Nice, in accordance with the conclusions of the European Council in Cologne;
> – a simplification of the Treaties with a view to making them clearer and better understood without changing their meaning;
> – the role of national parliaments in the European architecture.[163]

The Nice Treaty indeed envisaged yet another intergovernmental conference to amend the Treaties, reflecting 'the need to improve and to monitor the democratic legitimacy and transparency of the Union and its institutions, in order to bring them closer to the citizens of the Member States'.[164] The Lisbon Treaty – eventually – fulfilled the mandate for a comprehensive reform.

4. From Nice to Lisbon: The (New) European Union

Whereas the 1957 Rome Treaty was praised for 'its sober and precise legal wording',[165] every Treaty amendment since the Single European Act has been

---

of equality, the implementing arrangements for which shall be adopted by the Council, acting unanimously.'

[161] The Charter had been drafted by a special 'Convention' *outside* the Nice Intergovernmental Conference. On the drafting process, see G. de Búrca, 'The Drafting of the European Union Charter of Fundamental Rights' (2001) 26 *EL Rev.* 126.

[162] See Declaration No. 23 on the Future of the Union, para. 3.

[163] *Ibid.*, para. 5.   [164] *Ibid.*, para. 6.

[165] P. Pescatore, 'Some Critical Remarks on the "Single European Act"' (1987) 24 *CML Rev.* 9, 15.

criticised for the 'pragmatic' distortions introduced into the constitutional order of the European Community.[166] And while each political compromise admittedly advanced European integration, two decades of legal pragmatism had turned Europe's constitution into an 'accumulation of texts, breeding ever deepening intransparency'.[167] The European Treaties had become constitutional law full of historical experience – but without much legal logic.

This gloomy background provided the impulse for a major constitutional reform of the Union in the first decade of the twenty-first century. In the wake of the Nice Treaty's Declaration on the Future of the Union, the European Council convened in Laeken to issue a declaration on the Future of the European Union.[168] Among the four desirable aims, the Laeken Declaration identified the need for '[a] better division and definition of competence in the European Union', a '[s]implification of the Union's instruments', '[m]ore democracy, transparency and efficiency in the European Union' and a move '[t]owards a Constitution for European citizens'.[169]

How was this to be achieved? To pave the way for a *major* Treaty reform, the European Council decided to convene a Convention on the Future of Europe. The Convention was tasked 'to consider the key issues arising for the Union's future development and try to identify the various possible responses'. For that purpose, it was asked to 'draw up a final document', which would evolve into the 2004 Constitutional Treaty. Yet the Constitutional Treaty would never enter into force. It failed to win the ratification battles in France and the Netherlands. Despite this failure, many of its provisions have nonetheless survived into the Reform Treaty concluded at Lisbon.

---

[166] The Single European Act was famously criticised by Pescatore (*ibid.*, at 15). The eminent former judge confessed: 'I am among those who think that forgetting about the Single Act would be a lesser evil for our common future than ratification of this diplomatic document.' This document was described as 'a flood of verbose vagueness'. The Treaty on European Union found a memorable criticism in D. Curtin's phrase of the 'Europe of bits and pieces'. The Maastricht Treaty amendments were said to have 'no overriding and consistent constitutional philosophy behind the proposed reforms'. On the contrary, the European legal order was 'tinkered with in an arbitrary and *ad hoc* fashion by the intergovernmental negotiators in a manner which defied, in many respects, its underlying *constitutional* character' (see 'The Constitutional Structure of the Union: A Europe of Bits and Pieces' (1993) 30 *CML Rev.* 17, 17–18). For the Amsterdam Treaty it was said that 'the devil is not in the detail': 'The problem lies in the accumulation of texts, breeding ever deepening intransparency. Change which is not intelligible is likely to cause alienation' (see S. Weatherill, 'Flexibility or Fragmentation: Trends in European Integration', in J. Usher (ed.), *The State of the European Union* (Longman, 2000), 18). Finally, the Nice Treaty again encountered the strong voice of P. Pescatore, who raised the 'criticism of amateurishness' of the 'legal *bricolage* in the Nice documents' which constitute 'a patchwork of incoherent additions to the provisions of the EU and EC Treaties' (Guest Editorial, 'Nice – The Aftermath' (2001) 38 *CML Rev.* 265).

[167] Weatherill, 'Flexibility or Fragmentation' (n. 166 above), 8.

[168] Laeken Declaration of 15 December 2001 on the Future of the European Union.

[169] *Ibid.*

The Lisbon Treaty, while formally an amending Treaty, differs significantly from its predecessors. In substance, it is the – mildly moderated – 2004 Constitutional Treaty. And, while the Lisbon Treaty did not formally place the European Union onto a new constitutional foundation, its opening provisions already announced a dramatic constitutional decision: 'The Union shall replace and succeed the European Community'.[170] Was this the end of the pillar structure? Did the establishment of the 'new' European Union dissolve the 'old' European Union? And what were the institutional and constitutional changes brought about by the Lisbon Treaty? Before answering these questions, we need first to look at the (failed) Constitutional Treaty.

a. The (Failed) Constitutional Treaty: Formal 'Total Revision'

The Laeken European Council had charged a 'European Convention' with the task of identifying reform avenues for the future development of the Union.[171] The Convention would be chaired by a former French President, Valéry Giscard d'Estaing. It was to be composed of representatives from the Member States and the European institutions,[172] and led by a 'Praesidium'.[173] To facilitate its task, the convention organised a number of 'Working Groups',[174] which would prepare the intellectual ground for the plenary debate. The Convention eventually produced a *Draft* Constitutional Treaty, which was presented to the European Council in 2003. The subsequent Intergovernmental Conference made significant changes to the Draft Treaty,[175] and agreed on a final version in 2004.

---

[170] Art. 1(2)(b) Lisbon Treaty.

[171] On the work of the Convention and the 'accidental' creation of the Constitutional Treaty, see P. Norman, *The Accidental Constitution: The Making of Europe's Constitutional Treaty* (EuroComment, 2003).

[172] In addition to the Chairman (V. Giscard d'Estaing) and two Vice-Chairmen (G. Amato and J. L. Dehaene), the Convention was composed of 15 representatives from the national governments (one per State), 30 delegates from national parliaments (two per State), 16 members of the European Parliament and two Commission representatives. The (future) accession countries were represented in the same way as the Member States 'without, however, being able to prevent any consensus which may emerge among the Member States' (see Laeken Declaration, n. 168 above).

[173] The Praesidium was composed of the Chairman and the Vice-Chairmen, three government representatives, two national parliament representatives, two European Parliament representatives and two Commission representatives.

[174] The Convention established 11 'Working Groups': (I) 'Subsidiarity', (II) 'Charter/ECHR', (III) 'Legal Personality', (IV) 'National Parliaments', (V) 'Complementary Competences', (VI) 'Economic Governance', (VII) 'External Action', (VIII) 'Defence', (IX) 'Simplification', (X) 'Freedom, Security and Justice' and (XI) 'Social Europe'. For the working documents and final reports of the Convention Working Groups, see http://european-convention.eu.int/doc_wg.asp?lang=EN.

[175] On these changes, see P. Craig, *The Lisbon Treaty: Law, Politics, and Treaty Reform* (Oxford University Press, 2010), 16–20.

What was the constitutional structure of the (new) European Union? The 2004 Constitutional Treaty (CT) repealed all previous treaties,[176] and merged the pillar structure of the 'old' European Union to form a 'new' European Union.[177] The CT thus created *one* Union, with *one* legal personality, on the basis of *one* Treaty. The CT was thereby divided into four parts. Part I defined the values and objectives, competences and institutions, as well as instruments and procedures of the Union. Part II incorporated the Charter of Fundamental Rights into the Treaty. Part III spelled out the details of the various internal and external policies of the Union; and this included the former Second and Third Pillar policies of the 'old' Union. Finally, Part IV contained some general and final provisions.

The CT would, as an international treaty, need to be ratified by the Member States. Many of these States decided – in light of the 'constitutional' nature of the new Treaty – to submit their ratification to a referendum. This (national) constitutional choice was to provide direct democratic legitimacy to the European Union.[178] Yet, the strategy led to failure. The peoples of France and the Netherlands rejected the Constitutional Treaty in 2005. After the negative referenda, the Constitutional Treaty was put into a coma from which it was not to reawaken. Yet after a reflection period, the European Council agreed that 'after two years of uncertainty over the Union's treaty reform process, the time ha[d] come to resolve the issue and for the Union to move on'.[179] To this end, it called for an Intergovernmental Conference with the following mandate:

> The IGC is asked to draw up a Treaty (hereinafter called the 'Reform Treaty') amending the existing Treaties with a view to enhancing the efficiency and democratic legitimacy of the enlarged Union, as well as the coherence of its external action. The constitutional concept, which consisted in repealing all existing Treaties and replacing them by a single text called 'Constitution', is abandoned. The Reform Treaty will introduce into the existing Treaties, which remain in force, the innovations resulting from the 2004 IGC, as set out below in a detailed fashion.
>
> The Reform Treaty will contain two substantive clauses amending respectively the Treaty on the European Union (TEU) and the Treaty establishing the European Community (TEC). The TEU will keep its present name and the TEC will be called Treaty on the Functioning of the Union, the Union having a single legal personality.

---

[176] Art. IV-437 CT. This would have simplified matters significantly. In the words of J.-C. Piris, *The Lisbon Treaty: A Legal and Political Analysis* (Cambridge University Press, 2010), 20: 'Up until 2004, the original 1957 Treaties had been amended and complemented fifteen times. As a result, there were about 2,800 pages of primary law contained in seventeen Treaties or Acts[.]'

[177] Art. IV-438(1) CT: 'The European Union established by this Treaty shall be the successor to the European Union established by the Treaty on European Union and to the European Community.'

[178] Apart from two Member States that were constitutionally compelled to organise referenda (namely, Denmark and Ireland), seven additional Member States decided to go down the direct constitutional democracy road (i.e. France, Luxembourg, Poland, Portugal, Spain, the Netherlands, United Kingdom).

[179] European Council (Brussels, 21–22 June 2007), 'Presidency Conclusions' (2007) 3 *EU Bulletin* 1 at 8.

The word 'Community' will throughout be replaced by the word 'Union'; it will be stated that the two Treaties constitute the Treaties on which the Union is founded and that the Union replaces and succeeds the Community.[180]

The idea behind the mandate was simple. It consisted of abandoning the *form* of the CT,[181] while rescuing its *substance*.[182] The idea of a formal refounding of the European Union on the basis of a new Treaty was thus replaced with the idea of a substantive amendment of the existing Treaties. The CT had to drop its constitutional garb. In political terms, this window (un)dressing was necessary to justify a second attempt at Treaty reform. In legal terms, by contrast, 'none of the changes identified by the European Council were significant'.[183] Indeed, apart from some hasty and amateurish repackaging, the final 'Reform Treaty' would be 'the same in most important respects as the Constitutional Treaty'.[184]

The Reform Treaty was signed in December 2007 in Lisbon and was consequently baptised the 'Lisbon Treaty'. After ratification problems in Ireland,[185] Germany[186] and the Czech Republic,[187] the Lisbon Treaty entered into force in December 2009.

---

[180] CT, Annex I, paras. 1–2.

[181] This idea was spelled out in *ibid.*, para. 3: 'The TEU and the Treaty on the Functioning of the Union will not have a constitutional character. The terminology used throughout the Treaties will reflect this change: the term "Constitution" will not be used, the "Union Minister for Foreign Affairs" will be called High Representative of the Union for Foreign Affairs and Security Policy and the denominations "law" and "framework law" will be abandoned, the existing denominations "regulations", "directives" and "decisions" being retained. Likewise, there will be no article in the amended Treaties mentioning the symbols of the EU such as the flag, the anthem or the motto. Concerning the primacy of EU law, the IGC will adopt a Declaration recalling the existing case law of the EU Court of Justice.'

[182] *Ibid.*, para. 4.

[183] Craig, *Lisbon Treaty* (n. 175 above), 23.

[184] *Ibid.*, 24. According to Craig, the Reform Treaty 'replicated 90 per cent of what had been in the Constitutional Treaty' (*ibid.*, 31). The repacking was a result of the (political) compromise of keeping the 2004 Constitutional Treaty substantially intact, while producing a new treaty that formally looked different. On this dilemma, see *ibid.*, 26: 'The drafters of the Lisbon Treaty were therefore caught in a dilemma: the natural desire to frame the revised TEU so as to embrace the EU's important constitutional principles had to be tempered by the political need to produce a document that did not simply replicate Part I of the Constitutional Treaty.'

[185] After a first referendum had failed, the European Council promised Ireland a number of concessions (see European Council (Brussels, 11–12 December 2008), 'Presidency Conclusions' (2008) 12 *EU Bulletin* 8). The most significant of these was the promise that 'a decision will be taken, in accordance with the necessary legal procedures, to the effect that the Commission shall continue to include one national of each Member State' (*ibid.*, para. 2).

[186] On the Lisbon Decision of the German Constitutional Court, see Chapter 4, section 2(c).

[187] In order to remove the last hurdle to ratification, the European Council had to promise the Czech Republic an amendment to Protocol No. 30 on the Application of the Charter of Fundamental Rights (see European Council (Brussels, 29–30 October 2009), 'Presidency

b. The Lisbon Treaty: Substantive 'Total Revision'

It had been 'a long road from Nice to Lisbon'.[188] After four years lost on the Constitutional Treaty and four more years of suspension, the Lisbon Treaty embodied the strong desire 'to complete the process started by the Treaty of Amsterdam and by the Treaty of Nice with a view to enhancing the efficiency and democratic legitimacy of the Union and to improving the coherence of its action'.[189]

The Lisbon Treaty had reverted to the amendment technique. Instead of a formal 'total revision', it chose to build on the *acquis constitutionnel* created by the Rome Treaty establishing the European Community and the (Maastricht) Treaty establishing the European Union. But while the Lisbon Treaty merged both into a 'new' European Union, it retained a *dual* treaty base (Figure 1.3). This was – presumably – to underline its (formal) difference from the 2004 Constitutional Treaty. But, importantly, the dual treaty base no longer distinguished between a *Community* Treaty and a *Union* Treaty, as the new Union would be a single organisation. Substantively, *both* Treaties concern the European Union.

The division into two European Treaties follows a functional criterion. While the (new) Treaty on European Union contains the *general* provisions defining the Union, the Treaty on the Functioning of the European Union spells out specific provisions with regard to the Union institutions and policies. The structure of the Treaties is shown in Table 1.1.

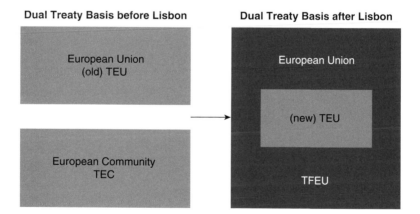

Figure 1.3 Dual Treaty Basis before and after Lisbon

Conclusions' (http://european-council.europa.eu/council-meetings/conclusions.aspx)). However, the current Czech government has opted out of this opt-out option.
[188] Craig, *Lisbon Treaty* (n. 175 above), 1.
[189] Lisbon Treaty – preamble 1.

Table 1.1 Structure of the TEU and TFEU

European Union		
EU Treaty	**FEU Treaty**	
Title I Common Provisions	Part I Principles	
Title II Democratic Principles	Part II Citizenship (Non-discrimination)	
Title III Institutions	Part III Union (Internal) Policies	
Title IV Enhanced Cooperation	Part IV Overseas Associations	
Title V External Action, and CFSP	Part V External Action	
Title VI Final Provisions	Part VI Institutions & Finances	
	Part VII General & Final Provisions	
Charter of Fundamental Rights		
Protocols (37)★		
Declarations (65)★★		

★According to Article 51 (new) TEU: 'The Protocols and Annexes to the Treaties shall form an integral part thereof.' And the best way to make sense of a Protocol is to see it as a legally binding 'footnote' to a particular provision of the Treaties.
★★Declarations are *not* an integral part of the Treaties, and are *not* legally binding. They only clarify the 'context' of a particular provision and, as such, may offer an interpretative aid.

This dual structure was shaped by the attempt of the Member States formally to 'repackage' the substance of the Constitutional Treaty. This 'restructuring' has led to a number of systemic inconsistencies. First, the institutional provisions are split over the two Treaties. Thus, Parts I and II as well as sections of Parts VI and VII of the TFEU should have been placed in the TEU. Second, because the Member States wished to underline the special status of the CFSP, this policy was not placed in Part V of the TFEU but instead inserted, as a separate title, into the TEU. This constitutional splitting of the Union's external relations provisions is unfortunate, and – oddity of oddities – places a single policy outside the TFEU. Third, instead of being an integral part of the TEU, the Charter of Fundamental Rights remains 'external' to the Treaties, while being recognised to 'have the same legal value as the Treaties'.[190]

Nonetheless, despite its choice for a dual treaty base, the Lisbon Treaty also contains elements that underline the 'unity' of the Treaty structure. First, both Treaties expressly confirm that they have the *same* legal value.[191] Second, the Protocols are attached to *both* Treaties – a break with a traditional constitutional

---

[190] Art. 6(1) (new) TEU.   [191] See Art. 1 TEU and Art. 1 TFEU.

technique. But, most importantly, the new European Union, while having two Treaties, has one single legal personality.[192]

What are the principal institutional and substantive changes brought about by the Lisbon Treaty? In line with the Laeken Declaration, the 2004 Constitutional Treaty and the 2007 Lisbon Treaty aimed at a better division and definition of Union competences. For that purpose, the TFEU contains a new title on 'categories and areas of Union competence'.[193] However, as a critical review of the title shows,[194] this reform objective has not been achieved. This negative outcome is however partly compensated for by the positive results with regard to the remaining three reform objectives. The Lisbon Treaty has satisfactorily simplified the Union instruments and lawmaking procedures. It has indeed abolished the 'old' Union instruments, such as 'common positions'; and it eliminated the 'cooperation' procedure that had existed since the Single European Act.

What about the third Laeken mandate, that is: '[m]ore democracy, transparency and efficiency in the European Union'? The Lisbon Treaty represents a dramatic step towards political union. The (new) Treaty on European Union now contains a separate title on 'democratic principles'.[195] The central provision here is Article 10 TEU, according to which '[t]he functioning of the Union shall be founded on representative democracy'.[196] Democratic representation is offered directly and indirectly. European citizens are 'directly represented at Union level in the European Parliament';[197] whereas they are indirectly represented through their Member States in the (European) Council.[198] This *dual* democratic legitimacy of the Union corresponds to its *federal* nature.[199] The Lisbon Treaty thereby enhances the direct representation of European citizens by significantly widening the powers of the European Parliament. Not only has 'co-decision' become the 'ordinary legislative procedure',[200] Parliament's decision-making powers with regard to executive, external and budgetary powers have also been significantly increased.[201]

Finally, what about the move '[t]owards a Constitution for European citizens'? The (Maastricht) European Union and the (Rome) European Community have now been merged into the (Lisbon) European Union. And, while the Union is still not formally based on a single Treaty, the Lisbon Treaty has successfully abolished the pillars of the (Maastricht) Union. The former 'Second Pillar' of the CFSP has been integrated into the (new) TEU. And, in its substance, the CFSP has been strengthened with regard to the Union's defence

---

[192] Art. 47 (new) TEU.   [193] Title I of Part I (Arts. 2–6) TFEU.

[194] R. Schütze, 'Lisbon and the Federal Order of Competences: A Prospective Analysis' (2008) 33 *EL Rev.* 709.

[195] See Title II of the (new) TEU.   [196] *Ibid.*, Art. 10(1).

[197] *Ibid.*, Art. 10(2).   [198] *Ibid.*, Art. 10(3).

[199] On this federal understanding, see Chapter 2, section 3.

[200] Art. 289 TFEU.

[201] For an analysis of these various powers, see Chapter 5, section 2(d).

policy.[202] (The strengthened role of a European defence policy induced the WEU to dissolve.)[203] With regard to the Third Pillar, the Lisbon Treaty transferred PJCC to the former First Pillar. The (Amsterdam) Third Pillar is thus 'reunited' with the rest of the original (Maastricht) pillar on Justice and Home Affairs, and both are now under the supranational roof of Title V of Part Three of the TFEU.[204]

Conclusion

In the first 60 years of its history, the European Union has evolved from a humble Community on coal and steel to a mature Union that is involved in almost all areas of modern life. The Union has, however, not only widened its jurisdictional and geographic scope, it has considerably deepened its supranational character – in relation to *both* normative *and* decisional supranationalism.[205]

This chapter has looked at four historical periods in the Union's evolution. The first two periods alone covered 40 years, and this is no accident, since the last 20 years have been a period of accelerated constitutional change. Treaty amendment followed Treaty amendment! The Lisbon Treaty is the last chapter in this constitutional chain novel. However, as section 4 has tried to show, it is a decisive chapter that has – if not in form, then in substance – reconstituted the European Union. This 'new' European Union differs in significant respects from the 'old' European Union founded by the Maastricht Treaty. Not only has the pillar structure disappeared, the Union's institutions as well as its powers and procedures have considerably changed. The European Union of today constitutes

---

[202] Art. 42(2) (new) TEU: 'The common security and defence policy shall include the progressive framing of a common Union defence policy. This will lead to a common defence, when the European Council, acting unanimously, so decides.' See also Art. 42(7) (new) TEU: 'If a Member State is the victim of armed aggression on its territory, the other Member States shall have towards it an obligation of aid and assistance by all the means in their power, in accordance with Article 51 of the United Nations Charter.'

[203] Statement of the Presidency of the Permanent Council of the WEU on behalf of the High Contracting Parties to the Modified Brussels Treaty – Belgium, France, Germany, Greece, Italy, Luxembourg, the Netherlands, Portugal, Spain and the United Kingdom (Brussels, 31 March 2010): 'The WEU has therefore accomplished its historical role. In this light we the States Parties to the Modified Brussels Treaty have collectively decided to terminate the Treaty, thereby effectively closing the organization, and in line with its article XII will notify the Treaty's depositary in accordance with national procedures.'

[204] This supranational roof came at the price of some intergovernmental characteristics, transitional provisions (see Title VII of Protocol No. 36 on Transitional Provisions), and 'differential integration' (see Protocol No. 21 On the Position of the United Kingdom and Ireland in respect of the Area of Freedom, Security and Justice). On the – complex – status of this policy area, see S. Peers, 'Mission Accomplished? EU Justice and Home Affairs Law after the Treaty of Lisbon' (2011) 48 *CML Rev.* 661.

[205] Contra J. Weiler, 'The Community System: The Dual Character of Supranationalism' (1981) 1 *YEL* 267. The Weiler thesis was already hard to defend before the Single European Act, but thereafter – and especially after the Maastricht Treaty – it became untenable.

a fairly 'compact' constitutional object. The sole satellite that still orbits around it is the European Atomic Energy Community;[206] and it is hoped that the Member States will – sooner rather than later – integrate that Community into the European Union.

The Lisbon Treaty will not be the last chapter of the European Union. The evolution of the European Union will of course continue. Constitutional change will need to follow social change. The Union must recognise this; or else it will be punished by life. What is remarkable, however, is that the method of constitutional change has itself changed over time. While at first organised by means of the Union's general competences,[207] formal Treaty amendment has become the preferred route after the Single European Act. The procedural hurdles for this are comparatively high,[208] but the Lisbon Treaty has tried to make that task a little easier. The Union legal order now recognises in Article 48 TEU two 'simplified revision procedures' in addition to the 'ordinary revision procedure'.[209] The ordinary revision here continues to require, after a complex preparatory stage,[210] the ratification of Treaty amendments 'by all the Member States in accordance with their respective constitutional requirements'.[211] The insistence on the express consent of all national parliaments or – where a referendum is constitutionally required – the national peoples will make this a steep route towards constitutional change.[212]

The two simplified revision procedures try to provide for an easier passage. But the first simplified procedure under Article 48(6) TEU hardly makes matters much simpler.[213] Although it leaves the decision to amend

---

[206] The Convention Working Group on 'Legal Personality' had generally argued in favour of merging Euratom into the new European Union (Final Report, CONV 305/02, 5); yet a minority in the Working Group had felt that the integration of Euratom was 'not absolutely essential given the specific nature of that Treaty' (*ibid.*, 3), while noting that the treaty-making powers of the Commission within the sectoral Community may justify institutional separation. This minority view was sadly followed.

[207] See R. Schütze, 'Organized Change towards an "Ever Closer Union": Art. 308 EC and the Limits to the Community's Legislative Competence' (2003) 22 *YEL* 79.

[208] See B. de Witte, 'Rules of Change in International Law: How Special Is the European Community?' (1994) 25 *Netherlands Yearbook of International Law* 299.

[209] Art. 48 (new) TEU. For an excellent overview of the new Treaty amendment rules, see S. Peers, 'The Future of EU Treaty Amendments' (2012) 31 *YEL* 17.

[210] This process may, or may not, involve the calling of a 'Convention'– depending on the extent of the proposed Treaty amendments, see Art. 48(3) (new) TEU, and will be followed by an intergovernmental conference.

[211] Art. 48(4) (new) TEU.

[212] The Lisbon Treaty did not replace the unanimity requirement by a qualified majority requirement. It only committed itself to a procedural obligation to 'rethink' Treaty amendments, where 'four fifths of the Member States have ratified it and one or more Member States have encountered difficulties in proceeding with ratification' (*ibid.*, para. 5).

[213] *Ibid.*, para. 6. The paragraph was used by the European Council for the first time in 2011 (see European Council Decision 2011/199 amending Art. 136 TFEU with regard to a stability mechanism for Member States whose currency is the euro ([2011] OJ L 91/1)).

Part III of the TFEU to the European Council, the amendment will only enter into force when approved by all the Member States 'in accordance with their respective constitutional requirements'. By contrast, the second simplified procedure allows the European Union – for a very small part of primary law[214] – to change its constitutional Treaties if backed up by the *tacit* consent of national *parliaments*.[215] This route allows for constitutional change through parliamentary *inaction*; and it textually appears to expressly exclude national referenda. This should indeed make future constitutional change easier and facilitates the constitutional capacity of the Union to adapt to social change.

FURTHER READING

Books

M. Andenas and J. Usher, *The Treaty of Nice and Beyond: Enlargement and Constitutional Reform* (Hart, 2003)

P. Craig, *The Lisbon Treaty: Law, Politics, and Treaty Reform* (Oxford University Press, 2010)

P. D. Dinan, *Europe Recast: A History of European Union* (Palgrave, 2004)

J. Gillingham, *European Integration, 1950–2003: Superstate or New Market Economy?* (Cambridge University Press, 2007)

A. G. Harryvan and J. van der Harst (eds.), *Documents on European Union* (St Martin's Press, 1997)

A. Milward, *The European Rescue of the Nation-State* (Routledge, 2000)

A. Moravcsik, *The Choice for Europe: Social Purpose & State Power from Messina to Maastricht* (Routledge, 1998)

P. Norman, *The Accidental Constitution* (EuroComment, 2003)

D. O'Keeffe and P. Twomey (eds.), *Legal Issues of the Maastricht Treaty* (Wiley, 1994)

D. O'Keeffe and P. Twomey (eds.), *Legal Issues of the Amsterdam Treaty* (Hart, 1999)

J.-C. Piris, *The Lisbon Treaty: A Legal and Political Analysis* (Cambridge University Press, 2010)

D. Urwin, *The Community of Europe: A History of European Integration since 1945* (Longman, 1994)

---

[214] Art. 48(7) (new) TEU. The paragraph only applies in two situations. First, '[w]here the Treaty on the Functioning of the European Union or Title V of this Treaty provides for the Council to act by unanimity in a given area or case, the European Council may adopt a decision authorising the Council to act by a qualified majority in that area or in that case.' (This however excludes decisions with military or defence implications.) Second, '[w]here the Treaty on the Functioning of the European Union provides for legislative acts to be adopted by the Council in accordance with a special legislative procedure, the European Council may adopt a decision allowing for the adoption of such acts in accordance with the ordinary legislative procedure.' However, it is important to note that Art. 353 TFEU sets external limits to Art. 48(7) (new) TEU.

[215] Art. 48(7) (new) TEU third indent.

Articles (and Chapters)

G. Bebr, 'The European Coal and Steel Community: A Political and Legal Innovation' (1953–4) 63 *Yale LJ* 1

G. Bebr, 'The European Defence Community and the Western European Union: An Agonizing Dilemma' (1954–5) 7 *Stanford Law Review* 169

D. Curtin, 'The Constitutional Structure of the Union: A Europe of Bits and Pieces' (1993) 30 *CML Rev.* 17

R. Efron and A. S. Nanes, 'The Common Market and Euratom Treaties: Supranationality and the Integration of Europe' (1957) 6 ICLQ 670

S. Peers, 'The Future of EU Treaty Amendments' (2012) 31 YEL 17

P. Pescatore, 'Some Critical Remarks on the "Single European Act"' (1987) 24 *CML Rev.* 9

A. H. Robertson, 'The European Political Community' (1952) 29 *BYIL* 383

A. H. Robertson, 'Legal Problems of European Integration' (1957) 91 *Recueil des Cours de l'Académie de la Haye* 105

L. Van Middelaar, 'Spanning the River: The Constitutional Crisis of 1965–1966 as the Genesis of Europe's Political Order' (2008) 4 *European Constitutional Law Review* 98

J. Weiler, 'The Transformation of Europe' (1990–1) 100 *Yale LJ* 2403

Cases on the Website

Case 26/62, *Van Gend en Loos*; Case 6/64, *Costa v. ENEL*; Case 120/78, *Cassis de Dijon*

2

Constitutional Nature
A Federation of States

Contents

Introduction

What is the European Union? Having started as an international organisation in 1952, should it still be described as such? Or, should it be seen as a State-in-the-making? In light of the developments discussed in Chapter 1, the Union occupies a place somewhere in between an international organisation of sovereign states and a nation state. This 'middle ground' between international and national organisation is however hard to conceive in terms of classic international law. Since the rise of the modern State system in the eighteenth century, we think of political communities exclusively in terms of sovereign States. An entity formed by States is therefore either a new sovereign State – as when England and Scotland formed Great Britain; or it is an international organisation of sovereign States, and the law between these sovereign States – international law – cannot be 'real' law because a sovereign State ultimately cannot be legally 'bound'. All relations between sovereign States must be voluntary and, as such, 'beyond' any public legal force.[1]

From the very beginning, this traditional idea of State sovereignty blocked a proper understanding of the nature of the European Union. The latter was said to have been 'established on the most advanced frontiers of the [international] law of peaceful cooperation'; and its principles of solidarity and integration had even taken it 'to the boundaries of federalism'.[2] But was the Union inside those boundaries or outside them? And what does federalism here mean? In the absence of a federal theory beyond the State, European thought invented a new word – supranationalism – and proudly announced the European Union to be *sui generis*. The Union was declared 'incomparable'; and the belief that Europe was incomparable ushered in the dark ages of European constitutional theory.[3] The *sui generis* idea is not a theory, because it refuses to search for commonalities.[4]

If the European Union was assuredly not a Federal *State*, could it be described as a Federation of *States*? This is the sole question this chapter wishes to address. It presents two – opposing – 'federal' perspectives that have been competing with each other over the past 200 years. Section 1 begins by introducing the older US American tradition, which has historically understood a Union of States as a third form of organisation between international and national law. Section 2 moves to the newer German federal tradition. Insisting on the indivisibility of sovereignty, this second tradition has led to the conceptual polarisation described above: a 'Union of States' is here either an international organisation – like the United Nations – or a (federally organised) Nation State – like Germany.

Sections 3 and 4 apply both alternative – theories to the European Union. From the perspective of the classic US tradition, the European Union can be seen as a Federation of States, whereas the German tradition reduces it to a (special) international organisation. Which is the better theory here? If legal theories are meant to explain legal practice, we shall see below that the second theory – insisting on the idea of State sovereignty – runs into serious explanatory difficulties and should consequently be discarded. The European Union is thus best understood as a 'Federation of States'. But let us tread slowly and start with a brief introduction to the constitutional history of the United States.

---

[1] In this context, see the famous remarks by E. de Vattel, *The Law of Nations* (translated: J. Chitty) (Johnson & Co., 1883), xiii: 'It is essential to every civil society (civitati) that each member have resigned a part of his right to the body of the society, and that there exist in it an authority capable of commanding all the members, of giving them laws, and of compelling those who should refuse to obey. Nothing of this kind can be conceived or supposed to subsist between nations. Each sovereign state claims, and actually possesses an absolute independence on all the others.'

[2] P. Pescatore, 'International Law and Community Law: A Comparative Analysis' (1970) 7 *CML Rev.* 167 at 182.

[3] While the 'classics' of European law had actively searched for comparisons with international and national phenomena (see E. Haas, *The Uniting of Europe* (Stanford University Press, 1968)), the legal comparative approach fell, with some exceptions, into a medieval slumber in the course of the 1980s.

[4] K. Popper, *The Logic of Scientific Discovery* (Routledge, 2002).

1. The American Tradition: Federalism as (Inter)national Law

The US federal tradition emerges with the 1787 Constitution of the United States of America. Having realised the weaknesses of the older 1777 US Constitution, deliberations on a 'more perfect union' had begun at a Constitutional Convention meeting in Philadelphia; and the Convention had proposed a new 'consolidated' Union. The Philadelphia proposal however triggered a heated debate on the nature of the 1787 Union. Those advocating greater centralisation thereby styled themselves as 'federalists'; and the papers that defended the new constitutional structure would become known as *The Federalist*.[5] By contrast, those insisting on the 'international' nature of the United States became known as '*anti-federalists*'. They were opposed to the 1787 Constitution and complained that the Philadelphia Convention had betrayed its mandate to 'preserv[e] the [*international*] form, which regards the Union as a *confederacy* of sovereign states'; 'instead of which, [it had] framed a *national* government, which regards the Unions as a *consolidation* of the States'.[6]

The response to this accusation – offered by James Madison – was brilliant and novel. He claimed that the 1787 Constitution neither created an international organisation, nor a nation state. Instead, it created a third political form: a Federation of States that was 'in between' an international and a national structure.

a. Madisonian Federalism: Three Analytical Dimensions

The view that the Union was an object that shared international and national elements is immortalised in *The Federalist No. 39* – written by James Madison. This master of constitutional analysis here explored the nature of the Union's legal order. Refusing to concentrate on the metaphysics of sovereignty, Madison singled out three analytical dimensions which – for convenience – may be called: the foundational, the institutional and the functional dimension. The first relates to the origin and character of the 1787 Constitution; the second concerns the composition of its governmental institutions; while the third deals with the scope and nature of the federal government's powers.

As regards the *foundational* dimension, the 1787 Constitution was clearly an *international* act. What did this mean? It meant that the Constitution would need to be ratified 'by the people, not as individuals composing one entire nation, but as composing the distinct and independent States to which they respectively belong'. The '*unanimous* assent of the several States' that wished to become parties was required. The Constitution would thus result 'neither from the decision of a *majority* of the people of the Union, nor from that of a

---

[5] A. Hamilton, J. Madison and J. Jay, *The Federalist*, ed. T. Ball (Cambridge University Press, 2003).

[6] *Ibid.*, 184.

majority of the States'.[7] 'Each State, in ratifying the Constitution, is considered as a sovereign body, independent of all others, and only to be bound by its own voluntary act.' The 1787 Constitution would therefore 'be [an *international*], and not a *national* act'.[8]

However, the new legal order differed from a classic international organisation in an important respect. Although the latter is ordinarily ratified by the State *legislatures*, the proposed Constitution was to be validated by 'the assent and ratification of the several States, *derived from the supreme authority in each State, the authority of the people themselves*'.[9] Instead of the State *governments* – the delegates of the people – each State *people* itself would have to ratify the Constitution. This is the meaning behind the famous phrase: 'We, the people'. However, it was not the 'American people', but the people(s) of the several States that would ordain the 1787 Constitution.[10] The direct authority from the (State) people(s) would set the Constitution above the State *governments*. And, in having the peoples of each State ratify the Constitution, the 1787 document would be a 'constitutional' – and not a 'legislative' – treaty.

What authority could amend the new Constitution once it had been 'ordained'? The 1787 Constitution would not require unanimity for amendment. The new amendment procedure was set out in Article V of the 1787 Constitution.[11] The provision stipulated that each proposed amendment would

---

[7]   *Ibid.* To bring the point home, Madison continues (*ibid.*, 185): 'Were the people regarded in this transaction as forming one nation, the will of the majority of the whole people of the United States would bind the minority, in the same manner as the majority in each State must bind the minority; and the will of the majority must be determined either by a comparison of the individual votes, or by considering the will of the majority of the States as evidence of the will of a majority of the people of the United States. Neither of these rules have been adopted.'

[8]   *Ibid.*, 185.   [9] *Ibid.*, 184 (emphasis added).

[10]   The phrase 'We, the people of the United States' simply referred to the idea that the people(s) in the States – not the State legislatures – had ratified the Constitution. Thus, the preamble of the 1780 Massachusetts Constitution, to offer an illustration, read: 'We, therefore, the people of Massachusetts'. The original 1787 draft preamble indeed read: 'We, the people of the States of New Hampshire, Massachusetts, Rhode-Island and Providence Plantations, Connecticut, New-York, New-Jersey, Pennsylvania, Delaware, Maryland, Virginia, North-Carolina, South-Carolina, and Georgia, do ordain, declare and establish the following constitution for the government of ourselves and our posterity.' However, due to the uncertainty over which of the 13 States would succeed in the ratification (according to Art. VII of the Constitution-to-be only nine States were required for the document to enter into force), the enumeration of the individuals States was dropped by the 'Committee of Style' (see M. Farrand, *The Framing of the Constitution of the United States* (Yale University Press, 1913), 190–1).

[11]   Art. V reads: 'The Congress, whenever two thirds of both Houses shall deem it necessary, shall propose Amendments to this Constitution, or, on the Application of the Legislatures of two thirds of the several States, shall call a Convention for proposing Amendments, which, in either Case, shall be valid to all Intents and Purposes, as part of this Constitution, when ratified by the Legislatures of three fourths of the several States, or by Conventions in three fourths thereof, as the one or the other Mode of Ratification may be proposed by the Congress[.]

have to be ratified by three-quarters of the States – represented by a State convention or by its State legislature.[12] Once the Constitution would enter into force, the power of amending it was thus 'neither wholly *national* nor wholly [*international*]'.[13]

Having analysed the origin and nature of the 1787 Constitution, Madison then moved to the second aspect of the 1787 constitutional structure. In relation to the *institutional* dimension, the following picture emerged. The legislature of the new Union was composed of two branches. The House of Representatives was elected by all the people of America as individuals and therefore was the 'national' branch of the central government.[14] The Senate, on the other hand, would represent the States as 'political and coequal societies'.[15] And in respecting their sovereign equality, the Senate was viewed as an international organ. Every law required the concurrence of a majority of the people and a majority of the States. Overall, the structure of the central government thus had 'a mixed character, presenting at least as many [*international*] as *national* features'.[16]

Finally, *The Federalist* analysed a third dimension of the new constitutional order. In terms of substance, the powers of the central government showed both international and national characteristics. In relation to their *scope*, they were surely not national, since the idea of a national government implied competence

---

[12] The structure of the amendment power led Dicey to conclude that 'the legal sovereignty of the United States resides in the States' governments as forming one aggregate body represented by three-fourths of the several States at any time belonging to the Union' (A. V. Dicey, *Introduction to the Study of the Law of the Constitution* (Liberty Fund, 1982), 81).

[13] Madison, *The Federalist No. 39* (n. 5 above), 186–7: 'Were it wholly national, the supreme and ultimate authority would reside in the *majority* of the people of the Union; and this authority would be competent at all times, like that of a majority of every national society, to alter or abolish its established government. Were it wholly [international], on the other hand, the concurrence of each State in the Union would be essential to every alteration that would be binding on all.'

[14] The 'national' structure of the House of Representatives would not be immediately created by the 1787 Constitution. Art. I, Section 4 stated: 'The Times, Places and Manner of holding Elections for Senators and Representatives, shall be prescribed in each State by the Legislature thereof; but Congress may at any time make or alter such Regulations, except as to the Place of choosing Senators.' In the words of H. Wechsler (see 'The Political Safeguards of Federalism: The Role of States in the Composition and Selection of the National Government' [1954] 54 *Columbia Law Review* 543 at 546): 'Though the House was meant to be the "grand depository of the democratic principle of the government", as distinguished from the Senate's function as the forum of the states, the people to be represented with due reference to their respective numbers were the people of the states.' The first national electoral law for the House would only be adopted in 1842.

[15] Madison, *The Federalist No. 39* (n. 5 above), 185. In *The Federalist No. 62*, Madison adds (*ibid.*, 301): 'In this spirit it may be remarked, that the equal vote allowed to each State is at once a constitutional recognition of the portion of sovereignty remaining in the individual States, and an instrument for preserving that residuary sovereignty. So far the equality ought to be no less acceptable to the large than to the small States; since they are not less solicitous to guard, by every possible expedient, against an improper consolidation of the States into one simple republic.'

[16] Madison, *The Federalist No. 39* (n. 5 above), 185.

over all objects of government. Thus, 'the proposed government cannot be deemed a *national* one; since its jurisdiction extends to certain enumerated objects only, and leaves to the several States a residuary and inviolable sovereignty over all other objects'.[17] However, the *nature* of the powers of the central government was 'national' in character. For the distinction between an international organisation and a national government was that 'in the former the powers operate on the political bodies composing the [organisation], in their political capacities; in the latter, on the individual citizens composing the nation, in their individual capacities'.[18] The 1787 Constitution allowed the central government to operate directly on individuals and thus fell on the national side.

In light of these three constitutional dimensions (see Table 2.1), Madison concluded that the overall constitutional structure of the 1787 Constitution was 'in strictness, neither a national nor [an international] Constitution, *but a composition of both*'.[19] The central government was a 'mixed government' that stood on 'middle ground'.[20]

b. The 'Mixed Constitution' and the Sovereignty Question

It was this *mixed* format of the constitutional structure of the United States of America that would soon come to be identified with the federal principle. A famous account was thereby offered by Alexis de Tocqueville, who introduced the new 'American' ideas to a broader European audience.[21] His influential book on the nature of the American Union also described it as a 'middle ground' between an international league and a national government.

[17] *Ibid.*, 186. *The Federalist No. 45* could justly claim that '[t]he powers delegated by the proposed Constitution to the federal government, are few and defined', whereas '[t]hose which are to remain in the State governments are numerous and indefinite' (*ibid.*, 227).
[18] Madison, *The Federalist No. 39*, 185. In *The Federalist No. 15*, we hear Hamilton say (*ibid.*, 67): 'The great and radical vice in the construction of the existing Confederation is in the principle of LEGISLATION for STATES or GOVERNMENTS, in their CORPORATE or COLLECTIVE CAPACITIES, and as contradistinguished from the INDIVIDUALS of which they consist. Though this principle does not run through all the powers delegated to the Union, yet it pervades and governs those on which the efficacy of the rest depends.' And in the words of the same author in *The Federalist No. 16* (*ibid.*, 74): 'It must stand in need of no intermediate legislations; but must itself be empowered to employ the arm of the ordinary magistrate to execute its own resolutions. The majesty of the national authority must be manifested through the medium of the courts of justice.'
[19] Madison, *The Federalist No. 39*, 187.
[20] *The Federalist No. 40* – Title; and Letter of J. Madison to G. Washington of 16 April 1787: 'Conceiving that an individual independence of the States is utterly irreconcilable with their aggregate sovereignty; and that a consolidation of the whole into one simple republic would be as inexpedient as it is unattainable, I have sought for some middle ground, which may at once support a due supremacy of the national authority, and not exclude the local authorities wherever they can be subordinately useful.'
[21] A. de Tocqueville, *Democracy in America*, ed. P. Bradley, 2 vols. (Vintage, 1954), I.

Table 2.1 Overview of *Federalist No. 39*

	International	**Federal**	**National**
Foundational Dimension	A 'Treaty' is ratified by each individual State.	A 'Constitutional Treaty' is ratified by the State peoples.	A 'Constitution' is adopted by the people.
Institutional Dimension	Each State is equally represented in a 'Council'.	Each State is represented in a Council; and each citizen is represented in Parliament.	Each citizen is equally represented in Parliament.
Functional Dimension	Acts are externally binding 'on' States.	Acts are binding on States or on individuals.	Acts are binding on individuals.
	The organisation has only limited powers.	The Union has only limited powers.	A sovereign State has unlimited powers.

For Tocqueville, the mixed nature of the American Union was particularly reflected in the composition of the central legislator. The American Union was neither a pure international organisation, in which the States would have remained on a footing of perfect – sovereign – equality, nor was it a national government; for if 'the inhabitants of the United States were to be considered as belonging to one and the same nation, it would be natural that the majority of the citizens of the Union should make the law'. The 1787 Constitution had chosen a 'middle course', '*which brought together by force two systems theoretically irreconcilable*'.[22]

This middle ground had also been reached in relation to the powers of government: 'The sovereignty of the United States is shared between the Union and the States, while in France it is undivided and compact.' 'The Americans have a Federal and the French a national Government.'[23] In fact, the unique aim of the 1787 Constitution 'was to divide the sovereign authority into two parts': 'In the one they placed the control of all the general interests of the Union, in the other the control of the special interests of its component States.'[24] The cardinal quality of the Union's powers was their direct effect: like a State government, the Union government could act directly on individuals.

Sovereignty – while ultimately residing somewhere – was thus seen as delegated and divided between *two* levels of government. Each State had given up part of its sovereignty, while the national government remained 'incomplete'. And, because both governments enjoyed powers that were 'sovereign', the new federalism was identified with the idea that '[t]wo sovereignties are necessarily in presence of each other'.[25] Federalism implied *dual* government, *dual* sovereignty and also *dual* citizenship.

---

[22] *Ibid.*, 122–3 (emphasis added).   [23] *Ibid.*, 128.
[24] *Ibid.*, 151.   [25] *Ibid.*, 172.

2. The German Tradition: International versus National Law

A victim of the nineteenth century's obsession with sovereign States,[26] German constitutional thought came to reject the idea of a divided or dual sovereignty. Sovereignty was seen as indivisible: in a Union of States, it could either lie with the States, in which case the Union was an international organisation; or sovereignty would lie with the Union, in which case the Union was a 'State'. Within this German tradition, federalism came thus to refer to the constitutional devolution of power within a sovereign *nation*.[27] A federation was a Federal *State*; and this 'national' reduction of the federal principle censored the very idea of a 'Federation *of States*'. To better explain this perspective, this section starts with an analysis of the conceptual polarisation between (international) Confederation and (national) Federation. Thereafter, we shall look at two early critics of the German constitutional tradition.

a. Conceptual Polarisation: 'Confederation' versus 'Federation'

German constitutional thought, like much European constitutional thought, insists on the indivisibility of sovereignty.[28] This idea of sovereignty here comes to operate as a prism within a Union of States: either the States have not transferred their sovereignty and thus remained sovereign; or they had transferred their sovereignty in which case the Union was a − new − sovereign State. The result is a conceptual 'polarisation' expressed in a distinction between two 'absolute' categories: *either* a Union of States was a 'Confederation of *States*' *or* it was a 'Federal *State*'. *Tertium non datur*: any third possibility was excluded.[29]

---

[26] M. Koskenniemi, *From Apology to Utopia* (Cambridge University Press, 2005), ch. 4.

[27] In the nineteenth century, Germany and Switzerland were Europe's 'federal' entities. Austria and Belgium would be added in the twentieth century. On the constitutional history of German federal thought, see E. Deuerlein, *Föderalismus: Die historischen und philosophischen Grundlagen des föderativen Prinzips* (List, 1972). The following section concentrates on German constitutional history; because it is this understanding that today informs much constitutional thinking in the world. See D. J. Elazar, *Constitutionalizing Globalization: The Postmodern Revival of Confederal Arrangements* (Rowman & Littlefield, 1998), 39: 'Federation, indeed, is federalism applied to constitutionally defuse power within the political system of a single nation. Federation became synonymous with modern federalism because the modern epoch was the era of the nation-state when, in most of the modern world, the ideal was to establish a single centralized state with indivisible sovereignty to serve single nations or peoples.'

[28] One British, one French and one German 'representative' will suffice to support this point: see Dicey, *Introduction to the Study of the Law of the Constitution* (n. 12 above), 3: 'Parliament is, under the British Constitution, an absolutely sovereign legislature'; R. Carré de Malberg, *Contribution à la Théorie Générale de l'État*, ed. E. Maulin (Dalloz, 2003), 139–40: 'La souveraineté est entière ou elle cesse de se concevoir. Parler de souveraineté restreinte, relative ou divisée, c'est commettre une contradiction in adjecto … Il n'est donc pas possible d'admettre dans l'État fédéral un partage de la souveraineté'; and P. Laband, *Das Staatsrecht des Deutschen Reiches* (Scientia, 1964), 73: 'die Souveränität eine Eigenschaft absoluten Charakters ist, die keine Steigerung und keine Verminderung zuläßt'.

[29] The logical device is also known as the 'law of the excluded middle'.

How did German federal thought define a 'confederation' or 'international organisation'? An (international) Union of States was said to be formed on the basis of an ordinary international treaty. Because it was an international treaty, the States had retained sovereignty and, therewith, the right to nullification and secession:

> Nullification and secession, absolutely prohibited within a unitary or federal State, follow logically from the nature of the Confederation as a treaty creature. A sovereign State cannot be bound unconditionally and permanently ... The Confederation is a creature of international law. However, international law knows no other legal subjects than States. The Confederation is not a State and can, consequently, not constitute a subject of international law.[30]

Since the Confederation was not a legal subject, it could not be the author of legal obligations; and it thus followed that the Member States *themselves* were the authors of the Union's commands.[31] The Union was thus regarded as possessing no powers of its own. It only 'pooled' and exercised *State* power. From this international law perspective, a Confederation was not an autonomous 'entity', but a mere 'relation' between sovereign States.

How did German federal thought define the concept of the 'Federal State'? The Federal State was regarded as a *State*; and, as such, it was sovereign – even if national unification had remained 'incomplete'. Because the Federal State was as sovereign as a unitary State, constitutional differences between the two types of States were downplayed to superficial 'marks of sovereignty'. It indeed became the task of German scholarship to make the 'Federal State' look like its unitary sisters. This was achieved through ingenious feats of legal 'reasoning'.

A first argument asserted that when forming the Union, the States had lost all their sovereignty. They had been 're-established' as '*Member* States' *by the Federal Constitution*.[32] But if the criterion of sovereignty could no longer be employed as the emblem of statehood, what justified calling these federated units 'States'? The search for a criterion that distinguished 'Member *States*' from 'administrative units' led German constitutional thought to insist on the existence of *exclusive* legislative powers.[33]

Let us look at a second argument that was developed to downplay the constitutional differences between a Federal State and a unitary State. In a Federal State powers are divided between the Federal State and its Member States. But if the characteristic element of a Member *State* was the possession of exclusive legislative power, how could the Federal State be said to be sovereign? The

---

[30] G. Jellinek, *Die Lehre von den Staatenverbindungen*, ed. W. Pauly (Keip, 1996), 175 and 178 (translated: R. Schütze).

[31] *Ibid.*, 176.

[32] A. Hänel, *Deutsches Staatsrecht* (Duncker & Humblot, 1892), 802–3.

[33] Jellinek, *Die Lehre von den Staatenverbindungen* (n. 30 above), 43–4.

German answer to this question was that all powers were ultimately derived from the Federal State, since it enjoyed 'competence-competence' (*Kompetenz-Kompetenz*).[34] This idea translated the unitary concept of sovereignty into a federal context: 'Whatever the actual distribution of competences, the Federal State retains its character as a sovereign State; and, as such, it potentially contains within itself all sovereign powers, even those whose autonomous exercise has been delegated to the Member States.'[35]

If the Federal State is sovereign, it must be empowered to *unilaterally* amend its constitution. '[T]he power to change its constitution follows from the very concept of the sovereign State.' 'A State, whose existence depends on the good will of its members, is not sovereign; for sovereignty means independence.'[36] The Federal State was, consequently, deemed to be empowered to 'nationalise' competences that were exclusively reserved to the Member States under the federal Constitution – even against the will of the federated States:

> The existence of the Member States in the Union is, as such, no absolute barrier to the federal will. Indeed, the option to transform the Member States into mere administrative units reveals, in the purest way, the sovereign nature of the Federal State … The negation of this legal option to transform the Federal State into a unitary State by means of constitutional amendment entails with it the negation of the sovereign and, therefore, state character of the Federal State.[37]

In the final analysis, the German tradition thus ultimately equates the Federal State with a constitutionally decentralised nation State.[38] Instead of the tripartite Madisonian classification, German thinking could only distinguish between two categories: an international organisation (confederation) or a nation state (federation) The difference between the two traditions can be seen in Figure 2.1.

b. Early Criticism: The (Missing) Federal Genus

The conceptual polarisation of the federal principle into two specific manifestations – (international) confederation and (national) federation – would structure

[34] One of the best discussions of the concept of *Kompetenz-Kompetenz* can be found in Hänel, *Deutsches Staatsrecht* (n. 32 above), 771–806.
[35] Jellinek, *Die Lehre von den Staatenverbindungen* (n. 30 above), 290–1 (translated: R. Schütze).
[36] *Ibid.*, 295–6 (translated: R. Schütze).
[37] *Ibid.*, 304 and 306 (translated: R. Schütze). This has never been accepted by US constitutionalism, see *Texas v. White* (1868) 74 US 700 at 725: 'The Constitution, in all its provisions, looks to an indestructible Union composed of indestructible States.' The rejection of an omnipotent Federal State can now also be found in the modern German Constitution. According to its Art. 79(3), constitutional '[a]mendments to this Basic Law affecting the division of the Federation into Länder, their participation on principle in the legislative process … shall be inadmissible'.
[38] H. Triepel, *Unitarismus und Föderalismus im Deutschen Reiche* (Mohr, 1907), 81.

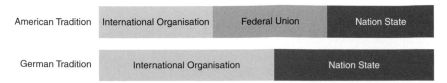

Figure 2.1 States Forming a Union

much of the twentieth century. And yet, there were two remarkable early critics of that tradition. They could not be more different as regards their legal and political outlook. Hans Kelsen *legally* approached the federal principle with the tools of his 'pure theory of law', while Carl Schmitt concentrated on the *political* nature of federal orders.[39]

In 1920, Kelsen torpedoed German federal thought in a path-breaking analysis of the principle of sovereignty and the nature of international law.[40] While remaining loyal to the idea of indivisible sovereignty,[41] Kelsen attacked the categorical distinction between confederation and Federal State. Legally, they had a similar structure. What distinguished the one from the other was only their degree of (de)centralisation. A Federal State was simply a more 'consolidated' or 'centralised' union than a confederation. One federal species would blend continuously into the other.[42]

What did this mean for the distinction between 'treaty' and 'constitution'? For Kelsen, 'treaty and constitution are not mutually exclusive concepts', since the content of a treaty may be a constitution. 'The Federal State may thus have a constitution and yet be founded on an international treaty as much as the confederation has its constitution that may also be created through a treaty.'[43] There was no objective or inherent distinction between 'treaty' and 'constitution' as regards their origin; what differed was the status given to them. Sovereignty lay in the eye of the beholder; and, for social communities, this was a question of social psychology.[44] The categorical distinction between 'treaty' and 'constitution', which was advocated by the German federal tradition, was based on a tautology:

> What matters is not, whether the treaty creates a legal order – every treaty does – but whether the legal order so created is considered as a partial legal order or as a total legal order. The decisive difference between the two lies in whether the juristic

---

[39] Neither of these two brilliant critiques of traditional German constitutional thought enjoyed much influence outside Germany after the Second World War. This is perhaps not surprising in the light of Schmitt's disgraceful post-Weimar biography. In Kelsen's case, the reason may lie in the lack of a translation of *Das Problem der Souveränität und die Theorie des Völkerrechts*.

[40] H. Kelsen, *Das Problem der Souveränität und die Theorie des Völkerrechts* (Mohr, 1920).

[41] *Ibid.*, 64–6.   [42] *Ibid.*, 195: 'eine Form kontinuierlich in die andere übergeht'.

[43] *Ibid.*

[44] This is, in my opinion, the very essence of Kelsen's theory of sovereignty and the 'basic' norm (*ibid.*, 15).

> construction of the binding force of the treaty … is considered to derive from a 'higher', that is a more general, legal order – in our case: from the legal norm 'pacta sunt servanda' of the international legal order; or, whether the juristic construction posits the legal order created by the treaty itself as the highest source. In the latter case, the binding force of the treaty order is derived from an 'originality hypothesis'. Thereby, one must not overlook that the treaty as such, that is, a meeting of wills, is never 'constitutive'. 'Constitutive', that is, the final source of legal validity and force, is in the former case the 'international law hypothesis', in other words, the idea that above the contracting parties stands a higher international legal order; and in the latter case the 'originality hypothesis'.
>
> When some refer to a treaty creating a Federal State as 'constitutive', this signifies nothing but a desire to dissociate the treaty from the international legal order – standing above all States and consequently also above the central legal order created by the Member States – by denying its foundational quality for the legal order of the Federal State. Better still, the hypothesis of the primacy of international law is rejected so as to posit the concrete treaty and the legal order it creates – a legal order, which from the perspective of international law, would only be a partial legal order – as sovereign, that is, as a State in the sense of the dominant sovereignty dogma. The primacy of this State legal order is thus presumed from the start[.][45]

This attack on the tautological nature of German federal thought was joined by a second – equally brilliant – critique: the federal theory of Carl Schmitt.[46] Schmitt agreed with Kelsen that the German debate had unduly concentrated on idealised differences between two *species* of the federal principle.[47] It had thereby forgotten to pay attention to the federal *genus* from which both species sprang. What were the *general* characteristics shared by the two *specific* manifestations of the federal principle? What had 'con*federation*' and '*Federal* State' in common? These questions centred on the 'federal' principle as such.

What, then, was federalism? A Federal Union was 'a permanent union based on a *voluntary* agreement whose object is the political preservation of its members'. The normative foundation for such a federal Union was a 'federal treaty'. The 'federal treaty' was a '*constitutional* treaty'. It was a treaty that 'changes the overall political status of each federated member in respect of this common aim'. A federal treaty was an international treaty of a constitutional nature.[48] 'Its conclusion is an act of the *pouvoir constituant*. Its content establishes the federal constitution and forms, at the same time, a *part of the constitution of every Member State*.'[49] The dual nature of each federation, standing on the middle ground

---

[45] H. Kelsen, *Allgemeine Staatslehre* (Springer, 1925), 197–8 (translated: R. Schütze).
[46] C. Schmitt, *Verfassungslehre* (Duncker & Humblot, 2003), Part IV: 'Verfassungslehre des Bundes', 361–91.
[47] *Ibid.*, 366.   [48] *Ibid.*, 367 and 368 (translated: R. Schütze):'zwischenstaatlicher Statusvertrag', 'Bundesvertrag' and 'Verfassungsvertrag'.
[49] *Ibid.*

between international and national order, was thus reflected in the dual nature of its foundational document. The 'federal treaty' stood in between an international treaty and a national constitution. Each federation was thus a creature of international *and* national law.[50]

What, then, distinguished a federation from an ordinary international organisation? Unlike an international league, every federal Union had 'a common will and, thus, its own *political* existence'.[51] What distinguished a federation from an ordinary State? Unlike a unitary State, the federation was characterised by a political *dualism*:

> In each federal union, two kinds of political bodies co-exist: the existence of the whole federal union and the individual existence of each federal member. Both kinds of political existence must remain coordinate in order for the federal union to remain alive.

Each federal Union thus permanently lives in an 'existential equilibrium'. 'Such an existential limbo will lead to many conflicts calling for decision.' Yet, for the political equilibrium to remain alive, the conflict over the locus of sovereignty must remain 'suspended'.[52] Where the sovereignty question is posed and – definitely – answered in favour of the Union, only it has political existence. The 'Union' is transformed into a sovereign State, whose legal structure may be federal but whose substance is not. Conversely, where the sovereignty question is posed and – definitely – answered in favour of the Member States, the political existence of the federation disappears and the Union dissolves into an international organisation.

What will this mean for the European Union? Let us now analyse the nature of that Union in light of the American and German traditions.

3. The European Union in Light of the American Tradition

The American tradition identified the 1787 United States with a 'mixed constitution' that lay between international and national organisation.

---

[50] *Ibid.*, 379: 'Jeder Bund ist als solcher sowohl völkerrechtliches wie staatsrechtliches Subjekt.'

[51] *Ibid.*, 371 (translated: R. Schütze, emphasis added). For Schmitt, the federation and its members are 'political' bodies. On Schmitt's definition of the 'political', see C. Schmitt, *Der Begriff des Politischen* (Duncker & Humblot, 1996).

[52] Schmitt, *Verfassungslehre* (n. 46 above), 376–8 (translated: R. Schütze). For that suspension to remain, a homogeneity of interests must be fostered. This had already been pointed out by de Tocqueville (n. 21 above), 175–6: 'Since legislators cannot prevent such dangerous collisions as occur between the two sovereignties which coexist in the Federal system, their first object must be, not only to dissuade the confederate States from warfare, but to encourage such dispositions as lead to peace.' 'A certain uniformity of civilization is not less necessary to the durability of a confederation than a uniformity of interests in the States which compose it.'

Within the classic period of European law, the European Union was also described as a hybrid that was placed 'between international and municipal law'.[53] 'The [Union] is a new structure in the marches between internal and international law.'[54] It 'is neither an international Confederation, nor a Federal State'. 'It simultaneously combines characteristics from both types of State relations and thus forms a *mixtum compositum*.'[55]

How did this mixed format express itself? What were its 'international' and 'national' features?[56] US constitutionalism offered a potent analytical approach to these questions. Refusing to concentrate on the metaphysics of sovereignty, three analytical dimensions had been singled out: the foundational, the institutional and the functional dimension. The first related to the origin and nature of the new legal order; the second concerned the composition of its 'government'; while the third dealt with the scope and nature of the federation's powers. This approach will now be applied to a legal analysis of the European Union.

a. Foundational Dimension: Europe's 'Constitutional Treaties'

The European Union was conceived as an international organisation. Its birth certificates are international treaties. Its formation had been 'international' – just like the American Union. However, unlike the American Union, the European Treaties were ratified by the national *legislatures* – not the national peoples – of its Member States. Genetically, they are therefore 'legislative' – not constitutional – treaties.[57]

---

[53] C. Sasse, 'The Common Market: Between International and Municipal Law' (1965–6) 75 *Yale LJ* 695; P. Hay, 'The Contribution of the European Communities to International Law' (1965) 59 *Proceedings of the American Society of International Law* 195 at 199: 'The contribution of the Communities for legal science is the breaking-up of the rigid dichotomy of national and international law.'

[54] E. Van Raalte, 'The Treaty Constituting the European Coal and Steel Community' (1952) 1 ICLQ 73 at 74.

[55] L.-J. Constantinesco, *Das Recht der Europäischen Gemeinschaften* (Nomos, 1977), 332 (translated: R. Schütze).

[56] In the following section, the terms 'international' and 'national' will be used as analytical terms. The former refers to a voluntary and horizontal structure recognising the sovereign equality of the States; the latter stands for the hierarchical and vertical structure within a unitary State. Even if the notion of 'unitary' is less charged with symbolic connotations than 'national', I shall use the latter term to facilitate a comparison with Madison's discussion of the mixed structure of the American Union.

[57] It is difficult – if not impossible – to accept that 'the founding treaties as well as each amendment agreed upon by the governments appear as the *direct expression* of the common will of the [national] peoples of the Union' (I. Pernice, 'Multilevel Constitutionalism and the Treaty of Amsterdam: European Constitution-making Revisited?' (1999) 36 *CML Rev.* 703 at 717 (emphasis added)). National ratifications are – with the exception of a few Member States – only indirect expressions of the common will of the national peoples of the Union. National consent is typically expressed through national legislatures. It is equally difficult to agree that these national ratifications should be regarded 'as a *common* exercise of constitution-making power by the peoples of the participating State' (*ibid.*, 717

Would this (legislative) 'treaty' origin rule out the idea of a European 'constitution'? This is not a matter of logical necessity. And, as soon as we accept that the status of a legal norm depends on the function a society gives it,[58] it is hard to deny that the European Treaties have been elevated to a constitutional status. They have evolved into a 'Treaty-Constitution'.[59] This emancipation has manifested itself in the following legal facts. First, in contrast to the normative regime governing international treaties, the European Court of Justice has insisted on the 'non-contractual' nature of European law: a Member State thus cannot invoke the breach of European law by another Member State to justify a derogation from its own obligations under the Treaties.[60]

Second, the European Court of Justice consolidated the direct applicability and supremacy of Union law over all national law.[61] This contrasts with classic international law, where the supremacy doctrine forms no part.[62] However, the absolute supremacy of European law has not been accepted by all Member States. In parallel with a *European* perspective, there coexists a *national* perspective on the supremacy issue.[63] But will the existence of a national perspective on the supremacy of European law not rule out the 'constitutional' or 'federal' character of the European Union? This is not the case. The ambivalence surrounding supremacy and sovereignty can be viewed as part and parcel of Europe's *federal* nature. The 'suspension' of the supremacy question in the European Union is the very proof of the *political* coexistence of *two* political bodies and thus evidence of Europe's living federalism.

Third, in establishing a direct link with individuals, Europe's constitutional order recognised from the very start an incipient form of European citizenship.[64] The latter was to be expressly acknowledged with the official introduction of a 'citizenship of the Union' in the Maastricht Treaty. According to Article 9 TEU '[e]very national of a Member State shall be a citizen of the Union'. And, in accordance with federal theory, every European will thus be a citizen of *two* political orders.

To conclude: in the eyes of the European Court of Justice and the majority of European scholars, the normative force of European law derives no longer from the normative foundations of international law. The ultimate normative base within Europe – its 'originality hypothesis' or '*Grundnorm*' – are the European

---

(emphasis added)). This theory does not explain how each unilateral national act ultimately transforms itself into a collective act.

[58] On this point, see the analysis by Kelsen, *Allgemeine Staatslehre* (n. 45 above).

[59] E. Stein uses the compound 'Treaty-Constitution' (see 'Toward Supremacy of Treaty-Constitution by Judicial Fiat: On the Margin of the Costa Case' (1964–5) 63 *Michigan Law Journal* 491).

[60] See Case 90–1/63, *Commission* v. *Luxembourg and Belgium* [1963] ECR 625.

[61] See Case 11/70, *Internationale Handelsgesellschaft mbH* v. *Einfuhr- und Vorratsstelle für Getreide und Futtermittel* [1970] ECR 1125.

[62] On this point, see Chapters 3 and 4.

[63] On this dual perspective on the supremacy question, see Chapter 4, sections 1 and 2.

[64] For the opposite view, see H. P. Ipsen, *Europäisches Gemeinschaftsrecht* (Mohr, 1972), 251.

Treaties as such. '[T]he E[U] Treaty, albeit concluded in the form of an international agreement, none the less constitutes the constitutional charter of a [Union] based on a rule of law[.]'[65]

But what about Treaty amendment? Treaty amendment continues to (ordinarily) require the ratification of all the Member States according to their respective national constitutional requirements.[66] Nevertheless: whereas the Member States − in the collective plural − remain the 'Masters of the Treaties', *individual* Member States have lost their 'competence-competence'. Legally, Member States are indeed no longer competent to determine *unilaterally* the limits of their own competences themselves.[67] And, as regards the right to withdrawal from the Union,[68] this is not an argument against the federal nature of the European *Union*, but merely an argument against the Union being a Federal *State*. For it is sovereign States that typically prohibit secession on the grounds that it violates their sovereign integrity.[69] By contrast, federal unions determine the beginning and end of membership by means of an international treaty with 'constitutional' effects.

b. Institutional Dimension: A European Union of States and People(s)

How are we to analyse the institutional dimension of the European Union? The Union's principal lawmaking organs today are the European Parliament and the Council. How should we characterise each of them alongside the international versus national spectrum? And what will it tell us about the nature of the European legislator?

The composition of the European Parliament has changed over time. Originally, it was an assembly of 'representatives of the *peoples of the States* brought together

---

[65] *Opinion 1/91* (EFTA) [1991] ECR I-6079, para. 21. See also, Case 294/83, *'Les Verts'* v. *Parliament* [1986] ECR 1339, para. 23: 'basic constitutional charter'.

[66] On the amendment provisions, see Chapter 1, Conclusion. The introduction of simplified revision procedures by the Lisbon Treaty has recently been associated with Union *Kompetenz-Kompetenz* (see G. Barrett, 'Creation's Final Laws: The Impact of the Treaty of Lisbon on the "Final Provisions" of the Earlier Treaties' (2008) 27 *YEL* 3 at 15: 'From the theoretical standpoint, all of these are of interest in that they confer a form of *Kompetenz-Kompetenz* on the European Union in that, for the first time they empower an institution of the Union itself − vis, the European Council − to amend the Treaties').

[67] A. von Bogdandy and J. Bast, 'The European Union's Vertical Order of Competences: The Current Law and Proposals for its Reform' (2002) 39 *CML Rev.* 227 at 237: '[T]he individual Member State has forfeited its right to determine its own competences (*Kompetenz-Kompetenz*) insofar as it is not permitted to extend its powers unilaterally to the detriment of the Union. While the Member States acting jointly as the Contracting Parties may amend the Treaties, transferring powers back to the Member States, they are bound by the procedures provided for in Article 48 TEU.'

[68] The right to withdrawal is now expressly enshrined in Art. 50(1) TEU: 'Any Member State may decide to withdraw from the Union in accordance with its own constitutional requirements.' For a long discussion of the provision in the context of Brexit, see Chapter 19.

[69] On secession in (inter)national law, see L. C. Buchheit, *Secession: The Legitimacy of Self-Determination* (Yale University Press, 1978).

in the Community'.[70] This designation was adequate as long as the Parliament consisted of 'delegates who shall be designated by the respective Parliaments from among their members in accordance with the procedure laid down by each Member State'.[71] However, the composition of the Parliament dramatically changed with the introduction of direct elections.[72] While there remain 'international' elements, its composition steadily evolved towards the 'national' pole. Today, the European Parliament *directly* represents – even if in a distorted way – a European people.[73] The Lisbon Treaty now expressly recognises this in Article 10(2) TEU: 'Citizens are directly represented at Union level in the European Parliament.' It is thus wrong to claim that the European Parliament represents the national *peoples* in their collective capacity. It represents a – constitutionally posited – European people. The Parliament's 'national' composition is reflected in its decision-making mode, which is majority voting.[74]

In terms of its composition, the Council is an 'international' organ. 'The Council shall consist of a representative of each Member State at ministerial level, who may commit the government of the Member State in question and cast its vote.'[75] Each national minister thus represents 'its' State government; and where decision-making is by unanimity, the sovereign equality of the Member States is respected. Yet, the European Treaties also envisage procedures that would break with the international idea of sovereign equality. From the very beginning, they permitted the Union to act by a (qualified) majority of States; and where a qualified majority sufficed, the Member States had weighed votes depending – roughly – on the size of their populations.[76] (Strictly speaking, the Council here does not represent the Member *States* – a notion that implies their *equality* – but it represents the national *peoples*.)[77] Formally, then, decision-making within the Council is neither completely international nor completely national, but a combination of both. It stands on federal middle ground.

The composition and operating mode of the European Parliament and the Council having been analysed, what – then – is the nature of the European legislator? According to the 'ordinary' legislative procedure, the Council decides

---

[70] Art. 137 EEC (emphasis added). France preferred this symbolic formulation. And to safeguard the indivisibility of the French Republic guaranteed under Art. 1 of the 1958 Constitution, the idea of a 'representative mandate' was also rejected by the Constitutional Council in its 1977 decision on the 1976 European Parliament Election Act (J. P. Jacqué, 'La Souveraineté française et l'élection du Parlement Européen au suffrage universel direct', in A. Bleckmann and G. Ress (eds.), *Souveränitätsverständnis in den Europäischen Gemeinschaften* (Nomos, 1980), 71).

[71] Art. 138 EEC.   [72] On this point, see Chapter 5, section 2(a).

[73] To this day, the European Treaties allocate a – neither equal nor proportional – number of parliamentary mandates to the Member States and there is still no uniform European electoral procedure. On the details, see *ibid*.

[74] Art. 231 TFEU: 'Save as otherwise provided in the Treaties, the European Parliament shall act by a majority of the votes cast.'

[75] Art. 16(2) TEU.   [76] On this point, see Chapter 5, section 4(c).

[77] For a similar conclusion albeit from a different perspective, see A. Peters, *Elemente einer Theorie der Verfassung Europas* (Duncker & Humblot, 2001), 563 and 566.

by a qualified majority and the European Parliament acts as 'co-legislator'.[78] The European legislator is here 'bicameral' and this constitutional structure 'reflects a subtle federal balance':

> Legislation comes into being through majority voting in the two houses of the legislature and only after the approval by both of them. One house represents the people in their capacity as citizens of the Union, the other house represents the component entities of the federation, the Member States, and – through them – the people in their capacity as citizens of the Member States.[79]

Europe's prevailing legislator is consequently a combination of 'national' and 'international' elements. While the Parliament represents a – constitutionally posited – European people, the Council represents the Member States and their peoples. This institutional arrangement reflects the *dual* basis of democratic legitimacy in the European Union.

c. Functional Dimension: The Division of Powers in Europe

What about the allocation of the functions of government? What kind of powers does the European Union enjoy? Within the internal sphere, Europe clearly enjoys significant legislative powers.[80] This is equally the case in the external sphere.[81] However, the European Union's powers remain enumerated powers. Its scope of government is 'incomplete'. The reach of Europe's powers is thus *not* 'national'– that is: sovereign – in scope.

But what is the nature of Europe's powers? When the European Union was born, the Treaties envisaged two instruments with direct effect on individuals. Regulations were to have direct and general application in all Member States.[82] Decisions allowed the Union to adopt directly applicable measures addressed to particular persons.[83] In making regulations and decisions directly applicable in domestic legal orders, the European Treaties thus recognised two 'national' instruments – one legislative, the other executive.

The European Union also possessed an 'international' instrument: the directive. In order to operate on individuals, the European command would need

---

[78] A. Dashwood, 'Community Legislative Procedures in the Era of the Treaty on European Union' (1994) 19 *EL Rev.* 343 at 362–3. 'The "product" of the procedure is an act adopted jointly by the European Parliament and the Council – in contrast to that of the consultation or cooperation-procedures, which is simply an act of the Council … the acts in question shall be signed by both the President of the European Parliament and the President of the Council, symbolising in the most concrete way possible the joint character of such acts.'

[79] K. Lenaerts, 'Federalism: Essential Concepts in Evolution – The Case of the European Union' (1998) 21 *Fordham International Law Journal* 746 at 763.

[80] On this point, see Chapter 7, section 1.   [81] On this point, see Chapter 8, section 1.

[82] See Art. 249(2) EC, and now: Art. 288(2) TFEU.

[83] See Art. 249(4) EC, and now: Art. 288(4) TFEU.

to be incorporated by the States. However, through a series of courageous rulings, the European Court of Justice partly transformed the directive's format by injecting 'national' elements. (As we shall see in Chapter 3, directives thus combine 'international' and 'national' features.[84] They are a form of 'incomplete legislation' and thus symbolically represent Europe's 'federal' middle ground.)

What about Europe's *executive* powers? While the Union had established its own enforcement machinery in some sectors, the direct administration of European legislation has remained an exception – even if Europe has enlarged its executive presence in recent years.[85] Indirect administration still characterises the Union legal order which continues to largely rely on its Member States to apply and implement European law.[86] The decentralised application of European law is effected through the supremacy principle: all organs of a Member State's administration – executive *and* judicial – must disapply conflicting national law in every individual case before them. Supremacy, in fact, primarily concerns the executive application of European law.[87] Unlike contemporary US federal doctrine,[88] European federalism even imposes a positive obligation on national administrations to implement European law. Thus, although national administrations are – from an institutional perspective – not integrated into the European administrative machinery, national administrations operate – from a functional perspective – as a decentralised European administration.

d. Overall Classification: The European Union on Federal 'Middle Ground'

In light of these three dimensions, how should we classify the European Union? Its formation was clearly international and its amendment still is. However, its international birth should not prejudge against the 'federal' or 'constitutional' status of the European Treaties. Was not the 1787 US *Federation* the result of an international act? And has not the 1949 German *Constitution* been ratified by the State legislatures?[89] The fact remains that the European legal order has adopted the 'originality hypothesis' and cut the umbilical cord with the international legal order. The Treaties *as such* – not international law – are posited at the origin of European law. Functionally, then, the European Union is based on a 'constitutional treaty' that stands on federal middle ground. The same conclusion was reached when analysing Europe's 'government'. The European Union's dominant legislative procedure strikes a federal balance between 'international'

---

[84] On the instrumental format of directives, see Chapter 3, section 3.

[85] On this point, see Chapter 9, sections 3 and 4.

[86] *Ibid.*   [87] On this point, see Chapter 4, section 1(b).

[88] On the 'no-commandeering rule' in US federalism, see D. Halberstam, 'Comparative Federalism and the Issue of Commandeering', in K. Nikolaidis and R. Howse (eds.), *The Federal Vision: Legitimacy and Levels of Governance in the United States and the European Union* (Oxford University Press, 2001), 213.

[89] Art. 144(1) of the German Constitution states: 'This Basic Law shall require ratification by the *parliaments* of two thirds of the German Länder in which it is initially to apply' (emphasis added).

and 'national' elements. And, while the scope of its powers is limited, the nature of the Union's powers is predominantly 'national'.

Overall, then, the legal structure of the European Union is 'in strictness, neither a national nor a[n] international Constitution, *but a composition of both*'.[90]

4. The European Union in Light of the German Tradition

European and especially German constitutionalism has historically insisted on the indivisibility of sovereignty. The *absolute* idea of sovereignty here operates as a prism that ignores all *relative* nuances within a mixed or dual legal structure. Where States form a union but retain their sovereignty, the object thereby created is an international organisation (confederation) regulated by international law. By contrast, where States transfer sovereignty to the centre, a new State emerges. Within this State – a Federal State if powers are territorially divided – the centre is solely sovereign and (potentially) omnicompetent.

What does this mean for an analysis of the legal nature of the European Union? When European thought began to apply its conceptual apparatus to the European Union, it noted that its theoretical categories could not explain the legal reality of European law. In the absence of a federal theory beyond the State, European thought invented a new word – supranationalism – and proudly announced the European Union to be *sui generis* (section (a)). In times of constitutional conflict, on the other hand, sovereignty thinking returned to the fore. The international law reading thereby received its classic expression in the debate surrounding the ratification of the Maastricht Treaty (section (b)).[91] The identification of the European Union with an international organisation led to three constitutional denials (section (c)): the European Union could have *no people, no constitution* and *no constitutionalism*.

a. *The* sui generis *'Theory': The 'Incomparable' European Union*

Europe's quest for a new word to describe the middle ground between international and national law would – at first – be answered by a novel concept: supranationalism. Europe was said to be a *sui generis* legal phenomenon. It was incomparable for 'it cannot be fitted into traditional categories of international or constitutional law'.[92]

---

[90] Hamilton, Madison and Jay, *The Federalist* (n. 5 above), 187.
[91] For this thesis, see D. Wyatt, 'New Legal Order, or Old' (1982) 7 *EL Rev.* 147; T. Schilling, 'The Autonomy of the Community Legal Order' (1996) 37 *Harvard International Law Journal* 389.
[92] H. L. Mason, *The European Coal and Steel Community: Experiment in Supranationalism* (Martinus Nijhoff, 1955), 126.

Was the European Union really a species without a genus? There are serious problems with the *sui generis* argument. First of all, it lacks analytical value since it is based on a conceptual tautology.[93] Worse, it 'not only fails to analyze but in fact asserts that no analysis is possible or worthwhile, it is in fact an "unsatisfying shrug"'.[94] Second, it only views the Union in *negative* terms − it is *neither* international organisation *nor* Federal State − and thus indirectly perpetuates the conceptual foundations of the European tradition.[95] And, in not providing any external standard, the *sui generis* formula cannot detect, let alone measure, the European Union's evolution. Thus, even where the European Community lost some of its 'supranational' features − as occurred in the transition from the ECSC to the E(E)C − *both* would be described as *sui generis*. But most important of all: the *sui generis* 'theory' is historically unfounded. All previously existing Unions of States lay between international and national law. More concretely, the power to adopt legislative norms binding on individuals − this acclaimed *sui generis* feature of Europe − cannot be the basis of its claim to specificity. The same lack of 'uniqueness' holds true for other normative or institutional features of the European Union.[96] And even if one sees Europe's *Sonderweg* − yet another way of celebrating the *sui generis* idea − in 'the combination of a "confederal" institutional arrangement and a "federal" legal arrangement',[97] this may not be too special after all.[98]

The *sui generis* 'theory' is indeed an introverted and unhistorical 'theory'. It poses − unsolvable − problems for an analysis of the political and constitutional *dualism* that characterises the European Union. For a tradition that (tacitly or expressly) relies on the − unitary − concept of sovereignty, the constitutional pluralism within the Union must be seen as a 'novelty' or 'aberration'. The absence of an 'Archimedean point' from which all legal authority can be explained has thus been − wrongly − hailed as a *sui generis* quality of

---

[93] P. Hay, *Federalism and Supranational Organisations* (University of Illinois Press, 1966), 37: 'It should be clear, however, that the term has neither analytic value of its own nor does it add in analysis: the characterization of the Communities as supranational and of their law as "supranational law" still says nothing about the nature of that law in relation either to national legal systems or to international law.'

[94] *Ibid.*, 44.

[95] For this brilliant point, see C. Schönberger, 'Die Europäische Union als Bund' (2004) 129 *Archiv des öffentlichen Rechts* 81 at 83.

[96] To give but one more illustration: Europe's supremacy principle is, in its structure, not unique. The Canadian doctrine of 'federal paramountcy' also requires only the 'disapplication' and not the 'invalidation' of conflicting provincial laws.

[97] J. Weiler, 'Federalism without Constitutionalism: Europe's Sonderweg', in K. Nikolaidis and R. Howse (eds.), *The Federal Vision: Legitimacy and Levels of Governance in the United States and the European Union* (Oxford University Press, 2001), 54 at 58.

[98] On this point, see P. Pescatore, *The Law of Integration: Emergence of a New Phenomenon in International Relations, Based on the Experience of the European Communities* (Sijthoff, 1974), 58.

the European Union.[99] Why not see the normative ambivalence surrounding sovereignty as part and parcel of Europe's *federal* nature? The *sui generis* 'theory' and the theory of constitutional pluralism indeed speak federal prose,[100] without – like Molière's Monsieur Jourdain – being aware of it.

In any event, the *sui generis* 'theory' of the European Union had always been a pragmatic tranquilliser. It did not prevent classificatory wars in times of constitutional conflict. And indeed: whenever the sovereignty question was posed, Europe's statist tradition would brush this pseudo-theory aside and insist on the international law nature of the Union.

b. The International Law Theory: The 'Maastricht Decision'

The ratification of the Maastricht Treaty was *the* 'constitutional moment' when the symbolic weight of European integration entered into the collective consciousness of European society. The ensuing legal debate crystallised into national constitutional reviews of the nature of the European Union. The most controversial and celebrated review was the 'Maastricht Decision' of the German Constitutional Court.[101]

The Maastricht Decision has structured the European constitutional debate for more than two decades.[102] The German Supreme Court had here posed the sovereignty question. Its central proposition was this: Europe's present *social* structure would set limits to the *constitutional* structure of the European Union;

---

[99]   See N. Walker, 'The Idea of Constitutional Pluralism' [2002] 65 MLR 317 at 338. This is how Walker, a leading figure of the 'constitutional pluralists', describes the origin of this 'new' constitutional philosophy: 'It is no coincidence that this literature has emerged out of the study of the constitutional dimension of EU law, for it is EU law which poses the most pressing paradigm-challenging test to what we might call constitutional monism. Constitutional monism merely grants a label to the defining assumption of constitutionalism in the Westphalian age … namely the idea that the sole centres or units of constitutional authorities are states. Constitutional pluralism, by contrast, recognizes that the European legal order inaugurated by the Treaty of Rome has developed beyond the traditional confines of inter-*national* law and now makes its own independent constitutional claims exist alongside the continuing claims of states' (*ibid.*, 337). This – 'Eurocentric' – view strikingly ignores the US experience, in which the Union *and* the States were seen to have 'constitutional' claims and in which the 'Union' was – traditionally – not (!) conceived in statist terms (see E. Zoeller, 'Aspects internationaux du droit constitutionnel. Contribution à la théorie de la féderation d'états' (2002) 194 *Recueil des Cours de l'Académie de la Haye* 43).

[100]   On the family resemblance between federalism and constitutional pluralism, see R. Schütze, 'Federalism as Constitutional Pluralism: "Letter from America"', in M. Avbelj and J. Komárek (eds.), *Constitutional Pluralism in the European Union and Beyond* (Hart 2012), 185.

[101]   BVerfGE 89, 155 (Maastricht Decision). The following discussion refers to the English translation of the judgment: [1994] CMLR 57 (Maastricht Decision), which can also be found on the textbook's website.

[102]   J. Baquero-Cruz, 'The Legacy of the Maastricht-Urteil and the Pluralist Movement' (2008) 14 ELJ 389.

and as long as there was no European people, there would be a legal limit to European integration.

How did the German Constitutional Court derive national limits to European integration? The Court based its reasoning on the democratic principle – *the* material principle of modern constitutional thought. How could European laws be legitimised from a democratic point of view? Two options here existed. First, European laws could be regarded as legitimised – directly or indirectly – through national democracy. Second, they could be legitimised by the existence of European democracy. As regards the first option, national democracy could only be *directly* safeguarded through unanimous voting in the Council. However, the rise of majority voting in the Council had increasingly allowed the European Union to adopt legislation against the will of national peoples.[103] European integration therefore imposed formidable limits on the effectiveness of *national* democracy. Yet, majority voting was necessary for European integration;[104] and this had been recognised by Germany's choice to transfer sovereign powers to Europe. The situation in which a Member State was outvoted in the Council could thus still be *indirectly* legitimised by reference to the national decision to open up to European integration. (That argument works only where the national decision is of a constitutional nature – as in the case of Article 23 of the German Constitution.) But even this decision was subject to the fundamental boundaries set by the national Constitution.[105]

How did the German Constitutional Court assess the second option – legitimation through a European democratic structure? The Court readily admitted that 'with the building-up of the functions and powers of the Union, it becomes increasingly necessary to allow the democratic legitimation and influence provided by way of national parliaments *to be accompanied* by a representation of the peoples of the Member States through a European Parliament as the source of a *supplementary* democratic support for the policies of the European Union'. Formal progress in this direction had been made through the establishment of European citizenship. This citizenship created a legal bond between Europe and its subjects, which 'although it does not have a tightness comparable to the common nationality of a single State, provides a legally binding expression of the degree of de facto community already in existence'.[106] But would this *constitutional* structure correspond to Europe's *social* structure? The existing democratic structure of the European Union

---

[103] Maastricht Decision (n. 101 above), 78.

[104] *Ibid.*, 86: 'Unanimity as a universal requirement would inevitably set the wills of the particular States above that of the Community of States itself and would put the very structure of such a community in doubt.'

[105] Art. 79(3) of the German Constitution states: 'Amendments to this Basic Law affecting the division of the Federation into Länder, their participation on principle in the legislative process, or the principles laid down in Articles 1 and 20 shall be inadmissible.'

[106] Maastricht Decision (n. 101 above) 86 (emphasis added).

would only work under certain social or '*pre*-legal' conditions. And, according to the Court, these social preconditions for constitutional democracy did not (yet) exist in Europe.[107]

The very purpose behind the European Union was to realise a 'Union of States' as '*an ever closer union of the peoples of Europe (organised as States) and not a State based on the people of one European nation*'.[108] The European Union was never to become a (federal) State. And from this negation, the German Constitutional Court drew its dramatic and (in)famous conclusions. First, the Union would need to recognise that the primary source of democratic legitimacy for European laws had remained the *national peoples*. Second, all legal authority of the European Union thus derived from the Member States. Third, European laws could consequently 'only have effects within the German sovereign sphere by virtue of the German instruction that its law is applied'. European norms required a national 'bridge' over which to enter into the domestic legal order. Fourth, where a European law went beyond this national scope, it could have no effects in the national legal order. Fifth, the ultimate arbiter of that question would be the Member States themselves, and in particular: their national Supreme Courts.

---

[107] Let us quote the contested para. 41 (*ibid.*, 87) in full. 'Democracy, if it is not to remain a merely formal principle of accountability, is dependent on the presence of certain pre-legal conditions, such as a continuous free debate between opposing social forces, interests and ideas, in which political goals also become clarified and change course and out of which comes a public opinion which forms the beginnings of political intentions. That also entails that the decision-making-processes of the organs exercising sovereign powers and the various political objectives pursued can be generally perceived and understood, and therefore that the citizen entitled to vote can communicate in his own language with the sovereign authority to which he is subject. Such factual conditions, in so far as they do not yet exist, can develop in the course of time within the institutional framework of the European Union ... Parties, associations, the press and broad casting organs are both a medium as well as a factor of this process, out of which a European public opinion may come into being[.]' The idea that no political system can operate without a broad consensus on the purposes of government by members of the polity is generally accepted. Only in passing did the German Constitutional Court seemingly define the substantive pre-conditions of democracy by a relative 'spiritual ... social ... and political' homogeneity of a people' (*ibid.*, 88). There is no trace in the judgment of an insistence on racial or ethnic homogeneity. Suggestions to the contrary, describing the German Court's position as one of 'organic ethno-culturalism' and as a 'worldview which ultimately informs ethnic cleansing' (see J. Weiler, 'Does Europe Need a Constitution? Demos, Telos and the German Maastricht Decision' (1995) 1 ELJ 219 at 251–2) are uninformed nonsense. Ironically, much of what Weiler pronounces to be 'his' civic theory of social and political commitment to shared values (*ibid.*, 253) is what we read in the German Constitutional Court's judgment.

[108] Maastricht Decision (n. 101 above), 89 (emphasis added). The Court continues the theme a little later: 'In any event the establishment of a "United States of Europe", in a way comparable to that in which the United States of America became a State, is not at present intended.' Incidentally, the German Supreme Court did, superficially, acknowledge the *sui generis* characteristics of the European Union by inventing a new term for the European Union – the 'Staatenverbund'.

In conclusion, *each* Member State had remained a master of the Treaties. Each of them had preserved 'the quality as a sovereign State in its own right and the status of sovereign equality with other States within the meaning of Article 2(1) of the United Nations Charter'.[109] European law was, in essence, international law.[110]

c. Europe's Statist Tradition Unearthed: Three Constitutional Denials

The constitutional conflict over the Maastricht Treaty on European Union had awoken old spirits: the belief in the sovereign nature of the nation state. The reactions to the Maastricht challenge were manifold and ranged from the placid and guided to the aggressive and misguided.[111] But underneath superficial differences, much of the ensuing constitutional debate would not escape the conceptual heritage of Europe's statist tradition.

The latent presence of this 'statist' tradition manifested itself in three constitutional denials: Europe was said to have *no* people, *no* constitution and *no* constitutionalism. These denials clearly derived from a deep-seated belief in the indivisibility of sovereignty. Because sovereignty could not be divided, it had to be in the possession of *either* the Union *or* the Member States; that is: *either* a European people *or* the national peoples. Depending on the locus of sovereignty, the European Union would be *either* based on a (national) constitution *or* an (international) treaty. And, even if Europe had a constitutional treaty, the lack of a 'constitutional demos' denied it a constitutionalism of its own.

Let us look at the underlying philosophical rationale for each of these denials, before subjecting each to constructive criticism.

Will a people – the 'constituency' for constitutional politics – precede its polity, or be a product of it? This question has received different philosophical and constitutional answers. To some, the 'people' will emerge only through subjection to a common sovereign.[112] To others, the 'people' will precede the State,

---

[109]   Maastricht Decision (n. 101 above), 91.

[110]   See Pernice, 'Multilevel Constitutionalism' (n. 57 above), 711: 'internationalist' view of the Court that 'treats [European] law as any other rule of international law'.

[111]   For a moderate and informed analysis in English, see U. Everling, 'The Maastricht Judgment of the German Federal Constitutional Court and its Significance for the Development of the European Union' (1994) 14 *YEL* 1. For the opposite, see Weiler, 'Does Europe Need a Constitution?' (n. 107 above).

[112]   See T. Hobbes, *Leviathan*, ed. R. Tuck (Cambridge University Press, 1996), 114 and 120: 'A Multitude of men, are made One Person, when they are by one man, or one Person, Represented; so that it be done with the consent of every one of that Multitude in particular. For it is the Unity of the Representer, not the Unity of the Represented, that Maketh the Person One … This done, the Multitude so united in one Person, is called a COMMONWEALTH, or in latine CIVITAS. This is the generation of that great LEVIATHAN, or rather (to speake more reverently) of that Mortall God, to which wee owe under the Immortal God, our peace and defence.' I am grateful to Q. Skinner for shedding much light on these passages.

for it is they who invest the government with its powers.[113] Most early modern European States were 'supra-national' in character in that they housed multiple 'nations' under one governmental roof.[114] However, with the rise of nationalism in the nineteenth century, States would come to be identified by their nation.[115] Multiple nations within one State came to be seen as an anomaly. This anomalous status was equally attached to the idea of 'dual citizenship': an individual should only be part of one political body.[116] (National) peoples thus came to be seen as mutually exclusive. Transposed to the context of the European Union, this meant that a European people could not exist alongside national peoples. (And European citizenship could not exist alongside national citizenship.) Both peoples would exclude – not complement – each other; and, as long as national peoples exist – as they do – a European people could not.

This brings us to the second denial: the absence of a European constitution. Under the doctrine of popular sovereignty, only a 'people' can formally 'constitute' itself into a legal sovereign. A constitution is regarded as a unilateral act of the '*pouvoir constituant*'; and it therefore follows:

> [I]t is inherent in a constitution in the full sense of the term that it goes back to an act taken by or at least attributed to the people, in which they attribute political capacity to themselves ... There is no such source for primary Union law. It goes back not to a European people but to the individual Member States, and remains dependent on them even after its entry into force. While nations give themselves a constitution, the European Union is given a constitution by third parties.[117]

And assuming, hypothetically, that a European people would in the future give the Union a constitution? Then, 'the Union would acquire competence to decide about competences (*Kompetenz-Kompetenz*)'. It would have the power to unilaterally change its constitution and would thus have turned itself from a confederation of States into a Federal State.[118] However, for the time

---

[113] The theory of popular sovereignty will typically distinguish between a 'people' (nation), on the one hand, and a 'subject' (citizen) on the other. The former refers to a community characterised by an emotion of solidarity that gives the group consciousness and identity. The latter refers to an individual's legal relation to his or her State. On these issues, see J. W. Salmond, 'Citizenship and Allegiance' (1901) 17 *Law Quarterly Review* 270.

[114] Before the 1789 French Revolution, French kings would refer to the 'peoples' of France (see B. Voyenne, *Histoire de l'Idée Fédéraliste: les Sources* (Presses d'Europe, 1973), 165). The United Kingdom is still a multi-demoi State that comprises the English, Scottish, Welsh and a part of the Irish nation (see M. Keating, *Plurinational Democracy: Stateless Nations in a Post-Sovereign Era* (Oxford University Press, 2001), 123: 'one of the most explicitly plurinational States in the world').

[115] On these issues generally, see E. Gellner, *Nations and Nationalism* (Wiley-Blackwell, 2006).

[116] O. Beaud, 'The Question of Nationality within a Federation: A Neglected Issue in Nationality Law', in R. Hansen and P. Weil (eds.), *Dual Nationality, Social Rights, and Federal Citizenship in the U.S. and Europe* (Berghahn, 2002), 317.

[117] D. Grimm, 'Does Europe Need a Constitution?' (1995) 1 ELJ 282 at 290.

[118] *Ibid.*, 299.

being, the Union is no State.[119] And, failing that, the European Union has no constitution.

Let us finally look at a third – milder – denial: 'The condition of Europe is not, as is often implied, that of constitutionalism without a constitution, but of a constitution without constitutionalism.'[120] (Paradoxically, this very same denial had been made in relation to the American Union in the eighteenth century.)[121] 'In federations, whether American or Australian, German or Canadian, the institutions of a federal state are situated in a constitutional framework which presupposes the existence of a "constitutional demos", a single *pouvoir constituant* made of the citizens of the federation in whose sovereignty, as a constituent power, and by whose supreme authority the specific constitutional arrangement is rooted.' 'In Europe, that precondition does not exist. Simply put, Europe's constitutional architecture has never been validated by a process of constitutional adoption by a European constitutional *demos*[.]'[122] And, in the absence of a unitary constitutional demos, Europe could have no constitutionalism.

What is common to these three denials? Each is rooted in the belief in sovereign states and based on the idea of indivisible sovereignty: a *unitary* people forms a *unitary* State on the basis of a *unitary* constitution. The inability to accept shared or divided sovereignty thus blinds the European tradition to the possibility of *federal* arrangements or a *duplex regimen* between peoples, States and constitutions. It is unable to envisage *two* peoples living in the same territory – yet, this is generally the case in federal unions.[123] It is unable to envisage *two* constitutional orders existing within the same territory – yet, this is generally the case in federal unions.[124] It is unable to envisage *two* governments operating in the same territory – yet, this is generally the case in federal unions. Finally, it is unable to envisage a compound *pouvoir constituant* of multiple *demoi* – yet, this is generally the case in federal unions.[125] The black-and-white logic of unitary

---

[119] This is universally accepted; see BVerfGE 22, 293 (EWG Verordnungen), 296: 'Die Gemeinschaft ist selbst kein Staat, auch kein Bundesstaat.'

[120] Weiler, 'Does Europe Need a Constitution' (n. 107 above), 220.

[121] Schmitt, *Verfassungslehre* (n. 46 above), 78: 'Den amerikanischen Verfassungen des 18. Jahrhunderts fehlt es an einer eigentlichen Verfassungstheorie.'

[122] Weiler, 'Federalism without Constitutionalism' (n. 97 above), 56–7.

[123] See Beaud, 'Question of Nationality' (n. 116 above), 320: 'Dual citizenship, essential to federations, is then nothing but the duplication of the fundamental law of duality of political entities constituting them. In contrast to the State, the federation here is characterised by a "political dualism".'

[124] Both US and German constitutionalism accept the idea of 'State Constitutions' in addition to the federal Constitution.

[125] When Professor Weiler confesses that 'I am unaware of any federal state, old or new, which does not presuppose the supreme authority and sovereignty of its federal demos' ('Federalism without Constitutionalism (n. 97 above), 57), we may draw his attention to his own academic home: the United States of America. Neither of the two Constitutions of the United States was ratified by a 'federal demos' in the form of 'the' American people. The Articles of Confederation were ratified by the State legislatures, while the 1787

constitutionalism is simply unable to capture the federal 'blue' on the international versus national spectrum.

The European Union's constitutionalism therefore must, in the future, be (re)constructed in federal terms. It is half-hearted to − enigmatically − claim that Europe has a constitution, but no constitutionalism. For once we admit that Europe has a constitution, who tells us so? National legal theory? International legal theory? Logically, the affirmation of a 'constitution' presumes the existence of a 'constitutionalism'; and only *a federal* constitutionalism can explain and give meaning to normative problems that arise in compound systems like the European Union.[126] And, once we apply *a federal* constitutionalism to the European Union, the above 'denials' are shown for what they are: *false problems*. They are created by a wrong constitutional theory. National constitutionalism simply cannot explain the 'dual nature' of federations as classical physics was unable to explain the dual nature of light.[127] By insisting that the European Union is *either* international *or* national, it denies its status as an (inter)national phenomenon.

d. Excursus: Europe's 'Democratic Deficit' as a 'False Problem'?

The classic illustration of the distorted European constitutional discourse is the debate on the European Union's 'democratic deficit'.[128] It is not difficult to find such a deficit if one measures decision-making in the Union against the unitary standard of a Nation State. There, all legislative decisions are theoretically legitimised by one source − 'the' people as represented in the national parliament. But is this − unitary − standard the appropriate yardstick for a *compound* body politic?

In a federal polity there are *two* arenas of democracy: the 'State demos' and the 'federal demos'. Both offer independent sources of democratic legitimacy; and a *federal* constitutionalism will need to take account of this *dual* legitimacy. One *functional* expression of this dualism is the division of legislative powers between

---

Constitution was ratified by the State peoples. And, as regards constitutional amendment, Art.V of the US Constitution still requires the concurrence of the federal demos − acting indirectly through its representatives − and three-quarters of the State demoi − acting either through their representatives or in conventions. More generally, in all (democratic) Federal Unions the *pouvoir constituant* should be a compound of the federal and the State demoi. Where the 'constitutional demos' is conceived in unitary terms, the federal Union loses its federal base (see Schmitt, *Verfassungslehre* (n. 46 above), 389).

[126] See my 'Constitutionalism and the European Union', in C. Barnard and S. Peers, *European Union Law* (Oxford University Press, 2017), 71.

[127] Classical physics insisted that a phenomenon must be either a particle or a wave; and it could not be both. Following the works of Einstein, modern physics now accepts the dual nature of light.

[128] The following discussion focuses on the constitutional aspect of the democratic deficit. It does not claim that there is no democratic deficit at the *social* level, such as the low degree of electoral participation or the quality of the public debate on Europe. Nor will it claim that the current constitutional structures could not be improved so as to increase democratic governance in the European Union.

the State demos and the federal demos. One *institutional* expression of this dual legitimacy is the compound nature of the central legislator. It is typically made up of *two* chambers; and, thus, every federal law is – ideally – legitimised by reference to *two* sources: the consent of the State peoples and the consent of the federal people. It is thus utterly mistaken to argue that '[t]rue federalism is fundamentally a non-majoritarian, or even anti-majoritarian, form of government since the component units often owe their autonomous existence to institutional arrangements that prevent the domination of minorities by majorities'.[129] Federalism is *not* inherently *non*-democratic.[130] It is – if based on the idea of government by the governed – inherently *demoi*-cratic.[131] The European Union is 'based on a *dual* structure of legitimacy: the totality of the Union's citizens, and the peoples of the European Union'. 'Elections provide *two* lines of democratic legitimacy for the Union's organizational structure. The European Parliament, which is based on elections by the totality of the Union's citizens, and the European Council as well as the Council, whose legitimacy is based on the Member States' democratically organized peoples[.]'[132] Duplex regimen, dual democracy.

[129]   G. Majone, 'Europe's "Democratic Deficit": The Question of Standards' (1998) 4 ELJ 5 at 11.

[130]   In this sense also, see R. A. Dahl, 'Federalism and the Democratic Process' in J. R. Pennock and J. W. Chapman (eds.), *Nomos XXV: Liberal Democracy* (New York University Press, 1983), 107: '[A]lthough in federal systems no single body of citizens can exercise control over the agenda, federalism is not for this reason less capable than a unitary system of meeting the criteria of the democratic process[.]'

[131]   K. Nicolaïdis, 'We the Peoples of Europe …' (2004) 83 *Foreign Affairs* 97 at 102. From this perspective, it is fundamentally mistaken to argue that 'the most legitimating element (from a "social" point of view) of the [Union] was the Luxembourg Accord and the veto power' as 'this device enabled the [Union] to legitimate its program and its legislation' (J. Weiler, 'The Transformation of Europe' (1990–1) 100 *Yale LJ* 2403 at 2473). This is mistaken in two ways. First, how can a unanimous decision of national ministers legitimate directly effective European laws? If European legislation affects European citizens *directly*, how can an *indirect* legitimatisation through national *executives* be sufficient? To solve this dilemma, Weiler refers to the underlying formal legitimacy of the founding Treaties that received national parliamentary consent and to the claim that national parliaments control their governments' ministers in the Council. However, the former argument cannot explain how an earlier parliament can bind its successors. (This normative problem may only be solved through the insertion of a clause into the national *constitution* that would legitimatise European integration.) And, even if we were to assume absolute control of national ministers by their national parliaments, *social* legitimacy is in any event co-dependent on 'system capacity'. Dahl explains this point as follows ('Federalism and the Democratic Process' (n. 130 above) at 105 – emphasis added): 'As Rousseau suggested long ago, it is necessarily the case that the greater the number of citizens, the smaller the weight of each citizen in determining the outcome … On the other hand, if a system is more democratic to the extent that it permits citizens to govern themselves on matters that are important to them, then in many circumstances a *larger system would be more democratic than a smaller one, since its capacity to cope with certain matters – defense and pollution, for example* – would be greater.'

[132]   A. von Bogdandy, 'A Disputed Idea Becomes Law: Remarks on European Democracy as a Legal Principle' in B. Kohler-Koch and B. Rittberger (eds.), *Debating the Democratic*

Finally, one *foundational* expression of this dual legitimacy is the – typically – compound nature of the federation's constituent power. The point has been well made in relation to the United States of America:

> Half a century ago J. Allen Smith wrote a book in which he bitterly criticized the undemocratic spirit of the American Scheme of government. In it he argued that a true democracy had to embrace the principle of majority rule … His criticism was justified, but only within his own frame of reference. It was phrased in the wrong terms. He was in fact criticising a federal system for serving the ends it was intended to serve … Nearly all governments that are called federal employ some device in the amending process to *prevent* a mere majority from changing the constitution … Does this prove federalism i[s] undemocratic? Certainly it does, if democracy be defined in terms of majority rule … They argue that the will of the majority is being thwarted and suggest by implication at least that this is ethically wrong; the term 'will of the majority' carries with it certain moral overtones in these days of enlightened democracy. But what the *ad hoc* majoritarians forget is that a federal [union] is a different thing, that it is not intended to operate according to a majority principle. We cannot apply the standard of unitary government to a federal [union]. If the opinion of a majority is a sufficient guide for public policy in a community then it is unlikely that a federal system will have been established in that community.[133]

How enlightening *comparative* constitutionalism can be! The discussion of the European Union's 'democratic deficit' indeed reveals a deficit in democratic theory.[134] The description of crisis reflects a crisis of description.[135] Indeed, '[t]he question about which standards should be employed to assess the democratic credentials of the EU crucially hinges on how the EU is conceptualized'.[136] The search for normative criteria to describe and evaluate the European Union will – eventually – lead to *a federal* constitutional theory.

Conclusion

What is the nature of the European Union? Can the Union be described as a federal Union? We saw above that the (older) US federal tradition easily classifies the European Union as a federal Union. The European Union has a mixed or compound nature; and, in combining international and national elements, it stands on federal 'middle ground'.

Legitimacy of the European Union (Rowman & Littlefield, 2007), 33 at 36–7 (emphasis added).

[133] W. S. Livingston, *Federalism and Constitutional Change* (Clarendon Press, 1956), 311–14.

[134] O. Beaud, 'Déficit politique ou déficit de la pensée politique?' (1995) 87 *Le Débat* 44.

[135] A. Winckler, 'Description d'une crise ou crise d'une description?' (1995) 87 *Le Débat* 59.

[136] B. Kohler-Koch and B. Rittberger, 'Charting Crowded Territory: Debating the Democratic Legitimacy of the European Union', in B. Kohler-Koch and B. Rittberger (eds.), *Debating the Democratic Legitimacy of the European Union* (Rowman & Littlefield, 2007), 1 at 4.

The federal label is – ironically – denied by Europe's own intellectual tradition. In pressing the federal principle into a national (State) format, the concept of federation is here reduced to that of a Federal State. And, while the creation of a Federal State may have been a long-term aim of a few idealists in the early years of European integration, the failure of the European Political Community in the 1950s caused the demise of federal 'ideology'.[137] The fall of federalism gave rise to the 'philosophy' of (neo-)functionalism,[138] which celebrated the Union as a *process* – a 'journey to an unknown destination'.[139]

Early commentators were nonetheless aware that the new European construct had moved onto the 'middle ground' between international and national law. Yet, Europe's conceptual tradition blocked the identification of that middle ground with the federal idea. Europe was celebrated as *sui generis*.[140] The *sui generis* 'theory' was, in any event, but a veneer. In times of constitutional conflict, Europe's old federal tradition returned from the depths and imposed its two polarised ideal types: Europe was either an international organisation or a Federal State; and since it was definitely not the latter, it was – by definition – the former.

What is the explanatory power of the international law thesis? Can it satisfactorily explain the legal and social reality within the European Union? In the last half a century, 'Little Europe' has emancipated itself from its humble birth and has grown into a mature entity: the European Union. The international law thesis thus runs into a great many explanatory difficulties. *Unlike* international doctrine predicts, the obligations imposed on the Member States are not interpreted restrictively. *Unlike* international doctrine predicts, the Member States are not allowed a free hand in how to execute their obligations. *Unlike* international doctrine predicts, the Member States cannot modify their obligations *inter se* through the conclusion of subsequent international treaties. In order to defend the international law hypothesis, its adherents must relegate the social reality of European law to a false appearance. European thought here refuses comparing the *ideal* with the *real*. But facts are stubborn things!

The *sui generis* thesis and the international law thesis had *both* caused the Union to disappear from the federal map. The federal idea however gradually returned. In a first step, it was accepted that the Union had borrowed the federal

---

[137]　M. Forsyth, 'The Political Theory of Federalism: The Relevance of Classical Approaches', in J. J. Hesse and V. Wright, *Federalizing Europe? The Costs, Benefits, and Preconditions of Federal Political Systems* (Oxford University Press, 1996), 25 at 26.

[138]　The functionalist classic is D. Mitrany, *A Working Peace System: An Argument for the Functional Development of International Organization* (National Peace Council, 1946). Neofunctionalism discards the belief in the automaticity of the integration process and emphasises the need to build new loyalties with strategic elites. The classic here is Haas, *Uniting of Europe* (n. 3 above).

[139]　A. Shonfield, *Journey to an Unknown Destination* (Penguin, 1973).

[140]　But how common exceptionalisms are! J. Calhoun described the 1787 US legal order as 'new, peculiar, and unprecedented' (see 'A Discourse on the Constitution and Government of the United States', in *Union and Liberty* (Liberty Fund, 1992), 117). The legal structure of the British Commonwealth has also been described as *sui generis*.

principle from the public law of federal States.[141] The European Union was said to be the 'classic case of federalism without federation'.[142] It had 'federal' features, but it was no 'federation'. Federation here still meant Federal State.[143] The word 'federal', by contrast, attached to a *function* and not to the *essence* of the organisation. (The adjective was allowed – adjectives refer to *attributes*, not to *essences* – but the noun was not.) In order for European constitutionalism to accept the idea of a 'Federation of States' a second step is therefore required. European constitutionalism needs to abandon its obsession with the idea of undivided sovereignty. It needs to accept that '[t]he law of integration rests on a premise quite unknown to so-called "classical" international law: that is the divisibility of sovereignty'.[144] The Union enjoys 'real powers stemming from a *limitation of sovereignty* or a transfer of powers from the States to the [Union]' through which, in turn, 'the Member States have *limited their sovereign rights*, albeit within limited fields'.[145]

The European Union is indeed based on a conception of divided sovereignty and is in strictness neither international nor national, 'but a composition of both'. It represents an (inter)national phenomenon that stands on – federal – middle ground. The best way to characterise the nature of the European Union is therefore as a Federation of States.

FURTHER READING

Books

M. Avbelj and J. Komárek, *Constitutional Pluralism in the European Union and Beyond* (Hart, 2012)

O. Beaud, *Théorie de la Fédération* (Presses Universitaires de France, 2009)

---

[141] Haas separated the idea of 'federation' from the notion of 'State' (*Uniting of Europe* (n. 3 above), 37) and could, consequently, speak of the 'federal attributes' (*ibid.*, 42) of the ECSC. The ECSC was, overall, described as a 'hybrid form, short of federation' (*ibid.*, 51), for it did not satisfy all the federal attributes believed by the author to be necessary for a federation to exist (*ibid.*, 59): 'While almost all the criteria point positively to federation, the remaining limits on the ability to implement decisions and to expand the scope of the system independently still suggest the characteristics of international organisation.'

[142] M. Burgess, *Federalism and the European Union: The Building of Europe 1950–2000* (Routledge, 2000), 28–9.

[143] See W. G. Friedmann, *The Changing Structure of International Law* (Stevens, 1964), 98: 'The [European] Treaties stop short of the establishment of a federation. They do not transfer to a federal sphere the general powers usually associated with a federal state[.]'

[144] Pescatore, *Law of Integration* (n. 98 above), 30. This corresponds to J. Fischer's vision: 'The completion of European integration can only be successfully conceived if it is done on the basis of a division of sovereignty between Europe and the nation-state. Precisely this is the idea underlying the concept of "subsidiarity", a subject that is currently being discussed by everyone and understood by virtually no one' ('From Confederacy to Federation: Thoughts on the Finality of European Integration', Speech at the Humboldt University in Berlin (12 May 2000)).

[145] Case 6/64, *Costa* v. *ENEL* [1964] ECR 585, 593 (emphasis added).

M. Burgess, *Federalism and the European Union: The Building of Europe 1950–2000* (Routledge, 2000)

E. Haas, *The Uniting of Europe* (Stanford University Press, 1968)

A. Hamilton, J. Madison and J. Jay, *The Federalist*, ed. T. Ball (Cambridge University Press, 2003)

P. Hay, *Federalism and Supranational Organisations* (University of Illinois Press, 1966)

G. Jellinek, *Die Lehre von den Staatenverbindungen* (Scientia, 1969)

H. Kelsen, *General Theory of Law and State* (Transaction, 2008)

K. Nikolaidis and R. Howse (eds.), *The Federal Vision: Legitimacy and Levels of Governance in the United States and the European Union* (Oxford University Press, 2001)

P. Pescatore, *The Law of Integration: Emergence of a New Phenomenon in International Relations, Based on the Experience of the European Communities* (Sijthoff, 1974)

B. Rosamond, *Theories of European Integration* (Palgrave, 2000)

J. Weiler, *The Constitution of Europe* (Cambridge University Press, 1999)

Articles (and Chapters)

D. Grimm, 'Does Europe Need a Constitution?' (1995) 1 ELJ 282

J. Habermas, 'Remarks on Dieter Grimm's "Does Europe Need a Constitution?"' (1995) 1 ELJ 303

K. Lenaerts, 'Federalism: Essential Concepts in Evolution – The Case of the European Union' (1998) 21 *Fordham International Law Journal* 746

K. Nicolaïdis, 'We the Peoples of Europe …' (2004) 83 *Foreign Affairs* 97

P. Pescatore, 'International Law and Community Law: A Comparative Analysis' (1970) 7 *CML Rev.* 167

C. Sasse, 'The Common Market: Between International and Municipal Law' (1965–6) 75 *Yale LJ* 695

C. Schmitt, 'Constitutional Theory of the Federation' in *Constitutional Theory* (Duke University Press, 2008), Part IV

R. Schütze, 'Constitutionalism and the European Union' in C. Barnard and S. Peers (eds.), *European Union Law* (Oxford University Press, 2017), 71

N. Walker, 'The Idea of Constitutional Pluralism' (2002) 65 *MLR* 317

J. Weiler, 'Federalism without Constitutionalism: Europe's Sonderweg' in K. Nikolaidis and R. Howse (eds.), *The Federal Vision: Legitimacy and Levels of Governance in the United States and the European Union* (Oxford University Press, 2001), 54

D. Wyatt, 'New Legal Order, or Old?' (1982) 7 *EL Rev.* 147

3

European Law I
Nature – Direct Effect

Contents

Introduction

Classic international law holds that each State can choose the relationship between its domestic law and international law. Two – constitutional – theories thereby exist: monism and dualism. Monist States make international law part of their domestic legal order. International law will here directly apply *as if* it were domestic law.[1] By contrast, dualist States consider international law separate from

---

[1] See Art. VI, Clause 2 of the United States Constitution (emphasis added): '[A]ll Treaties made, or which shall be made, under the Authority of the United States, *shall be the supreme Law of the Land*; and the Judges in every State shall be bound thereby, any Thing in the Constitution or Laws of any State to the Contrary notwithstanding.'

domestic law. International law is viewed as the law *between* States; national law is the law *within* a State. While international treaties are thus binding – externally – 'on' States, they cannot be binding 'in' States. International law needs to be 'transposed' or 'incorporated' into domestic law and may, at most, have *indirect* effects through the medium of national law. The dualist theory is based on a basic division of labour: international institutions apply international law, while national institutions apply national law. For an illustration of the two theories, see Figure 3.1.

Did the European Union leave the choice between monism and dualism to its Member States?[2] For dualist States, all European law would need to be 'incorporated' into national law before it could have domestic effects.[3] Here, there is no direct applicability of European law, as all European norms are mediated through national law and individuals will consequently never come into *direct* contact with European law. Where a Member State violates European law, this breach can only be established and remedied at the European level. The European Treaties indeed contained such an 'international' remedial machinery against recalcitrant Member States in the form of enforcement actions before the Court of Justice.[4] Another Member State or the Commission – but not individuals – could here bring an action to enforce their rights.

Did this not signal that the European Treaties were international treaties that tolerated the dualist approach? Not necessarily, for the Treaties also contained strong signals against the 'ordinary' international law reading. Not only was the Union entitled to adopt legal acts that were to be 'directly applicable *in* all Member States';[5] from the very beginning, the Treaties also contained a judicial

Figure 3.1 Monism and Dualism in National Law

[2] Under international law, the choice between monism and dualism is a 'national' choice. Thus, even where a State chooses the monist approach (like the United States), monism in this sense only means that international norms are *constitutionally* recognised as an autonomous legal source of *domestic* law. Dualism, by contrast, means that international norms will not automatically, that is: through a constitutional incorporation, become part of the national legal order. Each international treaty demands a separate legislative act 'incorporating' the international norm into domestic law. The difference between monism and dualism thus boils down to whether international law is incorporated via the constitution, as in the United States; or whether international treaties need to be validated by a special parliamentary command, as in the United Kingdom. The idea that monism means that States have no choice but to apply international law is not accepted in international law.

[3] For this dualist technique, see (amended) European Communities Act 1972 as well as the European Union Act 2011 – both discussed in the next chapter.

[4] On this point, see Chapter 10, section 3(a).

[5] Art. 288(2) TFEU.

mechanism that envisaged the direct application of European law by the national courts.[6] But regardless of the intention of the founding Member States, the European Court discarded any dualist reading of Union law in the most important case of European law: *Van Gend en Loos*.[7] The Court here cut the umbilical cord with classic international law by insisting that the European legal order was a 'new legal order'. In the famous words of the Court:

> The objective of the E[U] Treaty, which is to establish a common market, the functioning of which is of direct concern to interested parties in the [Union], implies that this Treaty is *more than an agreement which merely creates mutual obligations between the contracting States*. This view is confirmed by the preamble to the Treaty which refers not only to the governments but to peoples. It is also confirmed more specifically by the establishment of institutions endowed with sovereign rights, the exercise of which affects Member States and also their citizens. Furthermore, it must be noted that the nations of the States brought together in the [Union] are called upon to cooperate in the functioning of this [Union] through the intermediary of the European Parliament and the Economic and Social Committee.
>
> In addition the task assigned to the Court of Justice under Article [267 TFEU], the object of which is to secure uniform interpretation of the Treaty by national courts and tribunals, confirms that the States have acknowledged that [European] law has an authority which can be invoked by their nationals before those courts and tribunals. The conclusion to be drawn from this is that the [Union] constitutes a *new legal order of international law* for the benefit of which the States have limited their sovereign rights, albeit within limited fields, and the subjects of which comprise not only Member States but also their nationals. *Independently of the legislation of Member States*, [European] law therefore not only imposes obligations on individuals but is also intended to confer upon them rights which become part of their legal heritage.[8]

All judicial arguments here marshalled to justify a monistic reading of European law are debatable.[9] But with a stroke of the pen, the Court confirmed the independence of the European legal order from classic international law. Unlike ordinary international law, the European Treaties were more than agreements creating mutual obligations between States. European law was to be enforced in national courts – despite the parallel existence of an international enforcement machinery.[10] Individuals were subjects of European law and individual rights and obligations could consequently derive *directly* from European law.

---

[6] *Ibid.*, Art. 267. On the provision, see Chapter 10, section 4.

[7] Case 26/62, *Van Gend en Loos* v. *Netherlands Inland Revenue Administration* [1963] ECR (English Special Edition) 1.

[8] *Ibid.*, 12 (emphasis added).

[9] For a critical overview, see T. Arnull, *The European Union and Its Court of Justice* (Oxford University Press, 2006), 168ff.

[10] Case 26/62, *Van Gend en Loos*, 13. On the 'centralised' (international) enforcement methods within the EU legal order generally, see Chapter 10.

Importantly, *all* European law is directly applicable law,[11] and the European Union would therefore be able to *itself* determine the effect and nature of all European law within the national legal orders. The direct applicability of European law indeed allowed the Union *centrally* to develop two foundational doctrines of the European legal order: the doctrine of direct effect and the doctrine of supremacy. The present chapter deals with the doctrine of direct effect; Chapter 4 deals with the doctrine of supremacy.

What is the doctrine of direct effect? It is vital to understand that the Court's decision in favour of a monistic relationship between the European and the national legal orders did not mean that all European law would be directly effective, that is: enforceable by national courts or the national executive (see Figure 3.2). To be enforceable, a norm must be 'justiciable', that is: it must be capable of being applied by a public authority in a specific case.[12] But not all legal norms

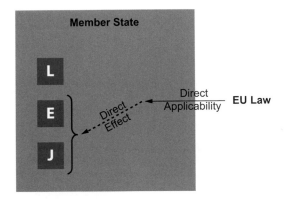

Figure 3.2 Direct Effect

[11] The direct applicability of the European Treaties is, at first sight, harder to justify, as many legal orders seem to 'transpose' them into national law. However, from a European constitutional perspective, the national ratification of a new draft (!) EU Treaty is not transposing EU primary law into national law. Indeed, after *Van Gend en Loos*, a fundamental distinction must be made between the individual national decision to ratify the (amendment to the) EU Treaties, and their coming into effect once all (!) the Member States have ratified them. For it is, importantly, solely the *collective* decision of all the Member States to agree to Treaty (amendments) that establishes the validity of the EU Treaties. Not the individual (national) ratification act but the collectivity of the Member States ratifying the Treaties underpins the validity of EU primary law; and, once that primary law exists, it is directly applicable in all the national legal orders. With the Lisbon Treaty, the distinction between the validity of EU primary law and national ratification has indeed gained further strength by means of the introduction of the simplified revision procedures set out in Art. 48(7) TEU. According to the latter, the European Union may – admittedly, for a very small part of primary law – change its Treaties if backed up by the *tacit* consent of national *parliaments*. This route allows for constitutional change through parliamentary *inaction*. And the validity and direct applicability of primary Union law is here clearly independent of any national ratification or transposition.

[12] On the application of the doctrine of direct effect to the national executive branch, see Conclusion below.

have this quality. For example, where a European norm requires Member States to establish a public fund to guarantee unpaid wages for insolvent private companies, yet leaves a wide margin of discretion to the Member States on how to achieve that end, this norm is not intended to have direct effects in a specific situation. While it binds the national *legislator*, the norm is not self-*executing*. The concept of direct applicability is thus wider than the concept of direct effect. Whereas the former refers to the *internal* effect of a European norm within national legal orders, the latter refers to the *individual* effect of a norm in specific cases.[13] Direct effect requires direct applicability, but not the other way around. However, the direct applicability of a norm only makes its direct effect *possible*.

After all these terminological preliminaries, when will European law have direct effect? And are there different types of direct effect? This chapter explores the doctrine of direct effect across the various sources of European law. It will start with the direct effect of the European Treaties in section 1. The European Treaties, as primarily law, also envisage the adoption of European secondary law. This secondary law may take various forms. These forms are defined in Article 288 TFEU,[14] which defines the Union's legal instruments and states:

> [1] To exercise the Union's competences, the institutions shall adopt regulations, directives, decisions, recommendations and opinions.
> [2] A regulation shall have general application. It shall be binding in its entirety and directly applicable in all Member States.
> [3] A directive shall be binding, as to the result to be achieved, upon each Member State to which it is addressed, but shall leave to the national authorities the choice of form and methods.
> [4] A decision shall be binding in its entirety. A decision which specifies those to whom it is addressed shall be binding only on them.
> [5] Recommendations and opinions shall have no binding force.

The provision acknowledges three binding legal instruments – regulations, directives and decisions – and two non-binding instruments.[15] Why was there a need for

---

[13] In this sense direct applicability is a 'federal' question as it relates to the effect of a 'foreign' norm in a domestic legal system, whereas direct effect is a 'separation-of-powers' question as it relates to the issue whether a norm is addressed to the legislature or the executive and judiciary.

[14] The institutional practice of Union decision-making has created a number of 'atypical' acts. For a discussion of atypical acts, see J. Klabbers, 'Informal Instruments before the European Court of Justice' (1994) 31 *CML Rev.* 997. But see also now: Art. 296 TFEU – third indent: 'When considering draft legislative acts, the European Parliament and the Council shall refrain from adopting acts not provided for by the relevant legislative procedure in the area in question.'

[15] Logic would dictate that non-binding acts are not binding. Yet, the European Court has accepted the possibility of their having some 'indirect' legal effect. In Case 322/88, *Grimaldi* v. *Fonds des maladies professionelles* [1989] ECR 4407, para. 18, the Court held

Table 3.1 EU Legislative Output: Legal Instruments (2015–17)

	2015	2016	2017
Regulations	1,282	1,216	1,117
Directives	38	41	32
Decisions	800	801	795
International treaties	41	66	74

three distinct binding instruments? The answer seems to lie in their specific – direct and indirect – effects in the national legal orders. While regulations and decisions were considered Union acts that directly establish legal norms (section 2), directives appeared to be designed as indirect forms of legislation (section 3).

Sadly, Article 288 TFEU is incomplete, for it only mentions the Union's *internal* instruments. A fourth binding instrument indeed needs to be 'read into' the list: international agreements. Union agreements are not only binding upon the institutions of the Union, but also '*on* its Member States'.[16] Did this mean that international agreements were an indirect form of external legislation, or could they be binding 'in' the Member States? Section 4 will analyse the doctrine of direct effects for international agreements.[17]

The extent to which the Union uses these various legal instruments can be seen in Table 3.1. It shows that – from a comparative point of view – regulations and decisions are the clearly dominating instruments of the Union. Directives, by contrast, represent a tiny fraction of the legal output of the Union today – an output that is even overshadowed by the number of international agreements yearly concluded by the Union with third States.

1. Primary Union Law: The Effect of the Treaties

The European Treaties are framework treaties. They establish the objectives of the European Union, and endow it with the powers to achieve these objectives.

---

that recommendations 'cannot be regarded as having no legal effect' as they 'supplement binding [European] provisions'. 'Non-binding' Union acts may, therefore, have legal 'side effects'. For an interesting overview, see L. Senden, *Soft Law in European Community Law: Its Relationship to Legislation* (Hart, 2004).

[16] Art. 216(2) TFEU.

[17] What this section will however not do is to explore the legal effects of decisions adopted by international organisations or bodies created by international agreements signed by the Union. The most prominent example here are so-called EEA decisions, that is: decisions adopted by the joint committee established by the EEA Agreement between the European Union and the EFTA States. For a brief analysis of the EEA arrangements, see (online) Chapter 18B, section 4(b/bb).

Many of the European policies in Part III of the TFEU thus simply set out the competences and procedures for future Union secondary law. The Treaties, as primary European law, only offer the constitutional bones. But could this constitutional 'skeleton' itself have direct effect? Would there be Treaty provisions that were sufficiently precise to give rise to rights that national courts could apply in specific situations?

The European Court affirmatively answered this question in *Van Gend en Loos*.[18] The case concerned a central objective of the European Union: the internal market. According to that central plank of the Treaties, the Union was to create a customs union between the Member States. Within a customs union, goods can move freely without any pecuniary charges levied when crossing borders. The Treaties had chosen to establish the customs union gradually; and to this effect ex-Article 12 EEC contained a standstill obligation:

> Member States shall refrain from introducing between themselves any new customs duties on imports or exports or any charges having equivalent effect, and from increasing those which they already apply in their trade with each other.[19]

The Netherlands appeared to have violated this provision, and, believing this to be the case, Van Gend & Loos – a Dutch importing company – brought proceedings in a Dutch court against the National Inland Revenue. The Dutch court had doubts about the admissibility and the substance of the case and referred a number of preliminary questions to the European Court of Justice.

Could a private party enforce an *international* treaty in a *national* court? And, if so, was this a question of national or European law? In the course of the proceedings before the European Court, the Dutch government heavily disputed that an individual could enforce a Treaty provision against its own government in a national court. Any alleged infringements had to be submitted to the European Court by the Commission or a Member State under the 'international' infringement procedures set out in Articles 258 and 259 TFEU.[20] The Belgian government, having intervened in the case, equally claimed that the question of what effect an international treaty had within the national legal order 'falls exclusively within the jurisdiction of the Netherlands court'.[21] Conversely, the Commission countered that 'the effects of the provisions of the Treaty on the national law of Member States cannot be determined by the actual national law of each of them but by the Treaty itself'.[22] And since ex-Article 12 EEC was 'clear and complete',

---

[18] Case 26/62, *Van Gend en Loos*.

[19] The provision has been repealed. Strictly speaking, it is therefore not correct to identify Art. 30 TEU as the successor provision, for the latter is based on ex-Arts. 13 and 16 EEC. The normative content of ex-Art. 12 EEC solely concerned the introduction of *new* customs duties; and therefore did not cover the abolition of existing tariff restrictions.

[20] Case 26/62, *Van Gend en Loos*, 6. On enforcement actions by the Commission, see Chapter 10, section 3(a).

[21] Case 26/62, *Van Gend en Loos*, 6.   [22] *Ibid*.

it was 'a rule of law capable of being effectively applied by the national court'.[23] The fact that the European provision was addressed to the Member States did 'not of itself take away from individuals who have an interest in it the right to require it to be applied in the national courts'.[24]

Two views thus competed before the Court. According to the dualist 'international' view, legal rights of private parties could 'not derive from the [Treaties] or the legal measures taken by the institutions, but [solely] from legal measures enacted by Member States'.[25] According to the monist 'constitutional' view, by contrast, European law was capable of directly creating individual rights. The Court famously favoured the second view. It followed from the 'spirit' of the Treaties that European law was no 'ordinary' international law. It would in itself be directly applicable in the national legal orders.

But when would a provision have direct effect, and thus entitle private parties to seek its application by a national court? Having briefly presented the general scheme of the Treaty in relation to customs duties,[26] the Court concentrated on the wording of ex-Article 12 EEC and found as follows:

> The wording of [ex-]Article 12 [EEC] contains a *clear and unconditional prohibition* which is not a positive but a *negative obligation*. This obligation, moreover, is *not qualified by any reservation on the part of the States, which would make its implementation conditional upon a positive legislative measure enacted under national law*. The very nature of this prohibition makes it ideally adapted to produce direct effects in the legal relationship between Member States and their subjects. The implementation of [ex-]Article 12 [EEC] does not require any legislative intervention on the part of the States. The fact that under this Article it is the Member States who are made the subject of the negative obligation does not imply that their nationals cannot benefit from this obligation.[27]

While somewhat repetitive, the test for direct effect is here clearly presented: wherever the Treaties contain a 'prohibition' that was 'clear' and 'unconditional', that prohibition would have direct effect. To be an unconditional prohibition thereby required two things. First, the European provision had to be an *automatic* prohibition, that is: it should not depend on subsequent positive legislation by the European Union. And, second, the prohibition should ideally be *absolute*, that is: 'not qualified by any reservation on the part of the States'.

This was a – very – strict test. But ex-Article 12 EEC was indeed 'ideally adapted' to satisfy this triple test. It was a clear prohibition and unconditional in the double sense outlined above. However, if the Court had insisted on a strict

---

[23]   *Ibid.*   [24]   *Ibid.*

[25]   This was the view of the German government (*ibid.*, 8).

[26]   The Court considered ex-Art. 12 EEC as an 'essential provision' in the general scheme of the Treaty as it relates to customs duties (*ibid.*, 12).

[27]   *Ibid.*, 13 (emphasis added).

application of all three criteria, very few provisions within the Treaties would have had direct effect. Yet the Court subsequently loosened the test considerably (section (a)). And, as we shall see in section (b) below, it clarified that the Treaties could be vertically and horizontally directly effective.

a. Direct Effect: From Strict to Lenient Test

The direct effect test set out in *Van Gend en Loos* was informed by three criteria. First, a provision had to be clear. Second, it had to be unconditional in the sense of being an automatic prohibition. And, third, this prohibition would need to be absolute, that is: not allow for reservations. In its subsequent jurisprudence, the Court expanded the concept of direct effect on all three fronts.

First, how clear would a prohibition have to be to be directly effective? Within the Treaties' title on the free movement of goods, we find the following famous prohibition: 'Quantitative restrictions on imports and all measures having equivalent effect shall be prohibited between Member States.'[28] Was this a clear prohibition? While the notion of 'quantitative restrictions' might have been − relatively − clear, what about 'measures having equivalent effect'? The Commission had realised the open-ended nature of the concept and offered some early semantic help.[29] And yet, despite all the uncertainty involved, the Court found that the provision had direct effect.[30]

The same lenient interpretation of what 'clear' meant was soon applied to even wider provisions. In *Defrenne*,[31] the Court analysed the following prohibition: '[e]ach Member State shall ensure that the principle of equal pay for male and female workers for equal work or work of equal value is applied'.[32] Was this a clear prohibition of discrimination? Confusingly, the Court found that the provision might and might not have direct effect. With regard to indirect discrimination, the Court considered the prohibition indeterminate, since it required 'the elaboration of criteria whose implementation necessitates the taking of appropriate measures at [European] and national level'.[33] Yet in respect of direct discrimination, the prohibition was directly effective.[34]

---

[28] Art. 34 TFEU.

[29] Directive 70/50/EEC on the abolition of measures which have an effect equivalent to quantitative restrictions on imports and are not covered by other provisions adopted in pursuance of the EEC Treaty [1970] OJ English Special Edition 17.

[30] Case 74/76, *Iannelli & Volpi SpA v. Ditta Paolo Meroni* [1977] ECR 557, para. 13: 'The prohibition of quantitative restrictions and measures having equivalent effect laid down in Article [34] of the [FEU] Treaty is mandatory and explicit and its implementation does not require any subsequent intervention of the Member States or [Union] institutions. The prohibition therefore has direct effect and creates individual rights which national courts must protect[.]'

[31] Case 43/75, *Defrenne v. Sabena* [1976] ECR 455, para. 19.

[32] Art. 157(1) TFEU.   [33] Case 43/75, *Defrenne v. Sabena*, para. 19.

[34] *Ibid.*, para. 24. However, the Court subsequently held the prohibition of indirect pay discrimination to be also directly effective, see Case 262/88, *Barber v. Guardian Royal Exchange Assurance Group* [1990] ECR I-1889, para. 37: '[Article 157(1)] applies directly to all forms

What about the second part of the direct effect test? When was a prohibition automatic? Would this be the case where the Treaties expressly acknowledged the need for positive legislative action by the Union to achieve a Union objective? For example, the Treaty chapter on the right of establishment contains not just a prohibition addressed to the Member States in Article 49 TFEU,[35] the subsequent Article 50 states:

> In order to attain freedom of establishment as regards a particular activity, the European Parliament and the Council, acting in accordance with the ordinary legislative procedure and after consulting the Economic and Social Committee, shall act by means of directives.

Would this not mean that the freedom of establishment was conditional on legislative action? In *Reyners*,[36] the Court rejected this argument. Despite the fact that the general scheme within the chapter on freedom of establishment contained a set of provisions that sought to achieve free movement through positive Union legislation,[37] the Court declared the European right of establishment in Article 49 TFEU to be directly effective. And the Court had no qualms about giving direct effect to the general prohibition on 'any discrimination on grounds of nationality'— despite the fact that Article 18 TFEU expressly called on the Union legislator to adopt rules 'designed to prohibit such discrimination'.[38]

Finally, what about the third requirement? Could *relative* prohibitions, even if clear, ever be directly effective? The prohibition on quantitative restrictions on imports, discussed above, is subject to a number of legitimate exceptions according to which it 'shall not preclude prohibitions or restrictions on imports, exports or goods in transit justified on grounds of public morality, public policy or public security'.[39] Was this then a prohibition that was 'not qualified by any

---

of discrimination which may be identified solely with the aid of the criteria of equal work and equal pay referred to by the article in question.' This generous reading was subsequently extended to the yet wider prohibition of 'any discrimination on grounds of nationality'; see Case C-85/96, *Martínez Sala* v. *Freistaat Bayern* [1998] ECR I-2691, para. 63.

[35] Art. 49(1) TFEU states: 'Within the framework of the provisions set out below, restrictions on the freedom of establishment of nationals of a Member State in the territory of another Member State shall be prohibited. Such prohibition shall also apply to restrictions on the setting-up of agencies, branches or subsidiaries by nationals of any Member State established in the territory of any Member State. Freedom of establishment shall include the right to take up and pursue activities as self-employed persons and to set up and manage undertakings, in particular companies or firms within the meaning of the second paragraph of Article 54, under the conditions laid down for its own nationals by the law of the country where such establishment is effected, subject to the provisions of the Chapter relating to capital.'

[36] Case 2/74, *Reyners* v. *Belgian State* [1974] ECR 631. For an excellent discussion of this question, see P. Craig, 'Once Upon a Time in the West: Direct Effect and the Federalisation of EEC Law' (1992) 12 *Oxford Journal of Legal Studies* 453 at 463–70.

[37] Case 2/74, *Reyners*, para. 32.

[38] Case 85/96, *Martínez Sala* v. *Freistaat Bayern*.   [39] Art. 36 TFEU.

reservation on the part of the States'? The Court found that this was indeed the case. For although these derogations would 'attach particular importance to the interests of Member States, it must be observed that they deal with exceptional cases which are clearly defined and which do not lend themselves to any wide interpretation'.[40] And since the application of these exceptions was 'subject to judicial control', a Member State's right to invoke them did not prevent the general prohibition 'from conferring on individuals rights which are enforceable by them and which the national courts must protect'.[41]

What, then, is the test for the direct effect of Treaty provisions in light of these – relaxing – developments? The simple test is this: a provision has direct effect when it is capable of being applied by a national court. Importantly, direct effect does *not* depend on a European norm granting a subjective right;[42] but on the contrary, the subjective right is a result of a directly effective norm.[43] Direct effect simply means that a norm can be 'invoked' in and applied by a court. And this is the case when the Court of Justice says it is! Today, almost all Treaty *prohibitions* have direct effect – even the most general ones. In *Mangold*,[44] the Court thus held that an – unwritten and vague – *general* principle of European law could have direct effect.

Should we embrace this development? We should, for the direct effect of a legal rule 'must be considered as being the normal condition of any rule of law'. The very questioning of the direct effect of European law was an 'infant disease' of the young European legal order.[45] And this infant disease has today – largely – been cured but for one area: the Common Foreign and Security Policy.

b. Dimensions: Vertical and Horizontal Direct Effect

Where a Treaty provision is directly effective, an individual can invoke European law in a national court (or administration). This will normally be as against the State. This situation is called 'vertical' effect, since the State is 'above' its subjects. But while a private party is in subordinate position vis-à-vis public authorities, it is in a coordinate position vis-à-vis other private parties. The legal effect of a norm between private parties is thus called 'horizontal' effect. And while there

---

[40] Case 13/68, *Salgoil* v. *Italian Ministry of Foreign Trade* [1968] ECR 453 at 463.

[41] Case 41/74, *van Duyn* v. *Home Office* [1974] ECR 1337, para. 7.

[42] For the opposite view, see K. Lenaerts and T. Corthaut, 'Of Birds and Hedges: The Role of Primacy in Invoking Norms of EU Law' (2006) 31 *EL Rev.* 287 at 310: direct effect 'is the technique which allows individuals to enforce a subjective right which is only available in the internal legal order in an instrument that comes from outside that order, against another (state or private) actor'.

[43] M. Ruffert, 'Rights and Remedies in European Community Law: A Comparative View' (1997) 34 *CML Rev.* 307 at 315.

[44] For a long discussion of this case, see section 3(b/bb).

[45] P. Pescatore, 'The Doctrine of "Direct Effect": An Infant Disease of Community Law' (1983) 8 *EL Rev.* 155.

has never been any doubt that Treaty provisions can be invoked in a vertical situation, there has been some discussion about their horizontal direct effects.

Should it make a difference whether European law is invoked in administrative proceedings against the Inland Revenue or in a civil dispute between two private parties? Should the Treaties be allowed to impose obligations on individuals? The Court in *Van Gend en Loos* had accepted this theoretical possibility.[46] And, indeed, the horizontal direct effect of Treaty provisions has never been in doubt for the Court.[47] A good illustration of the horizontal direct effect of Treaty provisions can be found in *Familiapress* v. *Bauer*.[48] The case concerned the interpretation of Article 34 TFEU prohibiting unjustified restriction on the free movement of goods. It arose in a *civil* dispute before the Vienna Commercial Court between Familiapress and a German competitor. The latter was accused of violating the Austrian Law on Unfair Competition by publishing prize crossword puzzles – a sales technique that was deemed unfair under Austrian law. Bauer defended itself in the national court by invoking Article 34 TFEU – claiming that the directly effective European right to free movement prevailed over the Austrian law. And the Court of Justice indeed found that a national law that constituted an unjustified restriction of trade would have to be disapplied in the civil proceedings.

The question whether a Treaty prohibition has horizontal direct effect must, however, be distinguished from the question of whether it also outlaws private party actions. For example, imagine that the rule prohibiting prize crossword puzzles had not been adopted by the Austrian legislature but by the Austrian Press Association – a private body regulating Austrian newspapers. Would this 'private' rule equally breach Article 34 TFEU? The latter is not simply a question of the *effect* of a provision, but rather of its personal scope.[49]

Many Treaty prohibitions are – expressly or implicitly – addressed to the State.[50] However, the Treaties equally contain provisions that are directly addressed to private parties.[51] The question whether a Treaty prohibition covers public as well as private actions is controversial. Should the 'equal pay for equal work' principle or the free movement rules – both *expressly* addressed to the Member

---

[46] Case 26/62, *Van Gend en Loos*, 12: '[European] law therefore not only imposes obligations on individuals ...'.

[47] Indeed, the direct effect of Art. 34 TFEU was expressly announced in a 'horizontal' case between two private parties; see Case 74/76, *Iannelli & Volpi* v. *Paolo Meroni*.

[48] Case C-368/95, *Vereinigte Familiapress Zeitungsverlags- und vertriebs GmbH* v. *Bauer Verlag* [1997] ECR I-3689.

[49] This point will be further discussed in the specific context of the free movement of goods, see Chapter 13, section 1(a).

[50] For example, Art. 157 TFEU states (emphasis added) that '[e]ach *Member State* shall ensure that the principle of equal pay for male and female workers for equal work or work of equal value is applied'; and Art. 34 TFEU prohibits restrictions on the free movement of goods 'between Member States'.

[51] Art. 101 TFEU prohibits 'all agreements between undertakings' that restrict competition within the internal market, and is thus addressed to private parties.

States – also *implicitly* apply to private associations and their actions? If so, the application of the Treaty will not just impose *indirect* obligations on individuals (when they lose their right to rely on a national law that violates European law); they will be *directly* prohibited from engaging in an activity. The Court has – in principle – confirmed that Treaty provisions, albeit addressed to the Member States, might cover private actions.[52] Thus in *Defrenne*, the Court found that the prohibition on pay discrimination between men and women could equally apply to private employers.[53] And, while the exact conditions remain uncertain,[54] the Court has confirmed and reconfirmed the inclusion of private actions within the free movement provisions.[55]

To distinguish the logical relations between the various constitutional concepts of direct applicability, direct effect – both vertical (VDE) and horizontal (HDE) – and private party actions, Figure 3.3 may be useful.

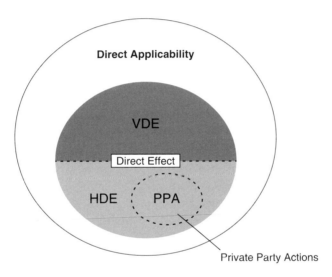

Figure 3.3 Direct Applicability, Direct Effect and Private Party Actions

---

[52] Case 36/74, *Walrave et al.* v. *Association Union cycliste international et al.* [1974] ECR 1405, para. 19: 'to limit the prohibitions in question to acts of a public authority would risk creating inequality in their application'.

[53] Case 43/75, *Defrenne*, para. 39: 'In fact, since Article [157 TFEU] is mandatory in nature, the prohibition on discrimination between men and women applies not only to the action of public authorities, but also extends to all agreements which are intended to regulate paid labour collectively, as well as to contracts between individuals.'

[54] The Court generally limits this application to 'private' rules that aim to regulate 'in a collective manner' (*ibid.*, para. 17). For somewhat more recent case law on the application of the free movement rules to private parties, see Case C-415/93, *Union Royale Belge des Sociétés de Football Association ASBL* v. *Jean-Marc Bosman* [1995] ECR I-4921.

[55] This has been confirmed for all four freedoms, with the possible exception of the provisions on goods. On the application of the free movement provisions in this context, see Chapter 13, section 1(a). For the same question in the context of EU fundamental rights, see Chapter 12, section 4(d).

2. Direct Union Law: Regulations and Decisions

When the European Union was created, the Treaties envisaged two instruments that were a priori directly applicable: regulations and decisions. A regulation would be an act of direct and general application in all Member States. It was designed as the legislative act of the Union. By contrast, a decision was originally seen as the executive instrument of the Union. It would directly apply to those to whom it was addressed.[56] Both instruments were predestined to have direct effects in the sense of allowing individuals to directly invoke them before national courts. Nonetheless, their precise effects have remained – partially – controversial. Would all provisions within a regulation be directly effective? And could decisions be generally applicable? Let us look at these questions in turn.

a. Regulations: The 'Legislative' Instrument

Article 288 defines a 'regulation' as follows:

> A regulation shall have general application. It shall be binding in its entirety and directly applicable in all Member States.[57]

This definition demands four things. First, regulations must be *generally* applicable. Second, they must be *entirely* binding. Third, they must be *directly* applicable, and that – fourth – in *all* Member States. This section starts by investigating characteristics one and four. It subsequently analyses the relationship between direct applicability and the question of direct effect.[58]

aa. General Application in All Member States

Regulations were designed to be an instrument of (material) legislation.[59] Their 'general application' was originally meant to distinguish them from the 'specific application' of decisions.

In *Zuckerfabrik Watenstedt GmbH* v. *Council*,[60] the European Court defined 'general' applicability as 'applicable to objectively determined situations and involves legal consequences for categories of persons viewed in a general and abstract manner'; yet conceded that a regulation would not lose its general nature 'because it may be possible to ascertain with a greater or lesser degree of accuracy

---

[56] The original Art. 189 EEC stated: 'A decision shall be binding in its entirety upon those to whom it is addressed.'

[57] Art. 288(2) TFEU.

[58] We shall analyse the 'second' element in Chapter 4, section 4(a/aa) when dealing with a regulation's pre-emptive capacity.

[59] Joined Cases 16–17/62, *Confédération Nationale des Producteurs de Fruits et de Légumes* v. *Council* [1962] ECR 471, para. 2. On the material concept of legislation, see Chapter 7, Introduction.

[60] Case 6/68, *Zuckerfabrik Watenstedt GmbH* v. *Council* [1968] ECR 409.

the number or even the identity of the persons to which it applies at any given time as long as there is no doubt that the measure is applicable as a result of an objective situation of law or of fact which it specifies'.[61] The crucial characteristic of a regulation – a characteristic that would give it a 'legislative' character – is thus the 'openness' of the group of persons to whom it applies. Where the group of persons is 'fixed in time' the act would not constitute a regulation but a bundle of individual decisions.[62]

Would all provisions within a regulation have to satisfy the general applicability test? The European Court has clarified that this is not the case. Not all provisions of a regulation must be general in character. Some provisions may indeed constitute individual decisions 'without prejudice to the question whether that measure considered in its entirety can be correctly called a regulation'.[63] This laxer threshold has also been applied to the geographical scope of regulations. Article 288 TFEU tells us that they must be applicable in all the Member States. However, the European Court sees a regulation's geographical applicability from an abstract perspective: while normatively valid in all Member States, its concrete application can be confined to a limited number of States.[64]

bb. Direct Application and Direct Effect

By making regulations directly applicable, the Treaties recognised from the very beginning a monistic connection between that Union act and the national legal orders. Regulations would be automatically binding *within* the Member States – a characteristic that distinguished them from ordinary international law. Regulations were thus 'a *direct source of rights and duties* for all those affected thereby, whether Member States or individuals, who are parties to legal relationships under [European] law'.[65] In 1958, this was extraordinary: the Union had been given the power to directly legislate for all individuals in the Member States.[66]

Would the direct application of regulations imply their direct effect? Direct applicability and direct effect are, as we saw above,[67] distinct concepts. The former refers to the *normative* validity of regulations within the national legal order. Direct applicability indeed simply means that no 'validating' national act is needed for European law to have effects within the domestic legal orders: 'The direct application of a Regulation means that its entry into force and its application in favour of those subject to it are independent of any measure of reception

---

[61] *Ibid.*, at 415.
[62] Joined Cases 41–4/70, *International Fruit Company and others* v. *Commission* [1971] ECR 411, esp. para. 17.
[63] Joined Cases 16–17/62, *Confédération Nationale des Producteurs de Fruits et Légumes*, para. 2.
[64] Case 64/69, *Compagnie Française commerciale et financière* v. *Commission* [1970] ECR 221.
[65] Case 106/77, *Amministrazione delle Finanze dello Stato* v. *Simmenthal SpA* [1978] ECR 629, paras. 14–15 (emphasis added).
[66] J.-V. Louis, *Les Règlements de la Communauté Économique Européenne* (Presses universitaires de Bruxelles, 1969), 16.
[67] See Introduction to this chapter.

into national law.'[68] Direct effect, on the other hand, refers to the ability of a norm to execute itself. Direct applicability thus only makes direct effect *possible*, but the former will not automatically imply the latter. The direct application of regulations thus 'leave[s] open the question whether a particular provision of a regulation has direct effect or not'.[69] In the words of an early commentator:

> Many provisions of regulations are liable to have direct effects and can be enforced by the courts. Other provisions, although they have become part of the domestic legal order as a result of the regulation's direct applicability, are binding for the national authorities only, without granting private persons the right to complain in the courts that the authorities have failed to fulfil these binding [Union] obligations. This is by no means an unrealistic conclusion. In every member State there consists quite a bit of law which is not enforceable in the courts, because these rules were not meant to give the private individual enforceable rights or because they are too vague or too incomplete to admit of judicial application.[70]

Direct effect is thus narrower than direct applicability. Not all provisions of a regulation will have to have direct effect. This has been expressly recognised by the Court.[71] In *Azienda Agricola Monte Arcosa*, the Court thus stated:

> [A]lthough, by virtue of the very nature of regulations and of their function in the system of sources of [European] law, the provisions of those regulations generally have immediate effect in the national legal systems without its being necessary for the national authorities to adopt measures of application, some of their provisions may none the less necessitate, for their implementation, the adoption of measures of application by the Member States … In the light of the discretion enjoyed by the Member States in respect of the implementation of those provisions, it cannot be held that individuals may derive rights from those provisions in the absence of measures of application adopted by the Member States.[72]

Legislative discretion left to the national level will thus prevent provisions within regulations from having direct effect, 'where the legislature of a Member State has not adopted the provisions necessary for their implementation in the

---

[68] Case 34/73, *Fratelli Variola SpA* v. *Amministrazione delle Finanze dello Stato* [1973] ECR 981, para. 10.

[69] P. Pescatore, *The Law of Integration: Emergence of a New Phenomenon in International Relations, Based on the Experience of the European Communities* (Sijthoff, 1974), 164.

[70] G. Winter, 'Direct Applicability and Direct Effect: Two Distinct and Different Concepts in Community Law' (1972) *CML Rev.* 425 at 436.

[71] See Case 230/78, *SpA Eridania-Zuccherifici nazionali and SpA Società Italiana per l'Industria degli Zuccheri* v. *Minister of Agriculture and Forestry, Minister for Industry, Trade and Craft Trades and SpA Zuccherifici Meridionali* [1979] ECR 2749; Case 137/80, *Commission* v. *Belgium* [1981] ECR 653; Case 72/85, *Commission* v. *The Netherlands* [1986] ECR 1219.

[72] Case C-403/98, *Azienda Agricola Monte Arcosa Srl* [2001] ECR I-103, paras. 26, 28.

national legal system'.[73] Regulations often explicitly call for the adoption of implementing measures.[74] But even if there is no express provision, Member States are under a general duty to implement non-directly effective provisions within regulations.[75] Yet non-directly effective provisions might still have indirect effects. These indirect effects have been extensively discussed in the context of directives, and will be treated there. Suffice to say here that the European Court applies the constitutional doctrines developed in the context of directives – such as the principle of consistent interpretation – also to provisions within regulations.[76]

b. Decisions: The Executive Instrument

Article 288 defines a Union 'decision' as follows:

> A decision shall be binding in its entirety. A decision which specifies those to whom it is addressed shall be binding only on them.[77]

The best way to make sense of this definition is to contrast it with that for regulations. Like a regulation, a decision shall be binding in its entirety. And like a regulation it will be directly applicable. However, unlike a regulation, a decision was originally not designed to be generally applicable;[78] yet, with time, European constitutional practice developed a non-addressed decision. This development

---

[73] *Ibid.*, para. 29.

[74] Art. 2(5) of Regulation 797/85 and Art. 5(5) of Regulation 2328/91 – at issue in *Azienda Agricola Monte Arcosa Srl* – indeed stated: 'Member States shall, for the purposes of this Regulation, define what is meant by the expression "farmer practising farming as his main occupation".' For an analysis of this practice, see R. Král, 'National Normative Implementation of EC Regulations: An Exceptional or Rather Common Matter?' (2008) 33 *EL Rev.* 243.

[75] For an implicit duty to adopt national implementing measures, see Case C-177/95, *Ebony Maritime et al.* v. *Prefetto della Provincia di Brindisi et al.* [1997] ECR I-1111, para. 35: '[T]he Court has consistently held that where a [Union] regulation does not specifically provide any penalty for an infringement or refers for that purpose to national laws, regulations and administrative provisions, Article [4(3) TEU] requires the Member States to take all measures necessary to guarantee the application and effectiveness of [European] law.'

[76] Case C-60/02, *Criminal proceedings against X* [2004] ECR I-651, paras. 61–3, esp. para. 62 (emphasis added): 'Even though in the case at issue in the main proceedings the [Union] rule in question is a regulation, which by its very nature does not require any national implementing measures, and not a directive, Article 11 of Regulation No 3295/94 empowers Member States to adopt penalties for infringements of Article 2 of that regulation, thereby making it possible to *transpose to the present case the Court's reasoning in respect of directives.*'

[77] Art. 288(4) TFEU.

[78] The old Art. 189 EEC stated: 'A decision shall be binding in its entirety upon those to whom it is addressed.'

is now recognised in Article 288(4) TFEU that allows for two types of decisions: decisions specifically applicable to those to whom it is addressed, and decisions that are generally applicable because they are not addressed to anybody specifically.

aa. *Specifically Addressed Decisions*

Decisions that mention an addressee shall only be binding on that person. Depending on whether the addressee(s) are private individuals or Member States, European law thereby distinguishes between individual decisions and State-addressed decisions.

Individual decisions are similar to national administrative acts. They are designed to execute a Union norm by applying it to an individual situation. A good illustration can be found in the context of competition law, where the Commission is empowered to prohibit anticompetitive agreements that negatively affect the internal market.[79] A decision that is addressed to a private party will only be binding on the addressee. However, this will not necessarily mean that it has no *horizontal* effects on other parties. Indeed, the European legal order expressly recognises that decisions addressed to one person may be of 'direct and individual concern' to another.[80] In such a situation this 'third person' is entitled to challenge the legality of that decision.[81]

State-addressed decisions constitute the second group of decisions specifically applicable to the addressee(s).[82] We find again a good illustration of this Union act in the context of competition law. Here the Union is empowered to prohibit State aid to undertakings that threaten to distort competition within the internal market.[83] What is the effect of a State-addressed decision in the national legal orders? Binding on the Member State(s) addressed, may it give direct rights to individuals? In *Grad* v. *Finanzamt Traunstein*,[84] the Court answered this question positively. The German government had claimed that State-addressed decisions cannot, unlike regulations, create rights for private persons. But the response of the European Court went the other way:

> [A]lthough it is true that by virtue of Article [288], regulations are directly applicable and therefore by virtue of their nature capable of producing direct effects, it does not follow from this that other categories of legal measures mentioned in that Article can

---

[79] Art. 101 TFEU.

[80] Art. 263[4] TFEU: 'Any natural or legal person may, under the conditions laid down in the first and second paragraphs, institute proceedings against an act addressed to that person or which is of direct and individual concern to them, and against a regulatory act which is of direct concern to them and does not entail implementing measures.'

[81] For this point, see Chapter 10, section 1(c).

[82] On this type of decision, see U. Mager, 'Die staatengerichtete Entscheidung als supranationale Handlungsform' (2001) 36 *Europarecht* 661.

[83] Art. 107 TFEU.

[84] Case 9/70, *Grad* v. *Finanzamt Traunstein* [1970] ECR 825.

> never produce similar effects. In particular, the provision according to which decisions are binding in their entirety on those to whom they are addressed enables the question to be put whether the obligation created by the Decision can only be invoked by the [Union] institutions against the addressee or whether such a right may possibly be exercised by all those who have an interest in the fulfilment of this obligation.
>
> It would be incompatible with the binding effect attributed to decisions by Article [288] to exclude in principle the possibility that persons affected may invoke the obligation imposed by a decision. Particularly in cases where, for example, the [Union] authorities by means of a decision have imposed an obligation on a Member State or all the Member States to act in a certain way, the effectiveness ('l'effect utile') of such a measure would be weakened if the nationals of that State could not invoke it in the courts and the national courts could not take it into consideration as part of [European] law. Although the effects of a decision may not be identical with those of a provision contained in a regulation, this difference does not exclude the possibility that the end result, namely the right of the individual to invoke the measures before the courts, may be the same as that of a directly applicable provision of a regulation.[85]

State-addressed decisions could, consequently, create rights for private citizens. They could have direct effect in certain circumstances. What were those circumstances? The Court insisted that the direct effect of a provision depended on 'the nature, background and wording of the provision'.[86] And indeed: the provision in question was a prohibition that was 'unconditional and sufficiently clear and precise to be capable of producing direct effects in the legal relationships between the Member States and those subject to their jurisdiction'.[87] This test came close – remarkably close – to the Court's direct effect test for Treaty provisions. But would this also imply – like for Treaty provisions – their horizontal direct effect? State-addressed decisions here seem to follow the legal character of directives,[88] which will be discussed in section 3.

bb. Non-addressed Decisions

While not expressly envisaged by the original Treaties, non-addressed decisions (decisions *sui generis*) had become a widespread constitutional phenomenon within the European Union.[89] The Lisbon Treaty has now 'officialised' them in Article 288 TFEU. But what is the function of these decisions? In the past,

---

[85]   *Ibid.*, para. 5.   [86]   *Ibid.*, para. 6.   [87]   *Ibid.*, para. 9.

[88]   See Case C-80/06, *Carp* v. *Ecorad* [2007] ECR I-4473, paras. 19ff., esp. para. 21: 'In accordance with Article [288], Decision 1999/93 is binding only upon the Member States, which, under Article 4 of that decision, are the sole addressees. Accordingly, the considerations underpinning the case-law referred to in the preceding paragraph with regard to directives apply *mutatis mutandis* to the question whether Decision 1999/93 may be relied upon as against an individual.'

[89]   For a historical and systematic analysis, see the groundbreaking work by J. Bast, *Grundbegriffe der Handlungsformen der EU: entwickelt am Beschluss als praxisgenerierter Handlungsform des Unions- und Gemeinschaftsrechts* (Springer, 2006).

the Union had recourse to these decisions – instead of regulations – to have an instrument that was directly applicable but lacked direct effect.

3. Indirect Union Law: Directives

The third binding instrument of the Union is the most mysterious one: the directive. According to Article 288 TFEU, a 'directive' is defined as follows:

> A directive shall be binding, as to the result to be achieved, upon each Member State to which it is addressed, but shall leave to the national authorities the choice of form and methods.[90]

This formulation suggested two things. First, directives appeared to be externally binding *on* States – not *within* States. On the basis of such a 'dualist' reading, directives would have no validity in the national legal orders. They seemed *not* to be directly applicable, and would thus need to be 'incorporated' or 'implemented' through national legislation. This dualist view was underlined by the fact that Member States were only bound as to the result to be achieved – for the obligation of result is common in classic international law.[91] Second, binding solely on the State(s) to which it was addressed, directives appeared to lack *general* application. Their general application could indeed only be achieved indirectly *via* national legislation transforming the European content into national form. Directives have consequently been described as 'indirect legislation'.[92]

But could this indirect Union law have direct effects? In a courageous line of jurisprudence, the Court confirmed that directives could – under certain circumstances – have direct effect and thus entitle individuals to have their European rights applied in national courts. But, if this was possible, would directives not become instruments of direct Union law, like regulations? The negative answer to this question will become clearer in this third section. Suffice to say here that the test for the direct effect of directives is subject to two additional limitations – one temporal, one normative. Direct effect would only arise *after* a Member State had failed properly to 'implement' the directive into national law, and then only in relation to the State authorities themselves. We shall analyse the conditions and limits for the direct effect of directives first, before exploring their potential indirect effects in national law.

---

[90] Art. 288(3) TFEU.
[91] For this view, see L.-J. Constantinesco, *Das Recht der Europäischen Gemeinschaften* (Nomos, 1977), 614. For a recent look at the various choices with regard to the methods of transposition, see R. Král, 'On the Choice of Methods of Transposition of EU Directives' (2016) 41 *EL Rev.* 220.
[92] Pescatore, 'Doctrine of "Direct Effect"' (n. 45 above) at 177.

a. Direct Effect and Directives: Conditions and Limits

That directives could directly give rise to rights that individuals could claim in national courts was accepted in *Van Duyn* v. *Home Office*.[93]

The case concerned a Dutch secretary, whose entry into the United Kingdom had been denied on the grounds that she was a member of the Church of Scientology. Britain had tried to justify this limitation on the free movement of workers by reference to an express derogation within the Treaties that allowed such restrictions on grounds of public policy and public security.[94] However, in an effort to harmonise national derogations from free movement, the Union had adopted a directive according to which '[m]easures taken on grounds of public policy or of public security shall be based exclusively on the *personal conduct of the individual concerned*'.[95] This outlawed national measures that limited free movement for generic reasons, such as membership of a disliked organisation. Unfortunately, the United Kingdom had not 'implemented' the directive into national law.

Could Van Duyn nonetheless directly invoke the directive against the British authorities? The Court of Justice found that this was indeed possible by emphasising the distinction between direct applicability and direct effect:

> [B]y virtue of the provisions of Article [288] regulations are directly applicable and, consequently, may by their very nature have direct effects, it does not follow from this that other categories of acts mentioned in that Article can never have similar effects. It would be incompatible with the binding effect attributed to a directive by Article [288] to exclude, in principle, the possibility that the obligation which it imposes may be invoked by those concerned. In particular, where the [Union] authorities have, by directive, imposed on Member States the obligation to pursue a particular course of conduct, the useful effect of such an act would be weakened if the individuals were prevented from relying on it before their national courts and if the latter were prevented from taking it into consideration as an element of [European] law. Article [267], which empowers national courts to refer to the Court questions concerning the validity and interpretation of all acts of the [Union] institutions, without distinction, implies furthermore that these acts may be invoked by individuals in the national courts.[96]

The Court here – rightly – emphasised the distinction between direct applicability and direct effect, yet – wrongly – defined the relationship between these two concepts in order to justify its conclusion. To brush aside the textual

---

[93] Case 41/74, *Van Duyn* v. *Home Office* [1974] ECR 1337.

[94] Art. 45(1) and (3) TFEU.

[95] Directive 64/221 on the coordination of special measures concerning the movement and residence of foreign nationals which are justified on grounds of public policy, public security or public health, OJ (English Special Edition): Chapter 1963–1964/117, Art. 3(1) (emphasis added).

[96] Case 41/74, *Van Duyn*, para. 12.

argument that regulations are directly applicable while directives are not, it wrongly alluded to the idea that direct effect without direct application was possible.[97] And the direct effect of directives was then justified by three distinct arguments. First, to exclude direct effect would be incompatible with the 'binding effect' of directives. Second, their 'useful effect' would be weakened if individuals could not invoke them in national courts. Third, since the preliminary reference procedure did not exclude directives, the latter must be capable of being invoked in national courts.

What was the constitutional value of these arguments? Argument one is a sleight of hand: the fact that a directive is not binding in *national law* is not 'incompatible' with its binding effect under *international law*. The second argument is strong, but not of a legal nature: to enhance the useful effect of a rule by making it more binding is a political argument. Finally, the third argument only begs the question: while it is true that the preliminary reference procedure generically refers to all 'acts of the institutions', it could be argued that only those acts that are directly effective can be referred. The decision in *Van Duyn* was right, but sadly without reason.

The lack of a convincing *legal* argument to justify the direct effect of directives soon prompted the Court to propose a fourth argument:

> A Member State which has not adopted the implementing measures required by the Directive in the prescribed periods may not rely, as against individuals, on its own failure to perform the obligations which the directive entails.[98]

This fourth reason has become known as the 'estoppel argument' – acknowledging its intellectual debt to English 'equity' law. A Member State that fails to implement its European obligations is 'stopped' from invoking that failure as a defence, and individuals are consequently – and collaterally – entitled to rely on the directive as against the State. Unlike the three original arguments, this fourth argument is *State*-centric. It locates the rationale for the direct effect of directives not in the nature of the instrument itself, but in the behaviour of the State.

This (behavioural) rationale would result in two important limitations on the direct effect of directives. For even if provisions within a directive were 'unconditional and sufficiently precise' 'those provisions may [only] be *relied upon by*

---

[97] In the words of J. Steiner: 'How can a law be enforceable by individuals within a Member-State if it is not regarded as incorporated in that State?' ('Direct Applicability in EEC: A Chameleon Concept' (1982) 98 *Law Quarterly Review* 229–48 at 234). The direct effect of a directive presupposes its direct application. And, indeed, ever since *Van Gend en Loos*, all directives must be regarded as directly applicable (see S. Prechal, *Directives in EC Law* (Oxford University Press, 2005), 92 and 229). For the same conclusion, see also C. Timmermans, 'Community Directives Revisited' (1997) 17 YEL 1–28 at 11–12.

[98] Case 148/78, *Ratti* [1979] ECR 1629, para. 22.

an individual against the State where that State fails to implement the Directive in national law *by the end of the period prescribed or where it fails to implement the directive correctly'*.[99] This direct effect test for directives therefore differed from that for ordinary Union law, as it added a temporal and a normative limitation. *Temporally*, the direct effect of directives could only arise *after* the failure of the State to implement the directive had occurred. Thus, before the end of the implementation period granted to Member States, no direct effect could take place. And even once this temporal condition had been satisfied, the direct effect would operate only as against the State. This *normative* limitation on the direct effect of directives has become famous as the 'no-horizontal-direct-effect rule'.

aa. The No-horizontal-direct-effect Rule

The Court's jurisprudence of the 1970s had extended the direct effect of Union law to directives. An individual could claim his European rights against a State that had failed to implement a directive into national law. This situation was one of 'vertical' direct effect. Could an individual equally invoke a directive against another private party? This 'horizontal' direct effect existed for direct Union law; yet should it be extended to directives?

The Court's famous answer is a resolute 'no': directives could not have horizontal direct effects. The 'no-horizontal-direct-effect rule' was first expressed in *Marshall*.[100] The Court here based its negative conclusion on a textual argument:

> [A]ccording to Article [288 TFEU] the binding nature of a directive, which constitutes the basis for the possibility of relying on the directive before a national court, exists only in relation to 'each member state to which it is addressed'. It follows that a directive may not of itself impose obligations on an individual and that a provision of a directive may not be relied upon as such against such a person.[101]

The absence of horizontal direct effect was confirmed in *Dori*.[102] A private company had approached Ms Dori for an English language correspondence course. The contract had been concluded in Milan's busy central railway station. A few days later, she changed her mind and tried to cancel the contract. A right of cancellation had been provided by the European directive on consumer contracts concluded outside business premises,[103] but Italy had not implemented the directive into national law. Could a private party nonetheless directly rely on the unimplemented directive against another private party? The Court was firm:

---

[99]   Case 80/86, *Kolpinghuis Nijmegen BV* [1987] ECR 3969, para. 7 (emphasis added).

[100] Case 152/84, *Marshall v. Southampton and South-West Hampshire Area Health Authority* [1986] ECR 723.

[101] *Ibid.*, para. 48.

[102] Case C-91/92, *Faccini Dori v. Recreb* [1994] ECR I-3325.

[103] Directive 85/577 concerning protection of the consumer in respect of contracts negotiated away from business premises ([1985] OJ L 372/31).

[A]s is clear from the judgment in *Marshall* ... the case-law on the possibility of relying on directives against State entities is based on the fact that under Article [288] a directive is binding only in relation to 'each Member State to which it is addressed'. That case-law seeks to prevent 'the State from taking advantage of its own failure to comply with [European] law' ... The effect of extending that case-law to the sphere of relations between individuals would be to recognise a power in the [Union] to enact obligations for individuals with immediate effect, whereas it has competence to do so only where it is empowered to adopt regulations. It follows that, in the absence of measures transposing the directive within the prescribed time-limit, consumers cannot derive from the directive itself a right of cancellation as against traders with whom they have concluded a contract or enforce such a right in a national court.[104]

This denial of any direct effect of directives in horizontal situations was grounded in three arguments.[105] First, a textual argument: a directive is binding in relation to each Member State to which it is addressed. (But had the Court not used this very same argument to establish the direct effect of directives in the first place?) Second, the estoppel argument: the direct effect for directives exists to prevent a State from taking advantage of its own failure to comply with European law. And since individuals were not responsible for the non-implementation of a directive, direct effect should not be extended to them. Third, a systematic argument: if horizontal direct effect were given to directives, the distinction between directives and regulations would disappear. This was a weak argument, for a directive's distinct character could be preserved in different ways.[106] In order to bolster its reasoning, the Court added a fourth argument in subsequent jurisprudence: legal certainty.[107] Since directives were not originally published, they must not impose obligations on those to whom they are not addressed. This argument has lost some of its force,[108] but continues to be very influential today.

All these arguments may be criticised.[109] But the Court of Justice has stuck to its conclusion: directives cannot *directly* impose obligations on individuals. They lack horizontal direct effect. This constitutional rule of European law has nonetheless been qualified by one limitation and one exception.

---

[104] Case C-91/92, *Dori*, paras. 22–5.

[105] The Court silently dropped the 'useful effect argument' as it would have worked towards the opposite conclusion.

[106] On this point, see R. Schütze, 'The Morphology of Legislative Power in the European Community: Legal Instruments and the Federal Division of Powers' (2006) 25 YEL 91.

[107] See Case C-201/02, *The Queen* v. *Secretary of State for Transport, Local Government and the Regions, ex p. Wells* [2004] ECR I-723, para. 56: 'the principle of legal certainty prevents directives from creating obligations for individuals'.

[108] The publication of directives is now, in principle, required by Art. 297 TFEU.

[109] For an excellent overview of the principal arguments, see P. Craig, 'The Legal Effect of Directives: Policy, Rules and Exceptions' (2009) 34 *EL Rev.* 349. But why does Professor Craig concentrate on arguments one and four, instead of paying close attention to the strongest of the Court's reasons in the form of argument two?

bb. The Limitation to the Rule: The Wide Definition of State (Actions)

One way to minimise the no-horizontal-direct-effect rule is to maximise the vertical direct effect of directives. The Court has done this by giving extremely extensive definitions to what constitutes the 'State', and what constitute 'public actions'.

What public authorities count as the 'State'? A minimal definition restricts the concept to a State's central organs. Because they failed to implement the directive, the estoppel argument suggested them to be vertically bound by the directive. Yet the Court has never accepted this consequence, and has endorsed a maximal definition of the State. It thus held that directly effective obligations 'are binding upon *all authorities of the Member States*'; and this included 'all organs of the administration, including decentralised authorities, such as municipalities',[110] even 'constitutionally independent' authorities.[111]

The best formulation of this maximalist approach was given in *Foster*.[112] Was the 'British Gas Corporation' – a statutory corporation for developing and maintaining gas supply – part of the British 'State'? The Court held this to be the case. Vertical direct effect would apply to any body 'whatever its legal form, which has been made responsible, pursuant to a measure adopted by the State, *for providing a public service under the control of the State and has for that purpose special powers* beyond those which result from the normal rules applicable in relations between individuals'.[113] This wide definition of the State consequently covers *private* bodies endowed with *public* functions.

This functional definition of the State, however, suggested that only 'public acts', that is: acts adopted in pursuit of a public function, would be covered. Yet there are situations where the State acts horizontally like a private person: it might conclude private contracts and employ private personnel. Would these 'private actions' be covered by the doctrine of vertical direct effect?

In *Marshall*, the plaintiff argued that the United Kingdom had not properly implemented the Equal Treatment Directive. But could an *employee* of the South-West Hampshire Area Health Authority invoke the direct effect of a directive against this State authority in this *horizontal* situation? The British government argued that direct effect would only apply 'against a Member State *qua* public authority and not against a Member State *qua* employer'. 'As an employer a State is no different from a private employer'; and '[i]t would not therefore be proper to put persons employed by the State in a better position than those who are employed by a private employer'.[114] This was an excellent argument, but the

---

[110] Case 103/88, *Costanzo SpA v. Comune di Milano* [1989] ECR 1839, para. 31 (emphasis added).

[111] Case 222/84, *Johnston v. Chief Constable of the Royal Ulster Constabulary* [1986] ECR 1651, para. 49.

[112] Case C-188/89, *Foster and others v. British Gas* [1990] ECR I-3313.

[113] *Ibid.*, para. 20 (emphasis added). For recent confirmations of that test, see Case C-46/15, *Ambisig Ambiente e Sistemas de Informação Geográfica*, EU:C:2016:530, para. 22; Case C-413/15, Farrell, EU:C:2017:745.

[114] Case 152/84, *Marshall*, para. 43.

Court would have none of it. According to the Court, an individual could rely on a directive as against the State 'regardless of the capacity in which the latter is acting, whether employer or public authority'.[115]

Vertical direct effect would thus not only apply to *private* parties exercising public functions, but also to public authorities engaged in *private* activities.[116] This double extension of the doctrine of vertical direct effect can be criticised for treating similar situations dissimilarly, for it creates a discriminatory limitation to the no-horizontal-direct-effect rule. However, the Court has recently confirmed that both extensions are an integral result of the *Foster* doctrine.[117]

cc. The Exception to the Rule: Incidental Horizontal Direct Effect

In the two previous scenarios, the Court respected the rule that directives could not have direct horizontal effects, but limited the rule's scope of application. Yet in some 'incidents', the Court has found a directive *directly* to affect the horizontal relations between private parties. This 'incidental' horizontal effect of directives must, despite some scholastic effort to the contrary,[118] be seen as an *exception* to the rule. The incidental horizontal direct effect cases indeed *violate* the rule that directives cannot negatively affect private parties. The two 'incidents' chiefly responsible for the doctrine of incidental horizontal direct effects here are *CIA Security* and *Unilever Italia*.

In *CIA Security* v. *Signalson and Securitel*,[119] the Court dealt with a dispute between three Belgian competitors whose business was the manufacture and sale of security systems. CIA Security had applied to a commercial court for orders requiring Signalson and Securitel to cease libel. The defendants had alleged that the plaintiff's alarm system did not satisfy Belgian security standards. This was indeed the case, but the Belgian legislation itself violated a European notification requirement established by Directive 83/189. But because the European norm was in a directive, this violation could – theoretically – not be invoked in a horizontal dispute between private parties. Or could it? The Court held as follows:

---

[115] *Ibid.*, para. 49.

[116] *Ibid.*, para. 51: 'The argument submitted by the United Kingdom that the possibility of relying on provisions of the Directive against the respondent qua organ of the State would give rise to an arbitrary and unfair distinction between the rights of State employees and those of private employees does not justify any other conclusion. Such a distinction may easily be avoided if the Member State concerned has correctly implemented the Directive in national law.'

[117] Case C-413/15, *Farrell*, where the Court was asked whether the traditional *Foster* definition consisted of two cumulative or two alternative criteria; and the Court expressly clarified that the latter was the case (*ibid.*, esp. para. 33).

[118] This phenomenon has been referred to as the: 'incidental' horizontal effect of directives (P. Craig and G. de Búrca, *EU Law* (Oxford University Press, 2011), 207ff.); 'horizontal side effects of direct effect' (Prechal, *Directives in EC Law* (n. 97 above), 261–70); and the 'disguised' vertical effect of directives (M. Dougan, 'The "Disguised" Vertical Direct Effect of Directives' (2000) 59 *Cambridge Law Journal* 586–612).

[119] Case C-194/94, *CIA Security* v. *Signalson and Securitel* [1996] ECR I-2201.

> Articles 8 and 9 of Directive 83/189 lay down a precise obligation on Member States to notify draft technical regulations to the Commission before they are adopted. Being, accordingly, *unconditional and sufficiently precise in terms of their content, those articles may be relied on by individuals before national courts.* It remains to examine the legal consequences to be drawn from a breach by Member States of their obligation to notify and, more precisely, whether Directive 83/189 is to be interpreted as meaning that a breach of the obligation to notify, constituting a procedural defect in the adoption of the technical regulations concerned, renders such technical regulations inapplicable so that they may not be enforced against individuals ... [I]t is undisputed that the aim of the directive is to protect freedom of movement for goods by means of preventive control and that the obligation to notify is essential for achieving such [Union] control. *The effectiveness of [Union] control will be that much greater if the directive is interpreted as meaning that breach of the obligation to notify constitutes a substantial procedural defect such as to render the technical regulations in question inapplicable to individuals.*[120]

CIA Security could thus rely on the directive as against its private competitors; and the national court had to 'decline to apply a national technical regulation which has not been notified in accordance with the directive'.[121] What else was this but horizontal direct effect?

This — puzzling — result was confirmed in *Unilever Italia v. Central Food.*[122] Unilever had supplied Central Food with olive oil that did not conform to Italian labelling legislation, and Central Food therefore refused to honour the sales contract between the two companies. Unilever, in turn, brought proceedings claiming that the Italian legislation violated Directive 83/189. The case was referred to the European Court of Justice, where the Italian and Danish governments intervened. Both governments protested that it was 'clear from settled case-law of the Court that a directive cannot of itself impose obligations on individuals and cannot therefore be relied on as such against them'.[123] But the Court's — strange — answer was again this:

> Whilst it is true, as observed by the Italian and Danish Governments, that a directive cannot of itself impose obligations on an individual and cannot therefore be relied on as such against an individual, that case-law does not apply where non-compliance with Article 8 or Article 9 of Directive 83/189, which *constitutes a substantial procedural defect*, renders a technical regulation adopted in breach of either of those articles inapplicable. In such circumstances, and unlike the case of non-transposition of directives with which the case-law cited by those two Governments is concerned, Directive 83/189 does not in any way define the substantive scope of the legal rule on the basis of which the national court must decide the case before it. It creates neither rights nor obligations for individuals.[124]

---

[120]   *Ibid.*, paras. 44–8 (emphasis added).   [121]   *Ibid.*, para. 55.
[122]   Case C-443/98, *Unilever Italia v. Central Food* [2000] ECR I-7535.
[123]   *Ibid.*, para. 35.   [124]   *Ibid.*, paras. 50–1 (emphasis added).

What did this mean? Could a 'substantial procedural effect' lead to the horizontal direct effect of the directive? Let us stick to hard facts. In both cases, the national court was required to disapply national legislation in *civil* proceedings between *private* parties. Did CIA Security and Unilever not 'win' a right from the directive to have national legislation disapplied; and did Signalson and Central Food not 'lose' the right to have national law applied? It seems impossible to deny that the directive *did* directly affect the rights and obligations of individuals. Even if it was addressed to the States by imposing a procedural obligation on them, it incidentally obliged private parties to accept forfeiting their national rights.

However, the exception to the no-horizontal-direct-effect rule has remained an exceptional exception.[125] But, even so, there are – strong – arguments for the Court to abandon its constitutional rule altogether.[126] And as we shall see in the Conclusion below, the entire debate surrounding directives might simply be the result of some linguistic confusion.

b. Indirect Effects through National and (Primary) European Law

aa. The Doctrine of Consistent Interpretation of National Law

Norms may have direct and indirect effects. A provision within a directive lacking direct effect may still have certain indirect effects in the national legal orders. The lack of direct effect means exactly that: a directive cannot itself – that is: *directly* – be invoked. However, a directive may still have indirect effects on the interpretation of national law. For the European Court has created a general duty on national courts (and administrations)[127] to interpret national law as far as possible in light of all European law.

---

[125] It may, at first sight, seem that the Court has broadened this exception to a second context in Case C-377/14, *Radlinger and Radlingerová v. Finway*, EU:C:2016:283. In this case, the plaintiff(s) had concluded an (unfair) credit agreement that the defendant sought to enforce. This credit agreement seemed to violate various EU consumer law directives; yet the national court had not investigated these, as there existed national legislation that did not permit a court to examine of its own motion the unfairness of contractual terms in this context. The Court of Justice found that this national rule itself violated the EU directives at issue (*ibid.*, paras. 54 and 66); but did this mean that the EU directives would need to be horizontally applied between the parties? The Court eschewed the answer. While invoking the *CIA/Unilever* idea that this was a situation in which 'a procedural rule [was] placed not on an individual but on the courts' (*ibid.*, para. 77), it nevertheless left open whether the obligation to apply the EU directives *ex officio* would have direct or only indirect effects on individuals (*ibid.*, paras. 79–80).

[126] See Opinion of Advocate General Jacobs in Case C-316/93, *Vaneetveld v. Le Foyer* [1994] ECR I-763, para. 31: '[I]t might well be conducive to greater legal certainty, and to a more coherent system, if the provisions of a directive were held in appropriate circumstances to be directly enforceable against individuals'; Craig, 'Legal Effect of Directives' (n. 109 above), 390: 'The rationales for the core rule that Directives do not have horizontal direct effect based on the Treaty text, legal certainty and the Regulations/Directives divide are unconvincing.'

[127] Case C-218/01, *Henkel v. Deutsches Patent- und Markenamt* [2004] ECR I-1725.

The doctrine of consistent interpretation was given an elaborate definition in *Von Colson*:

> [T]he Member States' obligation arising from a Directive to achieve the result envisaged by the Directive and their duty under Article [4(3) TEU] to take all appropriate measures, whether general or particular, to ensure the fulfilment of that obligation, is binding on all the authorities of Member States including, for matters within their jurisdiction, the courts. It follows that, in applying the national law in particular the provisions of a national law specifically introduced in order to implement [a Directive], national courts are required to interpret their national law in the light of the wording and the purpose of the Directive in order to achieve the result referred to in the third paragraph of Article [288].[128]

The duty of consistent interpretation is a duty to implement a directive by indirect means. Where a national legislator has *failed* to directly implement a directive, the task is (partly) transferred to the national judiciary. National courts are here under an obligation to 'implement' the directive judicially through a 'European' interpretation of national law. Temporally, the duty of consistent interpretation however only starts applying *after* the implementation period of the directive has passed.[129]

This duty of consistent interpretation applies regardless of 'whether the [national] provisions in question *were adopted before or after the directive*'.[130] The duty indeed extends to all national law – irrespective of whether the latter was intended to implement the directive. However, where domestic law had been specifically enacted to implement the directive, the national courts must operate under the particularly strong presumption 'that the Member State, following its exercise of the discretion afforded to it under that provision, had the intention of fulfilling entirely the obligations arising from the directive'.[131]

---

[128] Case 14/83, *Von Colson and Elisabeth Kamann* v. *Land Nordrhein-Westfalen* [1984] ECR 1891, para. 26. Because this paragraph was so important in defining the duty of consistent interpretation, it is sometimes referred to as the '*Von Colson* principle'.

[129] National courts are not required to interpret their national law in light of Union law *before* (!) the expiry of the implementation deadline. After Case C-212/04, *Adeneler and others* v. *Ellinikos Organismos Galaktos (ELOG)* [2006] ECR I-6057, there is no room for speculation on this issue: '[W]here a directive is transposed belatedly, the general obligation owed by national courts to interpret domestic law in conformity with the directive exists only once the period for its transposition has expired' (*ibid.*, para. 115). However, once a directive has been adopted, a Member State will be under the immediate constitutional obligation to 'refrain from taking any measures liable seriously to compromise the result prescribed' in the directive, see C-129/96, *Inter-Environnement Wallonie ASBL* v. *Region Wallonne* [1997] ECR 7411, para. 45. This obligation is independent of the doctrine of indirect effect.

[130] Case C-106/89, *Marleasing* v. *La Comercial Internacional de Alimentacion* [1990] ECR I-4135, para. 8 (emphasis added).

[131] Joined Cases C-397/01 to C-403/01, *Pfeiffer*, para. 112. For a more recent confirmation of this rule, see Case C-306/12, Spedition Welter, EU:C:2013:650, esp. para. 32: '[I]n

The duty of consistent interpretation leads to the *indirect* implementation of a directive. It can *indirectly* impose new obligations – both vertically and horizontally. An illustration of the horizontal *indirect* effect of directives can be seen in *Webb*.[132] The case concerned a claim by Mrs Webb against her employer. The latter had hired the plaintiff to replace a pregnant co-worker during her maternity leave. Two weeks after she had started work, Mrs Webb discovered that she was pregnant herself, and was dismissed for that reason. She brought proceedings before the Industrial Tribunal, pleading sex discrimination. The Industrial Tribunal rejected this on the grounds that the reason for her dismissal had not been her sex but her inability to fulfil the primary task for which she had been recruited. The case went on appeal to the (then) House of Lords, which confirmed the interpretation of national law but nonetheless harboured doubts about Britain's European obligations under the Equal Treatment Directive. On a preliminary reference, the European Court indeed found that there was sex discrimination under the directive and that the fact that Mrs Webb had been employed to replace another employee was irrelevant.[133] On receipt of the preliminary ruling, the House of Lords was thus required to change its previous interpretation of national law. Mrs Webb *won* a right, while her employer *lost* the right to dismiss her.

The doctrine of indirect effect here changed the horizontal relations between two private parties; and the duty of consistent interpretation has consequently been said to amount to '*de facto* (horizontal) direct effect of the directive'.[134] Normatively, this horizontal effect is however an *indirect* effect, as it operates through the medium of national law.

Are there limits to the duty of consistent interpretation? The duty is very demanding: national courts are required to interpret their national law '*as far as possible*, in the light of the wording and the purpose of the [Union act]'.[135] But what will 'as far as possible' mean? Should national courts be required to behave as if they were the national legislature? This might seriously undermine the (relatively) passive place reserved for judiciaries in most national constitutional orders. And the European legal order has therefore only asked national courts to adjust the interpretation of national law 'in so far as it is given discretion to do so *under national law*'.[136]

The European Court thus accepts that there exist established judicial methodologies within the Member States and has permitted national courts to limit themselves to 'the application of interpretative methods recognised by *national*

---

circumstances such as those of the case in the main proceedings, where national legislation reproduced word for word the provisions of Article 21(5) of the directive, the referring court is required, taking the whole body of domestic law into consideration and applying the interpretative methods recognised by domestic law, to interpret national law in a way that is compatible with the interpretation given to the directive by the Court.'

[132] Case C-32/93, *Webb* v. *EMO Air Cargo* [1994] ECR I-3567.

[133] *Ibid.*, paras. 26–8.   [134] Prechal, *Directives in EC Law* (n. 97 above), 211.

[135] Case C-106/89, *Marleasing*, para. 8 (emphasis added).

[136] Case C-14/83, *Von Colson*, para. 28 (emphasis added).

law'.[137] National courts are thus not obliged to 'invent' or 'import' novel interpretative methods.[138] However, within the discretion given to the judiciary under national constitutional law, the European doctrine of consistent interpretation requires the referring court 'to do whatever lies within its jurisdiction, having regard to the whole body of rules of national law'.[139]

Are there also European constitutional limits to the duty of the Union-conform interpretation of national law? The Court has clarified that the duty of consistent interpretation 'is limited by the general principles of law which form part of [European] law and in particular the principles of legal certainty and non-retroactivity'.[140] But, more importantly, the Court recognises that the clear and unambiguous wording of a national provision constitutes an absolute limit to its interpretation.[141] National courts are thus not required to interpret national law *contra legem*.[142] (This will however not protect 'established case-law' if the wording allows for an alternative interpretation.)[143] The duty of consistent interpretation would thus find a boundary in the clear wording of a provision. National courts are only required to interpret the text – and not to amend it! Textual amendments continue to be the task of the national legislatures – and not the national judiciaries.

bb. Indirect Effects through the Medium of European Law

The European Court has built an alternative – second – avenue to promote the indirect effect of directives. Instead of mediating their effect through *national*

---

[137]   Joined Cases C-397–403/01, *Pfeiffer,* para. 116 (emphasis added).

[138]   See M. Klammert, 'Judicial Implementation of Directives and Anticipatory Indirect Effect: Connecting the Dots' (2006) 43 *CML Rev.* 1251 at 1259. For the opposite view, see Prechal, *Directives in EC Law* (n. 97 above), 213.

[139]   Joined Cases C-397–403/01, *Pfeffer,* para. 118.

[140]   Case 80/86, *Kolpinghuis* [1987] ECR 3969, para. 13. This has been taken to imply that a Union-conform interpretation must not aggravate the criminal liability of a private party, as criminal law is subject to particularly strict rules of interpretation. For a general discussion here, see S. Drake, 'Twenty Years after *Von Colson*: The Impact of "Indirect Effect" on the Protection of the Individual's Community Rights' (2005) 30 *EL Rev.* 329.

[141]   Case C-555/07, *Kücükdeveci* v. *Swedex* [2010] ECR I-365, para. 49. See now also Case C-176/12, *Association de Médiation sociale,* EU: C: 2014: 2, 39.

[142]   Case C-212/04, *Adeneler* [2006] ECR I-5057, para. 110: 'It is true that the obligation on a national court to refer to the content of a directive when interpreting and applying the relevant rules of domestic law is limited by general principles of law, particularly those of legal certainty and non-retroactivity, and that obligation cannot serve as the basis for an interpretation of national law *contra legem*.' For a more recent case here, see: Case C-282/10, *Dominguez,* EU:C:2012:33.

[143]   Case C-441/14, *DI* v. *Estate of Rasmussen,* EU:C:2016:278, paras. 33–4: '[T]he requirement to interpret national law in conformity with EU law entails the obligation for national courts to change its established case-law, where necessary, if it is based on an interpretation of national law that is incompatible with the objectives of a directive. Accordingly, the national court cannot validly claim in the main proceedings that it is impossible for it to interpret the national provision at issue in a manner that is consistent with EU law by mere reason of the fact that it has consistently interpreted that provision in a manner that is incompatible with EU law.'

law, it indirectly translates their content into European law. How so? The way the Court has achieved this has been to capitalise on the general principles of European law. For the latter may — as primary Union law — have horizontal direct effect.[144]

This new avenue was opened in *Mangold*.[145] The case concerned the German law on Part-Time Working and Fixed-Term Contracts. The national employment law, transposing a European directive on the subject, permitted fixed-term employment contracts if the worker had reached the age of 52. However, the German law seemed to violate a second directive: Directive 2000/78 establishing a general framework for equal treatment in employment and occupation adopted to combat discrimination in the workplace. According to Article 6(1) of the directive, Member States could provide for differences in the workplace on grounds of age only if 'they are objectively and reasonably justified by a legitimate aim, including legitimate employment policy, labour market and vocational training objectives, and if the means of achieving that aim are appropriate and necessary'. In the present case, a German law firm had hired Mr Mangold, then aged 56, on a fixed-term employment contract. A few weeks after commencing employment, Mangold brought proceedings against his employer before the Munich Industrial Tribunal, where he claimed that the German law violated Directive 2000/78, as a disproportionate discrimination on grounds of age.

The argument was not only problematic because it was raised in *civil* proceedings between two *private* parties, which seemed to exclude the horizontal *direct* effect of Article 6(1). More importantly, since the implementation period of Directive 2000/78 had not yet expired, even the horizontal *indirect* effect of the directive could not be achieved through a 'Europe-consistent' interpretation of *national* law. Yet having found that the national law indeed violated the *substance* of the directive,[146] the Court was out to create a new way to review the legality of the German law. Instead of using the directive as such — directly or indirectly — it found a general principle of European constitutional law that stood *behind* the directive. That principle was the principle of non-discrimination on grounds of age. And it was *that* general principle that would bind the Member States when implementing European law.[147] From there, the Court reasoned as follows:

> Consequently, observance of the general principle of equal treatment, in particular in respect of age, cannot as such be conditional upon the expiry of the period allowed the Member States for the transposition of a directive intended to lay down a general framework for combating discrimination on the grounds of age ... In those circumstances it is the responsibility of the national court, hearing a dispute involving the principle of non-discrimination in respect of age, to provide, in a case within its

---

[144] On the normative quality of primary Union law, see section 1 above.
[145] Case C-144/04, *Mangold* v. *Helm* [2005] ECR I-9981.
[146] *Ibid.*, para. 65.
[147] On the so-called 'implementation situation', see Chapter 12, section 4(a).

> jurisdiction, the legal protection which individuals derive from the rules of [European] law and to ensure that those rules are fully effective, setting aside any provision of national law which may conflict with that law. Having regard to all the foregoing, the reply to be given to the [national court] must be that [European] law and, more particularly, *Article 6(1) of Directive 2000/78, must be interpreted as precluding a provision of domestic law such as that at issue in the main proceedings which author- ises, without restriction, unless there is a close connection with an earlier contract of employment of indefinite duration concluded with the same employer, the conclusion of fixed-term contracts of employment once the worker has reached the age of 52.*[148]

This judgment has been – very – controversial. But it is less the individ- ual components than their combination and context that was contentious. Past precedents had indeed established that the Union's (unwritten) general princi- ples might dynamically derive from the constitutional traditions of the Member States.[149] And the Court had previously found that provisions in a directive could be backed up by such a general principle.[150] It was also undisputed that general principles could apply to the Member States implementing European law and thereby have direct effect.[151] However, to use all elements in *this* context was potentially explosive. If this technique were generalised, the limitations inherent in the directive as an instrument of secondary law could be outflanked. The generalised use of primary law as the medium for secondary law was dangerous 'since the subsidiary applicability of the principles not only gives rise to a lack of legal certainty but also distorts the nature of the system of sources, converting typical [Union] acts into merely decorative rules which may be easily replaced by the general principles'.[152] Put succinctly: if a *special* directive is adopted to make a *general* principle sufficiently precise, how can the latter have direct effect while the former has not?

Yet to the chagrin of some,[153] the *Mangold* ruling was confirmed *and* consol- idated in *Kücükdeveci*.[154] This time, Germany was said to have violated Directive

---

[148] Case C-144/04, *Mangold*, paras. 76–8 (emphasis added).

[149] On this point, see Chapter 12, section 1(a). In the present case the 'genesis' of a general principle prohibiting age discrimination was indeed controversial. Apparently, only two national constitutions recognised such a principle (see Advocate General Mazák in Case C-411/05, *Palacios de la Villa* [2007] ECR I-8531).

[150] See Case 222/84, *Johnston* v. *Chief Constable*, para. 18: 'The requirement of judicial control stipulated by that article [of the directive] reflects a general principle of law which under- lies the constitutional traditions common to the Member States.'

[151] In the present case, the actual conclusion was nonetheless controversial (see M. Dougan, 'In Defence of Mangold?', in A. Arnull et al. (eds.), *A Constitutional Order of States? Essays in EU Law in Honour of Alan Dashwood* (Hart, 2011), 219).

[152] Joined Cases C-55-07 and C-56/07, *Michaeler et al.* v. *Amt für sozialen Arbeitsschutz Bozen* [2008] ECR I-3135, para. 21.

[153] For a piece of German angst, consider the decision of the German Constitutional Court in *Honeywell* discussed in Chapter 4, section 2(b).

[154] Case C-555/07, *Kücükdeveci* v. *Swedex* [2010] ECR I-365.

2000/78 by having discriminated against *younger* employees. The bone of contention was Article 622 of the German Civil Code, which established various notice periods depending on the duration of the employment relationship. However, the provision only started counting the duration after an employee had turned 25.[155] After ten years of service to a private company, Ms Kücükdeveci had been sacked. Having started work at the age of 18, her notice period was thus calculated on the basis of a three-year period. Believing that this *shorter* notice period for young employees was discriminatory, she brought an action before the Industrial Tribunal. On reference to the Court of Justice, that Court found the German law to violate the directive.[156] And since the implementation period for Directive 2000/78 had now expired, there was no *temporal* limit to establishing the indirect effect of the directive through national law.

But the indirect effect of the directive via the medium of national law now encountered an − insurmountable − *normative* limit. Because of its clarity and precision, the German legal provision was 'not open to an interpretation in conformity with Directive 2000/78'.[157] The indirect effect of the directive could thus not be established via the medium of national law, and the Court chose once more a general principle of European law as the medium for the content of the directive. The Court thus held that it was 'the general principle of European Union law prohibiting all discrimination on grounds of age, *as given expression in Directive 2000/78*, which must be the basis of the examination of whether European Union law precludes national legislation such as that at issue in the main proceedings'.[158] And where this general principle had been violated, it was the obligation of the national court to disapply any provision of national legislation contrary to that principle − regardless of whether private or public parties are involved.[159] Yet, crucially, the Court remained ambivalent about whether the general principle was violated *because* the directive had been violated.[160] The better view would here be that this is not the case. From a constitutional

---

[155]   The last sentence of Art. 622(2) of the German Civil Code states: 'In calculating the length of employment, periods prior to the completion of the employee's 25th year of age are not taken into account.'

[156]   Case C-555/07, *Kücükdeveci*, para. 43.

[157]   *Ibid.*, para. 49.

[158]   *Ibid.*, para. 27 (emphasis added), see also para. 50. The Court has subsequently clarified that for any general principle to have direct effect in a particular situation, 'that situation must also fall within the scope of the prohibition of discrimination laid down by Directive 2000/78' (see Case C-441/14, *DI* v. *Estate of Rasmussen*, EU:C:2016:278), para. 24). The general principle thus must always be 'mediated'.

[159]   Case C-555/07, *Kücükdeveci*, para. 51; Case C-441/14, *DI*, para. 36.

[160]   In *ibid.*, para. 43, the Court found that 'European Union law, more particularly the principle of non-discrimination on grounds of age as given expression by Directive 2000/78, must be interpreted as precluding national legislation, such as that at issue in the main proceedings'. But did this mean that the directive and the general principle were violated? In a later paragraph, the Court seems to leave the question to the national courts 'to ensure the full effectiveness of that law, disapplying *if need be* any provision of national legislation contrary to that principle' (para. 51, emphasis added).

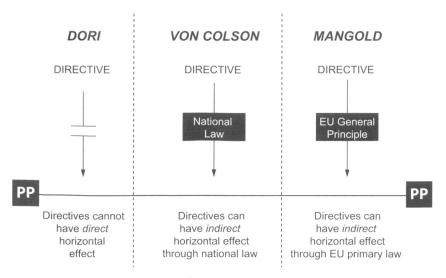

Figure 3.4 Indirect Effect in Proceedings Between Private Parties (PP)

perspective, the threshold for the violation of a general principle ought to be higher than that for a specific directive.[161]

4. External Union Law: International Agreements

In the 'globalised' world of the twenty-first century, international agreements have become important regulatory instruments. Instead of acting unilaterally, many States realise that the regulation of international trade or the environment requires a multilateral approach. And to facilitate international regulation, many legal orders have 'opened up' to international law and adopted a monist position. The European legal order has traditionally followed this monist approach. With regard to international agreements concluded by the Union, Article 216(2) TFEU states:

> Agreements concluded by the Union are binding upon the institutions of the Union and on its Member States.[162]

This definition suggested two things. First, international agreements were binding *in* the European legal order. And, indeed, the Court has expressly confirmed that international agreements 'form an integral part of the [European] legal system' from the date of their entry into force without the need for

---

[161]   The Court seems indeed to be moving in this direction, see Case C-147/08, *Römer v. Freie und Hansestadt Hamburg* [2011] ECR I-3591; Case C-176/12, *Association de médiation sociale v. Union locale des syndicats CGT and others*, EU: C: 2014: 2.

[162]   Emphasis added.

legislative acts of 'incorporation'.[163] Union agreements were external *Union law*. Second, these international agreements would also bind the Member States. And the Court here again favoured a monist philosophy. In treating international agreements as acts of the European institutions,[164] they would be regarded as European law; and as European law, they would be directly applicable 'in' the Member States. And, as directly applicable sources of European law, international agreements have the capacity to contain directly effective provisions that national courts must apply. When would such direct effects arise?

a. The Conditions of Direct Effect

Even in a monist legal order, not all international treaties will be directly effective.[165] The direct applicability of international agreements only makes them capable of having direct effects. Particular treaties may lack direct effect for 'when the terms of the stipulation import a contract, when either of the parties engages to perform a particular act, the treaty addresses itself to the political, not to the judicial department; and the legislature must execute the contract before it can become a rule for the Court'.[166] Where an international agreement asks for the adoption of implementing legislation it is indeed addressed to the legislative branch, and its norms will not be operational for the executive or the judiciary.

The question whether a Union agreement has direct effect has – again – been centralised by the European Court of Justice. The Court has justified this 'centralisation' by reference to the need to ensure legal uniformity in the European legal order. The effects of Union agreements may not be allowed to vary 'according to the effects in the internal legal order of each Member State which the law of that State assigns to international agreements'.[167] Once an agreement has thus been considered by the Court to unfold direct effects, it will be directly effective in the European as well as the national legal orders.

When will an international treaty have direct effects? The Court has devised a two-stage test.[168] In a first stage, it examines whether the agreement *as a whole* is capable of containing directly effective provisions. The signatory parties to the agreement may have positively settled this issue themselves.[169] If this is not the case, the Court will employ a 'policy test' that analyses the nature, purpose, spirit

---

[163]   Case 181/73, *Haegemann* v. *Belgium* [1974] ECR 449.

[164]   Case C-192/89, *Sevince* v. *Staatssecretaris van Justitie* [1990] ECR I-3461, para. 10.

[165]   C. M. Vazquez, 'Treaties as Law of the Land: The Supremacy Clause and the Judicial Enforcement of Treaties' (2008) 122 *Harvard Law Review* 599.

[166]   *Foster* v. *Neilson*, 27 US (2 Pet.) 253 at 314 (1829).

[167]   Case 104/81, *Hauptzollamt Mainz* v. *Kupferberg & Cie* [1982] ECR 3641, para. 14.

[168]   For an excellent analysis, see A. Peters, 'The Position of International Law within the European Community Legal Order' (1997) 40 *German Yearbook of International Law* 9–77 at 53–4 and 58–66.

[169]   Case 104/81, *Kupferberg*, para. 17.

or general scheme of the agreement.[170] This evaluation is inherently 'political', and the first part of the analysis is essentially a 'political question'. The conditions for the direct effect of external Union law here differ from the analysis of direct effect in the internal sphere, as internal law is automatically *presumed* to be *capable* of direct effect.

Where the 'political question' hurdle has been crossed, the Court will turn to examining the direct effect of a specific provision of the agreement.[171] The second stage of the test constitutes a classic direct effect analysis. Individual provisions must represent a 'clear and precise obligation which is not subject, in its implementation or effects, to the adoption of any subsequent measures'.[172] While the second stage of the test is thus identical to that for internal legislation, the actual results can vary. Identically worded provisions in internal and external legislation may not necessarily be given the same effect.[173]

In the past, the European Courts have generally been 'favourably disposed' towards the direct effect of Union agreements, and thus created an atmosphere of 'general receptiveness' to international law.[174] The classic exception to this constitutional rule is the WTO agreement.[175] The Union is a member of the World Trade Organization, and as such formally bound by its constituent agreements. Yet the Union Courts have persistently denied that agreement a safe passage through the first part of the direct effect test. The most famous judicial ruling in this respect is *Germany v. Council (Bananas)*;[176] yet, it was a later decision that clarified the constitutional rationale for the refusal to grant direct effect. In *Portugal v. Council*, the Court found it crucial to note that:

> Some of the contracting parties, which are among the most important commercial partners of the [Union], have concluded from the subject-matter and purpose of the WTO agreements that they are not among the rules applicable by their judicial organs

---

[170] See Joined Cases 21–24/72, *International Fruit Company NV and others* v. *Produktschap voor Groenten en Fruit* [1972] ECR 1219, para. 20; Case C-280/93, *Germany v. Council* [1993] ECR I-4973, para. 105.

[171] The two prongs of the test can be clearly seen in Case 104/81, *Kupferberg*. In paras. 18–22, the Court undertook the global policy test, while in paras. 23–7 it looked at the conditions for direct effectiveness of a specific provision.

[172] Case 12/86, *Demirel* v. *Stadt Schwäbisch Gmünd* [1987] ECR 3719, para. 14.

[173] J. H. J. Bourgeois, 'Effects of International Agreements in European Community Law: Are the Dice Cast?' (1983–4) 82 *Michigan Law Review* 1250–73 at 1261. See also the discussion on the pre-emptive effect of international treaties in Chapter 4, section 4(a/cc).

[174] P. Eeckhout, *External Relations of the European Union* (Oxford University Press, 2004), 301. This however appears to be in a process of change. On this development especially with regard to free trade agreements, see the excellent analysis by A. Semertzi, 'The Preclusion of Direct Effect in the Recently Concluded EU Free Trade Agreements' (2014) 51 *CML Rev.* 1125.

[175] P. Eeckhout, 'The Domestic Legal Status of the WTO Agreement: Interconnecting Legal System' (1997) 34 *CML Rev.* 11.

[176] Case C-280/93, *Germany v. Council* [1994] ECR I-4973.

> when reviewing the legality of their rules of domestic law. Admittedly, the fact that the courts of one of the parties consider that some of the provisions of the agreement concluded by the [Union] are of direct application whereas the courts of the other party do not recognise such direct application is not in itself such as to constitute a lack of reciprocity in the implementation of the agreement …
>
> However, the lack of reciprocity in that regard on the part of the [Union's] trading partners, in relation to the WTO agreements which are based on reciprocal and mutually advantageous arrangements and which must *ipso facto* be distinguished from agreements concluded by the [Union] … may lead to disuniform application of the WTO rules. *To accept that the role of ensuring that [European] law complies with those rules devolves directly on the [Union] judicature would deprive the legislative or executive organs of the [Union] of the scope for manoeuvre enjoyed by their counterparts in the [Union's] trading partners.*[177]

In light of the economic consequences of a finding of direct effect, the granting of such an effect to the WTO agreement was too political a question for the Court to decide. Not only was the agreement too 'political' in that it contained few hard-and-fast legal rules,[178] a unilateral decision to grant direct effect within the European legal order would have disadvantaged the Union vis-à-vis trading partners that had refused to allow for the agreement's enforceability in their domestic courts. The judicial self-restraint thus acknowledged that the constitutional prerogative for external relations lay primarily with the executive branch. Surprisingly, the Court's cautious approach to the WTO agreements, and their progeny,[179] has recently been extended into a second field.[180] And it seems likely that this less receptive approach will also apply to agreements concluded within the Union's Common Foreign and Security Policy. In light of the latter's specificity,[181] the Court might well find that the 'nature and broad logic' of CFSP agreements prevent their having direct effects within the Union legal order.

---

[177]   Case C-149/96, *Portuguese Republic* v. *Council of the European Union* [1999] ECR I-8395, paras. 43–6 (emphasis added).

[178]   For the GATT Agreement, see Joined Cases 21–24/72, *International Fruit Company*, para. 21: 'This agreement which, according to its preamble, is based on the principle of negotiations undertaken on the basis of "reciprocal and mutually advantageous arrangements" is characterised by the great flexibility of its provisions[.]'

[179]   For the lack of direct effect of WTO rulings in the Union legal order, see Case C-377/02, *Van Parys* [2005] ECR I-1465. On the relationship between the European Courts and decisions by international tribunals, see M. Bronckers, 'The Relationship of the EC Courts with Other International Tribunals. Non-committal, Respectful or Submissive?' (2007) 44 *CML Rev.* 601.

[180]   The Court dealt with the United Nations Convention on the Law of the Sea (UNCLOS), in Case C-308/06, *Intertanko et al.* v. *Secretary of State for Transport* [2008] ECR I-4057 and found (paras. 64–5): '[I]t must be found that UNCLOS does not establish rules intended to apply directly and immediately to individuals and to confer upon them rights or freedoms capable of being relied upon against States, irrespective of the attitude of the ship's flag State. It follows that the nature and the broad logic of UNCLOS prevent the Court from being able to assess the validity of a [Union] measure in the light of that Convention.'

[181]   On this point, see Chapter 8, sections 2(a) and 3(a).

b. The Dimensions of Direct Effect

What are the dimensions of direct effect for the Union's international agreements? Will a directly effective Union agreement be vertically *and* horizontally directly effective?[182]

Two constitutional options exist. First, international treaties can have horizontal direct effects. Then international agreements would come close to being 'external regulations'. Alternatively, the Union legal order could treat international agreements as 'external directives' and limit their direct effect to the vertical dimension. European citizens could then only invoke a directly effective provision of a Union agreement against the European institutions and the Member States, but they could not rely on a Union agreement in a private situation.

The Court has not expressly decided which option to follow. Yet, in *Polydor v. Harlequin* it seemed tacitly to assume the possibility of a horizontal direct effect of international agreements.[183] Doubts remained.[184] Yet the Court did not dispel them in *Sevince*.[185] However, the acceptance of the horizontal direct effect thesis has gained ground. In *Deutscher Handballbund eV v. Kolpak*,[186] the Court was asked whether rules drawn up by the German Handball Federation – a private club – would be discriminatory on grounds of nationality. The sports club had refused to grant Kolpak – a Slovakian national – the same rights as German players. This seemed to violate Article 38 of the Association Agreement between the Union and Slovakia stipulating that 'workers of Slovak Republic nationality legally employed in the territory of a Member State shall be free from any discrimination based on nationality, as regards working conditions, remuneration or dismissal, as compared to its own nationals'. The question, therefore, arose whether

---

[182] For a good new look at this question, see S. Gáspár-Szilágyi, 'The "Horizontal Direct Effect" of EU International Agreements: Is the Court Avoiding a Clear Answer?' (2015) 42 *Legal Issues of Economic Integration* 93. The following section will not explore the special constitutional principles governing the indirect effect of international agreements within the Union legal order. For a brief overview here, see R. Schütze, 'Direct and Indirect Effects of Union Law', in R. Schütze and T. Tridimas (eds.), *Oxford Principles of European Union Law – Volume I* (Oxford University Press, 2018), 265 at 296ff.

[183] Case 270/80, *Polydor and others v. Harlequin and others* [1982] ECR 329.

[184] These doubts inevitably gave rise to a good degree of academic speculation. In 1985, the following questions were put to H. J. Glaesner, the then Director General of the Legal Service of the Council, by the House of Lords Select Committee on the European Communities: 'You are well acquainted with the direct effect doctrine of internal provisions of the Treaty of Rome. As regards external provisions, [European] case law only supports direct effects which can be invoked against Member States. Is there any likelihood of it being extended to relations between private individuals …?' 'Would the distinction be likely to be that the Court would be more ready to grant an individual's right arising out of an external treaty … but would they hesitate to impose obligations on individuals arising out of those external treaties?' The Director-General could only answer: 'That is my feeling; it is not a philosophical consideration but a *feeling* of mine' (see Select Committee on the European Communities, *External Competence of the European Communities* [1984–5] Sixteenth Report (HMSO, 1985), 154 (emphasis added)).

[185] Case C-192/89, *Sevince*.

[186] Case C-438/00, *Deutscher Handballbund eV v. Maros Kolpak* [2003] ECR I-4135.

this article had 'effects *vis-à-vis third parties inasmuch as it does not apply solely to measures taken by the authorities but also extends to rules applying to employees that are collective in nature*'.[187] The Court thought that this could indeed be the case.[188] And in allowing the rules to apply directly to private parties, the Court presumed that the international agreement would be horizontally directly effective.

This implicit recognition of the horizontal direct effect of Union agreements has been confirmed outside the context of association agreements.[189] And in the absence of any mandatory constitutional reason to the contrary, this choice seems preferable. Like US constitutionalism, the European legal order should not exclude the horizontal direct effect of international treaties. The problems encountered in the context of European directives would be reproduced – if not multiplied – if the European Court were to split the direct effect of international treaties into two halves. Self-executing treaties should thus be able 'to establish rights *and duties* of individuals directly enforceable in domestic courts'.[190]

Conclusion

For a norm to be a legal norm it must be enforceable.[191] The very questioning of the direct effect of European law was indeed an 'infant disease' of a young legal order.[192] 'But now that [European] law has reached maturity, direct effect should be taken for granted, as a normal incident of an advanced constitutional order.'[193]

The evolution of the doctrine of direct effect, discussed in this chapter, indeed mirrors this maturation. Today's test for the direct effect of European law is an extremely lenient test. A provision has direct effect, where it is 'unconditional' and thus 'sufficiently clear and precise' – two conditions that probe whether a norm can (or should) be applied in court or whether it first needs legislative concretisation. All sources of European law have been considered to be capable of producing law with direct effects. And this direct effect normally applies vertically as well as horizontally.

The partial exception to this rule is the 'directive'. For directives, the Union legal order prefers their indirect effects.[194] '[W]herever a directive is correctly

---

[187]   *Ibid.*, para. 19 (emphasis added).

[188]   *Ibid.*, paras. 32 and 37.

[189]   See Case C-265/03, *Simutenkov* v. *Ministerio de Educacion y Cultura and Real Federacion Espanola de Futbol* [2005] ECR I-2579, where the Court confirmed *Deutscher Handballbund* in the context of the Partnership and Cooperation Agreement between the EC and the Russian Federation.

[190]   S. A. Riesenfeld, 'International Agreements' (1989) 14 *Yale Journal of International Law* 455–67 at 463 (emphasis added).

[191]   On the difference between (merely) 'moral' and (enforceable) 'legal' norms, see H. L. A. Hart, *The Concept of Law* (Clarendon Press, 1997).

[192]   Pescatore, 'Doctrine of "Direct Effect"' (n. 45 above).

[193]   A. Dashwood, 'From *Van Duyn* to *Mangold* via *Marshall*: Reducing Direct Effect to Absurdity' (2006–7) 9 CYELS 81.

[194]   Case 80/86, *Kolpinghuis*, para. 15: 'The question whether the provisions of a directive may be relied upon as such before a national court arises only if the Member State concerned

implemented, its effects extend to individuals *through the medium of the implementing measures adopted*.'[195] The Court even seems to insist on the mediated effect of directives for those parts of a directive that are directly effective.[196] The directive thus represents a form of 'background' or 'indirect' European law,[197] which is in permanent symbiosis with national (implementing) legislation.[198]

But even when directives have direct effect, they generally do not have horizontal direct effects. Why has the Court shown such 'childish' loyalty to the no-horizontal-direct-effect rule? Has that rule not created more constitutional problems than it solves? And is the Court perhaps discussing a 'false problem'? For if the Court simply wishes to say that an (unimplemented) directive may never directly prohibit *private* party actions, this does not mean that it cannot have horizontal direct effects in civil disputes challenging the legality of *State* actions.[199]

A final point still needs to be raised. Will the – direct or indirect – effects of European law be confined to the *judicial* application of European law? This argument has been made.[200] But this narrow view bangs its head against hard empirical facts.[201] It equally raises serious theoretical objections. For why should the recognition of an 'administrative direct effect' represent a 'constitutional

---

has not implemented the directive in national law within the prescribed period or has implemented the directive incorrectly.'

[195] Case 8/81, *Becker* v. *Finanzamt Münster-Innenstadt* [1982] ECR 53, para. 19 (emphasis added).

[196] Case 102/79, *Commission* v. *Belgium* [1980] ECR 1473, para. 12.

[197] Case C-298/89, *Gibraltar* v. *Council* [1993] ECR I-3605, para. 16 (emphasis added): 'normally a form of *indirect regulatory or legislative measure*'.

[198] The indirect effect of directives thereby never stops. Directives will always remain in the background as a form of 'fallback' legislation even where the national authorities have correctly implemented the directive; see Case 62/00, *Marks & Spencer plc* v. *Commissioners of Customs & Excise* [2002] ECR I-6325, paras. 27–8.

[199] This – much – simpler reading of the substance of the case law would bring directives close to the normative character of Art. 107 TFEU – prohibiting State aid. For while the provision can be invoked as against the State as well as against a private party, it cannot prohibit private aids by private companies.

[200] In this sense, see B. de Witte, 'Direct Effect, Supremacy and the Nature of the Legal Order', in P. Craig and G. de Búrca (eds.), *The Evolution of EU Law* (Oxford University Press, 1999), 177 at 193; and B. de Witte, 'Direct Effect, Primacy and the Nature of the Legal Order', in P. Craig and G. de Búrca (eds.), *The Evolution of EU Law* (Oxford University Press, 2011), 323 at 333.

[201] Among the myriad judgments, see Case 103/88, *Costanzo SpA* v. *Comune di Milano* [1989] ECR 1839, para. 31, where the Court found it 'contradictory to rule that an individual may rely upon the provisions of a directive which fulfil the conditions defined above in proceedings before the national courts seeking an order against the administrative authorities, and yet to hold that those authorities are under no obligation to apply the provisions of the directive and refrain from applying provisions of national law which conflict with them. It follows that when the conditions under which the Court has held that individuals may rely on the provisions of a directive before the national courts are met, all organs of the administration … are obliged to apply those provisions.' See also Case C-118/00, *Larsy and Inasti* [2001] ECR 5063.

enormity'?[202] In most national legal orders the courts are as subordinate to national legislation as the executive branch. They may 'interpret' national legislation, but must not amend it. And, once we accept that European law entitles all national courts – even the lowest court in the remotest part of the country – to challenge an act of parliament or the national constitution, is it really such an enormous step to demand the same of the executive? Would it not be absurd *not* to require national administrations to apply European law, but to allow for judicial challenges of the resulting administrative act? The conclusions of this chapter indeed extend to the administrative direct effects of European law.

FURTHER READING

Books

J. Bast, *Grundbegriffe der Handlungsformen der EU: entwickelt am Beschluss als praxisgenerierter Handlungsform des Unions- und Gemeinschaftsrechts* (Springer, 2006)

J.-V. Louis, *Les Règlement de la Communauté économique européenne* (Presses universitaires des Bruxelles, 1969)

M. Mendez, *The Legal Effects of EU Agreements* (Oxford University Press, 2013)

S. Prechal, *Directives in EC Law* (Oxford University Press, 2006)

A. Schrauwen and J. Prinssen, *Direct Effect: Rethinking a Classic of EC Legal Doctrine* (Europa Law Publishing, 2004)

Articles (and Chapters)

A. von Bogdandy, F. Arndt and J. Bast, 'Legal Instruments in European Union law and Their Reform: A Systematic Approach on an Empirical Basis' (2004) 23 YEL 91

J. H. J. Bourgeois, 'Effects of International Agreements in European Community Law: Are the Dice Cast?' (1983–4) 82 *Michigan Law Review* 1250

P. Craig, 'Once Upon a Time in the West: Direct Effect and the Federalisation of EEC Law' (1992) 12 *Oxford Journal of Legal Studies* 453

A. Dashwood, 'From *Van Duyn* to *Mangold* via *Marshall*: Reducing Direct Effect to Absurdity' (2006–7) 9 *CYELS* 81

M. Dougan, 'The "Disguised" Vertical Direct Effect of Directives' (2000) 59 *Cambridge Law Journal* 586

S. Drake, 'Twenty Years after *Von Colson*: The Impact of "Indirect Effect" on the Protection of the Individual's Community Rights' (2005) 30 *EL Rev.* 329

S. Gáspár-Szilágyi, 'The "Horizontal Direct Effect" of EU International Agreements: Is the Court Avoiding a Clear Answer?' (2015) 42 *Legal Issues of Economic Integration* 93

M. Klammert, 'Judicial Implementation of Directives and Anticipatory Indirect Effect: Connecting the Dots' (2006) 43 *CML Rev.* 1251

P. Pescatore, 'The Doctrine of "Direct Effect": An Infant Disease of Community Law' (1983) 8 *EL Rev.* 155

S. Prechal, 'Does Direct Effect Still Matter?' (2000) 37 *CML Rev.* 1047

---

[202]   De Witte, 'Direct Effect, Supremacy' (n. 200 above), 193.

J. Steiner, 'Direct Applicability in EEC Law: A Chameleon Concept' (1982) 98 *Law Quarterly Review* 229

S. Weatherill, 'Breach of Directives and Breach of Contract' (2001) 26 *EL Rev.* 177

G. Winter, 'Direct Applicability and Direct Effect: Two Distinct and Different Concepts in Community Law' (1972) *CML Rev.* 425

B. de Witte, 'Direct Effect, Primacy and the Nature of the Legal Order', in P. Craig and G. de Búrca (eds.), *The Evolution of EU Law* (Oxford University Press, 1999), 323

Cases on the Website

Case 26/62, *Van Gend en Loos*; Case 6/68, *Zuckerfabrik*; Case 9/70, *Grad*; Case 2/74 *Reyners*; Case 41/74, *Van Duyn*; Case 43/75, *Defrenne*; Case 270/80, *Polydor v. Harlequin*; Case 14/83, *Von Colson*; Case 152/84, *Marshall*; Case C-188/89, *Foster*; Case C-192/89, *Sevince*; Case C-91/92, *Faccini Dori*; Case C-32/93, *Webb*; Case C-280/93, *Germany v. Council (Bananas)*; Case C-194/94, *CIA Security*; Case C-368/95, *Familiapress v. Bauer*; Case C-149/96, *Portugal v. Council*; Case C-403/98, *Azienda Agricola*; Case C-443/98, *Unilever Italia*; Case C-438/00, *Deutscher Handallbund eV v. Kolpak*; Case C-144/04, *Mangold*; Case C-555/07, *Kucukdeveci*

4

European Law II
Nature – Supremacy/Pre-emption

Contents

Introduction

Since European law is directly applicable in the Member States, it must be recognised alongside national law by national authorities. And since European law can have direct effect, it might come into conflict with national law in a specific situation.[1] And where two legislative wills come into conflict, each legal order must determine *when* conflicts arise and *how* these conflicts are to be resolved.

---

[1] For the main theories on the relationship between direct effect and supremacy, see M. Dougan, 'When Worlds Collide! Competing Visions of the Relationship between

For the Union legal order, these two dimensions have indeed been developed. In Europe's constitutionalism they have been described as, respectively, the principle of pre-emption and the principle of supremacy: 'The problem of preemption consists in determining whether there exists a conflict between a national measure and a rule of [European] law. The problem of [supremacy] concerns the manner in which such a conflict, if it is found to exist, will be resolved.'[2] Pre-emption and supremacy thus represent 'two sides of the same coin'.[3] They are like Siamese twins: different though inseparable. There is no supremacy without pre-emption.

This chapter begins with an analysis of the supremacy doctrine. How supreme is European law? Will European law prevail over all national law? And what is the effect of the supremacy principle on national law? We shall see that there are *two* perspectives on the supremacy question. According to the *European* perspective, all Union law prevails over all national law. This 'absolute' view is not shared by the Member States. Indeed, according to their *national* perspective(s), the supremacy of European law is relative: some national law is considered to be beyond the supremacy of European law.

A third section then moves to the doctrine of pre-emption. This concept tells us to what extent European law 'displaces' national law; or, to put it the other way around: how much legislative space European law still leaves to the Member States. The Union legislator is generally free to choose to what extent it wishes to pre-empt national law within a certain area. However, there are two possible constitutional limits to this freedom. First, the type of *instrument* used – regulation, directive or international agreement – might limit the pre-emptive effect of Union law. And, second: the type of *competence* on which the Union act is based might determine the capacity of the Union legislator to pre-empt the Member States.

Direct Effect and Supremacy' (2007) 44 *CML Rev.* 931. This chapter, as will become clearer below, favours the view that supremacy requires direct effect. For where a European norm lacks direct effect, it cannot be applied in a specific case and for that reason cannot clash with a national norm. This is, in my view, also the traditional position of the European Court. The latter – for example – regularly holds that 'the question whether a national provision must be disapplied in as much as it conflicts with European Union law arises only if no compatible interpretation of that provision proves possible' (Case C-282/10 Dominguez, EU:C:2012:33, para. 23); and that seems to clearly suggest that, with regard to the indirect effect of, say, a European directive, it is not the doctrine of supremacy but another doctrine that applies. And it is that (!) other doctrine, for example, the duty of consistent interpretation derived from Art. 4(3) TEU that is here given direct effect in a specific case.

[2] M. Waelbroeck, 'The Emergent Doctrine of Community Preemption: Consent and Redelegation', in T. Sandalow and E. Stein (eds.), *Courts and Free Markets: Perspectives from the United States and Europe*, 2 vols. (Oxford University Press, 1982), II, 548–80, at 551.

[3] S. Krislov, C.-D. Ehlermann and J. Weiler, 'The Political Organs and the Decision-Making Process in the United States and the European Community', in M. Cappelletti, M. Seccombe and J. Weiler (eds.), *Integration through Law: Europe and the American Federal Experience*, 5 vols. (de Gruyter, 1986), I, 3 at 90.

1. The European Perspective: Absolute Supremacy

The resolution of legal conflicts requires a hierarchy of norms. Modern federal States typically resolve conflicts between federal and State legislation in favour of the former: federal law is supreme over State law.[4] This 'centralised solution' has become so engrained in our constitutional mentalities that we tend to forget that the 'decentralised solution' is also possible: local law may reign supreme over central law.[5] (Supremacy and direct effect are thus *not* different sides of the same coin. While the supremacy of a norm implies its direct effect, the direct effect of a norm will *not* imply its supremacy.)[6] Each compound legal order must thus determine which law prevails in the case of a normative conflict. The simplest supremacy format here is one that is absolute: all law from one legal order is superior to all law from the other. Absolute supremacy may here be given to the legal system of the smaller *or* the bigger political community. But between these two extremes lies a range of possible nuances.[7]

When the Union was born, the European Treaties did not expressly state the supremacy of European law.[8] Did this mean that supremacy was a matter to be determined by the national legal orders (decentralised solution)? Or was there a *Union* doctrine of supremacy (centralised solution)? And if the latter, how supreme would European law be over national law? Would it adopt an absolute doctrine, or would it permit areas in which national law could prevail over conflicting European law? And would the supremacy of European law lead to the 'invalidation' of State law; or would it only demand its 'disapplication'?

---

[4] Art. VI, Clause 2 of the US Constitution, for example, states: 'This Constitution, and the Laws of the United States which shall be made in pursuance thereof; and all treaties made, or which shall be made, under the Authority of the United States, shall be the supreme Law of the Land.'

[5] For a long time, the 'decentralised solution' structured federal relationships during the Middle Ages. Its constitutional spirit is best preserved in the old legal proverb: 'Town law breaks county law, county law breaks common law'. In the event of a legislative conflict, supremacy was thus given to the rule of the smaller political community.

[6] We can see direct effect without supremacy in the status given to customary international law in the British legal order.

[7] The status of international law in the German legal order depends on its legal source. While general principles of international law assume a hierarchical position between the German Constitution and federal legislation, international treaties have traditionally been placed at the hierarchical rank of normal legislation.

[8] The 2004 Constitutional Treaty *would* have added an express provision (Art. I-6 CT): 'The Constitution and law adopted by the institutions of the Union in exercising competences conferred on it shall have primacy over the law of the Member States.' However, the provision was not taken over by the Lisbon Treaty. Yet the latter has added Declaration 17 which states: 'The Conference recalls that, in accordance with well settled case law of the Court of Justice of the European Union, the Treaties and the law adopted by the Union on the basis of the Treaties have primacy over the law of Member States, under the conditions laid down by the said case law.'

Let us tackle these questions in two steps. We shall first look at the scope of the supremacy doctrine and see that the Union prefers an absolute principle: all European law prevails over all national law. However, the supremacy of European law will not affect the validity of national norms. This 'executive' nature of supremacy will be discussed in a second step.

a. The Absolute Scope of the Supremacy Principle

The dualist traditions within some Member States in 1958 posed a serious legal threat to the unity of the Union legal order.[9] Within dualist States, the status of European law is seen as depending on the national act 'transposing' the European Treaties. Where this was a parliamentary act, any subsequent parliamentary acts could – expressly or implicitly – repeal the transposition law. Within the British tradition, this follows from the classic doctrine of parliamentary sovereignty: an 'old' Parliament cannot bind a 'new' one. Any 'newer' parliamentary act will thus theoretically prevail over the 'older' 1972 European Communities Act. But the supremacy of European law may even be threatened in constitutionally monist States, because the supremacy of European law can here find a limit in the State's constitutional identity.

Would the European legal order insist that its law was to prevail over all national law, including national constitutions? The Court of Justice did just that in a series of foundational cases. But, while the establishment of Union supremacy over internal national law was swift, its extension over the international treaties of the Member States was much slower.

aa. Supremacy over Internal Laws of the Member States

Frightened by the decentralised solution to the supremacy issue, the Court centralised the question of supremacy quickly by turning it into a principle of Union law. In *Costa* v. *ENEL*,[10] the European judiciary was asked whether national legislation adopted *after* 1958 could prevail over the Treaties. The litigation involved an unsettled energy bill owed by Costa to the Italian National Electricity Board. The latter had been created by the 1962 Electricity Nationalisation Act, which was challenged by the plaintiff as a violation of the European Treaties. The Italian dualist tradition responded that the European Treaties – like ordinary international law – had been transposed by national legislation in 1957 that could – following international law logic – be derogated by subsequent national legislation.

Could the Member States thus unilaterally determine the status of European law in their national legal orders? The Court rejected this reading and distanced itself from the international law thesis:

---

[9] C. Sasse, 'The Common Market: Between International and Municipal Law' (1965–6) 75 *Yale LJ* 696–753.

[10] Case 6/64, *Costa* v. *ENEL* [1964] ECR 585.

By contrast with ordinary international treaties, the E[U] Treaty has created its own legal system which, on the entry into force of the Treaty, became an integral part of the legal systems of the Member States and which their courts are bound to apply ... The integration into the laws of each Member State of provisions which derive from the [Union], and more generally the terms and the spirit of the Treaty, make it impossible for the States, as a corollary, to accord precedence to a unilateral and subsequent measure over a legal system accepted by them on a basis of reciprocity. Such a measure cannot therefore be inconsistent with that legal system. The *executive force* of [European] law cannot vary from one State to another in deference to subsequent domestic laws, without jeopardising the attainment of the objectives of the Treaty ... It follows from all these observations that the law stemming from the Treaty, an independent source of law, could not, because of its special and original nature, be overridden by domestic legal provisions, however framed, without being deprived of its character as [European] law and without the legal basis of the [Union] itself being called into question.[11]

European law would need to reign supreme over national law, since its 'executive force' must not vary from one State to another. The supremacy of Union law could not be derived from classic international law;[12] and for that reason that Court had to declare the Union legal order autonomous from ordinary international law.

How supreme was European law? The fact that the European Treaties prevailed over national legislation did not automatically imply that *all* European law would prevail over *all* national law. Would the Court accept a 'nuanced' solution for certain national norms, such as national constitutional law? The European Court never accepted the relative scope of the supremacy doctrine. This was clarified in *Internationale Handelsgesellschaft*.[13] A German administrative court doubted that European legislation could violate fundamental rights granted by the German Constitution and raised this very question with the European Court of Justice. Were the fundamental structural principles of national constitutions, including human rights, beyond the scope of EU supremacy? The Court disagreed:

---

[11] *Ibid.*, 593–4 (emphasis added).

[12] Some legal scholars refer to the 'supremacy' of international law vis-à-vis national law (see F. Morgenstern, 'Judicial Practice and the Supremacy of International Law' (1950) 27 *BYIL* 42). However, the concept of supremacy is here used in an imprecise way. Legal supremacy stands for the priority of one norm over another. For this, two norms must conflict and, therefore, form part of an integrated legal order. Yet classic international law is based on the sovereignty of States and that implied a dualist relation with national law. Reference to the international law doctrine *pacta sunt servanda* will hardly help. The fact that a State cannot invoke its internal law to justify a breach of international obligations is not supremacy. Behind the doctrine of *pacta sunt servanda* stands the concept of legal responsibility: a State cannot – without legal responsibility – escape its international obligations. The duality of internal and international law is thereby maintained: the former cannot affect the latter (as the latter cannot affect the former).

[13] Case 11/70, *Internationale Handelsgesellschaft mbH* v. *Einfuhr- und Vorratsstelle für Getreide und Futtermittel* [1970] ECR 1125.

> Recourse to the legal rules or concepts of national law in order to judge the validity of measures adopted by the institutions of the [Union] would have an adverse effect on the uniformity and efficiency of [Union] law. The validity of such measures can only be judged in the light of [Union] law.[14]

The validity of Union law could thus not be affected – even by the most fundamental norms within the Member States. The Court's vision of the supremacy of European law over national law was an absolute one: 'The whole of [European] law prevails over the whole of national law.'[15]

bb. Supremacy over International Treaties of the Member States

While the Union doctrine of supremacy had quickly emerged with regard to national legislation,[16] its extension to international agreements of the Member States was much slower. From the very beginning, the Treaties here recognised an express exception to the supremacy of European law. According to Article 351 TFEU:

> The rights and obligations arising from agreements concluded before 1 January 1958 or, for acceding States, before the date of their accession, between one or more Member States on the one hand, and one or more third countries on the other, shall not be affected by the provisions of the Treaties.[17]

Article 351 here codified the 'supremacy' of *prior* international agreements of the Member States over conflicting European law. In the event of a conflict between the two, it was European law that could be disapplied *within the national legal orders*. Indeed, Article 351 'would not achieve its purpose if it did not imply a duty on the part of the institutions of the [Union] not to impede the performance of the obligations of Member States which stem from a prior

---

[14] *Ibid.*, para. 3.

[15] R. Kovar, 'The Relationship between Community Law and National Law', in EC Commission (ed.), *Thirty Years of Community Law* (EC Commission, 1981), 109 at 112–13.

[16] On the establishment of the *social* acceptance of the doctrine, see K. Alter, *Establishing the Supremacy of European Law: The Making of an International Rule of Law in Europe* (Oxford University Press, 2001).

[17] Para. 1. The provision continues (para. 2): 'To the extent that such agreements are not compatible with the Treaties, the Member State or States concerned shall take all appropriate steps to eliminate the incompatibilities established. Member States shall, where necessary, assist each other to this end and shall, where appropriate, adopt a common attitude.' On the scope of this obligation, see J. Klabbers, 'Moribund on the Fourth of July? The Court of Justice on Prior Agreements of the Member States' (2001) 26 *EL Rev.* 187; and R. Schütze, 'The "Succession Doctrine" and the European Union', in *Foreign Affairs and the EU Constitution* (Cambridge University Press, 2014), 91.

agreement'.[18] This was a severe incursion into the integrity of the European legal order, and as such had to be interpreted restrictively.[19]

But would there be internal or external limits to the 'supremacy' of prior international treaties of the Member States? The Court clarified that there existed internal limits to the provision. Article 351(1) would only allow Member States to implement their *obligations* towards *third* States.[20] Member States could thus not rely on Article 351 to enforce their rights; nor could they rely on the provision to fulfil their international obligations between themselves.

These internal limitations are complemented by external limitations. The Court clarified their existence in *Kadi*.[21] While admitting that Article 351 would justify even derogations from primary Union law, the Court insisted that the provision 'cannot, however, be understood to authorise any derogation from the principles of liberty, democracy and respect for human rights and fundamental freedoms enshrined in Article [2] [T]EU as a foundation of the Union'.[22] In the opinion of the Court, 'Article [351 TFEU] may in no circumstances permit any challenge to the principles that form part of the very foundations of the [Union] legal order.'[23] The Union's constitutional identity constituted a limit to the supremacy of prior international treaties concluded by the Member States.

But can the – limited – application of Article 351 TFEU be extended, by analogy, to *all* international agreements concluded by the Member States? The main constitutional thrust behind the argument is that it protects the effective exercise of the treaty-making powers of the Member States. For: 'otherwise the Member States could not conclude any international treaty without running

---

[18] Case 812/79, *Attorney General* v. *Juan C. Burgoa* [1980] ECR 2787, para. 9 (emphasis added). This was confirmed in Case C-158/91, *Criminal Proceedings against Jean-Claude Levy* [1993] ECR I-4287, para. 22: 'In view of the foregoing considerations, the answer to the question submitted for a preliminary ruling must be that the national court is under an obligation to ensure [that the relevant European legislation] … is fully complied with by refraining from applying any conflicting provision of national legislation, unless the application of such a provision is necessary in order to ensure the performance by the Member State concerned of obligations arising under an agreement concluded with non-member countries prior to the entry into force of the EEC Treaty.'

[19] Case C-324/93, *The Queen* v. *Secretary of State for Home Department, ex p. Evans Medical Ltd and Macfarlan Smith Ltd* [1995] ECR I-563, para. 32.

[20] Case 10/61, *Commission* v. *Italy* [1962] ECR 1, 10–11: '[T]he terms "rights and obligations" in Article [351] refer, as regards the "rights", to the rights of third countries and, as regards the "obligations", to the obligations of Member States and that, by virtue of the principles of international law, by assuming a new obligation which is incompatible with rights held under a prior treaty, a State ipso facto gives up the exercise of these rights to the extent necessary for the performance of its new obligation … In fact, in matters governed by the [European] Treat[ies], th[ese] Treat[ies] take precedence over agreements concluded between Member States before [their] entry into force[.]'

[21] Case C-402/05P, *Kadi and Al Barakaat International Foundation* v. *Council and Commission* [2008] ECR I-6351.

[22] *Ibid.*, para. 303.

[23] Case C-402/05P, *Kadi*, para. 304.

the risk of a subsequent conflict with [European] law'.[24] This idea has been criticised: there would be no reason why the normal constitutional principles characterising the relationship between European law and unilateral national acts should not also apply to subsequently concluded international agreements.[25] A middle position has proposed limiting the analogous application of Article 351 to situations where the conflict between post-accession international treaties of Member States and subsequently adopted European legislation was 'objectively unforeseeable' and could therefore not be expected.[26]

None of the proposals to extend Article 351 by analogy has however been mirrored in the jurisprudence of the European Court of Justice.[27] The Court has unconditionally upheld the supremacy of European law over international agreements concluded by the Member States after 1958 (or their date of accession).

In light of the potential international responsibility of the Member States, is this a fair constitutional solution? Should it indeed make a difference whether a rule is adopted by means of a unilateral national measure or by means of an international agreement with a third State? Constitutional solutions still need to be found to solve the Member States' dilemma of choosing between the Scylla of liability under the European Treaties and the Charybdis of international responsibility for breach of contract. Should the Union legal order, therefore, be given an *ex ante* authorisation mechanism for Member States' international agreements? Or should the Union share financial responsibility for breach of contract with the Member State concerned? These are difficult constitutional questions. They await future constitutional answers.[28]

b. The 'Executive' Nature of Supremacy: Disapplication, Not Invalidation

What are the legal consequences of the supremacy of European law over conflicting national law? Must a national court 'hold such provisions inapplicable to the extent to which they are incompatible with [European] law', or must it

---

[24] E. Pache and J. Bielitz, 'Das Verhältnis der EG zu den völkerrechtlichen Verträgen ihrer Mitgliedstaaten' (2006) 41 *Europarecht* 316 at 327 (my translation).

[25] E. Bülow, 'Die Anwendung des Gemeinschaftsrechts im Verhältnis zu Drittländern', in A. Clauder (ed.), *Einführung in die Rechtsfragen der europäischen Integration* (Europa Union Verlag, 1972), 52, 54.

[26] E.-U. Petersmann, 'Artikel 234', in H. Von der Groeben, J. Thiesing and C.-D. Ehlermann (eds.), *Kommentar zum EWG-Vertrag* (Nomos, 1991) 5725 at 5731 (para. 6).

[27] See Joined Cases C-176–7/97, *Commission v. Belgium and Luxembourg* [1998] ECR I-3557.

[28] For the time being, one legislative answer can be seen in the inclusion of 'savings' clauses in the relevant Union legislation. A good illustration of this technique is Art. 28 of Regulation 864/2007 on the law applicable to non-contractual obligations (Rome II) [2007] OJ L 199/40. This clause constitutes a legislative extension of Art. 351 TFEU: the Union legislation will not affect international agreements of the Member States with third States concluded after 1958 but before the time when the Regulation was adopted.

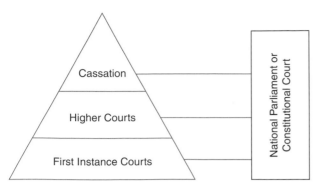

Figure 4.1 *Simmenthal* II: Centralised Constitutional Review

'declare them void'?[29] This question concerns the constitutional effect of the supremacy doctrine in the Member States.

The classic answer to these questions is found in *Simmenthal II*.[30] The issue raised in the national proceedings was this: 'what consequences flow from the direct applicability of a provision of [Union] law in the event of incompatibility with a subsequent legislative provision of a Member State'?[31] Within the Italian constitutional order, national legislation could be *repealed* solely by Parliament or the Supreme Court (see Figure 4.1). Would lower national courts thus have to wait until this happened and, in the meantime, apply national laws that violate Union laws?

Unsurprisingly, the European Court rejected such a reading. Appealing to the 'very foundations of the [Union]', the European Court stated that national courts were under a direct obligation to give immediate effect to European law. The supremacy of European law meant that 'rules of [European] law must be fully and uniformly applied in all the Member States from the date of their entry into force and for so long as they continue in force'.[32] But did this mean that the national court had to *repeal* the national law? According to one view, supremacy did indeed mean that national courts must declare conflicting national laws void. European law would 'break' national law.[33] Yet the Court preferred a milder – second – view:

---

[29]　This very question was raised in Case 34/67, *Firma Gebrüder Luck* v. *Hauptzollamt KölnRheinau* [1968] ECR 245.

[30]　Case 106/77, *Amministrazione delle Finanze dello Stato* v. *Simmenthal SpA* [1978] ECR 629. But see also Case 48/71, *Commission* v. *Italy* [1978] ECR 629

[31]　Case 106/77, *Simmenthal*, para. 13.

[32]　*Ibid.*, para. 14.

[33]　This is the very title of a German monograph by E. Grabitz, *Gemeinschaftsrecht bricht nationales Recht* (L. Appel, 1966). This position was shared by Hallstein: '[T]he supremacy of [European] law means essentially two things: its rules take precedence irrespective of the level of the two orders at which the conflict occurs, and further, [European] law *not only invalidates previous national law but also limits subsequent national legislation*' (W. Hallstein, quoted in Sasse, 'Common Market' (n. 9 above) at 717 (emphasis added)).

> [I]n accordance with the *principle of precedence* of [European] law, the relationship between provisions of the Treaty and directly applicable measures of the institutions on the one hand and the national law of the Member States on the other is such that those provisions and measures not only by their entry into force render *automatically inapplicable* any conflicting provision of current national law but – in so far as they are an integral part of, and take precedence in, the legal order applicable in the territory of each of the Member States – also preclude the valid adoption of new legislative measures to the extent to which they would be incompatible with [European] provisions.[34]

Where national measures conflict with European law, the supremacy of European law would thus not render them void, but only 'inapplicable'.[35] Not 'invalidation' but 'disapplication' was required of national courts, where European laws came into conflict with pre-existing national laws. Yet, in the above passage, the effect of the supremacy doctrine appeared stronger in relation to subsequent national legislation. Here, the Court said that the supremacy of European law would 'preclude the *valid adoption* of new legislative measures to the extent to which they would be incompatible with [European] provisions'.[36] Was this to imply that national legislators were not even *competent* to adopt national laws that would run counter to *existing* European law? Were these national laws void *ab initio*?[37]

In *Ministero delle Finanze* v. *IN. CO. GE. '90*,[38] the Commission picked up this second prong of the *Simmenthal* II ruling and argued that 'a Member State has *no power whatever to [subsequently] adopt* a fiscal provision that is incompatible with [European] law, with the result that such a provision … must be treated as *nonexistent*'.[39] But the European Court of Justice disagreed with this interpretation. Pointing out that *Simmenthal* II 'did not draw any distinction between preexisting and subsequently adopted national law',[40] the incompatibility of

---

[34] Case 106/77, *Simmenthal*, para. 17 (emphasis added).

[35] The Court's reference to 'directly applicable measures' was not designed to limit the supremacy of European law to regulations. The Union acts at issue in *Simmenthal* were, after all, directives. This point was clarified in subsequent jurisprudence: see Case 148/78, *Ratti* [1979] ECR 1629; Case 152/84, *Marshall* v. *Southampton and South-West Hampshire Area Health Authority* [1986] ECR 723.

[36] Case 106/77, *Simmenthal*, para. 17 (emphasis added).

[37] A. Barav, 'Les effets du droit communautaire directement applicable' (1978) 14 CDE 265–86 at 275–6; Grabitz, *Gemeinschaftsrecht* (n. 33 above) and Hallstein, quoted in Sasse, 'Common Market' (n. 9 above).

[38] Joined Cases C-10–22/97, *Ministero delle Finanze* v. *IN.CO.GE. '90 Srl and others* [1998] ECR I-6307.

[39] *Ibid.*, para. 18 (emphasis added).

[40] The *Simmenthal* II Court had indeed not envisaged two different consequences for the supremacy principle. While para. 17 appears to make a distinction depending on whether national legislation existed or not, the operative part of the judgment referred to both variants. It stated that a national court should refuse of its own motion to 'apply any conflicting provision of national legislation' (Case 106/77, *Simmenthal*, dictum).

subsequently adopted rules of national law with European law did not have the effect of rendering these rules non-existent.[41] National courts were thus only under an obligation to disapply a conflicting provision of national law – be it prior *or* subsequent to the Union law.[42]

What will this tell us about the nature of the supremacy principle? It tells us that the supremacy doctrine is about the 'executive force' of European law. The Union legal order, while integrated with the national legal orders, is not a 'unitary' legal order. European law leaves the 'validity' of national norms untouched; and will not negate the underlying legislative competence of the Member States. The supremacy principle is thus not addressed to the State legislatures, but to the national executive and judicial branches. (And, while the national *legislator* will be required to amend or repeal national provisions that give rise to legal uncertainty,[43] this secondary obligation is not a direct result of the supremacy doctrine but derives from Article 4(3) TEU.)[44] The executive force of European law thus generally leaves the normative validity of national law intact. National courts are not obliged to 'break' national law. They must only not apply it when in conflict with European law in a specific case.

This federal supremacy doctrine has a number of advantages. First, some national legal orders may not grant their (lower) courts the power to invalidate parliamentary laws. The question of who may invalidate national laws is thus left to the national legal order.[45] Second, comprehensive national laws

---

[41] Joined Cases C-10–22/97, *IN.CO.GE.*, paras. 20–1.

[42] The non-application of national laws in these cases is but a mandatory 'minimum requirement' set by the Union legal order. A national legal order can, if it so wishes, offer stricter consequences to protect the full effectiveness of European law: Case 34/67, *Firma Gebrüder Luck* v. *Hauptzollamt Koln-Rheinau* [1968] ECR 245, at 251: '[Although European law] has the effect of excluding the application of any national measure incompatible with it, the article does not restrict the powers of the competent national courts to apply, from among the various procedures available under national law, those which are appropriate for the purpose of protecting the individual rights conferred by [European] law.'

[43] See Case C-185/96, *Commission* v. *Hellenic Republic* [1998] ECR 6601, para. 32: 'On that point, suffice it to recall that, according to established case-law, the maintenance of national legislation which is in itself incompatible with [European] law, even if the Member State concerned acts in accordance with [European] law, gives rise to an ambiguous state of affairs by maintaining, as regards those subject to the law who are concerned, a state of uncertainty as to the possibilities for them of relying on [European] law.' See also Case 367/98, *Commission* v. *Portugal* [2002] ECR I-4731, esp. para. 41: 'The Court has consistently held that the incompatibility of provisions of national law with provisions of the Treaty, even those directly applicable, can be definitively eliminated only by means of binding domestic provisions having the same legal force as those which require to be amended.'

[44] See e.g. Case 74/86, *Commission* v. *Germany* [1988] ECR 2139, para. 12.

[45] Case C-314/08, *Filipiak* v. *Dyrektor Izby Skarbowej w Poznaniu* [2009] ECR I–11049, para. 82: 'Pursuant to the principle of the primacy of [European] law, a conflict between a provision of national law and a directly applicable provision of the Treaty is to be resolved by a national court applying [European] law, if necessary by refusing to apply the conflicting national provision, and not by a declaration that the national provision is invalid, the powers of authorities, courts and tribunals in that regard being a matter to be determined by each Member State.'

must only be disapplied to the extent to which they conflict with European law.[46] They will remain operable in purely internal situations. Third, once the Union act is repealed, national legislation may become fully operational again.[47]

2. The National Perspective: Relative Supremacy

The European Union is not a Federal State in which the sovereignty problem is solved. The European Union is a federal union of States.[48] Each federal union is characterised by a political dualism in which each citizen is a member of *two* political bodies. These *two* political bodies will compete for loyalty – and sometimes, the 'national' view on a political question may not correspond with the 'European' view on the matter. What happens when the political views of a Member State clash with those of the federal Union? Controversies over the supremacy of federal law are as old as the (modern) idea of federalism.[49] And, while the previous section exposed the European answer to the supremacy doctrine, this absolute vision is – unsurprisingly – not shared by the Member States.

There indeed exists a competing national view – or better: national views – on the supremacy issue. The extreme version of such a national view can be found in the (British) 2011 European Union Act. The latter unambiguously states as follows:

> Directly applicable or directly effective EU law (that is, the rights, powers, liabilities, obligations, restrictions, remedies and procedures referred to in section 2(1) of the European Communities Act 1972) falls to be recognised and available in law in the United Kingdom only by virtue of that Act or where it is required to be recognised and available in law by virtue of any other Act.[50]

---

[46] B. de Witte, 'Direct Effect, Supremacy and the Nature of the Legal Order', in P. Craig and G. de Búrca (eds.), *The Evolution of EU Law* (Oxford University Press, 1999), 177 at 190.

[47] *Ibid.*   [48] For an extensive discussion of this classification, see Chapter 2.

[49] R. Schütze, 'Federalism as Constitutional Pluralism: Letter from America', in J. Kommarek and M. Avbelj (eds.), *Constitutional Pluralism in the European Union and Beyond* (Hart, 2012), ch. 8.

[50] European Union Act 2011, s. 18. The text of s. 2(1) of the European Communities Act 1972 states: 'All such rights, powers, liabilities, obligations and restrictions from time to time created or arising by or under the Treaties, and all such remedies and procedures from time to time provided for by or under the Treaties, as in accordance with the Treaties are without further enactment to be given legal effect or used in the United Kingdom shall be recognised and available in law, and be enforced, allowed and followed accordingly; and the expression "enforceable EU right" and similar expressions shall be read as referring to one to which this subsection applies.' For a discussion of the complex relationship between European Union law and the doctrine of parliamentary sovereignty, see e.g. C. Turpin and A. Tomkins, *British Government and the Constitution: Text and Materials* (Cambridge University Press, 2011), 335ff.; A. Le Sueur et al., *Public Law: Text, Cases, and Materials* (Oxford University Press, 2013), 814ff.

A milder national perspective, on the other hand, accepts the supremacy of European law over national *legislation*; yet the supremacy of European law is still relative, since it is granted and limited by national *constitutional* law.

The national view(s) on the supremacy of European law have traditionally been expressed in three contexts.[51] First, some Member States – in particular their Supreme Courts – have fought a battle over human rights within the Union legal order. It was claimed that European law could not violate *national* fundamental rights. The same power has been claimed in a second context: ultra vires control. While the Member States here generally accept the supremacy of European law within *limited fields*, they contest that the European Union can exclusively delimit these fields. Finally, a third national claim goes even further than this and argues that there are absolute limits to European integration set by the 'constitutional identity' of each Member State. The following section will briefly introduce each of these three battles over the supremacy of European law by focusing predominantly on the conflict between the European Court of Justice and the German Constitutional Court.

a. Fundamental Rights Limits: The 'So-long' Jurisprudence

A strong national view on supremacy crystallised around *Internationale Handelsgesellschaft*.[52] For after the European Court of Justice had espoused its view on the absolute supremacy of European law, the case moved back to the German Constitutional Court.[53] The German Court now defined its perspective on the question. Could national constitutional law, especially national fundamental rights, affect the application of European law in the domestic legal order?

Famously, the German Constitutional Court rejected the European Court's absolute vision and replaced it with the counter-theory of the *relative* supremacy of European law. The reasoning of the German Court was as follows: while the German Constitution expressly allowed for the transfer of sovereign powers to the European Union in its Article 24,[54] such a transfer was itself limited by the

---

[51] The following section concentrates on the jurisprudence of the German Constitutional Court. This court has long been the most pressing and – perhaps – prestigious national court in the Union legal order. For the reaction of the French Supreme Courts, see R. Mehdi, 'French Supreme Courts and European Union Law: Between Historical Compromise and Accepted Loyalty' (2011) 48 *CML Rev.* 439. For the views of the Central European Constitutional Courts, see W. Sadurski, '"Solange, Chapter 3": Constitutional Courts in Central Europe – Democracy – European Union' (2008) 14 ELJ 1.

[52] Case 11/70, *Internationale Handelsgesellschaft mbH* v. *Einfuhr- und Vorratsstelle für Getreide und Futtermittel* [1970] ECR 1125.

[53] BVerfGE 37, 271 (*Solange I (Re Internationale Handelsgesellschaft)*). For an English translation, see [1974] 2 CMLR 540.

[54] Art. 24(1) of the German Constitution states: 'The Federation may by a law transfer sovereign powers to international organisations.' In the wake of the Maastricht Treaty, a new article was inserted into the German Constitution expressly dealing with the European Union (see Art. 23 German Constitution).

'constitutional identity' of the German State. Fundamental constitutional structures were thus beyond the supremacy of European law:

> The part of the Constitution dealing with fundamental rights is an *inalienable essential feature of the valid Constitution of the Federal Republic of Germany and one which forms part of the constitutional structure of the Constitution*. Article 24 of the Constitution does not without reservation allow it to be subjected to qualifications. In this, the present state of integration of the [Union] is of crucial importance. The [Union] still lacks … in particular a codified catalogue of fundamental rights, the substance of which is reliably and unambiguously fixed for the future in the same way as the substance of the Constitution … *So long as* this legal certainty, which is not guaranteed merely by the decisions of the European Court of Justice, favourable though these have been to fundamental rights, is not achieved in the course of the further integration of the [Union], the reservation derived from Article 24 of the Constitution applies … *Provisionally, therefore, in the hypothetical case of a conflict between [European] law and a part of national constitutional law or, more precisely, of the guarantees of fundamental rights in the Constitution, there arises the question of which system of law takes precedence, that is, ousts the other. In this conflict of norms, the guarantee of fundamental rights in the Constitution prevails* so long as *the competent organs of the [Union] have not removed the conflict of norms in accordance with the Treaty mechanism.*[55]

Thus, 'so long' as the European legal order had not developed an adequate standard of fundamental rights, the German Constitutional Court would 'disapply' European law that conflicted with the fundamental rights guaranteed in the German legal order.[56] There were consequently *national* limits to the supremacy of European law. However, these national limits were also *relative*, as they depended on the evolution and nature of European law. This was the very essence of the 'so long' formula: once the Union legal order had developed equivalent human rights guarantees, the German Constitutional Court would no longer challenge the supremacy of European law.

The Union legal order did indeed subsequently develop extensive human rights bill(s),[57] and the dispute over the supremacy doctrine was significantly softened in the aftermath of a second famous European case with a national coda. In *Wünsche Handelsgesellschaft*,[58] the German Constitutional Court not only

[55] *Solange I* [1974] CMLR 540 at 550–1, paras. 23–4 (emphasis added).
[56] The German Constitutional Court here adopted the doctrine that the supremacy of the German Constitution could only lead to a 'disapplication' and not an 'invalidation' of European law. The German Court thus 'never rules on the validity or invalidity of a rule of [European] law'; but '[a]t most, it can come to the conclusion that such a rule cannot be applied by the authorities or courts of the Federal Republic of Germany as far as it conflicts with a rule of the Constitution relating to fundamental rights' (*ibid.*, 552).
[57] On this point, see Chapter 12.
[58] BVerfGE 73, 339 (*Re Wünsche Handelsgesellschaft*)). For an English translation, see [1987] 3 CMLR 225.

recognised the creation of 'substantially similar' fundamental right guarantees, it drew a remarkably self-effacing conclusion from this:

> In view of those developments it must be held that, *so long as* the European [Union], and in particular the case law of the European Court, generally ensure an effective protection of fundamental rights as against the sovereign powers of the [Union] which is to be regarded as substantially similar to the protection of fundamental rights required unconditionally by the [German] Constitution, and in so far as they generally safeguard the essential content of fundamental rights, the Federal Constitutional Court will no longer exercise its jurisdiction to decide on the applicability of secondary [Union] legislation cited as the legal basis for any acts of German courts or authorities within the sovereign jurisdiction of the Federal Republic of Germany, and it will no longer review such legislation by the standard of the fundamental rights contained in the Constitution ...[59]

This judgment became known as 'So-Long II', for the German Constitutional Court again had recourse to this famous formulation in determining its relationship with European law. But importantly, this time the 'so-long' condition was inverted. The German Court promised not to question the supremacy of European law 'so long' as the latter guaranteed substantially similar fundamental rights to those recognised by the German Constitution. This was not an absolute promise to respect the absolute supremacy of European law, but a result of the Court's own relative supremacy doctrine having been fulfilled. 'So-Long II' thus only refined the national perspective on the limited supremacy of European law in 'So-Long I'.

b. Competence Limits I: From 'Maastricht' to 'Mangold'

With the constitutional conflict over fundamental rights settled, a second concern emerged: the ever-growing competences of the European Union. Who was to control and limit the scope of European law? Was it enough to have the *European* legislator centrally controlled by the *European* Court of Justice? Or should the national constitutional courts be entitled to a decentralised ultra vires review?

The European view on this is crystal clear: national courts cannot disapply – let alone invalidate – European law.[60] Yet, unsurprisingly, this absolute view has not been shared by all Member States. And it was again the German Constitutional Court that set the tone and the vocabulary of the constitutional debate. The ultra vires question was at the heart of its famous *Maastricht* decision that would subsequently be refined in *Honeywell* – the German reaction to the European Court's (in)famous decision in *Mangold*.

---

[59]   *Ibid.*, 265 (para. 48).
[60]   On the *Foto-Frost* doctrine, see Chapter 11, Introduction.

The German Court set out its ultra vires review doctrine in *Maastricht*.[61] Starting from the premise that the Union only had limited powers, the Court found that the Union ought not to be able to extend its own competences. While the Treaties allowed for teleological interpretation, there existed a clear dividing line 'between a legal development within the terms of the Treaties and a making of legal rules which breaks through its boundaries and is not covered by valid Treaty law'.[62] This led to the following conclusion:

> Thus, if European institutions or agencies were to treat or develop the Union Treaty in a way that was no longer covered by the Treaty in the form that is the basis for the Act of Accession, the resultant legislative instruments would not be legally binding within the sphere of German sovereignty. The German state organs would be prevented for constitutional reasons from applying them in Germany. Accordingly the Federal Constitutional Court will review legal instruments of European institutions and agencies to see whether they remain within the limits of the sovereign rights conferred on them or transgress them …
>
> Whereas a dynamic extension of the existing Treaties has so far been supported on the basis of an open-handed treatment of Article [352] of the [FEU] Treaty as a 'competence to round-off the Treaty' as a whole, and on the basis of considerations relating to the 'implied powers' of the [Union], and of Treaty interpretation as allowing maximum exploitation of [Union] powers (*'effet utile'*), in future it will have to be noted as regards interpretation of enabling provisions by [Union] institutions and agencies that the Union Treaty as a matter of principle distinguishes between the exercise of a sovereign power conferred for limited purposes and the amending of the Treaty, so that its interpretation may not have effects that are equivalent to an extension of the Treaty. Such an interpretation of enabling rules would not produce any binding effects for Germany.[63]

The German Constitutional Court thus threatened to disapply European law that it considered to have been adopted ultra vires.

This national review power was subsequently confirmed.[64] Yet, the doctrine was limited and refined in *Honeywell*.[65] The case resulted from a constitutional complaint that targeted the European Court's ruling in *Mangold*.[66] The plaintiff

---

[61] BVerfGE 89, 155 (*Maastricht Decision*). For an English translation, see [1994] 1 CMLR 57.
[62] *Ibid.*, 105 (para. 98).   [63] *Ibid.*, 105 (para. 99).
[64] BVerfGE 123, 267 (*Lisbon Decision*). For an English translation, see [2010] 3 CMLR 276. The Court here added a third sequel to its 'So-Long' jurisprudence (*ibid.*, 343): 'As long as, and insofar as, the principle of conferral is adhered to in an association of sovereign states with clear elements of executive and governmental cooperation, the legitimation provided by national parliaments and governments complemented and sustained by the directly elected European Parliament is sufficient in principle.'
[65] 2 BvR 2661/06 (*Re Honeywell*). For an English translation, see [2011] 1 CMLR 1067. For a discussion of the case, see M. Paydandeh, 'Constitutional Review of EU Law after *Honeywell*: Contextualising the Relationship between the German Constitutional Court and the EU Court of Justice' (2011) 48 *CML Rev.* 9.
[66] For an extensive discussion of the case, see Chapter 3, section 3(b/bb).

argued that the European Court's 'discovery' of a European principle that pro-hibited discrimination on grounds of age was ultra vires as it read something into the Treaties that was not there. In its decision, the German Constitutional Court confirmed its relative supremacy doctrine. It claimed the power to disapply European law that it considered not to be covered by the text of the Treaties. The principle of supremacy was thus not unlimited.[67] However, reminiscent of its judicial deference in *So-Long II*, the Court accepted a presumption that the Union would generally act within the scope of its competences:

> If each member State claimed to be able to decide through their own courts on the validity of legal acts by the Union, the primacy of application could be circumvented in practice, and the uniform application of Union law would be placed at risk. If however, on the other hand the Member States were completely to forgo ultra vires review, disposal of the treaty basis would be transferred to the Union bodies alone, even if their understanding of the law led in the practical outcome to an amendment of a Treaty or an expansion of competences. That in the borderline cases of possible transgression of competences on the part of the Union bodies – which is infrequent, as should be expected according to the institutional and procedural precautions of Union law – the [national] constitutional and the Union law perspective do not completely harmonise, is due to the circumstance that the Member States of the European Union also remain the masters of the Treaties ...
>
> Ultra vires review by the Federal Constitutional Court can moreover *only be considered if it is manifest* that acts of the European bodies and institutions have taken place outside the transferred competences. A breach of the principle of conferral is only manifest if the European bodies and institutions have transgressed the boundaries of their competences *in a manner specifically violating the principle of conferral*, the breach of competences is in other words sufficiently qualified. This means that the act of the authority of the European Union *must be manifestly in violation of competences* and that the impugned act is highly significant in the structure of competences between the Member States and the Union with regard to the principle of conferral and to the binding nature of the statute under the rule of law.[68]

This limits the national review of European law to 'specific' and 'manifest' violations of the principle of conferral. There was thus a *presumption that the Union institutions would generally act intra vires*; and only for clear and exceptional violations would the German Constitutional Court challenge the supremacy of European law. This has – so far – never happened.

But if the German court's behaviour was 'all bark and no bite',[69] another Supreme Court appears to have recently taken a bite and openly refused to

---

[67] *Honeywell* [2011] 1 CMLR 1067 at 1084 (para. 39): 'Unlike the primacy of application of federal law, as provided for by Article 31 of the Basic Law for the German legal system, the primacy of application of Union law cannot be comprehensive.' (It is ironic that this is said by a German *federal* court.)

[68] *Ibid.*, 1085–6 (paras. 42 and 46 (emphasis added)).

[69] C. U. Schmid, 'All Bark and No Bite: Notes on the Federal Constitutional Court's "Banana Decision"' (2001) 7 ELJ 95.

apply European Union law. Rebelling against the European Court's *Mangold* jurisprudence, the Danish Supreme Court has stated that the idea of a directly effective unwritten general principle of European law was not acceptable. In *Dansk Industri (Ajos)*,[70] it thus held:

> Following the EU Court of Justice's judgments in *Mangold*, C-144/04, EU:C:2005:709, *Kücükdeveci*, C-555/07, EU:C:2010:21, and the present case, we find that the principle prohibiting discrimination on grounds of age is a general principle of EU law which, according to the EU Court of Justice, is to be found in various international instruments and in the constitutional traditions common to the Member States. The EU Court of Justice does not refer to provisions in those treaties covered by the Law on Accession as a basis for the principle.
>
> Even though the principle is inferred from legal sources outside the EU Treaties, it is obvious that the three aforementioned judgments must be construed as involving an unwritten principle which applies at treaty level. *There is nothing in those judgments, however, to indicate that there is a specific treaty provision providing the basis for the principle. A situation such as this, in which a principle at treaty level under EU law is to have direct effect (thereby creating obligations) and be allowed to take precedence over conflicting Danish law in a dispute between individuals, without the principle having any basis in a specific treaty provision, is not foreseen in the Law on Accession ... It follows from the foregoing that, under the Law on Accession, principles developed or established on the basis of Article 6(3) TEU have not been made directly applicable in Denmark.*[71]

The Danish Supreme Court thus found that unwritten general principles of EU law could not have direct effect within Denmark, because the Danish Accession Law simply did not cover the European Court's *Mangold* jurisprudence.[72] The judgment is a novelty and has been criticised as a 'mutual disempowerment' and a 'breakdown of mutual trust' between the European Court of Justice and the Danish Supreme Court.[73]

---

[70]   Case 15/2014, *Dansk Industri, acting on behalf of Ajos* v. *Estate of A*. For an unofficial English translation, see the textbook's companion website. The case is a reaction to the ECJ case of the same name in which the Supreme Court had referred a number of preliminary questions to the ECJ, see: Case C-441/14, *Dansk Industri (DI), acting on behalf of Ajos A/S* v. *Estate of Karsten Eigil Rasmussen*, EU:C:2016:278.

[71]   *Ibid.*, pp. 45 and 47 (emphasis added).

[72]   This conclusion faces, in my view, a major obstacle that was identified by the Danish Supreme Court itself. The Danish Accession Law had been amended in 2008 to allow for the Lisbon Treaty and since *Mangold* had been decided in 2005, the 2008 Amendment had arguably absorbed and implicitly ratified that judicial development. The fact that the *Mangold* judgment was not expressly referred in the *travaux préparatoires* of the 2008 amendment cannot, in my view, change that conclusion. The Danish Supreme Court however held otherwise (*ibid.*, p. 47).

[73]   For an extensive discussion of the *Ajos* ruling, see M. Madsen, H. Olsen and U. Šadl, 'Competing Supremacies and Clashing Institutional Rationalities: The Danish Supreme Court's Decision in the *Ajos* Case and the National Limits of Judicial Cooperation' (2017)

c. Competence Limits II: National Constitutional Identities

The *Solange* jurisprudence as well as the *ultra vires* jurisprudence had both set *relative* limits to European integration: *so long as* the Union acknowledged fundamental rights and respected the competence limits *as set by the EU Treaties*, European law could be given supremacy over conflicting national law.

This integration-friendly position however received an absolute 'national' limit in a third famous judgment of the German Constitutional Court: the Lisbon Decision.[74] In this decision, the Court asserted that even in a situation where the German Parliament had agreed to a further transfer of competences to the Union, that (democratic) choice was limited by the 'constitutional identity' of the German State. What was this 'constitutional identity', and why could it not be limited? This was the answer given by the Constitutional Court:

> From the perspective of the principle of democracy, the violation of the constitutional identity codified in art. 79.3 of the Basic Law is at the same time an encroachment upon the constituent power of the people. *In this respect, the constituent power has not granted the representatives and bodies of the people a mandate to dispose of the identity of the constitution* … The safeguarding of sovereignty, demanded by the principle of democracy in the valid constitutional system prescribed by the Basic Law in a manner that is open to integration and to international law, does not mean that a pre-determined number or certain types of sovereign rights should remain in the hands of the state … *European unification on the basis of a treaty union of sovereign states may, however, not be achieved in such a way that not sufficient space is left to the Member States for the political formation of the economic, cultural and social living conditions* … Particularly sensitive for the ability of a constitutional state to democratically shape itself are decisions on substantive and formal criminal law (1), on the disposition of the monopoly on the use of force by the police within the state and by the military towards the exterior (2), fundamental fiscal decisions on public revenue and public expenditure, the latter being particularly motivated, inter alia, by social policy considerations (3), decisions on the shaping of living conditions in a social state (4) and decisions of particular cultural importance, for example on family law, the school and education system and on dealing with religious communities (5).[75]

Invoking the idea of (national) democracy, the German Constitutional Court here set absolute limits to European integration — at least European integration within the scope of the German Constitution. In order to remain a 'sovereign State' — what

---

23 ELJ 140; and U. Neergaard and K. Engsig Sørensen, 'Activist Infighting among Courts and Breakdown of Mutual Trust' (2017) 36 YEL 275.

[74] *Lisbon Decision* (n. 64 above). For an excellent analysis of the decision, see D. Thym, 'In the Name of Sovereign Statehood: A Critical Introduction to the Lisbon Judgment of the German Constitutional Court' (2009) 46 *CML Rev.* 1795.

[75] *Lisbon Decision* (n. 64 above), 332–41 (emphasis added). Article 79(3) of the German Constitution is the so-called 'Eternity Clause' and states: 'Amendments to this Basic Law affecting the division of the Federation into Länder, their participation in the legislative process, or the principles laid down in Articles 1 and 20 shall be inadmissible.'

an anachronistic idea in our global times! – national competences must guarantee that 'sufficient space' is left for the national legislature. And, in order to guarantee that guarantee, the German Court would engage in an 'identify review' that could, in the future, result in 'Union law being declared inapplicable in Germany'.[76]

3. Legislative Pre-emption: Nature and Effect

The contrast between the academic presence of the supremacy doctrine and the shadowy existence of the doctrine of pre-emption in the European law literature is arresting.[77] Everyone talks about supremacy but no one knows about pre-emption! One reason for the under-theorised nature of the pre-emption phenomenon has perhaps been a lack of clarity in distinguishing between the two doctrines. But though related, the two doctrines ought to be kept apart. Supremacy denotes the superior hierarchical status of the Union legal *order* over the national legal *orders* and thus gives Union law the *capacity* to pre-empt national law. The doctrine of pre-emption, on the other hand, denotes the *actual degree* to which national law will be set aside by European law.

The supremacy clause does not determine 'what constitutes a conflict between state and federal law; it merely serves as a traffic cop, mandating a federal law's survival instead of a state law's'.[78] Pre-emption, on the other hand, specifies when such conflicts have arisen, that is: to what extent Union law 'displaces' national law. The important question behind the doctrine of pre-emption is this: to what degree will European law displace national law on the same matter? The pre-emption doctrine is thus a 'relative' doctrine: not all European law pre-empts all national law.

The doctrine of pre-emption is essentially a doctrine of normative conflict. Conflicts arise where there is friction between two legal norms. The spectrum of conflict is open-ended and ranges from purely hypothetical frictions to literal contradictions between norms. There is no easy way to measure normative conflicts; and, in an attempt to classify degrees of normative conflict, pre-emption categories have been developed. Most pre-emption typologies will, to a great extent, be arbitrary classifications. They will only try to *reflect* the various judicial reasons and arguments created to explain why national law conflicts with European law. Sadly, unlike the US Supreme Court,[79] the European Court has yet to define and

---

[76]   *Ibid.*, 338. On the relationship between the identity review and the Court's *Solange* jurisprudence, see G. Anagnostaras, '*Solange III*? Fundamental Rights Protection under the National Identity Review' (2017) 42 *EL Rev.* 234.

[77]   For an illustration of this point, see P. Craig and G. de Búrca, *EU Law: Text, Cases and Materials* (Oxford University Press, 2015), which dedicates one (!) out of over 1,100 pages to the doctrine of pre-emption; yet spends 50 pages on the supremacy doctrine. The previous edition did not treat pre-emption at all.

[78]   S. C. Hoke, 'Preemption Pathologies and Civic Republican Values' (1991) 71 *Boston University Law Review* 685 at 755.

[79]   The US Supreme Court has summarised the different types of pre-emption in *Pacific Gas & Electric Co.* v. *State Energy Resources Conservation & Development Commission*, 461 US 190 (1983), 203–4 (quotations and references omitted) in the following manner: 'Congress' intent to supersede state law altogether may be found from a scheme of the

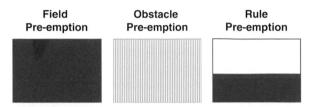

| Field
Pre-emption | Obstacle
Pre-emption | Rule
Pre-emption |

Figure 4.2 Pre-emption Types: Field, Obstacle, Rule Pre-emption

name a pre-emption typology for its legal order.[80] In linguistic alliance with US constitutionalism, we shall, therefore, analyse the European Court's jurisprudence through the lens of the three pre-emption categories developed in that Union, that is: field pre-emption, obstacle pre-emption, and rule pre-emption. A way to visualise these pre-emption categories is shown in Figure 4.2.

a. Field Pre-emption

Field pre-emption refers to those situations where the Court does not investigate any *material* normative conflict, but simply excludes the Member States on the grounds that the Union has exhaustively legislated for the field. This is the most powerful format of federal pre-emption: any national legislation within the occupied field is prohibited. The reason for the total exclusion lies in the perceived fear that *any* supplementary national action may endanger or interfere with the strict uniformity of Union law. Underlying the idea of field pre-emption is a purely abstract conflict criterion: national legislation conflicts with the *jurisdictional* objective of the Union legislator to establish an absolutely uniform legal standard.[81]

> federal regulation so pervasive as to make reasonable the inference that Congress left no room to supplement it, because the Act of Congress may touch a field in which the federal interest is so dominant that the federal system will be assumed to preclude enforcement of state laws on the same subject, or because the object sought to be obtained by federal law and the character of obligations imposed by it may reveal the same purpose … Even where Congress has not entirely displaced state regulation in a specific area, each state is preempted to the extent that it actually conflicts with federal law. Such a conflict arises when compliance with both federal and state regulations is a physical impossibility … or where state law stands as an obstacle to the accomplishment and execution of the full purpose and objectives of Congress.' The three identified pre-emption types are, respectively, field pre-emption, rule pre-emption and obstacle pre-emption.

[80] Unfortunately, the European Court has not (yet) committed itself to a principled pre-emption statement like *Pacific Gas & Electric Co.* v. *State Energy Resources Conservation & Development Commission.* It came close in Case 218/85, *Association comité économique agricole régional fruits et légumes de Bretagne* v. *A. Le Campion (CERAFEL)* [1986] ECR 3513. However, the Court has never extrapolated this pre-emption statement from its specific agricultural policy context. Moreover, not even in the agricultural context has *CERAFEL* become a standard point of reference in subsequent cases.

[81] The total prohibition for national legislators will thus to a certain extent reproduce the effects of a 'real' exclusive competence within the occupied field. On this point, see Chapter 7, section 2(a).

In order to illustrate the argumentative structure of field pre-emption, let us take a closer look at the jurisprudence of the European Court. In *Ratti*,[82] the ECJ found that a Union directive pre-empted any national measures falling within its scope. Member States were therefore 'not entitled to maintain, parallel with the rules laid down by the Directive for imports, different rules for the domestic market'. It was a consequence of the Union system that 'a Member State may not introduce into its national legislation conditions which are more restrictive than those laid down in the directive in question, or which are even more detailed *or in any event different*'.[83] The Union act represented an exhaustive set of rules, and, thus, totally pre-empted national legislators.

b. Obstacle Pre-emption

In contrast to field pre-emption, obstacle pre-emption – our second pre-emption category – requires some *material* conflict between European and national law. Unlike rule pre-emption, however, it refers to a form of argumentative reasoning that does not base the exclusionary effect of European law on the normative friction between a national law and *a particular European rule*. The Court will not go into the details of the legislative scheme, but will be content in finding that the national law somehow interferes with the proper functioning or impedes the objectives of the Union legislation. The burden of proof for finding a legislative conflict is, therefore, still relatively light.

Obstacle pre-emption reasoning can be found in *Bussone*.[84] In the '*absence of express provisions on the compatibility* with the organisation of the market established by [the] Regulation ... it is necessary to seek the solution to the question asked in the light of the aims and objectives of the regulations [as such]'. The Court noted that the Regulation did not seek to establish uniform prices, but that the organisation was 'based on freedom of commercial transactions under fair competitive conditions'. '[S]uch a scheme precludes the adoption of any national rules which may hinder, directly or indirectly, actually or potentially, trade within the [Union].'[85]

The Court here employed a functional conflict criterion to oust supplementary national legislation: those national measures that limit the scope, impede the functioning or jeopardise the aims of the European scheme will conflict with the latter. While not as abstract and potent as field pre-emption, the virility of this functional conflict criterion is nonetheless remarkable. Where the Court selects the 'affect' or 'obstacle' criterion, European law will widely pre-empt national legislation. Any national law that reduces the effectiveness of the Union system may be seen to be in conflict with European law.

---

[82] Case 148/78, *Ratti* [1979] ECR 1629.

[83] *Ibid.*, paras. 26–7 (emphasis added).

[84] Case 31/78, *Bussone* v. *Italian Ministry of Agriculture* [1978] ECR 2429.

[85] *Ibid.*, paras. 43, 46–7.

c. Rule Pre-emption

The most concrete form of conflict will occur where national legislation literally contradicts a *specific European rule*. Compliance with both sets of rules is (physically) impossible. This scenario can be described as rule pre-emption. The violation of Union legislation by the national measure follows from its contradicting a Union rule 'fairly interpreted'. Put negatively, where the national law does not contradict a specific Union provision, it will *not* be pre-empted.

We can find an illustration of this third type of pre-emption in *Gallaher*.[86] Article 3(3) of the Union Directive on the labelling of tobacco products had required that health warnings should cover 'at least 4% of the corresponding surface'. Reading the 'at least' qualification as a provision allowing for stricter national standards, the British government had tightened the obligation on manufacturers by stipulating that the specific warning ought to cover 6 per cent of the surfaces on which they are printed.

Was this higher national standard supplementing the European rule pre-empted and, thus, to be disapplied? The European Court did not think so in an answer that contrasts strikingly with its previous ruling in *Ratti*. Interpreting Articles 3 and 8 of the directive, the European Court found that '[t]he expression "at least" contained in both articles must be interpreted as meaning that, if they consider it necessary, Member States are at liberty to decide that the indications and warnings are to cover a greater surface area in view of the level of public awareness of the health risks associated with tobacco consumption'.[87] The Court – applying a rule pre-emption criterion – thus allowed the stricter national measure. The national law did not contradict the Union rule and the national rules were therefore not pre-empted by the European standard.

4. Constitutional Limits to Union Pre-emption

When exercising a competence, the Union legislator is generally free to determine to what extent it wishes to pre-empt national law. However, that legislative freedom could – theoretically – be restricted in two ways. First, it could make a difference if the Union legislator used a regulation instead of a directive as a Union act. For a long time, it was indeed thought that a regulation would automatically lead to field pre-emption, while a directive could never do so. We shall examine the pre-emptive capacity of the Union's various legal instruments and see that this view is – presently – mistaken.[88] However, a second constitutional limit to the pre-emptive effect of Union legislation might be found in the type of competence given to the Union.

Let us look at both (potential) limitations in turn.

---

[86] Case C-11/92, *The Queen v. Secretary of State for Health, ex p. Gallaher Ltd, Imperial Tobacco Ltd and Rothmans International Tobacco (UK) Ltd* [1993] ECR I-3545.

[87] *Ibid.*, para. 20.

[88] For an argument in favour of a reconceptualisation of the directive, see R. Schütze, 'The Morphology of Legislative Power in the European Community: Legal Instruments and the Federal Division of Powers' (2006) 25 *YEL* 91, conclusion.

a. Union Instruments and Their Pre-emptive Capacity

When the Union was born, its various legal instruments were seen to structure the vertical division of power between the European and the national level. Some early commentators thus argued that for each policy area the Treaty had fixed a specific format of legislative or regulatory intervention.[89] This reading of the various legal instruments has occasionally been expressed by the European Court of Justice.[90] Will this mean that the use of a particular instrument limits the Union legislator from pre-empting the Member States? This section investigates the *pre-emptive* quality of the Union's three 'regulatory' instruments: regulations, directives and international agreements.

aa. The Pre-emptive Capacity of Regulations

Regulations are binding in their entirety, and have been characterised as the 'most integrated form' of European legislation.[91] Typically considered to be the instrument of uniformity, will regulations automatically field pre-empt all national law within their scope of application?

The early jurisprudence of the ECJ indeed emphasised their field pre-emptive nature. In order to protect their 'direct applicability' within the national legal orders, the Court thus employed a strong pre-emption criterion. This initial approach is best illustrated in *Bollmann*.[92] Discussing the effect of a regulation on the legislative powers of the Member States, the ECJ found that since a regulation 'is directly applicable in all Member States, the latter, unless otherwise expressly provided, are precluded from taking steps, for the purposes of applying the regulation, which are *intended to alter its scope or supplement its provisions*'.[93] Early jurisprudence thus suggested that all national rules that fell within the scope of a regulation were automatically pre-empted.[94] Any supplementary national action would be prohibited.

It was this early jurisprudence that created the myth that regulations would automatically field pre-empt national law. Their direct applicability was wrongly associated with field pre-emption.[95] But subsequent jurisprudence quickly disapproved

---

[89] See P. Pescatore, *The Law of Integration: Emergence of a New Phenomenon in International Relations, Based on the Experience of the European Communities* (Sijthoff, 1974), 62–3; V. Constantinesco, *Compétences et pouvoirs dans les communautés européennes: contribution à l'étude de la nature juridique des communautés* (Pichon & Durand-Auzias, 1974), 85.

[90] Case C-91/92, *Faccini Dori v. Recreb* [1994] ECR I-3325.

[91] G. Gaja, P. Hay and R. D. Rotunda, 'Instruments for Legal Integration in the European Community: A Review', in M. Cappelletti, M. Seccombe and J. Weiler (eds.), *Integration through Law: Europe and the American Federal Experience*, 5 vols. (de Gruyter, 1986), I, 113 at 124.

[92] Case 40/69, *Hauptzollamt Hamburg Oberelbe v. Bollmann* [1970] ECR 69.

[93] *Ibid.*, para. 4 (emphasis added).

[94] Case 18/72, *Granaria v. Produktschap voor Veevoeder* [1972] ECR 1163, para. 16.

[95] 'This capacity to pre-empt or preclude national measures can be regarded as a characteristic peculiar to a Regulation (as opposed to any other form of [Union] legislation) and may shed some light on the nature of direct applicability under Article [288] of the Treaty' (M. Blumental, 'Implementing the Common Agricultural Policy: Aspects of the Limitations on the Powers of the Member States' (1984) 35 *Northern Ireland Legal Quarterly* 28–51 at 39).

of the simplistic correlation. In *Bussone*, the Court did not find the relevant regulation to field pre-empt national law, but analysed whether national laws were '*incompatible with the provisions of that regulation*'.[96] And in *Maris* v. *Rijksdienst voor Werknemerspensioenen*,[97] the Court clarified that this incompatibility could sometimes require a material conflict as a regulation would only preclude 'the application of any provisions of national law to a *different or contrary effect*'.[98] Regulations thus do not automatically field pre-empt. They will not always achieve 'exhaustive' legislation. On the contrary, a regulation may confine itself to laying down minimum standards.[99] It is thus misleading to classify regulations as instruments of strict uniformity.[100] While Member States are precluded from unilateral 'amendment' or 'selective application',[101] these constitutional obligations apply to all Union acts and do not specifically characterise the format of regulations.

bb. The Pre-emptive Capacity of Directives

Directives shall be binding 'as to the result to be achieved' and 'leave to the national authorities the choice of form and methods'.[102] Binding as to the result to be achieved, the instrument promised to respect the Member States' freedom to select a national path to a European end. The very term 'directive' suggested an act that would confine itself to 'directions', and the instrument's principal use for the harmonisation of *national* law reinforced that vision.

Do directives thus represent broad-brush 'directions' that guarantee a degree of national autonomy? An early academic school indeed argued this view.[103]

---

[96] Case 31/78, *Bussone* v. *Italian Ministry of Agriculture* [1978] ECR 2429, paras. 28–31.

[97] Case 55/77, *M. Maris, wife of R. Reboulet* v. *Rijksdienst voor Werknemerspensioenen* [1977] ECR 2327.

[98] *Ibid.*, paras. 17–18 (emphasis added).

[99] Council Regulation No. 259/93 on the supervision and control of shipments of waste within, into and out of the European Community ([1993] OJ L 30, p. 1) provides such an example of a 'minimum harmonisation' regulation. The regulation has been described as 'far from providing for a complete harmonisation of the rules governing the transfer of waste, and might in part even be regarded (in the words of one commentator) as an "organised renationalisation" of the subject' (Advocate General F. Jacobs, Case C-187/93, *Parliament* v. *Council* [1994] ECR I-2857, para. 22).

[100] Contra, J. A. Usher, *EC Institutions and Legislation* (Longman, 1998), 130: 'In effect Regulations could be said simply, if inelegantly, to amount to a "keep out" sign to national legislation.'

[101] Case 39/72, *Commission* v. *Italy* [1973] ECR 101, para. 20.

[102] Art. 288(3) TFEU.

[103] See R. W. Lauwaars, *Lawfulness and Legal Force of Community Decisions* (Sijthoff, 1973) 30–1 (emphasis added): 'But can this be carried so far that no freedom at all is left to the member States? In my opinion it follows from Art. [288] that the directive *as a whole* must allow member States the possibility of carrying out the rules embodied in the directive in their own way. A directive that constitutes a uniform law is not compatible with this requirement because, by definition, it places a duty on the member States to take over the uniform text and does not allow any freedom as to choice of form and method'; and Gaja, Hay and Rotunda, 'Instruments for Legal Integration' (n. 91 above), 133 (emphasis added): 'The detailed character of many provisions may be inconsistent with the *concept of directive* as defined in the [FEU] Treaty.'

These voices championed a constitutional frame limiting the directive's pre-emptive effect. To be a 'true' directive, it would need to leave a degree of legislative freedom, and as such could never field pre-empt national legislation within its scope of application. This position thus interpreted the directive in competence terms: the Union legislator would act ultra vires, if it went beyond the constitutional frame set by a directive. But when precisely the pre-emptive Rubicon was crossed remained shrouded in linguistic mist.

In any event, past constitutional practice within the Union legal order has never endorsed a constitutional limit to the pre-emptive effect of directives. On the contrary, in *Enka* the Court of Justice expressly recognised a directive's ability to be 'exhaustive' or 'complete' harmonisation, wherever strict legislative uniformity was necessary.[104] Directives can – and often do – occupy a regulatory field.[105] Their pre-emptive *capacity* therefore equals that of regulations. The national choice, referred to in Article 288[3] TFEU indeed only guarantees the power of Member States to implement the European *content* into national *form*: '[T]he choice is limited to the *kind* of measures to be taken; their *content* is entirely determined by the directive at issue. Thus the discretion as far as form and methods are concerned does not mean that Member States necessarily have a margin in terms of policy making.'[106]

cc. The Pre-emptive Capacity of International Agreements

The pre-emptive effect of Union agreements may be felt in two ways. First, directly effective Union agreements will pre-empt inconsistent *national* law.[107] But, second, self-executing international obligations of the Union will also pre-empt inconsistent *European* secondary law. The pre-emptive potential of international agreements over internal European law follows from the 'primacy' of the former over the latter.[108] For the Court considers international agreements of the Union hierarchically above ordinary Union secondary law.

---

[104] Case 38/77, *Enka BV* v. *Inspecteur der invoerrechten en accijnzen* [1977] ECR 2203, paras. 11–12: 'It emerges from the third paragraph of Article [288] of the Treaty that the choice left to the Member States as regards the form of the measures and the methods used in their adoption by the national authorities depends upon the result which the Council or the Commission wishes to see achieved. As regards the harmonisation of the provisions relating to customs matters laid down in the Member States by law, regulation or administrative action, in order to bring about the uniform application of the common customs tariff it may prove necessary to ensure the *absolute identity of those provisions*' (*ibid.*, paras. 11–12).

[105] E.g. Case 148/78, *Ratti* [1979] ECR 1629.

[106] S. Prechal, *Directives in EC Law* (Oxford University Press, 2005), 73.

[107] E.g. Case C-61/94, *Commission* v. *Germany (IDA)* [1996] ECR I-3989, where the European Court did find a national measure pre-empted by an international agreement. The agreement at stake was the international dairy agreement and the Court found 'that Article 6 of the annexes precluded the Federal Republic of Germany from authorising imports of dairy products, including those effected under inward processing relief arrangements, at prices lower than the minimum' (*ibid.*, para. 39).

[108] *Ibid.*, para. 52.

Let us solely concentrate on the first aspect: the pre-emptive ability of Union agreements in relation to *national* law. Will the pre-emptive effect of an international norm be the same as that of an identically worded provision within a regulation or a directive? The Court has responded to this question in an indirect manner. In *Polydor*,[109] it was asked to rule on the compatibility of the 1956 British Copyright Act with the agreement between the European Union and Portugal. The bilateral free trade agreement envisaged that quantitative restrictions on imports and all measures having an equivalent effect to quantitative restriction should be abolished, but exempted all those restrictions justified on the grounds of the protection of intellectual property. Two importers of pop music had been charged with infringement of Polydor's copyrights and had invoked the directly effective provisions of the Union agreement as a sword against the British law.

Would the Union agreement pre-empt the national measure? If the Court had projected the 'internal' Union standard established by its jurisprudence in relation to Articles 34–6 TFEU, the national measure would have been pre-empted. But the Court did not. It chose to interpret the identically worded provision in the Union agreement more restrictively.[110] Identical text will, therefore, not guarantee identical interpretation:

> [T]he fact that the provisions of an agreement and the corresponding [Union] provisions are identically worded does not mean that they must necessarily be interpreted identically. An international treaty is to be interpreted not only on the basis of its wording, but also in the light of its objectives.[111]

Context will thus prevail over text. The context or function of the international treaty will be decisive. Only where an international norm fulfils the 'same function' as the internal European norm, will the Court project the 'internal' pre-emptive effect to the international treaty.[112] But, while the Court may

---

[109]   Case 270/80, *Polydor and others* v. *Harlequin and others* [1982] ECR 329.

[110]   *Ibid.*, paras. 15, 18–19.

[111]   *Opinion 1/91* (EEA Draft Agreement) [1991] ECR I-6079, para. 14. In relation to the EEA, the Court found that it was 'established on the basis of an international treaty which, essentially, *merely creates rights and obligations as between the Contracting Parties* and provides for no transfer of sovereign rights to the inter-governmental institutions which it sets up' (*ibid.*, para. 20, emphasis added). The EU Treaty, by way of contrast, constituted 'the constitutional charter of a [Union] based on the rule of law', one of whose particular characteristics would be 'the direct effect of a whole series of provisions which are applicable to their nationals' (*ibid.*, para. 21).

[112]   An illustration can be found in Case 17/81, *Pabst & Richarz KG* v. *Hauptzollamt Oldenburg* [1982] ECR 1331, where the ECJ was asked to compare Art. 53(1) of the association agreement between the Union and Greece with the relevant provision in the TFEU: 'That provision, the wording of which is similar to that of Article [110] of the Treaty, fulfils, within the framework of the association between the [Union] and Greece, the

apply a milder form of pre-emption to international agreements, it has not announced any constitutional limits to the pre-emptive capacity of international agreements.

In sum, Union agreements have the capacity to pre-empt inconsistent national law. The pre-emptive potential of international agreements however appears to be milder than equivalently worded internal legislation. Only where the agreement has the same function as an internal European norm will the Court accept the same pre-emptive effect that would be triggered by identically worded European law.

b. Excursus: Competence Limits to Pre-emption

When legislating, the Union legislator is typically free to decide what pre-emption category it wishes to choose. Union discretion thus determines the degree to which national legislators are pre-empted by European legislation. However, there are legislative competences – to be discussed in Chapter 7 – that seem to restrict this liberty. For certain policy areas the Union legislator is indeed limited to setting minimum standards only. The constitutional relationship between the European and the national legislator is here essentially this: the EU Treaty guarantees the ability of the national legislator to adopt *higher* standards; and this seems to constitutionally rule out field pre-emption for these competences. A second variant of constitutionally limited pre-emption flows from the Union's 'complementary competences'. They will also be discussed in Chapter 7 and typically confine the Union legislator to adopt 'incentive measures' that exclude all harmonisation within the field.[113]

The central question for both types of competence is this: how much legislative space will the European Union need to leave to the national level? Do minimum harmonisation competences prevent the Union from ever laying down exhaustive standards with regard to a specific legislative *measure?* And can 'incentive measures' pre-empt national laws – even though a complementary competence excludes all harmonisation within the field? We shall explore these questions in Chapter 7 when looking specifically at the competence categories of the Union.

---

same function as that of Article [110] … It accordingly follows from the wording of Article 53(1), cited above, and from the objective and nature of the association agreement of which it forms part that that provision precludes a national system of relief from providing more favourable tax treatment for domestic spirits than for those imported from Greece' (*ibid.*, paras. 26–7). While the ECJ had found that the European Treaties and the EEA Treaty had different purposes and functions, the General Court seemed to favour a parallel interpretation of the EEA Agreement with identically worded provisions of the European Treaties and secondary law in Case T-115/94, *Opel Austria GmbH* v. *Council* [1997] ECR II-39.

[113] On this point, see Chapter 7, section 2(d).

Conclusion

The doctrine of direct effect demands that a national court *applies* European law; and the doctrine of supremacy demands that a national court *disapplies* national law that conflicts with European law. Direct effect and supremacy are nonetheless *not* twin doctrines. (There can be direct effect without supremacy.) The previous chapter explored the doctrine of direct effect, this chapter concentrated on the doctrine of supremacy and its twin doctrine: the doctrine of pre-emption. The doctrine of pre-emption determines to what extent national law must be disapplied or displaced. It is a theory of legislative conflict. The doctrine of supremacy is a theory of conflict resolution. The two doctrines are vital for any Union of States with overlapping legislative spheres.

For the European legal order, the supremacy of European law means that all Union law prevails over all national law. The absolute nature of the supremacy doctrine is, however, contested by the Member States. While they generally acknowledge the supremacy of European law, they have insisted on national constitutional limits. Is this relative nature of supremacy a 'novelty' or 'aberration'?[114] This view is introverted and unhistorical when compared with the constitutional experiences of the United States.[115] Indeed, the normative ambivalence surrounding the supremacy principle in the European Union is part and parcel of Europe's *federal* nature.[116]

What is the principle of pre-emption? As we saw above, the doctrine of pre-emption complements the supremacy of Union law. It determines when a conflict between Union law and national law has arisen; and this is a relative question. The question is not whether European law pre-empts national law but to what degree. Not all European law will thus displace all national law. So, when will a conflict between European and national law arise? There is no absolute answer to this question. The Union legislator and the European Court of Justice will not always attach the same conflict criterion to all European legislation. Sometimes a purely 'jurisdictional' conflict will be enough to pre-empt national law. In other cases, some material conflict with the European legislative scheme is necessary. Finally, the Court may insist on a direct conflict with a specific Union rule. In parallel to US constitutionalism we consequently distinguished three pre-emption categories within the Union legal order: field pre-emption, obstacle pre-emption and rule pre-emption.

---

[114] See N. Walker, 'The Idea of Constitutional Pluralism' (2002) 65 *MLR* 317 at 338. This terribly narrow-minded – 'Eurocentric' – view strikingly ignores the US experience, in which the Union and the States were seen to have 'constitutional' claims and in which the 'Union' was – traditionally – not (!) conceived in statist terms (see E. Zoeller, 'Aspects Internationaux du droit constitutionnel. Contribution à la théorie de la fédération d'états' (2002) 194 *Recueil des Cours de l'Académie de la Haye* 43).

[115] Schütze, 'Federalism as Constitutional Pluralism' (n. 49 above).

[116] On this point, see Chapter 2.

Are there any constitutional limits on the freedom of the Union legislator to pre-empt national law? We saw above that there may indeed exist limits that some competences impose; yet no such limits are inherent on the type of legislative instrument that the Union uses.

FURTHER READING

Books

K. Alter, *Establishing the Supremacy of European Law: The Making of an International Rule of Law in Europe* (Oxford University Press, 2001)

B. Davies, *Resisting the European Court of Justice: West Germany's Confrontation with European Law 1949–1979* (Cambridge University Press, 2014)

A. Oppenheimer, *The Relationship between European Community Law and National Law* (Cambridge University Press, 2004)

N. Walker (ed.), *Sovereignty in Transition* (Hart, 2003)

Articles (and Chapters)

P. Craig, 'Britain in the European Union', in J. Jowell and D. Oliver (eds.), *The Changing Constitution* (Oxford University Press, 2015), 104

M. Dougan, 'When Worlds Collide! Competing Visions of the Relationship between Direct Effect and Supremacy' (2007) 44 *CML Rev.* 931

U. Everling, 'The Maastricht Judgment of the German Federal Constitutional Court and Its Significance for the Development of the European Union' (1994) 14 YEL 1

J. Komárek, 'Czech Constitutional Court Playing with Matches: The Czech Constitutional Court Declares a Judgment of the Court of Justice of the EU Ultra Vires' (2012) 8 *European Constitutional Law Review* 323

R. Kovar, 'The Relationship between Community Law and National Law', in EC Commission (ed.), *Thirty Years of Community Law* (EC Commission, 1981), 109

K. Lenaerts and T. Corthaut, 'Of Birds and Hedges: The Role of Primacy in Invoking Norms of EU Law' (2006) 31 *EL Rev.* 287

M. Madsen, H. Olsen and U. Šadl, 'Competing Supremacies and Clashing Institutional Rationalities: The Danish Supreme Court's Decision in the *Ajos* Case and the National Limits of Judicial Cooperation' (2017) 23 ELJ 140

M. Paydandeh, 'Constitutional Review of EU Law after *Honeywell*: Contextualising the Relationship between the German Constitutional Court and the EU Court of Justice' (2011) 48 *CML Rev.* 9

W. Sadurski, '"Solange, Chapter 3": Constitutional Courts in Central Europe – Democracy – European Union' (2008) 14 ELJ 1

D. Thym, 'In the Name of Sovereign Statehood: A Critical Introduction to the *Lisbon* Judgment of the German Constitutional Court' (2009) 46 *CML Rev.* 1795

M. Waelbroeck, 'The Emergent Doctrine of Community Preemption: Consent and Redelegation', in T. Sandalow and E. Stein (eds.), *Courts and Free Markets:*

Perspectives from the United States and Europe, 2 vols. (Oxford University Press, 1982), II, 548

Cases on the Website

Case 6/64, *Costa* v. *ENEL*; Case 40/69, *Bollmann*; Case 11/70, *Internationale Handelsgesellschaft*; Case 38/77, *Enka*; Case 55/77, *Maris*; Case 106/77, *Simmenthal II*; Case 31/78, *Bussone*; Case 148/78, *Ratti*; Case 270/80, *Polydor*; Case C-11/92, *Gallaher*; Case C-350/92, *Spain* v. *Council*; Cases C-10–22/97, *INCOGE'90*; Case C-318/98, *Fornasar*; Case C-377/98, *Netherlands* v. *Parliament and Council*; Case C-402/05P, *Kadi*; German Constitutional Court Cases: *Wünsche Handellsgesellschaft, Maastricht, Honeywell, Lisbon*; Danish Supreme Court: *Dansk Industri*

5

Governmental Structure
Union Institutions I

Contents

Introduction

The creation of governmental institutions is *the* central task of all constitutions. Each political community needs institutions to govern its society; as each society needs common rules and a method for their making, execution and adjudication. It is no coincidence that the first three articles of the 1787 US Constitution establish and define – respectively – the 'Legislative Department', the 'Executive Department' and the 'Judicial Department'.

The European Treaties establish a number of European institutions to make, execute and adjudicate European law. The Union's institutions and their core tasks are defined in Title III of the Treaty on European Union. The central provision here is Article 13 TEU, which states:

> 1. The Union shall have an institutional framework which shall aim to promote its values, advance its objectives, serve its interests, those of its citizens and those of the Member States, and ensure the consistency, effectiveness and continuity of its policies and actions.
> The Union's institutions shall be:
> – the European Parliament,
> – the European Council,
> – the Council,
> – the European Commission (hereinafter referred to as 'the Commission'),
> – the Court of Justice of the European Union,
> – the European Central Bank,
> – the Court of Auditors.
> 2. Each institution shall act within the limits of the powers conferred on it in the Treaties, and in conformity with the procedures, conditions and objectives set out in them. The institutions shall practise mutual sincere cooperation …

The provision lists seven governmental institutions of the European Union. They constitute the core 'players' in the Union legal order.[1] What strikes the attentive eye first is the number of institutions: unlike a classic tripartite structure, the Union offers more than twice that number. Parliaments and courts are typically found in national legal orders, but the two institutions that do not – at first sight – seem to directly correspond to 'national' institutions are the (European) Council and the Commission. The name 'Council' represents a reminder of the 'international' origins of the European Union, but the institution can equally be found in the governmental structure of Federal States. It will be harder to find the name 'Commission' among the public institutions of States, where the executive is typically referred to as the 'government'. By contrast, central banks and courts of auditors again exist in many national legal orders.

---

[1] While the Treaties set up seven 'institutions', they also acknowledge the existence of other 'bodies'. First, according to Art. 13(4) TEU, the Parliament, the Council and the Commission 'shall be assisted by an Economic and Social Committee and a Committee of the Regions acting in an advisory capacity'. The composition and powers of the 'Economic and Social Committee' are set out in Arts. 301–4 TFEU. The composition and powers of the 'Committee of the Regions' are defined by Arts. 305–7 TFEU. In addition to the Union's 'Advisory Bodies', the Treaties equally acknowledge the existence of a 'European Investment Bank' (Arts. 308–9 TFEU; Protocol No. 5 on the Statute of the European Investment Bank).

Where do the Treaties define the Union institutions? The provisions on the Union institutions are split between the Treaty on European Union and the Treaty on the Functioning of the European Union as shown in Table 5.1.

What is the composition and task of each Union institution? Chapters 5 and 6 will provide an analysis of each institution alongside three dimensions: its *internal* structure, its *internal* decision-making procedures and finally its *internal* powers.[2] The *external* interactions *between* the various institutions will be discussed in Part II of this textbook— dealing with the powers and procedures of the *Union*. Can we nonetheless connect the institutions as 'organs' of the Union with their *external* interaction in a governmental function? And what does Article 13(2) TEU mean when insisting that each institution must act within the limits of its powers and according to the Treaties' procedures? Is this the separation-of-powers principle within the Union legal order? Let us look at this 'horizontal' question in section 1 of this chapter, before analysing the 'internal' structure of each institution in turn.

Table 5.1 Treaty Provisions on the Institutions

EU Treaty – Title III		FEU Treaty – Part VI – Title I – Chapter 1	
Article 13	Institutional Framework	Section 1	European Parliament (Articles 223–34)
Article 14	European Parliament		
Article 15	European Council	Section 2	European Council (Articles 235–6)
Article 16	Council		
Article 17	Commission	Section 3	Council (Articles 237–43)
Article 18	High Representative	Section 4	Commission (Articles244–50)
Article 19	Court of Justice	Section 5	Court of Justice (Articles 251–81)
		Section 6	European Central Bank (Articles 282–4)
		Section 7	Court of Auditors (Articles 285–7)
(Selected) Protocols: Protocol No. 3: Statute of the Court of Justice; Protocol No. 4: Statute of the ESCB and the ECB; Protocol No. 6: Location of the Seats of the Institutions, etc.			
(Internal) Rules of Procedure of the Institution European Parliament Rules of Procedure; (European) Council Rules of Procedure; European Commission Rules of Procedure; Court of Justice Rules of Procedure, etc.			

---

[2] Many of these 'internal' issues will be found in an institution's 'Rules of Procedure'. On the status of these procedural rules, see S. Lefevre, 'Rules of Procedure Do Matter: The Legal Status of the Institutions' Power of Self-organisation' (2005) 30 *EL Rev.* 802.

1. The 'Separation-of-Powers' Principle and the European Union

When in 1748, Montesquieu published *The Spirit of Laws*,[3] the enlightened aristocrat espoused his views on the division of powers in a chapter dedicated to 'The Constitution of England'.[4] Famously, three powers were identified:

> In every government there are three sorts of power: the legislative; the executive in respect to things dependent on the law of nations; and the executive in regard to matters that depend on the civil law. By virtue of the first, the prince or magistrate enacts temporary or perpetual laws, and amends or abrogates those that have been already enacted. By the second, he makes peace or war, sends or receives embassies, establishes the public security, and provides against invasions. By the third, he punishes criminals, or determines the disputes that arise between individuals. The latter we shall call the judiciary power ...[5]

Having identified three governmental 'powers' or functions, Montesquieu moved on to advocate their 'distribution' between different institutions:

> When the legislative and executive powers are united in the same person, or in the same body of magistrates, there can be no liberty; because apprehensions may arise, lest the same monarch or senate should enact tyrannical laws, to execute them in a tyrannical manner. Again, there is no liberty, if the judicial power be not separated from the legislative and executive. Were it joined with the legislative, the life and liberty of the subject would be exposed to arbitrary control; for the judge would be then the legislator. Were it joined to the executive power, the judge might behave with violence and oppression.[6]

Would the distribution of power mean that each power would need to be given to a 'separate' institution? Did the distribution of power thus lead to a *separation* of powers? This reading of Montesquieu's oracular passage appears – at first sight – to have been chosen by the founding fathers of the United States of America.[7] The idea behind the US constitutional structure seems to be that

---

[3] Charles de Secondat, Baron de Montesquieu, *The Spirit of Laws* (translated and edited by T. Nugent, and revised by J. Prichard) (Bell, 1914), available at www.constitution.org/cm/sol.htm.

[4] *Ibid.*, Book XI, ch. 6.   [5] *Ibid.*   [6] *Ibid.*

[7] On the impact of Montesquieu on the US Constitution, see J. Madison, *Federalist No. 47*, in A. Hamilton et al., *The Federalist*, ed. T. Ball (Cambridge University Press, 2003), 235: 'In order to form correct ideas on this important subject, it will be proper to investigate the sense in which the preservation of liberty requires that the three great departments of power should be separate and distinct. The oracle who is always consulted and cited on this subject is the celebrated Montesquieu.'

different governmental powers correlate with different institutions. Legislative powers are thus vested in 'Congress',[8] the executive power is vested in a 'President',[9] while the judicial power is vested in the 'Supreme Court'.[10]

But there is a second reading of the famous Montesquieu passage (see Figure 5.1). The distribution of powers here leads to a *combination* of powers. 'To form a moderate government, it is necessary to *combine* the several powers; to regulate, temper, and set them in motion; to give, as it were, ballast to one, in order to enable it to counterpoise the other.'[11] The exercise of the legislative function should thus ideally involve more than one institution:

> The legislative body being composed of two parts, they check one another by the mutual privilege of rejecting. They are both restrained by the executive power, as the executive is by the legislative. These three powers should naturally form a state of repose or inaction. But as there is a necessity for movement in the course of human affairs, they are forced to move, but still in concert.[12]

The idea behind this second conception of the separation-of-powers principle is thus a system of checks and balances. And it is this second conception of the separation-of-powers principle that informs the European Treaties.

The European Treaties indeed do not – unlike the US Constitution – discuss each institution within the context of one governmental function. Instead, the European Treaties adopted the opposite technique. Each institution has 'its' article in the Treaty on European Union, whose first section then describes the *combination*

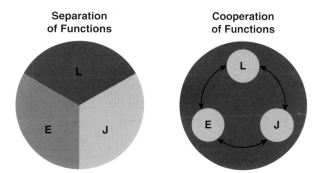

Separation of Functions   **Cooperation of Functions**

Figure 5.1 Separation-of-Power Models

---

[8] Art. I, section 1 US Constitution: 'All legislative Powers herein granted shall be vested in a Congress of the United States, which shall consist of a Senate and House of Representatives.'

[9] *Ibid.*, Art. II, section 1: 'The executive Power shall be vested in a President of the United States of America.'

[10] *Ibid.*, Art. III, section 1: 'The judicial Power of the United States, shall be vested in one Supreme Court, and in such inferior Courts as the Congress may from time to time ordain and establish.'

[11] Montesquieu, *Spirit of Laws* (n. 3 above), Book V, ch. 14.   [12] *Ibid.*

of governmental functions in which it partakes.[13] The European Treaties have indeed 'set up a system for distributing powers among different [Union] institutions, assigning to each institution its own role in the institutional structure of the [Union] and the accomplishment of the tasks entrusted to the [Union]'.[14] It is this conception of the separation-of-powers principle that informs Article 13(2) TEU. The provision is known as the principle of interinstitutional balance and reads:

> Each institution shall act within the limits of the powers conferred on it in the Treaties, and in conformity with the procedures, conditions and objectives set out in them. The institutions shall practice mutual sincere cooperation.

The provision contains three constitutional commands. First, each institution must act within its powers as defined by the Treaties. It is thus not possible for an institution to unilaterally *extend* its powers through constitutional practice.[15] Nor may an institution consensually *transfer* its powers to another institution – unless the Treaties expressly allow for such delegations of power. (The Union legal order has expressly permitted such delegations from the very beginning.)[16]

Second, '[o]bservance of the institutional balance means that each of the institutions must exercise its powers with due regard for the powers of the other institutions'.[17] This principle of 'mutual sincere cooperation' between the institutions in Article 13(2) TEU is the horizontal extension of the principle of sincere cooperation in Article 4(3) TEU.[18] One manifestation of this principle is interinstitutional agreements, in which the institutions agree to exercise 'their' powers in harmony with each other.[19]

---

[13] This is normally the first section of the TEU article dealing with the – respective – institution.

[14] Case C-70/88, *Parliament* v. *Council (Chernobyl)* [1990] ECR I-2041, para. 21.

[15] Case 149/85, *Wybot* v. *Faure* [1986] ECR 2391, esp. para. 23.

[16] On the delegation of legislative power, see Chapter 9, section 2(a).

[17] Case C-70/88, *Parliament* v. *Council*, para. 22; and see more recently Case C-133/06, *Parliament* v. *Council* [2008] ECR I-3189, para. 57.

[18] Art. 4(3) TEU only deals with the federal relations between the Union and its Member States. We shall analyse this provision in detail in Part II of the book.

[19] The Treaties envisage interinstitutional agreements for example in Art. 295 TFEU, which states: 'The European Parliament, the Council and the Commission shall consult each other and by common agreement make arrangements for their cooperation. To that end, they may, in compliance with the Treaties, conclude inter-institutional agreements which may be of a binding nature.' For a list of interinstitutional agreements concluded between 1958–2005, see W. Hummer, 'Annex: Interinstitutional Agreements Concluded During the Period 1958–2005' (2007) 13 ELJ 92. On the various 'theories' of the nature of inter-institutional agreements, see B. Driessen, 'Interinstitutional Conventions and Institutional Balance' (2008) 33 *EL Rev.* 550 at 551: 'Although such arrangements often do no more than lubricate interinstitutional relations, in many cases they affect the effective balance of influence between the institutions.'

Finally, each institution is embedded within the governmental procedures of the European Union. Thus, under the (ordinary) legislative procedure, three of the Union institutions will need to take part: the Commission must formally propose the legislative bill, and the Parliament as well as the Council must co-decide on its adoption. And even where an institution only needs to be 'consulted', this involvement through consultation 'represents an essential factor in the institutional balance intended by the Treat[ies]'.[20]

What types of governmental 'powers' or 'functions' may be identified for the European Union? Apart from defining what constitutes the legislative procedure(s),[21] the European Treaties do not formally classify the Union's governmental branches according to specific procedures. In line with classic constitutional thought, the Treaties continue to be based on an informal conception of governmental powers. The executive power thus relates to the competence of proposing and implementing laws, whereas the judicial power relates to the competence of arbitrating laws in court. In addition to the classic trinity, the European Union has, like many modern constitutions, come to also recognise a 'fourth power' that relates to international relations.[22] This fourth power is thereby located in between the legislative and the executive department,[23] for it involves both the adoption of important 'laws' and – in the worst case – the execution of wars against a third State. Finally, the European Union, again like many modern States, now also acknowledges a 'fifth power' relating to the public control of financial markets.[24] The task of central banks is to regulate and stabilise a polity's money supply.

How do the Union's institutions (and 'bodies') correlate with these five governmental powers so identified? It is important to keep in mind that '[t]he principle of institutional balance does not imply that the authors of the Treaties set up a balanced distribution of the powers, whereby the weight of each institution is the same as that of the others'.[25] It simply means that '[t]he Treaties set up a

---

[20] Case 138/79, *Roquette Frères* v. *Council (Isoglucose)* [1980] ECR 3333, para. 33.

[21] On what 'legislation' is, see Chapter 7, section 3.

[22] The recognition of foreign affairs as a public function distinct from the gestation of domestic affairs received its classic formulation in the political philosophy of John Locke. Locke had identified the 'federative power' as 'the power of war and peace, leagues and alliances, and all the transactions with all persons and communities without the commonwealth' (J. Locke, *Two Treaties of Government*, ed. P. Laslett (Cambridge University Press, 1985) 365, §146).

[23] Hamilton, *Federalist No. 75* (n. 7 above), 365 (emphasis added): 'Though several writers on the subject of government place that power in the class of executive authorities, yet this is evidently an arbitrary disposition; for if we attend carefully to its operation, it will be found to partake *more of the legislative than of the executive character*, though it does not seem strictly to fall within the definition of either of them … *The power in question seems therefore to form a distinct department, and to belong, properly, neither to the legislative nor to the executive.*'

[24] On the history of the Bank of England, see R. Roberts and D. Kynaston, *The Bank of England: Money, Power and Influence 1694–1994* (Oxford University Press, 1995); and on the creation of the US 'Federal Reserve System' in 1913, see A. Meltzer, *A History of the Federal Reserve*, 2 vols. (University of Chicago Press, 2004), I, 1913–51.

[25] J.-P. Jacque, 'The Principle of Institutional Balance' (2004) 41 *CML Rev.* 383.

Table 5.2 Union Institutions Correlating to Governmental Functions

Legislative	External	Executive	Judicial	Financial
Parliament	(European) Council	European Council	Court	Central Bank
Council	Parliament	Commission	Commission	Investment Bank

system for distributing powers among the different [Union] institutions, assigning each institution its own role in the institutional structure of the [Union] and the accomplishment of the tasks entrusted to the [Union]'.[26] Table 5.2 provides an overview of the *major* institutional participants that combine in each public function.

2. The European Parliament

Despite its formal place in the Treaties, the European Parliament has never been the Union's 'first' institution. For a long time it followed, in rank, behind the Council and the Commission. Parliament's original powers were indeed minimal. It was an 'auxiliary' organ that was to assist the institutional 'duopoly' of Council and Commission. This minimal role gradually increased from the 1970s onwards. The Budget Treaties gave it a say in the budgetary process, and subsequent Treaty amendments dramatically enhanced its role in the legislative process. Today the Parliament constitutes – with the Council – a chamber of the Union legislature. Directly elected by the European citizens,[27] Parliament constitutes not only the most democratic institution; in light of its elective 'appointment', it is also the most supranational institution of the European Union.

This section looks at four aspects of the European Parliament. First, we shall explore its formation through European elections. A second section analyses its internal structure. A third section presents its decision-making and voting rules. Finally, a fourth section provides an overview of Parliament's powers in the various governmental functions of the Union.

a. Formation: Electing Parliament

When the European Union was born, the 1952 Paris and 1957 Rome Treaties envisaged that its Parliament was to be composed of 'representatives of the peoples of the States'.[28] This characterisation corresponded to its formation because the European Parliament was not directly elected. It was to 'consist of delegates who shall be designated by the respective Parliaments from among their members

---

[26] Case C-70/88, *Parliament* v. *Council (Chernobyl)*, para. 21.
[27] Art. 10(2) TEU: 'Citizens are directly represented at Union level in the European Parliament.'
[28] Art. 137 EEC; see also Art. 20 ECSC.

in accordance with the procedure laid down by each Member State'.[29] European parliamentarians were thus – delegated – *national* parliamentarians. This formation method brought Parliament close to an (international) 'assembly', but the founding Treaties already breached the classic international law logic in two ways. First, they had abandoned the idea of a sovereign equality between the Member States by recognising different sizes for national parliamentary delegations.[30] And more importantly: both Treaties already envisaged that the European Parliament would eventually be formed through 'elections by direct universal suffrage in accordance with a uniform procedure in all Member States'.[31]

When did the transformation of the European Parliament from an 'assembly' of national parliamentarians into a directly elected 'parliament' take place? It took two decades before the Union's 1976 'Election Act' was adopted.[32] And ever since the first parliamentary elections in 1979, the European Parliament ceased to be composed of 'representatives of the peoples of the states'. The Lisbon Treaty has – belatedly – recognised this dramatic constitutional change. For it now characterises the European Parliament as being 'composed of representatives of the *Union's citizens*'.[33]

What is the size and composition of the European Parliament? How are elections conducted? And what is the status of a Member of the European Parliament (MEP)? Let us look at these questions in turn.

aa. Parliament's Size and Composition

The Treaties stipulate the following on the size and composition of the European Parliament:

> The European Parliament shall be composed of representatives of the Union's citizens. They shall not exceed seven hundred and fifty in number, plus the President. Representation of citizens shall be degressively proportional, with a minimum threshold of six members per Member State. No Member State shall be allocated more than ninety-six seats.

---

[29]   Art. 138 EEC; see also Art. 21 ECSC.

[30]   Originally, the EEC Treaty granted 36 delegates to Germany, France and Italy; 14 delegates to Belgium and the Netherlands; and six delegates to Luxembourg.

[31]   Art. 138(3) EEC: 'The [Parliament] shall draw up proposals for elections by direct universal suffrage in accordance with a uniform procedure in all Member States. The Council shall, acting unanimously, lay down the appropriate provisions, which it shall recommend to Member States for adoption in accordance with their respective constitutional requirements.' See also Art. 21(3) ECSC.

[32]   See: Act concerning the Election of the Members of the European Parliament by direct universal Suffrage. The Act was adopted in 1976 ([1976] OJ L 278/5). For an excellent discussion of the past and (possible) future of the Act, see S. Alonso de León, 'Four Decades of the European Electoral Law: A Look back and a Look ahead to an unfulfilled Ambition' (2017) 42 *EL Rev.* 353. In 2015, the European Parliament itself has strongly voiced its ambition to reform its electoral law before 2019; see Resolution of 11 November 2015 on the Reform of the Electoral Law of the European Union (2015/2035(INL)).

[33]   Art. 14(2) TEU (emphasis added).

> The European Council shall adopt by unanimity, on the initiative of the European Parliament and with its consent, a decision establishing the composition of the European Parliament, respecting the principles referred to in the first subparagraph.[34]

The European Parliament has a maximum size of 751 members. While relatively large in comparison with the (US) House of Representatives, it is still smaller than the (British) House of Lords.[35] The Treaties themselves no longer determine its composition.[36] It is the European Council that must decide on the national 'quotas' for the Union's parliamentary representatives. The distribution of seats must however be 'degressively proportional' within a range spanning from six to 96 seats. The European Council has indeed taken a formal decision on the principles governing the allocation of national 'quotas' within Parliament.[37] The concrete distribution of seats among Member States can be seen in Table 5.3.

The national 'quotas' for European parliamentary seats constitute a compromise between the *democratic* principle and the *federal* principle – two foundational constitutional principles of the European Union. The democratic principle here demands that each citizen in the Union has equal voting power ('one person, one vote'). By contrast, the federal principle pulls into the opposite directions by insisting on the political equality of States. The result of this compromise is the rejection of a *purely* proportional distribution of seats within the Union in favour of a *degressively* proportional system that takes account of the political existence of the Member States. The degressive element within that system unfortunately means that a Luxembourg citizen has ten times more voting power than a British, French or German citizen.

How are the *individual* members of Parliament elected? The Treaties solely provide us with the most general of rules: 'The members of the European Parliament

---

[34] *Ibid.*

[35] To compare: the (US) House of Representatives has 435 members. The (British) House of Commons is designed to have 650 members, while the (British) House of Lords has about 830 members.

[36] This had always been the case prior to the Lisbon Treaty. The composition of the Parliament has thus been 'de-constitutionalised'.

[37] European Council, Decision establishing the Composition of the European Parliament [2013] OJ L 181/57, esp. Art. 1: 'In the application of the principle of degressive proportionality provided for in the first subparagraph of Article 14(2) of the Treaty on European Union, the following principles shall apply: the allocation of seats in the European Parliament shall fully utilise the minimum and maximum numbers set by the Treaty on European Union in order to reflect as closely as possible the sizes of the respective populations of Member States; the ratio between the population and the number of seats of each Member State before rounding to whole numbers shall vary in relation to their respective populations in such a way that each Member of the European Parliament from a more populous Member State represents more citizens than each Member from a less populous Member State and, conversely, that the larger the population of a Member State, the greater its entitlement to a large number of seats.'

Table 5.3 Distribution of Seats in the European Parliament

Member State (Seats)		
Belgium (21)	Ireland (11)	Austria (18)
Bulgaria (17)	Italy (72+1★)	Poland (51)
Croatia (11)	Cyprus (6)	Portugal (21)
Czech Republic (21)	Latvia (8)	Romania (32)
Denmark (13)	Lithuania (11)	Slovenia (8)
Germany (96)	Luxembourg (6)	Slovakia (13)
Estonia (6)	Hungary (21)	Finland (13)
Greece (21)	Malta (6)	Sweden (20)
Spain (54)	Netherlands (26)	United Kingdom (73)
France (74)		

★This additional seat was added, as a result of Italian insistence, by the Lisbon Intergovernmental Council; see Declaration No. 4 on the composition of the European Parliament: 'The additional seat in the European Parliament will be attributed to Italy.' This is why the European Parliament has 751 and not 750 seats.

shall be elected for a term of five years by direct universal suffrage in a free and secret ballot.'[38] More precise rules are set out in the (amended) 1976 Election Act. Article 1 of the Act commands that the elections must be conducted 'on the basis of proportional representation'.[39] This outlaws the traditionally British election method of 'first past the post'.[40] The specifics of the election procedure are however principally left to the Member States.[41] European parliamentary elections thus still do not follow 'a uniform electoral procedure in all Member

[38] Art. 14(3) TEU.
[39] Art. 1(1) and (3) of the 1976 Election Act (n. 32 above).
[40] This condition had not been part of the original 1976 Election Act, but was added through a 2002 amendment. This amendment was considered necessary as, hitherto, the British majority voting system 'could alone alter the entire political balance in the European Parliament' (F. Jacobs et al., *The European Parliament* (Harper, 2005), 17). The best example of this distorting effect was the 1979 election to the European Parliament in which the British Conservatives won 60 out of 78 seats with merely 50 per cent of the vote (*ibid.*).
[41] Art. 8 of the 1976 Election Act: 'Subject to the provisions of this Act, the electoral procedure shall be governed in each Member State by its national provisions.' Under the Act, Member States are free to decide whether to establish national or local constituencies for elections to the European Parliament (*ibid.*, Art. 2), and whether to set a minimum threshold for the allocation of seats (*ibid.*, Art. 3). Moreover, each Member State can fix the date and times for the European elections, but this date must 'fall within the same period starting on a Thursday morning and ending on the following Sunday' for all Member States (*ibid.*, Art. 10(1)).

States', but are rather conducted 'in accordance with principles common to all Member States'.[42] The Treaties nonetheless insist on a second common constitutional rule:'every citizen of the Union residing in a Member State of which he is not a national shall have the right to vote and to stand as a candidate in elections to the European Parliament in the Member State in which he resides, under the same conditions as nationals of that State'.[43]

bb. Members of the European Parliament and Political Parties

For a long time, the 1976 Election Act solely governed the status of an MEP. It determined, *inter alia*, that members would enjoy the privileges and immunities of officials of the European Union.[44] It also established that membership of the European Parliament was incompatible with a parallel membership in a national government or parliament,[45] or with being a member of another European institution.

After years of debate and discontent, Parliament belatedly adopted its Statute for Members of the European Parliament.[46] The Statute 'lays down the regulations and general conditions governing the performance of the duties of members of the European Parliament'.[47] Accordingly, 'members shall be free and independent'.[48] They 'shall vote on an individual and personal basis', and shall thus 'not be bound by any instructions'.[49] Members are entitled to table proposals for Union

---

[42] Both alternatives are provided for in Art. 223(1) TFEU: 'The European Parliament shall draw up a proposal to lay down the provisions necessary for the election of its Members by direct universal suffrage in accordance with a uniform procedure in all Member States or in accordance with principles common to all Member States. The Council, acting unanimously in accordance with a special legislative procedure and after obtaining the consent of the European Parliament, which shall act by a majority of its component Members, shall lay down the necessary provisions. These provisions shall enter into force following their approval by the Member States in accordance with their respective constitutional requirements.'

[43] Art. 22(2) TFEU. However, the provision adds: 'This right shall be exercised subject to detailed arrangements adopted by the Council, acting unanimously in accordance with a special legislative procedure and after consulting the European Parliament; these arrangements may provide for derogations where warranted by problems specific to a Member State.'

[44] Art. 6(2) of the 1976 Election Act (n. 32 above).

[45] *Ibid.*, Art. 7.

[46] European Parliament, Decision 2005/684 adopting the Statute for Members of the European Parliament [2005] OJ L 262/1 (Annex 2). The legal basis for this type of act can now be found in Art. 223(2) TFEU: 'The European Parliament, acting by means of regulations on its own initiative in accordance with a special legislative procedure after seeking an opinion from the Commission and with the consent of the Council, shall lay down the regulations and general conditions governing the performance of the duties of its Members.'

[47] Art. 1 MEP Statute.

[48] *Ibid.*, Art. 2. This is repeated in Art. 6(1) of the 1976 Act: 'Members of the European Parliament shall vote on an individual and personal basis. They shall not be bound by any instructions and shall not receive a binding mandate.'

[49] Art. 3 MEP Statute.

acts,[50] and may form political groups.[51] They are to receive an 'appropriate salary to safeguard their independence',[52] and might get a pension.[53]

Members of Parliament will, as a rule, be members of a political party. Yet despite a considerable effort to nurture *European* parties,[54] European parliamentarians continue to be elected primarily as representatives of their *national* parties.[55] Members of Parliament will however often choose to join one of the European 'political groups'. (In reality, it is their national parties doing the joining for them.)[56] Parliament's Rules of Procedure stipulate that a political group must comprise a minimum number of 25 members and 'shall comprise Members elected in at least one-quarter of the Member States'.[57] The advantage of being within a political group is that they enjoy a privileged status within Parliament.

There presently exist seven political groups within the European Parliament: the European People's Party (EPP),[58] the Progressive Alliance of Socialists and

---

[50] *Ibid.*, Art. 5.   [51] *Ibid.*, Art. 8.

[52] *Ibid.*, Art. 9. Art. 10 fixes the salary as follows: 'The amount of the salary shall be 38.5 per cent of the basic salary of a judge of the Court of Justice of the European [Union].'

[53] *Ibid.*, Arts. 14ff.

[54] According to Art. 10(4) TEU: 'Political parties at European level contribute to forming European political awareness and to expressing the will of citizens of the Union.' The Treaties even contain a legal basis in Art. 224 TFEU for 'regulations governing political parties at European level referred to in Article 20(4) of the Treaty on European Union and in particular rules regarding their funding'. The legal basis has been used to adopt Regulation 1141/2014 on the statute and funding of European Political parties and European political foundations [2014] OJ L 317/1. The Regulation defines a 'political party' as an 'association of citizens', 'which pursues political objectives' and which is recognised or established within at least one Member State (*ibid.*, Art. 2). In order to register for the status as 'European Political Party' certain conditions must be satisfied (*ibid.*, Art. 3); and importantly they must commit to observe 'the values on which the Union is founded, as expressed in Article 2 TEU, namely respect for human dignity, freedom, democracy, equality, the rule of law and respect for human rights, including the rights of persons belonging to minorities' (*ibid.*, Art. 3(1)(c)). In order to control these conditions, and register new applicants, the Regulation has now established an 'Authority for European political parties and European political foundations', which decides on the registration and deregistration of European political parties (*ibid.*, Art. 6). If these conditions are fulfilled, the political party can – under certain conditions – apply for funding from the general budget of the European Union (*ibid.*, Art. 17).

[55] This led Hix to famously characterise European elections as 'second-order national contests' (S. Hix, *The Political System of the European Union* (Palgrave, 2005), 193).

[56] Each political group can itself decide on the membership in its Group Statute. For example, the European People's Party's Statute is based on the membership of national parties and distinguishes between 'Ordinary Member Parties' and 'Associated Member Parties'. According to Art. 5 of the Statute 'all members of the EPP Group in the European Parliament elected on a list of a member party are also members *ex officio* of the association'. However, parliamentarians who are not attached to any national party 'can become Individual Members of the association by decision of the Political Assembly on the proposal of the Presidency of the association' (*ibid.*).

[57] Rule 32(2) Parliament Rules of Procedure.

[58] For example, the French 'Republican' Party, as well as the German Party 'Christian Democratic Union' are members of this political group.

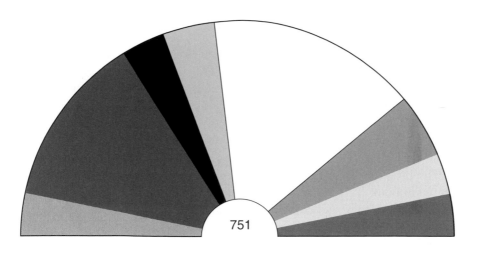

		EPP	Group of the European People's Party (Christian Democrats)	**221**	29.43%
	S&D	S&D	Group of the Progressive Alliance of Socialists and Democrats in the European Parliament	**191**	25.43%
		ECR	European Conservatives and Reformists	**70**	9.32%
		ALDE	Alliance of Liberals and Democrats for Europe	**67**	8.92%
		GUE/NGL	European United Left/Nordic Green Left	**52**	6.92%
		Greens/EFA	The Greens/European Free Alliance	**50**	6.66%
		EFDD	Europe of Freedom and Direct Democracy Group	**48**	6.39%
NI		**NI**	Non-attached Members – Members not belonging to any political group	**52**	6.92%

Figure 5.2 Distribution of Seats in the European Parliament (Political Parties)
(Source: European Parliament)

Democrats (S&D),[59] the European Conservatives and Reformists (ECR),[60] the Alliance of Liberals and Democrats for Europe (ALDE),[61] the European United Left–Nordic Green Left (GUE–NGL), the Greens–European Free Alliance (G–EFA) and the Europe of Freedom and Direct Democracy (EFDD). After the 2014 elections,[62] the distribution of seats among the political groups in the European Parliament is as shown in Figure 5.2.

[59] For example, the British 'Labour Party', the German 'Social Democratic Party' and the French 'Socialist Party' are members of this European political group.

[60] The British Conservative Party and Poland's 'Law and Justice' Party are members of this group.

[61] For example, the British 'Liberal Democrats', the French 'Democratic Movement' and the German 'Free Democratic Party' are members of this European political group.

[62] www.results–elections2014.eu/en/election-results-2014.html.

b. Internal Structure: Parliamentary Organs

Formally, Parliament must always act as the plenary. Yet it is entitled to organise itself internally and thus to establish a division of labour. According to Article 14(4) TEU, '[t]he European Parliament shall elect its President and its officers from among its members'. The various officers and their duties are laid down in Chapter 2 of Parliament's Rules of Procedure. According to its Rule 15, Parliament elects by secret ballot a President, 14 Vice-Presidents and five Quaestors.[63]

The President is the 'Speaker' of the European Parliament, whose duties are set out in Rule 22: 'The President shall direct all the activities of Parliament and its bodies.'[64] S/he is entitled 'to open, suspend and close sittings; to rule on the admissibility of amendments, on questions to the Council and Commission'; and s/he is also charged to 'maintain order, call upon speakers, close debates, put matters to the vote and announce the results of votes; and to refer to committees any communications that concern them'.[65] Finally, the President represents Parliament in interinstitutional or international relations.[66]

Parliament is also supported by a number of internal parliamentary organs. The 'Bureau' is the body formed by the President and the Vice-Presidents.[67] It is charged with taking decisions on financial and administrative matters concerning the internal organisation of Parliament and its Members.[68] The 'Conference of Presidents' is the organ that consists of the President and the Chairs of the Political Groups.[69] Importantly, it is the body that 'shall take decisions on the organization of Parliament's work and matters of legislative planning'.[70] It will thereby 'draw up the draft agenda of Parliament's part-sessions', and constitutes 'the authority responsible for the composition and competence of committees'.[71]

Committees constitute the most important 'decentralised' organs of Parliament. The two principal committee types are 'standing committees' and 'special committees'.[72] Standing committees are permanent committees. They are set up as thematically specialised bodies that concentrate on one area of parliamentary affairs.[73] With their mandates defined in the Parliament's Rules of Procedure,[74] Table 5.4 lists Parliament's Standing Committees.

Importantly, as committees functionally operate like miniature parliaments, all committees 'shall, as far as possible, reflect the composition of Parliament'.[75]

---

[63] The term of office for all three offices is two-and-a-half years (see Rule 19 Parliament Rules of Procedure).

[64] Rule 22(1) Parliament Rules of Procedure.

[65] *Ibid.*, Rule 22(2).   [66] *Ibid.*, Rule 22(4).   [67] *Ibid.*, Rule 24(1).

[68] *Ibid.*, Rule 25 – setting out the duties of the Bureau.

[69] *Ibid.*, Rule 26(1).

[70] *Ibid.*, Rule 27(2).

[71] *Ibid.*, Rule 27(6) and (7).

[72] *Ibid.*, Rules 196 and 197. 'Special committees' must generally expire after one year. For the detailed rules on Committees of Inquiry, see Rule 198.

[73] *Ibid.*, Rule 196.   [74] *Ibid.*, Annex V.   [75] *Ibid.*, Rule 199(1).

Table 5.4 Standing Committees of the European Parliament

Standing Committees			
Foreign Affairs	Economic and Monetary Affairs	Transport and Tourism	Legal Affairs
Development	Employment and Social Affairs	Regional Development	Civil Liberties, Justice and Home Affairs
International Trade	Environment, Public Health and Food Safety	Agriculture and Rural Development	Constitutional Affairs
Budgets	Industry, Research and Energy	Fisheries	Women's Rights and Gender Equality
Budgetary Control	Internal Market and Consumer	Culture and Education	Petitions

Committee members are elected after having been nominated by their political groups (or non-attached members). Standing committees have between 40 and 60 members, are headed by a 'Committee Chair', and are coordinated by 'Committee Coordinators'.[76] The duties of standing committees are thereby defined as follows: 'Standing committees shall examine questions referred to them by Parliament or, during an adjournment of the session, by the President on behalf of the Conference of Presidents.'[77] Voting within committees is by show of hands.[78] The responsibility for reporting back to the plenary is the task of a *rapporteur*. And this brings us to an important final point: committees only *prepare* decisions. For the task of deciding belongs – exclusively – to the plenary.

c. The Plenary: Decision-making and Voting

The Plenary is the formal decision-making 'organ' of the European Parliament. It is through the plenary that Parliament formally acts. The Treaties – anachronistically – determine that Parliament is to meet, as plenary, at least once a year to hold its annual session.[79] Parliament decided early on to divide its annual session

---

[76] *Ibid.*, Rule 205.

[77] *Ibid.*, Rule 201(1). According to Rule 201(2): 'Should two or more standing committees be competent to deal with a question, one committee shall be named as the committee responsible and the others as committees asked for opinions.'

[78] *Ibid.*, Rule 208.

[79] Art. 139 EEC. Today, Art. 229 TFEU states: 'The European Parliament shall hold an annual session. It shall meet, without requiring to be convened, on the second Tuesday in March. The European Parliament may meet in extraordinary part-session at the request of a majority of its component Members or at the request of the Council or of the Commission.'

into 12 'part-sessions' and to meet for a week every month. This choice has now been formally 'constitutionalised' by a Protocol attached to the Treaties.[80] These plenary sessions take place in Strasbourg — not in Brussels.

How does Parliament's plenary decide? Decision-making is governed by the general rule expressed in Article 231 TFEU: 'Save as otherwise provided in the Treaties, the European Parliament shall act by a majority of the *votes cast*. The Rules of Procedure shall determine the quorum.' These Rules define the quorum as 'one third of the component Members of Parliament'.[81]

What are the exceptions to the rule that Parliament decides by a majority of the votes cast? First, some Treaty articles qualify the majority by requiring that Parliament must decide by a majority of its *component* members. For example: the nominated Commission President 'shall be elected by the European Parliament by a majority of its *component members*'.[82] Second, some Treaty provisions require a doubly qualified majority. A good example can be found in a parliamentary motion censuring the Commission. Such a motion of censure requires a '*two-thirds majority* of the *votes* cast, representing the *majority of the component Members* of the European Parliament*'.[83]

The specifics of the voting procedure and the principles governing voting are set out in Rules 171–83 of the Parliament's Rules of Procedure. Parliament will generally vote by show of hands,[84] but 'voting by roll call' or electronic voting is also envisaged. In the former scenario, the individual votes of each parliamentarian will be recorded in the minutes.[85] In the latter scenario, 'only the numerical result of the vote shall be recorded'.[86]

Should a Parliament, which debates and votes in public, also be required to always record the votes of individual members? Two constitutional rationales compete in answering this question. From a democratic perspective, the 'transparency' of the vote is important in that it allows citizens to monitor their representatives. And, while the latter cannot be bound by instructions or a binding

---

[80] See Protocol No. 6 on the Location of the Seats of the Institutions: 'The European Parliament shall have its seat in Strasbourg where the 12 periods of monthly plenary sessions, including the budget session, shall be held. The periods of additional plenary sessions shall be held in Brussels. The committees of the European Parliament shall meet in Brussels. The General Secretariat of the European Parliament and its departments shall remain in Luxembourg.'

[81] Rule 168(2) Parliament Rules of Procedure. However, Rule 168(3) establishes the quorate nature of Parliament as a rebuttable presumption: 'All votes shall be valid whatever the number of voters unless the President, on request made before voting has begun by at least 40 members, establishes at the time of voting that the quorum is not present.'

[82] See Art. 17(7) TEU (emphasis added); Arts. 48 and 49 TEU; Arts. 223(1), 225, 226, 294(7) and 314(7) TFEU.

[83] Art. 234 TFEU (emphasis added). See also Art. 354 TFEU – last indent: 'For the purposes of Article 7 of the Treaty on European Union, the European Parliament shall act by a two-thirds majority of the votes cast, representing the majority of its component Members.'

[84] Rule 178(1) Parliament Rules of Procedure.

[85] *Ibid.*, Art. 180(4).   [86] *Ibid.*, Art. 181(2).

mandate,[87] citizens have at least a choice to 'deselect' their Member of Parliament in the following elections. On the other hand, an impersonal vote may better protect the independence of members of Parliament from less legitimate influences. These may be party-political pressures within Parliament or organised civil society in the form of corporatist lobbies.

d. Parliamentary Powers

When the Paris Treaty set up the European Parliament, its sole function was to exercise 'supervisory powers'.[88] Parliament was indeed a passive onlooker in the decision-making process within the first Community. The Rome Treaty expanded Parliament's function to 'advisory and supervisory powers'.[89] This recognised the active power of Parliament to be consulted on Commission proposals before their adoption by the Council.[90] After over 60 years of evolution and numerous amendments, the Treaty on European Union today defines the powers of the European Parliament in Article 14 TEU as follows:

> The European Parliament shall, jointly with the Council, exercise legislative and budgetary functions. It shall exercise functions of political control and consultation as laid down in the Treaties. It shall elect the President of the Commission.[91]

This definition distinguishes between four types of powers: legislative and budgetary powers as well as supervisory and elective powers.

aa. Legislative Powers

The European Parliament's principal power lies in the making of European laws. In the recent past, it has indeed evolved into a 'legislative powerhouse'.[92]

Its participation in the legislative process may take place at two moments in time. Parliament may informally propose new legislation.[93] However, it is not – unlike many national parliaments – entitled to formally propose bills. The task of making legislative proposals is, with minor exceptions, a constitutional prerogative of the Commission.[94]

---

[87] Art. 3 MEP Statute states: 'Members shall vote on an individual and personal basis. They shall not be bound by any instructions and shall not receive a binding mandate. Agreements concerning the way in which the mandate is to be exercised shall be null and void.'

[88] Art. 20 ECSC.   [89] Art. 137 EEC.

[90] Case 138/79, *Roquette Frères* v. *Council*.

[91] Art. 14(1) TEU.

[92] M. Kohler, 'European Governance and the European Parliament: From Talking Shop to Legislative Powerhouse' (2014) 52 *Journal of Common Market Studies* 600.

[93] Art. 225 TFEU: 'The European Parliament may, acting by a majority of its component Members, request the Commission to submit any appropriate proposal on matters on which it considers that a Union act is required for the purpose of implementing the Treaties. If the Commission does not submit a proposal, it shall inform the European Parliament of the reasons.'

[94] On this power, see Chapter 7, section 3.

The principal legislative involvement of Parliament thus starts after the Commission has submitted a proposal to the European legislature. Like other federal legal orders, the European legal order acknowledges a number of different legislative procedures. The Treaties now textually distinguish between the 'ordinary' legislative procedure and a number of 'special' legislative procedures. The former is defined as 'the joint adoption by the European Parliament and the Council' on a proposal from the Commission.[95] Special legislative procedures cover various degrees of parliamentary participation. Under the 'consent procedure' Parliament must give its consent before the Council can adopt European legislation.[96] Under the 'consultation procedure', by contrast, Parliament is not even entitled to do that. It merely needs to be consulted − a role that is closer to a supervisory than to a legislative function.[97] Exceptionally, a special legislative procedure may make Parliament the dominant legislative chamber.[98] These various procedures will be discussed in Chapter 7.

Importantly, Parliament's 'legislative' powers also extend to the external relations sphere. After Lisbon, Parliament has indeed become an important player in the conclusion of the Union's international agreements. This point will be discussed in Chapter 8.

bb. Budgetary Powers

National parliaments have historically been involved in the budgetary process because they were seen as legitimating the *raising* of revenue. In the words of the American colonists: 'No taxation without representation'. In the European Union, this picture is somewhat inverted. For, since Union revenue is fixed by the Council and the Member States,[99] the European Parliament's budgetary powers have not focused on the *income* side but on the *expenditure* side. Its powers have consequently been described as the 'reverse of those traditionally exercised by parliaments'.[100]

Be that as it may, Parliament's formal involvement in the Union budget started with the 1970 and 1975 Budget Treaties. They distinguished between compulsory and non-compulsory expenditure, with the latter being expenditure that

---

[95] Art. 289(1) TFEU.

[96] For example, Art. 19 TFEU, according to which 'the Council, acting unanimously in accordance with a special legislative procedure and after obtaining the consent of the European Parliament, may take appropriate action to combat discrimination based on sex, racial or ethnic origin, religion or belief, disability, age or sexual orientation'.

[97] For example, Art. 22(1) TFEU, which states: 'Every citizen of the Union residing in a Member State of which he is not a national shall have the right to vote and to stand as a candidate at municipal elections in the Member State in which he resides, under the same conditions as nationals of that State. This right shall be exercised subject to detailed arrangements adopted by the Council, acting unanimously in accordance with a special legislative procedure and after consulting the European Parliament[.]'

[98] For example, Art. 223(2) TFEU − granting Parliament the power, with the consent of the Council, to adopt a Statute for its Members.

[99] See Art. 311 TFEU on the 'Union's own resources'.

[100] D. Judge and D. Earnshaw, *The European Parliament* (Palgrave, 2008), 198.

would not result from compulsory financial commitments flowing from the application of European law. Parliament's powers were originally confined to this second category. The Lisbon Treaty has, however, abandoned the distinction between compulsory and non-compulsory expenditure, and Parliament has thus become an equal partner in establishing the Union's annual budget.[101]

cc. Supervisory Powers

A third parliamentary power is that of holding to account the executive. Parliamentary supervisory powers typically involve the power to debate, question and investigate.

A soft parliamentary power is the power to *debate*.[102] To that effect, the European Parliament is entitled to receive the 'general report on the activities of the Union' from the Commission,[103] which it 'shall discuss in open session'.[104] And, as regards the European Council, the Treaties require its President to 'present a report to the European Parliament after each of the meetings of the European Council'.[105] Similar obligations apply to the European Central Bank.[106]

The power to *question* the European executive is formally enshrined only for the Commission: 'The Commission shall reply orally or in writing to questions put to it by the European Parliament or by its Members.'[107] However, both the European Council and the Council have confirmed their willingness to be questioned by Parliament.[108] Early on, Parliament introduced the institution of 'Question Time' – modelled on the procedure within the British Parliament.[109] And under its own Rules of Procedure, Parliament is entitled to hold 'an extraordinary debate' on a 'matter of major interest relating to European Union policy'.[110]

---

[101] Art. 314 TFEU.

[102] In the area of the Union's common foreign and security policy, the parliamentary powers to question and debate are now expressly enshrined in Art. 36(2) TEU: 'The European Parliament may address questions or make recommendations to the Council or to the High Representative. Twice a year it shall hold a debate on progress in implementing the common foreign and security policy[.]'

[103] Art. 249(2) TFEU.

[104] *Ibid.*, Art. 233.

[105] Art. 15(6)(d) TEU.

[106] Art. 284(3) TFEU. See in particular the Interinstitutional Agreement between the European Parliament and the European Central Bank on the practical modalities of the exercise of democratic accountability and oversight over the exercise of the tasks conferred on the ECB within the framework of the Single Supervisory Mechanism [2013] OJ L 320/1.

[107] Art. 230 TFEU – second indent.

[108] The Council accepted this political obligation in 1973; see Jacobs et al., *European Parliament* (n. 40 above), 284.

[109] Rule 129 Parliament Rules of Procedure. For the acceptance of that obligation by the Commission, see Framework Agreement on relations between the European Parliament and the European Commission [2010] OJ L 304/47, para. 46.

[110] Rule 153 Parliament Rules of Procedure.

Parliament also enjoys the formal power to *investigate*. It is constitutionally entitled to set up temporary Committees of Inquiry to investigate alleged contraventions or maladministration in the implementation of European law.[111] These temporary committees complement Parliament's standing committees. They have been used, *inter alia*, to investigate the (mis)handling of the BSE crisis.[112]

Finally, European citizens have the general right to 'petition' the European Parliament.[113] And, according to a Scandinavian constitutional tradition, the European Parliament will also elect an 'ombudsman'. The European Ombudsman 'shall be empowered to receive complaints' from any citizen or Union resident 'concerning instances of maladministration in the activities of the Union institutions, bodies or agencies'. S/he 'shall conduct inquiries' on the basis of complaints addressed to her or him directly or through a Member of the European Parliament.[114]

dd. Elective Powers

Modern constitutionalism distinguishes between 'presidential' and 'parliamentary' systems. Within the former, the executive officers are independent from Parliament, whereas in the latter the executive is elected by Parliament. The European constitutional order sits somewhere 'in between'. Its executive was for a long time selected without any parliamentary involvement. This continues to be the case today for one branch of the Union executive: the European Council. However, as regards the Commission, the European Parliament has increasingly come to be involved in the appointment process. Today, Article 17 TEU describes the involvement of the European Parliament in the appointment of the Commission as follows:

> Taking into account the elections to the European Parliament and after having held the appropriate consultations, the European Council, acting by a qualified majority, shall propose to the European Parliament a candidate for President of the Commission. This candidate shall be elected by the European Parliament by a majority of its component members ... The Council, by common accord with the President-elect, shall adopt the list of the other persons whom it proposes for appointment as members of the Commission. They shall be selected, on the basis of the suggestions made by Member States ... The President, the High Representative of the Union for Foreign Affairs and Security Policy and the other members of the Commission shall

---

[111] Art. 226(1) TFEU. For a good overview of the history of these committees, see M. Shackleton, 'The European Parliament's New Committees of Inquiry: Tiger or Paper Tiger' (1998) 36 *Journal of Common Market Studies* 115.

[112] For the Report of the BSE Committee of Inquiry of the European Parliament, see K. Vincent, '"Mad Cows" and Eurocrats: Community Responses to the BSE Crisis' (2004) 10 ELJ 499.

[113] According to Art. 227 TFEU, any citizen or Union resident has the right to petition the European Parliament 'on any matter which comes within the Union's field or activity and which affects him, her or it directly'. See also Art. 20(2)(d) TFEU.

[114] Art. 228 TFEU.

be subject as a body to a vote of consent by the European Parliament. On the basis of this consent the Commission shall be appointed by the European Council, acting by a qualified majority.[115]

The appointment of the second branch of the European executive thus requires dual parliamentary consent.

Parliament must – first – 'elect' the President of the Commission. Controversy has thereby arisen whether the power to 'elect' also includes the power to 'nominate' the Commission President. During the last parliamentary elections, Parliament has indeed claimed this additional power by using the political concept of 'lead candidates' (in German: *Spitzenkandidaten*). According to this view, the 'lead candidate' of the political group that won the greatest number of seats within the Parliament should become the President of the Commission. From a democratic perspective, this argument must be lauded;[116] legally, on the other hand the parliamentary power to nominate the Commission Presidents seems to go against the express wording of Article 17 (7) TEU. The provisions grant the power of nomination to the European Council, which is only obliged to '[t]ak[e] into account the elections to the European Parliament' and to only 'consult[]' with the latter.

Be that as it may, Parliament must – second – also give its 'consent' to the Commission as a collective body as a whole. (Apart from the Commission's President, the European Parliament has consequently *not* got the power to confirm each and every Commissioner.)[117]

Once appointed, the Commission continues to 'be responsible to the European Parliament'.[118] Where its trust is lost, Parliament may vote on a motion of censure. If this vote of mistrust is carried, the Commission must resign as a body. The motion of collective censure here mirrors Parliament's appointment power, which is also focused on the Commission *as a collective body*. This blunt 'atomic option' has never been used.[119] However, unlike the appointment power, Parliament has been able to sharpen its tools of censure significantly by concluding a political agreement with the Commission. Accordingly, if Parliament expresses lack of confidence in an *individual* member of the Commission, the President of the Commission 'shall either require the resignation of that Member' or, after 'serious' consideration, explain the refusal to do so before Parliament.[120]

---

[115]   Art. 17(7) TEU.

[116]   For a very critical assessment of this claim, see M. Goldoni, 'Politicising EU Lawmaking? The *Spitzenkandidaten* Experiment as a Cautionary Tale' (2016) 22 ELJ 279.

[117]   However, Parliament may request each nominated Commissioner to appear before Parliament and to 'present' his or her views. This practice thus comes close to 'confirmation hearings' (Judge and Earnshaw, *European Parliament* (n. 100 above), 205).

[118]   Art. 17(8) TEU.

[119]   Once, the European Parliament came close to using this power when in 1999 it decided to censure the Santer Commission. However, the latter chose collectively to resign instead.

[120]   Framework Agreement (n. 109 above), para. 5. However, this rule has been contested by the Council; see Council statement concerning the framework agreement on relations between the European Parliament and the Commission [2010] OJ C 287/1.

While this is a much 'smarter sanction', it has also never been used due to the demanding voting threshold in Parliament.

Parliament is also involved in the appointment of other European officers. This holds true for the Court of Auditors,[121] the European Central Bank,[122] the European Ombudsman,[123] as well as some European Agencies.[124]

In light of all the elective (and censuring) power given to Parliament, one is justified in characterising the Union's governmental system as a 'semi-parliamentary democracy'.[125]

3. The European Council

The European Council originally developed outside the institutional framework of the European Union.[126] And, for some time, the Member States even tried to prevent the European Council from acting *within* the scope of the Treaties.[127] Since the 1992 Maastricht Treaty, the European Council has however steadily moved inside the institutional framework of the Union. And with the 2007 Lisbon Treaty, the European Council has finally become a formal institution of the European Union.[128] This formalisation recognises a substantive development in which the European Council had become 'the political backbone' of the European Union.[129]

The composition of the European Council is as simple as it is exclusive. It consists of the Heads of State or Government of the Member States.[130] With the Lisbon Treaty the European Council has its own President – who will be an additional member, as s/he cannot simultaneously serve as a Head of State or Government.[131] The President of the Commission shall also be a formal member.[132] However, neither the President of the European Council nor the

---

[121] Art. 286(2) TFEU.   [122] *Ibid.*, Art. 283(2).   [123] *Ibid.*, Art. 228(2).

[124] For example, Parliament is entitled to appoint two members to the Management Board of the European Environmental Agency; see Regulation No. 401/2009 on the European Environment Agency and the European Environment Information and Observation Network (Codified version) [2009] OJ L 126/13, Art. 8(1).

[125] P. Dann, 'European Parliament and Executive Federalism: Approaching a Parliament in a Semi-parliamentary Democracy' (2003) 9 ELJ 549.

[126] On the historical evolution of the European Council, see Chapter 1, section 2(c).

[127] European Council, 'Solemn Declaration on European Union (Stuttgart, 1983)' reproduced in A. G. Harryvan et al. (eds.), *Documents on European Union* (St Martin's Press, 1997), 215, para. 2.1.3: '[w]hen the European Council acts in matters within the scope of the European [Union], it does so in its capacity as the Council within the meaning of the Treaties'.

[128] Art. 13(1) TEU.

[129] J. Werts, *The European Council* (TMC Asser Institute, 1992), 296.

[130] Art. 15(2) TEU. The distinction between Heads of State or Government was originally made for France. For, under national constitutional law, the President, as Head of State, is principally charged with external relations powers. The situation is similar in Cyprus, Finland, Lithuania and – arguably – the Czech Republic and Poland.

[131] *Ibid.*, Art. 15(6) – last indent: 'The President of the European Council shall not hold a national office.'

[132] *Ibid.*, Art. 15(2).

Commission President enjoys a voting right.[133] They are thus not full members, but rather 'honorary' members of this Union institution. Their status is not so dissimilar to the High Representative of the Union for Foreign Affairs and Security Policy, who – while not even being a formal member of the European Council – shall nonetheless take part in its work.

The European Council shall meet twice every six months, but can have additional meetings when the situation so requires.[134] These regular meetings follow the seasons: there are spring, summer, autumn and winter meetings. These meetings were traditionally held in the Member State holding the Council Presidency. However, the European Council now 'shall meet in Brussels'.[135]

How will it decide? The decision-making process within the European Council is shrouded in secrecy, for its meetings are not public.[136] The default principle is set out in Article 15(4) TEU: 'Except where the Treaties provide otherwise, decisions of the European Council shall be taken by consensus.' The general rule is thus unanimity of all the Member States. However, there are some instances within the Treaties in which the European Council may act by a (qualified) majority of the Member States. In such a case, the Council's rules on what constitutes a qualified majority apply *mutatis mutandis* to the European Council.[137]

a. The President of the European Council

Traditionally, the European Council had a rotating presidency: every six months, the Head of State or Government of the State that held the Council Presidency was to be the President of the European Council. The Lisbon Treaty has given the European Council its own – permanent – President.[138]

The permanent President is elected by the European Council,[139] but cannot be elected from within the European Council. The period of office will be a (once renewable) term of two-and-a-half years.[140] This is a   relatively – short

---

[133] Art. 235(1) TFEU: 'Where the European Council decides by vote, its President and the President of the Commission shall not take part in the vote.'

[134] Art. 15(3) TEU. In urgent situations, the physical meeting can be replaced by a 'written procedure' (see Art. 7 European Council Rules of Procedure).

[135] Art. 1(2) European Council Rules of Procedure.

[136] *Ibid.*, Art. 4(3): 'Meetings of the European Council shall not be public.' However, according to Art. 10, the European Council may decide 'to make public the result of votes, as well as the statements in its minutes and the items in those minutes relating to the adoption of that decision'.

[137] Art. 235 TFEU: 'Article 16(4) of the Treaty on European Union and Article 238(2) of this Treaty apply to the European Council when it is acting by a qualified majority.'

[138] For a first analysis of this innovation, see H. de Waele and H. Broeksteeg, 'The Semipermanent European Council Presidency: Some Reflections on the Law and Early Practice' (2012) 49 *CML Rev.* 1039.

[139] Art. 15(5) TEU.

[140] *Ibid.* This has now happened with regard to the current President, see European Council Decision 2017/444 electing the President of the European Council ([2017] OJ L 67/87), Art. 1: 'Mr Donald TUSK is hereby re-elected President of the European Council for the period from 1 June 2017 until 30 November 2019.'

time when compared with other governmental offices within the European Union. Nonetheless, the advantages of a permanent President over a rotating presidency are considerable. First, the rotating presidency of six months was *very* short. A permanent President thus promises – more – permanence. Second, the idea of having the President or Prime Minister of a Member State act as President of the European Council had always been incongruous. How could the national loyalties of the highest *State* representative be harmoniously combined with the European obligation of standing above national interests? Third, the tasks of the President of the European Council have become far too demanding to be the subject of shared attention. The tasks of the President are today set out in Article 15(6) TEU:

> The President of the European Council:
> (a) Shall chair it and drive forward its work;
> (b) Shall ensure the preparation and continuity of the work of the European Council in cooperation with the President of the Commission, and on the basis of the work of the General Affairs Council;
> (c) Shall endeavour to facilitate cohesion and consensus within the European Council;
> (d) Shall present a report to the European Parliament after each of the meetings of the European Council.
>   The President of the European Council shall, at his level and in that capacity, ensure the external representation of the Union on issues concerning its common foreign and security policy, without prejudice to the powers of the High Representative of the Union for Foreign Affairs and Security Policy.[141]

The tasks of the President are not very specific. The President has primarily coordinating and representative functions. S/he represents the European Council as an institution within the Union. Outside the Union, s/he ensures the external representation of the Union with regard to the Union's CFSP – a task that is however shared with the High Representative for Foreign Affairs and Security Policy.[142] A picture of the current European Council President is provided in Figure 5.3.

b. The European Council: Functions and Powers

What are the functions and powers of the European Council? Article 15 TEU defines them as follows:

> The European Council shall provide the Union with the necessary impetus for its development and shall define the general political directions and priorities thereof.[143]

[141] These powers are further defined in Art. 2 of the European Council Rules of Procedure.
[142] On the High Representative, see section 4(b/cc) below.
[143] Art. 15(1) TEU.

Figure 5.3 European Council President: Donald Tusk

The political power to provide impulses and guidelines has been the traditional function of the European Council. It is the European Council whose Presidency Conclusions offer specific and regular stimuli to the development of the Union and its policies.[144] We find numerous expressions of this executive power of political guidance in the Treaties.[145] However, the definition given in Article 15 TEU is reductionist in that it concentrates on the European Council's *executive* function. Yet the European Council also exercises three important additional functions.

First, it is given a significant *constitutional* function. We have seen this above in relation to the simplified revision procedures.[146] And, in limited areas, the European Council is even given the power unilaterally to 'bridge' the procedural or competence limits established by the Treaties.[147] These '*passerelles*' (little bridges) provide the European Council with a partial competence-competence. Finally, the European Council agrees on the eligibility conditions for States hoping to become members of the Union.[148]

---

[144] On this point, see Chapter 9, section 1.

[145] For example, Art. 26(1) TEU: 'The European Council shall identify the Union's strategic interests, determine the objectives of and define general guidelines for the common foreign and security policy, including for matters with defence implications. It shall adopt the necessary decisions.'

[146] On the European Council's role within Art. 48 TEU, see Chapter 1, Conclusion.

[147] For an example of such a special 'bridge', see Art. 31(3) TEU, and Art. 86(4) TFEU.

[148] Art. 49 TEU. It is also charged to provide guidelines for the withdrawal of a Member State; see Art. 50(2) TEU. I shall look at this power, briefly, in the context of the Brexit chapter in this second edition (see Chapter 19).

Second, the European Council also has *institutional* functions. It can influence the composition of the European Parliament,[149] as well as that of the European Commission.[150] It shall adopt the various Council configurations and determine that body's presidency.[151] It shall appoint the High Representative of the Union for Foreign Affairs and Security Policy,[152] as well as the President (and the executive board) of the European Central Bank.[153]

Third, the European Council exercises *arbitration* powers and thus functions like an appeal 'court' in – very – specific situations.[154] We can find an illustration of this power in the context of the Union competence in the 'Area of Freedom, Security and Justice'.[155] The European Council is here empowered to suspend the legislative procedure to arbitrate between the Council and a Member State claiming that the draft European law 'would affect fundamental aspects of its criminal justice system'.[156]

By contrast, one of the functions that the European Council cannot exercise is to adopt legislative acts. Article 15 TEU is clear on this point: the European Council 'shall not exercise legislative functions'.[157] Nevertheless, and as we shall see below, the European Council has assumed quasi-regulatory functions in the context of 'economic and monetary policy'.[158]

4. The Council of Ministers

The 1957 Rome Treaty had originally charged the Council with the task of 'ensur[ing] that the objectives set out in this Treaty are attained'.[159] This task involved the exercise of legislative as well as executive functions. And, while other institutions would be involved in these functions, the Council was to be the central institution within the European Union. This has – over time – dramatically

---

[149]   Art. 14(2) TEU: 'The European Council shall adopt by unanimity, on the initiative of the European Parliament and with its consent, a decision establishing the composition of the European Parliament, respecting the principles referred to in the first subparagraph.'

[150]   Art. 17(5) TEU, as well as Art. 244 TFEU.

[151]   Art. 236 TFEU. For a detailed analysis, see section 4(a and b).

[152]   Art. 18(1) TEU.

[153]   Art. 283(2) TFEU.

[154]   Werts, *European Council* (n. 129 above), 299.

[155]   That is: Title V of Part III of the TFEU, Arts. 67–89 TFEU.

[156]   See Art. 82(3) TFEU: 'Where a member of the Council considers that a draft directive as referred to in paragraph 2 would affect fundamental aspects of its criminal justice system, it may request that the draft directive be referred to the European Council. In that case, the ordinary legislative procedure shall be suspended. After discussion, and in case of a consensus, the European Council shall, within four months of this suspension, refer the draft back to the Council, which shall terminate the suspension of the ordinary legislative procedure.'

[157]   Art. 15(1) TEU.

[158]   For a discussion of this (new) role, developed mainly after the financial crisis, see W. Wessels, *The European Council* (Palgrave, 2016), ch. 13. For a brief overview of the Union's policy in relation to economic and monetary union, see Chapter 18, section 1.

[159]   Art. 145 EEC.

changed with the rise of two rival institutions. On one side, the ascendancy of the European Parliament has limited the Council's legislative role within the Union; on the other side, the rise of the European Council has restricted the Council's executive powers. Today, the Council is best characterised as the 'federal' chamber within the Union legislature. It is the organ in which national ministers meet.

What is the composition of this federal chamber, and what is its internal structure? How will the Council decide – by unanimity or qualified majority? And what are the powers enjoyed by the Council? This fourth section addresses these questions in four subsections.

a. The Council: Composition and Configuration

Within the European Union, the Council is the institution of the Member States. Its intergovernmental character lies in its composition. The Treaty on European Union defines it as follows: 'The Council shall consist of a representative of each Member State at ministerial level, who may commit the government of the Member State in question and cast its vote.'[160] Within the Council, each national minister thus represents the interests of his Member State. These interests may vary depending on the subject matter decided in the Council. And indeed, depending on the subject matter at issue, there are different Council configurations.[161] And for each configuration, a different national minister will be representing his State.[162] While there is thus – legally – but one single Council, there are – politically – ten different Councils. The existing Council configurations are shown in Table 5.5.

What is the mandate of each Council configuration? The Treaties only define the task of the first two Council configurations.[163] The 'General Affairs Council' has one upward and one downward task. It must 'prepare and ensure the follow-up to meetings of the European Council'.[164] As regards its 'downward' task, it is charged to 'ensure consistency in the work of the different Council configurations' below the General Affairs Council.[165] The 'Foreign Affairs Council',

---

[160] Art. 16(2) TEU.

[161] Art. 16(6) TEU: 'The Council shall meet in different configurations, the list of which shall be adopted in accordance with Article 236 of the Treaty on the Functioning of the European Union.'

[162] Under the Rome Treaty, the dividing line between the European Council and the Council was not very clear, since the Council could then meet in the formation of Heads of State or Government (see A. Dashwood, 'Decision-making at the Summit' (2000) 3 *CYELS* 79). The illustrious club could thus transform itself – in an instant – from the European Council to the Council. With the Lisbon Treaty, this problem has disappeared, as the Treaties no longer expressly call for a Council configuration consisting of the Heads of State or Government.

[163] Art. 16(6) TEU.

[164] *Ibid*. For detailed rules on this task of the General Affairs Council, see Art. 2(2)–(4) Council Rules of Procedure.

[165] Art. 16(6) TEU.

Table 5.5 Council Configurations

Council Configurations
1 General Affairs
2 Foreign Affairs
3 Economic and Financial Affairs
4 Justice and Home Affairs
5 Employment, Social Policy, Health and Consumer Affairs
6 Competitiveness (Internal Market, Industry, Research and Space)
7 Transport, Telecommunications and Energy
8 Agriculture and Fisheries
9 Environment
10 Education, Youth, Culture and Sport

on the other hand, is required to 'elaborate the Union's external action on the basis of strategic guidelines laid down by the European Council and ensure that the Union's action is consistent'.[166] The thematic scope and functional task of the remaining Council configurations is constitutionally open. They will generally deal with the subjects falling within their thematic ambit.

b. Internal Structure and Organs

aa. The Presidency of the Council

The Council has no permanent President. Unlike the European Council, the Council operates in various configurations, and the task of presiding over these different configurations could not be given to one person. One therefore refers to the depersonalised office of the Council 'Presidency' as opposed to the President of the Council.

The Council Presidency is set out in Article 16(9) TEU:

> The Presidency of Council configurations, other than that of Foreign Affairs, shall be held by Member State representatives in the Council on the basis of equal rotation.

The Council Presidency is thus a *rotating* presidency. The modalities of the rotating presidency have changed with time. Originally, a single Member State held it for six months. This has given way to 'troika presidencies'. The Lisbon Treaty codifies these team presidencies. The Council Presidency 'shall be held by pre-established groups of three Member States for a period of eighteen

---

[166] *Ibid.*

months'.[167] And within the team of three States, each member of the group shall chair the respective Council configurations for a period of six months.[168] The great exception to the rotating presidency is the 'Foreign Affairs Council'. Here, the Treaty contains a special rule in Article 18 TEU – dealing with the office of the High Representative of the Union for Foreign Affairs and Security Policy: 'The High Representative shall preside over the Foreign Affairs Council.'[169]

The tasks of the Presidency are twofold. Externally, it is to represent the Council.[170] Internally, it is to prepare and chair the Council meetings. The team presidency is thereby charged to write a 'draft programme' for 18 months.[171] The individual Member State to hold office shall further establish 'draft agendas for Council meetings scheduled for the next six-month period' on the basis of the Council's draft programme.[172] Finally, the (relevant) chair of each Council configuration shall draw up the 'provisional agenda for each meeting'.[173] And, while the Council will need to approve the agenda at the beginning of each meeting,[174] the power to set the provisional agenda is remarkable. The provisional agenda must thereby have the following form:

> The provisional agenda shall be divided into two parts, dealing respectively with deliberations on the legislative and non-legislative activities. The first part shall be entitled 'Legislative deliberations' and the second 'Non-legislative activities'. The items appearing in each part of the provisional agenda shall be divided into A items and B items. Items for which approval by the Council is possible without discussion shall be entered as A items …[175]

The 'A items' constitute the vast majority of the agenda items.[176] They are effectively decided by the Council's committees, in particular the Committee of Permanent Representatives – to which we shall now turn.

---

[167] European Council Decision 2009/881 on the Exercise of the Presidency of the Council [2009] OJ L 315/50, Art. 1(1).

[168] *Ibid.*, Art. 1(2). Until 2020, the Council Presidency order thereby is as follows: Estonia, January–June 2018; Bulgaria, July–December 2018; Austria, January–June 2019; Romania, July–December 2019; Finland, January–June 2020.

[169] Art. 18(3) TEU. According to Art. 2(5) Council Rules of Procedure, the High Representative may, however, 'ask to be replaced by the member of that configuration representing the Member State holding the six-monthly presidency of the Council'.

[170] Art. 26 Council Rules of Procedure: 'The Council shall be represented before the European Parliament or its committees by the Presidency or, with the latter's agreement, by a member of the pre-established group of three Member States referred to in Article 1(4), by the following Presidency or by the Secretary-General.'

[171] *Ibid.*, Art. 2(6).   [172] *Ibid.*, Art. 2(7).   [173] *Ibid.*, Art. 3(1).   [174] *Ibid.*, Art. 3(7).

[175] *Ibid.*, Art. 3(6).

[176] According to F. Hayes-Renshaw and H. Wallace, *The Council of Ministers* (Palgrave, 2006), 77, some 85 per cent will be an 'A item'.

bb. 'Coreper' and Specialised Committees

The Council has, like the Parliament, developed committees to assist it. From the very beginning, a committee composed of representatives of the Member States would support the Council.[177] That committee was made permanent under the Rome Treaty.[178] The resultant 'Committee of *Permanent* Representatives' became known under its French acronym: 'Coreper'. The Permanent Representative is the ambassador of a Member State at the European Union. S/he is based in the national 'Permanent Representation to the European Union'.

Coreper has two parts: Coreper II represents the meeting of the ambassadors, while Coreper I – against all intuition – represents the meetings of their deputies. Both parts correspond to particular Council configurations. Coreper II prepares the first four Council configurations – that is the more important political decisions; whereas Coreper I prepares the more technical remainder.

The function of Coreper is vaguely defined in the Treaties: 'A Committee of Permanent Representatives of the Governments of the Member States shall be responsible for preparing the work of the Council.'[179] The abstract definition has been – somewhat – specified in the following way: 'All items on the agenda for a Council meeting shall be examined in advance by Coreper unless the latter decides otherwise. Coreper shall endeavour to reach agreement at its level to be submitted to the Council for adoption.'[180] In order to achieve that task, Coreper has set up 'working parties' below it.[181] (These working parties are composed of national civil servants operating on instructions from national ministries.) Where Coreper reaches agreement, the point will be classed as an 'A item' that will be rubber-stamped by the Council. Where it fails to agree in advance, a 'B item' will need to be expressly discussed by the ministers in the Council. (But, importantly, even for 'A items', Coreper is not formally entitled to take decisions itself. It merely 'prepares' and facilitates formal decision-making in the Council.)

The Treaties also acknowledge a number of specialised Council committees that complement Coreper. These committees are (primarily) advisory bodies. Five will be mentioned here. First, there is the Political and Security Committee

---

[177]   The Committee beneath the ECSC Council was called 'Commission de Coordination du Conseil des Ministres' (Cocor). Its members were not permanently residing in Brussels.

[178]   The Rome Treaty contained, unlike the Paris Treaty, an express legal basis for a Council Committee in Art. 151 EEC: 'The Council shall adopt its rules of procedure. These rules of procedure may provide for the setting up of a committee consisting of representatives of the Member States.' While the provision did not expressly mention that these representatives would be permanent representatives, this had been the intention of the Member States (E. Noel, 'The Committee of Permanent Representatives' (1967) 5 *Journal of Common Market Studies* 219). The Merger Treaty formally established the Committee of Permanent Representatives (*ibid.*, Art. 4).

[179]   Art. 16(7) TEU and Art. 240(1) TFEU. See also Art. 19 of the Council Rules of Procedure.

[180]   Art. 19(2) Council Rules of Procedure.

[181]   *Ibid.*, Art. 19(3). Under this paragraph, the General Secretariat is under an obligation to produce a list of these preparatory bodies.

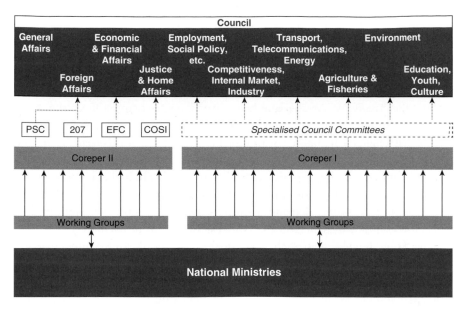

Figure 5.4 Preparatory Committees to the Council

(PSC) established in the context of the Common Foreign and Security Policy.[182] According to the Treaties, it shall *inter alia* 'monitor the international situation' and 'contribute to the definition of policies by delivering opinions to the Council'.[183] The Committee has become so important that the Member State representative delegated to it has become the third person with ambassadorial rank within the Permanent Representations. Second, there exists the 'Article 207 Committee'. The latter receives its name from the article under which it is established. Article 207 TFEU stipulates that in international negotiations between the European Union and third countries, the '[t]he Commission shall conduct these negotiations in consultation with a special committee appointed by the Council to assist the Commission'.[184] The following three committees deal with internal policies. A specialised Council committee is set up in the context of economic and monetary policy. The Economic and Financial Committee (EFC) is to 'promote coordination of the policies of Member States'.[185] Furthermore, '[a] standing committee shall be set up within the Council in order to ensure that operational cooperation on internal security is promoted and strengthened within the Union'.[186] This has since happened.[187] There are also specialised

---

[182] See Art. 38 TEU. See also Council Decision 2001/78 Setting up the Political and Security Committee [2001] OJ L 27/1.

[183] Art. 38 TEU.   [184] Art. 207(3) TFEU.

[185] *Ibid.*, Art. 134(1).   [186] *Ibid.*, Art. 71.

[187] See Council Decision 2010/131 on setting up the Standing Committee on operational cooperation on internal security (COSI) [2010] OJ L 52/50. According to Art. 1: 'The Standing Committee on operational cooperation on internal security (hereinafter referred to as "the Standing Committee") foreseen in Article 71 of the Treaty is hereby

committees with regard to Coreper I, the most important of which is the Special Committee on Agriculture (SCA).

cc. Excursus: The High Representative of Foreign Affairs and Security Policy

To help the Council Presidency within the Common Foreign and Security Policy, the Treaty of Amsterdam had created an 'assistant' office: the High Representative for the Common Foreign and Security Policy.[188] The Lisbon Treaty has changed its name into High Representative for *Foreign Affairs* and Security Policy. That change of name was designed to indicate a crucial institutional innovation: the 'personal union' of the (old) High Representative and the External Relations Commissioner. (This 'personal union' has not merged the two offices. It simply demands that the same person must hold *two* offices at once. Put colloquially, s/he will have to wear two institutional 'hats'.)

The High Representative shall conduct the Union's CFSP and chair the Foreign Affairs Council. In this capacity, s/he is subordinate to the Council.[189] The powers of the High Representative are defined in Article 27 TEU. The High Representative shall ensure the implementation of the decisions adopted by the European Council and the Council and make proposals for the development of that policy.[190] The High Representative will represent the Union for CFSP matters and shall express the Union's position in international organisations.[191] And to help fulfil her mandate, the High Representative will be assisted by the – newly created – European External Action Service (EEAS).[192] This is the diplomatic corps of the European Union.

---

set up within the Council.' Its tasks are defined in Art. 3, whose first paragraph reads: 'the Standing Committee shall facilitate and ensure effective operational cooperation and coordination under Title V of Part Three of the Treaty, including in areas covered by police and customs cooperation and by authorities responsible for the control and protection of external borders.' 'It shall also cover, where appropriate, judicial cooperation in criminal matters relevant to operational cooperation in the field of internal security.'

[188] See Art. 18(3) (old) EU: 'The Presidency shall be assisted by the Secretary-General of the Council who shall exercise the function of High Representative for the common foreign and security policy.'

[189] See Art. 18(2) TEU: 'as mandated by the Council'. As the High Representative is also the Commissioner for External Relations, she or he will be subordinate to the Commission President. According to Art. 18(4) TEU (emphasis added): 'In exercising these responsibilities within the Commission, and only for these responsibilities, the High Representative shall be bound by Commission procedures *to the extent that this is consistent with paragraphs 2 and 3.*'

[190] Art. 27(1) TEU.

[191] *Ibid.*, Art. 27(2).

[192] *Ibid.*, Art. 27(3). The EEAS was established by Council Decision 2010/427 establishing the organisation and functioning of the European External Action Service [2010] OJ L 201/30. On the establishment of the EEAS, see P. Koutrakos, 'Habemus European External Action Service' (2010) 35 *EL Rev.* 608; B. van Vooren, 'A Legal–Institutional Perspective on the European External Action Service' (2011) 48 *CML Rev.* 475.

c. Decision-making and Voting

The Council must – physically – meet in Brussels to make decisions.[193] The meetings are divided into two parts: one dealing with legislative activities, the other with non-legislative activities. When discussing legislation, the Council must meet in public.[194] The Commission will attend Council meetings.[195] However, it is not a formal member of the Council and is thus not entitled to vote. The quorum within the Council is as low as it is theoretical: a majority of the members of the Council are required to enable the Council to vote.[196]

Decision-making in the Council will take place in two principal forms: unanimous voting and majority voting. Unanimous voting requires the consent of all national ministers and is required in the Treaties for sensitive political questions.[197] Formal majority voting, however, represents the constitutional norm. The Treaties here distinguish between a simple and a qualified majority. 'Where it is required to act by a simple majority, the Council shall act by a majority of its component members.'[198] This form of majority vote is rare.[199] The constitutional default is indeed the qualified majority: 'The Council shall act by a qualified majority except where the Treaties provide otherwise.'[200]

What constitutes a qualified majority of Member States in the Council? This has been one of the most controversial constitutional concepts in the European Union. From the very beginning, the Treaties had instituted a system of *weighted votes*. Member States would thus not be 'sovereign equals' in the

---

[193] However, there exists an 'ordinary' and a 'simplified' written procedure established by Art. 12 Council Rules of Procedure.

[194] Art. 16(8) TEU and Art. 5(1). According to Art. 8, the deliberation of a non-legislative proposal must also be in public where 'an important new proposal' is at stake (*ibid.*, para. 1). Importantly, Art. 9 demands that 'the results of votes and explanations of votes by Council members', and the minutes, must always be made public.

[195] According to Art. 5(2) Council Rules of Procedure, the Council may however decide to deliberate without the Commission.

[196] *Ibid.*, Art. 11(4).

[197] Important examples of sensitive political issues still requiring unanimity are foreign affairs (see Chapter 8, section 3(a)), and 'the harmonisation of legislation concerning turnover taxes, excise duties and other forms of indirect taxation' (see Art. 113 TFEU). The Council will sometimes try to reach an informal 'consensus' so as to avoid a formal vote. On the distinction between consensus and unanimous voting, see S. Novak, 'The Silence of Ministers: Consensus and Blame Avoidance in the Council of the European Union' (2013) 51 *Journal of Common Market Studies* 1091, esp. 1092: 'Council members sometimes use consensus instead of voting to avoid backlash against members who oppose a particular matter. Formal voting would disclose the identity of opponents and open them up to criticism or retaliation by other participants in the decision-making process … The consensus method is used to preserve the silence of ministers. In other words, consensus is sometimes triggered by a strategy of blame avoidance.'

[198] Art. 238(1) TFEU.

[199] For example, Art. 150 TFEU. Most matters that allow for simple majority are (internal) procedural or institutional matters.

[200] Art. 16(3) TEU.

Table 5.6 Weighted Votes System within the Council (abolished)

Member States	Votes
Germany, France, Italy, United Kingdom	29
Spain, Poland	27
Romania	14
Netherlands	13
Belgium, Czech Republic, Greece, Hungary, Portugal	12
Austria, Bulgaria, Sweden	10
Croatia, Denmark, Ireland, Lithuania, Slovakia, Finland	7
Cyprus, Estonia, Latvia, Luxembourg, Slovenia	4
Malta	3
Qualified Majority: 260/352	

Council, but would possess a number of votes that correlated with the size of their population. The system of weighted votes that traditionally applied is set out in Table 5.6.

The weighting of votes was to some extent 'degressively proportional'. Indeed, the voting ratio between the biggest and the smallest state was ten to one – a ratio that is roughly similar to the degressively proportionate system for the European Parliament. However, the voting system also represented a system of symbolic compromises. For example: the four biggest Member States were all given the same number of votes – despite Germany's significantly greater demographic magnitude.[201]

In the past, this system of weighted votes was attacked from two sides: namely from the smaller Member States as well as the bigger Member States. The smaller Member States claimed that it favoured the bigger Member States and therefore insisted that the 260 votes must be cast by a majority of the States. The bigger Member States, by contrast, complained that the weighting unduly favoured smaller Member States and insisted on the political safeguard that the 260 votes cast in the Council correspond to 62 per cent of the total population of the Union. With these two qualifications taken into account, decision-making in the Council therefore traditionally demanded a *triple* majority: a (qualified) *majority* of the weighted votes had to be cast by a *majority* of the Member States representing a (qualified) *majority* of the Union population.

---

[201] According to the Union's official census figures (see Council Decision 2014/692 [2014] OJ L 289/18), the German population exceeds that of France – the second most populous State of the Union – by about 15 million people.

This triple majority system exclusively governed decision-making in the Union until 1 November 2014. From that date, a completely new system of voting applies in the Council. (However, until 31 March 2017, any Member State could insist on using the old system of voting in the Council.)[202] This revolutionary change is set out in Article 16(4) TEU, which states:

> As from 1 November 2014, a qualified majority shall be defined as at least 55 per cent of the members of the Council, comprising at least fifteen of them and representing Member States comprising at least 65 per cent of the population of the Union. A blocking minority must include at least four Council members, failing which the qualified majority shall be deemed attained. The other arrangements governing the qualified majority are laid down in Article 238(2) of the Treaty on the Functioning of the European Union.[203]

This new Lisbon voting arrangement here abolished the system of weighted votes in favour of a system that grants each State a single vote. In a Union of 28 States, 55 per cent of the Council members correspond to 16 States. But this majority is again qualified from two sides. The bigger Member States have insisted on a relatively high population majority behind the State majority. The population threshold of 65 per cent of the Union population would mean that any three of the four biggest States of the Union could theoretically block a Council decision (see Table 5.7). The smaller Member States have thus insisted on a qualification of the qualification. A qualified majority will be 'deemed attained', where fewer than four States try to block a Council decision.

The new Lisbon system of qualified majority voting was designed to replace the traditional triple majority with a simpler double majority. And yet the Member States – always fearful of abrupt changes – have agreed on two constitutional compromises that cushion the new system of qualified majority voting. First, the Member States have revived the 'Ioannina Compromise'.[204]

---

[202] Protocol No. 36 on Transitional Provisions, Art. 3(2). See also Declaration No. 7 on Art. 16(4) of the Treaty on European Union and Art. 238(2) of the Treaty on the Functioning of the European Union, in particular (draft) Arts. 1–3.

[203] The Treaty recognises an express exception to this in Art. 238(2) TFEU, which states: 'By way of derogation from Article 16(4) of the Treaty on European Union, as from 1 November 2014 and subject to the provisions laid down in the Protocol on transitional provisions, where the Council does not act on a proposal from the Commission or from the High Representative of the Union for Foreign Affairs and Security Policy, the qualified majority shall be defined as at least 72 per cent of the members of the Council, representing Member States comprising at least 65 per cent of the population of the Union.'

[204] The compromise was negotiated by the Member States' foreign ministers in Ioannina (Greece) – from where it takes its name. The compromise was designed to soften the transition from the Union of 12 to a Union of 15 Member States.

Table 5.7 Member State Population Sizes

Member State	Population (× 1,000)	(Potential) Blocking Minority	Population Majority (Potential)
Germany	80,523.7		
France	65,633.2		
United Kingdom	63,730.1		
Italy	59,685.2		
Spain	46,704.3		
Poland	38,533.3		
Romania	20,057.5		
Netherlands	16,779.6		
Belgium	11,161.6		
European Union (65%)	328,622.1		
European Union (35%)	176,950.4		

This was envisaged in a 'Declaration on Article 16(4)',[205] and is now codified in a Council Decision.[206]

According to the Ioannina Compromise, the Council is under an obligation – despite the formal existence of the double majority in Article 16(4) TEU – to continue deliberations, where one-quarter of the States or States representing one-fifth of the Union population oppose a decision.[207] The Council is here under the procedural duty to 'do all in its power' to reach – within a reasonable time – 'a satisfactory solution' to address the concerns by the blocking Member States.[208]

This soft mechanism is complemented by a hard mechanism to limit qualified majority voting in the Council. For the Treaties also recognise – regionally limited – versions of the 'Luxembourg Compromise'.[209] A patent illustration of this can be found in the context of the Union's Common Foreign and Security Policy. This contains the following provision: 'If a member of the Council declares that, for vital and stated reasons of national policy, it intends to oppose the adoption of a decision to be taken by qualified majority, a vote shall not be taken.'[210] And even if the matter may be referred to the European Council,[211]

---

[205] Declaration No. 7 on Art. 16(4) (n. 202 above) contains a draft Council Decision. And, in order to protect their voting rights, the Member States have even insisted on Protocol No. 9 on the Decision of the Council relating to the implementation of Art. 16(4) TEU and Art. 238(2) TFEU between 1 November 2014 and 31 March 2017 on the one hand, and as from 1 April 2017 on the other. The sole article of the Protocol states: 'Before the examination by the Council of any draft which would aim either at amending or abrogating the Decision or any of its provisions, or at modifying indirectly its scope or its meaning through the modification of another legal act of the Union, the European Council shall hold a preliminary deliberation on the said draft, acting by consensus in accordance with Art. 15(4) of the Treaty on European Union.'

[206] The Council formally adopted the decision in 2007 (see Council Decision 2009/857 [2009] OJ L 314/73).

[207] *Ibid.*, Art. 4.   [208] *Ibid.*, Art. 5.

[209] On the 'Luxembourg Compromise', see Chapter 1, section 2(b).   [210] Art. 31(2) TEU.

[211] On the appeal function of the European Council, see section 3(b).

that body will decide by unanimity.[212] A Member State can thus unilaterally block a Union decision on what it deems to be its vital interest.[213]

d. Functions and Powers

The Treaties summarise the functions and powers of the Council as follows:

> The Council shall, jointly with the European Parliament, exercise legislative and budgetary functions. It shall carry out policy-making and coordinating functions as laid down in the Treaties.[214]

Let us look at each of these four functions. First, traditionally, the Council has been at the core of the Union's legislative function. Prior to the rise of the European Parliament, the Council indeed was 'the' Union legislator. The Council is however today only a co-legislator, that is: a branch of the bicameral Union legislature.[215] And like Parliament, it must exercise its legislative function in public.[216] Second, Council and Parliament also share in the exercise of the budgetary function. What about the policymaking function? In this – third – respect, the European Council has overtaken the Council. The former now decides on the general policy choices, and the role of the Council has consequently been limited to specific policy choices that implement the general ones. Yet, these choices remain significant and the Council Presidency will set 'its' agenda.[217] Fourth, the Council has significant coordinating functions within the European Union. Thus, in the context of general economic policy, the Member States are required to 'regard their economic policies as a matter of common concern and shall coordinate them within the Council'.[218] The idea of an 'open method of coordination' indeed experienced a renaissance in the last decades.[219]

In addition to the four functions mentioned in Article 16 TEU, two additional functions must be added. First, the Council is still the dominant institution when

---

[212] Art. 31(2) TEU.

[213] For example, see Art. 48 TFEU in the context of the free movement of workers and important aspects of a Member State's social security system. The provision states: 'Where a member of the Council declares that a draft legislative act referred to in the first subparagraph would affect important aspects of its social security system, including its scope, cost or financial structure, or would affect the financial balance of that system, it may request that the matter be referred to the European Council.'

[214] Art. 16(1) TEU.

[215] On this point, see Chapter 7, section 3(a).

[216] Art. 16(8) TEU.

[217] For a soft expression of this power, see Art. 241 TFEU which entitles the Council to request the Commission to undertake studies and to submit any appropriate legislative proposals.

[218] Art. 121(1) TFEU.

[219] On the open method of coordination, see G. de Búrca, 'The Constitutional Challenge of New Governance in the European Union' (2003) 28 *EL Rev.* 814.

it comes to the conclusion of international agreements between the European Union and third countries.[220] Second, it can – occasionally – still act as the Union's executive branch. The Union can delegate implementing powers to the Council 'in duly justified specific cases' in any area of European law.[221] From a constitutional viewpoint, the exercise of the executive function by the Council is highly problematic. How can a part of the Union legislature exercise executive functions? This very possibility interferes with a foundational principle of modern constitutionalism: the idea of a separation of powers.

---

[220] On this point, see Chapter 8, section 3(b).
[221] Art. 291(2) TFEU. On this point, see Chapter 9, section 2(b).

6

Governmental Structure
Union Institutions II

Contents

1. The Commission

The technocratic character of the early European Union expressed itself in the name of a fourth institution: the Commission. The Commission constituted the centre of the European Coal and Steel Community, where it was 'to ensure that the objectives set out in [that] Treaty [were] attained'.[1] In the European

---

[1] Art. 8 ECSC.

Union, the role of the Commission is, however, 'marginalised' by the Parliament and the Council. With these two institutions constituting the Union legislature, the Commission is now firmly located in the executive branch. In guiding the Union, it – partly – acts like the Union's 'government'. This section analyses the composition and structure of the Commission, before looking at its internal decision-making procedures. The functions and powers of the Commission will be discussed next, before an excursus briefly presents European Agencies as auxiliary organs of the Commission.

a. Composition and Structure

The Commission consists of one national of each Member State.[2] Its members are chosen 'on the ground of their general competence and European commitment from persons whose independence is beyond doubt'.[3] The Commission's term of office is five years.[4] During this term, it must be 'completely independent'. Its members 'shall neither seek nor take instructions from any Government or other institution, body, office or entity'.[5] The Member States are under a duty to respect this independence.[6] Breach of the duty of independence may lead to a Commissioner being 'compulsorily retired'.[7]

How is the Commission selected? Originally, the Commission was 'appointed'.[8] The appointment procedure has subsequently given way to an election procedure. This election procedure has two stages. In a first stage, the President of the Commission will be elected. The President will have been

---

[2] Art. 17(4) TEU. The Lisbon Treaty textually limits this principle in a temporal sense. It would theoretically only apply until 31 October 2014. Thereafter, Art. 17(5) TEU states: 'As from 1 November 2014, the Commission shall consist of a number of members, including its President and the High Representative of the Union for Foreign Affairs and Security Policy, corresponding to two-thirds of the number of Member States, unless the European Council, acting unanimously, decides to alter this number.' The reduced Commission composition would be based on 'a system of strictly equal rotation between the Member States, reflecting the demographic and geographical range of all the Member States' (*ibid.*, and see also Art. 244 TFEU). This provision had been a centrepiece of the Lisbon Treaty, as it was designed to increase the effectiveness of the Commission by decreasing its membership. However, after the failure of the first Irish ratification referendum, the European Council decided to abandon this constitutional reform in order to please the Irish electorate; see Presidency Conclusions of 11–12 December 2008 (Document 17271/1/08 Rev 1). The fate of Art. 17(5) TEU is the best illustration of the worst dependence of the Union on individual Member States.

[3] Art. 17(3) TEU.

[4] *Ibid.*   [5] *Ibid.*

[6] Art. 245 TFEU – first indent.

[7] *Ibid.* – second indent. See also Art. 247 TFEU: 'If any Member of the Commission no longer fulfils the conditions required for the performance of his duties or if he has been guilty of serious misconduct, the Court of Justice may, on application by the Council acting by a simple majority or the Commission, compulsorily retire him.' On the replacement procedure, see *ibid.*, Art. 246.

[8] Arts. 9 and 10 ECSC.

Figure 6.1 European Commission President: Jean-Claude Juncker

nominated by the European Council '[t]aking into account the elections to the European Parliament', that is: in accordance with the latter's political majority.[9] The nominated candidate must then be 'elected' by the European Parliament. If not confirmed by Parliament, a new candidate needs to be found by the European Council.[10] The current Commission President can be seen in Figure 6.1.

After the election of the Commission President the second stage of the selection process begins. By common accord with the President, the Council will adopt a list of candidate Commissioners on the basis of suggestions made by the Member States.[11] With the list being agreed, the proposed Commission is subjected 'as a body to a vote of consent by the European Parliament', and on the basis of this election, the Commission shall be appointed by the European Council.[12] This complex and compound selection process constitutes a mixture of 'international' and 'national' elements. The Commission's democratic legitimacy thus derives partly from the Member States, and partly from the European Parliament.

---

[9] The term of the Commission runs roughly in parallel with that of the Parliament.

[10] Art. 17(7) TEU – first indent.

[11] *Ibid.* – second indent.

[12] *Ibid.* – third indent.

aa. The President and 'His' College

Whereas the Presidents of the Parliament and the Council are selected from 'within' the institution,[13] the Commission President helps in the selection of 'his' institution. This position as the 'Chief' Commissioner *above* 'his' college is clearly established by the Treaties.[14] 'The Members of the Commission shall carry out the duties devolved upon them by the President *under his authority*.'[15] In light of this political authority, the Commission is typically called after its President.[16]

The powers of the President are identified in Article 17(6) TEU, which reads:

> The President of the Commission shall:
> (a) lay down guidelines within which the Commission is to work;
> (b) decide on the internal organisation of the Commission, ensuring that it acts consistently, efficiently and as a collegiate body;
> (c) appoint Vice-Presidents, other than the High Representative of the Union for Foreign Affairs and Security Policy, from among the members of the Commission.
> A member of the Commission shall resign if the President so requests. The High Representative of the Union for Foreign Affairs and Security Policy shall resign, in accordance with the procedure set out in Article 18(1), if the President so requests.

The three powers of the President mentioned are formidable. First, s/he can lay down the political direction of the Commission in the form of strategic guidelines. This will normally happen at the beginning of a President's term of office.[17] The Presidential guidelines will subsequently be translated into the Commission's Annual Work Programme.[18] Second, the President is entitled to decide on the internal organisation of the Commission.[19] In the words of the Treaties: '[T]he responsibilities incumbent upon the Commission shall be structured and allocated among its members by its President.' The President is authorised to 'reshuffle the allocation of those responsibilities during the Commission's

---

[13] The same is true for the Court, see section 2(a) below. As regards the European Council, its President is also elected 'by' the institution, albeit not from 'within' the institution.

[14] N. Nugent, *The European Commission* (Palgrave, 2000), 68: 'The Commission President used to be thought of as *primus inter pares* in the College. Now, however, he is very much *primus.*'

[15] Art. 248 TFEU (emphasis added).

[16] For example: the last Commission was called the (second) 'Barroso Commission'.

[17] On this, see Chapter 9, section 1(a).

[18] For the Commission's Work Programme, see *ibid.*

[19] Due to its dual constitutional role, some special rules apply to the High Representative of the Union. Not only do the Treaties determine the latter's role within the Commission, the President will not be able *unilaterally* to ask for his or her resignation (see Art. 18(4) TEU: 'The High Representative shall be one of the Vice-Presidents of the Commission. He shall ensure the consistency of the Union's external action. He shall be responsible within the Commission for responsibilities incumbent on it in external relations and for coordinating other aspects of the Union's external action.')

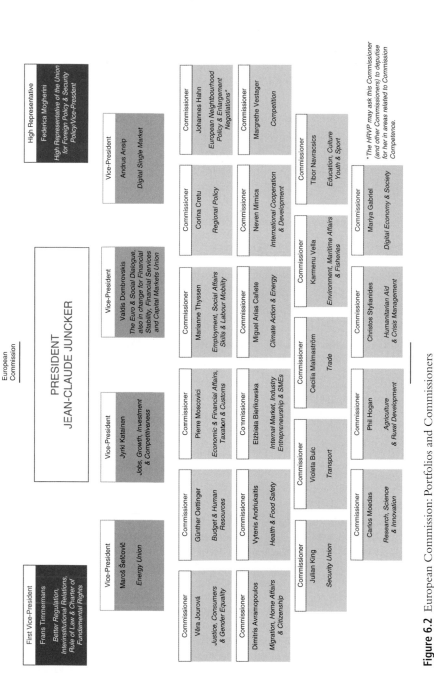

Figure 6.2 European Commission: Portfolios and Commissioners

term of office',[20] and may even ask a Commissioner to resign. Third, the President can appoint Vice-Presidents from 'within' the Commission. Finally, there is a fourth power not expressly mentioned in Article 17(6) TEU: 'The President shall represent the Commission.'[21]

What are the 'ministerial' responsibilities into which the present Commission is structured? Due to the requirement of one Commissioner per Member State, the 'Juncker Commission' had to divide the tasks of the European Union into 27 (!) 'portfolios'. Reflecting the priorities of the Union's current President, they are as set out in Figure 6.2.

Each Commissioner is responsible for his or her portfolio. Members of the Commission will thereby be assisted by their own cabinet.[22] And each cabinet will have an administrative head or *chef de cabinet*. An organisational novelty of the latest Commission is the idea of 'Project Teams', which combine various portfolios under the authority of a Vice-President of the Commission. The aim behind this administrative grouping seems to be the desire to set policy priorities from the very start, and to create more cohesion between various ministerial portfolios.[23]

bb. The Commission's Administrative Organs

The Commission has, just like the Parliament and the Council, an administrative infrastructure supporting the work of the College of Commissioners.

The administrative substructure is designed to 'assist' the Commission 'in the preparation and performance of its task, and in the implementation of its priorities and the political guidelines laid down by the President'.[24] It is divided into 'Directorates-General' and 'Services'. The former are specialised in specific policy areas and thus operate 'vertically'. The latter operate 'horizontally' in providing specialised services across all policy areas.[25]

The best way to understand 'Directorates-General' is to consider them as the Union equivalent of national 'ministries'. Staffed by European civil servants, there are presently 31 Directorates-General.[26] Importantly, these Directorates-General do not necessarily correspond with one 'Commissioner portfolio'. While there is

---

[20] Art. 248 TFEU.

[21] Art. 3(5) Commission Rules of Procedure.

[22] *Ibid.*, Art. 19(1): 'Members of the Commission shall have their own cabinet to assist them in their work and in preparing Commission decisions. The rules governing the composition and operation of the cabinets shall be laid down by the President.'

[23] The 'Project Teams' currently suggested, are: 'Jobs, Growth, Investment and Competitiveness', 'Digital Single Market', 'Energy Union', 'Euro and Social Dialogue', 'Better Regulation and Interinstitutional Relations', 'Budget and Human Resources' and 'Europe in the World'.

[24] Art. 21 Commission Rules of Procedure.

[25] This section will not look at the various services. The Commission distinguishes between 'General Services' (like the 'Secretariat General'), and 'Internal Services' (like the 'Legal Service' of the Commission). The functions of the former are set out in Art. 23(5) Commission Rules of Procedure. The functions of the latter are defined by Art. 23(4) Commission Rules of Procedure.

[26] See https://ec.europa.eu/info/departments_en.

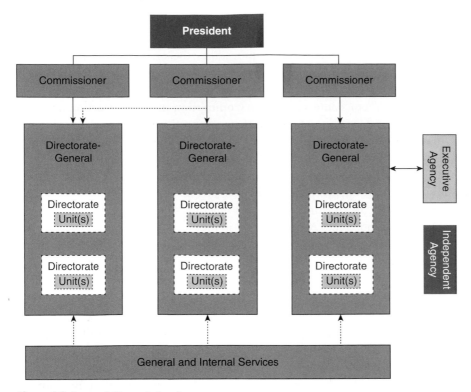

Figure 6.3 Internal Commission Structure

a direct correspondence in some areas, some Commissioner portfolios cut across
the subject matter of two or even more Directorates-General. Commissioners
are entitled to 'give instructions' to their Directorate(s)-General, with the latter
being obliged to 'provide them with all the information on their area of activity
necessary for them to exercise their responsibilities'.[27]

What is the structure *within* a Directorate-General? Each Directorate-General
is headed by a Director-General, who represents the main contact between
the Commission administration and the respective Commissioner(s). Each
Directorate-General is divided into directorates, and each directorate is divided
into units.[28] Units are headed by a Head of Unit and constitute the elementary
organisational entity within the Commission administration. An overview of the
internal Commission structure is provided in Figure 6.3.

b. Decision-making within the Commission

The Commission acts as a 'college', that is: as a collective body. The Treaties offer a
single article on decision-making within the Commission: 'The Commission shall
act by a majority of its Members.'[29] This is a devilishly simple and misleading picture.

[27] Art. 19(2) Commission Rules of Procedure.
[28] *Ibid.*, Art. 2 – second indent.
[29] Art. 250 TFEU.

It is complemented and corrected by the Commission's Rules of Procedure, which define the various decision-making procedures and their voting arrangements. The Rules distinguish between four procedures: the 'oral procedure', the 'written procedure', the 'empowerment procedure' and the 'delegation procedure'.[30]

The first two procedures require a decision by the College as a *collective* body. The oral procedure stipulates a Commission meeting. Meetings are 'private' and confidential,[31] and take place, as a general rule, at least once a week.[32] Commissioners are required to attend, but the President can release them from this duty in certain circumstances.[33] (However, to be quorate at least half of the Commissioners must be present.)[34] Decisions are principally taken by tacit consensus. However, decisions may be taken by majority vote if that is requested by a member.[35] To save time within the meeting, the Commission Agenda will typically be divided into A-items and B-items.[36]

To maximise time even further, the Commission is – under certain circumstances – entitled to dispense with a physical meeting and decide by means of the written procedure.[37] According to this procedure, a draft text is circulated to all Members of the Commission. Each Commissioner is entitled to make known any reservations within a time limit.[38] A decision is subsequently adopted if 'no Member has made or maintained a request for suspension up to the time limit set for the written procedure'.[39]

The oral and the written procedure were based on the principle of 'collegiality', that is: the collective decision-taking of the Commission. By contrast, the third and fourth procedures entitle the Commission to delegate power for the adoption of 'management or administrative measures' to individual officers. According to the 'empowerment procedure', the College can delegate power to one or more Commissioners.[40]

---

[30] Art. 4 Commission Rules of Procedure.
[31] *Ibid.*, Art. 9.   [32] *Ibid.*, Art. 5(2).   [33] *Ibid.*, Art. 5(3).   [34] *Ibid.*, Art. 7.
[35] *Ibid.*, Art. 8(2). A majority in this case requires the majority of its *component* members (*ibid.*, Art. 8(3)).
[36] Two days before the Commission College meets, the Commissioners' 'chiefs of cabinet' meet to discuss and resolve items in advance. The meeting of the 'chiefs of cabinets', which is chaired by the Secretary General of the Commission, thus operates like Coreper for the Council.
[37] Art. 12(1) Commission Rules of Procedure: 'The agreements of the Members of the Commission to a draft text from one or more of its Members may be obtained by means of written procedure, provided that the approval of the Legal Service and the agreement of the departments consulted in accordance with Article 23 of these Rules of Procedure has been obtained. Such approval and/or agreement may be replaced by an agreement between the Members of the Commission where a meeting of the College has decided, on a proposal from the President, to open a finalisation written procedure as provided for in the implementing rules.'
[38] Art. 12(2) Commission Rules of Procedure. Moreover, according to para. 3 '[a]ny Member of the Commission, may, in the course of the written procedure, request that the draft text be discussed'.
[39] *Ibid.*, Art. 12(4).   [40] *Ibid.*, Art. 13.

According to the 'delegation procedure', it can even delegate power to a Director-General. While this decentralised form of decision-taking is much more efficient, it doubtlessly undermines the principle of collegiality behind the Commission. The Court of Justice has therefore insisted on a constitutional balance between the theoretical principle of 'the equal participation of the Members of the Commission in the adoption of decisions' on the one hand,[41] and the practical principle of preventing 'collective deliberation from having a paralysing effect on the full Commission' on the other.[42] It has thus insisted on 'procedural' as well as 'substantive' guarantees for delegations of power. The former require that the decisions delegating authority are adopted at meetings of the Commission.[43] The latter insist that 'management of administrative measures' are not decisions of principle.[44]

c. Functions and Powers of the Commission

What are the functions and corresponding powers of the Commission in the governmental system of the European Union? The Treaties provide a concise constitutional overview of its tasks in Article 17 TEU:

> The Commission shall promote the general interest of the Union and take appropriate initiatives to that end. It shall ensure the application of the Treaties, and of measures adopted by the institutions pursuant to them. It shall oversee the application of Union law under the control of the Court of Justice of the European Union. It shall execute the budget and manage programmes. It shall exercise coordinating, executive and management functions, as laid down in the Treaties. With the exception of the common foreign and security policy, and other cases provided for in the Treaties, it shall ensure the Union's external representation. It shall initiate the Union's annual and multiannual programming with a view to achieving inter institutional agreements.[45]

The provision distinguishes six different functions. The first three functions constitute the Commission's core functions.

First, the Commission is tasked to 'promote the general interest of the Union' through initiatives. It is thus to act as a 'motor' of European integration. In order to fulfil this – governmental – function, the Commission is given the (almost) exclusive right to *formally* propose legislative bills:

[41] Case 5/85, *AKZO Chemie v. Commission* [1986] ECR 2585, para. 30.
[42] *Ibid.*, para. 31.
[43] *Ibid.*, para. 33.
[44] *Ibid.*, para. 37. In that case the Court of Justice found that a decision ordering an undertaking to submit to an investigation was a preparatory inquiry that was a measure of management (*ibid.*, para. 38). By contrast, in Case C-137/92P, *Commission v. BASF et al.* [1994] ECR I-2555, the Court held that a decision finding an infringement of Art. 114 TFEU was not a management decision (*ibid.*, para. 71).
[45] Art. 17(1) TEU.

> Union acts may only be adopted on the basis of a Commission proposal, except where the Treaties provide otherwise.[46]

The Commission's prerogative to propose legislation is a fundamental characteristic of the European constitutional order. The right of initiative extends to (multi)annual programming of the Union,[47] and embraces the power to make proposals for law reform.[48]

The second function of the Commission is to '*ensure* the application' of the Treaties. This function covers a number of powers – legislative and executive in nature. The Commission may thus be entitled to apply the Treaties by adopting secondary 'legislation'. These acts may be adopted directly under the Treaties;[49] or, under powers delegated to the Commission from the Union legislature.[50] In some areas the Commission may be granted the executive power to apply the Treaties itself. The direct enforcement of European law can best be seen in the context of European competition law,[51] where the Commission enjoys significant powers to fine – private or public – wrongdoers. These administrative penalties sanction the non-application of European law.

The third function of the Commission is to act as guardian of the Union. It shall thus '*oversee* the application' of European law. The Treaties indeed grant the Commission significant powers to act as 'police' and 'prosecutor' of the Union.

---

[46] Art. 17(2) TEU. For an exception, see Art. 76 TFEU on legislative measures in the field of police and judicial cooperation in criminal matters. We saw above that the Parliament or the Council can informally suggest legislative bills to the Commission. The European Council may also 'informally' suggest legislative initiatives; and there is even the possibility of European citizens to suggest legislative initiatives to the Commission. For an analysis of the so-called 'European Citizens' Initiative', see A. Karatzia, 'The European Citizens' Initiative and the EU Institutional Balance: On Realism and the Possibilities of Affecting EU Lawmaking' (2017) 54 *CML Rev.* 177.

[47] Under Art. 314(2) TFEU, the Commission is entitled to propose the draft budget: 'The Commission shall submit a proposal containing the draft budget to the European Parliament and to the Council not later than 1 September of the year preceding that in which the budget is to be implemented.'

[48] This is normally done through White Papers or Green Papers. For a famous White Paper, see EU Commission, Completing the Internal Market: White Paper from the Commission to the European Council (COM(85) 310). For a famous Green Paper, see EU Commission, Damages Actions for Breach of the EC Antitrust Rules (COM(2005) 672).

[49] See Art. 106(3) TFEU: 'The Commission shall ensure the application of the provisions of this Article and shall, where necessary, address appropriate directives or decisions to Member States.'

[50] On delegated legislation, see Chapter 9, section 2.

[51] See Art. 105(1) TFEU: '[T]he Commission shall ensure the application of the principles laid down in Articles 101 and 102. On application by a Member State or on its own initiative, and in cooperation with the competent authorities in the Member States, which shall give it their assistance, the Commission shall investigate cases of suspected infringement of these principles. If it finds that there has been an infringement, it shall propose appropriate measures to bring it to an end.'

The policing of European law involves the power to monitor and to investigate infringements of European law. These powers are – again – best defined in the context of European competition law.[52] Where an infringement of European law has been identified, the Commission may bring the matter before the Court of Justice. The Treaties thus give the Commission the power to bring infringement proceedings against Member States,[53] and other Union institutions.[54]

The remaining three functions mentioned by Article 17 TEU are less central to the Commission. They can be characterised as budgetary, coordinating and representative functions. First, the Commission shall execute the Union budget,[55] and thus manages most Union programmes. Second, the Commission is tasked – like most other institutions – to coordinate Union activities in some areas.[56]

Finally, the Commission shall 'ensure the Union's external representation'. This is a partial and partisan formulation. Indeed, the Commission is not the only external representative of the Union, as it must share this function with the President of the European Council as well as the High Representative of the Union. However, the Treaties do traditionally grant the Commission the power to act as external representative of the Union in the negotiation of international agreements.[57]

d. Excursus: European Agencies and the Commission

With the rise of the modern 'administrative state',[58] many legal orders have had to transfer governmental tasks to bodies not expressly mentioned in their

---

[52] See Regulation 1/2003 on the implementation of the rules on competition laid down in Arts. 81 and 82 of the Treaty [2003] OJ L 1/1, Chapter V: 'Powers of Investigation'. For a closer look at these provisions, see Chapter 17B, section 4.

[53] Art. 258 TFEU: 'If the Commission considers that a Member State has failed to fulfil an obligation under the Treaties, it shall deliver a reasoned opinion on the matter after giving the State concerned the opportunity to submit its observations. If the State concerned does not comply with the opinion within the period laid down by the Commission, the latter may bring the matter before the Court of Justice of the European Union.' For an extensive discussion of this, see Chapter 10, section 3(a).

[54] Art. 263 TFEU. The provision will be extensively discussed in Chapter 10, section 1.

[55] Art. 317 TFEU – first indent: 'The Commission shall implement the budget in cooperation with the Member States, in accordance with the provisions of the regulations made pursuant to Article 322, on its own responsibility and within the limits of the appropriations, having regard to the principles of sound financial management. Member States shall cooperate with the Commission to ensure that the appropriations are used in accordance with the principles of sound financial management.'

[56] For the Commission's powers of coordination, see for example: Art. 168(2) TFEU in the context of public health: 'The Commission may, in close contact with the Member States, take any useful initiative to promote such coordination, in particular initiatives aiming at the establishment of guidelines and indicators, the organisation of exchange of best practice, and the preparation of the necessary elements for periodic monitoring and evaluation.'

[57] On this point, see Chapter 8, section 3(b).

[58] On this point, see G. Lawson, 'The Rise and Rise of the Administrative State' (1993–4) 107 *Harvard Law Review* 1231.

constitutions. The rise of 'agencies' was a significant feature in the constitutional development of the United States in the first half of the last century;[59] and the European legal order followed this trend at the end of the twentieth century.[60] For, contrary to a widespread and misleading myth, the Commission administration constitutes – compared with State administrations – a small bureaucracy.[61] And despite a healthy growth in personnel over the past decades, the Commission would not be able to achieve all the tasks under the Treaties.

The European Union has therefore increasingly created 'European Agencies' to assist the Commission. For a long time, these agencies lived in the shadows of European Union law; and the Lisbon Treaty has only partially remedied this. For even if agencies are now expressly mentioned,[62] the EU Treaties still do not properly represent EU Agencies as a fundamental part of the institutional system of the Union.

What and where are the Union's agencies? EU Agencies were not created overnight, yet there continues to be a nocturnal air around

Table 6.1 (Selected) European Agencies and Decentralised Bodies

Agency	Country
European Fundamental Rights Agency (FRA)	Austria
European Defence Agency (EDA)	Belgium
European Environmental Agency (EEA)	Denmark
European Chemicals Agency (ECHA)	Finland
European Securities and Markets Agency (ESMA)	France
European Food Safety Authority (EFSA)	Italy
European Police Office (EUROPOL)	Netherlands
European Border and Coast Guard (FRONTEX)	Poland
European Union Intellectual Property Office (EUIPO)	Spain
European Medicines Agency (EMA)	United Kingdom

[59] P. Strauss, 'The Place of Agencies in Government: Separation of Powers and the Fourth Branch' (1984) 84 *Columbia Law Review* 573.

[60] While a few agencies had already emerged in the 1970s, there has been a real 'agencification' of the European legal order in the 1990s. Today, about 40 European Agencies exist in the most diverse areas of European law. For an inventory and functional typology of European Agencies, see S. Griller and A. Orator, 'Everything under Control? The "Way Forward" for European Agencies in the Footsteps of the Meroni Doctrine' (2010) 35 *EL Rev.* 3 at appendix.

[61] The figure of around 33,000 EU civil servants indeed compares rather favourably with the 420,000 British civil servants and the 78,000 civil servants just for London. And, to offer a private company comparison: JPMorgan employs more than 250,000 people.

[62] For example, Arts. 9 and 15 TEU; Art. 263 TFEU.

them. Not expressly mentioned in the Treaties, where did they come from? The answer lies in the fact that they are creatures of secondary Union law. The Union has created them by using its own legislative powers.[63] And, while there are constitutional limits to what powers can be delegated to European Agencies,[64] the Union has created many of them in the past decades (Table 6.1).

aa. European Agencies: Functions

What are the functions of European Agencies? Their primary function is to assist the Commission in its task to 'ensure' and 'oversee' the application of European law. Some EU Agencies are entitled to adopt binding decisions and thus apply European law directly.[65] Other EU Agencies are charged to prepare draft legislation for the Commission.[66] Many EU Agencies are simply information satellites: they are tasked to help the Commission in monitoring a policy area and to collect and coordinate information.[67] These three – and other – functions can be combined. We will further explore these administrative functions within the context of Chapter 9 on the Union's executive powers.

bb. European Agencies: Structure

What is the internal structure of a European Agency? And in what ways is it dependent on, or subordinate to, the Commission?

The Union legal order has no single answer to these questions. With regard to the structure of Commission agencies, the Union legal order generally distinguishes between two types of European Agencies: 'executive' agencies and 'independent' (or 'decentralised') agencies. Executive agencies are subordinate to the Commission and are governed by a single 'Statute'.[68] According to this Statute, executive agencies fall under the control and responsibility of the Commission,[69]

---

[63] Agencies are typically created on the basis of Arts. 114 or 352 TFEU – the Union's most general powers, which will be discussed in Chapter 7, section 1(b).

[64] On this point, see Chapter 9, section 2(d).

[65] For example: the European Securities and Markets Agency (ESMA); see Regulation 1095/2019 establishing a European Supervisory Authority (European Securities and Markets Authority), (2010) OJ L 331/84.

[66] For example: the European Medicines Agency; see Regulation 726/2004 laying down Union procedures for the authorisation and supervision of medicinal products for human and veterinary use and establishing a European Medicines Agency [2004] OJ L 136/1. According to the Regulation, the Agency only conducts the preparatory stages of a decision, while the Commission is entitled to take the final decision (*ibid.*, Art. 10(2)).

[67] For example: the European Union Agency for Fundamental Rights; see Regulation 168/2007 establishing a European Union Agency for Fundamental Rights [2007] OJ L 53/1.

[68] Regulation 58/2003 laying down the Statute for Executive Agencies to be entrusted with certain tasks in the management of Community Programmes [2003] OJ L 11/1.

[69] *Ibid.*, Art. 1: 'This Regulation lays down the statute of executive agencies to which the Commission, under its own control and responsibility, may entrust certain tasks relating to the management of [Union] programmes.'

and will have a limited lifetime.[70] They consist of a 'Steering Committee' and a 'Director',[71] which are appointed by the Commission.[72] The Commission is entitled to supervise executive agencies,[73] and it enjoys the power to 'review' and 'suspend' any of their acts.[74]

By contrast, a second class of EU Agencies is 'independent' from the Commission. This independence is both structural and functional. Independent agencies will typically consist of a 'Management Board' composed of one representative of each Member State and one (or two) representative(s) of the Commission.[75] They will be headed by an 'Executive Director', who is typically elected by the Management Board on a proposal from the Commission.[76] The Executive Director is, however, required to 'be completely independent in the performance of his or her duties', and this independence translates into a prohibition not to 'seek nor take instructions from any government or from any other body'.[77] In some EU Agencies, the Executive Director will be assisted by an 'Executive Board';[78] and some EU Agencies also have an internal 'Appeal Board' that is designed to offer an administrative review mechanism for private parties unhappy with a decision of the agency.[79]

Figure 6.4 Independent EU Agency Structure

---

[70] *Ibid.*, Art. 3.   [71] *Ibid.*, Art. 7.   [72] *Ibid.*, Arts. 8 and 10.

[73] *Ibid.*, Art. 20.   [74] *Ibid.*, Art. 22.

[75] For FRONTEX, see Regulation 2016/1624 on the European Border and Coast Guard (2016) OJ L 251/1, Art. 63. According to its Art. 67 the Board will typically decide by an absolute majority of its members but qualified majorities are also exceptionally envisaged. The Union has not yet developed a common structure for its various independent or decentralised agencies, but see: Joint Statement and Common Approach of the European Parliament, the Council and the European Commission on decentralised agencies – which can be found at: https://europa.eu/european-union/about-eu/agencies/overhaul_en.

[76] *Ibid.*, Art. 69.   [77] *Ibid.*, Art. 68(1).   [78] *Ibid.*, Art. 62(7).

[79] The best and most practical example here is EUIPO, whose complex appeal boards system is extremely important in the context of EU trade mark law. For an excellent overview of the various internal review mechanisms within EU Agencies, see M. Chamon, *EU Agencies: Legal and Political Limits to the Transformation of the EU Administration* (Oxford University Press, 2016), 338–46.

2. The Court of Justice of the European Union

'Tucked away in the fairyland Duchy of Luxembourg',[80] and housed in its 'palace', lies the Court of Justice of the European Union. The Court constitutes the judicial branch of the European Union. It is not a 'real' single court but an institution that is composed of various courts that are generically referred to as the Court of Justice of the European Union. This terminological roof includes the 'Court of Justice', the 'General Court' and any 'specialised courts' established within the Union legal order.[81]

The Court's task is to 'ensure that in the interpretation and application of the Treaties the law is observed'.[82] The Court of Justice of the European Union is, however, not the only one to interpret and apply European law. From the very beginning, the European legal order intended to recruit national courts in the interpretation and application of European law.[83] Indeed: from a functional perspective, national courts are thus decentralised 'European' courts. From an institutional perspective, however, they are distinct and there is no institutional bridge from the national courts to the European Court of Justice.[84]

In concentrating on the institution of the Court of Justice of the European Union, the following section will start out by analysing its judicial architecture. Subsections (b) and (c) look inside the judicial process and decision-making, and in particular judicial interpretation. Finally, subsection (d) briefly surveys the judicial powers of the Court.

a. Judicial Architecture: The European Court System

When the European Union was born, its judicial branch consisted of a single court: the 'Court of Justice'. The (then) Court was a 'one-stop shop'. All judicial affairs of the Union would pass through its corridors.

With its workload having risen to dizzying heights, the Court pressed the Member States to provide for a judicial 'assistant', and the Member States agreed to create a second court in the Single European Act. The latter granted the Council the power to 'attach to the Court of Justice a court with jurisdiction to hear and determine *at first instance*'.[85] Thanks to this definition, the newly created court was baptised the 'Court of First Instance'.[86] With the Lisbon Treaty, the Court has now been renamed as the 'General Court'. The reason for this change of name lies in the fact that the Court is no longer confined to first-instance cases. Instead, '[t]he General Court shall have jurisdiction to hear and determine actions or proceedings brought against decisions of the specialised courts'.[87]

---

[80]   E. Stein, 'Lawyers, Judges, and the Making of a Transnational Constitution' (1981) 75 AJIL 1.

[81]   Art. 19(1) TEU.   [82]   *Ibid.*

[83]   On this point, see Chapter 11.

[84]   There is no appeal from national courts to the European Courts. On this point, see again *ibid.*

[85]   Art. 11(1) SEA (emphasis added).

[86]   The Court was set up by Council Decision 88/591 establishing a Court of First Instance of the European Communities [1988] OJ L 319/1.

[87]   Art. 256(2) TFEU.

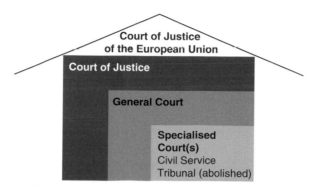

Figure 6.5 Structure of the Court of Justice of the European Union

What are the 'specialised courts' in the European Union? The Union had for about a decade one specialised court: the 'Civil Service Tribunal'.[88] The latter has however recently been abolished. But even in the absence of any actual 'specialised court', the Court of Justice of the European Union formally has a three-tiered system of courts.[89] The architecture of the Union's judicial branch is shown in Figure 6.5.

aa. *The Court of Justice: Composition and Structure*

'The Court of Justice shall consist of one judge from each Member State.'[90] They 'shall be chosen from persons whose independence is beyond doubt and who possess the qualifications required for appointment to the highest judicial office in their respective countries or who are juris consults of recognised competence'.[91]

In theory, judges are not unilaterally appointed by their Member State but rather by 'common accord of the governments of the Member States', and only after a hearing of an independent advisory panel.[92] Judges are indeed not representatives of their Member State and must be completely independent.[93] Their

---

[88] Council Decision 2004/752 establishing the European Union Civil Service Tribunal [2004] OJ L 333/7. See also N. Lavranos, 'The New Specialised Courts within the European Judicial System' (2005) 30 *EL Rev.* 261.

[89] In terms of the European Union's judicial reports, there are thus three different prefixes before a case. Cases before the Court of Justice are C-Cases, cases before the General Court are T-Cases (as the French name for the General Court is 'Tribunal'), and cases before the Civil Service Tribunal were F-Cases (stemming from the French 'fonction publique' for civil service).

[90] Art. 19(2) TEU.   [91] Art. 253 TFEU.

[92] *Ibid.* According to Art. 255 TFEU: 'A panel shall be set up in order to give an opinion on candidates' suitability to perform the duties of Judge and Advocate-General of the Court of Justice and the General Court before the governments of the Member States make the appointments referred to in Articles 253 and 254. The panel shall comprise seven persons chosen from among former members of the Court of Justice and the General Court, members of national supreme courts and lawyers of recognised competence, one of whom shall be proposed by the European Parliament. The Council shall adopt a decision establishing the panel's operating rules and a decision appointing its members. It shall act on the initiative of the President of the Court of Justice.' For a first analysis of this new form of judicial appointments, see T. Dumbrovsky et al., 'Judicial Appointments: The Article 255 TFEU Advisory Panel and Selection Procedures in the Member States' (2014) 51 *CML Rev.* 455.

[93] For detailed rules, see Art. 4 Court Statute.

term of appointment is for six years – a relatively short term for judges – that however can be renewed.[94] During their term of office they can only be dismissed by a unanimous decision of their peers.[95]

The judges compose the Court, but are not identical with it. The Court, as a formal institution, decides as a collective body that has its own President. In theory, the principle of collegiality should mean that the Court of Justice only decides in plenary session, that is: as a 'full court' of all judges. However, from the very beginning the Court was entitled to set up 'chambers'. This organisational device allows the Court to multiply into a variety of 'miniature courts'. For the Court's chambers enjoy – unlike parliamentary committees vis-à-vis Parliament's plenary – the powers of the full Court. The division into chambers thus allows the Court to spread its workload. And, indeed, the operation of the Court through chambers constitutes the norm for all categories of cases.[96] In the words of the Treaties: 'The Court of Justice *shall* sit in chambers or in a Grand Chamber', but exceptionally '*may also* sit as a full Court'.[97]

How many judges sit in a chamber, and how are they composed? Answers to these questions are provided in the Statute of the Court of Justice of the European Union, and the Rules of Procedure of the Court of Justice. According to the former, the Court will normally sit in chambers consisting of three and five judges.[98] Exceptionally, the Court can sit in a 'Grand Chamber' consisting of 15 judges, where a Member State or a Union institution as party to the proceedings so requests.[99] Very exceptionally, the Court shall sit as a 'full Court' in limited categories of constitutional cases.[100]

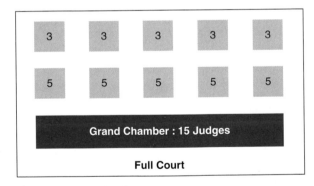

Figure 6.6 ECJ Chambers

---

[94] Art. 253(4) TFEU: 'Retiring Judges and Advocates-General may be reappointed.' According to para. [2]: '[e]very three years there shall be a partial replacement of the Judges and Advocates-General'. The relatively short term hardly constitutes a constitutional guarantee for independence but, as will be seen below, the independence of the Court is guaranteed by other devices, such as the collective and secret decision-making procedure.

[95] Art. 6 Court Statute.

[96] The original Art. 165(2) EEC had limited the ability to set up chambers for 'particular categories of cases', but the Maastricht Treaty removed that constitutional limitation.

[97] Art. 251 TFEU (emphasis added).   [98] Art. 16(1) Court Statute.

[99] *Ibid.*, Art. 16(2) and (3).   [100] *Ibid.*, Art. 16(4) and (5).

bb. *The Advocate General: Office and Function*

The Court 'shall be assisted by Advocates General'.[101] The institution of Advocate General is a trademark of the European judicial system.[102] Their number is currently set at 11.[103] They are appointed as officers of the Court,[104] but their duty is not to 'judge'. The Treaties define their function as follows: 'It shall be the duty of the Advocate General, acting with complete impartiality and independence, to make, in open court, reasoned submissions[.]'[105] According to this definition, an Advocate General is thus neither advocate nor general.[106] S/he is an independent adviser to the Court, who produces an 'opinion' that is not legally binding on the Court.[107] The opinion is designed to inform the Court of ways to decide a case and, in this respect, the Advocate General should act like an academic amicus curiae.[108]

Until recently, each case before the Court of Justice was preceded by the opinion of an Advocate General. However, according to the Court's new Statute, the Court 'may decide, after hearing the Advocate General, that the case shall be determined without a submission from the Advocate General'.[109] For the General Court, this absence is the constitutional rule. Only in exceptional cases will judgments of the General Court be preceded by the opinion of an Advocate General. And, according to the Statute of the Court, it is one of the 'judges' of the General Court who 'may be called to perform the task of an Advocate General'.[110] The Rules of Procedure of the General Court thereby indicate that this can happen 'if it is considered that the legal difficulty or the factual complexity of the case so requires'.[111]

---

[101] Art. 19(2) TEU.

[102] N. Burrows and R. Greaves, *The Advocate-General and EC Law* (Oxford University Press, 2007), 2.

[103] Art. 252(1) TFEU states: 'The Court of Justice shall be assisted by eight Advocates-General. Should the Court of Justice so request, the Council, acting unanimously, may increase the number of Advocates-General.' This increase has taken place through Council Decision 2013/336 [2013] OJ L 179/92.

[104] Art. 253 TFEU applies to judges as well as Advocates General.

[105] *Ibid.*, Art. 252(2).

[106] The title is thus 'a misnomer', since s/he 'is really no more an advocate than he is a general' (J. P. Warner as quoted in N. Brown and T. Kennedy, *The Court of Justice of the European Communities* (Sweet & Maxwell, 2000), 64).

[107] Famous examples, where the Court went against the Advocate General are Case 26/62, *Van Gend en Loos* v. *Netherlands Inland Revenue Administration* [1963] ECR 1; Case C-50/00P, *Unión de Pequeños Agricultores (UPA)* v. *Council* [2002] ECR I-6677.

[108] It is therefore deeply regrettable that, in recent decades, Advocates-General increasingly behave as if they were exclusive functionaries of the case law instead of acting as ambassadors between academia and the Court.

[109] Art. 20(5) Court Statute.

[110] *Ibid.*, Art. 49. According to the fourth indent of that article '[a] member called upon to perform the task of Advocate-General in a case may not take part in the judgment of the case'.

[111] *Ibid.*, Art. 30.

cc. *The General Court: Composition and Structure*

'The General Court shall include at least one judge per Member State.'[112] The exact number as set by the Statute today is 47 – a number that will increase to 'two judges per Member State as from 1 September 2019'.[113] The judges are to be chosen 'from persons whose independence is beyond doubt and who possess the ability required for appointment to *high* judicial office'.[114] Their (re)appointment is subject to the same rules as for the Court of Justice. The General Court also has its own President, whose election and functions are similar to his counterpart at the Court of Justice.

The General Court will – like the Court of Justice – also generally sit in chambers of three and five judges.[115] And, in exceptionally difficult or important cases, it may sit as a 'Grand Chamber'.[116] By contrast, in exceptionally easy circumstances, the General Court can also assign cases to a single-judge chamber.[117]

What is the jurisdiction of the General Court? Its jurisdiction has always been smaller than that of the Court of Justice. It was originally confined to first-instance cases brought directly by natural or legal persons.[118] Today, Article 256 TFEU distinguishes between three scenarios. First, the General Court will have jurisdiction to hear cases at first instance, with the exception of those cases assigned to a 'specialised court' or those cases reserved to the Court of Justice.[119] Second, the General Court will have jurisdiction to hear appeals against decisions of specialised courts. Third, the General Court *may* have jurisdiction for preliminary references from national courts in specific cases laid down by the Statute. (However, the General Court would here be entitled to decline jurisdiction and refer requests for a preliminary ruling to the Court of Justice, where it 'considers that the case requires a decision of principle likely to affect the unity or consistency of Union law'.)[120]

Decisions of the General Court can be 'appealed' or 'reviewed'. Appeals can be launched by any party that was (partly) unsuccessful.[121] However, appeals are limited to points of law and must be on the grounds of 'lack of competence', 'breach of procedure' or infringement of European law by the General Court.[122] If the appeal is well founded, the Court of Justice will 'quash' the decision of the General Court.[123] It can then choose one of two options. It may act like a 'court of cassation', that is: cancel the previous judgment and refer the case back to the

---

[112]   Art. 19(2) TEU.   [113]   Art. 48 Court Statute.   [114]   Art. 254(2) TFEU.

[115]   Art. 13 General Court Rules of Procedure.

[116]   *Ibid.*, Art. 14(2); Art. 28 (1): 'Whenever the legal difficulty or the importance of the case or special circumstances to justify, a case may be referred to the Grand Chamber[.]'

[117]   *Ibid.*, Art. 14(3).   [118]   Art. 11(1) SEA.

[119]   Art. 256(1) TFEU. One past exception were staff cases that fell within the first-instance jurisdiction of the Civil Service Tribunal. The Court of Justice enjoys a generally reserved first-instance jurisdiction for actions brought by a Member State or an institution for failure to act (see Art. 51 Court Statute).

[120]   Art. 256(3) TFEU – second indent.

[121]   Art. 56(2) Court Statute.   [122]   *Ibid.*, Art. 58.   [123]   *Ibid.*, Art. 61.

General Court. Alternatively, the Court of Justice can act as a 'court of revision' and give final judgment in the matter itself.[124]

Similar – but nonetheless distinct – are reviews. The Court of Justice is entitled to *review* a judgment of the General Court *on its own motion* in two situations. First, it can review a decision of the General Court, where that court acts in its own appellate capacity. Second, it can review a decision by the General Court where it gives a preliminary ruling for a national court.[125] However, in both situations review proceedings are limited to 'where there is a serious risk of the unity or consistency of Union law being affected'.[126]

dd. The 'Specialised Court(s)': The Civil Service Tribunal

Courts with special jurisdictions are a common phenomenon in many national legal orders. Judicial specialisation allows judges to develop and employ legal expertise in an area that requires special knowledge and expertise.

The EU Treaties do envisage the possibility of creating specialised courts below the General Court. Article 257 TFEU indeed entitles the European legislator to establish 'specialised courts attached to the General Court to hear and determine at first instance certain classes of action or proceedings brought in specific areas'.[127] The jurisdiction of any such specialised court will be defined in its constituting act, while its judges shall 'be chosen from persons whose independence is beyond doubt and who possess the ability required for appointment to judicial office'.[128] Unlike the judges at the higher European courts, they will not be appointed by common accord of the Member States but by the (unanimous) Council.[129]

What specialised jurisdictions can be created in the European legal order? The EU Treaties are here completely open. So far, however, only one specialised court has ever been established: the Civil Service Tribunal.[130] The Tribunal was originally charged to 'exercise at first instance jurisdiction in disputes between the Union and its servants'.[131] It consisted of seven judges,[132] who were appointed for six years by the Council.[133] Yet in a dramatic volte face, this first-and-only specialised EU court was abolished in 2016 (and its jurisdiction transferred to the General Court).[134] The reasons behind the dissolution of the

---

[124] Decisions of the Court of Justice in appeal cases are suffixed by a 'P' for the French 'pourvoi' (i.e. appeal). See for example: Joined cases C-402/05 P and C-415/05 P, *Kadi and Al Barakaat International Foundation* v. *Council and Commission* [2008] ECR I-6351.

[125] Art. 256(2) and (3) TFEU.

[126] *Ibid.* For the 'Review of Decisions of the General Court', see Title VI of the Rules of Procedure of the Court of Justice.

[127] Art. 257 TFEU – first indent.   [128] *Ibid.* – fourth indent.   [129] *Ibid.*

[130] Council Decision 2004/752 establishing the European Union Civil Service Tribunal [2004] OJ L 333/7 (repealed).

[131] Former Annex I of the Court Statute, Art. 1 (repealed).

[132] *Ibid.*, Art. 2 (repealed).   [133] Art. 257 TFEU – fourth indent.

[134] Regulation 2016/1192 on the transfer to the General Court of jurisdiction at first instance in disputes between the European Union and its servants, [2016] OJ L 200/137, Arts. 1 and 2.

Civil Service Tribunal are very controversial;[135] and in many respects, the 2016 reform is clearly 'in defiance of the letter if not the spirit of Article 257 TFEU, which specifically provides for the establishment of such specialized courts'.[136]

What are the future prospects for any other specialised courts in the Union legal order? The area in which the idea is most often invoked is intellectual property law, and in particular in relation to trade marks. The creation of a new specialised jurisdiction would here make enormous sense in light of the level of technical expertise needed for these cases; and the establishment of an Intellectual Property Court would also provide 'an exhaustive solution to the problem presented by the rapid increase of trade mark and design cases'.[137] In the 2016 judicial reform, this solution was however flatly rejected; and the Union legal order therefore lacks a specialised court today.

b. Judicial Procedure(s)

The procedure before the Court of Justice consists of two parts: a written part and an oral part.[138] The written part precedes the oral part and dominates the judicial procedure.

A case begins when brought before the Court by a written application by the applicant.[139] The application will then be served on the defendant, who may lodge a defence.[140] Each party has the right to reply to the other.[141] Thereafter, the Court takes over the initiative. Two steps structure the written procedure. First comes the assignment of the case. The Court will assign the case to a chamber or the full court – depending on the importance of the case.[142] It will also designate a 'Reporting Judge' and an Advocate General. They decide whether a preparatory inquiry needs to be held. This preparatory inquiry represents the second step. The Court may here, on its own motion or on application by a party,

---

[135] For an in-depth analysis of these 'reasons', see A. Alemanno and L. Pech, 'Thinking Justice outside the Docket: A Critical Assessment of the Reform of the EU's Court System' [2017] 54 *CML Rev.* 129.

[136] *Ibid.*, 134 as well as 151: 'a disguised constitutional reform of the EU's judiciary in breach of the "spirit of the Treaties"'. I could not agree more.

[137] J. Brinkhof and A. Ohly, 'Towards a Unified Patent Court in Europe', in A. Ohly and J. Pila (eds.,) *The Europeanization of Intellectual Property Law* (Oxford University Press, 2013), 199 at 219.

[138] For a legal definition, see Art. 20(2) Court Statute. This section will concentrate on the procedure(s) within the Court of Justice, and here in particular on direct actions.

[139] Art. 21 Court Statute. The provision, as well as Art. 120 of the Court Rules of Procedure, details the minimum information an application needs to contain.

[140] Art. 123 Court Rules of Procedure.

[141] *Ibid.*, Art. 126. The provision defines the response by the applicant as 'reply' and the subsequent response by the defendant as 'rejoinder'.

[142] *Ibid.*, Art. 60(1). The Court may also decide to 'join' cases on the grounds that they concern the same subject matter (*ibid.*, Art. 43). Famous examples include: Joined Cases C-46/93 and C-48/93, *Brasserie du Pêcheur SA* v. *Bundesrepublik Deutschland; The Queen* v. *Secretary of State for Transport, ex p. Factortame Ltd and others* [1996] ECR I-1029.

hear witnesses.[143] This leads to the oral part of the procedure.[144] The hearing of the parties will normally be in public,[145] where the judges are allowed to put questions to the parties. After the hearing, the Advocate General will deliver his opinion. And the final step is the judgment itself. It ends the case.[146]

How does the Court make a judgment? Judicial decision-making takes place in closed secrecy. The Court, in the formation that heard the case, here deliberates in secret.[147] The basis of the deliberation is not the opinion of the Advocate General, but a draft judgment prepared by the Reporting Judge. Every participating judge will state his or her opinion and the reasons behind it.[148] Voting will take place in reverse order of seniority – this is to prevent junior judges from being influenced by the opinion of their seniors. The final judgment will be reached by a majority of judges.[149]

This 'majority' decision is the only decision of the Court. For unlike the US Supreme Court, no dissenting opinions by a minority of judges are allowed. All judicial differences must thus be settled in the (majority) decision of the Court. This often turns a judgment into an 'edited collection', since disagreements within the Court must be settled by weaving diverse threads of reasoning into a single judicial texture. And the eclectic literary result may not be easy to understand! However, the collective and secret nature of the judgment is a shield protecting the independence of the European judiciary.

In addition to 'judgments', the Court also has the power to give 'orders' and 'opinions'. The former may result from an application for interim measures.[150] Interim measures are sometimes necessary, for actions brought before the Court have no suspensory effect.[151] An order will thus typically precede a judgment.[152] By contrast, 'opinions' of the Court can be requested in the context of international agreements.[153] Before the Union can conclude such an agreement, '[a] Member State, the European Parliament, the Council or the Commission may

---

[143]   Art. 66 Court Rules of Procedure.

[144]   For a brief overview here, see A. Rosas, 'Oral Hearings before the European Court of Justice' (2014) 21 *Maastricht Journal of European and Comparative Law* 596.

[145]   See Art. 31 Court Statute: 'The hearing in court shall be public, unless the Court of Justice, of its own motion or on application by the parties, decides otherwise for serious reasons.'

[146]   Art. 88 Court Rules of Procedure.

[147]   *Ibid.*, Art. 32(1): 'The deliberations of the Court shall be and shall remain secret.'

[148]   *Ibid.*, Art. 32(3).

[149]   *Ibid.*, Art. 32(4). There must always be an uneven number of voting judges. According to Art. 17(1) Court Statute, '[d]ecisions of the Court of Justice shall be valid only when an uneven number of its members is sitting in the deliberations'.

[150]   Art. 279 TFEU: 'The Court of Justice of the European Union may in any cases before it prescribe any necessary interim measures.'

[151]   *Ibid.*, Art. 278.

[152]   Orders are marked by an 'R' at the end of the case number, e.g. Case 27/76R, *United Brands* v. *Commission* [1976] ECR 425 preceding the judgment of the Court in Case 27/76, *United Brands* v. *Commission* [1978] ECR 207.

[153]   These 'Opinions' are not 'Cases' and are numbered separately, such as '*Opinion 1/94*'. For a list of the Court's 'Opinions', see Table of Cases 1(c).

obtain the opinion of the Court of Justice as to whether an agreement envisaged is compatible with the Treaties'.[154] The Court's opinion is here more than advisory, for where it is adverse 'the agreement envisaged may not enter into force unless it is amended or the Treaties are revised'.[155] The Court's opinions have indeed shaped the external relations law of the European Union.

c. Judicial Reasoning: Methods of Interpretation

Courts are not democratic institutions. Their decision-making ought thus not to be based on political expediency. And, in many modern societies, courts are therefore not allowed to make law.[156] They must only interpret and apply the law.

The Court of Justice of the European Union stands in this 'civilian' tradition. For according to Article 19 TEU the Court shall 'ensure that in the interpretation and application of the Treaties the law is observed'.[157] The European Court is here portrayed as an 'active' interpreter and as a 'passive' applier of European law. It must apply European law where its meaning is clear, and must interpret it where its meaning is not clear.

The process of interpretation is a process of expressing implicit meaning. It lies between art and science. It is creative in its construction of meaning; yet, by insisting on judicial 'rules' of construction, it has a scientific soul. The interpretation of law is thus the creation of legal meaning according to a judicial methodology. The judicial method 'justifies' a decision of a court.[158] A court must give 'grounds'– legal grounds – for its decisions.[159]

There are four common methods that judges use to justify their decisions. They are: historical interpretation, literal interpretation, systematic interpretation and teleological interpretation. There exists no hierarchy between these methods in the European legal order, and their parallel use may at times lead to conflicting results. Each method of interpretation grants a different degree of 'freedom' to the Court in deciding a case. The first two methods are 'conservative' methods, while the last two methods are 'progressive' methods of interpretation. A judicial preference for an interpretative method will thus prejudge the result of the interpretation.[160]

Theoretically, the smallest interpretative room is given by the historical method. Historical interpretation searches for the original meaning of a rule. However, a commitment to 'originalism' encounters problems. It presumes that

---

[154]   Art. 218(11) TFEU.   [155]   *Ibid.*

[156]   Exceptionally, some modern States recognise the lawmaking function of courts. The English common law system is the best example.

[157]   Art. 19(1) TEU.

[158]   On the notion of 'legal justification' in the European legal order, see J. Bengoetxea, *The Legal Reasoning of the European Court of Justice: Towards a European Jurisprudence* (Clarendon Press, 1993), ch. 5.

[159]   Art. 36 Court Statute: 'Judgments shall state the reasons on which they are based.'

[160]   In the beautifully paradoxical words of G. Radbruch: 'The interpretation is the result of its result.' See G. Radbruch, *Einführung in die Rechtswissenschaft* (Meyer, 1925), 129.

there was a clear meaning when the norm was created – which may not be the case.[161] And a historical reading of a norm may make it lose touch with the social reality to which it is to apply. Literal interpretation, by contrast, starts with the written text and gives it its (ordinary) contemporary meaning. The problem with the 'textualist' method in the European legal order is that there is not one single legal text. Systematic interpretation tries to construct the meaning of a norm by reference to its place within the general scheme of the legislative or constitutional system. Finally, teleological interpretation is the judicial method that allows a court to search for the purpose or spirit or useful effect – the *telos* – of a legal norm.

The European Court has used all four methods in its jurisprudence. But while occasionally using the historical method, the Court generally finds it paramount 'to consider the spirit, the general scheme and the wording of those provisions'.[162] Teleological and systematic consideration have indeed often trumped even the clear wording of a provision. This 'activist' jurisprudence has attracted severe criticism – from academics and politicians alike.[163]

d. Jurisdiction and Judicial Powers

The traditional role of courts in modern societies is to act as independent adjudicators between competing interests. Their jurisdiction may be compulsory, or not. The jurisdiction of the Court of Justice of the European Union is compulsory 'within the limits of the powers conferred on it in the Treaties'.[164] While compulsory, the Court's jurisdiction is thus limited. Based on the principle of conferral, the Court has no 'inherent' jurisdiction.

The functions and powers of the Court are classified in Article 19(3) TEU:

> The Court of Justice of the European Union shall, in accordance with the Treaties:
> (a) rule on actions brought by a Member State, an institution or a natural or legal person;
> (b) give preliminary rulings, at the request of courts or tribunals of the Member States, on the interpretation of Union law or the validity of acts adopted by the institutions;
> (c) rule in other cases provided for in the Treaties.

The provision classifies the judicial tasks by distinguishing between direct and indirect actions. The former are brought directly before the European Court. The latter arrive at the Court indirectly through preliminary references from national

---

[161] Constitutions (as well as legislation) are often the result of compromises. They take refuge in ambivalences and leave meaning to be defined in the future.

[162] *Van Gend en Loos*, 12.

[163] See H. Rasmussen, *On Law and Policy in the European Court of Justice: A Comparative Study in Judicial Policymaking* (Nijhoff, 1986).

[164] Art. 13(2) TEU.

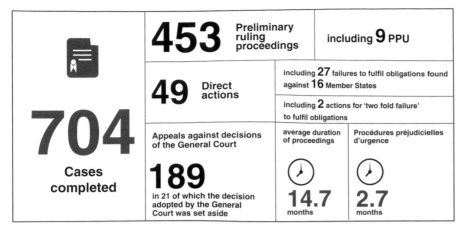

Figure 6.7 European Court of Justice: 'Fingerprint'

courts. The powers of the Court under the preliminary reference procedure are set out in a single article.[165] By contrast, there exist a number of direct actions in the Treaty on the Functioning of the European Union. This Treaty distinguishes between enforcement actions brought by the Commission or a Member State,[166] judicial review proceedings for action and inaction of the Union institutions,[167] actions for damages for the (non-)contractual liability of the Union,[168] as well as a few minor jurisdictional heads.[169] Figure 6.7 shows the judicial fingerprint of the European Court of Justice for the year 2016.[170] It shows Europe's highest court to be predominantly concerned with preliminary rulings – whereas direct actions are overwhelmingly a task for the General Court.[171]

In light of its broad jurisdiction, the Court of Justice of the European Union can be characterised as a 'constitutional', an 'administrative', an 'international' court as well as an 'industrial tribunal'. Its jurisdiction includes public and private matters; and the number of cases decided every year is staggering.

3. The European Central Bank

National central banks emerged in seventeenth-century Europe as public institutions to regulate the supply of money in the national market.[172] A European

---

[165] Art. 267 TFEU. The provision is analysed in Chapter 10, section 4.

[166] Arts. 258–60 TFEU. The provisions are analysed in Chapter 10, section 3.

[167] *Ibid.*, Arts. 263–6. The provisions are analysed in Chapter 10, sections 1 and 3.

[168] *Ibid.*, Arts. 268 and 340. The provisions are analysed in Chapter 10, section 2.

[169] *Ibid.*, Arts. 269–74.

[170] Court of Justice of the European Union, *Annual Report 2016: The Year in Review* (European Union, 2017), 28.

[171] In 2016, out of the 755 cases completed by the General Court, 645 were direct actions (*ibid.*, 30).

[172] Among the first 'central' banks to emerge were the Swedish Riksbank (1664) and the Bank of England (1694). On the legislative power of the US Congress to charter a national bank, see *McCulloch v. Maryland*, 17 US 316 (1819).

central bank had originally not been provided for in the Treaties. However, with the decision to move towards monetary union, a central institution was envisaged to regulate the money market in the European Union. The European Central Bank (ECB) came into formal existence in 1998, and assumed its formal functions on 1 January 1999 when the European currency – the euro – was introduced.

The status of the Bank within the institutional framework of the Union remained unclear for a long time. Prior to the Lisbon Treaty, it was not a formal 'institution' of the Union,[173] and its ambivalent legal status gave rise to a spirited academic debate. The debate has – partly – been ended by Article 13(1) TEU, which expressly identifies the ECB as an institution of the European Union. Nonetheless, the ECB is an institution with a special status that warrants a special analysis (see section (a)). Thereafter, we shall look at the composition and structure, decision-making procedure and functions of the ECB respectively (see sections (b)–(d)).

a. The Special Status of the ECB

Is the European Central Bank a *sui generis* institution of the Union? The argument has been made by reference to two of its 'special' characteristics. First, the European Central Bank is 'independent'.[174] Second, it is embedded in the European System of Central Banks (ESCB). This is a system composed of the ECB and the National Central Banks of the Member States whose currency is the euro;[175] and the Treaties formally assign the tasks of monetary policy to the ESCB and not directly to the ECB.[176]

Let us start by looking at the 'independent' status of the ECB. The ECB 'shall be independent in the exercise of its powers and in the management of its finances'; and the Union as well as the Member States must respect that independence.[177] Unlike any other Union institution, the Bank indeed has its own 'legal personality' that is distinct from the legal personality of the Union.[178] The Bank's special status originally gave rise to the theory that the ECB represented an 'independent specialised organisation of [Union] law' – like the European Atomic Community.[179] Yet the idea that the Bank was *legally* independent from

---

[173] Prior to the Lisbon Treaty, the legal existence of the ECB was provided for not in the article dealing with the institutions, but in a separate article; see Art. 8 EC: 'A European System of Central Banks (hereinafter referred to as "ESCB") and a European Central Bank (hereinafter referred to as "ECB") shall be established in accordance with the procedures laid down in this Treaty; they shall act within the limits of the powers conferred upon them by this Treaty and by the Statute of the ESCB and of the ECB (hereinafter referred to as "Statute of the ESCB") annexed thereto.'

[174] Art. 282(3) TFEU.   [175] *Ibid.*, Art. 282.   [176] *Ibid.*, Art. 127(2).   [177] *Ibid.*, Art. 282(3).

[178] *Ibid.*: 'The European Central Bank shall have legal personality.'

[179] C. Zilioli and M. Selmayr, *The Law of the European Central Bank* (Hart, 2001), 31. The practical consequence of that theory was that the ECB was assumed not to be directly bound by the objectives of the European Union. The sole 'Grundnorm' of the 'new Community' was price stability (*ibid.*, 35).

the European Union has been thoroughly rejected by the European Court of Justice. In *Commission* v. *European Central Bank*,[180] the Court unconditionally rejected the *legal* independence theory. The independence of the Bank only meant *political* independence.[181] And that political independence is not a unique feature of the Bank, but is shared by other Union institutions.[182]

What about the European Central Bank being part of a two-level structure within the European System of Central Banks? This – strange – constitutional structure must be understood against its historical background.[183] When the Member States decided to move towards monetary union, they had two alternatives. They could either dissolve the pre-existing National Central Banks and replace them with a – centralised – single European Central Bank; or they could create a decentralised structure within which the National Central Banks acted as agents of the ECB.

The Treaties have chosen the second option – an option that has many advantages.[184] However, this second option is *not* a federal option. National Central Banks are not in a federal relationship with the ECB. It is the ECB that *exclusively* governs within the European System of Central Banks. It is the ECB that can – exclusively – decide whether to exercise the powers granted to it by the Treaties itself 'or *through* the national central banks'.[185] And, when the ECB decides to 'have recourse to the national central banks',[186] the latter 'shall act in accordance with the guidelines and instructions of the ECB'.[187] National Central Banks are thus best seen as functionally integrated 'organs' of the ECB. They only enjoy 'delegated' powers under an exclusive EU competence, and not 'autonomous'

---

[180]   Case C-11/00, *Commission* v. *European Central Bank* [2003] ECR I-7147.

[181]   *Ibid.*, para. 134. For a criticism of that claim, see R. Smits, 'The European Central Bank's Independence and Its Relations with Economic Policy Makers' (2007–8) 31 *Fordham International Law Journal* 1614 at 1625: 'In a self-professed democracy, the idea of central bankers not being influenced by [Union] and State government members is absurd.'

[182]   Case C-11/00 (n. 180 above), para. 133: '[Union] institutions such as, notably, the Parliament, the Commission or the Court itself, enjoy independence and guarantees comparable in a number of respects to those thus afforded to the ECB. In that regard, reference may, for example, be made to Article [245 TFEU], which states that the Members of the Commission are, in the general interest of the [Union], to be completely independent in the performance of their duties. That provision states, in terms quite close to those used in [Article 130 TFEU], that in the performance of their duties the Members of the Commission are neither to seek nor to take instructions from any government or from any other body and, further, that each Member State undertakes not to seek to influence those Members in the performance of their tasks.'

[183]   For an excellent overview, see Zilioli and Selmayr, *Law of the European Central Bank* (n. 179 above), 54ff.

[184]   *Ibid.*, 57: 'The maintenance of the national central banks inside the ESCB was seen as an opportunity to found a new system on the experience, the traditions and the reputation of the national central banks[.]'

[185]   Art. 9(2) ECB Statute (emphasis added).

[186]   *Ibid.*, Art. 12(1) – third indent.   [187]   *Ibid.*, Art. 14(3).

national powers.[188] Within the scope of the Treaties, they are consequently agents of the ECB.[189] And the best way to characterise the ESCB is therefore to compare it to a *decentralised unitary* system – akin to the political system within the United Kingdom.[190]

In conclusion, how are we to characterise the ECB? Textually and functionally, the ECB is a 'formal' institution of the Union, albeit endowed with its own special characteristics.[191] While the ECB is organically separate from the National Central Banks, it functionally incorporates them as decentralised agents of the ECB. From this point of view, the ESCB is nothing but the ECB writ large.

b. Organs and Administrative Structure

The ECB has three central organs that are shown in Figure 6.8. Its two executive organs are the 'Executive Board' and the 'Supervisory Board'. Its principal regulatory organ is the 'Governing Council'.[192]

The Executive Board constitutes Europe's 'monetary executive'.[193] It comprises the President, the Vice-President and four additional members. The Executive Board is appointed by the European Council 'from among persons of recognised standing and professional experience in monetary or banking

---

[188] According to Art. 3(c) TFEU, 'monetary policy for the Member States whose currency is the euro' is an exclusive competence of the Union. It is for this reason that the ECB is entitled to even apply national (!) law transposing Union law (see Regulation 1024/2013 conferring specific tasks on the European Central Bank concerning policies relating to the prudential supervision of credit institutions [2013] OJ L 287/63). On exclusive competences and their meaning in the European legal order, see Chapter 7, section 2(a).

[189] The 'ECB agent' theory is supported by two additional arguments. First, according to Art. 35(6) ECB Statute, the Court of Justice will 'have jurisdiction in disputes concerning the fulfilment by a national central bank of obligations under the Treaties and the Statute'. Second, while national central banks 'may' perform additional functions to those specified in the European Treaties, the European Central Bank can prohibit them if it considers that they interfere with the objectives and tasks of the ESCB (see Art. 14(4) ECB Statute).

[190] On the constitutional 'devolution' of power from the Westminster Parliament, see V. Bogdanor, *Devolution in the United Kingdom* (Oxford University Press, 2001).

[191] For a much stronger thesis, see B. Krauskopf and C. Steven, 'The Institutional Framework of the European System of Central Banks: Legal Issues in the Practice of the First Ten Years of its Existence' (2009) 46 *CML Rev.* 1143 at 1149: 'The ECB has institutional features which set it distinctly apart from all the other EU institutions.'

[192] See Art. 129(1) TFEU as well as Art. 26 of Regulation 1024/2013 (n. 188 above). The Treaties mention a fourth – central but transitory – organ: the 'General Council' (see Art. 141(1) TFEU as well as Art. 44 of the ECB Statute). The General Council will comprise the President and Vice-President of the ECB and the Governors of all (!) the national central banks – even those not participating in monetary union. Art. 43 of the ECB Statute defines the tasks of the General Council as those that were formerly exercised by the European Monetary Institute (the predecessor of the ECB), which are further spelled out in Art. 46 of the ECB Statute.

[193] Zilioli and Selmayr, *Law of the European Central Bank* (n. 179 above), 84.

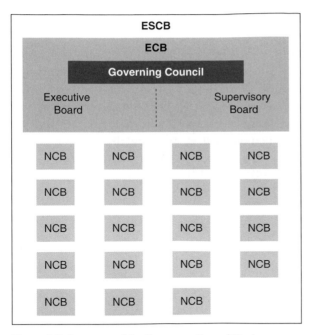

Figure 6.8 Structure of the European Central Bank

matters'.[194] The members of the Executive Board must perform their duties in complete independence.[195] Their term of office is eight years, and cannot be renewed.[196]

A second 'executive' organ is the 'Supervisory Board'. It is charged to assist the ECB with the specific task of supervising (big) banks so as to ensure the stability of the financial system within the Union.[197] It consists of a Chair and Vice Chair, four representatives of the ECB, as well as one representative from each participating Member State. Appointed for five years, the Chair will be chosen 'on the basis of an open selection procedure' from individuals of 'recognised standing and experience in banking and financial matters', who are not already members of the ECB. By contrast, the Vice Chair will be 'chosen from among the members of the Executive Board'.[198]

The Governing Council is Europe's monetary regulator. It comprises the members of the Executive Board and the governors of the National Central Banks of the euro-States.[199] Importantly, since the governors of the National Central Banks must not take instructions from their national governments,[200] they are *not* representatives of the Member States. They must act in the supranational interest of the European Union as a whole.[201] Governors of National

---

[194] Art. 283(2) TFEU.   [195] Art. 11 ECB Statute.   [196] *Ibid.*

[197] See Regulation 1024/2013 (n. 188 above), Art. 26(1).

[198] *Ibid.*, Art. 26(3); Art. 13(b) of ECB Rules of Procedure.

[199] Art. 283(1) TFEU.   [200] *Ibid.*, Art. 130.

[201] H. K. Scheller, *The European Central Bank* (ECB, 2004), 54.

Central Banks are thus unlike national ministers in the Council. They are not national representatives but representatives of the Union.

The central organs of the ECB are supported by a number of 'work units', and 'committees'.[202] Work units can be created by the Executive Board, and are 'under the managing direction' of the latter.[203] Work units within the ECB presently comprise 'Directorates-General' (for example: Financial Stability), and self-standing Directorates (for example: Internal Audit). With regard to committees, it is the Governing Council that will 'establish and dissolve' committees with particular mandates.[204] Committees are to be composed of up to two members from each of the National Central Banks (participating in the euro) and the ECB.

c. Internal Divisions and Decision-making

Who governs within the European Central Bank? The Governing Council is the central policymaking organ, which is charged to ensure that the tasks of the ECB are fulfilled. It will 'formulate the monetary policy of the Union, including, as appropriate, decisions relating to immediate monetary objectives, key interest rates and the supply of reserves in the ESCB, and shall establish the necessary guidelines for their implementation'.[205]

In the past, decision-making within the Governing Council was pleasantly straightforward: each member had one vote.[206] However, matters became more complex when the number of Member States that adopt the euro exceeded 18 in 2015. Here, the Statute envisages a – very – complex rotating system among national governors.[207] The Council will meet 'at least 10 times a year', and decisions are normally taken by simple majority.[208] Voting is confidential, but the Governing Council may decide to make the outcome of its deliberations public.[209] And, if the Governing Council resolves not to decide itself, it 'may delegate its normative powers to the Executive Board for the purpose of implementing its regulations and guidelines'.[210]

---

[202]   See www.ecb.europa.eu/ecb/orga/orgachart/html/index.en.html.

[203]   Art. 10 ECB Rules of Procedure (and see Decision of the European Central Bank 2004/257 [2004] OJ L 80/33).

[204]   Art. 9 ECB Rules of Procedure.

[205]   Art. 12(1) ECB Statute – first indent.

[206]   For particularly sensitive financial decisions, voting will be conducted through weighted votes. Votes will thereby 'be weighted according to the national central bank's shares in the subscribed capital of the ECB'. Obviously, the votes of the Executive Board will be zero (see Art. 10(3) ECB Statute).

[207]   The rotating system is set out in Art. 10(2) of the ECB Statute. A very useful visual chart for the rotation of voting rights in the Governing Council can be found at: www.ecb .europa.eu/ecb/orga/decisions/govc/html/votingrights.en.html.

[208]   Ibid., Art. 10(2) and (5). However, the Statute also envisages qualified majority voting, see ibid., Art. 10(3).

[209]   Ibid., Art. 10(4).

[210]   Art. 17(3) ECB Rules of Procedure.

What are the tasks of the Executive Board? In line with its 'executive' nature, it 'shall implement monetary policy in accordance with the guidelines and decisions laid down by the Governing Council'; and, in that executive capacity, it will also be the primary instructor for National Central Banks.[211] It will generally 'be responsible for the current business of the ECB'.[212] Decision-making in the Executive Board is done in person, with each person having one vote. Save as otherwise provided, the Executive Board will thereby act by a simple majority of the votes cast, with the President having a casting vote in the event of a tie.[213]

While the Executive Board thus primarily implements the Governing Council's monetary policy, the specific task of the 'Supervisory Board' is to assist the ECB in the prudential supervision of banks so as to guarantee 'the safety and soundness of credit institutions and the stability of the financial system within the Union'.[214] This second essential task – after monetary policy – is discharged in liaison with the Governing Council; yet the Union legal order here insists on a complete separation between the monetary and the supervisory functions of the ECB.[215] Decisions by the Supervisory Board will in general be taken by a simple majority of its members, but qualified majority voting also exists for certain areas.[216]

Finally, what are the tasks of the ECB President? S/he will have to chair the Governing Council and the Executive Board, and will represent the ECB externally.[217] External representation includes participation in Council meetings that discuss matters falling within the competences of the Bank.[218]

d. Functions and Powers

The ECB does not have the constitutional honour of its own article in the Treaty on European Union. This 'systemic' break in the arrangement of the institutional provisions is regrettable. In order to draw a picture of the functions and powers of the ECB, we must therefore look at the Treaty on the Functioning of the European Union.

The Treaties define the 'primary objective' of the European Central Bank as the maintenance of price stability.[219] This primary objective is not just a *primus inter pares*. While the ECB must also 'support the general economic policies in the Union', economic objectives are only secondary objectives that must be pursued '[w]ithout prejudice' to the monetary objective of price stability.[220]

---

[211] Art. 12(1) ECB Statute.   [212] *Ibid.*, Art. 11(6).   [213] *Ibid.*, Art. 11(5).

[214] Regulation, 1024/2013 (n. 188 above), Arts. 1 and 26.

[215] *Ibid.*, Art. 25(4): 'The ECB shall ensure that the operation of the Governing Council is completely differentiated as regards monetary and supervisory functions. Such differentiation shall include strictly separated meetings and agendas.'

[216] *Ibid.*, Art. 26(6) and (7).   [217] *Ibid.*, Art. 13 ECB Statute.

[218] Art. 284(2) TFEU.

[219] *Ibid.*, Art. 127(1), as well as *ibid.*, Art. 282(2). For a more extensive discussion of the powers of the ECB within the Economic and Monetary Union title of the TFEU, see Chapter 18, section 1.

[220] Art. 127(1) TFEU.

The primacy of price stability reflects modern economic thinking about the (limited) function of monetary policy.[221]

How is the ECB to achieve price stability? The Treaties answer this question indirectly by specifying a number of 'basic tasks'. The ECB must 'define and implement the monetary policy of the Union', 'conduct foreign-exchange operations', 'hold and manage the official foreign reserves of the Member States' and 'promote the smooth operation of payment systems'.[222] The most potent powers to achieve these tasks are the Bank's exclusive right to *authorise* the issue of euro banknotes, and to set interest rates.[223] Money supply within the Union (or rather the Euro Group)[224] is thus *centrally* determined by the ECB.

To partly regulate the demand side of the European currency, the Bank is equally involved in foreign exchange operations. However, the external relations powers of the Bank are subject to the special treaty-making procedure set out in Article 219 TFEU.[225] This makes the Council – not the ECB – the central player in the external sphere. The Bank is however entitled to recommend 'formal agreements on an exchange-rate system for the euro in relation to the currencies of third States' to the Council,[226] and must generally be consulted on monetary agreements.[227] This consultation requirement is extended to common positions within international financial institutions 'to secure the euro's place in the international monetary system'.[228]

Are there other functions of the ECB? With the creation of the banking union, the ECB has assumed a – secondary – function in the form of the supervision of (big) banks so as to ensure the stability of the financial system within the Union. Finally, a tertiary function lies in its advisory role to other Union institutions on 'areas falling within its responsibilities'.[229]

4. The Court of Auditors

Many constitutional orders subject public finances to an external audit.[230] In the Union legal order, the Court of Auditors was established by the 1975 Budget Treaty, and was elevated to a formal institution of the Union in the wake of the

---

[221]   Scheller, *European Central Bank* (n. 201 above), 45. But, of course, economic thinking is cyclical: what is 'orthodoxy' today may sooner or later become heterodoxy.

[222]   Art. 127(2) TFEU.

[223]   *Ibid.*, Art. 128(1) (emphasis added). The Member States may, however, issue euro coins, but the volume of the issue of euro coins is still subject to the approval of the ECB.

[224]   That is the name for the Member States participating in monetary union. The status of the so-called 'Euro Group' is clarified in Protocol No. 14 on the Euro Group. According to Art. 1, '[t]he Ministers of the Member States whose currency is the euro shall meet informally'. According to Art. 2, the Euro Group shall elect a president for two-and-a-half years.

[225]   On this point, see Chapter 8, section 3(b).   [226]   Art. 219(1) TFEU.

[227]   *Ibid.*, Art. 291(3).   [228]   *Ibid.*, Art. 138(1).

[229]   *Ibid.*, Art. 282(5): 'within the areas within its responsibilities, the European Central Bank shall be consulted on all proposed Union acts, and all proposals for regulation at national level, and may give an opinion'.

[230]   For the French 'Cour des Comptes', see www.ccomptes.fr/fr/CC/Accueil.html.

Maastricht Treaty. The name of this particular institution is partly misleading. The Court of Auditors is not a court in a judicial sense. It neither exercises judicial functions, nor is it staffed by lawyers.[231] The Court of Auditors is staffed by accountants, whose primary task is to 'carry out the Union's audit'.[232] Audit here means *external* audit, for each institution must internally audit itself.[233]

What is the structure and decision-making procedure of the Court? The Court consists of one national from each Member State. Members must be completely 'independent' and act 'in the Union's general interest'.[234] Membership is limited to persons who 'have belonged in their respective States to external audit bodies or who are especially qualified for this office'.[235] The Council – not the Member States – appoints members for a (renewable) term of six years.[236] The Court will – internally – elect its President.[237] The latter will 'call and chair the meetings of the Court', and 'represent the Court in its external relations'.[238] While the Court is divided into chambers,[239] it will normally act as a collegial body by a simple majority of its members.[240] Decisions of the Court shall be taken 'in formal session', but a written procedure may exceptionally apply.[241] However, for certain categories of reports the decision of a chamber might be sufficient.[242] Yet, all important reports must be adopted by the full Court.[243]

What are the functions and powers of the Court of Auditors? According to Article 287 TFEU, the Court of Auditors 'shall examine the accounts of all revenue

---

[231] However, this is the case in some Member States, and this may explain the naming of the respective national institutions as 'courts' (see N. Price, 'The Court of Auditors of the European Communities' (1982) 2 YEL 239).

[232] Art. 285 TFEU – first indent.

[233] Regulation 1605/2002 on the Financial Regulation applicable to the general budget of the European Communities ([2002] OJ L 248/1), ch. 3.

[234] Art. 285 TFEU – second indent. The duty is further defined in Art. 286(3) and (4) TFEU: 'In the performance of these duties, the Members of the Court of Auditors shall neither seek nor take instructions from any government or from any other body. The Members of the Court of Auditors shall refrain from any action incompatible with their duties. The Members of the Court of Auditors may not, during their term of office, engage in any other occupation, whether gainful or not. When entering upon their duties they shall give a solemn undertaking that, both during and after their term of office, they will respect the obligations arising therefrom and in particular their duty to behave with integrity and discretion as regards the acceptance, after they have ceased to hold office, of certain appointments or benefits.'

[235] *Ibid.*, Art. 286(1).   [236] *Ibid.*, Art. 286(2).   [237] *Ibid.*

[238] Rules of Procedure of the Court of Auditors (CoA), Art. 9(a) and (e).

[239] *Ibid.*, Art. 10. According to Art. 11 of Decision 26/2010 of the Court of Auditors implementing the Rules of Procedure, the Court has five chambers 'four Chambers with responsibility for specific areas of expenditure and for revenue (vertical Chambers), and one horizontal Chamber, known as the CEAD (Coordination, Communication, Evaluation, Assurance and Development) Chamber'.

[240] Art. 287(4) TFEU – third indent.

[241] Art. 19 CoA Rules of Procedure.   [242] *Ibid.*, Art. 26.

[243] Art. 64 of the Decision implementing the CoA Rules of Procedure (n. 239 above). This includes 'the Annual Report provided for in Article 287(4) TFEU' (a), 'the Statement of Assurance' (b), as well as certain categories of 'specific annual reports' (c).

and expenditure of the Union'.[244] And it shall additionally 'provide the European Parliament and the Council with a statement of assurance as to the reliability of the accounts and the legality and regularity of the underlying transactions'.[245] To fulfil its task, the Court will primarily audit the financial records of the Union. However, it is also entitled to perform 'on the spot' investigations 'on the premises of any body, office or agency which manages revenue or expenditure on behalf of the Union and in the Member States, including on the premises of any natural or legal person in receipt of payments from the budget'.[246] This wide investigative power includes the Member States – in their function of Union executive – as well as any individual recipient of Union funds. Yet the audit must here be carried out 'in liaison' with the competent national authorities.[247]

In examining the accounts, what standard is the Court to apply? Two constitutional options exist. *A formal* review will solely require an examination of the 'legality' of the Union's financing, that is: whether the accounts reflect all the revenue received and all expenditure incurred. By contrast, a *substantial* review will additionally examine the 'soundness' of public spending decisions, that is: whether the financial priorities of the Union guarantee 'value for money'. Substantive review is more intrusive, as it involves questioning the underlying political choices behind the budget.

The Union constitutional order has chosen this second option. The Court of Auditors must thus review whether the revenue and expenditure of the Union was 'lawful and regular', '*and* examine whether the financial management has been *sound*'.[248] The soundness of the Union's finances is thereby determined 'by reference to the principles of economy, efficiency and effectiveness'.[249]

The result of the audit will be published in an 'annual report' after the close of each financial year.[250] This annual report may be complemented by 'special reports' dealing with particular aspects of the Union budget.[251] The reports are designed to assist the European Parliament and the Council 'in exercising their powers of control over the implementation of the budget'.[252] And, since the Commission is primarily charged with the implementation of the Union budget, the reports will be primarily addressed to this Union institution.[253] They constitute a 'declaration of good conduct',[254] which – if missing – may lead to the fall of the Commission.[255]

---

[244]   Art. 287(1) TFEU.   [245] *Ibid.*   [246] *Ibid.*, Art. 287(3).   [247] *Ibid.*

[248]   *Ibid.*, Art. 287(2) (emphasis added).

[249]   Art. 27(1) Financial Regulation (n. 233 above).   [250] Art. 287(4) TFEU.

[251]   For example, see Special Report 3/2011 on 'The efficiency and effectiveness of EU contributions channelled through United Nations Organisations in conflict-affected countries' (see http://eca.europa.eu/portal/pls/portal/docs/1/7913076.PDF).

[252]   Art. 287(4) TFEU – fourth indent.

[253]   According to Art. 145(1) Financial Regulation (n. 233 above), if the accounts are regular and sound, the Parliament shall, upon recommendation by the Council and before 15 May of year *n+2*, give a discharge to the Commission in respect for the implementation of the budget of year *n*.

[254]   C. Kok, 'The Court of Auditors of the European Communities: "The Other European Court in Luxembourg"' (1989) 26 *CML Rev.* 345 at 350.

[255]   It was the Court of Auditor's Report on the 1996 Union budget that led to the fall of the Santer Commission.

Conclusion

This chapter, and the previous one, analysed the institutional structure of the European Union. We saw above that the Union is not based on the classic tripartite structure that became famous in the eighteenth century. The Union has seven 'institutions': the European Parliament, the European Council, the Council, the Commission, the Court of Justice of the European Union, the European Central Bank and the Court of Auditors. Each of these institutions is characterised by its distinct composition and its decision-making mode. According to these two dimensions, the Parliament, the Commission, the Court, the European Central Bank and the Court of Auditors are closer to the 'national' end of the spectrum; whereas the European Council and the Council are closer to its 'international' end.

Importantly, since the Union is based on the 'checks-and-balances' version of the separation-of-powers principle, each of the Union institutions shares in various governmental functions. This institutional power-sharing is indeed the very basis of the Union's system of checks and balances. What types of governmental 'powers' or 'functions' may be identified for the European Union? Chapter 5 identified five governmental functions: legislative, executive, judicial, external and financial functions. The legislative power relates to the competence of making laws. The executive power relates to the competence of proposing and implementing laws. The judicial power relates to the competence of adjudicating laws in court. A separate 'fourth power' relates to the external actions of a political community. Finally, a 'fifth power' relates to the public control of monetary markets.

Part II of this book will analyse the first four of these functions. What is the scope of the Union's powers and what legal procedures combine the various institutions into the exercise of these powers? Let us explore these questions by looking at each governmental power in turn.

FURTHER READING

Books

N. Brown and T. Kennedy, *The Court of Justice of the European Communities* (Sweet & Maxwell, 2000)

M. Chamon, *EU Agencies: Legal and Political Limits to the Transformation of the EU Administration* (Oxford University Press, 2016)

R. Corbett et al., *The European Parliament* (Harper, 2016)

F. Hayes-Renshaw and H. Wallace, *The Council of Ministers* (Palgrave, 2006)

S. Hix and B. Høyland, *The Political System of the European Union* (Palgrave, 2011)

D. Judge and D. Earnshaw, *The European Parliament* (Palgrave, 2008)

H. Kassim et al., *The European Commission of the Twenty-first Century* (Oxford University Press, 2013)

N. Nugent, *The Government and Politics of the European Union* (Palgrave, 2017)

N. Nugent and M. Rhinard, *The European Commission* (Palgrave, 2015)

G. Sabathil et al., *The European Commission* (Kogan Page, 2008)

S. Saurugger and F. Terpan, *The Court of Justice of the European Union and the Politics of Law* (Palgrave, 2016)

W. Wessels, *The European Council* (Palgrave, 2016)

M. Westlake and D. Galloway, *The Council of the European Union* (Harper, 2004)

C. Zilioli and M. Selmayr, *The Law of the European Central Bank* (Hart, 2001)

Articles (and Chapters)

S. Alonso de León, 'Four Decades of the European Electoral Act: A Look Back and a Look Ahead to an Unfulfilled Ambition' (2017) 42 *EL Rev.* 353

M. Chamon, 'The Institutional Balance, an Ill-Fated Principle of EU Law?' (2015) 21 *European Public Law* 371

E. Chiti, 'The Emergence of a Community Administration: The Case of European Agencies' (2000) 37 *CML Rev.* 309

M. Goldoni, 'Politicising EU Lawmaking? The *Spitzenkandidaten* Experiment as a Cautionary Tale' (2016) 22 ELJ 279

J.-P. Jacque, 'The Principle of Institutional Balance' (2004) 41 *CML Rev.* 383

M. Kohler, 'European Governance and the European Parliament: From Talking Shop to Legislative Powerhouse' (2014) 52 *Journal of Common Market Studies* 600

C. Kok, 'The Court of Auditors of the European Communities: "The Other European Court in Luxembourg"' (1989) 26 *CML Rev.* 345

B. Krauskopf and C. Steven, 'The Institutional Framework of the European System of Central Banks: Legal Issues in the Practice of the First Ten Years of its Existence' (2009) 46 *CML Rev.* 1143

S. Novak, 'The Silence of Ministers: Consensus and Blame Avoidance in the Council of the European Union' (2013) 51 *Journal of Common Market Studies* 1091

R. Smits, 'The European Central Bank's Independence and Its Relations with Economic Policy Makers' (2007–8) 31 *Fordham International Law Journal* 1614

H. de Waele and H. Broeksteeg, 'The Semi-permanent European Council Presidency: Some Reflections on the Law and Early Practice' (2012) 49 *CML Rev.* 1039

Part II Governmental Powers

Having analysed the constitutional foundations of the Union in Part I of the book, Part II explores the governmental functions of the Union. How and to what extent can the Union adopt legislation, and how will its legislative acts be executed and adjudicated? The Union legal order is a federal legal order that is based on the principle of conferral. According to this foundational principle, the Union can only act where the Treaties have conferred a power to do so. This power will determine the material scope within which the Union is entitled to act (competence) but also the manner in which it must act (procedure).

What is the extent of the Union's legislative powers and what are the procedures that need to be followed before Union legislation comes into being? Chapter 7 analyses these questions in depth. Chapter 8 looks at the foreign affairs powers of the Union and here, in particular, the creation of external 'legislation' in the form of international agreements. The executive branch is the subject of Chapter 9. We shall here discuss the powers to lead and enforce European law, while paying special attention to the Union system of executive federalism. This 'federal' solution can also be found in the context of the judicial function – discussed in Chapters 10 and 11. For in addition to the centralised adjudication of European law by the Union Courts, the direct effect of European law equally requires all national courts to act as decentralised 'Union' courts. A final chapter explores the judicial limits to all governmental powers: EU fundamental rights.

7

Legislative Powers
Competences and Procedures

Contents

Introduction

Each society needs common rules and mechanisms for their production. The concept of legislation is indeed central to all modern societies. It refers to the making of laws (*legis*).[1]

But what is 'legislation'? Two competing conceptions of legislation have emerged in modern constitutional thought. A *parliamentary* or *procedural*

---

[1] *Shorter Oxford English Dictionary.*

conception of legislation is tied to our modern understanding of *who* should be in charge of the legislative function. Legislation is here formally defined as every legal act adopted according to the (parliamentary) *legislative procedure*. This procedural conception of legislation has traditionally shaped British constitutional thought.[2] By contrast, a second conception defines *what* legislation should be, that is: legal rules with *general application*. This *material* or functional conception of legislation has shaped continental constitutional thought.[3] A material definition of legislation underpins phrases like 'delegated legislation' adopted by the executive.

Which of these traditions has informed European constitutionalism? The Union has traditionally followed a material definition.[4] However, with the Lisbon Treaty, a formal definition of legislative power has now been adopted. The Treaty on the Functioning of the European Union constitutionally defines:

> Legal acts adopted by legislative *procedure* shall constitute *legislative* acts.[5]

But what are the 'legislative' powers of the European Union? And what types of procedures are *legislative* procedures? This chapter answers these questions in four sections. Section 1 analyses the scope of the Union's legislative competences. This scope is limited, as the Union is not a sovereign State. Section 2 analyses the different categories of Union competences. Depending on what competence category is involved, the Union will enjoy distinct degrees of legislative power. Section 3 analyses the identity of the Union legislator. Various legislative procedures thereby determine how the Union must exercise its 'legislative' competences. Section 4 finally scrutinises the principle of subsidiarity as a constitutional principle that controls the exercise of the Union's shared legislative powers.

1. The Scope of Union Competences

When the British Parliament legislates, it need not 'justify' its acts. It is considered to enjoy a competence to do all things.[6] This 'omnipotence' is inherent in the idea of a *sovereign* parliament in a *sovereign* state. The European Union is

---

[2] For the British parliamentary definition of legislation, see A. V. Dicey, *Introduction to the Study of the Law of the Constitution* (Liberty Fund, 1982), esp. chs. I and II.

[3] For an excellent overview, see H. Schneider, *Gesetzgebung* (C. F. Müller, 1982).

[4] R. Schütze, 'The Morphology of Legislative Power in the European Community: Legal Instruments and the Federal Division of Powers' (2006) 25 YEL 91.

[5] Art. 289(3) TFEU (emphasis added).

[6] In the words of Dicey, *Introduction to the Study of the Law of the Constitution* (n. 2 above), 37–8: 'The principle of Parliamentary sovereignty means neither more nor less than this, namely that Parliament thus defined has, under the English constitution, the right to make or unmake any law whatever: and, further, that no person or body is recognised by the law of England as having a right to override or set aside the legislation of Parliament.'

neither 'sovereign' nor a 'state'. Its powers are *not inherent* powers. They must be *conferred* on it by the Member States in the European Treaties. This constitutional principle is called the 'principle of conferral'. The Treaty on European Union defines it as follows:

> Under the principle of conferral, the Union shall act only within the limits of the competences conferred upon it by the Member States in the Treaties to attain the objectives set out therein. Competences not conferred upon the Union in the Treaties remain with the Member States.[7]

The Treaties employ the notion of competence in various provisions. Nevertheless, there is no positive definition of the concept. So, what is a legislative competence? The best definition is this: a legislative competence is the *material field* within which an authority is entitled to legislate. What are these material fields in which the Union is entitled to legislate? The Treaties do *not* enumerate the Union's 'competences' in a single list. Instead, the Treaties pursue a different technique: they attribute legislative competence for each and every Union activity in the respective Treaty title. Each policy area contains a provision – sometimes more than one – on which Union legislation can be based. The various Union policies and internal actions of the Union are set out in Part III of the Treaty on the Functioning of the European Union (Table 7.1).[8]

The Treaties here present a picture of thematically limited competences in distinct policy areas. This picture is however – partly – misleading. Three legal developments significantly undermined the principle of conferral in the past; and these developments have led to widespread accusations that the European Union's competences are 'unlimited'. First, there has been a rise and general use of teleological interpretation. The Union's competences are often interpreted in such a way that they 'spill over' into policy areas that were – arguably – outside the Union's competence sphere. This 'spillover' effect can be particularly observed with regard to a second development: the rise of the Union's general competences. These are competences that are not confined to a specific 'thematic' area, but horizontally cut across various policy titles within the Treaties. The two most general Union competences thereby are: Articles 114 and 352 TFEU. The former can be found in Title VII and deals with the internal market; the latter is placed in the final provisions of the TFEU. Lastly, a third development has equally undermined the principle of conferral significantly: the doctrine of implied powers. However, that development will be looked at in Chapter 8 in the context of the Union's external powers.[9]

---

[7] Art. 5(2) TEU.

[8] And yet there exist some legal bases outside Part III of the TFEU, such as Art. 16(2) TFEU 'on rules relating to the protection of individuals with regard to the processing of personal data by Union institutions', and Art. 352 TFEU – the Union's most famous legal base.

[9] On this point, see Chapter 8, section 1(c/aa).

Table 7.1 Union Policies and Internal Actions

Part III TFEU – Union Policies and Internal Actions			
Title I	The Internal Market	Title XIII	Culture
Title II	Free Movement of Goods	Title XIV	Public Health
Title III	Agriculture and Fisheries	Title XV	Consumer Protection
Title IV	Free Movement of Persons, Services and Capital	Title XVI	Trans-European Networks
Title V	Area of Freedom, Security and Justice	Title XVII	Industry
Title VI	Transport	Title XVIII	Economic, Social and Territorial Cohesion
Title VII	Common Rules on Competition, Taxation and Approximation of Laws	Title XIX	Research and Technological Development and Space
Title VIII	Economic and Monetary Policy	Title XX	Environment
Title IX	Employment	Title XXI	Energy
Title X	Social Policy	Title XXII	Tourism
Title XI	The European Social Fund	Title XXIII	Civil Protection
Title XII	Education, Vocational Training, Youth and Sport	Title XXIV	Administrative Cooperation

Article 192
The European Parliament and the Council, acting in accordance with the ordinary legislative procedure ... shall decide what action is to be taken by the Union in order to achieve the objectives referred to in Article 191.

Title XX – Environment	
Article 191	Aims and Objectives
Article 192	**Legislative Competence**
Article 193	Powers of the Member States

a. Teleological Interpretation

The Union must act 'within the limits of the competences conferred upon it *by the Member States*'.[10] Did this mean that the *Member States* would be able to determine the scope of the Union's competences? A *strict* principle of conferral would indeed deny the Union the power autonomously to interpret its competences. But this solution encounters serious practical problems: how is the Union to work if every legislative bill would need to gain the consent of every national parliament? Classic international organisations solve this dilemma between theory and practice by insisting that the interpretation of international

---

[10] Art. 5(2) TEU (emphasis added).

treaties must be in line with the historical intentions of the Member States.[11] Legal competences will thus be interpreted restrictively. This restrictive interpretation is designed to preserve the sovereign rights of the States by preserving the historical meaning of the founding treaty.

By contrast, a *soft* principle of conferral allows for the teleological interpretation of competences. Instead of looking at the historical will of the founders, teleological interpretation asks what is the purpose – or *telos* – of a rule. It thus looks behind the legal text in search for a legal solution to a social problem that may not have been anticipated when the text was drafted. Teleological interpretation can therefore constitute a 'small' amendment of the original rule. It is potentially a method of incremental change that complements the – rare – qualitative changes following 'big' Treaty amendments.

Has the Union been able autonomously to interpret the scope of its competences, and if so how? After a brief period of following international law logic,[12] the Union embraced the constitutional technique of teleological interpretation. This technique can be seen in relation to the interpretation of the Union's *competences*, as well as in relation to the interpretation of European *legislation*.

The first situation is famously illustrated in the controversy surrounding the adoption of the (first) Working Time Directive.[13] The directive had been based on a provision within Title X on 'Social Policy'. That provision allowed the Union to 'encourage improvements, especially in the working environment, as regards the health and safety of workers'.[14] Would this competence entitle the Union to adopt legislation on the general organisation of working time?[15] The United Kingdom strongly contested this teleological reading. It claimed that there was no thematic link to health and safety, and that the Union legislator had therefore acted ultra vires. The Court, however, backed up the Union legislator. Its teleological reasoning was as follows:

---

[11]　In international law, this principle is called the '*in dubio mitius*' principle. In case of a doubt, the 'milder' interpretation should be preferred.

[12]　See e.g. Case 8/55, *Fédération Charbonnière de Belgique* v. *High Authority of the European Coal and Steel Community* [1955] ECR 245.

[13]　Case C-84/94, *United Kingdom of Great Britain and Northern Ireland* v. *Council (Working Time Directive)* [1996] ECR I-5755.

[14]　Ex-Art. 118a (1) EEC. This competence is today Art. 153(1)(a) TFEU, which allows the Union to support and implement the activities of the Member States as regards the 'improvement in particular of the working environment to protect workers' health and safety'.

[15]　Section II of Directive 93/104 regulated the minimum rest periods. Member States were obliged to introduce national laws to ensure that every worker is entitled to a minimum daily rest period of 11 consecutive hours per 24-hour period (*ibid.*, Art. 3), and to a rest break where the working day is longer than six hours (*ibid.*, Art. 4). Art. 5 granted a minimum uninterrupted rest period of 24 hours in each seven-day period, and determined that this period should in principle include Sunday. Art. 6 established a maximum weekly working time of 48 hours; and finally, the directive established four weeks' paid annual leave (*ibid.*, Art. 7).

> There is nothing in the wording of Article [153 TFEU] to indicate that the concepts of 'working environment', 'safety' and 'health' as used in that provision should, in the absence of other indications, be interpreted restrictively, and not as embracing all factors, physical or otherwise, capable of affecting the health and safety of the worker in his working environment, including in particular certain aspects of the organisation of working time.[16]

Apart from a few famous exceptions,[17] the European Court has indeed accepted all the teleological interpretations of Union competences by the Union legislator in the past.

More than that: the Court itself interprets Union legislation in a teleological manner. The classic case in this context is *Casagrande*.[18] In order to facilitate the free movement of persons in the internal market, the Union had adopted legislation designed to abolish discrimination between workers of different Member States as regards employment, remuneration and other conditions of work.[19] And to facilitate the integration of the worker and his family into the host state, Union legislation contained the following provision:

> The children of a national of a Member State who is or has been employed in the territory of another Member State *shall be admitted* to that State's general educational, apprenticeship and vocational training courses under the same conditions as the nationals of that State, if such children are residing in its territory. Member States shall encourage all efforts to enable such children to attend these courses under the best possible conditions.[20]

Would this provision entitle the son of an Italian worker employed in Germany to receive an educational grant for his studies? Literally interpreted, the provision exclusively covered the 'admission' of workers' children to the educational system of the host state. But the Court favoured a teleological interpretation that would maximise 'the useful effect' (*effet utile*) behind the Union law. And, since the purpose of the provision was 'to ensure that the children may take advantage on an equal footing of the educational and training

---

[16] Case C 84/94 (n. 13 above), para. 15. The Court, however, annulled the second sentence of Art. 5 of the directive that had tried to protect, in principle, Sunday as a weekly rest period. In the opinion of the Court, the Council had 'failed to explain why Sunday, as a weekly rest day, is more closely connected with the health and safety of workers than any other day of the week' (*ibid.*, para. 37).

[17] See e.g. Case C-376/98, *Germany v. Parliament and Council (Tobacco Advertising)* [2000] ECRI-8419. This famous exception will be discussed below.

[18] Case 9/74, *Casagrande v. Landeshauptstadt München* [1974] ECR 773.

[19] Regulation 1612/68 on freedom of movement for workers within the Community [1968] OJ English Special Edition 475.

[20] *Ibid.*, Art. 12 (emphasis added).

facilities available', it followed that the provision referred '*not only to rules relating to admission*, but also to general measures intended to facilitate educational attendance'.[21] Thus, despite the fact that the (then) Treaties did not confer an express competence in educational matters to the Union, the Court considered that national educational grants fell within the scope of European legislation. The teleological interpretation of Union legislation thus 'spilled over' into a sphere that the Member States had believed to have remained within their exclusive competence.

b. The General Competences of the Union

In principle, the European Treaties grant a specific competence to legislate within each policy area. We thus find the Union's competence on environmental protection, in the Treaty's title dedicated to the environment (Table 7.1). Yet in addition to these specific competences, the Union legislator also enjoys two general competences. These competences are not specific to a policy area but *horizontally* cut through the Union's sectoral policies; and they have even been used – or some might say abused – to develop policies not expressly mentioned in the Treaties. The two 'bad boys' in that context are Articles 114 and Article 352 TFEU. The former represents the Union's 'internal market competence'; the latter constitutes its 'residual competence'.

aa. The Internal Market Competence: Article 114

On the basis of Article 114 TFEU, the European Union is entitled to adopt measures for the approximation of national laws 'which have as their object the establishment and functioning of the internal market'. Already the wording of the competence betrays a significant difference to the Union's specific competences. For instead of a policy 'area' – like the environment – in which the Union is entitled to act, the competence is defined by means of an 'objective' – the internal market – that needs to be achieved. It is for this reason that Article 114 is sometimes characterised as a teleological competence; and it is for this reason also that the 'scope' of the competence is so elusive.

What is the scope of Article 114? In the past, the Union legislator has given an extremely wide interpretation of this general competence.[22] Its potentially unlimited scope is illustrated by *Spain v. Council*,[23] where the Court held that Article 114 could not only be used to generally legislate where there was a divergence of national laws on a given issue but that the Union could also legislate so as '*to prevent the heterogeneous development of national laws* leading to further disparities which would be likely to create obstacles to the free movement'.[24]

---

[21] Case 9/74, *Casagrande*, paras. 8–9 (emphasis added).

[22] For a more extensive discussion of the past and present interpretation of Art. 114 TFEU, see Chapter 14, section 1.

[23] Case C-350/92, *Spain v. Council* [1995] ECR I-1985.

[24] *Ibid.*, para. 35 (emphasis added).

The European legislator was thus entitled to prevent *future* obstacles to trade or a *potential* fragmentation of the internal market!

For a long time, the scope of the Union's internal market power therefore appeared devoid of constitutional boundaries. Yet the existence of such constitutional limits was famously confirmed in *Germany v. Parliament and Council (Tobacco Advertising)*.[25] The bone of contention here was a European directive that banned the advertising and sponsorship of tobacco products.[26] Could a prohibition or ban be based on the Union's internal market competence? Germany objected to the idea and argued that the Union's internal market power could only be used to *promote* trade in the internal market; and this was not so, where the Union legislation limited trade within the internal market by a total prohibition of tobacco advertising.[27] The Court accepted – to the surprise of many – the argument. It therefore annulled, for the first time in its history, European legislation on the grounds that it went beyond the Union's internal market power. Emphatically, the Court pointed out that the latter could not grant the Union an unlimited power to regulate the internal market:

> To construe that article as meaning that it vests in the [Union] legislature a general power to regulate the internal market would not only be contrary to the express wording of the provisions cited above but would also be incompatible with the principle embodied in Article [5 TEU] that the powers of the [Union] are limited to those specifically conferred on it. Moreover, a measure adopted on the basis of Article [114 TFEU] of the Treaty must genuinely have as its object the improvement of the conditions for the establishment and functioning of the internal market. If a mere finding of disparities between national rules and of the abstract risk of obstacles to the exercise of fundamental freedoms or of distortions of competition liable to result therefrom were sufficient to justify the choice of Article [114] as a legal basis, judicial review of compliance with the proper legal basis might be rendered nugatory.[28]

With *Tobacco Advertising*, the Court has come to insist on *three* constitutional limits on the Union's internal market power. First, a European law must *harmonise* national laws. Thus, Union legislation 'which leaves unchanged the different national laws already in existence, cannot be regarded as aiming to approximate the laws of the Member States'.[29] Second, a simple disparity in national laws will

---

[25] Case C-376/98, *Tobacco Advertising*.

[26] Directive 98/43/EC on the approximation of the laws, regulations and administrative provisions of the Member States relating to the advertising and sponsorship of tobacco products [1998] OJ L 213/9.

[27] Germany had pointed out that the sole form of advertising allowed under the directive was advertising at the point of sale, which only accounted for 2 per cent of the tobacco industry's advertising expenditure (Case C-376/98, *Tobacco Advertising*, para. 24).

[28] *Ibid.*, paras. 83–4.

[29] Case C-436/03, *European Parliament v. Council of the EU* [2006] ECR I-3733, para. 44.

not be enough to trigger the Union's general competence. The disparity must give rise to obstacles in trade or appreciable distortions in competition. Thus, while Article 114 TFEU can be used to 'harmonise' *future* disparities in national laws, it must be 'likely' that the divergent development of national laws leads to obstacles in trade.[30] Third, Union legislation must actually contribute to the elimination of obstacles to free movement or distortions of competition.[31]

These three constitutional limits to the Union's 'internal market power' have been confirmed *in abstracto*;[32] yet subsequent jurisprudence has led to fresh accusations that Article 114 grants the Union an (almost) unlimited competence.[33] The competence has thus recently been used to abolish roaming surcharges when mobile telephones are used abroad.[34] It has also been used to prohibit the sale of menthol cigarettes; while generally requiring tobacco manufacturers to have 65 per cent of the external surfaces of each cigarette packet be covered by health warnings.[35]

bb. The Residual Competence: Article 352

Article 352 TFEU constitutes the most general competence within the Treaties. Comparable to the 'Necessary and Proper Clause' in the US Constitution,[36] it states:

> If action by the Union should prove *necessary, within the framework of the policies defined in the Treaties, to attain one of the objectives set out in the Treaties, and the Treaties have not provided the necessary powers*, the Council, acting unanimously on a proposal from the Commission and after obtaining the consent of the European Parliament, shall adopt the appropriate measures. Where the measures in question are adopted by the Council in accordance with a special legislative procedure, it shall also act unanimously on a proposal from the Commission and after obtaining the consent of the European Parliament.[37]

[30] Case C–376/98, *Tobacco Advertising*, para. 86.

[31] Case C–491/01, *The Queen v. Secretary of State for Health, ex p. British American Tobacco(Investments) Ltd and Imperial Tobacco Ltd* [2002] ECR I-11453, para. 60.

[32] On this point, see *ibid.*, and Case C–380/03, *Germany v. Parliament and Council (Tobacco Advertising II)* [2006] ECR I-11573; and now: Case C–547/14, *Philip Morris Brands and others v. Secretary of State for Health*, EU:C:2016325.

[33] For a more detailed analysis, see Chapter 14, section 1.

[34] Regulation 531/2012 on roaming on public mobile communications networks within the Union, [2012] OJ L 172/10 (as amended). Art. 6a here abolished retail-roaming surcharges as from 15 June 2017.

[35] Directive 2014/40 on the approximation of the laws, regulations and administrative provisions of the Member States concerning the manufacture, presentation and sale of tobacco products and related products, [2014] OJ L 127/1, esp. Arts. 7 and 10. The Directive was unsuccessfully challenged in Case C–547/14, *Philip Morris* – a case that will be discussed in Chapter 14 in more detail.

[36] According to Art. I, s. 8, cl. 18 of the US Constitution, the American Union shall have the power '[t]o make all Laws which shall be necessary and proper for carrying into Execution the foregoing Powers, and all other Powers vested by this Constitution in the Government of the United States, or in any Department or Officer thereof'.

[37] Art. 352(1) TFEU (emphasis added).

The competence may be used to adopt legislation (as well as executive acts); and it may thereby be used in two ways. First, it can be employed in a policy title in which the Union is already given a specific competence, but where the latter is deemed insufficient to achieve a specific objective. Second, the residual competence can be used to develop a policy area that has no specific title within the Treaties (see Figure 7.1).

The textbook illustration for the second – and more dangerous – use of Article 352 is provided by the development of a Union environmental policy *prior* to its becoming an express Union competence through the Single European Act. For, stimulated by the political enthusiasm to develop such a European policy following the 1972 Paris Summit, the Commission and the Council indeed developed the policy without a specific competence title offered by the Treaties. The Member States themselves had here called on the Union institutions to make the widest possible use of all provisions of the Treaties, especially Article 352.[38] The 'indirect' development of a European environmental policy in the following years was indeed impressive.[39] It was only sidelined once the Union finally received an express competence in environmental matters in 1987.

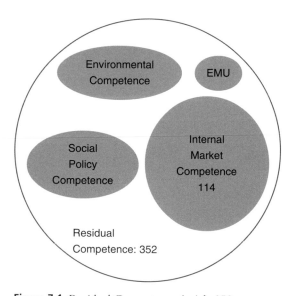

Figure 7.1 Residual Competence: Article 352

[38] The Declaration read: 'They [Heads of State or Government] agreed that in order to accomplish the tasks laid out in the different action programmes, it was advisable to use as widely as possible all the provisions of the Treaties *including* [*Article 352*]' (see European Council, First Summit Conference of the Enlarged Community; [1972] 10 *Bulletin of the European Communities*, 9 at 23 (emphasis added)).

[39] Prior to the entry into force of the SEA, a significant number of environment-related measures were adopted on the basis of Arts. 115 and 352, thus 'laying the foundation for the formation of a very specific [Union] environmental policy' (see F. Tschofen, 'Article 235 of the Treaty Establishing the European Economic Community: Potential Conflicts between the Dynamics of Lawmaking in the Community and National Constitutional Principles' (1991) 12 *Michigan Journal of International Law* 471 at 477).

Are there conceptual limits to Article 352? The provision establishes two textual limitations. First, '[m]easures based on this Article shall not entail harmonisation of Member States' laws or regulations in cases where the Treaties exclude such harmonisation'.[40] This precludes the use of the Union's residual competence in specific policy areas in which the Union is limited to merely 'complementing' national action.[41] Second, Article 352 'cannot serve as a basis for attaining objectives pertaining to the common foreign and security policy'.[42] This codifies past jurisprudence,[43] and is designed to protect the constitutional boundary drawn between the Treaty on European Union and the Treaty on the Functioning of the European Union.[44]

In addition to these express constitutional boundaries, the European Court has also recognised an *implied* limitation to the Union's residual competence. While accepting that Article 352 can be used for 'small' Treaty amendments, the Court has insisted that it could not be used to effect 'qualitative leaps' that constitute big changes to the constitutional identity of the European Union.[45] This was confirmed in *Opinion 2/94*.[46] The European Court had been requested to preview the Union's power to accede to the European Convention on Human Rights (ECHR) – at a time when there was no express power to do so in the Treaties.[47] The Court characterised the relationship between the Union's residual competence and the principle of conferral here as follows:

> Article [352] is designed to fill the gap where no specific provisions of the Treaty confer on the [Union] institutions express or implied powers to act, if such powers appear none the less to be necessary to enable the [Union] to carry out its functions with a view to attaining one of the objectives laid down by the Treaty. That provision, being an integral part of an institutional system based on the principle of conferred powers, cannot serve as a basis for widening the scope of [Union] powers *beyond the general framework* created by the provisions of the Treaty as a whole and, in particular, by those that define the *tasks* and the *activities* of the [Union]. On any view, Article [352] cannot be used as a basis for the adoption of provisions whose effect would, in substance, be to amend the Treaty without following the procedure which it provides for that purpose.[48]

[40] Art. 352(3) TFEU.

[41] On 'complementary' competences in the Union legal order that exclude all harmonisation, see section 2(d) below.

[42] Art. 352(4) TFEU.

[43] See Case C-402/05P, *Kadi et al.* v. *Council and Commission* [2008] ECR I-6351, paras. 198–9.

[44] See Art. 40 TEU. The provision will be extensively discussed in Chapter 8, section 1(d).

[45] A. Tizzano, 'The Powers of the Community', in Commission (ed.), *Thirty Years of Community Law* (Office for Official Publications of the EC, 1981), 43 at 58 9: 'To be more specific Article [352] cannot go beyond the bounds, described below, set by what has become known as the [European] constitution.' The author then lists three criteria, namely the 'observance of the principles essential to the organisation's structure', the 'observance of substantial principles of the [European] constitution' and the 'observance of the general principles of law laid down by the Court of Justice', thereby anticipating the ECJ's stance in *Opinion 2/94*.

[46] *Opinion 2/94* (Accession to the ECHR I) [1996] ECR I-1759.

[47] Following the Lisbon Treaty, the Union now has the express competence to accede to the Convention (see Art. 6(2) TEU). On this point, see Chapter 12, section 3(b).

[48] *Opinion 2/94* (n. 46 above), paras. 29–30 (emphasis added).

The general framework of the Treaty is here described as an outer jurisdictional boundary within which any legislative activity of the Union has to take place. The judicial reasoning in the second part of the judgment was then as follows. The Court found that the accession of the Union to the ECHR would have '*fundamental institutional implications* for the [Union] and for the Member States' and, since accession 'would be of *constitutional significance*', it would go beyond the scope of Article [352].[49]

Despite these – express and implied – conceptual limits, Article 352 has in the past been (almost) boundless. With the European Court granting the Union legislature (almost) complete freedom to interpret the scope of this competence, the only 'real' limit to Article 352 seems to lie in a political safeguard: unanimous voting in the Council. Yet even this political limit has increasingly come to be seen as insufficient. Fearful that a national minister would 'go native' when voting in Brussels, some Member States have thus established prior parliamentary authorisation mechanisms for Article 352. Following the lead from Germany,[50] the 2011 (British) European Union Act here insists as follows:

Section 8: Decisions under Article 352 TFEU

1. A Minister of the Crown may not vote in favour of or otherwise support an Article 352 decision unless one of subsections (3) to (5) is complied with in relation to the draft decision.
2. ...
3. This subsection is complied with if a draft decision is approved by Act of Parliament.
4. This subsection is complied with if –
   (a) in each House of Parliament a Minister of the Crown moves a motion that the House approves Her Majesty's Government's intention to support a specified draft decision and is of the opinion that the measure to which it relates is required as a matter of urgency, and
   (b) each House agrees to the motion without amendment.
5. This subsection is complied with if a Minister of the Crown has laid before Parliament a statement specifying a draft decision and stating that in the opinion of the Minister the decision relates only to one or more exempt purposes.[51]

---

[49] *Ibid.*, para. 35.

[50] In its Lisbon Decision, the German Constitutional Court referred to the 'indefinite' scope of Art. 352 TFEU, whose use – coming close to a Treaty amendment – would require the consent of the German Parliament, see BVerfGE 123, 267 (Lisbon), para. 328: 'Because of the indefinite nature of future application of the flexibility clause, its use constitutionally requires ratification by the German *Bundestag* and the *Bundesrat* on the basis of Article 23.1 second and third sentence of the Basic Law. The German representative in the Council may not express formal approval on behalf of the Federal Republic of Germany of a corresponding lawmaking proposal of the Commission as long as these constitutionally required preconditions are not met.'

[51] These exemptions are defined in para. 6: 'The exempt purposes are – (a) to make provision equivalent to that made by a measure previously adopted under Article 352 TFEU, other than an excepted measure; (b) to prolong or renew a measure previously adopted under that Article, other than an excepted measure; (c) to extend a measure previously adopted under that Article to another member State or other country; (d) to repeal existing measures adopted under that Article; (e) to consolidate existing measures adopted under that Article without any change of substance.'

2. Categories of Union Competences

The original Treaties did not specify the relationship between European and national competences.[52] They indeed betrayed no sign of a distinction between different competence categories.

Two competing conceptions therefore emerged in the early days of the Union legal order.[53] According to a first theory, all competences mentioned in the Treaties were exclusive competences. The Member States had fully 'transferred' their powers to the European Union,[54] and the division of powers between the Union and the Member States was thus based on a strict separation of competences.[55] An alternative second conception of the nature of Union competences also emerged in those early days: all the Union's powers were shared powers.[56] Member States had only renounced *their* exclusive right to act within their territory by permitting the Union to share in the exercise of public functions. The constitutional development of the European legal order was to take place between these two extreme conceptions. Different categories of Union competence were thus 'discovered' in the course of the 1970s.

What is the purpose of having different competence categories? Different types of competences constitutionally pitch the *relative degree of responsibility of two public authorities* within a material policy field. The respective differences are of a relational kind: exclusive competences 'exclude' the other authority from acting within the same policy area, while non-exclusive competences permit the coexistence of two legislators. Importantly, in order to provide a clear picture of the federal division of powers, each policy area should ideally correspond to one competence category.

What then are the competence categories developed in the European legal order? The Treaties today distinguish between various categories of Union competence in Article 2 TFEU. The provision reads as follows:

---

[52] J. V. Louis, 'Quelques réflexions sur la répartition des compétences entre la communauté européenne et ses états membres' (1979) 2 *Revue d'intégration européenne* 355 .

[53] For an early discussion of these two conceptions, see Tizzano, 'Powers of the Community' (n. 45 above), 63–7. Tizzano calls the first conception the 'federalist' view, the second conception the 'internationalist' view.

[54] This is the term used in Case 6/64, *Costa* v. *ENEL* [1964] ECR 585: 'By creating a [Union] of unlimited duration, having its own institutions, its own personality, its own legal capacity and capacity of representation on the international plane and, more particularly, *real powers stemming from a limitation of sovereignty or a transfer of powers from the States to the [Union]*, the Member States have limited their sovereign rights, albeit within limited fields, and have thus created a body of law which binds both their nationals and themselves' (emphasis added).

[55] The exclusivity thesis had been fuelled by early pronouncements of the European Court (see e.g. Case 30/59, *De Gezamenlijke Steenkolenmijnen in Limburg* v. *High Authority of the European Coal and Steel Community* [1961] ECR 1, para. 22: 'In the Community field, namely in respect of everything that pertains to the pursuit of the common objectives within the Common Market, the institutions of the Community have been endowed with exclusive authority'.).

[56] See e.g. H. P. Ipsen, *Europäisches Gemeinschaftsrecht* (J. C. B. Mohr, 1972), 432.

1. When the Treaties confer on the Union exclusive competence in a specific area, only the Union may legislate and adopt legally binding acts, the Member States being able to do so themselves only if so empowered by the Union or for the implementation of Union acts.

2. When the Treaties confer on the Union a competence shared with the Member States in a specific area, the Union and the Member States may legislate and adopt legally binding acts in that area. The Member States shall exercise their competence to the extent that the Union has not exercised its competence. The Member States shall again exercise their competence to the extent that the Union has decided to cease exercising its competence.

3. The Member States shall coordinate their economic and employment policies within arrangements as determined by this Treaty, which the Union shall have competence to provide.

4. The Union shall have competence, in accordance with the provisions of the Treaty on European Union, to define and implement a common foreign and security policy, including the progressive framing of a common defence policy.

5. In certain areas and under the conditions laid down in the Treaties, the Union shall have competence to carry out actions to support, coordinate or supplement the actions of the Member States, without thereby superseding their competence in these areas. Legally binding acts of the Union adopted on the basis of the provisions of the Treaties relating to these areas shall not entail harmonisation of Member States' laws or regulations.

The Treaties thus expressly recognise four general competence categories: exclusive competences, shared competences, coordinating competences and complementary competences (Figure 7.2); and Articles 3–6 TFEU correlate the various Union policies to a particular competence category. In addition, Article 2(4) TFEU acknowledges a separate competence category for the Union's common foreign and security policy. This section analyses the Union's internal competence categories, while the Union's CFSP competence will be discussed in Chapter 8.

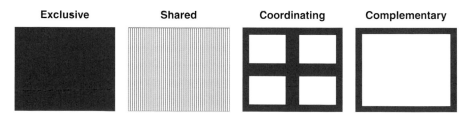

Figure 7.2 Competence Types

a. *Exclusive Competences: Article 3*

Exclusive powers are constitutionally guaranteed monopolies. Only one governmental level is entitled to act autonomously. Exclusive competences are thus double-edged provisions. Their positive side entitles one authority to act, while their negative side 'excludes' anybody else from acting autonomously within their scope. For the European legal order, exclusive competences are defined as areas, in which 'only the Union may legislate and adopt legally binding acts'. The Member States will only be able to act 'if so empowered by the Union or for the implementation of Union acts'[57].

What are the policy areas of constitutional exclusivity? In the past, the Court had accepted a number of competences to qualify under this type. The first exclusive competence was discovered in the context of the Common Commercial Policy (CCP). In *Opinion 1/75*,[58] the Court found that the existence of a merely shared competence within the field would 'compromise … the effective defence of the common interests of the [Union]'.[59] A second area of exclusive competence was soon discovered in relation to the conservation of biological resources of the sea. In *Commission* v. *United Kingdom*,[60] the Court found that Member States would 'no longer [be] entitled to exercise any power of their own in the matter of conservation measures in the waters under their jurisdiction'.[61]

Article 3 TFEU now expressly mentions five exclusive policy areas: (a) the customs union; (b) the establishment of the competition rules necessary for the functioning of the internal market; (c) monetary policy for the Member States whose currency is the euro; (d) the conservation of marine biological resources under the common fisheries policy; and (e) the common commercial policy.[62] In the light of the judicial status quo, this enumeration poses some problems,[63] but the Court has confirmed this list in the past.[64]

---

[57] Art. 2(1) TFEU.

[58] *Opinion 1/75* (Draft understanding on a local cost standard) [1975] ECR 1355.

[59] *Ibid.*, para. 13.

[60] Case 804/79, *Commission* v. *United Kingdom* [1981] ECR 1045.

[61] *Ibid.*, para. 18.   [62] Art. 3(1) TFEU.

[63] There was arguably no need to expressly mention the exclusive competence for the establishment of a customs union: on the one hand, the competence to establish *intra-Union* customs has been 'abolished'; and, regarding the *external* aspect of the customs union competence, on the other hand, the adoption of a common customs tariff is already covered by the Union's CCP competence. Second, what distinguishes the competition rules from the establishment of *all other rules* 'necessary for the functioning of the internal market'? The constitutional drafters seem to have fallen victim to a logical fallacy: these rules will not necessarily require the exclusion of all national action within their scope. Finally, subparagraph (d) codifies a constitutional chestnut that, in light of its subsequent judicial biography, could well have been (re)integrated into the European Union's *shared* agricultural competence. For a general discussion here, see R. Schütze, 'Dual Federalism Constitutionalised: The Emergence of Exclusive Competences in the EC Legal Order' (2007) 32 *EL Rev.* 3, 22–3.

[64] See Case C-550/07P, *Akzo Nobel Chemicals et al.* v. *Commission* (2010), ECR I-8301; Case C-370/12, *Pringle* v. *Ireland*, EU:C:2012:756.

b. Shared Competences: Article 4

aa. General Considerations

Shared competences are the 'ordinary' competences of the European Union. Unless the Treaties expressly provide otherwise, a Union competence will be shared.[65] Within a shared competence, 'the Union and the Member States may legislate';[66] yet according to the formulation in Article 2(2) TFEU both appear to be prohibited from acting at the same time:

> The Member States shall exercise their competence to the extent that the Union has not exercised its competence.

This formulation invokes the geometrical image of a divided field: the Member States may only legislate in that part which the European Union has not (yet) entered. Within one field, *either* the European Union *or* the Member States can exercise their shared competence.[67] But when viewed against the constitutional status quo ante, this is a misleading conception of shared competences. For, in the past 60 years, shared competences generally allowed the Union and the Member States to act in the same field at the same time. The exception to that rule concerned situations where the Union field pre-empted the Member States.[68] The formulation in Article 2(2) TFEU is based on that exception.[69] Will the technique of EU minimum harmonisation – allowing for higher national standards adopted in addition to the Union standards – thus be in danger? This seems doubtful, since the Treaties expressly identify minimum harmonisation competences as shared competences.[70]

Sadly, this pre-emption problem is not the only textual problem within Article 4 TFEU. For the provision recognises a special type of shared competence in Articles 4(3) and (4) TFEU. Both paragraphs separate the policy areas of research, technological development and space, as well as development cooperation and humanitarian aid from the 'normal' shared competences. What is so special about

---

[65]   Art. 4 TFEU states that EU competences will be shared 'where the Treaties confer on [the Union] a competence which does not relate to the areas referred to in Article 3 and 6', that is: areas of exclusive or complementary EU competence.

[66]   Art. 2(2) TFEU.

[67]   The Union may, however, decide to 'cease exercising its competence'. This reopening of legislative space arises 'when the relevant EU institutions decide to repeal a legislative act, in particular better to ensure constant respect for the principles of subsidiarity and proportionality'. See Declaration No. 18 'In relation to the delimitation of competences'.

[68]   On the various pre-emption types, see Chapter 4, section 3.

[69]   The Treaties however clarify that such field pre-emption would 'only' be taking place in relation to the legislative act (see Protocol No. 25 On the Exercise of Shared Competence: 'With reference to Article 2 of the Treaty on the Functioning of the European Union on shared competence, when the Union has taken action in a certain area, the scope of this exercise of competence only covers those elements governed by the Union act in question and therefore does not cover the whole [competence] area').

[70]   See Art. 4(2)(e) TFEU on the shared 'environment' competence.

these areas? According to paragraphs 3 and 4, the 'exercise of that competence shall not result in Member States being prevented from exercising theirs'. But since that qualification actually undermines the very essence of what constitutes a 'shared' competence, set out in Article 2(2) TFEU, these policy areas should never have been placed there. This special type of shared competence has been described as parallel competence.[71]

bb. Minimum Harmonisation Competences

Minimum harmonisation competences are shared competences that confine the Union to the adoption of minimum standards. The Union's environmental competence is in many respects paradigmatic for this type of shared competence. The Union here enjoys a shared competence under Article 192; yet Article 193 also states:

> The protective measures adopted pursuant to Article 192 shall not prevent any Member State from maintaining or introducing more stringent protective measures. Such measures must be compatible with the Treaties.

European legislation can thus only lay down minimum environmental standards that must permit national 'opt-ups'.[72] Yet the central question is this: must all EU environmental laws be minimum harmonisation measures; or does Article 193 only 'softly' require the Union legislator to leave some – abstractly defined – legislative space to the national legislators? Surprisingly, after almost three decades of constitutional practice, the issue has not been definitively resolved.

Two views are possible. According to a first view, Article 193 will not constitutionally prevent the Union legislator from adopting individual EU environmental laws that totally pre-empt all matters within their scope.[73] This first view therefore only assumes a strong *presumption* against field pre-emption, but the Union legislator faces no *constitutional limitation* to exhaustively harmonising a specific environmental issue. By contrast, a second view argues that Article 193 refers to every single piece of European legislation. Each Union act must thus leave a

---

[71] But even this definition is problematic, for it is simply difficult to imagine that a Union *legal* act has no limiting effect whatsoever on the powers of the Member States. Assuming, for example, that the European Union takes a legal position within the area of development cooperation. Should we believe that *all national measures adopted within this area will be permitted*, even if they actually hinder or impede the EU scheme? For, if this was the case, why was there any need for expressly requiring that 'in order to promote the complementarity and efficiency of their action, the Union and the Member States *shall* coordinate their policies on development cooperation and *shall* consult each other on their aid programmes' (Art. 210 TFEU (emphasis added))? How can two parallels 'complement' each other and why emphasise a duty of cooperation for two levels that supposedly could never come into conflict?

[72] This is different from the 'opt-out' mechanism in Art. 114(4)–(9) TFEU, which allows for a *derogation* from European legislation. See Chapter 14, section 1(d).

[73] J. H. Jans, *European Environmental Law* (Europa Law Publishing, 2000), 118.

degree of legislative space to the national legislators; and there are heavy legal arguments in favour of this *hard* constitutional solution. First, the very wording of Article 193 points in that direction. For the frame of reference for the higher national standard is not the Union's environmental *policy*, but the specific Union *measure(s)*. Second, from a teleological perspective, the aim of achieving a high level of protection within the Union would always be better served by allowing Member States to go beyond the compromise represented in the European legislation.[74] And, third, requiring the Union legislator to leave legislative space *within the scope of the European act*, would provide a concrete 'jurisdictional' standard that would better safeguard the Member States' legislative autonomy.

What are the judicial guidelines from the European Court of Justice? The nature of European environmental legislation has – partly – been addressed in the past;[75] and with *Azienda Agro-Zootecnica Franchini*,[76] the Court appears to favour the hard constitutional frame. The case concerned an Italian law under which it was forbidden to construct new wind turbines within a 500-metre buffer zone of a 'special protection area' – a prohibition that was claimed to violate a number of Union directives, *inter alia* the Birds and Habitats Directives. In its analysis of the stricter national law, the Court reasoned as follows:

> It should be noted in this regard that European Union rules do not seek to effect complete harmonisation in the area of the environment. Article 14 of the Birds Directive provides that Member States may introduce stricter protective measures than those provided for under that directive. *There is no provision in the Habitats Directive that is equivalent to Article 14 of the Birds Directive. Nevertheless, since that directive was adopted on the basis of Article 192 TFEU, it should be noted that Article 193 TFEU provides that Member States may adopt more stringent protective measures* ... It follows that legislation such as that at issue in the main proceedings which ... imposes an absolute prohibition on the construction of new wind turbines in those areas, pursues the same objectives as the Habitats Directive. To the extent that it provides for a stricter system of protection than that established by Article 6 of that directive, it therefore constitutes a more stringent protective measure within the meaning of Article 193 TFEU.[77]

---

[74] G. Winter, 'Die Sperrwirkung von Gemeinschaftssekundärrecht für einzelstaatliche Regelungen des Binnenmarkts mit besonderer Berücksichtigung von Art. 130 t EGV' [1998] 51 *Die öffentliche Verwaltung* 377 at 380.

[75] Case C-318/98, *Fornasar et al.* v. *Sante Chiarcosso* [2000] ECR I-4785; Case C-6/03, *Deponiezweckverband Eiterköpfe* v. *Land Rheinland-Pfalz* [2005] ECR I-2753.

[76] Case C-2/10, *Azienda Agro-Zootecnica Franchini sarl and Eolica di Altamura Srl* v. *Regione Puglia* [2011] ECR I-6561.

[77] *Ibid.*, paras. 48–52 (emphasis added).

The Court here suggests that even in the absence of a *legislative* clause expressly allowing for the adoption of stricter national standards, the Member States would always be allowed to go beyond the relevant Union legislation because of the *constitutional* guarantee offered in Article 193 TFEU.

c. Coordinating Competences: Article 5

Coordinating competences are defined in the third paragraph of Article 2 TFEU; and Article 5 TFEU places 'economic policy', 'employment policy' and 'social policy' within this category. The inspiration for this third category was the absence of a political consensus in the European Convention. Whereas one group wished to place economic and employment coordination within the category of shared competences, an opposing view advocated their classification as complementary competences. The Convention Presidium thus came to feel that 'the specific nature of the coordination of Member States' economic and employment policies merits a separate provision'.[78]

The constitutional character of coordinating competences remains largely undefined. From Articles 2 and 5 TFEU, we may solely deduce that the European Union has a competence to provide 'arrangements' for the Member States to exercise their competences in a coordinating manner. The Union's coordination effort may include the adoption of 'guidelines' and 'initiatives to ensure coordination'. It has been argued that the political genesis for this competence category should place it, on the normative spectrum, between shared and complementary competences.[79] If this systematic interpretation is accepted, coordinating competences would have to be normatively stronger than complementary competences. This would imply that the adoption of Union acts resulting in *some* degree of harmonisation would be constitutionally permitted under these competences.

d. Complementary Competences: Article 6

The term 'complementary competence' is not used in Article 2(5) TFEU. However, it appears to be the best way generically to refer to 'actions to support, coordinate or supplement the actions of the Member States'.[80] Article 6 TFEU lists seven areas: the protection and improvement of human health; industry; culture; tourism; education, vocational training, youth and sport; civil protection;

---

[78] The Presidium CONV 724/03 (Annex 2), p. 68. Arguably, the addition of a new competence type was unnecessary in light of Art. 2(6) TFEU. The provision states: 'The scope of and arrangements for exercising the Union's competences shall be determined by the provisions of the Treaties relating to each area.'

[79] In this sense, see P. Craig, 'Competence: Clarity, Conferral, Containment and Consideration' (2004) 29 *EL Rev.* 338.

[80] Art. 2(5) TFEU.

and administrative cooperation. Is this an exhaustive list? This should be the case in light of the residual character of shared competences.[81]

A good example of this competence type is the Union competence to protect human health, which is formulated as follows:

> Union action, which shall *complement* national policies, shall be directed towards improving public health, preventing physical and mental illness and diseases, and obviating sources of danger to physical and mental health … The Union shall encourage cooperation between the Member States in the areas referred to in this Article and, if necessary, lend support to their action. *It shall in particular encourage cooperation between the Member States to improve the complementarity of their health services in cross-border areas.*[82]

The contours of complementary competences are largely unexplored by jurisprudence. However, after the Lisbon reform, it now appears to be a defining characteristic of these competences that they do '*not entail harmonisation* of Member States' laws or regulations'.[83]

But what exactly is the prohibition of harmonisation here supposed to mean? Two views can be put forward. According to the first, the exclusion of harmonisation means that Union legislation must not affect *existing or future* national legislation. From this strict reading, the exclusion of harmonisation would consequently prohibit all pre-emptive effect to European legislation adopted under this competence type.[84] A second, less restrictive, view argues that the Union's legislative powers are only trimmed so as to prevent the de jure harmonisation of existing national legislation.[85] *Both* views appear, however, problematic. National legislators are – still – quicker in

---

[81] Prior to the Lisbon Treaty, the concept of complementary competence could be employed to refer to *two* types of competences. In the first group were those competences that constitutionally limit the European legislator to the adoption of minimum standards that could then be 'complemented' by higher national standards. The second group of 'complementary competences' expressly described the function of the Union legislator as 'complementing', 'supplementing' or 'supporting' national action by means of 'incentive measures' that would exclude all harmonisation within the field. Art. 2(5) TFEU restricts the definition of complementary competences to this second group. This definitional *fait accompli* places the first group into the residual category of shared competences. On the disadvantages of this terminological choice, see R. Schütze, 'Lisbon and the Federal Order of Competences: A Prospective Analysis' (2008) 33 *EL Rev.* 709, and Conclusion below.

[82] Art. 168(1) and (2) TFEU (emphasis added).

[83] *Ibid.*, Art. 2 (5) – second indent (emphasis added).

[84] See A. Bardenhewer-Rating and F. Niggermeier, 'Artikel 152', para. 20, in H. von der Groeben and J. Schwarze, *Kommentar zum Vertrag über die EU* (Nomos, 2003).

[85] For Lenaerts, 'incentive measures can be adopted in the form of Regulations, Directives, Decisions or atypical legal acts and are thus normal legislative acts of the [Union.]' '[T]he fact that a [European] incentive measure may have the indirect effect of harmonizing … does not necessarily mean that it conflicts with the prohibition on harmonization' (K. Lenaerts, 'Subsidiarity and Community Competence in the Field of Education' [1994–5] 1 *Columbia Journal of European Law* 1 at 13 and 15).

passing legislation than the Union legislator; and if a Member State thus wished to prevent Union action, it could be tempted to swiftly adopt a national law in the same area so as to 'block' future Union legislation.

3. Legislative Procedures: Ordinary and Special

British constitutionalism defines (primary) legislation as an act adopted by the Queen-in-Parliament. Behind this 'compound' legislator stands a legislative procedure. This legal procedure links the House of Commons, the House of Lords and the monarchy. EU constitutionalism also follows a procedural definition of legislative power. However, unlike British constitutional law, the Treaties expressly distinguish between two types of legislative procedures: an ordinary legislative procedure and special legislative procedures. Article 289 TFEU thus states:

> 1. The ordinary legislative procedure shall consist in the joint adoption by the European Parliament and the Council of a regulation, directive or decision on a proposal from the Commission. This procedure is defined in Article 294.
> 2. In the specific cases provided for by the Treaties, the adoption of a regulation, directive or decision by the European Parliament with the participation of the Council, or by the latter with the participation of the European Parliament, shall constitute a special legislative procedure.[86]

European 'legislation' is here – formally – defined as an act adopted by the bicameral Union legislator. (The Commission will ordinarily make legislative proposals, but this is not – strictly – an absolute characteristic of Union legislation.)[87] According to the *ordinary* legislative procedure, the European Parliament and the Council act as co-legislators with *symmetric* procedural rights. European legislation is therefore seen as the product of a 'joint adoption' by both institutions.

But the Treaties also recognise *special* legislative procedures. The defining characteristic of these special procedures is that they abandon the institutional equality of the European Parliament and the Council. Logically, then, Article 289(2) TFEU recognises two variants. In the first variant, the European Parliament acts as the dominant institution, with the mere 'participation' of the Council in the form of 'consent'.[88] The second variant inverts this relationship. The Council is

---

[86] Art. 289(1) and (2) TFEU.

[87] There is no mention of the Commission in Art. 289(2) TFEU, and Art. 289(4) TFEU adds: 'In the specific cases provided for by the Treaties, legislative acts may be adopted on the initiative of a group of Member States or of the European Parliament, on a recommendation from the European Central Bank or at the request of the Court of Justice or the European Investment Bank.'

[88] See *ibid.*, Arts. 223(2), 226 and 228. The procedure for the adoption of the Union budget is laid down in Art. 314 TFEU and will not be discussed here.

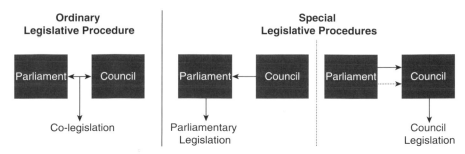

Figure 7.3 Structure of the union legislator

here the dominant institution, with the Parliament either participating through its 'consent',[89] or in the form of 'consultation'.[90] For an overview of the various legislative relations, see Figure 7.3.

What tells us when *which* legislative procedure applies? There is no constitutional rationale or procedure catalogue. Each legal basis within a policy area determines which procedure applies,[91] and whether that procedure is of a legislative nature. For example, the Union's internal market power in Article 114 TFEU states that the European Parliament and the Council shall act 'in accordance with the *ordinary legislative* procedure'. And the Treaty defines the ordinary legislative procedure in a section dedicated to the 'Procedures for the other Provisions'.[92] By contrast, there is no specific definition of what constitutes 'special' legislative procedures. They are thus defined in each specific legal basis. Article 352 TFEU – for example – allows for the adoption of Union measures 'in accordance with a *special legislative* procedure', and itself defines the latter as the Council acting unanimously after obtaining the consent of the European Parliament.

The following two subsections will analyse the ordinary and special legislative procedures in more detail.

a. The 'Ordinary' Legislative Procedure

aa. Constitutional Text: Formal Procedure

The ordinary legislative procedure has seven stages. Article 294 TFEU defines five stages; two additional stages are set out in Article 297 TFEU.

---

[89] See *ibid.*, Arts. 19(1), 25, 86(1), 223(1), 311, 312 and 352.

[90] See *ibid.*, Arts. 21(3), 22(1), 22(2), 23, 64(3), 77(3), 81(3), 87(3), 89, 113, 115, 118, 126, 127(6), 153(2), 182(4), 192(2), 203, 262, 308, 311, 349.

[91] Some legal bases require the consultation of an 'advisory' body. According to Art. 300 TFEU, the Union has two advisory bodies: the 'Economic and Social Committee', and the 'Committee of the Regions'. The former 'shall consist of representatives of organisations of employers, of the employed, and of other parties representative of civil society, notably in socioeconomic, civic, professional and cultural areas' (*ibid.*, para. 2), and its advisory powers are defined in Art. 304 TFEU. The Committee of the Regions consists of 'representatives of regional and local bodies who either hold a regional or local authority electoral mandate or are politically accountable to an elected assembly'. Its advisory powers are defined in Art. 307 TFEU.

[92] This is Part Six – Title I – Chapter 2 – Section 2 – Art. 294 TFEU.

Proposal stage. Under the ordinary legislative procedure, the Commission enjoys, with minor exceptions, the exclusive right to submit a legislative proposal.[93] This (executive) prerogative guarantees a significant agenda-setting power to the Commission. The Treaties partly protect this power from 'external' interferences by insisting that any amendment requires unanimity in the Council – an extremely high decisional hurdle.[94] And, as long as the Council has not acted, the Commission may alter its original proposal at will,[95] and can even decide to withdraw its proposal altogether. The Court has however clarified that especially the latter prerogative is subject to judicial review.[96]

First reading. The Commission proposal goes to the European Parliament. The Parliament will act by a majority of the votes cast,[97] that is: the majority of physically present members. It can reject the proposal, approve it, or – as a middle path – amend it. The bill then moves to the Council, which must act by a qualified majority of its members.[98] (It is here that the prerogative of the Commission to withdraw a proposal ends.) Where the Council agrees with Parliament's position, the bill is adopted with the first reading. Where it disagrees, the Council is called to provide its own position and communicate it, with reasons, to Parliament.

Second reading. The (amended) bill lies for the second time in Parliament's court; and Parliament has three choices as to what to do with it. Parliament may positively approve the Council's position by a majority of the votes cast;[99] or reject it by a majority of its component members.[100] Approval is thus easier than rejection.

---

[93] *Ibid.*, Art. 294(2). Para. 15 recognises exceptions to this rule in cases provided for in the Treaties. Perhaps the most significant exception is provided for by Art. 76 TFEU referring to legislative measures in the field of police and judicial cooperation in criminal matters.

[94] *Ibid.*, Art. 293(1).   [95] *Ibid.*, Art. 293(2).

[96] Case C-409/13, *Council* v. *Commission* (Right of Withdrawal), EU:C:2015:217. In this case, the Council argued 'that the Commission cannot derive from its right of legislative initiative enshrined in Article 17(2) TEU a symmetric right to withdraw a proposal' (*ibid.*, para. 33); and that a withdrawal out of 'pure political expediency' would 'be contrary to the principle of democracy' (*ibid.*, paras. 37–8) as well as the principle of sincere cooperation in Art. 13(2) TEU (*ibid.*, para. 47). The Court however principally rejected this view: 'contrary to the contentions of the Council and certain Member States, the Commission's power under the ordinary legislative procedure does not come down to submitting a proposal and, subsequently, promoting contact and seeking to reconcile the positions of the Parliament and the Council' (*ibid.*, 74). Therefore, as long as the Council had not formally acted, the Commission could not just alter its proposal but 'even, if need be, withdraw it' (*ibid.*). The Court nevertheless insisted that the Commission's decision to withdraw 'cannot, however, confer upon that institution a right of veto in the conduct of the legislative process' (*ibid.*, para. 75). It will therefore be subject to judicial review (*ibid.*, paras. 74–6). According to the Court, the Commission must show that the intended amendments of the Council and/ or the European Parliament would 'distort[] the proposal for a legislative act in a manner which prevents achievement of the objectives pursued by the proposal and which, therefore, deprives it of its *raison d'être*' (*ibid.*, para. 83).

[97] Art. 294(3) TFEU is silent on the voting regime within Parliament, and therefore Art. 231 TFEU applies: 'Save as otherwise provided in the Treaties, the European Parliament shall act by a majority of the votes cast. The rules of procedure shall determine the quorum.'

[98] Art. 294(4) and (5) TFEU is silent on the voting regime, and therefore Art. 16(4) TEU applies: 'The Council shall act by a qualified majority except where the Treaties provide otherwise.'

[99] *Ibid.*, Art. 294(7)(a).   [100] *Ibid.*, Art. 294(7)(b).

(This tendency is reinforced by assimilating passivity to approval.)[101] However, Parliament has a third choice: it may propose, by the majority of its component members, amendments to the Council's position.[102] The amended bill will be forwarded to the Council (and to the Commission which must deliver an opinion on the amendments). The bill is thus back in the Council's court, and the Council has two options. Where it approves all (!) of Parliament's amendments, the legislative act is adopted.[103] (The Council thereby acts by a qualified majority, unless the Commission disagrees with any of the amendments suggested by the Council or the Parliament.)[104] By contrast, where the Council cannot approve all of Parliament's amendments, the bill enters into the conciliation stage.[105]

Conciliation stage. This stage presents the last chance to rescue the legislative bill. As agreement within the 'formal' legislature has proved impossible, the Union legal order 'delegates' the power to draft a 'joint text' to a committee. This Committee is called the 'Conciliation Committee'.[106] The mandate of the Committee is restricted to reaching agreement on a joint text 'on the basis of the positions of the European Parliament and the Council at second reading'.[107] The Committee is composed of members representing the Council,[108] and an equal number of

---

[101] According to *ibid.*, Art. 294(7)(a) – second alternative, where the Parliament does not act within three months, 'the act shall be deemed to have been adopted in the wording which corresponds to the position of the Council'.

[102] *Ibid.*, Art. 294(7)(c). For an (internal) limitation on what types of amendments can be made, see Rule 69(2) of the Parliament's Rules of Procedure.

[103] Art. 294(8)(a) TFEU.   [104] *Ibid.*, Art. 294(9).   [105] *Ibid.*, Art. 294(8)(b).

[106] The Conciliation Committee is not a standing committee, but an ad hoc committee that 'is constituted separately for each legislative proposal requiring conciliation' (European Parliament, Codecision and Conciliation at: www.europarl.europa.eu/code/information/guide_en.pdf, 13).

[107] Art. 294(10) TFEU. However, the Court of Justice has been flexible and allowed the Conciliation Committee to find a joint text that goes beyond the common position after the second reading. See Case C-344/04, *The Queen on the application of International Air Transport Association et al.* v. *Department of Transport* [2006] ECR I-403, paras. 57–9: '[O]nce the Conciliation Committee has been convened, it has the task not of coming to an agreement on the amendments proposed by the Parliament but, as is clear from the very wording of Article [294 TFEU], "of reaching agreement on a joint text", by addressing, on the basis of the amendments proposed by the Parliament, the common position adopted by the Council. The wording of Article [294 TFEU] does not therefore itself include any restriction as to the content of the measures chosen that enable agreement to be reached on a joint text. In using the term "conciliation", the authors of the Treaty intended to make the procedure adopted effective and to confer a wide discretion on the Conciliation Committee. In adopting such a method for resolving disagreements, their very aim was that the points of view of the Parliament and the Council should be reconciled on the basis of examination of all the aspects of the disagreement, and with the active participation in the Conciliation Committee's proceedings of the Commission of the European Communities, which has the task of taking "all the necessary initiatives with a view to reconciling the positions of the … Parliament and the Council". In this light, taking account of the power to mediate thus conferred on the Commission and of the freedom which the Parliament and the Council finally have as to whether or not to accept the joint text approved by the Conciliation Committee, Article [294 TFEU] cannot be read as limiting on principle the power of that committee.'

[108] The Permanent Representative or his or her Deputy will typically represent the national ministers in the Council.

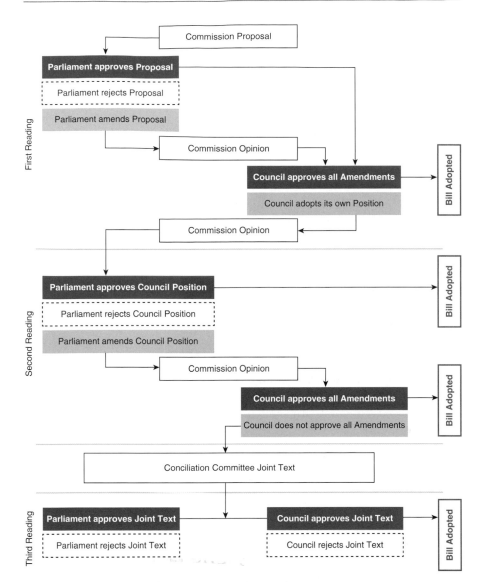

Figure 7.4 Ordinary Legislative Procedure under Article 294

members representing the European Parliament.[109] (The Commission will take part 'in' the committee, but is not a part 'of' the Committee. Its function is to be a mere catalyst for conciliation.)[110] The Committee indeed represents a 'miniature legislature'; and like its constitutional model, the Committee co-decides by a qualified majority of the Council representatives, and a majority of the representatives sent by Parliament. Where the Committee does not adopt a joint text, the legislative bill has failed. Where the Committee

---

[109] The parliamentary delegation must reflect the political composition of the formal Parliament (see Rule 71(2) of the Parliament's Rules of Procedure). It will normally include the three Vice-Presidents responsible for conciliation, the Rapporteur and Chair of the responsible parliamentary committee.

[110] Art. 294(11) TFEU. Formally, it will be the Commissioner responsible for the subject matter of the legislative bill, who will take part in the Conciliation Committee.

has managed to approve a joint text, the latter returns to the 'formal' Union legislator for a third reading.

Third reading. The 'formal' Union legislature must positively approve the joint text (without the power of amending it). The Parliament needs to endorse the joint text by a majority of the votes cast, whereas the Council must confirm the text by a qualified majority. Where one of the two chambers disagrees with the proposal made by the Conciliation Committee, the bill finally flounders. Where both chambers approve the text, the bill is adopted and now only needs to be 'signed' and 'published'.

Signing and publication. The last two stages before a bill becomes law are set out in Article 297 TFEU which states: 'Legislative acts adopted under the ordinary legislative procedure shall be signed by the President of the European Parliament and by the President of the Council'; and they shall subsequently 'be published in the Official Journal of the European Union'.[111] The publication requirement is a fundamental element of modern societies governed by the rule of law. Only 'public' legislative acts will have the force of law. The Union legal order also requires that all legislative acts 'shall state the reasons on which they are based and shall refer to any proposals, initiatives, recommendations, requests or opinions required by the Treaties'.[112] This formal 'duty to state reasons' can be judicially reviewed, and represents a hallmark of legislative rationality.

bb. Constitutional Practice: Informal Trilogues

Constitutional texts often only provide a stylised sketch of the formal relations between institutions. And this formal picture will need to be coloured and revised by informal constitutional practices. This is – very – much the case for the constitutional text governing the ordinary legislative procedure. The rudimentary status of the constitutional text is – self-consciously – recognised by the EU Treaties themselves,[113] and the importance of informal practices has been expressly acknowledged by the European institutions.[114]

The primary expression of these informal institutional arrangements is tripartite meetings called 'trilogues'. They combine the representatives of the three

---

[111]   *Ibid.*, Art. 297(1). For legislation, this will be the 'L' Series.

[112]   *Ibid.*, Art. 296 – second indent.

[113]   *Ibid.*, Art. 295 states: 'The European Parliament, the Council and the Commission shall consult each other and by common agreement make arrangements for their cooperation. To that end, they may, in compliance with the Treaties, conclude interinstitutional agreements which may be of a binding nature.'

[114]   See Interinstitutional Agreement between the European Parliament, the Council of the European Union and the European Commission on Better Law-Making (2016) OJ L123/1, esp. paras. 34–6: 'The European Parliament and the Council, in their capacity as co-legislators, agree on the importance of maintaining close contacts already in advance of interinstitutional negotiations, so as to achieve a better mutual understanding of their respective positions. To that end, in the context of the legislative process, they will facilitate mutual exchange of views and information, including by inviting representatives of the other institutions to informal exchanges of views on a regular basis. The European Parliament and the Council will, in the interest of efficiency, ensure a better

institutions involved in the legislative process – that is: Parliament, Council, and Commission – in 'informal' negotiations. Who are the respective representatives of the three institutions? This is a matter that can be decided by each institution itself. For the Parliament, it will *inter alia* involve the 'Rapporteur' and the Chair of the (standing) committee responsible. For the Council, its negotiating team has traditionally included the COREPER Representative of the Member State holding the Council Presidency, as well as the Chair of the relevant Council Working Group. The Commission will typically be represented by a negotiating team involving the responsible Directorate General.

What is the task of institutional trilogues? The trilogues system is designed to create informal bridges during the formal legislative procedure that open up 'possibilities for agreements at first and second reading stages, as well as contributing to the preparation of the work of the Conciliation Committee'.[115] Trilogues may thus be held 'at all stages of the [ordinary legislative] procedure'.[116] Indeed, a 'Joint Declaration' of the Union institutions contains respective commitments for each procedural stage. In order to facilitate a formal agreement within the Union legislator during the first reading (see Figure 7.5), informal agreements between the institutional representatives will thus be forwarded to Parliament or Council

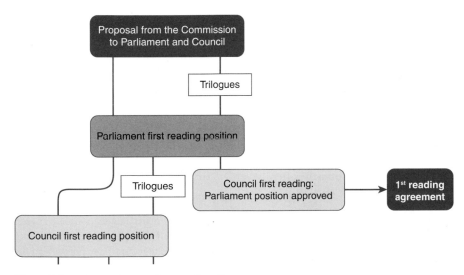

Figure 7.5 Trilogues during the First Reading

synchronisation of their treatment of legislative proposals. In particular, the European Parliament and the Council will compare indicative timetables for the various stages leading to the final adoption of each legislative proposal. Where appropriate, the three Institutions may agree to coordinate efforts to accelerate the legislative process while ensuring that the prerogatives of the co-legislators are respected and that the quality of legislation is preserved.'

[115] Joint Declaration on Practical Arrangements for the Codecision Procedure, [2007] OJ C 145/5, para. 7.

[116] *Ibid.*, para. 8.

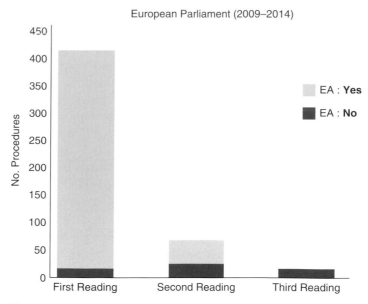

Figure 7.6 Early Agreements through Trilogues

respectively.[117] This equally applies to the second reading,[118] and to the conciliation stage.[119]

This strategy of informality has proved extremely successful (see Figure 7.6). It has indeed been so successful that '[c]odecision has *de facto* become a single-reading legislative proceed'.[120] And yet, there are serious constitutional problems. For informal trilogues should not be allowed to short-circuit the formal legislative procedure. Were this to happen, democratic deliberation within a fairly representative European Parliament would be replaced by the informal government of a small number of members of the three institutions (see Figure 7.7).[121] Representative democracy is here severely curtailed in the interest of efficiency.

---

[117] *Ibid.*, para. 14: 'Where an agreement is reached through informal negotiations in trilogues, the chair of Coreper shall forward, in a letter to the chair of the relevant parliamentary committee, details of the substance of the agreement, in the form of amendments to the Commission proposal. That letter shall indicate the Council's willingness to accept that outcome, subject to legal-linguistic verification, should it be confirmed by the vote in plenary. A copy of that letter shall be forwarded to the Commission.' For the inverted obligation, see *ibid.*, para. 18.

[118] *Ibid.*, para. 23.   [119] *Ibid.*, paras. 24–5.

[120] C. Roederer-Rynning and J. Greenwood, 'The Culture of Trilogues' (2015) 22 *Journal of European Public Policy* 1148. According to the authors, within the seventh European Parliament (2009–14), almost 90 per cent of all legislative acts adopted under the co-decision procedure were adopted at first reading.

[121] It goes without saying that Figure 7.7 is only a stylised illustration when it comes to the exact number of people involved in trilogues. According to one source, the European Parliament team may be between 20 to 30 persons, while the Council delegation may only have 1 to 3 (*ibid.*, 1155).

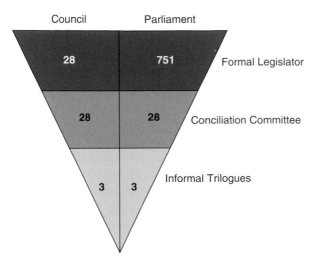

Council   Parliament

28	751	Formal Legislator
28	28	Conciliation Committee
3	3	Informal Trilogues

Figure 7.7 Declining Democratic Representation

The democratic deficit of the Union thus lies less in the *formal* structure of the Union legislator, but in its *informal* bypassing.[122]

b. The 'Special' Legislative Procedures

There is no general definition of what constitutes a 'special' legislative procedure in the Treaty section on procedures. They are indeed defined in each specific legislative competence. The Treaties thereby recognise three special legislative procedures. Unlike the ordinary procedure, Union legislation will here not be the result of a 'joint adoption' of the European Parliament and the Council. It will be adopted by *one* of the two institutions. In the first variant of Article 289(2) TFEU, this will be the Parliament; yet the Treaties still generally require the 'consent' of the Council. In the second variant of Article 289(2) TFEU, the Council will adopt the legislative act; yet, the Treaties will require either the 'consent' or 'consultation' of the Parliament. The first two special procedures may be characterised as the 'consent procedure', the third special procedure can be referred to as the 'consultation procedure'.

What are the characteristics of the 'consent procedure' and the 'consultation procedure'? The former requires one institution to consent to the legislative bill of the other. Consent is less than co-decision, for only the dominant institution will be able to determine the substantive content of the bill. The non-dominant institution will be forced to 'take it or leave it'. But this veto power is still – much – stronger than mere consultation. For, while the Court has recognised that consultation is 'an essential factor in the institutional balance intended by the Treaty',[123] consultation is nonetheless a mere 'formality'.[124] Because the formal

---

[122] For an excellent overview and critical analysis of the move towards informal politics, see C. Reh et al., 'The Informal Politics of Legislation: Explaining Secluded Decision Making in the European Union' (2013) 49 *Comparative Political Studies* 1112.

[123] Case 138/79, *Roquette Frères* v. *Council (Isoglucose)* [1980] ECR 3333, para. 33.

[124] The 'formality' still requires that the Council has to wait until Parliament has provided its opinion (see *ibid , para. 34.*): 'In that respect it is pertinent to point out that observance of that requirement implied that the Parliament has expressed its opinion. It is impossible to take the

obligation to consult will not mean that the adopting institution must take into account the substantive views of the other.[125]

4. The Principle of Subsidiarity

Subsidiarity – the quality of being 'subsidiary'– derives from *subsidium*. The Latin concept evolved in the military context. It represented an 'assistance' or 'aid' that stayed in the background. Figuratively, an entity is subsidiary where it provides a 'subsidy' – an assistance of subordinate or secondary importance. In political philosophy, the principle of subsidiarity came to represent the idea 'that a central authority should have a subsidiary function, performing only those tasks which cannot be performed effectively at a more immediate or local level'.[126] The principle thus has a positive and a negative aspect.[127] It positively encourages 'large associations' to assist smaller ones, where they need help; and it negatively discourages 'assign[ing] to a greater and higher association what lesser and subordinate organisations can do'. It is this dual character that has given the principle of subsidiarity its 'Janus-like' character.[128]

When did the subsidiarity principle become a constitutional principle of the European Union? The principle of subsidiarity surfaced in 1975,[129] but it would only find official expression in the context of the Union's environmental policy after the Single European Act (1986).[130] The Maastricht Treaty on European Union (1992) finally lifted the subsidiarity principle beyond its environmental confines. It became a general constitutional principle of the European Union. Today, the Treaty on European Union defines it in Article 5 whose third paragraph states:

> Under the principle of subsidiarity, in areas which do not fall within its exclusive competence, the Union shall act only if and in so far as the objectives of the proposed action cannot be sufficiently achieved by the Member States, either at central level or at regional and local level, but can rather, by reason of the scale or effects of the proposed action, be better achieved at Union level.

view that the requirement is satisfied by the Council's simply asking for the opinion.' On this point, see also Case C-65/93, *Parliament* v. *Council* [1995] ECR I-643. However, this case also established implied limitations on Parliament's prerogative (*ibid.*, paras. 27–8).

[125]   This was confirmed in Case C-417/93, *Parliament* v. *Council* [1995] ECR I-1185, esp. paras. 10–11.

[126]   *Oxford English Dictionary*: 'subsidiary' and 'subsidiarity'.

[127]   C. Calliess, *Subsidiaritäts- und Solidaritätsprinzip in der Europäischen Union* (Nomos, 1999), 26.

[128]   V. Constantinesco, 'Who's Afraid of Subsidiarity?' (1991) 11 YEL 33 at 35.

[129]   For a detailed textual genealogy of the subsidiarity principle in the European legal order, see R. Schütze, *From Dual to Cooperative Federalism: The Changing Structure of European Law* (Oxford University Press, 2009), 247ff.

[130]   The (then) newly inserted Art. 130 r (4) EEC restricted Community environmental legislation to those actions whose objectives could 'be attained better at Community level than at the level of the individual Member States'.

This definition clarifies that subsidiarity is only to apply within the sphere of the Union's non-exclusive powers and thus confirms that the European principle of subsidiarity is a principle of *cooperative* federalism.[131]

The Treaty definition of subsidiarity thereby builds on *two* tests. The first may be called the *national insufficiency test*. The Union can only act where the objectives of the proposed action could not be sufficiently achieved by the Member States (centrally or regionally). This appears to be an absolute standard. By contrast, a second test is a *comparative efficiency test*. The Union should not act unless it can *better* achieve the objectives of the proposed action. This appears to be based on a relative standard. The question that therefore arises is this: will the combination of these two tests mean that the Union would not be entitled to act where it is – in relative terms – better able to tackle a social problem, but where the Member States could – in absolute terms – still achieve the desired result?

This is indeed not the only textual problem with Article 5(3). For the formulation 'if and in so far' potentially offered *two* versions of the subsidiarity principle. The first version concentrates on the 'if' question by asking *whether* the Union should act. This has been defined as the principle of subsidiarity *in a strict sense*. The second version concentrates on the 'in so far' question by asking *how* the Union should act. This has been referred to as the principle of subsidiarity *in a wide sense*.[132]

The wording of Article 5(3) TEU is indeed a terrible textual failure. Too many political cooks seem to have spoiled the legal broth! In the past two decades, two – parallel – approaches have therefore evolved to give meaning to the subsidiarity principle. The first approach concentrates on the political safeguards of federalism. The second approach focuses on subsidiarity as an objective judicial standard.

a. Subsidiarity as a Political Safeguard of Federalism

Despite its literary presence,[133] the principle of subsidiarity has remained a subsidiary principle of European constitutionalism. The reason for its shadowy existence has been its lack of conceptual contours. If subsidiarity was everything to everyone, how should the Union apply it?

---

[131] On the meaning of that concept, see Schütze, *From Dual to Cooperative Federalism* (n. 129 above).

[132] K. Lenaerts, 'The Principle of Subsidiarity and the Environment in the European Union: Keeping the Balance of Federalism' (1994) 17 *Fordham International Law Journal* 846 at 875.

[133] From the – abundant – literature, see e.g. G. Berman, 'Taking Subsidiarity Seriously: Federalism in the European Community and the United States' (1994) 94 *Columbia Law Review* 331; N. Bernard, 'The Future of European Economic Law in the Light of the Principle of Subsidiarity' (1996) 33 *CML Rev.* 633; G. de Búrca, 'Reappraising Subsidiarity's Significance after Amsterdam', Harvard Jean Monnet Working Paper 1999/07; D. Z. Cass, 'The Word that Saves Maastricht? The Principle of Subsidiarity and the Division of Powers within the European Community' (1992) 29 *CML Rev.* 1107; Constantinesco, 'Who's Afraid of Subsidiarity?' (n. 128 above); G. Davies, 'Subsidiarity: The Wrong Idea, in the Wrong Place, at the Wrong Time' (2006) 43 *CML Rev.* 63.

To limit this semantic uncertainty, the Member States have tried to 'proceduralise' the principle. This attempt to develop subsidiarity into a political safeguard of federalism can be seen in Protocol No. 2 On the Application of the Principles of Subsidiarity and Proportionality. Importantly, the Protocol only applies to 'draft legislative acts',[134] that is: acts to be adopted under the ordinary or a special legislative procedure.[135]

The Protocol aims to establish 'a system of monitoring' the application of the principle. Each Union institution is called upon to ensure constant respect for the principle of subsidiarity.[136] And this means in particular that they must forward draft legislative acts to national parliaments.[137] These draft legislative acts must 'be justified' with regard to the principle of subsidiarity and proportionality.[138] This (procedural) duty to provide reasons is defined as follows:

> Any draft legislative act should contain a detailed statement making it possible to appraise compliance with the principles of subsidiarity and proportionality. This statement should contain some assessment of the proposal's financial impact and, in the case of a directive, of its implications for the rules to be put in place by Member States, including, where necessary, the regional legislation. The reasons for concluding that a Union objective can be better achieved at Union level shall be substantiated by qualitative and, wherever possible, quantitative indicators. Draft legislative acts shall take account of the need for any burden, whether financial or administrative, falling upon the Union, national governments, regional or local authorities, economic operators and citizens, to be minimised and commensurate with the objective to be achieved.[139]

How is this duty enforced? One solution here points to the European Court;[140] yet, the Protocol develops a second solution: the active involvement of national parliaments in the legislative procedure of the European Union.[141] The Treaty-makers hoped that this idea would kill two birds with one stone. The procedural involvement of national parliaments promised to strengthen the federal *and* the democratic safeguards within Europe.

---

[134] Art. 3 Protocol No. 2 On the Application of the Principles of Subsidiarity and Proportionality.

[135] However, this will not mean that the judicial principle of subsidiarity does not apply to other types of acts. On the application of the principle of subsidiarity to executive acts, see Chapter 9, section 3(b).

[136] Art. 1 of the Protocol.   [137] *Ibid.*, Art. 4.   [138] *Ibid.*, Art. 5.

[139] *Ibid.*

[140] *Ibid.*, Art. 8: 'The Court of Justice of the European Union shall have jurisdiction in actions on grounds of infringement of the principle of subsidiarity by a legislative act, brought in accordance with the rules laid down in Article 263 of the Treaty on the Functioning of the European Union by Member States, or notified by them in accordance with their legal order on behalf of their national Parliament or a chamber thereof.' For a discussion of the Court's deferential stance, see section 4(b) below.

[141] This function is acknowledged in Art. 12(b) TEU, which requests national parliaments to contribute to the good functioning of the Union 'by seeing to it that the principle of subsidiarity is respected in accordance with the procedures provided for in the Protocol on the application of the principles of subsidiarity and proportionality'.

But if national parliaments are to be the Union's 'watchdogs of subsidiarity',[142] would they enjoy a veto right (hard legislative solution) or only a monitoring right (soft legislative solution)? According to the Subsidiarity Protocol, each national parliament may within eight weeks produce a reasoned opinion stating why it considers that a European legislative draft does not comply with the principle of subsidiarity.[143] Each parliament will thereby have two votes.[144] Where the negative votes amount to one-third of all the votes allocated to the national parliaments, the European Union draft 'must be reviewed'. This is called the 'yellow card' mechanism, since the Union legislator 'may decide to maintain, amend or withdraw the draft'.[145]

The yellow card mechanism is strengthened in relation to proposals under the *ordinary* legislative procedure; albeit, here, only a majority of the votes allocated to the national parliaments will trigger it.[146] Under this 'orange card' mechanism, the Commission's justification for maintaining the proposal, as well as the reasoned opinions of the national parliaments, will be submitted to the Union legislator which will have to consider whether the proposal is compatible with the principle of subsidiarity. Where one of its chambers finds that the proposal violates the principle of subsidiarity, the proposal is rejected.[147] While this arrangement makes it – slightly – easier for the European Parliament to reject a legislative proposal on subsidiarity grounds, it might make it – ironically – more difficult for the Council to block a proposal on the basis of subsidiarity than on the basis of a proposal's lack of substantive merit.[148]

How successful has the yellow card mechanism been? From the very beginning, the subsidiarity mechanism has been said to 'add very little' to the federal control of the Union legislator.[149] Sparely successful in the past,[150] critics have pointed to a number of conceptual and practical inadequacies of the existing

---

[142] I. Cooper, 'The Watchdogs of Subsidiarity: National Parliaments and the Logic of Arguing in the EU' (2006) 44 *Journal of Common Market Studies* 281.

[143] Art. 6 Protocol No. 2 On the Application of the Principles of Subsidiarity and Proportionality.

[144] *Ibid.*, Art. 7(1).   [145] *Ibid.*, Art. 7(2).   [146] *Ibid.*, Art. 7(3).

[147] *Ibid.*, Art. 7(3)(b): 'if, by a majority of 55 per cent of the members of the Council or a majority of the votes cast in the European Parliament, the legislator is of the opinion that the proposal is not compatible with the principle of subsidiarity, the legislative proposal shall not be given further consideration'.

[148] For an analysis of this point, see G. Barrett, '"The King Is Dead, Long Live the King": The Recasting by the Treaty of Lisbon of the Provisions of the Constitutional Treaty concerning National Parliaments' (2008) 33 *EL Rev.* 66 at 80–1. In the light of the voting threshold, 'it seems fair to predict that blockade of legislative proposals under Article 7(2) is likely to be a highly exceptional and unusual situation'.

[149] See House of Commons, European Scrutiny Committee (Thirty-third Report: 2007– 8): 'Subsidiarity, National Parliaments and the Lisbon Treaty' (Stationary Office, 2008), para. 35.

[150] Only three yellow cards have so far been given to the Commission. For an analysis of the first activation of the yellow card mechanisms, see F. Fabbrini and K. Granat, '"Yellow Card, But No Foul": The Role of the National Parliaments under the Subsidiary Protocol and the Commission Proposal for an EU Regulation on the Right to Strike' (2013) 50 *CML Rev.* 115. The second activation of the yellow card mechanism concerned the Commission proposal

procedure;[151] and calls for a 'red card' mechanism have therefore been made.[152] These – tempting – calls should nevertheless be resisted: 'to give national parliaments what would amount to a veto over proposals would be incompatible with the Commission's constitutionally protected independence.'[153] Indeed, to turn national parliaments into 'co-legislators' in the making of European law would significantly aggravate the 'political interweaving' of the European and the national level and thereby deepen joint-decision traps.[154] The rejection of the hard veto solution is thus to be welcomed. The soft legislative solution allows national parliaments to channel and concentrate their scrutiny onto where it can be most useful and effective: on their respective national governments. Scrutiny of their actions in the Council constitutes a far superior control mechanism here.

b. Subsidiarity as a Judicial Safeguard of Federalism

After an 'initial review' at the 'political level', a second subsidiarity review lies with the EU judicature. The latter must thereby not only verify 'compliance with the procedural safeguards' within the Subsidiarity Protocol but it must also – and more importantly – verify 'compliance with the *substantive conditions*' set out in Article 5(3) TEU.[155]

   To what extent has the Court ensured that the Union legislator sufficiently justifies its acts by reference to the principle of subsidiarity? In *Germany v. Parliament and Council (Deposit Guarantee Scheme)*,[156] the German government claimed that the relevant Union act had violated the *procedural* obligation to state reasons.[157] The Union law had not explained how it was compatible with the principle of subsidiarity; and Germany insisted that it was necessary that 'the [Union] institutions

to create a European Public Prosecutor's Office, whereas the third yellow card concerned the Commission proposal to revise the 'Posted Workers Directive'. Yet, unlike in the first instance, the Commission decided to retain its original proposal in the second and third instance.

[151] See here in particular: D. Jancic, 'The Game of Cards: National Parliaments in the EU and the Future of the Early Warning Mechanism and the Political Dialogue' (2015) 52 *CML Rev.* 939.

[152] Most famously, this idea was championed by David Cameron in his attempt to renegotiate the British 'deal' with the European Union prior to the Brexit Referendum. For a brief analysis, see: http://blogs.lse.ac.uk/europpblog/2016/06/13/how-the-red-card-system-could-increase-the-power-of-national-parliaments-within-the-eu.

[153] A. Dashwood, 'The Relationship between the Member States and the European Union/Community' (2004) 41 *CML Rev.* 355 at 369. Similarly, S. Weatherill, 'Using National Parliaments to Improve Scrutiny of the Limits of EU Action' (2003) 28 *EL Rev.* 909 at 912.

[154] On the concept and shortfalls of 'political interweaving' (*Politikverflechtung*), see F. Scharpf, 'The Joint-decision Trap: Lessons from German Federalism and European Integration' (1988) 66 *Public Administration* 239.

[155] Case C-547/14, *Philip Morris Brands and others*, para. 217 (emphasis added).

[156] Case C-233/94, *Germany v. Parliament and Council (Deposit Guarantee Scheme)* [1997] ECRI-2405.

[157] On the duty to give reasons, see section 3 above. Germany made it an express point that it was this provision – and not the principle of subsidiarity as such – that it claimed had been violated (*ibid.*, para. 24).

must give detailed reasons to explain why only the [Union], to the exclusion of the Member States, is empowered to act in the area in question'. 'In the present case, the Directive does not indicate in what respects its objectives could not have been attained by action at Member State level or the grounds which militated in favour of [Union] action.'[158] The Court however gave short shrift to that accusation. Looking at the recitals of the Union law, the Court found that the Union legislator had given enough 'consideration' to the principle of subsidiarity.[159] Yet without any detailed analysis of whether or not the Member States or the Union should have been entitled to act, this was a *low* explanatory threshold indeed.

This low review standard vis-à-vis the procedural duty to state reasons has been confirmed,[160] especially in *Estonia* v. *Parliament and Council (Financial Statements)*.[161] In this case, Estonia had argued that 'the determination of compliance with the subsidiarity principle should have been made not for the [Union act] as a whole, but for each of its provisions individually';[162] yet the Court unconditionally rejected this argument by confirming that it was enough that 'the contested measure clearly discloses [its] essential objective' and that it would consequently 'be excessive to require a specific statement of reasons for each of the technical choices made'.[163]

Any substantive meaning of the subsidiarity principle is thus in the hands of the European Court of Justice. So how has the Court defined the relationship between the national insufficiency test and the comparative efficiency test? And has the Court favoured the restrictive or the wide meaning of subsidiarity?

There are surprisingly few judgments that offer a meaningful treatment of the principle of subsidiarity. In *United Kingdom* v. *Council (Working Time)*,[164] the United Kingdom had applied for the annulment of the Working Time Directive. The applicant claimed:

> [T]he [Union] legislature neither fully considered nor adequately demonstrated whether there were transnational aspects which could not be satisfactorily regulated by national measures, whether such measures would conflict with the requirements of the [Treaties] or significantly damage the interests of Member States or, finally, whether action at [European] level would provide clear benefits compared with action at national level.[165]

How did the Court respond? The Court offered an interpretation of subsidiarity that has structured the judicial vision of the principle ever since. It held:

---

[158] *Ibid.*, para. 23. [159] *Ibid.*, paras. 26–8.

[160] See Case C-377/98 *Netherlands* v. *Council & Parliament*, para. 33: 'Compliance with the principle of subsidiarity is necessarily implicit in the fifth, sixth and seventh recitals of the preamble to the Directive, which state that, in the absence of action at [European] level, the development of the laws and practices of the different Member States impedes the proper functioning of the internal market. It thus appears that the Directive states sufficient reasons on that point.'

[161] Case C-508/13, *Estonia* v. *Parliament and Council*, EU:C:2015:403.

[162] *Ibid.*, para. 51. [163] *Ibid.*, para. 60. [164] Case C-84/94 (n. 13 above).

[165] *Ibid.*, para. 46.

> Once the Council has found that it is necessary to improve the existing level of protection as regards the health and safety of workers and to harmonise the conditions in this area while maintaining the improvements made, achievement of that objective through the imposition of minimum requirements necessarily presupposes [Union]-wide action, which otherwise, as in this case, leaves the enactment of the detailed implementing provisions required largely to the Member States. The argument that the Council could not properly adopt measures as general and mandatory as those forming the subject-matter of the directive will be examined below in the context of the plea alleging infringement of the principle of proportionality.[166]

The quoted passage contained two fundamental choices. First, the Court assumed that where the Union had decided to 'harmonise' national laws, that objective necessarily presupposed Union legislation. This view answers the national insufficiency test with a mistaken tautology: only the Union can harmonise laws, and therefore the Member States already fail the first test!

But assuming the 'whether' of European action had been positively established, could the Union law go 'as far' as it had? This was the second crucial choice of the Court. It decided against the idea of subsidiarity in a wider sense. For, instead of analysing the intensity of the European intervention under Article 5(3) TEU, it chose to review it via the principle of proportionality under Article 5(4) TEU. And it is there that the Court made a third important choice. In analysing the proportionality of the Union law, it ruled that 'the Council must be allowed a wide discretion in an area which, as here, involves the legislature in making social policy choices and requires it to carry out complex assessments'. Judicial review would therefore be limited to examining whether the legislature's discretion 'has been vitiated by *manifest error or misuse of powers, or whether the institution concerned has manifestly exceeded the limits of its discretion*'.[167] The Court would thus again apply a *low* degree of judicial scrutiny.[168]

Choices one and three have been confirmed in subsequent jurisprudence. By concentrating on the national insufficiency test, the Court has short-circuited the comparative efficiency test.[169] It has not searched for qualitative or quantitative benefits of European laws, but confirmed its manifest error test – thus leaving subsidiarity to the political safeguards of federalism.

---

[166] *Ibid.*, para. 47.

[167] *Ibid.*, para. 58 (emphasis added).

[168] On the development of the judicial review standard for Union acts in this context, see G. de Búrca, 'The Principle of Proportionality and Its Application in EC Law' (1993) 13 YEL 105.

[169] See for example: Case C-491/01, *The Queen* v. *Secretary of State for Health, ex p. British American Tobacco(Investments) Ltd and Imperial Tobacco Ltd*, paras. 181–3: '[T]he Directive's objective is to eliminate the barriers raised by the differences which still exist between the Member States' laws, regulations and administrative provisions on the manufacture, presentation and sale of tobacco products, while ensuring a high level of health protection, in accordance with Article [114(3) TFEU]. Such an objective cannot be sufficiently achieved by the Member States individually and calls for action at [European] level, as demonstrated by the multifarious development of national laws in this case.' For a more recent application of this logic, see Case C-547/14, *Philip Morris Brands and others*, paras. 218–24.

By contrast, as regards the second choice, the Court has remained ambivalent. While in some cases it has incorporated the intensity question into its subsidiarity analysis,[170] other jurisprudence has kept the subsidiarity and the proportionality principles at arm's length.[171] What is the better option here? It has been argued that subsidiarity should be understood 'in a wider sense'.[172] It is indeed impossible to reduce subsidiarity to 'whether' the Union should exercise one of its competences. The distinction between 'competence' and 'subsidiarity' – between Article 5(2) and (3) TEU – will only make sense if the subsidiarity principle concentrates on the 'whether' of *the specific act at issue*. But the 'whether' and the 'how' of the specific action are inherently tied together. The principle of subsidiarity will thus ask *whether* the European legislator has *unnecessarily* restricted national autonomy. A subsidiarity analysis that will not question the *federal* proportionality of a European law is, by contrast, bound to remain an empty formalism. Subsidiarity properly understood *is* federal proportionality.[173]

Conclusion

The Union is not a sovereign State. Its legislative competences are 'enumerated' competences that are 'conferred' by the European Treaties. The majority of the Union's legislative competences are spread across Part III of the Treaty on the Functioning of the European Union. In each of its policy areas, the Union will typically be given a specific competence. Its competences are thus thematically limited; yet, as we saw above, the Union legislator has made wide use of its powers by interpreting them teleologically. In the past, the Union has also extensively used its general competences. Articles 114 and 352 TFEU indeed grant the Union two legislative competences that horizontally cut across (almost) all substantive policy areas. In their most dramatic form, they have even allowed the Union to develop policies that were not expressly mentioned in the Treaties.

But not all legislative competences of the Union provide it with the same legal power. The Union legal order recognises various competence categories. The EU Treaties distinguish between exclusive, shared, coordinating and

---

[170] In Case C-491/01 *The Queen* v. *Secretary of State for Health, ex p. British American Tobacco(Investments) Ltd and Imperial Tobacco*, the Court identified the 'intensity of the action undertaken by the [Union]' with the principle of subsidiarity and not the principle of proportionality (*ibid.*, para. 184). This acceptance of subsidiarity *sensu lato* can also be seen at work in Case C-55/06, *Arcor* v. *Germany* [2008] ECR I-2931, where the Court identified the principle of subsidiarity with the idea that 'the Member States retain the possibility to establish specific rules on the field in question' (*ibid.*, para. 144).

[171] See Case C-84/94, *United Kingdom* v. *Council (Working Time Directive)*; Case C-103/01 *Commission* v. *Germany*, para. 48.

[172] Schütze, *From Dual to Cooperative Federalism* (n. 129 above), 263ff. If subsidiarity was thus to be understood in a wider – substantive – sense, this would of course also allow national parliaments to explore the wider substantive implications of a draft legislative act, and therefore better reflect current constitutional practice.

[173] On the – liberal – principle of proportionality, see Chapter 10, section 1(b/bb).

complementary competences. Each competence category constitutionally distributes power between the Union and the Member States. Within its exclusive competences, the Union is exclusively competent to legislate; whereas it shares power with the Member States under its non-exclusive powers. We saw above that the Lisbon codification of the Union's competence categories is far from perfect. Sadly, the Treaties therefore still do not deliver clear principles for the European Union's federal order of competences.[174]

Who is the Union legislator? The Union legislator is a compound legislator. However, unlike the British constitutional order, there exists an 'ordinary' and three 'special' legislative procedures. All four procedures combine the European Parliament and the Council, but only under the ordinary legislative procedure are they co-authors with symmetric constitutional rights. Ordinary legislation needs to follow a complex formal procedure that may, in the most extreme situation, comprise three readings. In the past, the Union has however tried to adopt legislation after the first and the second reading; and, in order to achieve this result, it has used informal trilogues between the Parliament, the Council and the Commission. While these trilogues have been very successful, they contain the danger of short-circuiting the democratic representation underpinning the ordinary legislative procedure.

The Union legislator is – generally – a subsidiary legislator. The exercise of its non-exclusive competences is restricted by the principle of subsidiarity. The latter theoretically grants a constitutional advantage to national legislation in solving a social problem within the Union. In order to protect that constitutional advantage, the Union has employed two mechanisms. The first mechanism concentrates on the procedural involvement of national parliaments in the (political) principle of subsidiarity. The second mechanism focuses on judicial limits to the (legal) principle of subsidiarity.

Which mechanism works best? States can be partly protected by a procedural duty on the Union legislator to 'think hard' about subsidiarity. However, procedural obligations only provide *some* protection of State autonomy. The Court of Justice should thus be involved in setting a substantive subsidiarity standard. But would the setting of hard limits for the Union legislator not be inherently anti-democratic? This view is mistaken. For the democracy-centred rationale behind process constitutionalism is hard to apply to a federal context. Here the question is *not* whether a non-democratic court or a democratic parliament should decide, but whether the democratic majority of the *Union* or the democratic majority of a *State* should decide on the matter.

One final point needs to be made. In addition to the 'full' Union legislator, the Treaties also recognise the possibility of differentiated 'lawmaking' between some – but not all – Member States. The central provision governing this 'enhanced cooperation' can be found in Article 20 TEU, which states:

---

[174] Schütze, 'Lisbon and the Federal Order of Competences' (n. 81 above), 721; and now also S. Garben and I. Govaere, *The Division of Competences between the EU and the Member States* (Hart, 2017).

Member States which wish to establish enhanced cooperation between themselves within the framework of the Union's non-exclusive competences may make use of its institutions and exercise those competences by applying the relevant provisions of the Treaties ... The decision authorising enhanced cooperation shall be adopted by the Council as a last resort, when it has established that the objectives of such cooperation cannot be attained within a reasonable period by the Union as a whole, and provided that at least nine Member States participate in it.[175]

The Treaties here allow for a middle path between a single – centralised – solution for the Union as a whole and the diversity of – decentralised – national solution(s). For it allows a group of Member States to 'use' the Union institutions so as to adopt a *sui generis* 'Union' law that hierarchically stands below ordinary Union law.[176] However, this alternative solution will only be open 'as a last resort'. It can only be used when it has become clear that the adoption of 'proper' Union legislation for all Member States has definitely failed. The constitutional threshold is here very high with the European Court holding that 'only those situations in which it is *impossible to adopt such legislation in the foreseeable future* may give rise to the adoption of a decision authorizing enhanced cooperation'.[177]

FURTHER READING

Books

L. Azoulai (ed.), *The Question of Competence in the European Union* (Oxford University Press, 2014)

O. Costa and N. Black, *How the EU Really Works* (Routledge, 2014)

S. Garben and I. Govaere, *The Division of Competences between the EU and the Member States: Reflections on the Past, the Present and the Future* (Hart, 2017)

K. Granat, *The Principle of Subsidiarity and Its Enforcement in the EU Legal Order* (Hart, 2018)

S. Hix and B. Høyland, *The Political System of the European Union* (Palgrave, 2011)

B. Kohler-Koch and B. Rittberger, *Debating the Democratic Legitimacy of the European Union* (Rowman & Littlefield, 2007)

N. Nugent, *The Government and Politics of the European Union* (Palgrave, 2017)

R. Schütze, *From Dual to Cooperative Federalism: The Changing Structure of European Law* (Oxford University Press, 2009)

---

[175] Art. 20(1)–(2) TEU. The provision refers to Title III of Part VI (Arts. 326–34) of the TFEU for more detailed provisions. The provisions are excessively wordy and complex and are – very – rarely used. For an academic analysis of the first use of the provisions, see S. Peers, 'Divorce, European Style: The First Authorization of Enhanced Cooperation' (2010) 6 *European Constitutional Law Review* 339.

[176] Art. 326 TFEU – first indent: 'Any enhanced cooperation shall comply with the Treaties and Union law.'

[177] Joined Cases C-274–5/11, *Spain and Italy* v. *Council (Unitary Patent)* EU: C:2013:240, para. 50 (emphasis added).

Articles (and Chapters)

I. Cooper, 'The Watchdogs of Subsidiarity: National Parliaments and the Logic of Arguing in the EU' (2006) 44 *Journal of Common Market Studies* 281

P. Craig, 'Competence: Clarity, Conferral, Containment and Consideration' (2004) 29 *EL Rev.* 323

A. Dashwood, 'The Limits of European Community Powers' (1996) 21 *EL Rev.* 113

G. Davies, 'Subsidiarity: The Wrong Idea, in the Wrong Place, at the Wrong Time' (2006) 43 *CML Rev.* 63

D. Jancic, 'The Game of Cards: National Parliaments in the EU and the Future of the Early Warning Mechanism and the Political Dialogue' (2015) 52 *CML Rev.* 939

T. Konstadinides, 'Drawing the Line between Circumvention and Gap-filling: An Exploration of the Conceptual Limits of the Treaty's Flexibility Clause' (2012) 31 YEL 227

C. Reh et al., 'The Informal Politics of Legislation: Explaining Secluded Decision Making in the European Union' (2013) 49 *Comparative Political Studies* 1112

R. de Ruiter and C. Neuhold, 'Why Is Fast Track the Way to Go? Justification for Early Agreement in the Co-decision Procedure and their Effects' (2012) 18 ELJ 536

C. Roederer-Rynning and J. Greenwood, 'The Culture of Trilogues' (2015) 22 *Journal of European Public Policy* 1148

R. Schütze, 'Lisbon and the Federal Order of Competences: A Prospective Analysis' (2008) 33 *EL Rev.* 709

A. Tizzano, 'The Powers of the Community', in Commission (ed.), *Thirty Years of Community Law* (Office for Official Publications of the EC, 1981) 43

S. Weatherill, 'Competence Creep and Competence Control' (2004) 23 YEL 1

D. Wyatt, 'Community Competence to Regulate the Internal Market' (Oxford University Faculty of Law Research Paper 9/2007)

Cases on the Website

Case 9/74, *Casagrande; Opinion 1/75* (Local Cost Standard); Case 804/79, *Commission v. United Kingdom*; Case C-350/92, *Spain v. Council; Opinion 2/94* (Accession to the ECHR); Case C-84/94, *United Kingdom v. Council*; Case C-233/94, *Germany v. Parliament and Council*; Case C-376/98, *Tobacco Advertising*; Case C-2/10, *Azienda Agro-Zootecnica Franchini*; Case C-508/13, *Estonia v. Parliament and Council*

8

External Powers
Competences and Procedures

Contents

Introduction

The constitutional distinction between internal and external affairs emerges with the rise of the territorial State. With political communities becoming defined by geographical borders, foreign affairs henceforth refer to those matters that entail an 'external' dimension.[1] The recognition of foreign affairs as a distinct public function received its classic formulation in the political philosophy of John Locke. Locke classified all external competences under the name 'federative' power, that is: 'the power of war and peace, leagues and alliances, and all the transactions with all persons and communities *without the commonwealth*'.[2] This classic definition of the foreign affairs power identifies it with the power to decide over war and peace; and foreign affairs were consequently considered part of the executive power.[3] For relations between States were thought to have remained in a 'natural state'; and their 'law-less' character provided an argument against granting external powers to the legislative branch.

In the modern world, this reasoning is not as persuasive as 300 years ago. The idea that foreign affairs are all about war and peace has given way to a new understanding. For with the internationalisation of trade and commerce in the eighteenth and nineteenth centuries, a new foreign affairs occupation became consolidated: regulatory international agreements. The level of tariffs for goods needed to be regulated;[4] river navigation had to be coordinated;[5] and intellectual property rights required to be protected.[6] And the intense 'globalisation' and economic interdependence that started in the twentieth century have further intensified the need for – legal – cooperation between States. Today, much of the foreign affairs 'business' of modern States indeed concerns the conclusion of – economic – international agreements.

Yet, the Union is not a State – it is a Union of States. Is it nonetheless entitled to partake in the international affairs of the world? This depends – of course – on the structure of international law as well as the European Treaties themselves. The 1957 Treaty of Rome had already acknowledged the international personality of the European Community,[7] and the Treaty on European Union grants such legal personality to the Union.[8]

---

[1] 'Foreign' partly derives from the Latin '*foris*' meaning 'outside'.

[2] *Two Treatises of Government*, ed. P. Laslett (Cambridge University Press, 1988), 365, §146.

[3] Locke allocates this public function to the institution that exercises the executive function – the monarch (*ibid.*, §148). To minimise the danger of an armed conflict within the commonwealth, the use of force is to be monopolised in the hands of *one* institution. While the powers of internal execution and foreign policy are functionally distinct, they are united in the same institution for the sake of securing internal peace.

[4] For example: 1860 Anglo-French Trade Agreement (Cobden–Chevalier Treaty).

[5] For example: 1868 Rhine Navigation Convention.

[6] For example: 1883 Paris Convention for the Protection of Industrial Property.

[7] Ex-Art. 281 EC. By contrast, the legal personality of the (Maastricht) European Union had been in doubt. In theory, it had no legal personality, as there existed no legal provision for it. In constitutional practice, however, the (old) Union's international legal personality was implicit for it had been entitled to conclude international agreements under ex-Art. 24 (old) EU. For this old debate, see D. McGoldrick, *International Relations Law of the European Union* (Longman, 1997), ch. 2.

[8] Art. 47 TEU.

This chapter looks at the external powers and procedures of the European Union. Sadly, the Union suffers from a 'split personality' here because it has a split constitutional regime for foreign affairs. It has a general competence for its 'common foreign and security policy' (CFSP) within the TEU; and it enjoys various specific external powers within the TFEU. Sections 1 and 2 will analyse each of these competences and their respective nature. Section 3 looks at the procedural dimension of the external relations of the Union. How will the Union act, and which institutions need to cooperate for it to act? This depends on which of the two constitutional regimes applies. While Although the CFSP is still characterised by an 'executive' dominance, the procedures within the Union's special external powers are closer to the 'legislative' branch. Section 4 finally explores two constitutional safeguards regulating the exercise of shared external competences: mixed agreements, and the duty of loyal cooperation.

1. The External Competences of the Union

What are the Union's objectives as an actor on the international scene? Its external objectives are spelled out in Article 21 TEU. After a commitment to some 'universalist' values,[9] the provision commits the Union to a number of 'particular' objectives. These 'Union-specific' objectives are as follows:

> The Union shall define and pursue common policies and actions, and shall work for a high degree of cooperation in all fields of international relations, in order to:
> (a) safeguard its values, fundamental interests, security, independence and integrity;
> (b) consolidate and support democracy, the rule of law, human rights and the principles of international law;
> (c) preserve peace, prevent conflicts and strengthen international security, in accordance with the purposes and principles of the United Nations Charter, with the principles of the Helsinki Final Act and with the aims of the Charter of Paris, including those relating to external borders;
> (d) foster the sustainable economic, social and environmental development of developing countries, with the primary aim of eradicating poverty;
> (e) encourage the integration of all countries into the world economy, including through the progressive abolition of restrictions on international trade;
> (f) help develop international measures to preserve and improve the quality of the environment and the sustainable management of global natural resources, in order to ensure sustainable development;
> (g) assist populations, countries and regions confronting natural or man-made disasters; and
> (h) promote an international system based on stronger multilateral cooperation and good global governance.

---

[9] Art. 21(1) TEU: 'democracy, the rule of law, the universality and indivisibility of human rights and fundamental freedoms, respect for human dignity, the principles of equality and solidarity, and respect for the principles of the United Nations Charter and international law'.

In order to achieve these objectives, the Union cannot act as it pleases. In accordance with the principle of conferral – discussed in the previous chapter – the Union must act 'within the limits of the competences conferred upon it by the Member States in the Treaties'.[10] This principle indeed applies to 'both the internal action and the international action of the [Union]'.[11]

The competences of the Union on foreign affairs can generally be found in two constitutional sites, as shown in Table 8.1. Title V of the Treaty on European Union deals with the 'Common Foreign and Security Policy',[12] whereas Part V of the Treaty on the Functioning of the European Union enumerates various external policies within which the Union is entitled to act.[13] The relationship between both constitutional sites is complex, and, in some ways, they are 'living apart together'. They are living apart, as Article 40 TEU draws a constitutional dividing line between them; yet, they are also living together under a common roof, as the 'General Provisions on the Union's External Action' apply to both

Table 8.1 Union External Policies

EU Treaty – Title V: CFSP		FEU Treaty – Part V: External Action	
Chapter 1	General Provisions	Title I	General Provisions
Chapter 2	Specific Provisions on the CFSP	Title II	Common Commercial Policy
		Title III	Cooperation with Third Countries and Humanitarian Aid
Section 1	*Common Provisions*		
Section 2	*Common Security and Defence Policy*	Title IV	Restrictive Measures
		Title V	International Agreements
		Title VI	Relations with International Organisations and Third Countries and Union Delegations
		Title VII	Solidarity Clause

[10] Art. 5(2) TEU.

[11] *Opinion 2/94* (Accession to the ECHR) [1996] ECR I-1759, para. 24.

[12] The TEU's common provisions also contain two external competences for the Union. Art. 6(2) TEU empowers the Union to accede to the European Convention for the Protection of Human Rights and Fundamental Freedoms. The Union's 'Neighbourhood Policy' (ENP) finds its constitutional basis in Art. 8 TEU. The Union is here entitled to develop a 'special relationship' with neighbouring countries so as to establish 'an area of prosperity and good neighbourliness'. For a brief analysis of the ENP, see (online) Chapter 18B, section 4(c).

[13] A number of legal bases *outside* Part V of the TFEU also grant the Union external competences. For example, Art. 168(3) TFEU confers the power to adopt measures that foster cooperation with third countries and competent international organisations in the context of the Union's Public Health policy. For other express treaty-making competences, see Title XX on the environment, where the Union is given a competence to conclude environmental agreements with third States under Art. 191(4) TFEU.

of them.[14] This means that all of the Union's external actions must be guided by the same principles and objectives.

This section looks at the Union's general competence for its CFSP first of all, before analysing the main external competences conferred in the Treaty on the Functioning of the European Union. These competences are thematically arranged competences, yet there exists one exception: Article 216 TFEU. The provision grants the Union a 'residual' competence to conclude international agreements that horizontally cuts across all Union policies in the Treaty on the Functioning of the European Union. In some respects, it resembles Article 352 TFEU and warrants special attention. Finally, we shall also have a closer look at the complex relationship between the two external relations regimes within the two Treaties.

a. The Common Foreign and Security Policy

The general competence of the Union on foreign affairs can be found in Title V of the Treaty on European Union. The second chapter of this title deals with the Common Foreign and Security Policy. Article 24 TEU here grants the Union a general competence. It states:

> The Union's competence in matters of common foreign and security policy shall cover all areas of foreign policy and all questions relating to the Union's security, including the progressive framing of a common defence policy that might lead to a common defence.

This general competence is subsequently broken down into specific provisions dealing with the Union's power to adopt decisions. And with regard to the conclusion of international agreements, Article 37 TEU generally states:

> The Union may conclude agreements with one or more States or international organisations in areas covered by this Chapter.

The Common Security and Defence Policy (CSDP) is seen as 'an integral part' of the CFSP.[15] What is the scope of the CSDP? The latter 'shall provide the Union with an operational capacity', which the Union may use 'on missions outside the Union for peace-keeping, conflict prevention and strengthening

---

[14] Title V – Chapter 1 (Arts. 21 and 22) TEU. This is expressly confirmed for both constitutional sites in – respectively – Art. 23 TEU and Art. 205 TFEU. The latter states: 'The Union's action on the international scene, pursuant to this Part, shall be guided by the principles, pursue the objectives and be conducted in accordance with the general provisions laid down in Chapter 1 of Title V of the Treaty on European Union.'

[15] Art. 42(1) TEU.

international security in accordance with the principles of the United Nations Charter'.[16] The CSDP shall – in the future – also include the 'progressive framing of a common Union defence policy'.[17] Importantly however, Article 42 TEU contains a constitutional guarantee not to prejudice the neutrality of certain Member States, and to respect other Member States' obligations within the North Atlantic Treaty Organization (NATO).[18]

b. The Union's Special External Powers

Part V of the TFEU contains seven titles. After confirming the common principles and objectives of the Union's external action,[19] three titles deal with special external policies,[20] two titles concern institutional matters,[21] and one title establishes a 'Solidarity Clause'.[22]

The majority of the Union's external competences are found in Titles II–IV. However, we also find competences in the institutional provisions. Title V thus grants the Union a general competence to conclude international agreements,[23] and a special competence to conclude 'association agreements'.[24] Title VI moreover grants the Union a horizontal competence to establish and maintain cooperative relations 'as are appropriate' with international organisations, in particular the United Nations and the Council of Europe.[25]

Let us briefly look at the three titles dealing with specific external policies. Title II concerns the Union's Common Commercial Policy (CCP). This is the external expression of the Union's internal market. The Union is here tasked to represent the common commercial interests of the Member States on the international scene and to contribute to 'the harmonious development of world trade'.[26] Under

---

[16]   *Ibid.*   [17] Art. 42(2) TEU – first indent.   [18] *Ibid.* – second indent.

[19] Art. 205 TFEU.   [20] Part V – Titles II–IV of the TFEU.

[21] *Ibid.* – Titles I, V and VI.

[22] *Ibid.* – Title VII. Despite its position within Part V of the TFEU, the solidarity clause is not a 'real' external policy of the Union. It imposes an obligation on the Union and its Member States to act jointly 'if a Member State is the object of a terrorist attack or the victim of a natural or man-made disaster' (Art. 222(1) TFEU); and this situation may not necessarily have foreign implications for the European Union. However, there are intimate constitutional links with the Union's CFSP. For example, the Union is entitled to mobilise military resources made available by the Member States (*ibid.*).

[23] See Art. 216 TFEU (discussed below).

[24] See *ibid.*, Art. 217. These agreements are special agreements in that they create 'special, privileged links with a non-member country which must, at least to a certain extent, take part in the [Union] system' (see Case 12/86, *Demirel* v. *Stadt Schwäbisch Gmünd* [1987] ECR 3719, para. 9). The 'European Economic Area' Agreement between the European Union and Lichtenstein, Iceland and Norway is an association agreement. For a brief discussion of the EEA, see (online) Chapter 18B, section 4(b/bb).

[25] Art. 220 TFEU. The European Union is a – full or partial – member of a number of international organisations. For a list of these organisations and the respective status of the Union, see A. Missiroli, 'The New EU "Foreign Policy" System after Lisbon: A Work in Progress' (2010) 15 *European Foreign Affairs Review* 427 at 449ff.

[26] Art. 206 TFEU.

Article 207 TFEU, the Union is thereby entitled to adopt (unilateral) legislative acts,[27] and to conclude (bilateral or multilateral) international agreements.[28] The scope of the CCP covers all matters relating to trade in goods and services, commercial aspects of intellectual property, and foreign direct investment.[29]

Title III deals with three related but distinct external policies of the Union in three chapters. All three policies allow the Union to adopt unilateral measures,[30] and to conclude international agreements with third States.[31] Chapter 1 concerns 'Development Cooperation', whose primary objective is 'the reduction and, in the long term, the eradication of poverty' in developing countries.[32] Chapter 2 extends various forms of assistance to 'third countries other than developing counties'.[33] The Union's competence in respect of humanitarian aid can be found in Chapter 3 of this Title. It permits the Union to provide 'ad hoc assistance and relief and protection for people in third countries who are victims of natural or man-made disasters, in order to meet the humanitarian needs resulting from these different situations'.[34]

Finally, Title IV confers on the Union a competence to adopt economic sanctions. These are unilateral acts with a 'punitive' character. This competence has had an eventful constitutional history,[35] and still constitutes a strange animal. For according to Article 215 TFEU, the Union is not entitled to act on the basis of this competence alone. It can only exercise this competence *after* the Union has exercised its CFSP competence. The provision constitutes the central platform for the implementation of Resolutions of the Security Council of the United Nations.

Most of these external policies will be discussed – in much greater detail – in (online) Chapter 18B.

c. A 'Residual' Treaty Power: From ERTA to Article 216

Under the 1957 Rome Treaty, the European Union only enjoyed two express treaty-making powers: one with regard to the Common Commercial Policy, and the other with regard to Association Agreements.[36] In the absence of a general

---

[27] *Ibid.*, Art. 207(2): 'The European Parliament and the Council, acting by means of regulations in accordance with the ordinary legislative procedure, shall adopt the measures defining the framework for implementing the common commercial policy.'

[28] *Ibid.*, Art. 207(3).

[29] *Ibid.*, Art. 207(1). For a brief constitutional history of the scope of the CCP, see (online) Chapter 18B, section 1(a).

[30] See *ibid.*, Arts. 209(1), 212(2), 214(3).

[31] See *ibid.*, Arts. 209(2), 212(3), 214(4).

[32] *Ibid.*, Art. 208(1).   [33] *Ibid.*, Art. 212(1).   [34] *Ibid.*, Art. 214(1).

[35] For a good account of that constitutional history, see P. Koutrakos, *Trade, Foreign Policy and Defence in EU Constitutional Law: The Legal Regulation of Sanctions, Exports of Dual-use Goods and Armaments* (Hart, 2001), 58ff.

[36] Ex-Arts. 113 and 238 EEC.

'Treaty Power' of the Union,[37] the legal possibility of *implied* external powers was therefore vital for the young supranational creature eager to assert itself on the international stage. This possibility was famously accepted in *ERTA*.[38]

aa. ERTA *and the Doctrine of Implied Powers*

The legal background to the *ERTA* dispute is complex: the European Road Transport Agreement (ERTA, or under its French acronym: AETR) had been designed to harmonise certain social aspects of international road transport and involved a number of Member States as potential signatories. The negotiations had (re)started in 1967 and were conducted without involvement of the Union; yet before the conclusion of the negotiations, the Council enacted in 1969 a regulation dealing with the issue of road safety for the internal sphere of the Union. Since ERTA was nevertheless still seen to be an important step in the same direction on the larger international plane, the Member States involved in the ERTA negotiations agreed to coordinate their positions within the Council, with the presiding Member State acting as spokesman. The Commission felt excluded from its role as the Union's external broker, insisted on being involved in the negotiations and finally brought the matter before the European Court.

There the Commission argued that the Union's internal power over transport policy – set out in Article 91 TFEU – included the external power of treaty-making. This wide teleological interpretation was justified by reference to the argument that 'the full effect of this provision would be jeopardized if the powers which it confers, particularly that of laying down "any appropriate provisions", within the meaning of subparagraph (1)(c) of the article cited, did not extend to the conclusion of agreements with third countries'.[39] The Commission's argument thus emphasised the need for an additional policy instrument to implement its objectives under the Union's transport competence.

The Council opposed this interpretation contending that 'Article [91] relates only to measures *internal* to the [Union], and cannot be interpreted as authorizing the conclusion of international agreements'. The power to enter into agreements with third countries 'cannot be assumed in the absence of an express provision in the [Treaties]'.[40] However, in its judgment, the European Court famously sided with the Commission's extensive stance and held:

> To determine in a particular case the [Union's] authority to enter into international agreements, regard must be had to the whole scheme of the [Treaties] no less than to its substantive provisions. *Such authority arises not only from an express conferment*

---

[37] By contrast, Art. 101 Euratom Treaty grants that Community a general competence in para. 1: 'The Community may within the limits of its powers and jurisdiction, enter into obligations by concluding agreements or contracts with a third State, an international organisation or a national of a third State.'

[38] Case 22/70, *Commission v. Council (ERTA)* [1971] ECR 263.

[39] *Ibid.*, para. 7.   [40] *Ibid.*, paras. 9–10 (emphasis added).

> *by the [Treaties] – as is the case with Article [207] for tariff and trade agreements*
> *and with Article [217] for association agreements – but may equally flow from other*
> *provisions of the [Treaties] and from measures adopted, within the framework of*
> *those provisions, by the [Union] institutions …*
>
> According to Article [90], the objectives of the Treaty in matters of transport are
> to be pursued within the framework of a common policy. With this in view, Article
> [91(1)] directs the Council to lay down common rules and, in addition, 'any other
> appropriate provisions'. By the terms of subparagraph (a) of the same provision, those
> common rules are applicable 'to international transport to or from the territory of a
> Member State or passing across the territory of one or more Member States'. This
> provision is equally concerned with transport from or to third countries, as regards
> that part of the journey which takes place on [Union] territory. It thus assumes that
> the powers of the [Union] extend to relationships arising from international law, and
> hence involve the need in the sphere in question for agreements with the third coun-
> tries concerned.[41]

The passage clearly spoke the language of teleological interpretation: in the light of the general scheme of the Treaties, the Union's power to adopt 'any other appropriate provision' to give effect to the Union's transport policy objectives must be interpreted as including the legal power to enter international agreements.[42] This was subsequently confirmed in *Opinion 1/76*,[43] where the Court declared that

> [W]henever [European] law has created for the institutions of the [Union] pow-
> ers within its internal system for the purpose of attaining a specific objective, the
> [Union] has authority to enter into the international commitments necessary for the
> attainment of that objective even in the absence of an express provision in that
> connexion.[44]

bb. Article 216: Codifying ERTA?

The doctrine of implied treaty powers has had a complex and contradictory constitutional history.[45] The Lisbon Treaty has tried to codify the doctrine in Article 216 TFEU.[46] The provision states:

---

[41] *Ibid.*, paras. 15–16 and 23–7 (emphasis added).

[42] In the words of the *ERTA* Court: 'With regard to the implementation of the [Treaties] the system of internal [Union] measures may not therefore be separated from that of external relations' (*ibid.*, para. 19).

[43] *Opinion 1/76* (Draft Agreement for the Laying-up Fund for Inland Waterway Vessels) [1977] ECR 741.

[44] *Ibid.*, para. 3.

[45] See R. Schütze, *Foreign Affairs and the EU Constitution* (Cambridge University Press, 2014), ch. 7.

[46] See European Convention, 'Final Report Working Group VII – External Action' (CONV 459/02), para. 18: 'The Group saw merit in making explicit the jurisprudence of the Court[.]'

> The Union may conclude an agreement with one or more third countries or international organisations where the Treaties so provide or where the conclusion of an agreement is necessary in order to achieve, within the framework of the Union's policies, one of the objectives referred to in the Treaties, or is provided for in a legally binding Union act or is likely to affect common rules or alter their scope.[47]

While recognising the express treaty-making competences of the Union conferred elsewhere by the Treaties, the provision here grants the Union an additional residual competence to conclude international agreements in three situations.

The first alternative mentioned in Article 216(1) TFEU confers a treaty power to the Union 'where the conclusion of an agreement is necessary in order to achieve, within the framework of the Union's policies, *one of the objectives referred to in the Treaties*'. This formulation is – strikingly – similar to the one found in the Union's residual competence in Article 352 TFEU. Textually, this competence is thus wider than the judicial doctrine of parallel external powers as originally espoused in *ERTA*. For, as we saw above, the Court had there insisted that an external competence only derived from an internal *competence*; and that meant that no external competence could be derived from an internal *objective*.[48] Yet the first alternative in Article 216 suggests exactly that. The Court however seems to have recently clarified that we are only in the presence of sloppy drafting and that Article 216 TFEU indeed codifies the doctrine of parallel powers from *ERTA*.[49]

Article 216 mentions two additional situations. The Union will also be entitled to conclude international agreements, where this 'is provided for in a legally binding act or is likely to affect common rules or alter their scope'. Both alternatives make the existence of an external competence dependent on the existence of internal Union law. Two objections may be launched against this view. Theoretically, it is difficult to accept that the Union can expand its competences without Treaty amendment through the simple adoption of internal Union acts.[50] And, practically, it is hard to see how either alternative will ever go beyond

---

[47] Art. 216(1) TFEU.

[48] The classic doctrine of implied external powers, as defined in *Opinion 1/76*, thus stated that 'whenever [European] law has created for the institutions of the [Union] *powers* within its internal system for the purposes of attaining a specific objective, the [Union] has authority to enter into the international commitments necessary for the attainment of that objective even in the absence of an express provision in that connexion' (*Opinion 1/76* (Laying-up Fund) [1977] ECR 741, para. 3 – emphasis added). And, to make it even clearer, the Court continued to state that the external powers flowed 'by implication from the provisions of the Treaty creating the internal *power*' (*ibid.*, para. 4 – emphasis added).

[49] *Opinion 1/13* (Hague Convention), EU:C:2014:2303, para. 67.

[50] On the notion of *Kompetenz-Kompetenz*, see Chapter 2, section 2(a).

the first alternative.[51] In any event, as we shall see in section 2(b), it is likely that alternatives two and three were the result of a fundamental confusion within the minds of those drafting the text behind Article 216 TFEU.

d. The Relationship between the CFSP and the Special Competences

What is the constitutional relationship between the Union's general CFSP competence and its special competences listed in the external relations part of the Treaty on the Functioning of the European Union? While both are housed under the same common provisions, the borderline between the CFSP and the other external policies has always been hotly contested. The reason for this contestation lies in the distinct procedural regimes for each constitutional site. While the CFSP is still – principally – governed by an intergovernmental procedural regime, the Union's special external policies are supranational in character.[52]

The key provision governing the borderline between the intergovernmental CFSP and the supranational external Union policies is Article 40 TEU. The provision states:

> The implementation of the common foreign and security policy shall not affect the application of the procedures and the extent of the powers of the institutions laid down by the Treaties for the exercise of the Union competences referred to in Articles 3 to 6 of the Treaty on the Functioning of the European Union.
>
> Similarly, the implementation of the policies listed in those Articles shall not affect the application of the procedures and the extent of the powers of the institutions laid down by the Treaties for the exercise of the Union competences under this Chapter.

The first indent protects the Union's supranational procedures and powers. It is designed to prevent the (European) Council from using the Union's CFSP competences, where recourse to one of the Union's supranational competences

---

[51] In any event, the existence of the first alternative next to the second alternative should now – finally – put to rest the idea that the existence of (implied) treaty power depends on the existence of internal legislation. For a long time, the European Court was, however, undecided whether implied external powers were automatically implied from internal powers; or whether they were contingent on the actual exercise of these internal powers through the adoption of internal legislation. The better view had always insisted on parallel external powers running alongside the Union's internal powers without regard to European legislation (see E. Stein, 'External Relations of the European Community: Structure and Process' (1990) 1 *Collected Courses of the Academy of European Law* 115 at 146).

[52] On this point, see section 3.

is possible. This is indeed the traditional – and prior to Lisbon: exclusive – function of the provision.[53]

The Court has interpreted this aspect of Article 40 in *ECOWAS*.[54] The case involved a legal challenge to the constitutionality of Union acts combating the spread of small arms and light weapons in the Economic Community of Western African States (ECOWAS). Would these acts have to be adopted under the general CFSP competence or the Union's specific competence in development cooperation? The Court found that the acts pursued a general foreign affairs aim and a specific development cooperation objective. However, as long as the CFSP objective was only *incidental*, the Union could adopt its acts on the basis of its specific external competences. The decisive test was here akin to a 'centre of gravity' test.[55]

Has this result been 'amended' by the Lisbon Treaty? The Lisbon Treaty has added the second indent to Article 40 TEU. The provision now equally protects the intergovernmental CFSP from a supranational incursion through the Union's specific external competences. In its post-Lisbon jurisprudence, the Court has thereby clarified that this simply means that a 'centre of gravity' test will apply; and the new indent to Article 40 therefore seems to simply 'codify' the *ECOWAS* solution. The Court has thus held:

> If an examination of a European Union measure reveals that it pursues a twofold purpose or that it comprises two components and if one of these is identifiable as the main or predominant purpose or component, whereas the other is merely incidental, the act must be based on a single legal basis, namely that required by the main or predominant purpose or component.[56]

How best to characterise the constitutional relationship between the CFSP competence and the Union's special external powers? The Lisbon Treaty has abandoned the idea that the Union's CFSP objectives form a separate set of

---

[53] In order to protect the *acquis communautaire*, the (old) TEU provided that 'nothing in this Treaty shall affect the Treaties establishing the European Communities' (ex-Art. 47 (old) EU); and the Court of Justice was expressly called upon to police that border (see ex-Art. 46(f) (old) EU). For case law under the old provision, see Case C-170/96, *Commission v. Council (Airport Transit Visa)* [1998] ECR I-2763; Case C-176/03, *Commission v. Council (Environmental Criminal Penalties)* [2005] ECR I-7879; Case C-440/05, *Commission v. Council (Ship-Source Pollution)* [2007] ECR I-9097.

[54] Case C-91/05, *Commission v. Council (ECOWAS)* [2008] ECR I-3651.

[55] On the 'centre of gravity' test, see H. Cullen and A. Charlesworth, 'Diplomacy by Other Means: The Use of Legal Basis Litigation as a Political Strategy by the European Parliament and Member States' (1999) 36 *CML Rev.* 1243.

[56] *Parliament v. Council (Pirates II)*, EU:C:2016:435, para. 44. The Court added that where, exceptionally, there are two main purposes, without one being incidental to the other, then the Union would have to split the legal act into a CFSP act and a non-CFSP act.

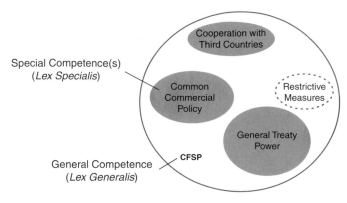

Figure 8.1 Relationships among Union External Competences

Union objectives;[57] and in light of the general nature of the CFSP, the latter should best be viewed as *lex generalis* to the *specialised* Union policies within Part V of the TFEU. The characterisation of the CFSP competence as *lex generalis* turns it into a subsidiary competence; and this subsidiary character establishes – with the exception of the Union competence on 'restrictive measures'[58] – a reciprocal relationship between the CFSP and the special external competences. The broader the interpretation given to the latter, the smaller the remaining scope of the CFSP competence. For an illustration of this relationship, see Figure 8.1.

2. The Nature of External Competences

What is the nature of the Union's external competences? What competence categories exist in the external sphere? With regard to their nature, the Treaties do not – as a rule – distinguish between internal and external competences. And indeed, within the areas of Union competences listed in Articles 3–6 TFEU, we find a number of external competences.[59] However, there are two exceptions to this constitutional rule. First, Article 2 TFEU specifically isolates the Union's CFSP competence from the ordinary competence categories – an arrangement that suggests a *sui generis* competence. Second, Article 3(2) TFEU provides a

---

57 This view can still be seen in Case C-402/05P, *Kadi and Al Barakaat International Foundation v. Council and Commission* [2008] ECR I-6351.

58 The availability of this competence depends on the CFSP competence having first been exercised.

59 For example, the common commercial policy is listed under the Union's exclusive competences (see Art. 3(1)(e) TFEU), environmental policy is listed as a shared competence (see Art. 191(4) TFEU: 'Within their respective spheres of competence, the Union and the Member States shall cooperate with third countries and with the competent international organisations. The arrangements for Union cooperation may be the subject of agreements between the Union and the third parties concerned'); and public health is listed as a complementary competence (see Art. 6(a) TFEU, and Art. 168(3) TFEU: 'The Union and the Member States shall foster cooperation with third countries and the competent international organisations in the sphere of public health').

source of exclusivity for the conclusion of international agreements that goes beyond the competence areas listed in Article 3(1) TFEU.

Let us look at both derogations from the 'ordinary' competence categories in turn.

a. The sui generis Nature of the CFSP Competence

The nature of the Union's CFSP competence has been a legal problem ever since its inception. According to an early view, law adopted under a CFSP competence was 'classic' international law that contrasted with supranational European law adopted under the 'ordinary' competences of the Union.[60] A second view, by contrast, argued that the CFSP competence was part of one and the same European legal order.[61]

The Lisbon Treaty has reinforced this second view. While recognising that the CFSP 'is subject to specific rules and procedures',[62] the Treaty on European Union and the Treaty on the Functioning of the European Union confirm that the two treaties 'have the same legal value'.[63] This includes secondary CFSP law. Indeed, the CFSP competence will be exercised by the 'ordinary' legal instruments of the Union legal order,[64] yet unlike 'ordinary' Union law, the direct effect of CFSP law appears to be exceptional.[65]

How shall we then best characterise the CFSP competence? The Treaties treat it as distinct from the Union competences referred to in Articles 3–6 TFEU.[66] But what is its exact nature? We might find a first answer to this question in Article 24 TEU dealing with the nature of the CFSP competence. The provision declares that '[t]he adoption of legislative acts shall be excluded' within the CFSP area. What will this mean? If the reference to 'legislative acts' were given

---

[60] M. Pechstein and C. Koenig, *Die Europäische Union* (Mohr Siebeck, 2000), 5ff. The thesis that Union law differed from Community law had gained support from ex-Art. 47 (old) EU, and Case C-402/05P, *Kadi*, para. 202: 'integrated but separate legal orders'.

[61] K. Lenaerts and T. Corthaut, 'Of Birds and Hedges: The Role of Primacy in Invoking Norms of EU Law' (2006) 31 *EL Rev.* 287 at 288.

[62] Art. 24(1) TEU.   [63] *Ibid.*, Art. 1 and Art. 1 TFEU.

[64] That is: decisions and international agreements. Prior to the Lisbon Treaty, the CFSP competence was to be exercised by a number of special legal instruments, such as 'joint actions' and 'common positions'.

[65] On the doctrine of 'direct effect' of European law, see Chapter 3. Direct effect is centrally determined by the European Courts. Yet the jurisdiction of the Court is generally excluded with respect to CFSP provisions and acts adopted on the basis of those provisions. The Treaties acknowledge only two express exceptions. First, CFSP law can be reviewed under Art. 40 TEU. Second, the Court has jurisdiction to review the legality of 'decisions providing for restrictive measures against natural or legal persons adopted by the Council on the basis of Chapter 2 of Title V of the Treaty on European Union' (see Art. 275(2) TFEU).

[66] Art. 40 TEU makes a clear distinction between the CFSP competence and 'the Union competences referred to in Articles 3–6 of the Treaty on the Functioning of the European Union'.

a formal meaning, that is: referring to acts adopted under a legislative procedure, then Article 24 TEU would state the obvious. Indeed, neither the ordinary nor any of the special legislative procedures apply within the CFSP. By contrast, if the formulation is given a material meaning, then Article 24 TEU signalled the exclusion of *generally* applicable CFSP norms.

A second key to the nature of CFSP competences might be found in Declaration 14 to the European Treaties, which underlines that the CFSP competence 'will not affect the existing legal basis, responsibilities, and powers of each Member State in relation to the formulation and conduct of its foreign policy, its national diplomatic service, relations with third countries and participation in international organisations'.[67] This formulation comes close to the idea of a parallel competence, but the better view insists that the CFSP competence is a 'special' or '*sui generis*' competence within the Union legal order.[68]

b. Article 3(2): Subsequently Exclusive Treaty Powers

We find a second exception to the 'ordinary' competence categories of the Union in Article 3(2) TFEU. The provision provides a special rule for the Union's competence to conclude international agreements. It states:

> The Union shall also have exclusive competence for the conclusion of an international agreement when its conclusion is provided for in a legislative act of the Union or is necessary to enable the Union to exercise its internal competence, or in so far as its conclusion may affect common rules or alter their scope.

In addition to the constitutionally fixed exclusive competences – mentioned in Article 3(1) – the Union legal order thus acknowledges the *dynamic* growth of its exclusive competences in the external sphere. Let us look at past constitutional practice in this context first, before questioning the constitutional theory underlying it.

aa. Three Lines of Exclusivity: Codifying Constitutional Practice?

According to Article 3(2), the Union may obtain exclusive treaty-making power, where one of three situations is fulfilled. These three situations are said to codify three famous judicial doctrines developed by the European Court prior to the Lisbon Treaty.[69]

According to the first situation, the Union enjoys an exclusive treaty making power when the conclusion of an international agreement 'is provided for in a

---

[67] Declaration No. 14 concerning the Common Foreign and Security Policy.

[68] M. Cremona, 'The Draft Constitutional Treaty: External Relations and External Action' (2003) 40 *CML Rev.* 1347 at 1354.

[69] On the three judicial doctrines, see R. Schütze, *Foreign Affairs and the EU Constitution* (Cambridge University Press, 2014), 256ff.

legislative act'. This formulation corresponds to the so-called 'WTO Doctrine' established in *Opinion 1/94* on the compatibility of the WTO Agreement with the Treaties.[70] The Court had here stated: '[w]henever the [Union] has concluded in its internal legislative acts provisions relating to the treatment of nationals of non-member countries or expressly conferred on the institutions powers to negotiate with non-member countries, it acquires exclusive external competence in the spheres covered by those acts'.[71] Article 3(2) codifies this judicial doctrine. However, the codification is more restrictive, as it excludes the first alternative ('provisions relating to the treatment of nationals of non-member countries') from its scope.

The second situation mentioned in Article 3(2) TFEU grants the Union an exclusive treaty power, where this 'is necessary to enable the Union to exercise its internal competence'. This formulation aims to codify the '*Opinion 1/76* Doctrine'.[72] In its past jurisprudence the Court had created a second line of subsequent exclusivity 'where the conclusion of an international agreement is necessary in order to achieve Treaty objectives *which cannot be attained by the adoption of autonomous rules*',[73] and where the achievement of an internal objective is 'inextricably linked' with the external sphere.[74] This restrictive definition however cannot be found in Article 3(2) TFEU. And, in its unqualified openness, the second situation comes close to the wording of the Union's 'residual' competence: Article 216 TFEU. The almost identical wording of Article 3(2) and Article 216 TFEU thus suggests that 'implied shared competence would disappear'; yet, this would be 'a wholly undesirable departure from the case law'.[75]

Finally, the third situation in Article 3(2) appears to refer to the Court's so-called '*ERTA* doctrine'. Under the *ERTA* doctrine,[76] the Member States are deprived of their treaty-making power whenever the exercise of those powers affects internal European law. Each time the Union 'adopts provisions laying down common rules, whatever form these may take, the Member States no longer have the right, acting individually or even collectively, to undertake obligations with third countries *which affect those rules*'.[77] The principle behind the *ERTA* doctrine is to prevent an international agreement concluded by the Member States from undermining 'the uniform and consistent application of the [Union] rules and the proper functioning of the system which they

---

[70] *Opinion 1/94* (WTO Agreement) [1994] ECR I-5267.   [71] *Ibid.*, para. 95.

[72] *Opinion 1/76* (Laying-up Fund) [1977] ECR 741. On the evolution of the *Opinion 1/76* doctrine, see Schütze, *Foreign Affairs* (n. 69 above), 258ff.

[73] *Opinion 2/92* (Third Revised Decision of the OECD on national treatment) [1995] ECR I-521, Part V, para. 4 (emphasis added).

[74] Case C-476/98, *Commission* v. *Germany (Open Skies)* [2002] ECR I-9855, para. 87.

[75] M. Cremona, 'A Constitutional Basis for Effective External Action? An Assessment of the Provisions on EU External Action in the Constitutional Treaty', EUI Working Paper 2006/30, 10. For a recent confirmation of this view, see Case C-600/14, *Germany* v. *Council*, EU:2017:935, esp. para. 51: '[T]he European Union may have an external competence that falls outside the situations laid down in Article 3(2) TFEU.'

[76] Case 22/70, *Commission* v. *Council*.   [77] *Ibid.*, para. 18 – emphasis added.

establish'.[78] Has Article 3(2) properly codified this third judicial line of exclusive powers? The third alternative in Article 3(2) – strangely – breaks the link between a *Member State* agreement and internal European law, and replaces it with an analysis of the effect of a *Union* agreement on European rules. But this simply is an 'editorial mistake', and the Court has clarified that the 'old' *ERTA* case law fully applies here.[79]

The practically most important situation within Article 3(2) is indeed this third situation. To what extent does the *ERTA* doctrine here 'pre-empt' the Member States from concluding international agreements on their own? In the past, the following criteria have come to guide the Court in its analysis. First, Article 3(2) is only triggered once the Union has adopted secondary law. The reference to 'common rules' being affected will not include primary law.[80] Second, in order to see if Article 3(2) applies, the Court will start to investigate to what extent internal Union law covers the scope of the envisaged international agreement. Third, if that is the case 'to a large extent', the Court will then look at whether there exists a risk that the Union common rules will be affected.[81] From here, the judicial analysis normally descends into an informed chaos in which the Court selects its precedents in a relatively arbitrary way so as to reach the result that it prefers. The Court has, for example, found that there need not be a contradiction between the envisaged international agreement and existing Union rules – alluding to the fact that something akin to field-pre-emption is taking place;[82] yet it has also held that Union rules will not be affected where they only lay down minimum rules – thereby allowing the Member States to be party to an international agreement that sets higher standards.[83]

bb. Subsequent Exclusivity: A Critical Analysis

The Treaties take great care to clarify that the question of Union competences is a 'constitutional' question. The competences of the Union should thus be increased solely by (ordinary) Treaty amendment.[84]

Should we not expect that the nature of a competence – that is: the degree to which Member States remain entitled to act – is also constitutionally fixed? In other words, is there not something strange in the idea that the Union can, without Treaty amendment, change its order of competences? As we saw above, this is not the position of the Lisbon Treaty, nor has it been that of the European Court:

---

[78] *Opinion 1/03* (Lugano Convention) [2006] ECR I-1145, para. 133.

[79] Case C-114/12 *Commission* v. *Council*, EU:C:2014:2151, esp. para. 66.

[80] This was recently confirmed, beyond doubt, in *Opinion 2/15* (Singapore), EU:C:2017:376, esp. paras. 234 and 235.

[81] See *Opinion 1/13* (Hague Convention), EU:C:2014:2303, paras. 83–4.

[82] See Case 114/12, *Commission* v. *Council*, para. 71; *Opinion 1/13* (Hague Convention), para. 85.

[83] *Opinion 2/91* (ILO Convention No. 170), [1993] ECR I-1061, esp. para. 18.

[84] On the idea of *Kompetenz- Kompetenz,* see Chapter 2, section 2(a).

> The exclusive or non-exclusive nature of the [Union]'s competence does not flow solely from the provisions of the Treaty but may also depend on the scope of the measures which have been adopted by the [Union] institutions for the application of those provisions and which are of such a kind as to deprive the Member States of an area of competence which they were able to exercise previously on a transitional basis.[85]

But even if Article 3(2) and the European Court embrace the idea of subsequently exclusive powers, should we uncritically accept this theory? A number of theoretical objections may indeed be advanced against it.[86] For identifying the effect of internal Union legislation with exclusive external competences raises serious objections from the perspective of the hierarchy of norms. The scope of the Union's exclusive competences is a constitutional question and, as such, it should – at least theoretically – only be extended by means of constitutional amendment. It thus seems a feat of legal alchemy to permit the Union to modify its order of competences, especially because this would allow the European legislator to escape the reach of the subsidiarity principle.[87] The exclusionary effect in the first and third situation in Article 3(2) indeed stem from the effect of Union legislation; and this legislative 'exclusivity' is more fragile than constitutionally exclusive powers, since it can again be repealed by a legislative act.

The two phenomena of constitutional and legislative exclusivity should therefore be kept apart. And while the Treaty-makers couched the effects mentioned in Article 3(2) TFEU in terms of exclusive competences, they should have been better expressed in the more nuanced vocabulary of the doctrine of legislative pre-emption.[88]

3. External Decision-making Procedures

How will the Union externally act, and through which procedures? This depends on the type of act adopted. An analysis of decision-making procedures within the Union's external powers must here distinguish between *unilateral acts* and *international agreements*.[89] Unilateral external acts are acts that are single-handedly adopted by the European Union but directed at a third party. Such unilateral acts might range from giving financial aid to a developing State to imposing

---

[85] *Opinion 2/91* (ILO Convention 170) [1993] ECR I-1061, para. 9. For a more recent confirmation that Art. 3(2) exclusive powers are not shared powers, see Case C-114/12, *Commission* v. *Council*, para. 73.

[86] Schütze, *Foreign Affairs* (n. 69 above), 269ff.

[87] C. Calliess, *Subsidiaritäts- und Solidaritätsprinzip in der Europäischen Union* (Nomos, 1999), 95.

[88] On the doctrine of pre-emption, see Chapter 4, section 3.

[89] This section will not deal with 'positions' adopted within an international organisation.

economic sanctions on a third country.[90] By contrast, international agreements are agreements between the Union and a third party, and thus require the consent of the latter. We find *both* instruments within both constitutional sites for external relations. However, while the constitutional regime for unilateral acts is fundamentally different between the CFSP and the specialised TFEU external policies, both share the same treaty-making procedure.

This third section looks at the procedural regime for unilateral acts and international agreements. With regard to unilateral acts, it will concentrate on the procedure for CFSP decisions only because unilateral acts adopted under the specialised external competences generally follow the (ordinary) legislative procedure;[91] and, as formal Union legislation, their adoption was already discussed in Chapter 7. All international agreements – including CFSP agreements – on the other hand, are concluded according to procedures found in the Treaty on the Functioning of the European Union. The 'ordinary' treaty-making procedure is here set out in Article 218 TFEU.

The provision constitutes the most important *procedural* link between the two external relations sites. Importantly, there are however also *personal* and *institutional* links between the CFSP and the Union's specialised external policies. The former is embodied in the person of the High Representative. The latter is expressed in Article 22 TEU – placed in the Chapter 'General Provisions on the Union's External Action'. According to this provision, the European Council must 'identify the strategic interests and objectives of the Union'. And these decisions on the strategic interests of the Union 'shall relate to the common foreign and security policy *and to other areas of the external action of the Union*'.[92] The European Council is thus the Union's – formal or informal – guide and pacemaker for all its external actions.[93]

a. CFSP Decision-making Procedures

The procedures for the adoption of unilateral CFSP acts are specific to the CFSP.[94] The specificity of CFSP procedures manifests itself in the institutional arrangements for decision-making, as well as the voting requirements in the

---

[90] Both of these external policies will be discussed in (online) Chapter 18B. For an example of a unilateral act imposing sanctions, see Council Regulation 833/2014 concerning restrictive measures in view of Russia's actions destabilising the situation in Ukraine [2014] OJ L 229/1.

[91] See Art. 207(2) TFEU (emphasis added): 'The European Parliament and the Council, acting by means of regulations in accordance with the *ordinary legislative procedure*, shall adopt the measures defining the framework for implementing the common commercial policy.'

[92] Emphasis added.

[93] The European Council indeed regularly decides on the strategic interests of the Union. It is interesting to note, however, that the European Council has come to prefer 'informal' strategies. On this point, see P. Eeckhout, *External Relations of the European Union* (Oxford University Press, 2004), 476–7.

[94] See Art. 24(1) TEU.

Council. Their 'intergovernmental' character differs significantly from the supra-national procedures governing all other external Union policies.

aa. Institutional Actors and Institutional Balance

The original institutional arrangements within the CFSP have rightly been criticised as 'confused'.[95] And, while the current Treaties have simplified some matters, the constitutional principles governing the institutional dimension within the CFSP remain complex.

The central *policy*maker is the European Council, which identifies the strategic interests and general guidelines for the CFSP. It acts by means of decisions on a recommendation from the Council.[96] These decisions not only set the direction of European foreign policy, but also its pace. (For decisions of the European Council will, as discussed below, have consequences for the voting arrangements in the Council.) The President of the European Council will 'at his level and in that capacity' ensure the external representation of the Union on issues concerning the CFSP without prejudice to the representational role of the High Representative of Foreign Affairs and Security Policy.[97]

The Council (here the Foreign Affairs Council) is the central *decision*-making body in the CFSP. It shall 'frame' the CFSP and 'take the decisions necessary for defining and implementing it' on the basis of the strategic interests and general guidelines adopted by the European Council.[98] (This central decision-making role extends to the conclusion of international agreements.)[99] The High Representative of Foreign Affairs and Security Policy, who will chair the Foreign Affairs Council, will generally assist the Council in its tasks.[100]

What is the role of the supranational Union institutions? The role of the Commission within the CFSP is minimal and ill defined. It 'may', with the High Representative, make joint proposals to the European Council on the strategic interests of the Union;[101] and it 'may' support proposals by the High Representative to the Council, but this joint right of initiative is shared with any Member State.[102] What is the role of the European Parliament? The role of the European Parliament is even smaller than that of the Commission. Its principal prerogative lies in being regularly consulted 'on the main aspects and the basic choices' within the CFSP and having its views taken into consideration.[103] Parliament can ask questions and make recommendations to the Council, and it must hold a debate, twice a year, on the state of the CFSP.[104]

---

[95] Eeckhout, *External Relations* (n. 93 above), 420.
[96] See Arts. 22(1) and 26(1) TEU.   [97] *Ibid.*, Art. 15(6).   [98] *Ibid.*, Art. 26(2).
[99] See Art. 218(2) TFEU: 'The Council shall authorise the opening of negotiations, adopt negotiating directives, authorise the signing of agreements and conclude them.'
[100] Art. 27(1) TEU.   [101] *Ibid.*, Art. 22(2).
[102] *Ibid.*, Art. 30. The Lisbon Treaty appears thus to have extinguished the Commission's autonomous right of initiative within the CFSP.
[103] *Ibid.*, Art. 36(1).   [104] *Ibid.*, Art. 36(2).

bb. *Voting Arrangements in the Council*

The Council is the central decision-taker within the CFSP. The Council voting rules are set out in Article 31 TEU. The general rule is that the Council acts unanimously. However, unlike other Union policies, the CFSP recognises the constitutional possibility of a 'constructive abstention'. It is constructive in that it allows the Council to act, despite the abstention of (a) Member State(s), by unanimity. The abstaining Member State, having made a formal declaration, is not obliged to apply the Union decision.[105]

In derogation from the unanimity rule, Article 31(2) enumerates a number of exceptional situations in which qualified majority voting applies. The Council can adopt a decision by qualified majority: (i) when it is based on a decision of the European Council; (ii) when it is based on a proposal from the High Representative following a specific request from the European Council; (iii) when it implements its own decisions; or (iv) when appointing a special representative (in accordance with Article 33 TEU).[106] This list of categories may be extended if the European Council so decides by unanimity.[107]

Importantly, what constitutes a qualified majority under Article 31 TEU differs according to the category involved. This follows from Article 238(2) TFEU,[108] which distinguishes between an 'ordinary' and a 'special' qualified majority for Council decisions, depending on whether the Council acts on a proposal from the High Representative. With the exception of category (ii), all CFSP decisions would thus seem to require a special qualified majority.

Finally, Article 31 TEU establishes two 'exceptions to the exception' of qualified majority voting. It sets two absolute limits to decisional supranationalism. The first is of a political nature, the second of a constitutional nature. The political limit incorporates the 'Luxembourg Compromise' into the CFSP.[109] Any Member State may 'for vital and stated reasons of national policy' declare that it opposes a decision to be taken by qualified majority voting.[110] By contrast, the second limit is of a constitutional nature: any qualified majority voting can never apply to decisions having military or defence implications.[111]

---

[105] This procedural mechanism finds a quantitative limit in one-third of the Member States comprising one-third of the population of the Union.

[106] Art. 33 TEU states: 'The Council may, on a proposal from the High Representative of the Union for Foreign Affairs and Security Policy, appoint a special representative with a mandate in relation to particular policy issues. The special representative shall carry out his mandate under the authority of the High Representative.'

[107] *Ibid.*, Art. 31(3).

[108] The provision states: 'By way of derogation from Article 16(4) of the Treaty on European Union, as from 1 November 2014 and subject to the provisions laid down in the Protocol on transitional provisions, where the Council does not act on a proposal from the Commission or from the High Representative of the Union for Foreign Affairs and Security Policy, the qualified majority shall be defined as at least 72 per cent of the members of the Council, representing Member States comprising at least 65 per cent of the population of the Union.'

[109] On the 'Luxembourg Compromise', see Chapter 1, section 2(b).

[110] Art. 31(2) TEU.   [111] *Ibid.*, Art. 31(5).

b. The (Ordinary) Treaty-making Procedure

The 'ordinary' procedure for the conclusion of international agreements by the Union is set out in Article 218 TFEU.[112]

The central institution within this procedure is the Council – not just as *primus inter pares* with Parliament but simply as *primus*. Article 218 indeed acknowledges the central role of the Council in all stages of the procedure:

> The Council shall authorise the opening of negotiations, adopt negotiating directives, authorise the signing of agreements and conclude them.[113]

The Council hereby acts by a qualified majority,[114] except in four situations. It needs the unanimous consent of all national ministers when the agreement covers an internal competence for which unanimity is required; unanimity is also needed for all association agreements, for all economic cooperation agreements with States that are candidates for Union accession, as well as in respect of the Union's accession agreement to the ECHR.[115]

Having recognised the primary role of the Council, Article 218 TFEU then defines the secondary roles of the other EU institutions in the various procedural stages of treaty-making (see Figure 8.2). The provision here distinguishes between the initiation stage and a negotiation stage (see section (aa)), as well as a signing and conclusion stage (see section (bb)). It also provides special rules for modifications and suspensions (see section (cc)). Exceptionally, the Union can become a party to international agreements without even having to conclude them. This – rare – phenomenon occurs, where the Union 'inherits' international agreements from its Member States through the doctrine of functional succession (see section (dd)).

---

[112]   Two special procedures are found in Arts. 207 and 219 TFEU. The former deals with trade agreements within the context of the Union's common commercial policy. Art. 207(3) here expressly clarifies that 'Article 218 shall apply, subject to the special provisions in this Article'. Art. 207 thus constitutes a *lex specialis* to the *lex generalis* of Art. 218. A second express derogation from the 'ordinary' procedure in Art. 218 is made for 'formal agreements on an exchange-rate system for the euro in relation to the currencies of third states' (see Art. 219(1): '[b]y way of derogation from Article 218'). Finally, with regard to non-binding 'informal' agreements between the Union and a third state, another procedure than Art. 218 TFEU may apply (see Case C-660/13, *Council* v. *Commission*, EU:C:2016:616).

[113]   Art. 218(2) TFEU.

[114]   Importantly, Art. 218 TFEU has not incorporated the old CFSP rule under ex-Art. 24(5) (old) EU, according to which a Member State would not be bound by an agreement to which its representative had not consented. However, the constitutional relationship between the general voting rules in Art. 218(8) TFEU and the special CFSP voting rules in Art. 31 TEU is not yet clarified. Whether special CFSP arrangements, such as the 'constructive abstention' or the 'emergency break', will apply to CFSP agreements remains to be seen. (However, importantly, unlike Art. 222(3) TFEU, no express mention is made of the applicability of the voting arrangements in Art. 31 TEU.)

[115]   Art. 218(8) TFEU.

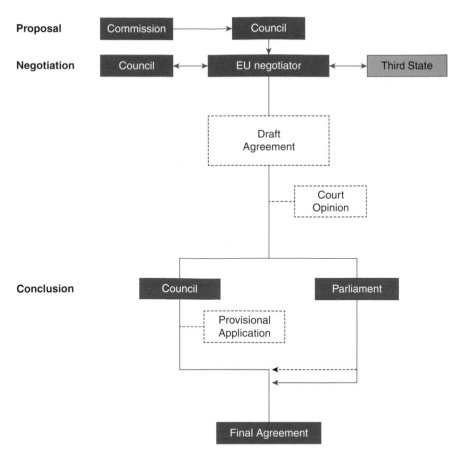

Figure 8.2 Treaty-making Procedure According to Article 218

aa. Initiation and Negotiation

Who can propose a new international agreement that the Union should conclude? Under Article 218(3), the Commission holds the exclusive right to make
recommendations for agreements that principally deal with non-CFSP matters.
By contrast, as regards subject matters that exclusively or principally fall within
the CFSP, it is the High Representative who must submit recommendations to
the Council. For matters falling partly within the CFSP and partly outside it,
there is also the possibility of 'joint proposals'.[116]

Acting on a recommendation, the Council may decide to open negotiations
and nominate the Union negotiator 'depending on the subject matter of the
agreement envisaged'.[117] This formulation is ambivalent. Textually, the phrase
suggests a liberal meaning. The Council can – but need not necessarily – appoint
the Commission as the Union negotiator for an agreement. According to this
reading the Commission will not automatically enjoy a prerogative to be the
Union's negotiator for non-CFSP agreements. However, a systematic reading of

[116] See Arts. 22(2) and 30(1) TEU.   [117] Art. 218(3) TFEU.

the phrase leads to a more restrictive meaning. For, if read in light of the juris-dictional division between the Commission and the High Representative at the recommendation stage, the Commission would be constitutionally entitled to be the Union negotiator for all Union agreements that 'exclusively or principally' fall into the Treaty on the Functioning of the European Union.[118] This is equally supported by teleological arguments.[119]

The Council will be able to address directives to the Union negotiator and to subject its powers to consultation with a special Council committee. Where the Commission is chosen as negotiator, it will thus not only need to be 'authorised' by the Council but would also need to conduct the negotiations under the con-trol of the Council. The Commission's powers are here between 'autonomous' and 'delegated' powers. They cannot be as autonomous as under the legislative procedure because neither the Council nor the Parliament can formally sug-gest amendments once the agreement is negotiated with a third State. The lower degree of Commission autonomy is furthermore justified by the fact that third parties are involved. (For the subsequent rejection of the negotiated agreement by the Council would indeed have 'external' negative repercussions.) The existence of a Council committee checking on the Commission creates, however, a 'two-front war' for the latter. That is, the Union negotiator has not only to externally negoti-ate with a third party, it also needs to internally deal with the Council.

To what extent may the Union negotiator – especially the Commission – be 'hamstrung' by the Council? This question received an interesting answer in *Commission v. Council (Emission Trading)*.[120] The Commission here sought the annulment of a Council negotiating mandate that it felt restricted its power to negotiate a greenhouse emissions-trading scheme with Australia too much. The Council directives for the Commission had stated as follows:

> A. Procedure for Negotiations
> 1. The Commission shall conduct negotiations in accordance with relevant Union legislation in force. *Where appropriate, detailed negotiation positions of the Union shall be established within the special committee referred to in [the man-date].* The Working Party on the Environment is designated as special committee to assist the Commission in this task …
> 3. *Each negotiating session shall be preceded by a meeting within the special com-mittee in order to identify the key issues and establish negotiating positions or guidance, as appropriate* …
> 4. The Commission shall report to the Council on the outcome of the negotia-tions after each negotiating session, and, in any event, at least quarterly. The Commission shall inform the Council and consult the special committee on any major problem that may arise during the negotiations.[121]

---

[118] In this sense, see Eeckhout, *External Relations* (n. 93 above), 196.
[119] According to Art. 17(1) TEU, it is the Commission that, with the exception of the CFSP, 'shall ensure the Union's external representation'.
[120] Case C-425/13 *Commission v. Council (Emission Trading)*, EU:C:2015:483.
[121] *Ibid.*, paras. 12 (emphasis added).

The Commission was deeply unhappy with all these conditions; yet the Court generally upheld the Council mandate – except with regard to the conditions set out in italics in the above quote. With regard to them, the Court held:

> [I]it is apparent from those provisions, constructed in the light of their wording and placed in their context, that their intention is that the negotiating positions have binding effects on the negotiator. It is contrary to Article 218(4) TFEU for the positions established by the special committee or, as the case may be, the Council itself to be binding in this way … *[W]hilst it is true that Article 218(4) TFEU authorizes the Council to draw up negotiating directives, it does not, on the other hand … invest that institution with the power to impose 'detailed negotiating positions' on the negotiator.* It follows that, by including those elements in the negotiating directives, the Council infringed the obligation laid down by Article 13(2) TEU to act within the limits of the powers conferred on it by Article 218(2) to (4) TFEU.[122]

The Council is thus not allowed to 'straitjacket' the Commission when negotiating international agreements with third countries. The Union negotiator must have a degree of autonomy, even if the Council can legitimately limit that autonomy to *some* extent.

What about Parliament? Parliament is not formally involved in the negotiation. However, Article 218(10) TFEU constitutionalises Parliament's right to be informed during all stages of the procedure. This right has the potential of anticipating the views of Parliament prior to the conclusion stage;[123] yet even in an area where Parliament will not be involved in the conclusion of the agreement, the Court has held that Parliament must always be 'immediately and fully informed' because its right to information ensures that 'Parliament is in a position to exercise democratic scrutiny of the European Union's external action' and 'more specifically, to verify that its powers are respected'.[124]

If any of the Union institutions involved (or any Member State) are unhappy with the negotiated agreement, it can challenge the 'constitutionality' of the

---

[122] *Ibid.*, paras. 87–91 (emphasis added).

[123] See Framework Agreement on Relations between the European Parliament and the European Commission, esp. Annex III. According to para. 3 of the Annex, '[t]he Commission shall take due account of Parliament's comments throughout the negotiations'.

[124] Case C-658/11, *Parliament v. Council (Pirates I)* EU: C: 2014: 2025, paras. 79 and 86. For an elaboration of the scope and nature of the obligation, see Case C-263/14 *Parliament v. Council (Pirates II)*. The Court here, *inter alia* clarified that the obligation to inform the Parliament lay on the Council – not the High Representative (*ibid.*, para. 73). And, with regard to the scope of the obligation to be informed, the Court held (*ibid.*, para. 76): '[W]ith respect to the scope of the information obligation covered by that provision, it must be stated that the procedure for negotiating and concluding international agreements laid down in Article 218 TFEU includes, inter alia, the authorization to open negotiations, the definition of the negotiating directives, the nomination of the Union negotiator and, in some cases, the designation of a special committee, the completion of negotiations, the authorization to sign the agreement, where necessary, the decision on the provisional application of the agreement before its entry into force and the conclusion of the agreement.'

draft agreement *prior* to its conclusion. This judicial 'preview' procedure can be found in Article 218(11) TFEU, which creates the jurisdiction of the Court of Justice for an 'Opinion' with regard to an international agreement.[125] This judicial preview can take place as soon as the agreement is 'envisaged' but it must be finished before the draft agreement is concluded.[126] Where this 'Opinion' leads to a finding that the negotiated agreement is not compatible with the Treaties, the agreement cannot enter into force – unless the EU Treaties themselves are amended.[127] The possibility of an *ex ante* 'review' of a draft agreement contrasts with the Court's ordinary *ex post* review powers for Union legislation.[128] However, the exception is – again – justified by the fact that third party rights under international law are involved. Indeed, it is a rule of international law that, once an agreement is validly concluded a contracting party generally cannot subsequently invoke internal constitutional problems to deny its binding effect.[129]

bb. Signing and Conclusion

The Council may sign and conclude the agreement after a proposal from the negotiator.[130] However, prior to the final conclusion of the agreement, the European Parliament must be involved. The rules on parliamentary participation in the conclusion of Union treaties are set out in Article 218(6) TFEU. The provision states:

> Except where agreements relate exclusively to the common foreign and security policy, the Council shall adopt the decision concluding the agreement:
> (a) after obtaining the consent of the European Parliament in the following cases:
>   (i) association agreements;

---

[125] Art. 218(11) TFEU. For a list of the Court's Opinions on international agreements, see Table of Cases 1(c).

[126] For a good discussion of the relevant case law with regard to the timing of the request for an opinion, see P. Eeckhout, *EU External Relations Law* (Oxford University Press, 2011), 268–74.

[127] This happened, for example, with regard to the European Convention on Human Rights in 1996 (see *Opinion 2/94* (Accession to ECHR) [1996] ECR I-1759). Prior to the Lisbon Treaty, accession to the Convention was thus unconstitutional. The Lisbon Treaty has amended the original Treaties, which now contain an express competence to accede to the ECHR in Art. 6(2) TEU.

[128] On *ex post* judicial review in the Union legal order, see Chapter 10, section 1.

[129] See Art. 46 Vienna Convention on the Law of Treaties: '(1) A State may not invoke the fact that its consent to be bound by a treaty has been expressed in violation of a provision of its internal law regarding competence to conclude treaties as invalidating its consent unless that violation was manifest and concerned a rule of its internal law of fundamental importance. (2) A violation is manifest if it would be objectively evident to any State conducting itself in the matter in accordance with normal practice and in good faith.'

[130] Art. 218(5) and (6) TFEU. The conclusion will usually be done by means of a Council Decision.

> (ii) agreement on Union accession to the European Convention for the Protection of Human Rights and Fundamental Freedoms;
> (iii) agreements establishing a specific institutional framework by organising cooperation procedures;
> (iv) agreements with important budgetary implications for the Union;
> (v) agreements covering fields to which either the ordinary legislative procedure applies, or the special legislative procedure where consent by the European Parliament is required.
> The European Parliament and the Council may, in an urgent situation, agree upon a time-limit for consent.
> (b) after consulting the European Parliament in other cases. The European Parliament shall deliver its opinion within a time-limit which the Council may set depending on the urgency of the matter. In the absence of an opinion within that time-limit, the Council may act.

The European Parliament will thus always be involved in the conclusion of Union agreements – except where the agreement *exclusively* relates to the CFSP. With this formulation, the TFEU seems, at first sight, to expressly allow for parliamentary involvement even with regard to agreements that do not exclusively but only principally relate to CFSP matters. Yet in *Parliament* v. *Council (Pirates I)*,[131] the Court unambiguously clarified that this is not the case. Insisting that Article 218 'establishes symmetry between the procedure for adopting EU measures internally and the procedure for adopting international agreements in order to guarantee that the Parliament and the Council enjoy the same powers in relation to a given field',[132] the Court here ruled that 'exclusively' actually means 'principally'. The fact that an EU agreement touched upon *some* matters falling within the TFEU was thus not enough to establish Parliament's right to be involved.[133]

For matters outside the CFSP, Article 218(6) then distinguishes between two forms of parliamentary participation: consent and consultation. The latter constitutes the residual category and applies to all agreements that do not require consent.

What are the – respective – procedural rules applying to parliamentary consent and consultation? The former requires Parliament to formally consent to the negotiated international treaty. Consent is here less than co-conclusion, as Parliament can only 'take or leave' the negotiated treaty. Its internal rules determine that Parliament must express consent 'in a single vote by a majority of the votes cast', and '[n]o amendments to the text of the agreement or protocol shall be admissible'.[134] The lack of formal amendment powers is regrettable. The simple power to veto an agreement has nevertheless proven to be (relatively) strong

---

[131] Case C-658/11.   [132] *Ibid.*, para. 56.
[133] *Ibid.*, paras. 58–62. This result has been confirmed in Case C-263/14 *Parliament* v. *Council (Pirates II)*, esp. para. 55.
[134] Rule 108(7) of the Parliament's Rules of Procedure.

in the past.[135] The parliamentary rights under the consultation procedure are, by contrast, much weaker. Although the Court has recognised that consultation is 'an essential factor in the institutional balance intended by the Treaty',[136] consultation is still a mere 'formality'.

What classes of international treaties require parliamentary consent under Article 218(6)(a)? The types of international agreements are enumerated in the form of five situations. The first, second and third categories may be explained by the constitutional idea of 'political treaties'.[137] For association agreements as well as institutional agreements – including the European Convention on Human Rights – will by definition express an important *political* choice with long-term consequences. For these fundamental political choices Parliament – the representative of the European citizens – must give its democratic consent. The fourth category represents a constitutional reflex that protects the special role the European Parliament enjoys in shaping the Union budget.[138]

Article 218(6)(a)(v) finally expands parliamentary consent to all agreements within policy areas that internally require parliamentary consent or co-decision. And, with this fifth category, parliamentary consent has become the constitutional rule. Nonetheless, the parallelism between the internal and external spheres is incomplete. For Parliament will *not* – as already mentioned above – enjoy the power of co-conclusion in areas in which the 'ordinary' legislative procedure applies. Its internal power to co-decision is reduced to a mere power of 'consent'. This structural 'democratic deficit' in the procedural regime for international agreements can be found in other constitutional orders of the world.[139] It is perhaps 'the' greatest democratic challenge of the modern world. For, in light of the often more than 1,000 pages that modern trade treaties typically cover, how can parliaments have any meaningful 'input' or 'control' here?

cc. Modification, Suspension (and Termination)

Article 218(7) TFEU deals with *modifications* of international agreements that have been successfully concluded. The Council may 'authorise the negotiator to approve on the Union's behalf modifications to the agreement where it provides for them to be adopted by a simplified procedure or by a body set up by the agreement'. (The Council can here again attach specific conditions to such an

---

[135] The European Parliament uses its negative veto rarely but regularly. It has for example rejected the first US–EU Swift agreement on 11 February 2010 and equally rejected the Anti-Counterfeiting Trade Agreement (ACTA) on 4 July 2012.

[136] Case 138/79, *Roquette Frères* v. *Council (Isoglucose)* [1980] 3333, para. 33.

[137] R. Jennings and S. Watts (eds.), *Oppenheim's International Law* (Oxford University Press, 2008), 211.

[138] For an extensive discussion of this category, see Case C-189/97, *Parliament* v. *Council (Mauritania Fisheries Agreement)* [1999] ECR I-4741.

[139] It can be found, for example, in the United States. According to Art. II, s. 2 of the US Constitution, it is the president who 'shall have Power, by and with the Advice and Consent of the Senate, to make Treaties, provided two thirds of the Senators present concur'. The American Parliament – the House of Representatives – is not formally involved.

authorisation.) In the absence of a specific authorisation for a simplified revision procedure, the ordinary treaty-making procedure will apply. This follows from a constitutional principle called *actus contrarius*. In order to modify an international agreement, the same procedure needs to be followed that led to the conclusion of the international agreement in the first place.

Article 218(9) TFEU deals with the *suspension* of an international agreement. The provision specifies that the Commission or the High Representative may propose to the Council the suspension of the agreement. And, while the provision does not expressly refer to the jurisdictional division between the two actors, as mentioned in Article 218(3) TFEU for the proposal stage, we should assume that this rule would apply analogously. The High Representative should thus solely be entitled to recommend suspension of international agreements that relate 'exclusively or principally' to the CFSP. Parliament is not expressly mentioned and will thus only have to be informed of the Council decision. This truncated procedure allows the Union quickly to decide on the (temporary) suspension of an agreement. However, this 'executive' decision without parliamentary consent distorts to some extent the institutional balance in the external relations field.

How are Union agreements *terminated*? Unfortunately, Article 218 TFEU does not expressly set out a procedural regime for the termination of a Union agreement. Two views are possible. The first view is again based on the idea of *actus contrarius:* the termination of an agreement would need to follow the very same procedure for its conclusion. This procedural parallelism has been contested by reference to the constitutional traditions of the Member States, which leave the termination decision principally in the hands of the executive.[140] A second view therefore reverts to the suspension procedure applied analogously.

dd. Union Succession to Member State Agreements

Can the Union be bound by agreements that it has not formally concluded? The counter-intuitive answer is indeed 'yes': under European law, the Union can be bound by agreements of its Member States where the former has succeeded the latter.[141]

The doctrine of Union succession to international agreements of the Member States is a doctrine of *functional* succession.[142] It is not based on a transfer of territory, but on a transfer of *functions*. The European Court announced this

---

[140] C. Tomuschat, 'Artikel 300 EG', in H. von der Groeben and J. Schwarze (eds.), *Kommentar zum Vertrag über die Europäische Union und zur Gründung der Europäischen Gemeinschaft*, 4 vols. (Nomos, 2004), IV, para. 61.

[141] For an overview, see R. Schütze, 'The "Succession Doctrine" and the European Union', in Schütze, *Foreign Affairs* (n. 69 above), 91.

[142] See P. Pescatore, *L'Ordre juridique des communautés européennes* (Presse Universitaire de Liège, 1975), 147–8 (my translation): '[B]y taking over, by virtue of the Treaties, certain competences and certain powers previously exercised by the Member States, the [Union] equally had to assume the international obligations that controlled the exercise of these competences and powers[.]'

European doctrine in relation to the General Agreement on Tariffs and Trade in *International Fruit*.[143] Formally, the Union was not a party to the international treaty, but the Court nonetheless found as follows:

> [I]n so far as under the [European] Treat[ies] the [Union] has *assumed the powers previously exercised by Member States* in the area covered by the General Agreement, the provisions of that agreement have the effect of binding the [Union].[144]

Functional succession here emanated from the exclusive nature of the Union's powers under the Common Commercial Policy (CCP). Since the Union had assumed the 'functions' previously exercised by the Member States in this area, it was entitled and obliged to also assume their international obligations.

For a long time after *International Fruit*, the succession doctrine remained quiet. But in the last decade it experienced a constitutional revival. This allowed the Court to define better the doctrine's contours. Three principles have traditionally governed functional succession in the European legal order. First, for the succession doctrine to come into operation *all* the Member States must be parties to an international treaty.[145] Second, *when* the international treaty is concluded is irrelevant. It will thus not matter whether the international treaty was concluded before or after the creation of the European Community in 1958.[146]

Third, the Union will only succeed to international treaties, where there is a '*full transfer of the powers* previously exercised by the Member States'.[147] The Union will thus not succeed to all international agreements concluded by all the Member States, but only to those where it has assumed an exclusive competence. Would the European succession doctrine thereby be confined to the sphere of the Union's *constitutionally* exclusive powers; or, would *legislative* exclusivity generated by Article 3(2) TFEU be sufficient? The Court has shown a preference for a succession doctrine that includes legislative exclusivity. In *Bogiatzi*,[148] the Court indeed found that a 'full transfer' could take place where the Member States were completely pre-empted within the substantive scope of the international treaty.

A fourth – radical – principle has recently been suggested in *Opinion 2/15*.[149] The Court here controversially found that where the Union has succeeded the Member States according to principles one to three, it also 'has competence to approve, by itself, a provision of an agreement concluded by it with a third State which stipulates that the commitments … in bilateral agreements previously

---

[143] Joined Cases 21–4/72, *International Fruit Company NV* v. *Produktschap voor Groenten en Fruit* [1972] ECR 1219.

[144] *Ibid.*, paras. 14–18 (emphasis added).

[145] Case C-188/07, *Commune de Mesquer* v. *Total* [2008] ECR I-4501.

[146] Case 308/06, *Intertanko and others* v. *Secretary of State for Transport* [2008] ECR I-4057.

[147] *Ibid.*, para. 4 (emphasis added).

[148] Case C-301/08, *Bogiatzi* v. *Deutscher Luftpool and others* [2009] ECR I-10185.

[149] *Opinion 2/15* (Singapore Free Trade Agreement).

concluded between Member States of the European Union and that third State must, upon entry into force of that agreement concluded by the European Union, be regarded as replaced by the latter'.[150] If that means what it seems to mean, then the doctrine of functional succession would no longer only have purely 'internal' effects within the Union legal order. It would, on the contrary, seem to entitle the *Union* to *externally* terminate the international agreements of the Member States previously concluded with that State.[151]

4. Sharing External Power: Constitutional Safeguards of Federalism

Member States are − as States − considered to be sovereign subjects of international law. From an international law perspective, they thus enjoy full external powers.

This simple solution however creates problems for unions of States; and two solutions have here been historically found. Within the US tradition, the Member States are completely 'closed' off from the international scene because the Union is seen as the sole bearer of external sovereignty.[152] By contrast, according to the German tradition, the Union and its Member States may both partake in international relations;[153] yet within such an 'open federation', the external relations of the Union and its Member States need to be coordinated so as to safeguard diplomatic and political consistency. The European Union has followed this second tradition. It is an open federation in which the Union and its Member States are active participants on the international scene.

How has the EU legal order coordinated the (potentially) dual presence of the Union and its Member States? The Union has followed two mechanisms. The first mechanism is a political safeguard that brings the Union and its Member States to the same negotiating table for an international agreement. This technique of cooperation is called a mixed agreement. By contrast, a second mechanism is 'internal' to the Union and imposes a 'duty of cooperation' on the Member States so as to guarantee 'unity in the international representation of the [Union]'.[154] And, while this duty − theoretically − operates on the Union as well as the Member States,[155] it has − practically − been solely used to facilitate the exercise of the Union's external powers on the international scene.

---

[150]   *Ibid.*, para. 249 (emphasis added).

[151]   As regards Member State agreements theoretically covered by Art. 351 TFEU, the Court additionally found that they would not deserve protection under the provision because 'that third state expressed the wish that those bilateral agreements come to an end upon the entry into force of the envisaged agreement'. On Art. 351 TFEU, see Chapter 4, section 1(a/bb).

[152]   For the US tradition of a 'closed federation', see R. Schütze, 'Federalism and Foreign Affairs: Mixity as an (Inter)national Phenomenon', in *Foreign Affairs and the EU Constitution* (Cambridge University Press, 2014), 175 at 177.

[153]   For the German tradition of an 'open federation', see *ibid.* at 185ff.

[154]   *Opinion 1/94* (WTO Agreement) (n. 70 above), para. 108.   [155]   *Ibid.*

a. Mixed Agreements: An International and Political Safeguard

Who can conclude international agreements that do not entirely fall into the competence sphere of the Union or the Member States? The traditional answer to that question has been that the Union *and* the Member States combine their external competences in the form of a *mixed* agreement – that is: an agreement to which both the Union and some or all of its Member States appear as contracting parties.[156] Mixity had originally been designed for a specific sector of European law.[157] However, it soon spread to become the hallmark of the European Union's foreign affairs federalism.[158]

The growth and success of mixed agreements in Europe's foreign affairs federalism may be accounted for by a number of reasons – internal and external to the Union legal order. First, mixed agreements would allow the Union and its Member States to complement their competences into a unitary whole that matched the external sovereignty of a third State. The division of treaty-making powers between them could then be reduced to an 'internal' Union affair.[159] Second, the uncertainty surrounding the nature and extent of the treaty-making powers of the young Union under international law originally provided an additional reason.[160] As long as it remained uncertain whether or how the Union could fulfil its international obligations, mixed agreements would provide legal

---

[156] Mixity normally extends to all phases of an international agreement and may thus add a pluralist dimension to the negotiation, conclusion and implementation stage. However, sometimes, the Member States authorise the Council to negotiate an international agreement on their behalf, e.g. Decision of the Representatives of the Governments of the Member States meeting in the Council authorizing the Presidency of the Council to negotiate, on behalf of the Member States, the provisions of a legally binding agreement on forests in Europe that fall within the competences of the Member States [2011] OJ L 285/1.

[157] Art. 102 Euratom Treaty: 'Agreements or contracts concluded with a third State, an international organisation or a national of a third State to which, in addition to the Community, one or more Member States are parties, shall not enter into force until the Commission has been notified by all the Member States concerned that those agreements or contracts have become applicable in accordance with the provisions of their respective national laws.'

[158] The first mixed agreement concluded by the EEC was the 1961 Agreement establishing an association between the European Economic Community and Greece [1963] OJ 26/294. For a now slightly outdated registry, see J. Heliskoski, *Mixed Agreements as a Technique for Organizing the International Relations of the European Community and its Member States* (Kluwer, 2001), 252–77, listing 154 mixed agreements concluded between 1961 and 2000.

[159] See Ruling 1/78 *(IAEA Convention)* [1978] ECR 2151, para. 35: 'It is sufficient to state to the other Contracting parties that the matter gives rise to a division of powers within the Community, it being understood that the exact nature of that division is a domestic question in which Third States have no need to intervene.'

[160] P. Pescatore, 'Les Relations extérieures des communautés européennes: contribution à la doctrine de la personalité des organisations internationales' (1961) 103 *Recueil des Cours* 1, 105.

Pure Union Agreement	**(Facultative) Mixed Agreement**	**(Compulsory) Mixed Agreement**
	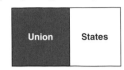	
European Union	European Union / Member States	Union / States
The Union enjoys exclusive competence(s) over the whole agreement.	The Union shares competence(s) with the Member States over the whole agreement.	The Member States enjoy an exclusive competence for a part of the agreement.

Figure 8.3 Mixed Agreements and Union Competences

security for third States by involving the Member States as international 'guarantors' of the Union obligation.[161]

The constitutional developments within the European legal order in the last four decades have weakened both rationales. Not only have the external powers of the Union been significantly expanded through the development of the doctrine of implied powers – now codified in Article 216 TFEU, its internal powers have been sharpened to guarantee the enforcement of Union agreements within the European legal order.[162] Today, the dominant – third – reason behind mixed agreements appears to be of a purely political nature: Member States insist on participating in their own name so as to remain 'visible' on the international scene.[163] Even for matters that fall squarely into the Union's shared competences, the Member States dislike being (en)closed behind a supranational veil. The Union legal order has consequently come to speak of 'facultative' as opposed to 'compulsory' mixed agreements (see Figure 8.3).[164]

How has the European Union reacted to the Member States' demand for mixed agreements? Shared competences should not, constitutionally, require mixed action.[165] For, within shared competences, the Union or the Member States can both act autonomously and conclude independent agreements; or,

---

[161] M. J. Dolmans, *Problems of Mixed Agreements: Division of Powers within the EEC and the Rights of Third States* (Asser Instituut, 1985), 95.

[162] On the direct and indirect effects of international agreement in the Union legal order, see Chapter 3, section 4.

[163] C. D. Ehlermann, 'Mixed Agreements: A List of Problems', in D. O'Keeffe and H. Schermers (eds.), *Mixed Agreements* (Kluwer, 1983), 3 at 6: 'Member States wish to continue to appear as contracting parties in order to remain visible and identifiable actors on the international scene. Individual participation is therefore seen as a way of defending and enhancing the prestige and influence of individual Member States.'

[164] The terminology was introduced by A. Rosas in his seminal 'Mixed Union – Mixed Agreements', in M. Koskenniemi (ed.), *International Law Aspects of the European Union* (Kluwer, 1998), 125.

[165] On the notion of shared competences in the Union legal order, see Chapter 7, section 2(b). On the traditional (non)existence of 'joint' competences within the Union legal order, see R. Schütze, 'The European Community's Federal Order of Competences: A Retrospective Analysis', in M. Dougan and S. Currie (eds.), *Fifty Years of the European Treaties: Looking Back and Thinking Forward* (Hart, 2009), 63, esp. 85–7.

if they so wish, they may also act jointly.[166] Indeed, it originally seemed that the European Court would demand specific *constitutional* justification for mixed external action in place of a pure Union agreement.[167] But in the last three decades, the Court of Justice has given its judicial blessing to the uncontrolled use of mixed agreement in areas of shared competences.[168] And, in *Opinion 2/15*, the Court even alluded to the idea that shared competences require joint action under a mixed agreement.[169] If that – wrong – idea becomes established jurisprudence, facultative mixity would have come to a sudden end!

The widespread use of mixed external action evinces a remarkable Union tolerance towards the Member States' international powers, as the practice of mixed agreements entails a significant *anti*-Union consequence. Because According to a European 'constitutional convention', the Council concludes mixed agreements on behalf of the Union only once *all* the Member States have themselves ratified the agreement in accordance with their constitutional traditions.[170] The convention boils down to requiring 'unanimous' consent before the Union can exercise its competence. The conventional arrangement thus prolongs the (in)famous Luxembourg Compromise in the external sphere. The constitutionally uncontrolled use of mixed agreements under the Union's shared powers has,

---

[166] See Case 316/91, *Parliament v. Council* [1994] ECR I-625, para. 26: 'The [Union's] competence in that field is not exclusive. The Member States are accordingly entitled to enter into commitments themselves vis-à-vis non-member States, either collectively or individually, or even jointly with the [Union].'

[167] *Opinion 1/76* (Laying-up Fund) [1977] ECR 741, paras. 6–8. The Court recognised that 'the danger of mixed agreements (and their attraction for Member States) lies in their tendency to over-emphasise at the expense of the [Union] the participation of the Member States as traditional international legal persons' (M. Cremona, 'The Doctrine of Exclusivity and the Position of Mixed Agreements in the External Relations of the European Community' (1982) 2 *Oxford Journal of Legal Studies* 393, 414).

[168] In the last 30 years, these 'facultative' mixed agreements – i.e. agreements in which the Union has competence to conclude the entire agreement – have become the prominent category of mixed agreements: 'Indeed, there is no decision from the Court under the EC Treaty where the explicit justification for recourse to the mixed procedure would have been the limited scope of [Union] competence – commonly regarded as the principal legal explanation for the practice of mixed agreements' (see Heliskoski, *Mixed Agreements* (n. 158 above), at 68).

[169] In *Opinion 2/15* (Singapore), para. 244, the Court found that because the Union 'only' had a shared competence, 'the envisaged agreement cannot be approved by the European Union alone'. I personally find this solution extremely problematic in light of the notion of 'shared competence'; and the Court appears to have partly backtracked from it now, see: Case 600/14, *Germany v. Council*, esp. para. 68. In this sense also, see Advocate General Wahl, *Opinion 3/15* (Farrell), para. 119: 'The choice between a mixed agreement or an EU-only agreement, when the subject matter of the agreement falls within an area of shared competence (or of parallel competence), is generally a matter for the discretion of the EU legislature.'

[170] The inspiration for this constitutional convention appears to lie in Art. 102 of the Euratom Treaty (n. 157 above). On the convention and ways to alleviate its consequences, see Eeckhout, *EU External Relations Law* (n. 93 above), 258–9.

unsurprisingly, been criticised as 'a way of whittling down systematically the personality and capacity of the [Union] as a representative of the collective interest'.[171]

On the other hand, mixed agreements can also – more positively – be seen as a way of safeguarding the role of national parliaments in EU treaty-making. For once the Union uses a mixed agreement, the conclusion of this agreement will not only require ratification by the European Parliament but also – subject to the constitutional traditions of the Member States – the ratification by every single national parliament and sometimes even regional parliaments. (How complex and uncertain this makes the EU ratification process can be seen in the drama surrounding the conclusion of the EU–Canada Trade Agreement that had originally been blocked by the Belgian region of Wallonia.)[172] The constitutional principles governing an 'incomplete' ratification of a mixed agreement have hardly been explored.[173]

b. The Duty of Cooperation: An Internal and Judicial Safeguard

The Member States' duty to cooperate loyally and sincerely informs all areas of European law.[174] However, the duty is particularly important in the external sphere.[175] And this is especially so where the Union and the Member States must coordinate their international powers under a mixed agreement.[176]

---

[171] P. Pescatore, '*Opinion 1/94* on "Conclusion" of the WTO Agreement: Is there an Escape from a Programmed Disaster?' (1999) 36 *CML Rev.* 387 at fn. 6. The criticism on mixed agreements has indeed been rich from the very beginning, see A. Barav, 'General Discussion', in C. W. A. Timmermans and E. L. M. Völker (eds.), *Division of Powers between the European Communities and their Member States in the Field of External Relations* (Kluwer, 1981), 144: '[M]ixed agreements are probably a necessary evil, part of the integration process, but nobody would like to see any more of them.'

[172] See *Financial Times*, 14 October 2016: 'Belgium's Walloon Parliament blocks EU–Canada free-trade deal'.

[173] But see now G. van der Loo and R. Wessel, 'The Non-Ratification of Mixed Agreements: Legal Consequences and Solutions' (2017) 54 *CML Rev.* 735.

[174] For the general duty, see Art. 4(3) TEU.

[175] For a special expression of the general duty of Art. 4(3) TEU in the CFSP area, see Art. 24(3) TEU: 'The Member States shall support the Union's external and security policy actively and unreservedly in a spirit of loyalty and mutual solidarity and shall comply with the Union's action in this area. The Member States shall work together to enhance and develop their mutual political solidarity. They shall refrain from any action which is contrary to the interests of the Union or likely to impair its effectiveness as a cohesive force in international relations.' For even more specific duties of cooperation, see Art. 32 TEU (consultation and coordination of national policies within the European Council and the Council) and Art. 34 TEU (coordination of Member States in international organisations).

[176] See Case 459/03, *Commission* v. *Ireland (Mox Plant)* [2006] ECR I-4657, paras. 175–6: 'The Court has also emphasised that the Member States and the [Union] institutions have an obligation of close cooperation in fulfilling the commitments undertaken by them under joint competence when they conclude a mixed agreement. That is in particular the position in the case of a dispute which, as in the present case, relates essentially to undertakings resulting from a mixed agreement which relates to an area, namely the protection and preservation of the marine environment, in which the respective areas of competence

However, while developed in the context of mixed agreements, this is not the only situation where the duty of cooperation has been given an active constitutional role.[177] For the Union legal order has equally had recourse to the duty of cooperation to facilitate the (autonomous) exercise of the *Union's* external competences. This facilitating role has been expressed in a positive and a negative manner. The positive aspect of the duty here demands that the Member States act as 'trustees of the Union interest'. By contrast, the negative aspect of the duty can place a limit on the Member States exercising their shared external competences. In this second role, the duty of cooperation operates – partly – as the 'reverse' of the principle of subsidiarity.[178]

aa. Member States as 'Trustees of the Union'

Classic international law is built on the idea of the sovereign State.[179] This State-centred structure of international law creates normative difficulties for non-State actors.[180] The European Union is a union of *States*, and as such still encounters normative hurdles when acting on the international scene. These normative hurdles have become fewer, but there remain situations in which the Union cannot externally act due to the partial blindness of international law towards compound subjects. And where the Union is – internationally – 'disabled' from exercising its competences, it will have to authorise its Member States to act on its behalf. This positive manifestation of the duty of cooperation is called the 'trustees doctrine'.[181]

of the [Union] and the Member States are liable to be closely interrelated, as is, moreover, evidenced by the Declaration of [Union] competence and the appendix thereto.' For an analysis of the duty of cooperation within the (mixed) WTO Agreement, see J. Heliskoski, 'The "Duty of Cooperation" between the European Community and its Member States within the World Trade Organization' (1997) 7 *Finnish Yearbook of International Law* 59.

[177] See Case 266/03, *Commission v. Luxembourg* [2005] ECR 4805, para. 58: 'That duty of genuine cooperation is of general application and does not depend either on whether the [Union] competence concerned is exclusive or on any right of the Member States to enter into obligations towards non-member countries.' For a general analysis of the duty in the external relations context, see M. Cremona, 'Defending the Community Interest: The Duties of Cooperation and Compliance', in M. Cremona and B. de Witte (eds.), *EU Foreign Relations Law: Constitutional Fundamentals* (Hart, 2008), 125; E. Neframi, 'The Duty of Loyalty: Rethinking Its Scope through Its Application in the Field of EU External Relations' (2010) 47 *CML Rev.* 323.

[178] I am aware that this is a controversial formulation as the subsidiarity principle may theoretically operate downwards *and upwards*. However, in the past, European law has mainly identified subsidiarity as a mechanism for protecting the exercise of State competences. And for that reason 'reverse subsidiarity' tries to capture the idea that the Court here uses the duty of cooperation to protect the exercise of Union competences.

[179] M. Koskenniemi, *From Apology to Utopia: The Structure of International Legal Argument* (Cambridge University Press, 2006).

[180] See Jennings and Watts, *Oppenheim* (n. 137 above), 245ff.

[181] For a first analysis of this doctrinal construction in the external sphere, see M. Cremona, 'Member States as Trustees of the Union Interest: Participating in International Agreements on Behalf of the European Union', in A. Arnull et al. (eds.), *A Constitutional Order of States: Essays in Honour of Alan Dashwood* (Hart, 2011), 435.

A good illustration of the trustees doctrine may be found in the context of the Union's inability to participate in international organisations. Many of these organisations still only allow sovereign States to become (active) members; and hence the European Union finds itself unable to exercise its competences in these international decision-making forums. An example of this state-centred membership is the International Labour Organization (ILO). Here, the Union cannot itself conclude international conventions and must thus rely on its Member States. The obligation to act as trustee of the Union thereby derives from the duty of cooperation:

> In this case, cooperation between the [Union] and the Member States is all the more necessary in view of the fact that the former cannot, as international law stands at present, itself conclude an ILO convention and must do so *through the medium of the Member States*.[182]

The Union must thus exercise its external competences indirectly, that is: through the Member States 'acting jointly in the [Union's] interest'.[183]

This idea was recently confirmed in the context of the International Organisation of Vine and Wine.[184] The Court here expressly clarified that the Union is entitled to adopt a common position for all the EU that would subsequently need 'to be adopted *on its behalf* in the body set up by that agreement, in particular *through the Member States which are party to that agreement acting jointly in its interest*'.[185]

bb. 'Reversed' Subsidiarity: Restrictions on the Exercise of Shared State Competences

In an area of shared competences both the Union and the Member States are entitled to act externally by – for example – concluding an international agreement with the United States. But due to the various procedural obstacles in the Union's treaty-making power, the Member States might be much quicker in exercising their shared competence. And third parties might indeed be more interested in 28 bilateral agreements than one Union agreement on a matter.[186]

In order to safeguard the 'unity in the international representation of the [Union]',[187] the Court has therefore developed a 'negative' aspect to the duty of cooperation. Where the international actions of a Member State might jeopardise the conclusion of a Union agreement, the Court has imposed specific obligations on the Member States. These obligations limit the exercise of their

---

[182] *Opinion 2/91* (ILO Convention 170) [1993] ECR I-1061, para. 37 (emphasis added).
[183] *Ibid.*, para. 5.   [184] Case C-399/12, *Germany v. Council (OIV)*, EU:C:2014, 2258.
[185] *Ibid.*, para. 52 (emphasis added).
[186] This approach might be inspired by the classic Roman strategy of '*divide et impera*', that is: divide and rule.
[187] *Opinion 1/94* (WTO Agreement) [1994] ECR I-5267, para. 108.

shared powers, and thus – to some extent – mirror and invert the principle of subsidiarity. And, like the principle of subsidiarity, the duty of cooperation has traditionally been thought to be of a 'procedural' nature.[188]

We find a good illustration of the negative duties imposed on the Member States when exercising their shared external competences in *Commission v. Luxembourg*.[189] Luxembourg had exercised its international treaty power to conclude a number of bilateral agreements with Eastern European States. The Commission was incensed, as it had already started its own negotiations for the Union as a whole. It thus complained that even if Luxembourg enjoyed a shared competence to conclude the agreements, '[t]he negotiation by the Commission of an agreement on behalf of the [Union] and its subsequent conclusion by the Council is inevitably made more difficult by interference from a Member State's own initiatives'.[190] The Union's position was claimed to have been weakened 'because the [Union] and its Member States appear fragmented'.[191] The Court adopted this view – but only partly:

> The adoption of a decision authorising the Commission to negotiate a multilateral agreement on behalf of the [Union] marks the start of a concerted [Union] action at international level and requires, for that purpose, *if not a duty of abstention on the part of the Member States, at the very least a duty of close cooperation* between the latter and the [Union] institutions in order to facilitate the achievement of the [Union] tasks and to ensure the coherence and consistency of the action and its international representation.[192]

Importantly, the Court did not condemn the exercise of Luxembourg's treaty power as such. Endowed with shared external power, Luxembourg could very well conclude bilateral agreements with third States. However, since the Commission had started a 'concerted [Union] action' for the conclusion of a Union agreement in this area, the Member State was under an obligation to cooperate and consult with the Commission. And, in not consulting the Union, Luxembourg had violated the duty of cooperation.[193] The duty of cooperation was thus primarily seen as a duty of information. It appeared to be *a procedural* duty of conduct, and not a substantive duty of result.

The purely procedural character of the duty was subsequently put into question. In *Commission v. Sweden*,[194] the Union institution brought proceedings against Sweden for 'splitting the international representation of the [Union] and

---

[188] Cremona, 'Defending the Community Interest' (n. 177 above), 168; Neframi, 'Duty of Loyalty' (n. 177 above), 355–6.
[189] Case 266/03, *Commission v. Luxembourg* [2005] ECR 4805.   [190] *Ibid.*, para. 53.
[191] *Ibid.*   [192] *Ibid.*, para. 60 (emphasis added).   [193] *Ibid.*, para. 61.
[194] Case C-246/07, *Commission v. Sweden* [2010] ECR I-3317. For an extensive analysis, see G. de Baere, '"O, Where Is Faith? O, Where Is Loyalty?" Some Thoughts on the Duty of Loyal Co-operation and the Union's External Environmental Competences in the Light of the PFOS Case' (2011) 36 *EL Rev.* 405.

compromising the unity achieved … during the first Conference of the Parties to [the Stockholm Convention on Persistent Organic Pollutants]'.[195] What had happened? Sweden had not abstained from making a proposal within the international conference, and the Commission claimed that this unilateral action violated the duty of cooperation. Sweden counterclaimed that it had given sufficient information to and consulted with the Union and the other Member States.[196]

But this time, this was not enough. After duly citing its case law, the Court moved to examine whether there existed a Union 'strategy' not to make a proposal.[197] And, in finding that such a Union strategy existed, and that Sweden had 'dissociated itself from a concerted common strategy within the Council',[198] the Court found that Sweden had violated the duty of cooperation. In a remarkable feat of judicial creativity, the Court now found that its past case law stood for the proposition that

> Member States are subject to special duties of action *and abstention* in a situation in which the Commission has submitted to the Council proposals which, although they have not been adopted by the Council, represent a point of departure for concerted [Union] action.[199]

This case might indeed be seen as the beginning of a *substantive* duty of cooperation. The Court was not satisfied with the procedural obligation to inform and consult, but prohibited the very exercise of a shared external competence by a Member State.

Are there dangers in a substantive reading of the duty of cooperation? While such a reading better protects the unity of external representation of the Union and its Member States, there is a danger for the autonomous exercise of the States' international powers.[200] It all depends on how early the duty to abstain from international action departing from the Union position starts. The temporal aspect of the duty will thus principally determine its substantive effect.

Conclusion

The European Union has international personality and indeed represents a significant international actor. Unlike its Member States, the Union is not regarded as a sovereign State in international law. The European Union is a union of States and, as such, it is a compound subject of international law.

The Union's external competences are conferred competences. For in the absence of external sovereignty, the Union must have power transferred to it by its Member States. What is the scope of the Union's competences? Section 1 analysed the dual constitutional regime for external competences, as the latter

---

[195] Case C-246/07, *Commission* v. *Sweden*, para. 44.   [196] *Ibid.*, para. 63.
[197] *Ibid.*, para. 76.   [198] *Ibid.*, para. 91.   [199] *Ibid.*, para. 103.
[200] Sweden rightly claimed that a substantive interpretation was 'likely to render shared competence in the case of mixed agreements meaningless' (*ibid.*, para. 63).

are generally found in two constitutional sites. Title V of the Treaty on European Union confers a general competence on the Union to deal with the Common Foreign and Security Policy. By contrast, Part V of the Treaty on the Functioning of the European Union enumerates a number of special competences in particular policy areas. In addition to these thematic competences, the Union is also given a 'residual' treaty-making power: Article 216 TFEU. We saw above that the provision attempts to codify the Court's jurisprudence on the Union's implied treaty-making powers. The provision is however a textual fiasco. For Article 216(1) appears to be – mistakenly – shaped by three principles created by the European Court in the context of the European Union's *exclusive* competences.

What is the nature of the Union's external competences? Can they be classified by means of the same categories that apply to the Union's legislative competences? We saw in section 2 that this is indeed generally the case. Yet, there are two constitutional exceptions. First, the character of the CFSP competence cannot be captured by the competence categories mentioned in Articles 3–6 TFEU. This follows implicitly from the – still – mysterious qualities of CFSP law, and expressly from Article 40 TEU. The CFSP competence is best seen as '*sui generis*' – a singular phenomenon that corresponds to the 'special' nature of the CFSP rules and procedures.[201] The second exception to the general competence categories of the Union is the idea of subsequently exclusive treaty-making powers. This idea derogates from the classification within the Union's legislative powers, whose exercise will not lead to an exclusive competence.[202] The idea of subsequent external exclusivity or 'exclusivity by exercise' had originally been developed by the European Court. The Lisbon Treaty has tried to codify past jurisprudence in the form of Article 3(2) TFEU. This codification is – again – not without problems, and it is – again – in the hands of the European judiciary to sharpen its contours in the future.

Section 3 analysed the decision-making procedures in the external relations of the Union. Which procedure thereby applies depends on two factors. First, is the measure to be adopted a unilateral act? Or is it an international agreement? If it is an international agreement, then the Treaties follow common treaty-making procedures. If it is a unilateral measure, then the Treaties distinguish between the two constitutional regimes for external relations. While acts adopted under the Union's special competences principally follow the (ordinary) legislative procedure, the procedure for unilateral CFSP acts is 'special'.[203] It has a special nature both in relation to the constitutional balance between the institutional actors involved, and the special voting arrangements in the Council. Both features turn the CFSP into an 'intergovernmental' area of European law that contrasts with the rest of the Union's 'supranational' decision-making procedures.

---

[201]   See Art. 24(1) TEU: 'The common foreign and security policy is subject to specific rules and procedures.'

[202]   The supremacy of European law leads to the 'pre-emption' of conflicting national law. For a discussion of this point, see Chapter 4, section 3.

[203]   See Art. 24(1) TEU.

These 'intergovernmental' elements are however less obvious in the procedure for treaty-making. For the Lisbon Treaty has 'unified' the procedural regimes for CFSP and non-CFSP treaties in Article 218 TFEU. The provision distinguishes between various stages. The negotiation of international treaties is thereby principally left in the hands of the Commission and the High Representative. The conclusion of the agreement is the task of the Council. However, Parliament will need to give its consent on a wide range of agreements; yet, as we saw above, consent is not co-decision. The external powers of the Parliament are thus lower than its internal powers.

Section 4 finally looked at constitutional devices designed to safeguard a degree of 'unity' in the external actions of the Union and its Member States. These devices are necessary as the European Union is an 'open federation'. In order to ensure external unity and consistency, the European legal order has principally had recourse to two constitutional mechanisms. Mixed agreements constitute an international law mechanism that brings the Union and the Member States (as well as third parties) to the same negotiating table. In an era of shared external powers,[204] mixed external action might not be mandatory; yet Member States have insisted on using mixed agreements as a political device. The second constitutional device is internal to the Union legal order. It is the duty of cooperation. While the duty is said to be reciprocal, it has principally been developed to facilitate the exercise of *Union* competences in the external sphere. The duty of cooperation has thereby been given a positive and a negative aspect. Positively, the Member States might be obliged to act as 'trustees of the Union interest' in international forums. Negatively, the duty has imposed obligations on the Member States when exercising their shared competences. This negative aspect is – to some extent – the opposite of the principle of subsidiarity. For the Member States are prevented from exercising their shared competence in order to prevent 'splitting the international representation of the [Union]'.[205]

FURTHER READING

Books

M. Cremona (ed.), *Developments in EU External Relations Law* (Oxford University Press, 2008)

M. Cremona and B. de Witte (eds.), *EU Foreign Relations Law: Constitutional Fundamentals* (Hart, 2008)

A. Dashwood and C. Hillion (eds.), *The General Law of EC External Relations* (Sweet & Maxwell, 2000)

P. Eeckhout, *EU External Relations Law* (Oxford University Press, 2011)

J. Heliskoski, *Mixed Agreements as a Technique for Organizing the International Relations of the European Community and its Member States* (Kluwer, 2001)

---

[204] See J. de la Rochère, 'L'ère des compétences partagées de l'étendue des compétences extérieures de la communauté européenne' (1995) 390 *Revue du Marché commun et de l'Union européenne* 461.

[205] Case C-246/07, *Commission v. Sweden*, para. 44.

P. Koutrakos, *EU International Relations Law* (Hart, 2015)

P. J. Kuijper et al., *The Law of EU External Relations: Cases, Materials, and Commentary on the EU as an International Legal Actor* (Oxford University Press, 2015)

D. McGoldrick, *International Relations Law of the European Union* (Longman, 1997)

R. Schütze, *Foreign Affairs and the EU Constitution* (Cambridge University Press, 2014)

B. Van Vooren and R. Wessel, *EU External Relations Law: Text, Cases and Materials* (Cambridge University Press, 2014)

Articles (and Chapters)

G. de Baere, '"O, Where Is Faith? O, Where Is Loyalty?" Some Thoughts on the Duty of Loyal Co-operation and the Union's External Environmental Competences in the Light of the PFOS Case' (2011) 36 *EL Rev.* 405

M. Cremona, 'Member States as Trustees of the Union Interest: Participating in International Agreements on Behalf of the European Union', in A. Arnull et al. (eds.), *A Constitutional Order of States: Essays in Honour of Alan Dashwood* (Hart, 2011), 435

A. Dashwood, 'The Attribution of External Relations Competence', in A. Dashwood and C. Hillion (eds.), *The General Law of EC External Relations* (Sweet & Maxwell, 2000), 115

C. D. Ehlermann, 'Mixed Agreements: A List of Problems', in D. O'Keeffe and H. Schermers (eds.), *Mixed Agreements* (Kluwer, 1983), 3

E. Neframi, 'The Duty of Loyalty: Rethinking Its Scope through Its Application in the Field of EU External Relations' (2010) 47 *CML Rev.* 323

A. Ott, 'The European Parliament's Role in EU Treaty-Making' (2016) 23 *Maastricht Journal of European and Comparative Law* 1009

A. Rosas, 'Mixed Union – Mixed Agreements', in M. Koskenniemi (ed.), *International Law Aspects of the European Union* (Kluwer, 1998), 125

R. Schütze, 'External Powers in the European Union: From "Cubist" Perspectives towards "Naturalist" Constitutional Principles?', in *Foreign Affairs and the EU Constitution* (Cambridge University Press, 2014), 237

E. Stein, 'External Relations of the European Community: Structure and Process' (1990) 1 *Collected Courses of the Academy of European Law* 115

D. Thym, 'Parliamentary Involvement in European International Relations', in M. Cremona and B. de Witte (eds.), *EU Foreign Relations Law: Constitutional Fundamentals* (Hart, 2008), 201

Cases on the Website

Case 22/70, *Commission v. Council (ERTA)*; Cases 21–24/72, *International Fruit*; Opinion 1/76 (Laying-up Fund); Opinion 2/91 (ILO Convention 170); Opinion 1/94 (WTO Agreement); Case C-266/03, *Commission v. Luxembourg*; Case C-91/05, *ECOWAS*; Case C-246/07, *Commission v. Sweden*; Case C-301/08, *Bogiatzi*; Case C-658/11, *Parliament v. Council (Pirates)*; Case C-425/13, *Commission v. Council*; Opinion 2/15 (Singapore)

9

Executive Powers
Competences and Procedures

Contents

Introduction

What are the 'executive' powers of the European Union? In many constitutions the executive branch has a residual character: anything that is *neither* legislative *nor* judicial is considered to fall within its scope. This *negative* definition of the executive function has historical reasons: the original purpose of the separation-of-powers principle was to *remove* powers from an almighty monarch to a parliament and the judiciary.

The problem with this negative definition however is its uncertain and relative nature; and serious attempts have therefore been made positively to identify 'prerogatives' of executive power. Outside the field of external relations,[1] two such prerogatives have traditionally been recognised. First, the executive power is – naturally – identified with the task of executing laws, and thus with the aim of maintaining internal peace.[2] The task of law enforcement is complemented by a second – seemingly contradictory – task.[3] Executive power is identified with the power to 'govern', that is: to lead and direct the political community. The executive branch is here the 'centre of impulse and decision'.[4] Despite their contradictory outlook, *both* traditional prerogatives of the executive – the reactive task to enforce laws and the active task to propose laws – are still based on a common idea: the executive enjoys the power of *decision*.

The power of decision is typically contrasted with the power to adopt legislation. For in the 'legislative State' of the nineteenth century all general legal norms should be adopted by Parliament.[5] This past ideal would however find limits in the normative needs of the 'administrative State' of the twentieth century.[6] Modern parliaments would simply have no time – nor expertise – to 'master all the details of tea chemistry and packaging in order to specify the precisely allowable limits of dust, artificial coloring, and the like that would affect suitability for consumption'.[7] Industrial societies required a 'motorised legislator';[8] and this secondary 'legislator' was found in the executive. The advent of the *legislating* executive 'constitutes one of the most important transformations of constitutionalism'.[9] In the administrative State the executive branch thus gains a third power: the power to adopt (delegated) legislation.[10]

A modern treatment of executive power should therefore include three core prerogatives of the executive. These three prerogatives are – in descending order: the *political* power to govern, the *legislative* power to adopt executive norms and the *administrative* power to enforce legislation.

---

[1] On the 'executive' elements within the Union's external powers, see Chapter 8, Introduction.

[2] This is the reason why J. Locke, *Two Treatises of Government* (Cambridge University Press, 1988), §148, recognising the distinctive character of the executive and the external function, nonetheless places both powers into the hands of a single person – the monarch.

[3] E. Zoller, *Droit constitutionnel* (Presses Universitaires de France, 1999), 425.

[4] L. Favoreu et al., *Droit constitutionnel* (Dalloz, 2002), 537.

[5] *Field* v. *Clark*, 143 US 649 (1892), 692.

[6] See G. Lawson, 'The Rise and Rise of the Administrative State' (1993–4) 107 *Harvard Law Review* 1231.

[7] W. Gellhorn and C. Byse, *Administrative Law: Cases and Comments* (Foundation Press, 1974), 62.

[8] C. Schmitt, *Die Lage der Europäischen Rechtswissenschaft* (Universitätsverlag Tübingen, 1950), 18.

[9] Zoller, *Droit constitutional* (n. 3 above), 436.

[10] H. W. R. Wade and C. F. Forsyth, *Administrative Law* (Oxford University Press, 2000), 839: 'there is no more characteristic administrative activity than *legislation*'; H. Pünder, 'Democratic Legitimation of Delegated Legislation: A Comparative View on the American, British and German Law' (2009) 58 ICLQ 353, esp. 355: 'in all countries compared, administrative law-making powers became the rule rather than the exception'.

This chapter discusses all three executive powers in the context of the European Union. Section 1 begins with an examination of the *political* power to act as government. We shall see that the 'steering' power of high politics belongs to two institutions within the Union: the European Council and the Commission. The Union 'government' is thus based on a 'dual executive'. Section 2 moves to an analysis of the (delegated) *legislative* powers of the Union executive. The central provisions here are Articles 290 and 291 TFEU. We shall see that the European legal order has allowed for wide delegations of power to the executive; while nonetheless insisting on substantive and procedural safeguards that protect two fundamental Union principles – federalism and democracy. Sections 3 and 4 look at the (administrative) enforcement powers of the Union. Based on the idea of 'executive federalism', the power to apply and enforce European law is here divided between the Union and the Member States. The Union can – exceptionally – execute its own law; yet the centralised administration is limited by the subsidiarity principle. And, as a rule, it is the Member States that execute Union law. This form of decentralised enforcement restricts the uniform effects of administrative decisions within the Union.

1. Governmental Powers: The Union's Dual Executive

The notion of 'government' is used in a wide and in a strict sense. In the wide sense, political communities are 'governed' by the totality of public institutions within society.[11] Yet in the strict sense of the word, they are 'governed' only by one of these institutions: the 'government'. The 'government' is that part of the executive that is charged with providing leadership and direction.[12] And depending on whether there exists one or two organs charged with political leadership within a society, we speak of a unitary or a dualist executive.[13] The US constitution is based on a unitary executive: all executive power is vested in one organ – the President of the United States.[14] By contrast, Britain and France are based on the idea of a dual executive. There are two institutions that are regarded as 'leading' the country. In monarchical Britain this is the (hereditary) Crown and its Cabinet; whereas in republican France this is the (elected) President and his/her 'Government'.[15]

The European Union is based on the idea of a dual executive. There are thus two institutions charged with 'governing' the European Union: the European

---

[11] This wide sense is used by the US Constitution (see Art. IV, s. 4: 'The United States shall guarantee to every State in this Union a Republican Form of Government').

[12] For this strict sense: see German Constitution, Chapter VI: 'The Federal Government'.

[13] Favoreu et al., *Droit constitutionnel* (n. 4 above), 539.

[14] For the US debate surrounding the 'unitary' executive, see S. Calabresi and K. Rhodes, 'The Structural Constitution: Unitary Executive, Plural Judiciary' (1992) 105 *Harvard Law Journal* 1153; L. Lessing and C. Sunstein, 'The President and the Administration' (1994) 94 *Columbia Law Review* 1.

[15] The 1958 French Constitution thus makes a clear distinction between the governmental powers of the President (Title II: Arts. 5–19), and those of the Government (Title III: Arts. 20–3).

Council and the Commission. The former is to 'provide the Union with the necessary impetus for its development' and to 'define the general political directions and priorities thereof'.[16] By contrast, the Commission is to 'promote the general interest of the Union and take appropriate initiatives to that end'.[17] *Both* institutions are consequently entitled and obliged to provide political leadership for the Union.

What are their – respective – legal instruments for such leadership? And are there (in)formal procedures that combine the European Council and the Commission in the exercise of their governmental powers? Let us explore these questions in this first section.

a. The Legal Instruments of Political Leadership

What are the *policy* instruments in the hands of the European Council and the Commission? The task of analysing political leadership in legal categories is difficult. Although political mechanisms tend to be fluid and situational, legal categories tend to be solid and permanent.

The task of the European Council is to act as 'initiator' and 'coordinator'. It will principally express its views through 'Presidency Conclusions',[18] and 'decisions'.[19] The precise legal character of the 'Conclusions' is unclear. However, what *is* clear is that they represent the highest political agreement of the Heads of State or Government of the Member States, and as such constitute a formidable political instrument to provide impulses and direction to the development of the European Union. Often, European Council Conclusions set the policy agenda for the Union for the mid-term future. They may cover both constitutional as well as substantive themes. With regard to the former, the European Council has indeed been the primary mover behind Treaty reform. With regard to the latter, the European Council has assumed a significant role in setting the legislative agenda for the Union. This may be illustrated by reference to the European Council's 'Strategic Agenda for the Union in Times of Change' – adopted as Presidency Conclusion in 2014.[20]

---

[16] Art. 15(1) TEU.   [17] *Ibid.*, Art. 17(1).

[18] For a list of Presidency Conclusions, see www.european-council.europa.eu/council-meetings/conclusions.

[19] For important European Council decisions in the context of external relations, see e.g. Common Strategy of the European Council on the Mediterranean region (2000/458/CFSP) [2000] OJ L 183/5.

[20] European Council Conclusions of 26/27 June 2014 (EUCO 79/14), Annex I (*ibid.*, 14): 'The May 2014 European elections open a new legislative cycle. This moment of political renewal comes precisely as our countries emerge from years of economic crisis and as public disenchantment with politics has grown. It is the right time to set out what we want the Union to focus on and how we want it to function. The European Council agreed today on five overarching priorities which will guide the work of the European Union over the next five years: stronger economies with more jobs; societies enabled to empower and protect; a secure energy and climate future; a trusted area of fundamental freedoms; effective joint action in the world.'

The Commission has developed a sophisticated variety of policy instruments.[21] After its election, the new Commission President will traditionally present his 'political guidelines' in which he sets out the priority areas for his term.[22] These strategic objectives will subsequently inform the Commission's annual 'work programmes'.[23] These work programmes will go beyond abstract priorities and typically contain a detailed annex with concrete legislative initiatives to be presented in the course of the year. (And in order to provide for a degree of interinstitutional cooperation, the Commission has agreed to present its work programme every year to the European Parliament and the Council and to 'duly take account' of their views and their requests for initiatives'.)[24] Finally, on the basis of the Commission's overall political strategies and work programmes, each Directorate-General will draft its own strategic and management plans.[25] An overview of the various policy instruments is shown in Table 9.1.

Table 9.1 'Soft' Instruments within the Executive Branch

	'Strategic' Instrument	'Administrative' Instrument
European Council	Presidency Conclusions	
European Commission	Political Guidelines	Annual Work Programmes
Directorate General	Strategic Plan	Management Plan

[21] For an overview, see https://ec.europa.eu/info/strategy/how-priorities-are-set_en.

[22] According to Art. 17(6)(a) TEU, the President shall 'lay down guidelines within which the Commission is to work'. For the political guidelines of the current 'Juncker Commission', see https://ec.europa.eu/commission/publications/president-junckers-political-guidelines_en.

[23] For the Commission's annual work programmes, see https://ec.europa.eu/info/publications/european-commission-work-programme_en. The 2017 Commission Work Programme thus states that '[i]n the coming year, the Commission will work in the framework of the 10 priorities outlined in the Political Guidelines – presented at the start of our mandate following discussions with the European Parliament and inspired by the European Council's "Strategic agenda for the Union in times of change" – to deliver a targeted and positive agenda that brings concrete results to protect, empower and defend citizens' (COM(2016) 710 final, 4).

[24] See 2016 Interinstitutional Agreement between the European Parliament, the Council of the European Union and the European Commission on Better Law-Making, [2016] OJ L 123/1, esp. para. 6. Moreover, according to para. 7 of the Agreement, the three Union institutions have agreed to commit to a 'joint declaration on annual interinstitutional programming' that is meant to 'set out broad objectives and priorities for the following year' (ibid., para. 7). The 2017 Joint Declaration on the EU's legislative priorities can be found at: https://ec.europa.eu/commission/publications/joint-declaration-eus-legislative-priorities-2017_en.

[25] For the list of strategic plans of the various Directorates-General, see: https://ec.europa.eu/info/publications/strategic-plans-2016–2020_en. For the various (annual) management plans, see: https://ec.europa.eu/info/publications/management-plans_en.

This ordinary policy cycle may – moreover – be complemented by extraordinary reform impulses, such as 'Action Programmes', 'Communications' or 'White Papers'.[26] These typically express a particular reform effort for a specific sector. They have been frequently employed in the past.

b. The Informal Procedure(s) of Government

How is the Union's dual executive working? Is there a strict division of powers between the European Council and the Commission? Or are both institutions cooperating in the joint task of government? The European Union has followed the second route – even if the legal procedures connecting its dual executive are not as formalised and 'legal' as in other areas of European law.

Many of the major policy initiatives within the Union originate in the Commission, yet are addressed to the European Council. For example: the 'Europe 2020' agenda was to provide the Union with an economic growth strategy for the next decade. It was originally devised by the Commission;[27] yet the Commission admitted that '[t]he European Council will have full ownership and be the focal point of the new strategy', and to that effect proposed to the European Council formally to endorse it. This indeed happened;[28] and it had happened similarly in the past.[29]

This upward cooperative process may be complemented by a downward process. For example: where the European Council has formally endorsed a general policy initiative, it may subsequently charge the Commission with the elaboration of specific policy initiatives. One prominent illustration of this institutional cooperation can be seen in the 'Stockholm Programme: An Open and Secure Europe Serving and Protecting Citizens'.[30] The Programme was established by the European Council, and constituted a multi-annual programme (2010–14) offering 'strategic guidelines for legislative and operational planning within the area of freedom, security and justice'.[31] One task within the Programme was 'Protecting Citizen's Rights in the Information Society',[32] in which the European Council recognised an individual's right to privacy. Acknowledging the executive prerogatives of the Commission within this area, the relevant passage of the Programme read as follows:

---

[26] For a list of Commission 'White Papers', see https://europa.eu/european-union/documents-publications/official-documents_en.

[27] Commission, Communication: A Strategy for smart, sustainable and inclusive growth, COM (2010) 2020 final.

[28] European Council, Presidency Conclusions (25/26 March 2010), and Presidency Conclusions (17 June 2010) – both available online (see n. 18 above).

[29] The most famous illustration is the 1985 Commission White Paper 'Completing the Internal Market' (COM (1985) 310 final), which was formally addressed to the European Council.

[30] European Council, *The Stockholm Programme – An Open and Secure Europe Serving and Protecting Citizens* [2010] OJ C 115/01.

[31] *Ibid.*, 4.   [32] *Ibid.*, 10.

The European Council invites the Commission to:
- evaluate the functioning of the various instruments on data protection and present, where necessary, further legislative and non-legislative initiatives to maintain the effective application of the above principles,
- propose a Recommendation for the negotiation of a data protection and, where necessary, data sharing agreements for law enforcement purposes with the United States of America, building on the work carried out by the EU–US High Level Contact Group on Information Sharing and Privacy and Personal Data Protection,
- consider core elements for data protection agreements with third countries for law enforcement purposes, which may include, where necessary, privately held data, based on a high level of data protection, improve compliance with the principles of data protection through the development of appropriate new technologies, improving cooperation between the public and private sectors, particularly in the field of research …

The Commission indeed followed the European Council's invitation and presented an 'Action Plan Implementing the Stockholm Programme',[33] where it committed itself to a concrete timetable for each of these policy initiatives.[34] And first fruits of this could soon be seen.[35]

The Stockholm Programme demonstrates that policy initiatives are often the result of a *dual* and *combined* executive impulse: the European Council may call on the Commission, and the Commission then calls on the European legislator.[36] The cooperative spirit between the European Council and the Commission will work particularly well where both follow similar political orientations. This may not necessarily be the case. For, as we saw above,[37] the European Council is not constitutionally free to 'appoint' the Commission of its political tastes. With the Commission being 'elected' by the European Parliament, the possibility thus arises that the political orientation of the latter – and hence that of the Commission – will not 'coincide' with that of the

---

[33] Commission, Communication: Delivering an Area of Freedom, Security and Justice for Europe's Citizens – Action Plan Implementing the Stockholm Programme (COM (2010) 171 final). For the general invitation by the European Council, see Presidency Conclusions (10/11 December 2009), 11 (para. 33): 'The European Council invites the Commission to present an Action Plan for implementing the Stockholm Programme, to be adopted at the latest in June 2010, and to submit a midterm review before 2012.'

[34] Commission, Action Plan (n. 33 above), Annex.

[35] Commission, Communication: 'A comprehensive approach on personal data protection in the European Union', COM(2010) 609 final. And see also Commission Decision 2010/87 on standard contractual clauses for the transfer of personal data to processors established in third countries under Directive 95/46/EC of the European Parliament and of the Council [2010] OJ L 39/5.

[36] For a constitutional link between the European Council and the Council, see Art. 16(6) TEU. The General Affairs Council is here charged to liaise with the European Council. On this point, see Chapter 5, section 4(a).

[37] On the selection of the Commission, see Chapter 6, section 1(a).

European Council. A 'conservative' European Council may thus have to collaborate with a 'labour' Commission. In this situation, the European Union's dual government will be subject to a political dynamic that is known in French constitutional law as 'cohabitation', that is: the coexistence of two politically opposed executives.[38]

2. Lawmaking Powers: Delegated and Implementing Acts

The advent of the legislating executive 'constitutes one of the most important transformations of constitutionalism'.[39] And indeed: within the Union legal order, executive rule-making accounts today for about 90 per cent of all lawmaking (see Table 9.2).

Executive legislation may thereby derive from two sources. It may be based on an 'autonomous' executive competence directly granted under the EU Treaties; or, it may be delegated to the executive on the basis of primary legislation. And from the very beginning, the European Treaties allowed for both: autonomous and delegated regulatory powers of the Commission.[40] The Treaty-makers had indeed anticipated that the Union legislator alone would not be able to legislate on all matters falling within the scope of the Treaties.[41]

Table 9.2 Legislative and Executive Acts (Numbers)

	2015	2016	2017
Legislative Acts (OLP)	60	72	73
Delegated	99	127	131
Implementing	873	832	903
Autonomous	611	590	618

---

[38] On this comparative constitutional point, see Favoreu et al., *Droit constitutionnel* (n. 4 above), 589ff.

[39] Zoller, *Droit constitutionnel* (n. 3 above), 436.

[40] In the Union legal order, we find a primary example of autonomous executive powers of the Commission in the field of EU competition law, see Art. 106(3) TFEU. By contrast, and in violation of the separation-of-powers principle, the EU Treaties still occasionally allow the Council to wield autonomous executive regulatory power. The most notorious example here is Art. 43 (3) TFEU, which entitles the Council to fix agricultural prices as well as the allocation of fishing opportunities in the Union. For a recent judicial discussion of the nature of the Council's 'implementing' power in both contexts, see respectively Case C-113/14, *Germany v. Parliament and Council*, EU:C:2016:635; Joined Cases C-124/13 and C-125/13, EU:C:2015:790.

[41] The E(E)C Treaty therefore already provided for the possibility of a transfer of legislative power to the Commission. Ex-Art. 211 EC entitled the Commission to 'exercise the powers conferred on it by the Council for the implementation of the rules laid down by the latter'.

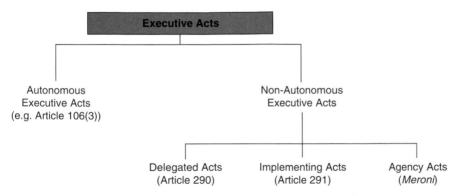

Figure 9.1 Types of Executive Acts

Would there be constitutional controls around delegated powers? The European legal order has indeed developed two constitutional safeguards to protect its foundational principles of federalism and democracy. Judicially, the Court of Justice has established a 'non-delegation' doctrine. In the name of democracy, the European legislator is here constitutionally prohibited from delegating *essential political choices* to the executive. Yet even within these substantive limits, the Union legislator has traditionally been unwilling to delegate power without some political control. From the very beginning, the Council – representing the Member States – would thus not delegate powers to the Commission – representing a supranational executive – unless the delegation was controlled by a (Council) committee. This system became known as 'Comitology'; and until the Lisbon Treaty, it was the sole political safeguard of federalism for executive lawmaking within the old 'Community' legal order.[42]

---

[42] For almost three decades, comitology had developed in the undergrowth of the Rome Treaty. It was only given textual foundations by the Single European Act. An amended ex-Art. 202 EC expressly provided that the Council should – except in 'specific cases'– 'confer on the Commission, in the acts which the Council adopts, powers for the implementation of the rules which the Council lays down'. The Council could thereby 'impose certain requirements in respect of the exercise of these powers'. This called for a comitology 'code' that would formally define the types of committees that could be used. The Council used this power three times: in 1987, 1999 and 2006. For the 1987 Comitology Decision, see Council Decision 87/373 laying down the procedures for the exercise of implementing powers conferred on the Commission [1987] OJ L 197/33. For the second Comitology Decision, see Council Decision 1999/468 laying down the procedures for the exercise of implementing powers conferred on the Commission [1999] OJ L 184/23. The 2006 Comitology Decision did not repeal its predecessor but amended it substantially: see Council Decision 2006/512 amending Decision 1999/468/EC laying down the procedures for the exercise of implementing powers conferred on the Commission [2006] OJ L 200/11. The most significant innovation here was the introduction of a new regulatory procedure: the 'regulatory procedure with scrutiny'. Art. 2(2) of the (amended) Comitology Decision defined its scope as follows: 'Where a basic instrument, adopted in accordance with the procedure referred to in [ex-] Article 251 of the [EC] Treaty, provides for the adoption of measures of general scope designed to amend non-essential elements of that instrument, *inter alia* by deleting some of those elements or by supplementing the

This has dramatically changed with the Lisbon Treaty. The latter has now split the 'old' constitutional regime for delegated lawmaking into two halves. The 'new' constitutional regime today distinguishes between a delegation of 'legislative' power – that is: the power to *amend* primary legislation – and a delegation of 'executive' power – that is, the power to *implement* primary legislation. Both forms of delegation identify the Commission as the principal delegee of Union power, yet they differ in the control mechanisms they establish vis-à-vis the exercise of delegated power. The delegation of *legislative* power is subject to the constitutional safeguards established in Article 290 TFEU (see section (a)). The delegation of implementing power is subject to the constitutional regime established by Article 291 TFEU (see section (b)).

a. The Delegation of 'Legislative' Power: Article 290

The constitutional regime for a delegation of legislative power to the Commission is set out in Article 290 TFEU. The legal conditions and limitations for this delegation are defined as follows:

> 1. A legislative act may delegate to the Commission the power to adopt non-legislative *acts of general application to supplement or amend certain non-essential elements of the legislative act*. The objectives, content, scope and duration of the delegation of power shall be explicitly defined in the legislative act. The essential elements of an area shall be reserved for the legislative act and accordingly shall not be subject of a delegation of power.
> 2. Legislative acts shall explicitly lay down the conditions to which the delegation is subject; these conditions may be as follows:
>   (a) the European Parliament or the Council may decide to revoke the delegation;
>   (b) the delegated act may enter into force only if no objection has been expressed by the European Parliament or the Council within a period set by the legislative act.
>   For the purposes of (a) and (b), the European Parliament shall act by a majority of its component members, and the Council by a qualified majority.[43]

A good illustration of the use of the provision can be found in the Union's Tobacco Sales Directive. As briefly mentioned in Chapter 7,[44] the Directive lays

---

instrument by the addition of new non-essential elements, those measures shall be adopted in accordance with the regulatory procedure with scrutiny.' The procedure was thus to apply to legislative powers delegated to the Commission under co-decision, that is, where the Council and the Parliament act as co-legislators. Yet, not all acts adopted by co-decision would be subject to the new procedure. It only covered 'measures of general scope', which would 'amend non-essential elements' of the primary legislation.

[43] Emphasis added.
[44] Directive 2014/40 on the approximation of the laws, regulations and administrative provisions of the Member States concerning the manufacture, presentation and sale of tobacco products and related products, [2014] OJ L 127/1. See Chapter 7, section 1(b/aa).

down (severe) requirements for tobacco products by, *inter alia* requiring that 65 per cent of the external surface of a packet be covered by health warnings. These health warnings must include a colour photograph chosen from a picture library. This picture library was however not part of the original Directive. The Union legislature had indeed delegated the power to 'establish and adapt the picture library' to the Commission,[45] which – acting under the powers granted by Article 290 TFEU – subsequently adopted such a library of picture warnings for tobacco products.[46]

aa. Delegated Acts: Amending or Supplementing

What is the scope of Article 290 TFEU? Is the provision restricted to acts adopted under the 'ordinary' legislative procedure?[47] Textually, the Treaty does not mandate this restriction; and to increase the ability of the Union legislator to concentrate on essential political matters, the better view suggests a wide understanding of 'legislative act' that includes the special legislative procedures.[48]

The scope of Article 290 thereby refers to two situations: a Commission act can either amend *or* supplement primary legislation. Is there any difference between these two methods? Despite strong arguments to the contrary, the Court has recently endorsed that there is. In *Parliament* v. *Commission (Connecting Europe Facility)*,[49] it accepted Parliament's argument that Article 290(1) TFEU introduced 'a clear distinction between the power to amend a legislative act and the power to supplement such an act'.[50] What was the nature of the distinction? For Parliament, the verb 'to amend' covered 'deletions, replacements and changes' to a legislative act, whereas the verb 'to supplement' would refer to 'the addition of new rules' that needed to be placed in 'a separate act which does not formally amend that act'.[51] The Court followed this formal distinction and underlined an important constitutional difference between amending and supplementing delegated acts. It held:

---

[45] *Ibid.*, Art. 10(3)(b).

[46] Commission Delegated Directive 2014/109 amending Annex II to Directive 2014/40 establishing the library of picture warnings to be used on tobacco products, (2014) OJ L360/22.

[47] On the distinction between the 'ordinary' legislative procedure and various 'special' legislative procedures, see Chapter 7, section 3.

[48] This position was advocated by the Commission; see Commission, Communication: 'Implementing Article 290 of the Treaty on the Functioning of the European Union', COM (2009) 673 final, 3: 'A delegation of power within the meaning of Article 290 is possible only in a legislative act. However, it makes little difference whether or not the legislative act was adopted jointly by Parliament and the Council, because Article 290 does not distinguish between the ordinary legislative procedure (formerly co-decision) and special legislative procedures.'

[49] Case C-286/14, *Parliament* v. *Commission*, EU:C:2016:183.

[50] *Ibid.*, para. 19.   [51] *Ibid.*

> [I]t follows from the wording 'to supplement or amend' that the two categories of delegated powers laid down in Article 290(1) TFEU are clearly distinguished. The delegation of a power to 'supplement' a legislative act is meant only to authorize the Commission to flesh out that act. Where the Commission exercises that power, *its authority is limited, in compliance with the entirety of the legislative act* … By contrast, the delegation of a power to 'amend' a legislative act aims to authorize the Commission to modify or repeal non-essential elements laid down by the legislature in that act. In cases where the Commission exercises that power, *it is not required to act in compliance with the elements that the authority conferred on it aims precisely to 'amend'.*[52]

The difference between an *amending* delegated act and a *supplementing* delegated act is here located in their different hierarchical relations to the primary act. Only the former can – unlike the latter – remove or alter substantive conditions within a primary act because it enjoys *hierarchical parity* with its parent legislative act. A supplementing act, by contrast, cannot amend the primary act and would therefore always have to be 'in compliance with the entirety of the legislative act'. In this view, the power to supplement is hierarchically subordinate to the power to amend (and of course the primary act); and their respective relations can be seen in Figure 9.2.

A delegated act supplementing a primary act could thus not change, say, the funding priorities for EU projects, whereas a delegated amending act potentially could; and because there is a constitutional difference in the two categories of delegated powers in Article 290 (1), the Court held that the choice between the two categories of delegated powers was not within the executive discretion of the Commission but required the EU legislature to expressly determine which of the two categories it wished to have used.[53] And in order to even better

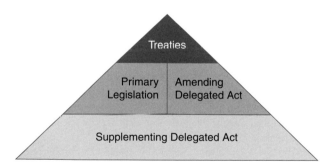

Figure 9.2 Normative Hierarchy among Delegated Acts

---

[52] Case C-286/14, *Parliament* v. *Commission*, paras. 40–2 (emphasis added).

[53] Ibid., para. 46. In the present case, the Court found that a provision authorising the Commission to adopt delegated acts 'detailing' funding priorities was an authorisation to 'supplement' but not to 'amend' (see esp. para. 50: 'Thus, by empowering the Commission to "detail" the funding priorities to be included in the work programmes referred to in

formally distinguish amending from supplementing delegated acts, the Court insisted that in the interest of 'regulatory clarity and transparency of the legislative process', all 'supplementing' acts needed to be free-standing acts.[54]

bb. *Judicial Safeguards: Constitutional Limits to Delegated Acts*

The ability to amend or supplement primary legislation is constitutionally limited in four ways. First, only the Commission – and not the Council[55] – may adopt delegated acts. Second, the Commission must adopt acts of 'general application', that is: acts that constitute material legislation.[56] Third, the European legislature cannot delegate to the Commission the power to adopt 'essential elements' of the legislative act. And, finally, the scope of delegated powers must be 'explicitly defined'.

Importantly, the third and the fourth criteria are distinct. The former constitutes an absolute limit to any delegation, while the latter only represents a relative limit that does not prevent the EU legislator from delegating as such. It only insists that the delegation is 'sufficiently precise, in that it must indicate clearly the limits of the power and must enable the Commission's use of the power to be reviewed by reference to objective criteria fixed by the EU legislature'.[57] Thus even where the Union has legitimately delegated *non*-essential elements to the Commission, the latter must of course act within the *expressly* delegated powers.

The most important constitutional limit is nevertheless imposed by the third condition. This 'essential elements' doctrine has a long history in the Union.[58] Its

---

Article 17 of Regulation No 1316/2013, Article 21(3) of that regulation authorises it not to amend elements already set out in that regulation, but to flesh out that regulation by developing details that were not defined by the legislature, while remaining obliged to comply with the provisions laid down by that regulation as a whole').

[54] The reasons for this result are spelled out in paras. 52–6 of the judgment and are highly complex.

[55] This had been possible under the Rome Treaty. For an analysis of delegations to the Council, see R. Schütze, '"Delegated" Legislation in the (New) European Union: A Constitutional Analysis' (2011) 74 MLR 661 at 672.

[56] On the notion of 'material' legislation as opposed to 'formal' legislation, see Chapter 7 – Introduction. In the past, 'implementation' under ex- Art. 202 EC comprised both general and specific acts; see Case 16/88, *Commission* v. *Council* [1989] ECR 3457, para. 11: 'The concept of implementation for the purposes of that article comprises both the drawing up of implementing rules and the application of rules to specific cases by means of acts of individual application.'

[57] For a recent case confirming this need for an 'express' and 'precise' delegation, see Case C-696/15P, *Czech Republic* v. *Commission*, EU:C:2017:595, esp. para. 49.

[58] Unfortunately, Art. 290 TFEU contains the seeds for two possible definitions of the 'essential elements' doctrine. A first formulation refers to 'non-essential elements *of the legislative act* (emphasis added), while the second formulation is broader and refers to the 'essential elements *of an area*' (emphasis added). This semantic ambivalence may well give rise to an uncertainty that has plagued the concept of 'minimum' standard in the context of shared competences. In that context it is not settled whether the Member States' power to adopt stricter measures must be viewed against each legislative act or against the policy area in general (see Chapter 7, section 2(b/bb)).

classic shape was given in *Köster*.[59] A German farmer had challenged the legality of a regulatory scheme established by the Commission that created import and export licences for cereals. It was alleged that 'the power to adopt the system in dispute belonged to the [Union legislator]', which should have acted according to the 'normal' legislative procedure established in Article 43 TFEU.[60] The Court disagreed: while basic elements of the policy area must be decided in accordance with the institutional balance prescribed by the Treaty, *non*-essential elements could be delegated and adopted by a simpler procedure. This followed from the scheme of the Treaty, and the common constitutional traditions of all the Member States.[61]

But what was the dividing line between 'basic elements' and 'non-essential' elements? In *Rey Soda*,[62] the Court tackled this question. Pointing to the institutional balance between the legislature and the Commission, the Court held that the delegation mandate 'must be interpreted strictly'; yet, despite this limitation, the Court insisted that 'the concept of implementation must be given a wide interpretation'.[63] Only the Commission would be able to continuously follow trends in agricultural markets and regulate quickly if the situation so required. The Union legislature was thus entitled 'to confer on the Commission *wide powers of discretion and action*'.[64] The scope of these – extensive – powers was to be judged in light of the objectives of the enabling act 'and less in terms of the literal meaning of the enabling word'.[65]

This flexible approach to the essential elements doctrine was refined in *Parliament* v. *Council (Schengen Borders Code)*.[66] Parliament here challenged an executive act adopted under powers delegated under the Schengen Borders Code.[67] The latter established rules for persons crossing an external border of the Union and was designed to combat illegal immigration. For that purpose, it wished to set up a system of border control and surveillance measures under Article 12. The provision stated:

> Border Surveillance
> 1   The main purpose of border surveillance shall be to prevent unauthorised border crossings, to counter cross-border criminality and to take measures against persons who have crossed the border illegally …

---

[59] Case 25/70, *Einfuhr- und Vorratsstelle für Getreide und Futtermittel* v. *Köster et Berodt & Co.* [1970] ECR 1161.

[60] *Ibid.*, para. 5.   [61] *Ibid.*, para. 6.

[62] Case 23/75, *Rey Soda* v. *Cassa Conguaglio Zucchero* [1975] ECR 1279.

[63] *Ibid.*, paras. 9–10.   [64] *Ibid.*, para. 11 (emphasis added).   [65] *Ibid.*, para. 14.

[66] Case C-355/10, *Parliament* v. *Council and Commission* EU:C:2012:516.

[67] Regulation 562/2006 establishing a [Union] Code on the Rules governing the movement of persons across borders (Schengen Borders Code) [2006] OJ L 105/1. The Regulation had been amended several times since 2009; and it originally used the pre-Lisbon arrangements for delegated acts. The following analysis has 'Lisbonised' the ruling.

> 2. The border guards shall use stationary or mobile units to carry out border surveillance. That surveillance shall be carried out in such a way as to prevent and discourage persons from circumventing the checks at border crossing points …
> 5. The Commission shall be empowered to adopt delegated acts in accordance with Article 33 concerning additional measures governing surveillance.

The Commission had exercised the power under Article 12(5) to lay down rules governing border guards when detecting suspicious ships at the Union's external sea borders. Parliament objected to these rules on the grounds that they breached the 'essential elements' doctrine: since the Schengen Borders Code was silent as to measures against ships at sea, this geographic extension was seen as an essential policy choice. Moreover, the delegated act laid down far-reaching enforcement measures without ensuring the rights of persons intercepted on the high seas, and it was therefore claimed to also interfere with the parliamentary prerogative to be involved in all essential political choices.

The Council objected to these arguments by claiming that 'the European Union legislature can itself fix the limits of the delegation, define what the essential aims of the basic legislation are and also decide the essential elements which cannot be delegated to the Commission'.[68] Yet unsurprisingly, the Court rejected the idea of a definitional carte blanche and seized the opportunity to give clearer contours to the 'essential elements' doctrine in the Union legal order. It held:

> According to settled case-law, the adoption of rules essential to the subject-matter envisaged is reserved to the legislature of the European Union. The essential rules governing the matter in question must be laid down in the basic legislation and may not be delegated. Thus, provisions which, in order to be adopted, require *political choices falling within the responsibilities of the European Union legislature cannot be delegated*. It follows from this that [delegated acts] cannot amend essential elements of basic legislation or supplement it by new essential elements. Ascertaining which elements of a matter must be categorised as essential is not – contrary to what the Council and the Commission claim – for the assessment of the European Union legislature alone, *but must be based on objective factors amenable to judicial review*. In that connection, it is necessary to take account of the characteristics and particularities of the domain concerned.[69]

Did the delegated powers with regard to border guards entail political choices? The Court indeed thought so:

---

[68] *Ibid.*, para. 45.   [69] *Ibid.*, paras. 64–8 (emphasis added).

> Depending on the political choices on the basis of which those rules are adopted, *the powers of the border guards may vary significantly*, and the exercise of those powers require authorisation, be an obligation or be prohibited, for example, in relation to applying enforcement measures, using force or conducting the persons apprehended to a specific location. In addition, where those powers concern the taking of measures against ships, their exercise is liable, depending on the scope of the powers, to interfere with the sovereign rights of third countries according to the flag flown by the ships concerned. *Thus, the adoption of such rules constitutes a major development in the SBC system.*
>
> Second, it is important to point out that provisions on conferring powers of public authority on border guards – such as the powers conferred in the contested decision, which include stopping persons apprehended, seizing vessels and conducting persons apprehended to a specific location – mean that *the fundamental rights of the persons concerned may be interfered with to such an extent that the involvement of the European Union legislature is required.*[70]

The Court concluded that the delegated act contained 'essential elements of external maritime border surveillance' and it was therefore a matter reserved for the Union legislature.[71]

This approach has become established jurisprudence.[72] The identification of an 'essential element' with a 'political choice' has indeed been regularly confirmed by the Court. The Court however continues to struggle identifying such a political choice. It has thereby developed a number of proxies such as the 'essential objective' of the basic act;[73] the need to have 'the conflicting interests at issue to be weighted up'; or, again, by reference to fundamental rights being affected 'to such an extent that the involvement of the EU legislature is required'.[74] The last proxy seems particularly unhelpful – not just because of its tautological nature, but because it entails the danger of colliding with a jurisprudential line developed under the EU Charter of Fundamental Rights.[75]

cc. Political Safeguards: Control Rights of the Legislator
What are the political safeguards that the Union legislator can impose to control delegated 'legislative' power? These are defined in the second paragraph of Article 290 TFEU.

---

[70] *Ibid.*, paras. 76–7 (emphasis added).   [71] *Ibid.*, paras. 78 and 79.

[72] See Case C-44/16P, *Dyson v. Commission*, EU:C:2017:357; Case C-696/15P *Czech Republic v. Commission*, EU:C:2017:595.

[73] Case C-44/16P, *Dyson v. Commission*, para. 64.

[74] Case C-696/15P, *Czech Republic v. Commission*, para. 78.

[75] On the tautological nature of this formulation, see D. Ritleng, 'The Reserved Domain of the Legislature: The Notion of "Essential Elements of an Area"', in C. F. Bergström and D. Ritleng, *Rulemaking by the European Commission* (Oxford University Press, 2016), 133 at 154. On the point whether any human rights violation must always be justified by a legislative act, see Chapter 12, section 2 (a/bb).

Legislative acts may allow the European Parliament or the Council 'to revoke the delegation' (subparagraph a), or to veto the adoption of the specific delegated act (subparagraph b). The Parliament must thereby act by a majority of its component members – which makes the control of the delegation slightly harder than the adoption of primary legislation.[76] The Council, by contrast, will act by a 'normal' qualified majority – which will make, where the legal basis in the Treaties requires unanimity, revocation easier than the adoption of primary legislation.

From a democratic point of view, Article 290 represents a revolution, when compared with the constitutional status quo within the 'old' Community. For the Rome Treaty had never acknowledged Parliament's *constitutional* right to control executive legislation.[77] (That right was reserved to the Council.) With the Lisbon Treaty, the Council *or* the European Parliament may – independently of each other – oppose or revoke delegated legislation. The parliamentary objection is thereby left to the institution's *political* discretion: Parliament thus need not point to special legal grounds to veto the Commission measure.[78] With regard to both alternatives mentioned in Article 290(2), the Lisbon amendments thus place the Parliament on a – roughly – equal footing with the Council in the political control of delegated acts. Delegated lawmaking by the Commission therefore today takes place 'in the shadow of a parliamentary veto'.[79]

Are the political safeguards of democracy and federalism in Article 290 the only ones; or may the Union legislator also insist on an *ex ante* influence through 'committees'? The provision contains no legal basis for the adoption of a 'comitology law'; and this constitutional absence should be seen as a deliberate choice. Admittedly, Article 290(2) uses the conditional 'may' in relation to the two political safeguards discussed above. However, this should not be interpreted to allow the European legislator carte blanche to determine, in each legislative act, which conditions to impose. The 'may' in Article 290(2) should simply be seen as allowing for the constitutional option of using *both* mechanisms or *none* in a legislative act; or of excluding either the European Parliament or the Council – depending on the *special* legislative procedure used.[80] This does not, of course, prevent the

---

[76] See Art. 231 TFEU: 'Save as otherwise provided in the Treaties, the European Parliament shall act by a majority of the votes cast.' For the application of this rule to the context of the ordinary legislative procedure, see Art. 294(13) TFEU.

[77] The 1999 Comitology system (as amended by the 2006 Comitology Decision) had provided for parliamentary involvement, but this had been a *legislative* concession by the Council.

[78] This had been the case under the 1999/2006 Comitology system (*ibid.*).

[79] J. Bast, 'New Categories of Acts after the Lisbon Reform: Dynamics of Parliamentarization in EU Law' (2012) 49 *CML Rev.* 885 at 918. For a first empirical analysis of legislative vetoes in the EU, see M. Kaeding and K. Stack, 'Legislative Scrutiny? The Political Economy and Practice of Legislative Vetoes in the European Union' (2015) 53 *JCMS* 1268. The study shows that there are hardly any vetoes by either Parliament or the Council.

[80] We should presume that where the primary legal base envisages the Council as the principal decision-maker, the (special) legislative act is unlikely to grant Parliament identical control powers for delegated acts.

Union legislature from requiring the Commission, in very technical areas of law, to base its delegated act on preliminary drafts (!) prepared by an EU Agency;[81] nor is the Commission prevented from consulting with (national) experts before it adopts a delegated act.[82]

b. The 'Conferral' of Executive Power: Article 291

The EU Treaties' regime for executive legislation is based on the idea that the nature of the constitutional control mechanism should take account of the nature of the power 'delegated'.[83] But if a delegation of *legislative* power is subject to the political control of the *legislature*, who is to control the exercise of *executive* or 'implementing power'?

The constitutional regime for 'implementing acts' is set out in Article 291 TFEU. The provision states:

> Where uniform conditions for implementing legally binding Union acts are needed, those acts shall confer implementing powers on the Commission, or, in duly justified specific cases and in the cases provided for in Articles 24 and 26 TEU, on the Council.[84]

The provision envisages the Commission *and the Council* as possible recipients of 'delegated' implementing power.[85] Strikingly, Article 291 does not mention substantive limits to such a conferral. Will the 'essential elements' principle or the specificity principle thus not apply? Or was this simply an editorial omission by the Treaty-makers? According to one view, the essential elements doctrine

---

[81] A good example here is the European Securities and Markets Authority (ESMA), which is tasked to develop 'draft regulatory technical standards' for the Commission when acting under Art. 290 TFEU. See here Art. 10 of Regulation 1095/2010 establishing a European Supervisory Authority, (2010) OJ L 331/84.

[82] Informally, the Commission has indeed agreed to consult with national experts in the preparation and drawing-up of delegated acts (see: Interinstitutional Agreement between the European Parliament, the Council of the European Union and the European Parliament on Better Law-Making, (2016) OJ L 123/1, esp. Annex: 'Common Understanding between the European Parliament, the Council and the Commission on Delegated Acts'). Importantly however, the Commission has emphasised '*that these experts will have a consultative rather than an institutional role in the decision-making procedure*' (Commission Communication (n. 48 above), 7).

[83] Again, despite the formal distinction between 'delegated' and 'implementing power', the acts adopted under Art. 291 TFEU are of course also the result of a 'delegation' in a primary act. On the material notion of 'legislation', see Chapter 7, Introduction.

[84] Art. 291(2) TFEU. Arts. 24 and 26 TEU are part of Common Foreign and Security Policy.

[85] The constitutional option of a 'self-delegation' by the Council has been rightly criticised as 'an anomaly in the overall picture of separation of functions' (K. Lenaerts and M. Desomer, 'Towards a Hierarchy of Legal Acts in the European Union? Simplification of Legal Instruments and Procedures' (2005) 11 ELJ 744, at 756).

must also be 'read into' Article 291,[86] while a second view claims that there is no need for such a doctrine because Article 291 should not be viewed from a *horizontal* separation-of-powers perspective but from a *vertical* division-of-powers perspective.[87] But be that as it may, delegations of implementing power under Article 291 have in the past been extremely generous,[88] and with regard to the – constitutional – requirement that 'uniform conditions for implementing legally binding Union acts *are needed*', the Court has again been generous by interpreting this subsidiarity-like requirement as if it fell within the political discretion of the Union.[89]

What about the political safeguards to control the exercise of implementing power? To control the exercise of implementing power by the Commission – but not the Council – the Union legislator has been called to 'lay down in advance the rules and general principles concerning mechanisms for control by Member States'.[90] This formulation stood in the constitutional tradition of the Rome Treaty; yet it appeared to give contradictory signals. On the one hand, it involves the Union legislator in the adoption of a future Comitology 'law': Council *and* Parliament 'acting by means of regulations in accordance with the ordinary legislative procedure' shall adopt the political control mechanisms for implementing powers. On the other hand, the provision charges the European legislator to establish 'mechanisms for control by *Member States*'. This formulation appears to exclude – as ultra vires – any direct participation of the Parliament (as well as the Council) in the control system.[91]

The 2011 Comitology Regulation has followed this second view.[92] The new system distinguishes between two procedures – the advisory procedure and

---

[86] In this sense, see H. Hofmann, 'Legislation, Delegation and Implementation under the Treaty of Lisbon: Typology Meets Reality' (2009) 14 ELJ 482; and see the excellent analysis by D. Ritleng, 'The Reserved Domain of the Legislature', in Bergström and Ritleng (eds.), *Rulemaking by the European Commission*, (n. 75 above), 133.

[87] For that argument, see Schütze, '"Delegated" Legislation' (n. 55 above). From this perspective, Ritleng's view that it simply cannot be true 'that the legislature's domain does not constitute a limit on the scope of implementing acts' is countered by the argument that the 'execution' of European law simply does not fall within the 'legislative' domain because implementing acts will, by definition, never touch 'essential elements'.

[88] Case C-65/13, *Parliament v. Commission (EURES)*, EU:C:2014:2289. The case involved the very generous delegation of implementing power, which simply stated: 'The Commission shall adopt measures pursuant to this Regulation for its implementation.'

[89] Case 427/12, *Commission v. Parliament & Council*, EU:C:2014:170, para.53.

[90] Art. 291(3) TFEU.

[91] See P. Craig, 'The Role of the European Parliament under the Lisbon Treaty', in S. Griller and J. Ziller (eds.), *The Lisbon Treaty: EU Constitutionalism without a Constitutional Treaty?* (Springer, 2008), 109 at 123.

[92] Regulation 182/2011 laying down the rules and general principles concerning mechanisms for control by Member States of the Commission's exercise of implementing powers [2011] OJ L 55/13. The Regulation is currently under review as the Commission has recently suggested 'targeted and limited amendments' to it (see COM(2017) 85 final, esp. 2).

the examination procedure – according to which the Commission can adopt implementing acts.[93] The Commission is not free to choose which procedure applies. On the contrary, the Comitology Regulation sets out the scope of the examination procedure with the advisory procedure constituting the residual category.[94] The examination procedure thereby applies to 'implementing acts of general scope', but will also cover individual measures in important policy areas of the Union.[95]

In what ways are the two procedures controlling the Commission's power to adopt implementing acts? Both procedures oblige the Commission to 'be assisted by a committee composed of representatives of the Member States'.[96] The Commission will thus have to submit draft acts to a committee. Under the advisory procedure, the opinion of the Committee is only 'advisory'. Where the advisory committee has a negative opinion, the Commission must take 'the utmost account of the conclusions' but may still adopt the implementing act anyway.[97] This freedom is restricted under the examination procedure. For while the Commission can adopt the act, where there is a positive or no opinion,[98] the Committee can veto a Commission act through a negative opinion.[99] Yet the Commission – as chair of the committee – can then still refer the draft act to an 'appeal committee' for further deliberation.[100] The appeal committee is composed in the same way as the examination committee;[101] and where it delivers a positive opinion, 'the Commission shall adopt the draft legislative acts'.[102] By contrast, where the appeal committee confirms the negative opinion, 'the Commission shall not adopt the draft legislative act'.[103] Schematically, the 'Comitology' regime under Article 291(3) TFEU is shown in Figure 9.3.

What is the role of the Union legislator in the control regime under Article 291 TFEU? The answer is that there is no direct role for either Parliament or Council. However, both are entitled to indicate to the Commission their belief that the draft act exceeds the implementing powers provided for in the primary

---

[93] *Ibid.*, recital 8.   [94] *Ibid.*, Art. 2.

[95] *Ibid.*, Art. 2(2). Subpara. (b) enumerates, *inter alia*, the common agricultural and fisheries policies and the common commercial policy.

[96] *Ibid.*, Art. 3(2).   [97] *Ibid.*, Art. 4(2).

[98] The rules as to when the Commission can adopt the act, where there is no opinion of the examination committee, are fairly complex. Art. 5(4) distinguishes between the general rule (subpara. 1) that allows the Commission to adopt the draft acts, and a number of exceptional cases (subpara. 2) in which silence is taken to be a negative opinion. Finally, Art. 5(5) contains a (very) special procedure for antidumping or countervailing measures.

[99] *Ibid.*, Art. 5(3): 'if the committee delivers a negative opinion, the Commission shall not adopt the draft implementing act'.

[100] *Ibid.*

[101] According to Art. 6(1) of the Regulation, the appeals committee shall decide by the majority provided for in Art. 5(1) Regulation, that is: according to 'the majority laid down in Article 16(4) and (5) of the Treaty on European Union and, where applicable, Article 238(3) TFEU'; and '[t]he votes of the representatives of the Member States within the committee shall be weighted in the manner set out in those Articles'.

[102] *Ibid.*, Art. 6(3) – first indent.   [103] *Ibid.*, Art. 6(3) – third indent.

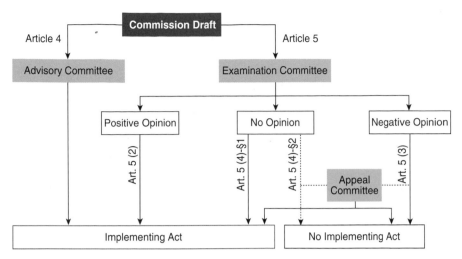

Figure 9.3 'Comitology' as Defined by Regulation 182/2011

act.[104] But this right of scrutiny is a 'soft' right. The Commission is not obliged to amend or withdraw its proposal. Yet, where the implementing act indeed exceeds the delegation mandate, both institutions will be entitled to apply for judicial review to have the act repealed on grounds of lack of competence.[105]

c. The Choice between Articles 290 and 291

What will the scope of Article 291 be? Will it be limited by the scope of Article 290? Or will the two provisions overlap? Will the Union legislator be able to freely choose whether it prefers a delegation under Article 290 or a delegation under Article 291?

A freedom of choice between Articles 290 and 291 contradicts the intention of the Treaty-makers;[106] and for the Commission, '[t]he authors of the new Treaty clearly intended the two articles to be mutually exclusive'.[107] What then are, according to this view, their respective spheres of application? The Commission has answered this question in the following way:

> [I]t should be noted that the authors of the new Treaty did not conceive the scope of the two articles in the same way. The concept of the delegated act is defined in terms of its scope and consequences – as a general measure that supplements or amends non-essential elements – whereas that of the implementing act, although never spelled out, is determined by its rationale – the need for uniform conditions for implementation. This discrepancy is due to the very different nature and scope

---

[104] *Ibid.*, Art. 11.
[105] On the availability of judicial review for lack of competence, see Chapter 10, section 1(b).
[106] See Final Report of Working Group IX (Simplification), CONV 424/02.
[107] European Commission, Communication: Implementing Art. 290 (n. 48 above), 3.

of the powers conferred on the Commission by the two provisions. When it receives the power to adopt delegated acts under Article 290 the Commission is authorised to supplement or amend the work of the legislator. Such a delegation is always discretionary: the legislator delegates its powers to the Commission in the interests of efficiency. In the system introduced by Article 291 the Commission does not exercise any 'quasi-legislative' power; its power is purely executive. The Member States are naturally responsible for implementing the legally binding acts of the European Union, but because it is necessary to have uniform conditions the Commission must exercise its executive power. Its intervention is not optional but compulsory, when the conditions of Article 291 are fulfilled.[108]

The argument advanced above is that Articles 290 and 291 follow different constitutional rationales. The former concerns the *voluntary* delegation of *legislative* power in the interest of efficiency – and thus deals with the *horizontal* separation of powers. By contrast, Article 291 concerns the *compulsory* delegation of *executive* power, where the national implementation leads to an unacceptable degree of diversity, and thus deals with the *vertical* separation of powers. Following this view, Article 291 must be placed within the constitutional context of 'executive federalism' within the European Union.[109] But even if the constitutional logic and values underlying Articles 290 and 291 are fundamentally different, does this mean that the two provisions never overlap and that the Union legislator has no freedom of choice between them?

The question received a first answer in *Commission* v. *Parliament & Council (Biocides)*.[110] The Commission had brought annulment proceedings against a legislative provision that delegated to it power under Article 291 as opposed to Article 290. Wishing to be empowered to adopt delegated – not implementing – acts, it repeated its view that the respective scopes of both provisions 'are different and mutually exclusive'. And insisting that the choice between a delegation under Article 290 and Article 291 must be based 'on objective and clear factors', it argued that the distinction between both provisions would hinge on the nature of the powers conferred. With respect to the latter criterion, it especially argued as follows:

If the purpose of those powers is to adopt non-essential rules of general application, *having the legal function of completing the normative framework of the legislative act concerned*, those rules supplement the legislative act in accordance with the first subparagraph of Article 290(1) TFEU. If, by contrast, those rules are *intended merely to give effect to the rules already laid down in the basic act* while ensuring uniform conditions of application within the European Union, they come under Article 291 TFEU. The exercise of implementing powers under Article 291 TFEU may in no way affect the content of the legislative act.[111]

---

[108]   *Ibid.*, 3–4.   [109]   On this point, see section 3 below.
[110]   Case 427/12, *Commission* v. *Parliament & Council*, EU:C:2014:170.   [111]   *Ibid.*, para. 23.

This suggested that the power under Article 290 was – constitutionally – greater than that under Article 291: the former could 'complete' (or amend) the normative framework of the legislative act, whereas the latter could merely 'give effect' to the legislative act; and since in the present case the contested provision required the 'greater' power under Article 290, the chosen method of delegation under Article 291 was unlawful.

The Court however rejected the idea of a clear dividing line between Articles 290 and 291. Finding that '*the EU legislature has discretion when it decides to confer a delegated power to the Commission pursuant to Article 290(1) TFEU or an implementing power pursuant to Article 291(2) TFEU*',[112] it limited its judicial review to 'manifest errors of assessment'.[113] The Court would thus principally respect the EU legislature's choice. In this case, the EU legislature could therefore 'reasonably' assume the view that the primary legislative act had laid down a 'complete legal framework' without the need for further amendment or supplementation.

This (relative) freedom of choice was recently confirmed in *Commission v. Parliament & Council (Visa Reciprocity)*.[114] This case involved EU legislation that exempted nationals of third countries from a visa requirement to enter the Union. The legislation contained an Annex in which it listed the countries exempted; yet it expressly made this exemption conditional on reciprocity: where a third State thus reintroduced a visa requirement for EU citizens, the Commission was entitled to temporarily suspend the visa waiver also on the Union side. This executive power had been delegated under Article 290 – a legislative decision that the Commission wished annulled, as it now preferred a delegation under Article 291.[115]

Analysing this legislative choice, the Court however confirmed that 'the EU legislature has discretion when it decides to confer on the Commission a delegated power pursuant to Article 290(1) TFEU or an implementing power pursuant to Article 291(2) TFEU'.[116] And expressly rejecting the Commission's argument that the extent of the discretionary power conferred on it was relevant, the Court found that the choice between Articles 290 and 291 solely depended on whether the contested act could be based on Article 290.[117] The Court here seems to altogether reject a review of whether the 'right' choice between Article 290 and 291 was made by simply testing whether – once the choice is made – the Commission was legally entitled to adopt the act it did under the chosen type of delegation.

This judicial minimalism in the review of the legislature's choice between Articles 290 and 291 is to be deeply regretted. Although there may be no hard

---

[112] *Ibid.*, para 40 (emphasis added).   [113] *Ibid.*

[114] Case C-88/14, *Commission* v. *Parliament & Council*, EU:C:2015:499.

[115] *Ibid.*, para. 11. The case is slightly more complicated, but I shall concentrate on the 'second stage' of the reciprocity mechanism. For an extensive analysis of the facts and context of the case, see M. Chamon, 'The Dividing Line between Delegated and Implementing Acts, Part Two' (2015) 52 *CML Rev* 1617.

[116] Case 427/12, *Commission* v. *Parliament & Council*, para. 28.

[117] *Ibid.*, para. 32. For a positive finding that this was the case, see *ibid.*, paras. 42–4.

conceptual difference between 'supplementing' legislative rules via Article 290 and 'specifying' (additional) implementing rules via Article 291,[118] there are important constitutional differences in the values protected by Articles 290 and 291. Article 290 is designed directly to protect *democratic* values, whereas Article 291 is primarily designed to protect *federal* values. And where the democratic safeguard of the essential elements doctrine in Article 290 is fulfilled, the Commission is immediately entitled to exercise its delegated powers to amend non-essential elements because the principle of *legislative* subsidiarity will have been satisfied by the basic legislative act.[119] By contrast, the Commission should not be automatically able to act under Article 291, as every exercise of Union implementing power under this provision ought still to be subject to the principle of *executive* subsidiarity.[120]

d. Delegating 'Implementing' Power to European Agencies

What about a delegation of power to European Agencies? Articles 290 and 291 are silent on this point. Does this mean that no legislative or executive power

---

[118] Bast, 'New Categories of Acts' (n. 79 above), 920. The Court has nevertheless come to mysteriously insist that under Art. 291 'the Commission may neither amend nor supplement the legislative act, even as to its non-essential elements' (Case C-65/13, *Parliament* v. *Commission (EURES)*, para. 45). Yet if implementation measures are meant to add 'further detail in relation to the framework' established in the legislative act (*ibid.*, para. 71), the material spheres of Arts. 290 and 291 are bound to overlap. This re-raises the problem of whether an 'essential elements' doctrine should apply to Art. 291 TFEU.

[119] The argument goes as follows: as the 'delegated act' only concerns 'non-essential' elements and since the delegation mandate must expressly and clearly specify the 'objectives, content, scope and duration of the delegation' (Art. 290(1) TFEU), all future delegated acts should be seen as covered by the subsidiarity analysis of the basic legislative act.

[120] On this point, see section 3(b) below. In this sense, see also the excellent analysis of Advocate General Cruz Villalón in Case 427/12, *Commission* v. *Parliament & Council*, esp. paras. 57 and 59: 'On the other hand, we should not lose sight of the fact that, ultimately, the distinction between delegated acts and implementing acts does not depend only on the difference between legislation (even if it is delegated) and implementation, but also on the fact that delegated acts are the product of the exercise of a normative competence belonging to the European Union itself, whereas implementing acts are the result of the (subsidiary) exercise by the Commission (or the Council) of a competence that belongs predominantly to the Member States … In the EU context, the question of normative force clearly arises in the case of Article 290 TFEU, which is concerned with the delegation to one institution of the powers that belong to other institutions of the European Union itself. In the case of Article 291 TFEU it is also necessary to use the criterion of normative force in order to establish whether the Commission (or the Council) has limited itself to "implementing" legally binding Union acts, but a preliminary question always arises, namely whether implementation falls to the European Union or to the Member States, and this will always depend on an objective factor over which the EU institutions have no control: the need for uniform conditions for implementation. In addition to the issue of the demarcation between the general and the specific, which is typical of legislative delegation and enabling, there is the issue of delimiting the competences of the European Union and the Member States.'

can be delegated to these bodies? With regard to a delegation of legislative power under Article 290, this is indeed the case, since the provision envisages the Commission as the sole recipient of the power to amend or supplement primary legislation. With regard to a delegation of executive power, on the other hand, a nuanced picture has emerged. Historically, the Union legal order has indeed heavily drawn on agencies to implement Union policies, yet it has traditionally not permitted a delegation of *any discretionary* executive powers to them.

This famous constitutional safeguard was established in *Meroni* v. *High Authority*.[121] The applicant here complained that the Commission had delegated 'powers conferred upon it by the Treaty, without subjecting their exercise to the conditions which the Treaty would have required if those powers had been exercised directly by it'.[122] The Court of Justice had little trouble in finding that this could not be done. For even if the delegation as such was constitutional, the Union 'could not confer upon the authority receiving the delegation powers different from those which the delegating authority itself received under the Treaty'.[123]

A second argument however then moved to an analysis of the constitutional limits to a delegation as such. And while noting that the ECSC Treaty did not provide any power to delegate,[124] the Court nonetheless found that such a constitutional possibility 'cannot be excluded'. It was inherent in the powers of the Commission 'to entrust certain powers to such bodies subject to conditions to be determined by it and subject to its supervision' if such delegation was necessary for the performance of the Union's tasks. These tasks were set out in Article 3 ECSC – a provision that laid down, however, 'very general objectives', which could not always be equally pursued. The Union thus had to make political choices, and these political choices could not be delegated to an agency:

> Reconciling the various objectives laid down in Article 3 [ECSC] implies a real discretion involving difficult choices, based on a consideration of the economic facts and circumstances in the light of which those choices are made. The consequences resulting from a delegation of powers are very different depending on whether it involves clearly defined executive powers the exercise of which can, therefore, be subject to strict review in the light of objective criteria determined by the delegating authority, *or whether it involves a discretionary power, implying a wide margin of discretion which may, according to the use which is made of it, make possible the execution of actual economic policy.* A delegation of the first kind cannot appreciably alter the consequences involved in the exercise of the powers concerned, whereas a delegation of the second kind, since it replaces the choices of the delegator by the choices of the delegate, brings about an actual transfer of responsibility.[125]

---

[121]   Case 9/56, *Meroni & Co., Industrie Metallurgische, SpA* v. *High Authority of the European Coal and Steel Community* [1958] ECR 133.

[122]   *Ibid.*, 146.   [123]   *Ibid.*, 150.

[124]   Art. 8 ECSC read: 'The [Commission] shall be responsible for assuring the fulfilment of the purposes stated in the present Treaty under the terms thereof.'

[125]   Case 9/56, *Meroni* v. *High Authority*, 152 (emphasis added).

This judgment clarified two things. First, a delegation to bodies not mentioned in the Treaties – even 'bodies established under private law' – was constitutionally possible. However, such delegations 'can only relate to clearly defined executive powers, the use of which must be entirely subject to the supervision of the [Commission]'.[126] This followed from the 'balance of powers which is characteristic of the institutional structure of the [Union]'. To delegate 'a discretionary power' to 'bodies other than those which the Treaty has established' would render that guarantee ineffective.

Subsequent judicial and academic commentary has concentrated on this last passage. *Meroni* came to stand for a constitutional non-delegation doctrine according to which the Union institutions could not delegate *any* discretionary power – let alone regulatory power – to European Agencies.[127] And while this expansive reading may not have been originally intended,[128] constitutional folklore has long paid homage to the '*Meroni* doctrine'. This constitutional choice has traditionally prevented European Agencies from exercising *regulatory* choices. For under the classic *Meroni* doctrine, European Agencies could only be empowered to adopt individually binding decisions to implement European norms.

After more than 50 years, this *Meroni* orthodoxy was suddenly left behind in *United Kingdom* v. *Parliament & Council (ESMA)*.[129] Britain here challenged a delegation of power to the European Securities and Markets Authority (ESMA). The relevant enabling legislation authorised ESMA to 'prohibit and impose conditions on the entry by natural or legal persons into a short sale or a transaction which creates, or relates to, a financial instrument', where there was a threat to the stability of financial markets within the Union.[130] Claiming that this gave the

---

[126] *Ibid.*

[127] The most drastic expression of this expansive reading of *Meroni* is Case 98/80, *Romano* v. *Institut national d'assurance maladie-invalidité* [1981] ECR 1241, para. 20: 'It follows both from Article [17] of the [EU] Treaty, and in particular by Articles [263] and [267] [TFEU], that a body such as the administrative commission may not be empowered by the Council to adopt acts having the force of law. Whilst a decision of the administrative commission may provide an aid to social security institutions responsible for applying [European] law in this field, it is not of such a nature as to require those institutions to use certain methods or adopt certain interpretations when they come to apply the [European] rules.'

[128] In Case 9/56, *Meroni*, the Court – repeatedly – referred to the '*wide* margin of discretion' that was delegated to the agency (*ibid.*, 153 and 154; emphasis added). A close historical analysis could thus narrow the ruling to an early expression of the 'basic elements' principle: the Commission was simply not allowed to delegate *basic* choices to an agency. The Court has itself (occasionally) signalled its willingness to limit the *Meroni* doctrine to a 'basic elements' doctrine for agencies (see Case C-164/98P, *DIR International Film Srl et al.* v. *Commission* [2000] ECR I-447); and albeit in a different context, Joined Cases C-154–5/04, *The Queen, ex p. National Association of Health Stores and others* v. *Secretary of State for Health* [2005] ECR I-6451, esp. para. 90.

[129] Case C-270/12, *United Kingdom* v. *Parliament & Council (ESMA)* EU:C:2014:18.

[130] Regulation 236/2012 on short selling and certain aspects of credit default swaps [2012] OJ L 86/1, Art. 28.

Agency 'a very large measure of discretion',[131] the Court was asked to annul the relevant delegation as a violation of the *Meroni* doctrine.

But, surprisingly, the Court did not annul the Union delegation. Consciously departing from the orthodox non-delegation doctrine for agencies, the Court now found it important to highlight 'that the bodies in question in *Meroni* v. *High Authority* were entities governed by private law, whereas ESMA is a European Union entity, created by the EU legislature'.[132] This seemed to confine the *Meroni* doctrine to private law bodies. With regard to Union agencies, on the other hand, the Court simply noted that the relevant Union legislation did 'not confer any autonomous power on that entity *that goes beyond the bounds of the regulatory framework established by the ESMA Regulation*';[133] and the Court here clearly seemed to accept the idea of agency discretion as long as that discretion was 'circumscribed', 'precisely delineated' and 'amenable to judicial review in the light of the objectives established by the delegating authority'.[134] Within such 'strictly circumscribed circumstances' – what terrible prose – the Agency would even be allowed to adopt measures of general application![135]

If confirmed, the *ESMA* judgment represents a radical departure from the classic *Meroni* doctrine, which could – in time – lead to the emergence of 'real' regulatory agencies within the Union legal order.

3. Administrative Powers I: Centralised Enforcement

With regard to the enforcement of Union law, Union of States may follow one of two constitutional models. According to the 'centralisation model', the administration of Union legislation is left to Union administrative authorities. In order to enforce its law, the Union thus establishes its own administrative infrastructure; and its executive competences here coincide with the legislative competences of the Union. This model has been adopted in the United States of America.[136] By contrast, the 'decentralisation model' leaves the execution of Union law to the Member States of the Union. The Union's executive competences are here smaller than its legislative competences. This system of decentralised execution is called 'executive federalism', and has traditionally been adopted in the Federal Republic of Germany.[137]

Which of the two models does the European Union follow? According to Article 291(1) TFEU, 'Member States shall adopt all measures of national law necessary to implement legally binding Union acts'; but where 'uniform

---

[131] Case C-270/12, *United Kingdom* v. *Parliament & Council*, paras. 28–32.   [132] *Ibid.*, para. 43.
[133] *Ibid.*, paras. 43–4 (emphasis added).   [134] *Ibid.*, paras. 45 and 53.
[135] *Ibid.*, para. 64. The Court – brilliantly – justifies its conclusion by pointing to Arts. 263 and 277, whose Lisbon (!) versions now indirectly suggest that Agencies may adopt generally binding measures.
[136] For an analysis of the centralisation model in the US, see R. Schütze, 'From Rome to Lisbon: "Executive Federalism" in the (New) European Union' (2010) 47 *CML Rev.* 1385 at 1387ff.
[137] For an analysis of the decentralisation model in Germany see *ibid.*, 1389ff.

conditions for implementing legally binding Union acts are needed', the Union shall adopt the executive act.[138] In the enforcement of European law, it is thus – primarily – the Member States that are called upon to execute European law. The execution of European law by the Union nevertheless constitutes a subsidiary – secondary – option. The European Union therefore appears to combine *both* federal models in its own constitutional brand. It partly adopts the US solution in which the Union's legislative and executive spheres coincide; but unlike US federalism, the Union's executive powers are subsidiary to the administrative powers of the Member States.

This section explores the centralised enforcement of Union legislation by the Union, whereas section 4 analyses the constitutional principles governing the decentralised enforcement of European law by the Member States.

a. The Scope of EU Administrative Competences

Administrative competences allow a public authority to apply a general norm to a specific situation. To what extent is the European Union empowered to directly apply its own legislative norms in specific situations?

When the European Union was first born, the European legal order had originally been conceived as a legislative system.[139] The vast majority of its competences were 'legislative' competences; while executive competences were expressly attributed in – very – few areas indeed.[140] Did this mean that in all areas that did not *expressly* confer administrative competences, the Union would have to rely on the State administrations to enforce European law? Or would the Union enjoy general or implied administrative competences to execute its own law in individual situations?

Two Union competences do potentially provide the Union with general administrative competences: Articles 114 and 352 TFEU.

The Union's internal market competence under Article 114 allows the Union to adopt 'measures for the approximation of the provisions laid down by law, regulation or administrative action in Member States'; and the power to adopt 'measures' appeared to include the power to adopt individual *decisions*. But how could an executive decision 'harmonise' national laws or administrative actions? In *Germany* v. *Council*,[141] this argument was placed on the judicial table in the context of the Product Safety Directive.[142] Germany argued that the power to

---

[138]   Art. 291(2) TFEU.

[139]   L. Azoulai, 'Pour un droit de l'execution de l'union européenne', in J. Dutheil de la Rochère (ed.), *L'Execution du droit de l'union: entre méchanismes communautaires et droit nationaux* (Bruylant, 2009), 1 at 2.

[140]   The 1957 Rome Treaty expressly mentioned only the power to adopt 'decisions' addressed to individuals in three areas: agriculture (ex- Art. 43 EEC), transport (ex- Arts. 79 and 80 EEC) and competition (ex- Arts. 85ff. EEC). The power to adopt decisions under the common commercial policy was implicit in ex- Art. 113(2) EEC.

[141]   Case C–359/92, *Germany* v. *Council* [1994] ECR I–3681.

[142]   Directive 92/59/EEC on general product safety [1992] OJ L 228, 24. The directive is now replaced by Directive 2001/95/EC on general product safety [2002] OJ L 11, 4.

'harmonise' legislation precluded the executive power to adopt individual decisions;[143] and since Article 9 of the relevant directive granted such a power in certain situations, the provision had to be void.[144] The Court held otherwise:

> The measures which the Council is empowered to take under that provision are aimed at 'the establishment and functioning of the internal market'. In certain fields, and particularly in that of product safety, the approximation of general laws alone may not be sufficient to ensure the unity of the market. Consequently, the concept of 'measures for the approximation' of legislation must be interpreted as encompassing the Council's power to lay down measures relating to a specific product or class of products and, if necessary, individual measures concerning those products.[145]

[143] Germany's principal argument in this respect is quoted in para. 17: 'The German Government objects to that argument essentially on the ground that the sole aim of … Article [114(1) TFEU] … is the approximation of laws and that those articles do not therefore confer power to apply the law to individual cases in the place of the national authorities, as permitted by Article 9 of the directive. The German Government further observes that the powers conferred upon the Commission by Article 9 thus exceed those which, in a federal state such as the Federal Republic of Germany, are enjoyed by the Bund in relation to the Länder, since, under the German Basic Law, the implementation of federal laws rests with the Länder. Lastly, the German Government submits that Article 9 cannot be regarded as constituting an implementing power, within the meaning of the third indent of [ex-] Article [202] of the [EC] Treaty, since that article does not embody a substantive power of its own, but merely authorises the Council to confer implementing powers on the Commission where a legal base exists in primary [European] law for the act to be implemented and its implementing measures.' This view was – partly – shared by Advocate General Jacobs (see Case C-359/92, *Germany* v. *Council*, at 3693, esp. para. 36).

[144] Art. 9 provided as follows: 'If the Commission becomes aware, through notification given by the Member States or through information provided by them, in particular under Article 7 or Article 8, of the existence of a serious and immediate risk from a product to the health and safety of consumers in various Member States and if: (a) one or more Member States have adopted measures entailing restrictions on the marketing of the product or requiring its withdrawal from the market, such as those provided for in Article 6(1)(d) to (h); (b) Member States differ on the adoption of measures to deal with the risk in question; (c) the risk cannot be dealt with, in view of the nature of the safety issue posed by the product and in a manner compatible with the urgency of the case, under the other procedures laid down by the specific [Union] legislation applicable to the product or category of products concerned; and (d) the risk can be eliminated effectively only by adopting appropriate measures applicable at [European] level, in order to ensure the protection of the health and safety of consumers and the proper functioning of the common market, the Commission, after consulting the Member States and at the request of at least one of them, may adopt a decision, in accordance with the procedure laid down in Article 11, requiring Member States to take temporary measures from among those listed in Article 6(1) (d) to (h).'

[145] Case C-359/92, *Germany* v. *Council*, para. 37. The Court also held Art. 9 of the directive to be a 'proportionate' executive power of the [Union] (*ibid.*, para. 46): 'Those powers are not excessive in relation to the objectives pursued. Contrary to the assertion made by the German Government, the infringement procedure laid down in Article [258] of the [FEU] Treaty does not permit the results set out in Article 9 of the directive to be achieved.'

Article 114 TFEU would thus entitle the Union to adopt individual decisions. Yet, since the judgment specifically dealt with *State* addressed decisions, the question remained whether Article 114 TFEU would also empower the Union to adopt decisions addressed to private individuals.

But subsequent jurisprudence has clarified that Article 114 TFEU could indeed be used for this purpose. The *cause célèbre* here is *United Kingdom* v. *Parliament and Council*.[146] The case concerned the validity of Regulation 2065/2003, which tried to ensure the effective functioning of the internal market through a European authorisation procedure for food products. The legislative measure delegated the power to grant or reject authorisations to the Commission;[147] and its decisions were addressed to individual applicants.[148] The British government protested: 'The legislative power conferred by Article [114] is a power to harmonise national laws, not a power to establish [Union] bodies or to confer tasks on such bodies, or to establish procedures for the approval of lists of authorised products.'[149] Yet in its judgment, the Court confirmed this very power. Article 114 TFEU could be used as a legal base for the power to adopt individual administrative decisions.[150]

Could Article 114 even be used to create the Union's own administrative infrastructure? The power of Article 114 to create a Union agency was indeed confirmed in *United Kingdom* v. *Parliament and Council (ENISA)*, where the Court expressly held:

> The legislature may deem it necessary to provide for the establishment of a [Union] body responsible for contributing to the implementation of a process of harmonisation in situations where, in order to facilitate the uniform implementation and application of acts based on that provision, the adoption of non-binding supporting and framework measures seems appropriate.[151]

An even more general constitutional basis for the adoption of administrative acts may be available to the European Union: Article 352 TFEU. The article allows the Union to 'adopt the appropriate *measures*', wherever this is necessary to attain one of the objectives set out in the Treaties. This power includes the competence to adopt administrative decisions; and the Court has clarified that this competence may also be used to complement a specific competence that did

---

[146] Case 66/04, *United Kingdom* v. *Parliament and Council* [2005] ECR I-10553.

[147] According to the authorisation procedure set out in Regulation 2065/2003 on smoke flavourings used or intended for use in or on foods [2003] OJ L309/1, Arts. 7–9.

[148] Art. 9(1)(b) of the Regulation; and see also Art. 11(1) of the Regulation.

[149] *Ibid.*, para. 18.

[150] *Ibid.*, para. 64. This has been subsequently confirmed in Case C-270/12, *United Kingdom* v. *Parliament and Council (ESMA)*, esp. paras. 103–17.

[151] Case C-217/04, *United Kingdom* v. *Parliament and Council (ENISA)* [2006] ECR I-3771, esp. para. 44.

not expressly provide for the centralised enforcement of European law.[152] The power to adopt administrative decisions can thus be derived – for almost every policy area within the scope of the Treaties – where this is deemed 'necessary'.[153] Article 352 indeed provides the Union with an *executive* competence reservoir that coincides with the scope of the Union's legislative powers.

b. The Nature of EU Administrative Competences

The Union acknowledges different types of competences with regard to its legislative and external powers. What about its executive powers, and here in particular: EU administrative powers? Constitutionally, there are strong reasons to assume that (almost) all administrative competences of the Union are shared competences.[154] Yet the exercise of these shared competences has significantly differed in the past.

aa. Shared Competences and the European Commission

EU competition law used to be 'the' famous illustration for the direct enforcement of Union law. The original enforcement system was centralised in the hands of the Commission and meant to guarantee the *uniform* application of the EU competition rules.[155] This centralised system was built around an authorisation procedure that left little space to national authorities. Drowning in individual notifications, the Commission lost much of its ability to police and prioritise over the years; and it therefore gradually started a number of decentralisation efforts that climaxed in the adoption of a new administrate arrangement in 2003.[156] This 'modern' system has created the 'European Competition Network'

---

[152] On the constitutional availability of Art. 352 TFEU in this situation, see R. Schütze, 'Organized Change towards an "Ever Closer Union": Article 308 EC and the Limits to the Community's Legislative Competence' (2003) 22 *YEL* 79 at 95: 'The Two Dimensions of Power: Regulatory Instruments and Article 308 EC'.

[153] On the (new) limits to Art. 352 TFEU, see Chapter 7, section 1(b/bb).

[154] One reason for this conclusion lies in the text of Art. 2 TFEU itself. The provision recognises that even within exclusive legislative competences of the Union, the Member States are entitled to act autonomously 'for the implementation of Union acts'. This theoretical result – exclusive legislative competence supported by a shared executive competence – reflects constitutional practice, compare only: Regulation 952/2013 laying down the Union Customs Code, (2013) OJ L 269/1.

[155] For an excellent discussion of the social and cultural reasons behind this desire for legal uniformity, see C.-D. Ehlermann, 'The Modernisation of EC Antitrust Policy: A Legal and Cultural Revolution' (2000) 37 *CML Rev.* 537 at 540: '[T]he dominant legal and administrative culture of the [EU] of the "Six" was still rather centralist. France was clearly the politically dominant Member State. French views heavily influenced [EU] legislation and administration … In addition, there were hardly any administrative structures in the Member States that would have allowed an efficient decentralized application of [EU] competition law in general … During the first decades of the [EU], there was no "competition culture" comparable to the one we have today.'

[156] Regulation 1/2003 on the implementation of the rules on competition laid down in Arts. [101 and 102] of the Treaty [2003] OJ L 1/1.

that has turned national competition authorities (NCAs) into important players in the (decentralised) enforcement of EU competition law.

What are the respective powers of the Commission vis-à-vis these national authorities?[157] Within the European Competition Network, the Commission is clearly set above the national authorities: once the Commission decides to initiate proceedings, the exercise of its (shared) competence 'shall relieve the competition authorities of the Member States of their competences'.[158] The Commission thus stands 'above' the NCAs, and its administrative 'supremacy' has been confirmed with regard to its power to issue decisions that the EU competition rules have not been violated.[159]

Are the Commission's (shared) administrative competences nevertheless subject to the principle of subsidiarity? We saw in Chapter 7 that the subsidiarity principle insists that the exercise of a shared competence by the Union is limited by reference to whether national actions are insufficient or comparatively less effective. The subsidiarity principle in Article 5(3) TEU thereby refers to any action by the Union; and this has – from the very beginning – been understood to include *administrative* actions.[160] What criteria has the Union legal order developed to clarify the contours of executive subsidiarity? In the context of European competition law, the Commission has specified when it wishes to centralise the administration of European law in the following way:

> The Commission is particularly well placed if one or several agreement(s) or practice(s), including networks of similar agreements or practices, *have effects on competition in more than three Member States* (cross-border markets covering more than three Member States or several national markets). Moreover, the Commission is particularly well placed to deal with a case if it is closely linked to other [Union] provisions which may be exclusively or more effectively applied by the Commission, if the [Union] interest requires the adoption of a Commission decision *to develop [Union] competition policy* when a new competition issue arises or *to ensure effective enforcement*.[161]

---

[157]   The legal principles with regard to the horizontal allocation of powers between NCAs have remained underdetermined. While encouraging horizontal cooperation, Union law appears to accept a system of parallel competences in which each national authority has the power – independent of each other – to unilaterally enforce EU competition law. See Commission Notice on Cooperation within the Network of Competition Authorities [2004] OJ C 101/03, esp. para. 5.

[158]   *Ibid.*, Art. 11(6).

[159]   Case C-375/09, *Prezes Urzędu Ochrony Konkurencji i Konsumentów* v. *Tele2 Polska sp. z o.o., devenue Netia SA* [2011] ECR I-3055; Case C-681/11, *Bundeswettbewerbsbehörde and Bundeskartellanwalt* v. *Schenker & Co. AG and Others*, EU:C:2013:404.

[160]   C. D. Ehlermann, 'Quelques réflexions sur la communication de la commission relative au principe de subsidiarité' (1992) *Revue du Marché Unique européen* 215. Importantly: executive subsidiarity here operates *independently* from the principle's application in the legislative sphere. Thus, even when *centralised legislative* action by the Union is justified under the subsidiarity principle, the latter may nonetheless mandate the *decentralised execution* of European legislation by the Member States.

[161]   Commission Notice (n. 157 above), paras. 14–15 (emphasis added).

The centralised administration of Union law is consequently mandated, where one of three – alternative – criteria is met. The first criterion relates to the *geographical scale* of the competition law problem. Where more than three Member States are concerned, administrative centralisation is deemed to be justified. This transborder element has close subsidiarity overtones in that it is associated with the 'national insufficiency' test.[162] The second criterion is, by contrast, of a *political* nature. Since the Commission is principally responsible for the development of European competition *policy*,[163] it must be able to decide important cases itself. The third criterion concerns the *effectiveness* of the competition law administration. This criterion is reminiscent of the 'comparative efficiency test' in Article 5(3) TEU. The Commission may thus centralise decision-making, where the national administrative authorities envisage conflicting or wrong decisions; or where a national authority unduly draws out proceedings in the case.[164]

Have the European Courts insisted on a judicial control of the subsidiarity principle? The issue did arise in *France Télécom* v. *Commission*.[165] A French undertaking had been subject to a Commission investigation and challenged its legality on the grounds that the French competition authority would have been better able to deal with the case. The Commission, on the other hand, insisted that the administrative system established by Regulation 1/2003 'preserve[d] the Commission's power to act at any time against any infringement of Articles [101 and 102 TFEU]'. Moreover, 'where the Commission has competence to apply the [FEU] Treaty directly in individual cases, the principle of subsidiarity cannot be interpreted in a manner that deprives it of such competence'.[166] In its judgment, the Court – wrongly – held that the subsidiarity principle could never limit the Commission's power to enforce the competition rules.[167] The judgment therefore represents a serious blow to the idea of an independent judicial analysis of executive subsidiarity.

bb. Shared Competences and European Agencies

What is the role of European Agencies in the administration of European law? We saw above that the power of EU Agencies has traditionally been severely limited. For under the classic *Meroni* doctrine, they were not entitled to exercise any discretionary or regulatory powers; and their tasks were therefore often confined to assisting the Commission or the relevant national authorities in the discharge of their administrative functions.

---

[162] On the two tests within the principle of subsidiarity, see Chapter 7, section 4.

[163] Commission Notice (n. 157 above), recital 43: 'Within the network of competition authorities the Commission, as the guardian of the Treaty, has the ultimate but not the sole responsibility for developing policy and safeguarding consistency when it comes to the application of European competition law.'

[164] *Ibid.*, para. 54.

[165] Case T-339/04, *France Télécom SA* v. *Commission* [2007] ECR II-521. The case is extensively discussed by F. Rizzuto, 'Parallel Competence and the Power of the EC Commission under Regulation 1/2003 According to the Court of First Instance' (2008) *ECLR* 286.

[166] Case T-339/04, *France Télécom*, paras. 72–3.   [167] *Ibid.*, para. 89.

A good illustration of this auxiliary role of EU Agencies is given by FRONTEX – the European Border and Coast Guard.[168] The Agency is tasked to manage, together with the respective national authorities, the external borders of the European Union including measures relating to the prevention and detection of migrant smuggling or trafficking.[169] The relationship between the EU Agency and the national authorities is thereby characterised as follows:

Shared Responsibility

1. The European Border and Coast Guard shall implement European integrated border management as a *shared responsibility of the Agency and of the national authorities responsible for border management*, including coast guards to the extent that they carry out maritime border surveillance operations and any other border control tasks. *Member States shall retain primary responsibility for the management of their sections of the external borders.*

2. Member States shall ensure the management of their external borders, *in their own interest and in the common interest of all Member States* in full compliance with Union law … in close cooperation with the Agency.

3. The Agency shall *support* the application of Union measures relating to the management of the external borders by *reinforcing, assessing and coordinating actions of Member States* in the implementation of those measures and in return.[170]

The provision clearly allocates primary administrative responsibility to the relevant Member State administrations, while allocating a merely 'supporting' role to the European Agency. The Agency will only act when a Member State has requested the Agency's 'assistance in implementing its obligations'; and the Agency's main responsibility thereby is to 'coordinate joint operations for one or more Member States' when an infringement of the EU border has been detected.[171] Indeed: while many EU Agencies today possess the power to adopt individual decisions vis-à-vis private parties and may even enjoy discretionary powers of a regulatory nature, their ordinary function is that of supporting or coordinating national agencies. When there has, however, been a failure of a national agency to properly implement European Union law, EU Agencies can assume a more central role and directly administer EU law themselves.[172]

---

[168] Regulation 2016/1624 on the European Border and Coast Guard, (2016) OJ L 251/1.

[169] *Ibid.*, Arts. 3 and 4(a).

[170] *Ibid.*, Art. 5 (emphasis added).

[171] *Ibid.*, Art. 14 (1) and (2)(b).

[172] For example: the European Securities and Markets Authority (ESMA) has the power to prohibit short-selling, which is however conditional on the fact that there exists 'a threat to the orderly functioning and integrity of financial markets' and 'no competent [national] authority has taken measures to address the threat' (Art. 28(2) of Regulation 236/2012 on short selling (n. 130 above)). For the same Art. 291-like subsidiarity mechanism, see also Art. 19 of the Frontex Regulation. The provision states that where, due to a failure of or a disproportionate challenge to a Member State, the control of the external borders is rendered ineffective, the Council may adopt implementing measures by 'requiring the Member State concerned to cooperate with the Agency in the implementation of those measures'.

4. Administrative Powers II: Decentralised Enforcement

Within the Union's system of executive federalism, it is primarily the Member States that are called upon to execute European law. This follows from the Union doctrines of direct effect and supremacy. The Court has thus unequivocally held that, with regard to directly effective Union law, 'all organs of the administration, including decentralized authorities such as municipalities, are obliged to apply those provisions';[173] and it has further clarified that this obligation also includes '[t]he duty to disapply national legislation which contravenes [Union] law'.[174] The doctrines of direct effect and supremacy – discussed in Chapters 3 and 4 – will thus indeed apply to national administrations.

This constitutional choice is, after the Lisbon Treaty, codified in Article 291(1), which states: 'Member States shall adopt all measures of national law necessary to implement legally binding Union acts'; and only where 'uniform conditions for implementing legally binding Union acts are needed', shall the Union itself adopt an executive act.[175] This choice in favour of the decentralised application of European law has two consequences. First, because the authorities that generally execute Union law are national authorities, it is *national* administrative law that governs the case; and, second, administrative decisions taken by national authorities will, as such, only be valid in the *national* territory.

The Union has tried to limit both consequences by placing them within a European constitutional frame. These constitutional limits make the decentralised application of European law by the Member States a form of executive *federalism*. The general constitutional principle governing the decentralised enforcement of European law is thereby laid down in Article 4(3) TEU. The provision states:

> The Member States shall take any appropriate measure, general or particular, to ensure fulfilment of the obligations arising out of the Treaties or resulting from the acts of the institutions of the Union.

This general duty has become known as the duty of loyal cooperation.[176]

---

[173] Case 103/88, *Costanzo SpA* v. *Comune di Milano* [1989] ECR 1839, para. 31.

[174] Case C-198/01, *CIF* v. *Autorità Garante della Concorrenza e del Mercato* [2003] ECR 8055, para. 49.

[175] Art. 291(2) TFEU.

[176] The duty was an early signal in favour of executive federalism; and the Court of Justice has positively confirmed that reading (see Joined Cases 89 and 91/86, *L'Étoile Commerciale and Comptoir National Technique Agricole (CNTA)* v. *Commission* [1987] ECR 3005, para. 11). See also Case C-476/93P, *Nutral* v. *Commission* [1995] ECR I-4125, para. 14: 'according to the institutional system of the [Union] and the rules governing relations between the [Union] and the Member States, it is for the latter, in the absence of any contrary provision of [European] law, to ensure that [Union] regulations, particularly those concerning the common agricultural policy, are implemented within their territory.'

a. National Administrative Autonomy (and Its Limits)

In enforcing European law, national authorities are subject to the duty of loyal cooperation. How has the Court of Justice interpreted this duty in the context of the Union's executive federalism?

The Court has started out by recognising, in principle, the procedural autonomy of the Member States in the enforcement of European law:

> Although under Article [4] of the [EU] Treaty the Member States are obliged to take all appropriate measures whether general or particular, to ensure fulfilment of the obligations arising out of the Treaty, it is for them to determine which institutions within the national system shall be empowered to adopt the said measures.[177]

More than that:

> Where national authorities are responsible for implementing a [Union] regulation it must be recognised that in principle this implementation takes place with due respect for the forms and procedures of national law.[178]

One expression of the principle of national procedural autonomy may be seen in the European 'no-commandeering' rule.[179] While not yet expressly confirmed by the European Courts, a Union decision may arguably never 'command' national executive officers directly. The formal addressee of a State-addressed decision always remains the *Member State as such*.[180]

In the past, the Union judiciary has implicitly adopted this position. For the Court has for example held that, within the decentralised enforcement, the Member States are entitled autonomously to interpret European rules, since 'the Commission has no power to take decisions on their interpretation but may only express an opinion which is not binding upon the national authorities'.[181]

---

[177]   Joined Cases 51–4/71, *International Fruit Company NV and others* v. *Produktschap voor groenten en fruit* [1971] ECR 1107, para. 3.

[178]   Case 39/70, *Norddeutsches Vieh- und Fleischkontor GmbH* v. *Hauptzollamt Hamburg-St Annen* [1971] ECR 49, para. 4. See also Joined Cases 205–15/82, *Deutsche Milchkontor GmbH and others* v. *Federal Republic of Germany* [1983] ECR 2633, para. 17: 'the national authorities when implementing [European] regulations act in accordance with the procedural and substantive rules of their own national law'.

[179]   For an analysis of the US principle of the same name, see D. Halberstam, 'Comparative Federalism and the Issue of Commandeering', in K. Nicolaidis and R. Howse (eds.), *The Federal Vision: Legitimacy and Levels of Governance in the US and the EU* (Oxford University Press, 2001).

[180]   For an excellent analysis of this point, see L. J. Constantinesco, *Das Recht der Europäischen Gemeinschaften* (Nomos, 1977), 299. For the opposite view, see T. von Danwitz, *Europäisches Verwaltungsrecht* (Springer, 2008), 626.

[181]   Case 133/79, *Sucrimex SA and Westzucker GmbH* v. *Commission* [1980] ECR 1299, para. 16. On the power of the Commission to decide on 'binding' interpretations of European law, see also Case 74/69, *Hauptzollamt Bremen-Freihafen* v. *Waren-Import-Gesellschaft Krohn & Co.* [1970] ECR 451, para. 9.

Textual ambivalences in EU legislation thus provide the national administrations – not the European administration – with the power to decide on the meaning of these provisions. And this signal may also be evidence of a more general constitutional rule that prohibits the Commission from issuing formal commands to national administrations. If that view is accepted, it follows that national administrative organs are not part of a hierarchically structured 'integrated administration'.[182] And where a national administration fails to execute European law, the Commission will have to initiate judicial enforcement proceedings against the *Member State*.[183]

But even if the Union executive cannot penetrate the administrative structures of its Member States, the procedural autonomy of the Member States is not absolute. It has to be reconciled with the need to apply Union law uniformly. What then are the constitutional limits imposed on the principle of national procedural autonomy? National administrative rules are subject to the constitutional principles of equivalence and effectiveness.[184] And, if these negative limits are not sufficient, the Union can harmonise national administrative procedures.[185]

What legal bases will the Union have to adopt common administrative procedures? The power to harmonise national administrative law has always been part of the Union's harmonisation power. And the competence to structure national administrative procedures has been widely used in the past.[186] The Lisbon Treaty

---

[182] On the conceptual relation between the power to issue administrative instructions and an integrated administration, see the brilliant analysis by G. Biaggini, *Theorie und Praxis des Verwaltungsrechts im Bundesstaat* (Helbing & Liechtenhahn, 1996).

[183] S. Kadelbach, 'European Administrative Law and the Law of a European Administration', in C. Joerges and R. Dehousse (eds.), *Good Governance in Europe's Integrated Market* (Oxford University Press, 2002), 167.

[184] Discussion of these two principles is typically confined to the context of *judicial* remedies; and they shall indeed be discussed in Chapter 11, sections 1 and 2. However, they equally apply – *mutatis mutandis* – to *administrative* remedies. The Court thus confirmed the principles of effectiveness and equivalence in Joined Cases 205–15/82, *Deutsche Milchkontor*, paras. 22–3, as well as in Case C-201/02, *The Queen on the application of Delena Wells* v. *Secretary of State for Transport* [2004] ECR I-723: '[U]nder Article [4(3) TEU] the competent authorities are obliged to take, within the sphere of their competence, all general or particular measures for remedying the failure to carry out an assessment of the environmental effects of a project as provided for in Article 2(1) of Directive 85/337. The detailed procedural rules applicable in that context are a matter for the domestic legal order of each Member State, under the principle of procedural autonomy of the Member States, provided that they are not less favourable than those governing similar domestic situations (principle of equivalence) and that they do not render impossible in practice or excessively difficult the exercise of rights conferred by the [European] legal order (principle of effectiveness).'

[185] Joined Cases 205–15/82, *Deutsche Milchkontor*, para. 24: 'if the disparities in the legislation of Member States proved to be such as to compromise the equal treatment of producers and traders in different Member States or distort or impair the functioning of the Common Market, it would be for the [Union] institutions to adopt the provisions needed to remedy such disparities'.

[186] For a good illustration of this, see Regulation 510/2006 on the protection of geographical indications and designations of origin for agricultural products and foodstuffs [2006] OJ

has also inserted a new special constitutional base: Article 197 TFEU. This article constitutes by itself Title XXIV dealing with the 'Administrative Cooperation' between the European Union and the Member States. The provision states:

> 1. Effective implementation of Union law by the Member States, which is essential for the proper functioning of the Union, shall be regarded as a matter of common interest.
> 2. The Union may support the efforts of Member States to improve their administrative capacity to implement Union law. Such action may include facilitating the exchange of information and of civil servants as well as supporting training schemes. No Member State shall be obliged to avail itself of such support. The European Parliament and the Council, acting by means of regulations in accordance with the ordinary legislative procedure, shall establish the necessary measures to this end, *excluding any harmonisation of the laws and regulations of the Member States* ...

The decentralised administration of Union law is – unsurprisingly – of central interest to the Union. To guarantee an effective administration, the Union may decide to 'support the efforts of Member States to improve their administrative capacity to implement Union law'. But this Union support is entirely voluntary, and the European legislation adopted under this competence must not entail 'any harmonisation of the laws and regulations of the Member States'.

This constitutional limitation is to be regretted. The trimming of the legal base to a 'complementary competence' may well have an ironic side effect.[187] In blocking the European streamlining of (inefficient) national administrations, the provision protects their formal organisational autonomy.[188] However, the refusal to allow for the harmonisation of national administrative capacities through Union legislation may indirectly favour the centralised intervention by the Union under Article 291(2) TFEU. Thus, in excluding the Union's competence to harmonise national administrative law, the authors of the Lisbon Treaty placed procedural autonomy over substantive autonomy. This constitutional choice

L 93/12. According to its Art. 5(5) 'the Member State shall initiate a national objection procedure ensuring adequate publication of the application and providing for a reasonable period within which any natural or legal person having a legitimate interest and established or resident on its territory may lodge an objection to the application'. Moreover: 'The Member State shall ensure that its favourable decision is made public and that any natural or legal person having a legitimate interest has means of appeal.' See also Directive 2002/21 on a common regulatory framework for electronic communications networks and services (Framework Directive) [2002] OJ L 108/33, esp. Arts. 3(2) and 4(1).

[187] The competence is mentioned as a complementary competence in Art. 6(g) TFEU.

[188] However, this protection will not be absolute: see Art. 197(3) TFEU: 'This Article shall be without prejudice to the obligations of the Member States to implement Union law or to the prerogatives and duties of the Commission. It shall also be without prejudice to other provisions of the Treaties providing for administrative cooperation among the Member States and between them and the Union.'

may – ironically – *reduce* the scope of the decentralised administration of Union law by the Member States.[189]

b. The Effects of National Administrative Acts

The decentralised execution of European law by the Member States means that an administrative decision taken by a national authority will, as such, only be binding within the Member State that adopted the decision.[190] This follows from the territoriality principle, according to which national powers can only unfold their effects within the national territory. Administrative decisions within a Member State, even when executing European law, will therefore in principle be adopted in complete isolation from other Member States. An administrative decision within one Member State thus has no automatic effects within another Member State.

The potential difficulties caused by diverse national administrative practices are clear. In the context of competition law, the Union is thus – for example – given the power to centralise the application of European law if there is a danger of administrative inconsistency between Member States. In other policy areas, the Union legislator has tried to build cooperative relationships between national authorities. These horizontal relationships are to facilitate the mutual recognition of national administrative acts enforcing European law. While not required automatically to give validity to administrative decisions of other Member States, national authorities may nonetheless be subject to procedural and substantive duties imposed by European law.[191] For example, as regards medicinal products for human use, the relevant European directive establishes a '[m]utual recognition procedure'.[192]

In other areas, the Union legislator has even granted automatic transnational validity to national administrative acts.[193] An illustration of this technique can

---

[189] To add a footnote to this conclusion: Art. 114 TFEU may – after Case C-376/98, *Germany v. Parliament and Council (Tobacco Advertising)* [2000] ECR I-8419 – still provide a legal basis for the harmonisation of national administrative provisions despite the existence of a 'saving clause' under Art. 197(2) TFEU. However, it may be doubted whether Art. 114 could ever be used to adopt a comprehensive 'European Administrative Code'. For an analysis of the constitution al competence to adopt such a code, see now P. Craig, 'A General Law on Administrative Procedure, Legislative Competence and Judicial Competence' (2013) 19 *European Public Law* 503.

[190] This means, for example, in the area of competition law, that there could – theoretically – be 28 NCAs that rule on the same matter of EU competition law (unless of course, the Commission takes the case). This system of 'parallel' administrative competences may lead to conflicts of (administrative) jurisdiction.

[191] This idea has been named 'reference model' and is extensively discussed by G. Sydow, *Verwaltungskooperation in der Europäischen Union* (Mohr Siebeck, 2004).

[192] Directive 2001/83 on the Community Code relating to medicinal products for human use [2001] OJ L 311/67.

[193] The term 'transnational validity' was coined by E. Schmidt-Aßmann, 'Verwaltung skooperation und Verwaltungskooperationsrecht in der Europäischen Verwaltung' (1996) 31 *Europarecht* 270.

be found in the Union Customs Code,[194] which grants Union-wide validity to national administrative acts.[195] We find similar investitures of transnational effects granted to national executive acts in other areas of European law.[196] However, national administrative acts with Union-wide effects still constitute very much the exception.[197]

Conclusion

This chapter analysed three core executive 'functions' within the European Union: the governmental, the legislative and the administrative function.

We found that the distribution of governmental powers is based on the idea of a dual executive. Two institutions are thus responsible for providing political impulses to the Union: the European Council and the Commission. From an international perspective, the former offers the highest political authority in the Union, as it assembles the highest national decision-makers in a European institution. The Commission constitutes, by contrast, the 'national' branch of the Union's dual executive. And it seems to have assumed a – functionally – subordinate position to the European Council. However, major policy initiatives may originate, as we saw above, in the Commission before they are formally endorsed by the European Council, and they often subsequently return to the Commission. Both branches of the Union executive thus cooperate in a complex constitutional relationship. That relationship will work best if both executive branches follow similar political orientations.

Section 2 analysed the 'lawmaking' powers of the Union executive. These powers are firmly in the hands of the Commission. They are exceptionally granted directly by the Treaties, but in the vast majority of cases they result from a delegation of powers. The Union legal order thereby distinguishes between two constitutional regimes for delegating lawmaking powers: Article 290 and Article 291 TFEU. Within the former, the Union legislator is entitled to delegate the power to amend or supplement primary legislation. This power is, however, limited by the 'essential element' doctrine, and either branch of the Union legislator is entitled to veto the resulting delegated acts.

By contrast, Article 291 TFEU allows for the conferral of 'implementing powers on the Commission'.[198] The provision does not mention any constitutional limits to the delegation mandate, but entitles the Union legislator to adopt 'the

---

[194]   Regulation 925/2013 laying down the Union Customs Code [2013] OJ L 269/1.

[195]   *Ibid.*, para. 26.

[196]   For example, Regulation 116/2009 on the export of cultural goods (Codified version) [2009] OJ L 39/1, makes the export of cultural goods outside the customs territory of the Union subject to an export licence and decrees that this licence shall be issued 'by a competent national authority' defined in Art. 2(2). Art. 2(3) then 'Europeanises' this national decision: 'The export licence shall be valid throughout the [Union]'.

[197]   This contrasts, as we shall see below, with the effects of national judgments in the Union legal order. See Chapter 11, section 4.

[198]   Art. 291(2) TFEU.

rules and general principles concerning mechanisms for control by Member States of the Commission's exercise of implementing powers'.[199] This power has been used in the form of Regulation 182/2011 – the 'Comitology Regulation'. Under that (post-Lisbon) comitology system, the Commission's implementing powers are subject to approval by a committee composed of Member State representatives. Depending on whether the advisory or examination procedure is applicable, the committee may or may not veto the Commission proposal.

Sections 3 and 4 looked at the third core executive function within the European Union. The power to 'administer' European law is shared between the Union and the Member States. Under this system of executive federalism, the Member States are primarily responsible for the administration of European law. However, the Union is entitled to establish a centralised enforcement machinery, '[w]here uniform conditions for implementing legally binding Union acts are needed'.[200] The Union's administrative powers are, however, subject to the principle of subsidiarity. This follows from Article 5(3) TEU, which subjects all Union action to this constitutional safeguard of federalism.

By contrast, in order to ensure a degree of uniformity in the decentralised enforcement of European law, the Union legal order has tried to place the national administrative autonomy into a Union constitutional frame. This has occasionally meant that national administrations must take the findings of other national administrations into account. Alternatively, the Court and the Union legislator have tried to establish European minimum standards that govern national administrative procedures. This has happened through positive harmonisation as well as the principles of equivalence and effectiveness. The two principles will be discussed in – much – more detail in Chapter 11 in the context of the decentralised enforcement of European law by national courts. The jurisprudence discussed there will also apply, *mutatis mutandis*, to the national implementation of Union law by the executive branch.

FURTHER READING

Books

C. F. Bergström, *Comitology: Delegation of Powers in the European Union and the Committee System* (Oxford University Press, 2005)

C. F. Bergström and D. Ritleng, *Rulemaking by the European Commission: The New System for Delegation of Powers* (Oxford University Press, 2016)

P. Craig, *EU Administrative Law* (Oxford University Press, 2012)

D. Curtin, *Executive Power of the European Union: Law, Practices, and the Living Constitution* (Oxford University Press, 2009)

T. von Danwitz, *Europäisches Verwaltungsrecht* (Springer, 2008)

H. Hofmann, G. Rowe and A. Türk, *Administrative Law and Policy of the European Union* (Oxford University Press, 2011)

J. Schwarze, *European Administrative Law* (Sweet & Maxwell, 2006)

---

[199] *Ibid.*, Art. 291(3).   [200] *Ibid.*, Art. 291(2).

Articles (and Chapters)

D. Adamski, 'The *ESMA* Doctrine: A Constitutional Revolution and the Economics of Delegation' (2014) 39 *EL Rev.* 812

J. Bast, 'New Categories of Acts after the Lisbon Reform: Dynamics of Parliamentarisation in EU Law' (2012) 49 *CML Rev.* 885

J. Bast, 'Is there a Hierarchy of Legislative, Delegated and Implementing Acts?', in C. F. Bergström and D. Ritleng, *Rulemaking by the European Commission: The New System for Delegation of Powers* (Oxford University Press, 2016), 157

M. Chamon, 'Institutional Balance and Community Method in the Implementation of EU Legislation following the Lisbon Treaty' (2016) 53 *CML Rev.* 1501

P. Craig, 'Delegated Acts, Implementing Acts and the New Comitology Regulation' (2011) 36 *EL Rev.* 671

D. Curtin, 'Political Executive Power', in *Executive Power of the European Union: Law, Practices, and the Living Constitution* (Oxford University Press, 2009), 69

B. Driessen, 'Delegated Legislation after the Treaty of Lisbon: An Analysis of Article 290 TFEU' (2010) 35 *EL Rev.* 837

V. Georgiev, 'Too Much Executive Power? Delegated Law-making and Comitology in Perspective (2013) 20 *Journal of European Public Policy* 535

S. Griller and A. Orator, 'Everything under Control? The "Way Forward" for European Agencies in the Footsteps of the Meroni Doctrine' (2010) 35 *EL Rev.* 3

D. Ritleng, The Reserved Domain of the Legislature: The Notion of 'Essential Elements of an Area', in C. F. Bergström and D. Ritleng, *Rulemaking by the European Commission: The New System for Delegation of Powers* (Oxford University Press, 2016), 133

R. Schütze, 'From Rome to Lisbon: "Executive Federalism" in the (New) European Union' (2010) 47 *CML Rev.* 1385

R. Schütze, '"Delegated" Legislation in the (New) European Union: A Constitutional Analysis' (2011) 74 MLR 661

Cases on the Website

Case 9/56, *Meroni*; Case 25/70, *Köster*; Case 23/75, *Rey Soda*; Case C-359/92, *Germany* v. *Council*; Case C-66/04, *United Kingdom* v. *Parliament and Council*; Case C-217/04, *United Kingdom* v. *Parliament and Council (ENISA)*; Case T-339/04, *France Telecom* v. *Commission*; Case C-355/10, *Parliament* v. *Council (Schengen Borders Code)*; Case C-270/12, *United Kingdom* v. *Parliament & Council (ESMA)*; Case C-427/12, *Commission* v. *Parliament & Council (Biocides)*; Case C-88/14, *Commission* v. *Parliament and Council (Visa Reciprocity)*; Case C-286/14, *Parliament* v. *Commission (Connecting Europe)*

10

Judicial Powers I
(Centralised) European Procedures

Introduction

When compared to the legislative and executive branches, the judiciary looks like a poor relation. For the classic civil law tradition reduces courts to 'the mouth that pronounces the words of the law',[1] and even the common law tradition finds that '[w]hoever attentively considers the different departments of power must perceive, that in a government in which they are separated from each other, the judiciary, from the nature of its functions, will always be *the least dangerous* to the political rights of the constitution'.[2] In the eyes of both traditions, the judiciary is thus 'the least dangerous branch'.[3]

This traditional view originates in the eighteenth century. It reduces the judiciary to its *adjudicatory* function, that is: the power to decide disputes between private parties. Yet this position was to change dramatically in the nineteenth and twentieth centuries.[4] Courts not only succeeded in imposing their control over the executive branch; some States even allowed for the constitutional review of legislation.[5] These judicial 'victories' over the executive and legislative branch were inspired by the idea that all public power should be subject to the 'rule of law'; and this idea would, in some legal orders, include the sanctioning power of the judiciary to order a State to make good damage caused by a public 'wrong'.[6]

A modern definition of the judicial function therefore needs to treat three core powers, which – in descending order – are: the power to *annul* legislative or executive acts, the power to *remedy* public wrongs and the power to *adjudicate* legal disputes between parties.

The following chapters explores these three judicial prerogatives within the Union legal order. Importantly: the judicial function is here 'split' between the Court of Justice of the European Union and the national courts. For the Union legal order decided, early on, to recruit national courts in the exercise of some judicial functions – and has thereby turned them into decentralised 'European'

---

[1] C. Montesquieu, *The Spirit of the Laws*, ed. and translated A. M. Cohler et al. (Cambridge University Press, 1989), 163.

[2] A. Hamilton, *Federalist 78* in A. Hamilton et al., *The Federalist*, ed. T. Ball (Cambridge University Press, 2003), 377 at 378. The quote continues: 'The judiciary … has no influence over either the sword or the purse; no direction either of the strength or of the wealth of the society, and can take no active resolution whatever. It may truly be said to have neither Force nor Will, but merely judgment; and must ultimately depend upon the aid of the executive arm even for the efficacy of its judgments.'

[3] For a famous analysis of this claim, see A. Bickel, *The Least Dangerous Branch: The Supreme Court at the Bar of Politics* (Yale University Press, 1986).

[4] For a comparative constitutional perspective on the rise of the judiciary, see M. Cappelletti, *Judicial Review in the Contemporary World* (Bobbs-Merrill, 1971).

[5] The US Supreme Court for example has, long ago, claimed the power to 'unmake' a law adopted by the legislature, see *Marbury* v. *Madison*, 5 US 137 (1803).

[6] This challenged the classic common law principle that the 'sovereign can do no wrong'. In the words of W. Blackstone, *Commentaries on the Laws of England* (Forgotten Books, 2010), Book III, ch. 17, 254: 'That the king can do no wrong, is a necessary and fundamental principle of the English constitution: meaning only, as has formerly been observed, that, in the first place, whatever may be amiss in the conduct of public affairs is not chargeable.'

courts. This judicial federalism has indeed been a cornerstone of the Union and will be discussed in Chapter 11.

This chapter, however, will concentrate on the 'centralised' powers of the Court of Justice of the European Union (see Figure 10.1). Section 1 starts with an analysis of its annulment power. The power of judicial review is the founding pillar of a Union 'based on the rule of law'.[7] Section 2 moves to the remedial power of the European Court,[8] and the question when the Union legislative or executive branches will be liable to pay damages for an illegal action. Finally, sections 3 and 4 investigate the Court's power to adjudicate disputes between parties. In addition to a number of direct actions (direct actions start directly in the European Court), the EU Treaties here envisage an indirect action starting in the national courts: the preliminary reference procedure. This procedure is the judicial cornerstone of the Union's cooperative federalism. For it combines the *central* interpretation of Union law by the Court of Justice with the *decentralised* application of European law by the national courts.

It goes without saying that this chapter cannot discuss all judicial competences of the European Court. An overview of the various judicial powers and procedures in the TFEU can nevertheless be found in Table 10.1.[9] Importantly, the EU Treaties here acknowledge two general jurisdictional limitations: Articles 275 and 276 TFEU. The former declares that the European Court will generally '*not* have jurisdiction with respect to the provisions relating to the common foreign and security policy nor with respect to acts adopted on the basis of those provisions'.[10] By contrast, the latter article decrees that the European Court 'shall have *no* jurisdiction to review the validity or proportionality of operations carried out by the police or other law-enforcement services of a Member State or the exercise of the responsibilities incumbent upon Member States with regard to the maintenance of law and order and the safeguarding of internal security'.[11] These two 'holes' in the judicial competences of the Court are deeply regrettable, for they effectively replace the 'rule of law' with the rule of the executive.

---

[7] Case 294/83, *Parti Écologiste 'Les Verts'* v. *European Parliament* [1986] ECR 1339, para. 23: 'The European [Union] is a [union] based on the rule of law, inasmuch as neither its Member States nor its institutions can avoid a review of the question whether the measures adopted by them are in conformity with the basic constitutional charter, the [Treaties].'

[8] The remedial powers of the national courts for breaches of European law by the Member States will be discussed in Chapter 11, section 3.

[9] Part Six – Title I – Chapter 1 – Section 5 TFEU. The section is – roughly – divided into an 'institutional' part (Arts. 251–7), and a 'competence and procedure' part (Arts. 258–81).

[10] *Ibid.*, Art. 275(1) (emphasis added). There are two exceptions within that exception. The first relates to the power of the Court to review the borderline, established by Art. 40 TEU, between the CFSP and the Union's special external policies. Second, a CFSP act is reviewable, where it is claimed to restrict the rights of a natural or legal person. The latter aspect will be discussed in (online) Chapter 18B, section 3(d).

[11] Art. 276 TFEU (emphasis added).

Table 10.1 Judicial Competences and Procedures

	Judicial Competences and Procedures (Articles 258–81 TFEU)		
Article 258	**Enforcement Action Brought by the Commission**	**Article 268**	**Jurisdiction in Damages Actions under Article 340**
Article 259	**Enforcement Action Brought by Another Member State**	Article 269	Jurisdiction for Article 7 TEU
Article 260	**Action for a Failure to Comply with a Court Judgment**	Article 270	Jurisdiction in Staff Cases
Article 261	Jurisdiction for Penalties in Regulations	Article 271	Jurisdiction for Cases Involving the European Investment Bank and the European Central Bank
Article 262	(Potential) Jurisdiction for Disputes Relating to European Intellectual Property Rights	Article 272	Jurisdiction Granted by Arbitration Clauses
Article 263	**Action for Judicial Review**	Article 273	Jurisdiction Granted by Special Agreement between the Member States
Article 264	Consequences of an Annulment Ruling	Article 274	Jurisdiction of National Courts Involving the Union
Article 265	**(Enforcement) Action for the Union's Failure to Act**	Article 275	Non-jurisdiction for the Union's CFSP
Article 266	Consequences of a Failure to Act Ruling	Article 276	Jurisdictional Limits within the Area of Freedom, Security and Justice
Article 267	**Preliminary Rulings**	**Article 277**	**Collateral (Judicial) Review for Acts of General Application...**
	Protocol No. 3 on the Statute of the Court of Justice of the European Union		
	Rules of Procedure of the Court of Justice		
	Rules of Procedure of the General Court		

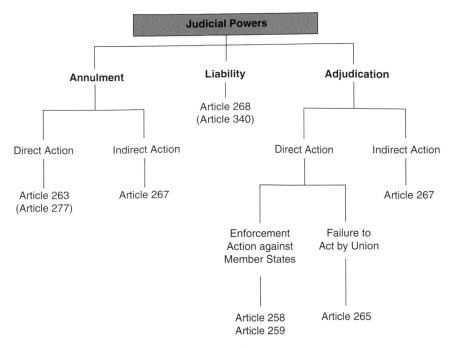

Figure 10.1 European Court: Powers (Flowchart)

1. Annulment Powers: Judicial Review

The most powerful prerogative of a court is the power to 'unmake' law, that is: to annul an act that was adopted by the legislative or executive branches. The competence and procedure for judicial review in the European Union legal order is set out in Article 263 TFEU. The provision reads:

[1] The Court of Justice of the European Union shall review the legality of legislative acts, of acts of the Council, of the Commission and of the European Central Bank, other than recommendations and opinions, and of acts of the European Parliament and of the European Council intended to produce legal effects vis-à-vis third parties. It shall also review the legality of acts of bodies, offices or agencies of the Union intended to produce legal effects vis-à-vis third parties.

[2] It shall for this purpose have jurisdiction in actions brought by a Member State, the European Parliament, the Council or the Commission on grounds of lack of competence, infringement of an essential procedural requirement, infringement of the Treaties or of any rule of law relating to their application, or misuse of powers.

[3] The Court shall have jurisdiction under the same conditions in actions brought by the Court of Auditors, by the European Central Bank and by the Committee of the Regions for the purpose of protecting their prerogatives.

> [4] Any natural or legal person may, under the conditions laid down in the first and second paragraphs, institute proceedings against an act addressed to that person or which is of direct and individual concern to them, and against a regulatory act which is of direct concern to them and does not entail implementing measures …
>
> [6] The proceedings provided for in this Article shall be instituted within two months of the publication of the measure, or of its notification to the plaintiff, or, in the absence thereof, of the day on which it came to the knowledge of the latter, as the case may be.[12]

Where an action for judicial review is well founded, the Court of Justice 'shall declare the acts concerned to be void'.[13] The Union will henceforth 'be required to take the necessary measures to comply with the judgment of the Court of Justice of the European Union';[14] and may even be subject to compensation for damage caused by the illegal act.[15]

What are the procedural requirements for a judicial review action? Article 263 follows a complex structure; and the easiest way to understand its logic is to break it down into four constituent components. Paragraph 1 concerns the question *whether* the Court has the power to review particular types of Union acts. Paragraph 2 tells us *why* there can be judicial review, that is: on what grounds one can challenge the legality of a European act. Paragraphs 2–4 concern the question of *who* may ask for judicial review and thereby distinguishes between three classes of applicants. Finally, paragraph 6 tells us *when* an application for review must be made, namely, within two months. After that, a Union act should – theoretically – be immune and permanent. (But, as we shall see below, while direct review is henceforth expired, an applicant may still be entitled to challenge the legality of a Union act *indirectly*.)

This section looks at the first three constitutional components before analysing the indirect routes to the judicial review of European law.

---

[12] The omitted para. 5 lays down special rules for Union agencies and bodies. It states: 'Acts setting up bodies, offices and agencies of the Union may lay down specific conditions and arrangements concerning actions brought by natural or legal persons against acts of these bodies, offices or agencies intended to produce legal effects in relation to them.' The following section will not deal with this special aspect of judicial review. Importantly, however, for some agencies, the review of an administrative decision may start internally with a 'Board of Appeal'. For an excellent analysis of this administrative review stage within agencies, see P. Chirulli and L. de Lucia, 'Specialised Adjudication in EU Administrative Law: The Boards of Appeal of EU Agencies' (2015) 40 *Europ EL Rev.* 832.

[13] Art. 264(1) TFEU. However, according to Art. 264(2) TFEU, the Court can – exceptionally – 'if it considers this necessary, state which of the effects of the act which it has declared void shall be considered as definitive'.

[14] *Ibid.*, Art. 266.

[15] *Ibid.*, Arts. 268 and 340. On this point, see section 2 below.

a. The Existence of a 'Reviewable' Act

Paragraph 1 determines whether there can be judicial review. This question has two dimensions. The first dimension relates to *whose* acts may be challenged; the second dimension clarifies *which* acts might be reviewed.

Whose acts can be challenged in judicial review proceedings? According to Article 263(1) TFEU, the Court is entitled to review 'legislative acts', that is: acts whose authors are the European Parliament and the Council both following the ordinary or a special legislative procedure. It can also review executive acts of all Union institutions and bodies – except for the Court of Auditors. By contrast, the Court cannot judicially review acts of the Member States. And this prohibition includes unilateral national acts, as well as international agreements of the Member States. (The European Treaties thus cannot – despite their being the foundation of European law – ever be reviewed by the Court.) So, even if national acts or international agreements of the Member States fall within the scope of European law, as collective acts of the Member States, they cannot be attributed to the Union institutions, and as such are beyond the review powers of the European Court.[16]

Which acts of the Union institutions can be reviewed? Instead of a positive definition, Article 263(1) only tells us which acts *cannot* be reviewed. Accordingly, there can be no judicial review for 'recommendations' or 'opinions'. The reason for this exclusion is that both instruments 'have no binding force',[17] and there is thus no need to challenge their *legality*.[18] The provision equally excludes judicial review for acts of the European Parliament, the European Council, and of other Union bodies not 'intended to produce legal effects vis-à-vis third parties'. The rationale behind this limitation is to exclude acts that are 'internal' to an institution. And despite being textually limited to *some* Union institutions, the requirement of an 'external' effect has been extended to all Union acts.

The Court has equally clarified that purely preparatory acts of the Commission or the Council cannot be challenged because 'an act is open to review only if it is a measure definitely laying down the position of the Commission or the Council'.[19] In a legislative or executive procedure involving several stages, all

---

[16] On the non-reviewability of international agreements concluded by the Member States, see Case C-146/13, *Spain* v. *Parliament and Council (Unitary Patent)*, EU:C:2015:298, esp. para. 101: '[I]t should be borne in mind that, in an action brought under Article 263 TFEU, the Court does not have jurisdiction to rule on the lawfulness of an international agreement concluded by Member States.' The use of so-called *inter se* agreements is thus one way to remove ECJ jurisdiction – unless the Court has specifically been granted jurisdiction under the international agreement itself.

[17] Art. 288(5) TFEU.

[18] Strangely, sometimes such 'soft law' may however have 'legal' effects. On this point, see L. Senden, *Soft Law in European Community Law* (Hart, 2004).

[19] Case 60/81, *International Business Machines (IBM)* v. *Commission* [1981] ECR 2639, para. 10.

preparatory acts are consequently considered 'internal' acts; and as such cannot be reviewed.[20]

But apart from these – minor – limitations, the Court has embraced a wide teleological definition of which acts may be reviewed. The nature of the (final) act would thereby be irrelevant. In *ERTA*,[21] the Court thus found:

> Since the only matters excluded from the scope of the action for annulment open to the Member States and the institutions are 'recommendations or opinions' – which by the final paragraph of Article [288 TFEU] are declared to have no binding force – Article [263 TFEU] treats as acts open to review by the Court all measures adopted by the institutions which are intended to have legal force. The objective of this review is to ensure, as required by Article [19 TEU], observance of the law in the interpretation and application of the Treaty. It would be inconsistent with this objective to interpret the conditions under which the action is admissible so restrictively as to limit the availability of this procedure merely to the categories of measures referred to by Article [288 TFEU]. An action for annulment must therefore be available in the case of all measures adopted by the institutions, whatever their nature or form, which are intended to have legal effects.[22]

The Court's wide review jurisdiction is however externally limited by Articles 275 and 276 TFEU – as discussed in the Introduction to this chapter, above.

b. Legitimate Grounds for Review

Not every reason is a sufficient reason to request judicial review. While the existence of judicial review is an essential element of all political orders subject to the 'rule of law', the extent of judicial review will differ depending on whether a procedural or a substantive version is chosen. The British legal order has traditionally followed a formal definition of the rule of law. Accordingly, courts are (chiefly) entitled to review whether in the adoption of an act the respective legislative or executive procedures have been followed.[23] The 'merit' or 'substance' of a legislative act is here beyond the review powers of the courts. By contrast, the US constitutional order has traditionally followed a *substantive* definition of the rule of law. Courts are also obliged to review the content of a legislative act, and, in particular, whether it violates fundamental human rights as guaranteed in the Constitution.

---

[20] However, the Court clarified that preparatory acts can indirectly be reviewed once the (final) 'external act' is challenged (*ibid.*, para. 12): 'Furthermore, it must be noted that whilst measures of a purely preparatory character may not themselves be the subject of an application for a declaration that they are void, any legal defects therein may be relied upon in an action directed against the definitive act for which they represent a preparatory step.'

[21] Case 22/70, *Commission v. Council (ERTA)* [1971] ECR 263.

[22] *Ibid.*, paras. 39–42.

[23] A. W. Bradley and K. D. Ewing, *Constitutional and Administrative Law* (Pearson, 2003), chs. 30 and 31.

Be that as it may, for the European legal order, Article 263(2) TFEU limits judicial review to four legitimate grounds: 'lack of competence', 'infringement of an essential procedural requirement', 'infringement of the Treaties or any rule of law relating to their application', and 'misuse of powers'. Do these reasons indicate whether the Union subscribes to a formal or substantive rule of law? Let us look at this general question first, before analysing the principle of proportionality as a specific ground of review.

aa. 'Formal' and 'Substantive' Grounds

The Union legal order recognises three 'formal' grounds of review.

First, a European act can be challenged on the grounds that the Union lacked the competence to adopt it. The ultra vires review of European law extends to all secondary and tertiary Union law. The review of the former originates in the principle of conferral.[24] Since the Union may only exercise those powers conferred on it by the Treaties, any action beyond these powers is ultra vires and thus voidable.[25] With regard to delegated legislation, the Court will not only review whether the delegate has acted within the scope of the powers delegated, but it must also ensure that the absolute limits to such a delegation have not been violated.[26] This follows not from the (vertical) principle of conferral, but from the (horizontal) principle protecting the institutional balance of powers within the Union.[27]

Second, a Union act can be challenged if it infringes an essential procedural requirement. According to this second ground of review, not all procedural irregularities may invalidate a Union act but only those that are 'essential'. When are 'essential' procedural requirements breached? The constitutional principles developed under this jurisdictional head are the result of an extensive 'legal basis litigation'.[28] An essential procedural step is breached when the Union adopts an act under a procedure that leaves out an institution that was entitled to be involved.[29] Alternatively, the Union may have adopted an act on the basis of a wrong voting arrangement *within* one institution. Thus, where the Council voted by unanimity instead of a qualified majority, an essential procedural requirement is breached.[30] By contrast, no essential procedural requirement is infringed when

---

[24] On the principle of conferral, see Chapter 7, section 1.

[25] The European Court has traditionally been reluctant to declare Union legislation void on the ground of lack of competence. This judicial passivity stemmed from the Court's unwillingness to interfere with a consensual decision of the Member States in the Council. On the 'culture of consent' after the Luxembourg compromise, see Chapter 1, section 2(b).

[26] On the delegation doctrine in the Union legal order, see Chapter 9, section 2.

[27] On the 'essential elements' principle, see Chapter 9, section 2(a/bb).

[28] On the phenomenon of 'legal basis litigation' in the Union legal order, see H. Cullen and A. Worth, 'Diplomacy by Other Means: The Use of Legal Basis Litigation as a Political Strategy by the European Parliament and Member States' (1999) 36 *CML Rev.* 1243.

[29] See Case 22/70, *Commission* v. *Council (ERTA)* [1971] ECR 263; Case C-70/88, *Parliament* v. *Council (Chernobyl)* [1990] ECR I-2041.

[30] See Case 68/86, *United Kingdom* v. *Council* [1988] ECR 855; Case C-300/89, *Commission* v. *Council* [1991] ECR I-2867.

the Union acts under a 'wrong' competence, which nonetheless envisages an identical legislative procedure.[31]

The third formal ground of review is 'misuse of powers', which has remained relatively obscure.[32] The subjective rationale behind it is the prohibition on pursuing a different objective from the one underpinning a legal competence.[33]

Finally, a Union act can be challenged on the grounds that it represents an 'infringement of the Treaties or any other rule of law relating to their application'. This constitutes a 'residual' ground of review. The European Court has used it as a constitutional pass-partout to import a range of 'unwritten' general principles into the Union legal order.[34] These principles include, most importantly, the principle of proportionality. With the introduction of these principles, the rule of law has received a *substantive* dimension in the European Union.[35] The most important expression of this substantive rule of law idea is the ability of the European Courts to review Union acts against EU fundamental rights.[36] They impose substantive limits on all governmental powers of the Union. In light of their importance, they will be dealt with extensively in Chapter 12.

bb. In Particular: The Proportionality Principle

The constitutional function of the proportionality principle is to protect liberal values.[37] It constitutes one of the 'oldest' general principles of the Union legal order.[38] Beginning its career as an unwritten principle, the proportionality principle is now codified in Article 5(4) TEU:

> Under the principle of proportionality, the content and form of Union action shall not exceed what is necessary to achieve the objectives of the Treaties.[39]

---

[31] Case 165/87, *Commission* v. *Council* [1988] ECR 5545, para. 19: 'only a purely formal defect which cannot make the measure void'.

[32] For a more extensive discussion of this ground of review, see H. Schermers and D. Waelbroeck, *Judicial Protection in the European Union* (Kluwer, 2001), 402ff.

[33] See Joined Cases 18 and 35/65, *Gutmann* v. *Commission* [1965] ECR 103.

[34] On the general principles in the Union legal order, see T. Tridimas, *The General Principles of EU Law* (Oxford University Press, 2007).

[35] For an express confirmation that the Union legal order subscribes to the substantive rule of law version, see Case C-367/95P, *Commission* v. *Sytraval and Brink's* [1998] ECR I-1719, para. 67; Case C-378/00, *Commission* v. *Parliament and Council* [2003] ECR I-937, para. 34.

[36] On the emergence of fundamental rights as general principles of Union law, see Chapter 12, section 1.

[37] On the origins of the proportionality principle, see J. Schwarze, *European Administrative Law* (Sweet & Maxwell, 2006), 678–9.

[38] An implicit acknowledgement of the principle may be found in Case 8/55, *Fédération Charbonnière de Belgique* v. *High Authority of the ECSC* [1955] ECR (English Special Edition) 245 at 306: 'not exceed the limits of what is strictly necessary'.

[39] The provision continues: 'The institutions of the Union shall apply the principle of proportionality as laid down in the Protocol on the application of the principles of subsidiarity and proportionality.'

The proportionality principle has been characterised as 'the most far-reaching ground for review', and 'the most potent weapon in the arsenal of the public law judge'.[40]

But how will the Court assess the proportionality of a Union act? In the past, the Court has developed a proportionality *test*. In its most elaborate form, the test follows a tripartite structure.[41] It analyses the *suitability, necessity* and *proportionality* (in the strict sense) of a Union act. However, the Court does not always distinguish between the second and third prongs.

Within its suitability review, the Court will check whether the European measure is suitable to achieve a given objective. This might be extremely straight-forward.[42] The necessity test is, on the other hand, more demanding. The Union will have to show that the act adopted represents the least restrictive means to achieve a given objective. Finally, even the least restrictive means to achieve a public policy objective might disproportionately interfere with EU fundamental rights. Proportionality in a strict sense thus weighs whether the burden imposed on an individual is excessive or not.

While this tripartite test may – in theory – be hard to satisfy, the Court has granted the Union a wide margin of appreciation wherever it enjoys a sphere of discretion. The legality of a discretionary Union act will thus only be affected 'if the measure is *manifestly inappropriate*'.[43] This relaxed standard of review has meant that the European Court rarely finds a Union measure to be disproportionately interfering with, say, fundamental rights.

We do, however, find a good illustration of a disproportionate Union act in *Kadi*.[44] In its fight against international terrorism, the Union had adopted a regulation freezing the assets of people suspected to be associated with Al-Qaida. The applicant alleged, *inter alia*, that the Union act disproportionately restricted his right to property. The Court held that the right to property was not absolute and 'the exercise of the right to property may be restricted, provided that those restrictions in fact correspond to objectives of public interest pursued by the [Union] and do not constitute, in relation to the aim pursued, a

---

[40] Tridimas, *General Principles* (n. 34 above), 140.

[41] See Case C-331/88, *The Queen* v. *Minister of Agriculture, Fisheries and Food and Secretary of State for Health, ex p. Fedesa and others* [1990] ECR I-4023, para. 13: '[T]he principle of proportionality is one of the general principles of [Union] law. By virtue of that principle, the lawfulness of the prohibition of an economic activity is subject to the condition that the prohibitory measures are appropriate and necessary in order to achieve the objectives legitimately pursued by the legislation in question; when there is a choice between several appropriate measures recourse must be had to the least onerous, and the disadvantages caused must not be disproportionate to the aims pursued.'

[42] For a rare example, where the test is not satisfied, see Case C-368/89, *Crispoltoni* v. *Fattoria autonoma tabacchi di Città di Castello* [1991] ECR I-3695, esp. para. 20.

[43] Case C-331/88, Fedesa (n. 41 above), para. 14 (emphasis added); Case C-122/95, *Germany* v. *Council (Bananas)* [1998] ECR I-973, para. 79.

[44] Case C-402/05P, *Kadi and Al Barakaat International Foundation* v. *Council and Commission* [2008] ECR I-6351.

disproportionate and intolerable interference, impairing the very substance of the right so guaranteed'.[45] And this required that 'a fair balance has been struck between the demands of the public interest and the interest of the individuals concerned'.[46] This fair balance had not been struck for the applicant; and the Union act would, so far as it concerned the applicant,[47] therefore have to be annulled.

c. Legal Standing before the European Court

The Treaties distinguish between three types of applicants in three distinct paragraphs of Article 263.

Paragraph 2 mentions the applicants who can always bring an action for judicial review. These 'privileged' applicants are: the Member States,[48] the European Parliament,[49] the Council and the Commission. The reason for their privileged status is that they are *ex officio* deemed to be affected by the adoption of every Union act.[50]

---

[45] *Ibid.*, para. 355.

[46] *Ibid.*, para. 360.

[47] *Ibid.*, paras. 371–2. However, the Court found that the Union act as such could, in principle, be justified (*ibid.*, para. 366).

[48] On the position of regions within Member States, see K. Lenaerts and N. Cambien, 'Regions and the European Courts: Giving Shape to the Regional Dimension of Member States' (2010) 35 *EL Rev.* 609.

[49] Under the original Rome Treaty, the European Parliament was not a privileged applicant. The reason for this lay in its mere 'consultative' role in the adoption of Union law. With the rise of parliamentary involvement after the Single European Act, this position became constitutionally problematic. How could Parliament cooperate or even co-decide in the legislative process, yet not be able to challenge an act that infringed its procedural prerogatives? To close this constitutional gap, the Court judicially 'amended' ex-Art. 173 EEC by giving the Parliament the status of a 'semi-privileged' applicant (see Case 70/88, *Parliament v. Council (Chernobyl)*, paras. 24–7: '[T]he Court cannot, of course, include the Parliament among the institutions which may bring an action under [ex-]Article 173 of the EEC Treaty or Article 146 of the Euratom Treaty without being required to demonstrate an interest in bringing an action. However, it is the Court's duty to ensure that the provisions of the Treaties concerning the institutional balance are fully applied and to see to it that the Parliament's prerogatives, like those of the other institutions, cannot be breached without it having available a legal remedy, among those laid down in the Treaties, which may be exercised in a certain and effective manner. The absence in the Treaties of any provision giving the Parliament the right to bring an action for annulment may constitute a procedural gap, but it cannot prevail over the fundamental interest in the maintenance and observance of the institutional balance laid down in the Treaties establishing the European Communities. Consequently, an action for annulment brought by the Parliament against an act of the Council or the Commission is admissible provided that the action seeks only to safeguard its prerogatives and that it is founded only on submissions alleging their infringement'). This status was codified in the Maastricht Treaty; and the Nice Treaty finally recognised Parliament's status as a fully privileged applicant under ex-Art. 230(2) EC.

[50] One notable absentee from the list of privileged applicants is the European Council. However, its interests are likely to be represented by the Council.

Paragraph 3 lists applicants that are 'semi-privileged'. These are the Court of Auditors, the European Central Bank and the Committee of the Regions.[51] They are 'partly privileged', as they may solely bring review proceedings 'for the purpose of protecting their prerogatives'.[52]

Paragraph 4 – finally – addresses the standing of natural or legal persons. These applicants are 'non-privileged' applicants, as they must demonstrate that the Union act affects them specifically. This fourth paragraph has been highly contested in the past 60 years. And, in order to make sense of the Court's past jurisprudence, we must start with a historical analysis of the 1957 'Rome formulation', before moving to the current 2007 'Lisbon formulation' of that paragraph.

aa. The Rome Formulation and its Judicial Interpretation

The Rome Treaty granted individual applicants the right to apply for judicial review in ex-Article 230 EC. Paragraph 4 of that provision stated:

> Any natural or legal person may … institute proceedings against a *decision* addressed to that person or against a *decision* which, although in the form of a regulation or *decision* addressed to another person, is of *direct and individual concern* to the former.[53]

This 'Rome formulation' must be understood against the background of two constitutional choices. *First*, the drafters of the Rome Treaty had wished to confine the standing of private parties to challenges of individual 'decisions', that is: administrative acts. The Rome Treaty thereby distinguished between three types of decisions: decisions addressed to the applicant, decisions addressed to another person, and decisions 'in the form of a regulation'. This third decision was a decision 'in substance', which had been put into the wrong legal form.[54] Judicial review was here desirable to avert an abuse of powers.

---

[51] On the right to consultation of the Committee of the Regions, see Art. 307 TFEU. And Art. 8(2) of Protocol No. 2 On the Application of the Principles of Subsidiarity and Proportionality states: 'In accordance with the rules laid down in the said Article, the Committee of the Regions may also bring such actions against legislative acts for the adoption of which the Treaty on the Functioning of the European Union provides that it be consulted.'

[52] For a definition of this phrase in the context of Parliament's struggle to protect its prerogatives before the Nice Treaty, see Case C-316/91, *Parliament* v. *Council* [1994] ECR I-625; Case C-187/93, *Parliament* v. *Council* [1994] ECR I-2857.

[53] Ex-Art. 230(4) EC (emphasis added).

[54] On the various instruments in the European legal order, see Chapter 3, Introduction. On the material distinction between 'decisions' and 'regulations', see Joined Cases 16–17/62, *Confédération nationale des producteurs de fruits et légumes and others* v. *Council* [1962] ECR 471, where the Court found that the Treaty 'makes a clear distinction between the concept of a 'decision' and that of a 'regulation' (*ibid.*, 478). Regulations were originally considered the sole 'generally applicable' instrument of the European Union, and their general character distinguished them from individual decisions. The crucial characteristic of a regulation was the 'openness' of the group of persons to whom it applied. Where the group of persons was 'fixed in time', the Court regarded the European act as a bundle of individual decisions

Second, not every challenge of a decision by private parties was permitted. Only those decisions that were of 'direct and individual concern' to a private party could be challenged. And, while this effect was presumed for decisions addressed to the applicant, it had to be proven for all other decisions. Private applicants were thus 'non-privileged' applicants in a dual sense. Not only could they *not* challenge all legal acts, they were – with the exception of decisions addressed to them – not presumed to have a legitimate interest in challenging the act.

Both constitutional choices severely restricted the standing of private parties and were heavily disputed. In the Union legal order prior to Lisbon, they were subject to an extensive judicial and academic commentary.[55]

In a first line of jurisprudence, the Court succeeded in significantly 'rewriting' ex-Article 230(4) EC by deserting the text's insistence on an (administrative) 'decision'. While it had originally paid homage to that text by denying private party review of generally applicable acts,[56] the Court famously abandoned its classic test and clarified that the general or specific nature of the Union act was irrelevant. In *Codorniu*,[57] the Court thus found:

> Although it is true that according to the criteria in the [fourth] paragraph of [ex-] Article [230] of the [EC] Treaty the contested provision is, by nature and by virtue of its sphere of application, of a legislative nature in that it applies to the traders concerned in general, that does not prevent it from being of individual concern to some of them.[58]

addressed to each member of the group (see Joined Cases 41–4/70, *International Fruit Company and others* v. *Commission* [1971] ECR 411, esp. para. 17).

[55] For the academic controversy (in chronological order), see A. Barav, 'Direct and Individual Concern: An Almost Insurmountable Barrier to the Admissibility of Individual Appeal to the EEC Court' (1974) 11 *CML Rev.* 191; H. Rasmussen, 'Why Is Article 173 Interpreted against Private Plaintiffs?' (1980) 5 *EL Rev.* 112; N. Neuwahl, 'Article 173 Paragraph 4 EC; Past, Present and Possible Future' (1996) 21 *EL Rev.* 17; A. Arnull, 'Private Applicants and the Action for Annulment since *Codorniu*' (2001) 38 *CML Rev.* 8; A. Ward, *Judicial Review and the Rights of Private Parties in EU Law* (Oxford University Press, 2007).

[56] The Court's classic test concentrated on whether – from a material point of view – the challenged act was a 'real' regulation. The 'test' is spelled out in Case 790/79, *Calpak* v. *Commission* [1980] ECR 1949, paras. 8–9: 'By virtue of the second paragraph of Article [288] of the Treaty [on the Functioning of the European Union] the criterion for distinguishing between a regulation and a decision is whether the measure at issue is of general application or not ... A provision which limits the granting of production aid for all producers in respect of a particular product to a uniform percentage of the quantity produced by them during a uniform preceding period is by nature a measure of general application within the meaning of Article [288] of the Treaty. In fact the measure applies to objectively determined situations and produces legal effects with regard to categories of persons described in a generalised and abstract manner. The nature of the measure as a regulation is not called into question by the mere fact that it is possible to determine the number or even the identity of the producers to be granted the aid which is limited thereby.'

[57] Case C-309/89, *Codorniu* v. *Council* [1994] ECR I-1853.

[58] *Ibid.*, para. 19. See also Case 76/01P, *Eurocoton et al.* v. *Council* [2003] ECR I-10091, para. 73: 'Although regulations imposing anti-dumping duties are legislative in nature and scope, in that they apply to all economic operators, they may nevertheless be of individual concern[.]'

This judicial 'amendment' cut the Gordian knot between the 'administrative' nature of an act and ex-Article 230(4) EC. Private parties could henceforth challenge *any* legal act – even generally applicable legislative acts like regulations or directives – as long as they could demonstrate 'direct and individual concern'.

This brings us to the second famous battleground under ex-Article 230(4) EC. What was the meaning of the 'direct and individual concern' formula?

The criterion of *direct* concern was taken to mean that the contested measure *as such* would have to directly affect the position of the applicant. This would *not* be the case, where the contested measure allowed for any form of discretionary implementation. Where an additional – and intervening – act was envisaged, there would thus be no 'direct' link between the measure and the applicant.[59] (In this case, the Union legal order would require the applicant to challenge the implementing measure – and not the 'parent' act.)

Sadly, the criterion of 'individual concern' was less straightforward. It was given an authoritative interpretation in *the* seminal case on the standing of private parties under ex-Article 230(4) EC: the *Plaumann* case. Plaumann, an importer of clementines, had challenged a Commission decision refusing to lower European customs duties on that fruit. But since the decision was not addressed to him – it was addressed to his Member State: Germany – he had to demonstrate that the decision was of 'individual concern' to him. The European Court defined the criterion as follows:

> Persons other than those to whom a decision is addressed may only claim to be individually concerned if that decision affects them by reason of certain attributes which are peculiar to them or by reason of circumstances in which they are differentiated from all other persons and by virtue of these factors distinguishes them individually just as in the case of the person addressed.[60]

This formulation became famous as the '*Plaumann* test'. If private applicants wish to challenge an act not addressed to them, it is not sufficient to rely on the adverse – absolute – effects that the act has on them. Instead, they must show that – relative to everybody else – the effects of the act are 'peculiar to them'. This *relational* standard insists that they must be 'differentiated from all other persons'. The applicants must be *singled* out as if they were specifically addressed.

---

[59]   See Case 294/83, *Les Verts*, para. 31: 'The contested measures are of direct concern to the applicant association. They constitute a complete set of rules which are sufficient in themselves and which require no implementing provisions.' In Case C-417/04P, *Regione Siciliana* v. *Commission* [2006] ECR I-3881, the Court however clarified that 'direct concern' was not about whether or not there – formally – needed to be additional implementing measures. It was only interested in whether the act directly determined – in a substantive sense – the situation of the applicant. Directives could thus be of direct concern – even if they always formally require implementation by the Member States (see Case T-135/96, *Union Européenne de l'artisanat et des petites et moyennes entreprises (UEAPME)* v. *Council* [1998] ECR II-02335).

[60]   Case 25/62, *Plaumann* v. *Commission* [1963] ECR 95 at 107.

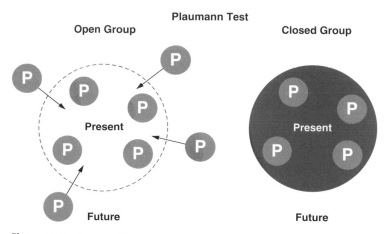

Figure 10.2 *Plaumann* Test

In the present case, the Court denied this *individual* concern, as Plaumann was seen to be only *generally* concerned 'as an importer of clementines, that is to say, by reason of a commercial activity which may at any time be practised by any person'.[61] The *Plaumann* test is therefore *very* strict: whenever a private party is a member of an 'open group' of persons — anybody could decide to become an importer of clementines tomorrow — legal standing under ex-Article 230(4) EC was denied.[62] A person would thus have to belong to a 'closed group' so as to be entitled to challenge a Union act (see Figure 10.2).

Unsurprisingly, this restrictive reading of private party standing was heavily criticised as an illiberal limitation on an individual's fundamental right to judicial review.[63] And the Court would partly soften its stance in specific are of European law.[64] However, it has refused to introduce a more general liberal approach to the standing of private applicants. In *Unión de Pequeños Agricultores (UPA)*,[65] the Court indeed expressly rejected the invitation to overrule its own jurisprudence on the – disingenuous – ground that '[w]hile it is, admittedly, possible to envisage

---

[61] *Ibid.*

[62] Even assuming that Plaumann was the only clementine importer in Germany at the time of the decision, the category of 'clementine importers' was open: future German importers could wish to get involved in the clementine trade. Will there ever be 'closed groups' in light of this definition? For the Court's approach in this respect, see Case 100/74, *CAM* v. *Commission* [1975] ECR 1393; Case 11/82, *Piraiki-Patraiki and others* v. *Commission* [1985] ECR 207.

[63] See Art. 6 of the European Convention on Human Rights: 'In the determination of his civil rights and obligations or of any criminal charge against him, everyone is entitled to a fair and public hearing within a reasonable time by an independent and impartial tribunal established by law.'

[64] This had happened – for example – in the area of European competition law; see Case 26/76, *Metro-SB-Großmärkte* v. *Commission* [1977] ECR 1875. For a recent analysis of the – softer – standing rules in the area of State aid, see S. Poli, 'The Legal Standing of Private Parties in the Area of State Aids after the Appeal in *Commission* v. *Kronoply/Kronotex*' (2012) 39 *Legal Issues of Economic Integration* 357.

[65] Case C-50/00, *Unión de Pequeños Agricultores (UPA)* v. *Council* [2002] ECR I-6677.

a system of judicial review of the legality of [Union] measures of general application different from that established by the founding Treaty and never amended as to its principles, it is for the Member States, if necessary, in accordance with Article 48 TEU, to reform the system currently in force'.[66]

Has this – requested – constitutional amendment taken place? Let us look at the Lisbon formulation dealing with the standing of private parties.

bb. *The Lisbon Formulation and Its Interpretative Problems*

The Lisbon Treaty has substantially amended the Rome formulation. The standing of private parties is now enshrined in Article 263(4) TFEU. The provision states:

> Any natural or legal person may … institute proceedings against an *act* addressed to that person or which is of *direct and individual concern* to them, and against a *regulatory act* which is of direct concern to them and does not entail implementing measures.[67]

The new formulation of paragraph 4 textually recognises the decoupling of private party standing from the nature of the Union act challenged. In codifying *Codorniu*, an individual can thus potentially challenge any Union 'act' with legal effects. However, depending on the nature of the act, Article 263(4) TFEU still distinguishes three scenarios.

First: decisions addressed to the applicant can automatically be challenged.

Second, with regard to 'regulatory' acts, a private party must prove 'direct concern'.[68] It also needs to prove that the act does not require implementing measures. This has introduced an additional formal hurdle that may not be easy to overcome.[69] For it seems that any type of act – even a formal communication –

---

[66] Case C-50/00, *UPA* v. *Council*, para. 45. The *Plaumann* test is a result of the Court's own interpretation of what 'individual concern' means, and the Court could have therefore – theoretically – 'overruled' itself. This has indeed happened in other areas of European law; see Joined Cases C-267/91 and C-268/91, *Criminal proceedings against Keck and Mithouard* [1993] ECR I-6097.

[67] Art. 263(4) TFEU (emphasis added).

[68] On the concept of 'direct concern' before the Lisbon amendments, see. above n. 59 The Court has confirmed that this jurisprudence also applies post-Lisbon, see Case T-262/10, *Microban* v. *Commission* [2011] ECR II-7697, para. 32: '[T]he concept of direct concern, as recently introduced in that provision cannot, in any event, be subject to a more restrictive interpretation than the notion of direct concern as it appeared in the fourth paragraph of [ex-]Article 230 EC.'

[69] The pre-Lisbon jurisprudence on 'direct concern' may explain why the Lisbon treaty-makers insisted on the further formal criterion that no implementing act be needed. As we saw in n. 59 above, the Court did not link direct concern with the question of whether or not an additional act of implementation was required. From this perspective, the new Art. 263(4) TFEU, and its insistence on the absence of any implementing act, signals the wish of the Lisbon Treaty-makers to return to a more restrictive – formal – position. And the post-Lisbon Court has indeed moved in this direction (see Case C-274/12P, *Telefónica* v. *Commission* EU:C:2013:852; Case C-553/14P, *Kyocera* v. *Commission*, EU:C:2015:805).

whether by the Union or the Member States can count as an implementing measure.[70]

Third, for all other acts, the applicant must continue to show 'direct *and* individual concern'. The Lisbon amendment has thus abandoned the requirement of 'individual concern' only for the second but not the third category of acts.

The dividing line between the second and third category was poised to become *the* post-Lisbon interpretative battlefield within Article 263(4) TFEU; and this dividing line is determined by the concept of 'regulatory act'.

What are 'regulatory acts'? The term is not defined in the EU Treaties. Two constitutional options exist. According to a first view, 'regulatory acts' are liberally defined as all 'generally applicable acts'.[71] This reading liberalises the standing of private applicants significantly, as the second category would cover all legislative as well as executive acts of a general nature. According to a second view, on the other hand, the concept of 'regulatory act' should be defined in contradistinction to 'legislative acts'. Regulatory acts are here understood as non-legislative general acts.[72] This view places acts adopted under the – ordinary or special – legislative procedure outside the second category. The judicial review of formal legislation would consequently require 'direct *and* individual concern', and would thus remain relatively immune from private party challenges.

Which of the two options should be chosen? Legally, the drafting history of Article 263(4) TFEU is inconclusive.[73] Nor do textual arguments clearly favour one view over the other.[74] And teleological arguments point in both directions – depending which *telos* one prefers. Those favouring individual rights will thus prefer the – wider – first view, whereas those wishing to protect democratic values will prefer the second – narrower – view.

---

[70] *Ibid.*, para. 55. This – tough – result should mean that a regulatory act adopted in the form of a 'directive' should never fall within the second class of acts within Art. 263(4), since they – by definition – always require a formal act of implementation by the Member States. On the format of the 'directive', see Chapter 3, section 3.

[71] See M. Dougan, 'The Treaty of Lisbon 2007: Winning Minds, Not Hearts' (2008) 45 *CML Rev.* 617; and J. Bast, 'Legal Instruments and Judicial Protection', in A. von Bogdandy and J. Bast (eds.), *Principles of European Constitutional Law* (Hart, 2009), 345 at 396.

[72] A. Ward, 'The Draft EU Constitution and Private Party Access to Judicial Review of EU Measures', in T. Tridimas and P. Nebbia (eds.), *European Union Law for the Twenty-first Century* (Hart, 2005), 201 at 221; A. Dashwood and A. Johnston, 'The Institutions of the Enlarged EU under the Regime of the Constitutional Treaty' (2004) 41 *CML Rev.* 1481 at 1509.

[73] Final Report of the Discussion Circle on the Court of Justice (CONV 636/03). See also M. Varju, 'The Debate on the Future of Standing under Article 230(4) TEC in the European Convention' (2004) 10 *European Public Law* 43.

[74] A comparison of the different language versions of Art. 263(4) TFEU is not conclusive. Systematic and textual arguments are equally inconclusive. For Art. 277 TFEU (on collateral review) uses the term 'act of general application' – a fact that could be taken to mean that the phrase 'regulatory act' is different. However, Art. 290 TFEU expressly uses the concept of 'non-legislative acts of general application'– which could, in turn, be taken to mean that 'regulatory act' in Art. 263(4) TFEU must mean something different here too.

How have the European Courts decided? In *Inuit I*,[75] the General Court sided with the second – narrower – view. The case involved a challenge by seal products traders to a Union regulation banning the marketing of such products in the internal market. Having been adopted on the basis of Article 114 TFEU, under the ordinary legislative procedure, the question arose as to what extent Union legislation could be challenged by interested private parties. After a comprehensive analysis of the various arguments for and against the inclusion of legislative acts into the category of regulatory acts, the General Court found the two classes of acts to be mutually exclusive. In the word of the Court:

> [I]t must be held that the meaning of 'regulatory act' for the purposes of the fourth paragraph of Article 263 TFEU must be understood as covering all acts of general application *apart from legislative acts*.[76]

The judgment was confirmed on appeal,[77] where the Court of Justice held as follows:

> [T]he purpose of the alteration to the right of natural and legal persons to institute legal proceedings, laid down in the fourth paragraph of [ex-]Article 230 EC, was to enable those persons to bring, under less stringent conditions, actions for annulment of acts of general application other than legislative acts. The General Court was therefore correct to conclude that the concept of 'regulatory act' provided for in the fourth paragraph of Article 263 TFEU does not encompass legislative acts.[78]

For private party challenges to legislative acts, the Union legal order therefore continues to require proof of a 'direct *and individual* concern' (see Figure 10.3). Reports on the death of *Plaumann* have also turned out to be greatly exaggerated.[79] For the Court in *Inuit I* expressly identified 'individual concern' under Article 263(4) TFEU with the *Plaumann* test. Rejecting the argument that the Lisbon Treaty makers had wished to replace the 'old' test with a 'new' less restrictive test, the Court here held:

> In that regard, it can be seen that the second limb of the fourth paragraph of Article 263 TFEU corresponds ... to the second limb of the fourth paragraph of [ex-]Article 230 EC. The wording of that provision has not been altered. Further, there is nothing

---

[75] Case T-18/10, *Inuit v. Parliament & Council*, [2011] ECR II-5599.

[76] *Ibid.*, para. 56 (emphasis added).

[77] Case C-583/11P, *Inuit v. Parliament & Council*, EU:C:2013:625.

[78] *Ibid.*, paras. 60–1.

[79] On the 'end' *of Plaumann*, see S. Balthasar, '*Locus standi* Rules for Challenges to Regulatory Acts by Private Applicants: The New Article 263(4) TFEU' (2010) 35 *EL Rev.* 542 at 548; M. Kottmann, '*Plaumanns* Ende: ein Vorschlag zu Art. 263 Abs. 4 AEUV' (2010) 70 *Zeitschrift für ausländisches öffentliches Recht und Völkerrecht* 547.

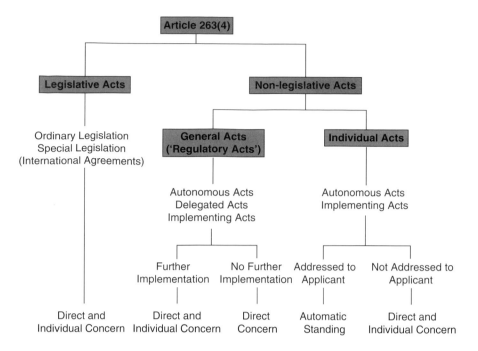

Figure 10.3 Types of Acts under Article 263(4)

to suggest that the authors of the Treaty of Lisbon had any intention of altering the scope of the conditions of admissibility already laid down in the fourth paragraph of [ex-]Article 230 EC … In those circumstances, it must be held that the content of the condition that the act of which annulment is sought should be of individual concern, as interpreted by the Court in its settled case-law since *Plaumann v Commission*, was not altered by the Treaty of Lisbon … According to that case-law, natural or legal persons satisfy the condition of individual concern only if the contested act affects them by reason of certain attributes which are peculiar to them or by reason of circumstances in which they are differentiated from all other persons, and by virtue of these factors distinguishes them individually just as in the case of the person addressed …[80]

The Court thus wishes to stick to *Plaumann*.[81] This however does not mean that there are no good arguments against it. The strongest critique of the *Plaumann* test has thereby come from the pen of Advocate General Jacobs. In *Unión de Pequeños Agricultores (UPA)*,[82] his learned opinion pointed to the test's

---

[80] Case C-583/11P, *Inuit*, paras. 70–2.

[81] For recent confirmations here, see Joined Cases C-191/14, C-192/14, C-295/14, C-389/14 and C-391/14 to C-393/14, *Borealis Polyolefine*, EU:C:2016:311; Case C-456/13P *T&L Sugars and others* v. *Commission*.

[82] Case C-50/00, *UPA*.

anomalous logic. It is indeed absurd that 'the greater the number of persons affected the less likely it is that effective judicial review is available'.[83] But what alternative test might then be suitable? 'The only satisfactory solution is therefore to recognise that an applicant is individually concerned by a [Union] measure where the measure has, or is liable to have, a *substantial adverse effect* on his interests.'[84] Yet as we saw above, the Court has rejected this reinterpretation on the formal ground that abandoning *Plaumann* would require Treaty amendment. However, the Court also provided a additional substantive ground to justify its restrictive stance towards private parties:

By Article [263] and Article [277], on the one hand, and by Article [267], on the other, the Treaty has established a complete system of legal remedies and procedures designed to ensure judicial review of the legality of acts of the institutions, and has entrusted such review to the [Union] Courts. Under that system, where natural or legal persons cannot, by reason of the conditions for admissibility laid down in the fourth paragraph of Article [263] of the Treaty, directly challenge [Union] measures of general application, they are able, depending on the case, either indirectly to plead the invalidity of such acts before the [European] Courts under Article [277] of the Treaty or to do so before the national courts and ask them, since they have no jurisdiction themselves to declare those measures invalid, to make a reference to the Court of Justice for a preliminary ruling on validity.[85]

The Court here justified its restrictive stance on the *direct* review of European law by pointing to its expansive stance on the *indirect* review of European law.[86] Let us look at this claim in more detail.

d. The Indirect Review of European Law

aa. Collateral Review: The Plea of Illegality

The first possibility of an indirect review of EU law can be found in the 'plea of illegality'.[87] Its procedure is set out in Article 277 TFEU:

---

[83] Opinion of Advocate General Jacobs, *ibid.*, para. 59.

[84] *Ibid.*, para. 102 (emphasis added).

[85] *Ibid.*, para. 40.

[86] *Ibid.*, paras. 41–2: 'Thus it is for the Member States to establish a system of legal remedies and procedures which ensure respect for the right to effective judicial protection. In that context, in accordance with the principle of sincere cooperation laid down in Article [4(3)] of the [EU] Treaty, national courts are required, so far as possible, to interpret and apply national procedural rules governing the exercise of rights of action in a way that enables natural and legal persons to challenge before the courts the legality of any decision or other national measure relative to the application to them of a [Union] act of general application, by pleading the invalidity of such an act.' This was confirmed in Case C-263/02P, *Commission* v. *Jégo-Quéré* [2004] ECR I-3425, paras. 31–2.

[87] For an academic discussion of this plea, see M. Vogt, 'Indirect Judicial Protection in EC Law: The Case of the Plea of Illegality' (2006) 31 *EL Rev.* 364.

> Notwithstanding the expiry of the period laid down in Article 263, sixth paragraph, any party may, in proceedings in which an act of general application adopted by an institution, body, office or agency of the Union is at issue, plead the grounds specified in Article 263, second paragraph, in order to invoke before the Court of Justice of the European Union the inapplicability of that act.

An applicant can thus invoke the illegality of a Union act 'of general application' in the course of proceedings for a – different – *direct action* under Article 263 TFEU. That is why this form of review is called 'collateral review'. The review is indeed not an independent action. The primary object of the review proceedings must be a *different* act.

This will typically be an act that implements the collaterally challenged 'parent' act. A good illustration of this technique can be found in the second *Inuit* case.[88] The applicants in *Inuit I* here challenged the Commission regulation implementing the Union legislation prohibiting trade in seal products within the internal market. This second challenge is – procedurally – easier in light of the fact that the Commission regulation represented a 'regulatory act' for which no individual concern had to be shown; and within the course of that second challenge, the applicants indeed tried – albeit unsuccessfully – to 'collaterally' challenge the legality of the parent – legislative – act.[89]

The constitutional advantage of the collateral review route may thus be twofold. It not only bypasses the two-month time limit under Article 263. It equally grants individuals the possibility of (indirectly) challenging legislative acts or regulatory acts that require further implementation.[90]

bb. Indirect Review through Preliminary Rulings

The second form of indirect review of European law may take place under the preliminary reference procedure – to be discussed in section 4 below. Under this

---

[88]   Case T-526/10, *Inuit v. Commission (Inuit II)* EU:T:2013:215; C-398/13P, *Inuit v. Commission (Inuit II P)*, EU:C:2015:535.

[89]   For an analysis of this dynamic, see A. Albors-Llorens, 'Remedies against the EU Institutions after Lisbon: An Era of Opportunity' (2012) 71 *Cambridge Law Journal* 507 at 529.

[90]   In the past, the Court has explained the advantages of the collateral review route as follows (Case 92/78, *Simmenthal v. Commission* [1979] ECR 777, paras. 37 and 41): 'Article [277] of the [FEU] Treaty gives expression to the general principle conferring upon any party to proceedings the right to challenge, for the purpose of obtaining the annulment of a decision of direct and individual concern to that party, the validity of previous acts of the institutions which form the legal basis of the decision which is being attacked, if that party was not entitled under Article [263] of the Treaty to bring a direct action challenging those acts by which it was thus affected without having been in a position to ask that they be declared void ... This wide interpretation of Article [277] derives from the need to provide those persons who are precluded by the [fourth] paragraph of Article [263] from instituting proceedings directly in respect of general acts with the benefit of a judicial review of them at the time when they are affected by implementing decisions which are of direct and individual concern to them.'

procedure, the European Court may also give rulings on 'the *validity* … of acts of the institutions, bodies, offices or agencies of the Union'.[91] The complementary nature of the indirect review route of Article 267 TFEU has been emphasised by the Court in *Les Verts*:

> [T]he European [Union] is a [Union] based on the rule of law, inasmuch as neither its Member States nor its institutions can avoid a review of the question whether the measures adopted by them are in conformity with the basic constitutional charter, the Treat[ies]. In particular, in Articles [263] and [277], on the one hand, and in Article [267], on the other, the Treaty established a complete system of legal remedies and procedures designed to permit the Court of Justice to review the legality of measures adopted by the institutions …
>
> Where the [Union] institutions are responsible for the administrative implementation of [European] measures, natural or legal persons may bring a direct action before the Court against implementing measures which are addressed to them or which are of direct and individual concern to them and, in support of such action, plead the illegality of the general measure on which they are based. Where implementation is a matter for the national authorities, such persons may plead the invalidity of general measures before the national courts and cause the latter to request the Court of Justice for a preliminary ruling.[92]

Individuals can thus challenge the legality of a Union act in national courts; and the indirect judicial review of Union acts through the preliminary reference procedure has indeed become the European Court's favoured option.

Why has the Court favoured the indirect review of European law under Article 267 over its direct review under Article 263? Under European law, the arguments in favour of the indirect review route are straightforward. Indirect challenges may be brought against *any* Union act – even those of a non-binding nature.[93] They can be brought on *any* grounds – even those outside Article 263(2). They can be launched by *anyone* – without regard to 'direct and individual concern'. And – finally – they can be brought at *any* time. (With regard to the last advantage, there exists however an important 'estoppel' exception. For in *TWD*, the Court insisted that where the applicant could 'without any doubt' have challenged a Union act directly under Article 263, it cannot subsequently ask for the indirect review of the measure via a preliminary reference.[94] The Court however interprets this '*TWD* principle' restrictively.)[95]

---

[91] Art. 267(1)(b) TFEU.

[92] Case 294/83, *Les Verts*, para. 23.

[93] Case 322/88, *Grimaldi* v. *Fonds des maladies professionnelles* [1989] ECR 4407, paras. 7–9.

[94] See Case C-263/02P, *Jégo Quéré*.

[95] See e.g. Case C-239/99, *Nachi* v. *Hauptzollamt Krefeld* [2001] ECR I-1197. For an analysis of the case law, see R. Schwensfeier, 'The *TWD* Principle Post-Lisbon' (2012) 37 *EL Rev.* 156.

Importantly, however, there are also serious disadvantages in the indirect review route via the preliminary reference procedure.[96] First, the latter can only be used if a national court has jurisdiction, and this may not be the case where there are no national implementing acts to challenge.[97] Second, the applicant may need to *breach* European law before challenging the legality of the act on which the illegal behaviour rests. Third, individual applicants in national courts have no 'right' to demand the indirect review of Union law by the European Court. Where the relevant national court entertains no doubts as to the validity of the Union act, no private party appeal to the European Court will be possible. We shall explore all of these points in greater detail further below in the context of the preliminary reference procedure.

2. Remedial Powers: Liability Actions

Where the Union legislature or executive has acted illegally, may the Court grant damages for losses incurred? The European Treaties do acknowledge an action for damages in Article 268 TFEU;[98] yet, for a strange reason the article refers to another provision: Article 340 TFEU, which reads:

> The contractual liability of the Union shall be governed by the law applicable to the contract in question.
>
> In the case of non-contractual liability, the Union shall, in accordance with the general principles common to the laws of the Member States, make good any damage caused by its institutions or by its servants in the performance of their duties.[99]

The provision distinguishes between *contractual* liability in paragraph 1, and *non-contractual* liability in paragraph 2. While the former is governed by national law, the latter is governed by European law. Paragraph 2 recognises that the Union can do 'wrong' either through its institutions or through its servants,[100] and that it will in this case be under an obligation to make good damage incurred.

What are the European constitutional principles underpinning an action for the non-contractual liability of the Union? Article 340[2] TFEU has had a colourful and complex constitutional history. It has not only been transformed

---

[96] For a brilliant and extensive analysis, see Opinion of Advocate General Jacobs in Case C-50/00, *UPA*, paras. 38–44.

[97] See Case C-263/02P, *Jégo Quéré*.

[98] Art. 268 TFEU: 'The Court of Justice of the European Union shall have jurisdiction in disputes relating to compensation for damage provided for in the second and third paragraphs of Article 340.'

[99] Art. 340(1) and (2) TFEU.

[100] As regards the Union's civil servants, only their 'official acts' will be attributed to the Union. With regard to their personal liability, Art. 340(4) TFEU states: 'The personal liability of its servants towards the Union shall be governed by the provisions laid down in their Staff Regulations or in the Conditions of Employment applicable to them.'

from a dependent action to an independent action, its substantial conditions have changed significantly. This section will briefly analyse the procedural and substantive conditions of Union liability actions.

a. Procedural Conditions: From Dependent to Independent Action

The action for damages under Article 340(2) TFEU started its life as a dependent action, that is: an action that hinged on the prior success of another action. In *Plaumann*, a case discussed in the previous section, a clementine importer had brought an annulment action against a Union decision while at the same time asking for compensation equivalent to the customs duties that had been paid as a consequence of the challenged European decision. However, as we saw above, the action for annulment failed due to the restrictive standing requirements under Article 263(4) TFEU; and the Court found that this would equally end the liability action for damages:

> In the present case, the contested decision has not been annulled. An administrative measure which has not been annulled cannot of itself constitute a wrongful act on the part of the administration inflicting damage upon those whom it affects. The latter cannot therefore claim damages by reason of that measure. The Court cannot by way of an action for compensation take steps which would nullify the legal effects of a decision which, as stated, has not been annulled.[101]

A liability action thus had to be preceded by a successful (!) annulment action. The *Plaumann* Court here insisted on a 'certificate of illegality' before even considering the substantive merits of Union liability.

This dramatically changed in *Lütticke*.[102] The case constitutes the 'declaration of independence' for liability actions:

> Article [340] was established by the Treaty as an independent form of action with a particular purpose to fulfil within the system of actions and subject to conditions for its use, conceived with a view to its specific purpose to fulfil within the system of actions and subject to conditions for its use, conceived with a view to its specific purpose.[103]

According to the Court, it would be contrary to 'the independent nature' of this action as well as to 'the efficacy of the general system of forms of action created by the Treaty' to deny admissibility of the damages action on the grounds that it might lead to a similar result as an annulment action.[104]

---

[101] Case 25/62, *Plaumann*, 108.

[102] Case 4/69, *Lütticke* v. *Commission* [1971] ECR 325.

[103] *Ibid.*, para. 6.

[104] *Ibid.* In the present case, the Court dealt with an infringement action for failure to act under Art. 265 TFEU (see section 3(b) below), but the same result applies to annulment

What are the procedural requirements for liability actions? The proceedings may be brought against any Union action or inaction that is claimed to have caused damage. The act (or omission) must normally be an 'official act', that is: it must be attributable to the Union.[105] Unlike Article 263 TFEU, there are no limitations on the potential applicants: anyone who feels 'wronged' by a Union (in)action may bring proceedings under Article 340(2) TFEU.[106]

Against whom does the action have to be brought? With the exception of the European Central Bank,[107] the provision only generically identifies the Union as the potential defendant. However, the Court has clarified that 'in the interests of a good administration of justice', the Union 'should be represented before the Court by the institution or institutions against which the matter giving rise to liability is alleged'.[108]

When will the action have to be brought? Unlike the strict two-month limitation period for annulment actions, liability actions can be brought within a five-year period.[109] The procedural requirements for liability actions are thus much more liberal than the procedural regime governing annulment actions.

---

actions; see Case 5/71, *Schöppenstedt* v. *Council* [1971] ECR 975, para. 3: 'The action for damages provided for by Articles [268] and [340], paragraph 2, of the Treaty was introduced as an autonomous form of action with a particular purpose to fulfil within the system of actions and subject to conditions on its use dictated by its specific nature. It differs from an application for annulment in that its end is not the abolition of a particular measure, but compensation for damage caused by an institution in the performance of its duties.'

[105] In the past, the European Court of Justice has insisted that the EU Treaties themselves – as collective acts of the Member States – cannot be the basis of a liability action (see Case 169/73, *Compagnie Continentale France* v. *Council* [1975] ECR 117, para. 16). For institutional acts, the Court has taken a teleological view on what constitutes the 'Union' (see Case C-370/89, *SGEEM & Etroy* v. *European Investment Bank* [1993] ECR I-2583). In the recent *Ledra* judgment (Joined Cases C-8/15P to C-10/15P, *Ledra and others* v. *Commission and European Central Bank*, EU:C:2016:701), the Court has further elaborated this teleological understanding.

[106] See Case 118/83, *CMC Cooperativa muratori e cementisti and others* v. *Commission* [1985] ECR 2325, para. 31: 'Any person who claims to have been injured by such acts or conduct must therefore have the possibility of bringing an action, if he is able to establish liability, that is, the existence of damage caused by an illegal act or by illegal conduct on the part of the [Union].' This also included the Member States (see A. Biondi and M. Farley, *The Right to Damages in European Law* (Kluwer, 2009), 88).

[107] Art. 340(3) TFEU. The provision specifically clarifies that the Bank *as such* – not the European Union – will be called to pay damages. The ECB has an independent personality (see Chapter 6, section 3(a)).

[108] Joined Cases 63–9/72, *Werhahn Hansamühle and others* v. *Council* [1973] ECR 1229, para. 7.

[109] Art. 46 Statute of the Court: 'Proceedings against the Union in matters arising from non-contractual liability shall be barred after a period of five years from the occurrence of the event giving rise thereto. The period of limitation shall be interrupted if proceedings are instituted before the Court of Justice or if prior to such proceedings an application is made by the aggrieved party to the relevant institution of the Union. In the latter event the proceedings must be instituted within the period of two months provided for in Article 263 of the Treaty on the Functioning of the European Union; the provisions of the second paragraph of Article 265 of the Treaty on the Functioning of the European

b. Substantive Conditions: From Schöppenstedt to Bergaderm

The constitutional regime governing the substantive conditions for liability actions may be divided into two historical phases. In the first phase, the European Court distinguished between 'administrative' and 'legislative' Union acts.[110] The former were subject to a relatively low liability threshold. The Union would be liable for (almost) any illegal action that had caused damage.[111] By contrast, legislative acts were subject to the so-called 'Schöppenstedt formula'.[112] This formula stated as follows:

> [W]here *legislative* action involving measures of economic policy is concerned, the [Union] does not incur non-contractual liability for damage suffered by individuals as a consequence of that action, by virtue of the provisions contained in Article [340], second paragraph, of the Treaty, *unless a sufficiently flagrant violation of a superior rule of law for the protection of the individual has occurred.*[113]

This formula made Union liability for legislative acts dependent on the breach of a 'superior rule' of Union law, whatever that meant,[114] which aimed to grant rights to individuals.[115] And the breach of that rule would have to be sufficiently serious.[116]

This test was significantly 'reformed' in *Bergaderm*.[117] The reason for this reform was the Court's wish to align the liability regime for breaches of European law

---

    Union shall apply where appropriate. This Article shall also apply to proceedings against the European Central Bank regarding non-contractual liability.'

[110] Tridimas, *General Principles* (n. 34 above), 478ff.

[111] See Case 145/83, *Adams* v. *Commission* [1985] ECR 3539, para. 44: '[B]y failing to make all reasonable efforts … the Commission has incurred liability towards the applicant in respect of that damage.' On the liability regime for administrative acts in this historical phase, see M. van der Woude, 'Liability for Administrative Acts under Article 215(2) EC', in T. Heukels and A. McDonnell (eds.), *The Action for Damages in Community Law* (Kluwer, 1997), 109–28.

[112] Case 5/71, *Schöppenstedt* v. *Council* [1971] ECR 975.

[113] *Ibid.*, para. 11 (emphasis added).

[114] On the concept of a 'superior rule', see Tridimas, *General Principles* (n. 37 above), 480–2.

[115] Case C-282/90, *Vreugdenhil BV* v. *Commission* [1992] ECR I-1937, paras. 20–1: 'In that context, it is sufficient to state that the aim of the system of the division of powers between the various [Union] institutions is to ensure that the balance between the institutions provided for in the Treaty is maintained, and not to protect individuals. Consequently, a failure to observe the balance between the institutions cannot be sufficient on its own to engage the [Union's] liability towards the traders concerned.'

[116] See Joined Cases 83 and 94/76, 4, 15 and 40/77, *Bayerische HNL Vermehrungsbetriebe and others* v. *Council and Commission* [1978] ECR 1209, para. 6: 'In a legislative field such as the one in question, in which one of the chief features is the exercise of a wide discretion essential for the implementation of the common agricultural policy, the [Union] does not therefore incur liability unless the institution concerned has manifestly and gravely disregarded the limits on the exercise of its powers.'

[117] Case C-352/98P, *Bergaderm et al.* v. *Commission* [2000] ECR I-5291.

by the Union with the liability regime governing breaches of European law by the Member States.[118] Today, European law confers a right to reparation:

> where three conditions are met: the rule of law infringed must be intended to confer rights on individuals; the breach must be sufficiently serious; and there must be a direct causal link between the breach of the obligation resting on the State and the damage sustained by the injured parties.[119]

Two important changes were reflected in the 'Bergaderm formula'.[120] First, the Court abandoned the distinction between 'administrative' and 'legislative' acts. The new test would apply to all Union acts regardless of their nature.[121]

Second, the Court dropped the idea that a 'superior rule' had to be infringed. Henceforth, it was only necessary to show that the Union had breached a rule intended to confer individual rights, that the breach was sufficiently serious, and that the breach had caused damage.[122] The second criterion is the most important one; and the decisive test for finding that a breach of European law was sufficiently serious was whether the Union 'manifestly and gravely disregarded the limits on its discretion'.[123]

One final question remains: can the Union ever be liable for *lawful* actions that nevertheless cause damage? Some legal orders indeed recognise governmental liability for lawful acts, where the latter demand a 'special sacrifice' from a limited category of persons. The early Union legal order seemed averse to

---

[118] *Ibid.*, para. 41. This inspiration was 'mutual' for, as we shall see in Chapter 11, section 3, the Court used Art. 340(2) TFEU as a rationale for the creation of a liability regime for the Member States.

[119] Case C-352/98P, *Bergaderm*, para. 42.

[120] See C. Hilson, 'The Role of Discretion in EC Law on Non-contractual Liability' (2005) 42 *CML Rev.* 676 at 682.

[121] Case C-352/98P, *Bergaderm*, para. 46. See also Case C-282/05P, *Holcim* v. *Commission* [2007] ECR I-2941, para. 48: 'The determining factor in deciding whether there has been such an infringement is not the general or individual nature of the act in question. Accordingly, the applicant is not justified in submitting that the criterion of a sufficiently serious breach of a rule of law applies only where a legislative act of the [Union] is at issue and is excluded when, as in the present case, an individual act is at issue.'

[122] For an overview of the three criteria in light of the case law, see K. Gutman, 'The Evolution of the Action for Damages against the European Union and its Place in the System of Judicial Protection (2011) 48 *CML Rev.* 695.

[123] Case C-352/98P, *Bergaderm*, para. 43. However, where there was no discretion, 'the mere infringement of [Union] law may be sufficient to establish the existence of a sufficiently serious breach' (*ibid.*, para. 44). For an extensive discussion on when the Commission commits a sufficiently serious breach in its assessment in the context of competition law, see Case T-351/03, *Schneider* v. *Commission* [2007] ECR II-2237.

[124] In the words of Case 5/71, *Schöppenstedt*, para. 11 (emphasis added): '[t]he non-contractual liability of the [Union] presupposes at the very least the *unlawful* nature of the act alleged to be the cause of the damage'.

this idea.[124] Yet in *Dorsch Consult*,[125] the General Court flirted with the possibility.[126] The Court of Justice has however put a – temporary – end to this in *FIAMM*.[127] It here held that by assuming 'the existence of a regime providing for non-contractual liability of the [Union] on account of the lawful pursuit by it of its activities falling within the legislative sphere, the [General Court] erred in law'.[128] The Union will therefore not be liable for damage caused by actions that it considers to be legal – even if they harm parties vested in the status quo.

3. Adjudicatory Powers I: Enforcement Actions

One of the essential tasks of courts is to apply and thereby enforce the law in disputes between private and public parties. This judicial form of law enforcement is 'reactive' because, unlike the 'active' enforcement by administrative authorities, it needs to be initiated by a party outside the court.

The adjudication of European law follows, like the administration of European law, a central and a decentralised route. The central route principally takes the form of two types of enforcement actions: enforcement actions against a Member State, and enforcement actions against the Union. With regard to the former, the Treaties allow the Commission or a Member State to bring proceedings, where they consider that a Member State has failed to fulfil an obligation under the Treaties. But the Treaties also establish an infringement procedure against the Union for a failure to act.

a. Enforcement Actions against Member States

Where a Member State breaches European law, the central way to 'enforce' the EU Treaties is to bring that State to the European Court.[129] As can be seen in

---

[125]   Case T-184/95, *Dorsch Consult* v. *Council and Commission* [1998] ECR II-667.

[126]   *Ibid.*, para. 80. '[I]n the event of the principle of [Union] liability for a lawful act being recognised in [European] law, such liability can be incurred only if the damage alleged, if deemed to constitute a "still subsisting injury", affects a particular circle of economic operators in a disproportionate manner by comparison with others (unusual damage) and exceeds the limits of the economic risks inherent in operating in the sector concerned (special damage), without the legislative measure that gave rise to the alleged damage being justified by a general economic interest.'

[127]   Case C-120/06P, *FIAMM et al.* v. *Council and Commission* [2008] ECR I-6513.

[128]   *Ibid.*, para. 179.

[129]   Exceptionally, and in the case of 'a serious and persistent breach' by a Member State of the values of the Union it is not the Court but the 'political forum' of the European Council that principally makes that determination (see Art. 7(2) TEU). Where such a serious and persistent breach is found, the membership rights of a State may be suspended (Art. 7(3) TEU). Art. 7 TEU stands behind the recent confrontations between the EU and Hungary and Poland; and it is by far the most dramatic 'enforcement' action that the Treaties know – albeit a political not a legal action. For a discussion of this extrajudicial enforcement mechanism, see C. Closas and D. Kochenov, *Reinforcing Rule of Law Oversight in the European Union* (Cambridge University Press, 2016).

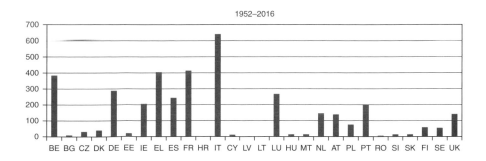

BE	BG	CZ	DK	DE	EE	IE	EL	ES	FR	HR	IT	CY	LV	LT	LU	HU	MT	NL	AT	PL	PT	RO	SI	SK	FI	SE	UK	Total
383	9	32	41	289	22	206	407	245	416	0	642	12	1	3	269	16	16	147	139	77	199	7	15	14	58	54	140	3,859

Figure 10.4 Infringement Proceedings Brought against Member States

Figure 10.4, this does not happen too often (even if it happens more often to some Member States).

The Union legal order envisages two potential applicants for enforcement actions against a failing Member State: the Commission and another Member State. The procedure governing the former scenario is set out in Article 258 TFEU; and the – almost – identical procedure governing the second scenario is set out in Article 259 TFEU. Both procedures are – partly – inspired by international law logic. For not only are individuals excluded from enforcing their rights under that procedure, the European Court cannot repeal national laws that violate European law. Its judgment will simply 'declare' that a violation of European law has taken place. However, as we shall see below, this declaration may be backed up by financial sanctions.

aa. The Procedural Conditions under Article 258

Enforcement actions against a Member State are 'the *ultima ratio* enabling the [Union] interests enshrined in the Treat[ies] to prevail over the inertia and resistance of Member States'.[130] They are typically brought by the Commission.[131] It is the Commission, acting in the general interest of the Union, that is charged with ensuring that the Member States give effect to European law.[132]

---

[130] Case 20/59, *Italy* v. *High Authority* [1960] ECR 325 at 339.

[131] The following section therefore concentrates on proceedings brought by the Commission. The procedure under Art. 259 TFEU, in any event, also requires Member States to bring the matter before the Commission (para. 2). However, unlike the procedural regime under Art. 258 TFEU, the matter will go to the Court even in the absence of a reasoned opinion by the Commission (para. 4). Member States very rarely bring actions against another Member State, but see Case C-145/04, *Spain* v. *United Kingdom* [2006] ECR I-7917.

[132] Case C-431/92, *Commission* v. *Germany* [1995] ECR I-2189, para. 21: 'In exercising its powers under Articles [17 TEU] and [258] of the [FEU] Treaty, the Commission does not have to show that there is a specific interest in bringing an action. Art. [258] is not

The procedural regime for enforcement actions brought by the Commission is set out in Article 258 TFEU, which states:

> If the Commission considers that a Member State has failed to fulfil an obligation under the Treaties, it shall deliver a reasoned opinion on the matter after giving the State concerned the opportunity to submit its observations. If the State concerned does not comply with the opinion within the period laid down by the Commission, the latter may bring the matter before the Court of Justice of the European Union.

The provision clarifies that before the Commission can bring the matter to the Court, it must pass through an administrative stage. The purpose of this pre-litigation stage is 'to give the Member State concerned an opportunity, on the one hand, to comply with its obligations under [European] law and, on the other, to avail itself of its right to defend itself against the complaints made by the Commission'.[133] This administrative stage expressly requires a 'reasoned opinion', and before that – even if not expressly mentioned in Article 258 – a 'letter of formal notice'.[134] In the 'letter of formal notice', the Commission will notify the State that it believes it to violate European law, and ask it to submit its observations. Where the Commission is not convinced by the explanations offered by a Member State, it will issue a 'reasoned opinion'; and after that second administrative stage,[135] it will go to court.

What violations of European law may be litigated under the enforcement procedure? With the general exceptions mentioned above,[136] the Commission can raise any violation of European law, including breaches of the Union's international agreements.[137] However, the breach must be committed by the 'State'.

---

intended to protect the Commission's own rights. The Commission's function, in the general interest of the [Union], is to ensure that the Member States give effect to the Treaty and the provisions adopted by the institutions thereunder and to obtain a declaration of any failure to fulfil the obligations deriving therefrom with a view to bringing it to an end.'

[133] Case 293/85, *Commission* v. *Belgium* [1988] ECR 305, para. 13.

[134] There are exceptions to this rule. The most important practical exception can be found in the shortened procedure in the context of the Union's state aid provisions (see Art. 108(2) TFEU).

[135] The Court has insisted that the Member State must – again – be given a reasonable period to correct its behaviour; see Case 293/85, *Commission* v. *Belgium* [1988] ECR 305, para. 14: '[T]he Commission must allow Member States a reasonable period to reply to the letter of formal notice and to comply with a reasoned opinion, or, where appropriate, to prepare their defence. In order to determine whether the period allowed is reasonable, account must be taken of all the circumstances of the case. Thus very short periods may be justified in particular circumstances, especially where there is an urgent need to remedy a breach or where the Member State concerned is fully aware of the Commission's views long before the procedure starts.'

[136] See Arts. 275 and 276 TFEU.

[137] Case C-61/94, *Commission* v. *Germany (IDA)* [1996] ECR I-3989.

This includes its legislature, its executive and – in theory – its judiciary.[138] The Member State will also be responsible for violations of Union law by territorially autonomous regions.[139] And even the behaviour of its nationals may – exceptionally – be attributed to the Member State.[140]

Are there any defences that a State may raise to justify its breach of European law? Early on, the Court clarified that breaches of European law by one Member State cannot justify breaches of another. In *Commission v. Luxembourg and Belgium*,[141] the defendants had argued that 'since international law allows a party, injured by the failure of another party to perform its obligations, to withhold performance of its own, the Commission has lost the right to plead infringement of the Treaty'.[142] The Court did not accept this 'international law' logic of the European Treaties. The Treaties were 'not limited to creating reciprocal obligations between the different natural and legal persons to whom [they are] applicable, but establish … a new legal order, which governs the powers, rights and obligations of the said persons, as well as the necessary procedures for taking cognisance of and penalising any breach of it'.[143] The binding effect of European law was thus comparable to the effect of ' 'institutional' law.[144] The Court has also denied the availability of 'internal' constitutional problems,[145] or budgetary restraints, as justifications.[146] However, one of the arguments that the Court has accepted in the past is the idea of *force majeure* in an emergency situation.[147]

bb. Judicial Enforcement through Financial Sanctions

The European Court is not entitled to nullify national laws that violate European law. It may only 'declare' national laws or practices incompatible with

---

[138]   The Court of Justice has been fairly reluctant to find that a national court has violated the Treaty. In the past, it has preferred to attribute the fact that a national judiciary persistently interpreted national law in a manner that violated European law to the *legislature's* failure to adopt clearer national laws; see Case C-129/00, *Commission v. Italy* [2003] ECR I-14637. On this point, see M. Taborowski, 'Infringement Proceedings and Non-compliant National Courts' (2012) 49 *CML Rev.* 1881.

[139]   See Case C-383/00, *Commission v. Germany* [2002] ECR I-4219, para. 18: 'the Court has repeatedly held that, a Member State may not plead provisions, practices or situations in its internal legal order, including those resulting from its federal organisation, in order to justify a failure to comply with the obligations'.

[140]   Case 249/81, *Commission v. Ireland (Buy Irish)* [1982] ECR 4005.

[141]   Joined Cases 90–1/63, *Commission v. Luxembourg and Belgium* [1964] ECR 625.

[142]   *Ibid.*, 631.   [143]   *Ibid.*

[144]   P. Pescatore, *The Law of Integration: Emergence of a New Phenomenon in International Relations Based on the Experience of the European Communities* (Sijthoff, 1974), 67 and 69.

[145]   See Case C-39/88, *Commission v. Ireland* [1990] ECR I-4271, para. 11: 'a Member State may not plead internal circumstances in order to justify a failure to comply with obligations and time-limits resulting from [European] law'.

[146]   See Case 30/72, *Commission v. Italy* [1973] ECR 161.

[147]   For an excellent discussion of the case law, see L. Prete and B. Smulders, 'The Coming of Age of Infringement Proceedings' (2010) 47 *CML Rev.* 9 at 44.

European law.[148] Where the Court has found that a Member State has failed to fulfil an obligation under the Treaties, 'the State shall be required to take the necessary measures to comply with the judgment of the Court'.[149] Inspired by international law logic, the European legal order here builds on the normative distinctiveness of European and national law. It remains within the competence of the Member States to remove national laws or practices that are incompatible with European law.

Nonetheless, the Union legal order may 'punish' violations by imposing financial sanctions on a recalcitrant State. The sanction regime for breaches by a Member State is set out in Article 260(2) and (3) TFEU. Importantly, financial sanctions will not automatically follow from every breach of European law. According to Article 260(2) TFEU, the Commission may only apply for a 'lump sum or penalty payment',[150] where a Member State has failed to comply with a *judgment of the Court*. The special enforcement action is thus confined to the enforcement of one type of Union act: Court judgments. And even in this limited situation, the Commission must bring a second (!) case before the Court.[151]

There is only one exception to the requirement of a second judgment. This 'exceptional' treatment corresponds to a not too exceptional situation: the failure of a Member State properly to transpose a 'directive'.[152] Where a Member State fails to fulfil its obligation 'to notify measures transposing a Directive adopted under a legislative procedure',[153] the Commission can apply for a financial sanction in the first enforcement action. The payment must take effect on the date set by the Court in its judgment, and is thus directed at this specific breach of European law.

b. Enforcement Actions against the Union: Failure to Act

Enforcement actions primarily target a Member State's failure to act (properly). However, 'infringement' proceedings may also be brought against Union

---

[148]   Cases 15 and 16/76, *France* v. *Commission* [1979] ECR 32.

[149]   Art. 260(1) TFEU.

[150]   The Court has held that Art. 265 allows it to impose a 'lump sum' *and* a 'penalty payment' at the same time (see Case C-304/02, *Commission* v. *France (French Fisheries II)* [2005] ECR I-6262). For one of the more spectacular orders, see Case C-196/13, *Commission* v. *Italy*, EU:C:2014:2407. For failure to comply with a 2007 judgment against Italy, the country was ordered to pay a lump sum of about €40 million and to make a regular penalty payment of the same amount for each six-month period of delay.

[151]   The Court has softened this procedural requirement somewhat by specifically punishing 'general and persistent' infringements; see Case C-494/01 *Commission* v. *Ireland (Irish Waste)* [2005] ECR I-3331. For an extensive discussion of this type of infringement, see P. Wennerås, 'A New Dawn for Commission Enforcement under Articles 226 and 228 EC: General and Persistent (GAP) Infringements, Lump Sums and Penalty Payments' (2006) 43 *CML Rev.* 31 at 33–50.

[152]   On the legal instrument 'directive', see Chapter 3, section 3.

[153]   Art. 260(3) TFEU. For a brief overview of the sanctioning activity under Art. 260(3), see E. Várnay, 'Sanctioning under Article 260(3) TFEU: Much Ado About Nothing?' (2017) 23 *European Public Law* 301.

institutions. Actions for failure to act are thereby governed by Article 265 TFEU, which states:

> Should the European Parliament, the European Council, the Council, the Commission or the European Central Bank, in infringement of the Treaties, fail to act, the Member States and the other institutions of the Union may bring an action before the Court of Justice of the European Union to have the infringement established. This Article shall apply, under the same conditions, to bodies, offices and agencies of the Union which fail to act.
>
> The action shall be admissible only if the institution, body, office or agency concerned has first been called upon to act. If, within two months of being so called upon, the institution, body, office or agency concerned has not defined its position, the action may be brought within a further period of two months.
>
> Any natural or legal person may, under the conditions laid down in the preceding paragraphs, complain to the Court that an institution, body, office or agency of the Union has failed to address to that person any act other than a recommendation or an opinion.

An action for failure to act may thus be brought against any Union institution or body – with the exception of the Court of Auditors and the European Court. It can be brought by another Union institution or body, a Member State as well as a private party. (And while Article 265 TFEU makes no express distinctions with regard to the standing requirements of public and private applicants, it seems that the Court mirrors its jurisprudence under Article 263(4) TFEU here.)[154]

---

[154] Despite the more restrictive wording ('failed to address to that person'), the Court is likely to read the 'direct and individual concern' criterion into Art. 265 TFEU. For past jurisprudence to that effect, see Case 247/87, *Star Fruit Co.* v. *Commission* [1989] ECR 291, para. 13: 'It must also be observed that in requesting the Commission to commence proceedings pursuant to Article [258] the applicant is in fact seeking the adoption of acts which are not of direct and individual concern to it within the meaning of the [fourth] paragraph of Article [263] and which it could not therefore challenge by means of an action for annulment in any event.' See also Case C-68/95, *T. Port GmbH & Co. KG* v. *Bundesanstalt für Landwirtschaft und Ernährung* [1996] ECR I-6065, para. 59: 'It is true that the third paragraph of Article [265] of the Treaty entitles legal and natural persons to bring an action for failure to act when an institution has failed to address to them any act other than a recommendation or an opinion. The Court has, however, held that Articles [263] and [265] merely prescribe one and the same method of recourse. It follows that, just as the fourth paragraph of Article [263] allows individuals to bring an action for annulment against a measure of an institution not addressed to them provided that the measure is of direct and individual concern to them, the third paragraph of Article [265] must be interpreted as also entitling them to bring an action for failure to act against an institution which they claim has failed to adopt a measure which would have concerned them in the same way. The possibility for individuals to assert their rights should not depend upon whether the institution concerned has acted or failed to act.'

What are the procedural stages of this action? As with enforcement actions against Member States, the procedure is divided into a (shortened) administrative and a judicial stage. The judicial stage will only commence once the relevant institution has been 'called upon to act', and has not 'defined its position' within two months.[155]

What types of 'inactions' can be challenged? In its early jurisprudence, the Court appeared to interpret the scope of Article 265 in parallel with the scope of Article 263.[156] This suggested that only those inactions with (external) legal effects might be challenged.[157] However, the wording of the provision points the other way – at least for non-private applicants. And this wider reading was indeed confirmed in *Parliament* v. *Council (Comitology)*,[158] where the Court found that '[t]here is no necessary link between the action for annulment and the action for failure to act'.[159] Actions for failure to act can thus also be brought in relation to 'preparatory acts'.[160] The material scope of Article 265 is, in this respect, wider than that of Article 263.

However, in one important respect the scope of Article 265 is much smaller than that of Article 263. For the European Court has added an 'unwritten' limitation that cannot be found in the text of Article 265. It insists that a finding of a failure to act requires the existence of an *obligation to act*. Where an institution has 'the right, but not the duty' to act, no failure to act can ever be established.[161] This is, for example, the case with regard to the Commission's competence to bring enforcement actions under Article 258 TFEU. Under this article 'the Commission is not bound to commence the proceedings provided for in that provision but in this regard has a discretion which excludes the right for individuals to require that institution to adopt a specific position'.[162] The existence of institutional discretion thus excludes an obligation to act.

In *Parliament* v. *Council (Common Transport Policy)*,[163] the Court offered further commentary on what the existence of an obligation to act requires. Parliament

---

[155] On what may count as a 'defined' position, see Case 377/87, *Parliament* v. *Council* [1988] ECR 4017; and Case C-25/91, *Pesqueras Echebastar* v. *Commission* [1993] ECR I-1719.

[156] Case 15/70, *Chevallery* v. *Commission* [1970] ECR 975, para. 6: '[T]he concept of a measure capable of giving rise to an action is identical in Articles [263] and [265], as both provisions merely prescribe one and the same method of recourse.'

[157] On this point, see section 1(a) above.

[158] Case 302/87, *Parliament* v. *Council* [1988] ECR 5615.

[159] *Ibid.*, para. 16: 'There is no necessary link between the action for annulment and the action for failure to act. This follows from the fact that the action for failure to act enables the European Parliament to induce the adoption of measures which cannot in all cases be the subject of an action for annulment.'

[160] Case 377/87, *Parliament* v. *Council* [1988] ECR 4017.

[161] Case 247/87, *Star Fruit Co.* v. *Commission*, esp. para. 12.

[162] *Ibid.*, para. 11. There is however a Commission duty to act on a complaint claiming a violation of EU competition law (see Case T-442/07, *Ryanair* v. *Commission* [2011] ECR II-333).

[163] Case 13/83, *Parliament* v. *Council* [1985] ECR 1513.

had brought proceedings against the Council claiming that it had failed to lay down a framework for a common transport policy. The Council responded by arguing that a failure to act under Article 265 'was designed for cases where the institution in question has a legal obligation to adopt a *specific* measure and that it is an inappropriate instrument for resolving cases involving the introduction of a whole system of measures within the framework of a complex legislative process'.[164] The Court joined the Council and rejected the idea that enforcement proceedings could be brought for a failure to fulfil the *general* obligation to develop a Union policy. The failure to act would have to be 'sufficiently defined'; and this would only be the case, where the missing Union act can be 'identified individually'.[165]

What are the consequences of an established failure to act on the part of the Union? According to Article 266, the institution 'whose failure to act has been declared contrary to the Treaties shall be required to take the necessary measures to comply with the judgment of the Court of Justice of the European Union'. And, in the absence of an express time limit for such compliance, the Court requires that the institution 'has a reasonable period for that purpose'.[166]

4. Adjudicatory Powers II: Preliminary Rulings

The European Court would not be able, on its own, to shoulder the adjudicatory task of deciding European law disputes. Yet, unlike the US constitutional order,[167] the European Union has not developed a parallel system of federal courts designed to apply Union law. The Union is based on a system of cooperative federalism: *all* national courts are entitled and obliged to apply European law to disputes before them.[168] The general role of national courts in the judicial application of European law will be extensively discussed in Chapter 11. This section however wishes to focus on the *Union* procedure that has allowed the

---

[164]   *Ibid.*, para. 29 (emphasis added).

[165]   *Ibid.*, para. 37. The Court thus held in para. 53 that 'the absence of a common policy which the Treaty requires to be brought into being does not in itself necessarily constitute a failure to act sufficiently specific in nature to form the subject of an action under Article [265]'.

[166]   *Ibid.*, para. 69.

[167]   On US judicial federalism, see R. H. Fallon et al., *Hart and Wechsler's the Federal Courts and the Federal System* (Foundation Press, 1996); E. Chemerinski, *Federal Jurisdiction* (Aspen, 2007).

[168]   We saw in Chapter 4 that this duty applies to every national court, see: Case 106/77, *Amministrazione delle Finanze dello Stato v. Simmenthal* [1978] ECR 629, para. 21: 'every national court must, in a case within its jurisdiction, apply [European] law in its entirety and protect rights which the latter confers on individuals'. On the 'cooperative' nature of the Art. 267 procedure, see recently Case C-160/14, *Ferreira da Silva e Brito and others v. Estado Português*, EU:C:2015:565, para. 37: '[T]he procedure laid down in Article 267 TFEU is an instrument for cooperation between the Court of Justice and the national courts[.]'

European Court of Justice to guarantee some uniformity in the decentralised adjudication of European law: the preliminary reference procedure.

From the beginning, the Treaties contained a mechanism for the interpretative assistance of national courts. Where national courts encounter problems relating to the interpretation of European law, they could ask 'preliminary questions' to the European Court. The questions are 'preliminary', since they *precede* the final application of European law by the national court. Thus, importantly: the European Court will not 'decide' the case. It is only *indirectly* involved in the judgment delivered by the national court; and for that reason preliminary rulings are called 'indirect actions'. The preliminary rulings procedure constitutes the cornerstone of the Union's judicial federalism; and this federalism is *cooperative* in nature because the European Court and the national courts collaborate in the adjudication of a single case.

The procedure for preliminary rulings is set out in Article 267 TFEU, which reads:

[1] The Court of Justice of the European Union shall have jurisdiction to give preliminary rulings concerning:
    (a)   the interpretation of the Treaties;
    (b)   the validity and interpretation of acts of the institutions, bodies, offices or agencies of the Union;
[2] Where such a question is raised before any court or tribunal of a Member State, that court or tribunal may, if it considers that a decision on the question is necessary to enable it to give judgment, request the Court to give a ruling thereon.
[3] Where any such question is raised in a case pending before a court or tribunal of a Member State against whose decisions there is no judicial remedy under national law, that court or tribunal shall bring the matter before the Court.[169]

The provision establishes a constitutional nexus between the central and the decentralised adjudication of European law. This section looks at four aspects of the procedure. We start by analysing the jurisdiction of the European Court under the preliminary reference procedure (paragraph 1). We then move to the conditions for a preliminary ruling (paragraph 2). A third step investigates which national courts are obliged to make a reference (paragraph 3). Finally, we shall analyse the nature and effect of preliminary rulings in the Union legal order.

---

[169]   The (omitted) fourth paragraph states: 'If such a question is raised in a case pending before a court or tribunal of a Member State with regard to a person in custody, the Court of Justice of the European Union shall act with the minimum of delay.' According to Art. 23a of the Court's Statute, there may exist an 'urgent preliminary procedure' (in French: 'procedure préjudicielle d'urgence' or 'PPU') in the area of freedom, security and justice. On the 'PPU', see C. Barnard, 'The PPU: Is It Worth the Candle? An Early Assessment' (2009) 34 *EL Rev.* 281.

a. Paragraph 1: The Jurisdiction of the European Court

The European Court's jurisdiction, set out in paragraph 1, covers all Union law – including international agreements of the Union.[170] It is however limited to *European* law: 'The Court is not entitled, within the framework of Article [267 TFEU] to interpret rules pertaining to national law.'[171] Nor can it theoretically give a ruling on the compatibility of national rules with Union law.

The Court's competence with regard to European law extends to questions pertaining to the 'validity and interpretation' of Unions law. Preliminary references may thus be made in relation to *two* judicial functions. They can concern the *validity* of Union law;[172] and in exercising its judicial review function, the European Court will be confined to providing a ruling on the validity of acts *below* the Treaties. National courts can however equally ask about the *interpretation* of European law. This includes all types of European law – ranging from the deepest constitutional foundations to the loftiest soft law.

The *application* of European law is – theoretically – not within the power of the Court. Article 267 'gives the Court *no jurisdiction to apply the Treat[ies] to a specific case*'.[173] However, the distinction between 'interpretation' and 'application' is sometimes hard to make. The Court has tried to explain it as follows:

> When it gives an interpretation of the Treat[ies] in a specific action pending before a national court, the Court limits itself to deducing the meaning of the [European] rules from the wording and spirit of the Treat[ies], it being left to the national court to apply in the particular case the rules which are thus interpreted.[174]

Theoretically, this should mean that the Court of Justice cannot decide whether a national law, in fact, violates Union law. And yet, the Court has often made this very assessment.[175]

A famous illustration of the blurred line between 'interpretation' and 'application' are the 'Sunday trading cases'.[176] Would the national prohibition on trading on Sundays conflict with the Union's internal market provisions? Preliminary

---

[170] Case 181/73, *Haegemann* [1974] ECR 449. On the more complex jurisdictional rules with regard to mixed agreements, see P. Koutrakos, 'The Interpretation of Mixed Agreements under the Preliminary Reference Procedure' (2002) 7 *European Foreign Affairs Review* 25.

[171] Case 75/63, *Hoekstra (née Unger)* [1964] ECR 177, para. 3.

[172] On this point, see section 1(d/bb) above.

[173] Case 6/64, *Costa* v. *ENEL* [1964] ECR 585 at 592 (emphasis added).

[174] Joined Cases 28–30/62, *Da Costa et al.* v. *Netherlands Inland Revenue Administration* [1963] ECR 31 at 38.

[175] For two excellent analyses of this category of cases, see G. Davies, 'The Division of Powers between the European Court of Justice and National Courts' *Constitutionalism Web-Papers* 3/2004 (SSRN Network: www.ssrn.com); T. Tridimas, 'Constitutional Review of Member State Action: The Virtues and Vices of an Incomplete Jurisdiction' (2011) 9 *International Journal of Constitutional Law* 737.

[176] See M. Jarvis, 'The *Sunday Trading* Episode: In Defence of the Euro-defence' (1995) 44 ICLQ 451.

references had been made by a number of English courts to obtain an interpretation of the EU Treaties' free movement of goods provisions. The Court found that national rules governing opening hours could be justified on public interest grounds, and originally asked the referring national court 'to ascertain whether the effects of such national rules exceed what is necessary to achieve the aim in view'.[177] Yet the decentralised application of this proportionality test led to judicial chaos in the United Kingdom. Simply put, different national courts decided differently! The European Court thus ultimately took matters into its own hands and centrally applied the proportionality test.[178] And, in holding that the British Sunday trading rules were not disproportionate interferences with the internal market, the Court crossed the line between 'interpretation' and 'application' of the Treaties.

b. Paragraph 2: The Conditions for a Preliminary Ruling

Article 267(2) TFEU defines the competence of national courts to refer preliminary questions. The provision allows 'any court or tribunal of a Member State' to ask a European law question that 'is necessary to enable it to give judgment'. Are there conditions on 'who' can refer 'what' question to the European Court? The two aspects have been subject to an extended judicial commentary and will be discussed in turn.

aa. 'Who': National Courts and Tribunals

The formulation 'court or tribunal' in Article 267 only refers to *judicial* authorities. This excludes *administrative* authorities, which have indeed been systematically excluded from the scope of the judicial cooperation procedure.[179]

---

[177] Case C-145/88, *Torfaen Borough Council* [1989] ECR I-3851, para. 15.

[178] Case C-169/91, *Stoke-on-Trent* v. *B&Q* [1992] ECR I-6635, paras. 12–14: 'As far as that principle is concerned, the Court stated in its judgment in the Torfaen Borough Council case that such rules were not prohibited by Article [34] of the [FEU] Treaty where the restrictive effects on [Union] trade which might result from them did not exceed the effects intrinsic to such rules and that the question whether the effects of those rules actually remained within that limit was a question of fact to be determined by the national court. In its judgments in the Conforama and Marchandise cases, however, the Court found it necessary to make clear, with regard to similar rules, that the restrictive effects on trade which might result from them did not appear to be excessive in relation to the aim pursued. The Court considered that it had all the information necessary for it to rule on the question of the proportionality of such rules and that it had to do so in order to enable national courts to assess their compatibility with [European] law in a uniform manner since such an assessment cannot be allowed to vary according to the findings of fact made by individual courts in particular cases.'

[179] See e.g. Case C-24/92, *Corbiau* [1993] ECR I-1277; Case C-53/03, *Syfait et al.* v. *GlaxoSmithKline* [2005] ECR I-4609.

But what exactly is a 'court or tribunal' that can refer questions to the Court of Justice? The Treaties provide no positive definition. Would the concept therefore fall within the competence of the Member States? Unsurprisingly, the European Court has not accepted this and has provided a European definition of the phrase. Its definition is extremely wide. In *Dorsch Consult*,[180] the Court thus held:

> In order to determine whether a body making a reference is a court or tribunal for the purposes of Article [267] of the Treaty, which is a question governed by [Union] law alone, the Court takes account of a number of factors, such as whether the body is established by law, whether it is permanent, whether its jurisdiction is compulsory, whether its procedure is inter partes, whether it applies rules of law and whether it is independent.[181]

The last criterion is often controlling. Therefore, an authority that is not independent from the State's administrative branch is not a court or tribunal in the meaning of European law.[182]

The enormous breadth of this definition is illustrated in *Broekmeulen*.[183] The plaintiff had obtained a medical degree from Belgium and tried to register as a 'General Practitioner' in the Netherlands. The registration was refused on the ground that Dutch professional qualifications were not satisfied. The plaintiff appealed before the 'Appeals Committee for General Medicine'– a professional body set up under private law. This Appeals Committee was not a court or tribunal under Dutch law. But would it nonetheless be a 'court or tribunal' under Article 267 (2); and, as such, be entitled to make a preliminary reference? The European Court found as follows:

> In order to deal with the question of the applicability in the present case of Article [267 TFEU], it should be noted that it is incumbent upon Member States to take the necessary steps to ensure that within their territory the provisions adopted by the [Union] institutions are implemented in their entirety. If, under the legal system of a Member State, the task of implementing such provisions is assigned to a professional body acting under a degree of governmental supervision, and if that body, in

---

[180]   Case C-54/96, *Dorsch Consult Ingenieugesellschaft* v. *Bundesbaugesellschaft Berlin* [1997] ECR I-4961.

[181]   *Ibid.*, para. 23.

[182]   Case C-53/03, *Syfait et al.* v. *GlaxoSmithKline*. NCAs are consequently not (!) allowed to use the Art. 267 procedure as they are considered to be part of the 'executive branch' – not the judicial branch. If they have a question with regard to EU competition law, they thus cannot ask the European Court of Justice but must, on the contrary, ask the European Commission for guidance. On the general question, whether NCAs should be considered 'courts or tribunals' in the sense of Art. 267, see A. Komninos, 'Article 234 EC and National Competition Authorities in the Era of Decentralisation' (2004) 29 *EL Rev.* 106.

[183]   Case 246/80, *Broekmeulen* v. *Huisarts Registratie Commissie* [1981] ECR 2311.

conjunction with the public authorities concerned, creates appeal procedures which may affect the exercise of rights granted by [European] law, it is imperative, in order to ensure the proper functioning of [Union] law, that the Court should have an opportunity of ruling on issues of interpretation and validity arising out of such proceedings. As a result of all the foregoing considerations and in the absence, in practice, of any right of appeal to the ordinary courts, the Appeals Committee, which operates with the consent of the public authorities and with their cooperation, and which, after an adversarial procedure, delivers decisions which are recognised as final, must, in a matter involving the application of [European] law, be considered as a court or tribunal of a Member State within the meaning of Article [267 TFEU].[184]

Can higher national courts limit the power of a lower national court to refer preliminary questions? The European legal order has given short shrift to any attempt to break the cooperative nexus between the European Court and *each level of the national judiciary*. In *Rheinmühlen*,[185] the Court thus held that 'a rule of national law whereby a court is bound on points of law by the rulings of a superior court cannot deprive the inferior courts of their power to refer to the Court questions of interpretation of [Union] law involving such rulings'.[186] For if inferior courts could not refer to the Court of Justice, 'the jurisdiction of the latter to give preliminary rulings and the application of [European] law *at all levels of the judicial systems* of the Member States would be compromised'.[187] Any national court or tribunal, at any level of the national judicial hierarchy, and at any stage of its judicial procedure, is thus entitled to refer a preliminary question to the European Court of Justice.[188] Even national rules allowing for an appeal against the decision of the national court to refer a preliminary question will violate 'the autonomous jurisdiction which Article [267 TFEU] confers on the referring court'.[189]

---

[184]   *Ibid.*, paras. 16–17.

[185]   Case 166/73, *Rheinmühlen-Düsseldorf* [1974] ECR 33.

[186]   *Ibid.*, para. 4.

[187]   *Ibid.* For a recent confirmation, see Case C-173/09, *Elchinov v. Natsionalna zdravnoosiguritelna kasa* [2010] ECR I-889; Case C-416/10, *Križan and others*, EU:C:2013:8.

[188]   This European entitlement cannot be transformed into a national obligation; see Case C-555/07, *Kücükdeveci v. Swedex* [2010] ECR I-365, para. 54: 'The possibility thus given to the national court by the second paragraph of Article 267 TFEU of asking the Court for a preliminary ruling before disapplying the national provision that is contrary to European Union law cannot, however, be transformed into an obligation because national law does not allow that court to disapply a provision it considers to be contrary to the constitution unless the provision has first been declared unconstitutional by the Constitutional Court. By reason of the principle of the primacy of European Union law, which extends also to the principle of non-discrimination on grounds of age, contrary national legislation which falls within the scope of European Union law must be disapplied.'

[189]   Case C-210/06, *Cartesio* [2008] ECR I-9641, para. 95: 'Where rules of national law apply which relate to the right of appeal against a decision making a reference for a preliminary ruling, and under those rules the main proceedings remain pending before the referring

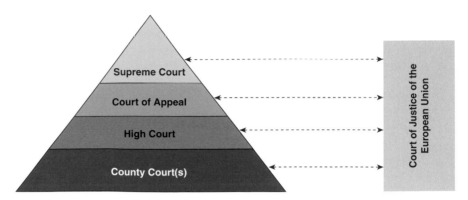

Figure 10.5 Preliminary Rulings under Article 267

For the English judicial hierarchy, the judicial federalism constructed by the European Court thus looks like Figure 10.5.

bb. 'What': Necessary Questions

National courts are entitled to request a preliminary ruling, where – within a pending case – there is a 'question' that they consider 'necessary' to give judgment.[190]

In the past, the European Court has been eager to encourage national courts to ask preliminary questions. For these questions offered the Court formidable opportunities to say what the European constitution 'is'.[191] Thus, even where questions were 'imperfectly formulated', the Court was willing to extract the 'right' ones.[192] Moreover, the Court will generally not 'criticise the grounds and purpose of the request for interpretation'.[193] In the words of a seminal judgment on the issue:

> court in their entirety, the order for reference alone being the subject of a limited appeal, the autonomous jurisdiction which Article [267 TFEU] confers on the referring court to make a reference to the Court would be called into question, if – by varying the order for reference, by setting it aside and by ordering the referring court to resume the proceedings – the appellate court could prevent the referring court from exercising the right, conferred on it by the [FEU] Treaty, to make a reference to the Court.'

[190] Case 338/85, *Pardini* v. *Ministero del Commercio con l'Estero and Banca Toscana* [1988] ECR 2041, para. 11: 'It follows that a national court or tribunal is not empowered to bring a matter before the Court by way of a reference for a preliminary ruling unless a dispute is pending before it in the context of which it is called upon to give a decision capable of taking into account the preliminary ruling. Conversely, the Court of Justice has no jurisdiction to hear a reference for a preliminary ruling when at the time it is made the procedure before the court making it has already been terminated.'

[191] In the famous phrase by C. E. Hughes (as quoted by E. Corwin, 'Curbing the Court' (1936) 26 *American Labor Legislation Review* 85): 'We are under a Constitution, but the Constitution is what the judges say it is[.]'

[192] Case 6/64, *Costa* v. *ENEL* [1964] ECR 585, 593: '[T]he Court has the power to extract from a question imperfectly formulated by the national court those questions which alone pertain to the interpretation of the Treaty.'

[193] *Ibid.*

> As regards the division of jurisdiction between national courts and the Court of Justice under Article [267] of the [FEU] Treaty the national court, which is alone in having a direct knowledge of the facts of the case and of the arguments put forward by the parties, and which will have to give judgment in the case, is in the best position to appreciate, with full knowledge of the matter before it, the relevance of the questions of law raised by the dispute before it and the necessity for a preliminary ruling so as to enable it to give judgment.[194]

Nonetheless, in very exceptional circumstances the Court will reject a request for a preliminary ruling. This happened in *Foglia v. Novello (No. 1)*,[195] where the Court insisted that questions referred to it must be raised in a 'genuine' dispute.[196] Where the parties to the national dispute agreed, in advance, on the desirable outcome, the Court will decline jurisdiction.[197] In a sequel to this case, the Court explained this jurisdictional limitation as follows:

> [T]he duty assigned to the Court by Article [267] is not that of delivering advisory opinions on general or hypothetical questions but of assisting in the administration of justice in the Member States. It accordingly does not have jurisdiction to reply to questions of interpretation which are submitted to it within the framework of procedural devices arranged by the parties in order to induce the Court to give its views on certain problems of [European] law which do not correspond to an objective requirement inherent in the resolution of a dispute.[198]

The Court of Justice has consequently imposed *some* jurisdictional control on requests for preliminary rulings. To prevent an abuse of the Article 267 procedure, the European Court will thus 'check, as all courts must, whether it has jurisdiction'.[199] Yet, the Court has been eager to emphasise that it wishes 'not

---

[194] Case 83/78, *Pigs Marketing Board* v. *Raymond Redmond* [1978] ECR 2347, para. 25.

[195] Case 104/79, *Foglia* v. *Novello* [1980] ECR 745.

[196] G. Bebr, 'The Existence of a Genuine Dispute: An Indispensable Precondition for the Jurisdiction of the Court under Article 177 EEC?' (1980) 17 *CML Rev.* 525.

[197] Case 104/79, *Foglia*, paras. 11–13: 'The duty of the Court of Justice under Article [267] of the [FEU] Treaty is to supply all courts in the [Union] with the information on the interpretation of [European] law which is necessary to enable them to settle *genuine* disputes which are brought before them. A situation in which the Court is obliged by the expedient of arrangements like those described above to give rulings would jeopardise the whole system of legal remedies available to private individuals to enable them to protect themselves against tax provisions which are contrary to the Treaty. This means that the questions asked by the national court, having regard to the circumstances of this case, do not fall within the framework of the duties of the Court of Justice under Article [267] of the Treaty. The Court has accordingly no jurisdiction to give a ruling on the question asked by the national court.'

[198] Case 244/80, *Foglia* v. *Novello (2)* [1981] ECR 3045, para. 18.

[199] *Ibid.*, para. 19.

in any way [to] trespass upon the prerogatives of the national courts';[200] and the Court here pledged to 'place as much reliance as possible upon the assessment by the national court of the extent to which the questions submitted are essential'.[201] The Court will therefore decline jurisdiction only very exceptionally:

> The presumption that questions referred by national courts for a preliminary ruling are relevant may be rebutted only in exceptional cases, where it is quite obvious that the interpretation of European Union law that is sought bears no relation to the actual facts of the main action or its purpose, where the problem is hypothetical, or where the Court does not have before it the factual or legal material necessary to give a useful answer to the questions submitted to it.[202]

There exists thus a 'presumption of relevance' that the EU law questions asked will be relevant for the national case at hand.[203]

c. Paragraph 3: The Obligation to Refer and 'Acte clair'

While any national court or tribunal 'may' refer a question to the European Court under paragraph 2, Article 267(3) TFEU imposes an obligation:

> Where any such question is raised in a case pending before a court or tribunal of a Member State against whose decisions there is no judicial remedy under national law, that court or tribunal shall bring the matter before the Court.

Certain courts therefore 'must' refer a question to the European Court. These courts are defined in Article 267(3) as courts 'against whose decisions there is no judicial remedy under national law'.

What will this formulation mean? Two theoretical options exist. Under an 'institutional' reading, the formulation refers to the highest judicial *institution* in the country. This would restrict the obligation to refer preliminary questions to a single court in a Member State – in the United Kingdom: the Supreme Court. By contrast, a 'procedural' reading links the definition of the court of last instance to the judicial *procedure* in the particular case. This broadens the obligation to refer to every national court whose decision cannot be appealed in the particular case.

---

[200] *Ibid.*, para. 18.   [201] *Ibid.*, para. 19.

[202] Case C-617/10, *Åklagaren* v. *Fransson* EU:C:2013:105, para. 40. For an illustration, where the Court found a preliminary question to be irrelevant, see e.g. Case C-618/10, *Banco Español de Crédito* EU:C:2012: 349, esp. paras. 78–9.

[203] Case 62/14, *Gauweiler and others* v. *Deutscher Bundestag*, EU:C:2015:400, para. 25. That there may nevertheless be a robust review of the admissibility of the preliminary ruling, see Case C-547/14, *Philip Morris Brands and Others*, EC:C:2016:325, paras. 29–53.

The Court of Justice has – from the very beginning – favoured the second reading.[204] The key concept in Article 267(3) is thereby the '*appealability*' of a judicial decision. What counts is the *ability* of the parties to appeal to a higher court. (The fact that the merits of the appeal are subject to a prior declaration of admissibility by a superior court will thereby not deprive the parties of that ability.)[205] Where an appeal is thus *procedurally* possible, the obligation under Article 267(3) will not apply.

Apart from the question as to what are courts 'against whose decisions there is no judicial remedy under national law', the wording of Article 267(3) appears relatively clear. Yet, this picture is – misleadingly – deceptive. For the European Court has judicially 'amended' the provision in two very significant ways.

The first 'amendment' relates to references on the validity of European law. And despite the restrictive wording of paragraph 3, the European Court has here insisted that *all* national courts – even courts that are not courts of last resort – are under an obligation to refer *when they are in doubt about the validity of a Union act*.[206] This *expansion* of the scope of Article 267(3) follows from the structure of the Union's judicial federalism, which grants the exclusive power to invalidate European law to the Court of Justice alone.[207]

By contrast, a second 'amendment' has limited the obligation to refer preliminary questions. This *limitation* follows from constitutional common sense. For to ask a question implies uncertainty as to the answer. And where the answer is 'clear', there may be no need to raise a question. Yet on its textual face, Article 267(3) treats national courts 'as perpetual children': they are forbidden from interpreting European law – even if the answers are crystal clear.[208] And in order to counter this, the Union legal order has imported a French legal doctrine under the name of *acte clair*.[209] The doctrine simply means that where it is *clear* how to *act*, a national court need not ask a preliminary question.

---

[204] The procedural theory received support in Case 6/64, *Costa* v. *ENEL* [1964] ECR 585, where the ECJ treated an Italian court of *first* instance as a court against whose decision there was no judicial remedy.

[205] Case C-99/00, *Lyckeskog* [2002] ECR I-4839, para. 16: 'Decisions of a national appellate court which can be challenged by the parties before a supreme court are not decisions of a court or tribunal of a Member State against whose decisions there is no judicial remedy under national law within the meaning of Article [267 TFEU]. The fact that examination of the merits of such appeals is subject to a prior declaration of admissibility by the Supreme Court does not have the effect of depriving the parties of a judicial remedy.' For a recent confirmation, see Case C-3/16, *Aquino* v. *Belgium*, EU:C:2017:209, paras. 35–6.

[206] See Case C-344/04, *The Queen on the application of International Air Transport Association et al.* v. *Department for Transport* [2006] ECR I-403, para. 30.

[207] On this point, see Chapter 11, Introduction.

[208] J. C. Cohen, 'The European Preliminary Reference and US Court Review of State Court Judgments: A Study in Comparative Judicial Federalism' (1996) *American Journal of Comparative Law* 421 at 438.

[209] There are different interpretations of the 'hidden' constitutional reasons behind the European *acte clair* doctrine. Some commentators have seen it in purely negative terms:

The doctrine of *acte clair* began its European career in *Da Costa*.[210] In this case, the Court held:

> [T]he authority of an interpretation under Article [267] already given by the Court may deprive the obligation of its purpose and thus empty it of its substance. Such is the case especially when the question raised is *materially identical* with a question which has already been the subject of a preliminary ruling in a similar case.[211]

The Court subsequently clarified that this also covered a second situation. Where the European Court had already given a negative answer to a question relating to the *validity* of a Union act, another national court need not raise the same question again.[212]

But general guidelines on the constitutional scope of the *acte clair* doctrine were only offered in *CILFIT*.[213] The Court here widened the doctrine to situations 'where previous decisions of the Court have already dealt with the *point of law* in question, irrespective of the nature of the proceedings which led to those decisions, even though the questions at issue are not strictly identical'.[214] Yet national courts would only be released from their obligation to refer questions under Article 267(3) TFEU, where certain conditions were fulfilled. In the words of the Court:

the European Court finally became resigned to the fact that national supreme courts did not honour their obligation to refer questions under Art. 267(3) TFEU, and the invention of the *acte clair* doctrine 'legalised' a (previously) illegal national practice. A second interpretation sees the doctrine in a positive light: the European Court rejected the idea of considering national supreme courts as less reliable than lower national courts in interpreting European law. The obligation to refer would thus only arise where there was a real European law 'question'. A third interpretation has seen the doctrine of *acte clair* as part of a 'give and take' strategy, according to which the Court gave more power to national courts so as to develop a doctrine of precedent. On the various readings, see H. Rasmussen, 'The European Court's *acte clair* Strategy in *CILFIT*' (1984) 10 *EL Rev.* 242.

[210] Cases 28–30/62, *Da Costa*.

[211] *Ibid.*, 38.

[212] Case 66/80, *International Chemical Corporation* [1981] ECR 1191, paras. 12–13: 'When the Court is moved under Article [267] to declare an act of one of the institutions to be void there are particularly imperative requirements concerning legal certainty in addition to those concerning the uniform application of [European] law. It follows from the very nature of such a declaration that a national court may not apply the act declared to be void without once more creating serious uncertainty as to the [European] law applicable. It follows therefrom that although a judgment of the Court given under Article [267] of the Treaty declaring an act of an institution, in particular a Council or Commission regulation, to be void is directly addressed only to the national court which brought the matter before the Court, it is sufficient reason for any other national court to regard that act as void for the purposes of a judgment which it has to give.'

[213] Case 283/81, *CILFIT and others* v. *Ministry of Health* [1982] ECR 3415.

[214] *Ibid.*, para. 14.

> [T]he correct application of [Union] law may be so obvious as to leave no scope for any reasonable doubt as to the matter in which the question raised is to be resolved. Before it comes to the conclusion that such is the case, the national court or tribunal must be convinced that the matter is equally obvious to the courts of the other Member States and to the Court of Justice. Only if those conditions are satisfied, may the national court or tribunal refrain from submitting the question to the Court of Justice and take upon itself the responsibility for resolving it. However, the existence of such a possibility must be assessed on the basis of the characteristic features of [European] law and the particular difficulties to which its interpretation gives rise.[215]

This is an extremely high threshold, which the Court linked to the fulfilment of a number of very (!) restrictive conditions.[216] These *CILFIT* conditions 'were designed to prevent national courts from abusing the doctrine in order to evade their obligation to seek a preliminary ruling where they are disinclined to adhere to the Court's case-law'.[217]

For a very long time, however, not much was known about the *CILFIT* conditions. In a recent judgment, the Court has helpfully added some clarity. In *Ferreira da Silva e Brito*,[218] the Court clarified that the existence of contradictory decisions of lower national courts was '*not* a conclusive factor capable of triggering the obligation set out in the third paragraph of Article 267 TFEU' because a higher court may still hold a distinct interpretation that it believes to be beyond reasonable doubt.[219] While disagreement *within one national legal* order is thus not a conclusive trigger, the Court of Justice nevertheless held that wherever there exists 'a great deal of uncertainty on the part of *many national courts and tribunals*', '[t]hat uncertainty shows not only that there are difficulties of interpretation, but

---

[215] *Ibid.*, paras. 16–17.

[216] *Ibid.*, paras. 18–20: 'To begin with, it must be borne in mind that [Union] legislation is drafted in several languages and that the different language versions are all equally authentic. An interpretation of a provision of [European] law thus involves a comparison of the different language versions. It must also be borne in mind, even where the different language versions are entirely in accord with one another, that [European] law uses terminology which is peculiar to it. Furthermore, it must be emphasised that legal concepts do not necessarily have the same meaning in [European] law and in the law of the various Member States. Finally, every provision of [European] law must be placed in its context and interpreted in the light of the provisions of [European] law as a whole, regard being had to the objectives thereof and to its state of evolution at the date on which the provision in question is to be applied.'

[217] K. Lenaerts et al., *EU Procedural Law* (Oxford University Press, 2014), 100.

[218] Case C-160/14, *Ferreira da Silva e Brito and others*.

[219] *Ibid.*, paras. 41–2 (emphasis added). Similarly, in Joined Cases C-72/14 and C-197/14, *X and van Dijk*, EU:C:2015:564, the Court held that the fact that a lower court had made a reference to the ECJ did not in itself mean that the *CILFIT* conditions were fulfilled because 'it is for the national courts alone against whose decision there is no judicial remedy under national law, to take upon themselves independently the responsibility for determining whether the case before them involves an "acte clair"' (*ibid.*, para. 59).

also that there is a risk of divergences in judicial decisions within the European Union'.[220] And, importantly, this was a question that the European Court itself felt very happy to – centrally – decide.[221] Far from indicating 'a considerable relaxation of the conditions of application of the *acte clair* exception' and an 'accrued decentralization in the interpretation of EU law', this recent development may indeed show the Court to police and restrict the CILFIT conditions much more willingly.[222]

d. The Legal Nature of Preliminary Rulings

What is the nature of preliminary rulings from the European Court? Preliminary references are not appeals. They are – principally – discretionary acts of a national court asking for interpretative help from the European Court. The decision to refer to the European Court of Justice thus lies entirely with the national court – not the parties to the dispute.[223] Once the European Court has given a preliminary ruling, this ruling will be binding. But *whom* will it bind – the parties to the national disputes or the national court(s)?

Preliminary rulings cannot bind the parties in the national dispute, since the European Court will not 'decide' their case. It is therefore misleading to even speak of a binding effect *inter partes* in the context of preliminary rulings.[224] The Court's rulings are addressed to the national court requesting the reference; and the Court has clarified that 'that ruling is binding on the national court as to the interpretation of the [Union] provisions and acts in question'.[225] Yet, will the binding effect of a preliminary ruling extend beyond the referring national court? In other words, is a preliminary ruling equivalent to a 'decision' addressed to a single court; or will the European Court's interpretation be generally binding on all national courts? The Court has long clarified that a preliminary ruling

---

[220] C-160/14, *Ferreira da Silva e Brito and others*, para. 43.

[221] *Ibid.*, para. 44. For the same 'centralised' application of the *CILFIT* criteria, see Case C-379/15, *Association France Nature Environnement v. Premier ministre and others*, EU:C:2016:603, esp. paras. 51–3.

[222] For the opposite conclusion, see A. Kornezov, 'The New Format of the *acte clair* Doctrine and Its Consequences' (2016) 53 *CMLR* 1317, esp. 1325 and 1341.

[223] Case C-2/06, *Kempter v. Hauptzollamt Hamburg-Jonas* [2008] ECR I-411, para. 41: 'the system established by Article [267 TFEU] with a view to ensuring that [European] law is interpreted uniformly in the Member States instituted direct cooperation between the Court of Justice and the national courts by means of a procedure which is completely independent of any initiative by the parties'. And para. 42: 'the system of references for a preliminary ruling is based on a dialogue between one court and another, the initiation of which depends entirely on the national court's assessment as to whether a reference is appropriate and necessary'.

[224] Contra: A. Toth, 'The Authority of Judgments of the European Court of Justice: Binding Force and Legal Effects' (1984) 4 YEL 1.

[225] Case 52/76, *Benedetti v. Munari* [1977] ECR 163, para. 26: 'that ruling is binding on the national court as to the interpretation of the [Union] provisions and acts in question'.

is *not* a 'decision'; indeed, it is not even seen as an (external) act of a Union institution.[226]

What then is the nature of preliminary rulings? The question has been hotly debated in the academic literature. And − again − we may contrast two views competing with each other. According to the common law view, preliminary rulings are legal precedents that generally bind all national courts. Judgments of the European Court are binding *erga omnes*.[227] This view typically links the rise of the doctrine of judicial precedent with the evolution of the doctrine of *acte clair*.[228] It is thereby claimed that the Court of Justice transformed its position vis-à-vis national courts from a *horizontal* and *bilateral* relationship to a *vertical* and *multilateral* one.[229]

The problem with this − masterful yet mistaken − theory is that the European Court subscribes to a second constitutional view: the civil law tradition. Accordingly, its judgments do not create 'new' legal rules but only clarify 'old' ones. In the words of the Court:

> The interpretation which, in the exercise of the jurisdiction conferred upon it by Article [267 TFEU], the Court of Justice gives to a rule of [European] law clarifies and defines where necessary the meaning and scope of that rule as it must be or ought to have been understood and applied from the time of its coming into force.[230]

The Court of Justice has thus adopted the − (in)famous − 'declaration theory'. Judgments only declare pre-existing positive law, and thus reach back in time to when the positive law was adopted. The vertical and multilateral effects of preliminary rulings are thus mediated through the positive law interpreted − and not, as the common law view asserts, through a doctrine of precedent.[231]

In light of the 'civilian' judicial philosophy of the European Court, its judgments are *not* generally binding.[232] There is no vertical or multilateral effect

---

[226] Case 69/85 (Order), *Wünsche Handelsgesellschaft* v. *Germany* [1986] ECR 947, para. 16.

[227] See A. Trabucchi, 'L'Effet *"erga omnes"* des décisions préjudicielles rendues par la cour de justice des communautés européennes' (1974) 10 *RTDE* 56.

[228] Rasmussen, 'European Court's *acte clair* Strategy' (n. 209 above).

[229] This view was popularised in P. Craig and G. de Búrca, *EU Law: Text, Cases and Materials* (Oxford University Press, 2007), 461.

[230] Case 61/79, *Amministrazione delle finanze dello Stato* v. *Denkavit* [1980] ECR 1205, para. 16; and somewhat more recently: Case C-453/00, *Kühne & Heitz* v. *Productschap voor Pluimvee en Eieren* [2004] ECR I-837, para. 21.

[231] Against this civilian background, the argument that the Treaty, by providing for the automatic operation of the obligation to refer, 'assumed that the Court's dicta under Article [267] were deprived of authority for any other court than the submitting one' (Rasmussen, 'European Court's *acte clair* Strategy' (n. 209 above) at 249), is flawed. And starting from this false premise, Rasmussen (over)interprets *CILFIT*.

[232] In this sense, see Toth, 'Authority of Judgments' (n. 224 above), 60: 'in the cases under discussion the Court itself has never meant to attribute, as is sometimes suggested, a general binding force to interpretative preliminary rulings'.

of judicial decisions as 'judgments of the European Courts are *not sources* but *authoritative evidences* of [European] law'. '[A]n interpretation given by the Court becomes an integral part of the provision interpreted and cannot fail to affect the legal position of all those who may derive rights and obligations from that provision.'[233]

Are there constitutional problems with the Union's civil law philosophy? Indeed, there are. For the 'declaratory' effect of preliminary rulings often generates 'retroactive' effects.[234] Indeed, in *Kühne & Heitz*,[235] the Court held that a (new) interpretation of European law must be applied 'even to legal relationships which arose or were formed before the Court gave its ruling on the question on interpretation'.[236] The Court has, however, recognised that its civil law philosophy must – occasionally – be tempered by the principles of legal certainty and financial equity.[237] It has therefore – exceptionally – limited the temporal effect of a preliminary ruling to an effect *ex nunc*, that is: an effect from the time of the ruling.[238] However, at the same time, the Court has clarified that legal certainty will not prevent the retrospective application of a (new) interpretation, where the judgment of a court of last instance 'was, in the light of a decision given by the Court subsequent to it, based on a misinterpretation of [European] law which was adopted without a question being referred to the Court for a preliminary ruling under the third paragraph of Article [267]'.[239]

Conclusion

The Court of Justice of the European Union has never just been 'the mouth of the law'. The Court's judicial powers are extensive – and the Court has extensively used them. Yet while the Court's judicial activism has been subject to heavy criticism,[240] the Court continues to be a 'court'; and as a court its powers are essentially 'passive' powers. This chapter looked at three judicial powers in the context of the Union legal order: the power to annul European law, the

---

[233]   *Ibid.*, 70 and 74.

[234]   On this point, see G. Bebr, 'Preliminary Rulings of the Court of Justice: Their Authority and Temporal Effect' (1981) 18 *CML Rev.* 475, esp. 491: 'The retroactive effect of a preliminary interpretative ruling is, according to the Court, the general rule.'

[235]   Case C-453/00, *Kühne & Heitz*.

[236]   *Ibid.*, para. 22.

[237]   For the former rationale, see Case C-2/06, *Kempter*; for the latter rationale, see Case 43/75, *Defrenne* v. *Sabena* [1976] ECR 455.

[238]   For an academic analysis here, see D. Düsterhaus, 'Eppur Si Muove! The Past, Present, and (Possible) Future of Temporal Limitations in the Preliminary Reference Procedure' (2017) 36 YEL 237.

[239]   Case C-2/06, *Kempter*, para. 39. For a critical analysis of this case, see A. Ward, 'Do unto Others as You Would Have Them Do unto You: "Willy Kempter" and the Duty to Raise EC Law in National Litigation' (2008) 33 *EL Rev.* 739.

[240]   See H. Rasmussen, *On Law and Policy in the European Court of Justice: A Comparative Study in Judicial Policymaking* (Nijhoff, 1986).

power to remedy illegal acts of the Union, and the power to enforce European law through adjudication, both directly in the European Court and indirectly through the national courts.

The Union is based on the rule of law inasmuch as the European Court is empowered to review the legality of European (secondary) law. The Union legal order has thereby opted for a strong 'rule of law' version. It allows the Court to review the formal and substantive legality of European law. One particularly important aspect of the substantive review of all Union law will be discussed in Chapter 12: judicial review in light of EU fundamental rights.

However, in the past, there existed severe procedural limitations on the right of individual applicants to request judicial review proceedings. Under the Rome Treaty, private parties were originally only entitled to challenge 'decisions' that were of 'direct and individual concern to them'. And while subsequent jurisprudence broadened their standing to the review of any Union act, the *Plaumann* formula restricted the right to judicial review to an exclusive set of private applicants. The Lisbon Treaty has only liberalised this procedural restriction for 'regulatory' acts.

Section 2 looked at the remedial powers of the European Court, while sections 3 and 4 analysed the application of European law through adjudication. With regard to the judicial adjudication of Union law, the Union has chosen a dual enforcement mechanism. First, it allows for the *central* adjudication of European law through actions directly brought before the Court of Justice of the European Union. The Treaties thereby distinguish between infringement actions against the Member States, and proceedings against the Union for a failure to act. However, second, the Union legal order also provides for the decentralised adjudication of European law in the national courts. From a functional perspective, national courts are thus – partly – European courts; and, in order to guarantee a degree of uniformity in the interpretation of European law, the EU Treaties provide for a 'preliminary reference procedure'. This is not an appeal procedure, but allows national courts to ask – if they want to – questions relating to the interpretation of European law. This – voluntary – cooperative arrangement is however replaced by a constitutional obligation for national courts of last resort.

The role of national courts in the exercise of the judicial function in the Union legal order cannot be overestimated. Their powers and procedures in the enforcement of Union law are the subject of the next chapter.

FURTHER READING

Books

A. Albors-Llorens, *Private Parties in European Community Law: Challenging Community Measures* (Clarendon Press, 1996)

S. Andersen, *The Enforcement of EU Law* (Oxford University Press, 2012)

A. Arnull, *The European Union and Its Court of Justice* (Oxford University Press, 2006)

A. Biondi and M. Farley, *The Right to Damages in European Law* (Kluwer, 2009)

M. Broberg and N. Fenger, *Preliminary References to the European Court of Justice* (Oxford University Press, 2014)

K. Lenaerts, I. Maselis and K. Gutman, *EU Procedural Law* (Oxford University Press, 2014)

L. Prete, *Infringement Proceedings in EU Law* (Kluwer, 2016)

T. Tridimas, *The General Principles of EU Law* (Oxford University Press, 2007)

A. Ward, *Judicial Review and the Rights of Private Parties in EU Law* (Oxford University Press, 2007)

Articles (and Chapters)

A. Albors-Llorens, 'Remedies against the EU Institutions after Lisbon: An Era of Opportunity' (2012) 71 *Cambridge Law Journal* 507

A. Arnull, 'Private Applicants and the Action for Annulment since *Codorniu*' (2001) 38 *CML Rev.* 8

S. Balthasar, '*Locus standi* Rules for Challenges to Regulatory Acts by Private Applicants: The New Article 263 (4) TFEU' (2010) 35 *EL Rev.* 542

J. Bast, 'Legal Instruments and Judicial Protection', in A. von Bogdandy and J. Bast (eds.), *Principles of European Constitutional Law* (Hart, 2009), 345

M. Broberg, '*Acte clair* Revisited' (2008) 45 *CML Rev.* 1383

K. Gutman, 'The Evolution of the Action for Damages against the European Union and Its Place in the System of Judicial Protection' (2011) 48 *CML Rev.* 695

L. Prete and B. Smulders, 'The Coming of Age of Infringement Proceedings' (2010) 47 *CML Rev.* 9

H. Rasmussen, 'The European Court's *Acte clair* Strategy in CILFIT' (1984) 10 *EL Rev.* 242

R. Schwensfeier, 'The *TWD* Principle Post-Lisbon' (2012) 37 *EL Rev.* 156

T. Tridimas, 'Knocking on Heaven's Door: Fragmentation, Efficiency and Defiance in the Preliminary Reference Ruling Procedure' (2003) 40 *CML Rev.* 9

J. Usher, 'Direct and Individual Concern: An Effective Remedy or a Conventional Solution?' (2003) 28 *EL Rev.* 575

M. Vogt, 'Indirect Judicial Protection in EC Law: The Case of the Plea of Illegality' (2006) 31 *EL Rev.* 364

P. Wennerås, 'Sanctions against Member States under Article 260 TFEU: Alive, But Not Kicking?' (2012) 49 *CML Rev.* 145

Cases on the Website

Case 25/62, *Plaumann*; Cases 28–30/62, *Da Costa*; Cases 31 and 33/62, *Lütticke*; Cases 90–1/63, *Commission v. Luxembourg and Belgium*; Case 22/70, *Commission v. Council (ERTA)*; Case 5/71, *Schöppenstedt*; Case 166/73, *Rheinmuhlen*; Case 104/79 *Foglia v. Novello (No. 1)*; Case 66/80, *International Chemical Corporation*; Case 246/80, *Broekmeulen*; Case 283/81, *CILFIT*; Case 13/83, *Parliament v. Council (Common Transport Policy)*; Case 294/83, *Les Verts*; Case 314/85, *Foto-Frost*; Case 302/87, *Parliament v. Council (Comitology)*; Case C-309/89, *Codorniu*; Case C-188/92, *TWD*; Case T-184/95, *Dorsch Consult*; Case C-352/98P, *Bergaderm*; Case C-50/00, *UPA*; Case C-453/00, *Kühne & Heitz*; Case C-402/05P, *Kadi*; Case C-120/06P, *FIAMM*; Case T-18/10, *Inuit I*; Case T-526/10, *Inuit II*; Case C-583/11P, *Inuit I-P*; Case C-160/14, *da Silva e Brito*

11

Judicial Powers II
(Decentralised) National Procedures

Introduction

National courts are the principal judicial enforcers of European law. 'Ever since *Van Gend en Loos* the Court has maintained that it is the task of the national courts to protect the rights of individuals under [Union] law and to give full effect to [Union] law provisions.'[1] Indeed, whenever European law is directly effective, national courts must apply it; and wherever a Union norm comes into conflict with national law, each national court must disapply the latter.[2]

---

[1] S. Prechal, 'National Courts in EU Judicial Structures' (2006) 25 *YEL* 429.

[2] On the principles of direct effect and supremacy, see Chapters 3 and 4.

The Union legal order thereby insists that nothing within the national judicial system must prevent national courts from exercising their functions as 'guardians' of the European judicial order.[3] In *Simmenthal*,[4] the Court thus held that each national court must be able to disapply national law – even where the national judicial system traditionally reserves that power to a central constitutional court:

> [E]very national court must, in a case within its jurisdiction, apply [Union] law in its entirety and protect rights which the latter confers on individuals and must accordingly set aside any provision of national law which may conflict with it, whether prior or subsequent to the [Union] rule. Accordingly any provision of a national legal system and any legislative, administrative or judicial practice which might impair the effectiveness of [European] law by withholding from the national court having jurisdiction to apply such law the power to do everything necessary at the moment of its application to set aside national legislative provisions which might prevent [Union] rules from having full force and effect are incompatible with those requirements which are the very essence of [Union] law.[5]

Functionally, the direct effect (and supremacy) of European law transform every single national court into a 'European' court. This decentralised system differs from the judicial system in the United States in which the application of federal law is principally left to 'federal' courts. Federal courts here apply federal law, while state courts apply state law. The European system, by contrast, is based on a philosophy of cooperative federalism: *all* national courts are entitled and obliged to apply European law to disputes before them. National courts are however not full European courts. Although they must interpret and apply European law, they are not empowered to annul a Union act. Within the Union legal order, this is an *exclusive* competence of the European Court:

> Since Article [263] gives the Court exclusive jurisdiction to declare void an act of a [Union] institution, the coherence of the system requires that where the validity of a [Union] act is challenged before a national court the power to declare that act invalid must also be reserved to the Court of Justice.[6]

---

[3] *Opinion 1/09* (Draft Agreement on the Creation of European and Community Patent Court) [2011] ECR I-1137, para. 66.

[4] Case 106/77, *Amministrazione delle Finanze dello Stato* v. *Simmenthal* [1978] ECR 629.

[5] *Ibid.*, paras. 21–2. For a recent confirmation, see e.g. Joined Cases C-188–9/10, *Melki & Abdeli* [2010] ECR I-5667, esp. para. 44.

[6] Case 314/85, *Foto-Frost* v. *Hauptzollamt Lübeck-Ost* [1987] ECR 4199, para. 17. See also Case C-461/03, *Schul Douane-expediteur* [2005] ECR I-10513. Under European law, national courts will thereby be entitled, under strict conditions, to grant interim relief (see Case C-466/93, *Atlanta Fruchthandelsgesellschaft mbH and others* v. *Bundesamt für Ernährung und Forstwirtschaft* [1995] ECR I-3799).

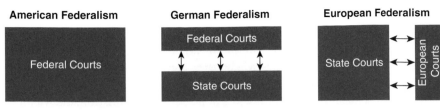

Figure 11.1 Judicial Federalism in Comparative Perspective

In opting for the decentralised judicial enforcement via state courts, the EU judicial system comes close to German judicial federalism; yet unlike the latter, state courts are not hierarchically subordinated. We saw in the previous chapter that there is no formal appeal procedure from the national to the European Courts, as the only procedural nexus here is the preliminary reference procedure. The relationship between national courts and the European Court is thus based on their *voluntary* cooperation. National courts are consequently only functionally – but not institutionally – Union courts (see Figure 11.1).

Has the Union therefore had to take State courts as it finds them? The Union legal order has indeed traditionally recognised the procedural autonomy of the judicial authorities of the Member States in the enforcement of European law:

> Where national authorities are responsible for implementing [European law] it must be recognised that in principle this implementation takes place with due respect for the forms and procedures of national law.[7]

This formulation has become known as the principle of 'national procedural autonomy'.[8] It essentially means that in the judicial enforcement of European law, the Union 'piggybacks' on the national judicial systems.[9] The danger of such 'piggybacking' is however that there may be situations in which there is a *European right* but no *national remedy* to enforce that right. But rights without remedies are like 'pie in the sky': a metaphysical meal. Each right should have its

---

[7] Case 39/70, *Norddeutsches Vieh- und Fleischkontor GmbH* v. *Hauptzollamt Hamburg-St Annen* [1971] ECR 49, para. 4.

[8] For a criticism of the notion, see C. N. Kakouris, 'Do the Member States Possess Judicial Procedural "Autonomy"?' (1997) 34 *CML Rev.* 1389 (arguing that the Court has never referred to the principle in its case law). However, the Court subsequently, and now regularly, recognised the principle in its case law; see Case C-201/02, *The Queen* v. *Secretary of State for Transport, ex p. Wells* [2004] ECR I-723, para. 67 (emphasis added): 'The detailed procedural rules applicable are a matter for the domestic legal order of each Member State, under the *principle of procedural autonomy of the Member States*'; and Joined Cases C-392/04 and C-422/04, *i-21 Germany & Arcor* v. *Germany* [2006] ECR I-8559, para. 57: 'principle of the procedural autonomy of the Member States'.

[9] K. Lenaerts et al., *EU Procedural Law* (Oxford University Press, 2014), 107.

remedy(ies);[10] and for that reason, the autonomy of national judicial procedures was never absolute. National procedural powers are thus not exclusive powers of the Member States;[11] and the Union has expressly recognised that it can harmonise national procedural laws where 'they are likely to distort or harm the functioning of the common market'.[12]

But did this mean that, in the absence of positive harmonisation, the Member States were absolutely free to determine how individuals could enforce their European rights in national courts? The Court has answered this question negatively. The core duty governing the decentralised enforcement of European law is thereby rooted in Article 4(3) TEU: the duty of 'sincere cooperation'.[13] This general duty is today complemented by Article 19(1), which states: 'Member States shall provide remedies sufficient to ensure effective legal protection in the fields covered by Union law.'

What does this mean? And to what extent does it limit the procedural autonomy of the Member States? This chapter explores these questions. We shall discuss two specific constitutional principles that the Court has derived from the general duty of sincere cooperation: the principle of equivalence and the principle of effectiveness. The classic expression of both can be found in *Rewe*:

> [I]n the absence of [European] rules on this subject, it is for the domestic legal system of each Member State to designate the courts having jurisdiction and to determine the procedural conditions governing actions at law intended to ensure the protection of the rights which citizens have derived from the direct effect of [European] law, it being understood that such conditions cannot be less favourable than those relating to similar actions of a domestic nature ... In the absence of such measures of

---

[10] Remedies might be said to fall into two broad categories. *Ex ante* remedies are to prevent the violation of a right (interim relief, injunctions), while *ex post* remedies are used to 'remedy' a violation that has already occurred (damages liability). On the many (unclear) meanings of 'remedy', see P. Birks, 'Rights, Wrongs, and Remedies' (2000) 20 *Oxford Journal of Legal Studies* 1 at 9ff.

[11] Contra: D. Simon, *Le Système juridique communautaire* (Presses Universitaires de France, 2001), 156: 'les Etats membres ont une competence exclusive pour determiner les organes qui seront chargés d'exécuter le droit communautaire'.

[12] Case 33/76, *Rewe-Zentralfinanz eG and Rewe-Zentral AG* v. *Landwirtschaftskammer für das Saarland* [1976] ECR 1989, para. 5: 'Where necessary, Articles [114 to 116 and 352 TFEU] enable appropriate measures to be taken to remedy differences between the provisions laid down by law, regulations or administrative action in Member States if they are likely to distort or harm the functioning of the common market. In the absence of such measures of harmonisation the right conferred by [European] law must be exercised before the national courts in accordance with the conditions laid down by national rules.'

[13] Art. 4(3) TEU states: 'Pursuant to the principle of sincere cooperation, the Union and the Member States shall, in full mutual respect, assist each other in carrying out tasks which flow from the Treaties. The Member States shall take any appropriate measure, general or particular, to ensure fulfilment of the obligations arising out of the Treaties or resulting from the acts of the institutions of the Union. The Member States shall facilitate the achievement of the Union's tasks and refrain from any measure which could jeopardise the attainment of the Union's objectives.'

harmonisation the right conferred by [European] law must [thus] be exercised before the national courts in accordance with the conditions laid down by national rules. The position would be different only if the [national rules] made it impossible in practice to exercise the rights which the national courts are obliged to protect.[14]

Even in the absence of European harmonisation, the procedural autonomy of the Member States was thus *relative*. National procedural rules could not make the enforcement of European rights less favourable than the enforcement of similar national rights. This prohibition of procedural discrimination was the principle of equivalence. But national procedural rules – even if not discriminatory – ought also not to make the enforcement of European rights 'impossible in practice'. This would become known as the principle of effectiveness. Both principles have led to a significant *judicial* harmonisation of national procedural laws,[15] and this chapter analyses their evolution in sections 1 and 2 below.

Section 3 turns to a third – famous – incursion into the procedural autonomy of national courts: the liability principle. While the previous two principles relied on the existence of *national* remedies for the enforcement of European law, this principle establishes a *European* remedy for proceedings in national courts. An individual can here, under certain conditions, claim compensatory damages resulting from a breach of European law. Importantly, the remedial competence of national courts is confined to *national* wrongs. They cannot give judgments on the non-contractual liability of the European Union. For the latter power is – like the power to annul Union law – an exclusive power of the Court of Justice of the European Union.[16]

Having analysed the three major constitutional principles governing the decentralised enforcement of European law 'in the absence of harmonisation', section 4 finally explores what happens in areas in which the Union has harmonised the remedial or jurisdictional competences of national courts. The most significant harmonisation here relates to the jurisdictional competences of

---

[14] Case 33/76, *Rewe*, para. 5. For the modern version, see Case C-312/93, *Peterbroeck, Van Campenhout & Cie* v. *Belgian State* [1995] ECR I-4599; Case C-61/14, *Orizzonte Salute – Studio Infermieristico Associato*, EU:C:2015:655, para. 46.

[15] The Court expressly refers to both principles: see Joined Cases C-392/04 and C-422/04 *i-21 Germany & Arcor* v. *Germany*, para. 57: '[A]ccording to settled case-law, in the absence of relevant [European] rules, the detailed procedural rules designed to ensure the protection of the rights which individuals acquire under [European] law are a matter for the domestic legal order of each Member State, under the principle of the procedural autonomy of the Member States, provided that they are not less favourable than those governing similar domestic situations (principle of equivalence) and that they do not render impossible in practice or excessively difficult the exercise of rights conferred by the [Union] legal order (principle of effectiveness).'

[16] See Joined Cases 106–20/87, *Asteris and others* [1988] ECR 5515, para. 15: '[T]he Court has exclusive jurisdiction pursuant to Article [268] of the [FEU] Treaty to hear actions for compensation brought against the [Union] under the second paragraph of Article [340] of the [FEU] Treaty.'

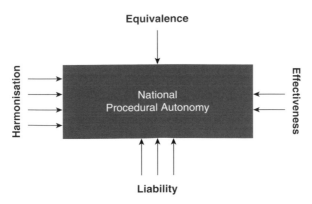

Figure 11.2 Limits on National Procedural Autonomy

national courts. This has allowed the Union to generally give national judgments transnational effects within the Union legal order. When, for example, will a judgment issued by a French or German court bind the judiciary in the United Kingdom? The most important Union harmonisation here relates to civil law but similar moves have been made in the context of criminal law.

1. The Equivalence Principle

The idea behind the principle of equivalence is straightforward: national procedures and remedies for the enforcement of European rights 'cannot be less favourable than those relating to similar actions of a domestic nature'.[17] When applying European law, national courts must act *as if* they were applying national law. National procedures and remedies must not discriminate between national and European rights. The equivalence principle simply demands that similar situations are treated similarly. It will consequently not affect the substance of national remedies. It only requires the *formal* extension of those remedies to 'similar' or 'equivalent' actions under European law. And, as such, the principle of equivalence is not too intrusive in the procedural autonomy of national courts.[18]

a. Non-discrimination: Extending National Remedies

A good example of the non-discrimination logic behind the equivalence principle can be seen in *i-21 Germany & Arcor* v. *Germany*.[19] The two plaintiffs were telecommunication companies that had paid licence fees to Germany. The

---

[17] Case 33/76, *Rewe*, para. 5.

[18] M. Dougan, *National Remedies before the Court of Justice: Issues of Harmonisation and Differentiation* (Hart, 2004), 26: 'Principles such as non-discrimination and equivalence implicitly assume that the remedies and procedural rules already provided under the domestic judicial orders are sufficient in scope and character to safeguard the exercise of the citizen's legal rights.'

[19] Joined Cases C-392/04 and C-422/04, *i-21 Germany & Arcor* v. *Germany*.

national fees had been calculated on the anticipated administrative costs of the respective national authority over a period of 30 years and were charged in advance. The companies successfully challenged the national law determining the assessment method before the Federal Administrative Court, which declared it to violate German constitutional law. The plaintiff companies then sought repayment of the fees they had already paid. However, the national court dismissed this second action on the grounds that the actual administrative decision had become final under national law. For under the German Administrative Procedure Act, a final administrative decision could only be challenged where the decision was 'downright intolerable'. For national law, this was not the case. But wondering whether it was required to apply a lower threshold for actions involving European law, the administrative court referred this question to the European Court.

Analysing the equivalence principle within this context, the European Court here held:

> [I]n relation to the principle of equivalence, this requires that all the rules applicable to appeals, including the prescribed timelimits, apply without distinction to appeals on the ground of infringement of [Union] law and to appeals on the ground of disregard of national law. It follows that, if the national rules applicable to appeals impose an obligation to withdraw an administrative act that is unlawful under domestic law, even though that act has become final, where to uphold that act would be 'downright intolerable', the same obligation to withdraw must exist under equivalent conditions in the case of an administrative act ... Where, pursuant to rules of national law, the authorities are required to withdraw an administrative decision which has become final if that decision is manifestly incompatible with domestic law, that same obligation must exist if the decision is manifestly incompatible with [Union] law.[20]

In the present case, the question whether the national decision was 'downright intolerable' or 'manifestly incompatible' with European law depended on the degree of clarity of the Union law at issue, and was an interpretative prerogative of the national court.[21] The European Court thus accepted the high *national* threshold for judicial challenges of final administrative acts, and demanded that it be applied, without discrimination, to European actions in national courts.

b. 'Similar' Actions: The Equivalence Test

The logic of non-discrimination requires that similar actions be treated similarly. But what are 'equivalent' or 'similar' actions? The devil always lies in the detail, and much case law on the equivalence principle has concentrated on this devilish question.

---

[20] *Ibid.*, paras. 62–3, 69.   [21] *Ibid.*, paras. 70–2.

In *Edis*,[22] a company had been required to pay a registration charge. Believing the charge to be contrary to European law, the plaintiff applied for a refund that was rejected by the Italian courts on the grounds that the limitation period for such refunds had expired. However, Italian law recognised various limitation periods – depending on whether the refund was due to be paid by public or private parties. The limitation period for public authorities was shorter than that for private parties. And this posed the following question: was the national court entitled to simply extend the national *public* refund procedure to charges in breach of European law; or was it required to apply the more generous *private* refund procedure? The Court answered as follows:

> Observance of the principle of equivalence implies, for its part, that the procedural rule at issue applies without distinction to actions alleging infringements of [Union] law and to those alleging infringements of national law, with respect to the same kind of charges or dues. *That principle cannot, however, be interpreted as obliging a Member State to extend its most favourable rules governing recovery under national law to all actions for repayment of charges or dues levied in breach of [European] law.* Thus, [European] law does not preclude the legislation of a Member State from laying down, alongside a limitation period applicable under the ordinary law to actions between private individuals for the recovery of sums paid but not due, special detailed rules, which are less favourable, governing claims and legal proceedings to challenge the imposition of charges and other levies. The position would be different only if those detailed rules applied solely to actions based on [European] law for the repayment of such charges or levies.[23]

In the present case, the 'equivalent' action was thus to be based on the national remedies that existed for refunds from *public* bodies. The existence of a more favourable limitation period for refunds from private parties was irrelevant, since the equivalence principle only required treating like actions alike. And the 'like' action in this case was the refund procedure applicable to a public body. The national procedural rules thus did not violate the principle of equivalence.[24]

But matters might not be so straightforward. In *Levez*,[25] the Employment Appeal Tribunal in London had asked the Court of Justice about the compatibility

---

[22] Case C-231/96, *Edilizia Industriale Siderurgica Srl (Edis)* v. *Ministero delle Finanze* [1998] ECR I-4951.

[23] *Ibid.*, paras. 36–7 (emphasis added).

[24] For a recent confirmation of this point, see Case C-61/14, *Orizzonte Salute – Studio Infermieristico Associato*, para. 67: '[T]he principle of equivalence requires that actions based on an infringement of national law and similar actions based on an infringement of EU law be treated equally and not that there be equal treatment of national procedural rules applicable to proceedings of a different nature such as civil proceedings, on the one hand, and administrative proceedings, on the other, or applicable to proceedings falling within two different branches of law.'

[25] Case C-326/96, *Levez* v. *Jennings (Harlow Pools) Ltd* [1998] ECR I-7835.

of section 2(5) of the 1970 Equal Pay Act with the equivalence principle. The national law provided that, in proceedings brought in respect of a failure to comply with the equal pay principle, women were not entitled to arrears of remuneration or damages of more than two years. The provision applied irrespective of whether a plaintiff enforced her *national* or *European* right to equal pay. Did this not mean that the equivalence principle was respected?

The European Court did *not* think so, as it questioned the underlying comparative base. As the national legislation was designed to implement the European right to equal pay, the Court held that the national law 'cannot therefore provide an appropriate ground of comparison against which to measure compliance with the principle of equivalence'.[26] Remedies for equal pay rights needed to be compared with national remedies for 'claims similar to those based on the Act', such as remedies for breach of a contract of employment or discrimination on grounds of race.[27] The equivalence principle indeed demanded the application of the more generous national remedies available under these more *general* national actions.

In conclusion, the equivalence principle requires national courts to ask, 'whether the actions concerned are similar as regards their purpose, cause of action and essential characteristics'.[28] This teleological comparability test might require the courts to look beyond the national procedural regime for a specific national or European right.

2. The Effectiveness Principle

From the very beginning, the European Court recognised the heightened tension between the (relative) procedural autonomy of the Member States and the principle of effectiveness. Although the equivalence principle simply required the *formal* extension of the *scope* of national remedies to equivalent European rights, the effectiveness principle appeared to ask national legal systems to provide for a *substantive* minimum *content* that would guarantee the enforcement of European rights in national courts. Thus, even where the equivalence principle would be of no assistance because no similar national remedy existed, the effectiveness principle could still require the strengthening of national remedies.

The power of the effectiveness principle to interfere with the principle of national procedural autonomy was therefore – from the start – much greater. Yet the European Court began to develop the principle from a minimal standard. National remedies would solely be found inefficient, where they 'made it *impossible* in practice to exercise the rights which the national courts are obliged to protect'.[29] This effectiveness standard has developed with time, and in various directions. For the sake of convenience, three historic standards may be

---

[26] *Ibid.*, para. 48.   [27] *Ibid.*, para. 49.

[28] Case C-78/98, *Preston et al.* v. *Wolverhampton Healthcare NHS Trust and others* [2000] ECR I-3201, para. 57: 'the national court must consider whether the actions concerned are similar as regards their purpose, cause of action and essential characteristics'.

[29] Case 33/76, *Rewe*, para. 5.

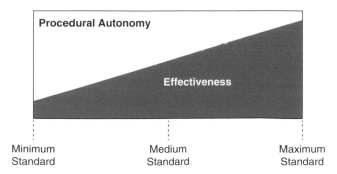

Figure 11.3 Standards of Effectiveness

distinguished. In addition to the minimum standard of practical impossibility, the Court has referred to the medium standard of an 'adequate' remedy,[30] and to the maximum standard guaranteeing the 'full effectiveness' of European law.[31] When and where do these three different standards apply? The Court's jurisprudence on this question has been disastrously unclear. The best way to analyse the cases is to identify general historical periods in addition to a variety of specific thematic lines.[32] This section indeed cannot do justice to the subtlety – or chaos – within this area of European law. We shall confine ourselves to outlining the three broad temporal periods in the general development of the effectiveness principle, and subsequently look inside one specific thematic line within the case law.

a. The Historical Evolution of the Effectiveness Standard

The academic literature on the effectiveness principle typically distinguishes between three – broadly defined – periods of evolution. A first period of *restraint* is replaced by a period of *intervention*, which is in turn replaced by a period of *balance*.[33] The three standards and their (inverse) relationship to the principle of national procedural autonomy can be seen in Figure 11.3.

aa. First Period: Judicial Restraint

In a first period, the European Court showed much restraint and respect towards the procedural autonomy of the Member States. The Court pursued a policy of judicial minimalism.[34] The standard for an 'effective remedy' was low and simply

---

[30] Case 14/83, *Von Colson*, para. 23.
[31] Case C-213/89, *The Queen v. Secretary of State for Transport, ex p. Factortame Ltd and others* [1990] ECR I-2433, para. 21.
[32] For illustrations of this – brilliant and necessary – approach, see Dougan, *National Remedies*, chs. 5–6; (n. 18 above); T. Tridimas, *The General Principles of EU Law* (Oxford University Press, 2006), ch. 9.
[33] A. Arnull, *The European Union and Its Court of Justice* (Oxford University Press, 2006), 268; Dougan, *National Remedies* (n. 18 above), 227; Tridimas, *General Principles* (n. 32 above), 420ff.
[34] A. Ward, *Judicial Review and the Rights of Private Parties in EC Law* (Oxford University Press, 2007), 87.

required that national judicial procedures must not make the enforcement of European rights (virtually) impossible.

This first period is exemplified by *Rewe*.[35] In that case, the plaintiff had applied for a refund of monies that had been charged in contravention of European law. The defendant accepted the illegality of the charges under European law, but counterclaimed that the limitation period for a refund, which existed under national law, had expired. The Court accepted that the existence of a *national* limitation period did not make the enforcement of *European* rights as such impossible and found for the defendant. The judgment was confirmed, in nearly identical terms, on the same day by a second case.[36] The Court's judicial minimalism was thereby premised on the hope of future legislative harmonisation by the Union.[37] And, with the latter not forthcoming,[38] the Court moved into a second phase in the evolution of the principle of effectiveness.

bb. Second Period: Judicial Intervention

In this second period, the Court developed a much more demanding standard of 'effectiveness'. In *Von Colson*,[39] two female job applicants for a warden position in an all-male prison had been rejected. The State prison service had indisputably discriminated against them on the grounds that they were women. Their European right to equal treatment had thus been violated, and the question arose how this violation could be remedied under national law. The remedy under German law exclusively allowed for damages, and these damages were furthermore restricted to the plaintiffs' travel expenses. Was this an effective remedy for the enforcement of their European rights? Or would European law require 'the employer in question to conclude a contract of employment with the candidate who was discriminated' against?[40]

The Court rejected this specific remedy.[41] For the enforcement of European law would 'not require any specific form of sanction for unlawful discrimination'.[42]

---

[35] Case 33/76, *Rewe*.

[36] Case 45/76, *Comet BV* v. *Produktschap voor Siergewassen*.

[37] Arnull, *European Union* (n. 33 above), 276 – referring to Case 130/79, *Express Dairy Foods Limited* v. *Intervention Board for Agricultural Produce* [1980] ECR 1887, para. 12: 'In the regrettable absence of [Union] provisions harmonising procedure and time-limits the Court finds this situation entails differences in treatment on a [European] scale. It is not for the Court to issue general rules of substance or procedural provisions which only the competent institutions may adopt.'

[38] For an exception to the rule, see Art. 6 of Directive 76/207 on the implementation of the principle of equal treatment for men and women as regards access to employment, vocational training and promotion, and working conditions [1976] OJ L 39/40. The provision stated: 'Member States shall introduce into their national legal systems such measures as are necessary to enable all persons who consider themselves wronged by failure to apply to them the principle of equal treatment within the meaning of Articles 3, 4 and 5 to pursue their claims by judicial process after possible recourse to other competent authorities.'

[39] Case 14/83, *Von Colson*.

[40] This was the first (preliminary) question asked by the German labour law court (*ibid.*, para. 6).

[41] *Ibid.*, para. 19.   [42] *Ibid.*, para. 23.

The Court nonetheless clarified that the effectiveness principle required that the national remedy 'be such as to guarantee real and effective judicial protection'.[43] The remedy would need to have 'a real deterrent effect on the employer', and in the context of a compensation claim this meant that the latter 'must in any event be *adequate* in relation to the damage sustained'.[44] Unsurprisingly, the German procedural rule that limited the compensation claim so dramatically did not satisfy this standard of effectiveness.[45]

Instead of a minimum standard, the Court here started to move to a standard that aspired *towards* the full effectiveness of European law. In *Dekker*,[46] the Court thus outlawed national procedural restrictions that 'weakened considerably'[47] the effectiveness of the European right to equal treatment; and in *Marshall II*,[48] it repeated its demand that where financial compensation was chosen to remedy a violation of European law, the compensatory damages 'must be *adequate*, in that it must enable the loss and damage actually sustained as a result of the discrimi-natory dismissal *to be made good in full*'.[49]

The most famous intervention in the procedural autonomy of a Member State is however reserved to another English case: *Factortame*.[50] The facts of the case were as follows: the appellant company was incorporated under English law, but most of its shareholders were Spanish nationals. It had registered fishing vessels under the 1894 Merchant Shipping Act – a practice that allowed its Spanish shareholders to benefit from the fishing quota allocated to Great Britain under the Union's common fishing policy. This practice of 'quota hopping' was targeted by the 1988 Merchant Shipping Act. This Act aimed at stopping Britain's quota being 'plundered' by 'vessels flying the British flag but lacking any genuine link with the United Kingdom'.[51] The 1988 Act consequently limited the rereg-istration of all vessels to vessels that were 'British owned' and controlled from within the United Kingdom. But this nationality requirement violated the non-discrimination principle on which the European internal market is founded, and Factortame challenged the compatibility of the 1988 Act with European law. In order to protect its European rights in the meantime, it applied for interim relief, since it found that it would become insolvent if the national legislation were immediately applied.

The case went to the (then) House of Lords; and the House of Lords did find that the substantive conditions for granting interim relief were in place but famously held that:

---

[43] *Ibid.*   [44] *Ibid.*   [45] *Ibid.*, para. 24.

[46] Case C-177/88, *Dekker* v. *Stichting Vormingscentrum voor Jong Volwassenen (VJV-Centrum) Plus* [1990] ECR I-3941.

[47] *Ibid.*, para. 24.

[48] Case C-271/91, *Marshall* v. *Southampton and South-West Hampshire Area Health Authority* [1993] ECR I-4367.

[49] *Ibid.*, para. 26 (emphasis added).

[50] Case C-213/89, *The Queen* v. *Secretary of State for Transport, ex p. Factortame Ltd and others* [1990] ECR I-2433.

[51] *Ibid.*, para. 4.

[U]nder national law, the English courts had no power to grant interim relief in a case such as the one before it … [as] the grant of such relief was precluded by the old common-law rule that an interim injunction may not be granted against the Crown, that is to say against the government, in conjunction with the presumption that an Act of Parliament is in conformity with [European] law until such time as a decision on its compatibility with that law has been given.[52]

Unsure whether this common law rule itself violated the effectiveness principle under European law, the House of Lords referred the case as a preliminary reference to Luxembourg. The European Court answered as follows:

[A]ny provision of a national legal system and any legislative, administrative or judicial practice which might impair the effectiveness of [European] law by withholding from the national court having jurisdiction to apply such law the power to do everything necessary at the moment of its application to set aside national legislative provisions which might prevent, even temporarily, [European] rules from having full force and effect are incompatible with those requirements, which are the very essence of [European] law. It must be added that the *full effectiveness* of [European] law would be just as much impaired if a rule of national law could prevent a court seised of a dispute governed by [European] law from granting interim relief in order *to ensure the full effectiveness of the judgment to be given on the existence of the rights claimed under [European] law*. It follows that a court which in those circumstances would grant interim relief, if it were not for a rule of national law, is obliged to set aside that rule.[53]

While short of creating a new remedy,[54] this came very close to demanding a maximum standard of effectiveness. Yet the Court soon withdrew from this highly interventionist stance and thereby entered into a third period in the evolution of the effectiveness principle.[55]

---

[52] *Ibid.*, para. 13.

[53] *Ibid.*, paras. 20–1 (emphasis added).

[54] A. G. Toth, 'Case Commentary' (1990) 27 *CML Rev.* 573 at 586: 'It follows that the judgment does not purport to lay down substantive conditions for the grant of interim protection, nor to define the measures that may be ordered. Still less does it require the national courts to devise interim relief where none exists. What it requires is that national courts should make use of any interim measure that is normally available under national law, in order to protect rights claimed under [European] law.'

[55] This section will *not* discuss the (in)famous *Emmott* judgment (see Case C-208/90, *Emmott v. Minister for Social Welfare and Attorney General* [1991] ECR I-4269), as the ruling should best be confined to the special context dealing with the nature of directives (*ibid.*, para. 17: 'Whilst the laying down of reasonable time-limits which, if unobserved, bar proceedings, in principle satisfies the two conditions mentioned above [i.e. the equivalence and effectiveness principles], account must nevertheless be taken of the particular nature of directives'). Moreover, the judgment was particularly motivated by a desire for substantive justice that clouded the judgment's formal legal value. The judgment's peculiar and special character

cc. Third Period: Judicial Balance

In this third period, the Court tried and – still – tries to find a balance between the minimum and the maximum standard of effectiveness.[56] The retreat from the second period of high intervention can be seen in *Steenhorst-Neerings*,[57] where the Court developed a distinction between national procedural rules whose effect was to totally *preclude* individuals from enforcing European rights and those national rules that merely *restrict* their remedies.[58]

In *Preston*,[59] the Court had again to deal with the 1970 Equal Pay Act whose s. 2(4) barred any claim that was not brought within a period of six months following cessation of employment. And, instead of concentrating on the 'full effectiveness' or 'adequacy' of the national remedy, the Court stated that '[s]uch a limitation period does not render impossible *or excessively difficult* the exercise of rights conferred by the [European] legal order and is not therefore liable to strike at the very essence of those rights'.[60] The Court here had recourse to a – stronger – alternative to the minimal impossibility standard: national procedures that would make the exercise of European rights 'excessively difficult' would fall foul of the principle of effectiveness.[61] This medium standard appeared to lie in between the minimum and the maximum standard.

When would this medium standard of effectiveness be violated? Instead of providing hard and fast rules, the Court has come to prefer a contextual test spelled out for the first time in *Peterbroeck*.[62] In order to discover whether a national procedural rule makes the enforcement of European rights 'excessively difficult', the Court analyses each case 'by reference to the role of that provision in the procedure, its progress and its special features, viewed as a whole, before

---

was indeed quickly realised by the Court (see Case C-410/92, *Johnson* v. *Chief Adjudication Officer* [1994] ECR I-5483, para. 26), which has, ever since, constructed it restrictively. On the – almost immediate – demise of *Emmott*, see M. Hoskins, 'Tilting the Balance: Supremacy and National Procedural Rules' (1996) 21 *EL Rev.* 365.

[56] F. G. Jacobs, 'Enforcing Community Rights and Obligations in National Courts: Striking the Balance', in A. Biondi and J. Lonbay (eds.), *Remedies for Breach of EC Law* (Wiley, 1996). See also Dougan, *National Remedies* (n. 18 above), 29: 'There has been a definite retreat back towards the orthodox presumption of national autonomy in the provision of judicial protection. But the contemporary principle of effectiveness surely remains more intrusive than the case law of the 1970s and early 1980s.'

[57] Case C-338/91, *Steenhorst-Neerings* v. *Bestuur van de Bedrijfsvereniging voor Detailhandel, Ambachten en Huisvrouwen* [1993] ECR I-5475.

[58] On the distinction, see Ward, *Judicial Review* (n. 34 above), 131. The distinction was elaborated in Case C-31/90, *Johnson* v. *Chief Adjudication Officer* [1991] ECR I-3723.

[59] Case C-78/98, *Preston et al.* v. *Wolverhampton Healthcare NHS Trust and others* [2000] ECR I-3201.

[60] *Ibid.*, para. 34 (emphasis added).

[61] For a recent confirmation of this 'excessively difficult' standard, see Case C-61/14, *Orizzonte Salute – Studio Infermieristico Associato*, para. 46; Case C-377/14, *Radlinger & Radlingerová* v. *Finway*, EU:C:2016:283, para. 50.

[62] Case C-312/93, *Peterbroeck, Van Campenhout & Cie SCS* v. *Belgian State* [1995] ECR I-4599.

the various national instances'.[63] It would thereby take into account 'the basic principles of the domestic judicial system, such as protection of the rights of the defence, the principle of legal certainty and the proper conduct of procedure'.[64] The results of this contextual test will be hard to predict as the Court emphasises the case-by-case nature of its analysis. Instead of hard rules, the Court's test is here based on a balancing act between different procedural interests – not dissimilar to a proportionality analysis.

May this balanced approach sometimes require national courts to create 'new remedies' for the enforcement of European rights? The obligation to create new remedies had been expressly rejected in the first historical phase of the effectiveness principle.[65] However, the Court appears to have confirmed this possibility within its third historical phase.

In *Unibet*,[66] the plaintiff sought a declaration by the Swedish courts that Swedish legislation violated the EU Treaties' free movement provisions. However, there existed no Swedish court procedure that allowed for an *abstract* review of national legislation in light of European law. An individual who wished to challenge a national rule would have to break national law first and then challenge it in national proceedings brought against him. Did the non-existence of a freestanding European review procedure violate the principle that there must be an effective remedy in national law?[67]

Synthesising the two previous periods of its case law, the Court emphasised that the Treaties were 'not intended to create new remedies in the national courts to ensure the observance of [European] law other than those already laid down by national law', *unless* 'it were apparent from the overall scheme of the national legal system in question that no legal remedy existed which made it possible to ensure, even indirectly, respect for an individual's rights under [European] law'.[68] Using its *Peterbroeck* test,[69] the Court found that there existed various indirect ways that did not make it 'excessively difficult' to challenge the compatibility of Swedish legislation with European law.[70] The request for a freestanding action was consequently denied. Yet, the Court had expressly accepted – for the first time – that the creation of new national remedies might exceptionally be required by the effectiveness principle.

Has the Lisbon Treaty changed the balance between the principle of national procedural autonomy and the effectiveness principle once more? The argument

---

63 *Ibid.*, para. 14.
64 *Ibid.* For a confirmation of this contextual test, see Case C-2/08, *Fallimento Olimpiclub*, EU:C:2009:506, esp. para. 27; Case C-377/14, *Radlinger & Radlingerová v. Finway*, para. 50.
65 Case 158/80, *Rewe-Handelsgesellschaft Nord mbH and Rewe-Markt Steffen v. Hauptzollamt Kiel (Butter-Cruises)* [1981] ECR 1805.
66 Case C-432/05, *Unibet v. Justitiekanslern* [2007] ECR I-2271. But see also Case C-253/00, *Muñoz & Superior Fruiticola v. Frumar & Redbridge Produce Marketing* [2002] ECR I-7289.
67 This was the first preliminary question in Case C-432/05, *Unibet*, para. 36.
68 *Ibid.*, paras. 40 and 41 (with reference to Case 158/80, *Rewe (Butter-Cruises)*).
69 Case 432/05, *Unibet*, para. 54 (with reference to Case C-312/93, *Peterbroeck*, para. 14).
70 Case 432/05, *Unibet*, para. 64.

could be made in light of the newly introduced Article 19(1) TEU and its insistence that 'Member States shall provide remedies sufficient to ensure effective legal protection in the fields covered by Union law'. However, the Court has recently confirmed the *Unibet* status quo.[71]

Constitutional continuity has also been confirmed with regard to the – after 2009 – binding EU Charter of Fundamental Rights. Although Article 47 EU Charter now expressly states that '[e]veryone whose rights and freedoms guaranteed by the law of the Union are violated has the right to an effective remedy before a tribunal', this right already existed prior to the Lisbon Treaty. And, while national courts are indeed bound by the provision when enforcing Union law,[72] the fundamental right to an effective remedy will only set an absolute minimum floor to national procedural systems.[73]

b. Procedural Limits to the Invocability of European Law

Having looked at the general evolution of the effectiveness standard in the previous section, this section will concentrate on a special thematic line within the latest historical period of the principle. This jurisprudential line concerns national procedural regimes governing the invocation of European law in national proceedings.

In many national legal orders, civil procedures are based on the principle that private parties are free to determine the content of their case.[74] The rationale behind this principle is private party autonomy. Unless a legal rule is seen as mandatorily applicable on grounds of public policy, a court may only apply those legal rules privately invoked. But even in administrative proceedings, a private party might sometimes be required to invoke its rights at the correct judicial stage. And where a party has failed to invoke a favourable right at first instance, but discovers its existence on appeal, legal certainty might prevent it from invoking it subsequently.

How have these principles been applied to the invocation of European law in national proceedings?[75] Will the effectiveness principle require national courts

---

[71]   Case C-583/11 P, *Inuit v. Parliament and Council*, EU:C:2013:625, paras. 103–4.

[72]   We shall see below that while EU fundamental rights are principally addressed to the Union institutions, national courts are also bound when implementing EU law. On this point, see Chapter 12, section 4.

[73]   See in particular Case C-279/09, *DEB v. Germany* [2010] ECR I-13849. For an excellent analysis of the (non-)relationship and differences between the principle of effectiveness and the principle of judicial protection in the EU Charter, see: J. Krommendijk, 'Is There Light on the Horizon? The Distinction between "*Rewe* effectiveness" and the Principle of Effective Judicial Protection in Article 47 of the Charter after *Orizzonte*' (2016) 53 *CML Rev.* 1395, esp. 1404ff.

[74]   On the distinction between 'adversarial' and 'inquisitorial' procedural systems, see M. Glendon et al., *Comparative Legal Traditions* (Thomson, 2007).

[75]   This *procedural* problem is distinct from the *structural* problem whether national courts might be prevented altogether from applying European law. For this structural problem within Europe's judicial federalism, see Chapter 10, section 4(b/aa).

to apply European law as a matter of public policy? Or has the European legal order followed a balanced approach according to which the national procedures apply unless they make the enforcement of European law excessively difficult?

These complex procedural questions were tackled in *Peterbroeck*.[76] The plaintiff claimed that a Belgian law violated its free movement rights. Unfortunately, the plea had not been raised in the first-instance proceedings; nor had it been invoked in the possible time limit prior to the appeal proceedings. Belgian procedural law consequently prevented the appeal court from considering the European law question; yet, thinking that this procedural limitation might itself violate European law, the national court referred a preliminary question to the Court of Justice.

In its answer, the European Court developed its contextual test to discover whether the application of national procedures rendered the application of European law 'excessively difficult'.[77] And the Court held that this was the case in the present context. Finding that the first-instance court had been unable to make a preliminary reference as it was not a 'court or tribunal' in the sense of Article 267 TFEU,[78] the time limit for raising new pleas prior to appeals was considered excessively short. The obligation not to raise points of European law of its own motion thus did 'not appear to be reasonably justifiable by principles such as the requirement of legal certainty or the proper conduct of procedure'.[79]

But did this mean that national courts were positively required, as a matter of general principle, to invoke European law *ex officio*? In a judgment delivered on the very same day, the Court answered this question in the negative. In *Van Schijndel*,[80] the Court added an important caveat to the effectiveness principle. The Court held:

> [T]he domestic law principle that in civil proceedings a court must or may raise points of its own motion is limited by its obligation to keep to the subject-matter of the dispute and to base its decision on the facts put before it. That limitation is justified by the principle that, in a civil suit, it is for the parties to take the initiative, the court being able to act of its own motion only in exceptional cases where the public interest requires its intervention. That principle reflects conceptions prevailing in most of the Member States as to the relations between the State and the individual; it safeguards the rights of the defence; and it ensures proper conduct of proceedings by, in particular, protecting them from the delays inherent in the examination of new pleas.[81]

---

[76] Case C-312/93, *Peterbroeck*.

[77] On this point, see *ibid*.

[78] *Ibid*., para. 17.   [79] *Ibid*., para. 20.

[80] Joined Cases C-430/93 and C-431/93, *Van Schijndel and Johannes Nicolaas Cornelis van Veen* v. *Stichting Pensioenfonds voor Fysiotherapeuten* [1995] ECR I-4705.

[81] *Ibid*., paras. 20–1. See also Case C-126/97, *Eco Swiss China Time Ltd* v. *Benetton International NV* [1999] ECR I-3055, para. 46: 'Moreover, domestic procedural rules which, upon the expiry of that period, restrict the possibility of applying for annulment of a subsequent arbitration award proceeding upon an interim arbitration award which is in the nature

This suggests that while the equivalence principle may oblige national courts to raise European law of their own motion,[82] the effectiveness principle hardly ever will. The Court will here only challenge national procedural rules that make the enforcement of European rights 'virtually impossible or excessively difficult'.[83]

This medium standard of effectiveness was subsequently confirmed and refined.[84] And we find a good clarification and classification of the case law within this jurisprudential line in *Van der Weerd*.[85] The Court here expressly distinguished *Peterbroeck* as a special case 'by reasons of circumstances peculiar to the dispute which led to the applicant in the main proceedings being deprived of the opportunity to rely effectively on the incompatibility of a domestic provision with [European] law'.[86] But more importantly: the Court identified two key factors in determining when it considers the effectiveness principle to demand the *ex officio* application of European law. First, it emphasised that it would be hesitant to interfere with the procedural autonomy of the national court, where the parties had 'a genuine opportunity to raise a plea based on [Union] law'.[87] National courts will therefore generally not be asked to forsake their passive role in private law actions. However, second, the question whether an *ex officio* application of EU law was constitutionally required was dependent on the importance of the respective European law at issue.

This second factor explains why the Court has been much more demanding in cases involving consumer protection.[88] For the Court treats this area of

---

of a final award, because it has become res judicata, are justified by the basic principles of the national judicial system, such as the principle of legal certainty and acceptance of res judicata, which is an expression of that principle.'

[82] Joined Cases C-430/93 and C-431/93, *Van Schijndel*, para. 13: 'Where, by virtue of domestic law, courts or tribunals must raise of their own motion points of law based on binding domestic rules which have not been raised by the parties, such an obligation also exists where binding [European] rules are concerned.'

[83] Case C-40/08, *Asturcom Telecomunicaciones v. Rodríguez Nogueira* [2009] ECR I-9579, para. 46.

[84] See Case C-126/97, *Eco Swiss China Time*; Case C-240/98, *Océano Grupo Editorial v. Rocío Murciano Quintero* [2000] ECR I-4941; Joined Cases C-397/98 and C-410/98, *Metallgesellschaft et al. v. Commissioners of Inland Revenue et al.* [2001] ECR I-1727; Case C-2/06, *Kempter v. Hauptzollamt Hamburg-Jonas* [2008] ECR I-411.

[85] Case C-222/05, *Van der Weerd et al. v. Minister van Landbouw, Natuur en Voedselkwaliteit* [2007] ECR I-4233.

[86] *Ibid.*, para. 40.

[87] *Ibid.*, para. 41.

[88] See Case C-243/08, *Pannon v. Erzsébet Sustikné Győrfi* [2009] ECR I-4713. The judgment was subsequently confirmed in Case C-618/10, *Banco Espanol de Crédito* EU:C:2012:349. In Case C-377/14, *Radlinger & Radlingerová v. Finway*, the Court has even referred to the obligation to assess of its own motion EU consumer law as 'settled case-law of the Court' and held that 'the imbalance which exists between the consumer and the seller or supplier may be corrected by the court hearing such disputes only by positive action unconnected with the actual parties to the contract' (*ibid.*, paras. 52–3). The exact constitutional principles within this area are not too clear however. For an overview of the relevant case law, see M. Ebers, 'From *Océano* to *Asturcom*: Mandatory Consumer Law, *ex officio* Application

European law as an expression of 'European public policy'. The same approach seems to apply to EU competition law, which the Court considers 'a matter of public policy which must be automatically applied by national courts'.[89]

3. The Liability Principle

The original European Treaties appeared to exclusively accept national remedies when it came to the decentralised enforcement of European law. For the EU Treaties were apparently 'not intended to create new remedies in the national courts to ensure the observance of [Union] law other than those already laid down by national law'.[90] This apparent competence limit was to protect the procedural autonomy of the Member States. For even if the Court had pushed for a degree of (judicial) harmonisation in the decentralised enforcement of European law via the principles of equivalence and effectiveness, it would be *national* remedies whose scope or substance was extended.

But what would happen if no national remedy existed at all? Would the non-existence of such a national remedy not be an absolute barrier to the enforcement of a European right? Theoretically, this should indeed be the end of the story; yet in what was perceived as a dramatic turn of events, the European Court renounced its earlier position and proclaimed a *European* remedy for breaches of European law in *Francovich*.[91] The Court now insisted that in certain situations individuals must always be able to sue, where the State was liable for losses caused by its violation of European law.[92]

What are the conditions for State liability in the European Union? Will every breach trigger the liability principle? We shall look at these questions first, before analysing whether the principle only applies against the State or also captures private party actions. The Court indeed appears to have extended the liability principle from violations of European law by public authorities to breaches of European law by private parties.

a. State Liability: The Francovich Doctrine

Under the principle of effectiveness, national remedies must not make the enforcement of European law excessively difficult. But this did not mean that *States* would have to compensate all damage resulting from their breaches of

of European Union Law and *res judicata*' (2010) *European Review of Private Law* 823; H.-W. Micklitz and N. Reich, 'The Court and Sleeping Beauty: The Revival of the Unfair Terms Directive (UTD)' (2014) 51 *CML Rev.* 771 at 780ff.
[89] Case C-295/04, *Manfredi* v. *Lloyd Adriatico Assicurazioni SpA* [2006] ECR I-6619, para. 31.
[90] Case 158/80, *Rewe (Butter-Cruises)*. We saw above that the Court appears to have recently changed its view with regard to the principle of effectiveness.
[91] Joined Cases C-6/90 and C-9/90, *Francovich and Bonifaci et al.* v. *Italy* [1991] ECR I-5357.
[92] This European remedy contrasts favourably with the absence of such a remedy in the US legal order. In the United States, the doctrine of 'sovereign immunity' offers the Member States a shield against liability actions for damages resulting from a violation of Union law.

European law. The essential question for a long time therefore was 'whether [European] law requires the national courts to acknowledge a right to damages vested in the victims of the violation of [European] law and to order public authorities, found to have infringed [European] law, to pay compensation to such persons, and if so, in which circumstances and according to which criteria'.[93]

For a long time, the Court had been ambivalent towards this question. While in one case it had positively found that a State's violation of European law required it '*to make reparation* for any unlawful consequences which may have ensued',[94] in another case it held that if 'damage has been caused through an infringement of [European] law the State is liable to the injured party of the consequences *in the context of the provisions of national law on the liability of the State*'.[95] Did this mean that the liability of the State depended on the existence of such a remedy in *national* law?[96] Or, did the Court have an independent *European* remedy in mind? This question was long undecided – even if for a clairvoyant observer there was 'little doubt that one future day the European Court will be asked to say, straightforwardly, whether [European] law requires a remedy in damages to be made available in the national courts'.[97]

This day came on 8 January 1990. On that day, the Court received a series of preliminary questions in *Francovich and others* v. *Italy*.[98] The facts of the case are memorably sad.[99] Italy had flagrantly flouted its obligations under the EU Treaties by failing to implement a European directive designed to protect employees in the event of their employer's insolvency.[100] The directive had required Member States to pass national legislation guaranteeing the payment of outstanding wages. Francovich had been employed by an Italian company, but had hardly received any wages. Having brought proceedings against his employer, the latter had gone insolvent. For that reason he brought a separate action against the Italian State to cover his losses. In the course of these second proceedings, the national court asked the European Court whether the State itself would be obliged to cover the losses of the employees. The European Court found that the directive had left the Member States a 'broad discretion with regard to the organisation, operation and

---

[93] A. Barav, 'Damages in the Domestic Courts for Breach of Community Law by National Public Authorities', in H. G. Schermers et al. (eds.), *Non-contractual Liability of the European Communities* (Nijhoff, 1988), 149.

[94] Case 6/60, *Humblet* v. *Belgium* [1960] ECR (English Special Edition) 559 at 569 (emphasis added).

[95] Case 60/75, *Russo* v. *Azienda di Stato per gli interventi sul mercato agricolo* [1976] ECR 45, para. 9 (emphasis added).

[96] For an (outdated) overview of the damages provisions in national law, see N. Green and A. Barav, 'Damages in the National Courts for Breach of Community Law' (1986) 6 *YEL* 55.

[97] Barav, 'Damages in the Domestic Courts' (n. 93 above), 165.

[98] Joined Cases C-6/90 and C-9/90, *Francovich*.

[99] Opinion of Advocate General Mischo (*ibid.*, para. 1): 'Rarely has the Court been called upon to decide a case in which the adverse consequences for the individuals concerned of failure to implement a directive were as shocking as in the case now before us.'

[100] The Court had already expressly condemned this failure in Case 22/87, *Commission* v. *Italian Republic* [1989] ECR 143.

financing of the guarantee institutions', and it therefore lacked direct effect.[101] It followed that 'the persons concerned cannot enforce those rights against the State before the national courts where no implementing measures are adopted within the prescribed period'.[102]

But this was not the end of the story! The Court – unhappy with the negative result flowing from the lack of direct effect – continued:

> [T]he principle whereby a State must be liable for loss and damage caused to individuals as a result of breaches of [European] law for which the State can be held responsible is inherent in the system of the Treaty. A further basis for the obligation of Member States to make good such loss and damage is to be found in Article [4(3)] of the Treaty [on European Union], under which the Member States are required to take all appropriate measures, whether general or particular, to ensure fulfilment of their obligations under [European] law. Among these is the obligation to nullify the unlawful consequences of a breach of [European] law. It follows from all the foregoing that it is a principle of [European] law that the Member States are obliged to make good loss and damage caused to individuals by breaches of [European] law for which they can be held responsible.[103]

The European Court here took a qualitative leap in the context of remedies. Up to this point, it could still be argued that the principle of national procedural autonomy precluded the creation of new – European – remedies, as the principles of equivalence and effectiveness solely required the extension of *national* remedies to violations of European law. With *Francovich* the Court clarified that the right to reparation for such violations was 'a right founded directly on [European] law'.[104] The action for State liability was thus a *European* remedy that had to be made available in the national courts.[105]

How did the Court justify this 'revolutionary' result? It had recourse to the usual constitutional suspects: the special nature of the European Treaties and the general duty under Article 4(3) TEU. A more sophisticated justification was added by a later judgment. In *Brasserie du Pêcheur*,[106] the Court thus found:

> Since the Treaty contains no provision expressly and specifically governing the consequences of breaches of [European] law by Member States, it is for the Court, in pursuance of the task conferred on it by Article [19] of the [EU] Treaty of ensuring that in the interpretation and application of the Treaty the law is observed, to rule on such a question in accordance with generally accepted methods of interpretation, in particular by reference to the fundamental principles of the [Union] legal

---

[101] Joined Cases C-6/90 and C-9/90, *Francovich*, para. 25.

[102] *Ibid.*, para. 27.   [103] *Ibid.*, paras. 33–7.   [104] *Ibid.*, para. 41.

[105] On the application of this new principle in the United Kingdom, see J. Convery, 'State Liability in the United Kingdom after *Brasserie du Pêcheur*' (1997) 34 *CML Rev.* 603.

[106] Joined Cases C-46/93 and C-48/93, *Brasserie du Pêcheur SA* v. *Bundesrepublik Deutschland and the Queen* v. *Secretary of State for Transport, ex p. Factortame Ltd and others* [1996] ECR I-1029.

> system and, where necessary, general principles common to the legal systems of the Member States. Indeed, it is to the general principles common to the laws of the Member States that the second paragraph of Article [340] of the [FEU] Treaty refers as the basis of the non-contractual liability of the [Union] for damage caused by its institutions or by its servants in the performance of their duties. The principle of the non-contractual liability of the [Union] expressly laid down in Article [340] of the [FEU] Treaty is simply an expression of the general principle familiar to the legal systems of the Member States that an unlawful act or omission gives rise to an obligation to make good the damage caused. That provision also reflects the obligation on public authorities to make good damage caused in the performance of their duties.[107]

The principle of State liability was thus rooted in the constitutional traditions common to the Member States and was equally recognised in the principle of *Union* liability for breaches of European law.[108] There was consequently a parallel between *State* liability and *Union* liability for tortious acts of public authorities; and this parallelism would have a decisive effect on the conditions for State liability for breaches of European law.

aa. The Three Conditions for State Liability

Having created the liability principle for State actions, the *Francovich* Court nonetheless made the principle dependent on the fulfilment of three conditions:

> The first of those conditions is that the result prescribed by the directive should entail the grant of rights to individuals. The second condition is that it should be possible to identify the content of those rights on the basis of the provisions of the directive. Finally, the third condition is the existence of a causal link between the breach of the State's obligation and the loss and damage suffered by the injured parties. Those conditions are sufficient to give rise to a right on the part of individuals to obtain reparation, a right founded directly on [European] law.[109]

The original liability test was thus as follows: European law must have been intended to grant individual rights, and these rights would – despite their potential lack of direct effect – have to be identifiable.[110] If this was the case, and

---

[107]   *Ibid.*, paras. 27–9.

[108]   On this point, see Chapter 10, section 2.

[109]   Joined Cases C-6/90 and C-9/90, *Francovich*, paras. 40–1.

[110]   For an analysis of this criterion, see Dougan, *National Remedies* (n. 18 above), 238ff. For a case in which the European Court found that a directive did not grant rights, see Case C-222/02, *Paul et al. v. Germany* [2004] ECR I-9425, para. 51: 'Under those conditions, and for the same reasons as those underlying the answers given above, the directives cannot be regarded as conferring on individuals, in the event that their deposits are unavailable as a result of defective supervision on the part of the competent national authorities, rights capable of giving rise to liability on the part of the State on the basis of [European] law.'

if European law was breached by a Member State not guaranteeing these rights, any loss that was caused by that breach could be reclaimed by the individual.[111] On its face, this test appeared to be complete and therefore one of *strict* liability: any breach of an identifiable European right would lead to State liability. But the Court subsequently clarified that this was *not* the case. The *Francovich* test was confined to the specific context of a flagrant non-implementation of a European directive.

Drawing on its jurisprudence on *Union* liability, the Court indeed introduced a much more restrictive principle of State liability in *Brasserie du Pêcheur*.[112] For the Court here clarified that State liability was to be confined to 'sufficiently serious' breaches. To cover up the fact that it had implicitly added a 'fourth' condition to its *Francovich* test, the Court replaced the new condition with the second criterion of its 'old' test. The new liability test could thus continue to insist on three – necessary and sufficient – conditions. However, it now read as follows:

> [European] law confers a right to reparation where three conditions are met: the rule of law infringed must be intended to confer rights on individuals; the breach must be sufficiently serious; and there must be a direct causal link between the breach of the obligation resting on the State and the damage sustained by the injured parties.[113]

The Court justified its limitation of State liability to 'sufficiently serious' breaches by reference to the wide discretion that Member States might enjoy, especially when exercising legislative powers. The 'limited liability' of the legislature is indeed a common constitutional tradition of the Member States and equally applies to the Union legislature. Where legislative functions are concerned, Member States 'must not be hindered by the prospect of actions for damages'.[114] The special democratic legitimacy attached to parliamentary legislation here provides an argument against public liability for breaches of private rights, 'unless the institution concerned has manifestly and gravely disregarded the limits on the exercise of its powers'.[115] And in analysing whether a breach was sufficiently serious in the sense of a 'manifest ... and grave ... disregard ...',

---

[111] For an analysis of this criterion, see Tridimas, *General Principles* (n. 32 above), 529–33. See particularly: Case C-319/96, *Brinkmann Tabakfabriken GmbH* v. *Skatteministeriet* [1998] ECR I-5255.

[112] Joined Cases C-46/93 and C-48/93, *Brasserie du Pêcheur*, para. 42: 'The protection of the rights which individuals derive from [European] law cannot vary depending on whether a national authority or a [Union] authority is responsible for the damage.'

[113] *Ibid.*, para. 51.

[114] *Ibid.*, para. 45.

[115] *Ibid.* See also Case C-392/93, *The Queen* v. *HM Treasury, ex p. British Telecommunications* [1996] ECR I-10631, para. 42.

the Court would balance a number of diverse factors,[116] such as the degree of discretion enjoyed by the Member States as well as the clarity of the Union norm breached.

Unfortunately, there are very few hard and fast rules to determine when a breach is sufficiently serious. Indeed, the second criterion of the *Brasserie* test has been subject to much uncertainty. Would the manifest and grave disregard test only apply to the legislative function? The Court appears to have answered this question in *Hedley Lomas*,[117] when dealing with the failure of the national *executive* to correctly apply European law. The Court here found:

> [W]here, at the time when it committed the infringement, the Member State in question was not called upon to make any legislative choices and had only considerably reduced, or even no, discretion, the mere infringement of [European] law may be sufficient to establish the existence of a sufficiently serious breach.[118]

This confirmed the potential liability of the executive branch and clarified that the less the discretion enjoyed by the latter, the more likely would be the liability of a State.[119] The Court here indeed seemed to acknowledge two alternatives within the second *Brasserie* condition – depending whether the State violated European law via its legislative or executive branch. The existence of these two alternatives would be confirmed in *Larsy*,[120] where the Court found:

> [A] breach of [European] law is sufficiently serious where a Member State, in the exercise of its legislative powers, has manifestly and gravely disregarded the limits on its powers and, secondly, that where, at the time when it committed the infringement, the Member State in question had only considerably reduced, or even no, discretion, the mere infringement of [European] law may be sufficient to establish the existence of a sufficiently serious breach.[121]

[116] Joined Cases C-46/93 and C-48/93, *Brasserie du Pêcheur*, para. 56: 'The factors which the competent court may take into consideration include the clarity and precision of the rule breached, the measure of discretion left by that rule to the national or [Union] authorities, whether the infringement and the damage caused was intentional or involuntary, whether any error of law was excusable or inexcusable, the fact that the position taken by a [Union] institution may have contributed towards the omission, and the adoption or retention of national measures or practices contrary to [European] law.'

[117] Case C-5/94, *The Queen v. Ministry of Agriculture, Fisheries and Food, ex p. Hedley Lomas* [1996] ECR I-2553.

[118] *Ibid.*, para. 28.

[119] Case C-424/97, *Haim v. Kassenzahnärztliche Vereinigung Nordrhein* [2000] ECR I-5123, para. 38. See also Case C-470/03, *A. G. M.-COS.MET et al. v. Suomen Valtio et al.* [2007] ECR I-2749.

[120] Case C-118/00, *Larsy v. Institut national d'assurances sociales pour travailleurs indépendants* [2001] ECR I-5063.

[121] *Ibid.*, para. 38.

With regard to executive breaches, the threshold for establishing state liability is thus much lower than the liability threshold for legislative actions. While the incorrect *application* of a clear European norm by the national executive will incur strict liability, the incorrect *implementation* of a directive by the national legislature may not.[122] However, the European Court strictly distinguishes the *incorrect* implementation of a directive from its *non*-implementation. The use of a stricter liability regime for legislative non-action makes much sense, for the failure of the State cannot be excused by reference to the *exercise* of legislative discretion. The Court has consequently held that the non-implementation of a directive could *per se* constitute a sufficiently serious breach.[123]

What about the third branch of government? Was the extension of State liability to national courts 'unthinkable'?[124] And, if it were not, would the Court extend its ordinary constitutional principles to judicial breaches of European law? The unthinkable thought deserves a special section.

bb. State Liability for Judicial Breaches of European Law

Common-sense intuition identifies the 'State' with its legislative and executive branches. The 'State' generally acts through its Parliament and its government or administration. Yet there exists of course a third power within the State: the judiciary. The benign neglect of the 'least dangerous branch' stems from two reductionist perceptions. First, the judiciary is reduced to a passive organ that merely represents the 'mouth of the law'.[125] Second, its independence from the legislature and executive is mistaken as an independence from the State. Both perceptions are of course misleading: for in adjudicating disputes between private parties and in controlling the other State branches, the judiciary exercises *State* functions. And, like the national executive, the national judiciary may breach European law by misapplying it in the national legal order. This misapplication could – theoretically – constitute a violation that triggers State liability under EU law.

---

[122] Joined Cases C-283 and C-291–2/94, *Denkavit et al.* v. *Bundesamt für Finanzen* [1996] ECR I-4845.

[123] Case C-178/94, *Dillenkofer* v. *Germany* [1996] ECR I-4845, para. 29: 'failure to take any measure to transpose a directive in order to achieve the result it prescribes within the period laid down for that purpose constitutes per se a serious breach of [European] law and consequently gives rise to a right of reparation for individuals suffering injury if the result prescribed by the directive entails the grant to individuals of rights whose content is identifiable and a causal link exists between the breach of the State's obligation and the loss and damage suffered'. Interestingly, as Tridimas points out, this may not necessarily be the case as a Member State may believe that its existing laws already fulfil the requirements of a directive (*General Principles* (n. 32 above), 506).

[124] H. Toner, 'Thinking the Unthinkable? State Liability for Judicial Acts after *Factortame* (III)' (1997) 17 YEL 165.

[125] Charles de Secondat, Baron de Montesquieu, *The Spirit of Laws* (translated and edited by T. Nugent, and revised by J. Prichard) (Bell, 1914); available at: www.constitution.org/cm/sol.htm), Book XI, ch. 6.

This theoretical possibility had implicitly been recognised by the *Brasserie* Court.[126] And the practical possibility was confirmed in *Köbler*.[127] Austrian legislation had granted a special length-of-service increment to professors having taught for 15 years at Austrian universities, without taking into account any service spent at universities of other Member States. The plaintiff – a university professor having taught abroad – brought an action before the Austrian Supreme Administrative Court, claiming that his free movement rights had been violated. Despite being a court 'against whose decision there is no judicial remedy under national law', the Supreme Administrative Court did not request a preliminary ruling from the Court of Justice as it – wrongly – believed the answer to the preliminary question to be clear.[128] As a consequence, it – wrongly – decided that the Austrian norm did not violate the plaintiff's directly effective free movement rights.

Not being able to appeal against the final decision, Köbler brought a new action for damages in a (lower) civil court. In the course of these civil proceedings, the national court asked the European Court of Justice whether the principle of State liability for breaches of European law extended to (wrong) judicial decisions. And the positive response was as follows:

> In the light of the essential role played by the judiciary in the protection of the rights derived by individuals from [European] rules, the full effectiveness of those rules would be called in question and the protection of those rights would be weakened if individuals were precluded from being able, under certain conditions, to obtain reparation when their rights are affected by an infringement of [European] law attributable to a decision of a court of a Member State adjudicating at last instance. It must be stressed, in that context, that a court adjudicating at last instance is by definition the last judicial body before which individuals may assert the rights conferred on them by [European] law. Since an infringement of those rights by a final decision of such a court cannot thereafter normally be corrected, individuals cannot be deprived of the possibility of rendering the State liable in order in that way to obtain legal protection of their rights.[129]

The liability for damages would thereby not undermine the independence of the judiciary. For the principle of State liability 'concerns not the personal

---

[126] The Court had here clarified that the principle of State liability 'holds good for any case in which a Member State breaches [European] law, *whatever the organ of the State* whose act or omission was responsible for the breach' (Joined Cases C-46/93 and C-48/93, *Brasserie du Pêcheur*, para. 32, emphasis added).

[127] Case C-224/01, *Köbler v. Austria* [2003] ECR I-10239. The facts of the case were slightly more complex than presented here. For a fuller discussion of the case, see M. Breuer, 'State Liability for Judicial Wrongs and Community Law: The Case of *Gerhard Köbler v. Austria*' (2004) 29 *EL Rev.* 243.

[128] On the obligation to refer preliminary questions for courts of last resort under Art. 267(3) TFEU and the *acte clair* doctrine, see Chapter 10, section 4(c).

[129] Case C-224/01, *Köbler*, paras. 33–4.

liability of the judge but that of the State'.[130] Nor would the idea of State liability for wrong judicial decisions call into question the constitutional principle of *res judicata*. After all, the *Francovich* remedy would not revise the judicial decision of a court, but provide damages for the wrong – final – judgment. The principle of State liability meant 'reparation, but not revision of the judicial decision which was responsible for the damage'.[131] But what if revision through an appeal was still possible in the national legal order? Will State liability for judicial acts of lower courts provide a complementary remedy? In line with the general character of State liability as a remedy of last resort,[132] this should be denied. The *Köbler* Court indeed appeared to confine the liability principle to national courts against whose decision there was no appeal.[133]

Having thus confirmed the possibility of *Francovich* liability for final courts,[134] would the substantive conditions for this liability differ from the ordinary criteria established in *Brasserie du Pêcheur?* The Court found that this was not the case: State liability for judicial decisions would be 'governed by the same conditions'.[135] What did this mean for the second prong of the *Brasserie* test requiring a 'sufficiently serious' breach of European law? For the Court this meant that State liability for a judicial decision would only arise 'in the *exceptional* case where the court has manifestly infringed the applicable law'.[136] And this depended on, *inter alia*, 'the degree of clarity and precision of the rule infringed, whether the infringement was intentional, whether the error of law was excusable or inexcusable'.[137] The Court thus aligned its test for judicial acts with the test for (discretionary) legislative acts. For unlike (non-discretionary) executive acts, liability for judicial behaviour could not simply be established by a misapplication of European law. Liability was limited to exceptional circumstances, where a *manifest* infringement of European law had occurred; and this was in particular the case, where the national court had disregarded the settled jurisprudence of the ECJ.[138]

---

[130] *Ibid.*, para. 42.   [131] *Ibid.*, para. 39.

[132] On this point, see Conclusion below.

[133] Case C-224/01, *Köbler*, para. 53 (emphasis added): 'State liability for an infringement of [European] law by a decision of a national court adjudicating *at last instance* can be incurred only in the exceptional case where the court has manifestly infringed the applicable law.'

[134] *Köbler* itself was subsequently confirmed in Case C-173/03, *Traghetti del Mediterraneo* v. *Italy* [2006] ECR I-5177.

[135] Case C-224/01, *Köbler*, para. 52. And the Court clarified in Case C-173/03, *Traghetti del Mediterraneo* that 'under no circumstances may such criteria impose requirements stricter than that of a manifest infringement of the applicable law, as set out in paragraphs 53 to 56 of the *Köbler* judgment' (*ibid.*, para. 44), and that European law thus 'precludes national legislation which limits such liability solely to cases of intentional fault' (*ibid.*, para. 46). For a discussion of this decision, see B. Beutler, 'State Liability for Breaches of Community Law by National Courts: Is the Requirement of a Manifest Infringement of the Applicable Law an Insurmountable Obstacle?' (2009) 46 *CML Rev.* 773.

[136] Case C-224/01, *Köbler*, para. 53.

[137] *Ibid.*, para. 55.   [138] *Ibid.*, para. 56.

In the present case, these conditions were not met. For although the Supreme Administrative Court had wrongly interpreted European law, its incorrect application of the Treaty was not 'manifest in nature' and thus did not constitute a sufficiently serious breach of European law.[139]

b. Private Liability: The Courage Doctrine

The idea of 'State liability' applies – it almost goes without saying – where the *State* is liable for a breach of European law. This *vertical* dimension of the liability principle has long been established, but what about the principle's *horizontal* dimension? While the principles of equivalence and effectiveness may require that breaches of European law by private parties be adequately compensated under *national* remedial law, will there be a *European* remedy according to which individuals are liable to pay damages for the losses suffered by other private parties?[140] From the very beginning, the Union legal order envisaged that European law could directly impose obligations on individuals.[141] But did this imply that a failure to fulfil these obligations could trigger the secondary obligation to make good the damage suffered by others?

The Court has given an ambivalent answer to this question in *Courage* v. *Crehan*.[142] The case concerned European competition law, which directly imposes obligations on private parties not to conclude anticompetitive agreements under Article 101 TFEU.[143] The plaintiff had brought an action against a public house tenant for the recovery of unpaid deliveries of beer. The tenant attacked the underlying beer-supply agreement by arguing that it was void as an anticompetitive restriction, and counterclaimed damages that resulted from the illegal agreement. However, under English law a party to an illegal agreement was not entitled to claim damages; and so the Court of Appeal raised the question whether this absolute bar to compensation itself violated European law. The European Court considered the issue as follows:

---

[139] *Ibid.*, paras. 120–4. For a similar result, see more recently Case C-168/15, *Tomášová* v. *Slovenská republika – Ministerstvo spravodlivosti SR*, EU:C:2016:602.

[140] In favour of this proposition, see Opinion of Advocate General van Gerven in Case C-128/92, *H. J. Banks & Co. Ltd* v. *British Coal Corporation* [1994] ECR I-1209, paras. 40–1: '[T]he question arises whether the value of the *Francovich* judgment as a precedent extends to action by an individual (or undertaking) against another individual (or undertaking) for damages in respect of breach by the latter of a Treaty provision which also has direct effect in relations between individuals … In my view, that question must be answered in the affirmative[.]'

[141] On this point, see Chapter 3, Introduction.

[142] Case C-453/99, *Courage* v. *Crehan* [2001] ECR I-6297.

[143] Art. 101(1) TFEU states: 'The following shall be prohibited as incompatible with the internal market: all agreements between undertakings, decisions by associations of undertakings and concerted practices which may affect trade between Member States and which have as their object or effect the prevention, restriction or distortion of competition within the internal market[.]'

The full effectiveness of Article [101] of the [FEU] Treaty and, in particular, the practical effect of the prohibition laid down in Article [101(1)] would be put at risk if it were not open to any individual to claim damages for loss caused to him by a contract or by conduct liable to restrict or distort competition. Indeed, the existence of such a right strengthens the working of the [European] competition rules and discourages agreements or practices, which are frequently covert, which are liable to restrict or distort competition. From that point of view, actions for damages before the national courts can make a significant contribution to the maintenance of effective competition in the [Union]. There should not therefore be any absolute bar to such an action being brought by a party to a contract which would be held to violate the competition rules.[144]

The Court here insisted on damages for losses suffered by a breach of European competition law by a private party. But was this a *national* or a *European* remedy? The original ambivalence surrounding the principle of State liability now embraced the principle of private liability.[145]

Did *Courage* represent a horizontal extension of the liability principle? On a minimal reading, the ruling could be regarded as a simple application of the principle of effectiveness.[146] After all, the last sentence of the above passage seemed to outlaw a restriction to a *national* remedy. And the Court did not place its reasoning inside the *Brasserie* test. On a maximal reading, by contrast, *Courage* could be seen as a new constitutional doctrine that establishes a European remedy against private parties violating European law.[147] The constitutional language and spirit of the ruling indeed pointed towards a new and independent source of liability.[148] And the Court did not place its reasoning into the analytical framework governing the effectiveness principle.

---

[144] Case C-453/99, *Courage*, paras. 26–7.

[145] For an early expression of this ambivalence, see O. Odudu and J. Edelman, 'Compensatory Damages for Breach of Article 81' (2002) 27 *EL Rev.* 327 at 336: 'Though, on its face, *Courage* does not suggest that a new remedy should be created to protect [European] rights, simply that existing national remedies should not be denied, *Courage* can be read as supporting the idea that compensatory damages must generally be provided for breach of Article [101], and must be available to all those who have suffered from the breach.'

[146] Dougan, *National Remedies* (n. 18 above), 379 (pointing to the absolute bar on one party seeking compensation).

[147] N. Reich, "The "Courage" Doctrine: Encouraging or Discouraging Compensation for Antitrust Injuries?' (2005) 42 *CML Rev.* 35 at 38; A. Komninos, 'Civil Antitrust Remedies between Community and National Law', in C. Barnard and O. Odudu (eds.), *The Outer Limits of European Law* (Hart, 2009), 363 at 383: 'The enunciation of a [European] right in damages and, by implication, of a principle of civil liability of individuals for breaches of [European] law, is a logical consequence of the Court's abundant case law on state liability, and reflects a more general principle of [European] law that, everyone is bound to make good loss or damage arising as a result of his conduct in breach of a legal duty.'

[148] Case C-453/99, *Courage*, para. 19.

If we accept the wider reading of *Courage*, what conditions should the Court apply to private party violations of European law? If *Courage* was the private *Francovich*, then *Manfredi* is the private *Brasserie*. In *Manfredi*,[149] Italian consumers had brought an action against their insurance companies. They claimed that those companies had engaged in anticompetitive behaviour; and, as a result of this breach of the European competition rules, their car insurance was on average 20 per cent higher than the normal price would have been. Could they ask for damages?

The Court here repeated that 'the practical effect of Article [101(1)] would be put at risk if it were not open to any individual to claim damages for loss caused to him by a contract or by conduct liable to restrict or distort competition'; and concluded that therefore 'any individual can claim compensation for the harm suffered where there is a causal relationship between that harm and an agreement or practice prohibited under Article [101 TFEU]'.[150] This sounded like a strict liability test, for there was no express reference to a sufficiently serious breach. Had the Court thus dropped the second *Brasserie* criterion, because the European competition rules were unconditional and sufficiently clear so that 'the mere infringement of [European] law may be sufficient to establish the existence of a sufficiently serious breach'?[151] The Court has remained ambivalent on this issue. Indeed, it has generally left the detailed procedural framework to national law.[152]

The existence of a general liability test for public and private violations of European law is thus in doubt. But even if *Courage* is eventually integrated into a unified liability test, it is important to underline that the private liability doctrine should be confined to breaches of obligations directly addressed to individuals.[153] Only where European law directly regulates private party actions should the *Courage* doctrine apply. Private liability ought thus never to originate in breaches of obligations addressed to public authorities − even if they have horizontal direct effect.[154] Not horizontal direct effect, but the narrower criterion of whether a European norm addresses private party actions should constitute the unwritten premise of private party liability. The *Courage* doctrine should thus be confined to breaches of a − very − qualified part of European law.

---

[149] Joined Cases C-295/04 to C-298/04, *Manfredi et al.* v. *Lloyd Adriatico Assicurazioni et al.* [2006] ECR I-6619.

[150] *Ibid.*, para. 61. For a more recent conformation of this approach, see Case C-557/12, *Kone and others* v. *ÖBB Infrastrukur*, EU:C:2014:1317.

[151] Case C-5/94, *Hedley Lomas*, para. 28.

[152] Joined Cases C-295/04 to C-298/04, *Manfredi*, para. 62. On this point with regard to *Francovich* liability more generally, see n. 197ff. below.

[153] Similarly: S. Drake, 'Scope of *Courage* and the Principle of "Individual Liability' for Damages: Further Development of the Principle of Effective Judicial Protection by the Court of Justice' (2006) 31 *EL Rev.* 841 at 861.

[154] On the distinction between horizontal direct effect and private party actions, see Chapter 3, section 1(b).

4. European Harmonisation: Judicial Cooperation

Let us recall the core principle governing the decentralised enforcement of European law by national courts:

> [I]n the absence of [European] rules on this subject, it is for the domestic legal system of each Member State to designate the courts having jurisdiction and to determine the procedural conditions governing actions at law intended to ensure the protection of the rights which citizens have derived from the direct effect of [European] law … In the absence of such measures of harmonisation the right conferred by [European] law must [thus] be exercised before the national courts in accordance with the conditions laid down by national rules.[155]

We saw above that this national procedural autonomy was however only relative; and the first three sections of this chapter explored three constitutional principles that have come to limit the procedural autonomy of national courts. Importantly: these three principles – the principles of equivalence, effectiveness and liability – generally come to operate *in the absence of any European harmonisation*. Whenever European harmonisation has taken place, on the other hand, our three constitutional principles may be replaced by more specific EU legislative rules.

The process of procedural harmonisation has however been slow and piecemeal. In the past decades, the Union has only managed to harmonise national procedural laws in a small number of substantive areas[156] while also only providing a small number of general 'EU remedies' in civil (and criminal) proceedings.[157]

The primary focus of the Union's harmonisation effort has thereby been on the jurisdictional coordination of national courts. What is the problem here? According to the idea of national sovereignty, national courts

---

[155] Case 33/76, *Rewe*, para. 5.

[156] One of the more advanced areas here is EU competition law, see Directive 2014/104 on certain rules governing actions for damages under national law for infringement of the competition law provisions of the Member States and of the European Union [2014] OJ L 349/1. For an analysis of the directive, see N. Dunne, '*Courage* and Compromise: The Directive on Antitrust Damages' (2015) 40 *EL Rev.* 581; and more generally: M. Bergström et al. (eds.), *Harmonising EU Competition Litigation: The New Directive and Beyond* (Hart, 2016). Apart from EU competition law, there are also other substantive areas in which the Union has specifically tried to harmonise national procedural laws, yet even here, 'the most common approach was – and indeed remains – to include at most only a limited number of enforcement-related provisions in acts that primarily deal with substantive matters' (F. G. Wilman, 'The End of the Absence? The Growing Body of EU Legislation on Private Enforcement and the Main Remedies It provides for' (2016) 53 *CML Rev.* 887 at 893).

[157] With regard to civil law 'EU remedies', see E. Storskrubb, *Civil Procedure and EU Law: A Policy Area Uncovered* (Oxford University Press, 2008). For an overview of EU legislation in criminal proceedings, see V. Mitsilegas, *EU Criminal Law after Lisbon* (Hart, 2016), chs. 6–7.

may – theoretically – claim 'universal' jurisdiction for all legal problems in the world.[158] In the context of the European Union, does that means that an EU citizen could go to any national court when enforcing her EU rights? Imagine the following scenario: a German consumer, living in the United Kingdom, has bought a product from a French business that has violated the EU competition rules: can she go to an English court to ask for damages? Or is she obliged to seek redress in a French or a German court?

This question concerns the horizontal division of jurisdictional competences between national courts; and EU harmonisation has here been adopted to 'federally' coordinate them so as to prevent 'parallel proceedings' on the same subject matter. EU harmonisation in this context is not concerned with the question of whether a national legal order offers efficient remedies for the enforcement of EU law. It rather concerns the preliminary question *which* national legal order will have jurisdiction; and this question is, in turn, important because the Union legal order has tied this jurisdictional question to the idea of judicial cooperation and the mutual recognition of national judgments in the Union.

a. Cooperation and Mutual Recognition in Civil Matters

The Union competence with regard to judicial cooperation in civil matters can be found in Article 81 TFEU.[159] It states:

> 1. The Union shall develop judicial cooperation in civil matters having cross-border implications, based on the principle of mutual recognition of judgments and of decisions in extrajudicial cases. Such cooperation may include the adoption of measures for the approximation of the laws and regulations of the Member States.

---

[158] Many national legal orders have nevertheless recognised self-imposed restrictions especially with regard to civil law. These limits are laid down in a State's 'private international law' legislation. For an analysis of the English 'private international law', see P. Torremans et al. (eds.), *Cheshire, North & Fawcett on Private International Law* (Oxford University Press, 2017).

[159] The provision constitutes, on its own, Ch. 3 ('Judicial Cooperation in Civil Matters') of Title V ('Area of Freedom, Security and Justice') of the TFEU. Importantly, all acts adopted within Title V will generally not bind the United Kingdom and Ireland (see: Protocol No. 21 on the Position of the United Kingdom and Ireland in Respect of the Area of Freedom, Security and Justice). Despite this general opt-out, the Protocol has allowed the UK and Ireland to 'opt in' to individual measures (*ibid.*, Arts. 3 and 4), and the two States have indeed, with very few exceptions, made use of this for the legislation adopted under Art. 81 TFEU. A more complex situation, applies to Denmark, which also benefits from a general opt-out (see Protocol No. 22 on the Position of Denmark). Yet instead of generally opting back into EU secondary law, Denmark has preferred to generally stay out. The major exception here is an international agreement concluded with the EU on 'jurisdiction and the recognition and enforcement of judgments in civil and commercial matters' ([2005] OJ L 299/62). This Agreement extends, de facto, the Brussels I Regulation to Denmark.

2. For the purposes of paragraph 1, the European Parliament and the Council, acting in accordance with the ordinary legislative procedure, shall adopt measures, particularly when necessary for the proper functioning of the internal market, aimed at ensuring:
   (a) the mutual recognition and enforcement between Member States of judgments and of decisions in extrajudicial cases …
   (c) the compatibility of the rules applicable in the Member States concerning conflict of laws and of jurisdiction …
3. Notwithstanding paragraph 2, measures concerning family law with cross-border implications shall be established by the Council, acting in accordance with a special legislative procedure. The Council shall act unanimously after consulting the European Parliament …

The provision constitutes the modern fountain of 'EU private international law'.[160] It explicitly deals with 'civil' law matters and therefore excludes all public law, including administrative and criminal law. Article 81 thereby expressly distinguishes between general civil law in paragraph 2 and the special case of family law in paragraph 3; and with regard to both, the Union has further distinguished between the *jurisdictional* question of 'mutual recognition and enforcement', on the one hand, and the *substantive* question as to which national law applies ('conflicts of laws'), on the other.

This two-times-two division is today reflected in four famous regulations that constitute the legislative core within this area of European law. These four Regulations derive their names from two important and beautiful European cities: Brussels and Rome; with the two 'Brussels Regulations' dealing with jurisdiction, and the two 'Rome Regulations' dealing with the substantive question which national (civil) law applies (see Table 11.1).

The following section concentrates on the general principles governing civil and commercial law under the Brussels I Regulation.

aa. *Dividing Competences between National Courts*
The Brussels I Regulation generally deals with 'civil and commercial matters';[161] and its central aim is expressed as follows:

---

[160] The historical evolution of EU private international law is fairly complex. For general treatments here, see M. Bogdan, *Concise Introduction to EU Private International Law* (Europa Law, 2015); and P. Stone, *EU Private International Law* (Elgar, 2014). Importantly, EU private international law is not confined to dealing with the enforcement of substantive European law in national courts. It more generally determines whether a national court has jurisdiction and which national law applies in a specific case.

[161] Certain civil and commercial matters are expressly excluded from the scope of the Regulation, see Art. 1 (2). The provision principally excludes family law matters (subparas. a and e), insolvency proceedings (subpara. b), arbitration (subpara. d) and succession (subpara. f).

> In the interests of the harmonious administration of justice it is necessary to minimise the possibility of concurrent proceedings and to ensure that irreconcilable judgments will not be given in different Member States. There should be a clear and effective mechanism for resolving cases of *lis pendens* and related actions, and for obviating problems flowing from national differences as to the determination of the time when a case is regarded as pending.[162]

In order to achieve this aim, the Regulation lays down a number of (default) rules.[163] Where the parties have not contractually settled on a specific court, the Regulation holds 'that jurisdiction is generally based on the defendant's domicile'.[164] Article 4 of the Regulation confirms that 'persons domiciled in a Member State shall, whatever their nationality, be sued in the courts of that Member States'.[165]

This general rule means two things. First, it clarifies that it is not 'nationality' but 'domicile' that is important; and, second, it gives clear preference to the

Table 11.1 EU Private International Law (Selection)

Brussels I Regulation	Regulation 1215/2012 on jurisdiction and the recognition and enforcement of judgments in civil and commercial matters (recast)
Brussels II Regulation	Regulation 2201/2003 concerning jurisdiction and the recognition and enforcement of judgments in matrimonial matters and the matters of parental responsibility
Rome I Regulation	Regulation 593/2008 on the law applicable to contractual obligations
Rome II Regulation	Regulation 864/2007 on the law applicable to non-contractual obligations
Other Regulations	Regulation 1259/2010 implementing enhanced cooperation in the area of the law applicable to divorce and legal separation (Rome III)
	Regulation 650/2012 on jurisdiction, applicable law, recognition and enforcement of decisions and acceptance and enforcement

---

[162] Brussels I Regulation, recital 21.

[163] The Brussels I Regulation is – like much private law – only default legislation in that the private parties can specifically decide to conclude a special contract that determines which court they would like to give jurisdiction to (*ibid.*, Art. 25). For an academic treatment of these 'choice-of-court' agreements, see T. Hartley, *Choice-of-Court Agreements under the European and International Instruments* (Oxford University Press, 2013).

[164] Brussels I Regulation, recital 15.

[165] *Ibid.*, Art. 4. The question of what counts as being 'domiciled' in a Member State is generally left to each Member State (*ibid.*, Art. 62: 'In order to determine whether a party is domiciled in the Member State whose courts are seized of the matter, the court shall apply its internal law'); yet with regard to legal persons, Art. 63 contains a number of EU specific rules.

defendant as opposed to the *plaintiff* by generally forcing the latter to go to the courts of the Member State of his opponent.

And yet there are two major exceptions to this rule. For a number of areas, such as contract and tort claims,[166] insurance contracts,[167] consumer contracts[168] and employment contracts,[169] the Union grants a parallel competence to other national courts. With regard to consumer contacts, for example, the Regulation states that, if certain conditions are fulfilled,[170] the consumer has a choice:

> A consumer may bring proceedings against the other party to a contract either in the courts of the Member State in which that party is domiciled or, regardless of the domicile of the other party, in the courts for the place where the consumer is domiciled.[171]

But more importantly still: for some matters, the Brussels I Regulation designates a jurisdiction as exclusively competent that is not related to the domicile of either the defendant or the plaintiff. These heads of 'exclusive jurisdiction' are set out in Article 24 of the Regulation,[172] and whenever they apply, the general or special jurisdictions discussed above are suspended. For example: with regard to immovable property, it will always be the national courts in which that property is located that enjoy exclusive jurisdiction within the Union.

How does the Regulation deal with jurisdictional conflicts where two or more national courts claim jurisdiction simultaneously? For matters falling within an exclusive jurisdictional competence, the Regulation unequivocally states:

---

[166] *Ibid.*, s. 2, esp. Art. 7.　[167] *Ibid.*, s. 3 (Arts. 10–16).

[168] *Ibid.*, s. 4 (Arts. 17–19).　[169] *Ibid.*, s. 5 (Arts. 20–3).

[170] The conditions for consumer contracts are set out in Art. 17 of the Regulation, and the most important condition here is the situation described in Art. 17(1)(c). The consumer's 'home' courts will thus only have (parallel) jurisdiction, where the seller either has a commercial presence in that State, or where s/he has been specifically 'directing' her commercial activities to that State. On the notion of 'directing', see Joined Cases C-585/08 and C-144/09, *Pammer* v. *Reederei Schlüter* and *Hotel Alpenhof* v. *Heller* [2010] ECR I-12527.

[171] Brussels I Regulation, Art. 18(1).

[172] The provision states: 'The following courts of a Member State shall have exclusive jurisdiction, regardless of the domicile of the parties: (1) in proceedings which have as their object rights in rem in immovable property or tenancies of immovable property, the courts of the Member State in which the property is situated … (2) in proceedings which have as their object the validity of the constitution, the nullity or the dissolution of companies or other legal persons or associations of natural or legal persons … (3) in proceedings which have as their object the validity of entries in public registers, the courts of the Member State in which the register is kept; (4) in proceedings concerned with the registration or validity of patents, trade marks, designs, or other similar rights required to be deposited or registered … (5) in proceedings concerned with the enforcement of judgments, the courts of the Member State in which the judgment has been or is to be enforced.'

> Where a court of a Member State is seised of a claim which is principally con-
> cerned with a matter over which the courts of another Member State have exclusive
> jurisdiction by virtue of Article 24, it shall declare of its own motion that it has no
> jurisdiction.[173]

With regard to non-exclusive parallel competences, on the other hand, the Regulation establishes the following rule (*lis pendens*):

> [W]here proceedings involving the same cause of action and between the same
> parties are brought in the courts of different Member States, any court other than
> the court first seised shall of its own motion stay its proceedings until such time as
> the jurisdiction of the court first seised is established … Where the jurisdiction of the
> court first seised is established, any court other than the court first seised shall decline
> jurisdiction in favour of that court.[174]

The Regulation here establishes a first-seized-first-jurisdiction rule. Whichever court is first seized must first determine whether it is competent under the Brussels I Regulation. Any other – second – court must wait until that first court has made that determination; and only after the first court has itself rejected its jurisdiction, may it resume jurisdiction under the Regulation. This first-come-first-jurisdiction rule is open to abuse;[175] yet the European Court has clarified that a second-seized court cannot issue anti-suit injunctions to stop a parallel trial abroad,[176] nor can it under any circumstances review the jurisdiction of a court in another Member State.[177]

The jurisdictional autonomy of each and every national court has been justi-fied in *Gasser* as follows:

> [T]he Brussels [Regulation] is necessarily based on the trust which the [Member
> States] accord to each other's legal systems and judicial institutions. It is that mutual
> trust which has enabled a compulsory system of jurisdiction to be established, which

---

[173]   *Ibid.*, Art. 27.   [174]   *Ibid.*, Art. 29(1) and (3).

[175]   Where a dispute between two private parties arises, one party might be tempted to start proceedings, out of the blue, in a Member States that has no link whatsoever to the civil dispute with the sole aim of delaying the proceedings. Due to the legendary slowness of the Italian legal system, this strategic move has been called the 'Italian torpedo'. A party here commences proceedings in an Italian court which might take years to find that it is ultimately not competent.

[176]   Case 159/02, *Turner* v. *Grovit* [2004] ECR I-3565, esp. para 28: 'In so far as the conduct for which the defendant is criticized consists in recourse to the jurisdiction of the court of another Member State, the judgment made as to the abusive nature of that conduct implies an assessment of the appropriateness of bringing proceedings before a court of another Member State. Such an assessment runs counter to the principle of mutual trust[.]'

[177]   Brussels I Regulation, Art. 45(3): '[T]he jurisdiction of the court of origin may not be reviewed'.

all the courts within the purview of the [Regulation] are required to respect, and as a corollary the waiver by those States of the right to apply their internal rules on recognition and enforcement of foreign judgments in favour of a simplified mechanism for the recognition and enforcement of judgments.[178]

bb. Mutual Recognition of National Judgments

The Brussels I Regulation is a 'double instrument'. It regulates not only the jurisdiction of national courts within the European Union but also the recognition and enforcement of their judgments.[179] Indeed: the rationale behind centrally determining the horizontal division of powers between national courts has always been to facilitate the mutual recognition and enforcement of their judgments. The simple rules within the Brussels Regulation here are these:

A judgment given in a Member State shall be recognised in the other Member States without any special procedure being required.[180]

And:

A judgment given in a Member State which is enforceable in that Member State shall be enforceable in the other Member States without any declaration of enforceability being required.[181]

A national judgment given in one Member State will thus generally enjoy the force of *res judicata* in all other Member States of the Union; and '[u]nder no circumstances may a judgment given in a Member State be reviewed as to its substance in the Member State addressed'.[182] This mutual juridical recognition is however not absolute. For the Brussels I Regulation recognises a number of (limited) exceptions – the most important of which are a violation of the jurisdictional rules of the Brussels Regulation and overriding public policy considerations.[183] Yet absent such specific grounds, a judgment given by a French or German court will be 'binding' and 'enforceable' in all other Member States. The mutual recognition of civil law judgments indeed constitutes one of the cornerstones of the judicial federalism established by the Union. It finds a – weaker – expression in criminal law to which we must now turn.

---

[178] Case C-116/02, *Gasser* v. *MISAT* [2003] ECR I-14694, para. 72.

[179] Bogdan, *EU Private International Law* (n. 160 above), 33.

[180] Brussels I Regulation, Art. 36 (1).

[181] *Ibid.*, Art. 39.   [182] *Ibid.*, Art. 52.

[183] The various grounds are listed in Art. 45 of the Regulation. For an extensive discussion here, see Stone, *EU Private International Law* (n. 160 above), 230–45.

b. Cooperation and Mutual Recognition in Criminal Matters

The Union competence(s) with regard to judicial cooperation in criminal matters are found in Articles 82–6 TFEU.[184] The central provision here states:

> Judicial cooperation in criminal matters in the Union shall be based on the principle of mutual recognition of judgments and judicial decisions and shall include the approximation of the laws and regulations of the Member States in the areas referred to in paragraph 2 and in Article 83.
>
> The European Parliament and the Council, acting in accordance with the ordinary legislative procedure, shall adopt measures to:
> (a) lay down rules and procedures for ensuring recognition throughout the Union of all forms of judgments and judicial decisions;
> (b) prevent and settle conflicts of jurisdiction between Member States …
> (d) Facilitate cooperation between judicial or equivalent authorities of the Member States in relation to proceedings in criminal matters and the enforcement of decisions.[185]

The provision deals, among other things, with the jurisdiction of national courts and the mutual recognition of their judgments in the context of criminal law. Like in the area of civil law, there may again be a number of situations where more than one Member State claims jurisdiction for a particular criminal act; and this is particularly problematic in criminal law because most legal orders accept the principle that a crime cannot be judged twice (in Latin: *ne bis in idem*).

The Union has nevertheless not been very successful in removing conflicts of criminal law jurisdiction.[186] It has perhaps been slightly more successful with regard to the 'mutual recognition' of national judgments; yet this success has not been through Union legislation adopted on the basis of Articles 82–3 TFEU but – anachronistically – through an international agreement between the Member States.[187] The latter here states:

> A person whose trial has been finally disposed of in one Contracting Party may not be prosecuted in another Contracting Party for the same acts provided that, if a penalty has been imposed, it has been enforced, is actually in the process of being enforced or can no longer be enforced under the laws of the sentencing Contracting Party.[188]

---

[184] The provisions constitute Ch. 4 ('Judicial Cooperation in Criminal Matters') of Title V ('Area of Freedom, Security and Justice') of the TFEU. Importantly, Protocol No. 21 On the Position of the United Kingdom and Ireland in Respect of the Area of Freedom, Security and Justice and Protocol No. 22 On the Position of Denmark (see n. 159 above for both) will of course apply here too.

[185] Art. 82 (1) TFEU.

[186] For a critical analysis of the EU efforts here, see S. Peers, *EU Justice and Home Affairs: Volume II: EU Criminal Law, Policing, and Civil Law* (Oxford University Press, 2016), 228ff.

[187] This international agreement is the Schengen Convention Implementing the Schengen Agreement [2000] OJ L 239/19.

[188] Schengen Implementing Convention, Art. 54.

In interpreting this provision, the European Court has clarified that its main purpose is 'that no one is prosecuted on the same facts in several Member States on account of his having exercised his right to freedom of movement'.[189] This European *ne bis in idem* principle thereby applies regardless of whether or not there has been any prior harmonisation of national criminal law;[190] and while the precise contours of the *ne bis in idem* principle continue to be litigated,[191] its 'constitutional' core is nevertheless clear: a judgment given by one national court must, in principle, be recognised by all other Member States.

This principle of mutual recognition can also be found in relation to the preparation and execution of a judgment. And the Union has here adopted its most controversial criminal law measure: the European Arrest Warrant (EAW).[192] The EWA is 'a *judicial* decision issued by a Member State with a view to the arrest and surrender by another Member Sate of a requested person, for the purposes of conducting a criminal prosecution or executing a custodial sentence or detention order'.[193] The EWA has consequently a pre-trial and post-trial function; and its controversial heart lies in the idea that a Member State must surrender any person – even one of its nationals – where that person has been charged or judged with a crime that may not be punishable in the surrendering State.[194] The EWA however allows for a range of mandatory and optional exceptions that permit non-execution;[195] but the Court has held that this list of exceptions is exhaustive. The Court justifies this result again by reference to the idea of 'mutual trust' on which the principle of mutual recognition in general, and the EAW in particular, is based.[196]

Conclusion

Functionally, national courts are Union courts; yet the decentralised adjudication of European law by national courts means that the procedural regime for the enforcement of European rights is principally left to the Member States.

---

[189] Joined cases C-187/01 and C-385/01, *Gözütok and Brügge* [2003] ECR I-1345, para. 38.

[190] *Ibid.*, para. 32.

[191] For an analysis of the past jurisprudence here, see C. Janssens, *The Principle of Mutual Recognition in EU Law* (Oxford University Press, 2013), 132–65. For a recent case, see Case C-486/14, *Kossowski*, EU:C:2016:483.

[192] Framework Decision 2002/584/JHA on the European Arrest Warrant and the surrender procedures between Member States (2002) OJ L 190/1. The EWA was adopted prior to the Lisbon Treaty and it was therefore adopted by means of a legal instrument that was only known in the former 'third pillar' of the pre-Lisbon European Union. For an academic analysis of the EWA, see E. Herlin-Karnell, 'From Mutual Trust to the Full Effectiveness of EU Law: 10 Years of the European Arrest Warrant' (2013) 38 *EL Rev.* 79.

[193] Framework Decision 2002/584 (EAW), Art. 1(1) (emphasis added).

[194] The abolition of the requirement of 'double criminality' can be found in *ibid.*, Art. 2(2). It expands to the 32 most dangerous crimes.

[195] *Ibid.*, Arts. 3–4a.

[196] See Joined Cases C-404/15 and C-659/15 PPU, *Pál Aranyosi and Robert Căldăraru v. Generalstaatsanwaltschaft Bremen*, EU:C:2016:198, esp. paras. 77–8.

This rule of 'national procedural autonomy' is however qualified by four principles. First, in the presence of European harmonisation, national courts must of course apply the procedural arrangements offered by European law. But even in the absence of European harmonisation, the European legal order has asked national courts to provide national remedies to prevent or discourage breaches of European law. The two key constitutional principles judicially developed by the Court of Justice here are the equivalence and the effectiveness principles. The former requests national courts to extend existing national remedies to similar European actions. The latter demands that these national remedies must not make the enforcement of European law 'excessively difficult'. Finally, there is a last limitation: the liability principle. The *Francovich* doctrine obliges national courts to provide for damages that compensate for losses resulting from (sufficiently serious) breaches of European law by a Member State. *Courage* may be seen as the horizontal extension of this principle, but the jury on this point is still out.

What is the relationship between national remedies and the *Francovich* remedy? The Court seems to treat the latter as a remedy of last resort.[197] We saw a specific expression of this relation in the *Köbler* rule that the availability of appeal procedures under national law precludes State liability for judicial breaches of European law. However, this will not mean that national and European remedies do not complement each other. Indeed, the specific procedural regime for the EU remedy of State liability is governed by national rules. The enforcement of the *Francovich* 'remedy' in the national courts will thus itself be subject to the principles of equivalence and effectiveness.[198]

Let us look at one last point: what is the relationship between *Francovich* liability and direct effect? From the early days of this remedy, the Court has been clear that an individual may have a right to damages even for violations of directly effective norms of European law.[199] Thus, the fact that an action can be brought

---

[197] See Case C-91/92, *Faccini Dori* v. *Recreb* [1994] ECR I-3325, para. 27: 'If the result prescribed by the directive cannot be achieved by way of interpretation, it should also be borne in mind that, in terms of the judgment in Joined Cases C-6/90 and C-9/90, *Francovich and others* v. *Italy* [1991] ECR I-5357, paragraph 39, [European] law requires the Member States to make good damage caused to individuals through failure to transpose a directive, provided that three conditions are fulfilled.'

[198] On the *Francovich* remedy being put into a national procedural context, see Case C-168/15, *Tomášová*, para. 38: '[W]here the conditions for a State to incur liability are satisfied, a matter which it is for the national courts to determine, it is on the basis of national law that the State must make reparation for the consequences of the loss or damage caused, provided that the conditions laid down by national law in respect of reparation of loss or damage are not less favourable than those relating to similar domestic claims (principle of equivalence) and are not so framed as to make it, in practice, impossible or excessively difficult to obtain reparation (principle of effectiveness).'

[199] Joined Cases C-46/93 and C-48/93, *Brasserie du Pêcheur*, paras. 20 and 22: 'The Court has consistently held that the right of individuals to rely on the directly effective provisions of the Treaty before national courts is only a minimum guarantee and is not sufficient in

to force a national administration to apply European law is no barrier for the availability of this secondary remedy.[200] This makes profound sense as the application of European law may only operate prospectively, whereas the compensation for past misapplications of European law works retrospectively. However, there can – of course – be liability without direct effect; and the State obligation to make good any damage caused by a serious breach of European law will often be the only option for an individual who cannot rely on the – vertical or horizontal – direct effect of European law.

The final section of this chapter explored to what extent the EU has coordinated national jurisdictions. The Brussels I Regulation here determines, with regard to cross-border disputes in civil matters, which national court should have competence; and once this is done, a judgment rendered by that national court must in general be recognised and enforced in all other Member States. Within the context of criminal law, similar principles have been established – yet, as we shall see below, they have generated a range of human rights issues in the Union legal order.

FURTHER READING

Books

M. Bogdan, *Concise Introduction to EU Private International Law* (Europa Law, 2015)

M. Claes, *The National Courts' Mandate in the European Constitution* (Hart, 2005)

M. Dougan, *National Remedies before the Court of Justice: Issues of Harmonisation and Differentiation* (Hart, 2004),

C. Janssens, *The Principle of Mutual Recognition in EU Law* (Oxford University Press, 2013)

C. Kilpatrick et al. (eds.), *The Future of Remedies in Europe* (Hart, 2000)

K. Lenaerts, I. Maselis and K. Gutman, *EU Procedural Law* (Oxford University Press, 2014)

V. Mitsilegas, *EU Criminal Law After Lisbon: Rights and the Transformation of Justice in Europe* (Hart, 2016)

S. Peers, *EU Justice and Home Affairs Law – Volume II: EU Criminal Law, Policing, and Civil Law* (Oxford University Press, 2016)

A. M. Slaughter, A. Stone Sweet and J. Weiler, *The European Courts and National Courts: Doctrine and Jurisprudence: Legal Change in its Social Context* (Hart, 1998)

P. Stone, *EU Private International Law* (Elgar 2016)

E. Storskrubb, *Civil Procedure and EU Law: A Policy Area Uncovered* (Oxford University Press, 2008)

---

itself to ensure the full and complete implementation of the Treaty … It is all the more so in the event of an infringement of a right directly conferred by a [European] provision upon which individuals are entitled to rely before the national courts. In that event the right to reparation is the necessary corollary of the direct effect of the [European] provisions whose breach caused the damage sustained.'

[200] See also Case C-150/99, *Sweden v. Stockhold Lindöpark* [2001] ECR I-493, para. 35.

Articles (and Chapters)

A. Arnull, 'The Principle of Effective Judicial Protection in EU Law: An Unruly Horse?' (2011) 36 *EL Rev.* 51

B. Beutler, 'State Liability for Breaches of Community Law by National Courts: Is the Requirement of a Manifest Infringement of the Applicable Law an Insurmountable Obstacle?' [2009] 46 *CML Rev.* 773

J. Convery, 'State Liability in the United Kingdom after *Brasserie du Pêcheur* [1997] 34 *CML Rev.* 603

M. Dougan, 'The Vicissitudes of Life at the Coalface: Remedies and Procedures for Enforcing Union Law before the National Courts', in P. Craig and G. de Búrca, *The Evolution of EU Law* (Oxford University Press, 2011), 407

W. van Gerven, 'Of Rights, Remedies and Procedures' (2000) 37 *CML Rev.* 501

B. Hess, The Brussels I Regulation: Recent Case Law of the Court of Justice and the Commission's Proposed Recast, (2012) 49 *CML Rev.* 1075

C. N. Kakouris, 'Do the Member States Possess Judicial Procedural "Autonomy"?' (1997) 34 *CML Rev.* 1389

J. Komarek, 'Federal Elements in the Community Judicial System: Building Coherence in the Community Legal System' (2005) 42 *CML Rev.* 9

R. Lauwaars, 'The Application of Community Law by National Courts *ex officio*' (2007–2008) 31 *Fordham International Law Journal* 1161

S. Prechal, 'Community Law in National Courts: The Lessons from *Van Schijndel*' (1998) 35 *CML Rev.* 681

N. Reich, 'The "*Courage*" Doctrine: Encouraging or Discouraging Compensation for Antitrust Injuries?' (2005) 42 *CML Rev.* 35

J. Steiner, 'From Direct Effect to *Francovich*: Shifting Means of Enforcement of Community Law' (1993) 18 *EL Rev.* 3

F. G. Wilman, 'The End of the Absence? The growing Body of EU Legislation on Private Enforcement and the Main Remedies It provides for' (2016) 53 *CML Rev.* 887

Cases on the Webpage

Case 26/62, *Van Gend en Loos*; Case 33/76, *Rewe*; Case 106/77, *Simmenthal II*; Case 14/83, *Von Colson*; Case 177/88, *Dekker*; Case C-213/89, *Factortame*; Joined Cases C-6 and 9/90, *Francovich*; Case C-271/91, *Marshall II*; Case C-338/91, *Steenhorst-Neerings*; Joined Cases C-46 and 48/93; *Brasserie du Pêcheur*; Case C-312/93, *Peterbroeck*; Joined Cases C-430–1/93, *Van Schijndel*; Case C-5/94, *Hedley Lomas*; Case C-231/96, *Edis*; Case C-326/96, *Levez*; Case C-78/98, *Preston*; Case C-453/99, *Courage*; Case C-118/00, *Larsy*; Case C-224/01, *Köbler*; Case C-116/02, *Gasser*; Joined Cases C-295–8/04, *Manfredi*; Joined Cases C-392 and 422/04, *i-22 Germany & Arcor* v. *Germany*; Case C-222/05, *Van der Weerd*; Case C-432/05, *Unibet*

12

Judicial Powers III
EU Fundamental Rights

Contents

Introduction

The protection of human rights is a central task of many judiciaries.[1] Judicial review in light of fundamental human rights may here be limited to the review of the executive;[2] yet in its expansive form, it includes the judicial review of legislative acts.[3] The European Union follows this second tradition. Fundamental rights set substantive – judicial – limits to all governmental powers and processes within the Union. They indeed constitute one of the most popular grounds of judicial review in actions challenging the validity of European Union law.

What are the sources of human rights in the Union legal order? Despite the absence of a 'bill of rights' in the original Treaties,[4] three sources for EU fundamental rights were subsequently developed. The European Court first began distilling fundamental rights from the constitutional traditions of the Member States. This *unwritten* bill of rights was inspired and informed by a second bill of rights: the European Convention on Human Rights. This *external* bill of rights was subsequently matched by a – third – *written* bill of rights specifically drafted for the European Union: the EU Charter of Fundamental Rights.

These three sources of EU fundamental rights are now expressly referred to – in reverse order – in Article 6 of the Treaty on European Union. The provision reads:

> 1. The Union recognises the rights, freedoms and principles set out in the Charter of Fundamental Rights of the European Union of 7 December 2000, as adopted at Strasbourg, on 12 December 2007, which shall have the same legal value as the Treaties ...
> 2. The Union shall accede to the European Convention for the Protection of Human Rights and Fundamental Freedoms. Such accession shall not affect the Union's competences as defined in the Treaties.
> 3. Fundamental rights, as guaranteed by the European Convention for the Protection of Human Rights and Fundamental Freedoms and as they result from the constitutional traditions common to the Member States, shall constitute general principles of the Union's law.

This chapter investigates each of the Union's three bills of rights and the constitutional principles that govern them. Section 1 starts with the discovery of an 'unwritten' bill of rights in the form of general principles of European

---

[1] On human rights as constitutional rights, see A. Sajó, *Limiting Government* (Central European University Press, 1999), ch. 8; and on the role of the judiciary in this context, see M. Cappelletti, *Judicial Review in the Contemporary World* (Bobbs-Merrill, 1971).

[2] For the classic doctrine of parliamentary sovereignty in the United Kingdom, see A. V. Dicey, *Introduction to the Study of the Law of the Constitution* (Liberty Fund, 1982).

[3] On the idea of human rights as 'outside' majoritarian (democratic) politics, see Sajó, *Limiting Government* (n. 1 above), ch. 2, 5ff.

[4] P. Pescatore, 'Les Droits de l'homme et l'intégration européenne' (1968) 4 *Cahiers du droit européen* 629.

law. Section 2 then moves to an analysis of the Union's 'written' bill of rights:
the EU Charter of Fundamental Rights, which was adopted to codify existing human rights in the Union legal order. Section 3 investigates the formal
relationship between the Union and the European Convention on Human
Rights. Finally, section 4 explores the relationship between all three bills of
rights and the Member States. It will be seen that *each* of the three Union
bills applies, at least to some extent, also to the Member States. *National* courts
may thus be obliged to review the legality of *national* law also in light of EU
fundamental rights.

1. The 'Unwritten' Bill of Rights: Human Rights as 'General Principles'

Neither the 1951 Paris Treaty nor the 1957 Rome Treaty contained any express
references to human rights.[5] The silence of the former could be explained by its
limited scope. The silence of the latter, by contrast, could have its origin in the
cautious climate following the failure of the 'European Political Community'.[6]
With political union having failed, the 'grander' project of a human rights bill
was replaced by the 'smaller' project of economic integration.[7]

  Be that as it may, the European Court would – within the first two decades – develop an (unwritten) bill of rights for the European Union.[8] These
fundamental rights would be *European* rights, that is: rights that were *independent* from national constitutions. The discovery of human rights as general
principles of European law will be discussed first. Thereafter, this section
discusses possible structural limits to EU human rights in the form of international obligations flowing from the United Nations Charter.

---

[5] For speculations on the historical reasons for this absence, see P. Pescatore, 'The Context
and Significance of Fundamental Rights in the Law of the European Communities' (1981)
2 *Human Rights Journal* 295. For a new look at the historical material, see G. de Búrca, 'The
Evolution of EU Human Rights Law', in P. Craig and G. de Búrca (eds.), *The Evolution of
EU Law* (Oxford University Press, 2011), 465.

[6] On the European Political Community, see Chapter 1, section 1(b). This grand project had
asked the (proposed) Community 'to contribute towards the protection of human rights
and fundamental freedoms in the Member States' (Art. 2), and would have integrated the
European Convention on Human Rights into the Community legal order (Art. 3).

[7] Pescatore, 'Context and Significance' (n. 5 above), 296.

[8] The judicial motifs of the European Court in developing human rights are controversially
discussed in the literature. It seems accepted that the Court discovered human rights as
general principles – at least partly – in defence to national Supreme Courts challenging the
absolute supremacy of European law (see Chapter 4, section 2). Apart from this 'defensive'
use, the Court has been accused of an 'offensive use' in the sense of 'employ[ing] fundamental rights instrumentally' by 'clearly subordinat[ing] human rights to the end of closer
economic integration in the [Union]' (see J. Coppel and A. O'Neill, 'The European Court
of Justice: Taking Rights Seriously?' (1992) 29 *CML Rev.* 669, 670 and 692). This 'offensive'
thesis has – rightly – been refuted (see J. H. H. Weiler and N. Lockhart, '"Taking Rights
Seriously" Seriously: The European Court and Its Fundamental Rights Jurisprudence'
(1995) 32 *CML Rev.* 51 (pt. I) and 579 (pt. II)).

a. The Birth of EU Fundamental Rights

The birth of EU fundamental rights did not happen overnight. The Court had been invited – as long ago as 1958 – to judicially review a Union act in light of fundamental rights.

In *Stork*,[9] the applicant had challenged a European decision on the grounds that the Commission had infringed *German* fundamental rights. In the absence of a European bill of rights, this claim drew on the so-called 'mortgage theory'. According to this theory, the powers conferred on the European Union were tied to a human rights 'mortgage'. *National* fundamental rights would bind the *European* Union, since the Member States could not have created an organisation with more powers than themselves.[10] When they thus transferred powers to the Union, the very transfer was subject to the respective 'constitutional tradition' of each Member State. This argument was however – correctly[11] – rejected by the Court. The task of the Union institutions was to apply European laws 'without regard for their validity under national law'.[12] National fundamental rights could thus be *no direct* source of EU fundamental rights.

This position of the European Union towards *national* fundamental rights indeed never changed. However, the Court's view has significantly evolved with regard to the existence of implied *European* fundamental rights. Having originally found that European law did 'not contain any general principle, *express or otherwise*, guaranteeing the maintenance of vested rights',[13] the Court subsequently discovered 'fundamental human rights enshrined in the general principles of [European] law'.[14] This new position was spelled out in *Internationale Handelsgesellschaft*.[15] The Court here – again – rejected the applicability of national fundamental rights to European law, as this would challenge the supremacy of European over national law; yet the judgment now also confirmed the existence of an 'analogous guarantee' in European Union law. To quote the famous passage in full:

[9] Case 1/58, *Stork & Cie* v. *High Authority of the European Coal and Steel Community* [1958] ECR (English Special Edition) 17.

[10] As the Latin legal proverb makes clear: '*Nemo dat quod non habet*'.

[11] For a criticism of the 'mortgage theory', see H. G. Schermers, 'The European Communities Bound by Fundamental Rights' (1990) 27 *CML Rev.* 249, 251.

[12] Case 1/58, *Stork* v. *High Authority*, 26: 'Under Article 8 of the [ECSC] Treaty the [Commission] is only required to apply Community law. It is not competent to apply the national law of the Member States. Similarly, under Article 31 the Court is only required to ensure that in the interpretation and application of the Treaty, and of rules laid down for implementation thereof, the law is observed. It is not normally required to rule on provisions of national law. Consequently, the [Commission] is not empowered to examine a ground of complaint which maintains that, when it adopted its decision, it infringed principles of German constitutional law (in particular Articles 2 and 12 of the Basic Law).'

[13] Joined Cases 36–8/59 and 40/59, *Geitling Ruhrkohlen-Verkaufsgesellschaft mbH, Mausegatt Ruhrkohlen-Verkaufsgesellschaft mbH and I. Nold KG* v. *High Authority of the European Coal and Steel Community* [1959] ECR (English Special Edition) 423, 439 (emphasis added).

[14] Case 29/69, *Stauder* v. *City of Ulm* [1969] ECR 419, para. 7.

[15] Case 11/70, *Internationale Handelsgesellschaft mbH* v. *Einfuhr- und Vorratsstelle für Getreide und Futtermittel* [1979] ECR 1125.

> [T]he law stemming from the Treaty, an independent source of law, cannot because of its very nature be overridden by rules of national law, however framed, without being deprived of its character as [Union] law and without the legal basis of the [Union] itself being called in question. Therefore the validity of a [Union] measure or its effect within a Member State cannot be affected by allegations that it runs counter to either fundamental rights as formulated by the constitution of that State or the principles of a national constitutional structure. However, an examination should be made as to whether or not any analogous guarantee inherent in [Union] law has been disregarded. *In fact, respect for fundamental rights forms an integral part of the general principles of law protected by the Court of Justice. The protection of such rights, whilst inspired by the constitutional traditions common to the Member States, must be ensured within the framework of the structure and objectives of the [Union].*[16]

From this moment, fundamental rights were seen as an integral part of the general principles of European Union law. They were '*inspired* by the constitutional traditions *common* to the Member States', with the latter representing an *indirect* source for the Union's fundamental rights.

But what was the exact nature of this indirect relationship between national human rights and European human rights? And how would the former influence the latter? A constitutional clarification was offered in *Nold*.[17] Drawing on its previous jurisprudence, the Court held:

> [F]undamental rights form an integral part of the general principles of law, the observance of which it ensures. In safeguarding these rights, the Court is bound to draw *inspiration* from constitutional traditions common to the Member States, and it cannot therefore uphold measures which are incompatible with fundamental rights recognised and protected by the constitutions of those States. Similarly, international treaties for the protection of human rights on which the Member States have collaborated or of which they are signatories, can supply *guidelines* which should be followed within the framework of [European] law.[18]

In searching for fundamental rights inside the general principles of European law, the Court would thus draw 'inspiration' from the common constitutional traditions of the Member States. One – ingenious – way of identifying an 'agreement' between the various national constitutional traditions was to use international *agreements* of the Member States. And one such international agreement in place then was the European Convention on Human Rights. Having been

---

[16] *Ibid.*, paras. 3–4 (emphasis added).
[17] Case 4/73, *Nold* v. *Commission* [1974] ECR 491.
[18] *Ibid.*, para. 13 (emphasis added).

ratified by all Member States and dealing specially with human rights,[19] the Convention would soon assume a 'particular significance' in identifying fundamental rights for the European Union.[20] And yet, none of this conclusively characterised the legal relationship between European human rights, national human rights and the European Convention on Human Rights.

Let us therefore look at the question of the Union human rights standard first, before analysing the judicial doctrines governing limits to EU human rights.

aa. The European Standard – An 'Autonomous' Standard

Human rights express the fundamental values of a society. Each society may wish to protect distinct values and give them a distinct level of protection.[21] Not all societies may thus choose to protect a constitutional 'right to work',[22] while most liberal societies will protect 'liberty'; yet, the level at which liberty is protected might vary.[23]

Which fundamental rights exist in the European Union, and what is their level of protection? From the very beginning, the Court of Justice felt not completely free to invent an unwritten bill of rights. Instead, and in the words of the famous *Nold* passage, the Court was '*bound to* draw inspiration from constitutional traditions common to the Member States'.[24] But how binding would that inspiration be? Could the Court discover human rights that not all Member States recognise as a national human right? And would the Court consider itself under an obligation to use a particular standard for a human right?

---

[19] When the E(E)C Treaty entered into force on 1 January 1958, five of its Member States were already parties to the European Convention for the Protection of Human Rights and Fundamental Freedoms, signed in Rome on 4 November 1950. Ever since France joined the Convention system in 1974, all EU Member States have also been members of the European Convention legal order. For an early reference to the Convention in the jurisprudence of the Court, see Case 36/75, *Rutili* v. *Ministre de l'intérieur* [1975] ECR 1219, para. 32.

[20] See Joined Cases 46/87 and 227/88, *Höchst* v. *Commission* [1989] ECR 2859, para. 13: 'The Court has consistently held that fundamental rights are an integral part of the general principles of law the observance of which the Court ensures, in accordance with constitutional traditions common to the Member States, and the international treaties on which the Member States have collaborated or of which they are signatories. The European Convention for the Protection of Human Rights and Fundamental Freedoms of 4 November 1950 (hereinafter referred to as "the European Convention on Human Rights") is of particular significance in that regard.'

[21] 'Constitutions are not mere copies of a universalist ideal, they also reflect the idiosyncratic choices and preferences of the constituents and are the highest legal expression of the country's value system.' See B. de Witte, 'Community Law and National Constitutional Values' (1991–2) 2 *Legal Issues of Economic Integration* 1 at 7.

[22] Art. 4 of the Italian Constitution states: 'The Republic recognises the right of all citizens to work and promotes those conditions which render this right effective.'

[23] To illustrate this point with a famous joke: 'In Germany everything is forbidden, unless something is specifically allowed, whereas in Britain everything which is not specifically forbidden, is allowed.' (The joke goes on to claim that: 'In France everything is allowed, even if it is forbidden; and in Italy everything is allowed, especially when it is forbidden.')

[24] Case 4/73, *Nold*, para. 13 (emphasis added).

The relationship between the Union standard and the various national standards is not an easy one. Would the obligation to draw inspiration from the constitutional traditions *common* to the States not imply a common *minimum* standard? Serious practical problems follow from this view. For, if the European Union consistently adopted the lowest common human rights denominator to assess the legality of its acts, this would inevitably lead to charges that the European Court refuses to take human rights seriously.[25] Should the Union thus favour the *maximum* standard among the Member States,[26] as 'the most liberal interpretation must prevail'?[27] This time, there are serious theoretical problems with this view. For the maximalist approach assumes that courts always balance private rights against public interests. But this is not necessarily the case;[28] and, in any event, the maximum standard is subject to a 'communitarian critique' that insists that the public interest should also be taken seriously.[29] The Court has consequently rejected both approaches.

What about the European Convention on Human Rights (ECHR) as a – common – Union standard? What indeed is the status of the Convention in the Union legal order? The relationship between the European Union and the European Convention has remained ambivalent. The Court of Justice has not found the ECHR to be formally binding on the Union;[30] and it has never considered itself materially bound by the interpretation given to the Convention by the European Court of Human Rights. This interpretative freedom has created the possibility of a distinct *Union* standard for fundamental rights; yet it equally entails the danger of diverging interpretations of the European Convention in Strasbourg and Luxembourg.[31]

---

[25] For an early (implicit) rejection of the minimalist approach, see Case 44/79, *Hauer* v. *Land Rheinland-Pfalz* [1979] ECR 3727, para. 32 (emphasis added) – suggesting that a fundamental right only needs to be protected in '*several* Member States'.

[26] In favour of a maximalist approach, see L. Besselink, 'Entrapped by the Maximum Standard: On Fundamental Rights, Pluralism and Subsidiarity in the European Union' (1998) 35 *CML Rev.* 629.

[27] This 'Dworkinian' language comes from Case 29/69, *Stauder*, para. 4.

[28] The Court of Justice was faced with such a right–right conflict in Case C-159/90, *Society for the Protection of Unborn Children Ireland Ltd* v. *Stephen Grogan and others* [1991] ECR I-4685, but (in)famously refused to decide the case for lack of jurisdiction.

[29] J. Weiler, 'Fundamental Rights and Fundamental Boundaries: On Standards and Values in the Protection of Human Rights', in N. Neuwahl and A. Rosas (eds.), *The European Union and Human Rights* (Brill, 1995), 51 at 61: 'If the ECJ were to adopt a maximalist approach this would simply mean that for the [Union] in each and every area the balance would be most restrictive on the public and general interest. A maximalist approach to human rights would result in a minimalist approach to [Union] government.'

[30] See Case 4/73, *Nold*. On the idea that Member State treaties are binding on the Union, see Chapter 8, section 3(b/dd).

[31] See Joined Cases 46/87 and 227/88, *Höchst AG* v. *Commission* [1989] ECR 2859. For an excellent analysis, see R. Lawson, 'Confusion and Conflict? Diverging Interpretations of the European Convention on Human Rights in Strasbourg and Luxembourg', in R. Lawson and M. de Blois (eds.), *The Dynamics of the Protection of Human Rights in Europe*, 3 vols. (Martinus Nijhoff, 1994), III, 219 esp. 234–50.

Has the Lisbon Treaty changed this ambivalent relationship overnight? Today, there are strong textual reasons for claiming that the European Convention is *materially* binding on the Union.[32] For according to the (new) Article 6(3) TEU, fundamental rights as guaranteed by the Convention '*shall constitute general principles of the Union's law*'.[33] Will this formulation not mean that all Convention rights *are* general principles of Union law? If so, the Convention standard would henceforth provide a direct standard for the Union (see Figure 12.1). But if this route were chosen, the Convention standard would – presumably – only provide a *minimum* standard for the Union's general principles.[34]

In conclusion, the Union standard for the protection of fundamental rights is an *autonomous* standard. While drawing inspiration from the constitutional traditions common to the Member States and the European Convention on Human Rights, the Court of Justice has – so far – not considered itself directly bound by a particular national or international standard. The Court has therefore remained free to distil and protect what it sees as the shared values among the majority of people(s) within the Union and thereby assisted – dialectically – in the establishment of a shared identity for the people(s) of Europe.[35]

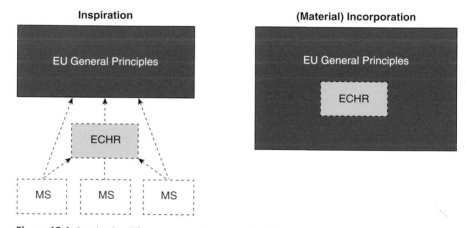

Figure 12.1 Inspiration Theory versus Incorporation Theory

---

[32] In Case C-617/10, *Åklagaren* v. *Fransson* EU: C: 2013: 105, the Court has however confirmed that the ECHR would – even after Lisbon – not be formally (!) binding on the Union (*ibid.*, para. 44): '[I]t is to be remembered that whilst, as Article 6(3) TEU confirms, fundamental rights recognised by the ECHR constitute general principles of the European Union's law and whilst Article 52(3) of the Charter requires rights contained in the Charter which correspond to rights guaranteed by the ECHR to be given the same meaning and scope as those laid down by the ECHR, the latter does not constitute, as long as the European Union has not acceded to it, a legal instrument which has been formally incorporated into European Union law.'

[33] Art. 6(3) TEU (emphasis added).

[34] This is the solution that appears to have been chosen for the Charter, see section 2 below.

[35] T. Tridimas, 'Judicial Federalism and the European Court of Justice', in J. Fedtke and B. S. Markesinis (eds.), *Patterns of Federalism and Regionalism: Lessons for the UK* (Hart, 2006), 149 at 150 – referring to the contribution of the judicial process 'to the emergence of a European *demos*'.

bb. Limitations, and 'Limitations on Limitations'

Within the European constitutional tradition, some rights are absolute rights. They cannot – under any circumstances – be legitimately limited.[36] However, most fundamental rights are *relative* rights that may be limited in accordance with a public interest. Private property may thus be taxed, and individual freedom be restricted – *if* such actions are justified by the common good.

Has the European legal order recognised such limits to human rights? From the very beginning, the Court indeed clarified that human rights are 'far from constituting unfettered prerogatives',[37] and that they may thus be subject 'to limitations laid down in accordance with the public interest'.[38] Nonetheless, liberal societies would cease to be liberal if they permitted unlimited limitations to human rights. Many legal orders therefore recognise limitations on public interest limitations. These 'limitations on limitations' to fundamental rights restrictions can be relative or absolute in nature (see Figure 12.2).

According to the principle of proportionality, each restriction of a fundamental right must always be 'proportionate' in relation to the public interest pursued.[39] The principle of proportionality is thus a *relative* principle. It balances interests: the greater the public interest protected, the greater the right restrictions permitted. In order to limit this relativist logic, a second principle may come into play.

According to the 'essential core' doctrine any limitation of human rights – even proportionate ones – must never undermine the 'very substance' of a

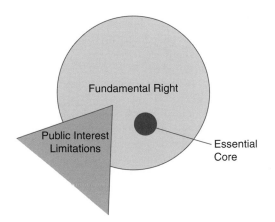

Figure 12.2 Rights Limitations: Relative and Absolute

---

[36] The European Court of Justice followed this tradition and recognised the existence of absolute rights in Case C-112/00, *Schmidberger* [2003] ECR I-5659, para. 80: 'the right to life or the prohibition of torture and inhuman or degrading treatment or punishment, which admit of no restriction'.

[37] Case 4/73, *Nold* v. *Commission*, para. 14.

[38] *Ibid.*

[39] Case 44/79, *Hauer*, para. 23.

fundamental right. This sets an *absolute* limit to all governmental actions by identifying an 'untouchable' core within a fundamental right. Yet while the principle of proportionality is almost omnipresent in the jurisprudence of the Court,[40] the existence of an 'essential core' doctrine is still unclear.[41]

The Court appears to have finally confirmed the existence of an 'essential core' doctrine in *Zambrano*.[42] Two Columbian parents challenged the rejection of their Belgian residency permits on the grounds that their children had been born in Belgium and thereby assumed Belgian and thus European citizenship.[43] And since minor children would inevitably have to follow their parents, the question arose whether the latter's deportation would violate their children's fundamental status as European citizens. The Court here held that the Belgian measures violated the Treaties, as they would 'have the effect of depriving citizens of the Union of the genuine enjoyment of the *substance of the rights* conferred by virtue of their status of citizens of the Union'.[44] The recognition of an untouchable 'substance' of a fundamental right here functioned like the essential core doctrine. In subsequent jurisprudence, the Court has however clarified that it will give a narrow construction of what constitutes the 'substance' of Union citizenship. The expulsion of a third-country husband will thus not as such constitute an unjustifiable limitation on the right to family life, where it does not force the Union citizen herself to leave the Union territory.[45]

---

[40] On the proportionality principle, see also Chapter 10, section 1(b/bb).

[41] The European Courts appear to implicitly accept the doctrine; see Case 4/73, *Nold*, 14: 'Within the [Union] legal order it likewise seems legitimate that these rights should, of necessity, be subject to certain limits justified by the overall objectives pursued by the [Union], on condition that the substance of these rights is left untouched'.

[42] Case C-34/09, *Zambrano* v. *Office national de l'emploi* [2011] ECR I-1177. Admittedly, there are many questions that this – excessively – short case raises (see 'Editorial: Seven Questions for Seven Paragraphs' (2011) *EL Rev.* 161).

[43] According to Art. 20(1) TFEU: 'Citizenship of the Union is hereby established. Every person holding the nationality of a Member State shall be a citizen of the Union. Citizenship of the Union shall be additional to and not replace national citizenship.'

[44] Case C-34/09, *Zambrano*, para. 42 (emphasis added); and see also para. 44: 'In those circumstances, those citizens of the Union would, as a result, be unable to exercise the substance of the rights conferred on them by virtue of their status as citizens of the Union.' See also Case C-86/12, *Alokpa & Moudoulou* v. *Ministre du Travail, de l'Emploi et de l'Immigration*, EU:C:2013:645.

[45] See Case C-434/09, *McCarthy* v. *Secretary of State for the Home Department* [2011] ECR I-3375; Case C-256/11, *Dereci* v. *Bundesministerium für Inneres* [2011] ECR I-11315. For an analysis of these cases, see S. Adam and P. van Elsuwege, 'Citizenship and the Federal Balance between the European Union and Its Member States: Comment on *Dereci*' (2012) 37 *EL Rev.* 176. For more recent case law, see Case C-165/14, *Rendón Marín* v. *Administración del Estado*, EU:C:2016:675; Case C-304/14, *Secretary of State for the Home Department* v. *CS*, EU:C:2016:674. The last judgment is especially problematic, as it seems to suggest that the essential core of a right can somehow be limited if that limitation is proportionate (*ibid.*, para. 50).

b. United Nations Law: External Limits to European Human Rights?

The European legal order is a constitutional order based on the rule of law.[46] This implies that an individual, where legitimately concerned,[47] must be able to challenge the legality of a European act on the basis that his human rights have been violated. Should there be exceptions to this rule, especially in the context of foreign affairs? This question is controversially debated in comparative constitutionalism; and it has, in the context of the European Union, received much attention in a special form: will *European* fundamental rights be limited by *international* obligations flowing from the United Nations Charter?

The classic answer to this question was offered by *Bosphorus*.[48] The case dealt with a European regulation implementing the United Nations embargo against the Federal Republic of Yugoslavia.[49] Protesting that its fundamental right to property was violated, the plaintiff judicially challenged the European act; and the Court had no qualms in judicially reviewing the European legislation – even if a lower review standard was applied.[50] The constitutional message behind the classic approach was clear: where the Member States decided to fulfil their international obligations under the United Nations qua European law, they would have to comply with the constitutional principles of the Union legal order and, in particular: European human rights.

This classic approach was however challenged by the General Court in 2005 by *Kadi*.[51] The applicant was a presumed Taliban terrorist, whose financial assets had been frozen as a result of European legislation that reproduced UN Security Council Resolutions.[52] Kadi claimed that his fundamental

---

[46] Case 294/83, *Parti Écologiste 'Les Verts'* v. *European Parliament* [1986] ECR 1339.

[47] On the judicial standing of private parties in the Union legal order, see Chapter 10, section 1(c).

[48] Case C-84/95, *Bosphorus Hava Yollari Turizm ve Ticaret AS* v. *Minister for Transport, Energy and Communications and others* [1996] ECR I-3953.

[49] Council Regulation 990/93 concerning trade between the European Economic Community and the Federal Republic of Yugoslavia (Serbia and Montenegro) [1993] OJ L 102, 14) was based on UN Security Council Resolution 820 (1993).

[50] For a critique of the standard of review, see I. Canor, '"Can Two Walk Together, Except They Be Agreed?" The Relationship between International Law and European Law: The Incorporation of United Nations Sanctions against Yugoslavia into European Community Law through the Perspective of the European Court of Justice' (1998) 35 *CML Rev.* 137–87.

[51] Case T-315/01, *Kadi* v. *Council and Commission* [2005] ECR II-3649.

[52] The legal challenge principally concerned Council Regulation 881/2002 imposing certain specific restrictive measures directed against certain persons and entities associated with Usama bin Laden, the Al-Qaida network and the Taliban, and repealing Regulation 467/2001 [2002] OJ L 139/9. The Regulation aimed to implement UN Security Council Resolution 1390 (2002) laying down the measures to be directed against Usama bin Laden, members of the Al-Qaida network and the Taliban and other associated individuals, groups, undertakings and entities.

rights of due process and property had been violated. The Union organs intervened in the proceedings and argued – to the surprise of many – that '*the Charter of the United Nations prevail[s] over every other obligation of international, [European] or domestic law*' to the effect that European human rights should be inoperative.[53]

To the even greater surprise – if not shock – of European constitutional scholars,[54] the General Court accepted this argument. How did the Court come to this conclusion? It had recourse to a version of the 'succession doctrine', according to which the Union may be bound by the international obligations of its Member States.[55] While this conclusion was in itself highly controversial, the dangerous part of the judgment related to the consequences of that conclusion. For the General Court recognised 'structural limits, imposed by general international law' on the judicial review powers of the European Court.[56] In the words of the Court:

> Any review of the internal lawfulness of the contested regulation, especially having regard to the provisions or general principles of [European] law relating to the protection of fundamental rights, would therefore imply that the Court is to consider, indirectly, the lawfulness of those [United Nations] resolutions. In that hypothetical situation, in fact, the origin of the illegality alleged by the applicant would have to be sought, not in the adoption of the contested regulation but in the resolutions of the Security Council which imposed the sanctions. In particular, if the Court were to annul the contested regulation, as the applicant claims it should, although that regulation seems to be imposed by international law, on the ground that that act infringes his fundamental rights which are protected by the [Union] legal order, such annulment would indirectly mean that the resolutions of the Security Council concerned themselves infringe those fundamental rights.[57]

The General Court thus declined jurisdiction to directly review European legislation *because it would entail an indirect review of the United Nations resolutions*. The justification for this self-abdication was that United Nations law was binding on all Union institutions, including the European Courts.

---

[53]   Case T-315/01, *Kadi*, paras. 156 and 177 (emphasis added).

[54]   P. Eeckhout, *Does Europe's Constitution Stop at the Water's Edge: Law and Policy in the EU's External Relations* (Europa Law, 2005); and R. Schütze, 'On "Middle Ground": The European Community and Public International Law', EUI Working Paper 2007/13.

[55]   Case T-315/01, *Kadi*, paras. 193ff. On the doctrine, see Chapter 8, section 3(b/dd).

[56]   Case T-315/01, *Kadi*, para. 212.

[57]   *Ibid.*, paras. 215–16 (references omitted).

From a constitutional perspective, this reasoning was prisoner to a number of serious mistakes.[58] And in its appeal judgment,[59] the Court of Justice remedied these constitutional blunders and safely returned to the traditional *Bosphorus* approach. The Court held:

> [T]he obligations imposed by an international agreement cannot have the effect of prejudicing the constitutional principles of the [European Treaties], which include the principle that all [Union] acts must respect fundamental rights, that respect constituting a condition of their lawfulness which it is for the Court to review in the framework of the complete system of legal remedies established by the Treat[ies].[60]

The United Nations Charter, while having 'special importance' within the European legal order,[61] would thus not be different from other international agreements.[62] Like 'ordinary' international agreements, the United Nations Charter might – if materially binding – have primacy over European legislation but '[t]hat primacy at the level of [European] law would not, however, extend to primary law, in particular to the general principles of which fundamental rights form part'.[63] European human rights would thus *not* find an external structural limit in the international obligations stemming from the United Nations.[64] The Union was firmly based on the rule of law, and this meant that all European legislation – regardless of its 'domestic' or international origin – would be limited by the respect for fundamental human rights.

---

[58] First, even if one assumes that the Union succeeded the Member States and was thus bound by United Nations law, the hierarchical status of international agreements is *below* the European Treaties. It would thus be European human rights that limit international agreements – not the other way around. The Court's position was equally based on a second mistake: the General Court believed the United Nations Charter prevails over every international and domestic obligation (*ibid.*, para. 181). But this is simply wrong with regard to the 'domestic law' part. The United Nations has never claimed 'supremacy' within domestic legal orders, and after the constitutionalisation of the European Union legal order, the latter now constitutes such a 'domestic' legal order vis-à-vis international law.

[59] Case C-402/05P, *Kadi and Al Barakaat International Foundation* v. *Council and Commission* [2008] ECR I-6351.

[60] *Ibid.*, para. 285.

[61] *Ibid.*, para. 294.

[62] *Ibid.*, para. 300: '[I]mmunity from jurisdiction for a [Union] measure like the contested regulation, as a corollary of the principle of the primacy at the level of international law of obligations under the Charter of the United Nations, especially those relating to the implementation of resolutions of the Security Council adopted under Chapter VII of the Charter, cannot find a basis in the [European Treaties].'

[63] *Ibid.*, para. 308.

[64] *Ibid.*, para. 327.

2. The 'Written' Bill of Rights: The Charter of Fundamental Rights

The desire for a *written* bill of rights for the European Union first expressed itself, by the end of the 1970s, in arguments favouring accession to the European Convention on Human Rights.[65] Yet an alternative strategy became prominent in the late twentieth century: the Union's own bill of rights.

The initiative for a 'Charter of Fundamental Rights' came from the European Council, which transferred the drafting mandate to a 'European Convention'.[66] The idea behind an internal Union codification was to strengthen the protection of fundamental rights in Europe 'by making those rights more visible in a Charter'.[67] The Charter was proclaimed in 2000, but it was then *not* legally binding. Its status was similar to the European Convention on Human Rights: it provided an informal *inspiration* but imposed no formal obligation on the European Union.[68] This ambivalent status was immediately perceived as a constitutional problem.[69] But it took almost a decade before the Lisbon Treaty recognised the Charter as having 'the same legal value as the Treaties'.

This second section looks at the structure and content of the Charter, before investigating its relationship with the European Treaties. The relationship is complex, since Article 6(1) TEU 'appends' the – amended[70] – Charter to the European Treaties. Not unlike the US 'Bill of Rights',[71] the Charter is thus placed *outside* the Union's general constitutional structure.

a. The Charter: Structure and Content

The Charter 'reaffirms' the rights that result 'in particular' from the constitutional traditions common to the Member States, the European Convention on

---

[65] Commission, 'Memorandum on the Accession of the European Communities to the European Convention for the Protection of Human Rights and Fundamental Freedoms' (1979) *Bulletin of the European Communities* – Supplement 2/79, esp. 11ff.

[66] On the drafting process, see G. de Búrca, 'The Drafting of the European Union Charter of Fundamental Rights' (2001) 26 *EL Rev.* 126.

[67] Charter, preamble 4. For a criticism of the idea of codification, see J. Weiler, 'Does the European Union Truly Need a Charter of Rights' (2000) 6 ELJ 95 at 96: '[B]y drafting a list, we will be jettisoning one of the truly original features of the current constitutional architecture in the field of human rights – the ability to use the legal system of each of the Member States as an organic and living laboratory of human rights protection which then, case by case, can be adapted and adopted for the needs of the Union by the European Court in dialogue with its national counterparts.' The argument however – wrongly – assumed that the EU Charter would replace the Court's general principles jurisprudence.

[68] See Case C-540/03, *Parliament v. Council* [2006] ECR I-5769, para. 38: 'the Charter is not a legally binding instrument'.

[69] The Charter was announced at the Nice European Council, and its status was one of the questions in the 2000 Nice 'Declaration on the Future of the Union'.

[70] The 'Convention' drafting the 'Constitutional Treaty' amended the Charter. The amended version was first published in [2007] OJ C 303/1 and can now be found in [2010] OJ C 83/389.

[71] The US 'Bill of Rights' is the name given to the first ten amendments to the 1787 US Constitution.

Human Rights and the general principles of European law.[72] This formulation suggests two things. First, the Charter aims to codify existing fundamental rights and was thus not intended to create 'new' ones. And, second, it codifies European rights from *various* sources – and thus not solely the general principles found in the European Treaties. To help identify the source(s) behind individual Charter articles, the Member States decided to give the Charter its own commentary: the 'Explanations'.[73] These 'Explanations' are not strictly legally binding, but they must be given 'due regard' in the interpretation of the Charter.[74]

The structure of the Charter is shown in Table 12.1. The Charter divides the Union's fundamental rights into six classes. The classic liberal rights are covered by Titles I to III as well as Title VI. The controversial Title IV codifies the rights of workers; yet, provision is here also made for the protection of the family and the right to healthcare.[75] Title V deals with 'citizens' rights', that is: rights that a

Table 12.1 Structure of the EU Charter

EU Charter of Fundamental Rights
Preamble
Title I – Dignity
Title II – Freedoms
Title III – Equality
Title IV – Solidarity
Title V – Citizens' Rights
Title VI – Justice
Title VII – General Provisions Article 51 – Field of Application Article 52 – Scope and Interpretation of Rights and Principles Article 53 – Level of Protection Article 54 – Prohibition of Abuse of Rights
Protocol No. 30 on Poland & the United Kingdom
Explanations

[72] Charter, preamble 5.

[73] Art. 6(1) TEU – second indent. These so-called 'Explanations' are published in [2007] OJ C 303/17.

[74] Art. 6(1) TEU and Art. 52(7) Charter: 'The explanations drawn up as a way of providing guidance in the interpretation of this Charter shall be given due regard by the courts of the Union and of the Member States.'

[75] See, respectively: Arts. 33 and 35 of the Charter.

polity provides exclusively to its members.[76] This includes the right to vote and to stand as a candidate in elections.[77]

The general principles on the interpretation and application of the Charter are finally set out in Title VII. These general provisions establish four fundamental principles. First, the Charter is addressed to the Union and will only exceptionally apply to the Member States.[78] Second, not all provisions within the Charter are 'rights', that is: directly effective entitlements for individuals. Third, the rights within the Charter can, within limits, be restricted by Union legislation.[79] Fourth, the Charter tries to establish harmonious relations with the European Treaties and the European Convention, as well as the constitutional traditions common to the Member States.[80] In the context of the present section, principles two, three and four warrant special attention.[81]

aa. (Hard) Rights and (Soft) Principles

It is important to note that the Charter makes a distinction between 'rights' and 'principles'. The Charter indeed expressly recognises the separate existence of 'principles' in Title VII.[82]

The distinction between rights and principles seems to contradict the jurisprudence of the Court with regard to fundamental *rights* as general *principles* in the context of the European Treaties. Yet what the Charter here means is that only those provisions that have direct effect will be 'rights' in that they can be invoked before a court. Not all provisions within the Charter are rights in this strict sense. Indeed, the Court has found that Charter provisions that are not unconditional and sufficiently precise would require (legislative) concretisation before they can become effective.[83]

What are these principles in the Charter, and what is their effect? The 'Explanations' offer a number of illustrations, for example: Article 37 of the Charter dealing with 'Environmental Protection'. The provision reads: 'A high

---

[76] Not all rights in this title appear to be citizens' rights. For example, Art. 41 of the Charter protecting the 'right to good administration' states (emphasis added): '*Every person* has the right to have his or her affairs handled impartially, fairly and within a reasonable time by the institutions, bodies, offices and agencies of the Union.'

[77] Art. 39 Charter.

[78] *Ibid.*, Art. 51.

[79] *Ibid.*, Art. 52(1).

[80] *Ibid.*, Art. 52(2)–(4) and (6).

[81] Principle one will be discussed in section 4(b) below.

[82] Arts. 51(1) and 52(5) of the Charter. For a good discussion of these provisions, and the case law here, see J. Krommendijk, 'Principled Silence or Mere Silence on Principles? The Role of the EU Charter's Principles in the Case Law of the European Court of Justice' (2015) 11 *European Constitutional Law Review* 321.

[83] See e.g. Case C-176/12, *Association de médiation sociale* v. *Union locale des syndicats CGT and others*, EU:C:2014:2, paras. 45 and 48: 'It is therefore clear from the wording of Article 27 of the Charter that, for this article to be fully effective, it must be given more specific expression in European Union or national law … Accordingly, Article 27 of the Charter cannot, as such, be invoked in a dispute, such as that in the main proceedings[.]'

level of environmental protection and the improvement of the quality of the environment *must be integrated into the policies of the Union* and ensured in accordance with the principle of sustainable development.'[84] This wording contrasts strikingly with that of a classic right provision. For it constitutes less a *limit* to governmental action than an *aim* for governmental action. Principles indeed come close to orienting objectives, which 'do not however give rise to direct claims for positive action by the Union institutions'.[85] They are not subjective rights, but objective guidelines that need to be observed.[86] Thus:

> The provisions of this Charter which contain principles may be implemented by legislative and executive acts taken by institutions … They shall be judicially cognisable only in the interpretation of such acts and in the ruling on their legality.[87]

The difference between rights and principles is thus one between a hard and a soft judicial claim. An individual will not have an (individual) right to a high level of environmental protection, but in line with the classic task of legal principles,[88] the courts must generally draw 'inspiration' from the Union principles when interpreting European law.

How is one to distinguish between 'rights' and 'principles'? Sadly, the Charter offers no catalogue of principles. Nor are its principles neatly grouped into a section within each substantive title. And even the wording of a particular article will not conclusively reveal whether it contains a right or a principle. But most confusingly, even a single article 'may contain both elements of a right and of a principle'.[89] How is this possible? The best way to make sense of this is to see rights and principles not as mutually exclusive concepts, but as distinct yet overlapping legal constructs.[90] 'Rights' are situational crystallisations of principles, and therefore derive from principles. A good illustration may be offered by Article 33 of the Charter on the status of the family and its relation to professional life as pictured by Figure 12.3.

bb. Limitations, and 'Limitations on Limitations'

Every legal order protecting fundamental rights recognises that some rights can be limited to safeguard the general interest. For written bills of rights, these limitations are often specifically recognised for each constitutional right. While

---

[84] Emphasis added.
[85] 'Explanations' (n. 73 above), 35.
[86] Art. 51(1) of the Charter: 'respect the rights, observe the principles'.
[87] *Ibid.*, Art. 52(5).
[88] See R. Dworkin, *Taking Rights Seriously* (Duckworth, 1996).
[89] 'Explanations' (n. 73 above), 35.
[90] In this sense, see R. Alexy, *A Theory of Constitutional Rights* (Oxford University Press, 2002), 47 – using the Wittgensteinian concept of 'family resemblance' to describe the relationship between 'rights' and 'principles'.

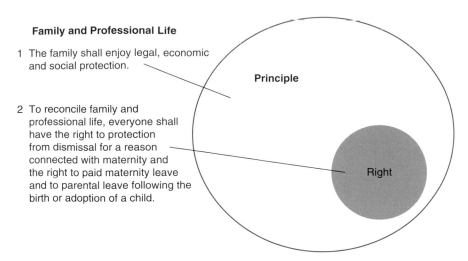

Family and Professional Life

1 The family shall enjoy legal, economic and social protection.

2 To reconcile family and professional life, everyone shall have the right to protection from dismissal for a reason connected with maternity and the right to paid maternity leave and to parental leave following the birth or adoption of a child.

Principle

Right

Figure 12.3 Principles and Rights within the Charter

the Charter follows this technique for some articles,[91] it also contains a provision that establishes general rules for limitations to all fundamental rights.

These general rules are set out in Article 52 of the Charter. The provision states:

> Any limitation on the exercise of the rights and freedoms recognised by this Charter must be *provided for by law* and *respect the essence of those rights and freedoms*. Subject to the principle of *proportionality*, limitations may be made only if they are necessary and genuinely meet objectives of general interest recognised by the Union or the need to protect the rights and freedoms of others.[92]

The provision subjects all limitations to EU Charter rights to three constitutional principles.

First, any limitation of fundamental rights must be provided for 'by law'. This (new Lisbon) requirement seems to prohibit, out of hand, human rights violations that are the result of individual acts based on *autonomous* executive powers.[93] The Court has confirmed this in *Knauf Gips* v. *Commission*.[94]

The problem is still this: will a limitation of someone's fundamental rights require the (democratic) legitimacy behind *formal* legislation? Put differently:

---

[91] See Art. 17 (Right to Property) of the Charter, which states in para. 1: 'No one may be deprived of his or her possessions, except in the public interest and in the cases and under the conditions provided for by law, subject to fair compensation being paid in good time for their loss. The use of property may be regulated by law in so far as is necessary for the general interest.'

[92] *Ibid.*, Art. 52(1) (emphasis added).

[93] On autonomous executive acts, see Chapter 9, section 2.

[94] Case C-407/08P, *Knauf Gips* v. *Commission* [2010] ECR I-6371, esp. paras. 91–2.

must every 'law' limiting a fundamental right be adopted under a 'legislative procedure'?[95] This view would significantly affect the balance between fundamental rights and the (democratic) pursuit of the common good. For if Article 52 outlaws all limitations of fundamental rights that are the result of *delegated* executive acts, much of the governmental machinery of the Union would come to a halt.

In order to prevent such a 'petrification' of the executive branch, the Court has rejected a formal concept of 'law'. Its material reading of the phrase 'provided for by law' was confirmed in *Schecke & Eifert*.[96] The case concerned two farmers who had received money under the Union's Common Agricultural Policy (CAP). One of the conditions for the receipt of money was the requirement to consent to the publication of information on the beneficiaries of the aid. This requirement had been established by a Union regulation adopted by the Council (!), which was subsequently implemented by a Commission (!) regulation. The two farmers claimed, *inter alia*, that their fundamental right to the protection of personal data under Article 8 of the Charter had been infringed;[97] and the question arose whether the publication of their names was 'provided for by law'. The Court indeed held that this was the case by simply pointing to the Commission (!) regulation requiring such publication.[98]

In light of this judgment, the best reading of the first requirement in Article 52 EU Charter is therefore this: the requirement that each limitation of a fundamental right be 'provided for by law' does not require direct *democratic* legitimation of all fundamental right interferences.[99] The provision rather insists on the *liberal* demand that all such interferences are rooted in a generally applicable norm. The generality of the norm is here a guarantee against arbitrary interferences that violate the central pillar of modern liberalism: equality before the law.

---

[95] In favour of this view, see D. Triantafyllou, 'The European Charter of Fundamental Rights and the "Rule of Law": Restricting Fundamental Rights by Reference' (2002) 39 *CML Rev.* 53–64 at 61: 'Accordingly, references to "law" made by the Charter should ideally require a co-deciding participation of the European Parliament'.

[96] Joined Cases C-92–3/09, *Schecke & Eifert* v. *Land Hessen* [2010] ECR I-11063.

[97] Art. 8(1) EU Charter states: 'Everyone has the right to the protection of personal data concerning him or her.'

[98] Joined Cases C-92–3/09, *Schecke & Eifert*, para. 66: 'First, it is common ground that the interference arising from the publication on a website of data by name relating to the beneficiaries concerned must be regarded as "provided for by law" within the meaning of Article 52(1) of the Charter. Articles 1(1) and 2 of Regulation No. 259/2008 expressly provide for such publication.'

[99] In this sense, see also Case C-130/10, *Parliament* v. *Council*, EU:C:2012:472, esp. para. 83: 'So far as concerns the Parliament's argument that it would be contrary to Union law for it to be possible for measures to be adopted that impinge directly on the fundamental rights of individuals and groups by means of a procedure excluding the Parliament's participation, it is to be noted that the duty to respect fundamental rights is imposed, in accordance with Article 51(1) of the Charter of Fundamental Rights of the European Union, on all the institutions and bodies of the Union.' The Court has now also expressly confirmed that an international agreement may constitute a 'law' for the purposes of Art. 52 of the EU Charter, see: *Opinion 1/15*, EU:C:2017:592, esp. paras. 145–6. The reasoning here comes nevertheless suspiciously close to requiring a formal legislative act – at least for the internal sphere.

Be that as it may, Article 52(1) of the Charter mentions, of course, two additional limitations on limitations. Most importantly: Article 52 has confirmed the independent existence of an absolute limit to public interferences into fundamental rights by insisting that each limitation must always 'respect the essence' of the right in question. The codification of the 'essential core' doctrine is to be welcomed; and its independence from the principle of proportionality has been consistently confirmed.[100]

Finally, and according to the principle of proportionality, each restriction of fundamental rights must be necessary in light of the general interest of the Union or the rights of others. This imposes an obligation on the Union to balance the various rights and interests at stake. In *Digital Rights Ireland*, for example, the Court found that Union Directive 2006/24 on data retention could not be justified on public security grounds. In the words of the Court:

> As regards the necessity for the retention of data required by Directive 2006/24, it must be held that the fight against serious crime, in particular against organised crime and terrorism, is indeed of the utmost importance in order to ensure public security and its effectiveness may depend to a great extent on the use of modern investigation techniques ... In this respect, it must be noted, first, that Directive 2006/24 covers, in a generalised manner, all persons and all means of electronic communication as well as all traffic data without any differentiation, limitation or exception being made in the light of the objective of fighting against serious crime ... It follows from the above that Directive 2006/24 does not lay down clear and precise rules governing the extent of the interference with the fundamental rights enshrined in Articles 7 and 8 of the Charter. It must therefore be held that Directive 2006/24 entails a wide-ranging and particularly serious interference with those fundamental rights in the legal order of the EU, without such an interference being precisely circumscribed by provisions to ensure that it is actually limited to what is strictly necessary ... Having regard to all the foregoing considerations, it must be held that, by adopting Directive 2006/24, the EU legislature has exceeded the limits imposed by compliance with the principle of proportionality in the light of Articles 7, 8 and 52(1) of the Charter.[101]

The Court consequently annulled the relevant Union legislation because it constituted a disproportionate interference with EU fundamental rights.

---

[100] Case C-293/12, *Digital Rights Ireland Ltd v. Minister for Communications, Marine and Natural Resources*. The Court here clearly distinguished between a violation of the essential core doctrine (*ibid.*, paras. 39–40) and a breach of the principle of proportionality (*ibid.*, paras. 45–69). For more recent confirmation, see Case C-547/14, *Philip Morris and others v. Secretary of State for Health*, EC:C:2016:325, esp. para. 151.

[101] Case C-293/12, *Digital Rights Ireland Ltd*, paras. 51–69. Arts. 7 and 8 of the Charter deal, respectively, with the respect for private and family life and the protection of personal data.

b. Relations with the European Treaties (and the European Convention)

aa. Harmonious Relations with the European Treaties

The EU Charter has come to be the focal point for all judicial analysis of fundamental rights violations in the Union legal order. Instead of referring back to the older (unwritten) general principles, the Court now prefers to start with the Charter. The Charter is however not 'inside' the Treaties but 'outside' them. The question therefore arises as to its relationship with the European Treaties. According to Article 6(1) TEU, the Charter has the same legal value as the Treaties and its relationship to them is governed by Title VII of the Charter. Article 52(2) here specifically governs the relationship between the Charter and the Treaties. It states:

> Rights recognised by this Charter for which provision is made in the Treaties shall be exercised under the conditions and within the limits defined by those Treaties.

The Charter thus adopts the Latin rule of *lex specialis derogat lex generalis*: the more specific – constitutional – law controls the more general law. Where the Charter codifies a fundamental right or freedom from the Treaties, the EU Treaties will have precedence and the Court is likely to confine its analysis to the provision(s) in the Treaties only.[102]

But this elegant theoretical solution suffers from practical uncertainties. How are we to identify the rights the Charter 'recognises' as (unwritten) fundamental rights within the European Treaties? The 'Explanations' are not of much assistance. A question to be resolved in future jurisprudence will thus be this: has the Charter recognised rights from the constitutional traditions of the Member States *outside* those recognised as general principles within the European Treaties?[103] If that was the case, those Charter rights would not be subject to the conditions and limits defined by the Treaties. And even where a Charter right does correspond to a general principle in the Treaties, the latter could have a narrower scope than the corresponding right in the Charter. In such cases, the question

---

[102] Case C-233/12, *Gardella* v. *INPS*, EU:C:2013:449, esp. paras. 39 and 41: 'In that vein, Article 15(2) of the Charter reiterates *inter alia* the free movement of workers guaranteed by Article 45 TFEU, as confirmed by the explanations relating to that provision … Consequently, in order to answer the questions referred, an analysis of Articles 45 TFEU and 48 TFEU is sufficient.'

[103] Art. 52(4) of the Charter states: 'In so far as this Charter recognises fundamental rights as they result from the constitutional traditions common to the Member States, those rights shall be interpreted in harmony with those traditions.' The 'Explanations' (n. 73 above), 34, tell us that Art. 52(4) has been based on the wording of Art. 6(3) TEU and demands that 'rather than following a rigid approach of "a lowest common denominator", the Charter rights concerned should be interpreted in a way offering a high standard of protection which is adequate for the law of the Union and in harmony with the common constitutional traditions'.

arises whether the entire Charter right is subject to the limitations established by the Treaties for the general principle.[104]

bb. Harmonious Relations with the European Convention

The Charter's relation to the European Convention is even more puzzling. The Charter seemingly offers a simple solution in its Article 52(3):

> In so far as this Charter contains rights which correspond to rights guaranteed by the Convention for the Protection of Human Rights and Fundamental Freedoms, the meaning and scope of those rights shall be the same as those laid down by the said Convention. This provision shall not prevent Union law providing more extensive protection.

The provision appears to *materially* incorporate the European Convention on Human Rights into the Charter. On its surface, the first sentence of the provision thereby extends the *lex specialis* rule established in the previous paragraph for the European Treaties. It thus seems that for those Charter rights that correspond to Convention rights, the conditions and limits of the latter will apply.[105] But the logic of Convention precedence is contradicted by the second sentence. For if we allow Charter rights to adopt a higher standard of protection than that established in the European Convention,[106] it must be the Charter that constitutes the *lex specialis* for the European Union.

The wording of Article 52(3) is thus – highly – ambivalent. The best way to resolve the textual contradiction is to interpret the provision to simply mean that

---

[104] This excellent point is made by K. Lenaerts and E. de Smijter, 'A "Bill of Rights" for the European Union' (2001) 38 *CML Rev.* 273, 282–4. The authors compare the scope of the respective non-discrimination rights of the Charter (Art. 21 of the Charter) with that of the Treaties (Art. 19 TFEU). The scope of the former seems thereby broader than the scope of the latter. The question therefore arises whether the Court will subject the 'additional' scope of Art. 21 of the Charter to the conditions set out in the TFEU. The same question potentially arises in the context of the freedom to conduct a business within the Charter (Art. 16 of the Charter) and its relationship to the free movement provisions within the TFEU.

[105] The 'Explanations' (n. 73 above), 33, contain a list of rights that 'at the present stage' must be regarded as corresponding to rights in the ECHR. For a recent case on the first sentence of Art. 52(3) Charter, see Case C-279/09, *Deutsche Energiehandels- und Beratungsgesellschaft mbH*.

[106] It has been argued that this contradiction would dissolve if 'Union law' is understood as referring to the European Treaties or European legislation – and not to the Charter (T. Schmitz, 'Die Grundrechtscharta als Teil der Verfassung der Europäischen Union' [2004] *Europarecht* 691 at 710). But there are serious textual, historical and teleological arguments against this view. First, why should Art. 52(3) of the Charter not deal with the relationship between the Charter and the ECHR? Put differently, if the second sentence were confined to the higher standard established by the European Treaties, why was this not clarified in Art. 6(2) TEU or Art. 6(3) TEU? Second, historically, the European Convention Working Group had expressly argued for a higher standard within the Charter (see Working Group II (Final Report) (2002) CONV 354/02, 7: 'The second sentence of

'the level of protection afforded by the Charter may never be lower than that guaranteed by the ECHR'.[107] Convention rights will thus offer a baseline – a minimum standard – for Charter rights.

3. The 'External' Bill of Rights: The European Convention on Human Rights

The discovery of an unwritten bill of rights and the creation of a written bill of rights for the Union have been 'internal' achievements. They did 'not result in any form of external supervision being exercised over the Union's institutions'.[108] Indeed, until recently, the Union was not a party to a single international human rights treaty.[109] And, by preferring *its* internal human rights over any external international standard, the Court has been accused of a 'chauvinist' and 'paro- chial' attitude.[110]

This bleak picture *is* distorted – at the very least, when it comes to one international human rights treaty that has always provided an external standard to the European Union: the European Convention on Human Rights. From the very beginning, the Court of Justice took the Convention very seriously,[111]

Article 52 §3 of the Charter serves to clarify that this article does not prevent more exten- sive protection already achieved or which may subsequently be provided for (i) in Union legislation and (ii) in some articles of the Charter which, although based on the ECHR, go beyond the ECHR because Union law acquis had already reached a higher level of protection (e.g. Article 47 on effective judicial protection, or Article 50 on the right not to be punished twice for the same offence). Thus, the guaranteed rights in the Charter reflect higher levels of protection in existing Union law'). Third, there are good teleological arguments for allowing a higher Charter standard (see D. Chalmers et al., *European Union Law* (Cambridge University Press, 2010), 244: 'The ECHR covers forty-six states. It is committed to a less intense form of political integration and governs a more diverse array of situations than the European Union. It is not clear that the judgments of a court such as the European Court of Human Rights, operating in that context, should be accepted almost unquestioningly').

[107] 'Explanations' (n. 73 above), 33. The 'Explanations' subsequently distinguish between a list of Charter rights 'where both the meaning and the scope are the same as the correspond- ing Articles of the ECHR', and those Charter rights 'where the meaning is the same as the corresponding Articles of the ECHR, but where the scope is wider' (*ibid.*, 33–4).

[108] I. de Jesús Butler and O. de Schutter, 'Binding the EU to International Human Rights Law' (2008) 27 YEL 277 at 278. This statement is correct only if limited to *direct* external supervision.

[109] *Ibid.*, 298. The Union has now acceded to the United Nations Convention on the Rights of Persons with Disabilities, see [2010] OJ L 23/35. On the negotiating history of the Convention, see G. de Búrca, 'The European Union in the Negotiation of the UN Disability Convention' (2010) 35 *EL Rev.* 174.

[110] G. de Búrca, 'The European Court of Justice and the International Legal Order after *Kadi*' (2010) 51 *Harvard International Law Journal* 1. In a later publication, Professor de Búrca softens her charge that the European Union ignores or snubs international or regional human rights law, see de Búrca, 'Evolution' (n. 5 above), 489.

[111] See S. Douglas-Scott, 'A Tale of Two Courts: Luxembourg, Strasbourg and the Growing European Human Rights Acquis' (2006) 43 *CML Rev.* 629. And in the words of a distin- guished judge of the Court: '[C]ontrary to what sometimes seems to be assumed in the

sometimes even too seriously.[112] The Union has for a long time indeed acted *as if* it was bound by the ECHR,[113] and even the ECHR has developed some form of external review of Union acts. Nonetheless, there *are* still many complexities and shortcomings in the Union's relations to the European Convention as long as the Union is not formally bound by it. In the words of the Court:

> [I]t is to be remembered that whilst, as Article 6(3) TEU confirms, fundamental rights recognised by the ECHR constitute general principles of the European Union's law and whilst Article 52(3) of the Charter requires rights contained in the Charter which correspond to rights guaranteed by the ECHR to be given the same meaning and scope as those laid down by the ECHR, *the latter does not constitute, as long as the European Union has not acceded to it, a legal instrument which has been formally incorporated into European Union law.*[114]

This third section explores the external Convention standard before and after Union accession in a first step. Thereafter, we shall quickly look at the accession (pre)conditions imposed by the Union legal order.

a. The European Convention Standard for Union Acts

aa. Before Accession: (Limited) Indirect Review

The Union is not a formal party to the European Convention. And the European Convention system has not found the European Union to have 'succeeded' its Member States.[115] Could the Member States thus escape their international obligations under the Convention by transferring decision-making powers to the European Union? In order to avoid a normative vacuum, the European

---

legal literature, I am not aware of a single case where the ECJ has gone clearly against an interpretation advanced by the European Court of Human Rights.' See A. Rosas, 'The European Court of Justice in Context: Forms and Patterns of Judicial Dialogue' (2007) 1 *European Journal of Legal Studies* 1 at 10.

[112] See Case C-145/04, *Spain* v. *United Kingdom* [2006] ECR I-7917. In that case, Spain had – rightly – argued that the extension of the right to vote in elections to the European Parliament to persons who are not citizens of a Member State violates Art. 20 TFEU. Yet the Court, expressing '[a]t the outset' (*Ibid.*, para. 60) its wish to comply with the judgment of the European Court of Human Rights in *Matthews* v. *United Kingdom* [1999] 28 EHRR 361, misinterpreted the federal foundations of the European Union to pursue this aim to the end (paras. 94–5).

[113] There however seems to be a decline in the material use of the ECHR as a point of reference after the adoption of the EU Charter (see G. de Búrca, 'After the EU Charter of Fundamental Rights: The Court of Justice as a Human rights Adjudicator?' (2013) 20 *Maastricht Journal of European and Comparative Law* 168).

[114] For this pertinent reminder, see Case C-617/10, *Åklagaren* v. *Hans Åkerberg Fransson*, EU:C:2013:105, para. 44 (emphasis added).

[115] *Confédération Française Démocratique du Travail* v. *European Communities (alternatively, their Member States)* [1978] 13 DR 231, 240: 'In so far as the application is directed against the European [Union] as such the Commission points out that the European [Union] [is]

Convention system has developed a form of *indirect* judicial review of Union acts.

This indirect review is based on the doctrine of (limited) State responsibility for acts of the Union. This complex construction draws on the idea of a human rights mortgage: the ECHR Member States cannot transfer powers to the EU without being bound – at least to some extent – by the European Convention to which they are formal parties. In *M & Co.* v. *Germany*,[116] the European Commission of Human Rights thus found that, whereas 'the Convention does not prohibit a Member State from transferring powers to international organisations', '*a transfer of powers does not necessarily exclude a State's responsibility under the Convention with regard to the exercise of the transferred powers*'.[117] This would however not mean that the State was to be held responsible for all actions of the Union, because: 'it would be contrary to the very idea of transferring powers to an international organisation to hold the Member States responsible … in each individual case'.[118] And consistent with its chosen emphasis on *State* responsibility, the Convention system would therefore not concentrate on a concrete Union act, but on the States' decision to transfer powers to the Union. This transfer of powers was thereby deemed 'not incompatible with the Convention provided that within that organisation fundamental rights will receive *an equivalent protection*'.[119]

In *Bosphorus*,[120] the European Court of Human Rights justified this 'middle ground' position as follows:

> The Convention does not, on the one hand, prohibit Contracting Parties from transferring sovereign power to an international (including a supranational) organisation in order to pursue co-operation in certain fields of activity. Moreover, even as the holder of such transferred sovereign power, that organisation is not itself held responsible under the Convention for proceedings before, or decisions of, its organs as long as it is not a Contracting Party. On the other hand, it has also been accepted that a Contracting Party is responsible under Article 1 of the Convention for all acts and omissions of its organs regardless of whether the act or omission in question was a consequence of domestic law or of the necessity to comply with international legal obligations. Article 1 makes no distinction as to the type of rule or measure concerned and does not exclude any part of a Contracting Party's 'jurisdiction' from scrutiny under the Convention.
>
> *In reconciling both these positions and thereby establishing the extent to which a State's action can be justified by its compliance with obligations flowing from its*

not a Contracting Party to the European Convention on Human Rights (Art 66 of the Convention). To this extent the consideration of the applicant's complaint lies outside the Commission's jurisdiction ratione personae.'

[116] *M& Co.* v. *Federal Republic of Germany* (1990) 64 DR 138.

[117] *Ibid.*, 145 (emphasis added).

[118] *Ibid.*, 146.

[119] *Ibid.*, 145 (emphasis added).

[120] *Bosphorus Hava Yollari Turizm ve Ticaret Anonim Sirketi* v. *Ireland* [2006] 42 EHRR 1.

> *membership of an international organisation to which it has transferred part of its sovereignty, the Court has recognised that absolving Contracting States completely from their Convention responsibility in the areas covered by such a transfer would be incompatible with the purpose and object of the Convention ... In the Court's view, State action taken in compliance with such legal obligations is justified as long as the relevant organisation is considered to protect fundamental rights, as regards both the substantive guarantees offered and the mechanisms controlling their observance, in a manner which can be considered at least equivalent to that for which the Convention provides. By 'equivalent' the Court means 'comparable'; any requirement that the organisation's protection be 'identical' could run counter to the interest of international co-operation pursued.*[121]

In its indirect review of Union acts (via its Member States), the Convention Court would thus not apply its 'normal' standard.[122] Because the Union protected human rights in an 'equivalent' manner to that of the Convention, the European Court of Human Rights would operate a 'presumption' that the States had not violated the Convention by transferring powers to the European Union. This presumption translates into a lower review standard for acts adopted by the European Union,[123] since the presumption of equivalent protection will only be rebutted where the actual treatment of human rights within the Union was 'manifestly deficient'.[124]

This lower review standard represents a compromise between two extremes: no control (as the Union is not a Convention member) and full control; and this compromise has been said to be 'the price for Strasbourg achieving a level of control over the EU, while respecting its autonomy as a separate legal order'.[125]

---

[121] *Ibid.*, paras. 152–5 (emphasis added).

[122] For a criticism of this point, see Joint Concurring Opinion of Judges Rozakis et al. (*ibid.* paras. 3–4): 'The right of individual application is one of the basic obligations assumed by the States on ratifying the Convention. It is therefore difficult to accept that they should have been able to reduce the effectiveness of this right for persons within their jurisdiction on the ground that they have transferred certain powers to the European [Union]. For the Court to leave to the [Union's] judicial system the task of ensuring "equivalent protection" without retaining a means of verifying on a case-by-case basis that that protection is indeed "equivalent", would be tantamount to consenting tacitly to substitution, in the field of [European] law, of Convention standards by a [Union] standard which might be inspired by Convention standards but whose equivalence with the latter would no longer be subject to authorised scrutiny ... In spite of its relatively undefined nature, the criterion "manifestly deficient" appears to establish a relatively low threshold, which is in marked contrast to the supervision generally carried out under the European Convention on Human Rights.'

[123] J. Callewaert, 'The European Convention on Human Rights and European Union Law: A Long Way to Harmony' [2009] *European Human Rights Law Review* 768, 773: 'through the *Bosphorus*-presumption and its tolerance as regards "non manifest" deficiencies, the protection of fundamental rights under [European] law is policed with less strictness than under the Convention'.

[124] *Bosphorus* (n. 120 above), paras. 156–7.

[125] Douglas-Scott, 'Tale of Two Courts' (n. 111 above), 639.

Under the European Convention, Member States are consequently not responsible for every European Union act that – theoretically – violates the European Convention.

When can a Member State benefit from the *Bosphorus* presumption, and when not? The Convention system has introduced an important distinction in this context: where a Member State executes compulsory or non-discretionary Union acts, it would benefit from limited review; whereas voluntary or discretionary State acts would be subject to a full review. For all EU primary law, the Member States will thus be directly and fully responsible because European primary law is freely 'authored' by the Member States – not the European Union.[126] European secondary law, by contrast, is always 'authored' by the Union; yet the *Bosphorus* presumption will here only apply to 'fully determined' European Union acts, that is: acts that do not involve any discretionary implementation by the Member States. Where Union secondary law offers Member States a choice on how to implement Union law, these discretionary national acts are national acts – not Union acts – and therefore subject to a full Convention review.[127]

bb. *After Accession: (Full) Direct Review*

The present Strasbourg jurispsrudence privileges the Union in not subjecting it to the full external review by the European Court of Human Rights. This privilege is not the result of the Union being a 'model' member. Instead it results from the Union *not* being a formal member of the European Convention system.

Will the presumption that the Union – in principle – complics with the European Convention disappear with accession? It seems compelling that the *Bosphorus* presumption will cease once the Union accedes to the Convention. For '[b]y acceding to the Convention, the European Union will have agreed to have its legal system measured by the human rights standards of the ECHR', and will 'therefore no longer deserve special treatment'.[128] The replacement of an *indirect* review by a *direct* review should therefore – at least in theory – lead to the replacement of the *limited* review by a *full* review. Yet the life of law is not always logical, and the Strasbourg Court may well decide to cherish past experiences by applying a lower review standard to the (acceded) European Union.

---

[126] On the European law principles governing the authorship of an act, see R. Schütze, 'The Morphology of Legislative Powers in the European Community: Legal Instruments and the Federal Division of Powers' (2006) 25 YEL 91, 98ff.

[127] *Bosphorus* (n. 120 above), paras. 148 and 157.

[128] T. Lock, 'EU Accession to the ECHR: Implications for Judicial Review in Strasbourg' (2010) 35 *EL Rev.* 777 at 798. See also O. de Schutter, '*Bosphorus* Post-Accession: Redefining the Relationship between the European Court of Human Rights and the Parties to the Convention', in V. Kosta et al. (eds.), *The EU Accession to the ECHR* (Hart, 2014), 177: 'This chapter argues that there will be no argument to justify the survival of the doctrine in its current form following the accession of the EU to the ECHR[.]'

What seems however certain is that accession will widen the scope of application of the European Convention to all Union actions. As we saw above, the external review of Union acts prior to accession depended on the Member States implementing Union acts; and this, by definition, required that a *Member State* had acted in some way and thereby exercised 'its' authority (even if this national authority was confined to non-discretionary choices). By contrast, in situations where the Union institutions had acted directly upon an individual without any mediating Member State measure, this Union act could not – even indirectly – be reviewed.[129] For in the absence of a connecting factor to one of the signatory States, the Union act was outside the Convention's jurisdiction.[130] This should definitely change once the Union accedes to the Convention. Henceforth all Union actions that directly enforce European law would fall within the jurisdiction of the Strasbourg Court.

b. Union Accession to the European Convention: Preconditions

The EU Commission has, long ago, suggested that an accession to the Convention should be pursued.[131] But under the original Treaties, the European Union lacked the express power to conclude human rights treaties. The Commission had thus proposed using the Union's general competence: Article 352 TFEU; yet – famously – the Court rejected this strategy in *Opinion 2/94*.[132] Since accession by the Union would have '*fundamental institutional implications*' for the Union and its Member States, it would go beyond the scope of Article 352 TFEU.[133] Only a subsequent Treaty amendment could provide the Union with the power of accession.

This power has now been granted by the Lisbon amendment. According to Article 6(2) TEU, the European Union 'shall accede to the European Convention for the Protection of Human Rights and Fundamental Freedoms'. The 'shall' formulation indicates that the Union is even constitutionally obliged to become a member of this organisation.[134] However, membership must not 'affect the Union's competences as defined in the Treaties';[135] and, even more importantly, Union accession to the European Convention needs to pay due regard to the 'specific characteristics of the Union and Union law'.[136] These constitutional

---

[129] See *Connolly v. Fifteen Member States of the European Union* (Application No. 73274/01).
[130] Art. 1 of the ECHR states: 'The High Contracting Parties shall secure to everyone within their jurisdiction the rights and freedoms defined in Section I of this Convention.'
[131] Commission, 'Memorandum' (n. 65 above).
[132] *Opinion 2/94* (Accession to ECHR) [1996] ECR I-1759.
[133] *Ibid.*, paras. 35–6 (emphasis added). On this point, see: Chapter 7, section 1(b/bb).
[134] Membership of the European Convention is now open to the European Union. For a long time, accession to the European Convention was confined to States (see Art. 4 of the Statute of the Council of Europe). This has recently changed with the amendment to Art. 59 of the Convention, para. 2 of which now states: 'The European Union may accede to this Convention.'
[135] Art. 6(2) TEU.
[136] Protocol No. 8 relating to Art. 6(2) of the Treaty on European Union on the Accession of the Union to the European Convention on the Protection of Human Rights and

preconditions have recently been given a controversial interpretation in *Opinion 2/13* (Accession to the ECHR II).

aa. Union Accession I: Constitutional Preconditions

No Opinion by the Court has generated more – negative – commentary in recent years than *Opinion 2/13*.[137] The Court had been asked to preview the constitutionality of an agreement negotiated between the Union and the ECHR Member States that would have affected the accession of the Union. And, infamously, the Court gave a resounding 'no'. This 'no' went against the three principal Union institutions as well as the absolute majority of Member States,[138] and yet: the Court was, with regard to its overall result, correct to find that the (draft) accession agreement violated the 'specific characteristics of the Union and Union law'.[139]

What was the main problem for the Court? The Court recalled that the Union is not a State; and that its legal order was a 'new kind of legal order' that was neither international nor national in nature.[140] The special characteristics of the Union were thereby partly manifested in the horizontal relations between the Member States and found particular expression in the principle of mutual

---

Fundamental Freedoms, Art. 1. According to the provision, this duty includes in particular: '(a) the specific arrangements for the Union's possible participation in the control bodies of the European Convention'; and, '(b) the mechanisms necessary to ensure that proceedings by non-Member States and individual applications are correctly addressed to Member States and/or the Union as appropriate'. According to Art. 2: 'The agreement referred to in Article 1 shall ensure that accession of the Union shall not affect the competences of the Union or the powers of its institutions. It shall ensure that nothing therein affects the situation of Member States in relation to the European Convention, in particular in relation to the Protocols thereto, measures taken by Member States derogating from the European Convention in accordance with Article 15 thereof and reservations to the European Convention made by Member States in accordance with Article 57 thereof.'

[137] For a selection of the numerous academic discussions, see Editorial, 'The EU's Accession to ECHR – a "NO" from ECJ!' (2015) 52 *CML Rev.* 1; P. Gragl, 'The Reasonableness of Jealousy: *Opinion 2/13* and EU Accession to the ECHR' (2015) 15 *European Yearbook on Human Rights* 27; T. Lock, 'The Future of the European Union's Accession to the European Convention of Human Rights after *Opinion 2/13*: Is It Still Possible and Is It Still Desirable?' (2015) 11 *European Constitutional Law Review* 239; B. de Witte and S. Imamovic, '*Opinion 2/13* on Accession to the ECHR: Defending the EU Legal Order against a Foreign Human Rights Court' (2015) 40 *EL Rev* 683.

[138] The Commission, the Parliament, the Council as well as 24(!) Member States had all intervened and pleaded in favour of accession.

[139] This does not mean that one must agree with all aspects, formal or substantive, of the Opinion. Especially the discussions with regard to Art. 53 of the EU Charter (*ibid.*, paras. 179–90) and the preliminary ruling mechanism (*ibid.*, paras. 196–200) are, in my view, weak. By contrast, the Court's arguments with regard to the CFSP are, in my view, rather convincing. For as long as the Member States are unwilling to grant the ECJ jurisdiction on CFSP matters, it would be incongruous to confer such jurisdiction 'exclusively on an international court which is outside the institutional and judicial framework of the EU' (*ibid.*, para. 256).

[140] *Ibid.*, paras. 156–8.

trust and mutual recognition.[141] These – federal – principles constitute, as we saw in Chapter 11, a key founding stone of the Union legal order. The principle of mutual recognition demands that Member States must generally accept the decisions of other Member States *as if they had adopted these decisions themselves.* For example: Germany cannot, in principle, refuse to recognise a decision of a French court because it believes that the decision of the latter violates fundamental human rights; and, according to the ECJ, this logic would have been undermined by the draft accession agreement:

> [W]hen implementing EU law, the Member States may, under EU law, be required to presume that fundamental rights have been observed by the other Member States, so that not only may they not demand a higher level of national protection of fundamental rights from another Member State than that provided by EU law, but, save in exceptional cases, they may not check whether that other Member State has actually, in a specific case, observed the fundamental rights guaranteed by the EU.
>
> The approach adopted in the agreement envisaged, which is to treat the EU as a State and to give it a role identical in every respect to that of any other Contracting Party, specifically disregards the intrinsic nature of the EU and, in particular, fails to take into consideration the fact that the Member States have, by reason of their membership of the EU, accepted that relations between them as regards the matters covered by the transfer of powers from the Member States to the EU are governed by EU law to the exclusion, if EU law so requires, of any other law. *In so far as the ECHR would, in requiring the EU and the Member States to be considered Contracting Parties not only in their relations with Contracting Parties which are not Member States of the EU but also in their relations with each other, including where such relations are governed by EU law, require a Member State to check that another Member State has observed fundamental rights, even though EU law imposes an obligation of mutual trust between those Member States, accession is liable to upset the underlying balance of the EU and undermine the autonomy of EU law.*[142]

The passage is problematic because the Court was wrong to insinuate that the problem with the accession agreement lay in the fact that it 'treat[ed] the EU as a State and to give it a role identical in every respect to that of any other Contracting Party'. Indeed, the opposite was the case. For the true problem with the agreement was treating the Member States (!) like any third contracting party – without due regard to their being *Member* States of the European Union. While a third State may thus need to check compliance with the ECHR standard when it extradites one of its nationals, within a federal Union – which

---

[141]   *Ibid.*, para. 168 (emphasis added): 'This legal structure is based on the fundamental premise that each Member State shares with all the other Member States, *and recognises that they share with it*, a set of common values on which the EU is founded, as stated in Article 2 TEU. That premise implies and justifies the existence of mutual trust between the Member States that those values will be recognised and, therefore, *that the law of the EU that implements them will be respected.*'

[142]   *Ibid.*, paras. 192–4 (emphasis added).

is itself (eventually) bound by the ECHR – this obligation undermines the principle of mutual recognition and trust. And in the eyes of the Court it was this lack of federal sensitivity towards the Member States as *States within the European Union* that was 'liable adversely to affect the specific characteristics of EU law and its autonomy'.[143]

If that reading is accepted, the problem with the accession agreement was not that it treated the EU like a State but rather that it treated it too much like an international organisation of 'sovereign' contracting parties. That is, instead of allowing Member States to mutually trust each other within a federal Union of States and blame the Union for failures in the principle of mutual trust, the accession agreement overemphasised the independent contracting status of each State. For many a human rights lawyer, this view has been hard to swallow.[144] And it is difficult to see how a new accession agreement would soon emerge on the horizon.

bb. Union Accession II: Procedural Conditions

How would a – future – negotiated accession agreement be concluded? On the Union side, accession will principally depend on the Member States of the Union:

> The Council shall ... act unanimously for the agreement on accession of the Union to the European Convention for the Protection of Human Rights and Fundamental Freedoms; the decision concluding this agreement shall enter into force after it has been approved by the Member states in accordance with their respective constitutional requirements.[145]

The Council will thus have to agree unanimously, having previously obtained the consent of the European Parliament,[146] and unlike ordinary international agreements of the Union, the Union decision concluding the accession agreement will – like a mixed agreement – only come into force once each and every Member State has ratified it. The Member States will therefore be able to block Union accession twice: once in the Council and once outside it. And while they technically are under a constitutional obligation to consent to accession as members of the Council, this is not the case for the second consent. For the duty to accede to the Convention expressed in Article 6(2) TEU will only bind the Union – and its institutions – but not the Member States.

---

[143] *Ibid.*, para. 200.

[144] For a good overview of some of the – truly exaggerated – claims, and in particular the accusation that the ECJ was a 'danger to human rights protection' (see Gragl, 'Reasonableness of Jealousy' (n. 137 above)).

[145] Art. 218(8) TFEU – second indent.

[146] *Ibid.*, Art. 218(6)(a)(ii).

4. The 'Incorporation Doctrine': EU Fundamental Rights and National Law

European fundamental rights are of course binding on the *European* Union to which they are addressed.[147] Yet will they also bind the Member States?

Two options here exist. According to a 'separation model', European fundamental rights exclusively apply to the Union, while national fundamental rights exclusively apply to the Member States.[148] By contrast, according to an 'incorporation model', European fundamental rights are 'incorporated' into the national legal orders and thus apply to European as well as national authorities by virtue of the fact that they always concern *Union* rights that must be guaranteed regardless of who interferes with them.

The European Union has, like the United States today,[149] chosen a solution in between these two extremes. While rejecting 'total' incorporation, it has developed a doctrine of 'selective' incorporation whereby EU fundamental rights may – in certain situations – directly apply to the Member States.[150] This fourth – and final – section analyses those situations in which the Union's three bills of rights have been found to apply to national authorities.

a. Incorporation and General Principles: Implementation and Derogation

The incorporation doctrine started out in the context of the Union's general principles jurisprudence. The need for such a doctrine in this context could have been doubtful in light of the fact that EU fundamental rights here are a product of the common constitutional traditions of the Member States. How can there be a need for incorporation? The answer lies in the Union's autonomous human rights standard that may be higher than a particular national

---

[147] Fundamental rights can of course be invoked against the Union legislature as well as the Union executive; and as regards the latter, the Court has recently held that EU fundamental rights will even bind the Union institutions when acting 'outside the EU legal framework' (see Joined Cases C-8/15P to C-10/15P, *Ledra and others* v. *Commission and European Central Bank*, EU:C:2016:701, para. 67). The Court here held that whenever the Commission acts – even outside EU law – it would be bound by EU fundamental rights.

[148] This separation model originally applied in US constitutionalism, because the federal Bill of Rights was here seen to be exclusively addressed to the Union; and it therefore could not bind the States, see *Barron* v. *Mayor of Baltimore*, 32 US (7 Pet) 243 (1833).

[149] With the rise of the doctrine of incorporation in the early twentieth century, the US (federal) Bill of Rights started to be considered to also apply to the States. See *Gitlow* v. *New York* 268 US 652 (1925). For a comparison between the US and the European incorporation doctrines, see R. Schütze, 'European Fundamental Rights and the Member States: From "Selective" to "Total" Incorporation?' (2011–12) 14 *CYELS* 337.

[150] The question of incorporation is distinct from the question of direct effect. The doctrine of direct effect concerns the question whether provisions are sufficiently clear and precise. If they are, fundamental rights (like any ordinary European law) will need to be applied by the executive and judicial branches. By contrast, the doctrine of incorporation concerns the addressee, that is the question *against whom* they can be applied, in this case: whether European human rights may – exceptionally – also be addressed to the Member States.

standard.[151] National legislation may thus respect national human rights, and yet violate the (higher) European standard. The Court has thus indeed invented an 'incorporation doctrine' for the general principles of the Union legal order. However, this European incorporation doctrine is 'selective' in that it only applies in two situations. The first situation concerns the implementation of European law (implementation situation). The second situation concerns derogations from European law (derogation situation).

The Court expressly confirmed that EU human rights bind national authorities when implementing European law in *Wachauf*.[152] European fundamental rights would be 'binding on the Member States when they *implement* [European] rules'.[153] What is the constitutional rationale behind this? Incorporation has here been justified on the grounds that the Member States functionally act as the Union's decentralised executive branch.[154] It would be – black – magic, so the argument goes, if the Union could escape its human rights control by leaving the implementation of controversial European policies to the Member States. Individuals will thus be entitled to challenge national acts executing European law if they violate fundamental European rights. But while this is a reasonable rationale in situations in which the Member States strictly execute European law to the letter, should it also extend to situations where the Member States are left with autonomous discretion? This tricky question appears, in principle, to be answered in the positive.[155]

---

[151] On this point, see section 1(a/aa) above.

[152] Case 5/88, *Wachauf v. Bundesamt für Ernährung und Forstwirtschaft* [1989] ECR 2609. The idea had been implicit in the (earlier) *Rutili* ruling.

[153] Case 5/88, *Wachauf*, para. 19 (emphasis added).

[154] On the Member States acting as the Union executive, see Chapter 9, section 4.

[155] Three cases support this point. In Case 5/88, *Wachauf*, the Court expressly referred to the margin of appreciation left to the Member States in the implementation of European law (para. 22): 'The [Union] regulations in question accordingly leave the competent national authorities a sufficiently wide margin of appreciation to enable them to apply those rules in a manner consistent with the requirements of the protection of fundamental rights, either by giving the lessee the opportunity of keeping all or part of the reference quantity if he intends to continue milk production, or by compensating him if he undertakes to abandon such production definitively.' Second, in Case C-2/92, *The Queen v. Ministry of Agriculture, Fisheries and Food, ex p. Dennis Clifford Bostock* [1994] ECR I-955), the plaintiff brought proceedings against the British Ministry of Agriculture, arguing that the United Kingdom had violated his property rights by failing to implement a compensation scheme for outgoing tenants and thus wrongly implementing European agricultural legislation. While finding that the European legislation did not require such a compensation scheme, the Court nonetheless examined whether European fundamental rights had been violated by the national legislation. This was confirmed in Case C-275/06, *Promusicae v. Telefónica de España* [2008] ECR I-271. The case will be discussed in section 4(b/aa) below. However, there are also judicial authorities against extending the implementing situation to cases where the Member States go beyond minimum harmonisation; see Case C-2/97, *Società italiana petroli SpA (IP) v. Borsana* [1998] ECR I-8597, esp. para. 40: 'Since the legislation at issue is a more stringent measure for the protection of working

The Court has also come to accept a second situation in which European human rights are 'incorporated'. This is the case when Member States 'derogate' from European law. This 'derogation situation' was first accepted in *ERT*.[156] The plaintiff had been granted an exclusive licence under Greek law to broadcast television programmes, which had been violated by a local television station. In the course of national proceedings, the defendant claimed that the Greek law restricted its freedom to provide services protected under the European Treaties and also violated its fundamental right to freedom of expression. In a preliminary ruling, the European Court held that where a Member State relied on European law 'in order to justify rules which are likely to obstruct the exercise of the freedom to provide services, such justification, provided by [Union] law, must be interpreted in the light of the general principles of law *and in particular fundamental rights*'.[157] In this *derogating* situation, national rules would be subject to European fundamental rights, in this case: freedom of expression.

The Court's judgment in *ERT* was a silent revolution, since it implicitly over-ruled an earlier decision to the contrary.[158] The constitutional rationale behind the derogation situation however remains contested.[159] Moreover, the *ERT* judgment was – as many revolutions are – ambivalent about its ambit. Would European human rights apply to national measures even outside the 'derogation situation'? A wider rationale had indeed been suggested in one part of the *ERT* judgment that simply spoke of national rules falling within the scope of European law.[160]

And while it is clear that a national law must first fall within the scope of European law,[161] the relationship between the derogation rationale and the wider

---

conditions compatible with the Treaty and results from the exercise by a Member State of the powers it has retained pursuant to Article [153] of the [FEU] Treaty, it is not for the Court to rule on whether such legislation and the penalties imposed therein are compatible with the principle of proportionality'; Case C-6/03, *Deponiezweckverband Eiterköpfe* v. *Land Rheinland-Pfalz* [2005] ECR I-2753.

[156] Case C-260/89, *Elliniki Radiophonia Tiléorassi (ERT) et al.* v. *Dimotiki Etairia Pliroforissis and Sotirios Kouvelas and Nicolaos Avdellas et al.* [1991] ECR I-2925.

[157] *Ibid.*, para. 43 (emphasis added).

[158] In Cases 60 and 61/84, *Cinéthèque SA and others* v. *Fédération nationale des cinémas français* [1985] ECR 2605.

[159] See in particular F. Jacobs, 'Human Rights in the European Union: The Role of the Court of Justice' [2001] *EL Rev.* 331 at 336–7; P. M. Huber, 'The Unitary Effect of the Community's Fundamental Rights: The *ERT*-Doctrine Needs to Be Revisited' (2008) 14 *European Public Law* 323 at 328: 'Though this concept is approved from various sides, it is neither methodologically nor dogmatically convincing.'

[160] Case C-260/89, *ERT*, para. 42: '[W]here such rules do fall within the scope of [European] law, and reference is made to the Court for a preliminary ruling, it must provide all the criteria of interpretation needed by the national court to determine whether those rules are compatible with the fundamental rights the observance of which the Court ensures and which derive in particular from the European Convention on Human Rights.' In the subsequent paragraph the Court then refers to the derogation rationale as a 'particular' expression of this wider rationale.

[161] See Case C-159/90, *Grogan*, in which the Court declared that the defendants could not invoke their European fundamental right to freedom of expression against Irish legislation

scope rationale has never been conclusively resolved.[162] And even if the wider rationale is the right one, the question remains what exactly is meant by the phrase 'the scope of European law'. Various meanings here compete with each other. First, the Court may identify the scope of European law with the scope of existing European *legislation*.[163] Second, the formulation could refer to the Union's *legislative competences*.[164] (This would broaden the applicability of incorporation to areas in which the Union has not yet adopted positive legislation.) Finally, the Court might wish to include all situations that fall within the scope of the Treaties, *period*.

b. *Incorporation and the Charter of Fundamental Rights*

aa. *General Rules for All Member States*
Will the 'Charter of Fundamental Rights *of the European Union*' be binding on the Member States? The Charter answers this question in Article 51 establishing its field of application:

> prohibiting activities assisting abortion. According to the European Court, the defendants had not distributed information on abortion clinics on behalf of those clinics and it *thus followed that* 'the link between the activity of the students' associations of which Mr Grogan and the other defendants are officers and medical terminations of pregnancies carried out in clinics in another Member State is too tenuous for the prohibition on the distribution of information to be capable of being regarded as a restriction within the meaning of ... the Treaty' (*ibid.*, para. 24). The national legislation thus lay outside the scope of European law (*ibid.*, para. 31).

[162] See Case C-299/95, *Kremzow* v. *Austria* [1997] ECR I-2629, para. 16: 'The appellant in the main proceedings is an Austrian national whose situation is not connected in any way with any of the situations contemplated by the Treaty provisions on freedom of movement for persons. Whilst any deprivation of liberty may impede the person concerned from exercising his right to free movement, the Court has held that a purely hypothetical prospect of exercising that right does not establish a sufficient connection with [European] law to justify the application of [European] provisions[.]'

[163] See Case C-309/96, *Annibaldi* v. *Sindaco del Comune di Guidonia and Presidente Regione Lazio* [1997] ECR I-7493, paras. 21 and 24: 'Against that background, it is clear, first of all, that there is nothing in the present case to suggest that the Regional Law was intended to implement a provision of [Union] law either in the sphere of agriculture or in that of the environment or culture ... Accordingly, as [European] law stands at present, national legislation such as the Regional Law, which establishes a nature and archaeological park in order to protect and enhance the value of the environment and the cultural heritage of the area concerned, applies to a situation which does not fall within the scope of [European] law.' See also Case C-323/08 *Rodríguez Mayor* v. *Herencia yacente de Rafael de las Heras Dávila* [2009] ECR I-11621, para. 59: 'However, as is clear from the findings relating to the first two questions, a situation such as that at issue in the dispute in the main proceedings does not fall within the scope of Directive 98/59, or, accordingly, within that of [Union] law.'

[164] This appears to be the meaning of the phrase in Joined Cases 60–1/84, *Cinéthèque*, para. 26: 'Although it is true that it is the duty of this Court to ensure observance of fundamental rights in the field of [European] law, it has no power to examine the compatibility with the European Convention of national legislation which concerns, as in this case, an area which falls within the jurisdiction of the national legislator.'

> The provisions of this Charter are addressed to the institutions, bodies, offices and agencies of the Union with due regard for the principle of subsidiarity *and to the Member States only when they are implementing Union law*. They shall therefore respect the rights, observe the principles and promote the application thereof in accordance with their respective powers and respecting the limits of the powers of the Union as conferred on it in the Treaties.[165]

The provision clarifies that the Charter is in principle addressed to the Union, and will only exceptionally apply to the Member States 'when they are *implementing* Union law'. This codifies the *Wachauf* jurisprudence. The article is, however, silent on the second scenario: the derogation situation.

Is the incorporation doctrine under the Charter thus more 'selective'? The 'Explanations' relating to the Charter are inconclusive. They state: 'As regards the Member States, it follows unambiguously [*sic*] from the case-law of the Court of Justice that the requirement to respect fundamental rights defined in the context of the Union is only binding on the Member States *when they are in the scope of Union law*.'[166] The 'Explanations' then substantiate this statement by referring *both* to *Wachauf* and *ERT*; yet ultimately revert to a formulation according to which European fundamental rights 'are binding on Member States when they *implement* [Union] rules'.[167]

In light of this devilish inconsistency, the 'Explanations' have not much value. The wording of Article 51, on the other hand, is crystal clear and could have proven an insurmountable textual barrier.[168] But it seems that the Court has elected to extend its 'general principles' jurisprudence also to the Charter. In *Fransson*,[169] the Court thus gave an extremely broad reading to the 'incorporation situation' within Article 51 of the Charter. It held:

> [T]he Charter's field of application so far as concerns action of the Member States is defined in Article 51(1) thereof, according to which the provisions of the Charter are addressed to the Member States only when they are implementing European Union law. That article of the Charter thus confirms the Court's case-law relating to the

---

[165]   Art. 51(1) of the Charter (emphasis added).
[166]   'Explanations' (n. 73 above), 32 (emphasis added).
[167]   *Ibid.* (emphasis added). The 'Explanations' here quote Case C-292/97, *Karlsson* [2000] ECR I-2737, para. 37 (itself referring to Case C-2/92, *Bostock*, para. 16).
[168]   This view is taken by C. Barnard, 'The "Opt-Out" for the UK and Poland from the Charter of Fundamental Rights: Triumph of Rhetoric over Reality?', in S. Griller and J. Ziller (eds.), *The Lisbon Treaty: EU Constitutionalism without a Constitutional Treaty?* (Springer, 2008), 256 at 263: 'Even if the explanations are wider, it is unlikely that they will be used to contradict the express wording of the Charter since the Explanations are merely guidance on the interpretation of the Charter. The Charter will therefore apply to states only when implementing [European] law[.]'
[169]   Case C-617/10, *Åklagaren v. Fransson*, EU:C:2013:105.

extent to which actions of the Member States must comply with the requirements flowing from the fundamental rights guaranteed in the legal order of the European Union.

The Court's settled case-law indeed states, in essence, that the fundamental rights guaranteed in the legal order of the European Union are applicable in all situations governed by European Union law, but not outside such situations. In this respect the Court has already observed that it has no power to examine the compatibility with the Charter of national legislation lying outside the scope of European Union law. On the other hand, if such legislation falls within the scope of European Union law, the Court, when requested to give a preliminary ruling, must provide all the guidance as to interpretation needed in order for the national court to determine whether that legislation is compatible with the fundamental rights the observance of which the Court ensures (see *inter alia*, to this effect, Case C-260/89 ERT [1991] I-2925) ... *Since the fundamental rights guaranteed by the Charter must therefore be complied with where national legislation falls within the scope of European Union law, situations cannot exist which are covered in that way by European Union law without those fundamental rights being applicable. The applicability of European Union law entails applicability of the fundamental rights guaranteed by the Charter.*[170]

In the present case, the Court thus found – over the protesting Member States – that the relevant national measure had to be judicially reviewed in light of EU fundamental rights because it was 'connected' to European Union law.[171] This seems to identify 'implementation' with any action within the scope of Union law – a reading that would naturally include the derogation situation. But more than that: the 'all situations governed by EU law' formulation comes close to a form of total incorporation, admittedly, within the scope of EU law.[172]

What does this generous incorporation doctrine mean for the relationship between the (incorporated) European and a *higher* national human rights standard? What happens, for example, where a Member State, when implementing European law, respects the European standard but violates a higher national standard? Should European law here prevent a Member State from applying its higher standard to a situation governed by European law? The problem seems to be addressed by Article 53 of the Charter, which states:

Nothing in this Charter shall be interpreted as restricting or adversely affecting human rights and fundamental freedoms as recognised, in their respective field of application, by Union law ... and by the Member States' constitutions.

---

[170]   *Ibid.*, paras. 17–19 and 21.   [171]   *Ibid.*, para. 24.

[172]   For a recent use of the broad 'all situations' formulation, see Case C-685/15, *Online Games and others*, EU:C:2017:452, para. 55: '[Art. 51(1) of the Charter] confirms the Court's settled case-law, which states that the fundamental rights guaranteed in the legal order of the European Union are applicable in all situations governed by EU law.'

The provision has been said to challenge the supremacy of European law,[173] yet the Court has expressly rejected this reading in *Melloni*.[174] The Spanish Constitutional Court here made a preliminary reference to the European Court of Justice about the possibility of refusing to execute a European Arrest Warrant. The wish not to extradite the Italian defendant stemmed from the Spanish constitutional order insisting on an opportunity for retrial in cases where the original conviction had been given *in absentia*. This opportunity did not exist in Italy, and the question thus arose whether the higher Spanish fundamental right could be invoked under Article 53 of the Charter to disapply the Union obligation under the European arrest warrant.

The European Court of Justice had none of it:

> The interpretation envisaged by the national court at the outset is that Article 53 of the Charter gives general authorisation to a Member State to apply the standard of protection of fundamental rights guaranteed by its constitution when that standard is higher than that deriving from the Charter and, where necessary, to give it priority over the application of provisions of EU law. Such an interpretation would, in particular, allow a Member State to make the execution of a European arrest warrant issued for the purposes of executing a sentence rendered in absentia subject to conditions intended to avoid an interpretation which restricts or adversely affects fundamental rights recognised by its constitution … Such an interpretation of Article 53 of the Charter cannot be accepted. That interpretation of Article 53 of the Charter would undermine the principle of the primacy of EU law inasmuch as it would allow a Member State to disapply EU legal rules which are fully in compliance with the Charter where they infringe the fundamental rights guaranteed by that State's constitution.[175]

Is Article 53 EU Charter therefore a – legally – meaningless political 'inkblot'?[176] This is not necessarily so, when viewed from the – right – perspective of the principle of pre-emption. Article 53 here simply states that a higher national human rights standard will not be pre-empted by a lower European standard as regards the validity of *national* law.

An illustration of the parallel application of European and national fundamental rights can be seen in *Promusicae* v. *Telefónica de España*.[177] Representing producers and publishers of musical recordings, the plaintiff had asked the defendant to disclose the identities and physical addresses of persons whom it provided with Internet services. These persons were believed to have used

---

[173] For a discussion of this point, see J. B. Liisberg, 'Does the EU Charter of Fundamental Rights Threaten the Supremacy of Community Law?' (2001) 38 *CML Rev.* 1171.

[174] Case C-399/11, *Melloni* v. *Ministerio Fiscal*, EU:C:2013:107. For an extensive discussion of the case, and its context, see L. Besselink, 'The Parameters of Constitutional Conflict after *Melloni*' (2014) 39 *EL Rev.* 531.

[175] Case C-399/11, Melloni, paras. 56–8 (emphasis added).

[176] Liisberg, 'EU Charter of Fundamental Rights' (n. 173 above) at 1198.

[177] Case C-275/06, *Promusicae* v. *Telefónica de España*.

the KaZaA file exchange programme, thereby infringing intellectual property rights. The defendant refused the request on the grounds that under Spanish law such a disclosure was solely authorised in criminal – not civil – proceedings. Promusicae responded that the national law implemented European law, and it consequently had to respect the European fundamental right to property.

The question before the European Court therefore was this: must Articles 17 and 47 of the Charter 'be interpreted as requiring Member States to lay down, in order to ensure effective protection of copyright, an obligation to communicate personal data in the context of civil proceedings'?[178] Not only did the Court find that there was no such obligation, it added that the existing European legislation would 'not preclude the possibility for the Member States of laying down an obligation to disclose personal data in the context of civil proceedings'.[179] A higher national standard for the protection of property was thus *not* prohibited. However, this higher national standard would need to be balanced against 'a further [European] fundamental right, namely the right that guarantees protection of personal data and hence of private life'.[180] And it was the obligation of the national court to reconcile the two fundamental rights by striking 'a fair balance' between them.[181]

This jurisprudence has been confirmed in *Fransson*.[182] The decisive criterion as to when a higher national fundamental right standard may still apply in a situation governed by EU law seems therefore to be whether EU law entirely or partially 'determines' (or 'pre-empts') a situation. Where it completely pre-empts national law, the higher national standard cannot apply. By contrast, where EU law leaves a margin of discretion to national law and that national law does not conflict with European law, the higher national standard will be allowed.

bb. *Special Rules for Poland and the United Kingdom*

The general rules governing the relationship between the Charter and the Member States are qualified for Poland and the United Kingdom. The two States have a special Protocol that governs the application of the Charter to them.[183]

---

[178]   *Ibid.*, para. 41. Arts. 17 and 47 of the Charter protect, respectively, the right of property and the right of an effective remedy.

[179]   *Ibid.*, para. 54.

[180]   *Ibid.*, para. 63.

[181]   *Ibid.*, paras. 65 and 68.

[182]   Case C–617/10, *Åklagaren* v. *Fransson*, esp. para. 29.

[183]   Protocol No. 30 on the Application of the Charter of Fundamental Rights of the European Union to Poland and to the United Kingdom. The European Council had originally agreed that the Czech Republic would be added to Protocol No. 30; see European Council (29–30 October 2009), Presidency Conclusions – Annex I: (Draft) Protocol on the Application of the Charter of Fundamental Rights of the European Union to the Czech Republic. However, the current Czech government appears to have formally withdrawn the request to be included in Protocol No. 30.

The Protocol is not a full 'opt-out' from the Charter. It expressly requires 'the Charter to be applied and interpreted by the courts of Poland and the United Kingdom'.[184] The Court has confirmed this reading in *NS*: 'Protocol (No. 30) does not call into question the applicability of the Charter in the United Kingdom or in Poland.'[185] However, opinions differ as to whether the Protocol constitutes a simple clarification for the two States – not unlike the 'Explanations';[186] or whether it does indeed represent a *partial* opt-out by establishing special principles for the two countries.[187]

The two Articles that make up the Protocol state:

Article 1

1. The Charter does not extend the ability of the Court of Justice of the European Union, or any court or tribunal of Poland or of the United Kingdom, to find that the laws, regulations or administrative provisions, practices or action of Poland or of the United Kingdom are inconsistent with the fundamental rights, freedoms and principles that it reaffirms.
2. In particular, and for the avoidance of doubt, nothing in Title IV of the Charter creates justiciable rights applicable to Poland or the United Kingdom except in so far as Poland or the United Kingdom has provided for such rights in its national law.

And:

Article 2

To the extent that a provision of the Charter refers to national laws and practices, it shall only apply to Poland or the United Kingdom to the extent that the rights or principles that it contains are recognised in the law or practices of Poland or of the United Kingdom.

In what ways, if any, do the two articles establish special rules qualifying any incorporation under Article 51 of the Charter? According to Article 1(1) of the Protocol, the Charter must not *extend* the review powers of the national courts to find national laws of these States incompatible with European rights. This

---

[184] Protocol No. 30, preamble 3.

[185] Joined Cases C-411/10 and C-493/10, *NS* v. *Secretary of State for the Home Department* [2011] ECR I-13905, para. 119.

[186] Protocol No. 30, preamble 8: 'Noting the wish of Poland and the United Kingdom to clarify certain aspects of the application of the Charter'. For a sceptical view on the purpose of the Protocol, see M. Dougan, 'The Treaty of Lisbon 2007: Winning Minds, Not Hearts' (2008) 45 *CML Rev.* 617 at 670: '[T]he Protocol's primary purpose is to serve as an effective political response to a serious failure of public discourse. Indeed, the Protocol emerges as a fantasy solution to a fantasy problem[.]'

[187] *Ibid.*, preamble 10: 'Reaffirming that references in this Protocol to the operation of specific provisions of the Charter are strictly without prejudice to the operation of other provisions of the Charter.'

provision appears to assume that the Charter rights go beyond the status quo offered by the Union's unwritten bill of rights. This is not (yet) certain, but if the Court were to find Charter rights that did not correspond to human rights in the Treaties, then Poland and the United Kingdom would not be bound by these 'additional' rights when implementing European law.[188] The Protocol would consequently constitute a *partial* opt-out from the Charter. This is repeated 'for the avoidance of any doubt' in the context of the 'solidarity' rights in Article 1(2).[189]

But what is the constitutional purpose behind Article 2 of the Protocol? In order to understand this provision, we need to keep in mind that some Charter rights expressly refer to 'national laws governing the exercise' of a European right.[190] Take for example the 'right to marry and right to found a family' – a right of particular concern to Poland.[191] According to Article 9 of the Charter '[t]he right to marry and the right to found a family shall be guaranteed in accordance with the national laws governing the exercise of these rights'.

Assume that the Court confirms the existence of a directly effective European right that would, in implementing situations, bind the Member States. Would 28 different national laws govern the exercise of this right? Or would the Court revert to the *common* constitutional traditions of the Member States? And even if the former were the case, could a couple consisting of a Spaniard and a Pole claim a right to celebrate their same-sex marriage – a marriage that is allowed in Spain but prohibited in Poland? To avoid any normative confusion, Article 2 of the Protocol thus clarifies that any reference to national laws and practices only refers to 'law or practices of Poland or of the United Kingdom'.

---

[188]   It is not yet certain whether the Court will follow this logic. In Joined Cases C-411/10 and C-493/10, *NS*, the Court seemed to reduce Art. 1(1) to a simple explanation of Art. 51 (*ibid.*, para. 120): 'Article 1(1) of Protocol (No 30) explains Article 51 of the Charter with regard to the scope thereof and does not intend to exempt the Republic of Poland or the United Kingdom from the obligation to comply with the provisions of the Charter or to prevent a court of one of those Member States from ensuring compliance with those provisions.'

[189]   And yet, this might only be true for Britain as Declaration No. 62 looks like a Polish 'opt-out' from the opt-out in Protocol No. 30. It states: 'Poland declares that, having regard to the tradition of social movement of "Solidarity" and its significant contribution to the struggle for social and labour rights, it fully respects social and labour rights, as established by European Union law, and in particular reaffirmed in Title IV of the Charter of Fundamental Rights of the European Union.'

[190]   The following Charter rights use this phrase: Art. 9 – 'Right to marry and to found a family'; Art. 10 – 'Freedom of thought, conscience, and religion'; Art. 14 – 'Right to education'; Art. 16 – 'Freedom to conduct a business'; Art. 27 – 'Workers' right to information and consultation within the undertaking'; Art. 28 – 'Right of collective bargaining and action'; Art. 30 – 'Protection in the event of unjustified dismissal'; Art. 34 – 'Social security and social assistance'; Art. 35 – 'Health care'; Art. 36 – 'Access to services of general economic interest'.

[191]   Declaration No. 61 by the Republic of Poland on the Charter of Fundamental Rights of the European Union: 'The Charter does not affect in any way the right of Member States to legislate in the sphere of public morality, family law, as well as the protection of human dignity and respect for human physical and moral integrity.'

c. Incorporation and the European Convention on Human Rights?

All Member States are formal parties to the European Convention, and therefore directly bound by it. Is there thus any need for an incorporation doctrine once the European Union accedes to the ECHR?

The answer is – surprisingly – 'Yes'. For while the substantive human rights standard established by the Convention is, after accession, likely to be the same for the Union and its Member States, the formal legal effects of the Convention will differ. As an international agreement, the European Convention currently only binds the Member States under classic international law; and under classic international law, States remain free as to which domestic legal status to grant to an international treaty. For a majority of Member States,[192] the Convention indeed only enjoys a status equivalent to national legislation, that is: it is placed *below* the national constitution. In the event of a conflict between a European Convention right and a national constitution, the latter will prevail.[193]

This normative hierarchy will change when the Union becomes a party to the European Convention. For once the Convention has become binding on the Union, it will also bind the Member States qua European law. This follows from Article 216 TFEU, according to which '[a]greements concluded by the Union are binding upon the institutions of the Union *and on its Member States*'.[194] The provision 'incorporates' all Union agreements into the national legal orders.[195] The European Convention will thus be *doubly* binding on the Member States: they are *directly* bound as parties to the Convention and *indirectly* bound as members of the Union. And, with regard to the binding effect of the Convention qua European law, the Convention will have a hierarchical status *above* the national constitutions.

d. Excursus: Human Rights and Private Party Actions

This section has so far explored whether national authorities could be subject to EU fundamental rights. A very different question however is this: should fundamental rights also apply to private parties?

---

[192] On this point, see N. Krisch, 'The Open Architecture of European Human Rights Law' (2008) 71 MLR 183 at 197: '[F]rom the perspective of the domestic courts national constitutional norms emerge as ultimately superior to European human rights norms and national courts as the final authorities in determining their relationship. This seems to hold more broadly: asked about their relationship to Strasbourg, 21 out of 32 responding European constitutional courts declared themselves not bound by ECtHR rulings.'

[193] For the German legal order, see the relatively recent confirmation by the German Constitutional Court in *Görgülü* (2 BvR 1481/04) available in English, at: www.bverfg .de/entscheidungen/rs20041014_2bvr148104en.html.

[194] Emphasis added.

[195] A. Peters, 'The Position of International Law within the European Community Legal Order' (1997) 40 *German Yearbook of International Law* 9–78 at 34: 'transposing international law into [European] law strengthens international rules by allowing them to partake in the special effects of [European] law'.

Traditionally, fundamental rights are solely addressed to public authorities. They are designed to protect private individuals against *public* power; and, as such, they will not address situations in which a private party violates another private party's fundamental rights. But if a private company systematically pays women less than men, does this not also violate the fundamental principle of equal treatment? For many legal orders, the answer here depends on the comparability of private and public conduct. Although State action generally covers everyone, private actions may only apply to a limited number of persons; and in safeguarding private choices – even morally indefensible ones – classic constitutional doctrine generally denies the *direct* application of fundamental rights to private parties. Nonetheless, in seeing fundamental rights as objective values, some constitutional orders accept their *indirect* or *limited* direct application.[196]

How has the European constitutional order solved this question? Some articles of the European Treaties have indeed been found to address private as well as public parties.[197] By contrast, the European Convention on Human Rights is not addressed to private actions; and the argument has been extended to the Charter.[198] Yet even if the Charter does not directly apply to private parties, it may, as we saw above, still have an indirect effect whenever the Court uses it to interpret European primary or secondary law.

Conclusion

The protection of human rights is a central task of the European judiciary. Unfortunately, the Union has not reserved one place for human rights, but has instead developed three bills of rights. Its unwritten bill of rights results from the general principles of Union law; the Charter of Fundamental Rights adds a written bill of rights for the Union; and the European Convention on Human Rights has provided an external bill of rights – even prior to formal accession by the Union. This chapter has analysed these three bills of rights and their respective relations to each other. The picture shown in Figure 12.4 has thereby emerged.

The EU's human rights 'surplus' has created a range of technical problems. We saw above, that the complexity of the Union's fundamental rights regime is

---

[196] For German constitutionalism, see BVerfGE 7, 198 (*Lüth*).

[197] See Art. 157 TFEU on the right to equal pay, which the Court held to apply to private parties in Case 43/75, *Defrenne* v. *Sabena* [1976] ECR 455, para. 39: 'The prohibition on discrimination between men and women applies not only to the action of public authorities, but also extends to all agreements which are intended to regulate paid labour collectively, as well as to contracts between individuals.'

[198] P. Craig, *The Lisbon Treaty: Law, Politics, and Treaty Reform* (Oxford University Press, 2010): '[The Charter] will not bind private parties such as employers.' If this view is accepted, there will indeed exist 'an uneasy tension in normative terms between the solely vertical scope of the Charter rights, when compared to the vertical and horizontal scope of some Treaty articles' (*ibid.*, 209).

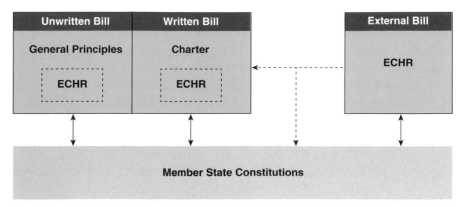

Figure 12.4 Relationship between the Union's Three 'Bills of Rights'

mainly rooted in the parallel coexistence of three sources of fundamental rights. For even if the EU Charter has become the primary instrument for the judicial review on fundamental right grounds, the relationship between the Charter and the EU Treaties (and the ECHR) is still not perfectly clarified. With regard to the EU Treaties, it thus continues to be unclear to what extent the more specific provisions within the Treaties will always determine the substantive outcome in a human rights challenge; and, as regards the ECHR, there remains some doubt as to what extent the Treaties and the Charter are (materially) bound by the Convention standard.

A second major complexity has arisen out of the coexistence of European and national fundamental rights. For instead of choosing either a simple separation model or a simple incorporation model, the Union has chosen a selective incorporation model according to which the Member States are *sometimes* bound by EU fundamental rights. Unlike the US legal order, incorporation thereby does not depend on *which* fundamental right is at stake but rather depends on the *situation* in which a Member State acts. Classically, if a State adopts national measures to implement or derogate from European law, it will be bound by EU fundamental rights; and nationals of that Member State can thus invoke these EU fundamental rights against their own State.

FURTHER READING

Books

P. Alston (ed.), *The EU and Human Rights* (Oxford University Press, 1999)

E. Ellis (ed.), *The Principle of Proportionality in the Laws of Europe* (Hart, 1999)

S. Morano-Foadi and L. Vickers, *Fundamental Rights in the EU: A Matter for Two Courts* (Hart, 2017)

S. Peers et al. (eds.), *The EU Charter of Fundamental Rights: A Commentary* (Hart, 2014)

T. Tridimas, *The General Principles of EU Law* (Oxford University Press, 2007)

S. de Vries et al. (eds.), *The Protection of Fundamental Rights in the EU After Lisbon* (Hart, 2013)

S. de Vries et al. (eds.), *The EU Charter of Fundamental rights as a Binding Instrument* (Hart, 2015)

A. Williams, *EU Human Rights Policies: A Study in Irony* (Oxford University Press, 2004)

Articles (and Chapters)

L. Besselink, 'Entrapped by the Maximum Standard: On Fundamental Rights, Pluralism and Subsidiarity in the European Union' (1998) 35 *CML Rev.* 629

G. de Búrca, 'The Evolution of EU Human Rights Law', in P. Craig and G. de Búrca (eds.), *The Evolution of EU Law* (Oxford University Press, 2011), 465

J. Coppel and A. O'Neill, 'The European Court of Justice: Taking Rights Seriously?' (1992) 29 *CML Rev.* 669

C. Costello, 'The *Bosphorus* Ruling of the European Court of Human Rights: Fundamental Rights and Blurred Boundaries in Europe' (2006) 6 *Human Rights Law Review* 87

S. Douglas-Scott, 'A Tale of Two Courts: Luxembourg, Strasbourg and the Growing European Human Rights Acquis' (2006) 43 *CML Rev.* 629

J. Krommendijk, 'Principled Silence or Mere Silence on Principles? The Role of the EU Charter's Principles in the Case Law of the Court of Justice' (2015) 11 *European Constitutional Law Review* 321

K. Lenaerts, 'Exploring the Limits of the EU Charter of Fundamental Rights' (2012) 8 *European Constitutional Law Review* 375

J. B. Liisberg, 'Does the EU Charter of Fundamental Rights Threaten the Supremacy of Community Law?' (2001) 38 *CML Rev.* 1171

T. Lock, 'The Future of the European Union's Accession to the European Convention on Human Rights after *Opinion 2/13*: Is It Still Possible and Is It Still Desirable?' (2015) 11 *European Constitutional Law Review* 239

D. Triantafyllou, 'The European Charter of Fundamental Rights and the "Rule of Law": Restricting Fundamental Rights by Reference' (2002) 39 *CML Rev.* 53

J. Weiler, 'Fundamental Rights and Fundamental Boundaries: On Standards and Values in the Protection of Human Rights', in N. Neuwahl and A. Rosas (eds.), *The European Union and Human Rights* (Brill, 1995), 51

J. Weiler, 'Does the European Union Truly Need a Charter of Rights' (2000) 6 ELJ 95

Cases on the Webpage

Case 1/58, *Stork*; Case 11/70, *Internationale Handelsgesellschaft*; Case 4/73, *Nold*; Case 5/88, *Wachauf*; Case C-260/89, *ERT*; Case C-84/95, *Bosphorus*; Case C-402/05P, *Kadi*; Case C-275/06, *Promusicae* v. *Telefonica*; Case C-34/09, *Zambrano*; Case C-407/08P, *Knaut Gips*; Joined Cases C-92–3/09, *Schecke & Eifert*; Joined Cases C-411 and 493/10, *NS*; Case C-617/10, *Fransson*; Case C-399/11, *Melloni*; Case C-293/12, *Digital Rights Ireland*; *Opinion 2/13* (ECHR Accession II)

Part III Substantive Law

This final Part III explores the substantive law of the European Union. When the Union was founded, its central substantive aim was the creation of a 'common' or 'internal' market between the Member States. Such an internal market was to go well beyond a free trade area or a customs union. Free trade areas and customs unions are areas in which a group of States abolishes, between themselves, tariffs and quantitative restrictions to inter-State trade in goods. The European Union however wished to go further. Its aim was to create an internal market as an area without internal frontiers to the free movement of goods, persons, services and capital.

To establish these four fundamental freedoms, the EU Treaties pursue a dual strategy: negative and positive integration. Negative integration refers to the judicial removal of illegal national barriers to trade, whereas positive integration means Union legislation that 'harmonises' national laws. Chapters 13 and 14 will explore both strategies in the context of the free movement of goods. Chapter 15 will analyse to what extent persons – natural persons and companies – can freely move within the Union, while Chapter 16 will look at the free movement of services and capital within the internal market.

If the core historical task of the Union has been to *create* the internal market, a second central task today is to *regulate* that market. The most important Union policy with regard to private companies has here traditionally been EU competition law – which will be discussed in Chapter 17. But the Union has also come to positively regulate many more substantive policy areas, and Chapter 18 provides a short overview of four 'representative' internal policies in which the Union plays a major legislative or executive role today.

13

Free Movement of Goods I
Negative Integration

Contents

Introduction

From the very beginning, *the* central task of the European Union was the creation of a 'common' or 'internal' market.[1] This is 'an area without internal frontiers in which the free movement of *goods, persons, services* and *capital* is ensured'.[2] The Union's 'internal market' would thus comprise *four* fundamental freedoms and involve 'the elimination of all obstacles to intra-[Union] trade in order to merge the national markets into a single market bringing about conditions as close as possible to those of a genuine internal market'.[3]

The economic advantages of uniting various national markets into a common market are manifold. Economic growth and efficiency gains will result from a better division of labour *between nations* through which comparative advantages can be exploited.[4] States have however not unconditionally followed the promises of free trade in the past. On the contrary, the better part of the history of Europe is a history of economic 'nationalism'. Each State has been 'protective' of its own national economy and erected trade barriers, such as 'customs duties' or 'quantitative restrictions'. The elimination of such national 'protectionism' was the primary aim behind the creation of the EU 'internal market'.

How could the Union create a 'single' internal market out of 'diverse' national markets? To create a common market, the EU Treaties pursue a dual strategy: negative and positive integration.[5] The Union was first charged to 'free' the internal market from unjustified national barriers to trade in goods, persons, services and capital; and, in order to create these four 'fundamental freedoms', the Treaties contained four prohibitions 'negating' illegitimate obstacles to intra-Union trade. This strategy of *negative* integration is complemented by a – second – strategy: *positive* integration. The Union is here charged to adopt positive legislation to remove obstacles to intra-Union trade arising from the diversity of national legislation. For that purpose, the Treaties conferred a number of legislative 'internal market' competences to the Union. The most general of these competences can be found in Title VII of the TFEU; and the most important

---

[1] See ex-Art. 2 ECSC and ex-Art. 2 EEC. The latter stated: 'The Community shall have as its task, by establishing a common market and progressively approximating the economic policies of Member States, to promote throughout the Community, a harmonious development of economic activities, a continuous and balanced expansion, an increase in stability, an accelerated raising of the standard of living and closer relations between the states belonging to it.' The notions of 'common market', 'internal market' and 'single market' are here used interchangeably. On the history of each specific expression, see K. Mortelmans, 'The Common Market, the Internal Market and the Single Market: What's in a Market?' (1998) 35 *CML Rev.* 101.

[2] Art. 26(2) TFEU.

[3] Case 15/81, *Gaston Schul Douane Expediteur BV* v. *Inspecteur der Invoerrechten en Accijnzen, Roosendaal* [1982] ECR 1409, para. 33.

[4] The two classic studies here are A. Smith, *Wealth of Nations* (Oxford University Press, 1998); and D. Ricardo, *The Principles of Political Economy and Taxation* (Dover Publications, 2004).

[5] J. Pinder, 'Positive and Negative Integration: Some Problems of Economic Union in the EEC' (1968) 24 *World Today* 88.

Table 13.1 Internal Market – Overview

TFEU – Part III: Internal Market Provisions	
Title I: The Internal Market	
Title II: Free Movement of Goods *Chapter 1: The Customs Union* *Chapter 2: Customs Cooperation* *Chapter 3: Prohibition of QRs* Title III: Agriculture & Fisheries	Title IV: Persons, Services & Capital *Chapter 1: Workers* *Chapter 2: Establishment* *Chapter 3: Services* *Chapter 4: Capital*
Title VII: Competition, Taxation & Approximation of Law	

provision here is Article 114, which entitles the Union to adopt harmonisation measures that 'have as their object the establishment and functioning of the internal market'.[6] The EU Treaty provisions governing the internal market are set out in Table 13.1.

Chapters 13 and 14 will, respectively, explore the spheres of negative and positive integration in the context of the free movement of goods. The free movement of goods has traditionally been the most important fundamental freedom within the internal market. Chapter 13 here analyses the constitutional regime of 'negative integration'; and in many respects, that regime has been 'path-breaking'. It has for a long time provided the general 'model' that would be followed by the other three freedoms. Section 1 therefore uses the free movement of goods provisions to introduce and present the general jurisdictional problems governing all (!) four fundamental freedoms and the 'structure' of negative integration generally.

Sections 2–4 subsequently concentrate on the specific substantive regime for goods. This regime is – sadly – split over two sites within Part III of the TFEU (see Table 13.2). It finds its principal place in Title II governing the free movement of goods, which is complemented by a chapter on 'Tax Provisions' within Title VII. With regard to goods, the Treaties expressly distinguish between *fiscal* restrictions and *regulatory* restrictions. Section 2 deals with fiscal restrictions, that is: pecuniary charges that are specifically imposed on imports. By contrast, regulatory measures are measures that limit market access by 'regulatory' means, and section 3 explores the multitude of possible regulatory restrictions, such as product requirements. Section 4 finally looks at possible justifications for such regulatory restrictions.

1. Negative Integration: Jurisdictional Questions

The EU Treaties set out four fundamental freedoms that prohibit unjustified restrictions to the free movement of goods, persons, services and capital. The Court has clarified that all fundamental freedoms are clear, unconditional and

---

[6] Art. 114 TFEU.

Table 13.2 Free Movement of Goods – Details

Title II: Free Movement of Goods	Title VII: Competition, Taxation, Approximation
Chapter 1: Customs Union	**Chapter 1: Rules on Competition**
Article 30: Prohibition on CD and CEE	**Chapter 2: Tax Provisions**
Article 31: Common Customs Tariff	Article 110: Prohibition of Discriminatory Taxes
Article 32: Commission Duties	Article 111: Repayment of Internal Taxes
Chapter 2: Customs Cooperation	Article 112: Countervailing Charges
Chapter 3: Quantitative Restrictions	Article 113: Harmonisation of Indirect Taxes
Article 34: Prohibition of QR and MEE on Imports	**Chapter 3: Approximation of Laws**
Article 35: Prohibition of QR and MEE on Exports	
Article 36: Justifications	
Article 37: State Monopolies of a Commercial Character	

precise, and thus give rise to direct effect.[7] The four fundamental freedoms can therefore be enforced as European rights in national courts. This constitutional choice has turned the European (and national) judiciary into the champion of negative integration. The court(s) here 'free' national markets from illegal barriers to trade and, as we shall see below, much of the 'internal market law' is consequently 'case law' developed by the European Courts.

What is the jurisdictional scope of this negative integration? This section explores four aspects of the scope of negative integration through the prism of the free movement of goods.[8] First, will the free movement provisions only outlaw *public* measures that hinder trade or would they also cover *private* party actions?

---

[7] In the course of time, all internal market freedoms have been declared directly effective. For the free movement of goods, see Art. 30 TFEU (see Case 77/72, *Capolongo* [1973] ECR 611); Art. 34 TFEU (Case 8/74, *Dassonville* [1974] ECR 837); Art. 35 TFEU (Case 83/78, *Pigs Marketing Board* v. *Raymond Redmond* [1978] ECR 2347); Art. 110 TFEU (Case 27/67, *Fink-Frucht* v. *Hauptzollamt München-Landsbergerstrasse* [1967] ECR 223). For the free movement of persons, see Art. 45 (Case 41/74, *Van Duyn* v. *Home Office* [1974] ECR 1337); Art. 49 TFEU (Case 2/74, *Reyners* v. *Belgium* [1974] ECR 631); and Art. 21 TFEU (Case C-413/99, *Baumbast and R* v. *Secretary of State for the Home Department* [2002] ECR I-7091). For the free movement of services, see Art. 56 (Case 33/74, *Van Binsbergen* [1974] ECR 1299). For the free movement of capital, see Art. 63 (Joined Cases C-163/94, C-165/94 and C-250/94, *Sanz de Lera and others* [1995] ECR I-4821). On the constitutional concept of direct effect, see Chapter 3.

[8] Just to repeat, the arguments within this first section apply, *mutatis mutandis*, to the three other freedoms, that is: persons (Chapter 15) as well as services and capital (Chapter 16).

Second, are the free movement provisions confined to outlawing national measures that discriminate between foreign and domestic goods or would they also extend to non-discriminatory measures? The third and the fourth aspects finally analyse two possible limits to negative integration. We shall see that the Union has been particularly maladroit here. It has persistently rejected a *de minimis* test for minor restrictions; yet it is more willing to exclude 'purely internal situations' from the scope of negative integration.

a. 'Personal' Scope: 'State Measures' and 'Private Party Actions'

Who is the addressee of negative integration? Whose measures may fall foul of the four fundamental freedoms? Among the various provisions on the free movement of goods, the only one that reveals its addressee is Article 110. The latter demands that '*[n]o Member State*' shall impose discriminatory taxes on foreign goods and therefore suggests that only *State* measures would be covered by the provision. By contrast, all other provisions do not disclose to whom they are addressed. Using the passive voice, they simply state that customs duties and quantitative restrictions '*shall be prohibited* between Member States' and that left open the question of whether these prohibitions were confined to *State measures* or whether they would also extend to *private measures* that restricted intra–Union trade.[9]

The question of whether the fundamental freedoms outlaw only State measures or private actions is traditionally referred to as the question of horizontal direct effect.[10] This is however misleading: for the concept of horizontal direct effect refers to the 'effect' of a *Union* measure in national proceedings between private parties and not to the – more restrictive – question of whether private party actions themselves are covered. There is indeed a fundamental difference between whether a Union provision can be invoked in national proceedings and whether, say, an Irish supermarket's refusal to sell French products violates the free movement provisions (see Figure 13.1).[11]

---

[9]   Admittedly, the EEC Treaty did originally contain clearer language with regard to quantitative restrictions, in ex-Art. 31 EEC. For the latter stated (emphasis added): '*Member States* shall refrain from introducing between themselves any new quantitative restrictions or measures having equivalent effect.'

[10] J. B. Cruz, 'Free Movement and Private Autonomy' (1999) 24 *EL Rev.* 603; J. Snell, 'Private Parties and the Free Movement of Goods and Services', in M. Andenas and W.-H. Roth, *Services and Free Movement in EU Law* (Oxford University Press, 2003), 211; C. Krenn, 'A Missing Piece in the Horizontal Effect "Jigsaw": Horizontal Direct Effect and the Free Movement of Goods' (2012) 49 *CML Rev.* 177S; S. Enchelmaier, 'Horizontality: The Application of the Four Freedoms to Restrictions Imposed by Private Parties', in P. Koutrakos and J. Snell, *Research Handbook on the Law of the EU's Internal Market* (Elgar, 2017), 54.

[11] On the distinction between horizontal direct effect and private party actions, see Chapter 3, section 1(b).

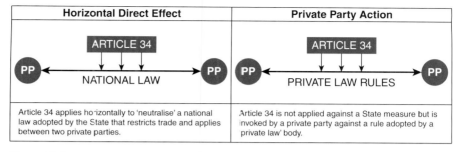

Figure 13.1 HDE and PPA under Article 34

The question of whether the free movement provisions cover private actions has been controversial. For *some* fundamental freedoms it is judicially settled. In *Walrave*,[12] the Court thus clarified for the free movement of persons and services that:

> [The freedoms do] not only apply to the action of public authorities but extend[] like-wise to rules of any other nature aimed at regulating in a collective manner gainful employment and the provision of services. The abolition as between Member States of obstacles to freedom of movement for persons and to freedom to provide services, which are fundamental objectives of the [Union] contained in Article [3] of the [EU] Treaty, would be compromised if the abolition of barriers of national origin could be neutralized by obstacles resulting from the exercise of their legal autonomy by associations or organizations which do not come under public law.[13]

The Court here extended the scope of two fundamental freedoms to private party actions; yet the ruling also suggested that the freedoms would not capture all private actions. They were confined to private party actions that were '*regulating in a collective manner*'. The refusal by one German law firm to, say, hire British graduates would thus escape negative integration, while a collective decision by the German Law Society to discriminate against British graduates might not.

Surprisingly, for the free movement of goods, the Court has traditionally been unwilling to extend the scope of negative integration beyond State measures.[14]

---

[12] Case 36/74, *Walrave and Koch* v. *Association Union cycliste international* [1974] ECR 1405.

[13] *Ibid.*, paras. 17–18. For the horizontal application of the free movement of persons and services provisions, see also Case C-415/93. *Union royale belge des sociétés de football association ASBL* v. *Jean-Marc Bosman* [1995] ECR I-4921; Case C-438/05, *International Transport Workers' Federation and Finnish Seamen's Union* v. *Viking* [2007] ECR I-10779, para. 33: 'according to settled case-law, Articles [45], [49] and [56] [TFEU] do not apply only to the actions of public authorities but extend also to rules of any other nature aimed at regulating in a collective manner gainful employment, self-employment and the provision of services'.

[14] The exceptional jurisprudential line that is sometimes invoked regards intellectual property rights; yet the better view here holds that the Court reviews the underlying State legislation (see D. T. Keeling, *Intellectual Property Rights in EU Law, I: Free Movement and Competition Law* (Oxford University Press, 2004), 176. For a discussion of this line of cases, see section 4(d) below.

In *Vlaamse Reisbureaus*, it thus held that this freedom concerned '*only public measures* and not the conduct of undertakings.'[15] This indeed became the orthodox solution for the free movement of goods. Yet the Court has nonetheless given an extremely broad definition of State measures. These measures would include all acts adopted by the central, regional or local authorities;[16] and the exercise of *public* functions by an *independent* professional body would equally be caught.[17] Actions by private bodies, by contrast, would only be held to violate the free movement of goods provisions, where they could be indirectly attributed to the State. For example, when the Irish State financed a private company to run a 'Buy Irish' advertisement campaign, the Court simply held:

> In the circumstances the … activities in question amount to the establishment of a national practice, introduced by the Irish Government and prosecuted with its assistance, the potential effect of which on imports from other Member States is comparable to that resulting from government measures of a binding nature.[18]

This logic of 'vicarious liability' also applies where it can be shown that a Member State 'fails to adopt adequate measures to prevent obstacles to the free movement of goods that are created'.[19] In *Schmidberger*,[20] the Court thus held that a demonstration, organised by private parties, that blocked an important trade route between Italy and Austria could violate Article 34:

---

[15] Case 311/85, *Vlaamse Reisbureaus* v. *ASBL Sociale Dienst van de Plaatselijke en Gewestelijke Overheidsdiensten* [1987] ECR 3801, para. 30 (emphasis added). See also Case C–159/00, *Sapod Audic* v. *EcoEmballages* [2002] ECR I–5031, para. 74: '[T]hat latter obligation arises out of a private contract between the parties to the main proceedings. Such a contractual provision cannot be regarded as a barrier to trade for the purposes of Article [34] of the Treaty since it was not imposed by a Member State but agreed between individuals.'

[16] Case 45/87, *Commission* v. *Ireland* [1988] ECR 4929; Joined Cases C–1/90 and C–176/90, *Aragonesa de Publicidad Exterior and others* v. *Departamento de Sanidad y Seguridad Social de la Generalitat de Cataluña* [1990] ECR I–4151.

[17] Joined Cases 266–7/87, *The Queen* v. *Royal Pharmaceutical Society of Great Britain, ex p. Association of Pharmaceutical Importers and others* [1989] ECR 1295, para. 15. See also Case C–292/92, *Hünermund and others* v. *Landesapothekerkammer Baden-Württemberg* [1993] ECR I–6787, para. 15.

[18] Case 249/81, *Commission* v. *Ireland* [1982] ECR 4005, esp. para. 27. See also Case 222/82, *Apple and Pear Development* v. *Lewis and others* [1983] ECR 4083.

[19] Case C–265/95, *Commission* v. *France (Strawberries)* [1997] ECR I–6959, para. 31. The Court here however clarified that it was only the combination of Art. 34 TFEU and Art. 4(3) TEU that allowed this 'vicarious liability' to work, see *ibid.* 32: 'Article [34 TFEU] therefore requires the Member States not merely themselves to abstain from adopting measures or engaging in conduct liable to constitute an obstacle to trade but also, when read with Article [4(3) TEU], to take all necessary and appropriate measures to ensure that that fundamental freedom is respected on their territory.'

[20] Case C–112/00, *Schmidberger and others* v. *Austria* [2003] ECR I–5659.

> [A]s an indispensable instrument for the realisation of a market without internal frontiers, Article [34] does not prohibit only measures emanating from the State which, in themselves, create restrictions on trade between Member States. *It also applies where a Member State abstains from adopting the measures required in order to deal with obstacles to the free movement of goods which are not caused by the State.* The fact that a Member State abstains from taking action or, as the case may be, fails to adopt adequate measures to prevent obstacles to the free movement of goods that are created, in particular, by actions by private individuals on its territory aimed at products originating in other Member States is just as likely to obstruct intra-[Union] trade as is a positive act ... It follows that, in a situation such as that at issue in the main proceedings, *where the competent national authorities are faced with restrictions on the effective exercise of a fundamental freedom enshrined in the Treaty, such as the free movement of goods, which result from actions taken by individuals, they are required to take adequate steps to ensure that freedom in the Member State concerned*[.][21]

This extensive definition of 'State actions' has come to indirectly cover some situations, where private party actions are at stake; yet, as mentioned above, it seemed for a long time that the free movement of goods provisions could not directly capture private party actions.

This orthodoxy has recently been challenged in *Fra.bo*.[22] The case concerned a *private* law body responsible in Germany for certifying the technical appropriateness of copper fittings. Having refused to certify the products of Fra.bo, an Italian company, the latter claimed that this decision prevented it from selling its products on the German market. The German certification body objected to the claim by pointing out that 'it is not bound by the provisions governing the free movement of goods and that only the Federal Republic of Germany is required to answer for any infringements of Article [34]'.[23] Yet while acknowledging the financial and political independence of the private body, the Court – surprisingly – found it nevertheless to be bound by the provision. Even if there existed another way to obtain certification,[24] the Court considered that the certification body 'in reality holds the *power to regulate the entry into the German market*'.[25] Sadly, the Court neither clarified whether it had overruled its previous jurisprudence with regard to goods nor expressly referred to its *Walrave* jurisprudence. Yet it seems that private party actions that regulate in a collective manner the free movement of goods will henceforth also fall within the scope of negative integration.

---

[21] *Ibid.*, paras. 57–62 (emphasis added).

[22] Case C-171/11, *Fra.bo SpA v. Deutsche Vereinigung des Gas- und Wasserfaches eV (DVGW)* EU:C:2012:453. For an excellent discussion of this ruling and its context, see G. van Harten and T. Nauta, 'Towards Horizontal Direct Effect for the Free Movement of Goods? Comment on *Fra.bo*' (2013) 38 *EL Rev.* 677.

[23] Case C-171/11, *Fra.bo*, para. 14.   [24] *Ibid.*, para. 29.   [25] *Ibid.*, para. 31.

b. Material Scope: Discrimination and Restriction Tests

To what extent should the Union remove national trade barriers through negative integration? This is the central question governing all internal market law. Its answer depends on what kind of internal market one wants; and three normative internal market models can indeed be distinguished. These three ideal-typical models are: the 'international' model, the 'federal' model and the 'national' model.[26]

Under the (modern) international model,[27] each State contractually commits itself to limiting its *external* sovereignty by opening its *external* borders to foreign goods, while it fully retains internal sovereignty over 'its' national market. This idea has become known as the principle of 'host state' control. It allows the importing – that is: the host – state to impose its domestic laws on foreign goods; yet it must not discriminate against imports. The prohibition of discrimination quintessentially requires States not to establish a set of rules that *distinctly* apply to imports. Within the international model, the frame of reference for discrimination is always the 'host state'. Discriminatory effects must flow from the *national measure adopted by the host state*; whereas a 'discrimination' flowing from a diversity of national regulations is not covered. The constitutional demand behind the international model is the full assimilation of foreign goods under host state rule. They are entitled to 'national treatment' in all respects – but nothing more.

The 'federal' market model, on the other hand, is based on the principle that within a 'common market' States must also lose a part of their *internal* sovereignty over 'their' national market. In line with the Union principle of mutual recognition, goods are generally entitled to move freely within the common market once they comply with the law of their home state. (The host state is thus, in principle, no longer allowed to impose its internal sovereignty over imports because they already have been regulated by another 'sovereign'.) The transition from host state to home state control within the federal model thus signifies a dramatic loss of regulatory power for the host state. The federal model is thereby not concerned with the question whether or not the host state discriminates against imports; it rather examines whether *the extension of host state laws to imports imposes a 'restriction' or 'obstacle' to intra-Union trade*. Such a restriction or obstacle is seen to arise because the good is subject to two – or in the worst-case scenario: 28 – different national 'sovereigns'.

Finally, according to the 'national' market model, all trade restrictions that are above a – legislative or judicial – Union standard must be removed. The constitutional regime of the 'common market' is here completely assimilated to that of a 'national market'. Where a State adopts rules that are higher than the Union standard, this higher state standard will violate the free movement

---

[26] For a different construction of economic ideal types within the internal market, see M. Maduro, *We the Court: The European Court of Justice and the European Economic Constitution* (Hart, 1998), esp. ch. 4.

[27] On the distinction between the 'classic' and the 'modern' international model, see R. Schütze, *From International to Federal Market* (Oxford University Press, 2017), ch. 1.

Table 13.3 Market Models and Tests

	International Model	Federal Model	National Model
Principle	Host State Rule	Home State Rule	Union Rule
Test	Direct or indirect 'discrimination' of imports	'Restrictions' to trade arising from national disparities	'Restrictions' to freedom of trade

provisions – even when this standard is applied to a State's own 'home' production. The constitutional rationale within this third model is thus not one that
identifies obstacles to trade resulting from disparities between different national
legislations. It is not a relative test that balances the jurisdictional claims of the
home state against those of the host state. On the contrary, it is based on an
absolute economic criterion: *where a State law reduces the volume of trade within the
internal market disproportionately*, it will – in principle – violate the free movement
provisions.

Which one of these three models has the European Union adopted? The
wording of the free movement provisions offers diverse suggestions. While one
provision is clearly based on the international model,[28] others seemed neutral
as to which model is to apply.[29] The Union legal order has in in the past used
all three models. And, having generally started from an international model
based on a *discrimination test*, it subsequently introduced a federal model based
on outlawing *restrictions* arising from regulatory disparities between Member
States. This federal model has become predominant in today's internal market;
yet within the case law of the Court, we also find glimpses of a national model
based on an absolute restriction of trade test.[30] Table 13.3 provides some benchmarks for the analysis of internal market law by linking our three models to three
principles and three tests. These tests have, albeit in various forms and shapes,
emerged with regard to all four fundamental freedoms; and they will thus give us
a good indication to what extent the internal market is 'integrated' with regard
to a particular fundamental freedom.

c. *Constitutional Limits I:* De minimis *and Remoteness*

The Union is a federation of States that is based on the principle of enumerated powers. The scope of the free movement provisions must consequently

---

[28] Art. 110(1) TFEU states: 'No Member State shall impose, directly or indirectly, on the products of other Member States any internal taxation of any kind in excess of that imposed
directly or indirectly on similar domestic products.'

[29] *Ibid.*, Art. 34 states: 'Quantitative restrictions on imports and all measures having equivalent
effect shall be prohibited between Member States.'

[30] With regard to *ibid.*, Art. 30, see e.g. Case C-163/90, *Administration des Douanes et Droits
Indirects* v. *Legros* [1992] ECR I-4625. The national model also surfaced in relation to Art.
34 in the *Sunday Trading* cases – to be discussed below.

also be limited; and in the past, there have been various attempts to identify these constitutional limits. These limits are easiest to find under the international model: for if only national measures that discriminate against imports are prohibited, then all non-discriminatory national measures are outside the scope of negative integration. Constitutional limits are however much harder to identify within a federal or national understanding of the internal market. Indeed, once non-discriminatory measures fall within the scope of the negative integration sphere, the question arises where exactly the Union liberalisation powers stop and where the protected regulatory powers of the Member States begin.

One way to limit the scope of market liberalisation would be through a quantitative criterion. If there existed a minimum threshold – say, a certain trade volume in foreign goods – that needed to be crossed before the free movement provisions applied, anything below that bar could simply be considered too minimal for the Union to get involved. Such a *de minimis* test would be straightforward and safeguard the regulatory powers of the Member States; yet the Court has – unlike in other areas of Union law[31] – persistently refused to read a *de minimis* rule into its free movement provisions.[32] With regard to customs duties, it has thus held that '[t]he very low rate of the charge cannot change its character with regard to the principles of the Treaty which for the purpose of determining the legality of those charges, do not admit of the substitution of quantitative criteria for those based on the nature of the charge'.[33] This refusal to establish quantitative criteria was subsequently confirmed for regulatory barriers in *Van de Haar*:

> It must be emphasized in that connection that Article [34] of the Treaty does not distinguish between measures having an effect equivalent to quantitative restrictions according to the degree to which trade between Member States is affected. If a national measure is capable of hindering imports it must be regarded as a measure having an effect equivalent to a quantitative restriction, *even though the hindrance is slight* ...[34]

This principle applies to all free movement law.[35] But, while categorically rejecting a quantitative *de minimis* rule, the Court has occasionally used a *qualitative* criterion to exclude situations that it considers too remote from the scope

---

[31] For an overview of the *de minimis* rule in the context of EU competition law, see Chapter 17, section 2(a)(dd).

[32] For an analysis of the case law here, see M. Jansson and H. Kalimo, '*De minimis* Meets "Market Access": Transformations in the Substance – and the Syntax – of EU Free Movement Law' (2014) 51 *CML Rev.* 523.

[33] Case 24/68, *Commission* v. *Italy (Statistical Levy)* [1969] ECR 193, para. 14.

[34] Joined Cases 177–8/82, *Van den Haar and others* [1984] ECR 1797, para. 13 (emphasis added).

[35] Case C-49/89, *Corsica Ferries France* v. *Direction générale des douanes françaises* [1989] ECR I-441, para. 8: 'As the Court has decided on various occasions, the articles of the [EU Treaties] concerning the free movement of goods, persons, services and capital are fundamental [Union] provisions and any restriction, even minor, of that freedom is prohibited.'

of its free movement rules.[36] It has thus held in *Kranz* that where the effects on intra-Union trade were 'too uncertain and indirect', the Court would not classify a national measure as a restriction on the free movement of goods.[37] While very uncertain and indirect, the remoteness criterion has the advantage that it is capable of capturing actual or potential effects on intra-Union trade. This allows the Court to scrutinise national legislation that may have a minimal – or no – effect in the actual case yet which might potentially affect a much broader category of traders in a serious manner.

d. Constitutional Limits II: Purely Internal Situations

One constitutional limit that applies to all four freedoms is their inability to penetrate into 'purely internal situations'. The Court derives this limit to the free movement provisions from their purpose to deal with *cross*-border situations. The limitation is designed to allow Member States some regulatory space in situations that lack a Union dimension and it therefore shares a family resemblance with the principle of subsidiarity.[38] Thus: when a *British* national challenges *British* legislation without ever having moved out of *Britain*, the free movement provisions will be of no avail because they cannot be applied 'to situations which are *wholly internal to a Member State*, in other words, where there is no factor connecting them to any of the situations envisaged by [Union] law'.[39] With regard to goods in particular, the Court has thus held that 'the application of the *Netherlands* legislation to the sale in the *Netherlands* of [goods] produced in *that country* is in no way linked to the importation or exportation of goods and does not therefore fall within the scope of [the Treaties]'.[40]

Despite its undoubted merits, the disadvantage of the 'purely internal situation' doctrine is that it can give rise to a phenomenon called 'reverse discrimination'.[41] It occurs when the federal model governs the scope of negative

---

[36]   On this point, see E. Spaventa, 'The Outer Limits of the Treaty Free Movement Provisions: Some Reflections on the Significance of *Keck,* Remoteness and *Deliège*', in C. Barnard and O. Odudu (eds.), *The Outer Limits of European Law* (Hart, 2009), 245.

[37]   Case C-69/88, *Krantz v. Ontvanger der Directe Belastingen and Netherlands State* [1990] ECR I-583, para. 11. See also Case C-379/92, *Peralta* [1994] ECR I-3453, para. 24.

[38]   On the principle of subsidiarity, see Chapter 7, section 4. For its application to the European Court of Justice, see T. Horsley, 'Subsidiarity and the European Court of Justice: Missing Pieces in the Subsidiarity Jigsaw?' (2012) 50 *Journal of Common Market Studies* 267.

[39]   Case 175/78, *Saunders* [1979] ECR 1129, para. (emphasis added).

[40]   Case 286/81, *Oosthoek* [1982] ECR 4575, para. (emphasis added).

[41]   For academic discussions of this phenomenon, see E. Cannizzaro, 'Producing "Reverse Discrimination" through the Exercise of EC Competences' (1997) 17 *YEL* 29; M. Poiares Maduro, 'The Scope of European Remedies: The Case of Purely Internal Situations and Reverse Discrimination', in C. Kilpatrick et al. (eds.), *The Future of Remedies in Europe* (Hart, 2000), 117; C. Dautricourt and S. Thomas, 'Reverse Discrimination and Free Movement of Persons under Community Law: All for Ulysses, Nothing for Penelope?' (2009) 34 *EL Rev.* 433; and A. Tryfonidou, *Reverse Discrimination in EC Law* (Kluwer, 2009).

integration. The latter requires, as we saw above, each Member State to accept, as regulatory equivalents, the national standards of every other Member State; and the situation may thus arise that the (more expensive) products of high regulation Member States compete against the (less expensive) goods of low regulation Member States.

A good example of this regulatory competition is *Cassis de Dijon* – a case that we will extensively discuss below.[42] Germany here tried to extend its higher consumer protection standard to French imports but due to the principle of mutual recognition, it was not allowed to do so; yet, because it continued to apply its higher standard to German goods, the latter suffered a 'discriminatory' disadvantage vis-à-vis French imports. Reverse discrimination thus takes place where a Member State with a higher regulatory standard chooses to impose that standard on its own goods (purely internal situation), while foreign imports are allowed to benefit from the European principle of mutual recognition.[43]

In order to partly mitigate the effects of the phenomenon of reverse discrimination, the Court has nonetheless come to adopt an extremely restrictive interpretation of what constitutes a 'purely internal situation'.[44] It has thus given a very wide interpretation of what constitutes cross-border movement;[45] while it has also come to dissociate itself from the requirement that each individual case needs to – factually – contain a cross-border element. In *Pistre*,[46] the Court indeed dismissed the French government's objection that the case fell outside the scope of Union law because '*the facts in question in the main proceedings* are confined to French territory since the prosecutions in question have been brought against French nationals and concern French products marketed on French territory'.[47] Finding that the contested national measure potentially applied to foreign products, the Court insisted that the free movement provisions '*cannot be considered inapplicable simply because all the facts of the specific case before the national court are confined to a single Member State*'.[48] With this ruling, the Court thus

---

[42] Case 120/78, *Rewe-Zentral AG* v. *Bundesmonopolverwaltung für Branntwein (Cassis de Dijon)* [1979] ECR 649.

[43] See also Case 178/84, *Commission* v. *Germany (Beer Purity)* [1987] ECR 1227. The Court has unambiguously clarified that such reverse discrimination does not fall within the scope of negative integration (see Case 98/86, *Mathot* [1987] ECR 809).

[44] For an extensive discussion of the Court's approaches, see Tryfonidou, *Reverse Discrimination* (n. 41 above), ch. 3.

[45] For a discussion of this point in the context of the free movement of persons, see N. Nic Shuibhne, 'Free Movement of Persons and the Wholly Internal Rule: Time to Move On?' (2002) 39 *CML Rev.* 731.

[46] Joined Cases C-321–4/94, *Pistre and others* [1997] ECR I-2343.

[47] *Ibid.*, para. 41 (emphasis added).

[48] *Ibid.*, para. 44 (emphasis added). For a confirmation of this rule, see Case C-184/96, *Commission* v. *France (Foie gras)* [1998] ECR I-6197; Case C-448/98, *Guimont* [2000] ECR I-10663.

pushed the jurisdictional limits of the free movement provisions significantly into what seemed to be a purely internal situation. For it clarified that it was not the facts of the specific case but the character of the national measure that determined when the free movement provisions would apply.[49]

2. Fiscal Barriers: Customs Duties and Discriminatory Taxation

a. Fiscal Barriers I: Customs Duties and Equivalent Charges

Customs duties are the classic weapon of the protectionist State. They are traditionally employed to 'protect' domestic goods against cheaper imports. Customs duties here operate like a 'countervailing' charge or tax that is typically demanded at the national border. Yet within a customs union, these pecuniary charges are prohibited.

The European Union's internal market is based on a customs union.[50] Article 30 TFEU consequently outlaws customs duties in the following simple and uncompromising way:

> Customs duties on imports and exports and charges having equivalent effect shall be prohibited between Member States. The prohibition shall also apply to customs duties of a fiscal nature.

Textually, the provision applies to duties and charges on imports and exports – with no exceptions being made.[51] And the fact that Article 30 constitutes an absolute prohibition has indeed been confirmed, as section (aa) below will show; yet, as section (bb) reveals, the Court has nevertheless allowed for objective justifications that may exceptionally permit charges imposed by Member States.

aa. Article 30: An Absolute Prohibition

What is a customs duty? With no formal definition in the EU Treaties, the Court has defined the concept in a general way. A customs duty is:

> any pecuniary charge, however small and whatever its designation and mode of application, which is imposed on goods by reason of the fact that they cross a frontier.[52]

---

[49] See A. Tryfonidou, 'The Outer Limits of Article 28 EC: Purely Internal Situations and the Development of the Court's Approach through the Years', in Barnard and Odudu, *Outer Limits of European Law* (n. 36 above), at 208.

[50] Art. 28 TFEU: 'The Union shall comprise a customs union[.]'

[51] According to Art. 28(2) TFEU, the prohibition even applies 'to products coming from third countries which are in free circulation in Member States'. On the meaning of this clause, see Schütze, *International to Federal Market* (n. 27 above), 187–97.

[52] Case 24/68, *Commission v. Italy (Statistical Levy)*, para. 7.

The Treaties do however not only outlaw customs duties in this strict sense. For Article 30 extends the prohibition to 'charges having equivalent effect' (CEE); and in *Commission v. Italy*,[53] the Court defined a CEE as

> any charge which, by altering the price of an article exported, has the same restrictive effect on the free circulation of that article as a customs duty.[54]

The purpose of the charge is thereby irrelevant, as Article 30 'ma[de] no distinction based on the purpose of the duties and charges the abolition of which it requires'.[55] All that mattered was the effect of a charge, and even the smallest of effects would matter.[56]

Would Article 30 nonetheless require a *protectionist* effect, that is: an effect that protected domestic goods? Despite a brief flirtation with a protectionist rationale,[57] the Court has chosen a different standard. The mere presence of a restricting effect on the free movement of goods will trigger Article 30 – a constitutional choice that was made in *Statistical Levy*.[58] Italy had imposed a levy on goods leaving (or entering) Italy for the purpose of collecting statistical data. Since the levy applied universally to all goods crossing the national border, Italy argued that the measure could not constitute a CEE 'since any protection of domestic production or discrimination is eliminated'.[59] The Court disagreed:

> [T]he purpose of the abolition of customs barriers is not merely to eliminate their protective nature, as the Treaty sought on the contrary to give general scope and effect to the rule on the elimination of customs duties and charges having equivalent effect, in order to ensure the free movement of goods. It follows from the system as a whole and from the general and absolute nature of the prohibition of any customs duty applicable to goods moving between Member States that customs duties are prohibited independently of any consideration of the purpose for which they were introduced and the destination of the revenue obtained therefrom.[60]

Statistical Levy thus clarified that Article 30 outlawed *all* restrictions – including restrictions devoid of a protectionist effect.[61] The 'general and absolute nature of the prohibition of any customs duties' was confirmed in subsequent jurisprudence.[62] '[A]ny pecuniary charge – however small – imposed on goods

---

[53] Case 7/68, 423, *Commission v. Italy (Art Treasures)* [1968] ECR 423.

[54] *Ibid.*, 429.   [55] *Ibid.*

[56] Case 24/68, *Commission v. Italy (Statistical Levy)*, para. 14: 'The very low rate of the charge cannot change its character with regard to the principles of the Treaty[.]'

[57] Case 2 and 3/62, *Commission v. Luxembourg and Belgium* [1962] ECR 425, 432.

[58] Case 24/68, *Commission v. Italy (Statistical Levy)*.

[59] *Ibid.*, para. 12.   [60] *Ibid.*, paras. 6–7.   [61] *Ibid.*, para. 9.

[62] Case 2/69, *Sociaal Fonds voor de Diamantarbeiders v. S.A. Ch. Brachfeld & Sons and Chougol Diamond Co.* [1969] ECR 211.

by reason of the fact that they cross a frontier constitutes an obstacle to the movement of such goods.'[63] And such an obstacle remained an obstacle 'even if it is not imposed for the benefit of the State, is not discriminatory or protective in effect or if the product on which the charge is imposed is not in competition with any domestic product'.[64]

This absolute restriction rationale underlying Article 30 clearly stemmed from the material scope of Article 30. For the prohibition appeared to only outlaw national measures that imposed a charge on the frontier-crossing of goods; and these measures are – by definition – distinctly applicable to imports or exports.

This also explains an important conceptual limit to the scope of Article 30. For if it only applies to measures that apply at the national border, it cannot cover *internal* taxation. The question thus arises of when a fiscal charge constitutes an 'external' customs duty, and when it constitutes an internal tax.[65] In its past jurisprudence, the Court has tried to answer this question by excluding from the scope of Article 30 'financial charges within a general system of internal taxation *applying systematically to domestic and imported products according to the same criteria.*[66]

This – convincing – external limit to Article 30 has, however, been overruled by a short string of cases dealing with non-discriminatory customs charges *within* Member States. In *Legros,*[67] the Court was asked to deal with a 'regional' customs charge that was levied when goods were imported into Réunion – an island in the Indian Ocean that constitutes an overseas department of France. In the view of the Court, such a 'regional' charge was 'as serious as a charge levied at the national frontier by reason of the introduction of the product into the whole territory of a Member State'.[68] The Court subsequently clarified this ruling in

---

[63] *Ibid.,* para. 11/14.

[64] *Ibid.,* paras. 15/18. See also Case C-72/03, *Carbonati Apuani Srl* v. *Comune di Carrara* [2004] ECR I-8027.

[65] Since the Treaty only outlaws *discriminatory* internal taxes, the answer to this question will conclusively determine the legality of non-discriminatory fiscal charges. On this point, see section 2(b) below.

[66] Case 77/72, *Capolongo* v. *Azienda Agricole* [1973] ECR 611, para. 12 (emphasis added). The Court however qualified this exclusion of generally applicable tax measures by insisting (*ibid.,* paras. 13–14) that 'when such a financial charge or duty is intended exclusively to support activities which specifically profit taxed domestic products, it can follow that the general duty levied according to the same criteria on the imported product and the domestic product nevertheless constitutes for the former a net supplementary tax burden, whilst for the latter it constitutes in reality a set-off against benefits or aids previously received … Consequently, a duty within the general system of internal taxation applying systematically to domestic and imported products according to the same criteria, can nevertheless constitute a charge having an effect equivalent to a customs duty on imports, when such contribution is intended exclusively to support activities which specifically benefit the taxed domestic product.'

[67] Case C-163/90, *Administration des Douanes et Droits Indirects* v. *Léopold Legros and others* [1992] ECR I-4625.

[68] *Ibid.,* para. 16.

Lancry,[69] where it held that the said regional charges would even violate Article 30 when imposed on products of the 'home' State. The reasoning of the Court is worth quoting in full:

> The unity of the [Union] customs territory is undermined by the establishment of a regional customs frontier just the same, whether the products on which a charge is levied by reason of the fact that they cross a frontier are domestic products or come from other Member States. Furthermore, the obstacle to the free movement of goods created by the imposition on domestic products of a charge levied by reason of their crossing that frontier is no less serious than that created by the collection of a charge of the same kind on products from another Member State.
>
> Since the very principle of a customs union covers all trade in goods, as provided for by Article [28 TFEU], *it requires the free movement of goods generally, as opposed to inter-State trade alone*, to be ensured within the union. Although Article [28ff.] makes express reference only to trade between Member States, that is because it was assumed that there were no charges exhibiting the features of a customs duty in existence within the Member States. Since the absence of such charges is an essential precondition for the attainment of a customs union covering all trade in goods, it follows that they are likewise prohibited by Article [30].[70]

The Court here interpreted Article 30 in light of the 'national' market model that is disconnected from inter-State trade. This reasoning has been heavily attacked;[71] and yet, the Court has confirmed it in later jurisprudence.[72] Any customs duty, whether imposed at a national border between Member States or at a regional border within a Member State, is thus prohibited – unless it can exceptionally be justified.

bb. Objective 'Justifications'

May a State, exceptionally, impose customs duties in certain situations? There are no express justifications for fiscal barriers to trade in goods. This absence contrasts with the presence of such justifications for regulatory barriers in Article 36.[73]

Could the latter provision apply by analogy to fiscal barriers? In *Commission v. Italy*,[74] Italy tried to justify a charge on the export of goods with artistic or historical value by pointing to Article 36. Yet the Court rejected this reasoning. Exceptions to the free movement of goods had to be interpreted restrictively; and with regard to Article 36 this meant that it 'is not possible to apply the exception laid down in the latter provision to measures which fall outside the

---

[69] Joined Cases C-363/93, C-407–11/93, *Lancry SA* v. *Direction Générale des Douanes and others* [1994] ECR I-3957.

[70] *Ibid.*, paras. 27–9.

[71] For an excellent criticism of this approach, see Advocate General M. Poiares Maduro in Case C-72/03, *Carbonati Apuani Srl* v. *Comune di Carrara* [2004] ECR I-8027, paras. 44–50.

[72] *Ibid.* See also Case C-293/02, *Jersey Produce Marketing Organisation Ltd* v. *States of Jersey and Jersey Potato Export Marketing Board* [2005] ECR I-9542.

[73] For the text of Art. 36 and its interpretation, see section 4(a) below.

[74] Case 7/68, *Commission* v. *Italy (Art Treasures)*.

scope of the prohibitions referred to in the chapter relating to the elimination of quantitative restrictions between Member States'.[75] Article 36 was thus confined to *regulatory* restrictions and could not be extended to *fiscal* charges. And since there were no specific justifications for measures falling into Article 30, the Court concluded that the provision 'does not permit of any exceptions'.[76]

The Court however subsequently recognised two *implied* exceptions. The first exception relates to the situation where a fiscal charge constitutes consideration for a service rendered. In *Statistical Levy*,[77] the Italian government had argued that its wish to create statistical data for imports and exports generally benefited individual traders, and that this commercial advantage 'justifies their paying for this public service' as a quid pro quo.[78] The Court indeed accepted the abstract idea;[79] yet it gave it an extremely restrictive interpretation. In the present case, it thus found against Italy, since the charge was not consideration for a *specific* service benefiting *individual traders*. The statistical information was only 'beneficial to the economy as a whole', and the advantage was thus 'so general' that the charge could not be regarded 'as the consideration for a *specific* benefit'.[80]

This line of argument was confirmed in *Bresciani*.[81] The Court here held that compulsory health inspections on imported (raw) cowhides could not be seen as a specific service for individual importers. The Court thereby found it of no relevance that the duty at issue was proportionate to the costs of the compulsory health inspections, since the inspections were conducted in the general public interest and should consequently be financed by the public purse.[82]

The second – implied – exception from the absolute prohibition of fiscal charges are charges that a Member State levies as compensation for frontier checks *that are required under European law*. The rationale behind this exception is that the Member States here act on behalf of the Union, and in a manner that facilitates the free movement of goods. In *Bauhuis*,[83] the Court had to deal

---

[75]   *Ibid.*, 430.

[76]   Case 24/68, *Commission v. Italy (Statistical Levy)*, para. 10; Case 2/69, *Sociaal Fonds voor de Diamantarbeiders v. S.A. Ch. Brachfeld*, paras. 19 and 21.

[77]   Case 24/68, *Commission v. Italy (Statistical Levy)*.   [78]   *Ibid.*, para. 15.

[79]   *Ibid.*, para. 11: 'Although it is not impossible that in certain circumstances a specific service actually rendered may form consideration for a possible proportional payment for the service in question, this may only apply in specific cases which cannot lead to the circumvention of the provisions of [Art. 30] of the Treaty.'

[80]   *Ibid.*, para. 16 (emphasis added). See also Case 39/73, *Rewe-Zentralfinanz eGmbH v. Direktor der Landwirtschaftskammer Westfalen-Lippe* [1973] ECR 1039, esp. para. 4.

[81]   Case 87/75, *Bresciani v. Amministrazione Italiana delle Finanze* [1976] ECR 129.

[82]   *Ibid.*, para. 10: 'Nor, in determining the effects of the duty on the free movement of goods, is it of any importance that a duty of the type at issue is proportionate to the costs of a compulsory public health inspection carried out on entry of the goods. The activity of the administration of the State intended to maintain a public health inspection system imposed in the general interest cannot be regarded as a service rendered to the importer such as to justify the imposition of a pecuniary charge. If, accordingly, public health inspections are still justified at the end of the transitional period, the costs which they occasion must be met by the general public which, as a whole, benefits from the free movement of [Union] goods.'

[83]   Case 46/76, *Bauhuis v. The Netherlands* [1977] ECR 5.

with a Union law that required veterinary and public health inspections by the exporting Member State so as to make multiple frontier inspections by the importing Member State(s) unnecessary. Finding such health inspections to be not unilaterally imposed by a Member State but reflecting 'the general interest of the [Union]',[84] the Court held that they would not hinder trade in goods. Since the Member States here act as the decentralised Union administration,[85] national charges for these 'Union' inspections were thus legal.

The conditions for this 'Bauhuis justification' were subsequently developed in Commission v. Germany.[86] The Court here established the following test for national inspection fees:

> [S]uch fees may not be classified as charges having an effect equivalent to a customs duty if the following conditions are satisfied: (a) they do not exceed the actual costs of the inspections in connection with which they are charged; (b) the inspections in question are obligatory and uniform for all the products concerned in the [Union]; (c) they are prescribed by [European] law in the general interest of the [Union]; (d) they promote the free movement of goods, in particular by neutralizing obstacles which could arise from unilateral measures of inspection adopted in accordance with Article 36 of the Treaty.[87]

b. Fiscal Barriers II: Discriminatory Taxation

With regard to fiscal barriers, the prohibition of customs duties and the prohibition of discriminatory taxation are two sides of the same coin. In the Union legal order, Article 110 TFEU is designed to complement Article 30 TFEU:

> Article [110] supplement[s], within the system of the Treaty, the provisions on the abolition of customs duties and charges having equivalent effect. [Its] aim is to ensure free movement of goods between the Member States in normal conditions of competition by the elimination of all forms of protection which result from the application of internal taxation which discriminates against products from other Member States. Accordingly, Article [110] must guarantee the complete neutrality of internal taxation as regards competition between domestic products and products imported from other Member States.[88]

Due to their complementary roles, the material scopes of Articles 30 and 110 are however fundamentally different. The former catches national measures that impose a charge on goods when crossing an *external* (national) frontier; whereas Article 110 was to apply where foreign goods are subject to *internal* taxation.

---

[84] *Ibid.*, para. 29.
[85] On executive federalism and the duty of the Member States to indirectly administer EU law, see Chapter 9, section 4.
[86] Case 18/87, *Commission* v. *Germany* [1988] ECR 5427.   [87] *Ibid.*, para. 8.
[88] Case 193/85, *Cooperativa Co-Frutta Srl* v. *Amministrazione delle finanze dello Stato* [1987] ECR 2085, para 25.

Like two sides of the same coin, the two prohibitions within Articles 30 and 110 were thus bound together yet mutually exclusive.[89]

The difference in their thematic scope also seemed to imply a fundamental difference with regard to the constitutional test applicable within each prohibition. Article 30 was based, as we saw above, on an (absolute) restriction test for distinctly applicable measures. Article 110, on the other hand, is centred on a (relative) discrimination test for indistinctly applicable measures, that is measures that apply both to foreign *and* domestic goods.

Article 110 states:

> [1] No Member State shall impose, directly or indirectly, on the products of other Member States any internal taxation of any kind *in excess of* that imposed directly or indirectly on similar domestic products.
>
> [2] Furthermore, no Member State shall impose on the products of other Member States any internal taxation of such a nature to afford *indirect protection* to other products.

The text of Article 110 here clarifies that it only applies to taxes on *goods*, that is: indirect taxes;[90] and despite its clear wording, the Court has found the provision to apply to taxes on goods imported as well as exported.[91]

---

[89] Case C-78/90, *Compagnie Commerciale de l'Ouest and others* v. *Receveur Principal des Douanes de La Pallice Port* [1992] ECR I-1847, para. 22: 'The provisions on charges having equivalent effect and those on discriminatory internal taxation cannot be applied together. The scope of each of those provisions must therefore be defined.' And see already Case 94/74, *IGAV* v. *ENCC* [1975] ECR 699, para. 13: 'One and the same scheme of taxation cannot, under the system of the Treaty, belong simultaneously to both categories mentioned, having regard to the fact that the charges referred to in Article [30] must be purely and simply abolished whilst, for the purpose of applying internal taxation, Article [110] provides solely for the elimination of any form of discrimination, direct or indirect, in the treatment of the domestic products of the member States and of products originating in other Member States.' Nonetheless, when a charge falls into Art. 30 and when into Art. 110 may sometimes not be an easy question.

[90] Case 20/76, *Schöttle & Söhne OHG* v. *Finanzamt Freudenstadt* [1977] ECR 247.

[91] Case 142/77, *Statens Kontrol med ædle Metaller* v. *Larsen* [1978] ECR I-1543, paras. 21–5: 'The wording of Article [110] refers only to the discriminatory application of systems of internal taxation to products imported from other Member States. The application of the same systems of taxation to exports is referred to in Articles [111–12] from the point of view of the repayment of excessive taxation which may distort conditions of trade within the common market. It follows from a comparison of those provisions that the aim of the Treaty in this field is to guarantee generally the neutrality of systems of internal taxation with regard to intra-[Union] trade whenever an economic transaction going beyond the frontiers of a Member State at the same time constitutes the chargeable event giving rise to a fiscal charge within the context of such a system. It therefore seems necessary to interpret Article [110] as meaning that the rule against discrimination which forms the basis of that provision also applies when the export of a product constitutes, within the context of a system of internal taxation, the chargeable event giving rise to a fiscal charge. It would in fact be incompatible with the system of the tax provisions laid down in the Treaty to acknowledge that Member States, in the absence of an express prohibition laid down in the Treaty, are free to apply in a discriminatory manner a system of internal taxation to products intended for export to other Member States.'

According to the structure of Article 110, the provision thereby outlaws two types of national taxes. Paragraph 1 declares illegal all national tax laws that *discriminate* between foreign and domestic goods. Discrimination here means that 'similar' foreign goods are treated dissimilarly. Paragraph 2 then covers a second variant of fiscal protectionism. Strictly speaking, it is not based on a discrimination rationale, since its scope is wider than outlawing the dissimilar treatment of 'similar' goods.[92] Yet by prohibiting the 'indirect protection to other products', the better view regards Article 110(2) as outlawing all general forms of discrimination; and the relationship between the two paragraphs may thus best be described as one of *lex specialis* to *lex generalis*.[93] However, by insisting on proof of a protectionist effect paragraph 2 is stricter than paragraph 1,[94] as the latter will not require evidence of such an effect.

aa. Paragraph 1: Discrimination against 'Similar' Foreign Goods

Article 110(1) prohibits foreign goods being taxed 'in excess of' similar domestic goods. This outlaws internal taxes that discriminate between national and imported products. This might occur through direct or indirect means. Direct discrimination takes place where national tax legislation *legally* disadvantages foreign goods by – for example – imposing a higher tax rate than that for domestic goods.[95] Indirect discrimination occurs where the same national tax formally applies to both foreign and domestic goods, but materially imposes a *heavier* fiscal burden on the former.

An excellent illustration of an indirectly discriminatory tax can be seen in *Commission* v. *France*.[96] The Commission had brought enforcement proceedings

---

[92] On the two distinct tests for Art. 110(1) and (2) TFEU, see Case 27/67, *Fink-Frucht GmbH* v. *Hauptzollamt München-Landsbergerstrasse* [1967] ECR 223 at 233: 'Whereas the first paragraph of Article [110] only prohibits taxation in so far as it exceeds a clearly defined level, the prohibition laid down in the second paragraph is based on the protective effect of the taxation in question to the exclusion of any exact standard of reference. A tax must therefore be considered as incompatible with the Treaty if it is capable of having the effect referred to above.' The Court will consequently start its analysis with the first variant in Art. 110, and only where the goods are found not to be 'similar' will it move to the residual variant in paragraph 2. For unlike the second paragraph of the provision, Art. 110(1) presumes the discrimination to be protectionist. However, the probation of discriminatory taxation will only apply where foreign goods are taxed 'in excess of' domestic goods. Reverse discrimination is thus theoretically possible, and has indeed been accepted (see *ibid.*).

[93] Case 193/85, *Co-Frutta* [1987] ECR 2085, para. 19: '[W]here the requirement of similarity prescribed by the first paragraph of Article [110] is not fulfilled, the second paragraph of that article is intended to cover all forms of indirect tax protection in the case of products which, without being similar within the meaning of the first paragraph of Article [110], are nevertheless in competition, even partial, indirect or potential competition, with each other.'

[94] See Case C-167/05, *Commission* v. *Sweden* [2008] ECR I-2127.

[95] See Case 57/65, *Lütticke GmbH* v. *Hauptzollamt Sarrelouis* [1966] ECR 205; Case 148/77, *Hansen & Balle* v. *Hauptzollamt de Flensburg* [1978] ECR 1787.

[96] Case C-302/00, *Commission* v. *France (Dark Tobacco)* [2002] ECR I-2055.

against France on the grounds that its differential tax on light-tobacco and dark-tobacco cigarettes violated Article 110. Having found that the two types of cigarettes were indeed 'similar',[97] the Court moved on to address the issue of discrimination and here found as follows:

> Although [the French tax] does not establish any formal distinction according to the origin of the products, it adjusts the system of taxation in such a way that the cigarettes falling within the most favourable tax category come almost exclusively from domestic production whereas almost all imported products come within the least advantageous category. Those features of the system are not nullified by the fact that a very small fraction of imported cigarettes come within the most favourable category whereas, conversely, a certain proportion of domestic production comes within the same tax category as imported cigarettes. It appears, therefore, that the system of taxation is designed in such a way as to benefit a typical domestic product and handicaps imported cigarettes to the same extent.[98]

The judgment brilliantly explicates the concept of indirect discrimination (and also confirmed that fiscal measures may not be justified by reference to the express justifications reserved for regulatory measures in Article 36 TFEU).[99] Where similar goods were treated dissimilarly, a violation of Article 110 had occurred.

The central key to Article 110(1) lies in the concept of 'similarity'. When are domestic and foreign goods *similar*? Early on, the Court clarified that similarity is wider than identity;[100] and that similarity relates to *comparability*.[101] Comparability here means that two goods 'have similar characteristics and meet the same needs from the point of view of consumers'.[102] But are 'whisky' and 'cognac' comparable drinks?[103] In a series of cases, the Court has established criteria to determine when two products are 'similar' and when they are not. The Court has thereby endorsed a 'broad interpretation of the concept of similarity'

---

[97] *Ibid.*, paras. 22ff.   [98] *Ibid.*, para. 30.

[99] *Ibid.*, paras. 32–3: 'Without explicitly invoking Article [36], the French Government argues that [the French tax system] is conducive to the protection of human health and life. In this regard, it is sufficient to point out that Article [36] of the [FEU] Treaty must be interpreted strictly and thus cannot be understood as authorising measures of a different nature from the quantitative restrictions on imports and exports and measures having equivalent effect laid down by Articles [34 and 35 TFEU].'

[100] See Case 148/77, *Hansen & Balle*, para. 19: 'The application of that provision is based not on a strict requirement that the products should be identical but on their "similarity".'

[101] See Case 168/78, *Commission v. France (Whisky v. Cognac)* [1980] ECR 347, para. 5.

[102] Case 45/75, *Rewe-Zentrale des Lebensmittel-Großhandels GmbH v. Hauptzollamt Landau/Pfalz* [1976] ECR 181.

[103] Case 168/78, *Commission v. France (Whisky v. Cognac)*.

that will nonetheless take account of 'objective' differences between two seem-ingly similar products.[104]

An excellent illustration of this approach is *Humblot*.[105] Monsieur Humblot had acquired a (German) Mercedes car in France. The car possessed 36 CV (fis-cal horsepower) and he had to pay a special tax imposed by the French Revenue Code, which distinguished between a progressive annual tax for cars up to 16 CV and a single special tax for cars above this rate. The special tax was nearly five times higher than the highest rate of the general progressive tax. And as France did not produce any cars above 16 CV, the question arose whether the special tax was 'in excess of' the national tax on domestic goods. But are small (French) cars comparable to big (German) cars? The French government defended its internal tax regime by arguing that 'the special tax is charged solely on luxury vehi-cles, which are *not similar*, within the meaning of the first paragraph of Article [110] to cars liable to the differential tax'.[106] The Court disagreed. For while it acknowledged the power of the Member States to 'subject products such as cars to a system of road tax which increases progressively in amount depending on an *objective criterion*, such as the power rating',[107] the French tax system did not do so and thus (indirectly) discriminated against foreign cars.[108]

What 'objective' criteria may be used fiscally to distinguish between seem-ingly similar products? This question is – misleadingly – called the question of 'objective justification'.[109] What stands behind this misnomer is the idea that while a national tax system must be neutral towards foreign goods, it can dis-criminate between goods 'on the basis of objective criteria'.[110] Thus, where a Member State discriminates on the basis of a regional policy objective, such a public policy objective will not amount to protectionist discrimination. The dis-crimination is here 'justified' by 'objective' criteria that distinguish two products.

---

[104] Case 243/84, *John Walker v. Ministeriet for Skatter og Afgifter* [1986] ECR 875, para. 11. 'The Court endorsed a broad interpretation of the concept of similarity in its judgments … and assessed the similarity of the products not according to whether they were strictly identical, but according to whether their use was similar and comparable. Consequently, in order to determine whether products are similar it is necessary first to consider certain objective characteristics of both categories of beverages, such as their origin, the method of manufacture and their organoleptic properties, in particular taste and alcohol content, and secondly to consider whether or not both categories of beverages are capable of meeting the same needs from the point of view of consumers.'

[105] Case 112/84, *Humblot v. Directeur des services fiscaux* [1985] ECR 1367.

[106] *Ibid.*, para. 9.   [107] *Ibid.*, para. 12.

[108] While the Court was coy with regard to the exact violation, the case appears to acknowledge a partial violation of Art. 110(1) in para. 14. For a subsequent case on the – reformed – French car tax system, see Case 433/85, *Feldain v. Directeur des services fiscaux du département du Haut-Rhin* [1987] ECR 3521.

[109] Case 21/79, *Commission v. Italy (Regenerated Oil)* [1980] ECR 1. The term is used *ibid.*, para. 16: 'objectively justified'.

[110] Case 243/84, *John Walker v. Ministeriet for Skatter og Afgifter*, para. 23.

This can be seen in *Commission v. France (Natural Sweet Wines)*.[111] The Commission had brought proceedings against a French tax scheme that exempted naturally sweet wines from the higher consumption duty on liqueur wines. The French government defended this differential treatment by pointing to the fact that 'natural sweet wines are made in regions characterized by low rainfall and relatively poor soil, in which the difficulty of growing other crops means that the local economy depends heavily on their production'.[112] This regional policy objective gave preferential treatment to a 'traditional and customary production' over similar goods resulting from industrial production. And this 'objective' criterion was not discriminating against foreign goods.[113]

bb. Paragraph 2: Protection against 'Competing' Foreign Goods

Even when an internal tax does not discriminate against 'similar' domestic products, it might still fall within the second paragraph of Article 110. For in the words of the Court:

> The second paragraph of Article [110] is complementary to the first. It prohibits the imposition of any internal taxation which imposes a higher charge on an imported than a domestic product which competes with the imported product, although it is not similar to it within the meaning of the first paragraph of Article [110]. The prohibition also applies in the absence of direct competition where the internal taxation subjects the imported product to a specific fiscal charge in such a way as to protect certain activities distinct from those used in the manufacture of the imported product. However, the said second paragraph is only applicable when the various economic relationships envisaged by it are not merely fortuitous, but lasting and characteristic.[114]

Strictly speaking, the rationale behind Article 110(2) is broader than a prohibition on discriminatory taxation. (For the idea of discrimination implies treating similar products dissimilarly. And where there are no similar domestic products, there cannot be discrimination.)[115] Yet the better way is to see Article 110(2) as an extension of the discrimination rationale in Article 110(1). Its reach is simply wider when outlawing all internal taxes that grant 'indirect protection' to domestic goods. For the provision here targets national taxes *that generally disadvantage foreign goods*. The Court has however held that such indirect protection can only occur when domestic goods are *in competition* with imported goods.[116]

---

[111]   Case 196/85, *Commission v. France (Natural Sweet Wines)* [1987] ECR 1597.

[112]   *Ibid.*, para. 9.

[113]   *Ibid.*, para. 10. See also Case 132/88, *Commission v. Greece* [1990] ECR I-1567; Case 213/96, *Outokumpu* [1998] ECR I-1777.

[114]   Case 27/67, *Fink-Frucht GmbH v. Hauptzollamt München-Landsbergerstrasse*, [1968] ECR 327, Summary Point 5.

[115]   Case 184/85, *Commission v. Italy (Bananas)* [1987] ECR 2013.

[116]   Where this is not the case, Art. 110(2) will indeed not apply; see Case C-47/88, *Commission v. Denmark* [1990] ECR I-4509; Case C-383/01, *DeDanskeBilimportorer v. Skatteministeriet, Toldog Skattestyrelsen* [2003] ECR I-6065.

And Article 110(2) consequently requires two elements to be fulfilled before a national tax is found to hinder the free movement of goods. First, the national law will tax *competing* goods differently and, second, this differentiation indirectly *protects* national goods and thus indirectly 'discriminates' against foreign goods.

When will two goods be in competition? Within Article 110(2), the Court has generally adopted a flexible approach. This can be seen in *Commission v. United Kingdom (Beer & Wine)*.[117] The Commission had brought infringement proceedings against Great Britain in the belief that its tax regime for wine granted indirect protection to British beer. The national tax on wine was indeed significantly higher than that on beer, and as Britain produced very little wine but a lot of beer, the suspicion of indirect protectionism arose. Britain counterclaimed that there was no competitive relationship between beer and wine, and that there could thus be no such protectionist effect. Not only were the two products 'entirely different' with regard to their production and price structure,[118] the goods would hardly ever be substituted by consumers.[119] The Court was not impressed with this line of argument, and espoused a dynamic understanding of product substitution:

> In order to determine the existence of a competitive relationship under the second paragraph of Article [110], it is necessary to consider not only the present state of the market but also the possibilities for development within the context of the free movement of goods at the [Union] level and the further potential for the substitution of products for one another which may be revealed by intensification of trade, so as fully to develop the complementary features of the economies of the Member States in accordance with the objectives laid down by Article [3] of the [EU] Treaty … For the purpose of measuring the degree of substitution, it is impossible to restrict oneself to consumer habits in a Member State or in a given region. In fact, those habits, which are essentially variable in time and space, cannot be considered to be a fixed rule; the tax policy of a Member State must not therefore crystallize given consumer habits so as to consolidate an advantage acquired by national industries concerned to comply with them.[120]

The Court here brilliantly attacked the chicken-and-egg problem within Article 110(2). For two goods might not presently be in competition *because* of the artificial price differences created by internal taxation. The British argument that its tax policy only reflected a social habit in which beer was mass-consumed,

---

[117] Case 170/78, *Commission v. United Kingdom (Beer & Wine, Interim Judgment)* [1980] ECR 417.

[118] *Ibid.*, para. 13.

[119] *Ibid.*: 'As regards consumer habits, the Government of the United Kingdom states that in accordance with long-established tradition in the United Kingdom, beer is a popular drink consumed preferably in public-houses or in connexion with work; domestic consumption and consumption with meals is negligible. In contrast, the consumption of wine is more unusual and special from the point of view of social custom.'

[120] *Ibid.*, paras. 6 and 14.

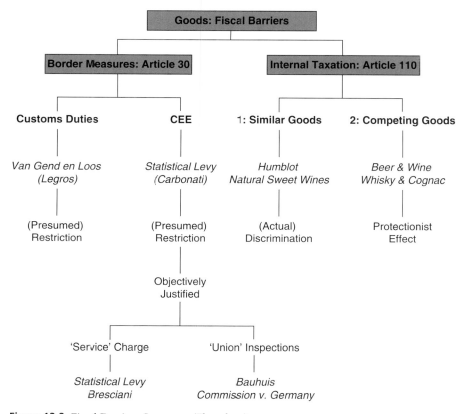

Figure 13.2 Fiscal Barriers: Summary (Flowchart)

while wine was an 'elitist' drink, disregarded the fact that the social habit might itself – at least partly – be the product of its fiscal policy. And once this fiscal policy disappeared, beer and wine *could* be in competition. This *dynamic* understanding of product substitutability acknowledges the ability of fiscal regimes to *dynamically* shape consumer preferences.

Once a foreign product has been found to be in competition with a domestic product, the Court will then investigate whether the national tax regime generates a protectionist effect. In the above case, the Court indeed found that the higher tax burden on wine would afford protection to domestic beer production.[121] And in another case, involving 'drinks in Luxembourg',[122] the Court considered a clear protectionist effect to exist where 'an essential part of domestic production' came within the most favourable tax category whereas competing products – 'almost all of which [were] imported from other Member States'– were subject to higher taxation.[123] In its subsequent jurisprudence, the

---

[121] Case 170/78, *Commission* v. *United Kingdom (Beer & Wine, Final Judgment)* [1983] ECR 2265, para. 27.

[122] G. Rodrigues Iglesias, 'Drinks in Luxembourg: Alcoholic Beverages and the Case Law of the European Court of Justice', in D. O Keeffe (ed.), *Judicial Review in European Union Law: Liber amicorum in Honour of Lord Slynn of Hadley* (Kluwer, 2000), 523.

[123] Case 168/78, *Commission* v. *France (Whisky* v. *Cognac)*, para. 41.

Court has nonetheless tried to establish a more nuanced economic analysis to determine when a protectionist effect is present and when not.[124]

3. Regulatory Barriers I: Prohibitions

Regulatory barriers are legal obstacles to trade that cannot be overcome by the payment of money.[125] They potentially range from a complete ban on (foreign) products to the partial restriction of a product's use.

What types of regulatory barriers to the free movement of goods do the Treaties prohibit? The Treaty regime for regulatory barriers is set out in Chapter 3 of Title II. The chapter outlaws quantitative restrictions on imports (Article 34) and exports (Article 35); yet it also contains a provision according to which restrictions on imports or exports can be justified (Article 36) by specific public interests.

Two features of this constitutional arrangement strike the attentive eye. First, unlike the legal regime governing customs duties, the Treaties expressly distinguish between *two* prohibitions: one for imports, and one for exports. And, second, the constitutional regime for regulatory barriers expressly allows for public policy exceptions. This section deals with the first feature and analyses the respective prohibitions of quantitative restrictions on imports and exports. Section 4 will then examine the express (and implied) justifications for regulatory restrictions on the free movement of goods.

a. Quantitative Restrictions on Imports: Article 34

The central provision governing regulatory barriers to imports is Article 34. It states:

> Quantitative restrictions on imports and all measures having equivalent effect shall be prohibited between Member States.

The core of this prohibition consists of the concept of 'quantitative restrictions'. These are restrictions that limit the quantity of imported goods to a fixed amount.[126] Quantitative restrictions are thus *quotas*, which – in their most extreme form – amount to a total ban.[127] Import quotas operate as absolute

---

[124] Case 167/05, *Commission* v. *Sweden (Beer & Wine)* [2008] ECR I-2127.

[125] See Case 74/76, *Iannelli & Volpi* v. *Meroni* [1977] ECR 557, para. 9: 'However wide the field of application of Article [34] may be, it nevertheless does not include obstacles to trade covered by other provisions of the Treaty … Thus obstacles which are of a fiscal nature or have equivalent effect and are covered by Articles [30 and 110] of the Treaty do not fall within the prohibition in Article [34].'

[126] See Case 2/73, *Geddo* v. *Ente Nazionale Risi* [1973] ECR 865, para. 7: 'The prohibition on quantitative restrictions covers measures which amount to a total or a partial restraint of, according to the circumstances, imports, exports, or goods in transit.'

[127] Case 34/79, *Regina* v. *Henn and Darby* [1979] ECR 3795, para. 12: '[P]rohibition on imports … is the most extreme form of restriction.'

frontier barriers: once a quota for a product is exhausted, foreign imports cannot legally enter the domestic market.

The text of Article 34 equally covers – like Article 30 on customs duties – a second form of measures called 'measures having an equivalent effect to quantitative restrictions' (MEEQRs); and it is this category that has been at the centre of much judicial attention in the past half-century. Within a long and complex jurisprudential history, four periods can be identified that mark the evolution of the concept of MEEQRs.

aa. First Period: Dassonville and 'Border Measures'

Dassonville is one of the most misunderstood cases in the history of European law.[128] The judgment can indeed only be understood when placed in the conceptual context of its time. This historical context was governed by the international model of the internal market.

This international model was reflected in the first Commission definition of MEEQRs in Directive 70/50.[129] This liberalisation Directive distinguished between two types of such measures: distinctly applicable measures and indistinctly applicable measures. The former were subject to Article 2 of the Directive, which stated:

> This Directive covers measures, other than those applicable equally to domestic or imported products, which hinder imports which could otherwise take place, including measures which make importation more difficult or costly than the disposal of domestic production … The measures referred to must be taken to include those measures which:
>
> (a) lay down, *for imported products only*, minimum or maximum prices below or above which imports are prohibited, reduced or made subject to conditions liable to hinder importation;
> (b) lay down *less favourable prices for imported products* than for domestic products;
> (c) fix profit margins or any other price components *for imported products only* or fix these differently for domestic products and for imported products, to the detriment of the latter;
> (d) preclude any increase in the price *of the imported product* corresponding to the supplementary costs and charges inherent in importation;
> (e) fix the prices of products *solely on the basis of the cost price or the quality of domestic products* at such a level as to create a hindrance to importation[.][130]

---

[128] R. Schütze, 'Framing *Dassonville*: Text and Context in European Law' (Cambridge University Press, in preparation). For a typical misreading of the case, see e.g. J. Weiler, 'The Constitution of the Common Market Place: Text and Context in the Evolution of the Free Movement of Goods', in P. Craig and G. de Búrca (eds.), *The Evolution of EU Law* (Oxford University Press, 1999), 349.

[129] Directive 70/50 on the abolition of measures which have an effect equivalent to quantitative restrictions on imports and are not covered by other provisions adopted in pursuance of the EEC Treaty [1970] OJ L 13/29.

[130] *Ibid.*, Art. 2(a)–(e) (emphasis added).

By contrast, national measures that were indistinctly or 'applicable equally' were, in principle, not prohibited.[131] However, Article 3 of the Directive exceptionally extended the concept of MEEQRs to certain equally applicable measures:

> This Directive also covers measures governing the marketing of products which deal, in particular, with shape, size, weight, composition, presentation, identification or putting up and which are equally applicable to domestic and imported products, *where the restrictive effect of such measures on the free movement of goods exceeds the effects intrinsic to trade rules.*
>
> This is the case, in particular, where:
> – the restrictive effects on the free movement of goods are out of proportion to their purpose;
> – the same objective can be attained by other means which are less of a hindrance to trade.[132]

Directive 70/50 was informed by a fundamental constitutional choice. Unlike import-related measures, product requirements equally applicable to domestic and imported goods were – in principle – considered outside the scope of Article 34. For their restrictive effects on the free movement of goods were not seen as a consequence of individual State measures, but were regarded as '*inherent in the disparities* between rules applied by Member States'.[133] And these legislative disparities should not be removed by negative integration but would need to be removed through the Union's positive harmonisation powers.[134] Article 34 thus primarily targeted national rules which *themselves* discriminated – directly or indirectly – against imports. Where, on the other hand, the restrictive effect of a measure lay not in the national measure itself but in its being different from other national rules, the restrictive effect could not be attributed to a single Member State but was inherent in the disparities between rules applied by different Member States. Such equally applicable marketing measures could only *exceptionally* fall within the scope of Article 34, where they had 'a restrictive effect on the free movement of goods *over and above that which is intrinsic to such rules*'.[135]

It is against this background that the Court gave its ruling in *Dassonville*.[136] The case involved the legality of Belgian rules that made the importation (or sale) of Scotch whisky dependent on having a 'certificate of origin' from the British customs authorities. Dassonville had imported a consignment of Johnnie Walker without the required certificate and was thus duly prosecuted by the Belgian authorities. In the context of a preliminary ruling, the Belgian court asked whether the certification requirement constituted an MEEQR and the Court's famous answer was this:

---

[131] *Ibid.*, recital 8.   [132] Emphasis added.   [133] *Ibid.* (emphasis added).
[134] On the scope of Art. 114 TFEU, see Chapter 14, section 1.
[135] Directive 70/50 (n. 129 above), recital 9 (emphasis added).
[136] Case 8/74, *Procureur du Roi* v. *Dassonville* [1974] ECR 837.

> *All trading rules enacted by Member States which are capable of hindering, directly or indirectly, actually or potentially, intra-[Union] trade are to be considered as measures having an effect equivalent to quantitative restrictions.* In the absence of a [Union] system guaranteeing for consumers the authenticity of a product's designation of origin, if a Member State takes measures to prevent unfair practices in this connexion, it is however subject to the condition that these measures should be reasonable and that the means of proof required should not act as a hindrance to trade between Member States and should, in consequence, be accessible to all [Union citizens].[137]

On its surface, the ruling did not distinguish between equally (indistinctly) and non-equally (distinctly) applicable rules. On the contrary, it outlawed '[a]ll trading rules' that would 'directly or indirectly, actually or potentially' hinder intra-Union trade. This formulation became known as the '*Dassonville* formula'; and it has traditionally been understood as a radical confirmation of a national market model for Article 34.[128] Nothing, however, could be further from the truth, since the judgment originally focused – like Directive 70/50 – on *international* trading rules; and it may best be seen as a judicial complement to the Directive.[139]

bb. Second Period: Cassis and 'Product Requirements'

The most important case in all free movement law – perhaps in all European Union law – is *Cassis de Dijon*.[140] The case concerned a German law that fixed the minimum alcohol strength of liqueurs at 25 per cent. This national rule prohibited the sale of 'Cassis de Dijon' as a 'liqueur' in Germany, since the distinguished French drink had an alcohol content below 20 per cent. Formally, the national measure applied equally to foreign and domestic goods; and – in line with previous case law – the question thus arose whether this product requirement had a disproportionately restrictive effect in the sense of Article 3 of Directive 70/50. The Court gave the following famous answer:

> Obstacles to movement within the [Union] resulting from disparities between national laws relating to the marketing of the products in question must be accepted in so far as those provisions may be recognized as being necessary in order to satisfy mandatory requirements relating in particular to the effectiveness of fiscal supervision, the protection of public health, the fairness of commercial transactions and the defence of the consumer ...
>
> [T]he requirements relating to the minimum alcohol content of alcoholic beverages do not serve a purpose which is in the general interest and such as to take

---

[137] *Ibid.*, paras. 5–6.

[138] E.g. Weiler, 'Constitution of the Common Market Place' (n. 128 above).

[139] For an elaboration of this argument, see Schütze, From *International to Federal Market* (n. 27 above), ch. 3.

[140] Case 120/78, *Rewe-Zentral AG* v. *Bundesmonopolverwaltung für Branntwein* [1979] ECR 649.

> precedence over the requirements of the free movement of goods, which constitutes one of the fundamental rules of the [Union] ... There is therefore no valid reason why, provided that they have been lawfully produced and marketed in one of the Member States, alcoholic beverages should not be introduced into any other Member State; the sale of such products may not be subject to a legal prohibition on the marketing of beverages with an alcohol content lower than the limit set by the national rules.[141]

While the judgment can, superficially, be aligned with the formal logic behind Directive 70/50, it implicitly overruled its – central – substantive presumption, namely, that trade restrictions flowing from disparities between equally applicable product requirements would only *exceptionally* qualify as MEEQRs. From now on, a different logic applied: *unless* there were mandatory requirements in the general interest that the host State could invoke, the latter was *not* entitled to impose its domestic product standards on imported goods. This presumption has become known as the 'principle of mutual recognition'.

This principle constitutes the – federal – cornerstone of the EU internal market. It simply means that Member States must, in principle, mutually recognise each other's product standards. It is this principle of mutual recognition that turns the presumption of legality for product requirements – established by Directive 70/50 – into a presumption of illegality. For *unless the host State can justify the imposition of its product rules, the extension of these rules to imports will violate Article 34. Cassis* here fundamentally changes the economic principle underlying Article 34 from host State to home State rule; and thereby triggered a transition from an international to a federal model of integration.

Part and parcel of this federal model is the possibility of 'reverse discrimination'.[142] It arises when a Member State is prevented from imposing *its* national rules to imported goods within its market but nonetheless applies *its* stricter standards to *its* domestic goods. The discrimination is here 'reversed' because – unlike a typical protectionist State – the application of national legislation leads to an economically disadvantageous situation for domestic goods. *Cassis de Dijon* itself offered a good illustration of such reverse discrimination. For if the minimum alcohol requirement applied to German liqueurs only, imported – French – liqueurs could enjoy a competitive advantage over the more expensive German goods.

How has the European Court dealt with reverse discrimination? In order to protect the legislative competence of each State with regard to its own goods, the Court has clarified that Article 34 cannot be used to challenge reverse discrimination. Dealing with a Belgian law that required – solely – Belgian butter to indicate the name and address of the producer, the Court thus held in *Mathot*:

---

[141] *Ibid.*, paras. 8 and 14.
[142] On the idea of reverse discrimination, see section 1(d) above.

> With regard to Article [34] of the [FEU] Treaty, it must be emphasized that the purpose of that provision is to eliminate obstacles to the importation of goods *and not to ensure that goods of national origin always enjoy the same treatment as imported goods* ... [A]nd even if there is discrimination against domestically-produced butter, such a difference of treatment can in no circumstances restrict the importation of butter or prejudice the marketing of imported butter. Article [34] of the [FEU] Treaty is not therefore infringed by such rules.[143]

Be that as it may, a significant consequence of *Cassis* was that the discrimination rationale for identifying MEEQRs became sidelined. For product requirements were 'non-discriminatory' measures.[144] And with the discrimination rationale weakened, the question gradually arose whether all sorts of non-discriminatory measures that hindered trade could fall into Article 34.

cc. Third Period: Keck and 'Selling Arrangements'

In a third period of the case law, the Court seemed to indeed favour this – broader – view – a view that was directly inspired by a national market model of integration. A striking illustration of this trend is *Torfaen*.[145] The case formed part of the (in)famous *Sunday Trading* cases.[146] It had been brought by Torfaen Borough Council, which alleged that B&Q had infringed the 1950 (British) Shops Act by trading on Sunday. The defendant counterclaimed that the British restriction on opening times of shops was an MEEQR. How so? It was simply argued that the national law reduced the absolute amount of total sales; and since a percentage of these sales were foreign goods, the Sunday trading ban

---

[143]   Case 98/86, *Criminal Proceedings against Mathot*, paras. 7–8 (emphasis added).

[144]   See Case 788/79, *Criminal Proceedings against Gilli and Andres* [1980] ECR 2071). Even if the extension of the host State's product requirements to imports imposes a 'dual burden' on imported goods because they have to comply with the home state and the host state rules, the 'discriminatory' effect cannot be attributed to the host State rule alone. It rather results from the 'disparities' in national product requirements between the host and the home State. And, since this disparity cannot be attributed to a single State, these situations are better not viewed in light of the concept of discrimination. This is not uncontroversial. For some academic authors, all of the free movement case law can 'be analysed within the framework of a unitary anti-discrimination principle' (see N. Bernard, 'Discrimination and Free Movement in EC Law' (1996) 45 ICLQ 82 at 97). For a later assertion of this view, see N. Nic Shuibhne, 'The Free Movement of Goods and Article 28 EC: An Evolving Framework' (2002) 27 *EL Rev.* 408, esp. 410: 'By introducing the fallacy of "non-discrimination" in *Cassis*, when what was at issue was really indirect discrimination, the Court initiated a misapplication of the discrimination lexicon[.]' Personally, I find this view very hard to accept – both from a descriptive as well as a normative perspective. Descriptively, it contradicts the terminological classification used by the Court. Normatively, it alludes to a single anti-discrimination principle, which – in my opinion – neglects the evolution of the latter from an international to a federal philosophy.

[145]   Case 145/88, *Torfaen Borough Council* v. *B&Q* [1989] ECR 3851.

[146]   For an analysis of these cases, see C. Barnard, '*Sunday Trading*: A Drama in Five Acts' (1994) 57 *MLR* 449; A. Arnull, 'What Shall We Do on Sunday?' (1991) 16 *EL Rev.* 112.

constituted a restriction on imports! And, drawing on its jurisprudential line on sales restrictions,[147] the Court indeed held that the Shops Act would constitute an MEEQR if 'the effects of such national rules exceed what is necessary to achieve the aim in view'.[148]

The ruling signalled that any national law could potentially constitute an MEEQR where it was seen as unnecessarily restrictive of trade; and it encouraged commercial traders to challenge virtually all national rules that somehow fell into the *Dassonville* formula.[149] Flooded with cases, it gradually dawned on the Court that its jurisprudence had gone too far; and soon enough, it announced an unprecedented retreat in *Keck*.

In *Keck*,[150] criminal proceedings had been brought against a supermarket manager who had allowed products to be sold at a loss. This form of sales promotion was prohibited in France, but Keck argued that the prohibition constituted – à la Sunday Trading cases – an MEEQR because it restricted intra-Union trade in goods.[151] To the surprise of many, the Court disagreed. While confirming the *Dassonville* formula, it insisted that certain measures would only fall foul of Article 34 if they were discriminatory:

> National legislation imposing a general prohibition on resale at a loss is not designed to regulate trade in goods between Member States. Such legislation may, admittedly, restrict the volume of sales, and hence the volume of sales of products from other Member States, in so far as it deprives traders of a method of sales promotion. But the question remains whether such a possibility is sufficient to characterize the legislation in question as a measure having equivalent effect to a quantitative restriction on imports …
>
> It is established by the case-law beginning with 'Cassis de Dijon' that, in the absence of harmonization of legislation, obstacles to free movement of goods which are the consequence of applying, to goods coming from other Member States where they are lawfully manufactured and marketed, rules that lay down requirements to be met by such goods (such as those relating to designation, form, size, weight, composition, presentation, labelling, packaging) constitute measures of equivalent effect prohibited by Article [34]. This is so even if those rules apply without distinction to all products unless their application can be justified by a public-interest objective taking precedence over the free movement of goods. *By contrast, contrary to what has previously been decided, the application to products from other Member States of national provisions restricting or prohibiting certain selling arrangements is not such as to hinder directly or indirectly, actually or potentially, trade between Member*

---

[147] For an extensive discussion of this point, see Schütze, *From International to Federal Market* (n. 27 above), 143–9.

[148] Case 145/88, *Torfaen*, para. 15. The Court expressly referred to Art. 3 of Directive 70/50 (n. 129 above) as inspiration for this test.

[149] See D. Chalmers, 'Free Movement of Goods within the European Community: An Unhealthy Addiction to Scotch Whisky' 42 (1993) ICLQ 269.

[150] Joined Cases C-267–8/91, *Criminal Proceedings against Keck and Mithouard* [1993] ECR I-6097.

[151] *Ibid.*, para. 3.

> *States within the meaning of the* Dassonville *judgment, so long as those provisions apply to all relevant traders operating within the national territory and so long as they affect in the same manner, in law and in fact, the marketing of domestic products and of those from other Member States.*[152]

The case constituted a symbolic revolution. Drawing a distinction between product requirements and 'selling arrangements',[153] *Keck* clarified that the latter would only constitute MEEQRs where they discriminated against the marketing of foreign goods. Only *discriminatory* selling arrangements would violate the free movement of goods provisions. By contrast, and in line with *Cassis de Dijon*, *non*-discriminatory product requirements would still fall within the scope of Article 34. And in the face of two different constitutional tests for internal measures within Article 34, the distinction between product requirements and selling arrangements became *the* classificatory battle in the post-*Keck* jurisprudence.

A good illustration of this debate can be seen in *Familiapress* v. *Bauer*.[154] The case pitched an Austrian newspaper publisher against a German competitor that had used prize-winning crossword puzzles in its publications. This sales technique was prohibited in Austria and when the German newspapers were sold there, Familiapress brought proceedings against Bauer. The latter counterclaimed that the Austrian measure constituted an MEEQR and the question arose whether it constituted a selling arrangement in the meaning of the *Keck* judgment. Before the Court of Justice, the Austrian government relied on this view but the Court did not think so:

> The Austrian Government maintains that the prohibition at issue falls outside Article [34] of the Treaty. In its view, the possibility of offering readers of a periodical the chance to take part in prize competitions s merely a method of promoting sales and hence a selling arrangement within the meaning of the judgment in *Keck and Mithouard*. The Court finds that, even though the relevant national legislation is directed against a method of sales promotion, in this case it bears on the actual content of the products, in so far as the competitions in question form an integral part of the magazine in which they appear. As a result, the national legislation in question as applied to the facts of the case is not concerned with a selling arrangement within the meaning of the judgment in *Keck and Mithouard*.[155]

This located the distinction between selling arrangements and product requirements in the 'physical integrity' of the imported good: any national rule that would 'bear[] on the actual content of the product[]' would *not* constitute a

---

[152] *Ibid.*, paras. 12–16 (emphasis added).
[153] The distinction had been – academically – suggested by E. White, 'In Search of the Limits of Article 30 of the EEC Treaty' (1989) 26 *CML Rev.* 235.
[154] See Case C-368/95, *Familiapress* v. *Bauer Verlag* [1997] ECR I-3689.
[155] *Ibid.*, paras. 10–11.

selling arrangement under the *Keck* jurisprudential line.[156] As the Austrian rule in the present case did touch on the actual content of the product, the measure would be a product requirement and its extension to foreign goods was consequently prohibited – even if the national law was non-discriminatory in nature. By contrast, where a measure is classified as a selling arrangement, the Court will need to investigate whether it discriminates or not; and the Court has linked this question with two criteria set out in *Keck*. First, is the measure indistinctly applicable? Second, if so, would it '*affect in the same manner, in law and in fact, the marketing of domestic products and of those from other Member States*'?[157] Only were both criteria are fulfilled will the national law escape Article 34 as a non-discriminatory selling arrangement. While the first question is thereby a simple matter of law,[158] the latter may be a complex matter of fact, and the Court here applies intense judicial scrutiny.

dd. *Fourth Period:* Italian Trailers *and 'Consumer Restrictions'*

'Product requirements' and 'selling arrangements' are only two categories of national measures that potentially constitute MEEQRs. Other categories may of course equally fall foul of the provision. For example: 'border measures', such as import licenses, have always been considered to fall within the scope of Article 34. Yet for a very long time it seemed that all MEEQRs would need to be national laws that somehow interfered with the commercial chain leading from *production* and *trading* to the *selling* of a good. Rules that limited the *consumer* use of a good appeared to be outside the scope of Article 34.

Should national laws that ban smoking in restaurants and pubs be within or without the scope of Article 34? And, if they are within, what test should here apply? The Court gave some answers to these questions in *Italian Trailers*.[159] The case involved a provision within the Italian Highway Code that prohibited the use of trailers on motorcycles and mopeds. The Commission considered the provision to constitute an MEEQR and brought proceedings against Italy. Italy defended itself by insisting that 'a rule concerning use is covered by Article [34 TFEU] only if it prohibits all uses of a product or its only use, if the product only has one', whereas 'if there is a discretion as to the possible uses of the product, the situation no longer falls under Article [34]'.[160]

---

[156] See Case C-470/93, *Verein gegen Unwesen in Handel und Gewerbe Köln e.V. v. Mars GmbH* [1995] ECR I-1923, where the Court implicitly held that a rule that would 'compel the importer to adjust the presentation of his products according to the place where they are to be marketed' would not be a selling arrangement (*ibid.*, paras. 13–14).

[157] *Keck* (n. 150 above), para. 16 (emphasis added).

[158] For a distinctly applicable selling arrangement that the Court outlawed, see Case C-531/07, *Fachverband der Buch- und Medienwirtschaft v. LIBRO Handelsgesellschaft mbH* [2009] ECR I-3717.

[159] Case C-110/05, *Commission v. Italy (Italian Trailers)* [2009] ECR I-519. For general academic analyses of the 'consumer restriction' cases, see P. Oliver, 'Of Trailers and Jet Skis: Is the Case Law on Article 34 TFEU Hurtling in a New Direction' (2010) 33 *Fordham International Law Journal* 1423.

[160] Case C-110/05, *Commission v. Italy (Italian Trailers)*, para. 19.

In its ruling, the Court picked up this distinction and differentiated between trailers for general use and trailers specifically designed for motorcycles.[161] With regard to the latter, the question was this: would the *prohibition* on using motor trailers on a public highway constitute an MEEQR? The Court answered this question positively:

> It should be noted in that regard that a prohibition on the use of a product in the territory of a Member State has a considerable influence on the behaviour of con-sumers, which, in its turn, affects the access of that product to the market of that Member State. *Consumers, knowing that they are not permitted to use their motor-cycle with a trailer specially designed for it, have practically no interest in buying such a trailer.* Thus, Article 56 of the Highway Code prevents a demand from existing in the market at issue for such trailers and therefore hinders their importation. It fol-lows that the prohibition laid down in Article 56 of the Highway Code, to the extent that its effect is to hinder access to the Italian market for trailers which are specially designed for motorcycles and are lawfully produced and marketed in Member States other than the Italian Republic, constitutes a measure having equivalent effect to quantitative restrictions on imports within the meaning of Article [34 TFEU], unless it can be justified objectively.[162]

The judicial reasoning here stepped outside the dichotomy of *Cassis*-related 'product requirements' and *Keck*-defined 'selling arrangements'. The Italian meas-ure was in fact neither; and faced with this new category of measures, the Court promoted a new test to centre stage. This new test was a 'market-access' test.

This new test was confirmed in *Mickelsson*.[163] The case involved a Swedish restriction on the use of personal watercraft (jet skis). The skis could only be used on either generally navigable waters or on specifically designated waterways. This restriction had been violated by the defendants; and in the course of crimi-nal proceedings, they pleaded that the Swedish legislation constituted a violation of Article 34 TFEU. In its reply to the preliminary question, the Court built on its market-access test for consumer use restriction as follows:

> Even if the national regulations at issue *do not have the aim or effect of treating goods coming from other Member States less favourably*, which is for the national court to ascertain, the restriction which they impose on the use of a product in the territory of a Member State may, depending on its scope, have a considerable influ-ence on the behaviour of consumers, which may, in turn, affect the access of that product to the market of that Member State. Consumers, knowing that the use permitted by such regulations is very limited, have only a limited interest in buying that product.
>
> In that regard, where the national regulations for the designation of navigable waters and waterways have the *effect of preventing users of personal watercraft*

---

[161] *Ibid.*, paras. 51ff.   [162] *Ibid.*, paras. 56–8 (emphasis added).
[163] Case C-142/05, *Åklagaren* v. *Mickelsson and Roos* [2009] ECR I-4273.

> *from using them for the specific and inherent purposes for which they were intended or of greatly restricting their use, which is for the national court to ascertain, such regulations have the effect of hindering the access to the domestic market in question for those goods and therefore constitute, save where there is a justification pursuant to Article [36] or there are overriding public interest requirements, measures having equivalent effect to quantitative restrictions on imports prohibited by Article [34].*[164]

The Court here confirmed that there was no need to show discrimination; nor was there any reference to the principle of mutual recognition. The market-access test simply focused on whether the national rules totally or 'greatly' prevented consumers from using products that were lawfully produced in the European Union. This market-access test was informed by a *national* market philosophy, albeit one that was qualified by a substantial – qualitative – threshold.[165]

In the immediate post-*Trailer* jurisprudence, this market-access test appears to have become the dominant rationale underlying Article 34 – even in areas in which alternative jurisprudential lines provided relatively safe identical solutions. The question has therefore been raised whether the Court has abandoned its *Keck* jurisprudence;[166] but the even more important question was henceforth this: what is the relationship between the various tests developed in the Court's jurisprudence

ee. Towards a Unitary Doctrinal Framework?

In its preliminary observations in *Italian Trailers*, the Court represented its existing case law as follows:

> It should be recalled that, according to settled case-law, all trading rules enacted by Member States which are capable of hindering, directly or indirectly, actually or potentially, intra-[Union] trade are to be considered as measures having an effect

---

[164] *Ibid.*, paras. 26–8 (emphasis added).

[165] In this sense, see P. Wennerås and K. Bøe Moen, 'Selling Arrangements, Keeping *Keck*' (2010) 35 *EL Rev.* 387 at 395: 'Judging from the norms set out and applied in *Italian Trailers* and *Mickelsson and Roos* it appears that the threshold inherent in the market hindrance test is high, and that it is significantly more qualified than the "substantial" market access test first proposed by Advocate General Jacobs in *Leclerc-Siplec* and nurtured by Advocates General and academics ever since.'

[166] For this argument, see E. Spaventa, 'Leaving *Keck* Behind? The Free Movement of Goods after the Rulings in *Commission* v. *Italy and Mickelsson and Roos*' (2009) 34 *EL Rev* 914 at 915 and 929: '[F]or sure, the Court did not openly overrule *Keck*, and yet the market access formula might suggest, in fact if not in law, the end of the *Keck* dichotomy … the *Keck* distinction based on the type of rules is no longer relevant; what matters is the effect of the rules on market access.' Yet some doubts about the demise of Keck surfaced quickly: see Case C-531/07, *Fachverband der Buch- und Medienwirtschaft* v. *LIBRO* [2009] ECR I-3717; Case C-108/09, *Ker-Optika bt* v. *ÀNTSZ Dél-dunántúli Regionális Intézete* [2010] ECR I-12213.

> equivalent to quantitative restrictions and are, on that basis, prohibited by Article [34]. It is also apparent from settled case-law that Article [34] reflects the obligation to respect the principles of non-discrimination and of mutual recognition of products lawfully manufactured and marketed in other Member States, as well as the principle of ensuring free access of [European] products to national markets.[167]

The scope of Article 34, as jurisdictionally defined by the *Dassonville* formula, is here broken down into three principles that determine the material scope of the provisions: the *international* principle of non-discrimination, the *federal* principle of mutual recognition and the *national* principle of free market access.

But how did these three principles relate to each other? Two possibilities here exist (see Figure 13.3). According to the (traditional) *category approach*, each of the three principles correlates with a specific category of measure. National rules affecting selling arrangements would thus be – exclusively – tested against a discrimination test, product requirements would be subject to the principle of mutual recognition, and consumer restrictions fall – exclusively – under the market-access test. The market-access test will here consequently only apply to measures that are neither subject to the *Keck* nor *Cassis* line; and non-discriminatory selling arrangements would therefore not fall foul of Article 34 via the market-access test. By contrast, according to a *unitary approach*, the Court could theoretically regard the three principles as generally applicable principles that each concretise Article 34 for all categories of measures. Any national measure that potentially hindered trade according to the *Dassonville* formula would thus have to be tested against each of the three principles – vertically ranging from the international discrimination test to the national market-access test.

Which of the two approaches has the Court favoured in its *post-Trailers* jurisprudence? The judicial signals are still very uncertain,[168] and we will have to wait for more conclusive answers from the Court.

b. Quantitative Restrictions on Exports: Article 35

The wording of Article 35 mirrors that of Article 34:

> Quantitative restrictions on exports, and all measures having equivalent effect, shall be prohibited between Member States.

[167] Case C-110/05, *Italian Trailers*, paras. 33–4 (with references to *Dassonville, Sandoz, Cassis* and *Keck*).

[168] For an analysis of the recent jurisprudence and its criticism, see R. Schütze, 'Of Types and Tests: Towards a Unitary Doctrinal Framework for Article 34 TFEU?' (2016) 41 *EL Rev.* 826.

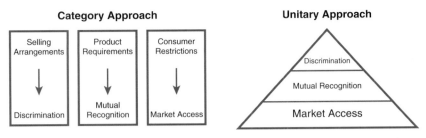

Figure 13.3 Two Possible Approaches to Article 34

Would it therefore not be logical if the constitutional principles governing quantitative restrictions on exports mirrored those on imports? This argument will work for (international) trade rules, such as export licences,[169] yet – importantly – not for others. The reason for this asymmetry is the fact that the scope of Article 35 is indirectly limited by the scope of Article 34. For if the *Cassis* principle of mutual recognition is to work, the product standards of the home State must be presumed legitimate. With regard to product requirements, the Court has consequently interpreted Article 35 to include only those national laws that specifically discriminate against exports.

This logical extension of *Cassis* was made in *Groenveld*.[170] A wholesaler of horsemeat had challenged the legality of a Dutch law prohibiting the (industrial) production of horsemeat sausages. The law had been adopted in order to protect Dutch meat exports in light of the fact that the consumption of horsemeat was not allowed in the national markets of some important trading partners. The Court held that the prohibition on the (industrial) production of horsemeat sausages did not constitute an MEEQR on exports:

> [Article 35] concerns national measures which have as their specific object or effect the restriction of patterns of exports and thereby *the establishment of a difference in treatment between the domestic trade of a Member State and its export trade in such a way as to provide a particular advantage for national production or for the domestic market of the State in question at the expense of the production or of the trade of other Member States.* This is not so in the case of a prohibition like that in question which is applied objectively to the production of goods of a certain kind without drawing a distinction depending on whether such goods are intended for the national market or for export.[171]

Equally applicable *product requirements* would thus *not* constitute MEEQRs on exports. After all, *Cassis* had held that it fell within the responsibility of the home

---

[169] See Case 53/76, *Procureur de la République de Besançon* v. *Les Sieurs Bouhelier and others* [1977] ECR 197; Case C-5/94, *The Queen* v. *Ministry of Agriculture, Fisheries and Food, ex p. Hedley Lomas (Ireland)* [1996] ECR I-2553.

[170] Case 15/79, *Groenveld* v. *Produktschap voor Vee en Vlees* [1979] ECR 3409.

[171] *Ibid.*, para. 7 (emphasis added).

State to set down these rules and that it was only the extension of the host State's product requirements that would constitute an MEEQR under Article 34.

But did this mean that Article 35 could never apply to equally applicable national laws? And what test would the Court apply for Article 35? It took almost 30 years before the Court gave an answer to these question in *Gysbrechts*.[172] The case involved a Belgian law that prohibited distance-selling contracts from forcing the consumer to provide her credit card number before a period of seven working days (within which withdrawal from the contract was possible).[173] Was this 'selling arrangement' an MEEQR on exports? The Court found that the national measure did indeed 'deprive the traders concerned of an efficient tool with which to guard against the risk of non-payment', which therefore restricted trade. Yet in light of the measure being equally applicable, did it fulfil the *Groenveld* formula?[174] The Court found that this was indeed the case: the national measure was an MEEQR since 'its actual effect is none the less greater on goods leaving the market of the exporting Member State than on the marketing of goods in the domestic market of that Member State'.[175] Equally applicable measures may thus constitute MEEQRs on exports, where they indirectly discriminate.

The judicial language from *Groenveld* to *Gysbrechts* indeed suggests that Article 35 is based on a discrimination test. This contrasts with the more liberal regime governing the other fundamental freedoms, and the argument has therefore been made to include non-discriminatory measures in the scope of Article 35.[176]

4. Regulatory Barriers II: Justifications

a. *General Aspects I: Grounds of Justification*

From the very beginning, the Treaty acknowledged that some quantitative restrictions or measures having equivalent effect could be justified on public policy grounds. This express acknowledgement reflects the fact that *regulatory* measures often pursue a legitimate *regulatory* interest. These legitimate interests are set out in Article 36. It states:

---

[172]   Case C-205/07, *Gysbrechts and Santurel Inter* [2008] ECR I-9947. For an analysis of this case, see M. Szydlo, 'Export Restrictions within the Structure of Free Movement of Goods: Reconsideration of an Old Paradigm' (2010) 47 *CML Rev.* 753; A. Dawes, 'A Freedom Reborn? The New Yet Unclear Scope of Article 29 EC' (2009) 34 *EL Rev.* 639.

[173]   Case C-205/07, *Gysbrechts*, para. 13.

[174]   The Court expressly confirmed Case 15/79, *Groenveld* in Case C-205/07, *Gysbrechts*, para. 40.

[175]   Case C-205/07, *Gysbrechts*, para. 43. This point was explained in para. 42: 'As is clear from the order for reference, the consequences of such a prohibition are generally more significant in cross-border sales made directly to consumers, in particular, in sales made by means of the internet, by reason, inter alia, of the obstacles to bringing any legal proceedings in another Member State against consumers who default, especially when the sales involve relatively small sums.'

[176]   Szydlo, 'Export Restrictions' (n. 172 above), 789.

The provisions of Articles 34 and 35 shall not preclude prohibitions or restrictions on imports, exports or goods in transit justified on grounds of public morality, public policy or public security; the protection of health and life of humans, animals or plants; the protection of national treasures possessing artistic, historic or archaeological value; or the protection of industrial and commercial property. Such prohibitions or restrictions shall not, however, constitute a means of arbitrary discrimination or a disguised restriction on trade between Member States.

The provision here expressly exempts national laws that hinder the free movement of goods on six grounds. Member States may invoke 'public morality'– for example – to justify trade restrictions on the importation of pornographic goods.[177] They may refer to 'public policy' reasons, *inter alia* to protect the right to mint coinage.[178] A State has been entitled to plead 'public security' to justify restrictions on imports of petroleum products to guarantee a degree of national energy independence.[179] Scientific uncertainty about a product's impact on the health of humans (or animals and plants) can justify a national trade restriction.[180] The export of national treasures can also be blocked.[181] Finally, a State is allowed to limit intra-Union trade to protect intellectual property rights.[182]

The Court has found this list to be exhaustive: the exceptions listed in Article 36 'cannot be extended to cases other than those specifically laid down'.[183] The Court has consequently held Article 36 not to cover consumer protection.[184] And, more generally: it has found that since Article 36 'constitutes a derogation from the basic rule that all obstacles to the free movement of goods between Member States shall be eliminated', it 'must be interpreted strictly'.[185] Yet, despite limiting the scope of Article 36 so significantly, the Court has ever since *Cassis de Dijon* allowed for implied derogations.

---

[177] See Case 34/79, *Regina* v. *Henn and Darby*.

[178] See Case 7/78, *R.* v. *Thompson, Johnson & Woodiwiss* [1978] ECR 2247.

[179] See Case 72/83, *Campus Oil and others* v. *Minister for Industry and Energy and others* [1984] ECR 2727.

[180] This is the most popular and most important ground of justification for goods, see e.g. Case 104/75, *de Peijper* para. 15: 'health and life of humans rank first among the property or interests protected by Article 36'.

[181] According to P. Oliver et al., *Free Movement of Goods in the European Union* (Hart, 2010), 281 there is no case law on the direct application of this ground.

[182] See Case 192/73, *Van Zuylen frères* v. *Hag AG* [1974] ECR 731.

[183] Case 113/80, *Commission* v. *Ireland (Irish Souvenirs)* [1981] ECR 1625, para. 7.

[184] See Case 229/83, *Édouard Leclerc and others* v. *SARL 'Au blé vert' and others* [1985] ECR 1, para. 30: 'Since it derogates from a fundamental rule of the Treaty, Article 36 must be interpreted strictly and cannot be extended to cover objectives not expressly enumerated therein. Neither the safeguarding of consumers' interests nor the protection of creativity and cultural diversity in the realm of publishing is mentioned in Article 36. It follows that the justification put forward by the French Government cannot be accepted.'

[185] Case 46/76, *Bauhuis*, para. 12.

aa. *Mandatory Requirements and* Cassis de Dijon

Why would the Court be strict on the *express* policy grounds mentioned in Article 36 and yet allow for *implied* – additional – grounds of justification at the same time?

The explanation behind this apparent paradox is that Article 36 was originally designed against the backdrop of the international market model within which it was to apply to discriminatory national measures. But once Article 34 was seen – after *Cassis* – to cover non-discriminatory measures, the Court was caught in a dilemma: on the one hand, it wished to recognise that the expansion of the material scope of Article 34 had to trigger a – simultaneous – expansion of the potential grounds of justification; yet, on the other hand, that expansion could not take place within Article 36 because that might invite the Member States to use the new grounds also for discriminatory measures and thereby undermine the Court's tough stance here. The way out of this dilemma was daring but ingenious: the Court simply deposited a second justificatory route but only for those measures that fell outside the international market model. With the emergence of the federal model in *Cassis*, the Court thus began to exempt obstacles to the free movement of goods that were

> necessary in order to satisfy *mandatory requirements* relating in particular to the effectiveness of fiscal supervision, the protection of public health, the fairness of commercial transactions and the defence of the consumer.[186]

These additional justifications were originally called 'mandatory requirements'; but the Court increasingly refers to them as 'imperative requirements' or 'overriding reason[s] relating to the public interest'.[187] They constitute an – unlimited – addition to the express grounds of justification in Article 36 (see Table 13.4).[188]

bb. *Mandatory Requirements: From Non-Discrimination to Discrimination?*

In its classic jurisprudence, the Court insisted from the very start that mandatory requirements might solely justify national laws 'which apply *without discrimination to both domestic and imported products*'.[189] This was famously confirmed in *Commission v. Ireland* (*Irish Souvenirs*).[190] Ireland had here required that all

---

[186] *Cassis de Dijon* (n. 140 above), para. 8 (emphasis added).

[187] *Italian Trailers* (n. 159 above), paras. 59–60.

[188] This list is very long and includes, *inter alia*: consumer protection (see Case 178/84, *Commission v. Germany* [1987] ECR 1227); the protection of the environment (see Case 302/86, *Commission v. Denmark* [1988] ECR 4607); fiscal supervision and public health (see *Cassis de Dijon* (n. 140 above); social cultural specificity (see *Torfaen Borough Council v. B&Q* (n. 145 above), the diversity of the press (see Case C-368/95, *Familiapress v. Bauer* (n.154 above)); fundamental rights generally (see Case C-112/00, *Schmidberger v. Austria* [2003] ECR I-5659 and many others).

[189] Case 788/79, *Gilli and Andres*, para. 6 (emphasis added).

[190] Case 113/80, *Commission v. Ireland*.

Table 13.4 Justificatory Grounds

Discriminatory Measures	Non-discriminatory Measures
Express Grounds: Article 36 (Limited)	**'Imperative Requirements' (Unlimited)**
Public Morality	Consumer Protection
Public Policy	Environmental Protection
Public Security	Fiscal Supervision
Health Protection	Public Health
National Treasures	Socio-cultural Specificity
Intellectual Property	Press Diversity
	Human Rights Protection …

imported jewellery was to bear a designation of origin or the word 'foreign'. This was a clearly discriminatory measure that violated Article 34, but Ireland contended that the measure was justified in the interest of consumer protection.[191] In light of the discriminatory nature of the Irish law the Court held otherwise:

> In view of the fact that neither the protection of consumers nor the fairness of commercial transactions is included amongst the exceptions set out in Article 36, those grounds cannot be relied upon as such in connexion with that article.[192]

Discriminatory national measures could therefore only be justified by reference to the express – and exhaustive – list of public policy grounds in Article 36,[193] while imperative requirements would be confined to non-discriminatory rules.[194]

This distinction between two different justificatory routes has been criticised;[195] and the Court has sometimes tried to evade it by sharp scholastic means,[196] or by bluntly fudging the issue of the (non-)discriminatory character of a national measure.[197] In more recent jurisprudence, the Court even appears to have come to accept that discriminatory measures may (sometimes) be justified by imperative requirements.

[191] *Ibid.*, para. 5.   [192] *Ibid.*, para. 8.   [193] *Ibid.*, para. 11.
[194] *Ibid.*, para. 10.
[195] See Advocate General F. Jacobs in Case C-379/98, *Preussen Elektra* v. *Schleswag* [2001] ECR I-2099, paras. 227ff.
[196] See Case C-2/90, *Commission* v. *Belgium (Walloon Waste)* [1992] ECR I-4431.
[197] Case C-379/98, *Preussen Elektra* v. *Schleswag*. See also: Case C-54/05, *Commission* v. *Finland*; Case C-531/07, *Fachverband der Buch- und Medienwirtschaft* v. *LIBRO Handelsgesellschaft mbH*.

One of the interesting questions in this context is whether selling arrangements that fall within the scope of Article 34 may ever be justified by imperative requirements. Theoretically, this should not be the case if constitutional logic is followed. (As we saw above, solely *discriminatory* selling arrangements can constitute MEEQRs.) Selling arrangements that violate Article 34 should thus, in theory, solely be justifiable on the grounds mentioned in Article 36. However, the Court has given reason to believe that a softer rule might sometimes apply in practice. It has thus held in *Agostini* that a discriminatory advertising ban could be justified when the latter 'is necessary to satisfy *overriding requirements of general public importance* or one of the aims listed in Article 36 of the [FEU] Treaty'.[198] A similar problem surrounds Article 35 after *Gysbrechts*.[199] In light of this confusion, there is indeed 'strong normative appeal to a model whereby all types of justification are in principle available, but according to which the presence of discrimination would make the job of the [national] regulator in showing that the chosen scheme is lawful particularly onerous'.[200]

b. General Aspects II: Proportionality of National Standards

The fact that a national restriction comes under one of the express or implied grounds of justification is only a first step. The last sentence of Article 36 additionally stipulates that such a restriction 'shall not, however, constitute a means of arbitrary discrimination or a disguised restriction on trade between Member States'. The Court has read this to require the 'proportionality' of the national measure:

> [T]he principle of proportionality which underlies the last sentence of Article 36 of the Treaty requires that the power of the Member States to prohibit imports of the products in question from other Member States should be *restricted to what is necessary to attain the legitimate aim* ...[201]

---

[198] See Case C-34/95, *Konsumentombudsmannen* v. *De Agostini* [1997] ECR I-3843, paras. 39–45 (emphasis added): '[T]he Court held that legislation which prohibits television advertising in a particular sector concerns selling arrangements for products belonging to that sector in that it prohibits a particular form of promotion of a particular method of marketing products ... Consequently, an outright ban on advertising aimed at children less than 12 years of age and of misleading advertising, as provided for by the Swedish legislation, is not covered by Article [34] of the Treaty, unless it is shown that the ban does not affect in the same way, in fact and in law, the marketing of national products and of products from other Member States. In the latter case, it is for the national court to determine whether the ban is necessary to satisfy *overriding requirements of general public importance* or one of the aims listed in Article 36 of the [FEU] Treaty if it is proportionate to that purpose and if those aims or requirements could not have been attained or fulfilled by measures less restrictive of intra-[Union] trade.'

[199] The Court here explored consumer protection as a legitimate justification (paras. 48ff.), even though the measure was (indirectly) discriminatory.

[200] S. Weatherill, 'Free Movement of Goods' (2012) 61 ICLQ 541 at 544.

[201] Case 174/82, *Sandoz* [1983] ECR 2445, para. 18.

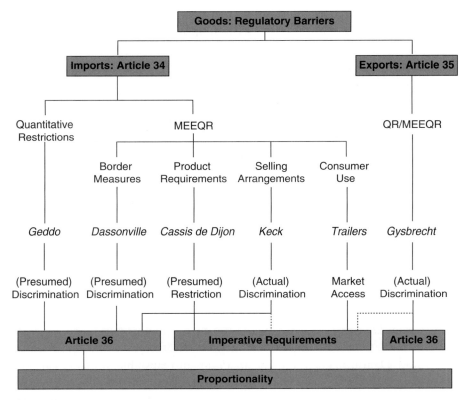

Figure 13.4 Regulatory Barriers: Summary (Flowchart)

This necessity test has been unconditionally extended to mandatory or imperative requirements.[202] The proportionality requirement indeed constitutes a general aspect of all express or implied justifications.[203] In its most elaborate form, it requires proof that the national measure is suitable, necessary and proportionate (in a strict sense). However, the Court often reduces its proportionality test to a 'necessity' analysis and here insists that the public interest pursued 'must not be attainable by measures which are less restrictive of such trade'.[204]

This least-restrictive-means test constitutes the heart of the proportionality requirement. Behind it stands a complex question: what standard of protection

---

[202] Case 120/78, *Rewe-Zentral* v. *Bundesmonopolverwaltung für Branntwein*; Case 261/81, *Rau Lebensmittelwerke* v. *De Smedt* [1982] ECR 3961, para. 12: 'It is also necessary for such rules to be proportionate to the aim in view.'

[203] The Union legal order has also developed a third general aspect limiting the use of justifications under Art. 36: Union human rights. These will limit the power of the Member States to use the Treaties derogation (see Case C-260/89, *ERT* [1991] ECR I-2925). For a discussion of the '*ERT* principle', see Chapter 12, section 4(a).

[204] See Case C-389/96, *Aher-Waggon GmbH* v. *Germany* [1998] ECR I-4473, para. 20. See Case 261/81, *Rau* v. *De Smedt* [1982] ECR 3961, para. 12: 'It is also necessary for such rules to be proportionate to the aim in view. If a Member State has a choice between various measures to attain the same objective it should choose the means which least restricts the free movement of goods.'

should the proportionality test be based on? If the British legislature favours a high level of public morality and bans all pornography, should it matter that other Member States do not prefer to stand on such high moral ground? Or, should Germany be allowed to insist on 'beer purity' as the highest standard of consumer protection, while other Member States allow their beer to be brewed with artificial ingredients? The question of proportionality is here intrinsically linked to the question of the desirable (national) standard of protection.

Would the Court use the host or the home State's regulatory standard as its baseline? Unfortunately, this is a question to which the Court has not given consistent answers.[205] On the one hand, the Court pays regular respect to the idea that 'th[e] degree of protection may vary from one Member State to the other, Member States must be allowed a margin of appreciation and, consequently, the fact that one Member State imposes less strict rules than another Member State does not mean that the latter's rules are disproportionate'.[206] On the other hand, however, the Court has struck down a higher national standard in some areas by applying a stricter level of judicial scrutiny.

We thus find acceptance of a host State's (high) national standard in *Henn & Darby*.[207] The case concerned the importation of pornographic films and magazines from Denmark, which violated the British import ban on such goods. Could this national law be justified on grounds of public morality, or would the 'lower' Danish standard provide an argument that public morality can survive in a society that is more permissive of pornography? The Court chose the higher British standard as its baseline. It held that it was, as a rule, 'for each Member State to determine in accordance with its own scale of values and in the form selected by it the requirements of public morality in its territory'.[208] This choice in favour of the host standard rule did however not mean that the importing State was entitled to discriminate against foreign goods. For the Court subsequently clarified that 'a Member State may not rely on grounds of public morality in order to prohibit the importation of goods from other Member States *when its legislation contains no prohibition on the manufacture or marketing of the same goods on its territory*'.[209] Yet this limitation would nonetheless not 'preclude the authorities of the Member State concerned from applying to those goods, once imported, the same restrictions on marketing

---

[205] On this point, see G. de Búrca, 'The Principle of Proportionality and Its Application in EC Law' (1993) 13 *YEL* 105.

[206] *Italian Trailers* (n. 159 above), para. 65. See also Case C-394/97, *Sami Heinonen* [1999] ECR I-3599, para. 43: 'It should be pointed out that the Member States, which retain exclusive competence as regards the maintenance of public order and the safeguarding of internal security, enjoy a margin of discretion in determining, according to particular social circumstances and to the importance attached by those States to a legitimate objective under [Union] law, such as the campaign against various forms of criminality linked to the consumption of alcohol, the measures which are likely to achieve concrete results.'

[207] Case 34/79, *Regina* v. *Henn and Darby*.   [208] *Ibid.*, para. 15.

[209] Case 121/85, *Conegate* v. *HM Customs & Excise* [1986] ECR 1007, para. 16 (emphasis added).

which are applied to similar products manufactured and marketed within the country'.[210]

By contrast, the Court has *not* deferred to the high host-state standard in other areas. One of these areas in which the Court has judicially developed its own 'European' (federal) standard is consumer protection.

c. In Particular: Consumer Protection and 'European' Standards

Ever since *Cassis*, the Court has emphasised that regulatory trade barriers could be justified on the grounds that 'suitable information is conveyed to the [consumer]'.[211] The public policy defence of 'consumer protection' has indeed become one of the most prominent imperative requirements for the free movement of goods. And unlike the more deferential approach shown vis-à-vis other public interests, the Court has here adopted a 'tough' stance towards unreasonably high host State standards.[212] This tough stance towards overly protective national laws is designed to break open traditional production and marketing rules, where the latter had crystallised into (national) consumer expectations and contained the potential of dividing the internal market.

The most famous case – certainly for Germany – in this context is *Commission v. Germany (Beer Purity)*.[213] The Court here flatly rejected the claim that the traditional German law confining the designation 'beer' to beverages brewed without artificial additives was a proportionate means of consumer protection.[214] Pointing to its dynamic consumer perception – developed under Article 110 – the Court simply found that German consumers could be sufficiently protected by suitable labelling requirements.[215] In the Court's view, a high national consumer standard must never 'crystallize given consumer habits so as to consolidate an advantage acquired by national industries concerned to comply with them'.[216] The Court thus discarded the German maximalist consumer standard and instead developed its own standard of the (reasonably) informed consumer.

This 'European' consumer standard was further developed in *Mars*.[217] The case concerned a complaint launched by a consumer association against the US

---

[210] *Ibid.*, para. 21.   [211] *Cassis de Dijon* (n. 140 above), para. 13.

[212] For an analysis of the case law here, see S. Weatherill, 'Recent Case Law Concerning the Free Movement of Goods: Mapping the Frontiers of Market Deregulation' (1999) 36 *CML Rev.* 51; S. Weatherill, *EU Consumer Law and Policy* (Edward Elgar, 2013), ch. 2.

[213] Case 178/84, *Commission v. Germany (Beer Purity)* (n.188 above). For Italians, a probably even more famous case is Case 407/85, *3 Glocken*. The passionate opinion of Advocate General Mancini is a delicious meal for any European lawyer!

[214] *Beer Purity* (n. 188 above), para. 53: '[I]n so far as the German rules on additives in beer entail a general ban on additives, their application to beers imported from other Member States is contrary to the requirements of [Union] law as laid down in the case-law of the Court, since that prohibition is contrary to the principle of proportionality.'

[215] *Ibid.*, para. 35.

[216] *Ibid.*, para. 32. The Court expressly referred to Case 170/78, *Commission v. United Kingdom*.

[217] Case C-470/93, *Verein gegen Unwesen in Handel und Gewerbe Köln e. V. v. Mars* [1995] ECR I-1923.

sweets manufacturer, whose ice-cream bars were presented with wrappers of '+10%'. The plaintiff argued that the presentation gave the consumer the false impression that the bars had been increased by the quantity corresponding to the coloured part of the wrapping, which was – unsurprisingly – significantly bigger that 10 per cent. Was a national law that protected the consumer against this form of commercial marketing a proportionate restriction on the free movement of goods? The Court's succinct answer was as follows:

> It is accepted by all the parties that the '+ 10%' marking is accurate in itself. However, it is contended that the measure in question is justified because a not insignificant number of consumers will be induced into believing, by the band bearing the '+ 10%' marking, which occupies more than 10% of the total surface area of the wrapping, that the increase is larger than that represented. Such a justification cannot be accepted. *Reasonably circumspect consumers* may be deemed to know that there is not necessarily a link between the size of publicity markings relating to an increase in a product's quantity and the size of that increase.[218]

German consumer law was thus found to be disproportionately protective, since its protective standard was seen to be too high when compared to the Union standard. This Union standard of the 'average consumer who is reasonably well informed and reasonably observant and circumspect' has become a permanent feature of the Court's case law in this context.[219] Yet the Court will – exceptionally – also allow for higher national consumer standards, where social or linguistic factors make a national or social group particularly vulnerable.[220] In these situations, the obstacle to the free movement of goods can only be removed by means of positive integration.[221]

d. In Particular: Intellectual Property Justifications

The most complex and commercially most significant justification mentioned in Article 36 is 'the protection of industrial and commercial property' – in short, intellectual property rights.

Intellectual property rights are designed to encourage creativity and research by protecting the commercial fruits of an idea or of a reputation. The two basic manifestations here are patents and trade marks. Both forms of intellectual property grant their owners an 'exclusive' right. In the case of patents, this is the exclusive right to manufacture a product; in the case of trade marks, the exclusive

---

[218] *Ibid.*, paras. 21–4 (emphasis added).
[219] Case C-210/96, *Gut Springenheide v. Oberkreisdirektor des Kreises Steinfurt* [1998] ECR I-4657, para. 31; Case C-220/98, *Estée Lauder Cosmetics* [2000] ECR I-117, para. 27.
[220] Case C-220/98, *Estée Lauder*, paras. 29–31.
[221] On the general harmonisation competence and consumer protection, see Chapter 14, section 1; and on the Union's special consumer policy competence, see Chapter 18, section 3.

right relates to the marketing of the good.[222] Traditionally, these exclusivity rights were granted by Member States; and they therefore posed serious problems for the construction of a European internal market. For intellectual property rights entitle their owner to legally exclude the production or marketing of the same product – even if that product was legally produced in another Member State.

How has the Court solved the tension between private property rights and the internal market?[223] The original Treaties contained, in Article 345 TFEU, some language suggesting that European law was supposed to leave these rights alone;[224] yet, their inclusion in Article 36 indicated that they could potentially fall within Article 34. In its jurisprudence, the Court has tried to solve this tension by developing a general European standard on what constitutes a legitimate exercise of national intellectual property rights (see section (aa)). It has subsequently concretised this standard in a variety of contexts, and in particular with regard to the doctrine of Union exhaustion (see section (bb)) as well as the judicial doctrine of confusion (see section (cc)).

aa. (Il)legitimate 'Exercises': The 'Specific Subject Matter' Doctrine

The Court has unconditionally clarified that intellectual property rights may be limited by European law. To justify this result in the face of Article 345, it has introduced a dichotomy between the 'existence' and the 'exercise' of intellectual property rights.[225] The Court here pays lip service to Article 345 by claiming to leave the *existence* of national property rights untouched, yet it easily finds that Union law can restrict their *exercise*. This distinction is, in many ways, a false distinction and it has rightly been criticised.[226]

Be that as it may, once the Court had found that Article 34 may outlaw certain exercises of intellectual property rights and that Article 36 solely justifies 'legitimate' exercises, it had to define what these legitimate exercises are. In order to do this, the Court created a doctrine that has come to be known as the 'specific subject matter' doctrine. The latter is an (indirect) expression of the principle of proportionality. In *Centrafarm* v. *Sterling Drug*, the Court explained this point as follows:

---

[222] A third type of intellectual property is copyright. It allows the owner of a work of art to control its reproduction and exploitation. After a long period of ambivalence, the Court confirmed that copyrights would fall under Art. 36 in Joined Cases C-92/92 and C-326/92, *Phil Collins and others* [1993] ECR I-5145 – despite the textual reference to 'industrial and commercial property' in that provision.

[223] For general overviews of these questions, see Keeling, *Intellectual Property Rights* (n. 14 above), I; P. Oliver et al., *Oliver on Free Movement of Goods in the European Union* (Oxford University Press, 2010), ch. 9.

[224] Art. 345 TFEU states: 'The Treaties shall in no way prejudice the rules in Member States governing the system of property ownership.'

[225] The distinction was first introduced in the context of competition law (see Joined Cases 56 and 58–64, *Établissements Consten S.à.R.L. and Grundig-Verkaufs-GmbH* v. *Commission* [1966] ECR 299). It was subsequently transferred to the free movement of goods context.

[226] For an overview of the criticism, see Keeling, *Intellectual Property Rights* (n. 14 above), I, 54ff.

As a result of the provisions in the Treaty relating to the free movement of goods and in particular of Article [34], quantitative restrictions on imports and all measures having equivalent effect are prohibited between Member States. By Article 36 these provisions shall nevertheless not include prohibitions or restrictions on imports justified on grounds of the protection of industrial or commercial property. Nevertheless, it is clear from this same Article, in particular its second sentence, as well as from the context, that whilst the Treaty does not affect the existence of rights recognized by the legislation of a Member State in matters of industrial and commercial property, yet the exercise of these rights may nevertheless, depending on the circumstances, be affected by the prohibitions in the Treaty. Inasmuch as it provides an exception to one of the fundamental principles of the Common Market, *Article 36 in fact only admits of derogations from the free movement of goods where such derogations are justified for the purpose of safeguarding rights which constitute the specific subject matter of this property.*[227]

In essence: intellectual property rights – or better: their use – will only be justified under Article 36 when they concern the 'specific subject matter' of that intellectual property right. (The 'specific subject matter' formulation is an – embarrassingly bad – English translation of the French phrase '*objet spécifique*', which really means specific 'objective' or 'purpose'.)

For each particular property right, the Court therefore had to define the specific subject matter or purpose. With regard to patents, this was done as follows:

In relation to patents, the specific subject matter of the industrial property is the guarantee that the patentee, to reward the creative effort of the inventor, has the exclusive right to use an invention with a view to manufacturing industrial products and *putting them into circulation for the first time, either directly or by the grant of licences to third parties, as well as the right to oppose infringements.*[228]

For trade marks, on the other hand, the Court held:

In relation to trade marks, the specific subject-matter of the industrial property is the guarantee that the owner of the trade mark has the exclusive right to use that trade mark, *for the purpose of putting products protected by the trade mark into circulation for the first time, and is therefore intended to protect him against competitors wishing to take advantage of the status and reputation of the trade mark by selling products illegally bearing that trade mark.*[229]

These two definitions of the specific subject matter of patents and trade marks, respectively, bring us to a first problem that Union law had to face when

---

[227] Case 15/74, *Centrafarm and de Peijper* v. *Sterling Drug* [1974] ECR 1147, paras. 5–8 (emphasis added).

[228] *Ibid.*, para. 9.

[229] Case 16/74, *Centrafarm and de Peijper* v. *Winthrop*, para. 8 (emphasis added).

balancing the interests of the free movement of goods against the protection of intellectual property rights. This problem is commonly referred to as the doctrine of exhaustion. A second problem relates specifically to trade marks. For their specific function is not only the right of first sale but also to 'guarantee the origin of the trade-marked product to the consumer or ultimate user, by enabling him without any possibility of confusion to distinguish that product from products which have another origin'.[230]

bb. The Exhaustion of Rights Doctrine

National laws usually grant a patent or trade mark owner control of the production or marketing of a product until its first sale. These exclusive rights are normally exhausted when the goods have been consensually placed on the *national* market. However, within the internal market, the question arises whether European law demands that the rights should also be exhausted when goods are placed within the broader *Union* market. This problem is referred to as the question of Union exhaustion; and the Court has indeed insisted that Union exhaustion can take place for the entire Union market but only under the condition that the right-holder has *consensually placed the goods into free circulation in another (!) Member State*.

An excellent illustration of this Union doctrine of exhaustion is *Centrafarm v. Sterling Drug*.[231] The case involved an US company – Sterling Drug – who held parallel patents for the sale of pharmaceutical goods in several States of the European Union. Due to governmental price restrictions in the United Kingdom, British drugs were (then) much cheaper than Dutch drugs and a third party – Centrafarm – decided to exploit these price differences by importing British products into the Dutch market. The sale of these imports was opposed on the basis of Sterling's Dutch patent, since the patent holder had not itself placed the goods on the Dutch market. The Court however famously felt that this exercise of a patent right was not covered by its specific subject matter and held:

> An obstacle to the free movement of goods may arise out of the existence, within a national legislation concerning industrial and commercial property, of provisions laying down that a patentee's right is not exhausted when the product protected by the patent is marketed in another Member State, with the result that the patentee can prevent importation of the product into his own Member State when it has been marketed in another State. Whereas an obstacle to the free movement of goods of this kind may be justified on the ground of protection of industrial property where such protection is invoked against a product coming from a Member State where it is not patentable and has been manufactured by third parties without the consent

---

[230]   Case 102/77, *Hoffmann-La Roche & Co. AG v. Centrafarm Vertriebsgesellschaft* [1978] ECR 1139, para. 7.

[231]   Case 15/74, *Centrafarm v. Sterling Drug*, EU:C:1974:114.

> of the patentee and in cases where there exist patents, the original proprietors of which are legally and economically independent, a derogation from the principle of the free movement of goods *is not, however, justified where the product has been put onto the market in a legal manner, by the patentee himself or with his consent, in the Member State from which it has been imported*, in particular in the case of a proprietor of parallel patents.[232]

The Court here established the doctrine of Union exhaustion for patents (and this was subsequently extended to trade marks).[233] A patent holder is consequently not allowed to (ab)use his property right to block imports that he himself had placed on the market of the exporting State. The rationale for the exhaustion doctrine is as beautiful as it is simple: a person that has 'consented' to benefit from the internal market cannot subsequently plead national property rights to shield against competition from the internal market. The key characteristic for Union exhaustion is thus the *consensual* marketing *in another Member State*.

But what counts as 'consent'? In its complex jurisprudence, the Court has had to specify when it felt consent had been given. It has clarified that for exhaustion to take place it did not matter whether the goods could be legally patented in the exporting Member State.[234] However, consent will not be seen as given, where another Member State orders the production of goods on the basis of a compulsory licence.[235] Nor will consent be considered as given where identical trade marks have the same origin but are used by two independent undertakings.[236]

---

[232] *Ibid.*, paras. 10–11 (emphasis added).

[233] Case 16/74, *Centrafarm and de Peijper* v. *Winthrop*, paras. 9–11.

[234] Case 187/80, *Merck* v. *Stephar and others* [1981] ECR 2063, esp. para. 11: 'It is for the proprietor of the patent to decide, in the light of all the circumstances, under what conditions he will market his product, including the possibility of marketing it in a Member State where the law does not provide patent protection for the product in question. If he decides to do so he must then accept the consequences of his choice as regards the free movement of the product within the Common Market, which is a fundamental principle forming part of the legal and economic circumstances which must be taken into account by the proprietor of the patent in determining the manner in which his exclusive right will be exercised.'

[235] Case 19/84, *Pharmon* v. *Hoechst* [1985] ECR 2281. See also Case C-30/90, *Commission* v. *UK* [1992] ECR I-829, where the Court held that these compulsory licences may themselves constitute an MEEQR.

[236] Case C-10/89, *SA CNL-SUCAL NV* v. *HAG (Hag II)* [1990] ECR I-3711. The ruling is famous because it overruled the previously established 'common origin doctrine' that originally provided an exception to the consent requirement (see Case 192/73, *Van Zuylen* v. *HAG (Hag I)* [1974] ECR 731). On the rise and fall of the common origin doctrine, see R. Joliet and D. Keeling, 'Trade Mark Law and the Free Movement of Goods: The Overruling of the Judgment in "*Hag I*" (1991) 22 *International Review of Industrial Property and Copyright* 303.

Finally, consent will not be seen as given where the goods are marketed outside the internal market. For, while insisting on *Union* exhaustion, the Union has rejected the idea of an *international* exhaustion of rights.[237]

cc. *Trade Marks and the Question of Consumer Confusion*

'Since the dawn of capitalism, honest traders have sought to distinguish their goods from goods produced by other persons by affixing distinguishing signs to them. Equally ancient, no doubt, is the practice, on the part of dishonest traders, of imitating such signs in an attempt to pass off their goods as the goods of the more successful trader with an established reputation.'[238] One of the special purposes of trade mark law is to prevent such 'passing-off'. It aims to protect the commercial reputation of an honest trader and wishes to protect the consumer against the possibility of confusion.

The question of 'confusing' trade marks has been one of the trickiest questions under Article 36. For confusion may not only result from dishonest traders but might have a completely innocent origin when, say, a British trade mark 'clashes' with a German one. This happened in *Terrapin* v. *Terronova*.[239] The case involved the appeal by the owner of the British trade mark 'Terrapin' against a decision of a German court finding that it was confusingly similar to the existing German trade mark 'Terranova'. There had obviously been no dishonest intent to freeride on the commercial reputation of the latter, and the question therefore arose whether the free movement of goods should prevail over obstacles created by the disparity of national trade mark registrations. The Court did not think so:

> [I]n the present state of [European Union] law an industrial or commercial property right legally acquired in a Member State may legally be used to prevent under the first sentence of Article 36 of the Treaty the import of products marketed under a name giving rise to confusion where the rights in question have been acquired by different and independent proprietors under different national laws. If in such a case the principle of the free movement of goods were to prevail over the protection given by the respective national laws, the specific objective of industrial and commercial property rights would be undermined.[240]

---

[237] Where the goods are marketed outside the internal market, the exhaustion doctrine will not apply – unless the Union has concluded an international agreement that extends the doctrine to the territory of the third parties. This has, for example, happened in the EEA Agreement. The Court has also clarified that Member States cannot adopt a doctrine of international exhaustion in Case C-355/96, *Silhouette International Schmied GmbH & Co. KG* v. *Hartlauer* [1998] ECR I-4799. For a discussion of this controversial decision, see D. O'Keeffe and B. Keane, 'The Shadow of Silhouette' (1999/2000) 19 *YEL* 139.

[238] Keeling, *Intellectual Property Rights*, I (n. 14 above), 147.

[239] Case 119/75, *Terrapin (Overseas) Ltd* v. *Terranova Industrie CA Kapferer & Co.* [1976] ECR 1039.

[240] *Ibid.*, para. 7.

This 'conservative' judgment was confirmed in *Deutsche Renault* v. *Audi*.[241] The case concerned a dispute over the respective use of the trade marks 'Quadra' and 'Quattro'. The Court underlined once more that the criteria for a risk of confusion would essentially be 'a matter of national law'.[242] (This deferential attitude towards national law was a result of the absence of Union harmonisation with regard to trade marks. A substantial degree of harmonisation was however subsequently achieved by the Trade Mark Directive.)[243]

Conclusion

This chapter has tried to kill two birds with one stone. Its general aim was to provide a general overview of the scope and nature of negative integration. We saw above that the scope of negative integration is in the hands of the European Court(s). All fundamental freedoms have direct effect and can thus be used as European rights against conflicting national laws. They also seem to apply to private 'laws' – at least where the latter collectively regulate a social issue in a manner that hinders intra-Union trade.

The material scope of the free movement rules is however less clear. Having started as an 'international' organisation, the Union has originally followed the international model of free trade; yet, with time, it has increasingly employed a federal model. With the constitutional rationale behind negative integration changing, the question about the 'boundaries' or limits of the internal market has become ever more prominent. Union law has here not yet found any convincing solutions, apart from a very weak 'remoteness rule' and the idea that 'purely internal situations' are beyond the scope of negative integration.

The special aim of this chapter has been to explore the degree of negative integration for the free movement of goods. The constitutional regime governing this 'first' freedom is textually more complex than that for all other three freedoms. For unlike the other three freedoms, which only contain one single prohibition of illegal trade barriers, the EU Treaties distinguish, in the context of goods, between fiscal and regulatory barriers; and for fiscal barriers, the Treaties further distinguish between customs charges and internal taxation.

For customs charges, prohibited under Article 30, the Court insists on an absolute prohibition that today even applies to non-discriminatory charges *within* Member States. By contrast, the prohibition of discriminatory tax measures under Article 110 still requires discrimination. For regulatory measures, the Court's rationale has changed over time, and Article 34 now seems to comprise a number of tests that apply to different categories of national measures. For product requirements, the Court has, ever since *Cassis de Dijon*, applied a federal model based on home State rule. For selling arrangements, on the other

---

[241] Case C-317/91, *Deutsche Renault* v. *Audi* [1993] ECR I-6227.

[242] *Ibid.*, para. 31.

[243] On the positive harmonisation effort in the context of intellectual property rights in general, see Chapter 14, section 2(b).

hand, it has reverted to a discrimination test that is based on host State rule; and this rationale equally informs Article 35 with regard to exports. For consumer restrictions, finally, it operates a market-access test that comes very close to a 'national' reading of the internal market. The relationship between the various tests within Article 34 is not yet clear; yet there might be reasons to believe that the Court is gradually moving away from its older category approach and towards a more unitary approach.

Finally, this chapter also explored to what extent Member States can justify trade barriers to the free movement of goods. We saw in section 2 that despite the absence of express justifications for fiscal restrictions, the Court has allowed the idea of an 'objective justification'. Express justifications however only exist with regard to regulatory trade barriers and are found in Article 36. These grounds have been enriched by implied justifications called 'imperative requirements'. The latter will however – in theory – only apply to non-discriminatory restrictions.

The central problem with regard to justifying national restrictions is however not so much the grounds of justification but the standard against which national restrictions are reviewed. The Court has here followed a differentiated approach. For some grounds, it has permitted a wide margin of discretion to the 'host' State; while for others, it has applied a strict proportionality test that outlaws any national laws above a certain 'European' standard. This European standard is a judicially 'engineered' standard. It is often complemented by a harmonised standard laid down by the Union legislator. This second strategy of – positive – market integration will be discussed in the next chapter.

FURTHER READING

Books

C. Barnard, *The Substantive Law of the EU: The Four Freedoms* (Oxford University Press, 2016)

L. Gormley, *EU Law of Free Movement of Goods and Customs Union* (Oxford University Press, 2009)

D. T. Keeling, *Intellectual Property Rights in EU Law, I: Free Movement and Competition Law* (Oxford University Press, 2003)

N. Nic Shuibhne, *The Coherence of EU Free Movement Law: Constitutional Responsibility and the Court of Justice* (Oxford University Press, 2013)

P. Oliver (ed.), *Oliver on Free Movement of Goods in the European Union* (Hart, 2010)

M. Poiares Maduro, *We the Court* (Hart, 1998)

R. Schütze, *From International to Federal Market: The Changing Structure of European Law* (Oxford University Press, 2017)

J. Snell, *Goods and Services in EC Law: A Study of the Relationship between the Freedoms* (Oxford University Press, 2002)

A. Tryfonidou. *Reverse Discrimination in EC Law* (Kluwer, 2009)

S. Weatherill, *The Internal Market as a Legal Concept* (Oxford University Press, 2017)

F. Weiss and C. Kaupa, *European Union Internal Market Law* (Cambridge University Press, 2014)

Articles (and Chapters)

R. Barents, 'Charges of Equivalent Effect to Customs Duties' (1978) 15 *CML Rev.* 415

D. Chalmers, 'Free Movement of Goods within the European Community: An Unhealthy Addiction to Scotch Whisky?' (1993) 42 ICLQ 269

M. Danusso and R. Denton, 'Does the European Court of Justice Look for a Protectionist Motive under Article 95?' (1990) 17 *Legal Issues of European Integration* 67

A. Easson, 'Fiscal Discrimination: New Perspectives on Article 95 of the EEC Treaty' (1981) 18 *CML Rev.* 521

A. Easson, 'Cheaper Wine or Dearer Beer? Article 95 Again' (1984) 9 *EL Rev.* 57

S. Enchelmaier, '"Moped Trailers", "Mickelsson & Roos", "Gysbrechts": The ECJ's Case Law on Goods Keeps on Moving' (2010) 29 YEL 190

S. Enchelmaier, 'Horizontality: The Application of the Four Freedoms to Restrictions Imposed by Private Parties', in P. Koutrakos and J. Snell, *Research Handbook on the Law of the EU's Internal Market* (Elgar, 2017)

U. Loewenheim, 'Intellectual Property before the European Court of Justice' (1995) 26 *International Review of Industrial Property and Copyright Law* 829

R. Schütze, 'Of Types and Tests: Towards a Unitary Doctrinal Framework for Article 34 TFEU?' (2016) 41 *EL Rev.* 826

J. Snell, 'The Notion of Market Access: A Concept or a Slogan?' (2010) 47 *CML Rev.* 437

E. Spaventa, 'Leaving *Keck* Behind? The Free Movement of Goods after the Rulings in *Commission* v. *Italy and Mickelsson and Roos*' (2009) 34 *EL Rev.* 914

M. Szydło, 'Export Restrictions within the Structure of Free Movement of Goods: Reconsideration of an Old Paradigm' (2010) 47 *CML Rev.* 753

S. Weatherill, 'After *Keck*: Some Thoughts on How to Clarify the Clarification' (1996) 33 *CML Rev.* 885

E. White, 'In Search of the Limits of Article 30 of the EEC Treaty' (1989) 26 *CML Rev.* 235

Cases on the Website

Case 7/68, *Commission* v. *Italy (Art Treasures)*; Case 24/68, *Commission* v. *Italy (Statistical Levy)*; Case 8/74, *Dassonville*; Case 15/74, *Centrafarm*; Case 36/74, *Walrave*; Case 87/75, *Bresciani*; Case 119/75, *Terrapin*; Case 46/76, *Bauhuis*; Case 120/78, *Cassis de Dijon*; Case 170/78, *Commission* v. *United Kingdom (Beer & Wine)*; Case 15/79, *Groenveld*; Case 34/79, *Henn and Darby*; Case 113/80, *Commission* v. *Ireland*; Cases 177 and 178/82, *Van de Haar*; Case 112/84, *Humblot*; Case 178/84, *Commission* v. *Germany (Beer Purity)*; Case 196/85, *Commission* v. *France (Natural Sweet Wines)*; Case 311/85, *Vlaamse Reisbureaus*; Case 98/86, *Mathot*; Case 18/87, *Commission* v. *Germany*; Case 69/88, *Krantz*; Case 145/88, *Torfaen*; Case C-163/90, *Legros*; Cases C-267 and 268/91, *Keck*; Case C-317/91, *Deutsche Renault* v. *Audi*; Joined Cases C-363, 407–11/93, *Lancry*; Case C-470/93, *Mars*; Joined Cases C-321–4/94, *Pistre and others*; Case C-34/95, *Agostini*; Case C-368/95, *Familiapress* v. *Bauer*; Case C-112/00, *Schmidberger*; Case C-302/00, *Commission* v. *France (Dark Tobacco)*; Case C-110/05, *Commission* v. *Italy (Italian Trailers)*; Case C-142/05, *Mickelson*; Case C-205/07, *Gysbrechts*; Case C-171/11, *Fra.bo*

14

Free Movement of Goods II
Positive Integration

Introduction

The gradual integration of the various the national markets into a 'common' or 'internal' European market can be achieved by two complementary mechanisms. First, the Treaties may themselves 'negate' certain national barriers to intra-Union trade. For the free movement of goods, this form of negative integration was discussed in the previous chapter. A second technique is 'positive integration': the Union here adopts positive legislation to – partly or exhaustively – remove obstacles to trade arising from the differences in national laws.

This idea of integration through legislation stands behind Article 26 TFEU, which states:

> The Union shall adopt measures with the aim of establishing or ensuring the functioning of the internal market, in accordance with the relevant provisions of the Treaties.[1]

Legislative competences for positive integration are placed within the specific policy areas of the Union.[2] However, the Treaties also contain a number of horizontal competences that generally allow the Union to create an 'internal market'. These 'internal market' competences can be found in Chapter 3 of Title VII of the TFEU. They have been the bedrock of the Union's positive integration programme. Articles 114 and 115 here provide the Union with a legislative competence 'for the approximation of the provisions laid down by law, regulation or administrative action in Member States *which have as their object the establishment and functioning of the internal market*'.[3]

These two general internal market competences apply to all four fundamental freedoms.[4] They are complemented by three more 'specific' internal market competences. With regard to fiscal measures, Article 113 allows the Union to harmonise legislation on 'forms of *indirect taxation* to the extent that such harmonisation is necessary to ensure the establishment and functioning of the internal market and to avoid distortions of competition'. By contrast, Article 116 targets distortions of competition, while Article 118 empowers the Union '[i]n the context of the establishment and functioning of the internal market' to 'establish measures for the creation of European intellectual property rights'.[5] An overview of these competences can be found in Table 14.1.

Table 14.1 Harmonisation Competences

Chapter 2: Tax Provisions		Chapter 3: Approximation of Laws	
Article 110	Discriminatory Taxation	Article 114	General Competence I
Article 111	Export Repayments	Article 115	General Competence II
Article 112	Export Repayments Approval	Article 116	Specific Competence: Competition
Article 113	Specific Competence: Taxes	Article 117	Commission Consultation
		Article 118	Specific Competence: Intellectual Property

[1] Art. 26(1) TFEU.   [2] On this point, see Chapter 7.
[3] Art. 114(1) TFEU (emphasis added).
[4] According to *ibid.*, Art. 26(2): '[t]he internal market shall comprise an area without internal frontiers in which the free movement of goods, persons, services and capital is ensured in accordance with the provisions of the Treaties'.
[5] *Ibid.*, Art. 118(1).

This chapter explores the constitutional principles and limits governing positive integration. Section 1 analyses the scope and nature of the general internal market competence(s): Articles 114 and 115. We shall see there that the Union has an – almost – unlimited competence to harmonise national laws that affect the establishment or functioning of the internal market. Section 2 looks at the more limited special competences given to the Union in Articles 113 and 118. Section 3 investigates how the Union can use its internal market competences, as the Union may exercise its powers through distinct harmonisation methods. Section 4 finally offers an excursion into a particular – yet fundamentally important – aspect of positive integration in the internal market: the Common Agricultural Policy.

1. Internal Market Competences I: General Competences

Originally, the sole competences for the 'internal market' were Articles 115 and 116 TFEU. The former entitled the European Union to 'issue *directives* for the *approximation* of such provisions laid down by law, regulation or administrative action in Member States as *directly affect* the establishment or functioning of the common market'.[6] Article 116 TFEU, by contrast, was more specific. It allowed the Union to issue directives where a difference between national laws 'is distorting the conditions of competition in the internal market'.[7]

Article 115 soon turned out to be legally 'quite simply unlimited'.[8] Yet the competence had an important *political* limit: it required unanimity in the Council; and this political safeguard substantially limited the exercise of the Union's internal market competence in its early life.[9] This however dramatically changed after the Single European Act. The latter provided Article 115 with a 'brilliant assistant': Article 114.[10] The new constitutional neighbour textually widened the Union's internal market competence;[11] and – importantly – it no longer required a unanimous decision of all Member States. Today Article 114 states:

---

[6] Emphasis added.

[7] The competence was thus designed as the positive integration platform for the EU's competition policy; yet despite its more specific focus, it soon declined into practical oblivion. U. Everling, 'Zur Funktion der Rechtsangleichung inder Europäischen Gemeinschaft:vom Abbau der Verzerrungen zur Schaffung des Binnenmarktes', in F. Capotorti et al. (eds.), *Du droit international au droit de l'intégration: liber amicorum Pierre Pescatore* (Nomos, 1987), 227 at 232.

[8] P. Leleux, 'Le Rapprochement des législations dans la communauté economique européenne' (1968) 4 *CDE* 129 at 138. On the function and scope of Art. 115 TFEU in the Union legal order, see F. Marx, *Funktion und Grenzen der Rechtsangleichung nach Art. 100 EWG-Vertrag* (Heymann, 1976); C. Eiden, *Die Rechtsangleichung gemäß Art. 100 des EWG-Vertrages* (Duncker & Humblot, 1984).

[9] On this point, see A. Dashwood, 'Hastening Slowly: The Community's Path towards Harmonization', in H. Wallace, W. Wallace and C. Webb (eds.), *Policy-making in the European Community* (Wiley & Sons, 1983), 177.

[10] D. Vignes, 'The Harmonisation of National Legislation and the EEC' (1990) 15 *EL Rev.* 358 at 367.

[11] Constitutionally, Art. 114 TFEU no longer contained the – by now obsolete – references to 'directives' as instruments of harmonisation; nor did it mention the 'direct [e]ffect' of national laws on the internal market.

1. Save where otherwise provided in the Treaties, the following provisions shall apply for the achievement of the objectives set out in Article 26. The European Parliament and the Council shall, acting in accordance with the ordinary legislative procedure and after consulting the Economic and Social Committee, adopt the measures for the approximation of the provisions laid down by law, regulation or administrative action in Member States which have as their object the establishment and functioning of the internal market.

2. Paragraph 1 shall not apply to fiscal provisions, to those relating to the free movement of persons nor to those relating to the rights and interests of employed persons.

3. The Commission, in its proposals envisaged in paragraph 1 concerning health, safety, environmental protection and consumer protection, will take as a base a high level of protection, taking account in particular of any new development based on scientific facts. Within their respective powers, the European Parliament and the Council will also seek to achieve this objective ...[12]

This gave the Union legislator a horizontal competence, save where otherwise provided,[13] to harmonise national laws that affected the internal market. Positive harmonisation could thereby be adopted by a qualified majority of the Member States. This departure from the unanimity requirement within the Council would however not extend to all areas within the internal market. Indeed Article 114(2) expressly states that Article 114(1) would 'not apply to fiscal provisions, to those relating to the free movement of persons nor to those relating to the rights and interests of employed persons'. (These politically 'sensitive' matters would continue to fall under Article 115 TFEU or one of the specific legal competences within the relevant Treaty titles.) A fear of 'unqualified' qualified majority voting also led to the inclusion of two further qualifications. First, Article 114(3) obliges the Commission to base its legislative proposals on a 'high level of protection' with regard to these interests; and, second, Article 114(4)–(5) TFEU – quoted below – allowed, for the first time in the Union's history, for differential positive integration.[14]

---

[12] *Ibid.*, Art. 114(1)–(3). For the text of paras. 4 and 5, see section 1(d) below.
[13] On the 'residual' nature of Art. 114, see section 1(c) below.
[14] For the historical justification of these paragraphs, see Advocate General G. Tesauro in Case C-41/93, *France v. Commission* [1994] ECR I-1829, para. 4: 'The possibility granted to a Member State of continuing to apply its own national rules, even though the matter has been harmonized at [Union] level, is intended to ensure "reinforced" protection of certain particularly important interests and, above all, to answer the preoccupations expressed by a number of countries during the negotiations leading up to the Single Act to the effect that any harmonization adopted by a majority vote might result in a diminution of the degree of protection enjoyed by such interests at national level. In other words, the provision represents a "counterweight" to offset the relinquishment of the principle of unanimity with regard to the adoption of measures necessary for the creation and operation of the internal market, in the cases provided for in Article [114(1)].'

Table 14.2 Harmonisation Measures (Selection)

Product Requirements	Consumer Protection
General Product Safety (Directive 2001/95)	Unfair Terms in Consumer Contracts (Directive 1993/13)
Registration, Evaluation, Authorization and Restriction of Chemicals (REACH) (Regulation 1907/2006)	Consumer Sales (Directive 1999/44)
Toy Safety (Directive 2009/48)	Unfair Commercial Practices (Directive2005/29)
Notification of Technical Standards (Directive 2015/1535)	Misleading and Comparative Advertising (Directive 2006/114)
Novel Foods and Food Ingredients (Regulation 2015/2283)	Consumer Credit (Directive 2008/48)
Trade Marks (Directive 2015/2436)	Consumer Rights (Directive 2011/83)

Despite these qualifications, Article 114 is (with Article 352) the broadest competence of the Union. Indeed, its horizontal and supranational nature have turned Article 114 into 'the' constitutional base for the Union's positive integration programme. For illustrative purposes, a selection of some important harmonisation measures is provided in Table 14.2.

This section wishes to explore, in a more detailed way than Chapter 7, the scope of Article 114 TFEU. Sections (a) and (b) start by analysing the concept of 'harmonisation' and the substantive conditions that need to be satisfied before the Union is entitled to activate its 'internal market' competence. Thereafter, section (c) investigates potential limits imposed by other competences within the Treaties; whereas section (d) looks at the derogations expressly set out in Article 114(4)–(5) TFEU.

a. The Concept of 'Approximation' or 'Harmonisation'

The Union's internal market competences are based on the idea of 'approximation' or 'harmonisation'. Would this idea require the existence of national laws *before* and *after* the Union legislation?

For a long time, European law indeed strongly linked the concept of harmonisation to the *subsequent* existence of national laws. This was originally the result of the harmonisation instrument of the 'directive'.[15] Directives require Member States to adopt national legislation that implements the Union command. A directive thus results in 'harmonised' *national* rules; and it consequently seemed that the *subsequent* existence of national rules was a conceptual minimum within

---

[15] According to Art. 288(3) TFEU, '[a] directive shall be binding, as to the result to be achieved, upon each Member State to which it is addressed, but shall leave to the national authorities the choice of form and methods'. On the Union instrument of the 'directive', see Chapter 3, section 3.

the notion of harmonisation. This however changed with the Single European Act, when Article 114 TFEU 'decoupled' the idea of harmonisation from the 'directive'. The Union could henceforth adopt any measure under its internal market competence – and this included 'regulations' as instruments of *direct* Union legislation.[16]

What about the *prior* existence of national laws as a precondition for Article 114 TFEU? This question was the subject of *Spain v. Council*.[17] The European legislator here believed the national protection for medicinal patents to be insufficient, and had therefore created a supplementary EU protection certificate on the basis of Article 114 that could be granted under the same conditions as national patents. Two major constitutional hurdles seemed to oppose the legality of this European law. First, could Article 114 be used to create *new* property rights; or could it only harmonise *existing* rights?[18] Second, since at the time of the adoption of the Union law only *two* Member States had legislation concerning a supplementary certificate, could one speak of a harmonisation of national laws here?

The Court took the first hurdle by force. It simply rejected the claim that the European law created a new right.[19] Concentrating on the second hurdle, the Court then addressed the question of whether Article 114 required the *pre*-existence of diverse national laws before Union harmonisation could take place; and in the eyes of the Court, this was not the case. The Union could use its internal market competence equally 'to *prevent the heterogeneous development of national laws* leading to further disparities which would be likely to create obstacles to the free movement of medicinal products within the [Union] and thus directly affect the establishment and the functioning of the internal market'.[20] The Union was thus entitled to use its harmonisation power to prevent the *future* adoption of diverse national laws so as to prevent *future* obstacles to trade![21]

This judicial ruling was confirmed in *Vodafone*;[22] and it seems to have emptied the concept of harmonisation of almost any content.

---

[16] On the Union instrument of 'regulation', see Chapter 3, section 2.

[17] Case C-350/92, *Spain v. Council* [1995] ECR I-1985.

[18] The Court has indeed found that Union legislation that creates 'new' rights will have to be based on Art. 352 TFEU, see *Spain v. Council* (n. 17 above), para. 23 (with reference to *Opinion 1/94* (Competence of the Community to conclude international agreements concerning services and the protection of intellectual property) [1994] ECR I-5267, para. 59).

[19] *Spain v. Council* (n. 17 above), para. 27.

[20] *Ibid.*, para. 35 (emphasis added).

[21] On the idea of 'preventive' harmonisation in the internal market, see M. Seidel, 'Präventive Rechtsangleichung im Bereich des Gemeinsamen Marktes' (2006) 41 *Europarecht* 26. For some limits, see however Case C-436/03, *Parliament and Council* [2006] ECR I-3733, para. 44. The Court here confirmed and extended the point made in relation to intellectual property law.

[22] Case C-58/08, *Vodafone and others v. Secretary of State for Business, Enterprise and Regulatory Reform* [2010] ECR I-4999.

b. The 'Establishment' or 'Functioning' of the Internal Market

The Union's internal market competence is a horizontal competence. It is horizontal because it is not thematically limited to a particular policy area. Article 114 applies to *any* national measure that somehow affects the establishment or functioning of the internal market.[23]

This horizontal scope thereby refers to two alternatives. The first alternative deals with the 'establishment' of the internal market and concerns obstacles to free movement. The second alternative refers to the 'functioning' of the internal market and addresses distortions of competition resulting from disparities between national laws. Importantly: the combination of these two objectives means that the scope of positive integration under Article 114 TFEU is wider than the scope of negative integration under Article 34 TFEU.[24]

To what extent would Union legislation have to serve the 'establishment' or 'functioning' of the internal market? Until the end of the twentieth century, the jurisprudence of the Court unequivocally confirmed the widest possible reading of the Union's general harmonisation competence: almost anything, it seemed, could be based on Article 114. This perception significantly changed with *Germany* v. *Parliament and Council (Tobacco Advertising)*.[25]

aa. The Tobacco Advertising *Judgment: A Turning Point*

Tobacco Advertising famously confirmed the existence of constitutional limits for Article 114. The bone of contention here was a Union law that banned the advertising and sponsorship of tobacco products.[26] Germany disliked the idea and claimed that a prohibition or even a ban of a product could never be based on the Union's internal market competence. Article 114 could only be used to 'establish' trade and this was not the case, where Union legislation *prohibited* trade.[27] And while admitting that Article 114 could, in the alternative, still potentially be used to

---

[23] S. Weatherill, 'The Limits of Legislative Harmonization Ten Years after *Tobacco Advertising*: How the Court's Case Law Has Become a "Drafting Guide"' (2011) 12 *German Law Journal* 827 at 831: 'Article [114] is functionally driven: any national measure may be harmonized provided that leads to an improvement in the functioning of the internal market envisaged by Article 26 TFEU[.]'

[24] This means that even where a national law is outside the scope of Art. 34 TFEU – such as non-discriminatory selling arrangements after *Keck* (see Chapter 13, section 3(a/cc)), these selling arrangements could be harmonised under Art. 114 TFEU if they affect the functioning of the internal market. For an overview of the debate on the (only partial) connection between Arts. 34 and 114 TFEU, see G. Davies, 'Can Selling Arrangements Be Harmonised?' (2005) 30 *EL Rev.* 370.

[25] Case C-376/98, *Germany* v. *Parliament and Council (Tobacco Advertising)* [2000] ECR I-8419.

[26] Directive 98/43 on the approximation of the laws, regulations and administrative provisions of the Member States relating to the advertising and sponsorship of tobacco products [1998] OJ L 213/9.

[27] Germany had pointed out that the sole form of advertising allowed under the directive was advertising at the point of sale, which only accounted for 2 per cent of the tobacco industry's advertising expenditure (Case C-376/98, *Tobacco Advertising*, para. 24).

ensure the proper functioning of the internal market, this second alternative within Article 114 should only apply to cases where the distortion was 'considerable'.[28]

The Court accepted – to the surprise of many – these arguments and annulled, for the first time in its history, a Union law on the grounds that it went beyond the internal market competence. Emphatically, the Court underlined that Article 114 could not grant the Union an unlimited power to regulate the internal market:

> To construe that article as meaning that it vests in the [Union] legislature a general power to regulate the internal market would not only be contrary to the express wording of the provisions cited above but would also be incompatible with the principle embodied in Article [5 TEU] that the powers of the [Union] are limited to those specifically conferred on it. Moreover, a measure adopted on the basis of Article [114] of the Treaty must genuinely have as its object the improvement of the conditions for the establishment and functioning of the internal market. If a mere finding of disparities between national rules and of the abstract risk of obstacles to the exercise of fundamental freedoms or of distortions of competition liable to result therefrom were sufficient to justify the choice of Article [114] as a legal basis, judicial review of compliance with the proper legal basis might be rendered nugatory.[29]

What conclusions did the Court draw from this statement of principle? The Court split its ruling into an 'establishment' and a 'functioning' part and analysed, in turn, the two alternative applications of the Union's harmonisation competence.

Regarding the elimination of obstacles to free movement, the Court now qualified its generous ruling in *Spain* v. *Council*.[30] While accepting that 'recourse to Article [114] as a legal basis is possible if the aim is to prevent the emergence of future obstacles to trade resulting from multifarious development of national laws', the Court nonetheless insisted that '*the emergence of such obstacles must be likely* and the measure in question must be designed to prevent them'.[31] Were future obstacles to intra-Union trade in tobacco advertising likely? The Court accepted this for press products; yet 'for numerous types of advertising of tobacco products', the prohibition within the directive 'cannot be justified by the need to eliminate obstacles to the free movement of advertising media or the freedom to provide services in the field of advertising'.[32] The Union legislature had thus not been entitled to rely on its internal market power on the grounds that the measure would eliminate obstacles to free movement.

---

[28] Case C-376/98, *Tobacco Advertising*, para. 29. There was previous case law to support this claim, e.g. Case 91/79, *Commission* v. *Italy*, para. 8; Case C-300/89, *Commission* v. *Council (Titanium Dioxide)*, para. 23.

[29] Case C-376/98, *Tobacco Advertising*, paras. 83–4 (emphasis added).

[30] Case C-350/92, *Spain* v. *Council*.

[31] Case C-376/98, *Tobacco Advertising*, para. 86 (emphasis added).

[32] *Ibid.*, paras. 97 and 99.

But recourse to the competence could possibly still be justified by means of the second alternative in Article 114: the elimination of distortions of competition. In previous jurisprudence, the Court had indeed interpreted this condition widely by allowing all harmonising measures that 'deal with disparities between the laws of the Member States in areas where such disparities are liable to create or maintain distorted conditions of competition'.[33] This suggested that *any* disparities in national laws liable to create *any* distortion of competition could be harmonised.

Yet *Tobacco Advertising* now corrected this excessive reading also for the 'functioning' part of the internal market competence. For the Court here accepted Germany's invitation: distortions of competition would have to be *appreciable* to entitle the Union to act under Article 114. Constitutionally, the Union legislator was thus not entitled to pass laws under Article 114 'with a view to eliminating the smallest distortions of competition'.[34] And since the national laws at issue had only a 'remote and indirect' effect on competition, disparities between them could not lead to distortions that were appreciable.[35] The directive was thus not (!) legitimately based on the second alternative of the internal market competence either and the Court consequently annulled the European directive.

bb. Post-Tobacco Advertising *Developments: Back to Square One?*
With *Tobacco Advertising* the Court expressly accepted *some* limits to the Union's internal market power.

First, a simple disparity in national laws would theoretically not be enough to trigger the Union's harmonisation competence. The disparity must either give rise to obstacles in trade or lead to appreciable distortions in competition. And while Article 114 could still be used to harmonise *future* disparities in national laws, it had to be 'likely' that this divergent development led to obstacles in trade or appreciable distortions of competition. (The Court has, occasionally, come to verbalise this requirement by extending the constitutional criterion of a 'direct effect' on the internal market – textually mandated only in Article 115 TFEU – to Article 114 TFEU.)[36]

Second, the Union measure must *actually contribute* to the elimination of obstacles to trade or distortions of competition,[37] and where this is not the case

---

[33] See Case C-300/89, *Commission* v. *Council (Titanium Dioxide)* [1991] ECR I-2867, para. 15.

[34] Case C-376/98, *Tobacco Advertising*, para. 107.   [35] *Ibid.*, para. 109.

[36] See Case C-210/03, *Swedish Match* [2004] ECR I-11893, para. 29; Case C-380/03, *Germany* v. *Parliament and Council (Tobacco Advertising II)* [2006] ECR I-11573, para. 37. See also Case C-58/08, *The Queen, on the application of Vodafone Ltd and others* v. *Secretary of State for Business, Enterprise and Regulatory Reform* [2010] ECR I-4999, para. 32: 'While a mere finding of disparities between national rules and the abstract risk of infringements of fundamental freedoms or distortion of competition is not sufficient to justify the choice of Article [114 TFEU] as a legal basis, the [Union] legislature may have recourse to it in particular where there are differences between national rules which are such as to obstruct the fundamental freedoms and thus have a direct effect on the functioning of the internal market.'

[37] Case C-491/01, *British American Tobacco* [2002] ECR I-11453, para. 60.

the Union measure is not a measure of positive integration and will thus be annulled.

These two constitutional limits to the Union's 'internal market' competence have been confirmed *in abstracto* by subsequent jurisprudence;[38] yet, their concrete application has led to renewed accusations that Article 114 grants the Union an unlimited competence for the internal market.

A good illustration of this erosion of *Tobacco Advertising* is *Philip Morris*.[39] The case concerned a legal challenge to the Union directive on the manufacture and labelling of tobacco products (the Tobacco Sales Directive).[40] The applicants argued that a number of provisions within the Directive could not have been based on Article 114 because they would not facilitate trade or remove distortions of competition. Apart from attacking the Union labelling requirement that demanded that 65 per cent of the front and the back surface be covered by health warnings, the core target here was Article 7 of the directive which required that 'Member States shall prohibit the placing on the market of tobacco products with a characterising flavour'. This meant, *inter alia* that 'menthol cigarettes' could no longer be sold, and the question arose how such an elimination of trade could be characterised as a facilitation of trade. Yet the Court, referring to its older jurisprudence, curtly argued as follows:

> [I]t is foreseeable, with a sufficient degree of probability, that in the absence of measures at EU level, the relevant national rules could develop in divergent ways, including with regard to the use of menthol. Article 7 of Directive 2014/40, in prohibiting the placing on the market of tobacco products with a characterising flavour, guards precisely against such divergences in the rules of the Member States. *According to the case-law … recourse to Article 114 TFEU as a legal basis is possible if the aim is to prevent the emergence of future obstacles to trade as a result of divergences in national laws, when the emergence of such obstacles is likely and the harmonisation measure adopted is designed to prevent them … It should also be recalled that, according to the case-law cited … the measures that may be adopted on the basis of Article 114 TFEU can consist, inter alia, in prohibiting, provisionally or definitively, the marketing of a product or products.* It follows that removing divergences between the national rules concerning the composition of tobacco products, or preventing those rules from developing in divergent ways, including by means of an EU-wide prohibition of certain additives, is intended to facilitate the smooth functioning of the internal market for the products concerned.[41]

---

[38] For the relevant case law, see e.g. n. 36 above.

[39] Case C-547/14, *Philip Morris Brands SARL and Others* v. *Secretary of State for Health*, EU:C:2016:325. The case was flanked by two additional challenges, and decided on the same day, namely Case C-358/14, *Poland* v. *Parliament and Council*, EU:C:2016: 323; Case C-477/14, *Pillbox 38* v. *Secretary of State for Health*, EU:C:2016:324.

[40] Directive 2014/40 on the approximation of the laws, regulations and administrative provisions of the Member States concerning the manufacture, presentation and sale of tobacco products [2014] OJ L127/1.

[41] Case C-547/14, *Philip Morris Brands*, paras. 120–5 (emphasis added).

This seems to – radically – put *Tobacco Advertising* into question; and we need to see how the future will develop here.

c. Relationship to Other Competences: Article 114(2) and Beyond

Article 114 TFEU presents itself with an understatement. With false modesty, it states that it only applies 'save where otherwise provided in the Treaties'. This is deeply misleading, for it suggests that the provision is but a residual competence that only applies where no more specific legal competence is available.[42] The question thus arises when the Union can actually use its general internal market competence under Article 114 and when it must use – say – its special environmental competence, if it wishes to set environmental standards for industrial machinery.

Had the Court taken a strict view on Article 114, hardly any matters may have fallen within its scope. Yet the Court treats Article 114 TFEU like a 'normal' competence. This was confirmed in *Titanium Dioxide*.[43] The Court here acknowledged that internal market measures would typically have a dual aim, namely an internal market aim as well as a specific *substantive* policy aim.[44] And in deciding whether or not Article 114 or a specific legal competence applies, the Court would have recourse to a 'centre of gravity' doctrine.[45] The latter makes the choice of competence dependent on whether the Union measure principally deals with the internal market or with the more specific substantive interest.

There are however two qualifications to this picture. First, Article 114 itself expressly excludes three matters from its legislative scope because it states in paragraph 2 that it 'shall not apply to *fiscal* provisions, to those relating to the *free movement of persons* nor to those relating to the *rights and interests of employed persons*'.

These three areas can never be harmonised on the basis of Article 114. If Union legislation is here deemed necessary, this will have to be done either under Article 115 TFEU – requiring unanimity – or one of the special substantive competences dealing with taxation, the free movement of persons, or employment. In the past, the Court has given a broad interpretation to the excluded

---

[42] This is however the case for Art. 352 TFEU. For an analysis of this point, see R. Schütze, 'Organized Change towards an "Ever Closer Union": Article 308 EC and the Limits of the Community's Legislative Competence' (2003) 22 *YEL* 79 at 99ff.

[43] Case C-300/89, *Commission v. Council (Titanium Dioxide)*.   [44] *Ibid.*, para. 11.

[45] See Case C-155/91, *Commission v. Council (Waste)* [1993] ECR I-939; Case C-187/93, *Parliament v. Council (Waste II)* [1994] ECR I-2857. For an academic analysis of the phenomenon of legal basis litigation, esp. in relation to Art. 114 TFEU, see R. Barents, 'The Internal Market Unlimited: Some Observations on the Legal Basis of Community Legislation' (1993) 30 *CML Rev.* 85; H. Cullen and A. Charlesworth, 'Diplomacy by Other Means: The Use of Legal Basis Litigation as a Political Strategy by the European Parliament and Member States' (1999) 36 *CML Rev.* 1243.

policy fields in Article 114(2).[46] But is the list in Article 114(2) exhaustive? The Court has indeed held this to be the case.

The Member States have nonetheless tried to 'shield' other special Union competences from the general internal market competence. How so? In their capacity as Masters of the Treaties, they have increasingly included clauses within specific policy areas that expressly exclude the harmonisation of national laws within a specific policy area. For example: under its 'public health' competence in Article 168, the Union is entitled to adopt health measures but only '*excluding any harmonisation* of the laws and regulations of the Member States'.[47]

These clauses limit the ability of the Union legislator to adopt harmonisation measures under these special competences, but do they also limit the scope of Article 114? The European Court appears to have expressed a negative view in *Tobacco Advertising*.[48] Germany had here partly challenged the use of Article 114 for the Tobacco Advertising Directive on the grounds that the directive was a 'health measure' and that it should therefore have been based on Article 168 TFEU; and since the latter excluded any harmonisation, the directive should be annulled.

The Court however rejected this argument in full. While admitting that '[t]he national measures *affected* [were] to a large extent inspired by public health policy objectives',[49] the Court clarified that the exclusion of harmonisation in Article 168(5) did 'not mean that harmonising measures adopted on the basis of other provisions of the Treaty cannot have any impact on the protection of human health'.[50] '[T]he [Union] legislature cannot be prevented from relying on that legal basis on the ground that public health protection is a decisive factor in the choices to be made'.[51] The exclusion of harmonisation in a complementary competence of the Union cannot therefore operate as a limitation on Article 114 TFEU.

d. 'Opting Up': The Derogations in Article 114(4) and (5)

Once the Union has adopted a harmonisation measure, all national rules that conflict with the Union measure will have to be disapplied. This follows from the supremacy of European law. When Article 114 TFEU was drafted, some Member States therefore feared that the introduction of qualified majority

---

[46] For a wide and teleological interpretation of the phrase 'fiscal provisions' in Art. 114(2) TFEU, see Case C-338/01, *Commission v. Council* [2004] ECR I-4829, para. 63: 'With regard to the interpretation of the words "fiscal provisions", there is nothing in the Treaty to indicate how that concept should be construed. It is, however, necessary to point out that, by reason of their general character, those words cover not only all areas of taxation, without drawing any distinction between the types of duties or taxes concerned, but also all aspects of taxation, whether material rules or procedural rules.' The ruling was confirmed in Case C-533/03, *Commission v. Council* [2006] ECR I-1025, esp. para. 4.

[47] Art. 168(5) TFEU (emphasis added).

[48] Case C-376/98, *Germany v. Council (Tobacco Advertising)*.

[49] *Ibid.*, para. 76 (emphasis added).   [50] *Ibid.*, para. 78.   [51] *Ibid.*, para. 88.

voting in the Council could undermine their higher national standards in politically sensitive areas; and they consequently insisted on a constitutional mechanism that allowed them to 'justify' these – derogating – national laws. This was greeted with theoretical outrage;[52] yet the practical consequences of the 'public policy' justifications in Article 114(4)–(5) have been very limited. Drafted in parallel with Article 36 TFEU, the fourth and fifth paragraph of Article 114 state:

> 4. If, after the adoption of a harmonisation measure by the European Parliament and the Council, by the Council or by the Commission, a Member State deems it necessary to *maintain* national provisions *on grounds of major needs referred to in Article 36, or relating to the protection of the environment or the working environment*, it shall notify the Commission of these provisions as well as the grounds for maintaining them.
> 5. Moreover, without prejudice to paragraph 4, if, after the adoption of a harmonisation measure by the European Parliament and the Council, by the Council or by the Commission, a Member State deems it necessary to *introduce* national provisions based on *new scientific evidence relating to the protection of the environment or the working environment on grounds of a problem specific to that Member State arising after the adoption of the harmonisation measure*, it shall notify the Commission of the envisaged provisions as well as the grounds for introducing them.

The two paragraphs allow a Member State to either 'maintain' or 'introduce' national measures that 'conflict' with the harmonised Union measure. Importantly, conflict here means that a Member State *does not comply with Union legislation adopted under Article 114*. Articles 114(4) and (5) TFEU thus do not cover situations where a Member State is entitled – under the harmonisation measure – to adopt stricter or higher national norms.[53] They exclusively refer to the situation, where a Member State would 'breach' Union legislation by insisting on a standard that is *higher* than the – mandatory and exhaustive – Union standard. Article 114(4) thereby covers the situation where a Member State wishes to 'maintain' – existing – national laws, whereas Article 114(5) refers to the power of Member States to 'introduce' – new – national laws. Both situations are subject to an administrative procedure conducted by the Commission,[54] which can subsequently be reviewed by the European Court.[55]

---

[52] P. Pescatore, 'Some Critical Remarks on the "Single European Act"' (1987) 24 *CML Rev.* 9; C.-D. Ehlermann, 'The Internal Market Following the Single European Act' (1987) 24 *CML Rev.* 361.

[53] On the various harmonisation techniques, see section 3 below.

[54] For the elaborate administrative and procedural regime, see Art. 114(6)–(8) TFEU. For an overview of these provisions, see N. de Sadeleer, 'Procedures for Derogation from the Principle of Approximation of Laws under Article 95 EC' (2003) 40 *CML Rev.* 889.

[55] Art. 114(9) TFEU provides: 'By way of derogation from the procedure laid down in Articles 258 and 259, the Commission and any Member State may bring the matter directly before the Court of Justice of the European Union if it considers that another Member State is making improper use of the powers provided for in this Article.'

Article 114(4) entitles a Member State to apply to the Commission for permission to maintain its higher laws '*on grounds of major needs referred to in Article 36, or relating to the protection of the environment or the working environment*'.[56] The list of public interest grounds is here limited to the express public interest derogations for the free movement of goods and two – and only two – unwritten imperative requirements recognised by the Court.[57] By contrast, Article 114(5) does not mention the public policy grounds in Article 36. It insists on new scientific evidence and even demands a problem specific to a Member State. Article 114(5) thus appeared from the very beginning much stricter than Article 114(4). This view was judicially confirmed in *Denmark* v. *Commission*,[58] where the Court held as follows:

> The difference between the two situations envisaged in Article [114] is that, in the first, the national provisions predate the harmonisation measure. They are thus known to the [Union] legislature, but the legislature cannot or does not seek to be guided by them for the purpose of harmonisation. It is therefore considered acceptable for the Member State to request that its own rules remain in force …
>
> By contrast, in the second situation, the adoption of new national legislation *is more likely to jeopardise harmonisation.* The [Union] institutions could not, by definition, have taken account of the national text when drawing up the harmonisation measure. In that case, the requirements referred to in Article [36 TFEU] are not taken into account, and only grounds relating to protection of the environment or the working environment are accepted, on condition that the Member State provides new scientific evidence and that the need to introduce new national provisions results from a problem specific to the Member State concerned arising after the adoption of the harmonisation measure.
>
> It follows that neither the wording of Article [114(4) TFEU] nor the broad logic of that article as a whole entails a requirement that the applicant Member State prove that maintaining the national provisions which it notifies to the Commission is justified by a problem specific to that Member State … Analogous considerations apply to the requirement for new scientific evidence. That condition is imposed under Article [114(5) TFEU] for the introduction of new derogating national provisions, but it is not laid down in Article [114(4) TFEU] for the maintenance of existing derogating national provisions. It is not one of the conditions imposed for maintaining such provisions.[59]

The Court here found that the Commission was entitled, in the exercise of its administrative discretion, to be much stricter in granting derogations under Article 114(5).

This was reconfirmed in subsequent administrative and judicial practice. In *Upper Austria* v. *Commission*,[60] Austria had applied for a specific derogation under

---

[56]   Emphasis added.
[57]   On these imperative requirements, see Chapter 13, section 4(a).
[58]   Case C-3/00, *Denmark* v. *Commission* [2003] ECR I-2643.   [59]   *Ibid.*, paras. 58–62.
[60]   Joined Cases T-366/03 and T-235/04, *Land Oberösterreich and Republic of Austria v. Commission* [2005] ECR II-4005.

Article 114(5) in relation to the Union directive on genetically modified organisms (GMOs). The Austrian measure intended to prohibit the cultivation of seed composed of or containing GMOs as well as the breeding of transgenic animals. The Commission however refused to allow the stricter national law on the grounds that 'Austria failed to provide new scientific evidence or demonstrate that a specific problem in [that country] arose'.[61] Austria appealed to the General Court against that administrative decision, and this gave the Court an opportunity to explain the criteria in Article 114(5).

The Court unambiguously clarified that the criteria of 'new scientific evidence' and the existence of 'a problem specific to the Member State' were cumulative conditions;[62] and that the burden of proof for both criteria squarely lay with the Member State concerned.[63] Unhappy with this ruling, Austria subsequently appealed to the Court of Justice. However, the latter equally confirmed the Commission decision, yet additionally alluded that the reference to a 'specific' national problem would not require the existence of a 'unique' problem within one Member State.[64]

This liberal reading of the 'specificity' criterion was elaborated in *Netherlands v. Commission (Air Pollution)*.[65] The case concerned the rejection by the Commission of an application for a derogation under Article 114(5) with regard to the Union directive on air pollution by emissions from motor vehicles. The Dutch authorities had wished to introduce a more restrictive new law that would require the insertion of a filter reducing pollution below the Union level. The Commission had rejected this wish for a stricter national environmental law on the grounds that the Netherlands had failed to show a 'specific' Dutch pollution problem. The administrative decision was appealed.

This challenge gave the General Court an excellent opportunity to shed new light on the purpose behind Article 114(5) in general and its second criterion in particular. The Court thereby clarified that Article 114(5) was designed to apply in cases 'where a new phenomenon arises in all or part of a Member State's territory' and where an amendment to Union legislation was unsuitable due to the local nature of the problem or the long delays in passing such legislation.[66]

This view provided the key to the notion of 'specificity':

> By referring to the case of a problem specific to a Member State which has arisen after the adoption of a [Union] harmonisation measure, Article [114(5) TFEU] therefore excludes the possibility of national provisions being introduced based upon it which derogate from harmonised rules in order to deal with a general environmental danger in the [Union]. Any problem which arises in terms which are on the whole comparable throughout the Member States and which lends itself, therefore,

---

[61] *Ibid.*, para. 15.   [62] *Ibid.*, para. 54.   [63] *Ibid.*, para. 63.

[64] Joined Cases C-439/05 P and C-454/05 P, *Land Oberösterreich and Republic of Austria* v. *Commission* [2007] ECR I-7141, paras. 65ff.

[65] Case T-182/06, *Netherlands* v. *Commission* [2007] ECR II-1983.   [66] *Ibid.*, para. 61.

> to harmonised solutions at [Union] level is general in nature and is, consequently, not specific within the meaning of Article [114(5) TFEU]. It is therefore necessary, in order correctly to interpret Article [114(5) TFEU], to envisage the requirement of national specificity of a problem essentially from the angle of the aptness or inaptness of the harmonisation of the applicable [Union] rules to confront adequately the difficulties encountered locally, since the established inaptness of those rules justifies the introduction of national measures.[67]

The Court consequently found in favour of the Dutch government's contention and confirmed that 'for a problem to be specific to a Member State within the meaning of the relevant provision, it is not necessary that it is the result of an environmental danger within that State alone'.[68]

2. Internal Market Competences II: 'Special' Competences

a. Tax Harmonisation: In Particular, Article 113

From the very beginning, the Treaty contained one competence that expressly envisaged the harmonisation of national taxation. It can today be found in Article 113 TFEU and states:

> The Council shall, acting *unanimously* in accordance with a special legislative procedure and after consulting the European Parliament and the Economic and Social Committee, adopt provisions for the *harmonisation of legislation concerning turnover taxes, excise duties and other forms of indirect taxation* to the extent that such harmonisation is necessary to ensure the establishment and the functioning of the internal market and to avoid distortion of competition.[69]

The provision allows the Union, when backed up by the unanimous consent of all national governments in the Council, to harmonise all forms of 'indirect taxation'. Indirect taxes are taxes that are imposed indirectly. (While direct taxes look at the value added by a production *activity*, indirect taxes impose a tax on a product's *price*. Indirect taxes are therefore consumption or consumer taxes. They are collected from the person who is not directly responsible for the economic change that is taxed.) The two principal forms of indirect taxation expressly mentioned by Article 113 are turnover (sales) taxes and excise duties. The founding fathers regarded these two indirect taxes as 'a matter of primary

---

[67] *Ibid.*, paras. 61–4.

[68] *Ibid.*, para. 65. The case was subsequently appealed to the ECJ, which overturned the General Court but on a different point of law (see Case C-405/07P, *Netherlands* v. *Commission* [2008] ECR I-8301).

[69] Art. 113 TFEU (emphasis added).

importance',[70] because they posed a particularly serious danger for the establishment and functioning of the internal market.

In the past, the Union has slowly engaged in the harmonisation of both forms of indirect taxes. With regard to turnover taxation, it has thereby followed the French tradition and adopted a Union-wide system of value added tax (VAT). This system is codified in Directive 2006/112 'on the common system of value added tax'.[71] VAT is here defined as the application to goods (and services) of 'a general tax on consumption exactly proportional to the price of the goods'.[72] The standard rate for that tax is currently 15 per cent.[73] The rate is however a minimum rate that allows Member States to charge a higher VAT rate in their territory.[74]

In addition to VAT, the Union may also harmonise special consumer taxes. These excise duties are 'a modern version of ancient taxes' ('excises').[75] They are typically imposed on 'sensitive' or 'luxury' goods like tobacco and alcohol. Traditionally, the level at which these taxes were pitched has differed significantly in the Member States. The Union has therefore adopted a number of harmonisation measures.[76] These measures establish – again – only minimum tax rates.[77] They consequently allow the Member States to exercise their 'sovereign' right to impose higher duties if they consider this appropriate in light of their socio-economic choices.

The wording of Article 113 conceptually excludes the harmonisation of *direct* taxes, such as income and corporation tax. It is nonetheless important to recall that the harmonisation of direct taxes is not beyond the scope of positive integration as such. Although the second paragraph of Article 114 TFEU excludes their harmonisation by qualified majority, these taxes may still be harmonised by a unanimous Council on the basis of Article 115 TFEU.

---

[70] European Communities, *The Value-Added Tax in the European Community* (European Communities, 1970), 3: 'It seems clear from the marked difference between the approach to harmonisation of indirect taxes on the one hand, and of direct taxes on the other, that the authors of the Rome Treaty regarded harmonisation of turnover taxes and excise duties as a matter of primary importance.'

[71] Directive 2006/112 on the common system of value added tax [2006] OJ L 347/1.

[72] *Ibid.*, Art. 1(2).

[73] *Ibid.*, Art. 97: 'From 1 January 2016 until 31 December 2017, the standard rate may not be lower than 15%.' The directive however also recognises a number of reduced rates and also allows for exemptions.

[74] The highest VAT (standard) rate in a Member State is currently set at 27 per cent in Hungary.

[75] D. W. Williams, *EC Tax Law* (Longman, 1998), 93.

[76] For alcoholic beverages, see Directive 92/83 on the harmonisation of the structures of excise duties on alcohol and alcoholic beverages [1992] OJ L 316/21; for manufactured tobacco, see Directive 2011/64 on the structure and rates of excise duty applied to manufactured tobacco [2011] OJ L 176/24. Common rules for all these products are set out in Directive 2008/118 concerning the general arrangements for excise duty [2009] OJ L 9/12.

[77] These 'minimum' levels can still be very high. For cigarettes, for example, the overall excise duty 'shall represent at least 57% of the weighted average retail selling price of cigarettes released for consumption' (see Directive 2011/64, Art. 10).

Table 14.3 Corporate Tax Rates – National Differences

Lowest Tax Member States		Higher Tax Member States	
Hungary	9%	Malta	35%
Bulgaria	10%	Belgium	34%
Cyprus	12%	France	33%
Ireland	12%	Germany	30%
Latvia	15%	Luxembourg	29%
Lithuania	15%	Greece	25%
United Kingdom: 19%			

In sum, all tax harmonisation is subject to a 'fiscal veto'. Each Member State thus continues to protect its political 'sovereignty' over taxation. This fiscal veto has made the harmonisation of taxation very difficult. EU legislation in this area is indeed piecemeal and thin. The main pressing issue for the future would probably be the harmonisation of corporate tax.[78] The latter differs significantly between the Member States (see Table 14.3), which leads to significant distortions in the functioning of the internal market. Yet instead of harmonising a common – minimum – corporation tax, the Union has here relied on the idea of a fiscal competition between the national legal orders.

b. Intellectual Property Harmonisation: In Particular, Article 118

The 'territorial' nature of intellectual property rights divides the internal market into separate national markets. Early on, the Union therefore tried to engage in forms of (international) harmonisation.[79] And, despite the existence of Union competences to harmonise intellectual property rights from the beginning,[80] the Union has only actively engaged in the supranational harmonisation of intellectual property rights with the introduction of Article 114 TFEU (following the Single

---

[78] For an overview of the harmonisation efforts here, see D. Pîrvu, *Corporate Tax Harmonisation in the European Union* (Palgrave, 2012).

[79] The two prominent forms of international harmonisation are the European Patent Convention (1973), which created the European Patent Office and whose signatory States extend beyond the Union Member States. The second international convention was confined to the Member States of the Union and was called the Community Patent Convention (1975). The Convention was meant to create a unitary Community patent within the Community but never entered into force.

[80] The Court has confirmed that the Union has competence to harmonise intellectual property rights under Arts. 115 and 352 TFEU (see *Opinion 1/94* (WTO Agreement) [1994] ECR I-5267, para. 59).

European Act).[81] The provision has been vital for the harmonisation of all national laws governing patents,[82] and trade marks.[83]

Nonetheless, the Court has traditionally insisted on a solid limit to Article 114. It has clarified that the competence must be used to harmonise *national* intellectual property rights; and that it cannot be used to create a 'Union' intellectual property right. This was confirmed in *Opinion 1/94*,[84] where the Court expressly held that Article 114 was not available 'for creating new rights superimposed on national rights' and that – in an absence of any specific competence in the Treaties – the sole constitutional basis to create such Union intellectual property rights was Article 352 TFEU.[85] The Union's residual competence has indeed been used to create a '[Union] Trade Mark'.[86]

Yet the unanimity requirement in Article 352 has been a major hurdle for the creation of other intellectual property rights and, in particular, a Union patent. The Lisbon Treaty tried to remedy this by inserting Article 118 TFEU. The provision grants an express legal basis for the creation of Union intellectual property rights and states:

---

[81] For an overview of the legislative measures adopted in the field of intellectual property rights generally, see Sir R. Arnold, 'An Overview of European Harmonisation Measures in Intellectual Property Law', in A. Ohly and J. Pila (eds.), *The Europeanization of Intellectual Property Law* (Oxford University Press, 2013), 25.

[82] See Regulation 1768/92 concerning the creation of a supplementary protection certificate for medicinal products [1992] OJ L 182/1. This was the Regulation at issue in *Spain* v. *Council* (n. 17 above). The Regulation was replaced by Regulation 469/2009, [2009] OJ L152/1.

[83] See Directive 89/104 to approximate the laws of the Member States relating to trade marks [1989] OJ L 40/1. It has now been replaced by Directive 2015/2436 to approximate the laws of the Member States relating to trade marks ('Trade Mark Directive') [2015] OJ L 336/1. For the extensive case law generated by the older Trade Mark Directive(s), see M. Leistner, 'Harmonization of Intellectual Property Law in Europe: The European Court of Justice's Trade Mark Case Law 2004–2007' (2008) 45 *CML Rev.* 69; and A. Kur, 'Harmonization of Intellectual Property Law in Europe: The ECJ's Trade Mark Case Law 2008–2012' (2013) 50 *CML Rev.* 773.

[84] *Opinion 1/94* (n. 18 above).

[85] *Ibid.*, para. 59. This ruling was confirmed in Case C-377/98, *Netherlands* v. *Parliament and Council* [2001] ECR I-7079, where the Netherlands had challenged the legality of Directive 98/44 on the legal protection of biotechnological inventions [1998] OJ L 213/13. The central argument here was that the directive did not harmonise national patent laws but created a European patent – a view that was rejected by the Court (*ibid.*, para. 25).

[86] Regulation 40/94 on the [Union] trade mark [1994] OJ L 11/1, which has now been replaced by Regulation 2017/1001 on the European Union trade mark [2017] OJ L 154/1. The Union trade mark is defined in Art. 1 as follows: '1. A trade mark for goods or services which is registered in accordance with the conditions contained in this Regulation and in the manner herein provided is hereinafter referred to as a "European Union trade mark" ("EU trade mark"). 2. An EU trade mark shall have a unitary character. It shall have equal effect throughout the Union: it shall not be registered, transferred or surrendered or be the subject of a decision revoking the rights of the proprietor or declaring it invalid, nor shall its use be prohibited, save in respect of the whole Union. This principle shall apply unless otherwise provided in this Regulation.'

In the context of the establishment and functioning of the internal market, the European Parliament and the Council, acting in accordance with the ordinary legislative procedure, shall establish *measures for the creation of European intellectual property rights to provide uniform protection of intellectual property rights throughout the Union* and for the *setting up of centralised Union-wide authorisation, coordination and supervision arrangements.*

The Council, acting in accordance with a special legislative procedure, shall by means of regulations establish *language arrangements for the European intellectual property rights*. The Council shall act unanimously after consulting the European Parliament.[87]

The provision allows the Union to adopt legislation for the creation and enforcement of *European* intellectual property rights. (Its wording and teleological spirit thus command that it cannot be used as a legal basis for the harmonisation of *national* intellectual property rights. Here, Article 114 will continue to apply.)

Article 118 TFEU was used to create a 'European patent'.[88] Ideas for such a unitary patent have spanned numerous decades, yet the unanimity requirement in Article 352 had led to 'a long history of fruitless proposals and failed initiatives'.[89] And, ironically, despite the possibility of qualified majority voting offered by Article 118(1), the unanimity requirement in Article 118(2) with regard to the 'language requirements for the intellectual property rights' has meant that the Union patent could only be adopted after an authorisation to use the constitutional mechanism of enhanced cooperation.[90]

The European patent is a patent that is not subject to national patent laws. It is a patent with a 'unitary effect' and 'a unitary character' that provides 'uniform protection' with 'equal effect on all the participating Member States'.[91] It operates in the same way as the 'EU Trade Mark' in that it removes the 'barrier of territoriality of the rights conferred on the proprietors' that 'cannot be removed by approximation of laws'.[92]Importantly, however, both the 'EU Trade Mark' and

---

[87] Art. 118 TFEU (emphasis added).

[88] Regulation 1257/2012 implementing enhanced cooperation in the area of the creation of unitary patent protection [2012] OJ L 361/1.

[89] C. Seville, 'Developments (and Non-Developments) in the Harmonization of EU Intellectual Property Law' (2008–9) 11 CYELS 89 at 113.

[90] The constitutional mechanism of enhanced cooperation allows some Member States to use the Union institutions to adopt special Union law that just applies to them. The mechanism is generally laid down in Title Three of Part VI of the TFEU. For a brief overview, see Chapter 7, Conclusion.

[91] Regulation 1257/2012, Art. 3(2). The patent is however not directly granted by the Union as such, but the Union has delegated this power to the European Patent Office – that is, an international organisation set up by the European Patent Convention. For a first analysis of the EU patent, see S. Peers, 'The Constitutional Implication of the EU Patent' (2011) 7 *European Constitutional Law Review* 229.

[92] Trade Mark Regulation 2017/1001 (n. 86 above), recital 5.

the 'European Patent' do 'not replace the laws of the Member States'. National laws are still available 'for those undertakings which do not want protection of their trade marks [and patents] at [Union] level'.[93]

3. Harmonisation Methods: 'Old' and 'New' Approaches

The Union's internal market competences are shared competences.[94] Unlike exclusive competences, shared competences allow the *Union and the Member States* to act within a field:

> When the Treaties confer on the Union a competence shared with the Member States in a specific area, the Union and the Member States may legislate and adopt legally binding acts in that area.[95]

Within shared competences, European and national legislation may thus come into conflict; and in the event of such a legislative conflict, Union law will – according to the Union doctrine of supremacy – prevail over national law. However, not every exercise of a shared competence by the Union legislator will necessarily pre-empt national law. In the past, the Union has indeed developed different harmonisation methods. The use of any such method is not constitutionally prescribed by Articles 114ff. It falls within the political discretion of the Union legislator. In some situations, the Union may wish to completely harmonise an area and totally pre-empt all national action within the harmonised field. Member States are here excluded because the Union legislation 'occupies the field'. By contrast, the Union may decide to only lay down minimum standards that permit – higher – national standards. Here, European law does only partially pre-empt the Member States and Union and national law 'cooperate' with each other.

How has the Union exercised its harmonisation competences in the past? The answer to this question has changed over time. The present section will explore this in relation to the free movement of goods and, in particular, the harmonisation of product requirements.[96] We shall see that the Union originally preferred 'complete' or 'total' harmonisation. This 'old approach' to harmonisation was replaced by a 'new approach' in which the Union began to increasingly have recourse to minimum harmonisation. But before we analyse this shift in more detail, let us quickly survey the three principal harmonization methods that the Union has used in its past legislative practice.

---

[93] *Ibid.*, recital 8.

[94] See Art. 4(2)(a) TFEU. For a discussion of the nature of shared competences, see Chapter 7, section 2.

[95] See Art. 2(2) TFEU.

[96] Technical barriers have been said to represent the 'paradigm case for harmonization' that 'provide[s] the yardstick by which the harmonization programme as a whole has to be judged' (Dashwood, 'Hastening Slowly' (n. 9 above), 183–4).

a. Harmonisation Methods and Pre-emption Types

The Union has traditionally had recourse to three principal harmonisation methods: complete harmonisation, optional harmonisation and minimum harmonisation.[97] Importantly: all three harmonisation methods refer to the 'intensity' – not the 'scope'[98] – of a harmonisation measure.

Complete harmonisation exists where the Union exhaustively and fully regulates a matter within the scope of a Union measure. The Union here assumes full responsibility to deal with all issues within the legislative act to the exclusion of all national law. Within the context of product requirements, three elements have characterised complete harmonisation. First, the relevant act lays down rules that define a 'European' product standard. Second, the Union act contains a clause obliging the Member States to permit the free circulation of products conforming to the Union standard (the free movement clause); and, finally, it also contains a clause that prohibits the marketing of all non-conforming products (the exclusivity clause).[99] Under complete harmonization, European products thus *replace* national products. Complete or full harmonisation is here meant to create a 'level playing field' on which all economic actors within the Union would operate under equally competitive conditions in the internal market.

Optional harmonisation represents a second classic harmonisation method. Here, the EU lays down a Union standard, compliance with which will guarantee free movement within the internal market;[100] yet the European standard is optional in that it leaves a choice to manufacturers. They can adopt the Union standard and benefit from unlimited free movement in the internal market; or

---

[97] Some go so far as to list five distinct methods of harmonisation (see P. J. Slot, 'Harmonisation' (1996) 21 *EL Rev.* 378).

[98] The *scope* of a legislative act sets jurisdictional limits to the Union rules. It determines the legislative 'field'. Matters found to lie outside the legislative field of a harmonisation measure remain *non*-harmonised and thus within the residual powers of the Member States. Where European law does not harmonise all aspects within a policy area, Union terminology speaks of *partial harmonisation*. Here, the scope of a Union measure is viewed against the harmonisation effort in the entire economic policy field. Partial harmonisation, as non-harmonisation, may even be expressed *within* a single Union law. The most well-known example is the development risk defence in the Product Liability Directive, [1985] OJ L 210/29. The directive purports to harmonise the different liability regimes within the Member States, while at the same time leaving it to the Member States whether to allow for a development risk defence for manufacturers. The defence represents a non-harmonised provision that was consciously placed *outside* the scope of the Union measure. For a discussion of the directive and the development risk defence, see Chapter 18, section 3(d).

[99] E.g. Directive 76/768 on the approximation of the laws of the Member States relating to cosmetic products [1976] OJ L 262/169, Art. 3: 'Member States shall take all necessary measures to ensure that only cosmetic products which conform to the provisions of this Directive and its Annexes may be put on the market.'

[100] E.g. Directive 70/220 on the approximation of the laws of the Member States relating to measures to be taken against air pollution by gases from positive-ingestion engines of motor vehicles [1970] OJ 76/1.

they can stick to their national standards but then risk that their goods may not be marketable in another Member State. Unlike complete harmonisation, optional harmonisation will thus not prohibit the marketing of non-conforming goods.[101] It rather creates *two* markets that exist alongside each other. For in addition to a national market for traditional goods there also exists a European market in 'Euro' goods. For these harmonised goods, optional harmonisation establishes, like complete harmonisation, an absolute Union standard that cannot be limited by national legislation.

Minimum harmonisation constitutes the third classic harmonisation method. The idea behind minimum harmonisation is that even once the Union has adopted a Union standard that applies to all manufacturers within the Union, the Member States remain entitled to adopt *stricter* national standards for their domestic products. Unlike optional harmonisation, the Union standard is compulsory; yet unlike complete harmonisation, this compulsory standard is not fully pre-empting national legislation. Minimum harmonisation only sets a mandatory floor that will allow for *upward* legislative flexibility. Under this harmonisation method, the Union and the national level act as co-legislators in the regulation of product requirements. The Member States are allowed to preserve their traditional products; yet they must also allow all goods that comply with the minimum Union standard into their domestic market. Importantly: the concept of minimum harmonisation will, thereby, not imply a European commitment to the lowest national standard within the Union.[102]

b. Harmonisation under the 'Old Approach'

Has the Union preferred one harmonisation approach over the other? In its early life, it indeed preferred a complete approach to harmonisation that would come into play whenever differences in national laws created obstacles to intra-Union trade.

The 'epic' scope of this original harmonisation programme can be seen reflected in the Council's 'General Programme for the Elimination of Technical Barriers to Trade arising from disparate National Regulations'.[103] It can also be found in Directive 70/50 – discussed in the previous chapter.[104] For the Commission here believed that all national 'measures governing the marketing of products which

---

[101] J. Currall, 'Some Aspects of the Relation between Articles 30–36 and Article 100 of the EEC Treaty, with a Closer Look at Optional Harmonisation' (1984) 4 *YEL* 169 at 179.

[102] The European Court has been explicit about this point in Case C-84/94, *United Kingdom of Great Britain and Northern Ireland* v. *Council of the European Union* [1996] ECR I-5755, paras. 17 and 56.

[103] The programme was adopted in 1969 and envisaged a three-stage package of measures to be completed by 1970. However, only one-third of the envisaged directives were adopted by 1973, see: K. A. Armstrong and S. Bulmer, *The Governance of the Single European Market* (Manchester University Press, 1997), esp. ch. 6.

[104] Directive 70/50 on the provisions of [ex-]Art. 33(7), on the abolition of measures which have an effect equivalent to quantitative restrictions on imports and are not covered by other provisions adopted in pursuance of the EEC Treaty [1970] OJ L 13/29.

deal, in particular, with shape, size, weight, composition, presentation, identification or putting up' would have to be harmonised under Article 114 because national disparities in such rules generally fell outside the scope of Article 34.[105] The problem with this idea lay thereby less in the – ambitious – scope of the early harmonisation programme but rather in its chosen method. For under the old approach to harmonisation, the Union preferred full harmonisation with almost all Union laws based on complete (or optional) harmonisation.[106] This led to the so-called 'vertical' approach to harmonisation according to which every single product needed to be harmonised individually – potentially ranging from light bulbs to bananas.

This 'complete' or 'vertical' approach to harmonisation had direct consequences for the legislative space left to Member States. A brief look at the jurisprudence of the time will indeed be revealing. For example: in *Ratti*,[107] national criminal proceedings had been brought against the head of an Italian undertaking manufacturing solvents and varnishes. Italian legislation had obliged the manufacturers of those products to affix labels indicating the total percentage of particular substances. Having violated the national law, Ratti claimed that the latter breached the relevant Union harmonisation measure. The Union act had been adopted on the basis of Article 115 in light of 'considerable differences' in the national legal orders that had created barriers to trade and thus 'directly affected the establishment and functioning of the market in dangerous preparations such as solvents';[108] and to eliminate these differences, the relevant Union directive prohibited Member States from 'restrict[ing] or imped[ing] on the grounds of classification, packaging or labelling the placing on the market of dangerous preparations which satisfy the requirements of the Directive'.[109]

And, in line with its aim to establish complete harmonisation, the Member States were consequently:

> not entitled to maintain, parallel with the rules laid down by the Directive for imports, different rules for the domestic market. Thus it is a consequence of the system introduced by [Union harmonisation] that a Member State may not introduce into its national legislation conditions which are more restrictive than those laid down in the Directive in question, or which are even more detailed or in any event different, as regards the classification, packaging and labelling of solvents and that this prohibition on the imposition of restrictions not provided for applies both to the direct marketing of the products on the home market and to imported products.[110]

---

[105] *Ibid.*, recital 9. The presumption of legality for national product requirements would be neutralised where the restrictive effect on the free movement of goods exceeded the effects intrinsic to trade rules. For a longer discussion of this point, see Chapter 13, section 3(a/aa).

[106] R. H. Lauwaars, 'The "Model Directive" on Technical Harmonization', in R. Bieber et al. (eds.), *1992: One European Market* (Nomos, 1998), 156.

[107] Case 148/78, *Ratti* [1979] ECR 1629.   [108] *Ibid.*, paras. 10–11.

[109] Directive 73/173 on the approximation of Member States' laws, regulations and administrative provisions relating to the classification, packaging and labelling of dangerous preparations (solvents) [1973] OJ L 189/7, Art. 8.

[110] *Ibid.*, paras. 26–7.

Stricter national provisions were here not permitted, since they went beyond the terms laid down by Union harmonisation.[111]

But even if the national law violated the Union directive, could it nonetheless be justified under Article 36? Could a Member State retain its stricter national laws on the basis that the obstacles to the free movement of goods they created were justified by reference to public policy interests? Consistent with its earlier ruling in *Simmenthal*,[112] the Court clarified that this was not possible once the Union had exercised its harmonisation competence through total harmonisation:

> [W]hen, pursuant to [Article 115] of the Treaty, [Union] directives provide for the harmonization of measures necessary to ensure the protection of the health of humans and animals and establish [Union] procedures to supervise compliance therewith, recourse to [Article 36] ceases to be justified.[113]

National measures within the scope of the directive could thus no longer be justified by reference to Article 36 TFEU. Within its field of application, the Union legislation would provide *all* the answers and pre-empt *all* national laws.

The constitutional principles structuring the relationship between European and national legislation were further developed in subsequent jurisprudence. In *Commission* v. *Kingdom of Denmark*,[114] the Court scrutinised the relationship between the Union directive on the classification, packaging and labelling of dangerous substances and preparations and Danish legislation. The directive had been adopted to strengthen the protection of human health and the environment against potential risks which could arise from the placing on the market of new substances.[115] The core of the Union law was a notification

---

[111]   *Ibid.*, para. 33.

[112]   See Case 35/76, *Simmenthal SpA* v. *Ministere des finances italien* [1976] ECR 1871. According to the famous phrase of this first *Simmenthal* ruling, '[Article 36 TFEU] is not designed to reserve certain matters to the exclusive jurisdiction of Member States but permits national laws to derogate from the principle of the free movement of goods to the extent to which such derogation is and continues to be justified for the attainment of the objectives referred to in that article' (*ibid.*, para. 14). Subsequent jurisprudence on the meaning of the *Simmenthal* ruling however clarified that not all types of harmonisation measures would block Art. 36 TFEU. Only in cases of complete harmonisation would the Member States cease to be entitled to justify national measures hindering trade by recourse to that article, see Case C-39/90, *Denkavit Futtermittel GmbH* v. *Land Baden-Württemberg* [1991] ECR I-3069, para. 19: '[R]ecourse to [Article 36] ceases to be justified only if, pursuant to [Articles 114/115], [Union] directives provide for the complete harmonization of national laws. It must therefore be accepted that where the approximation of the laws of the Member States has not yet been achieved in a given field the corresponding national laws may place obstacles in the way of the principle of free movement in so far as the obstacles in question are justified by one of the grounds set out in [Article 36] of the Treaty or by imperative requirements.'

[113]   Case 148/78, *Ratti*, para. 36.

[114]   Case 278/85, *Commission* v. *Denmark* [1987] ECR 4069.

[115]   Directive 79/831 on the approximation of the laws, regulations and administrative provisions relating to the classification, packaging and labelling of dangerous substances [1997] OJ L 259/10, recital 1.

requirement imposed on the manufacturer or importer of those substances. The Danish government had extended this mechanism and imposed *a stricter* national standard. The Commission brought proceedings for wrongful implementation; and the Danes defended themselves by denying that the provision was contrary to the directive because the national rule was only '*wider than that provided for in the Directive*'.[116] Stricter national health and environmental standards, the Danish government held, could not be in conflict with the European legislation since the former pursued the same objective as the latter.

The Court disagreed. It noted that the harmonisation here was designed to pursue two objectives: the protection of humans and the environment *as well as* the elimination of obstacles to intra-Union trade in dangerous substances,[117] and it therefore held:

> [T]he [Union] legislature has laid down an exhaustive set of rules governing the notification, classification, packaging and labelling of substances, both old and new, and that it has not left to the Member States any scope to introduce other measures in their national legislation … [T]he protection of man and the environment is only one of the objectives of the Directive; the other objective is to eliminate obstacles to trade in the substances in question within the [Union]. Consequently, the rules of the Directive relating to notification are not meant to be rules providing a minimum degree of protection which leaves the Member States free to widen the obligation provided for therein, but are intended to be exhaustive.[118]

Stricter national standards would thus fall foul, because they departed from the uniform Union standard.[119] The ideal behind complete harmonisation is thus total uniformity within the internal market. Once the Union legislator has adopted common rules, they should provide the *exclusive* standard within the field.

c. Harmonisation under the 'New Approach'

The old approach to harmonisation gradually grinded towards a hold at the end of the 1970s. The *complete* harmonisation of *all* national differences in product standards appeared increasingly unachievable, especially as many Member States

---

[116]   Case 278/85, *Commission* v. *Denmark*, para 15.

[117]   *Ibid.*, para. 16.   [118]   *Ibid.*, paras. 12 and 22.

[119]   In this respect, see Case 815/79, *Cremonini and Vrankovich* [1980] ECR 3583, para. 6: 'The Directive was adopted on the basis of [Article 115] of the Treaty and aims to secure the approximation of the provisions laid down by law, regulation or administrative action of the Member States to the extent to which such provisions are likely to form technical obstacles to trade in such equipment. The purpose of such a directive would be frustrated if the competent national authorities in the exercise of the powers reserved to them relating to the form and method of implementing the Directive did not keep within the limits of the discretion outlined by this Directive, because any overstepping of these limits might create new disparities and therefore fresh barriers to trade and as a result prevent the free movement of goods in a field in which the [Union] legislature had adopted provisions in order to ensure such freedom.'

had come to creatively use product standards as a way of protecting their national economies in the wake of a severe economic crisis. This neo-protectionism sealed the fate of the 'old' approach to harmonisation; and in order to rescue the internal market – and with it the European Union – a new solution had to be quickly found. A first step towards a new solution was famously suggested by the European Court. For, with *Cassis de Dijon*, the Court proposed to dramatically limit the scope of the harmonisation programme of the Union (see section (aa)). Yet the Union legislature went further and eventually also dropped its commitment to complete harmonisation by adopting a 'new approach' to harmonisation that prioritised minimum harmonisation (see section (bb)).

aa. Cassis de Dijon *and the 'New Strategy'*

New momentum in the internal market arrived in the form of a judicial tonic: *Cassis de Dijon*.[120] The judgment famously elevated the principle of mutual recognition – and the underlying idea of home State control – to a general constitutional principle of the internal market. The idea behind *Cassis de Dijon* was that, absent Union harmonisation, mutual recognition of national legislation would provide a second-best solution.[121] Yet importantly, *Cassis* was no rallying cry for absolute mutual recognition. The presumption of functional equivalence among national laws had limits. Member States could invoke mandatory requirements to justify host State control in certain circumstances. Nevertheless, the Court had showed its intent to judicially remove obstacles arising from disparities in product requirements. It was a broadside against recalcitrant States: if positive integration was not forthcoming, the Court would push the internal market through the process of negative integration.

The *Cassis* revolution had immediate consequences in the political sphere. For the Union executive decided to align the scope of the Union's harmonisation programme to the *Cassis* approach.[122] The emergence of the principle of home state control and the idea of mutual recognition had 'enlarged' the scope of negative integration; and the scope of Europe's positive harmonisation programme could consequently be limited. In 1980, the European Commission spelled out this new harmonisation strategy in a Communication on the consequences of *Cassis de Dijon*.[123] Acknowledging the judicial lead that the application of

---

[120] Case 120/78, *Rewe-Zentral AG* v. *Bundesmonopolverwaltung für Branntwein (Cassis de Dijon)* [1979] ECR 649.

[121] The Court's (sad) reminder of the absence of common rules on the production and marketing of alcohol at the time of *Cassis de Dijon* points at the *auxiliary* character of the solution found. Only as long as the Union was unable to act would the national legislation of the home State enjoy presumption of validity throughout the common market. Once the Union had adopted common rules harmonising the disparate national technical standards, the EU regime would prevail. According to this reading, the principle of mutual recognition had a temporary status. It was the 'second-best' option pending harmonisation of the relevant field.

[122] For a detailed account, see K. Alter and S. Meunier-Aitsahalia, 'Judicial Politics in the European Community' (1994–5) 26 *Comparative Political Studies* 535.

[123] Communication concerning the Consequences of the Judgment given by the Court of Justice on 20 February 1979 in Case 120/78 (*Cassis de Dijon*) [1980] OJ C 256/2.

national product requirements to imports would constitute an unlawful obstacle to intra-Union trade, it here concluded:

> The Commission's work of harmonization will henceforth have to be directed mainly at national laws having an impact on the functioning of the common market where barriers to trade to be removed arise from national provisions which are admissible under the criteria set by the Court.[124]

The scope of positive integration could consequently be dramatically reduced. Instead of harmonising all differences in national laws, say on product requirements, the Commission would from now on confine its legislative ambitions to those national product requirements that could be *justified* under Article 36 TFEU or mandatory requirements. Union harmonisation would therefore only take place where the mutual recognition of national standards under *Cassis de Dijon* had failed. This new strategy elevated the principle of mutual recognition to the cornerstone of the – federal – internal market. Positive integration through harmonisation here becomes a second-best solution that only applies where the functional equivalence of national legislation had been shown *not* to work.

bb. The 'New Approach' and Horizontal Legislation

This new strategy was complemented by two significant reforms in the legislative sphere. The first is of a constitutional nature: Article 114, introduced with the Single European Act, henceforth allowed for qualified majority voting when it came to Union harmonisation measures. But equally important was a second development: a change in the Union's harmonisation methodology. This 'new approach' to harmonisation is manifest in the White Paper 'Completing the Internal Market'.[125]

What were the changes by the White Paper? First and foremost, it consolidated the constitutional value of the principle of mutual recognition as expressed by *Cassis de Dijon*: '[T]he general principle should be approved that, if a product is lawfully manufactured and marketed in one Member State, there is no reason why it should not be sold freely throughout the [Union]'. National product laws that protect public interests 'essentially come down to the same thing, and so should normally be accorded recognition in all Member States.'[126] Yet the

---

[124] *Ibid.*

[125] European Commission, 'Completing the Internal Market: White Paper from the Commission to the European Council' COM (1985) 310. The Annex of the White Paper listed more than 300 Commission proposals and a concrete timetable for their adoption. However, as an astute observer remarked: 'The merit of the White Paper is not the assiduous compilation of 300 topics for harmonization directives, but the renunciation of more than 1000 directives which would have been necessary according to the traditional internal market strategies' (H. Schmitt von Sydow, 'The Basic Strategies of the Commission's White Paper', in R. Bieber et al. (eds.), *1992: One European Market* (Nomos, 1988), 79 at 91–2).

[126] White Paper: 'Completing the Internal Market' (n. 125 above), point 58.

real innovation of the White Paper lay in the conception of a 'new approach to technical harmonisation'.[127] Legislative harmonisation of product requirements would – henceforth – be restricted to essential health and safety requirements:

> [W]here barriers to trade are created by *justified* divergent national regulations concerning the health and safety of citizens and consumer and environmental protection, legislative harmonization will be confined to laying down the *essential requirements*, conformity to which will entitle a product to free movement within the [Union].[128]

The idea behind this new approach is that the Union abandons its focus on adopting binding *product* requirements for the Union market. (The task of setting – voluntary – European product norms would henceforth mainly be left to private standard-setting bodies.)[129] Instead, the Union harmonisation programme is refocused on setting essential health and safety standards that harmonise not the products as such but the quality standard they must at least meet in order to travel freely within the internal market. This move from a vertical (product-related) approach towards a horizontal approach to harmonisation ultimately led to the rise of minimum harmonisation.

An excellent illustration of this rise is offered by *Gallaher*.[130] Imperial Tobacco and Rothmans International Tobacco had brought proceedings before the High Court of England to obtain a declaration that certain provisions of the British Tobacco Products Labelling (Safety) Regulations 1991 infringed the (then) Union Tobacco Labelling Directive.[131] Article 3(3) of the Union directive stipulated that health warnings be printed 'so that at least 4% of the corresponding surface is covered', while its Article 8 stated that 'Member States may not, for reasons of labelling, prohibit or restrict the sale of products which comply with this Directive'. Referring to the 'at least' formula, the British government had tightened the obligation on manufacturers by requiring that the specific warning ought to at least cover 6 per cent of the surfaces on which they were printed.

---

[127] The new approach had been predefined by the Council Resolution on a New Approach to Technical Harmonization and Standards [1985] OJ C 136/1.

[128] White Paper: 'Completing the Internal Market' (n. 125 above), point 68.

[129] Directive 83/189 laying down a procedure for the provision of information in the field of technical standards and regulations [1985] OJ L 109/8. The directive was repealed and replaced by Directive 98/34, which has now itself been replaced by Directive 2015/1535 laying down a procedure for the provision of information in the field of technical standards and regulations and of rules on information Society services [2015] OJ L 241/1. The Court of Justice has ruled, with regard to the predecessor provision, that the notification obligation is directly effective – even in horizontal situations (see Case C-194/94, *CIA Security International SA* v. *Signalson SA and Securitel SPRL* [1996] ECR I-2201). For a long discussion of this case, see Chapter 3, section 3(a/cc).

[130] Case C-11/92, *The Queen* v. *Secretary of State for Health, ex p. Gallaher Ltd, Imperial Tobacco Ltd and Rothmans International Tobacco (UK) Ltd* [1993] ECR I-3545.

[131] Directive 89/622 on the approximation of laws, regulations and administrative provisions of the Member States concerning the labelling of tobacco products [1989] OJ L 359/1. This old measure has since been replaced by Directive 2014/40 (n. 40 above) – discussed above.

Could this be done? Two tobacco companies contested this and argued that the Union harmonisation measure left no discretion to national legislators to adopt stricter national standards. The Court was therefore asked to rule on the compatibility of the stricter national requirements with the Union measure, and its answer contrasts strikingly with its earlier ruling in *Ratti*. The Court now read Article 8 of the directive as relating only to imports and acknowledged the existence of an implied power to establish stricter standards for national products. Interpreting Articles 3 and 8 of the directive, the European Court found:

> It should be borne in mind that the directive, which was adopted pursuant to [Article 114], is designed to eliminate barriers to trade which might arise as a result of differences in national provisions on the labelling of tobacco products and thereby impede the establishment and operation of the internal market. With that end in view, the directive contains common rules concerning the health warnings to appear on the unit packet of tobacco products and the indications of the tar and nicotine yields to appear on cigarette packets ...
>
> The expression 'at least' contained in both articles must be interpreted as meaning that, if they consider it necessary, Member States are at liberty to decide that the indications and warnings are to cover a greater surface area in view of the level of public awareness of the health risks associated with tobacco consumption ... [T]his interpretation of the provisions may imply less favourable treatment for national products in comparison with imported products and leaves in existence some inequalities in conditions of competition. However, those consequences are attributable to the degree of harmonization sought by the provisions in question, which lay down *minimum* requirements.[132]

The Court – following the Union legislator – thus allowed for stricter national standards. Such standards should, nonetheless, not restrict intra-Union trade, and could consequently not be applied to imported goods. This followed from the aim of the directive to eliminate barriers to trade and from Article 8 thereof:

> Member States which have made use of the powers conferred by the provisions containing minimum requirements cannot, according to Article 8 of the Directive, prohibit or restrict the sale within their territory of products imported from other Member States which comply with the Directive.[133]

The constitutional regime for minimum harmonisation has recently been confirmed for the (new) 2014 Tobacco Sales Directive.[134] The Union here accepts that a Member State can go beyond the 'harmonised' Union standard, but that it could only enforce its national choice against its own citizens. This form of minimum harmonisation has today become a widespread feature of Union legislation generally. Its success is rooted in combining a degree of European unity with a degree of national diversity in the internal market.

---

[132] *Ibid.*, paras. 10, 20 and 22 (emphasis added).   [133] *Ibid.*, para. 16.
[134] Case C-547/14, *Philip Morris* v. *Secretary of State*, esp. paras. 66–84.

4. In Particular: The Common Agricultural Policy

In the aftermath of the Second World War, agricultural production in Europe was characterised by economic insufficiency and most European States therefore established national policies that actively intervened in the market to ensure a degree of national sufficiency. Two options therefore existed when the European Union was created. The EU Treaties could exclude agricultural products from the liberal principles of the internal market so as to protect these national agricultural policies; or, alternatively, the Treaties could include agriculture, yet replace the *national* agricultural policies with a *common* agricultural policy.[135] The first option proved unacceptable to the 'agricultural' countries in Europe, and in particular France. Freedom of movement for industrial products without free movement for agricultural goods was feared to tilt the balance in favour of German industrial trade.[136] The Treaties consequently did include agricultural goods within the scope of the internal market; yet – in the light of their special status – established a special regime for them.

This special constitutional regime is placed in a separate title dealing with agriculture. It is 'sandwiched' between Title II on the free movement of (industrial) goods and Title IV on free movement of persons, services and capital. Title III here deals with the Common Agricultural Policy (CAP), which now expressly includes the Common Fisheries Policy.[137]

The content of Title III can be in seen in Table 14.4. Article 38 here confirms that '[t]he internal market shall extend to agriculture, fisheries and trade in agricultural products';[138] yet it immediately clarifies that this extension of the internal market principles would only apply '[s]ave as otherwise provided in 39 to 44'.[139] The agricultural regime indeed constitutes a collective *lex specialis* in the law of the internal market. The reason behind the special status given to agricultural trade was the strong nexus that was seen to exist between the common *market* and the common *policy*. This constitutional link between negative and positive

---

[135] Less integrated economic unions – such as free trade areas or customs unions typically leave agriculture outside their scope. For an excellent introduction into the 'historical' birth conditions of the Common Agricultural Policy, see M. Melchior, 'The Common Agricultural Policy', in Commission (ed.), *Thirty Years of Community Law* (Office for Official Publications of the EC, 1981), 437–8.

[136] For an analysis of the geopolitical situation, see A. Moravcik, *The Choice for Europe: Social Purpose and State Power from Messina to Maastricht* (Cornell University Press, 1998), ch. 2.

[137] The Common Fisheries Policy (CFP) has, since its inception, been an integral part of the CAP. The Lisbon Treaty has made this even more explicit by adding 'Fisheries' to the 'Agriculture' Title. For an overview of the Common Fisheries Policy, see R. Churchill and D. Owen, *The EC Common Fisheries Policy* (Oxford University Press, 2010); J. Wakefield, 'Fisheries: A Failure of Values' (2009) 46 *CML Rev.* 431.

[138] Art. 38(1) TFEU. The Treaty thereby defines agricultural products as follows: '"Agricultural products" means the products of the soil, of stockfarming and of fisheries and products of first-stage processing directly related to these products.' Art. 38(3) subsequently refers to the more elaborate list in Annex I of the Treaties.

[139] *Ibid.*, Art. 38(2).

Table 14.4 Treaty Title on Agriculture

Title III: Agriculture (and Fisheries)	
Article 38	Special Status of Agricultural Goods within the Internal Market
Article 39	Objectives of the Common Agricultural Policy
Article 40	Common Organisation of Agricultural Markets
Article 41	Flanking Policies (vocational training, research, consumption)
Article 42	Relationship to EU Competition Law
Article 43	Legislative Competence for CAP Measures
Article 44	National Market Organisations (and countervailing charges)

integration is indeed expressly made in Article 38(4), which states: 'The operation and development of the internal *market* for agricultural products *must be
accompanied* by the establishment of a common agricultural *policy*.'[140] The close
connection between negative and positive integration predestined EU agricultural law to become the 'most developed and coherent field of [European] law'.[141]

The objectives of the CAP are listed in Article 39 TFEU. They include, in particular, the increase of agricultural productivity, the guarantee of a fair standard
of living for farmers, and the stabilisation of agricultural markets.[142] These objectives have been interpreted to give wide discretion to the Union legislator.[143]
In order to attain these objectives, the Treaty thereby anticipated 'a common
organisation of agricultural markets' in Article 40 TFEU.[144] The provision was
not designed as a legal basis but instead set out three forms in which a common
agricultural policy could be achieved. It states:

> 1. In order to attain the objectives set out in Article 39, a common organisation of
>   agricultural markets shall be established. This organisation shall take one of the
>   following forms, depending on the product concerned:
>   (a) common rules on competition;
>   (b) compulsory coordination of the various national market organisations;
>   (c) *a European market organisation*.

---

[140]   Art. 38(4) TFEU (emphasis added).
[141]   R. Barents, *The Agricultural Law of the EC* (Kluwer, 1994), 366. This gave rise to the common belief that once the Union had intervened through the setting up of a CMO, the
Union competence would become 'exclusive' through an 'occupation of the field'. Today,
this debate is clearly settled in favour of a shared competence (see Art. 4(2)(d) TFEU).
[142]   Art. 39(1)(a)–(c) TFEU. For an analysis of the objectives and their relation to each other,
see J. A. McMahon, 'Chasing a Moving Target through a Thick Fog: Questioning the
Objectives of the Common Agricultural Policy', in N. Nic Shuibhne and L. W. Gormley
(eds.), *From Single Market to Economic Union: Essays in Memory of John A. Usher* (Oxford
University Press, 2012), 267.
[143]   See Case 114/76, *Bela-Mühle* v. *Grows-Farm* [1977] ECR 1211; Case 44/79, *Hauer* v. *Land
Rheinland-Pfalz* [1979] ECR 3727.
[144]   Art. 40(1) TFEU.

> 2. The common organisation established in accordance with paragraph 1 may include all measures required to attain the objectives set out in Article 39, *in particular regulation of prices, aids for the production and marketing of the various products, storage and carryover arrangements and common machinery for stabilising imports or exports.* The common organisation shall be limited to pursuit of the objectives set out in Article 39 and shall exclude any discrimination between producers or consumers within the Union. Any common price policy shall be based on common criteria and uniform methods of calculation.[145]

The distinction in Article 40(1) between three forms of organising agricultural markets would however be of little importance. In the past, the European legislator 'invariably' favoured the third option: a European or common market organisation (CMO).[146] The traditional heart of most CMOs was thereby the 'price mechanism', that is: the idea that the Union could set a common price for each agricultural product. It was this regulatory mechanism that led to an extremely centralised approach for agricultural goods. Section (a) looks at this 'old approach', whereas section (b) explores how it has gradually given way to a 'new approach' to agricultural harmonisation.

a. The 'Old' CAP: Vertical Harmonisation

aa. Product Support through Common Prices

The Union legal order has traditionally followed a 'vertical' approach to the regulation of agricultural products. CMOs would be established for individual agricultural goods on the basis of Article 43 TFEU;[147] and this was in fact achieved for most products. Each common market organisation was designed to form a comprehensive regulatory code for the product(s) to which it applied. A list of the 'classic' CMOs is provided in Table 14.5

The Treaty thereby provided the Union legislator with a wide spectrum of regulatory methods: it was entitled to adopt '*all* measures required to attain the

---

[145] Emphasis added. The third paragraph adds: 'In order to enable the common organisation referred to in paragraph 1 to attain its objectives, one or more agricultural guidance and guarantee funds may be set up.'

[146] F. G. Snyder, *Law of the Common Agricultural Policy* (Sweet & Maxwell, 1985), 71. Constitutional practice has preferred the expression common market organisation for a regulatory regime that combined elements from each method (see Melchior, 'Common Agricultural Policy' (n. 135 above), 443).

[147] Art. 43 TFEU contains two legal bases – one in Art. 43(2) and one in Art. 43(3). The former allows the European Parliament and the Council, in accordance with the ordinary legislative procedure to 'establish the common organisation of agricultural markets provided for in Article 40(1)'; whereas the latter allows the Council(!) to 'adopt measures on fixing of prices, levies, aid and quantitative limitations and on the fixing and allocation of fishing opportunities'.

Table 14.5 Common Market Organisations

(Specific) Common Market Organisations under the CAP		
Bananas	Hops Raw	Tobacco
Beef and Veal	Live Trees and Other Plants	Rice
Cereals	Milk and Milk Products	Seeds
Dried Fodder	Olive Oil and Table Olives	Sheepmeat and Goatmeat
Eggs	Pigmeat	Sugar
Flax and Hemp	Poultrymeat	Wine
Fruit & Vegetables	Processed Fruit & Vegetables	Annex II Products
	Fisheries	

objectives set out in Article 39'.[148] And, in order to manage production, the Union originally concentrated on the regulation of agricultural prices. The central idea behind price regulation was the 'market principle'.[149] According to that principle agricultural producers had to obtain an adequate income from the market and not – at least not directly – from the Union. To secure the growth of the agricultural sector and to stabilise product markets, a sophisticated intervention system was established to keep Union agricultural prices at a constant level. The regulation of common prices eventually evolved into 'the' policy instrument of the CAP.[150] The resulting complexity had important consequences for the division of legislative powers between the Union and the Member States.

bb. Legislative Pre-emption through 'Common Market Organisations'

To what extent could national legislators still tinker with a common market organisation? The constitutional principles governing Union harmonisation inside common market organisations came to the fore in *Galli*.[151] An Italian decree tried to control the prices of goods produced or distributed by large firms. Criminal proceedings had been brought against Galli, who sold cereals

---

[148]   Art. 40(2) TFEU.

[149]   Melchior, 'Common Agricultural Policy' (n. 135 above), 439. The principle has been defined as guaranteeing a 'market to which every producer has free access and whose operation is regulated only by the measures provided for by the common organization' (see Case 218/85, *Association comité économique agricole régional fruits et légumes de Bretagne v. A. Le Campion (CERAFEL)* [1986] ECR 3513, para. 20). In the words of F. Snyder, the reference to the market principle is 'at best confusing' as it – misleadingly – 'implies that CAP prices are determined by supply and demand, whereas in fact are determined by negotiation and then administered' (*Law of the Common Agricultural Policy* (n. 146 above), fnn. 6 and 105). Public authorities would be authorised to intervene in the common market to adjust the balance between supply and demand so as to keep prices at the desired level.

[150]   Barents, *Agricultural Law of the EC* (n. 141 above), 89.

[151]   Case 31/74, *Galli* [1975] ECR 47.

in contravention of that national law. In a preliminary reference, the European Court of Justice was asked to review the national measure in the light of the Regulation setting up a common market organisation in cereals.[152] Having been adopted within the framework of Article 40 TFEU, the Union legislator had here aimed to establish a 'single market' in cereals.[153] A 'central place' within that system was held by a price mechanism,[154] whose importance and function was explained as follows:

> The purpose of this price system is to make possible complete freedom of trade within the [Union] and to regulate external trade accordingly, all in accordance with the objectives pursued by the common agricultural policy. *So as to ensure the freedom of internal trade the Regulation comprises a set of rules intended to eliminate both the obstacles to free movement of goods and all distortions in intra-[Union] trade due to market intervention by Member States other than that authorized by the Regulation itself* ... Such a system excludes any national system of regulation *impeding directly or indirectly, actually or potentially, trade within the [Union]*. Consequently, as concerns more particularly the price system, any national provisions, the effect of which is to distort the formation of prices as brought about within the framework of the [Union] provisions applicable, are incompatible with the Regulation.[155]

The Court thus concluded that 'Member States can no longer interfere through national provisions taken unilaterally in the machinery of price formation established under the common organization.'[156] National legislation affecting prices would automatically conflict with the common market organisation. The reason given by the Court for this wide pre-emptive effect was that the Union legislator had intended to create a single market characterised by 'complete freedom of trade' in which 'all distortions' of competition due to national legislation were eliminated.

This nexus between the desire to create a 'single market' in a product and the establishment of common market organisation was reinforced in subsequent jurisprudence. Importantly, however, the Union legal order has here not generally insisted on automatic field pre-emption. Not every CMO constituted a complete system that would exhaustively regulate all aspects falling within its scope.[157] The Court instead cultivated an aggressive variant of obstacle pre-emption to oust any supplementary national legislation that it felt interfered with the functioning of the common market organisation established by Union legislation.

---

[152] Regulation 120/67 on the common organisation of the market in cereals [1967] OJ L 117/29.

[153] Case 31/74, *Galli*, para. 8

[154] *Ibid.*, para. 10. [155] *Ibid.*, paras. 11–16 (emphasis added). [156] *Ibid.*, paras. 29–30.

[157] For the standard formulation, see Case 16/83, *Prantl* [1984] ECR 1299, para. 13: '[O]nce rules on the common organization of the market may be regarded as forming a complete system, the Member States no longer have competence in that field unless the [Union] provides otherwise.'

This strong obstacle pre-emption standard held sway over the CAP for over four decades.[158] Emphasising the unity of the common market, the Court thus traditionally insisted that a CMO would try to recreate the 'conditions for trade within the [Union] similar to those existing in a national market'.[159] National measures that impeded the proper functioning of the CMO or jeopardised its aims would be pre-empted.

The clearest expression of this aggressive pre-emption standard emerges in *Compassion*.[160] The case had been brought by the Royal Society for the Prevention of Cruelty to Animals against the British minister of agriculture, who had rejected the request to ban the export of calves into Member States that allowed for the rearing of calves in 'veal crates'. Asked whether this potential trade restriction would interfere with the common market organisation in beef and veal, the Court confirmed that 'where there is a regulation on the common organisation of the market in a given sector, the Member States are under an obligation to refrain from taking any measures which might undermine or create exceptions to it'. In other words: '[r]ules which interfere with the proper functioning of a common organisation of the market are also incompatible with such common organisation, even if the matter in question has not been exhaustively regulated by it'.[161] Such would be the case for a ban on the export of calves, since the latter 'would have a considerable impact on the formation of market prices, which would interfere with the proper functioning of the common organisation of the market'.[162]

b. The 'New' CAP: Towards Horizontal Harmonisation

Why was there such a need for legislative uniformity under the (old) CAP? The insistence on uniformity in EU agricultural law was a direct result of the Union's intervention method.[163] The fragility of the price mechanism required that any national legislation that would potentially affect it had to be banned as an unlawful interference with the Union regulatory regime. In the Court's own words:

---

[158] For a relatively recent case, see, e.g., Case C-22/99, *Bertinetto and Biraghi* [2000] ECR I-7629.

[159] Case 4/79, *Société coopérative 'Providence agricole de la Champagne'* v. *Office national interprofessionnel des céréales (ONIC)* [1980] ECR 2823, para. 25.

[160] Case C-1/96, *The Queen* v. *Minister of Agriculture, Fisheries and Food, ex p. Compassion in World Farming Ltd* [1998] ECR I-1251.

[161] *Ibid.*, para. 41.   [162] *Ibid.*, para. 44.

[163] Barents, *Agricultural Law of the EC* (n. 141 above), 367: 'The uniformity principle has decisively influenced the structure of [EU] agricultural law. It explains, inter alia, why the position of the operator under the market and price policy is almost exclusively a matter of [Union] law and why, in general, the role of the Member States is limited to the strict application of the [Union] legislation. Moreover, this feature has significantly contributed to the legalistic structure of this field of law, as any divergent practice on the level may undermine its effectiveness and thus has to be prevented by the laying down of [Union] rules. The result is a strong centralization of agricultural legislation[.]'

[I]n a sector covered by a common organisation, a fortiori where that organisation is based on a common pricing system, Member States can no longer take action, through national provisions taken unilaterally, affecting the machinery of price formation at the production and marketing stages established under the common organisation.[164]

The vertical approach, combined with the price support system, brought the CAP close to a total or complete harmonisation approach in which European law was – almost – exclusively governing agricultural products.

The problem with this 'centralist' solution was that it created more problems than it solved. Indeed, while the 'old' CAP had been conceived in the context of agricultural insufficiency, the situation had dramatically changed when modern agricultural production methods led to an impressive agricultural surplus in the Union. Yet due to the high price level for agricultural products within the internal market, this surplus could not be sold off on the world market. And the resulting 'butter mountains' and 'wine lakes' increasingly became a symbol of the excesses of the Union's public intervention system.

By the end of the 1980s, internal and external pressure on the CAP had increased to such an extent that reform seemed inevitable. The process of structural change gradually started in 1992 with the (limited) 'MacSharry reforms'. A more comprehensive reform was subsequently suggested in the 'Agenda 2000'.[165] The Commission felt it was 'now time to formulate concrete proposals to reshape the common agricultural policy and prepare it for the next century' and proposed a generalised shift 'from price support to direct payments'.[166] The Agenda 2000 proposals thereby structured the CAP into two 'pillars': income support and rural development.[167] Reforms in both pillars would be reviewed in 2002, when the Commission undertook a 'mid-term review'.[168] The review urged the Union to 'complet[e] the shift from product to producer support with the introduction of a decoupled system of payments per farm'.[169] This reform ambition bore first fruits in 2003, and is today reflected in Regulation 1307/2013.[170] The Regulation creates 'common rules on payments granted *directly* to farmers', and thereby distinguishes between 'a basic payment' and a number of special additional payments.[171]

---

[164] Case C-283/03, *A. H. Kuipers* v. *Productschap Zuivel* [2005] ECR I-4255, para. 42.

[165] Agenda 2000 for a stronger and wider Union, COM (1997) 2000 final (Volume I), Bulletin of the European Union, Supplement 5/97.   [166] *Ibid.*, 26–9.

[167] The major legislative fruit of the second pillar is today Regulation 1305/2013 on support for rural development by the European Fund for Rural Development [2013] OJ L 347/487.

[168] Commission, 'Communication: Mid-Term Review of the Common Agricultural Policy' COM (2002) 394 final.   [169] *Ibid.*, 3.

[170] Regulation 1307/2013 establishing rules for direct payments to farmers under support schemes within the framework of the Common Agricultural Policy [2013] OJ L 347/608.

[171] *Ibid.*, Art. 1. Art. 5 of the Regulation thereby refers to Regulation 1306/2013 as providing the substantive rules governing the financing and management of these payments (see Regulation 1306/2013 on the financing, management and monitoring of the Common Agricultural Policy [2013] OJ L 347549).

This move to 'decouple' the CAP from the price mechanism and product support is complemented by a move towards horizontal legislation for all common market organisations. Regulation 1308/2013 today achieves the feat of bringing all existing 21 sectoral market organisations under the umbrella of a single common market organisation. The 'Single Common Market Organisation' establishes a common legislative framework for 'all agricultural products' to which the European Treaties apply.[172] The Single CMO Regulation is structured in six parts. Part I sets out the introductory provisions (Articles 1–7). Part II constitutes the lion's part and deals with the 'Internal Market' (Articles 8–175). (Importantly, the new Regulation has here not completely replaced the idea of product support via a price mechanism. Instead it has established moderated common rules for public intervention and aid schemes.) This part however also lays down the various marketing standards for agricultural products. Part III concerns trade with third countries (Articles 176–205), whereas Part IV sets out special rules on competition (Articles 206–18). Parts V–VI conclude with some general and final provisions (Articles 219–32).

What will the effect of these reforms be on the ability of the Member States to supplement agricultural Union legislation? The reforms have been said to 'have a substantial effect on the structure and features of [European] agricultural law';[173] and '[a]s a consequence, [Union] agricultural law will lose to an increasing extent its rather uniform character resulting from the formal equality brought about by price intervention'.[174] It seems indeed reasonable to think that the 'new approach' for the CAP will – like the new approach for 'product requirements' discussed in the previous section – lead to a breaking-up of previously pre-empted fields. The harmonisation approach, here too, would have moved from (near) complete harmonisation to minimum harmonisation.

Conclusion

This chapter has tried to explore the scope and nature of positive integration within the internal market. While focusing on the free movement of goods, the principles discussed within this chapter will apply, *mutatis mutandis*, to the other three freedoms.

What is the scope of positive integration? Section 1 explored the limits to the Union's internal market competences. We saw there that the Union has not been eager to limit its harmonisation competences. It has refused to give a specific

---

[172] Single CMO Regulation, recital (3): 'This Regulation should apply to all agricultural products listed in Annex I to the Treaty on the European Union (TEU) and to the Treaty on the Functioning of the European Union (TFEU) (together, "the Treaties") in order to ensure the existence of a common organisation of the market for all such products, as required by Article 40(1) TFEU.'

[173] Barents, *Agricultural Law of the EC* (n. 141 above), 365.

[174] *Ibid.*, 371.

content to the technique of 'harmonisation', and it has traditionally interpreted the requirement that the harmonisation must serve the establishment or functioning of the internal market extremely widely. An important – symbolic – turning point did however occur with *Tobacco Advertising*. The Court here annulled for the first time a Union measure on the grounds that it was not covered by the general competence under Article 114. Importantly, the Union's general harmonisation competence is however not limited by specific legislative competences within the Treaties that exclude any harmonisation. Wherever the centre of gravity of a Union act falls onto the internal market side, legislative harmonisation under Article 114 is possible.

To what extent has the Union used its harmonisation competences? The Union legislator has principally a choice whether to fully or minimally harmonise a given matter. According to the 'old approach' to harmonisation, it originally preferred total harmonisation whereby the Union measure field pre-empted the Member States. After *Cassis de Dijon*, a new approach to harmonisation gradually emerged. It is based on the idea of minimum harmonisation that permits the Member States to complement the Union standard by higher national standards. This shift from 'full' to 'minimum' harmonisation was explored in section 3 in the context of the harmonisation of product requirements. The move away from Union centralisation has taken much longer in the context of the Common Agricultural Policy. Here, the close connection between negative and positive integration meant that the Union has traditionally preferred (near) complete harmonisation so as to guarantee 'free' trade of agricultural products governed by a common market organisation. This 'socialist' approach to production is however gradually changing and the shared CAP competence appears to be increasingly exercised through horizontal legislation.

FURTHER READING

Books

R. Barents, *The Agricultural Law of the EC* (Kluwer, 1994)

C. Barnard and J. Scott, *The Law of the Single European Market: Unpacking the Premises* (Hart, 2002)

R. Bieber et al. (eds.), *1992: One European Market* (Nomos, 1988)

M. Egan, *Constructing a European Market: Standards, Regulation and Governance* (Oxford University Press, 2001)

J. A. McMahon, *EU Agricultural Law* (Oxford University Press, 2007)

I. Maletic, *The Law and Policy of Harmonisation in Europe's Internal Market* (Edward Elgar, 2013)

R. Schütze, *From Dual to Cooperative Federalism: The Changing Structure of European Law* (Oxford University Press, 2009)

P. Syrpis, *The Judiciary, the Legislature and the EU Internal Market* (Cambridge University Press, 2012)

B. J. M. Terra and P. J. Wattel, *European Tax Law* (Kluwer, 2012)

S. Weatherill, *Law and Integration in the European Union* (Clarendon, 1995)

D. Williams, *EC Tax Law* (Longman, 1998)

Articles (and Chapters)

K. Alter and S. Meunier-Aitsahalia, 'Judicial Politics in the European Community' (1994–5) 26 *Comparative Political Studies* 535

Sir R. Arnold, 'An Overview of European Harmonisation Measures in Intellectual Property Law', in A. Ohly and J. Pila (eds.), *The Europeanization of Intellectual Property Law* (Oxford University Press, 2013), 25

R. Barents, 'The Internal Market Unlimited: Some Observations on the Legal Basis of Community Legislation' (1993) 30 *CML Rev.* 85

A. Dashwood, 'Hastening Slowly: The Community's Path towards Harmonization', in H. Wallace, W. Wallace and C. Webb (eds.), *Policy-making in the European Community* (Wiley & Sons, 1983), 177

G. Davies, 'Can Selling Arrangements Be Harmonised?' (2005) 30 *EL Rev.* 37

M. Dougan, 'Minimum Harmonization and the Internal Market' (2000) 37 *CML Rev.* 853

C.-D. Ehlermann, 'The Internal Market following the Single European Act' (1987) 24 *CML Rev.* 361

P. Pescatore, 'Some Critical Remarks on the "Single European Act"' (1987) 24 *CML Rev.* 9

N. de Sadeleer, 'Procedures for Derogation from the Principle of Approximation of Laws under Article 95 EC' (2003) 40 *CML Rev.* 889

C. Seville, 'Developments (and Non-developments) in the Harmonization of EU Intellectual Property Law' (2008–9) 11 *CYELS* 89

P. J. Slot, 'Harmonisation' (1996) 21 *EL Rev.* 378

S. Weatherill, 'The Limits of Legislative Harmonization Ten Years after *Tobacco Advertising*: How the Court's Case Law Has Become a "Drafting Guide"' (2011) 12 *German Law Journal* 827

Cases on the Website

Case 31/74, *Galli*; Case 35/76, *Simmenthal*; Case 120/78, *Cassis de Dijon*; Case 148/78, *Ratti*; Case 278/85, *Commission v. Denmark*; Case C-300/89, *Commission v. Council (Titanium Dioxide)*; Case C-11/92, *Gallaher*; Case C-350/92, *Spain v. Council*; Case C-359/92, *Germany v. Council; Opinion 1/94* (WTO Agreement); Case C-1/96, *Compassion*; Case C-376/98, *Germany v. Parliament and Council (Tobacco Advertising)*; Case C-3/00, *Denmark v. Commission*; Joined Cases T-366/03 and T-235/04, *Upper Austria v. Commission*; Case C-66/04 *United Kingdom v. Parliament and Council*; Case T-182/06, *Netherlands v. Commission (Air Pollution)*; Case C-58/08, *Vodafone*; Case C-547/14, *Philip Morris*

15

Free Movement of Persons
Workers and Beyond

Contents

Introduction

Going beyond an internal market in goods, the EU Treaties also envisage the free movement of persons. This constitutional choice was originally inspired by an economic rationale. The second fundamental freedom had been created to assist people wishing to work in another Member State and was consequently confined to economically active persons. The Treaties thereby distinguished between two classes of economic migrants: 'employed' and 'self-employed' persons; and the Treaty Title dealing with the movement of persons today still addresses 'Workers' and the 'Right of Establishment' in two separate chapters. The establishment chapter thereby not only covers natural persons but also, importantly, the rights of companies.

With subsequent Treaty amendments, these two special chapters were nevertheless complemented by the 'horizontal' rules on Union citizenship; and with the introduction of the citizenship provisions, the Union has (partially) cut the economic link that traditionally connected persons to EU free movement rights. The Union's citizenship rules grant every citizen the (limited) 'right to move and reside freely within the territory of the Member States'.[1]

What is the scope of these three sources of rights with regard to the free movement of persons? This chapter hopes to explore each source individually as well as the horizontal connections between them. Sections 1 and 2 analyse the special free movement rights for economically active persons; that is: workers and self-employed professionals, while section 3 specifically explores the free movement rights of companies (and their subsidiaries). An overview of the relevant Treaty provisions can be found in Table 15.1.

When compared to the free movement of goods provisions – discussed in Chapter 13 – two fundamental differences can here immediately be noted. First, the free movement of persons provisions do not expressly distinguish between regulatory and fiscal barriers to trade; and the Court has confirmed that both fall within the same free movement provisions.[2] Second, and again unlike the free movement of goods, the Treaty chapters on workers and establishment only each contain *one* central prohibition outlawing restrictions on the free movement of persons.

---

[1] Art. 21(1) TFEU. A similar right is enshrined in Art. 45 EU Charter of Fundamental Rights.

[2] See Case C-204/90, *Bachmann* v. *Belgium* [1992] ECR I-249; Case C-279/93, *Finanzamt Köln-Altstadt* v. *Schumacker* [1995] ECR I-225; Case C-80/94, *Wielockx* v. *Inspecteur der Directe Belastingen* [1995] ECR I-2493. For an analysis of these cases, see F. Vanistendael, 'The Consequences of *Schumacker* and *Wielockx*: Two Steps Forward in the Tax Procession of Echternach' (1996) 33 *CML Rev.* 255.

Table 15.1 Free Movement of Persons – Overview

Treaty Rules on the Free Movement of Persons	
Citizenship Rights (Articles 20–5)	
Free Movement of Workers	**Freedom of Establishment**
Article 45 Prohibition on (Unjustified) Restrictions	Article 49 Prohibition on National Restrictions
Article 46 Union Competence: Free Movement of Workers	Article 50 Union Competence: Freedom of Establishment
Article 47 Duty to Encourage the Exchange of Young Workers	Article 51 Official Authority Exception for Self-employed Persons
Article 48 Union Competence: Social Security	Article 52 Legitimate Justifications for National Restrictions
	Article 53 Union Competence: Mutual Recognition
	Article 54 Legal Persons (Companies)
	Article 55 Establishment through Participation in a Company's Capital
Secondary Law (Selection)	
Regulation 492/2011 on the Freedom of Movement of Workers Regulation 883/2004 on the Coordination of National Social Security Systems Directive 2005/36 on the Mutual Recognition of Professional Qualifications Directive 2004/38 on the Rights of Citizens (Citizenship Directive)	

The concentration of all 'negative' integration into a single provision for workers and a single provision for the self-employed appears to make the legal regime governing the free movement of persons much less complex than the fragmented constitutional regime governing the free movement of goods. Yet, beware: the opposite is the case! The high complexity within this area of EU law thereby stems from two roots. First, each of the Treaty chapters contains a number of special harmonisation competences to positively assist the Union to establish the free movement of persons. These competences have been widely exercised; and for this reason, the Union law governing persons is a rich and complex amalgam of primary and secondary law. However, the complexity within this area also has a second root: the existence of general free movement rights granted to all European citizens. Section 4 explores these general rights and their relationship to the special movement rights for workers and the self-employed.

Section 5 – finally – analyses the horizontal rules that govern the various justifications for national restrictions on the free movement of persons. In addition to the ordinary public policy justifications, the main derogation here is a public service exception that allows Member States to restrict access to professions that are linked to the exercise of public authority.

In order to better distinguish the various elements and overlapping aspects of the free movement of persons provisions, Figure 15.1 offers a first schematic arrangement that should be kept in mind when studying this chapter.

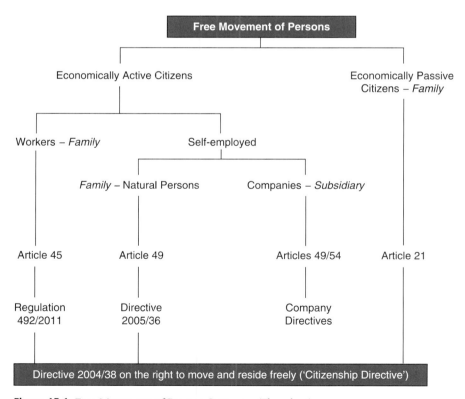

Figure 15.1 Free Movement of Persons: Summary (Flowchart)

1. Free Movement of Workers

The Treaty on the Functioning of the European Union contains a single provision that governs national restrictions and possible justifications to the free movement of workers. The text of Article 45 reads as follows:

1. Freedom of movement for workers shall be secured within the Union.
2. Such freedom of movement shall entail the abolition of any discrimination based on nationality between workers of the Member States as regards employment, remuneration and other conditions of work and employment.
3. It shall entail the right, subject to limitations justified on grounds of public policy, public security or public health:
    (a) to accept offers of employment actually made;
    (b) to move freely within the territory of Member States for this purpose;
    (c) to stay in a Member State for the purpose of employment in accordance with the provisions governing the employment of nationals of that State laid down by law, regulation or administrative action;
    (d) to remain in the territory of a Member State after having been employed in that State, subject to conditions which shall be embodied in regulations to be drawn up by the Commission.
4. The provisions of this Article shall not apply to employment in the public service.

The Court has held that the provision has direct effect.[3] It will thus grant Union rights that individuals can invoke when they wish to challenge State measures (as well as collective private actions).[4]

Unlike the free movement of goods provisions, which distinguish between import and export restrictions, Articles 45 is silent as to whether it covers host state as well as home state laws; yet the Court has found that the provision indeed covers 'import' as well as 'export' restrictions. A Member State thus cannot – without justification – prevent its nationals from seeking employment in another

---

[3] See especially Case 41/74, *Van Duyn* v. *Home Office* [1974] ECR 1337, esp. paras. 6–7: 'These provisions impose on Member States a precise obligation which does not require the adoption of any further measure on the part of the [Union] institutions or of the Member States and which leaves them, in relation to its implementation, no discretionary power. Paragraph 3, which defines the rights implied by the principle of freedom of movement for workers, subjects them to limitations justified on grounds of public policy, public security or public health. The application of these limitations is, however, subject to judicial control, so that a Member State's right to invoke the limitations does not prevent the provisions of Article [45], which enshrine the principle of freedom of movement for workers, from conferring on individuals rights which are enforceable by them and which the national courts must protect.'

[4] Case 36/74, *Walrave and Koch* v. *Association union cycliste internationale* [1974] ECR 1405, para. 17; Case C-415/93, *Union royale belge des sociétés de football association ASBL* v. *Jean-Marc Bosman* [1995] ECR I-4921.

Member State,[5] or to disadvantage them for doing so;[6] and the Court has also clarified that any national having once exercised his free movement rights can invoke them against his own State and within his own State.[7]

Many of the rights workers enjoy under Article 45 are codified in Union legislation. For under Article 46, the Union is entitled to 'issue directives or make regulations setting out the measures required to bring about freedom of movement for workers, as defined in Article 45'. The two most important pieces of legislation in this context are Regulation 492/2011 'on freedom of movement of workers within the Union' (the 'Workers Regulation'),[8] and Directive 2004/38 'on the right of citizens and their family members to move and reside freely within the territory of the Member States' (the 'Citizenship Directive).[9] In combination with Article 45 TFEU, both Union acts have given concrete content to the personal and material scope of the rights granted to workers in the European Union.

a. Personal Scope I: 'Workers' and Quasi-workers

aa. Employment: A Minimalist Definition

When is a person a 'worker'? Will part-time work be sufficient? Are persons searching for work already 'workers'? These questions concern the personal scope of Article 45. The latter defines the categories of persons falling within the scope of the provision. The Court of Justice has insisted that it alone enjoys the 'hermeneutic monopoly' to determine the scope of the term 'worker'.[10] It has held:

---

[5] See Case C-18/95, *Terhoeve* [1999] ECR I-345, para. 38: '[N]ationals of Member States have in particular the right, which they derive directly from the Treaty, to leave their State of origin to enter the territory of another Member State and reside there in order there to pursue an economic activity.'

[6] See Case C-515/14, *Commission* v. *Cyprus*, EU:C:2016:30. The case will be discussed below.

[7] See Case C-419/92, *Scholz* v. *Opera Universitaria di Cagliari and Cinzia Porcedda* [1994] ECR I-505, para. 9: 'Any [Union] national who, irrespective of his place of residence and his nationality, has exercised the right to freedom of movement for workers and who has been employed in another Member State, falls within the scope of the aforesaid provisions'. However, importantly, like all free movement rules, Arts. 45 and 49 TFEU will not apply to 'purely internal situations' (see e.g. Case 175/78, *The Queen* v. *Saunders* [1979] ECR 1129). On the 'purely internal situation' limitation in general, see Chapter 13, section 1(d).

[8] Regulation 492/2011 on freedom of movement for workers within the Union [2011] OJ L141/1. The regulation is supported by Regulation 2014/54 on measures facilitating the exercise of rights conferred on workers [2014] OJ L 128/8.

[9] Directive 2004/38 on the right of citizens of the Union and their family members to move and reside freely within the territory of the Member States ('Citizenship Directive') [2004] OJ L 158/77.

[10] F. Mancini, 'The Free Movement of Workers in the Case-Law of the European Court of Justice', in D. Curtin and D. O'Keeffe (eds.), *Constitutional Adjudication in the European Community and National Law* (Butterworths, 1992), 67.

> If the definition of this term were a matter within the competence of national law, it would therefore be possible for each Member State to modify the meaning of the concept of 'migrant worker' and to eliminate at will the protection afforded by the Treaty to certain categories of persons.[11]

The concept of 'worker' is thus a European concept, as 'the Treaty would be frustrated if the meaning of such a term could be unilaterally fixed and modified by national law'.[12]

What, then, is the European scope of the concept of 'worker'? The Court has given it a broad definition in *Lawrie-Blum*:

> The concept must be defined in accordance with objective criteria which distinguish the employment relationship by reference to the rights and duties of the persons concerned. The essential feature of an employment relationship, however, is that *for a certain period of time a person performs services for and under the direction of another person in return for which he receives remuneration*.[13]

This definition contained three criteria. First, a person would have to be 'settled' in the (host) State.[14] Second, the person would have to be under the direction of someone else; and, third, consideration for this subordination was the payment of remuneration.[15]

What form of remuneration would be required to trigger the scope of Article 45? In *Levin*,[16] a British national was refused a residence permit in the Netherlands on the grounds that she was not engaged in full-time work that provided her with remuneration 'commensurate with the means of subsistence considered as necessary by the legislation of the Member State'.[17] Would the rights under Article 45 thus depend on receiving a minimum salary within the host Member State? The Court, anxious to avoid a definition of 'worker' that differed depending on the Member State involved, held otherwise:

---

[11] Case 75/63, *Hoekstra (née Unger)* v. *Bestuur der Bedrijfsvereniging voor Detailhandel en Ambachten* [1964] ECR 177, 184.

[12] *Ibid.* For a recent confirmation, see Case C-143/16, *Abercrombie & Fitch Italia* v. *Bordonaro*, EU:C:2017:566, para. 19: '[T]hat concept has a specific independent meaning and must not be interpreted narrowly.'

[13] Case 66/85, *Lawrie-Blum* v. *Land Baden-Württemberg* [1986] ECR 2121, para. 17 (emphasis added).

[14] This requirement of 'permanency' distinguishes 'workers' under Art. 45 TFEU from 'posted workers' who fall within the scope of the free movement of services. On 'posted workers' as a distinct category, see Chapter 16, section 2(a).

[15] In this sense, see Case C-456/02, *Trojani* v. *Centre public d'aide sociale de Bruxelles* [2004] ECR I-7573, para. 22: 'the constituent elements of any paid employment relationship, namely subordination and the payment of remuneration'.

[16] Case 53/81, *Levin* v. *Staatssecretaris van Justitie* [1982] ECR 1035.

[17] *Ibid.*, para. 10.

> Since part-time employment, although it may provide an income lower than what is considered to be the minimum required for subsistence, constitutes for a large number of persons an effective means of improving their living conditions, the effectiveness of [Union] law would be impaired and the achievement of the objectives of the Treaty would be jeopardized if the enjoyment of rights conferred by the principle of freedom of movement for workers were reserved solely to persons engaged in full-time employment and earning, as a result, a wage at least equivalent to the guaranteed minimum wage in the sector under consideration …
>
> In this regard no distinction may be made between those who wish to make do with their income from such an activity and those who supplement that income with other income, whether the latter is derived from property or from the employment of a member of their family who accompanies them. *It should however be stated that whilst part-time employment is not excluded from the field of application of the rules on freedom of movement for workers, those rules cover only the pursuit of effective and genuine activities, to the exclusion of activities on such a small scale as to be regarded as purely marginal and ancillary.*[18]

The Court here defined a 'worker' as a person remunerated for an 'effective and genuine' activity. Under this minimalist definition, the number of working hours and the level of remuneration is irrelevant, except where the activity is so small that it is 'purely marginal and ancillary'. Subsequent jurisprudence has consolidated this minimalist standard.[19] It thus confirmed that benefits in kind could be considered 'remuneration' as long as the work done was 'capable of being regarded as forming part of the normal labour market'.[20]

But what about people who could not support themselves in the host State? The Court has here insisted that even where a person needs financial assistance *from the State* to supplement his or her income, this would still be irrelevant for the status as a 'worker' as long as s/he was engaged in an effective and genuine activity.[21]

An 'effective and genuine' activity is thus the conceptual core of the personal scope of Article 45. It covers full-time, part-time, occasional and even zero-hour

---

[18] *Ibid.*, paras. 15–17 (emphasis added).

[19] See Case 139/85, *Kempf* v. *Staatssecretaris van Justitie* [1986] ECR 1741; Case 344/87, *Bettray* v. *Staatssecretaris van Justitie* [1989] ECR 1621; Case C-456/02 *Trojani*.

[20] Case C-456/02 *Trojani*, para. 24.

[21] Case 139/85, *Kempf* v. *Staatssecretaris van Justitie*, para. 14: 'It follows that the rules on this topic must be interpreted as meaning that a person in effective and genuine part-time employment cannot be excluded from their sphere of application merely because the remuneration he derives from it is below the level of the minimum means of subsistence and he seeks to supplement it by other lawful means of subsistence. In that regard it is irrelevant whether those supplementary means of subsistence are derived from property or from the employment of a member of his family, as was the case in *Levin*, or whether, as in this instance, they are obtained from financial assistance drawn from the public funds of the Member State in which he resides, provided that the effective and genuine nature of his work is established.'

work as long as there is an employment relationship with regard to work that is 'not purely marginal or ancillary'.

bb. *Beyond Employment: Former Workers and Job-seekers*

The Court's minimalist definition of 'worker' has given an extremely broad personal scope to Article 45; but it still hinged on the *presence* of a genuine employment relationship. Would Article 45 however equally cover people searching for *future* employment, or persons who had been in *past* employment?

The Court has indeed found these 'quasi-workers' to fall into the personal scope of Article 45. For former employees this solution is suggested by the provision itself;[22] and the Court has emphatically confirmed this solution in *Lair*.[23] A French national had brought proceedings against a German university for refusing to award her a maintenance grant. This was a social advantage which a worker would have been entitled to claim under Article 45.[24] Could Mrs Lair claim this right *after* having ceased to work in the host State? Three Member States intervened in the case and argued that 'a person loses the status of worker, on which the social advantages depend, when, in the host State, [s]he gives up either [her] previous occupational activity or, if unemployed, [her] search for employment in order to pursue full-time studies'.[25] The Court disagreed:

> Although the wording of those provisions does not provide an express answer to that question, there is nevertheless a basis in [Union] law for the view that the rights guaranteed to migrant workers do not necessarily depend on the actual or continuing existence of an employment relationship … Persons who have previously pursued in the host Member State an effective and genuine activity as an employed person as defined by the Court but who are no longer employed are nevertheless considered to be workers under certain provisions of [Union] law …
>
> It is therefore clear that migrant workers are guaranteed certain rights linked to the status of worker even when they are no longer in an employment relationship. In the field of grants for university education, such a link between the status of worker and a grant awarded for maintenance and training with a view to the pursuit of university studies does, however, presuppose some continuity between the previous occupational activity and the course of study; there must be a relationship between the purpose of the studies and the previous occupational activity.[26]

---

[22] Art. 45(3)(d) TFEU expressly refers to the right 'to remain in the territory of a Member State after having been employed in that State, subject to conditions which shall be embodied in regulations to be drawn up by the Commission'.

[23] Case 39/86, *Lair* v. *Universität Hannover* [1988] ECR 3161.

[24] *Ibid.*, para. 28. On the material scope of Art. 45 TFEU and the notion of social advantage under Art. 7(2) of Regulation 492/2011, see section 1(c) below.

[25] Case 39/86, *Lair* v. *Universität Hannover*, paras. 31–7.

[26] *Ibid.*, para. 36.

Non-employed persons could thus continue to enjoy worker rights; yet these rights required 'some continuity' with the previous occupational activity. This qualification was to prevent abuses of the host State's social welfare system.[27]

With regard to retired pensioners, the Court has also held that 'the fact that a person is no longer in an employment relationship does not deny him certain guaranteed rights which are linked to the status of a worker and that a retirement pension, whose grant is dependent on the prior existence of an employment relationship, which has come to an end, falls within that category of rights'.[28] Pensioners who previously worked in a Member State other than their own, are thus constitutionally entitled to stay. By contrast, pensioners who never 'worked' outside their home state and only moved to another Member State after they retired 'cannot therefore rely on the free movement guaranteed by Article 45 TFEU'.[29]

What about persons seeking future employment? The Court has expressly expanded the personal scope of Article 45 to job-seekers in *Antonissen*.[30] The case arose from a preliminary question by an English High Court on the compatibility of a British law permitting the deportation of foreigners who were unemployed. The British government had argued that 'according to the strict wording of Article [45] of the Treaty, [Union] nationals are given the right to move freely within the territory of the Member States for the purpose only of accepting offers of employment actually made (Article [45(3)(a) and (b)]) whilst the right to stay in the territory of a Member State is stated to be for the purpose of employment (Article [45(3)(c)])'.[31]

The Court unequivocally rejected this view by insisting that 'a strict interpretation of Article [45(3)] would jeopardize the actual chances that a national of a Member State who is seeking employment will find it in another Member State, and would, as a result, make that provision ineffective'.[32] The enumeration within Article 45(3) was non-exhaustive, and included the right of job-seekers 'to move freely within the territory of the other Member States and to stay there for the purposes of seeking employment'.[33]

The Union has however accepted temporal and material limitations to the extension of the status of 'worker' to a job-seeker. First, it has clarified that Member States may adopt *temporal* limitations. In *Antonissen*, the Court thus allowed national measures that restrict the right to stay within the

---

[27] Case 39/86, *Lair v. Universität Hannover*, para. 43. In Case 197/86, *Brown v. Secretary of State for Scotland* [1988] ECR 3205, the Court thus imposed strict requirements when a former worker was entitled to educational rights, such as a grant for university studies.

[28] Case C-300/15, *Kohl and Kohl-Schlesser*, EU:C:2016:361, para. 25 (with reference to prior case law).

[29] *Ibid.*, para. 26 (with references to previous case law). Such pensioners will however potentially benefit from their free movement rights as European citizens under Art. 21 TFEU (*ibid.*, para. 27).

[30] Case C-292/89, *The Queen v. Immigration Appeal Tribunal, ex p. Antonissen* [1991] ECR I-745.

[31] *Ibid.*, para. 9.   [32] *Ibid.*, para. 12.   [33] *Ibid.*, para. 13.

host State to 'a reasonable time'.[34] Second, the Union has also allowed for material limitations. In *Lebon*, it was thus held that '[t]hose who move in search of employment qualify for equal treatment only as regards *access to employ-ment* in accordance with Article[45]of the[FEU]Treaty'.[35] Unlike full workers, job-seekers were consequently not entitled to a fully fledged right to equal treatment with regard to all social and tax advantages offered by the host State. This severe qualification was somewhat softened in *Collins*,[36] where the Court found that foreign job-seekers could request unemployment benefits as the latter were intended to 'facilitate *access to employment* in the labour market'.[37] The ruling has thus narrowed the gap in the material scope of Article 45 for workers and quasi-workers.

b. Personal Scope II: Family Members

While the text of Article 45 does not mention any other beneficiaries than 'workers', it was never in doubt that the right of free movement covered – albeit in an indirect and derivative way – family members. A worker willing to move to another Member State would be entitled to bring his family.[38]

Union law even grants a worker's family members 'their' own rights to reside and work in the territory of the host State. These 'family member' rights were originally laid down in a specific Union act governing the mobility of workers.[39] With the exception of one single right (the education of workers' children) in

---

[34] *Ibid.*, para. 16. The Court was still eager to add: 'if after the expiry of that period the per-son concerned provides evidence that he is continuing to seek employment and that he has genuine chances of being engaged' (*ibid.*), the job-seeker could not be forced to leave the territory of the host Member State. This jurisprudence was subsequently codified and expanded in the Citizenship Directive, whose Art. 7(3) deals specifically with the reten-tion of the status as worker by 'a Union citizen who is no longer a worker'. The provision extends the status of worker in the following situations: '(a) he/she is temporarily unable to work as the result of an illness or accident; (b) he/she is in duly recorded involuntary unemployment after having been employed for more than one year and has registered as a job-seeker with the relevant employment office; (c) he/she is in duly recorded invol-untary unemployment after completing a fixed-term employment contract of less than a year or after having become involuntarily unemployed during the first twelve months and has registered as a job-seeker with the relevant employment office. In this case, the status of worker shall be retained for no less than six months; (d) he/she embarks on vocational training. Unless he/she is involuntarily unemployed, the retention of the status of worker shall require the training to be related to the previous employment.'

[35] Case 316/85, *Centre public d'aide sociale de Courcelles* v. *Lebon* [1987] ECR 2811, para. 26.

[36] Case C-138/02, *Collins* v. *Secretary of State for Work and Pensions* [2004] ECR I-2703.

[37] *Ibid.*, para. 63. This was confirmed in Case C-258/04, *Office national de l'emploi* v. *Ioannis Ioannidis* [2005] ECR I-8275, para. 22; Joined Cases C-22–3/08, *Vatsouras and others* v. *Arbeitsgemeinschaft (ARGE) Nürnberg 900* [2009] ECR I-4585, esp. para. 37.

[38] See Case 249/86, *Commission* v. *Germany* [1989] ECR 1263.

[39] Regulation 1612/68 on freedom of movement for workers within the Community [1968] OJ English Special Edition 475, Arts. 10–12. The Regulation has been replaced by Regulation 492/2011 (n. 8 above).

the Workers Regulation,[40] the Citizenship Directive has today absorbed these family rights.

The Court has however, in the past, established a number of important principles in the specific context of the free movement of workers. For example, it has clarified that 'family member rights are *indirect rights*' that derive from the 'primary' right granted to the worker. Family members will therefore 'qualify only *indirectly* for the equal treatment accorded to the worker himself'; and where a worker's child ceases to be protected qua the worker – say, he or she has reached maturity and independence – it would no longer be able to claim any derived rights under Article 45 TFEU and secondary law.[41]

The Court has nonetheless loosened the dependency of family members on the rights of the worker in *Baumbast*.[42] In this case, a German father had lived in the United Kingdom with his wife and two daughters for a considerable period of time; yet his request for a renewal of their residence permit was rejected by the Secretary of State on the grounds that he was no longer a 'worker'. Mr Baumbast appealed to the Immigration Appeal Tribunal, which requested a preliminary reference ruling on the extent to which (what is now) Regulation 492/2011 granted rights to family members even after the employment relationship had ended. In particular, could Baumbast's small daughters continue their schooling in the United Kingdom? The Court here held that the Regulation would indeed

> ensure that children of a [Union] worker can, even if he has ceased to pursue the activity of an employed person in the host Member State, undertake and, where appropriate, complete their education in that Member State … just like the status of migrant worker itself, the rights enjoyed by members of a [Union] worker's family under Regulation [492/2011] can, in certain circumstances, continue to exist even after the employment relationship has ended.[43]

The case thus stands, among other things, for the confirmation that a worker's family members may, in some circumstances, continue to enjoy secondary

---

[40] Art. 10 of Regulation 492/2011 ('Workers' Families') states: 'The children of a national of a Member State who is or has been employed in the territory of another Member State shall be admitted to that State's general educational, apprenticeship and vocational training courses under the same conditions as the nationals of that State, if such children are residing in its territory. Member States shall encourage all efforts to enable such children to attend these courses under the best possible conditions.' It was the predecessor of this provision that was given a broad teleological interpretation in Case 9/74, *Casagrande* v. *Landeshauptstadt München* [1974] ECR 773.

[41] Case 316/85, *Centre public d'aide sociale de Courcelles* v. *Marie-Christine Lebon* [1987] ECR 2811, paras. 12–14 (emphasis added).

[42] Case C-413/99, *Baumbast and R* v. *Secretary of State for the Home Department* [2002] ECR I-7091.

[43] *Ibid.*, paras. 69–70.

Union rights despite the fact that the primary right-holder has ceased to be a migrant worker in the host State.[44] This jurisprudence has also been codified in the Citizenship Directive.[45]

c. Material Scope: Discrimination and Beyond

Which rights will workers enjoy on the basis of Article 45 TFEU and Union legislation? Article 45(2) expressly refers to 'the abolition of any discrimination based on nationality between workers of the Member States as regards employment, remuneration and other conditions of work and employment'; and Article 45(3) clarifies that this 'shall entail the right' to accept offers, to move freely and to stay within the territory of a Member State for that purpose.

These textual bones were given flesh by two central pieces of Union legislation: the Citizenship Directive (Directive 2004/38) and the Workers Regulation (Regulation 492/2011). With regard to workers, the latter is the more important one as it sets out the specific rights for workers and their families.[46] In addition to outlawing access restrictions to the labour market of the host State,[47] the Regulation also confirms the principle of equal treatment during an employment relationship. The central provision here is Article 7, which states:

[44] In this case, the Court even accepted the possibility that the primary right-holder might derive residency rights from his dependent children, but only if s/he is the 'primary carer' of the children (see *ibid.*, para. 75: 'In the light of the foregoing, the answer to the second question must be that where children have the right to reside in a host Member State in order to attend general educational courses pursuant to [Article 10 of Regulation 492/11], that provision must be interpreted as entitling the parent who is the primary carer of those children, irrespective of his nationality, to reside with them in order to facilitate the exercise of that right notwithstanding the fact that the parents have meanwhile divorced or that the parent who has the status of citizen of the European Union has ceased to be a migrant worker in the host Member State'). In this case, the primary carer was Mrs Baumbast, which left Mr Baumbast to search for an alternative way to obtain residency rights. He eventually found them under the citizenship provisions of the Treaty. On this aspect of the ruling, see section 4(a) below.

[45] See now generally Arts. 12 and 13 of Citizenship Directive (n. 9 above) respectively dealing with the 'Retention of the right of residence by family members in the event of death or departure of the Union citizen' and the 'Retention of the right of residence by family members in the event of divorce, annulment of marriage or termination of registered partnership'.

[46] Regulation 492/2011 (n. 8 above). The Regulation has three chapters. Ch. 1 deals with 'Equality, Equal Treatment and Workers' Families'. Ch. 2 concerns 'Clearance of Vacancies and Applications for Employment'. Finally, Ch. 3 sets up a 'Committee for ensuring close cooperation between the Member States in matters concerning the freedom of movement of workers and their employment'. The principal rights are set out in Ch. 1 of the Regulation, which is divided into three sections: s. 1 is on 'Eligibility for Employment' (Arts. 1–6); s. 2 deals with 'Employment and Equality of Treatment' (Arts. 7–9); while s. 3 concerns 'Workers' Families' (Art. 10).

[47] See Art. 4(1) of the Regulation: 'Provisions laid down by law, regulation or administrative action of the Member States which restrict by number or percentage the employment of foreign nationals in any undertaking, branch of activity or region, or at a national level, shall not apply to nationals of the other Member States.'

> 1. A worker who is a national of a Member State may not, in the territory of another Member State, be *treated differently from national workers by reason of his nationality* in respect of any conditions of employment and work, in particular as regards remuneration, dismissal, and, should he become unemployed, reinstatement or re-employment.
> 2. He shall enjoy the *same social and tax advantages as national workers*.[48]

Despite the direct effect of Article 45 TFEU, Article 7 of the Regulation plays a profound role in the case law. It provides a negative expression of the equal treatment principle in paragraph 1, and a positive expression of that principle in paragraph 2.

aa. Discriminatory Measures I: Article 7(1) of the Regulation

Is Article 7(1) inspired by a discrimination rationale? And, if so, which one? It is clear that the provision captures direct discrimination, like lower pay for foreign workers. In *Sotgiu*,[49] the Court also clarified that the formulation 'by reason of his nationality' was not confined to direct discrimination.

> The rules regarding equality of treatment, both in the Treaty and in Article 7 of Regulation [492/2011], forbid not only overt discrimination by reason of nationality but also *all covert forms of discrimination* which, by the application of other criteria of differentiation, lead in fact to the same result.[50]

Article 7(1) of the Regulation thus covers direct and indirect discrimination. Subsequent jurisprudence thereby crystallised two situations in which national laws would appear to be *indirectly* discriminatory.[51] The first situation concerns national laws that 'although applicable irrespective of nationality' nonetheless 'affect essentially migrant workers or the great majority of those affected are migrant workers'.[52] Where national legislation treats workers differently on grounds of their origin or residence, this *could* be 'tantamount, as regards their practical effect, to discrimination on the grounds of nationality'.[53] By contrast, the second situation arises where national laws 'are indistinctly applicable but can more easily be satisfied by national workers than by migrant workers or where there is a risk that they may operate to the particular detriment of migrant workers'.[54] Unless the differential treatment can here be objectively justified, both types of national laws would violate Article 7(1) of the Regulation.

---

[48] *Ibid.*, Art. 7 (emphasis added).
[49] Case 152/73, *Sotgiu* v. *Deutsche Bundespost* [1974] ECR 153.
[50] *Ibid.*, para. 11 (emphasis added).
[51] See Case C-237/94, *O'Flynn* v. *Adjudication Officer* [1996] ECR I-2617.
[52] *Ibid.*, para. 18 (with extensive references to the case law).
[53] *Ibid.*   [54] *Ibid.* (with extensive references to the case law).

The discrimination logic governing Article 7(1) was recently confirmed in *Landeskliniken*.[55] Dealing with a promotion scheme for employees of a local authority that was tied to periods of service completed with that authority, the Court summarised its jurisprudence neatly as follows:

> Article 7(1) of Regulation No 492/2011 constitutes merely the specific expression of the principle of non-discrimination laid down in Article 45(2) TFEU within the specific field of conditions of employment and work and must therefore be interpreted in the same way as Article 45(2) TFEU ... The equal treatment rule laid down in Article 45 TFEU and in Article 7 of Regulation No 492/2011 prohibits not only overt discrimination by reason of nationality but also all covert forms of discrimination which, through the application of other distinguishing criteria, lead in fact to the same result.
>
> Unless objectively justified and proportionate to the aim pursued, a provision of national law – even if it applies regardless of nationality – must be regarded as indirectly discriminatory if it is intrinsically liable to affect migrant workers more than national workers and if there is a consequent risk that it will place the former at a particular disadvantage. *In order for a measure to be treated as being indirectly discriminatory, it is not necessary for it to have the effect of placing at an advantage all the nationals of the State in question or of placing at a disadvantage only nationals of other Member States, but not nationals of the State in question.*
>
> In the present case, by refusing to take into account in their entirety any relevant periods of service that a migrant worker has completed with an employer established in a Member State other than the Republic of Austria, the national legislation at issue in the main proceedings is liable to affect migrant workers more than national workers, placing the former at a particular disadvantage as they will in all likelihood have accrued professional experience in a Member State other than the Republic of Austria[.][56]

bb. *Discriminatory Measures II: Article 7 (2) of the Regulation*

A positive expression of the equal treatment rights for migrant workers is set out in Article 7(2) of the Regulation. Foreign workers are here granted 'the same social and tax advantages as national workers'.[57] This provision was originally given a restrictive interpretation which limited the benefits in Article 7(2) to those that 'being connected with employment, are to benefit the workers themselves'.[58] Subsequently, however, the notion of 'social advantage' received a wide teleological meaning. In *Cristini*,[59] the Court found the phrase to refer to

---

[55] Case C-514/12, *Zentralbetriebsrat der gemeinnützigen Salzburger Landeskliniken Betriebs* v. *Land Salzburg*, EU:C:2013:799.

[56] *Ibid.*, paras. 23–8 (emphasis added).

[57] In Case 316/85, *Centre public d'aide sociale de Courcelles* v. *Lebon* [1987] ECR 2811, the Court originally excluded job-seekers from the scope of Art. 7(2) of then (ex-)Regulation 1612/68. This judgment has, however, been partly overruled in Case C-138/02, *Collins* v. *Secretary of State for Work and Pensions* [2004] ECR I-2703.

[58] Case 76/72, *Michel S.* v. *Fonds national de reclassement social des handicaps* [1973] ECR 457, para. 9.

[59] Case 32/75, *Cristini* v. *SNCF* [1975] ECR 1085.

'all social and tax advantages, *whether or not attached to the contract of employment*';[60] and this included travel reductions in fares for large families offered by the State.

This definition was confirmed in *Lair*.[61] The Court here broadened the concept of social advantage to all advantages which entailed 'the possibility of improving [a worker's] living and working conditions and promoting his social advancement'.[62] This included all advantages that

> are generally granted to national workers primarily because of their status as workers or by virtue of the mere fact of their residence on the national territory and whose extension to workers who are nationals of other Member States therefore seems likely to facilitate the mobility of such workers within the [Union].[63]

However, as under Article 7(1) of the Regulation, Member States are entitled to justify differential treatment 'if it is based on objective considerations that are independent of the nationality of the persons concerned and proportionate to the legitimate aim of the national provisions'.[64] A residence requirement might thus be legitimate, where a Member States wishes 'to ensure that there is a *genuine* link between an applicant for an allowance in the nature of a social advantage within the meaning of Article 7(2) of Regulation'.[65]

cc. Non-discriminatory Measures adopted by Member States

What about *non*-discriminatory restrictions to the free movement of workers? While much of the case law on workers focuses on discriminatory national laws, the Court accepts that non-discriminatory measures can equally fall within the scope of Article 45 TFEU:

> It is settled case-law that Article [45 TFEU] prohibits not only all discrimination, direct or indirect, based on nationality, but also national rules which are applicable irrespective of the nationality of the workers concerned but impede their freedom of movement.[66]

---

[60] *Ibid.*, para. 13 (emphasis added).
[61] Case 39/86 *Lair* v. *Universität Hannover*. [62] *Ibid.*, para. 20.
[63] *Ibid.*, para. 21. The Court has thus refused to consider a World War service invalidity pension as a social advantage (see Case 207/78, *Even and ONPTS* [1979] ECR 2019, para. 24: 'Such a benefit, which is based on a scheme of national recognition, cannot therefore be considered as an advantage granted to a national worker by reason primarily of his status of worker or resident on the national territory and for that reason does not fulfil the essential characteristics of the "social advantages" referred to in Art. 7(2) of Regulation [492/211]').
[64] Case C-138/02, *Collins* v. *Secretary of State for Work and Pensions*, para. 66.
[65] *Ibid.*, para. 67. On the 'real link' jurisprudence, see C. O'Brian, 'Real Links, Abstract Rights and False Alarms: The Relationship between the ECJ's "Real Link" Case Law and National Solidarity' (2008) 33 *EL Rev.* 643.
[66] Case C-464/02, *Commission* v. *Denmark* [2005] ECR I-7929, para. 45.

The famous confirmation of that possibility is *Bosman*.[67] The case concerned a professional football rule according to which a footballer could not be employed by another club unless the latter paid a transfer or training fee. This was a non-discriminatory rule that applied to nationals and non-nationals alike. Nonetheless, the Court here found:

> Provisions which preclude or deter a national of a Member State from leaving his country of origin in order to exercise his right to freedom of movement therefore constitute an obstacle to that freedom even if they apply without regard to the nationality of the workers concerned … Since they provide that a professional footballer may not pursue his activity with a new club established in another Member State unless it has paid his former club a transfer fee agreed upon between the two clubs or determined in accordance with the regulations of the sporting associations, the said rules constitute an obstacle to freedom of movement for workers.[68]

Expressly rejecting a comparison to the Court's *Keck* judgment, because the contested rules would '*directly affect players' access to the employment market in other Member States*',[69] the Court here found that the national rules violated Article 45 and thus needed justification.

The Union has thus embraced a 'federal' integration model for the free movement of workers. It curbs the internal sovereignty of each Member State – even with regard to its own citizens – when the national rule adopted hinders access to the labour market of other Member States. In *Commission* v. *Cyprus*,[70] the Court for example condemned a national rule according to which a Cypriot civil servant would lose his future pension rights if s/he resigned from her employment before the age of 45 – regardless of whether s/he left for a job abroad or a private job in Cyprus. In the words of the Court:

> While the legislation at issue in the present case applies both to Cypriot civil servants choosing to resign in order to work in the private sector in their Member State of origin and to those resigning and leaving that Member State in order to work in another Member State, within an EU institution or other international organisation, the fact remains that that legislation may restrict the freedom of movement of the latter category of civil servants *preventing or deterring them from leaving their Member State of origin to take up employment in another Member State* … Such legislation directly affects the access of Cypriot civil servants to the employment market in Member States other than the Republic of Cyprus and is thus *capable of impeding freedom of movement for workers*.[71]

---

[67] Case C-415/93, *Union royale belge des sociétés de football association ASBL* v. *Jean-Marc Bosman*.

[68] *Ibid.*, paras. 96 and 100.

[69] *Ibid.*, para. 103 (emphasis added). On this point, see also Case C-176/96, *Lehtonen et al.* v. *Fédération royale belge des sociétés de basket-ball* [2000] ECR I-2681, paras. 49–50.

[70] Case C-515/14, *Commission* v. *Cyprus*.

[71] *Ibid.*, para. 47 (emphasis added).

d. Positive Integration: National Social Security Systems

With the rise of the 'welfare State' in the twentieth century, many States set up schemes designed to guarantee the social protection of workers.[72] The central aim of these welfare schemes is to provide social guarantees against the eventuality of not being able to make a living through labour. The two traditional ways to achieve this aim are 'social insurance' and 'social assistance'. Insurance-based systems rely on social contributions by active workers (and their employers). They are often compulsory and will typically provide coverage against the worst forms of work-related risks, such as accidents, sickness or unemployment. By contrast, assistance-based models are designed to offer a (flat) minimum rate of financial help. They are financed by the public purse through general taxation.

National social security systems generally only pay benefits to workers employed or resident in their State. This 'principle of territoriality' however poses serious problems for the free movement of workers. From the very beginning, the Treaties therefore contained a legislative competence to coordinate the national social security systems. It can today be found in Article 48, which states:

> The European Parliament and the Council shall, acting in accordance with the ordinary legislative procedure, adopt such measures in the field of social security as are necessary to provide freedom of movement for workers; to this end, they shall make arrangements to secure for employed and self-employed[73] migrant workers and their dependants:
> (a) aggregation, for the purpose of acquiring and retaining the right to benefit and of calculating the amount of benefit, of all periods taken into account under the laws of the several countries;
> (b) payment of benefits to persons resident in territories of Member States.

[72] The birth of the modern social security system is often credited to the German Chancellor Bismarck (1815–98), who introduced it into Imperial Germany at the end of the nineteenth century. For the birth of social security in the United States, see the 1934 US Social Security Act.

[73] The original provision within the E(E)C Treaty only referred to workers in the traditional sense, and for that reason the Union had to have recourse to Art. 352 TFEU to adopt social security legislation that would also cover self-employed persons. Since the Lisbon Treaty, the concept of 'worker' in Art. 48 TFEU is however wider than that of Art. 45 TFEU, as it now also includes self-employed 'workers'. The legislation adopted under Art. 48 TFEU can thus cover the free movement of workers, freedom of establishment and services for natural persons without having recourse to Art. 352 TFEU. However, in order to capture non-economically active migrants, the residual competence would still be needed.

Due to the financial implications involved, this competence is a 'sensitive' competence for the Member States.[74] It has traditionally been used to adopt 'coordination' measures, that is: measures that do not attempt to harmonise the diverse national security systems but rather – more modestly – try to coordinate their (personal) scope of application.[75]

aa. National Coordination: Regulation 883/2004

The coordination of the national social security systems is today achieved by Regulation 883/2004.[76] The core rationale underlying the Regulation is this:

> It is necessary to subject persons moving within the [Union] to the social security scheme of only one single Member State in order to avoid overlapping of the applicable provisions of national legislation and the complications which could result therefrom. Within the [Union] there is in principle no justification for making social security rights dependent on the place of residence of the person concerned; nevertheless, in specific cases, in particular as regards special benefits linked to the economic and social context of the person involved, the place of residence could be taken into account.[77]

---

[74] For that reason, Art. 48 [2] TFEU contains an additional federal safeguard, which states: 'Where a member of the Council declares that a draft legislative act referred to in the first subparagraph would affect important aspects of its social security system, including its scope, cost or financial structure, or would affect the financial balance of that system, it may request that the matter be referred to the European Council. In that case, the ordinary legislative procedure shall be suspended. After discussion, the European Council shall, within four months of this suspension, either: (a) refer the draft back to the Council, which shall terminate the suspension of the ordinary legislative procedure; or (b) take no action or request the Commission to submit a new proposal; in that case, the act originally proposed shall be deemed not to have been adopted.'

[75] See R. Cornelissen, 'The Principle of Territoriality and the Community Regulations on Social Security' (1996) 33 *CML Rev.* 439 at 443: 'It is clear that the Regulations pursue only a limited objective; they in no way affect the freedom of Member States to determine the rules of their own social security systems'; and Joined Cases C-611–12/10, *Hudzinski v. Agentur für Arbeit Wesel – Familienkasse and others* EU:C:2012:339, para. 42: '[S]ince Article 48 TFEU provides for the coordination, and not the harmonization, of the legislation of the Member States, substantive and procedural differences between the social security schemes of individual Member States, and hence in the rights of persons who are insured persons there, are unaffected by that provision, as each Member State retains the power to determine in its legislation, in compliance with EU law, the conditions pursuant to which benefits may be granted under a social security scheme.'

[76] Regulation 883/2004 on the coordination of social security systems [2004] OJ L 166/1. The famous predecessor here was Regulation 1408/71 on the application of social security schemes to employed persons and their families moving within the Community [1971] OJ English Special Edition 416. For a comprehensive account of both Regulations and the case law thereunder, see J. Pennings, *European Social Security Law* (Intersentia, 2010).

[77] Regulation 883/2004, preambles 15 and 16.

The structure and content of the Regulation is complex and can be found in Table 15.2. The Regulation defines its material scope by reference to the types of social security benefit it covers;[78] and, importantly, the Regulation does not apply to social assistance.[79] The distinction between *social security* (covered) and *social assistance* (not covered) is thus vital.[80] When the Union was founded, that distinction was relatively clear in all Member States: a social security system referred to the insurance system funded by worker and employer contributions that guaranteed a 'right' to payment, whereas social assistance referred to a non-contributory and need-based payment by the State so as to provide a minimum standard of living.

This clear distinction has however gradually become blurred – partly thanks to the European Court's expansive definition of social security benefits.[81] The Union legislator has subsequently codified this development and the (recast) Regulation today expressly includes – in addition to social security benefits – the new category of 'special non-contributory cash benefits' (in Chapter 9 of Title III). These benefits are non-contributory benefits because they are not

Table 15.2 Regulation 883/2004 – Structure

Regulation – Titles		Title III – Chapters	
Title I	General Provisions (Articles 1–10)	Chapter 1	Sickness, maternity and equivalent paternity benefits (Articles 17–35)
Title II	Determination of the Legislation Applicable (Articles 11–16)	Chapter 2	Benefits in respect of accidents at work and occupational diseases (Articles 36–41)
Title III	Special Provisions Concerning the Various Categories of Benefits (Articles 17–70)	Chapter 3	Death grants (Articles 42–3)
		Chapter 4	Invalidity benefits (Articles 44–9)
Title IV	Administrative Commission and Advisory Committee (Articles 71–5)	Chapter 5	Old-age and survivors' pensions (Articles 50–60)
Title V	Miscellaneous Provisions (Articles 76–86)	Chapter 6	Unemployment benefits (Articles 61–5)
Title VI	Transitional and Final Provisions (Articles 87–91)	Chapter 7	Pre-retirement benefits (Article 66)
Annexes I–XI		Chapter 8	Family benefits (Articles 67–9)
		Chapter 9	Special non-contributory cash benefits (Article 70)

---

[78] *Ibid.*, Article 3.   [79] *Ibid.*, Art. 3(5).

[80] For a recent case dealing with the question whether 'child tax credit' is one or the other, see Case C-308/14, *European Commission* v. *United Kingdom*, EU:C:2016:436.

[81] For a good and (brief) overview of the older and newer case law, see M. Cousins, 'Social Security, Social Assistance, and "Special Non-Contributory Benefits": The Never-Ending Story (2007) 9 *European Journal of Social Security* 95.

financed by personal contributions but by general taxation; and they are 'special' because their purpose comes close to that of a social security system.[82] However, unlike social security benefits that can generally be 'exported' when the worker moves to another Member State, special non-contributory benefits, by contrast, 'shall be provided exclusively in the Member State in which the persons reside'.[83] A Member State is thus, under the Regulation, entitled to "cut" these special benefits if the claimant wishes to move to other Member State.

Once a benefit falls within the scope of the Regulation, what happens? The principal aim of the Regulation is *not to harmonise* national benefits but to *coordinate* them. It thus does not limit a Member State's ability to define the *material* scope of any of its social security benefits; yet it does limits its ability to freely determine their personal scope.

The four core principles of Union coordination must be seen in this light. First, according to the principle of equal treatment, *foreign* workers will generally 'enjoy the same benefits and be subject to the same obligations under the legislation of [the competent] Member State as the nationals thereof'.[84] Second, according to the principle of *aggregation*, Member States are under the general obligation to 'take into account periods of insurance, employment, self-employment or residence completed under the legislation of any other Member State as though they were periods competed under the legislation which it applies'.[85] Third, according to the *no-overlap* principle, the Regulation will, as a

---

[82] Regulation 883/2004, Art. 70 thereby defines these benefits as follows: 'For the purposes of this Chapter, "special non-contributory cash benefits" means those which: (a) are intended to provide either: (i) supplementary, substitute or ancillary cover against the risks covered by the branches of social security referred to in Article 3(1), and which guarantee the persons concerned a minimum subsistence income having regard to the economic and social situation in the Member State concerned; or (ii) solely specific protection for the disabled, closely linked to the said person's social environment in the Member State concerned, and (b) where the financing exclusively derives from compulsory taxation intended to cover general public expenditure and the conditions for providing and for calculating the benefits are not dependent on any contribution in respect of the beneficiary. However, benefits provided to supplement a contributory benefit shall not be considered to be contributory benefits for this reason alone, and (c) are listed in Annex X.' For an excellent analysis of the case law and problems generated by these 'mixed' benefits, see A. P. van der Mei, 'Regulation 1408/71 and Coordination of Special Non-contributory Benefit Schemes' (2002) 27 *EL Rev.* 551.

[83] Regulation 883/2004, Art. 70(4). This rule of non-exportability has made the distinction between social security benefit proper and special non-contributory benefit a hard line to draw, see Case C-215/99, *Jauch* v. *Pensionsversicherungsanstalt der Arbeiter* [2001] ECR I-1901; Case C-43/99, *Leclere and Deaconescu* v. *Caisse nationale des prestations familiales* [2001] ECR I-4265; Case C-406/04, *De Cuyper* v. *Office national de l'emploi* [2006] ECR I-6947.

[84] Regulation 883/2004, Art. 4.

[85] *Ibid.*, Art. 6. As Cornelissen, 'Principle of Territoriality' (n. 75 above), 451 explains: 'A worker who claims an old-age pension after having worked for 14 years in Italy and 4 years in Germany fulfils neither the conditions under Italian legislation for an Italian pension (15 to 20 years of insurance are needed in Italy to be entitled to a pension) nor the conditions under German legislation for a German pension (a minimum of 5 years is needed in Germany). In order to avoid these consequences of the "principle of territoriality", the Regulations provide for the aggregation of periods of insurance completed in the Member States.'

rule, 'neither confer nor maintain the right to several benefits of the same kind for one and the same period of compulsory insurance'.[86] Finally, and relatedly, according to the *single-legislation* principle, persons to whom the Regulation applies 'shall be subject to the legislation of a single Member State only'.[87] It is the last principle that is of particular interest.

bb. In Particular: The 'Single-Legislation' Principle

A worker that resides in one Member States but works in another could be tempted to apply for the same social security benefits in two different Member States. By contrast, a Member State might, in such a situation, be more than happy to point to the other (!) Member State having to pay a benefit. In order to avoid such temptations, the Regulations sets out detailed rules on which State is competent and is thereby based on the principle that only one Member State is competent. For workers this will generally be the State of employment;[88] yet there are many special additional rules that are laid down in Title II of the Regulation (Articles 11–16).

The Court has traditionally insisted on a strict interpretation of the single-legislation principle. It has thus held:

> The provisions of Title II [of Regulation 883/2004] constitute a complete system of conflict rules the effect of which is to *divest the legislature of each Member State of the power to determine the ambit and the conditions for the application of its national legislation so far as the persons who are subject thereto and the territory within which the provisions of national law take effect are concerned.*[89]

Put differently: since only one State is exclusively competent to grant social security benefits, a worker should never be entitled to any benefits from more than one State because the very intention behind the Regulation is 'to prevent the concurrent application of a number of national legislative systems and the complications which might ensure'.[90]

This rule has however been softened in *Bosmann*.[91] Mrs Bosmann originally worked in Germany, where both of her children studied at university. Having paid German income tax, she was entitled to German child benefits; yet once she took up a new post in the Netherlands, the German authorities discontinued

---

[86] Regulation 883/2004, Art. 10.   [87] *Ibid.*, Art. 11(1).

[88] This principle is called the *lex loci laboris* and is established in Art. 11(3)(a) of Regulation 883/2004. For a critical assessment of the principle, see F. Pennings, 'Coordination of Social Security on the Basis of the State-of-employment Principle: Time for an Alternative?' (2005) 42 *CML Rev.* 67.

[89] Case 302/84, *Ten Holder* v. *Bestuur van de Nieuwe Algemene Bedrijfsvereniging* [1986] ECR 1821, para. 21 (emphasis added). This formula has become a standard formula in EU social security law.

[90] Case C-275/96, *Kuusijärvi* v. *Riksförsäkringsverket* [1998] ECR I-3419, para. 28.

[91] Case C-352/06, *Brigitte Bosmann* v. *Bundesagentur für Arbeit – Familienkasse Aachen* [2008] ECR I-3827.

these benefits on the grounds that Dutch legislation was now exclusively competent with regard to these benefits. The Dutch legislation however did not grant any child benefits to children aged over 18, and Bosmann therefore brought proceedings to force the German authorities to pay the benefit. In its ruling, the Court of Justice now held that 'the Member State of residence cannot be deprived of the right to grant child benefit to those resident within its territory'; yet it also insisted that Union law could 'not require the competent German authorities to grant Mrs Bosmann the family benefit in question'.[92]

The Court here established that the single-legislation principle is not 'prohibitively' exclusive. A Member State that is technically not the 'competent' State under the Regulation consequently 'has the power, but not the obligation' to grant social security benefits.[93] This exception (!) to the single State principle has been confirmed in subsequent jurisprudence.[94]

2. Establishment I: Natural Persons

Freedom of establishment constitutes the second source of European rights concerning the free movement of persons. It guarantees the free movement of *self-employed* persons (and companies). In order to achieve this aim, the relevant Treaty chapter contains a central prohibition on illegal national barriers. It can be found in Article 49 and states:

> Within the framework of the provisions set out below, restrictions on the freedom of establishment of nationals of a Member State in the territory of another Member State shall be prohibited. Such prohibition shall also apply to restrictions on the setting-up of agencies, branches or subsidiaries by nationals of any Member State established in the territory of any Member State.
>
> Freedom of establishment shall include the right to take up and pursue activities as self-employed persons and to set up and manage undertakings, in particular companies or firms within the meaning of the second paragraph of Article 54, under the conditions laid down for its own nationals by the law of the country where such establishment is effected, subject to the provisions of the Chapter relating to capital.

The provision has been given direct effect.[95] It will thus autonomously grant European rights to individuals and will be discussed in section (a) below. Article 49 is complemented by two legislative competences designed to push for positive

---

[92] *Ibid.*, paras. 27 and 31.

[93] Joined Cases C-611–12/10, *Hudzinski* v. *Agentur für Arbeit Wesel* and *Wawrzyniak* v. *Agentur für Arbeit Mönchengladbach* EU:C:2012:339.

[94] See Case C-611–12/10, *Hudzinski*; Case C-394/13, *B*, EU:C:2014:2199; C-382/13, *Franzen and others*, EU:C:2015:261. For a first discussion of this move 'from possibility to duty', see N. Rennuy, 'The Emergence of a Parallel System of Social Security Coordination' (2013) 50 *CML Rev.* 1221 at 1247ff.

[95] The provision was given direct effect in Case 2/74, *Reyners* v. *Belgium* [1974] ECR 631. On this controversial constitutional choice, see Chapter 3, section 1(a).

integration in this area. According to Article 50, the Union may generally adopt legislative measures 'in order to attain freedom of establishment as regards a particular activity'.[96] Furthermore, Article 53 specifically grants the Union a competence to adopt 'directives for the mutual recognition of diplomas, certificates and other evidence of formal qualifications and for the coordination of the provisions laid down by law, regulation or administrative action in Member States concerning the taking-up and pursuit of activities as self-employed persons'.[97] While unable to deal with the various legislative instruments in this context, section (b) below analyses the most important instrument – certainly for lawyers – here.

a. Negative Integration under Article 49

aa. Personal Scope: Self-employed Persons

The personal scope of Article 49 captures 'self-employed' persons.[98] Like workers, these self-employed persons will need to be engaged in a genuine economic activity. However, unlike workers, self-employed persons will not work under the direction of an employer and will not receive a 'salary' compensating for their 'subordination'. The personal scopes of Articles 45 and 49 are thus 'mutually exclusive'.[99] The definition of 'worker' thereby negatively determines the personal scope of the freedom of establishment. Importantly, self-employed persons might be natural or legal persons, for Article 54 TFEU expressly provides that the freedom of establishment covers companies and firms.[100]

Self-employed persons (and companies) will typically produce goods or perform services. And while there are no delineation problems with regard to goods, the Union legal order has had to delimit the personal scope of Article 49 from the perspective of the free movement of services because this third freedom protects, among other things, persons offering a service in another State.[101]

What, then, is the characteristic feature underlying the freedom of establishment? In *Gebhard*, the Court has identified it as follows:

> The right of establishment, provided for in Articles [49] to [54] of the Treaty, is granted both to legal persons within the meaning of Article [54] and to natural persons who are nationals of a Member State of the [Union]. Subject to the exceptions and conditions laid down, it allows all types of self-employed activity to be taken up and pursued on the territory of any other Member State, undertakings to be formed and operated, and agencies, branches or subsidiaries to be set up …

---

[96] Art. 50(1) TFEU.   [97] *Ibid.*, Art. 53(1).

[98] The personal scope of Art. 49 TFEU also covers the family members of self-employed persons. For the general rules on family member rights, see section 1(b) above.

[99] Case C-55/94, *Gebhard* v. *Consiglio dell'Ordine degli Avvocati e Procuratori di Milano* [1995] ECR I-4165, para. 20.

[100] This aspect of the freedom of establishment will be explored in section 3 below.

[101] According to Art. 56 TFEU, 'restrictions on freedom to provide services within the Union shall be prohibited in respect of nationals of Member States who are established in a Member State other than that of the person for whom the services are intended'.

> The concept of establishment within the meaning of the Treaty is therefore a very broad one, allowing a [Union] national to participate, on a stable and continuous basis, in the economic life of a Member State other than his State of origin and to profit there from, so contributing to economic and social interpenetration within the [Union] in the sphere of activities as self-employed persons. In contrast, where the provider of services moves to another Member State, the provisions of the chapter on services, in particular the third paragraph of Article [57], envisage that he is to pursue his activity there on a temporary basis.[102]

The decisive criterion distinguishing 'established' service providers from 'temporary' service providers is thus the 'stable and continuous basis' on which the former participate in the economy of the host Member State. A 'stable and continuous' presence will trigger the personal scope of the freedom of establishment. However, importantly, the concept of establishment will not require exclusive presence in the host State (as this would rule out secondary establishment). While the applicability of Article 49 is determined by the 'duration', 'regularity, periodicity or continuity' of the services provided,[103] such a presence will not even need to take the form of a 'branch' or 'agency' but may consist of an 'office'.[104]

Importantly, and despite its unfortunate wording, Article 49 does not only apply to 'restrictions on the freedom of establishment of nationals of a Member State in the territory of another Member State', but will also prohibit restrictions imposed on nationals by their *own State*. This double function of Article 49 was clarified in *Knoors*.[105] In this case a Dutch national, who had qualified and worked as a plumber in Belgium, wished to return to the Netherlands. Knoors applied to the competent Dutch authorities for authorisation to carry on his profession in his country of origin; yet the authorisation was refused on the grounds that he did not possess the necessary Dutch qualifications. Could Article 49 TFEU here be used by a national against his own State? The Court indeed held this to be the case:

> Although it is true that the provisions of the Treaty relating to establishment... cannot be applied to situations which are purely internal to a Member State, the position nevertheless remains that the reference in Art. [49] to 'nationals of a Member State' who wish to establish themselves 'in the territory of another Member State' cannot be interpreted in such a way as to exclude from the benefit of [Union] law a given Member State's own nationals when the latter, owing to the fact that they have

---

[102] Case C-55/94, *Gebhard*, paras. 23–6 (emphasis added). The third paragraph of Art. 57 TFEU states that '[w]ithout prejudice to the provisions of the Chapter relating to the right of establishment, the person providing a service may, in order to do so, temporarily pursue his activity in the Member State where the service is provided, under the same conditions as are imposed by that State on its own nationals'.

[103] Case C-55/94, *Gebhard*, para. 27.

[104] See Case 205/84, *Commission* v. *Germany* [1986] ECR 3755, para. 21.

[105] See Case 115/78, *Knoors* v. *Staatssecretaris van Economische Zaken* [1979] ECR 399.

lawfully resided on the territory of another Member State and have there acquired a trade qualification which is recognized by the provisions of [Union] law, are, with regard to their state of origin, in a situation which may be assimilated to that of any other person enjoying the rights and liberties guaranteed by the Treaty.[106]

The scope of the freedom of establishment thus covers – like the free movement of workers – not only restrictions by the host State but also restrictions by the home State under the condition that the national of the latter either wishes to leave or has already exercised his freedom of movement.

bb. Material Scope: Discrimination and Beyond

Article 49 prohibits 'restrictions' on the freedom of establishment. The prohibition thereby expressly covers primary and secondary establishment. Primary establishment occurs where a person establishes himself for the first time. The right to establishment is, however, 'not confined to the right to create a single establishment within the [Union]', but includes the 'freedom to set up and maintain, subject to observance of the professional rules of conduct, more than one place of work within the [Union]'.[107] Secondary establishment therefore covers 'the setting-up of agencies, branches or subsidiaries by nationals of any Member State [already] established in the territory *of any Member State*'.[108]

Which types of restrictions on primary or secondary establishment will Article 49 prohibit? The wording of the provision clearly covers discriminatory measures. This includes *directly* discriminatory national laws,[109] and equally prohibits *indirect* discrimination on grounds of nationality.[110]

A good illustration for direct discrimination is offered in *Reyners*.[111] The plaintiff had been born in Brussels to Dutch parents and had retained his Dutch nationality. Having been resident in Belgium all his life, he had received his legal education there and had graduated with a Belgian law degree. Yet when applying to become a barrister, his application was denied because a 1919 Belgian law stated that only Belgian nationals could exercise the legal profession. Such a direct discrimination on ground of nationality was clearly in breach of Article 49 TFEU.

A good illustration for indirect discrimination can be found in *Klopp*.[112] The case involved a German barrister registered with the Düsseldorf (Germany) bar, who had applied for secondary registration at the Paris (France) bar. His

---

[106] *Ibid.*, para. 24. For a recent confirmation of this rule, see Case C-386/14, *Groupe Steria* v. *Ministère des Finances et des Comptes publics*, EU:C:2015:524, para. 14.

[107] Case 107/83, *Ordre des avocats au Barreau de Paris* v. *Klopp* [1984] ECR 2971, para. 19.

[108] Art. 49 TFEU – first indent (emphasis added).

[109] See Case 2/74, *Reyners* v. *Belgium*; Case C-221/89, *The Queen* v. *Secretary of State for Transport, ex p. Factortame (Factortame II)* [1991] ECR I-3905.

[110] Case 71/76, *Thieffry* v. *Conseil de l'ordre des avocats à la cour de Paris* [1977] ECR 765; Case C-64/08, *Engelmann* [2010] ECR I-8219.

[111] Case 2/74, Reyners v. Belgium [1974] ECR 631.

[112] Case 107/83, *Ordre des avocats au Barreau de Paris* v. *Onno Klopp* [1984] ECR 2971.

application there was however rejected on the grounds that he did not satisfy the French law on barristers that required them to join or establish a set of chambers in one place only. This law was not directly discriminatory, since it also applied to French barristers; yet the Court had no problem in finding an indirect discrimination to have taken place:

> It should be emphasized that under the second paragraph of Article [49] freedom of establishment includes access to and the pursuit of the activities of self-employed persons 'under the conditions laid down for its own nationals by the law of the country where such establishment is effected'. It follows from that provision and its context that in the absence of specific [Union] rules on the matter each Member State is free to regulate the exercise of the legal profession in its territory. Nevertheless that rule does not mean that the legislation of a Member State may require a lawyer to have only one establishment throughout the [Union] territory. Such a restrictive interpretation would mean that a lawyer once established in a particular Member State would be able to enjoy the freedom of the Treaty to establish himself in another Member State only at the price of abandoning the establishment he already had.[113]

Whether the scope of Article 49 also covered non-discriminatory measures remained uncertain for some time.[114] In *Vlassopoulou*,[115] the Court had to deal with a Greek lawyer asking for permission to practise at the German bar. The relevant State ministry rejected her request out of hand, since she did not possess the qualifying German law degrees. She appealed on the grounds that the Justice Ministry should have taken into account that she had a German law doctorate and had practised German law as a paralegal for about five years. The Court agreed:

> [E]ven if applied without any discrimination on the basis of nationality, national requirements concerning qualifications may have the effect of hindering nationals of the other Member States in the exercise of their right of establishment guaranteed to them by Article [49 TFEU]. That could be the case if the national rules in question took no account of the knowledge and qualifications already acquired by the person concerned in another Member State.[116]

This — almost casual — inclusion of non-discriminatory measures into the scope of Article 49 was confirmed in *Gebhard*.[117] The case involved a German lawyer who had, this time, practised law in Italy under the title 'avvocato' without being formally admitted to the Italian bar. This violated the relevant national rules on the organisation of the legal profession; and the Court here unambiguously held that despite their 'non-discriminatory' character, the national rules violated Article 49 because they were 'liable to hinder or make less attractive' the freedom of establishment.[118] This market-access formula potentially covers all

---

[113]   *Ibid.*, paras. 17–18.
[114]   See Case 221/85, *Commission* v. *Belgium* [1987] ECR 719.
[115]   Case C-340/89, *Vlassopoulou* v. *Ministerium für Justiz, Bundes- und Europaangelegenheiten Baden-Württemberg* [1991] ECR I-2357.
[116]   *Ibid.*, para. 15.   [117]   Case C-55/94, *Gebhard*.   [118]   *Ibid.*, para. 37.

types of regulatory barriers. It could thus be seen as an expression of a 'national' reading of Article 49; yet the Court has often insisted that national measures must hinder '[a]ccess to the market' of *foreign* establishments,[119] which builds on a 'federal' model of negative integration in this context.

The potency of the *Gebhard* formula 'liable to hinder or make less attractive' in deregulating national rules is nevertheless impressive. It can clearly be seen in *Blanco Pérez*.[120] Spanish legislation had stipulated that anyone wishing to open a new pharmacy could not do so without authorisation. Potential pharmacists needed to apply for a licence, which was only granted for a particular territorial area and according to the following rule: a new pharmacy could only be opened where it would be servicing a population of 2,800; and, where that number was surpassed, each pharmacy would still need to be at a minimum 250 metres from all others. This was clearly a non-discriminatory rule that applied to foreign and national pharmacists alike; yet the Court still found a violation of Article 49 TFEU that required justification. It held:

> A national rule which makes the establishment of an undertaking from another Member State conditional upon the issue of prior authorisation falls within that category, since it is capable of hindering the exercise by that undertaking of freedom of establishment by preventing it from freely pursuing its activities through a fixed place of business … Secondly, that legislation allows, in each pharmaceutical area, only one pharmacy to be set up per unit of population of 2 800, the opening of a supplementary pharmacy not being permitted until that threshold has been exceeded, when a new pharmacy can be set up for the fraction over 2 000 inhabitants. Thirdly, that legislation precludes pharmacists from being able to pursue an independent economic activity in the premises of their choice, since they are required, in general, to observe a minimum distance of 250 metres in relation to existing pharmacies. *The effect of such rules is to hinder and render less attractive the exercise by pharmacists from other Member States of their activities on Spanish territory through a fixed place of business. Consequently, national legislation such as that at issue in the cases before the referring court constitutes a restriction on the freedom of establishment within the meaning of Article 49 TFEU.*[121]

---

[119] Case C-442/02, *Caixa Bank France* v. *Ministère de l'Économie, des Finances et de l'Industrie* [2004] ECR I-8961, para. 14; and also Case C-400/08, *Commission* v. *Spain* [2011] ECR I-1915, para. 64: 'In that context, it should be borne in mind that the concept of "restriction" for the purposes of Article [49 TFEU] covers measures taken by a Member State which, although applicable without distinction, affect access to the market for undertakings from other Member States and thereby hinder intra-[Union] trade.' For an analysis of the case law on persons in light of the market-access test, see E. Spaventa, *Free Movement of Persons in the European Union: Barriers to Movement in their Constitutional Context* (Kluwer, 2007), ch. 5.

[120] Joined Cases C-570/07 and C-571/07, *Blanco Pérez and Chao Gómez* v. *Consejería de Salud y Servicios Sanitarios and Principado de Asturias* [2010] ECR I-4629.

[121] *Ibid.*, paras. 54–60 (emphasis added). Having found a violation of Art. 49 TFEU, the Court then subjected the national rules to a thorough justification analysis. On the grounds and standard of justification within this context, see section 5 below.

b. Positive Integration under Article 53

The Union enjoys a special competence in Article 53 TFEU for the adoption of directives on the mutual recognition of formal qualifications and the coordination of provisions concerning the taking up of professional activities.[122]

The Union here originally adopted a range of sectoral directives on regulated professions like architects, doctors and lawyers. Recognising the disadvantages of such a vertical (profession-by-profession) approach to harmonisation, the Union gradually began to switch to a more horizontal approach in the context of higher-education diplomas.[123] This horizontal approach culminated in the adoption of Directive 2005/36 on the recognition of professional qualifications;[124] as well as Directive 2006/123 on services in the internal market.[125] And, while the latter shall interest us in the next chapter,[126] the former needs to be analysed in some detail here.

aa. Horizontal Harmonisation: Mutual Recognition of Professional Qualifications

The Professional Qualifications Recognition Directive consolidates and reorganises many older (vertical) measures under a single roof. The Directive is long and complex. Its structure can be seen in Table 15.3. Its central purpose is said to be this:

> This Directive establishes rules according to which a Member State which makes access to or pursuit of a regulated profession in its territory contingent upon possession of specific professional qualifications (referred to hereinafter as the host Member State) shall recognise professional qualifications obtained in one or more other Member States (referred to hereinafter as the home Member State) and which allow the holder of the said qualifications to pursue the same profession there, for access to and pursuit of that profession.[127]

---

[122] Art. 53(1) TFEU.

[123] Ex-Directive 89/48 on a general system for the recognition of higher-education diplomas awarded on completion of professional education and training of at least three years' duration [1989] OJ L 19/16.

[124] Directive 2005/36 on the recognition of professional qualifications [2005] OJ L 255/22. The directive was adopted not only under Art. 53 TFEU but also with the assistance of Arts. 46 TFEU (workers) and Art. 62 TFEU (services); and it thus applies not just to the freedom of establishment.

[125] Directive 2006/123 on services in the internal market [2006] OJ L 376/36.

[126] The 'Services Directive' deals – unsurprisingly – primarily with the provision of services. However, partly based on Art. 53 TFEU, is also contains a chapter on the 'Establishment' of service providers and therefore represents a legislative specification of Art. 49 TFEU. The case law under this chapter of the directive has therefore run in parallel with the 'constitutional' case law under Art. 49 TFEU (see, e.g., Case C-293/14, *Hiebler* v. *Schlagbauer*, EU:C:2015:843 – which is very similar to the legal issues in Joined Cases C-570/07 and C-571/07, *Blanco Pérez and Chao Gómez*).

[127] Directive 2005/36, Art. 1.

Table 15.3 Directive 2005/36 – Structure

Regulation – Titles		Title III – Chapter III – Sections	
Title I	General Provisions	Section 1	General Provisions
Title II	Free Provision of Services	Section 2	Doctors of Medicine
Title III	**Freedom of Establishment**	Section 3	General Care Nurses
	Chapter I: General System	Section 4	Dental Practitioners
	Chapter II: Professional Experience	Section 5	Veterinary Surgeons
	Chapter III: Minimum Coordination	Section 6	Midwives
	Chapter IV Common Provisions	Section 7	Pharmacists
Title IV	Detailed Rules for Pursuing the Profession	Section 8	Architects
Title V	Administrative Cooperation		
Title VI	Other Provisions		

Regulated professions are professions whose access is regulated by public or private law rules. Depending on which kind of regulated profession is at stake, the Directive distinguishes between three techniques of recognition. These three techniques are set out in three chapters in Title III of the Directive. Chapter I sets out a general system of recognition, which is complemented by a special regime for the recognition of professional experience (Chapter II) and an (automatic) recognition regime following the coordination of minimum training conditions (Chapter III).

The first recognition technique represents the residual technique, as it will apply 'to all professions which are not covered by Chapters II and III'.[128] The basic rule here is expressed in Article 13. It requires Member States to mutually recognise a professional qualification or professional experience vis-à-vis applicants possessing a formal qualification issued by another Member State or an 'attestation of competence'. A Member State may however impose compensation measures under Article 14 of the Directive. The provision states:

> Article 13 does not preclude the host Member State from requiring the applicant to complete an adaptation period of up to three years or to take an aptitude test if:
> (a) the duration of the training of which he provides evidence under the terms of Article 13, paragraph 1 or 2, is at least one year shorter than that required by the host Member State;
> (b) the training he has received covers substantially different matters than those covered by the evidence of formal qualifications required in the host Member State;
> (c) the regulated profession in the host Member State comprises one or more regulated professional activities which do not exist in the corresponding profession

---

[128] *Ibid.*, Art. 10.

in the applicant's home Member State within the meaning of Article 4(2), and that difference consists in specific training which is required in the host Member State and which covers substantially different matters from those covered by the applicant's attestation of competence or evidence of formal qualifications.

A more generous recognition regime is applied to professions covered by Chapters II and III. The latter lays down common rules for certain types of professions that make the recognition of national titles automatic. The Court has indeed held that anyone meeting the common requirements set out in the Directive cannot be subject to additional national requirements.[129]

bb. Vertical Harmonisation: Free Movement of Lawyers?

Despite its general scope, the Professional Qualifications Directive does not cover all regulated professions. For example: the legal profession continues to be subject to a set of specific Union directives.[130] The central instrument of vertical harmonisation here is Directive 98/5, which aims to facilitate the establishment of lawyers in a Member State other than that in which they originally qualified.[131]

Studying law, unlike studying medicine, continues to be a very 'national' affair with a legal syllabus full of national subjects. And, as long as, say, English tort law is very different from, French or German tort law, the mutual recognition of legal qualifications will encounter steep obstacles. However, there are of course also common areas of knowledge – European law being one example – in which there exist 'transferable skills', and the Union legislator has tried to capitalise on these common skills and adopted a (relatively) flexible learning-by-doing approach for lawyers wishing to establish themselves in another Member State.

---

[129] For architects, see Case C-365/13, *Ordre des architectes* v. *Belgium*, EU:C:2014:280, esp. para. 24: 'It follows that the system of automatic recognition of professional qualifications provided for, as regards the profession of architect, in Articles 21, 46 and 49 of Directive 2005/36 leaves the Member States no discretion.'

[130] For an academic analysis of the various legal instruments in this context, see J. Lombay, 'Assessing the European Market for Legal Services: Development in the Free Movement of Lawyers in the European Union' (2010) 33 *Fordham International Law Journal* 1629; G. Muller, 'Free Movement of Lawyers within the EU Internal Market: Achievements and Remaining Challenges' (2015) 26 *European Business Law Review* 355.

[131] See Directive 98/5 to facilitate practice of the profession of lawyer on a permanent basis in a Member State other than that in which the qualification was obtained [1998] OJ L 77/36. The following section will not deal with not-yet-fully qualified lawyers. The controversial question here has been whether a law graduate of State A can go to State B to get his professional qualification only to return to State A and practise there as a fully qualified lawyer. (In the past, the most prominent State B has been Spain as it traditionally did not require a professional practice component to become a lawyer but simply deferred to a university degree in law.) For a case here, see Joined Cases C-58/13 and C-59/13, *Torresi and Torresi* v. *Consiglio dell'Ordine degli Avvocati di Macerata*, EU:C:2014:2088.

According to Directive 98/5, any fully qualified lawyer may establish herself in another Member State under her home-country professional title and there may, under certain conditions, immediately give advice on her home state law, European and international law – and even the law of the host state.[132] After a period of practice of three years in the host state, a foreign lawyer can then apply to be admitted to the legal profession of the host state and may even be entitled to practise there under the professional title of the host state.[133]

3. Establishment II: Companies

The 'establishment' chapter within the European Treaties expressly covers companies. The wording of Article 49 TFEU already confirms that the right of establishment prohibits 'restrictions on the setting-up of agencies, branches or subsidiaries by nationals of any Member State established in the territory of any Member State',[134] while it equally protects the right 'to set up and manage undertakings, in particular companies or firms'.[135] Article 50 TFEU then gives the Union a special legislative competence in the field of company mobility. Article 54 TFEU finally removes all doubts. For the provision states:

> Companies or firms formed in accordance with the law of a Member State and having their registered office, central administration or principal place of business within the Union shall, for the purposes of this Chapter, be treated in the same way as natural persons who are nationals of Member States.
>
> 'Companies or firms' means companies or firms constituted under civil or commercial law, including cooperative societies, and other legal persons governed by public or private law, save for those which are non-profit-making.[136]

The provision unconditionally extends the personal scope of the freedom of establishment to legal persons. These legal persons must however be profit-oriented companies (or firms);[137] and they must be formed in

---

[132] *Ibid.*, Arts. 2 and 5.

[133] *Ibid.*, Art. 10, which details a number of different scenarios. On the relationship between the provision and the Professional Qualifications Recognition Directive, see Case C-359/09, *Ebert* v. *Budapesti Ügyvédi Kamara* [2011] ECR I-269.

[134] Art. 49 TFEU – first indent.   [135] *Ibid.* – second indent.

[136] *Ibid.*, Art. 54 (emphasis added). The provision is complemented by *ibid.*, Art. 55, which states: 'Member States shall accord nationals of the other Member States the same treatment as their own nationals as regards participation in the capital of companies or firms within the meaning of Article 54, without prejudice to the application of the other provisions of the Treaties.' On the right to buy shares and its relation to the freedom of establishment and capital, see Chapter 16, section 3(d/aa).

[137] V. Edwards, *EC Company Law* (Oxford University Press, 1999), 338: 'The reference to firms is misleading to common law lawyers, suggesting as it does non-corporate entities: the terms of the Article suggest that only entities with a legal personality are covered, and thus that, for example, English law partnerships are not within the scope of the provisions (although of course the partners, qua natural persons, will be able to invoke freedom of establishment in their own right).'

accordance with the national law of a Member State,[138] while also having some corporate connection with the Union.[139]

Article 54 TFEU appears to leave the personal scope of the freedom of establishment for companies entirely to the Member States. Did this mean that each Member State could unilaterally determine which companies would benefit from a corporate personality within its territory? The question as to the personal scope of corporate mobility has troubled European law for a long time (section (a)). It precedes the question about the material scope of Article 49 TFEU with regard to companies (section (b)). Section 3(c) explores the abuse-of-rights doctrine in the context of secondary establishment, while section 3(d) analyses the extent to which the Union has engaged in the positive integration of national company laws.

a. Personal Scope: The Definition of 'Companies'

Companies are legal persons formed to undertake a business activity. These 'undertakings' may be conducted in a variety of legal forms. The predominant form has historically been the 'limited liability company'. Emerging in the nineteenth century, this corporate form allows the shareholders of the company to limit their personal liabilities for debts incurred by the company to the amount of share capital paid into the company capital. This separation of corporate and personal liability is designed to encourage individual investment; yet, the limitation of liability contains – of course – a risk for creditors of the company.[140] For that reason, national company laws will often make the grant of this corporate form dependent, as a quid pro quo, on the fulfilment of a number of conditions. These national conditions often vary, and the question may thus arise whether an English company is allowed to establish itself in France or Germany – even if it does not fulfil *their* respective national company laws.

Unlike many concepts used by the Treaties, the concept of 'company' appeared to be no 'Union concept'. Article 54 TFEU indeed unconditionally defers to the Member States with regard to the creation of national companies.[141] And when the Union was founded in 1957, two philosophies on the formation and

---

[138] This was expressly confirmed in Case C-47/12, *Kronos* v. *Finanzamt Leverkusen*, EU:C:2014:2200. In this case, the Court was asked whether a US firm could benefit from the EU free movement provisions, and the Court was categorical (*ibid.*, para. 46): '[A] company or firm which is not formed in accordance with the law of a Member State cannot enjoy freedom of establishment.' This solution was all the more important as the US firm had been (mutually) recognised under German law but the Court found that this would still not grant it free movement rights under Art. 49 TFEU (*ibid.*, para. 50).

[139] This second condition mentioned in Art. 54 TFEU seems to exclude third-country letter-box companies that have no genuine connection with the Union economy.

[140] On the doctrine of corporate personality in the United Kingdom, see *Salomon* v. *A. Salomon & Co. Ltd* [1897] AC 22. For a historical overview of the rise of the limited company, see T. Hadden, *Company Law and Capitalism* (Weidenfeld & Nicolson, 1977).

[141] The original Rome Treaty however contained a provision that asked the Member States to negotiate and conclude separate international agreements on, *inter alia* 'the mutual recognition of companies or firms' and 'the retention of legal personality in the event of transfer of their seat from one country to another' (see ex-Art. 293 EC). The Member States indeed

recognition of companies coexisted in the Member States.[142] According to the 'real seat theory', a company could only become a legal person if it had its central administration or principal place of business within the Member State in which it wished to incorporate. The seat theory thus insists on a 'physical' link between the (national) legal personality of a company and its primary residence.[143] By contrast, the 'incorporation theory' dispenses with this physical link and simply grants legal personality to all companies properly incorporated under national law. The nationality of a company is here solely determined by its law of incorporation and its 'registered office'.[144]

The Treaties recognise both theories in Article 54 TFEU. Did the reference to companies being 'formed in accordance with the law of a *Member State*' however mean that *any* State could impose *any* conditions? Let us look at this question first.

aa. *Home State Restrictions and* Daily Mail

To what extent can the home State define and restrict the formation of a company? The question received a first answer in *Daily Mail*.[145] In this case, the Court had to deal with a British condition that made the 'life' of a British company moving abroad subject to the consent of the British government. This condition did not directly stem from British company law, which – adopting the incorporation doctrine – allows its companies to establish their central management and control outside the United Kingdom.[146] However, British tax legislation had indirectly tied the corporate status to residency by requiring that a British company could only move abroad with the consent of the Treasury.[147] The applicant had wished to move to the Netherlands to avoid paying corporation tax and thus challenged the British residency requirement on the grounds that it interfered with its right of establishment. It claimed that it had 'the same right of primary establishment in another Member State as is conferred on natural persons by Article [49]'.[148]

The Court did not object to the idea that the freedom of establishment applied to restrictions on the emigration (or 'export') of companies imposed by the home State. Yet it did not find such a restriction in place. In the view of the Court, the British law did not stand in the way of a transfer of the old business to a newly incorporated company in another Member State. For it only

---

signed such a Convention on the Mutual Recognition of Companies and Bodies Corporate in 1968, yet the Convention never entered into force due to the failure of the Netherlands to ratify the Convention. Ex-Art. 293 EC was deleted by the Lisbon Treaty.

[142] For an excellent discussion of the question from a variety of perspectives, see C. H. Panayi, 'Corporate Mobility in Private International Law and European Community Law: Debunking Some Myths' (2009) 28 *YEL* 123.

[143] The seat theory has been traditionally championed by Germany.

[144] The incorporation theory has been traditionally championed by the Netherlands and has received significant support with the accession of the United Kingdom.

[145] Case 81/87, *The Queen* v. *HM Treasury and Commissioners of Inland Revenue, ex p. Daily Mail and General Trust* [1988] ECR 5483.

[146] *Ibid.*, para. 3.   [147] *Ibid.*, para. 5.   [148] *Ibid.*, para. 12.

required Treasury consent 'where such a company seeks to transfer its central management and control out of the United Kingdom *while maintaining its legal personality and its status as a United Kingdom company*'.[149] Stated in more general terms, the Court here confirmed the 'neutrality' of the European Treaties with regard to the status of national companies:

> [U]nlike natural persons, companies are creatures of the law and, in the present state of [Union] law, creatures of national law. They exist only by virtue of the varying national legislation which determines their incorporation and functioning … the legislation of the Member States varies widely in regard to both the factor providing a connection to the national territory required for the incorporation of a company and the question whether a company incorporated under the legislation of a Member State may subsequently modify that connecting factor. Certain States require that not merely the registered office but also the real head office, that is to say the central administration of the company, should be situated on their territory, and the removal of the central administration from that territory thus presupposes the winding-up of the company with all the consequences that winding-up entails in company law and tax law. The legislation of other States permits companies to transfer their central administration to a foreign country but certain of them, such as the United Kingdom, make that right subject to certain restrictions, and the legal consequences of a transfer, particularly in regard to taxation, vary from one Member State to another.
>
> *The Treaty has taken account of that variety in national legislation. In defining, in Article [54], the companies which enjoy the right of establishment, the Treaty places on the same footing, as connecting factors, the registered office, central administration and principal place of business of a company …* It must therefore be held that the Treaty regards the differences in national legislation concerning the required connecting factor and the question whether – and if so how – the registered office or real head office of a company incorporated under national law may be transferred from one Member State to another as problems which are not resolved by the rules concerning the right of establishment but must be dealt with by future legislation or conventions. *Under those circumstances, Articles [49] and [54] of the Treaty cannot be interpreted as conferring on companies incorporated under the law of a Member State a right to transfer their central management and control and their central administration to another Member State while retaining their status as companies incorporated under the legislation of the first Member State.*[150]

The Court thus leaves the 'status' of a company entirely in the hands of its home State. The complete freedom of national legislators to define the 'status' of a company, that is: the conditions as to how a company is created

---

[149] *Ibid.*, para. 18 (emphasis added).

[150] *Ibid.*, paras. 19–24 (emphasis added). The Court here expressly pointed to Art. 50(2)(g) TFEU and ex-Art. 293 EC as a potential legal basis for the European or international harmonisation.

and how it loses its right to life, was subsequently confirmed in *Cartesio*.[151] A Member State may therefore legitimately hold that a company loses its corporate status – its 'personality' and 'nationality' – when moving its residence abroad. This is in striking contrast to Union law governing the free movement of natural persons; but this difference was justified by reference to the fact that as long as companies continue to be 'creatures of national law', it is national law – not European law – that defines their coming into and out of existence.

bb. *Host State Restrictions and* Centros

The central question after *Daily Mail* was this: did Article 54's deference to national company law cover the *home* State as well as the *host* State? Could the latter also impose its national conditions on the status of (foreign) companies; or would European law only defer to the 'company' definition of the home State?

In its jurisprudence, the Court has clarified that the reference to the formation of a company 'in accordance with the law of a Member State' exclusively referred to the law of the State in which the company was *first* incorporated. The (more restrictive) company law of the host State will thus not benefit from Article 54 TFEU. The case that famously elucidates this 'first formation' principle is *Centros*.[152] It concerned the refusal by the Danish Companies Board to register a branch of a foreign company called Centros that had been incorporated as an English limited liability company. The Danish authorities argued that since Centros did not engage in any business activities in the United Kingdom but conducted all its trade in Denmark, it was Denmark – and not the United Kingdom – that should be regarded as the (home) State of primary establishment.

The Court famously rejected this argument. It laconically pointed out that the company had already been 'formed in accordance with the law of a Member State' and that it was 'immaterial that the company was formed in the first Member State only for the purpose of establishing itself in the second, where its main, or indeed entire, business is to be conducted'.[153] The 'status' of Centros as an English company could thus not be affected by the fact that its central

---

[151]   Case C-210/06, *Cartesio* [2008] ECR I-9641, esp. paras. 104–10. The Court here went against its much more (neo-)liberal Advocate General, who had advised the Court to overrule *Daily Mail* in the following words (*ibid.*, para. 31): 'In sum, it is impossible, in my view, to argue on the basis of the current state of [Union] law that Member States enjoy an absolute freedom to determine the "life and death" of companies constituted under their domestic law, irrespective of the consequences for the freedom of establishment. Otherwise, Member States would have *carte blanche* to impose a "death sentence" on a company constituted under its laws just because it had decided to exercise the freedom of establishment.'

[152]   Case C-212/97, *Centros Ltd v. Erhvervs- og Selskabsstyrelsen*.

[153]   *Ibid.*, para. 17.

administration and principal place of business was in another Member State. English company law would exclusively determine the status of the company. The absolute priority granted to the company law of first incorporation was subsequently confirmed.[154]

In sum, in the absence of Union legislation, Article 54 entitles the Member States to determine the personal scope of Article 49. The concept of a 'company' is left to national law; yet the Court has clarified that the determining law is only the law of the 'home State'– that is, the State of first incorporation. It exclusively falls within the competence of that State to define the conditions for the life and death of a company; and since these conditions concern the *formal status* of the company as such, they are not regarded as substantive restrictions falling within the material scope of Article 49. However, the Court has been eager to point out that any national restriction that does '*not* affect [the] status of a company incorporated under [national] law' will not benefit from Article 54's deference to national company law. It will instead be examined under Article 49.[155]

b. Material Scope: Primary and Secondary Establishment

Article 49 TFEU expressly mentions two aspects of the freedom of establishment with regard to companies. It not only positively guarantees the right 'to set up and manage' companies (primary establishment). It also negatively prohibits 'restrictions on the setting-up of agencies, branches or subsidiaries by nationals of any Member State established in the territory of any Member State' (secondary establishment). The material scope of Article 49 TFEU thereby captures restrictions on the *emigration* ('export') and the *immigration* ('import') of companies

---

[154] Case C-208/00, *Überseering BV* v. *Nordic Construction Company* [2002] ECR 9919. It is important to keep in mind that the Court's *Centros* jurisprudence has not sounded a death knell to the real-seat theory followed by some Member States. The Union is still neutral as to whether a State follows the incorporation of the seat theory, and where a company has been first registered in a Member State – like Germany or Hungary – that follows the seat theory, the company will lose its status as a company under Art. 54 TFEU where it moves its central administration outside its State of incorporation (see Case C-210/06, *Cartesio*). However, a seat-theory State will not be able to impose its corporate philosophy on a company first registered within a jurisdiction that follows the more liberal incorporation theory (see Case C-208/00, *Überseing*)

[155] Case C-371/10, *National Grid Indus BV* v. *Inspecteur van de Belastingdienst Rijnmond/kantoor Rotterdam* [2011] ECR I-12273, esp. paras. 31–2: 'The national legislation at issue in the main proceedings does not concern the determination of the conditions required by a Member State of a company incorporated under its law for that company to be able to retain its status of a company of that Member State after transferring its place of effective management to another Member State.' For a discussion of the case, see R. Kok, 'Exit Taxes for Companies in the European Union after National Grid Indus' (2012) 21 *EC Tax Review* 200. The issue has more recently been confirmed in Case C-594/14, *Kornhaas* v. *Dithmar*, EU:C:2015:806, where the Court also denied the existence of a violation of Art. 54 TFEU because the German law at issue 'in no way concerned the formation of a company in a given Member State or its subsequent establishment in another Member State' (*ibid.*, para. 28). Once these two cases are seen as exclusively dealing with Art. 54 TFEU, it might then go too far to assume that they somehow signal the arrival of a *Keck*-like approach to establishment. For that interesting argument, see W.-G. Ringe, '*Kornhaas* and the Challenge of Applying *Keck* in Establishment' (2017) 42 *EL Rev.* 270.

issued by either the home or the host State.[156] And, as already explained above, Article 49 captures regulatory as well as fiscal measures.[157]

The central question behind the material scope of Article 49 is whether it is confined to discriminatory measures or whether it also captures non-discriminatory restrictions on the primary or secondary establishment of companies. The language of Article 49 here gives ambivalent signals: the right to primary establishment seems to only protect against discrimination ('under the conditions laid down for its own nationals by the law of the country where such establishment is effected'), while the right to secondary establishment speaks the language of a restriction test that goes beyond discrimination.

aa. Primary Establishment: A Discrimination Test?

Despite the fact that Article 54 grants 'immunity' to national laws defining the status of the company, there will surely be national measures dealing with primary establishment that fall within the scope of Article 49.

An excellent illustration of a discriminatory national measure here is offered by *Factortame II*.[158] The case concerned the rights of Spanish nationals to have their fishing ships entered in the British register. Following a statutory reform designed to prevent the use of the British fishing quota by foreign nationals, the Merchant Shipping Act 1988 limited the registration of British fishing vessels to those ships that were 'British-owned', 'managed, and its operations ... directed and controlled, from within the United Kingdom', and where the 'charterer, manager or operator of the vessel' was British.[159]

---

[156]   That Art. 49 TFEU protects against restrictions on the emigration and immigration of companies was clarified in Case 81/87, *Daily Mail*, para. 16: 'Even though those provisions are directed mainly to ensuring that foreign nationals and companies are treated in the host Member State in the same way as nationals of that State, they also prohibit the Member State of origin from hindering the establishment in another Member State of one of its nationals or of a company incorporated under its legislation which comes within the definition contained in Article [54]. As the Commission rightly observed, the rights guaranteed by Articles [49ff.] would be rendered meaningless if the Member State of origin could prohibit undertakings from leaving in order to establish themselves in another Member State.' See also Case C-446/03, *Marks & Spencer v. David Halsey (Her Majesty's Inspector of Taxes* [2005] ECR I-10837, para. 31: 'Even though, according to their wording, the provisions concerning freedom of establishment are directed to ensuring that foreign nationals and companies are treated in the host Member State in the same way as nationals of that State, they also prohibit the Member State of origin from hindering the establishment in another Member State of one of its nationals or of a company incorporated under its legislation.'

[157]   Famous 'fiscal' cases are Case 81/87, *Daily Mail* as well as Case C-446/03, *Marks & Spencer*. For an extensive analysis of the EU and corporate tax law, see C. H. Panayi, *European Union Corporate Tax Law* (Cambridge University Press, 2013).

[158]   Case C-221/89, *The Queen v. Secretary of State for Transport, ex p. Factortame Ltd and others* [1991] ECR I-3905.

[159]   *Ibid.*, para. 6.

That looked like a textbook case of discrimination; and, indeed, after having made a formal concession to the retained powers of Member States under international law to determine the 'nationality' of their ships,[160] the Court found that these residual powers would have to be exercised consistently with Union law.[161] This meant that a condition that 'stipulates that where a vessel is owned or chartered by natural persons they must be of a particular nationality and where it is owned or chartered by a company the shareholders and directors must be of that nationality is contrary to Article [49] of the Treaty'.[162] The same held true for the residence requirement, imposed by the second condition, which was found to be – indirectly – discriminatory.[163]

One of the most controversial questions on primary establishment concerns the situation where a company wishes to 'exit' its home State so as to 'reincorporate' or 'convert' into a company formed under the national laws of a second State.[164] Not covered by the immunity granted by Article 54 TFEU,[165] the Court has held the requirement to be liquidated before its departure to be 'a barrier to the actual conversion of such a company … [which] constitutes a restriction on the freedom of establishment of the company concerned'.[166] On the other hand, the Court has insisted that Article 49 grants no absolute right to corporate conversion. The possibility of such a conversion will be governed by

---

[160]   *Ibid.*, para. 13.   [161]   *Ibid.*, para. 14; see also paras. 26–9.   [162]   *Ibid.*, para. 30.

[163]   *Ibid.*, para. 32: 'As for the requirement for the owners, charterers, managers and operators of the vessel and, in the case of a company, the shareholders and directors to be resident and domiciled in the Member State in which the vessel is to be registered, it must be held that such a requirement, which is not justified by the rights and obligations created by the grant of a national flag to a vessel, results in discrimination on grounds of nationality. The great majority of nationals of the Member State in question are resident and domiciled in that State and therefore meet that requirement automatically, whereas nationals of other Member States would, in most cases, have to move their residence and domicile to that State in order to comply with the requirements of its legislation. It follows that such a requirement is contrary to Article [49].'

[164]   For an analysis of this particular question, see O. Mörsdorf, 'The Legal Mobility of Companies within the European Union through Cross-border Conversion' (2012) 49 *CML Rev.* 629.

[165]   See Case C-210/06, *Cartesio*, paras. 111–12: '[T]he situation where the seat of a company incorporated under the law of one Member State is transferred to another Member State with no change as regards the law which governs that company falls to be distinguished from the situation where a company governed by the law of one Member State moves to another Member State with an attendant change as regards the national law applicable, since in the latter situation the company is converted into a form of company which is governed by the law of the Member State to which it has moved. In fact, in that latter case, the power referred to in paragraph 110 above, far from implying that national legislation on the incorporation and winding-up of companies enjoys any form of immunity from the rules of the [FEU] Treaty on freedom of establishment, cannot, in particular, justify the Member State of incorporation, by requiring the winding-up or liquidation of the company, in preventing that company from converting itself into a company governed by the law of the other Member State, to the extent that it is permitted under that law to do so.'

[166]   *Ibid.*, para. 113. For a recent confirmation of this rule, see Case C-106/16, *Polbud-Wykonawstwo*, EU:C:2017:807.

the law of the second (new) home State 'to the extent that it is permitted under that law to do so';[167] and only where the latter allows such conversions for its own national companies can a foreign company insist on equal treatment under Article 49 TFEU.[168]

National measures limiting primary establishment therefore appear to be principally subject to a discrimination test.[169]

bb. Secondary Establishment: A Restriction Test

Secondary establishment concerns 'the setting-up of agencies, branches or subsidiaries' of a company. These legal forms of secondary establishment are not exhaustive: any permanent presence in another Member State may be covered.[170]

All of these forms equally benefit from Article 49 TFEU. A Member State is thus prohibited from giving preference to a particular form of secondary establishment. This was authoritatively confirmed in *Commission* v. *France (Avoir Fiscal)*.[171] The case concerned a tax credit that was offered to all insurance companies whose registered office was in France. The allowance covered French companies as well as foreign subsidiaries – as opposed to agencies or branches – set up in France by foreign companies.[172] Claiming that this discriminated against foreign insurance companies, the Commission brought proceedings on the grounds that the national law 'constitute[d] an indirect restriction on the freedom to set up secondary establishment[s]'.[173] The Court agreed that there was discrimination between national and foreign companies,[174] and found that 'the fact that insurance companies whose registered office is situated in another Member State are at liberty to establish themselves by setting up a subsidiary in order to have

---

[167] Case C-210/06, *Cartesio*, para. 112.

[168] Case C-378/10, *VALE*, EU:C:2012:440, paras. 32–3: 'It is thus apparent that the expression "to the extent that it is permitted under that law to do so", in paragraph 112 of *Cartesio*, cannot be understood as seeking to remove, from the outset, the legislation of the host Member State on company conversions from the scope of the provisions of the Treaty on the Functioning of the European Union governing the freedom of establishment, but as reflecting the mere consideration that a company established in accordance with national law exists only on the basis of the national legislation which "permits" the incorporation of the company, provided the conditions laid down to that effect are satisfied. In the light of the foregoing, the Court concludes that national legislation which enables national companies to convert, but does not allow companies governed by the law of another Member State to do so, falls within the scope of Articles 49 TFEU and 54 TFEU.'

[169] For a discrimination rationale, see Case C-411/03, *Sevic Systems* [2005] ECR I-10805, esp. para. 22. For an extensive discussion of *Sevic* in the context of the freedom of corporate establishment, see T. Papadopoulos, 'EU Regulatory Approaches to Cross-border Mergers: Exercising the Right of Establishment' (2011) 36 *EL Rev.* 71.

[170] Case 205/84, *Commission* v. *Germany* [1986] ECR 3755, esp. para. 21.

[171] Case 270/83, *Commission* v. *France (Avoir Fiscal)* [1986] ECR 273.

[172] *Ibid.*, para. 6. In legal terminology, a subsidiary company is a company that will be established under the company laws of the host State.

[173] *Ibid.*, para. 7.

[174] On the discrimination test applied by the Court in this case, see *ibid.*, paras. 19–20.

the benefit of the tax credit cannot justify different treatment' since '*[t]he second sentence of the first paragraph of Article [49] expressly leaves traders free to choose the appropriate legal form in which to pursue their activities in another Member State*'.[175]

This case, like many others,[176] had been based on a discrimination rationale. After *Centros*,[177] there can however be no doubt that non-discriminatory restrictions on secondary establishments will equally be caught by Article 49 TFEU. As we saw above, the Danish authorities had here refused to register a branch of an English company on the grounds that it did all its business in Denmark and that it had been set up as an English company for the sole purpose of avoiding the Danish minimum share capital requirements. Having framed the case as one of secondary establishment,[178] the Court had no qualms to view the refusal to register a Danish branch as 'an obstacle to the exercise of the freedom [of establishment]'.[179] The fact that the national legislation on minimum capital equally applied to Danish companies and thus 'applied in a non-discriminatory manner' was no defence.[180]

This inclusion of non-discriminatory measures is clearly confirmed in the Court's post-*Centros* jurisprudence. In *Inspire Art*,[181] the Dutch legislator had extended the Dutch company rules on minimum share capital and a director's liability to 'formally foreign' companies. The Court again was adamant: making the Dutch legislation mandatory for a branch of a foreign company had 'the effect of *impeding the exercise* by those companies of the freedom of establishment conferred by the Treaty'.[182] This obstacle-focused language was subsequently refined,[183] and the Court has recently confirmed that it is 'settled case law that all measures which prohibit, impede or render less attractive the exercise of the freedom of establishment must be regarded as restriction[s] on that freedom'.[184]

---

[175] *Ibid.*, para. 22 (emphasis added).

[176] See e.g. Case 79/85, *Segers* v. *Bestuur van de Bedrijfsvereniging voor Bank- en Verzekeringswezen, Groothandel en Vrije Beroepen* [1986] ECR 2375; Case C-3/88, *Commission* v. *Italy* [1989] I-ECR 4035, para. 8: 'According to the Court's case-law the principle of equal treatment, of which Articles [49] and [56] of the Treaty embody specific instances, prohibits not only overt discrimination by reason of nationality but also all covert forms of discrimination which, by the application of other criteria of differentiation, lead in fact to the same result.' Writing in 1999, Edwards, *EC Company Law* (n. 137 above), 364, still noted that 'in contrast to the case-law on individuals' freedom of establishment, the case-law on corporate freedom of establishment appears to have little evolved towards a restriction-based analysis'.

[177] Case C-212/97, *Centros*. According to J. Borg-Barthet, *The Governing Law of Companies* (Hart, 2012), 113: '*Centros* was to the freedom of corporate establishment what *Cassis* was to the free movement of goods.'

[178] On this point see section 3(c) below.

[179] Case C-212/97, *Centros*, para. 22.

[180] *Ibid.*, para. 34. The Court referred to its *Gebhard* test and found the national measures could not be justified by imperative requirements in the general interest (*ibid.*, paras. 35–8).

[181] Case C-167/01, *Kamer van Koophandel en Fabrieken voor Amsterdam* v. *Inspire Art* [2003] ECR I-10155.

[182] *Ibid.*, para. 101 (emphasis added).

[183] Case C-442/02, *Caixa Bank France*; Case C-371/10, *National Grid Indus*.

[184] *Ibid.*, para. 36.

How potent this 'prohibit, impede or render less attractive' formula is can be seen in *AGET Iraklis*.[185] The case involved a challenge by the principal shareholder of a French multinational company to Greek legislation regulating collective redundancies. Under Greek labour law, collective redundancies by any company required the prior approval of the relevant minister; and, if the latter refused to authorise such redundancies, they simply could not take place. For the Court this was a serious violation of the exercise of the right of secondary establishment:

> Such exercise also entails, in principle, the freedom to determine the nature and extent of the economic activity that will be carried out in the host Member State, in particular the size of the fixed establishments and the number of workers required for that purpose ... [U]nder the legislation at issue in the main proceedings it is the very ability of such an establishment to effect collective redundancies that is subject, in this instance, to a requirement that there be no opposition on the part of the competent public authority ... National legislation such as that at issue in the main proceedings is thus such as to render access to the Greek market less attractive ... Accordingly, it must be held that such national legislation is liable to constitute a serious obstacle to the exercise of freedom of establishment in Greece.[186]

The case comes dangerously close to a 'national' model of negative integration, and it is hoped that the Court will not repeat its *Sunday Trading* mistakes here.[187]

c. 'Letter-box Companies': The Doctrine of 'Abuse of Rights'

The Court's generous jurisprudence on secondary establishment, combined with its deference to national law when it comes to company incorporations, has created a 'market' for company laws in Europe. Potential entrepreneurs are permitted to choose in which jurisdiction to incorporate their business, and this choice will be protected throughout the Union and for the entire life of the company.

The ability of individuals to freely select a particular company law regime has led to a 'regulatory competition' between national legal orders.[188] This

---

[185] Case C-201/15, *Anonymi Geniki Etairia Tsimenton Iraklis (AGET Iraklis)* v. *Ypourgos Ergasias, Koinonikis Asfalisis kai Koinonikis Allilengyis*, EU:C:2016:972.

[186] *Ibid.*, paras. 53–7.

[187] On the *Sunday Trading* cases within the context of the free movement of goods, see Chapter 13, section 3(a/cc).

[188] See J. Armour and W.-G. Ringe, 'European Company Law 1999–2010: Renaissance and Crisis' (2011) 48 *CML Rev.* 142: '[T]he judicial development of corporate freedom of establishment triggered large-scale use of foreign company laws by entrepreneurs incorporating new businesses ... The jurisdiction of choice for these entrepreneurs was mostly the UK, where no minimum capital is required for a private company ... The massive migration of entrepreneurs from continental European countries in the years 2003–2006 put lawmakers in those countries under pressure. Virtually all major jurisdictions responded to the market pressure in an attempt to make their company law system more appealing to businesses and to retain incorporations.' On the idea of regulatory competition in company law, see also S. Deakin, 'Two Types of Regulatory Competition: Competitive Federalism Versus Reflexive Harmonisation' (1999) 2 *CYELS* 231; W. Schön, 'Playing Different Games? Regulatory Competition in Tax and Company Law Compared' (2005) 42 *CML Rev.* 331.

competition among States however entails the danger of a 'race to the bottom' for company laws. Inspired by the (bad) example of Delaware in the United States, this 'competitive' effect on the mandatory requirements imposed on companies has been termed the 'Delaware effect'.[189] The starkest manifestation of this Delaware effect is a home State that harbours a myriad of 'letter-box companies', that is: companies whose only 'physical' presence within that State is a brass plate attached to a solicitor's office.

In order to protect third parties − such as creditors − against these 'shell companies', host States with higher company law standards have traditionally responded in three ways. Some States have simply insisted that the company must reincorporate in the 'host' State if the company has its central 'seat' of business there. This first solution has, as we saw above, been prohibited by the European Court of Justice.[190] Some States have therefore built on a second solution: the doctrine of 'formally foreign' or 'pseudo-foreign' companies.[191] A host State here formally recognises the foreign company as a legal person but still imposes some material conditions on it; yet again, the Court has not been willing to accept this solution. Where Member States wish to impose their higher capital requirements on foreign companies, they would have to justify their higher standard by reference to overriding reasons relating to the public interest − a route that will typically fail.[192] The Court has however recognised a third 'special' justification for national legislation designed to fight letter-box companies. This third doctrine is called the 'abuse of right' doctrine.[193]

How effective has this third solution been in the fight against shell companies? The Court has come to define the parameters of the 'abuse doctrine' in a very restrictive manner. In *Centros*, it indeed rejected the Danish argument that the English company was a mere letter-box company that had been created for the sole purpose of circumventing the Danish protection of company creditors. The Court here held:

---

[189] For US discussion of this phenomenon, see W. L. Cary, 'Federalism and Corporate Law: Reflections upon Delaware' (1974) 83 *Yale LJ* 663; R. Drury, 'The Regulation and Recognition of Foreign Corporations: Responses to the "Delaware Syndrome"' (1998) 57 *Cambridge Law Journal* 165.

[190] Case C-212/97, *Centros*.

[191] For an early exposition in the US context, see E. R. Latty, 'Pseudo-Foreign Corporations' (1955) 65 *Yale LJ* 137. The doctrine of a formally foreign company was used by the Netherlands in Case C-167/01, *Inspire* Art.

[192] Case C-167/01, *Inspire Art*, para. 132.

[193] The Court has developed the doctrine into a general weapon against the excessive use of free movement law, see e.g. Case 33/74, *van Binsbergen* [1974] ECR 1299; Case 115/78, *Knoors*; Case C-110/99, *Emsland-Stärke GmbH* v. *Hauptzollamt Hamburg-Jonas* [2000] ECR I-11569. For academic commentaries of the general doctrine, see L. Neville Brown, 'Is There a General Principle of Abuse of Rights in Community Law?', in D. Curtin and T. Heukels (eds.), *Institutional Dynamics of European Integration − Essays in Honour of Henry G. Schermers*, 3 vols. (Martinus Nijhoff, 1994), II, 511; K. Sorenson, 'Abuse of Rights in Community Law: A Principle of Substance or Merely Rhetoric? (2006) 43 *CML Rev.* 423. See also R. de la Feria and S. Vogenauer, *Prohibition of Abuse of Law: A New General Principle of EU Law?* (Hart, 2011).

> [I]t is immaterial that the company was formed in the first Member State only for the purpose of establishing itself in the second, where its main, or indeed entire, business is to be conducted.[194]

And, while admitting that Union law recognised an abuse doctrine, the latter would only allow Member States 'to prevent individuals from *improperly or fraudulently* taking advantage of provisions of [European] law'.[195] However:

> [T]he fact that a national of a Member state who wishes to set up a company chooses to form it in the Member State whose rules of company law seem to him the least restrictive and to set up branches in other Member States cannot, in itself, constitute an abuse of the right of establishment.[196]

This reasoning was victim to a serious intellectual shortcut. Even if the Court was right to protect the ability of *English* company law to define the status of *English* companies, it could have conditioned a company's European right to *secondary* establishment to it being still *established* in the first State. After all, does the wording of Article 49[1] TFEU not itself seem to make the freedom of secondary establishment dependent on being (primarily) 'established' in the territory of another Member State? And since the Court normally defines 'establishment' as '*the actual pursuit of an economic activity through a fixed establishment in another Member State for an indefinite period*',[197] it could have used this substantive test to remove companies that have no (or minimal) business within their State of incorporation.[198] Yet the Court chose not to do so; and by not demanding any economic connection between the State of incorporation and the company, it almost entirely closed off the abuse-of-rights doctrine for letter-box companies.

[194]   Case C-212/97, *Centros*, para. 17 (with reference to *Segers*).
[195]   *Ibid.*, para. 24 (with reference *inter alia* to *Binsbergen*).
[196]   *Ibid.*, para. 27 (emphasis added).
[197]   For this substantial reading of establishment, see *Factortame II* (n. 109 above), paras. 19–21: 'At the hearing, the Commission argued that the registration of a vessel constituted in itself an act of establishment within the meaning of Article [49] *et seq.* of the Treaty and that therefore the rules on freedom of establishment were applicable. It must be observed in that regard that the concept of establishment within the meaning of Article [49] *et seq.* of the Treaty involves the actual pursuit of an economic activity through a fixed establishment in another Member State for an indefinite period. Consequently, the registration of a vessel does not necessarily involve establishment within the meaning of the Treaty, in particular where the vessel is not used to pursue an economic activity or where the application for registration is made by or on behalf of a person who is not established, and has no intention of becoming established, in the State concerned.'
[198]   Importantly, this qualitative threshold would be lower than the substantive threshold demanded by the real-seat theory. For whereas the latter insists on linking primary establishment with the business's *principal* place of trade, the former only insists on there being *some* genuine economic activity.

This overly restrictive definition of the doctrine was somewhat broadened in *Cadbury Schweppes*.[199] The case involved British legislation designed to fight corporate tax avoidance. Tax avoidance is – unlike tax evasion – the legal use of international and national tax arrangements to reduce one's tax burden. Established in the United Kingdom, Cadbury-Schweppes had set up two (controlled) subsidiaries in Ireland where the corporate tax rate was 10 per cent, that is: less than 75 per cent of the British rate. To prevent any tax abuse, the British Parliament had adopted legislation on 'controlled foreign companies', which provided that the parent company could be taxed on the profit of the subsidiary in the United Kingdom unless the subsidiary engaged in genuine trading activities.[200]

Could this be done under European Union law? While confirming its ruling in *Centros* and finding a restriction on secondary establishment in place,[201] the Court nonetheless found that this restriction could be justified:

> [A] national measure restricting freedom of establishment may be justified where it specifically relates to *wholly artificial arrangements aimed at circumventing the application of the legislation of the Member State concerned* ... It follows that, in order for a restriction on the freedom of establishment to be justified on the ground of prevention of abusive practices, the specific objective of such a restriction must be to *prevent conduct involving the creation of wholly artificial arrangements which do not reflect economic reality, with a view to escaping the tax normally due on the profits generated by activities carried out on national territory.*[202]

Such a 'wholly artificial' arrangement would especially exist where the secondary establishment did not involve a '*genuine economic activity*'.[203] An abuse of rights could here be found, when the company did derive an artificial advantage from this arrangement (subjective element) that was not covered by the objective of the free movement provisions (objective element).[204]

---

[199] Case C-196/04, *Cadbury Schweppes plc and Cadbury Schweppes Overseas Ltd* v. *Commissioners of Inland Revenue* [2006] ECR I-7995.

[200] For a summary of the British legislation, see *ibid.*, paras. 3–12.

[201] *Ibid.*, paras. 30–46.   [202] *Ibid.*, paras. 51 and 55 (emphasis added).

[203] *Ibid.*, para. 54 (emphasis added).

[204] *Ibid.*, para. 64. The Court imported this two-elements test from its previous ruling in Case C-110/99, *Emsland-Stärke*, where it defined its abuse-of-rights test as follows (*ibid.*, paras. 52–3): 'A finding of an abuse requires, first, a combination of objective circumstances in which, despite formal observance of the conditions laid down by the [Union] rules, the purpose of those rules has not been achieved. It requires, second, a subjective element consisting in the intention to obtain an advantage from the [Union] rules by creating artificially the conditions laid down for obtaining it. The existence of that subjective element can be established, inter alia, by evidence of collusion between the [Union] exporter receiving the refunds and the importer of the goods in the non-member country.' For an analysis of the '*Emsland-Stärke*' test, see P. Koutrakos, 'The *Emsland-Stärke* Abuse of Law Test in the Law of Agriculture and Free Movement of Goods', in R. de la Feria and S. Vogenauer (eds.), *Prohibition of Abuse of Law: A New General Principle of EU Law?* (Hart, 2011), 203.

This elusive test draws a fine line between the formal use and the material abuse of the freedom of establishment. While a company cannot be prevented from profiting from the advantages flowing from the internal market – even if that means that it 'avoids' national legislation,[205] its conduct can be prohibited by a Member State when the objective pursued by the freedom of establishment is not achieved. The Court has here applied a strict standard.[206]

d. Positive Integration: Article 50(2)(g) and Beyond

aa. Harmonisation: Company Law Directives

The chapter on establishment contains, as we saw above, a number of special legislative competences for the adoption of Union secondary law. With regard to the free movement of companies, Article 50(2) TFEU thereby allows the Union in particular to adopt directives, in accordance with the ordinary legislative procedure,[207] in order to create the freedom of establishment:

> (f) by effecting the progressive abolition of restrictions on freedom of establishment in every branch of activity under consideration, both as regards the conditions for setting up agencies, branches or subsidiaries in the territory of a Member State and as regards the subsidiaries in the territory of a Member State and as regards the conditions governing the entry of personnel belonging to the main establishment into managerial or supervisory posts in such agencies, branches or subsidiaries;
>
> (g) by coordinating to the necessary extent the safeguards which, for the protection of the interests of members and others, are required by Member States of companies or firms within the meaning of the second paragraph of Article 54 with a view to making such safeguards equivalent throughout the Union …

Thanks to the liberal jurisprudence of the European Court with regard to the freedom of secondary establishment, Article 50(2)(f) TFEU has hardly played any role in the past. By contrast, the centrality of Article 50(2)(g) TFEU for the

---

[205] See e.g. Case C-196/04, *Cadbury Schweppes*, para. 36: '[T]he fact that a [Union] national, whether a natural or a legal person, sought to profit from tax advantages in force in a Member State other than his State of residence cannot in itself deprive him of the right to rely on the provisions of the Treaty.'

[206] E.g. Case C-182/08, *Glaxo Wellcome* v. *Finanzamt München II* [2009] ECR I-8591, esp. para. 100: 'To the extent that the application of legislation such as that at issue in the main proceedings cannot be limited to wholly artificial arrangements, established on the basis of objective elements, but covers all cases in which a resident taxpayer has acquired shares in a resident company from a non-resident shareholder at a price which, for whatever reason, exceeds the nominal value of those shares, the effects of such legislation exceed what is necessary in order to attain the objective of preventing wholly artificial arrangements which do not reflect economic reality and whose only purpose is unduly to obtain a tax advantage.'

[207] Art. 50(1) TFEU.

positive integration in this field cannot be overestimated. It has been the true fountain of a 'European company law', which has come to inform many areas of national company law.[208] What is the scope of this legislative competence? The provision refers to national laws 'for the protection of members *and* others' and thus covers company law safeguards with regard to shareholders as well as third parties, such as creditors. These national safeguards would need to be 'coordinat[ed]' so as to make them 'equivalent throughout the Union'.

Despite its unfortunate wording, Article 50(2)(g) TFEU is no coordinating competence. On the contrary, it constitutes a shared competence that allows the Union to *harmonise* national company law '[i]n order to attain freedom of establishment'.[209] The reference to the 'attainment' of the internal market for companies could however have been taken to only cover the 'establishment' of the internal market and to thus exclude the adoption of harmonisation measures whose object was the 'functioning' of the internal market. That would have made the scope of Article 50(2)(g) significantly smaller than the scope of Article 114 TFEU – which, as we saw above, covers both aspects of the internal market.[210] The Court seems to have however rejected this narrow reading. In *Daihatsu*,[211] it thus suggested that the competence also related to the approximation of national laws to the extent required for the functioning of the internal market.[212] In any event, it has constructed Article 50(2)(g) extremely broadly.[213]

How has the Union exercised this competence? Historically, EU company law directives were 'numbered' but the Union legislator has recently abandoned this practice (see Table 15.4). The various company law directives thereby deal with such central company law issues as the validity of obligations entered into by a company,[214] the compulsory disclosure of certain documents,[215] its capital maintenance and alteration;[216] or the regulation of its

---

[208] For an overview of the field of European company law, see e.g. V. Edwards, *EC Company Law* (Oxford University Press, 1999); S. Grundmann, *European Company Law* (Intersentia, 2012).

[209] Art. 50(1) TFEU. The Court has confirmed that Art. 50(2)(g) TFEU can be used 'to achieve complete harmonisation' (Case C-212/97, *Centros*, para. 28) and has indeed found some company law directives to exhaustively harmonise a field (see Case C-167/01, *Inspire Art*, para. 69).

[210] On the scope of Art. 114 TFEU, see Chapter 14, section 1.

[211] Case C-97/96, *Verband deutscher Daihatsu-Händler eV* v. *Daihatsu Deutschland GmbH* [1997] ECR I-6843.

[212] *Ibid.*, para. 18.

[213] J. Wouters, 'European Company Law: *Quo vadis?*' (2000) 37 *CML Rev.* 257 at 270: 'Any link [directives] have with the realization of freedom of establishment for companies is at best indirect; the emphasis is entirely on legislative policy aims of equivalent protection for shareholders and creditors in the common market.' Nonetheless, where the Union legislator finds that Art. 50(2)(g) is not sufficient, it has added Art. 114 TFEU; see Directive 2007/36 on the exercise of certain rights of shareholders in listed companies [2007] OJ L 184/17.

[214] Directive 2017/1132 relating to certain aspects of company law (codification) [2017] OJ L 169/46, Title I – Chapter II.

[215] *Ibid.*, Title I – Ch. III.   [216] *Ibid.*, Title I – Ch. IV.

Table 15.4 EU Company Law Directives (Historical Selection)

EU Company Legislation	
First Company Law Directive (1968)	Eighth Company Law Directive (1984)
Second Company Law Directive (1976)	Ninth Company Law Directive (failed)
Third Company Law Directive (1978)	Tenth Company Law Directive (recast)
Fourth Company Law Directive (1978)	Eleventh Company Law Directive (1989)
Fifth Company Law Directive (failed)	Twelfth Company Law Directive (1989)
Sixth Company Law Directive (1982)	Thirteenth Company Law Directive (recast)
Seventh Company Law Directive (1983)	Fourteenth Company Law Directive (draft)

annual financial statements.[217] They determine the information to be included in a public company's statute,[218] impose certain requirements with regard to their share capital[219] and grant certain Union rights to shareholders in listed companies.[220] The Union has also branched out into more specific issues. It has thus adopted legislation on the regulation of company mergers,[221] and it has equally laid down the parameters for (hostile) takeover bids.[222] Some of these aspects have now been codified into Directive 2017/1132 relating to certain aspects of company law.[223]

bb. In Particular: European Corporate Forms

Article 50(2)(g) only provides the Union with a competence to *harmonise* the national laws governing companies formed in accordance with national law. It will not allow the Union to create European companies. This has been clarified, albeit indirectly, in *Parliament* v. *Council (European Cooperative Society)*.[224] If the Union therefore wishes to create novel – European – corporate forms, it

---

[217] Directive 2013/34 on the annual financial statements, consolidated financial statements and related reports of certain types of undertakings [2013] OJ L 182/19.

[218] *Ibid.*, esp. Arts. 2–3.   [219] *Ibid.*, esp. Arts. 6–9.

[220] Directive 2007/36 on the exercise of certain rights of shareholders in listed companies [2007] OJ L 184/17.

[221] Directive 2017/1132 (n. 213 above), Title II.

[222] Directive 2004/25 on takeover bids [2004] OJ L 142/12. For an analysis of the directive, see G. Kemperink and J. Struyck, 'The Thirteenth Company Law Directive and Competing Bids' (2008) 45 *CML Rev.* 93.

[223] Directive 2017/1132 (n. 213 above). The Directive now provides a common roof for six previous sectoral directives, including the Sixth and Eleventh Company Law Directives.

[224] Case C-436/03, *Parliament* v. *Council* [2006] ECR I-3733, where the Court found that Art. 114 TFEU could not even serve as an appropriate legal base, see *ibid.*, para. 44: 'In those circumstances, the contested regulation, which leaves unchanged the different national laws already in existence, cannot be regarded as aiming to approximate the laws of the Member States applicable to cooperative societies, but has as its purpose the creation of a new form of cooperative society in addition to the national forms.'

needs to have recourse to Article 352 TFEU – the Union's most general legislative base.[225] In the past, the Union has indeed used this competence to create three supranational corporate forms.[226] They are: the European Economic
Interest Grouping,[227] the European Company (*Societas Europaea* (SE))[228] and the
European Cooperative Society (SCE).[229]

The rationale behind the creation of European corporate forms is to overcome the limitations of the national corporate form. They are designed as corporate vehicles for cross-border businesses, and their statutes typically require a
cross-border element.[230] A good illustration of the advantages of a supranational
form is offered in the 'European Company'.[231] Its existence has been justified as
follows:

> It is essential to ensure as far as possible that the economic unit and the legal unit
> of business in the [Union] coincide. For that purpose, provision should be made for
> the creation, *side by side with companies governed by a particular national law*, of
> companies formed and carrying on business under the law created by a [Union]
> Regulation applicable in all Member States. The provisions of such a Regulation will
> permit the creation and management of *companies with a European dimension*, free
> from the obstacles arising from the disparities and the limited territorial application
> of national company law.[232]

This passage clarified that the European Company was not to replace national
companies but was merely designed as an instrument of optional harmonisation.[233]
The instrument could be used by companies with a 'European dimension' – a
criterion that the statute subsequently defines by a number of conditions that
show that the European Company is a company for public companies.[234]

---

[225] *Ibid.*, para. 46.
[226] For an excellent overview of this area, see H. Fleischer, 'Supranational Corporate Forms
    in the European Union: Prolegomena to a Theory on Supranational Forms of Association'
    (2010) 47 *CML Rev.* 1671.
[227] Regulation 2137/85 on the European Economic Interest Grouping (EEIG) [1985] OJ L
    199/1.
[228] Regulation 2157/2001 on the Statute for a European Company (SE) [2001] OJ L 294/1.
[229] Regulation 1435/2003 on the Statute for a European Cooperative Society (SCE) [2003]
    OJ L 207/1.
[230] Fleischer, 'Supranational Corporate Forms' (n. 225 above), 1689 and 1707.
[231] For an early analysis, see V. Edwards, 'The European Company: Essential Tool or Eviscerated
    Dream' (2003) 40 *CML Rev.* 443; M. Siems, 'The Impact of the European Company (SE)
    on Legal Culture' (2005) 30 *EL Rev.* 431.
[232] Regulation 2157/2001 (n. 227 above), preamble (6) and (7) (emphasis added).
[233] On the harmonisation technique of optional harmonisation, see Chapter 14, section 3.
[234] Only a number of public limited liability companies, with two of them governed by the
    law of different Member States, may merge to form a European Company (*ibid.*, Art. 2),
    which itself will be a public limited liability company (*ibid.*, Art. 3) whose share capital
    shall not be less than €120,000 (*ibid.*, Art. 4).

4. Horizontal Rules I: European Citizenship

Free movement law governing persons has become considerably more complex with the introduction of Union citizenship by the 1992 Maastricht Treaty.[235] Placed within Part II of the TFEU,[236] the Treaty today acknowledges that '[e]very person holding the nationality of a Member State shall be a citizen of the Union' and that Union citizenship grants a number of rights to all 'Europeans'.[237] With regard to free movement specifically, Article 21 TFEU here states:

> 1. Every citizen of the Union shall have the right to move and reside freely within the territory of the Member States, subject to the limitations and conditions laid down in the Treaties and by the measures adopted to give them effect.
> 2. If action by the Union should prove necessary to attain this objective and the Treaties have not provided the necessary powers, the European Parliament and the Council, acting in accordance with the ordinary legislative procedure, may adopt provisions with a view to facilitating the exercise of the rights referred to in paragraph 1.[238]

The central question behind paragraph 1 has been whether the provision grants a directly effective right to all Union citizens that is independent from the free movement of workers and freedom of establishment discussed above. Is there such a third – general – right to move freely within the Union (section (a))? Regardless of whether or not there exists such a constitutional right under Article 21(1), Article 21(2) grants the Union a legislative competence, and this competence has been used to adopt the 'Citizenship' Directive.[239] This Directive fleshes out the free movement rights for all categories of natural persons within the Union (section (b)). Importantly, companies are not covered by the citizenship provisions (see Figure 15.2).

---

[235] For an early analysis of these provisions, see C. Closa, 'The Concept of Citizenship in the Treaty on European Union' (1992) 29 *CML Rev.* 1137. And for an excellent re-evaluation, see D. Kochenov, 'Ius Tractum of Many Faces: European Citizenship and the Difficult Relationship between Status and Rights' (2009) 15 *Columbia Journal of European Law* 169.

[236] Part II is entitled: 'Non-discrimination and Citizenship of the Union', and the citizenship provisions can be found in Arts. 20–5 TFEU.

[237] Art. 20(1) TFEU.

[238] *Ibid.*, Art. 21(3) provides a special Union competence for measures concerning social security or social protection. It states: 'For the same purposes as those referred to in paragraph 1 and if the Treaties have not provided the necessary powers, the Council, acting in accordance with a special legislative procedure, may adopt measures concerning social security or social protection. The Council shall act unanimously after consulting the European Parliament.'

[239] Directive 2004/58 on the right of citizens of the Union and their family members to move and reside freely within the territory of the Member States [2004] OJ L 229/35. The directive was adopted on the legal bases of Art. 18 TFEU (non-discrimination), Art. 46 TFEU (workers), Art. 50 TFEU (establishment) and Art. 59 TFEU (services).

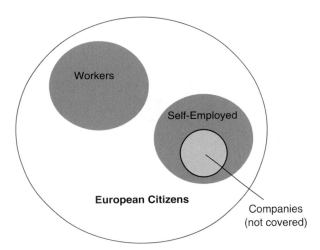

Figure 15.2 Citizenship Provisions – Coverage

a. European Citizenship: A Third Source of Movement Rights

Would Article 21(1) TFEU be directly effective, and therefore grant general movement rights to all European citizens? Having approached the matter in various indirect ways,[240] the Court finally gave a straight answer in *Baumbast*.[241] The case concerned the fight of a German father to stay with his daughters in the United Kingdom while they continued their education in a British school. The fundamental question put before the European Court was this: would a Union citizen, who no longer enjoyed a right of residence as a migrant worker, nonetheless enjoy an independent right of residence on the basis of Article 21(1) alone?

The United Kingdom government vehemently rejected this view. '[A] right of residence cannot be derived directly from Article [21(1) TFEU]', because '[t]he limitations and conditions referred to in that paragraph show that it is not intended to be a free-standing provision'.[242] The Court famously found otherwise:

> [T]he Treaty on European Union does not require that citizens of the Union pursue a professional or trade activity, whether as an employed or self-employed person, in order to enjoy the rights provided in Part Two of the [FEU] Treaty, on citizenship of the Union. Furthermore, there is nothing in the text of that Treaty to permit the conclusion

---

[240] See Case C-85/96, *Martínez Sala* v. *Freistaat Bayern* [1998] ECR I-2691; Case C-184/99, *Grzelczyk* v. *Centre public d'aide sociale d'Ottignies-Louvain-la-Neuve* [2001] ECR I-6193. In the latter case the Court famously held (*ibid.*, para. 31) that 'Union citizenship is destined to be the fundamental status of nationals of the Member States'. For an analysis of the case law here, see E. Spaventa, 'Seeing the Wood Despite the Trees? On the Scope of Union Citizenship and Its Constitutional Effects' (2008) 45 *CML Rev.* 13.

[241] Case C-413/99, *Baumbast and R* v. *Secretary of State for the Home Department.* The facts of the case are presented in section 1(b) above.

[242] *Ibid.*, para. 78.

that citizens of the Union who have established themselves in another Member State in order to carry on an activity as an employed person there are deprived, where that activity comes to an end, of the rights which are conferred on them by the [FEU] Treaty by virtue of that citizenship. *As regards, in particular, the right to reside within the territory of the Member States under Article [21(1)] that right is conferred directly on every citizen of the Union by a clear and precise provision of [that] Treaty.* Purely as a national of a Member State, and consequently a citizen of the Union, Mr Baumbast therefore has the right to rely on Article [21(1)].

Admittedly, that right for citizens of the Union to reside within the territory of another Member State is conferred subject to the limitations and conditions laid down by the [Treaties] and by the measures adopted to give it effect. However, the application of the limitations and conditions acknowledged in Article [21(1)] in respect of the exercise of that right of residence is subject to judicial review. Consequently, any limitations and conditions imposed on that right do not prevent the provisions of Article [21(1)] from conferring on individuals rights which are enforceable by them and which the national courts must protect.[243]

The Court here clarified four things. First, Article 21(1) was directly effective and would thus grant general movement rights that could be invoked against national law. The fact that these rights were subject to limitations and conditions was no barrier to their direct effect. Second, the personal scope of the citizenship provisions did not depend on the economic status of a person: Europeans enjoyed free movement rights as citizenship rights; and citizenship was a 'fundamental status' independent of someone's past or present economic position.[244] Third, with regard to their personal scope, the citizenship provisions would be residual provisions. They would only apply whenever one of the specialised movement regimes was inapplicable.[245] Fourth, a limitation on citizenship rights was possible but would be subject to judicial review; and where these limitations were disproportionate, the Court could strike them down on the basis of Article 21(1).[246]

We can clearly see this reasoning at work in *Prinz*.[247] The case concerned a German student who had lived with her family in Tunisia for a decade before returning to Germany for the last two years of her secondary education. Having obtained her A-levels in Germany, she immediately commenced her studies at the Erasmus University Rotterdam (Netherlands) for which she was awarded a

---

[243] *Ibid.*, paras. 83–6 (emphasis added).   [244] *Ibid.*, para. 82.

[245] For a subsequent confirmation, see Case C-632/13, *Skatteverket* v. *Hirvonen*, EU:C:2015:765.

[246] *Ibid.*, paras. 91–3. For subsequent confirmations and refinements of *Baumbast*, see e.g. Case C-200/02, *Zhu and Chen* v. *Secretary of State for the Home Department* [2004] ECR I-9925; Case C-34/09, *Zambrano* v. *ONEM* [2011] ECR I-1177.

[247] Joined Cases C-523/11 and C-585/11, *Prinz* v. *Region Hannover* and *Philipp Seeberger* v. *Studentenwerk Heidelberg*, EU:C:2013:524. For a first analysis of the case, see O. Neuvonen, 'In Search of (Even) More Substance for the "Real Link" Test: Comment on *Prinz* and *Seeberger*' (2014) 39 *EL Rev.* 125.

German educational grant for one year. However, when asking for an extension of that maintenance grant to cover the entire duration of her university studies, her application was rejected on the grounds that such an unlimited education grant depended on prior continuous residence in Germany for a minimum of three years. The administrative decision was challenged before a national court, which asked the European Court whether this residency requirement was a disproportionate restriction of Article 21 TFEU. And, in light of its past jurisprudence, the Court lost no time in finding such a restriction.[248]

b. Citizenship Directive: Substantive Content

The directive on the right of citizens to move and reside freely within the Union was adopted to codify in 'a single legislative act' the various secondary sources governing the free movement of persons.[249] It was designed to lay down, in a horizontal manner, 'the conditions governing the exercise of the right of free movement and residence within the territory of the Member States by Union citizens' (and their family members).[250]

The directive thereby contains five substantive chapters. Chapter II concerns the rights of exit and entry (Articles 4–5). Chapter III details the rights of residence (Articles 6–15). Chapter IV lays down rules for the right of permanent residence (Articles 16–21). Chapter V assembles provisions that are common to the right of (temporary) residence and permanent residence (Articles 22–6). Finally, Chapter VI provides detailed rules on legitimate restrictions to the right of entry and residence on grounds of public policy, public security or public health (Articles 27–33).

Let us explore the residency rights the Directive grants first, before looking at its equal treatment provisions in a second step.

[248] *Prinz* (n. 246 above), paras. 31–2: 'It must be stated that a condition of uninterrupted residence of three years, like that laid down in Article 16(3) of the BAföG, even though it applies without distinction to German nationals and other citizens of the European Union, constitutes a restriction on the right to freedom of movement and residence enjoyed by all citizens of the Union pursuant to Article 21 TFEU. Such a condition is likely to dissuade nationals, such as the applicants in the main proceedings, from exercising their right to freedom of movement and residence in another Member State, given the impact that exercising that freedom is likely to have on the right to the education or training grant.'

[249] Directive 2004/38 (n. 9 above), preamble 4. Prior to the Citizenship Directive, and in addition to various specific legislative measures for economically active citizens, the Union had adopted three residency directives for non-economically active persons; see Directive 90/364 (general residence right [1990] OJ L 180/26), Directive 90/365 (retired persons' residence [1990] OJ L 180/28), and Directive 90/366 (student residence [1990] OJ L 180/30). The Student Directive was subsequently declared void (see Case C-295/90, *Parliament v. Council* [1992] ECR I-4193), and replaced by Directive 93/96 on the right of residence for students ([1993] OJ L 317/59).

[250] Family members are defined in Art. 2(2). The group of beneficiaries is extended by Art. 3(2) to persons that are not entitled to free movement and residency but whose entry and residency the host State is obliged to facilitate. For an overview, see Table 15.5.

aa. *Residency Rights for Union Citizens (and Their Families)*

The directive distinguishes *three classes* of residency rights for EU citizens (and their family members).

According to Article 6, all Union citizens will have the short-term right to reside in the territory of another Member State for a period of up to three months 'as long as they do not become an unreasonable burden on the social assistance system of the host Member State'.[251]

A strengthened – second – class of residency rights is established by Article 7, whose first paragraph reads:

> All Union citizens shall have the right of resicence on the territory of another Member State for a period of longer than three months if they:
> (a) are workers or self-employed persons in the host Member State; or
> (b) have sufficient resources for themselves and their family members not to become a burden on the social assistance system of the host Member State during their period of residence and have comprehensive sickness insurance cover in the host Member State; or
> (c) – are enrolled at a private or public establishment, accredited or financed by the host Member State on the basis of its legislation or administrative practice, for the principal purpose of following a course of study, including vocational training; and
> – have comprehensive sickness insurance cover in the host Member State and assure the relevant national authority, by means of a declaration or by such equivalent means as they may choose, that they have sufficient resources for themselves and their family members not to become a burden on the social assistance system of the host Member State during their period of residence[.]

The provision acknowledges three categories of persons that will benefit from mid-term residency rights. Subparagraph (a) refers to the two groups of economically active migrants expressly recognised by the Treaties.[252] This is extended to all persons with 'sufficient resources' and with 'comprehensive sickness insurance' (subparagraph (b)),[253] with students benefiting from a slightly more generous treatment (subparagraph (c)).

---

[251] *Ibid.*, Art. 14(1).

[252] Art. 7(3) of the directive codifies previous case law according to which Union citizens who are no longer working or self-employed 'shall retain the status of worker or self-employed' in certain circumstances. For a discussion of this point, see 'quasi-worker', section 1(a/bb) above.

[253] Art. 8(4) of the directive thereby partly defines 'sufficient resources' by stating: 'Member States may not lay down a fixed amount which they regard as "sufficient resources", but they must take into account the personal situation of the person concerned. In all cases this amount shall not be higher than the threshold below which nationals of the host Member State become eligible for social assistance, or, where this criterion is not applicable, higher than the minimum social security pension paid by the host Member State.'

Table 15.5 Family Members and Other Beneficiaries

Family Members: Article 2(2)	Discretionary Residence: Article 3(2)
– Spouse – Partner with whom the Union citizen has contracted a registered partnership, on the basis of the legislation of a Member State, if the legislation of the host Member State treats registered partnerships as equivalent to marriage and in accordance with the conditions laid down in the relevant legislation of the host Member State – Direct descendants who are under the age of 21 or are dependants and those of the spouse or partner – Dependent direct relatives in the ascending line and those of the spouse or partner	– Any other family members, irrespective of their nationality, not falling under the definition in point 2 of Article 2 who, in the country from which they have come, are dependants or members of the household of the Union citizen having the primary right of residence, or where serious health grounds strictly require the personal care of the family member by the Union citizen – The partner with whom the Union citizen has a durable relationship, duly attested

Finally, the directive grants a third class of right: the 'right of permanent residence' in certain situations. The general rules for this are laid down in Article 16, which confers such a right to every Union citizen after lawful presence in the host State 'for a continuous period of five years'.[254] Importantly, this right of long-term residency is *independent of the economic status and the financial means of the person concerned*. It is also granted to family members.[255] Continuity of residence will thereby not be interrupted 'by temporary absences not exceeding a total of six months a year'.[256] And once acquired, 'the right of permanent residence shall be lost only through absence from the host Member State for a period exceeding two consecutive years'.[257]

bb. Beyond Residency: Equal Treatment

Once a person is legally resident in another Member State, the Directive expressly grants this person a right to equal treatment in Article 24. The provision states:

> 1. Subject to such specific provisions as are expressly provided for in the Treaty and secondary law, all Union citizens residing on the basis of this Directive in the territory of the host Member State shall enjoy equal treatment with the nationals of that Member State within the scope of the Treaty. The benefit of this right shall

---

[254] *Ibid.*, Art. 16(1). Art. 17 thereby establishes a more preferable regime for former workers or self-employed persons, and Art. 18 deals with the acquisition of the right of permanent residence by certain family members.

[255] *Ibid.*, Art. 16(2).

[256] *Ibid.*, Art. 16(3). The provision also contains special exceptions for absences for special reasons, such as military service or maternity leave.

[257] *Ibid.*, Art. 16(4).

> be extended to family members who are not nationals of a Member State and who have the right of residence or permanent residence.
> 2. By way of derogation from paragraph 1, the host Member State shall not be obliged to confer entitlement to social assistance during the first three months of residence ... nor shall it be obliged, prior to acquisition of the right of permanent residence, to grant maintenance aid for studies, including vocational training, consisting in student grants or student loans to persons other than workers, self-employed persons, persons who retain such status and members of their families.

Let us look at the provision in a bit more detail. Article 24(1) represents an equal treatment clause that however only applies to 'Union citizens residing on the basis of this Directive'. What does this mean? The connection between lawful residence and equal treatment had been made by the European Court in the past;[258] but in *Dano* it was shown to be an absolutely essential precondition for equal treatment.[259]

Dano involved a Romanian national who had moved to Germany, where she had been residing with her sister for more than three years and without ever having worked there. She had applied for social assistance and, when the latter was rejected, brought proceedings on the basis Article 24. In its ruling, the Court confirmed the link between lawful residence and equal treatment,[260] and when examining the three classes of residency rights set out in Article 7 of the directive – discussed above – found that Ms Dano fell into none: she had stayed in Germany longer than three months but fewer than five years; and she could therefore only qualify for the second class of residency right; yet since she was neither economically active nor in possession of 'sufficient resources ... not to become a burden on the social assistance system of the host Member State', the Court found that she did not enjoy any residency rights under Article 7(1)(b). For that reason, she also could not claim social benefits under Article 24(1) of the directive:

> A Member State must therefore have the possibility, pursuant to Article 7 of Directive 2004/38, of refusing to grant social benefits to economically inactive Union citizens who exercise their right to freedom of movement solely in order to obtain another Member State's social assistance although they do not have sufficient resources to claim a right of residence. To deny the Member State concerned that possibility would ... have the consequence that persons who, upon arriving in the territory of another Member State, do not have sufficient resources to provide for themselves would have them automatically, through the grant of a special non-contributory cash benefit which is intended to cover the beneficiary's subsistence costs.[261]

[258]   See Case C-85/96, *Martínez Sala*; Case C-184/99, *Grzelczyk*; Case C-209/03, *Bidar* [2005] ECR I-2119.

[259]   Case C-333/13, *Dano and Dano* v. *Jobcenter Leipzig*, EU:C:2014:2358.

[260]   *Ibid.*, para. 69.

[261]   *Ibid.*, paras. 78–9.

The Court here dealt a severe blow to what is colloquially called 'welfare tourism'; and its protective stance towards the Member States welfare competences was subsequently confirmed.[262]

By contrast, once an EU citizen is lawfully resident, a Member State is required to treat all legally resident Union citizens within its territory like its own nationals.[263] This general principle is, however, as Article 24(1) underlines, subject to such 'specific provisions as are expressly provided for in the Treaty and secondary law'. Moreover, the Union legislator has expressly – and controversially – derogated from the equal treatment principle in Article 24(2) with regard to social assistance within the first three months (and maintenance grants for students).

What counts as 'social assistance' here? The Court's definition of the term has been strongly driven by teleological considerations. In *Brey*,[264] it comprehensively defined social assistance as follows:

> [T]he concept must be interpreted as covering all assistance introduced by the public authorities, whether at national, regional or local level, that can be claimed by an individual who does not have resources sufficient to meet his own basic needs and the needs of his family and who, by reason of that fact, may become a burden on the public finances of the host Member State during his period of residence which could have consequences for the overall level of assistance which may be granted by that State.[265]

The exclusion of social assistance in Article 24(2) was principally designed to exclude unemployment benefit within the first three months in the host State. Yet such a right had been judicially accepted in *Collins*,[266] and the question therefore arose whether the *legislative* exclusion of social assistance in Article 24(2) would violate the *constitutional* right to equal treatment directly granted under Article 45(2) TFEU. The Court has ducked this question in *Vatsouras and Koupatantze*.[267] Somewhat mischievously, it here held that '[b]enefits of a financial nature which, independent of their status under national law, are intended to facilitate access to the labour market cannot be regarded as constituting "social assistance" within

---

262 Case C-67/14 *Jobcenter Berlin Neukölln* v. *Alimanovic*, EU:C:2015:597; Case C-299/14, *Jobcenter Kreis Recklinghausen, García-Nieto and others*, EU:C:2016:114.

263 See Case C-456/02, *Trojani*, para. 40.

264 Case C-140/12, *Pensionsversicherungsanstalt* v. *Brey*, EU:C:2013:565.

265 *Ibid.*, para. 61.

266 Case C-138/02, *Collins* v. *Secretary of State for Work and Pensions*.

267 Joined Cases C-22–3/08, *Vatsouras and Koupatantze* v. *Arbeitsgemeinschaft (ARGE) Nürnberg 900* [2009] ECR I-4585. For a critical analysis of this ruling, see E. Fahey, 'Interpretative Legitimacy and the Distinction between "Social Assistance" and "Work Seekers Allowance"' (2009) 34 *EL Rev.* 933.

the meaning of Article 24(2) of Directive 2004/38'.[268] These – unbelievably bold – semantic acrobatics may have saved the Union legislator. They have however come at the price of significantly compromising the clarity and consistency of European secondary law.

5. Horizontal Rules II: Justifications and Derogations

a. *General Justifications: Express and Implied Public Policy Grounds*

As with the free movement of goods, all restrictions on the free movement of persons can potentially be justified on the basis of legitimate public interests. For workers, Article 45(3) thus expressly allows for 'limitations justified *on grounds of public policy, public security or public health*'. For the freedom of establishment, Article 52 permits the 'special treatment for foreign nationals on grounds of *public policy, public security or public health*'.

Directive 2004/38 has now partly codified the case law generated under both constitutional justification clauses, while also extending these justifications horizontally to all Union citizens falling within the personal scope of the Directive. The public policy justifications for restrictions on the right of residence and equal treatment are thereby found in Chapter VI of the Citizenship Directive. Article 27 of the Directive here expressly acknowledges the power of the Member States to 'restrict the freedom of movement and residence of Union citizens and their family members, irrespective of nationality, on grounds of public policy, public security or public health'.

With regard to the first two public interest grounds, the Directive further clarifies that national restrictions must 'be based exclusively on the personal conduct of the individual concerned',[269] and that this personal conduct 'must represent a genuine, present and sufficiently serious threat affecting one of the fundamental interests of society'.[270] With regard to public health, Article 29 of the Directive subsequently determines that only 'diseases with epidemic potential' and the like will justify measures restricting free movement.[271] The remainder of this part of the Directive then deals with special issues, and in particular the procedural safeguards against expulsions.

---

[268] *Vatsouras and Koupatantze* (n. 266 above), para. 45. The Court has subsequently held that the German 'subsistence allowance' that is given to persons to cover the minimum costs to lead a decent life was not (!) a benefit 'intended to facilitate access to the labour market' and thus fell outside the *Vatsouras* exception to Art. 24(2) of the directive (see Case C-67/14, *Jobcenter Berlin Neukölln* v. *Alimanovic*, paras. 44–6).

[269] Directive 2004/38, Art. 27(2) – first indent. For an early judicial definition of what constitutes personal conduct, see Case 41/74, *Van Duyn* v. *Home Office*.

[270] Directive 2004/38, Art. 27(2) – second indent. For an early judicial definition of what constitutes a 'present' threat, see Case 30/77, *Régina* v. *Pierre Bouchereau* [1977] ECR 1999.

[271] Directive 2004/38, Art. 29(1).

Is this list of public policy justifications in the Treaties and the Citizenship Directive exhaustive? The Court has held that discriminatory measures – whether direct or indirect – can indeed solely be justified by reference to the express justifications recognised by the Treaty (and secondary law).[272] Yet as soon as the Court acknowledged that non-discriminatory measures could potentially violate the free movement provisions, it also recognised – just like for the free movement of goods – the existence of additional – implied – justifications. These implied justifications are called 'imperative requirements' or 'overriding requirements' relating to the public interest.[273] And as with the free movement of goods, the Court here accepts an unlimited and thus extremely wide range of imperative requirements.[274]

The constitutional principles governing these imperative requirements are set out in *Gebhard*,[275] where the Court held:

> [N]ational measures liable to hinder or make less attractive the exercise of fundamental freedoms guaranteed by the Treaty must fulfil four conditions: they must be applied in a non-discriminatory manner; they must be justified by imperative requirements in the general interest; they must be suitable for securing the attainment of the objective which they pursue; and they must not go beyond what is necessary in order to attain it.[276]

Imperative requirements offered by the Member States may thus only justify non-discriminatory restrictions to the free movement of persons and will be subject to the principle of proportionality. The case law on the free movement of goods here generally applies analogously.[277]

---

[272] See Case C-64/08, *Engelmann* [2010] ECR I-8219, para. 34; and more recently Case C-375/14, *Laezza*, EU:C:2016:60, para. 25. However, with regard to fiscal restrictions to the free movement of persons, the Court seems to be more relaxed, and has here partly allowed implied imperative grounds to be invoked to justify discriminatory measures.

[273] The terminology of the Court is – sadly – not uniform; see Case C-212/97, *Centros* v. *Erhvervs- og Selskabsstyrelsen* [1999] ECR I-1459, para. 32 ('imperative requirements'); Case C-442/02, *Caixa Bank France* v. *Ministère de l'Économie, des Finances et de l'Industrie* [2004] ECR I-8961, para. 17 ('overriding requirements'). Sometimes, the Court even replaces 'requirements' with 'reasons' (see Case C-446/03, *Marks & Spencer plc* v. *David Halsey (Her Majesty's Inspector of Taxes)* [2005] ECR I-10837, para. 35 ('imperative reasons')).

[274] Such imperative requirements include consumer protection (see Case 220/83, *Commission* v. *France* [1986] ECR 3663), environmental protection (see Case C-17/00, *De Coster* [2001] ECR I-9445), and many, many more. In light of the list that Barnard has collected (The Substantive Law of the EU: The Four Freedoms (Oxford University Press, 2016), 483–7), it seems almost anything can be invoked!

[275] Case C-55/94, *Gebhard* v. *Consiglio dell'Ordine degli Avvocati e Procuratori di Milano* [1995] ECR I-4165.

[276] *Ibid.*, para. 37.

[277] On imperative requirements and the principle of proportionality in the context of the free movement of goods, see Chapter 13, section 4(a/b).

Within the context of the free movement of EU citizens, the Court has nevertheless developed a special way to analyse the proportionality of national restrictions. For it here often embeds its proportionality analysis into the question whether the EU citizen has a sufficient link of integration with the host society. And while this sufficient link is, 'according to settled case law', presumed for persons economically active in the host state, this is not necessarily the case for non-economically active citizens,[278] such as students. In *Prinz*,[279] the Court thus conceded that a Member State was entitled to prevent unreasonable burdens on the public purse, and the Court accepted that education grants could be limited to persons 'who have demonstrated a certain degree of integration into the society of that State'.[280] And it is here that the Court applies its proportionality test by insisting that

> [T]he proof required to demonstrate the genuine link must not be too exclusive in nature or unduly favour one element which is not necessarily representative of the real and effective degree of connection between the claimant and this Member State.[281]

This however was the case in *Prinz*. The Court here found that the German residency requirement violated Article 21 TFEU because it was 'too general and exclusive, and goes beyond what is necessary to achieve the objectives pursued and cannot, therefore, be regarded as proportionate'.[282]

b. Special Derogation: The Public Service Exception

States may wish to reserve 'State jobs' for their nationals; and the EU Treaties do concede such a public service exception for restrictions on the free movement of persons. For workers, we find this special derogation in Article 45(4) TFEU, which states that '[t]he provisions of this Article shall not apply to *employment in the public service*'.[283] For the freedom of establishment this special limitation can be found in Article 51 which excludes activities 'connected, even occasionally, with the *exercise of official authority*'.

On their surface, both Treaty provisions appear to exclude different things from their respective scopes. For workers, the wording of Article 45 suggests that all employment in State institutions can be excluded, and it therefore seems

---

[278]   Case C-238/15, *Bragança Linares Verruga and others* v. *Ministre de l'Enseignement supérieur et de la Recherche*, EU:C:2016, 949, para. 49.

[279]   Joined Cases C-523/11 and C-585/11, *Prinz*.

[280]   *Ibid.*, para. 36.   [281]   *Ibid.*, para. 37.

[282]   *Ibid.*, para. 40.   [283]   Emphasis added.

based on an *institutional* definition of what the public service exception is. By contrast, the provision on establishment in Article 51 seems to adopt a *functional* definition that does focus on whether public functions are exercised.[284]

Despite their textual differences, the Court has opted for a uniform definition for both derogations. This choice in favour of a single – functional – definition of 'public service' can be seen in *Commission v. Belgium*.[285] The Court here held in the context of Article 45(4) TFEU as follows:

> [D]etermining the sphere of application of Article [45(4)] raises special difficulties since in the various Member States authorities acting under powers conferred by public law have assumed responsibilities of an economic and social nature or are involved in activities which are not identifiable with the functions which are typical of the public service yet which by their nature still come under the sphere of application of the Treaty. In these circumstances the effect of extending the exception contained in Article [45(4)] to posts which, whilst coming under the State or other organizations governed by public law, still do not involve any association with tasks belonging to the public service properly so called, would be to remove a considerable number of posts from the ambit of the principles set out in the Treaty and to create inequalities between Member States according to the different ways in which the state and certain sectors of economic life are organized.[286]

Because the meaning of the concept 'public service' required a 'uniform interpretation',[287] the Court has consequently rejected an institutional (national) definition and favours a functional (European) definition in Article 45(4). In *Sotgiu*,[288] the Court thus clarified that it was of 'no interest whether a worker is engaged as a workman (*ouvrier*), a clerk (*employé*) or an official (*fonctionnaire*) or even whether the terms on which he is employed come under public or private law'.[289] As

---

[284] This functional definition was confirmed by the Court in Case 2/74, *Reyners*, paras. 44–5 (emphasis added): 'The first paragraph of Article [51] must enable Member States to exclude non-nationals from taking up functions involving the exercise of official authority, which are connected with one of the activities of self-employed persons provided for in Article [49]. This need is fully satisfied when the exclusion of nationals is limited to those activities which, taken on their own, constitute a direct and specific connection with the exercise of official authority.'

[285] Case 149/79, *Commission v. Belgium* [1980] ECR 3881. See also Case C-473/93, *Commission v. Luxembourg* [1996] ECR I-3207, esp. para. 27: 'the criterion for determining whether Article [45](4) of the Treaty is applicable must be functional and must take account of the nature of the tasks and responsibilities inherent in the post, in order to ensure the effectiveness and scope of the provisions of the Treaty on freedom of movement of workers'.

[286] Case 149/79, *Commission v. Belgium*, para. 11.

[287] *Ibid.*, para. 12.

[288] Case 152/73, *Sotgiu v. Deutsche Bundespost*.

[289] *Ibid.*, para. 5.

these designations could 'be varied at the whim of national legislatures', they could not provide a criterion for the interpretation of European law.[290]

What, then, is the substantive meaning of the Union concept of 'public service'? In *Reyners*,[291] the Court had been asked if the entire legal profession could be covered by the public service exception. The Court disagreed. The exclusion of an entire profession was only permissible where the professionals would be bound to constantly come into direct contact with the exercise of official authority;[292] and this was – despite regular and organic contacts with the judicial system – not the case of lawyers:

> Professional activities involving contacts, even regular and organic, with the courts, including even compulsory cooperation in their functioning, do not constitute, as such, connexion with the exercise of official authority. The most typical activities of the profession of avocat, in particular, such as consultation and legal assistance and also representation and the defence of parties in court, even when the intervention or assistance of the avocat is compulsory or is a legal monopoly, cannot be considered as connected with the exercise of official authority. The exercise of these activities leaves the discretion of judicial authority and the free exercise of judicial power intact.[293]

The exclusion of entire posts or professions 'depend[ed] on whether or not the posts in question *are typical of the specific activities of the public service* in so far as the exercise of powers conferred by public law and responsibility for safeguarding the general interest of the State are vested in it'.[294] The Court has indeed subjected its functional test to 'very strict conditions'.[295] It has emphasised that the public service exception 'must be restricted to activities which in themselves are directly and specifically connected with the exercise of official authority'.[296] The work must involve '*a special relationship of allegiance* to the State and reciprocity of rights and duties which form the foundation of the bond of nationality'.[297] The simple transfer of some public powers to employees is not enough. It is necessary that these public powers are exercised '*on a regular basis by those holders and do not represent a very minor part of their activities*'.[298]

---

[290] *Ibid.*

[291] Case 2/74, *Reyners* v. *Belgium* [1974] ECR 631.

[292] *Ibid.*, paras. 45–7.

[293] *Ibid.*, paras. 51–3.

[294] Case 149/79, *Commission* v. *Belgium*, para. 12 (emphasis added).

[295] Case 66/85, *Lawrie-Blum* v. *Land Baden-Württemberg* [1986] ECR 2121, para. 28.

[296] Case C-61/08, *Commission* v. *Greece (Notaries)* [2011] ECR I-4399, para. 71; Case C-160/08, *Commission* v. *Germany (Ambulances)* [2010] ECR I-3713, para. 57.

[297] Case 149/79, *Commission* v. *Belgium*, para. 10 (emphasis added).

[298] Case C-47/02, *Anker and others* v. *Germany* [2003] ECR I-10447, para. 63 (emphasis added). And despite the express reference to the lower threshold of 'occasional' exercises of public powers in Art. 51 TFEU, the case law on that provision appears to run in parallel to that on Art. 45(4). For a recent confirmation of this view, see Case C-392/15, *Commission* v. *Hungary*, EU:C:2017:73, whose paras. 107–8 summarise the existing case law.

In a separate jurisprudential line, the Court has also clarified that the public service exception only justifies restrictions on the *access* to – but not discriminations inside – a position involving public power. Thus, where foreigners have been admitted to a public service post, they will benefit from the equal treatment principle. In the words of the Court, Article 45(4) 'cannot justify discriminatory measures':

> The interests which this derogation allows Member States to protect are satisfied by the opportunity of restricting admission of foreign nationals to certain activities in the public service ... The very fact that they have been admitted shows indeed that those interests which justify the exceptions to the principle of non-discrimination permitted by Article [45(4)] are not at issue.[299]

The reasoning under Article 45(4) applies, *mutatis mutandis*, to Article 51 and restrictions to professions involving public power.

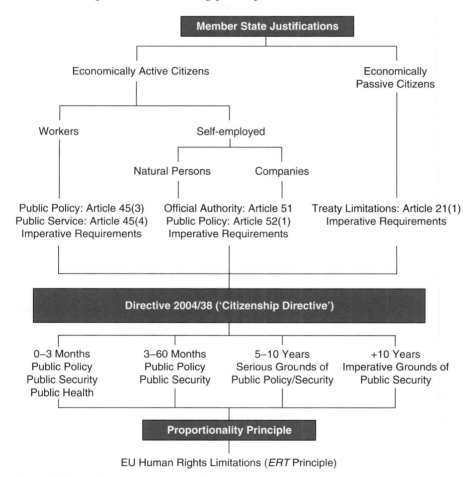

Figure 15.3 Justifications: Summary (Flowchart)

[299] Case 152/73, *Sotgiu* v. *Deutsche Bundespost*, para. 4; Case C-20/16, *Bechtel* v. *Finanzamt Offenburg*, EU:C:2017:488, esp. para. 35.

Conclusion

This has been a long chapter; and the reason for its length is that the free movement of persons is a complex fundamental freedom. It not only comprises the free movement of workers and the freedom of establishment for the self-employed as well as companies, but the European Treaties also grant a (limited) movement right to all citizens of the Union. These three distinct constitutional sources of free movement rights for persons were discussed in this chapter. Each of the three sources is complemented by – vertical or horizontal – secondary law; and the interplay between negative and positive integration has resulted in a mixture of primary and secondary Union law that makes this area of European law so rich in technical nuances.

In order to navigate these technical waters, two elements – one qualitative, one quantitative – should be kept in mind. First, despite the introduction of the horizontal provisions on Union citizenship, the Union legal order continues to *qualitatively* distinguish between categories of person exercising movement rights. Economically active Union 'workers' and 'professionals' will thus generally be entitled to full assimilation into the host State, while non-economically active citizens will not. Within the latter category, the Union has moreover adopted a *quantitative* approach.[300] The number of rights that a migrant Union citizen can claim will depend on the degree of his or her integration into the host society. A Member State may thus insist on a 'genuine link' between the migrant and the host society; yet that link must 'not be too exclusive in nature or unduly favour one element which is not necessarily representative of the real and effective degree of connection between the claimant and this Member State'.[301]

Restrictions on citizenship mobility must thus be justified and proportionate restrictions. And, in light of the restriction test developed for all three constitutional sources on the free movement of persons, the qualitative and quantitative distinctions will indeed be particularly important at the justification level. The EU Treaties and the Citizenship Directive therefore make the public policy grounds available and the review standard applicable dependent on the category of citizen involved and the length of time spent in the host State (see Figure 15.3).

How successful has the free movement of (natural) persons been in the past? In contrast to the phenomenal success of the free movement of goods, the free movement of persons has traditionally not been very successful in quantitative terms. With only around 3 per cent of EU citizens using their free movement rights, the migration levels between Member States are disappointingly low.

---

[300] Barnard, *Substantive Law* (n. 273 above), 358.
[301] Joined Cases C-523/11 and C-585/11, *Prinz*, para. 37.

FURTHER READING

Books

C. Barnard, *The Substantive Law of the EU: The Four Freedoms* (Oxford University Press, 2016)

J. Borg-Barthet, *The Governing Law of Companies in EU Law* (Hart, 2012)

V. Edwards, *EC Company Law* (Oxford University Press, 1999)

M. Fuchs and R. Cornelissen, *EU Social Security Law* (Beck-Hart-Nomos, 2015)

S. Grundmann, *European Company Law* (Intersentia, 2011)

A. P. van der Mei, *Free Movement of Persons within the European Community: Cross-border Access to Public Benefits* (Hart, 2003)

J. Pennings, *European Social Security Law* (Intersentia, 2015)

E. Spaventa, *Free Movement of Persons in the European Union: Barriers to Movement in their Constitutional Context* (Kluwer, 2007)

A. Tryfonidou, *The Impact of Union Citizenship on the EU's Market Freedoms* (Hart, 2016)

F. Weiss and C. Kaupa, *European Union Internal Market Law* (Cambridge University Press, 2014)

Articles (and Chapters)

J. Armour and W.-G. Ringe, 'European Company Law 1999–2010: Renaissance and Crisis' (2011) 48 *CML Rev.* 142

M. Dougan, 'The Constitutional Dimension to the Case Law on Union Citizenship' (2006) 31 *EL Rev.* 613

E. Fahey, 'Interpretive Legitimacy and the Distinction between "Social Assistance" and "Work-seekers' Allowance": Comment on "Vatsouras"' (2009) 34 *EL Rev.* 933

H. Fleischer, 'Supranational Corporate Forms in the European Union: Prolegomena to a Theory on Supranational Forms of Association' (2010) 47 *CML Rev.* 1671

D. Kochenov, 'The Essence of EU Citizenship Emerging from the Last Ten Years of Academic Debate: Beyond the Cherry Blossoms and the Moon?' (2013) 62 ICLQ 97

C. O'Brien, 'Real Links, Abstract Rights and False Alarms: The Relationship between the ECJ's "Real Link" Case Law and National Solidarity' (2008) 33 *EL Rev.* 643

N. Rennuy, 'The Emergence of a Parallel System of Social Security Coordination' (2013) 50 *CML Rev.* 1221

W.-H. Roth, 'From "*Centros*" to "*Überseering*": Free Movement of Companies, Private International Law, and Community Law' (2003) 52 ICLQ 177

E. Spaventa, 'From "*Gebhard*" to "*Carpenter*": Towards a (Non-)economic European Constitution' (2004) 41 *CML Rev.* 743

A. Tryfonidou, 'In Search of the Aim of the EC Free Movement of Persons Provisions: Has the Court of Justice Missed the Point?' (2009) 46 *CML Rev.* 1591

D. Thym, 'The Elusive Limits of Solidarity: Residence Rights of and Social Benefits for Economically Inactive Union Citizens' (2015) 52 *CML Rev.* 17

Cases on the Website

Case 152/73, *Sotgiu*; Case 2/74, *Reyners*; Case 32/75, *Cristini*; Case 115/78, *Knoors*; Case 149/79, *Commission v. Belgium*; Case 53/81, *Levin*; Case 107/83, *Klopp*; Case 270/83, *Commission v. France (Avoir Fiscal)*; Case 66/85, *Lawrie Blum*; Case 316/85, *Lebon*; Case 39/86, *Lair*; Case 81/87, *Daily Mail*; Case C-221/89, *Factortame II*; Case C-292/89, *Antonissen*; Case C-340/89, *Vlassopoulou*; Case C-415/93, *Bosman*; Case C-55/94, *Gebhard*; Case C-97/96, *Daihatsu*; Case C-212/97, *Centros*; Case C-413/99, *Baumbast*; Case C-167/01, *Inspire Art*; Case C-138/02, *Collins*; Case C-436/03, *Parliament v. Council (European Cooperative Society)*; Case C-196/04, *Cadbury Schweppes*; Case C-210/06, *Cartesio*; Case C-570/07, *Blanco Pérez*; Joined Cases C-22–3/08, *Vatsouras and Koupatentze*; Joined Cases C-611–12/10, *Hudzinski*; Joined Cases C-523 and 585/11, *Prinz*; Case C-140/12, *Brey*; Case C-514/12, *Landeskliniken*; Case C-333/13, *Dano*

16

Free Movement of Services and Capital

Contents

Introduction

In the first half of the twenty-first century, services (and capital) have moved to the heart of the European economy.[1] Yet the Treaty freedoms dealing with

---

[1] V. Hatzopoulos, *Regulating Services in the European Union* (Oxford University Press, 2012), vii: 'Over 70 per cent of Member States' GDP comes from the provision of services. About the

Table 16.1 Internal Market – Overview

TFEU – Part III: Internal Market Provisions	
Title I: The Internal Market	
Title II: Free Movement of Goods	Title IV: Persons, Services & Capital
Chapter 1: The Customs Union	Chapter 1: Workers
Chapter 2: Customs Cooperation	Chapter 2: Establishment
Chapter 3: Prohibition of QRs	Chapter 3: Services
Title III: Agriculture & Fisheries	Chapter 4: Capital

the liberalisation of services and capital long suffered from a 'shadow exist-ence'.[2] The nocturnal status of the third and the fourth freedoms thereby stemmed from different constitutional causes. For services, it lay in the ambiv-alent status of the services provisions. The Treaties appeared to treat them as a 'subordinate' freedom – the services chapter only applies 'in so far as [services] are not governed by the provisions relating to the freedom of movement for goods, capital and persons'.[3] The nocturnal existence of the capital chapter originated from a different constitutional cause. Its 'backwardness' stemmed from the fact that the original capital provisions had left the liberalisation effort entirely in the hands of the Union legislator. This predominance of positive integration only changed with the 1992 Treaty on European Union. The latter radically redrafted the capital chapter; and its provisions would henceforth be directly effective – belatedly giving rise to the forces of nega-tive integration.

This fourth and final chapter on the Union's internal market explores the third and the fourth freedom of movement: the freedom of services and the freedom of capital (Table 16.1). Section 1 analyses the general aspects of the free movement of services. We shall see there that the Court has significantly pushed negative integration through a restriction rationale; yet the Union has also followed a positive integration path in the form of the 'Services Directive'. Section 2 moves to two special – and very controversial – services regimes, namely that for posted workers and that for public services. By contrast, sec-tions 3 and 4 deal with the free movement of capital – with the former section analysing the scope of the (negative) freedom, whereas the latter surveys the various grounds on which restrictions to the free movement of capital may be justified.

---

same percentage accounts to the actual level of employment in services, while the numbers climb to over 95 per cent when it comes to the creation of new employment.'
[2] For services, see W.-H. Roth, 'The European Economic Community's Law on Services: Harmonisation' (1988) 25 *CML Rev.* 35.
[3] Art. 57[1] TFEU.

1. Services I: General Regime

Despite its slow start, the free movement of services is today one of the most progressive freedoms. Its central prohibition can be found in Article 56 TFEU, which states:

> Within the framework of the provisions set out below, restrictions on freedom to *provide* services within the Union shall be prohibited in respect of *nationals of Member States who are established in a Member State other than that of the person for whom the services are intended.*[4]

The provision is complemented by Article 57 TFEU, which provides a constitutional clarification of what is – and what is not – supposed to be covered by the prohibition. It thereby defines services as follows:

> Services shall be considered to be 'services' within the meaning of the Treaties where they are normally *provided for remuneration*, in so far as they are not governed by the provisions relating to freedom of movement for goods, capital and persons.
>   'Services' shall in particular include:
> (a) activities of an industrial character;
> (b) activities of a commercial character;
> (c) activities of craftsmen;
> (d) activities of the professions.
> Without prejudice to the provisions of the Chapter relating to the right of establishment, the person providing a service may, in order to do so, *temporarily pursue his activity* in the Member State where the service is provided, *under the same conditions as are imposed by that State on its own nationals.*[5]

Two 'existential' questions lay in these two articles. First, what was the relationship between the freedom of services and the other freedoms, especially the freedom of establishment; and, second, what was the 'personal scope' of the freedom of services? Was it the service itself or the provider of the service? On the one hand, Article 57 defined a service as an 'activity'– an immaterial 'object' that is not a 'good'– but, on the other hand, Article 56 seemed to textually outlaw only those limitations that would affect the service *provider*. The central prohibition in Article 56 indeed appeared to primarily protect the free movement of a person, who could – according to Article 57 TFEU – 'temporarily pursue his activity in the Member State where the service is provided, under the same conditions as are imposed by that State on its own nationals'.

---

[4] Art. 56[1] TFEU (emphasis added). The second indent offers a legislative competence to the Union to extend the provisions of the services chapter 'to nationals of a third country who provide services and who are established within the Union'.
[5] Art. 57 TFEU (emphasis added).

Table 16.2 Services Provisions – Overview

TFEU Services Chapter	
Article 56	General Prohibition on Restrictions on Services
Article 57	Definition(s) of Services and General Relations to the Other Freedoms
Article 58	Special Relations to the Transport Title and the Capital Freedom
Article 59	Legislative Competence (liberalisation directives)
Article 60	Legal Competence for Commission Recommendations
Article 61	Prohibition of Discrimination (in the presence of service restrictions)
Article 62	Cross-references to Chapter on Establishment ('official authority exception', 'policy justifications', 'mutual recognition' and 'legal persons')
Protocol No. 26 'On Services of General Interest'	
Secondary Law (Selection) Directive 2006/123 on Services in the Internal Market Directive 96/71 on Posted Workers Directive 2011/24 on Patients' Rights in Cross-border Healthcare	

This first section hopes to explore these general questions and to offer an overview of the dramatic advancement of this third freedom. The progress of negative integration here has also been accompanied by positive integration, and the most important measure in this context is the controversial 'Services Directive'. Section 2 subsequently moves to two special aspects of the Union regime governing services. We shall investigate the special regime for 'posted workers', which – unlike the term suggests – is not subject to the free movement of workers provisions. The second special regime concerns the provision of 'public services', that is: services that the general public is entitled to have guaranteed by the State.

What this chapter will however not explore are the (written and unwritten) public policy justifications for restrictions on services because Article 62 TFEU here simply cross-references to the chapter on establishment; and the analysis made there will indeed apply, *mutatis mutandis*, to services.[6]

a. *Negative Integration: The Prohibition in Article 56*

aa. *Personal Scope I: Beneficiaries and Addressees*

Article 56 prohibits 'restrictions on freedom to provide services within the Union' and the Court has declared the provision to be directly effective.[7]

---

[6] For an analysis of the justifications available for restrictions to the free movement of persons, and the freedom of establishment particularly, see Chapter 15, section 5. For a special analysis of justifications for services restrictions, see Hatzopoulos, 'Regulating Services' (n. 1 above), ch. 4; S. O'Leary and J. Fernandez-Martin, 'Judicially Created Exceptions to Free Provisions of Services' in M. Andenas and W.-H. Roth (eds.), *Services and Free Movement in EU Law* (Oxford University Press, 2002), 163.

[7] Case 33/74, *Van Binsbergen v. Bestuur van de Bedrijfsvereniging voor de Metaalnijverheid* [1974] ECR 1299, para. 26.

What is the 'personal' scope of the prohibition? The provision gives a right to *self*-employed service *providers* – not workers. However: in what situations? Article 56 appears to envisage only one single situation: a person (or company) established in one Member State moves abroad to provide a service to a person in another Member State. The Court has however clarified that Article 56 covers two additional situations. It will also apply where the *recipient* of the service moves to the Member State of the service provider; and, third, it will also apply where neither the provider nor the recipient moves but the service *itself* moves across national borders.

That Article 56 would also cover the second situation was famously established in *Luisi and Carbone*, where the Court held:

> By virtue of Article [56] of the Treaty, restrictions on freedom to provide such services are to be abolished in respect of nationals of Member States who are established in a Member State other than that of the person for whom the service is intended. In order to enable services to be provided, the person providing the service may go to the Member State where the person for whom it is provided, is established *or else the latter may go to the State in which the person providing the service is established*. Whilst the former case is expressly mentioned in the third paragraph of Article [57], which permits the person providing the service to pursue his activity temporarily in the Member State where the service is provided, *the latter case is the necessary corollary thereof, which fulfils the objective of liberalizing all gainful activity not covered by the free movement of goods, persons and capital*.[8]

The application of Article 56 to the third situation was confirmed in *Alpine Investments*.[9] The case involved the advertising of financial services through the sales technique of 'cold calling'. A Dutch company had here called *potential* recipients of financial services in other Member States. This technique had been prohibited by the Netherlands following numerous complaints by investors having made bad investments. Challenging the prohibition in a national court, Alpine Investments argued that since its services were also offered to foreign investors, the prohibition of cold calling violated the free provision of services as guaranteed in the EU Treaties. In a preliminary ruling, the ECJ agreed by not only clarifying that potential service recipients would be covered but that neither the service provider nor the recipient had to physically move:

---

[8] See Case 286/82, *Luisi and Carbone* v. *Ministero del Tesoro* [1984] ECR 377, para. 10 (emphasis added). For subsequent confirmation, see e.g. Case C-372/04, *Watts* v. *Bedford Primary Care Trust and Secretary of State for Health* [2006] ECR I-4325; and Case C-342/15, *Piringer*, EU:C:2017:196, where the Court refers to this second situation as the '"passive" freedom to provide services' (*ibid.*, para. 35).

[9] See Case C-384/93, *Alpine Investments BV* v. *Minister van Financiën* [1995] ECR I-1141; Case C-60/00, *Carpenter* v. *Secretary of State for the Home Department* [2002] I-6279; Case C-342/14, *X-Steuerberatungsgesellschaft* v. *Finanzamt Hannover-Nord*, EU:C:2015:827.

First, [the national court] asks whether the fact that the services in question are just offers without, as yet, an identifiable recipient of the service precludes application of Article [56] of the Treaty. The freedom to provide services would become illusory if national rules were at liberty to restrict offers of services. *The prior existence of an identifiable recipient cannot therefore be a condition for application of the provisions on the freedom to provide services.*

The second aspect of the question is whether Article [56] covers services which the provider offers by telephone to persons established in another Member State and which he provides without moving from the Member State in which he is established. *In this case, the offers of services are made by a provider established in one Member State to a potential recipient established in another Member State. It follows from the express terms of Article [56] that there is therefore a provision of services within the meaning of that provision.*[10]

Article 56 consequently outlaws restrictions imposed by the host State as well as by the home State; and as with the free movement of persons, a single prohibition thus applies to 'import' as well as 'export' restrictions alike.[11]

Having looked at the 'beneficiary' side of Article 56, which addressees are caught by the personal scope of the provision? The personal scope of Article 56 not only captures restrictions adopted by public authorities but – again like the free movement of persons – may equally apply to actions by private parties. The potential inclusion of private party actions was indeed established for both freedoms in *Walrave and Koch*.[12] The Court here expressly held:

Prohibition of such discrimination does not only apply to the action of public authorities but extends likewise to rules of any other nature aimed at regulating in a collective manner gainful employment and the provision of services ... Since, moreover, working conditions in the various Member States are governed sometimes by means of provisions laid down by law or regulation and sometimes by agreements and other acts concluded or adopted by private persons, to limit the prohibitions in question to acts of a public authority would risk creating inequality in their application. Although the third paragraph of Article [57], and Article[] [60], specifically relate, as regards the provision of services, to the abolition of measures by the State, this fact does not defeat the general nature of the terms of Article [56], which makes no distinction between the source of the restrictions to be abolished.[13]

---

[10] Case C-384/93, *Alpine Investments*, paras. 18–21 (emphasis added).

[11] For restrictions imposed by the 'home' State, see e.g. *ibid.*, para. 30: '[T]hat provision covers not only restrictions laid down by the State of destination but also those laid down by the State of origin. As the Court has frequently held, the right freely to provide services may be relied on by an undertaking as against the State in which it is established if the services are provided for persons established in another Member State.'

[12] Case 36/74, *Walrave and Koch* v. *Association Union cycliste internationale* [1974] ECR 1405.

[13] *Ibid.*, paras. 17–19. For a general discussion of the personal scope of the free movement provisions, see Chapter 13, section 1(a).

The inclusion of private party actions that 'regulat[e] in a collective matter' the provision of services has been a permanent feature of the provision. The Court has thereby given a wide reading to the regulatory function rationale. In *Laval*,[14] it thus held that collective *strike actions*, taken by a trade union to bring pressure on a foreign service provider, could fall within the personal scope of Article 56.

bb. Personal Scope II: The Concept of 'Services'

The object behind Article 56 is the 'freedom to provide services'. This formulation textually covers the 'provider' of the service as well as the 'service' itself. Both aspects can indeed be combined once we identify the protective aim of Article 56 in the freedom to engage in a particular economic *activity*. The central aim behind the freedom of services is to outlaw restrictions on economic activities, that is: activities that are 'normally provided for remuneration'.

This laconic definition, found in Article 57, has been subject to intense judicial examination. Would it include services that are illegal in the host State; and what about services whose remuneration was not direct consideration? The Court has answered both questions affirmatively and thereby established an enormously broad concept of 'services'. With regard to socially 'contentious' services, like prostitution or abortion, the Court has thus insisted in *Grogan* that where an activity is 'lawfully practiced in *several* Member States', the immoral or illegal status of the service in one or more State(s) will not prevent the Court from holding that a 'service' within the meaning of Article 57 TFEU has been rendered.[15]

A similarly liberal stance has developed with regard to the requirement of remuneration. Originally, the Court had here however started with a more conservative definition. In *Humbel*,[16] it had still insisted that the essential characteristic of remuneration was that 'it constitutes *consideration* for the service in question, and is normally agreed upon *between the provider and the recipient of the service*'.[17] This restrictive definition was subsequently opened on either side. The Court thus clarified that 'consideration' must be read in the broadest possible sense:

---

[14] Case C–341/05, *Laval un Partneri Ltd* v. *Svenska* [2007] ECR I-11767. For an excellent contextual discussion of the case from the point of view of direct effect, see A. Dashwood, '*Viking* and *Laval*: Issues of Horizontal Direct Effect' (2007–8) 10 CYELS 525.

[15] Case C–159/90, *Grogan* [1991] ECR I-4685, para. 18. The Court has explained this choice as follows: 'It is not for the Court to substitute its assessment for that of the legislature in those Member States where the activities in question are practised legally' (*ibid.*, para. 20). This controversial choice has been confirmed in subsequent jurisprudence, see e.g. Case C–275/92, *Her Majesty's Customs and Excise* v. *Schindler and Schindler* [1994] ECR I-1039; Case C–268/99, *Jany and others* v. *Staatssecretaris van Justitie* [2001] ECR I-8615, paras. 56–7: 'So far as concerns the question of the immorality of that activity, raised by the referring court, it must also be borne in mind that, as the Court has already held, it is not for the Court to substitute its own assessment for that of the legislatures of the Member States where an allegedly immoral activity is practised legally. Far from being prohibited in all Member States, prostitution is tolerated, even regulated, by most of those States, notably the Member State concerned in the present case.'

[16] Case 263/86, *Belgian State* v. *Humbel and others* [1988] ECR 5365 637.

[17] *Ibid.*, para. 17 (emphasis added).

> [T]he decisive factor which brings an activity within the ambit of the Treaty provisions on the freedom to provide services is its economic character, that is to say, the activity must not be provided for nothing.[18]

This liberal definition simply equates the requirement of 'remuneration' with that of an 'economic' activity. And the Court has even dropped the idea that the service provider need be directly paid by the recipient. Where a third party – like an insurance fund – indirectly pays for medical expenses incurred, the treatment will still be seen as a 'remunerated' service.[19]

In light of this wide definition of the personal scope of Article 56, how has the Court 'delineated' the freedom to provide services from the other three freedoms? The wording of Article 57[3] here suggested that the service chapter would only apply to situations '*in so far as they are not governed* by the provisions relating to freedom of movement for goods, capital and persons'. This assigned a subordinate and residual character to the freedom to provide services.

While the Court originally followed this textual lead,[20] it decisively rejected the idea of a subordinate freedom in *Fidium Finanz*.[21] The Court here insisted that Article 57 '*does not establish any order of priority between the freedom to provide services and the other fundamental freedoms*'.[22] Where a national measure related to the freedom to provide services and to another freedom, it was 'necessary to consider to what extent the exercise of those fundamental liberties is affected and whether, in the circumstances of the main proceedings, one of those prevails over the other'.[23] This 'centre of gravity' approach elevates the freedom to

---

[18] Case C-281/06, *Jundt* v. *Finanzamt Offenburg* [2007] ECR I-12231, para. 32; see also Case C-159/90, *Grogan*.

[19] Case C-157/99, *Peerbooms* v. *Stichting CZ Groep Zorgverzekeringen* [2001] ECR I-5473, esp. para. 56: '[T]he fact that hospital medical treatment is financed directly by the sickness insurance funds on the basis of agreements and pre-set scales of fees is not in any event such as to remove such treatment from the sphere of services within the meaning of Article [57] of the Treaty'. See more generally: Case 352/85, *Bond van Adverteerders and others* [1988] ECR 2085, para. 16, and Joined Cases C-51/96 and C-191/97, *Deliège* [2000] ECR I-2549, para. 56: '[Services] may fall within the scope of Article [56] of the Treaty even if some of those services are not paid for by those for whom they are performed.'

[20] Case 205/84, *Commission* v. *Germany (Insurance)* [1986] ECR 3755.

[21] Case C-452/04, *Fidium Finanz AG* v. *Bundesanstalt für Finanzdienstleistungsaufsicht* [2006] ECR I-9521.

[22] *Ibid.*, para. 32.

[23] *Ibid.*, para. 34. This has been confirmed in Case C-602/10, *Volksbank Romania* EU:C:2012:443, para. 70: 'Where a national measure relates to both the freedom to provide services and the free movement of capital, it is necessary to consider to what extent the exercise of those fundamental freedoms is affected and whether, in the circumstances of the main proceedings, one of them prevails over the other. The Court will in principle examine the measure in dispute in relation to only one of those two freedoms if it appears, in the circumstances of the case, that one of them is entirely secondary in relation to the other and may be considered together with it (Case C-452/04, *Fidium Finanz* [2006] ECR I-9521, paragraph 34).'

provide services to the same rank as the other freedoms – a position that has intensified the 'delineation' problems with the other three freedoms.[24]

Delineation problems are nevertheless particularly pronounced with regard to the freedom of establishment. Here the Court originally followed its traditional view on the residual and subordinate nature of the services provisions. Thus, wherever a company maintained a permanent presence in the host State, the matter fell into the freedom of establishment and the company 'cannot therefore avail itself of Articles [56 and 57] with regard to its activities in the Member State in question'.[25] This view was (partly) confirmed in *Gebhard*;[26] yet the Court here also accepted that a service provider is entitled to equip himself with some form of infrastructure in the host State. The principal criterion to distinguish between establishment and services would be whether the activities were carried out 'on a temporary basis'.[27] (This view accords with Article 57[3] TFEU, which refers to the criterion of time to distinguish the right of establishment from the right to provide services.)

In subsequent jurisprudence, the Court has however prudently refused to put a definite time limit on when the provision of services becomes (primary or secondary) establishment. Its casuistic and service-friendly approach is best illustrated in *Schnitzer*,[28] where the Court found:

> [S]ervices within the meaning of the Treaty may cover services varying widely in nature, including services which are provided over an extended period, even over several years … Services within the meaning of the Treaty may likewise be constituted by services which a business established in a Member State supplies with a greater or lesser degree of frequency or regularity, even over an extended period, to persons established in one or more other Member States, for example the giving of advice or information for remuneration. No provision of the Treaty affords a means of determining, in an abstract manner, the duration or frequency beyond which the supply of a service or of a certain type of service in another Member State can no longer be regarded as the provision of services within the meaning of the Treaty.[29]

This extremely wide and open definition of services only encounters one categorical limit, namely where the provider (or recipient) of the service 'establishes his *principal* residence, on a permanent basis, or in any event without there being a foreseeable limit to the duration of that residence, in the territory of another Member State'.[30] This – wide – reading of 'services' excludes only situations of

---

[24] For an extensive analysis of these delineation problems, see V. Hatzopoulos, 'The Case Law of the ECJ Concerning the Free Provision of Services: 2000–2005' (2006) 43 *CML Rev.* 923 esp. 948ff.

[25] Case 205/84, *Commission* v. *Germany (Insurance)*, para. 21.

[26] Case C-55/94, *Gebhard* v. *Consiglio dell'Ordine degli Avvocati e Procuratori di Milano* [1995] ECR I-4165, esp. paras. 20 and 22.

[27] *Ibid.*, para. 26   [28] Case C-215/01, *Schnitzer* [2003] ECR I-14847.   [29] *Ibid.*, paras. 30–1.

[30] Case C-208/07, *von Chamier-Glisczinski* v. *Deutsche Angestellten-Krankenkasse* [2009] ECR I-6095, para. 75, and see also Case C-70/95, *Sodemore* v. *Regione Lombardia* [1997] ECR I-3395, para. 38: 'establishes his *principal* residence' for an 'indefinite period' in the host State.

primary establishment from the scope of Article 57; and this gives 'a clear priority' to the rules on services over those on (secondary) establishment.[31] It seems, therefore, that the Court has managed to turn the Treaty text on the relationship between the two freedoms on its head!

Why is the distinction between the freedom of establishment and the free provision of services so important? The reason is this:

> [A] Member State may *not make the provision of services in its territory subject to compliance with all the conditions required for establishment* and thereby deprive of all practical effectiveness the provisions of the Treaty whose object is, precisely, to guarantee the freedom to provide services.[32]

The rights granted under the freedom of services are consequently perceived as wider than the rights under the freedom of establishment. For, where a person does not wish to establish herself in the territory of the host State, she cannot be expected to entertain such a close relationship with the legal order of that State as someone who decides to stay there permanently.

cc. Material Scope: Discrimination and Beyond

What 'material scope' does Article 56 have? In other words: what types of national measures fall foul of the freedom to provide services? Like the free movement of persons, the provision covers regulatory as well as fiscal measures.[33] But would Article 56 cover discriminatory as well as non-discriminatory measures? The text of Article 56 suggests that only discriminatory restrictions are covered; yet this narrow reading seems to be contradicted by Article 61, which mysteriously refers to 'restrictions on freedom to provide services'.

With the Treaty text pointing in different directions, it was up to the Court to determine the degree of negative integration. The Court thereby started out with a classic discrimination rationale. Article 56 would outlaw all restrictions that were based on the nationality or the residence of the service provider.[34]

---

[31] V. Hatzopoulos, 'The Court's Approach to Services (2006–2012): From Case Law to Case Load?' (2013) 50 *CML Rev.* 459 at 464: 'Hence, especially in relation to the freedom of establishment, a clear priority is being drawn in the Court's recent case law, in favour of the rules on services.'

[32] Case C-76/90, *Säger v. Dennemeyer* [1991] ECR I-4221, para. 13 (emphasis added).

[33] The services provisions cover, like the free movement of persons provisions, 'regulatory' as well as 'fiscal' measures; see e.g. Case C-134/03, *Viacom Outdoor Srl v. Giotto Immobilier* [2005] ECR I-1167; Case C-544/03, *Mobistar SA v. Commune de Fléron* [2005] ECR I-7723.

[34] See e.g. Case 33/74, *Van Binsbergen*, para. 10; Case 36/74, *Walrave*, para. 17; Case 15/78, *Société générale alsacienne de banque v. Koestler* [1978] ECR 1971, para. 5: '[T]he Treaty, whilst it prohibits discrimination, does not impose any obligation to treat a foreigner providing services more favourably, with reference to his domestic law, than a person providing services established in the Member State where the services have been provided.' For a classic discrimination reading of Art. 56, see G. Marenco, 'The Notion of Restriction on the

With regard to residence requirements in particular, the Court thus found that they would 'have the result of depriving Article [56] of all useful effect, in view that the precise object of that Article is to abolish restrictions on freedom to provide services imposed on persons who are not established in the State where the service is to be provided'.[35]

The Court has however not stopped here. Realising that the freedom to provide services would have to be wider than the freedom of establishment, the Court in *Säger* expressly confirmed that Article 56 went beyond discrimination:

> Article [56] requires not only the elimination of all discrimination against a person providing services on the ground of his nationality but also the abolition of any restriction, *even if it applies without distinction* to national providers of services and to those of other Member States, *when it is liable to prohibit or otherwise impede the activities of a provider of services* established in another Member State where it lawfully provides similar services.[36]

This *Säger* formula clearly states that Article 56 would cover discriminatory and non-discriminatory measures.[37] The inclusion of non-discriminatory measures into the scope of Article 56 was however limited. For the Court insisted that they must actually restrict cross-border services.[38] The Court has equally clarified that a national measure will not constitute a restriction 'solely by virtue of the fact that other Member States apply less strict rules to providers of similar services established in their territory'.[39] The non-discriminatory measure must 'affect access to the market' and 'thereby hinder intra-[Union] trade'.[40]

This 'market-access' test is distinct from a double-burden test, since it does not build on the idea of (primary) home State control and the principle of mutual recognition. However, like the double-burden test, it rejects the idea

---

Freedom of Establishment and Provision of Services in the Case Law of the Court' (1991) 11 *YEL* 111.

[35] Case 33/74, *Van Binsbergen*, para. 11. See also Case 205/84, *Commission v. Germany (Insurance)*, esp. para. 52: 'If the requirement of an authorization constitutes a restriction on the freedom to provide services, the requirement of a permanent establishment is the very negation of that freedom.'

[36] Case C-76/90, *Säger*, para. 12.

[37] The *Säger* formula has become a standard formula, see Joined Cases C-344/13 and C-367/13, *Blanco and Fabretti* v. *Agenzia delle Entrate*, EU:C:2014:2311, para. 26; Case C-342/15, *Piringer*, para. 49. In line with the settled case law on establishment (see Chapter 15, section 5(a)), the distinction between discriminatory and non-discriminatory measures determines whether in addition to the Treaty's express justifications Member States can also refer to unwritten imperative requirements or overriding reasons in the public interest (see Joined Cases C-344/13 and C-367/13, *Blanco and Fabretti* v. *Agenzia delle Entrate*, para. 38; Case C-375/14, *Laezza*, EU:C:2016:60, para. 26).

[38] Case C-384/93, *Alpine Investments*, para. 35.

[39] *Ibid.*, para. 27. See also Case C-518/06, *Commission v. Italy* [2009] ECR I-3491, para. 63.

[40] *Ibid.*, para. 64.

of (primary) host State control. The question that has, in the past, been hotly debated is whether the restriction test under Article 56 allows the host State – like under the free movement of goods – a *Keck*-like exception.[41] For while not having expressly acknowledged the idea of 'selling arrangements' for services, the Court has expressly excluded from the scope of Article 56 'measures, the only effect of which is to create additional costs in respect of services in question and which affect in the same way the provision of services between Member States and that within one Member State'.[42] But this simply seems to insist on a 'federal' as opposed to a 'national' – model of integration; since the Court here merely underlines that the hindering effect caused by the national measure must be greater for *inter*-State trade than for *intra*-State trade.

b. Positive Integration: The Services Directive

The Union is entitled under Article 59 TFEU to adopt legislation designed to 'achieve the liberalisation of a *specific* service' by means of directives.[43] This is the sole legislative competence within the services chapter. On the basis of its word-ing, it appears to confine positive integration to a vertical approach: each and every service would need to be harmonised individually.[44] A vertical approach has indeed been applied to a range of sector-specific service industries, such as audiovisual media services,[45] as well as healthcare services.[46]

This vertical approach has however been complemented by a horizontal approach that tries to regulate general aspects for all services. What is the legisla-tive competence here? Thanks to the cross-referencing done by Article 62 TFEU, the services chapter can here employ the 'services' of two legislative competences

---

[41] The argument had been advanced in Case C–384/93, *Alpine Investments*, but the Court distinguished the national measure at issue from a selling arrangement (*ibid.*, para. 36: 'Such a prohibition is not analogous to the legislation concerning selling arrangements held in *Keck and Mithouard* to fall outside the scope of Article [34] of the Treaty'). According to some authors, the distinction between product requirements and selling arrangements cannot be transposed to the field of services, while others have argued that the Court may eventually accept an extension of *Keck* to the freedom to provide services (see M. Maduro, 'The Sage of Article 30 EC Treaty: To Be Continued' (1998) 5 *Maastricht Journal of European and Comparative Law* 298). For an extensive discussion of these issues, see J. Luís da Cruz Vilaça, 'On the Application of *Keck* in the Field of Free Provision of Services', in M. Andenas and W.-H. Roth (eds.), *Services and Free Movement in EU Law* (Oxford University Press, 2002), 25; D. Doukas, 'Untying the Market Access Knot: Advertising Restrictions and the Free Movement of Goods and Services' (2006–7) 9 *CYELS* 177.
[42] Case C–544/03, *Mobistar SA* v. *Commune de Fléron*, para. 31.
[43] Art. 59(1) TFEU (emphasis added).
[44] On the distinction between a vertical and a horizontal approach to harmonisation, see Chapter 14, section 4(a) and (b).
[45] Directive 2010/13 on the coordination of certain provisions laid down by law, regulation or administrative action in Member States concerning the provision of audiovisual media services (Audiovisual Media Services Directive) [2010] OJ L 95/1.
[46] Directive 2011/24 on the application of patients' rights in cross-border healthcare [2011] OJ L 88/45.

placed in the establishment chapter.[47] Those legal competences allow the Union
– additionally – to 'issue directives for the coordination' of justified restrictions,[48]
and to 'issue directives for the mutual recognition of diplomas, certificates and
other evidence of formal qualifications' and for the coordination of national laws
'concerning the taking-up and pursuit of activities as self-employed persons'.[49]
And it is these cross-references to Articles 52 and 53 TFEU that have allowed the
Union to adopt horizontal harmonisation measures in the context of services.
The most important 'horizontal' measure here is Directive 2006/123 on services
within the internal market ('Services Directive').[50]

The Services Directive has been very controversial. It has been said to be 'the
most widely and passionately discussed text of secondary [*sic*] legislation in the
history of the EU'.[51] Passions indeed ran so high that very few of the reasons
behind the Directive are still within it. The central pillar within the original draft
had been the home State ('country of origin') principle, according to which
Member States were required to 'ensure that [service] providers are subject only
to the national provisions of their Member State of origin'.[52] The idea that
the home State is the sole regulator of a service did however encounter criticism from the European Parliament, especially because the (original) Services
Directive effected hardly any substantial harmonisation to lift all national laws to
a commonly agreed standard.[53] The danger of such unconditional liberalisation
was the spectre of 'social dumping', that is: the undercutting of a host State's
higher social costs by service providers operating from home states with lower
social costs.[54]

After substantial amendments, the final version of the Services Directive now
looks like a meagre version of its controversial predecessor. It still aims to liberalise the 'services' market by legislative means;[55] yet it seems to do so in a much

---

[47]   The 'common' use of these legal competences for establishment and services indeed makes
much sense, since both freedoms overlap within these two areas. Not only does the services chapter generically incorporate the public policy justifications from the establishment chapter (see Chapter 15, section 5), but the regulation of professional activities will
indeed affect both freedoms equally.

[48]   Art. 62 TFEU in combination with Art. 52(2) TFEU.

[49]   *Ibid*.

[50]   Directive 2006/123 on services in the internal market [2006] OJ 376/36. The directive
was based on Art. 62 in combination with Art. 53 TFEU.

[51]   V. Hatzopoulos, 'Assessing the Services Directive 2006/123' (2007–8) 10 CYELS 215 at
236. On the negotiating history of the directive, see J. Flower, 'European Legislation: The
Services Directive' (2006–7) 9 CYELS 217.

[52]   Art. 16(1) of the original draft proposed by the Commission ('Bolkenstein draft'). For a discussion, see C. Barnard, *The Substantive Law of the EU* (Oxford University Press, 2013), 439.

[53]   Hatzopoulus, 'Assessing the Services Directive' (n. 51 above), 238.

[54]   The best expression of this idea in the United Kingdom is the by now proverbial 'Polish
plumber', see http://en.wikipedia.org/wiki/Polish_Plumber.

[55]   The directive describes its aims in preambles 5 and 6: 'It is therefore necessary to remove
barriers to the freedom of establishment for providers in Member States and barriers to
the free movement of services between Member States and to guarantee recipients and
providers the legal certainty necessary for the exercise in practice of those two fundamental

softer and less general manner. Not only has the material scope of the Directive been reduced through a range of derogations for specific service sectors,[56] the Directive will also not interfere with more specific Union legislation.[57]

The Services Directive today contains eight chapters. Chapters I and VIII set out general and final provisions. Chapter II deals with 'Administrative Simplification' and asks the Member States to simplify or abolish unnecessary national measures regulating services. Chapter III addresses the freedom of establishment.[58] This might, at first glance, seem an unusual chapter within a directive on services; yet in light of the partial overlap between the establishment and the services chapters within the Treaties, this makes practical sense. Chapter IV represents the heart of the Directive and concerns the free movement of services. It is complemented by Chapter V on the quality of services. Finally, Chapters VI and VII concern – respectively – administrative cooperation and a convergence programme between the Member States.

For the liberalisation of services, the fundamental chapter within the directive undoubtedly is Chapter IV (Table 16.3). It constitutes the legislative equivalent of the services chapter within the FEU Treaty. Its central provision is Article 16(1) and states:

> Member States shall respect the right of providers to provide services in a Member State other than that in which they are established. *The Member State in which the service is provided shall ensure free access to and free exercise of a service activity within its territory.* Member States shall not make access to or exercise of a service

freedoms of the Treaty … Those barriers cannot be removed solely by relying on direct application of Articles [49] and [56] of the Treaty, since, on the one hand, addressing them on a case-by-case basis through infringement procedures against the Member State concerned would, especially following enlargement, be extremely complicated for national and [Union] institutions, and, on the other hand, the lifting of many barriers requires prior coordination of national legal schemes, including the setting up of administrative cooperation.'

[56] *Ibid.*, Art. 2(2). The most remarkable exemptions are financial services (Art. 2(2)(b)), healthcare services (Art. 2(2)(f)) and social services (Art. 2(2)(j)). Moreover, Art. 2(3) equally excludes the entire field of taxation from the scope of the directive.

[57] *Ibid.*, Art. 3. Art. 3(1) thereby states in particular: 'If the provisions of this Directive conflict with a provision of another [Union] act governing specific aspects of access to or exercise of a service activity in specific sectors or for specific professions, the provision of the other [Union] act shall prevail and shall apply to those specific sectors or professions. These include: (a) Directive 96/71 [concerning the posting of workers in the framework of the provision of services]; (b) Regulation 1408/71 [on the application of social security schemes to employed persons, to self-employed persons and to members of their families moving within the Union];(c) Council Directive 89/552 on the coordination of certain provisions laid down by law, regulation or administrative action in Member States concerning the pursuit of television broadcasting activities; (d) Directive 2005/36 [on the recognition of professional qualifications].'

[58] This chapter has generated much of the case law under the Services Directive, see Case C-293/14, *Hiebler v. Schlagbauer*, EU:C:2015:843; Joined Cases 340/14 and C-341/14, *Trijber & Harmsen*, EU:C:2015:641.

activity in their territory subject to compliance with any requirements which do not respect the following principles:

(a) *non-discrimination*: the requirement may be neither directly nor indirectly discriminatory with regard to nationality or, in the case of legal persons, with regard to the Member State in which they are established;

(b) necessity [*sic*]: the requirement must be justified for reasons of public policy, public security, public health or the protection of the environment;

(c) proportionality: the requirement must be suitable for attaining the objective pursued, and must not go beyond what is necessary to attain that objective.[59]

Textually, the provision differs in a number of interesting ways from Articles 56ff. of the Treaty. First, unlike Article 56 TFEU, the scope of Article 16 of the Services Directive appears to be smaller. For the rights of recipients of services are expressly covered by a separate provision in the Directive's services chapter.[60] Second, unlike Article 56 TFEU, Article 16(1) of the Directive expressly lays down a test by which to assess restrictions. Any national requirement that hinders the 'free access to and free exercise of a service activity' would be caught by the provision. This is close to the Court's jurisprudence and might indeed eventually be interpreted in light of a 'home State principle'.[61] Third, with regard to justifications, Article 16(1) mentions that any national restriction will have to be 'justified by reasons of public policy, public security, public health or the protection of the environment'.[62] This duplicates the Treaty text on express derogation with the addition of environmental protection. However, it omits the unwritten imperative requirements developed by the Court. Being silent on these, there are

Table 16.3 Services Directive – Chapter IV

Services Directive: Chapter IV – Free Movement of Services	
Article 16	Freedom to Provide Services
Article 17	Additional Derogations from the Freedom to Provide Services
Article 18	Case-by-case Derogations
Article 19	Rights of Recipients of Services
Article 20	Non-discrimination
Article 21	Assistance for Recipients

[59] Emphasis added. The reference in Art. 16(1)(b) to 'necessity' is an editorial mistake and should have referred to 'justification'.

[60] See *ibid.*, Art. 19.

[61] In this sense, see C. Barnard, 'Unravelling the Services Directive' (2008) 45 *CML Rev.* 323 at 362.

[62] With regard to public safety, Art. 18 of the directive provides an – exceptional – additional justification. For Art. 18(1) here states: 'By way of derogation from Article 16, and in exceptional circumstances only, a Member State may, in respect of a provider established in another Member State, take measures relating to the safety of services.'

strong arguments that the Union legislator may have abolished them for service restrictions falling within Article 16 of the Directive.[63] Finally, by making non-discrimination a general requirement – even at the justification stage – it could be argued that discriminatory measures can never be justified.

These readings of Article 16 of the Directive have not yet been conclusively confirmed. But if the Court were to disallow all unwritten justifications and all discriminatory measures (even if adopted on the grounds of public policy), the liberalising potential of the directive would go far beyond the primary law established by Articles 56ff. of the TFEU.[64]

2. Services II: Special Regimes

a. Service Providers and Posted Workers

One of the special legal questions within the services chapter, and one with an enormous political dimension, is whether service providers established in one State are entitled to bring their *employed staff* into the host State; and, if this is the case, whether these 'posted workers' will be subject to the labour laws of the home or the host State. Importantly, this question is not a question that falls within the Treaty provisions dealing with the free movement of workers. Posted workers are not seeking to *permanently* enter the host State's labour market. They are workers who are *temporarily* employed in the host State by a *foreign* service provider established in another State.

Would the personal scope of Article 56 TFEU cover employed persons,[65] especially where they are seen as part of the 'infrastructure' of a company providing

---

[63] The argument that this is a simple oversight by the Union legislator is hard to make, since the Service Directive expressly allows for overriding reasons relating to the public interest in its Chapter III on Establishment (*ibid.*, Arts. 9(1)(b)) and 10(2)(b)). The Court has, rather unthankfully, left this question open in Case C-179/14, *Commission* v. *Hungary*, EU:C:2016:108, esp. para. 116; yet in an earlier case, albeit with regard to another provision within the Directive. it expressly held that 'even though Article 52(1) TFEU allows Member States to justify, on any of the grounds listed in that provision, national measures constituting a restriction on the freedom of establishment, that does not prevent the EU legislature, when adopting secondary legislation, such as Directive 2006/213, giving effect to a fundamental freedom enshrined in the FEU Treaty, from restricting certain derogations, especially when, as in the present case, the relevant provision of secondary law merely reiterates settled case-law to the effect that a requirement such as that at issue in the main proceedings is incompatible with the fundamental freedoms on which economic operators can rely' (*ibid.*, para. 40). That argument could, by analogy, be extended to Art. 16 of the directive.

[64] There are nevertheless a number of important 'additional derogations' from Art. 16 of the directive listed in its Art. 17. For regulated professions, for example, Art. 17(6) of the Services Directive states that restrictions on the freedom to provide services will fall outside the scope of Art. 16. Where a tax consultancy company thus offers services in a (host) Member State in which these services are regulated, the Services Directive will not apply (see Case C-342/14, *X-Steuerberatungsgesellschaft* v. *Finanzamt Hannover-Nord*, esp. para. 26).

[65] The personal scope of Art. 56 TFEU only covers self-employed persons (or companies) – not employed workers. Posted workers are thus not direct right-holders under Art. 56.

services in another Member State? Would Article 56 TFEU allow a service provider to 'post' – less expensive – workers from its home State instead of using the host State's local labour force? The Court has confirmed that the freedom of services covers posted workers in *Rush Portuguesa*.[56] It here held:

> Article[s] [56] and [57] of the Treaty therefore preclude a Member State from prohibiting a person providing services established in another Member State from moving freely on its territory with all his staff and preclude that Member State from making the movement of staff in question subject to restrictions …[67]

The Court has however added a fundamental caveat to this liberal interpretation of Article 56. For it admitted that this liberal reading would

> not preclude [host] Member States from extending their legislation, or collective labour agreements entered into by both sides of industry, to any person who is employed, *even temporarily*, within their territory, *no matter in which country the employer is established*.[68]

This caveat appeared to categorically exempt national labour laws from the scope of Article 56; yet the Court subsequently clarified that this was not the case. While the host State would generally be entitled to apply its local labour laws to temporarily posted foreign workers, this extension could violate Article 56 TFEU unless it was justified under the 'overriding reason relating to the public interest' of the protection of workers.[69] National labour laws of the host State would consequently not be immune from the services provisions but needed to be proportionate; yet with *Rush Portuguesa*, there existed a general presumption that the imposition of the host State's labour laws would generally be justified.

---

[66] Case C-113/89, *Rush Portuguesa Ld^a v. Office national d'immigration* [1990] ECR I-1417. The Court has also clarified that the labour force employed may even include third-country nationals, where they are legally resident and have a work permit in the 'home' State of the service provider (see Case C-43/93, *Vander Elst* v. *Office des Migrations Internationales* [1994] ECR I-3803).

[67] Case C-113/89, para. 12.   [68] *Ibid.*, para. 17 (emphasis added).

[69] Case C-272/94, *Guiot and Climatec* [1996] ECR I-1905; Case C-165/98, *Mazzoleni and Inter Surveillance Assistance* [2001] ECR I-2189, esp. paras. 27–30: 'The overriding reasons relating to the public interest which have been recognised by the Court include the protection of workers. As regards more specifically national provisions relating to minimum wages, such as those at issue in the main proceedings, it is clear from the case-law of the Court that [Union] law does not preclude Member States from extending their legislation, or collective labour agreements entered into by both sides of industry, relating to minimum wages, to any person who is employed, even temporarily, within their territory, regardless of the country in which the employer is established. It follows that the provisions of a Member State's legislation or collective labour agreements which guarantee minimum wages may in principle be applied to employers providing services within the territory of that State, regardless of the country in which the employer is established. It

This legal solution was subsequently codified into Directive 96/71 concerning the posting of workers ('Posted Workers Directive').[70] The Directive is not intended to 'harmonise' but to 'coordinate' national labour laws 'in order to lay down *a nucleus of mandatory rules for minimum protection* to be observed in the host country by employers who post workers to perform temporary work in the territory of a Member State where the services are provided'.[71] This aim is to be achieved by Article 3 of the Directive, which states:

> Member States shall ensure that, whatever the law applicable to the employment relationship, the undertakings referred to in Article 1(1) guarantee workers posted to their territory the terms and conditions of employment covering the following matters which, *in the Member State where the work is carried out*, are laid down:
> − by law, regulation or administrative provision, and/or
> − by collective agreements or arbitration awards which have been declared *universally applicable within the meaning of paragraph 8*, insofar as they concern [all building work]:
>   (a) maximum work periods and minimum rest periods;
>   (b) minimum paid annual holidays;
>   (c) the minimum rates of pay, including overtime rates; this point does not apply to supplementary occupational retirement pension schemes;
>   (d) the conditions of hiring-out of workers, in particular the supply of workers by temporary employment undertakings;
>   (e) health, safety and hygiene at work;
>   (f) protective measures with regard to the terms and conditions of employment of pregnant women or women who have recently given birth, of children and of young people;
>   (g) equality of treatment between men and women and other provisions on non-discrimination.
> For the purposes of this Directive, the concept of minimum rates of pay referred to in paragraph 1(c) is defined by the national law and/or practice of the Member State to whose territory the worker is posted.[72]

follows that [Union] law does not preclude a Member State from requiring an undertaking established in another Member State which provides services in the territory of the first State to pay its workers the minimum remuneration fixed by the national rules of that State. However, there may be circumstances in which the application of such rules would be neither necessary nor proportionate to the objective pursued, namely the protection of the workers concerned.'

[70] Directive 96/71 concerning the posting of workers in the framework of the provision of services, [1997] OJ L 18/1. The directive was based on Art. 62 in combination with 53(1) TFEU. For an early and excellent analysis of the directive, see P. Davies, 'Posted Workers: Single Market or Protection of National Labour Law Systems?' (1997) 34 *CML Rev.* 571. The directive was left unaffected by the Services Directive, as the latter gives priority to the Posted Workers Directive (see Art. 3(1)(a) as well as Art. 17(2) of the Services Directive).

[71] Directive 96/71, preamble 13 (emphasis added).

[72] *Ibid.*, Art. 3(1) (emphasis added). Art. 1(1) of the directive refers to undertakings that are established in the Union that post workers to the territory of another Member States. The three situations in which they may occur are set out in Art. 1(3) of the directive.

The provision deals with the terms and conditions of employment. According to the Court, it pursues a dual objective:

> [T]he first subparagraph of Article 3(1) of Directive 96/71 pursues a dual objective. First, it seeks to ensure a climate of fair competition between national undertakings and undertakings which provide services transnationally, inasmuch as it requires the latter to afford their workers, as regards a limited list of matters, the terms and conditions of employment laid down in the host Member State. Secondly, that provision aims to ensure that posted workers will have the rules of the host Member State for minimum protection as regards the terms and conditions of employment relating to those matters applied to them while they work on a temporary basis in the territory of that Member State.[73]

Article 3 of the Posted Workers Directive indeed confirms the ability of the host State to extend the hard core of its mandatory labour laws to any foreign services provider. These labour laws will principally be laid down in (public) national measures; yet in the case of building work, they can also be found in (private) collective agreements wherever they are 'universally applicable'.[74]

Is the list of 'core' provisions in Article 3(1) exhaustive? The directive suggests a negative answer. Not only does Article 3(7) appear to allow for higher national labour standards;[75] Article 3(10) permits Member States to apply 'terms and conditions of employment on matters *other than those referred to in the first subparagraph of paragraph 1* in the case of *public policy* provisions'.[76] Strangely, the Court has nonetheless held that Article 3(1) indeed provides an exhaustive list; and that the public policy exception in Article 3(10) needs to be interpreted restrictively.

The two cases that establish these severe and complementary limitations are *Laval* and *Commission* v. *Luxembourg (Posted Workers)*.[77] In *Laval*, a Latvian company of that name had posted 35 workers from Latvia to Sweden to work on a construction site near Stockholm. The Swedish building workers' union had approached Laval to negotiate a collective agreement for an hourly wage of about £13, which was almost twice as much as the Latvian salary level. Laval refused and became the subject of an industrial action that was challenged in the Swedish labour courts. The latter made a preliminary reference to the European Court of Justice, which had to decide on the compatibility of the strike action with the Posted Workers Directive and Article 56 TFEU. In its ruling, the Court established a number of important things.

---

[73] Case C-396/13, *Sähköalojen ammattiliitto ry* v. *Elektrobudowa Spolka Akcyjna*, EU:C:2015:86, para. 30.

[74] Directive 96/71, Art. 3(8). The provision defines 'universally applicable' as agreements or awards 'which must be observed by all undertakings in the geographical area and in the profession or industry concerned'. The Court enforces this condition strictly (see Case C-341/05, *Laval un Partneri Ltd* v. *Svenska*; Case C-346/06, *Rüffert* v. *Land Niedersachsen* [2008] ECR I-1989).

[75] Directive 96/71, Art. 3(7) states that Art. 3(1) 'shall not prevent application of terms and conditions of employment which are more favourable to workers'.

[76] *Ibid.*, Art. 3(10) (emphasis added).   [77] Case C-341/05, *Laval un Partneri Ltd* v. *Svenska*.

First, the Court found that the directive 'did not harmonise the material content' of the mandatory rules of minimum protection mentioned in Article 3(1).[78] It thus fell within the competence of the Member States to determine, for example, the substantive level of the national minimum wage.[79]

Second, where a Member State had not generally made one of the requirements in Article 3(1) applicable to all undertakings within its territory, it was not entitled on a case-by-case basis to insist on these requirements.[80]

Third, and regardless of Article 3(7), 'the level of protection which must be guaranteed to workers posted to the territory of the host Member State is limited, in principle, to that provided for in Article 3(1), first subparagraph, (a) to (g) of Directive 96/71'.[81] Apart from the exception in Article 3(10), this meant that the list in Article 3(1) was exhaustive.

Fourth, because the collective action organised by the trade union was not legitimate under the Directive, the strike action constituted a restriction on the freedom to provide services that needed to be justified.[82]

In *Commission* v. *Luxembourg*,[83] the Court added a fifth and final element. Not only did 'Article 3(1) set … out an exhaustive list of the matters in respect of which the Member States may give priority to the rules in force in the host

[78] *Ibid.*, para. 60.

[79] This has been repeatedly confirmed. See Case C-522/12, *Isbir* v. *DB Services*, EU:C:2013:711, esp. para. 37: 'Directive 96/71 does not itself provide any substantive definition of the minimum wage. The task of defining what are the constituent elements of the minimum wage, for the application of that directive, therefore comes within the scope of the law of the Member State concerned, but only in so far as that definition, deriving from the legislation or relevant national collective agreements, or as interpreted by the national courts, does not have the effect of impeding the free movement of services between Member States.'

[80] *Ibid.*, para. 71: 'It must therefore be concluded at this stage that a Member State in which the minimum rates of pay are not determined in accordance with one of the means provided for in Article 3(1) and (8) of Directive 96/71 is not entitled, pursuant to that directive, to impose on undertakings established in other Member States, in the framework of the transnational provision of services, negotiation at the place of work, on a case-by-case basis, having regard to the qualifications and tasks of the employees, so that the undertakings concerned may ascertain the wages which they are to pay their posted workers.' See also Case C-522/12, *Isbir* v. *DB Services*, EU:C:2014:149, para. 37.

[81] Case C-341/05, *Laval un Partneri Ltd* v. *Svenska*, para. 81. In the present case, there existed no 'universally applicable' collective agreement; nor had the Swedish government invoked Art. 3(10) of the directive and for that reason the provision was not relevant (*ibid.*, para. 84). The exhaustive nature of Art. 3(1) has subsequently been confirmed in Case C-346/06, *Rüffert*.

[82] The Court here reconfirmed that private party actions – here a strike action by a Union – could fall into the personal scope of Art. 56 TFEU and that the strike action constituted a restriction of the provision of services, see Case C-341/05, *Laval*, para. 99. And while the Court agreed that 'the right to take collective action for the protection of the workers of the host State against possible social dumping may constitute an overriding reason of public interest within the meaning of the case-law of the Court' (*ibid.*, para. 103), the Court still found that the collective action could not be justified in the present case (*ibid.*, paras. 104–10).

[83] Case C-319/06, *Commission* v. *Luxembourg* [2008] ECR I-4323.

Member State',[84] the public policy exception in Article 3(10) was 'a derogation from the fundamental principle of freedom to provide services which must be interpreted strictly' and whose scope 'cannot be determined unilaterally by the Member States'.[85]

In sum, the Court has provided a minimalist definition of the exceptions within the Posted Workers Directive so as to maximise its liberalising effect.

b. Service Recipients and 'Public' Services

The idea of public services reaches back to Roman times;[86] yet, it is only with the rise of the welfare State in the (early) twentieth century that the concept received its modern form. Public services here come to be seen as services that the State is obliged to offer its citizens so as to allow them to live a decent life.[87] Public services thereby not only refer to State activities designed to 'protect' the liberty and property of the citizenry. They include the positive provision of essential public 'goods' such as education and health.

Would these 'public services' be services in the meaning of primary or secondary Union law? The Services Directive finds a – relatively – clear answer to this question: it simply excludes public services from its scope.[88] The EU Treaties however do not offer such a clear-cut rule. While they do recognise the special place of public services of a general *economic* interest,[89] *non*-economic public services have been said to be beyond the scope of Union law.[90]

---

[84] *Ibid.*, para. 26.   [85] *Ibid.*, para. 30.

[86] F. Löwenberg, *Service public and öffentliche Dienstleistungen in Europa* (Berliner Wissenschaftsverlag, 2011), 67.

[87] The 'father' of the French 'School of Public Service' is L. Duguit, who established the idea with *Les transformations du droit public* (Nabu Press, 2010). For the 'German' equivalent, see E. Forsthoff, *Der Staat der Industriegesellschaft* (Beck, 1971).

[88] For the Services Directive, see n. 50 above. The directive expressly states in its Art. 2(2) that it will not apply to, *inter alia*, 'non-economic services of general interest' (a); 'healthcare services whether or not they are provided via healthcare facilities, and regardless of the ways in which they are organised and financed at national level or whether they are public or private' (f); or 'social services relating to social housing, childcare and support of families and persons permanently or temporarily in need which are provided by the State, by providers mandated by the State or by charities recognised as such by the State' (j). Moreover, Art. 17 provides for an additional derogation by stating that Art. 16 shall not apply 'to services of general economic interest which are provided in another Member State'.

[89] See Art. 14 TFEU. The provision states that 'the Union and the Member States, each within their respective powers and within the scope of application of the Treaties, shall take care that such services operate on the basis of principles and conditions, particularly economic and financial conditions, which enable them to fulfil their missions'. The provision has been complemented by Protocol No. 26 On Services of General Interest. The Protocol will be discussed in greater detail in (online) Chapter 17B, section 1(b).

[90] *Ibid.*, Art. 2: 'The provisions of the Treaties do not affect in any way the competence of Member States to provide, commission and organise non-economic services of general interest.'

Does this exemption mean that States could impose restrictions on foreigners attempting to receive services financed by the public purse? An indicative answer to this question may be provided by Article 51 TFEU.[91] The latter limits the application of the services provisions in the context of activities that 'are connected, even occasionally, with the exercise of official authority'. Yet the Court has, as we saw above,[92] imposed very strict conditions on this derogation and insisted on 'a special relationship of allegiance to the State and reciprocity of rights and duties which form the foundation of the bond of nationality'.[93] Education and health services will generally not fall into this restrictive definition;[94] and public services not covered by Article 51 would therefore, it seems, be subject to Article 56.[95]

Does this mean that any EU national can freely travel to another Member State and receive public services there? What about State services that are publicly financed and even 'free of charge'? The question to what extent service recipients are covered by Article 56 has received a complex judicial answer. In *Humbel*,[96] the Court had to deal with this issue in an educational context. French parents had sent their son to a Belgian secondary school which requested an enrolment fee that was not charged to Belgian students. This was a clearly discriminatory measure that would however only fall within the scope of Article 56 if the State school were seen as offering a 'service' within the meaning of the Treaty. The Court rejected this view by pointing to the essential characteristic of remuneration, which:

> lies in the fact that it constitutes consideration for the service in question, and is normally agreed upon between the provider and the recipient of the service. That characteristic is, however, absent in the case of courses provided under the national education system. First of all, the State, in establishing and maintaining such a system, *is not seeking to engage in a gainful activity but is fulfilling its duties towards its own population in the social, cultural and educational fields.* Secondly, the system in question is, as a general rule, *funded from the public purse and not by pupils or their parents.* The nature of the activity is not affected by the fact that pupils or their parents must sometimes pay teaching or enrolment fees in order to make a certain contribution to the operating expenses of the system.[97]

The ruling appeared to exclude all publicly funded 'services' from the scope of Article 56 TFEU. This view was confirmed in a case involving university

---

[91] The provision applies to the services chapter by means of the cross-reference in Art. 62 TFEU.

[92] See Chapter 15, section 5(b).

[93] Case 149/79, *Commission v. Belgium* [1980] ECR 3881, para. 10.

[94] See Case 66/85, *Lawrie-Blum* v. *Land Baden-Württemberg* [1986] ECR 2121 (State school teacher); and Case 307/84, *Commission* v. *France* [1986] ECR 1725 (nurses).

[95] See Case 155/73, *Sacchi* [1974] ECR 409; Case C-260/89, *ERT* [1991] ECR I-2925.

[96] Case 263/86, *Belgium* v. *Humbel* [1988] ECR 5365.

[97] *Ibid.*, paras. 17–19 (emphasis added).

education, where the Court equally made the availability of Article 56 dependent on the service being '*essentially funded out of private funds*'.[98]

This relatively clear exclusion of publicly financed services from the scope of Article 56 has however been qualified in a second context: public health services.[99] Should publicly funded national health systems fall within or without the services provisions? In *Peerbooms*,[100] the Court held that a medical treatment received abroad would be a service – even if a social security institution would subsequently reimburse that payment:

> [A] medical service provided in one Member State and paid for by the patient should not cease to fall within the scope of the freedom to provide services guaranteed by the Treaty merely because reimbursement of the costs of the treatment involved is applied for under another Member State's sickness insurance legislation.[101]

While the ruling could, perhaps, still be squared with the Court's wide notion of remuneration, discussed above, *Watts* subsequently clarified that even systems that are fully funded through national taxation – like the British NHS – would fall within the scope of Article 56 TFEU.[102] Wherever the patient is called upon to pay for her medical treatment abroad, that treatment would be considered a service (even if she would be fully reimbursed by the public purse):

> Article [56] applies where a patient such as Mrs Watts receives medical services in a hospital environment for consideration in a Member State other than her State of residence, regardless of the way in which the national system with which that person is registered and from which reimbursement of the cost of those services is

---

[98] Case C-109/92, *Wirth* v. *Landeshauptstadt Hannover* [1993] ECR I-6447, para. 17 (emphasis added). For a very good overview of the (early) education cases, see G. Davies, 'Welfare as a Service' (2002) 29 *Legal Issues of Economic Integration* 27. See also Case C-56/09, *Zanotti* v. *Agenzia delle Entrate* [2010] ECR I-4517, esp. para. 32: 'However, the Court has held that courses offered by educational establishments essentially financed by private funds, in particular by students and their parents, constitute services within the meaning of Article [57], since the aim of those establishments is to offer a service for remuneration.'

[99] While private healthcare constitutes a service within the meaning of Art. 57 TFEU, this had not been clear for public healthcare. For an overview of the cases and problems involved here, see e.g. V. Hatzopoulos, 'Killing National Health and Insurance Systems but Healing Patients?' (2002) 39 *CML Rev.* 683; T. Hervey, 'The Current Legal Framework on the Right to Seek Health Care Abroad in the European Union' (2006–7) 9 CYELS 261. The Union legislator has tried to coordinate this area through Union legislation, see Directive 2011/24 on the Application of Patients' Rights in Cross-border Healthcare (n. 46 above). For a critical overview of the directive, see S. De La Rosa, 'The Directive on Cross-border Healthcare or the Art of Codifying Complex Case Law' (2012) 49 *CML Rev.* 15.

[100] Case C-157/99, *Geraets-Smits* v. *Stichting Ziekenfonds VGZ* and *H. T. M. Peerbooms* v. *Stichting CZ Groep Zorgverzekeringen* [2001] ECR I-5473.

[101] *Ibid.*, para. 55.   [102] Case C-372/04, *Watts*.

subsequently sought operates. It must therefore be found that a situation such as that which gave rise to the dispute in the main proceedings, in which a person whose state of health necessitates hospital treatment goes to another Member State and there receives the treatment in question for consideration, falls within the scope of the Treaty provisions on the freedom to provide services, there being no need in the present case to determine whether the provision of hospital treatment in the context of a national health service such as the NHS is in itself a service within the meaning of those provisions.[103]

Having thus confirmed that medical services offered by public health systems fall within the scope of the freedom of services, the central question has been whether a State can make the reimbursement of medical expenses incurred abroad conditional on an authorisation procedure. In other words, can a State in which the public service is offered free of charge impose conditions on the reimbursement of patients who wish to go abroad to receive the service in another Member State? The Court has found such authorisation procedures to constitute restrictions on the freedom of services.[104]

However, it has been relatively generous in offering States opportunities to justify these restrictions. In *Watts*,[105] a British patient wished to receive a 'hip replacement' from the NHS but, when confronted with a very long waiting list, she went to France without authorisation and subsequently asked for reimbursement. In this case, the Court identified two justificatory routes for such authorisation requirements. First, a Member State could invoke 'the risk of seriously undermining the financial balance of a social security system' as an overriding reason in the general interest. Second, it could rely on public health grounds in relation to 'the objective of maintaining a balanced medical and hospital service open to all' as well as 'the maintenance of treatment capacity or medical competence on the national territory'.[106] These grounds were nonetheless subject to a proportionality analysis. This meant, in particular, that unacceptably long waiting

---

[103]   *Ibid.*, paras. 90–1.

[104]   See e.g. Case C-158/96, *Kohll* v. *Union des caisses de maladie* [1998] ECR I-1931, paras. 33–5: 'It should be noted that, according to the Court's case-law, Article [56] of the Treaty precludes the application of any national rules which have the effect of making the provision of services between Member States more difficult than the provision of services purely within one Member State. While the national rules at issue in the main proceedings do not deprive insured persons of the possibility of approaching a provider of services established in another Member State, they do nevertheless make reimbursement of the costs incurred in that Member State subject to prior authorisation, and deny such reimbursement to insured persons who have not obtained that authorisation. Costs incurred in the State of insurance are not, however, subject to that authorisation. Consequently, such rules deter insured persons from approaching providers of medical services established in another Member State and constitute, for them and their patients, a barrier to freedom to provide services.' See also, Case C-157/99, *Peerboom*, para. 69; Case C-372/04, *Watts*, para. 94.

[105]   Case C-372/04, *Watts*.

[106]   *Ibid.*, paras. 103–5.

lists would entitle a patient to have her authorisation to receive medical treat-ment abroad approved by the national authorities of the home State.[107]

3. Capital I: Scope and Nature

Capital is – in theory – the most 'mobile' factor of production. Thanks to its 'fluid' nature, it can potentially move with tremendous speed across national bor-ders. In order to limit its volatile nature, States have traditionally tried to control capital movements into and out of their jurisdiction.

When the European Union was born, national capital controls were fully in place; yet the Member States promised in the EU Treaties to 'progressively abol-ish between themselves all restrictions on the movement of capital belonging to persons resident in Member States'.[108] The free movement of capital was to be the fourth – and final – freedom within the Union's 'internal market'. Yet when compared to its three sisters, it had been conceived in strikingly weaker terms. The freedom of capital indeed originally appeared to be 'an anomaly amongst the fundamental freedoms'.[109] For the Treaties envisaged that capital restrictions between the Member States would only be removed through positive integra-tion, and then only 'to the extent necessary to ensure the proper functioning of the common market'.[110] (With regard to exchange measures, the Member States were even only required to 'endeavour to avoid' introducing new restrictions on the movement of capital.)[111] These vague and conditional commitments meant that the original capital provisions lacked direct effect.[112]

---

[107] *Ibid.*, para. 123: 'Where the delay arising from such waiting lists appears to exceed an acceptable time having regard to an objective medical assessment of the abovementioned circumstances, the competent institution may not refuse the authorisation sought on the grounds of the existence of those waiting lists, an alleged distortion of the normal order of priorities linked to the relative urgency of the cases to be treated, the fact that the hospital treatment provided under the national system in question is free of charge, the obligation to make available specific funds to reimburse the cost of treatment to be provided in another Member State and/or a comparison between the cost of that treatment and that of equivalent treatment in the competent Member State.' For a confirmation of the *Watts* approach, see Case C-268/13, Petru, EU:C:2014:2271.

[108] Ex-Art. 67(1) EEC.

[109] L. Flynn, 'Coming of Age: The Free Movement of Capital Case Law 1993–2002' (2002) 39 *CML Rev.* 773.

[110] See ex-Art. 67 EEC. See also ex-Art. 69 EEC.   [111] Ex-Art. 71 EEC.

[112] The Court rejected the direct effect of the old free movement of capital provisions in Case 203/80, *Casati* [1981] ECR 2595, esp. paras. 9–11: 'At present, it cannot be denied that complete freedom of movement of capital may undermine the economic policy of one of the Member States or create an imbalance in its balance of payments, thereby impairing the proper functioning of the Common Market. For those reasons, [ex-]Article 67(1) [EEC] differs from the provisions on the free movement of goods, persons and services … The scope of that restriction, which remained in force after the expiry of the transitional period, varies in time and depends on an assessment of the requirements of the Common Market and on an appraisal of both the advantages and risks which liberalization might entail for the latter, having regard to the stage it has reached and, in particular, to the level of integration attained in matters in respect of which capital

In the absence of direct effect, capital liberalisation would have to progress through positive – and not negative – integration. However, the positive integration of this fourth freedom proved slow.[113] Its legislative implementation would only gather pace in the aftermath of the White Paper 'Completing the Internal Market'.[114] The central legislative measure here was Directive 88/361,[115] which established the free movement of capital within the Union. The Directive would later on provide the blueprint for a – constitutional – reform of the capital chapter by the 1992 Maastricht Treaty.[116] The 'old' provisions were replaced by an (almost) completely new set of rules.[117] This 'dramatic metamorphosis' turned the capital provisions from a 'weakly worded' freedom to 'a powerful liberalizing force both within and outside the EU'.[118]

The provisions governing the capital freedom can today be found in four Articles within Chapter 4 of Title IV ('Free Movement of Persons, Services and Capital') of the TFEU. They are laid out in Table 16.4.

This section explores the nature and scope of the prohibition in Article 63. It starts with the question whether, and to what extent, Article 63 has been given direct effect. It then moves to an analysis of its internal and external limits and, in particular, the notions of 'capital' and 'restriction'. Section 4 subsequently surveys the various available justifications for restrictions on the free movement of capital. The freedom of capital indeed acknowledges a number of very particular exceptions that cannot be found within the other three fundamental freedoms. These special justifications respond to the especially mobile character of capital.

movements are particularly significant. Such an assessment is, first and foremost, a matter for the Council, in accordance with the procedure provided for by [ex-]Article 69 [EEC].' For an analysis of the case, see M. Peterson, 'Capital Movements and Payments under the EEC Treaty after *Casati*' (1982) 7 *EL Rev.* 167; J.-V. Louis, 'Free Movement of Capital in the Community: The *Casati* Judgment' (1982) 19 *CML Rev.* 443.

[113]   See First Directive for the implementation of [ex-]Art 67(1) EEC [1959–62] OJ English Special Edition 49; Second Council 63/21 Directive adding to and amending the First Directive for the implementation of Art. 67 of the Treaty [1963–4] OJ English Special Edition 5.

[114]   Commission, 'White Paper: Completing the Internal Market', COM (85) 310 final.

[115]   Directive 88/361 for the implementation of Art. 67 of the Treaty [1988] OJ L 178/18. Art. 1 required: 'Member States shall abolish restrictions on movement of capital taking place between persons resident in Member States.' The Court has had no hesitation in considering Art. 1 to be directly effective; see Joined Cases C-358/93 and C-416/93, *Aldo Bordessa and others* [1995] ECR I-361, para. 33: 'The requirement under Article 1 of the Directive for Member States to abolish all restrictions on movements of capital is precise and unconditional and does not require a specific implementing measure.'

[116]   S. Mohamed, *European Community Law on the Free Movement of Capital and EMU* (Kluwer, 1999), 24–5: 'The original rules on capital movement were subject to greater changes … than any other economic freedoms. The original Treaty provisions on capital, even though subject to some minor amendments by the Single European Act, survived until they were replaced completely by a new set of rules in 1994.'

[117]   J. Usher, 'The Evolution of the Free Movement of Capital' (2008) 31 *Fordham International Law Journal*, 1533.

[118]   J. Snell, 'Free Movement of Capital: Evolution as a Non-linear Process', in P. Craig and G. de Búrca (eds.), *The Evolution of EU Law* (Oxford University Press, 2011), 547 at 548.

Table 16.4 Capital Provisions – Overview

Title IV – Chapter 4: Capital and Payments	
Article 63	Prohibition on Capital (and Payment) Restrictions
Article 64	Third-county Exception(s)
Article 65	Justification(s) for National Restrictions
Article 66	Exceptional Safeguard Measures for Third-country Capital
Protocol No. 32 on the Acquisition of Property in Denmark	
Secondary Law: Directive 88/361 on the Implementation of Article [63] Directive 77/799 on Mutual Assistance in the Sphere of Taxation & Insurance	

a. The Direct Effect of Article 63

The central prohibition governing the free movement of capital is found in Article 63 TFEU. It states:

> Within the framework of the provisions set out in this Chapter, *all restrictions on the movement of capital between Member States and between Member States and third countries shall be prohibited.*[119]

This appeared to be a clear and unconditional provision; and indeed the Court had held its legislative predecessor in Directive 88/361 to have direct effect.[120] However, the Directive had been confined to *intra*-Union situations, whereas Article 63(1) TFEU also covered capital movement to and from third States. And considering the wider scope of Article 63, the question arose whether the provisions could also have direct effect in situations that involved third countries.

Should the Union grant EU rights to third-country nationals to challenge Member State laws that restrict the free movement of capital? The extension of a fundamental freedom to third countries is 'unique amongst the internal market freedoms'.[121] It has been said to constitute a 'revolutionary departure from the

---

[119] Art. 63(1) TFEU (emphasis added). This prohibition of capital restrictions is extended to restrictions on 'payments', that is: the financial consideration for a concrete legal transaction. The 1957 EEC Treaty had originally dealt with restrictions on payments in a separate part of the Treaty (see ex-Arts. 104–9 EEC). The central provision was here contained in ex-Art. 106(1) EEC and stated: 'Each Member State undertakes to authorise, in the currency of the Member State in which the creditor or the beneficiary resides, any payments connected with the movement of goods, services or capital, and any transfers of capital and earnings, to the extent that the movement of goods, services, capital and persons between Member States has been liberalised pursuant to this Treaty.' Prior to the 1992 Maastricht reforms, the distinction between 'capital' and 'payment' was thus important.

[120] Joined Cases C-358/93 and C-416/93, *Aldo Bordessa and others*.

[121] Flynn, 'Coming of Age' (n. 109 above), 785.

original Treaty framework'.[122] Although the capacity of a third-country national to be the bearer of free movement rights is not unknown within Union law, in the context of the freedom of capital it gains a new dimension.[123]

This extension of capital movements between Member States *and third countries* is nonetheless conditioned by Article 64 TFEU. The provision not only exempts (certain) national measures adopted before 31 December 1993 from the scope of Article 63 TFEU;[124] it ultimately leaves the degree of capital liberalisations vis-à-vis third countries to the Union legislator. The provision states:

> Whilst endeavouring to achieve the objective of free movement of capital between Member States and third countries to the greatest extent possible and without prejudice to the other Chapters of the Treaties, the European Parliament and the Council, acting in accordance with the ordinary legislative procedure, shall adopt the measures on the movement of capital to or from third countries involving direct investment – including investment in real estate – establishment, the provision of financial services or the admission of securities to capital markets.[125]

The legislative competence to progressively *liberalise* capital movements vis-à-vis third States in Article 64(2) TFEU is further complemented by a legislative competence to 'adopt measures which constitute a step *backwards* in Union law as regards the liberalisation of the movement of capital to or from third countries' in Article 64(3) TFEU.[126]

With these two major qualifications to Article 63, would the Court nonetheless find that Article 63 was directly effective with regard to capital movements vis-à-vis third countries? Surprisingly, the Court did find the extra-Union aspect of Article 63 to have direct effects. In *Sanz de Lera*,[127] it held:

---

[122]   Mohamed, *European Community Law* (n. 116 above), 216.
[123]   For unlike third-country goods that may circulate freely once they have already entered into the internal market (see Art. 28(2) TFEU), Art. 63 TFEU provided a constitutional weapon to *bring capital into or out of the internal market*!
[124]   Art. 64(1) TFEU states: 'The provisions of Article 63 shall be without prejudice to the application to third countries of any restrictions which exist on 31 December 1993 under national or Union law adopted in respect of the movement of capital to or from third countries involving direct investment – including in real estate – establishment, the provision of financial services or the admission of securities to capital markets. In respect of restrictions existing under national law in Bulgaria, Estonia and Hungary, the relevant date shall be 31 December 1999.'
[125]   *Ibid.*, Art. 64(2).
[126]   Art. 64(2) TFEU thereby provides for a differential decision-making procedure for third-country measures. Liberalisation measures only require a qualified majority in the Council, while a unanimous decision is required for further capital restrictions under Art. 64(3) TFEU.
[127]   Joined Cases C-163/94, C-165/94 and C-250/94, *Sanz de Lera and others* [1995] ECR I-4821.

Article [63(1)] of the Treaty lays down a clear and unconditional prohibition for which no implementing measure is needed. The expression 'within the framework of the provisions set out in this Chapter' in Article [63] relates to the whole chapter in which it appears. The provision must therefore be interpreted in that context ... The exception provided for in Article [64(1)] of the Treaty concerning the application to non-member countries of the restrictions existing on 31 December 1993 under national law or [Union] law regarding the capital movements listed in it to or from non-member countries is precisely worded, with the result that no latitude is granted to the Member States or the [Union] legislature regarding either the date of applicability of the restrictions or the categories of capital movements which may be subject to restrictions. Furthermore, the power to adopt measures granted to the Council by Article [64(2)] of the Treaty relates only to the categories of capital movements to or from non-member countries listed in that provision. Nor is the adoption of such measures a prerequisite for implementing the prohibition laid down in Article [63(1)] of the Treaty, *since that provision relates to restrictions that do not come within the scope of Article [64(1)] of the Treaty.*[128]

The Court consequently found that all of Article 63 conferred directly enforceable rights on individuals — even with regard to capital movements from or to third States. The Court has also confirmed that Article 63 has the same material scope for intra-Union and extra-Union capital movements, since it has insisted that the same notion of capital restriction would apply in both situations.[129]

What, then, is the material scope of Article 63? Let us explore the notion of 'capital' first before investigating the concept of 'restriction' in a second step.

b. The (Elusive) Concept of 'Capital'

The Treaty chapter on capital focuses — like the free movement of goods — on the movement of an object. This protected object is called 'capital'. Capital

---

[128] *Ibid.*, paras. 41–6 (emphasis added). This has been expressly confirmed in Case C–101/05, *Skatteverket* v. *A* [2007] ECR I-11531, where Germany had argued that the direct effect of Art. 63 TFEU was excluded for those categories of capital movements mentioned in Art. 64(1) TFEU. The argument was however expressly rejected by the Court with reference to *Sanz de Lera and others*, paras. 25–6.

[129] Case C–101/05, *Scatteverket*, where a number of governments had argued 'that the concept of restriction on the movement of capital cannot be interpreted in the same manner with regard to relations between Member States and third countries as it is with regard to relations between Member States' (*ibid.*, para. 28). The Court roundly rejected this view in para. 31: '[E]ven if the liberalisation of the movement of capital with third countries may pursue objectives other than that of establishing the internal market, such as, in particular, that of ensuring the credibility of the single [Union] currency on world financial markets and maintaining financial centres with a world-wide dimension within the Member States, it is clear that, when the principle of free movement of capital was extended, pursuant to Article [63], to movement of capital between third countries and the Member States, the latter chose to enshrine that principle in that article and in the same terms for movements of capital taking place within the [Union] and those relating to relations with third countries.'

constitutes the defining characteristic of the modern economic system.[130] It is a commonly used concept that lacks a commonly agreed definition. A conceptual core may however be found by contrasting 'capital' with 'consumption'. Capital can be negatively defined as all that wealth that is not consumed but 'invested'.[131] Capital thus relates to financial investments. Yet there are a thousand ways to invest money; and, sadly, the Treaties do not offer much constitutional guidance as to what the Union legal order considers capital.

The task of determining the conceptual boundaries of the notion of capital was thus in the hand of the Union legislature and the Court. The former has used this power in the past by adopting a legislative definition of the concept in an annex to Directive 88/361.[132] It contains a 'nomenclature' of capital movements, which the Court has accepted as of an 'indicative value'.[133] The directive thereby lists a number of capital categories under various headings (see Table 16.5). Common categories thereby are 'direct investments',[134] 'investments in real estate'[135] and 'operations in securities' dealt with on the capital or money market.[136] However, almost any money – received or spent – will come under the free movement of capital. The nomenclature offered by the directive is not exhaustive, and the Court has confirmed its willingness to go beyond the broad categories within the directive.[137] The notion of capital within the Union legal order has consequently been given an open and expansive scope – a scope that

[130] K. Marx, *Capital* (Oxford Paperbacks, abridged edn, 2008).

[131] In this sense, albeit in a different context, see Joined Cases 286/82 and 26/83, *Luisi and Carbone*, para. 21: 'the movements of capital covered by Article [63] are financial operations essentially concerned with the investment of funds in question rather than remuneration for a service'.

[132] Directive 88/361 (n. 115 above), Annex I: 'Nomenclature of the Capital Movements referred to in Article 1 of the Directive'.

[133] See Case C-222/97, *Trummer and others* [1999] ECR I-1661, para. 20: 'It should be noted in that connection that the [FEU] Treaty does not define the terms "movements of capital" and "payments". However, inasmuch as Article [63] substantially reproduces the contents of Article 1 of Directive 88/36, and even though that directive was adopted on the basis of [ex-]Articles 69 and 70(1) of the EEC Treaty, which have since been replaced by Article [63] *et seq.* of the [FEU] Treaty, the nomenclature in respect of movements of capital annexed to Directive 88/361 still has the same indicative value, for the purposes of defining the notion of capital movements, as it did before the entry into force of Article [63] *et seq.*, subject to the qualification, contained in the introduction to the nomenclature, that the list set out therein is not exhaustive.'

[134] Directive 88/361 (n. 115 above), Annex I – Heading I; see Case C-54/99, *Association Eglise de scientologie de Paris and Scientology International Reserves Trust* v. *The Prime Minister* [2000] ECR I-1335.

[135] Directive 88/361 (n. 115 above), Annex I – Heading II; see Case C-302/97, *Konle* v. *Austria* [1999] ECR I-3099.

[136] Directive 88/361 (n. 115 above), Annex I – Headings III and V; see the 'Golden Share' cases (n. 146 below).

[137] When dealing with 'dividends' on shares in a foreign company, the Court thus held that '[a]lthough receipt of dividends is not expressly mentioned in the nomenclature annexed to Directive 88/361 as "capital movements", it necessarily presupposes participation in new or existing undertakings referred to in Heading I(2) of the nomenclature' (see Case C-35/98, *Staatssecretaris van Financiën* v. *B. G. M. Verkooijen* [2000] ECR I-4071, para. 28).

Table 16.5 Capital Nomenclature

	Directive 88/361 – Annex I: Nomenclature of Capital Movements
I.	Direct Investments
II.	Investments in Real Estate
III.	Operations in Securities
IV.	Operations in Collective Investment Undertakings
V.	Operations in Securities and Other Instruments Normally Dealt with on the Money Market
VI.	Operations in Current and Deposit Accounts with Financial Institutions
VII.	Credits Related to Commercial Transactions or to the Provision of Services
VIII.	Financial Loans and Credits
IX.	Sureties, Other Guarantees and Rights of Pledge
X.	Transfers in Performance or Insurance Contracts
XI.	Personal Capital Movements (Inheritances, Dowries)
XII.	Physical Import and Export of Financial Assets

comprises a myriad of economic but also some 'non-economic' activities, such as financial gifts or personal inheritances.[138]

c. Capital Restrictions: Discrimination and Beyond

Article 63 TFEU prohibits 'all *restrictions* on the movement of capital'.[139] This refers to both import as well as export restrictions; and the notion of restriction covers regulatory as well as fiscal measures.

What types of restrictions will be covered by the provisions? The Court has clarified that Article 63 definitely includes all discriminatory measures that hinder the free movement of capital;[140] and in particular: capital authorisation

---

[138] See Case C-67/08, *Block* v. *Finanzamt Kaufbeuren* [2009] ECR I-883; Case C133/13, Q, EU:C:2014:2460.

[139] Art. 63(1) TFEU.

[140] Case C-302/97, *Konle* v. *Austria*, paras. 23–4: 'Section 10(2) of the TGVG 1993, which exempts only Austrian nationals from having to obtain authorization before acquiring a plot of land which is built on and thus from having to demonstrate, to that end, that the planned acquisition will not be used to establish a secondary residence, creates a discriminatory restriction against nationals of other Member States in respect of capital movements between Member States. Such discrimination is prohibited by Article [63] of the Treaty, unless it is justified on grounds permitted by the Treaty.' See also Case C-279/00, *Commission* v. *Italy* [2002] ECR I-1425, para. 37: 'Secondly, the obligation to establish a guarantee with a credit institution having its registered office or a branch office on Italian territory, as follows from Article 2(2)(c) of Law No. 196/97, is a restriction on capital movements within the meaning of Article [63(1)], in so far as it impedes an undertaking wishing to carry on the business of providing temporary labour in Italy from putting forward, in order to obtain the licence required for that purpose, a guarantee established with a credit institution established in another Member State.'

requirements.[141] However, the text of Article 63 clearly suggests that the freedom of capital could go beyond discrimination. This has indeed been confirmed by the Court with regard to regulatory measures (section (aa)); yet with regard to fiscal measures, a discrimination test still applies (section (bb)).

aa. Non-discriminatory Capital Restrictions

That Article 63 could cover non-discriminatory capital restrictions was confirmed in *Sandoz*.[142] The Court here dealt with Austrian legislation imposing a stamp duty of 0.8 per cent on any loan. Sandoz challenged the national measure by claiming that the imposition of a stamp duty 'constituted an obstacle to the free movement of capital between a borrower residing in Austria and a lender established in another Member State which was likely to deter the borrower from turning to such a lender'.[143] The Austrian Finance Minister objected that the national law '*did not discriminate against lenders established in a Member State other than that of the borrower*'.[144] The Court however held that this was irrelevant:

> [L]egislation such as that at issue in the main proceedings deprives residents of a Member State of the possibility of benefiting from the absence of taxation which may be associated with loans obtained outside the national territory. Accordingly, such a measure is likely to deter residents from obtaining loans from persons established in other Member States.[145]

The inclusion of non-discriminatory measures within the scope of Article 63 was – famously – confirmed in the 'Golden Share' cases.[146] These cases arose in the aftermath of a neo-liberal wave at the turn of the twenty-first century in

---

[141] Joined Cases C-163/94, C-165/94 and C-250/94, *Sanz de Lera and others* [1995] ECR I-4821, paras. 24 and 25; Case C-54/99, *Scientology*, para. 14: 'A provision of national law which makes a direct foreign investment subject to prior authorisation constitutes a restriction on the movement of capital within the meaning of Article [63(1)] of the Treaty.'

[142] Case C-439/97, *Sandoz GmbH* v. *Finanzlandesdirektion für Wien* [1999] ECR I-7041. See also T. Horsley, 'The Concept of an Obstacle to Intra-EU Capital Movement', in N. Nic Shuibhne and L. W. Gormley (eds.), *From Single Market to Economic Union: Essays in Memory of John A. Usher* (Oxford University Press, 2012), 155 at 165: 'The ruling in *Sandoz* represents, in the area of direct taxation, the high-water mark in the Court's review of non-discriminatory national rules as obstacles to intra-EU movement.' For a brilliant criticism of the ruling, see K. Banks, 'The Application of the Fundamental Freedoms to Member State Tax Measures: Guarding against Protectionism or Second-guessing National Policy Choices?' (2008) 33 *EL Rev.* 482.

[143] Case C-439/97, *Sandoz*, para. 14.   [144] *Ibid.*, para. 15 (emphasis added).

[145] *Ibid.*, para. 19. For a similar formulation, see Case C-478/98, *Commission* v. *Belgium* [2000] ECR I-7587, para. 18: 'Measures taken by a Member State which are liable to dissuade its residents from obtaining loans or making investments in other Member States constitute restrictions on movements of capital within the meaning of that provision.'

[146] The 'Golden Share' cases are Case C-367/98, *Commission* v. *Portugal* (*Golden Shares I*) [2002] ECR I-4731; Case C-483/99, *Commission* v. *France* (*Golden Shares II/ElfAquitaine*) [2002] ECR I-4781; Case C-503/99, *Commission* v. *Belgium* (*Golden Shares III*) [2002] ECR I-4809; Case C-98/01, *Commission* v. *United Kingdom* (*BAA*) [2003] ECR I-4641;

which many European States decided to reprivatise formerly nationalised companies. Fearful of losing all influence over their freshly denationalised industries, many States however tried to retain a degree of control by either restricting the sale of shares to particular investors or by issuing 'golden shares'.

An excellent illustration of the first method can be found in *Commission* v. *Portugal*.[147] The case concerned a Portuguese reprivatisation law that had been adopted to reduce the role of the State in the national economy. The Portuguese legislation however insisted that any natural or legal person acquiring more than 10 per cent of the voting capital within a privatised company would need to obtain the prior authorisation of the Minister for Financial Affairs.[148] Portugal claimed that this was a non-discriminatory measure that fell outside Article 63,[149] but the Court identified a restriction of the free movement of capital:

> Even though the rules in issue may not give rise to unequal treatment, they are liable to impede the acquisition of shares in the undertakings concerned and to dissuade investors in other Member States from investing in the capital of those undertakings. They are therefore liable, as a result, to render the free movement of capital illusory. In those circumstances, the rules in issue must be regarded as a restriction on the movement of capital within the meaning of Article 73b of the Treaty. It is therefore necessary to consider whether, and on what basis, that restriction may be justified.[150]

We find a good illustration of the second control method is *Commission* v. *United Kingdom*.[151] The case involved the 1986 'Airport Act' that privatised the British Airport Authority (BAA); yet permitted the Secretary of State for Transport to retain a 'One Pound Special Share'. This special share allowed its owner to veto important business decisions within the – now private – company.[152] Repeating that Article 63 TFEU would 'go … beyond the mere elimination of unequal treatment, on grounds of nationality, as between operators on the financial markets', the Court had again no qualms about considering the government's 'golden share' a restriction on the free movement of capital.[153]

Joined Cases C-282–3/04, *Commission* v. *Netherlands* (*KPN/TPG*) [2006] ECR I-9141; Case C-112/05, *Commission* v. *Germany* (*VW*) [2007] ECR I-8995; Joined Cases C-463–4/04, *Federconsumatori and others* v. *Comune di Milano* [2007] ECR I-10419; more recently, Case C-171/08, *Commission* v. *Portugal* (*Commission* v. *Portugal I*) [2010] ECR I-6817; Case C-543/08, *Commission* v. *Portugal* (*Commission* v. *Portugal II*) [2010] ECR I-11241.

[147] Case C-367/98, *Commission* v. *Portugal*.

[148] *Ibid.*, para. 14. The law even contained a discriminatory provision according to which 'maximum permitted participation by foreign entities in the capital of companies whose re-privatisation has been completed shall henceforth be fixed at 25%, save where a higher limit has previously been fixed by the legislation providing for their re-privatisation'. This direct form of discrimination was easily disposed of by the Court (*ibid.*, paras. 40–2) and does not interest us here.

[149] *Ibid.*, para. 43.   [150] *Ibid.*, paras. 45–6.

[151] Case C-98/01, *Commission* v. *United Kingdom* (*BAA*).   [152] *Ibid.*, paras. 8–12.

[153] *Ibid.*, para. 44. The case also involved a limitation on the share capital per person, but the Court could here simply rely on its first golden share judgment.

This judicial intolerance towards 'golden shares' for public authorities in private companies reached a climax in *Commission* v. *Germany*.[154] The case concerned the German privatisation law for Volkswagen – one of the major German car manufacturers. Ingeniously, the German government had here not issued a 'golden share' that would directly allow it to veto business decisions. Instead, the national law neutrally required that all fundamental company decisions would need to be backed by more than four-fifths of the share capital, and that no single person could exercise voting rights beyond one-fifth of the share capital. On its face, the law thus did not grant any special legal rights to the German authorities. However, when looking behind the text of the Volkswagen law, the Court found that only a single shareholder owned 20 per cent of the share capital: the (regional) State of Lower Saxony. The national law thus exploited a *factual* 'situation' that allowed 'State authorities to procure for themselves a blocking minority allowing them to oppose important resolutions', which was 'liable to deter direct investors from other Member States'.[155]

The Volkswagen ruling left many questions on the relationship between Article 63 TFEU and State involvement in the running of a national company unanswered;[156] yet the Court has, on the other hand, clearly confirmed that national rules guaranteeing public ownership of a certain industry and prohibiting its privatisation fall within the scope of Article 63 TFEU.[157]

bb. Fiscal Measures: A Discrimination Test

A sizeable class of cases under Article 63 concern fiscal measures on direct taxation.[158] Where these fiscal measures – directly or indirectly – discriminate against foreign capital, they will constitute a capital restriction that needs to be justified by the Member State concerned.

---

[154]   Case C-112/05, *Commission* v. *Germany* (*VW*).

[155]   *Ibid.*, paras. 50–2.

[156]   A few years ago, the Court tried to clarify the extent of this potentially revolutionary ruling, see: Case C-95/12, *Commission* v. *Germany* (*VW II*) EU:C:2013:676. The case concerned the amended Volkswagen law, which had removed the voting cap yet retained the 80 per cent voting majority for important company decisions. This retention of the especially low blocking minority was challenged by the Commission; yet the Court here insisted that it was only the combination of the 20 per cent voting cap and the 20 per cent blocking minority that had fallen foul of Art. 63 TFEU in the previous *Volkswagen* case. On the generally – unclear – relations between national company law and the EU free movement of capital provisions, see W.-G. Ringe, 'Company Law and Free Movement of Capital' (2010) 69 *Cambridge Law Journal* 378; C. Gerner-Beuerle, 'Shareholders between the Market and the State: The VW Law and Other Interventions in the Market Economy' (2012) 49 *CML Rev.* 97.

[157]   Joined Cases C-105/12 to C-107/12, *The Netherlands* v. *Essent and others*, EU:C:2013:677, para. 38: '[T]he prohibition of privatisation falls within the scope of Article 63 TFEU and must be examined in the light of that article.'

[158]   For an excellent analysis of the place of direct tax measures in the internal market generally, see S. Kingston, 'The Boundaries of Sovereignty: The ECJ's Controversial Role Applying Internal Market Law to Direct Tax Measures' (2006–7) 9 CYELS 287.

The Court has thereby developed a very broad notion of indirect discrimination. For example: in *Van Caster*,[159] Germany had established a tax regime for investment funds that distinguished between 'white funds' and 'black funds'. In the former case, an investment fund had offered all the information required by the German tax authorities and was consequently subject to the general rules of taxation. Where, by contrast, a fund had not complied with the German transparency rules, a flat income tax rate was applied. This flat rate could, in good economic years, be more favourable than the general tax regime; yet it could also, in bad economic years, 'result in an overstatement of the taxpayer's real income' especially 'where interest rates remain low over a long period'.[160]

Was this flat rate for 'black funds', which applied to resident and non-resident investments alike, a capital restriction falling within the scope of Article 63? The Court held this to be the case in the following words:

> Such a flat-rate tax is ... likely to deter such a taxpayer from investing in funds which do not satisfy the obligations under that provision of national law. As the German Government stated at the hearing, choosing to comply or not with these obligations is a matter for investment funds and depends, in particular, on their desire to obtain clients in Germany. Accordingly, by their nature, those obligations are unlikely to be complied with by an investment fund which is not active in the German market and does not actively target that market ... Since such funds are generally non-resident funds, it should be noted that the national legislation at issue in the main proceedings is likely to deter a German investor from acquiring holdings in a non-resident investment fund ... Such legislation constitutes, therefore, a restriction on the free movement of capital which is prohibited, in principle, by Article 63 TFEU.[161]

Importantly: while using the formal language of 'restriction', the Court's substantive reasoning is here nonetheless based on a discrimination rationale. Yet what about non-discriminatory national measures that hinder the free movement of capital not because they themselves discriminate but because they create dual tax burdens? Would the unlimited double taxation by two distinct Member States violate Article 63?

A typical example of a dual tax scenario is offered in *Verkooijen*.[162] A Dutch employee of a Belgian company had received company shares as part of an employees' savings plan. The dividend earned on these shares was subject to 25 per cent dividend tax in Belgium. It was also subject to income tax in the Netherlands – despite the fact that the Dutch rules exempted dividends received from Dutch companies from income tax. Mr Verkooijen claimed that the limitation of the income tax exemption to national companies violated the free movement of capital, and the Court agreed:

---

[159] Case C-326/12, *Van Caster and Van Caster* v. *Finanzamt Essen-Süd*, EU:C:2014:2269.

[160] *Ibid.*, para. 27.

[161] *Ibid.*, paras. 34–8. This approach was confirmed by Case C-560/13, *Finanzamt Ulm* v. *Wagner-Raith*, EU:C:2015:357.

[162] Case C-35/98, *Staatssecretaris van Financiën* v. *B. G. M. Verkooijen*.

> Such a provision also has a restrictive effect as regards companies established in other Member States: it constitutes an obstacle to the raising of capital in the Netherlands *since the dividends which such companies pay to Netherlands residents receive less favourable tax treatment than dividends distributed by a company established in the Netherlands*, so that their shares are less attractive to investors residing in the Netherlands than shares in companies which have their seat in that Member State.[163]

The Court here outlawed a national tax measure that differentiated between 'national' and 'foreign' dividends and thus merely provided a warning shot to all *discriminatory* elements *within* national fiscal systems. Yet the ruling again left open the question of whether the existence of dual taxation – dividend tax in Belgium combined with income tax in the Netherlands – would itself be a restriction on the free movement of capital.

Could 'dual' (fiscal) burdens violate Article 63 as much as dual (regulatory) burdens would violate Article 34? This question was finally posed in *Kerckhaert*.[164] The case concerned a Belgian resident who had received dividends from a French company. These dividends had been taxed at the rate of 15 per cent in France, yet they were equally subject to Belgian income tax at the rate of 25 per cent – without the possibility of having the French tax 'set off' against the Belgian tax. The applicants in the case thus argued that since their 'French' dividends were taxed twice, the Belgian tax legislation constituted a restriction on the free movement of capital that fell foul of Article 63 TFEU.

Would the (unlimited) dual taxation of capital violate the free movement principle behind the internal market? In the context of regulatory barriers to goods, the answer after *Cassis de Dijon* is crystal clear: the dual regulation by the home and the host State violates free movement law – unless it is justified by means of imperative requirements of the public interest. Yet the Court rejected the mutual recognition logic in the present case, and insisted that only discriminatory taxation would fall within the scope of Article 63. In the opinion of the Court, the adverse consequences flowing from the imposition of the – second but neutral – Belgian tax simply resulted 'from the exercise *in parallel by two Member States of their fiscal sovereignty*'.[165]

The Court subsequently repeated this solution in *Test Claimants (II)*:

> [S]ince European Union law, as it currently stands does not lay down any general criteria for the attribution of areas of competence between the Member States in relation to the elimination of double taxation within the European Union, each

---

[163] *Ibid.*, paras. 34–5 (emphasis added). The ruling was confirmed in Case C-319/02, *Manninen* [2004] ECR I-7477, esp. paras. 20 and 23.

[164] Case C-513/04, *Kerckhaert and Morres* v. *Belgische Staat* [2006] ECR I-10967. For an extensive discussion of the case, see G. Kofler and R. Mason, 'Double Taxation: A European "Switch in Time"?' (2007) 14 *Columbia Journal of European Law* 63 at 74ff.

[165] Case C-513/04, *Kerckhaert*, para. 20.

Member State remains free to organise its system for taxing distributed profits, provided, however, that the system in question does not entail discrimination prohibited by the FEU Treaty.[166]

In conclusion, with regard to direct taxation, the Court has thus rejected the 'federal' model of integration for the free movement of capital and instead prefers an 'international' model that is still based on the fiscal sovereignty of the Member States. According to the international model, the Member States are solely prohibited from adopting (nationally) discriminatory measures.[167] A direct tax will thus only violate Article 63 TFEU if it *itself* offers a less favourable treatment to foreign capital. In the absence of positive harmonisation, each Member State can therefore apply its tax system to capital coming within its jurisdiction, as long as this tax system is 'neutral' and 'coherent'. This can, for example, mean that a person may have to pay inheritance tax twice – once in Germany and once in Spain.[168] For in the absence of Union legislation providing for general criteria for the apportionment of national taxes, it is purely in the hands of the Member States to eliminate double taxation through international agreements between themselves.[169]

This international solution for fiscal measures radically contrasts with the rejection of 'regulatory sovereignty' in *Cassis de Dijon*. It is however in line with the Union's treatment of indirect taxes under Article 110 TFEU – discussed in Chapter 13.

---

[166] Case C–35/11, *Test Claimants in the FII Group Litigation* v. *Commissioners of Inland Revenue and the Commissioners for Her Majesty's Revenue & Customs* EU:C:2012:707, para. 40. This phrase has become a 'formula' that is now generally quoted by the Court.

[167] Kingston, 'Boundaries of Sovereignty' (n. 158 above). 309: '[I]t would seem that the discrimination-based approach is, for now, winning the day, with the Court using a discrimination analysis[.]'

[168] This happened in Case C–67/08, *Block* v. *Finanzamt Kaufbeuren* [2009] ECR I-883, where the Court again held (*ibid.*, paras. 30–1): '[Union] law, in the current stage of its development and in a situation such as that in the main proceedings, does not lay down any general criteria for the attribution of areas of competence between the Member States in relation to the elimination of double taxation within the European [Union] … It follows from this that, in the current stage of the development of Community law, the Member States enjoy a certain autonomy in this area provided they comply with Community law, and are not obliged therefore to adapt their own tax systems to the different systems of tax of the other Member States in order, inter alia, to eliminate the double taxation arising from the exercise in parallel by those Member States of their fiscal sovereignty.'

[169] On the status of these double taxation agreements in the Union legal order, see R. Schütze, 'European Law and Member State Agreements: An Ambivalent Relationship?', in *Foreign Affairs and the EU Constitution* (Cambridge University Press, 2014), 120 esp. at 150ff. Since then, the Court has further clarified the status of double-taxation treaties in Case C–176/15, *Riskin & Timmermans* v. *Belgium*, EU:C:2016:488.

d. External Limits: Capital and the Other Freedoms

Are silver coins or banknotes transported from one Member State to another State protected by the chapter on capital or *goods*?[170] The question whether and when a given situation is governed by which freedom has been particularly important in the context of the free movement of capital. Because as the pre-Maastricht capital provisions originally lacked direct effect, the question of whether a case was governed by the free movement of capital or not determined whether an individual could use the EU Treaties to challenge national measures restricting intra-Union trade. And while this normative weakness has today been removed, the free movement of capital provisions continue to be 'special' in one particular aspect: unlike the three other freedoms, Article 63 extends to restrictions between Member States and *third countries*.[171] The importation of silver coins from a third country into the internal market may thus be protected – or not – depending on whether the freedom of capital or the freedom of goods applies to the case.

The principles governing the scope of the freedom of capital in relation to the other freedoms are complex, especially in relation to the freedom of establishment (section (aa)) and the free movement of services (section (bb)). Let us look at both borderlines in turn.

aa. Relationship to the Freedom of Establishment

The EU Treaties expressly acknowledge the potential overlap between the freedom of capital and the freedom of establishment. The freedom of establishment is made 'subject to the provisions of the Chapter relating to capital',[172] while the provisions on capital 'shall be without prejudice to the applicability of restrictions on the right of establishment which are compatible with the Treaties'.[173]

Did this indicate that both freedoms could simultaneously apply? The question has been intensely debated, especially over national rules restricting direct investments in foreign companies. In a complex web of diverse jurisprudential lines, the Court here generally prefers to apply one freedom only;[174] and it

---

[170] The Court has made its classification dependent on whether the coins (or banknotes) are still used as legal tender or not; see Case 7/78, *Regina* v. *Thomson* [1978] ECR 2247, para. 26: 'Silver alloy coins which are legal tender in a Member State are, by their very nature, to be regarded as means of payment and it follows that their transfer does not fall within the provisions of Articles [34 *et seq.*] of the Treaty.' See also Case C-416/93, *Bordessa*, para. 13: '[T]he physical transfer of assets falls not under Articles [34] and [56] but under Article [63] and the Directive implementing that provision.'

[171] On this point, see section 3(a) above.

[172] Art. 49 TFEU – second indent.

[173] *Ibid.*, Art. 65(2). The Nomenclature Annex of Directive 88/361 defines 'direct investment' as '[e]stablishment and extension of branches or new undertakings belonging solely to the person providing the capital' as well as the '[p]articipation in new or existing undertaking with a view to establishing or maintaining lasting economic links'.

[174] Case C-42/07, *Liga Portuguesa de Futebol Profissional*, EU:C:2009:519, para. 47: 'Where a national measure relates to several fundamental freedoms at the same time, the Court will in principle examine the measure in relation to only one of those freedoms if it appears,

thereby draws a dividing line between the freedom of establishment and the free movement of capital where the investor has gained 'definite influence' in the foreign company.[175] Where this is the case, the freedom of establishment applies, and an examination of the freedom of capital has been held unnecessary.[176]

The exclusion of direct investments that provide definite managerial control from the scope of the free movement of capital makes enormous sense from the Union point of view.[177] For the opposite result would mean that the freedom of capital – indirectly – grants 'establishment' rights to third-country nationals; and this would undermine the personal scope of Article 49 which is confined to nationals of the Member States.[178] While a third country person or company is thus constitutionally entitled to 'invest' in the European Union, it does not enjoy freedom of establishment – even indirectly under the free movement of capital provisions.[179] To put this in concrete terms: a Saudi prince is constitutionally entitled to invest in a European football club under Article 63 but he has no constitutional right under Article 49 to buy and assume 'definite influence' over it.

---

in the circumstances of the case, that the other freedoms are entirely secondary in relation to the first and may be considered together with it.'

[175] Case C-251/98, *Baars* v. *Inspecteur der Belastingen* [2000] ECR I-2787, esp. para. 21: 'A 100% holding in the capital of a company having its seat in another Member State undoubtedly brings such a taxpayer within the scope of application of the Treaty provisions on the right of establishment.' See also Case C-436/00, *X and Y* [2002] ECR I-10829; Case C-196/04, *Cadbury Schweppes* v. *Commissioners of Inland Revenue* [2006] ECR I-7995. The Court has also clarified that where the national legislation only concerns the relations within a group of companies, then this would fall within the freedom of establishment; see *Cadbury Schweppes* (*ibid.*, para. 32); Case C-284/06, *Finanzamt Hamburg-Am Tierpark* v. *Burda* [2008] ECR I-4571, para. 68: 'It follows from settled case-law that, in so far as any given national rules concern only relationships within a group of companies, they primarily affect the freedom of establishment.'

[176] Case C-196/04, *Cadbury Schweppes*, para. 33: 'If, as submitted by the applicants in the main proceedings and Ireland, that legislation has restrictive effects on the free movement of services and the free movement of capital, such effects are an unavoidable consequence of any restriction on freedom of establishment and do not justify, in any event, an independent examination of that legislation in the light of Articles [56] and [63].'

[177] From the point of view of a third-country investor, the dividing line between a 'definite influence' investment and a passive (portfolio) investment has the ironic side effect that the higher the investment the lower the level of protection.

[178] With regard to companies, see Case C-47/12, *Kronos International* v. *Finanzamt Leverkusen*, para. 46: '[A] company or form which is not formed in accordance with the law of a Member State cannot enjoy freedom of establishment.'

[179] *Ibid.*, para. 53: 'It should also be noted that the Court has held that, since the Treaty does not extend freedom of establishment to third countries, it is important to ensure that the interpretation of Article 63(1) TFEU as regards relations with third countries does not enable economic operators who do not fall within the limits of the territorial scope of freedom of establishment to profit from that freedom.'

By contrast, the Court has held that where a national restriction concerns 'ordinary shareholder[s]',[180] the free movement of capital will principally apply. And it has again favoured the application of only one freedom by holding that there is 'no need for a separate examination of the measures at issue in the light of the Treaty rules concerning freedom of establishment', where the establishment restriction was 'a direct consequence of the obstacles to the free movement of capital' to which it is 'inextricably linked'.[181]

The judicial solution championed by the Court here comes close to a centre-of-gravity approach, which makes the *exclusive* application of one freedom over the other dependent on which is the *primary* freedom affected.[182] This solution however encounters problems where national legislation equally applies to all forms of investments. The Court has thus indicated that it would be willing to concede the parallel application of the freedom of establishment and the free movement of capital in situations where '[n]ational legislation [is] not intended to apply only to those shareholdings which enable the holder to have a definite influence on a company's decisions and to determine its activities but which applies irrespective of the size of the holding which the shareholder has in a company'.[183]

However, the Court has also clarified that the parallel application of both freedoms is confined to situations that concern *intra*-Union capital movements. Where, by contrast, a third-country restriction is concerned, only the free movement of capital can apply. The Court has confirmed this in *Test Claimants (II)*.[184] National legislation that concerns shareholdings granting a definite influence over a company will thus completely fall outside the free movement provisions as 'neither Article 49 TFEU nor Article 63 TFEU may be relied upon', whereas national rules that do not apply exclusively to situations of definite influence must be assessed in light of Article 63 only.[185] The reason for this external limitation of Article 63 was ably explained by the Court as follows:

---

[180] Case C-35/98, *Verkooijen*, para. 64.

[181] Case C-367/98, *Commission* v. *Portugal*, para. 56.

[182] This approach had been championed by Advocate General Albers in Case C-251/98, *Baars*, paras. 26–30.

[183] Case C-326/07, *Commission* v. *Italy* [2009] ECR I-2291, para. 36; Case C-157/05, *Holböck* v. *Finanzamt Salzburg-Land* [2007] ECR I-4051. Did this mean that a third-country investor could use the capital provisions to achieve a hostile takeover of a Union company, where the national legislation generically applied to all investors? The question is still unresolved. However, in subsequent cases, the Court appears to moderately backtrack by looking – if possible – at the specific facts of the individual case. See e.g. Case C-284/06, *Burda*; Case C-310/09, *Ministre du Budget, des Comptes publics et de la Fonction publique* v. *Accor* [2011] ECR I-8115, paras. 31–8. For a brief analysis of these cases, see D. S. Smit, 'EU Freedoms, Non-EU Countries and Company Taxation: An Overview and Future Prospects' (2012) *EC Tax Law* 223.

[184] Case C-35/11, *Test Claimants in the FII Group Litigation*. For an extensive analysis of the case, as well as the general problems underlying this area, see R. Murphy, 'Why Does Tax Have to Be So Taxing? The Court Revisits the Franked Investment Income Litigation' (2013) 38 *EL Rev.* 695.

[185] Case C-35/11, *Test Claimants (II)*, paras. 98–9.

Since the Treaty does not extend freedom of establishment to third countries, it is important to ensure that the interpretation of Article 63(1) TFEU as regards relations with third countries does not enable economic operators who do not fall within the limits of the territorial scope of freedom of establishment to profit from that freedom.[186]

bb. Relationship to the Free Movement of Services

What about the freedom of services? The Treaties originally appeared to treat services as a residual category; yet, as we saw above, the Court has raised the status of the services provisions to an independent freedom.[187] The question has thus arisen whether the freedoms of services and capital may also be applied in parallel or not.

While a parallel application is not unknown,[188] the Court has also privileged a centre-of-gravity approach here. In *Fidum*,[189] the German financial authorities had refused to grant authorisation to a Swiss company offering credit to customers in Germany and the question arose of whether the situation was covered by the free movement of services or capital. The Court held as follows:

Contrary to the chapter of the Treaty concerning the free movement of capital, the chapter regulating the freedom to provide services does not contain any provision which enables service providers in non-member countries and established outside the European Union to rely on those provisions ... Thus, the question arises as to the delimitation of and the relationship between, first, the Treaty provisions concerning the freedom to provide services and, second, those governing the free movement of capital ... Where a national measure relates to the freedom to provide services and the free movement of capital at the same time, it is necessary to consider to what extent the exercise of those fundamental liberties is affected and whether, in the circumstances of the main proceedings, one of those prevails over the other. The Court will in principle examine the measure in dispute in relation to *only one of those two freedoms if it appears, in the circumstances of the case, that one of them is entirely secondary in relation to the other and may be considered together with it.*[190]

---

[186] *Ibid.*, para. 100.   [187] On this point, see section 1(a/bb) above.

[188] In Case C-484/93, *Svensson and Gustavsson* v. *Ministre du Logement et de l'Urbanisme* [1995] ECR I-3955, the Court found a violation of the free movement of capital provisions (*ibid.*, para. 10) and a violation of the scope of the free movement of services (*ibid.*, para. 12). See also Case C-279/00, *Commission* v. *Italy* [2002] ECR I-1425, para. 41: 'It follows from all the preceding considerations that, by requiring undertakings engaged in the provision of temporary labour which are established in other Member States to maintain their registered office or a branch office on Italian territory, and to lodge a guarantee of ITL 700 million with a credit institution having its registered office or a branch office on Italian territory, the Italian Republic has failed to fulfil its obligations under Articles [56] and [63].'

[189] Case C-452/04, *Fidium Finanz*.

[190] *Ibid.*, paras. 25, 27 and 34 (emphasis added).

The choice of which freedom applies was – as the Court points out – of fundamental importance, since the case involved a company established in a third State (Switzerland). The Treaties would here only apply if the free movement of capital were concerned; and the rejection of the parallel application of the free movement of capital in the present case stemmed from the wish to 'prevent … the extension of all the internal market freedoms to third country situations via the back door of the free movement of capital'.[191] Using a centre of-gravity approach, the Court consequently found that the freedom of services was 'predominant' and that the restrictions on the freedom of capital were 'merely an inevitable consequence of the restriction imposed on the provision of services'.[192] The Swiss company therefore had no constitutional right to offer its financial services in a Member State of the European Union.

4. Capital II: Justifications (and Derogations)

As with the other three fundamental freedoms, the EU Treaties recognise that capital restrictions imposed by the Member States may be justified by reference to certain public interests. The express justifications for such capital restrictions are enumerated in Article 65(1) TFEU:

> The provisions of Article 63 shall be without prejudice to the right of Member States:
> (a) to apply the relevant provisions of their tax law which distinguish between tax-payers who are not in the same situation with regard to their place of residence or with regard to the place where their capital is invested;
> (b) to take all requisite measures to prevent infringements of national law and regulations, in particular in the field of taxation and the prudential supervision of financial institutions, or to lay down procedures for the declaration of capital movements for purposes of administrative or statistical information, or to take measures which are justified on grounds of public policy or public security.

The first subparagraph permits national tax laws that historically apply differentiated rates to (permanently) resident and non-resident taxpayers.[193] This justification is specific to the free movement of capital, which here – again – pays homage to the idea of the fiscal 'sovereignty' of the Member States.[194] The second subparagraph refers to a number of specific administrative justifications

---

[191] Snell, 'Free Movement of Capital' (n. 118 above), 571. For a strong criticism of the 'either/or' centre-of-gravity theory, see S. Hindelang, *The Free Movement of Capital and Foreign Direct Investment: The Scope of Protection in EU Law* (Oxford University Press, 2009), esp. 111. For the author, the application of the 'exclusivity theory' 'would be devastating when it comes to third country capital movement'.

[192] Case C-452/04, *Fidium Finanz*, para. 49.

[193] Usher, 'Evolution of the Free Movement of Capital' (n. 117 above), 1549.

[194] This idea is even reinforced for restrictive tax measures adopted by Member States towards third countries in Art. 65(4) TFEU.

for capital restrictions but also lists some of the Treaties' general public policy justifications.

The justifications in Article 65(1)(a) and (b) TFEU are both subject to the principle, mentioned in Article 65(3) TFEU, that they must never 'constitute a means of arbitrary discrimination or a disguised restriction on the free movement of capital'.[195] And the Court has also clarified that as 'derogations from the fundamental principle of free movement of capital', they must 'be interpreted strictly' and in particular that 'their scope cannot be determined unilaterally by each Member State without any control by the [Union] institutions'.[196] In the past, this control has been mainly exercised by the Court. For the Union legislator has – apart from a few notable exceptions – hardly harmonised matters within this field.[197]

a. Express Justifications I: Tax Discriminations under Article 65(1)(a)

The Court traditionally treats fiscal measures in a distinct way. We have seen this distinctiveness already in the context of Article 63 TFEU, where the Court insists that only discriminatory taxes are prohibited. Discrimination within national tax systems will thereby typically be indirect discrimination. For many national tax systems determine their tax rates or tax benefits not according to the nationality of the taxpayer but according to its residency.

But is a residency requirement not *ipso facto* discriminatory? The Court gave a first – negative – answer in *Schumacker*.[198] The case involved a German tax benefit that had not been granted to a person who was (partly) taxed but not resident in Germany; and while admitting that a residency criterion '*may* constitute indirect discrimination by reason of nationality', the Court here held that in the context of (direct) taxation 'the situations of residents and of non-residents are not, as a rule, comparable'.[199] There was therefore – as a rule – no discrimination, where a national tax system generally differentiated between resident and non-resident taxpayers. However, the Court added an important qualification: where '[t]here is no objective difference between the situations of such a non-resident and a resident',[200] the differential treatment by a Member State would be discriminatory and thus needed to be justified.[201]

---

[195] Art. 65(3) TFEU.

[196] Case C-54/99, *Eglise de scientologie*, para. 17. In this particular case, the Court held in the context of the public policy and security justification that they 'may be relied on only if there is a genuine and sufficiently serious threat to a fundamental interest of society'.

[197] For a light degree of positive integration in the field of capital movements, see however Directive 2003/48 on taxation of savings income in the form of interest payments [2003] OJ L 157/38; Regulation 1889/2005 on controls of cash entering or leaving the Community [2005] OJ L 309/9; Directive 2005/60 on the prevention of the use of the financial system for the purpose of money laundering and terrorist financing [2005] OJ L 309/15; Directive 2008/7 concerning indirect taxes on the raising of capital [2008] OJ L 46/11.

[198] Case C-279/93, *Finanzamt Köln-Altstadt v. Schumacker* [1995] ECR I-225.

[199] *Ibid.*, paras. 29 and 31.   [200] *Ibid.*, para. 37.   [201] *Ibid.*, para. 39.

But will such discriminatory measures then not always be justified by Article 65(1)(a)? After all, the provision generically refers to all national tax laws that 'distinguish between taxpayers who are not in the same situation *with regard to their place of residence or with regard to the place where their capital is invested*'.[202]

The question has received – strong – negative responses in *Verkooijen* and *Manninen*.[203] Both cases concerned the refusal to grant tax benefit on the grounds that the taxpayer was not resident in the benefit-granting Member State. And instead of viewing Article 65(1)(a) as a justification designed to apply to such discriminatory tax measures, the Court – ingeniously, yet somewhat mischievously – held that that specific justification must not constitute 'a means of arbitrary discrimination'. In its view, only objectively comparable situations could fall within the scope of the justification:

> Article [65(1)(a)] of the Treaty, which, as a derogation from the fundamental principle of the free movement of capital, must be interpreted strictly, cannot be interpreted as meaning that any tax legislation making a distinction between taxpayers by reference to the place where they invest their capital is automatically compatible with the Treaty. The derogation in Article [65(1)(a) TFEU] is itself limited by Article [65(3) TFEU] which provides that the national provisions referred to in Article [65(1)] 'shall not constitute a means of arbitrary discrimination or a disguised restriction on the free movement of capital and payments as defined in Article [63]'. A distinction must therefore be made between unequal treatment which is permitted under Article [65(1)(a) TFEU] and arbitrary discrimination which is prohibited by Article [65(3)] … to be capable of being regarded as compatible with the Treaty provisions on the free movement of capital, the difference in treatment must concern situations which are not objectively comparable or be justified by overriding reasons in the general interest, such as the need to safeguard the coherence of the tax system.[204]

This interpretation ultimately denies Article 65(1)(a) its quality as an independent justification.[205] If the provision could not be used to justify the different treatment of 'objectively comparable' situations, what could it do? (Had

202 Emphasis added. According to Declaration No. 7 on '[ex-]Article 73(d) of the Treaty establishing the European Community' annexed to the Final Act of the Treaty on European Union, the provision is however said to be restricted to national tax measures that were in force at the time. 'The Conference affirms that the right of Member States to apply the relevant provisions of their tax law as referred to in [ex-]Article 73(d)(1)(a) of this Treaty will apply only with respect to the relevant provisions which exist at the end of 1993.' Apparently a second phrase was subsequently added: 'However, this Declaration shall apply only to capital movements between Member States and to payments effected between Member States.' The Declaration is quoted in Mohamed, *European Community Law* (n. 116 above), 144.

203 Case C-35/98, *Staatssecretaris van Financiën v. B. G. M. Verkooijen*; Case C-319/02, *Manninen* [2004] ECR I-7477.

204 *Ibid.*, paras. 28–9.

205 S. Peers, 'Free Movement of Capital: Learning Lessons or Slipping on Spilt Milk', in C. Barnard and J. Scott (eds.), *The Law of the Single European Market: Unpacking the Premises* (Hart, 2002), 333 at 348: 'The Court has therefore interpreted the Treaty wording intended

the *Schumacker* ruling not said that unless 'objectively comparable', a residency criterion would not even constitute discrimination and thus not fall within the scope of Article 63 TFEU in the first place?) The Court here seems to have completely closed off the scope for Article 65(1)(a), as a residency requirement for objectively comparable situations will always be treated as 'arbitrary' and may thus never be justified on the basis of Article 65(1)(a)!

Perhaps realising that its ruling effectively removes one of the express justifications for national tax laws, the Court however 'generously' opened the constitutional avenue of 'overriding reason in the general interest' to these discriminatory tax measures. A residency requirement could thus potentially be justified by pleading the cohesion of the national tax system. However, this compensatory move blurred the district justificatory regimes for discriminatory and non-discriminatory measures.

b. Express Justifications II: Article 65(1)(b)

Unlike the 'public policy' justifications available to the other three fundamental freedoms, Article 65(1)(b) only mentions 'public policy' and 'public security'.[206] This reduced list excludes 'public morality' and 'public health' as well as other common justifications usually available for national restrictions to free movement.

The provision does however contain two additional justifications. Member States are allowed 'to take all requisite measures to *prevent infringements of national law and regulations, in particular* in the field of taxation and the prudential supervision of financial institutions, or to lay down procedures for the *declaration* of capital movements for purposes of administrative or statistical information'.[207] The special emphasis on infringement prevention and declaration procedures in this context corresponds to the particularly 'fluid' and potentially 'clandestine' nature of capital movements.

The Court has given a broad reading of these special grounds in Article 65(1)(b). In *Sandoz*,[208] it held a fiscal measure justified '[s]ince the effect of such a measure is to compel such persons to pay the duty, it prevents taxable persons from evading the requirements of domestic tax legislation through the exercise of freedom of movement of capital guaranteed by Article [63(1)] of the Treaty'.[209] Effective fiscal supervision and the prevention of tax evasion

---

to *protect* tax discrimination in the sphere of free movement of capital to mean exactly the opposite. While such an interpretation secures a uniform application of the Treaty freedoms as regards tax exceptions, it appears to flaunt the deliberate intentions of Treaty drafters.'

[206] See respectively Case C-54/99, *Eglise de Scientologie*; Case C-423/98, *Albore* [2000] ECR I-5965. With regard to 'public policy' exceptions, the Court has 'transposed its jurisprudence developed within the ambits of other freedoms to that of capital movement' (Hindelang, *Free Movement of Capital* (n. 191 above), 225).

[207] Emphasis added.

[208] Case C-439/97, *Sandoz* v. *Finanzlandesdirektion für Wien, Niederösterreich und Burgenland*.

[209] *Ibid.*, para. 24. For a biting criticism of this reasoning, see Banks, 'Application of the Fundamental Freedoms' (n. 142 above), 494.

will thus fall within the scope of the justification.[210] Moreover, the Court has clarified that preventive measures are not confined to the field of taxation. Underlining the open-ended nature of Article 65(1)(b), the Court confirmed in *Bordessa* that 'other measures are also permitted in so far as they are designed to prevent illegal activities of comparable seriousness, such as money laundering, drug trafficking or terrorism'.[211]

Unlike its broad approach to the *grounds* of justification here, the Court has however been very strict with regard to what constitutes a 'proportionate' restriction.[212] The Court has thus almost automatically found authorisation requirements for capital movements – unlike mere 'declaration' requirements – disproportionate. In the view of the Court '[a] requirement of that nature would cause the exercise of the free movement of capital to be subject to the discretion of the administrative authorities and thus be such as to render that freedom illusory'.[213] The Court has however, exceptionally, allowed authorisation requirements with regard to immovable property. In *Kronle*,[214] the Court thus conceded that a declaration procedure sometimes 'does not, therefore, in itself enable the aim pursued to be achieved in the context of a procedure for prior authorization'; and that 'Member States must also be able to take measures where a breach of the agreed declaration is duly established after the property has been acquired.'[215]

c. Implied Justifications: Imperative Requirements

The Court has left no doubt that restrictions on the free movement of capital may in some circumstances be justified 'by reasons referred to in Article [65(1)] *or by overriding requirements of the general interest*'.[216] And while the Court has insisted that 'economic grounds can never serve as justification for obstacles prohibited by the Treaty',[217] the overriding requirements may also be as broad and variegated as the imperative requirements under the free movement of goods.[218]

A central uncertainty governing these overriding requirements is however whether they are restricted to non-discriminatory measures or not. In a number of cases, the Court seems to have insisted that discriminatory measures may only be 'justified on grounds permitted by the Treaty' and that the implied 'overriding interests of the public interest' can only be invoked for a national measure '*if it*

---

[210] Joined Cases C-163/94, C-165/94 and C-250/94, *Sanz de Lera*, para. 22.

[211] Joined Cases C-358/93 and C-416/93, *Bordessa and others*, para. 21.

[212] For a good application of the proportionality principle, see Case C-112/05, *Commission v. Germany (Volkswagen)*.

[213] Joined Cases C-358/93 and C-416/93, *Bordessa and others*, para. 25; Joined Cases C-163/94, C-165/94; C-250/94, *Sanz de Lera*.

[214] Case C-302/97, *Konle v. Austria*.   [215] *Ibid.*, para. 46.

[216] Case C-367/98, *Commission v. Portugal (Golden Shares I)*, para. 49 (emphasis added).

[217] *Ibid.*, para. 52. See also Case C-436/00, *X&Y*, para. 50.

[218] See e.g. Case C-302/97, *Konle v. Austria*, where the Court held 'town and country planning' to constitute such an overriding requirement (*ibid.*, para. 40).

is not applied in a discriminatory manner.[219] However, as we saw above, the Court appears to have abandoned the distinction between discriminatory and non-discriminatory measures for at least one overriding requirement: the 'cohesion of the national tax system'.

The cohesion of the national tax system constitutes one of the most important overriding requirements in the context of capital restrictions.[220] The Court has clarified that this ground is distinct from pleading the prevention of the reduction in tax revenue. For while the latter 'cannot be regarded as a matter of overriding general interest',[221] the Court has accepted that the internal logic of the national tax system may require that the grant of a particular tax benefit be 'directly linked' to offsetting another tax imposed on resident taxpayers.[222] In protecting the internal coherence of the national tax system, the Court has however given a restrictive interpretation to what constitutes such a 'direct link'. In *Verkooijen*, it rejected the existence of a direct link between a tax benefit and a second tax, where there 'are two separate taxes levied on different taxpayers'.[223] And while the Court generally allows fiscal cohesion to be pleaded in the fight against tax circumvention, it seems to exclude national tax measures that are 'not specifically designed to exclude from a tax advantage purely artificial schemes designed to circumvent [national] tax law'.[224]

---

[219] *Ibid.*, paras. 24 and 40 (emphasis added). See also Joined Cases C-515/99, C-519–24/99 and C-526–40/99, *Reisch and others* v. *Bürgermeister der Landeshauptstadt Salzburg and others* [2002] ECR I-2157, para. 33: 'Such restrictions may nevertheless be permitted if the national rules pursue, in a non-discriminatory way, an objective in the public interest and if they observe the principle of proportionality, that is if the same result could not be achieved by other less restrictive measures.'

[220] The justification was originally developed in Case C-204/90, *Bachmann* v. *Belgium* [1992] ECR I-249; and Case C-300/90, *Commission* v. *Belgium* [1992] ECR I-305 in the context of the free movement of workers.

[221] Case C-436/00, *X&Y*, para. 50; Case C-35/98, *Verkooijen*, para. 59.

[222] See e.g. Case C-204/90, *Bachmann* v. *Belgium*; Case C-300/90, *Commission* v. *Belgium*; Case C-35/98, *Verkooijen*; Case C-436/00, *X&Y*.

[223] Case C-35/98, *Verkooijen*, para. 58. In Case C-319/02, *Manninen*, the Court however seems to have accepted the possibility of a direct link between two taxes paid by two different taxpayers. The Finnish government had here claimed (*ibid.*, para. 41) that 'if a tax credit were to be granted to the recipients of dividends paid by a Swedish company to shareholders who were fully taxable in Finland, the authorities of that Member State would be obliged to grant a tax advantage in relation to corporation tax that was not levied by that State, thereby threatening the cohesion of the national tax system'. The Court however responded as follows (*ibid.*, para. 45): 'Even if that tax legislation is thus based on a link between the tax advantage and the offsetting tax levy, in providing that the tax credit granted to the shareholder fully taxable in Finland is to be calculated by reference to the corporation tax due from the company established in that Member State on the profits which it distributes, such legislation does not appear to be necessary in order to preserve the cohesion of the Finnish tax system.' One commentator has consequently remarked that '[i]t is not clear whether the criteria "one and the same taxpayer" and "the same tax" are cumulative' (D. Weber, *Tax Avoidance and the EC Treaty Freedoms: A Study on the Limitations under European Law to the Prevention of Tax Avoidance* (Kluwer, 2005), 243).

[224] Case C-436/00, *X&Y*, para. 61.

d. Special Derogations for Third-country Restrictions

The extension of the freedom of capital to third countries constitutes a unique departure from the Treaty framework governing the internal market. We saw above that this has not prevented the Court from declaring Article 63(1) directly effective vis-à-vis third-country movements and to insist that the same concept of 'restriction' was to apply in this context. Nonetheless, it is 'not unreasonable' to expect the Union 'to prescribe a lesser degree of liberalisation towards third countries' than among its own Member States.[225] In the absence of a Union power to 'harmonise' third-country legislation, the Union should indeed resist 'the wholesale unilateral extension of capital freedom to third countries': '[i]n the absence of a level playing-field in the global financial market, such a generous unilateral move can distort the harmonious development of its internal financial market'.[226] The EU Treaties partly heed these warnings by offering special justifications to national restrictions on third country capital.

aa. Special Grounds of Justification

The Union legal order has indeed enumerated a number of special derogations that allow Member States to maintain national restrictions on capital movements from or to third countries that would not be allowed in an intra-Union context.

The EU Treaties expressly mention three such special derogations for third-country capital. First, there is the so-called 'grandfather clause' in Article 64(1) TFEU. It expressly excludes certain classes of third-country capital restrictions that existed before a particular date:

> The provisions of Article 63 shall be without prejudice to the application to third countries of any restrictions which exist on 31 December 1993 under national or Union law adopted in respect of the movement of capital to or from third countries involving direct investment – including in real estate – establishment, the provision of financial services or the admission of securities to capital markets. In respect of restrictions existing under national law in Bulgaria, Estonia and Hungary, the relevant date shall be 31 December 1999.

This special derogation allows the Member States – and the Union(!) – to maintain capital restrictions vis-à-vis third countries that existed prior to 1 January 1994 (or 1 January 2000). Being 'unreserved … and indefinite', it constitutes 'the most general and broad-based exception' to the free movement of capital in the Treaties.[227] And while the Union can remove these capital restrictions by means of Union legislation under Article 64(2) TFEU, it may equally decide to add new Union restrictions under Article 64(3) TFEU.[228]

---

[225]   Mohamed, *European Community Law* (n. 116 above), 216.   [226]   *Ibid.*

[227]   Hindelang, *Free Movement of Capital* (n. 191 above), 277. For an extensive interpretation of this provision, see Case C-302/97, *Konle* v. *Austria*; C-157/05, *Holböck* v. *Finanzamt Salzburg-Land*.

[228]   For an analysis of Art. 64(2)–(3) TFEU, see above.

A second special derogation for capital movements from or to third countries can be found in Article 65(4) TFEU. It allows the Union

> to adopt a decision stating that restrictive tax measures adopted by a Member State concerning one or more third countries are to be considered compatible with the Treaties in so far as they are justified by one of the objectives of the Union and compatible with the proper functioning of the internal market.

This legal basis allows the Union to adopt an *executive* decision that determines that a national capital restriction is justified – even where a *judicial* interpretation of Article 65 TFEU may come to the opposite conclusion.[229] This executive interference into the province of the judiciary, while not unknown in other areas of Union law, constitutes a serious breach of the separation-of-powers principle.[230]

Finally, the Treaties allow for a third derogation that is known as a 'safeguard clause' under international economic law. Following Article 66 TFEU, where capital movements (potentially) cause 'serious difficulties for the operation of economic and monetary union' the Union is exceptionally entitled to adopt 'safeguard measures with regard to third countries for a period not exceeding six months if such measures are strictly necessary'. The provision allows the Union to adopt temporary measures in an economic emergency situation.

bb. Special Standard(s) of Justification

In addition to these three special grounds, the Court has also acknowledged a special – lower – justificatory standard for third-country capital restrictions. In *Test Claimants II*, the Court expressly held:

> [I]t may be that a Member State will be able to demonstrate that a restriction on capital movements to or from non-member countries is justified for a particular reason in circumstances where that reason would not constitute a valid justification for a restriction on capital movements between Member States.[231]

---

[229]   According to Snell, 'Free Movement of Capital' (n. 118 above), 553 this is 'remarkable' in that it allows the Council to make a political determination of what should be a judicial determination by the Court. This provision introduced by the Lisbon Treaty 'demonstrates a distrust of the Court on the part of the Member States' (*ibid.*, 554).

[230]   See R. Murphy, 'Changing Treaty and Changing Economic Context: The Dynamic Relationship of the Legislature and the Judiciary in the Pursuit of Capital Liberalization', in P. Syrpis (ed.), *The Judiciary, the Legislature and the EU Internal Market* (Cambridge University Press, 2012), 274 at 294–5: '[T]he newly inserted Article 65(4) TFEU has the potential to muddy the waters between the legislature [*sic*] and the judiciary. Traditionally it is the Court that is accused of "judicial law making". In the context of this new Article, an accusation of "legislative [*sic*] adjudicating" could be levelled at the Council.'

[231]   See Case C-446/04, *Test Claimants* [2006] ECR I-11753, para. 171.

We can see why this may be the case in *Skatteverket*.[232] The case involved the refusal of the Swedish authorities to grant a tax exemption to dividends that were paid by a company established in a third country (here, Switzerland). This refusal was explained on the grounds of guaranteeing the effectiveness of fiscal supervision. This overriding requirement would generally fail in an intra-Union context,[233] where the Court has subjected it to a strict proportionality review. This strict review is the result of the existence of Union legislation facilitating the fiscal supervision between Member States.[234] However, 'movement of capital to or from third countries takes place in a different legal context from that which occurs in the [Union]',[235] and the Court in particular held that 'the taxation by a Member State of economic activities having cross-border aspects which take place within the [Union] is not always comparable to that of economic activities involving relations between Member States and third countries'.[236]

The strict proportionality review in an intra-Union context will thus *not* automatically be transposed to an extra-Union context. For whereas the Union can facilitate cross-border fiscal supervision *between the Member States* through Union legislation, no such 'federal' cooperation exists with third States; and in the absence of positive integration with third States, Member States will consequently be subject to a lower degree of negative integration.[237] National capital restrictions on third-country capital can thus be justified, where intra-Union restrictions could not.

---

[232] Case C-101/05, *Skatteverket* v. *A*.

[233] See D. S. Smit, 'EU Freedoms, Non-EU Countries and Company Taxation: An Overview and Future Prospect' (2012) 21 *EC Tax Review* 233 at 243: 'The CJEU has accepted the need for effective fiscal supervision in the abstract as a justification for a restrictive tax measure, but has nonetheless rejected such a defence, on grounds of proportionality, in virtually each concrete case in an intra-Union context.'

[234] Directive 2011/16 on administrative cooperation in the field of taxation [2011] OJ L 64/1. The directive has been adopted on the basis of Articles 113 and 115 TFEU and lays down a mandatory information exchange system between the Member States. Its Art. 8 (1) states: 'The competent authority of each Member State shall, by automatic exchange, communicate to the competent authority of any other Member State, information regarding taxable periods as from 1 January 2014 that is available concerning residents in that other Member State, on the following specific categories of income and capital as they are to be understood under the national legislation of the Member State which communicates the information: (a) income from employment; (b) director's fees; (c) life insurance products not covered by other Union legal instruments on exchange of information and other similar measures; (d) pensions; (e) ownership of and income from immovable property.'

[235] Case C-101/05, *Skatteverket* v. *A*, para. 36.   [236] *Ibid.*, para. 37.

[237] *Ibid.*, paras. 60–1: 'However, that case-law, which relates to restrictions on the exercise of freedom of movement within the [Union], cannot be transposed in its entirety to movements of capital between Member States and third countries, since such movements take place in a different legal context from that of the cases which gave rise to the judgments referred to in the two preceding paragraphs. In the first place, relations between the Member States take place against a common legal background, characterised by the existence of [Union] legislation, such as Directive 77/799, which laid down reciprocal

Table 16.6 Justification Grounds: General and Special

General Justifications	
Article 65(1)(a)	Tax differentiation on grounds of residency
Article 65(1)(b)	Public policy Public security Infringement prevention in the field of taxation Prudential supervision of financial institutions' Declaration Procedures
Overriding Reasons	Fiscal cohesion Town & country planning Minority shareholder protection etc.
Article 75	Antiterrorist measures
Third-country Specific Justifications	
Article 64(1)	'Grandfather clause' for past capital restrictions
Article 65(4)	Restrictive tax measures vis-à-vis third countries
Article 66	Safeguard clause for balance of payments difficulties

Conclusion

In comparison to the free movement of goods and persons, the free movement of services and capital are 'latecomer' freedoms. For a long time, they were seen as 'underdeveloped' when compared to the internal market principles created for the first two freedoms.

This has dramatically changed in the last two decades. Services have become hugely important for the national economies of the Member States and the Union market. The Court has recognised this shift in the real world and has judicially pressed the services provisions to the forefront of negative integration.

> obligations of mutual assistance. Even if, in the fields governed by that directive, the obligation to provide assistance is not unlimited, the fact remains that that directive established a framework for cooperation between the competent authorities of the Member States which does not exist between those authorities and the competent authorities of a third country where the latter has given no undertaking of mutual assistance.' For a criticism of the Court's approach and an argument in favour of mutual recognition also in a third-country context, see Hindelang, *Free Movement of Capital* (n. 191 above), 243: 'In the context of the proportionality test, attention should also be directed towards the operation of the "second Cassis principle" in a third country context. In an intra-[Union] context, the "second Cassis principle", also called the "principle of mutual recognition" or the "principle of functional parallelism", gives rise to the rebuttable presumption within the proportionality test that once a capital movement has complied with the rules and regulations in one Member State, further measures by other Member States are not necessary to protect their interest … Due to the applicability of the freedom of capital movements to third countries, the principle of "functional parallelism" must in general also be valid in these situations with one self-evident modification: that the principle, like the freedom itself, applies only unilaterally.'

Covering import and export restrictions of a regulatory and fiscal nature, the third freedom embraces discriminatory as well as non-discriminatory restrictions. The judicial forces of negative integration have been complemented by Union harmonisation, and in particular the Services Directive. The latter has been extremely controversial in its advocacy of the 'home State' principle and its federal model of integration; yet many of its provisions still need to be given concrete content by the European Courts in the future.

This chapter has also explored two 'special' services regimes, namely the Union rules governing 'posted workers' and the constitutional principles governing 'public' services. These two special aspects of the freedom of services are particularly sensitive for the Member States' social systems. For an extensive interpretation of the posted workers provisions may lead to social dumping, whereas public services usually affect the public purse.

The second part of this chapter explored the freedom of capital. On a normative level, this fourth freedom was originally very different from its three older sisters. For the capital provisions originally lacked direct effect and the Court could thus not judicially push the negative integration of national capital markets. This changed with the 1992 Maastricht Treaty, which radically transformed the textual base of the fourth freedom. The latter became directly effective and today covers discriminatory as well as non-discriminatory restrictions on the free movement of capital. The freedom of capital is thereby the sole freedom that can apply to intra-Union as well as extra-Union restrictions. The extension to third-country capital restrictions adopted by the Member States makes a clear delineation between this fourth freedom and the three other freedoms essential; and, as we saw above, the Court has tried to set external limits to the free movement of capital provisions in light of the other freedoms.

Be that as it may, we also saw above that the freedom of capital makes a clear distinction between 'regulatory' and 'fiscal' measures. With regard to the former, the Court applies a restriction test that does not require discrimination, whereas with regard to the latter, it does insist on direct or indirect discrimination. This 'conservative' approach to fiscal restrictions on the free movement of capital means that *Cassis*-type dual burdens will not be caught by Article 63 TFEU as the Court here protects the parallel exercise of the fiscal 'sovereignty' of Member States.[238] This approach parallels Article 110 TFEU in the context of goods; and it leaves the removal of non-discriminatory obstacles to the Union legislator. The progress of positive integration and the move to a 'capital markets union' has however been incredibly slow.[239] The reason for this slowness lies especially in the unanimity rule applicable to fiscal harmonisation.[240]

---

[238] While not expressly discussed for the other three freedoms, this fiscal exceptionalism applies here too (see R. Schütze, *From International to Federal Market: The Changing Structure of European Law* (Oxford University Press, 2017), ch. 6).

[239] For a recent overview of (non-)progress towards a 'capital markets union', see N. Moloney, 'Capital Markets Union: "Ever Closer Union" for the EU Financial System?' (2016) 41 *EL Rev.* 307.

[240] For a discussion of Art. 113 TFEU, see Chapter 14, section 2(a).

FURTHER READING

Books

M. Andenas and W.-H. Roth, *Services and Free Movement in EU Law* (Oxford University Press, 2003)

C. Barnard, *The Substantive Law of the EU: The Four Freedoms* (Oxford University Press, 2016)

V. Hatzopoulos, *Regulating Services in the European Union* (Oxford University Press, 2012)

S. Hindelang, *The Free Movement of Capital and Foreign Direct Investment: The Scope of Protection in EU Law* (Oxford University Press, 2009)

S. Mohamed, *European Community Law on the Free Movement of Capital and EMU* (Brill, 1999)

J. Snell, *Goods and Services in EC Law: A Study of the Relationship between the Freedoms* (Oxford University Press, 2002)

F. Weiss and C. Kaupa, *European Union Internal Market Law* (Cambridge University Press, 2014)

Articles (and Chapters)

C. Barnard, 'Unravelling the Services Directive' (2008) 45 *CML Rev.* 323

A. Cordewener, 'Free Movement of Capital between EU Member States and Third Countries: How Far Has the Door Been Closed?' (2009) 18 *EC Tax Review* 260

G. Davies, 'Welfare as a Service' (2002) 29 *Legal Issues of Economic Integration* 27

P. Davies, 'Posted Workers: Single Market or Protection of National Labour Law Systems?' (1997) 34 *CML Rev.* 571

S. Enchelmaier, 'Always at Your Service (Within Limits): The ECJ's Case Law on Article 56 TFEU (2006–11)' (2011) 36 *EL Rev.* 615

S. Evju, 'Revisiting the Posted Workers Directive: Conflict of Laws and Laws in Conflict' (2009–10) 12 CYELS 151

V. Hatzopoulos, 'The Court's Approach to Services (2006–2012): From Case Law to Case Load?' (2013) 50 *CML Rev.* 459

S. Kingston, 'The Boundaries of Sovereignty: The ECJ's Controversial Role Applying Internal Market Law to Direct Tax Measures' (2006–7) 9 CYELS 287

N. Moloney, 'Capital Markets Union: "Ever Closer Union" for the EU Financial System?' (2016) 41 *EL Rev.* 307

R. Murphy, 'Changing Treaty and Changing Economic Context: The Dynamic Relationship of the Legislature and the Judiciary in the Pursuit of Capital Liberalization', in P. Syrpis (ed.), *The Judiciary, the Legislature and the EU Internal Market* (Cambridge University Press, 2012), 274

S. O'Leary and J. Fernandez-Martin, 'Judicially Created Exceptions to Free Provisions of Services', in M. Andenas and W.-H. Roth (eds.), *Services and Free Movement in EU Law* (Oxford University Press, 2002), 163

S. Peers, 'Free Movement of Capital: Learning Lessons or Slipping on Spilt Milk', in C. Barnard and J. Scott (eds.), *The Law of the Single European Market: Unpacking the Premises* (Hart, 2002), 333

J. Snell, 'Free Movement of Capital: Evolution as a Non-linear Process', in P. Craig and G. de Búrca (eds.), *The Evolution of EU Law* (Oxford University Press, 2011) 547

E. Spaventa, 'Public Services and European Law: Looking for Boundaries' (2002/3) 5 *CYELS* 271

R. Zahn, 'Revision of the Posted Workers Directive: A Europeanisation Perspective' (2017) 19 *CYELS* [online]

Cases on the Website

Case 36/74, *Walrave and Koch*; Case 120/78, *Cassis de Dijon*; Case 286/82, *Luisi and Carbone*; Case 263/86, *Humbel*; Case C-113/89, *Rush Portuguesa*; Case C-76/90, *Säger*; Case C-159/90, *Grogan*; Joined Cases C-267–8/91, *Keck*; Case C-279/93, *Schumacker*; Case C-384/93, *Alpine Investments*; Case C-55/94, *Gebhard*; Joined Cases C-163, 165 and 250/94, *Sanz de Lera*; Case C-302/97, *Kronle*; Case C-439/97, *Sandoz*; Case C-35/98, *Verkooijen*; Case C-367/98, *Commission v. Portugal (Golden Shares I)*; Case C-157/99, *Peerbooms*; Case C-98/01, *Commission v. United Kingdom (BAA)*; Case C-215/01, *Schnitzer*; Case C-372/04, *Watts*; Case C-452/04, *Fidium Finanz*; Case C-513/04, *Kerckhaert*; Case C-101/05, *Skatteverket*; Case C-112/05, *Commission v. Germany (VW)*; Case C-341/05, *Laval*; Case C-319/06, *Commission v. Luxembourg (Posted Workers)*; Case C-35/11, *Test Claimants II*; Case C-326/12, *Van Caster*; Case C-396/13, *Sähköalojen*

17

Competition Law
Private Undertakings

Contents

Introduction

Competitive markets are markets in which economic rivalry enhances efficiency. Market 'forces' determine the winners and losers of this rivalry, and competition will – ultimately – force inefficient losers out of the market.

Who, however, forces the winner(s) to act efficiently? By the end of the nineteenth century, this question was first raised in the United States. After a period of intense competition 'the winning firms were seeking instruments to assure themselves of an easier life';[1] and they started to use – among other things – the common law 'trust' to coordinate their behaviour within the market. To counter the anticompetitive effects of these trusts, the US legislator adopted the first competition law of the modern world: the Sherman Antitrust Act (1890). It attacked the two cardinal sins within all competition law: anticompetitive agreements, and monopolistic markets.[2] The meaning of what 'competition' is has nonetheless remained controversial; and two basic 'schools' have here traditionally 'competed' with each other. Following the 'Harvard School', competition law is to prevent harm to consumers (exploitative offences) as well as harm to competitors (exclusionary offences), whereas the 'Chicago School' sees the enhancement of 'consumer welfare' as the sole objective of competition law.[3]

---

[1] G. Amato, *Antitrust and the Bounds of Power: The Dilemma of Liberal Democracy in the History of the Market* (Hart, 1997), 8.

[2] The Act was named after Senator John Sherman, who proposed it. Section 1 here states: 'Every contract, combination in the form of trust or otherwise, or conspiracy, in restraint of trade or commerce among the several States, or with foreign nations, is declared to be illegal[.]' And section 2, by contrast, states: 'Every person who shall monopolize, or attempt to monopolize, or combine or conspire with any other person or persons, to monopolize any part of the trade or commerce among the several States, or with foreign nations, shall be deemed guilty of a felony[.]'

[3] For a presentation of the two schools, see G. Monti, *EC Competition Law* (Cambridge University Press, 2007), 57–68.

The US experience has significantly shaped the competition law of the European Union;[4] yet the inclusion of a EU Treaty chapter on competition law was originally rooted not so much in competition concerns as such. It was rather the 'general agreement that the elimination of tariff barriers would not achieve its objectives if private agreements of economically powerful firms were permitted to be used to manipulate the flow of trade'.[5] The primary function of EU competition law was therefore originally seen in the removal of private party actions that would

> tend to restore the national divisions in trade between Member States [and] might be such as to frustrate the most fundamental objectives of the [Union]. The Treaty, whose preamble and content aim at abolishing the barriers between States, and which in several provisions gives evidence of a stern attitude with regard to their reappearance, could not allow undertakings to reconstruct such barriers.[6]

EU competition law was thus — at first — primarily conceived as a complement to the internal market.[7] This also explains the position of the competition provisions within the EU Treaties. They are found in Chapter 1 of Title VII of the TFEU that deals principally with internal market matters. The chapter is divided into two sections — one dealing with classic competition law, that is: '[r]ules applying to undertakings'; the other with public interferences in the market through '[a]ids granted by States'. Table 17.1 provides an overview of the various competition rules within the EU Treaties. Both sections contain one or two (directly effective) prohibitions, as well as a Union competence for the adoption of Union secondary law. The legislative competence(s) have been used to some extent, yet EU competition law is equally governed by a wide range of soft-law instruments adopted by the executive.

---

4 On the direct influence of US law and its indirect influence via German law, see D. Gerber, *Law and Competition in Twentieth-century Europe: Protecting Prometheus* (Oxford University Press, 2001).

5 *Ibid.*, 343.

6 Case 56 and 58/64, *Consten and Grundig* v. *Commission* [1964] ECR 299 at 340.

7 This link between the internal market and EU competition law continues to be textually anchored in the Treaties. According to Art. 3(3) TEU (emphasis added), '[t]he Union shall establish an internal market. It shall work for the sustainable development of Europe based on balanced economic growth and price stability, [and] a highly *competitive* social market economy, aiming at full employment and social progress'. The meaning of the provision is clarified in Protocol No. 27 On the Internal Market and Competition, according to which 'the internal market as set out in Art. 3 of the Treaty on European Union *includes a system ensuring that competition is not distorted*' (emphasis added). And within the Treaty on the Functioning of the European Union, Art. 3(1)(b) grants the Union an exclusive competence for 'the establishing of the competition rules necessary for the functioning of the *internal market*' (emphasis added).

Table 17.1 Competition Rules – Overview

FEU Treaty – Title VII – Chapter 1	
Section 1: Rules Applying to Undertakings	**Section 2: Aids Granted by States**
Article 101: Anticompetitive Agreements	Article 107: State Aid Prohibition
Article 102: Abuse of a Dominant Position	Article 108: Commission Powers
Article 103: Competition Legislation I	Article 109: Competition Legislation II
Article 104: 'Transitional' Provisions	
Article 105: Commission Powers	
Article 106: Public Undertakings (and Public Services)	
Competition Secondary & Soft Law (Selection) Block Exemption Regulations (esp. Regulation 330/2100 on Vertical Agreements) Regulation 139/2004 on the control of concentrations between undertakings (EUMR) Guidelines on Horizontal Agreements Guidelines on Vertical Agreements Guidelines on the Application of Article 101(3) TFEU etc.	

This chapter concentrates on private undertakings. The relevant Treaty section here is built upon three pillars. The first pillar deals with anticompetitive cartels and can be found in Article 101. The second pillar concerns situations where a dominant undertaking abuses its market power and is dealt with in Article 102. The third pillar is unfortunately invisible, for when the Treaties were concluded, they did not mention the control of mergers. This constitutional gap has never been closed by subsequent Treaty amendments; yet it has received a legislative filling in the form of the EU Merger Regulation (EUMR).

Let us discuss, step by step, these three pillars of 'private' competition law.

1. Cartels I: Jurisdictional Aspects

The first pillar of European competition law is Article 101. It outlaws anticompetitive collusions between undertakings, that is: 'cartels'. Historically, this form of illegal behaviour has been the most dangerous anticompetitive practice.

The prohibition on any collusion between undertakings to restrict competition in the internal market is set out in Article 101. It states:

> 1. The following shall be prohibited as incompatible with the internal market: all agreements between undertakings, decisions by associations of undertakings and concerted practices which may affect trade between Member States and which have as their object or effect the prevention, restriction or distortion of competition within the internal market …

2. Any agreements or decisions prohibited pursuant to this Article shall be auto-matically void.
3. The provisions of paragraph 1 may, however, be declared inapplicable in the case of:
    –   any agreement or category of agreements between undertakings,
    –   any decision or category of decisions by associations of undertakings,
    –   any concerted practice or category of concerted practices, which contrib-utes to improving the production or distribution of goods or to promoting technical or economic progress, while allowing consumers a fair share of the resulting benefit, and which does not:
        (a) impose on the undertakings concerned restrictions which are not indis-pensable to the attainment of these objectives;
        (b) afford such undertakings the possibility of eliminating competition in respect of a substantial part of the products in question.

Article 101 follows a tripartite structure. Paragraph 1 prohibits as incompatible with the internal market collusions between undertakings that are anticompeti-tive by object or effect if they affect trade between Member States. Paragraph 3 exonerates certain collusions that are justified by their overall pro-competitive effects for the Union economy. In between this dual structure of prohibition and justification – oddly – lies paragraph 2, which determines that illegal collusive practices are automatically void and thus cannot be enforced in court.[8]

This section analyses paragraph 1 of Article 101. We start by considering the kinds of undertakings and the types of collusive behaviour caught by Article 101(1), and we also look at the requirement of an 'effect on trade between Member States'. All three criteria are 'jurisdictional' criteria,[9] as they do not define an illegal behaviour as such, but merely trigger the applicability of Article 101. The two 'substantive' criteria within Article 101 are found in the requirement of an *anti*competitive collusion in Article 101(1), and its potential *pro*-competitive justifications in Article 101(3). These two substantive criteria, as well as two par-ticular forms of agreements, will be discussed in section 2.

a. The Concept of 'Undertaking'

The English word 'undertaking' has traditionally not meant what the European Treaties want it to mean.[10] The word is a translation from the German and

---

[8] This is not the sole consequence of a violation of Art. 101 TFEU. The Union has typically used its powers to impose significant fines on undertakings violating the provision. On the enforcement of European competition law generally, see W. Wils, *Principles of European Antitrust Enforcement* (Hart, 2005).

[9] In this sense, see O. Odudu, *The Boundaries of EC Competition Law* (Oxford University Press, 2006), 58.

[10] In its sinister and saddest form, the word refers to the preparations for a funeral service. For the notion of undertaking in that context, see Case 30/87, *Bodson* v. *SA Pompes funèbres des régions libérées* [1988] ECR 2479.

French equivalents, and was deliberately chosen to avoid pre-existing meanings in British company law.[11] According to the famous definition in *Höfner and Elser*, the concept of undertaking means this:

> [T]he concept of an undertaking encompasses every entity engaged in an economic activity, regardless of the legal status of the entity and the way in which it is financed[.][12]

This definition ties the notion of undertaking to an *activity*; and this *functional* definition broadens the personal scope of the competition rules to include entities that may – formally – not be regarded as companies. It catches natural persons,[13] and includes 'professionals' – like barristers.[14] Even the 'State', and its public bodies, may sometimes be regarded as an undertaking, where they engage in an economic activity.[15] The advantage of this broad functional definition is its flexibility; its disadvantage is its uncertainty. Indeed, depending on the context, an entity may or may not be an 'undertaking' within the meaning of EU competition law in particular situations.[16]

What, then, are economic activities? The Court has consistently held that 'any activity consisting in offering goods or services on a given market is an economic activity'.[17] This comprehensive definition will nevertheless find a limit when public functions are exercised. In *Poucet & Pistre*,[18] the Court thus refused to consider organisations managing a public social security system as 'undertakings' because their activities were 'based on the principle of national solidarity' and 'entirely non-profit-making'.[19] A private body will thus not count as an undertaking, where it is engaged in 'a task in the public interest which forms

---

[11] R. Lane, *EC Competition Law* (Longman, 2001), 33.

[12] Case C-41/90, *Höfner and Elser* v. *Macrotron* [1991] ECR I-1979, para. 21.

[13] See Case 170/83, *Hydrotherm* v. *Compact* [1984] ECR 2999, para. 11.

[14] See Case C-309/99, *Wouters et al.* v. *Algemene Raad van de Nederlandse Orde van Advocaten* [2002] ECR I-1577, para. 49.

[15] See Case 118/85, *Commission* v. *Italy* [1987] ECR 2599, esp. para. 7: '[T]he State may act either by exercising public powers or by carrying on economic activities of an industrial or commercial nature by offering goods and services on the market. In order to make such a distinction, it is therefore necessary, in each case, to consider the activities exercised by the State and to determine the category to which those activities belong.'

[16] Advocate General F. Jacobs, Case C-475/99, *Firma Ambulanz Glöckner* v. *Landkreis Südwestpfalz* [2001] ECR I-8089, para. 72: '[T]he notion of undertaking is a relative concept in the sense that a given entity might be regarded as an undertaking for one part of its activities while the rest falls outside the competition rules.'

[17] Case C-180/98, *Pavlov and others* v. *Stichting Pensioenfonds Medische Specialisten* [2000] ECR I-6451, para. 75.

[18] Joined Cases C-159–60/91, *Poucet & Pistre* [1993] ECR I-637.

[19] *Ibid.*, paras. 18–19. This was confirmed in Joined Cases C-264/01, C-306/01 and C-354–5/01, *AOK Bundesverband and others* [2004] ECR I-2493. But see also Case C-67/96, *Albany International BV* v. *Stichting Bedrijfspensioenfonds Textielindustrie* [1999] ECR I-5751. The latter case has been particularly controversial.

part of the essential functions of the State'.[20] What counts as an essential public function is however not always easy to tell. The Court has refused to be bound by a 'historical' or 'traditional' understanding of public services. In *Höfner & Elser* it consequently found that '[t]he fact that employment procurement activities are normally entrusted to public agencies cannot affect the economic nature of such activities', since '[e]mployment procurement has not always been, and is not necessarily, carried out by public entities'.[21]

In conclusion, then, the Court has so far not found a convincing definition of what counts as an economic activity;[22] and this is particularly true for the question when a public authority is engaged in an economic activity.[23]

b. The 'Single Economic Unit' Doctrine

Article 101 covers collusions *between* undertakings. It requires the combined effort of a number of undertakings. The prohibited action under Article 101 must therefore be *bilateral* or *multilateral* – and not unilateral, that is: 'within' a single undertaking. The Court has persistently held that Article 101 does not apply to the 'internal' relationships within an undertaking. The relationship between a company and its workers is consequently outside the scope of Article 101. For even if workers are engaged in an economic activity, their 'services' are considered as 'incorporated into the undertaking' with whom they 'form an economic unit'.[24]

This 'single economic unit' doctrine is not confined to relationships within one legal entity.[25] It can equally cover relationships between – legally – independent undertakings if they form part of a corporate group. A 'group' or 'concern' is a collection of 'parent' and 'subsidiary' companies that operate as a single economic unit (see Figure 17.1). This single-economic-unit doctrine was clarified in *Centrafarm and de Peijper*,[26] where the Court expressly held:

---

[20] Case C-343/95, *Calì & Figli Srl* v. *Servizi ecologici porto di Genova* [1997] ECR I-1547, esp. paras. 22–3: 'The anti-pollution surveillance for which SEPG was responsible in the oil port of Genoa is a task in the public interest which forms part of the essential functions of the State as regards protection of the environment in maritime areas. Such surveillance is connected by its nature, its aim and the rules to which it is subject with the exercise of powers relating to the protection of the environment which are typically those of a public authority. It is not of an economic nature justifying the application of the Treaty rules on competition.'

[21] Case C-41/90, *Höfner and Elser* v. *Macrotron*.

[22] For an academic analysis of the case law, see O. Odudu, 'The Meaning of Undertaking within 81 EC' (2006) 7 *CYELS* 211.

[23] See Case C-205/03 P, *FENIN* [2005] ECR I-6295. For an extensive discussion of the latter – very controversial – case, see M. Krajewski and M. Farley, 'Non-economic Activities in Upstream and Downstream Markets and the Scope of Competition Law after *FENIN*' (2007) 32 *EL Rev.* 111.

[24] Case C-22/98, *Becu and others* [1999] ECR I-5665, para. 26.

[25] For an overview of the doctrine, see O. Odudu and D. Bailey, 'The Single Economic Entity Doctrine in EU Competition Law' (2014) 51 *CML Rev.* 1721.

[26] Case 15/74, *Centrafarm BV and Adriaan de Peijper* v. *Sterling Drug* [1974] ECR 1147.

> [Article 101] is not concerned with agreements or concerted practices between undertakings belonging to the same concern and having the status of parent company and subsidiary, *if the undertakings form an economic unit within which the subsidiary has no real freedom to determine its course of action on the market,* and if the agreements or practices are concerned merely with the internal allocation of tasks as between the undertakings.[27]

The case clarified that Article 101 could not apply to relationships within groups of undertakings, and thereby underlined that the key for the provisions' non-application was the *economic* dependence of two – legally independent – undertakings. Economic dependence here exists when 'the *subsidiaries do not enjoy real autonomy in determining their course of action in the market, but carry out the instructions issued to them by the parent company controlling them*'.[28]

The key element within the single economic unit doctrine is consequently the question of 'control'. Where a 'parent' company does control its subsidiary 'child', economic dependence exists, and their behaviour falls outside the scope of Article 101. 'Control' is a matter of fact to be decided in each individual case; and the Court will here particularly look to 'the economic, organisational and legal links' between two companies.[29] The Union Courts have however accepted a legal presumption that a parent company holding 100 per cent of the capital of a subsidiary exercises decisive influence over the latter;[30] but even

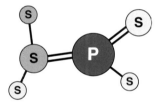

Figure 17.1 Economic Group with Parent (P) and Subsidiaries (S)

---

[27] *Ibid.*, para. 41 (emphasis added). See Case 22/71, *Béguelin Import Co.* v. *S.A.G.L. Import Export* [1971] ECR 949.

[28] Case C-73/95 P, *Viho* v. *Commission* [1996] ECR I-5457, para. 16.

[29] Case C-97/08 P, *Akzo Nobel NV and others* v. *Commission* [2009] ECR I-8237, para. 58.

[30] *Ibid.*, paras. 60–1: 'In the specific case where a parent company has a 100% shareholding in a subsidiary which has infringed the [EU] competition rules, first, the parent company can exercise a decisive influence over the conduct of the subsidiary and, second, there is a rebuttable presumption that the parent company does in fact exercise a decisive influence over the conduct of its subsidiary. In those circumstances, it is sufficient for the Commission to prove that the subsidiary is wholly owned by the parent company in order to presume that the parent exercises a decisive influence over the commercial policy of the subsidiary. The Commission will be able to regard the parent company as jointly and severally liable for the payment of the fine imposed on its subsidiary, unless the parent company, which has the burden of rebutting that presumption, adduces sufficient evidence to show that its subsidiary acts independently on the market.' See also more recently, Case C-501/11 P, *Schindler and others* v. *Commission*, EU:C:2013:522.

where an undertaking holds much less than 100 per cent of the shareholdings of another undertaking, the latter might still be under the control of the former.

c. Forms of Collusion: Agreements and Beyond

What types of collusions are covered by Article 101? The provision refers to three types of collusions: 'agreements between undertakings, decisions by associations of undertakings and concerted practices'.

Agreements are the most straightforward category. The Union concept of 'agreement' has been given an extremely wide scope.[31] The Union legal order is here not interested whether the agreement formally constitutes a 'contract' under national law. What counts is 'a concurrence of wills' between economic operators.[32]

But Article 101 also catches 'concerted practices'. This second category of collusion is the most mysterious one. It is designed to capture practices falling short of an agreement.

Finally, Article 101 also covers 'decisions of associations of undertakings'. This third category of collusion catches institutionalised cartels.[33] It clarified that undertakings cannot escape the scope of Article 101 by substituting *multilateral* collusion between them by establishing an association that would adopt *unilateral* decisions on their behalf.

Let us explore the notions of 'agreement' and 'concerted practice' in more detail.

aa. Agreements I: Horizontal and Vertical Agreements

One of the central concerns within the early Union legal order was the question whether Article 101 covered only 'horizontal' or also 'vertical' agreements (see Figure 17.2). Horizontal agreements are agreements between undertakings that are competing against each other, that is: companies placed at the same commercial level. Vertical agreements, by contrast, are agreements between undertakings at different levels of the commercial chain, that is agreements between companies not competing against each other.

Since Article 101 prohibits anticompetitive agreements, would it not follow that only 'horizontal' agreements between *competitors* are covered? This logic is not without its problems. For while vertical agreements between a producer (P) and a distributor (D) may increase economic efficiency through a division

---

[31] For an analysis of the concept of 'agreement', see J. Shaw, 'The Concept of Agreement in Article 85 EEC' (1991) 16 *EL Rev.* 262.

[32] See Case T-41/96, *Bayer AG* v. *Commission* [2000] ECR II-3383, para. 69; Case C-2 and 3/01 P, *Bundesverband der Arzneimittel-Importeure and Commission* v. *Bayer* [2004] ECR I-23, para. 97.

[33] This may include professional bodies, such as the Bar Council. See Case C-309/99, *Wouters et al.* v. *Algemene Raad van de Nederlandse Orde van Advocaten.* For a more recent judgment here, see Case T-111/08, *MasterCard and others* v. *Commission* [2009] ECR I-5655.

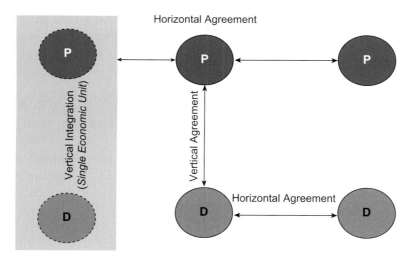

Figure 17.2 Horizontal and Vertical Agreements

of labour, they can also significantly harm the consumer through a restriction of price competition.

Would such vertical agreements fall within the jurisdictional scope of Article 101? The European Court has – famously and positively – answered this question in *Consten and Grundig* v. *Commission*.[34] The German producer Grundig had concluded a distribution agreement for the French market with Consten. The Commission claimed that the agreement breached European competition law. The applicants counterclaimed that the Union lacked jurisdiction under Article 101 as 'distributorship contracts do not constitute "agreements between undertakings" within the meaning of that provision, since the parties are not on a footing of equality'.[35] The Court disagreed:

> Article [101] refers in a general way to all agreements which distort competition within the common market and does not lay down any distinction between those agreements based on whether they are made between competitors operating at the same level in the economic process or between non-competing persons operating at different levels. In principle, no distinction can be made where the Treaty does not make any distinction.
>
> Furthermore, the possible application of Article [101] to a sole distributorship contract cannot be excluded merely because the grantor and the concessionaire are not competitors *inter se* and not on a footing of equality. Competition may be distorted within the meaning of Article [101(1)] not only by agreements which limit it as between the parties, but also by agreements which prevent or restrict competition which might take place between one of them and third parties. For this purpose, it is irrelevant whether the parties to the agreement are or are not on a footing of equality

[34] Case 56 and 58/64, *Consten and Grundig* v. *Commission* [1964] ECR 299.
[35] *Ibid.*, 339.

as regards their position and function in the economy. This applies all the more, since, by such an agreement, the parties might seek, by preventing or limiting the competition of third parties in respect of the products, to create or guarantee for their benefit an unjustified advantage at the expense of the consumer or user, contrary to the general aims of Article [101].[36]

The arguments in favour of including vertical agreements here were textual and teleological. Within its text, Article 101 indeed did not make a distinction between horizontal and vertical agreements, and it thus seemed to generically cover both types. Teleologically, moreover, Article 101 was said to not only protect against restrictions of competition imposed on the distributor, but it would equally protect third parties – namely, consumers and competitors; and since vertical agreements could create unjustified disadvantages for these third parties, they would have to be within the jurisdiction of European competition law.[37]

bb. Agreements II: 'Tacit Acquiescence' versus 'Unilateral Conduct'

Every agreement – whether horizontal or vertical – must be concluded through the consent between the parties. It must be formed by a concurrence of *two* wills. The idea of an 'agreement' will thus find a limit where one party *unilaterally* imposes its will on the other. Yet there may sometimes be a fine line between tacit *acceptance* and unilateral *imposition*; and the European Courts have struggled to demarcate this line for the Union legal order.[38]

The reason for this fuzziness lies in what the Courts call 'apparently unilateral' behaviour in continuous contractual relations between two parties. A good illustration of such 'apparently unilateral behaviour' can be found in *Ford v. Commission*.[39] The US car manufacturer had established a selective distribution system in Europe, especially in Britain and Germany, through a 'main dealer agreement'. That agreement originally allowed German distributors to order right-hand as well as left-hand drive cars. However, as the prices for Ford cars on the British market suddenly increased significantly, British customers began buying cars from German dealers; and afraid that its British distributor would suffer the consequences, Ford notified its German dealers that it would no longer accept their orders for right-hand drive cars. These would now be exclusively reserved for the British market.

---

[36] *Ibid.*

[37] This second argument was an important one: vertical agreements would need to be within the scope of Art. 101 TFEU because they could have an anticompetitive effect both with regard to intra-brand competition – that is: price competition between distributors – but also inter-brand competition between different producers. On the distinction between inter-brand and intra-brand competition, see section 2(a/aa) below.

[38] See Case 107/82, *AEG* v. *Commission* [1983] ECR 3151; Joined Cases 25–6/84, *Ford-Werke AG and Ford of Europe Inc.* v. *Commission* [1985] ECR 2725; Case C-70/93, *BMW* v. *ALD Auto-Leasing* [1995] ECR I-3439.

[39] Joined Cases 25–6/84, *Ford-Werke AG and Ford of Europe Inc.* v. *Commission*.

Was the decision to discontinue supplies to the German dealers an agreement? Ford claimed that the discontinuance decision was of a unilateral nature; and since 'a unilateral act cannot be included among agreements', it would fall outside the scope of Article 101.[40] The Court held otherwise:

> Such a decision on the part of the manufacturer does not constitute, on the part of the undertaking, a unilateral act which, as the applicants claim, would be exempt from the prohibition contained in Article [101(1)] of the Treaty. On the contrary, *it forms part of the contractual relations between the undertaking and its dealers.*[41]

This extremely generous interpretation of 'consent' has nevertheless encountered some limits. In *Bayer* v. *Commission*,[42] a German pharmaceutical company used its distribution system to market Adalat – a medical product designed to treat cardiovascular disease. The price of the product differed significantly as it was indirectly fixed by the respective national health authorities. The prices fixed by the Spanish and French health services were thereby on average 40 per cent lower than prices in the United Kingdom; and following commercial logic, Spanish and French wholesalers began exporting to the British market. With its British dealer registering an enormous loss of turnover, Bayer decided to stop delivering large orders to Spanish and French wholesalers. Instead, it provided them with the quantities that it thought would saturate their national markets.

Was this indirect export restriction based on a consensual agreement? The General Court rejected this view. While accepting that 'apparently unilateral conduct' can qualify as an agreement, the latter required – as a conceptual minimum – the '*existence of an acquiescence by the other partners, express or implied, in the attitude adopted by the manufacturer*'.[43] And, in the present case, tacit acquiescence was missing.[44] For the mere continuation of the business relationship could not as such be tacit acquiescence. The judgment was confirmed on appeal,[45] where the European Court concisely clarified the situation as follows:

> The mere concomitant existence of an agreement which is in itself neutral and a measure restricting competition that has been imposed unilaterally does not amount to an agreement prohibited by that provision.[46]

---

[40] *Ibid.*, para. 15.   [41] *Ibid.*, para. 21 (emphasis added).
[42] Case T-41/96, *Bayer AG* v. *Commission*.
[43] *Ibid.*, para. 72 (emphasis added).
[44] *Ibid.*, paras. 151ff.: 'Examination of the attitude and actual conduct of the wholesalers shows that the Commission has no foundation for claiming that they aligned themselves on the applicant's policy designed to reduce parallel imports ... [T]he wholesalers continued to try to obtain packets of Adalat for export and persisted in that line of activity, even if, for that purpose, they considered it more productive to use different systems to obtain supplies, namely the system of distributing orders intended for export among the various agencies on the one hand, and that of placing orders indirectly through small wholesalers on the other.'
[45] Cases C-2 and 3/01 P, *Bundesverband der Arzneimittel-Importeure and Commission* v. *Bayer*.
[46] *Ibid.*, para. 141.

Put the other way around: for an 'apparently unilateral' measure to become part of a continuous contractual relationship, the other party must – at the very least – tacitly acquiesce. And this tacit acquiescence must be shown through actual compliance with the 'apparently unilateral' measure.

cc. Concerted Practices and Parallel Conduct

The conclusion of an agreement is the primary form of collusion between undertakings. A second – less concrete – form mentioned in Article 101(1) is 'concerted practices'.[47] The concept was designed as a safety net to catch all forms of collusive behaviour falling short of an agreement. The European Court indeed identifies the aim behind the concept as follows:

> [T]he object is to bring within the prohibition of that Article a form of coordination between undertakings which, without having reached the stage where an agreement properly so-called has been concluded, knowingly substitutes practical cooperation between them for the risk of competition.[48]

The heart of a concerted practice is thus the practical 'coordination' between undertakings. Unlike agreements, this coordination is however not consensually 'agreed':

> By its very nature, then, a concerted practice does not have all the elements of a contract but may inter alia arise out of coordination which becomes apparent from the behaviour of the participants.[49]

The concept of a concerted practice is thus wider and vaguer than that of an agreement; yet the two concepts are not mutually exclusive.[50]

Tacit collusion or coordination will often be the result of an oligopolistic market structure. That is, due to the existence of very few undertakings in the market, the strategic behaviour of each market player is here 'known' to the others; and since a price increase by a single undertaking would shift its market share to its competitors, undertakings may 'tacitly' decide to raise prices in parallel.

While the Court has held that such 'parallel behaviour may not itself be identified with a concerted practice, *it may however amount to strong evidence of such*

---

47 For academic analysis of this concept, see V. Korah, 'Concerted Practices' (1973) 36 MLR 220; A. Jones, '*Woodpulp*: Concerted Practice and/or Conscious Parallelism' (1993) 6 ECLR 273; G. Van Gerven and E. N. Varona, 'The *Wood Pulp* Case and the Future of Concerted Practices' (1994) 31 *CML Rev.* 575.

48 Case 48/69, *Imperial Chemical Industries v. Commission* [1972] ECR 619, para. 64; Case C-49/92 P, *Commission v. Anic Partecipazioni* [1999] ECR I-4125, para. 115.

49 Case 48/69, *Imperial Chemical Industries v. Commission*, para. 65.

50 See Case C-49/92 P, *Commission v. Anic Partecipazioni* [1999] ECR I-4125, para. 132: '[W]hilst the concepts of an agreement and of a concerted practice have particularly different elements, they are not mutually incompatible.'

a practice if it leads to conditions of competition which do not correspond to the normal conditions of the market'.[51] The Court has therefore found that, while every producer is free to change his prices, it is nevertheless contrary to Article 101 'for a producer to cooperate with his competitors, in any way whatsoever, in order to determine a coordinated course of action relating to a price increase and to ensure its success by prior elimination of all uncertainty as to each other's conduct regarding the essential elements of that action, such as the amount, subject-matter, date and place of the increases'.[52]

The Court however keeps insisting that not all 'parallel behaviour' between undertakings will be identified with a concerted practice. Parallel behaviour that directly follows from market forces would be beyond reproach. Article 101 would 'not deprive economic operators of the right to adapt themselves intelligently to the existing and anticipated conduct of their competitors'.[53] Behaviour in line with a competitor's interests will therefore not, as such, constitute a sufficient claim to a concerted practice. Absent any 'direct or indirect contact',[54] undertakings are allowed to align their commercial behaviour to the 'logic' of the market.[55] The problem may however lie in the very – corrupted – logic of oligopolistic markets; and for that reason the dividing line between (illegal) concerted practices and (legal) parallel conduct continues to be difficult to draw.

d. (Potential) Effect on Trade between Member States

Not all agreements will fall within the jurisdictional scope of Article 101.[56] Article 101 only catches agreements that may 'affect trade between Member States'.

What is the point behind this jurisdictional limitation around Article 101? The answer lies – partly – in the principle of conferral. The *European* Union should only concern itself with agreements that have a *European* dimension. This European dimension here shows itself through a (potential) effect on trade *between* Member States. In the words of the European Court:

---

[51] Case 48/69, *Imperial Chemical Industries*, para. 66 (emphasis added).

[52] *Ibid.*, para. 118.

[53] Joined Cases 40–8/73, 50/73, 54–6/73, 111/73, 113–14/73, *Coöperatieve Vereniging 'Suiker Unie' UA and others v. Commission* [1975] ECR 1663, para. 174; Case C-49/92 P, *Commission v. Anic Partecipazioni*, para. 117.

[54] Joined Cases 40–8/73, 50/73, 54–6/73, 111/73, 113–14/73, *'Suiker Unie' v. Commission*, paras. 27 and 174; Case C-49/92 P, *Commission v. Anic Partecipazioni*, para. 117.

[55] The evidentiary burden on the Commission is very high; see Joined Cases C-89/85, C-104/85, C-114/85, C-116–17/85 and C-125–9/85, *Ahlström Osakeyhtiö and others v. Commission* [1993] ECR I-1307, para. 71: '[P]arallel conduct cannot be regarded as furnishing proof of concertation unless concertation is the only plausible explanation for such conduct.'

[56] The following sections refer to 'agreements', but the analysis applies, *mutatis mutandis*, to decisions of associations of undertakings, and concerted practices.

> The concept of an agreement 'which may affect trade between Member States' is intended to define, in the law governing cartels, the boundary between the areas respectively covered by [European] law and national law. It is only to the extent to which the agreement may affect trade between Member States that the deterioration in competition caused by the agreement falls under the prohibition of [European] law contained in Article [101]; otherwise it escapes that prohibition.[57]

Agreements must thus have an *inter-State* dimension – otherwise they will be outside the sphere of European competition law. But what is this 'European' sphere of competition law? The jurisdictional scope of Article 101 has been – very – expansively interpreted. What was important here was whether:

> [T]he agreement is capable of constituting a *threat, either direct or indirect, actual or potential, to freedom of trade between Member States* in a manner which might harm the attainment of the objectives of a single market between States.[58]

This formula originated in *Société Technique Minière*, where the Court held that Article 101 requires proof 'that the agreement in question may have an influence, direct or indirect, actual or potential, on the *pattern of trade between Member States*'.[59] This 'pattern-of-trade' test is extremely broad as it captures both quantitative as well as qualitative changes to trade.[60]

The fact that an agreement relates to a single Member State will thereby not necessarily mean that Article 101 is not applicable.[61] Nonetheless, not all effects on inter-State trade will trigger Article 101. For the effects 'must not be insignificant';[62] and the Commission will indeed only police agreements that *appreciably* affect intra-Union trade.[63] According to its 'non-appreciably-affecting-trade'

---

[57] Case 56 and 58/64, *Consten and Grundig* v. *Commission*, 341.

[58] Ibid., 341 (emphasis added).

[59] Case 56/65, *Société Technique Minière* v. *Maschinenbau Ulm* [1965] ECR 235 at 249 (emphasis added).

[60] For a general analysis of this criterion, see J. Faull, 'Effect on Trade between Member States' (1999) 26 *Fordham Corporate Law Institute* 481; Commission, 'Guidelines on the Effect on Trade Concept Contained in Articles [101 and 102] of the Treaty' [2004] OJ C 101/81.

[61] See C-125/07 P, *Erste Group Bank* v. *Commission* [2009] ECR I-8681, para. 3; Case 246/86, *Belasco and others* v. *Commission* [1989] ECR 2117, para. 38: 'Accordingly, although the contested agreement relates only to the marketing of products in a single Member State, it must be held to be capable of influencing intra-[Union] trade.'

[62] Case C-306/96, *Javico International and Javico AG* v. *Yves Saint Laurent Parfums SA (YSLP)* [1998] ECR I-1983, para. 16 (with reference to Case 5/69, *Völk* v. *Vervaecke* [1969] ECR 295).

[63] The Commission makes a clear distinction between an appreciable effect on inter-State *trade* on the one hand, and appreciable restrictions on *competition* on the other. The former will be discussed here, while the latter will be discussed in section 2(a/dd) below.

(NAAT) rule,[64] agreements will generally not fall within the jurisdictional scope of Article 101 if two cumulative conditions are met. First, '[t]he aggregate market share of the parties on any relevant market within the [Union] affected by the agreement does not exceed 5%'; and, second, 'the aggregate annual [Union] turnover of the undertakings concerned in the products covered by the agreement does not exceed 40 million euro'.[65] However, the Commission has recalled that '[t]he assessment of appreciability depends on the circumstances of each individual case, in particular the nature of the agreement and practice, the nature of the products covered and the market position of the undertakings concerned'.[66] And it equally agrees that each agreement will need to 'be considered in the economic and legal context in which they occur', and that it will thus 'be necessary to have regard to any *cumulative* effects of parallel networks of similar agreements'.[67]

2. Cartels II: Substantive Aspects

a. Restrictions of Competition: Anticompetitive Object or Effect

In order for an agreement to violate Article 101(1), it must be anticompetitive; that is: it must be a 'prevention, restriction or distortion of competition'.[68]

The meaning of 'restriction of competition' in this context has been very controversial. If it simply referred to a restriction of the *individual* freedom to trade, then all binding agreements would be anticompetitive, for '[t]o bind, to restrain, is of their very essence'.[69] This individualist definition of restriction has however never been dominant in the Union legal order.[70] A second

---

[64] Commission, 'Guidelines on the Effect on Trade Concept' (n. 60 above), para. 50.

[65] *Ibid.*, para. 52.   [66] *Ibid.*, para. 45.

[67] *Ibid.*, para. 49 (emphasis added). When examining the effect on trade between Member States, the Court will take into account whether or not the agreement forms part of a broader network of agreements. This 'contextual' view of agreements was further developed in *Delimitis* (Case C-234/89, *Delimitis* v. *Henninger Bräu* [1991] ECR I-935). The case arose out of a dispute between the plaintiff publican and the brewery Henninger and turned on the legality of a beer supply agreement. Could a single agreement concluded by a local pub with a local brewery have an effect in intra-Union trade? On the surface, this seemed unlikely; yet the Court placed the agreement within the network of agreements to which it belonged and held that 'the *cumulative effect of several similar agreements* constitutes one factor amongst others in ascertaining whether, by way of a possible alteration of competition, trade between Member States is capable of being affected' (*ibid.*, para. 14 (emphasis added)). It was consequently necessary to analyse the effects of all beer supply agreements within the network to see if the single agreement contributed to a cumulative effect that had an inter-State dimension.

[68] This formulation covers hypothetical, quantitative and qualitative limitations of competition. In this section, 'restriction' of competition will be employed as a generic term.

[69] See *Chicago Board of Trade v. United States*, 246 US 231 (1918) 238.

[70] The early case law may however be read as unduly concentrating on the freedom of individuals; see E. Rousseva, *Rethinking Exclusionary Abuses in EU Competition Law* (Hart, 2010), 83ff.

view has therefore argued that Article 101 protects the *structural* freedom offered by the market to – actual or potential – competitors. This view emphasises the exclusionary effects of restrictions of competition and corresponds to the 'Harvard School'.[71] A third view has finally imported the 'Chicago School' into the debate on the scope of Article 101(1). It argues that the prohibition should exclusively outlaw 'exploitative effects' in the form of allocative inefficiencies to consumer welfare.[72] The case law of the European Courts has been closest to the second view – even if the European Commission has at one time tried hard to move towards the third view.[73]

This subsection analyses four aspects of what constitutes a restriction of competition in the Union legal order. We start by looking at the various dimensions of competition, before examining the two modes of violating Article 101(1) – that is: restrictions by 'object or effect'. This includes an analysis of whether the 'ancillary restraints' doctrine represents a 'rule of reason' in disguise. Finally, we shall briefly look at the *de minimis* limitation on restrictions of competition.

aa. Two Dimensions: Inter-brand and Intra-brand Competition

A restriction of competition is primarily a restriction between competitors. Early on however, the European Court confirmed that competition could be restricted by horizontal as well as vertical agreements.[74] But was this solely an admission that vertical agreements could restrict inter-brand competition, that is: competition between producers of different brands? Or did the inclusion of vertical agreements into the scope of Article 101(1) signal that *intra*-brand competition – that is: competition between distributors of the same brand – was independently protected?

The European Court has preferred the second reading. The Union legal order consequently recognises two independent dimensions of competition: inter-brand and intra-brand competition. In *Consten and Grundig*,[75] the Court thus rejected the plaintiffs' argument that there could be no restriction of competition through vertical agreements:

---

[71] The 'European' equivalent of the 'Harvard School' is the 'Freiberg School', which has become famous for its 'ordo-liberalism'. For a concise overview of the philosophical positions of that school, see D. Gerber, 'Constitutionalizing the Economy: German Neoliberalism, Competition Law and the "New Europe"'' (1994) 42 *American Journal of Comparative Law* 25.

[72] Odudu, *Boundaries of EC Competition Law* (n. 9 above), 102.

[73] See Commission, 'Guidelines on the Application of Article [101(3)] of the Treaty' [2004] OJ C 101/97. However, see also Joined Cases C-501/06 P, C-513/06 P, C-515/06 P and C-519/06 P, *GlaxoSmithKline and others* v. *Commission* [2009] ECR I-9291, where the Court rejected the 'Chicagoisation' of European competition law.

[74] For a discussion of this point, see section 1(c/aa) above.

[75] Case 56 and 58/64, *Consten and Grundig* v. *Commission*.

> The principle of freedom of competition concerns the various stages and manifes-
> tations of competition. Although competition between producers is generally more
> noticeable than that between distributors of products of the same make, it does not
> thereby follow that an agreement tending to restrict the latter kind of competition
> should escape the prohibition of Article [101(1)] merely because it might increase
> the former.[76]

Would every restriction of competition through vertical agreements violate
Article 101(1)? In a later decision, the Court recognised that a pro-competitive
effect in inter-brand competition might come at the price of a restriction of
intra-brand competition. This holistic approach can be seen in *Société Technique
Minière*,[77] where the Court found an exclusive distribution agreement *not* to
violate Article 101 on the following ground:

> The competition in question must be understood within the actual context in
> which it would occur in the absence of the agreement in dispute. In particular it
> may be doubted whether there is an interference with competition if the said agree-
> ment seems really necessary for the penetration of a new area by an undertaking.
> Therefore, in order to decide whether an agreement containing a clause 'granting an
> exclusive right of sale' is to be considered as prohibited by reason of its object or of
> its effect, it is appropriate to take into account in particular the nature and quantity,
> limited or otherwise, of the products covered by the agreement, [and] *the position
> and importance of the grantor and the concessionaire on the market for the products
> concerned* ...[78]

Whether there exists a restriction of competition will thus have to be evaluated alongside both 'brand' dimensions. The Commission appears to share this
holistic approach.[79]

bb. *Restrictions by Object: European 'per se Rules'*

An agreement may fall within Article 101(1) if it is anticompetitive by 'object
or effect'. These are alternative conditions.[80] The fulfilment of one will fulfil
Article 101(1).

The possibility of violating EU competition law 'by object' will not mean that
purely imaginary restrictions 'intended' in the future are covered. The reference

---

[76] *Ibid.*, 342. And in a later part of the judgment (*ibid.*, 343), the Court provided the rationale
for this choice: 'Because of the considerable impact of distribution costs on the aggregate
cost price, it seems important that competition between dealers should also be stimulated.
The efforts of the dealer are stimulated by competition between distributors of products of
the same make.'

[77] Case 56/65, *Société Technique Minière* v. *Maschinenbau Ulm*.

[78] *Ibid.*, 250 (emphasis added).

[79] Commission, 'Guidelines on Article [101(3)]' (n. 73 above), paras. 17ff.

[80] Case 56/65, *Société Technique Minière* v. *Maschinenbau Ulm*, 249.

to the purpose of an agreement must not be misunderstood as referring to the subjective intentions of the parties. On the contrary, it refers to the *objective content* of the agreement. It is designed to identify certain 'hard-core restrictions' within an agreement. These 'hard core restrictions' need not be subjected to a detailed effects analysis, as they can simply be presumed to be 'sufficiently deleterious' to competition.[81] In this sense, restrictions by object operate as '*per se* rules', that is: rules whose existence 'as such' constitutes a breach of EU competition law. The advantage of such '*per se*' rules or hard-core restrictions is 'judicial economy'. Instead of a substantive analysis of the anticompetitive effects of an agreement, the Court saves time by concentrating on the 'form' of certain contractual clauses.

What are the hard-core restrictions that the Union legal order considers restrictions by object? Various contractual clauses have been given this status – in both horizontal and vertical agreements. With regard to horizontal agreements, they have been said to include price-fixing clauses,[82] output-limiting clauses,[83] and market-sharing clauses.[84] With regard to vertical agreements, restrictions by object will be presumed to exist when the agreement contains a clause that imposed a fixed (minimum) resale price,[85] or grants absolute territorial protection to a distributor.[86]

The last restriction by object has been the most contentious one. And the classic case here is – once more – *Consten and Grundig*.[87] Grundig had appointed Consten its exclusive distributor in France. Consten had thereby promised to market and service the German products in France – a potentially costly commitment. In exchange, Grundig agreed not to deliver its goods to

---

[81] *Ibid.*, 249; Case 56 and 58/64, *Consten and Grundig* v. *Commission*, 342: 'Besides, for the purpose of applying Article [101(1)], there is no need to take account of the concrete effects of an agreement once it appears that it has as its object the prevention, restriction or distortion of competition.' See also Case C-8/08, *T-Mobile Netherlands and others* v. *Raad van bestuur van de Nederlandse Mededingingsautoriteit* [2009] ECR I-4529, para. 29: 'by their very nature, as being injurious to the proper functioning of normal competition'. For an analysis of the case law here, see D. Bailey, 'Restrictions of Competition by Object under Article 101 TFEU' (2012) 49 *CML Rev.* 559. In light of some recent case law, it has been argued that the Court has taken a wrong turn, see C. I. Nagy, 'The New Concept of Anti-Competitive Object: A Loose Cannon in EU Competition Law' (2015) 36 ECLR 154.

[82] See Art. 101(1)(a): 'directly or indirectly fix purchase or selling prices or any other trading conditions'; and see in particular Case 48/69, *Imperial Chemical Industries* v. *Commission*.

[83] See Art. 101(1)(b): 'limit or control production, markets, technical development, or investment', and see in particular Case 41/69, *Chemiefarma* v. *Commission*.

[84] See Art. 101(1)(c): 'share markets or sources of supply'; and see in particular Joined Cases 40–8/73, 50/73, 54–6/73, 111/73, 113–14/73, '*Suiker Unie*' v. *Commission*.

[85] See Case 243/83, *Binon & Cie* v. *Agence et messageries de la presse* [1985] ECR 2015; Art. 4(a) of (Commission) Regulation 330/2010 on the application of Art. 101(3) of the Treaty on the Functioning of the European Union to categories of vertical agreements and concerted practices [2010] OJ L 102/1.

[86] See Case 56 and 58/64, *Consten and Grundig*; Art. 4(b) of (Commission) Regulation 330/2010.

[87] Case 56 and 58/64, *Consten and Grundig* v. *Commission*.

other traders on the French market, and it also agreed to contractually prohibit its German wholesalers from exporting goods into France. This level of territorial protection was *relative*, since it solely applied to Grundig's own distribution system. Yet in order to prevent 'parallel traders'– that is: third parties trading in parallel to the official distribution channels – from selling their products in France, Grundig granted an intellectual property right to Consten. This intellectual property right established *absolute* territorial protection for Consten. For not a single trader within France could legally sell Grundig products without the official distributor's consent. In the eyes of the European Court, such an agreement establishing absolute territorial protection betrayed a clear wish of the parties 'to eliminate any possibility of competition at the wholesale level',[88] and thus constituted an agreement that had as its *object* the restriction of competition.[89]

cc. Restrictions by Effect: A European 'Rule of Reason'?

Where agreements do not contain clauses that are '*per se*' restrictions of competition, Article 101(1) requires proof of the agreement's anticompetitive *effect*.[90]

The central question here is: will the prohibition be triggered as soon as an agreement contains clauses that have *some* anticompetitive effects; or, will it only apply to agreements that are *overall* anticompetitive? Put differently: should Article 101(1) catch agreements that limit – in absolute terms – production, yet which nevertheless enhance – in relative terms – competition, say, through the development of a new product? The wording of Article 101(1) suggests an absolute test. The view has however been voiced that an absolute test is overinclusive and should be replaced by a relative test that weighs the anticompetitive effects of an agreement against its pro-competitive effects.

This debate on whether Article 101(1) follows an absolute or a relative test has been associated with the US doctrine of a 'rule of reason'. According to the latter, the absolute prohibition of anticompetitive agreements will not apply to reasonable restrictions of trade. Should such an implied limitation also apply to Article 101(1) – even though the article already recognises an express justification in Article 101(3)? The existence of such a rule of reason doctrine has been

---

[88] *Ibid.*, 343.

[89] For a confirmation of this 'tough' view on restrictions of parallel trade as a restriction by object, see Joined Cases C-501/06 P, C-513/06 P, C-515/06 P and C-519/06 P, *GlaxoSmithKline and others* v. *Commission* – which overruled the General Court's attempt to soften that principle of European competition law in Case T-168/01, *GlaxoSmithKline Services* v. *Commission* [2006] ECR II-2969. For an analysis of the case, see C. Petrucci, 'Parallel Trade of Pharmaceutical Products: The ECJ Finally Speaks – Comment on *GlaxoSmithKline*' (2010) 35 *EL Rev.* 275.

[90] In order to assess the effect of an individual agreement *on* the market, the Court will analyse the agreement's position *within* the market. It thereby applies a contextual approach that places an individual agreement within its economic context. Where an agreement forms part of a network of agreements, the Courts may thus look at the 'cumulative' effects within the market. On this 'economic' contextualism, see in particular Case C-234/89, *Delimitis* v. *Henninger Bräu*.

hotly debated in European law circles.[91] And the debate is not just theoretical: the constitutional choice concerning whether there exists a rule of reason in Article 101(1) may have significant practical consequences.[92]

What have the European Courts said? They have given ambivalent signals. For while the Courts – in theory – deny the existence of a rule of reason under Article 101(1),[93] there are some jurisprudential lines that come very close to a practical application of the doctrine. For example: did the European Court not insist that a restriction of competition was not anticompetitive if '*necessary* for the penetration of a new area by an undertaking'?[94] Was this balancing of anticompetitive effects against pro-competitive effects not a rule of reason in disguise? The European Courts have denied this, and have instead developed alternative doctrines to explain their reasoning.

The most famous doctrine in this respect is the doctrine of ancillary restraints. Three cases may explain this doctrine in more detail. In *Remia and Nutricia*,[95] the Court had to deal with the legality of a 'non-compete clause'. These clauses prevent the seller of a business from competing with the buyer within a period of time after the sale. This is undoubtedly a restriction of competition on the part of the seller; yet very few undertakings would be willing to purchase a business without a guarantee that its previous owner will temporarily stay out of the market. Finding that transfer agreements generally 'contribute to the promotion of competition because they lead to an increase in the number of undertakings in the market', the Court recognised that without the non-compete clause, 'the agreement for the transfer of the undertaking could not be given effect'.[96] All ancillary restrictions within an overall pro-competitive agreement would fall outside the scope of Article 101(1).

This ancillary restraints doctrine was confirmed in *Pronuptia* in the context of a franchise agreement,[97] and it received its most elaborate form in *Métropole Télévision*.[98] The General Court here held:

[91] See Odudu, *Boundaries of EC Competition Law* (n. 9 above); R. Nazzini, 'Article 81 EC between Time Present and Time Past: A Normative Critique of "Restrictions of Competition" in EU Law' (2006) 43 *CML Rev.* 497.

[92] It will be seen below that Art. 101(3) is not a 'neutral' exemption for pro-competitive agreements, since it makes the exemption dependent on the fulfilment of four conditions.

[93] See Case T-112/99, *Métropole Télévision (M6) and others* v. *Commission* [2001] ECR II-2459; T-328/03, *O2 (Germany)* v. *Commission* [2006] ECR II-1231. For an extended discussion of the second case, see M. Marquis, '*O2 (Germany)* v. *Commission* and the Exotic Mysteries of Article 81(1) EC' (2007) 32 *EL Rev.* 29.

[94] See Case 56/65, *Société Technique Minière* v. *Maschinenbau Ulm*, 250 (emphasis added).

[95] Case 42/84, *Remia and others* v. *Commission* [1985] ECR 2545.

[96] *Ibid.*, para. 19.

[97] Case 161/84, *Pronuptia de Paris* v. *Pronuptia de Paris Irmgard Schillgallis* [1986] ECR 353, paras. 16ff. (esp. 17–18): '[T]he franchisor must be able to take the measures necessary for maintaining the identity and reputation of the network bearing his business name or symbol. It follows that provisions which establish the means of control necessary for that purpose do not constitute restrictions on competition for the purposes of Article [101(1)]. The same is true of the franchisee's obligation to apply the business methods developed by the franchisor and to use the know-how provided.'

[98] Case T-112/99, *Métropole Télévision (M6)* v. *Commission*.

> In [EU] competition law the concept of an 'ancillary restriction' covers any restriction which is directly related and necessary to the implementation of a main operation … The condition that a restriction be necessary implies a two-fold examination. It is necessary to establish, first, whether the restriction is objectively necessary for the implementation of the main operation and, second, whether it is proportionate to it. As regards the objective necessity of a restriction, it must be observed that inasmuch as … the existence of a rule of reason in [European] competition law cannot be upheld, it would be wrong, when classifying ancillary restrictions, to interpret the requirement for objective necessity as implying a need to weigh the pro- and anti-competitive effects of an agreement. Such an analysis can take place only in the specific framework of Article [101(3)] of the [FEU] Treaty.[99]

The (European) doctrine of ancillary restraints thus differs from the (US) rule of reason in that it will not involve a concrete balancing of the pro-competitive and anticompetitive effects of the agreement. The operation of the doctrine is, according to the Court, 'relatively abstract'.[100] It only tolerates contractual clauses restricting competition without which 'the main agreement is *difficult or even impossible to implement*'.[101] Thus: only *objectively necessary restrictions* of competition within an overall pro-competitive agreement will be accepted. These objectively necessary restrictions must moreover be 'ancillary', that is: 'subordinate' to the main object of the agreement.

dd. Non-appreciable Restrictions: The de minimis Rule

According to the common law principle *de minimis non curat lex*, the law should not concern itself with trifles. Translated into the present context, the European Court has declared that it will not use Article 101 to establish 'perfect competition'.[102] Minor market imperfections will thus be tolerated. Restrictions of competition will only fall within Article 101(1), where they do so 'to an appreciable extent'.[103] This is called the *de minimis* rule.

According to the Court, *de minimis* is measured not in quantitative or qualitative trade terms, but depends on the relevant market share. This view is supported by the Commission, which has offered guidance in its 'De Minimis Notice'.[104] The Notice is designed to 'indicate[], with the help of market share thresholds, the

---

[99]   *Ibid.*, para. 104 (references omitted).

[100] *Ibid.*, para. 109.

[101] *Ibid.* (emphasis added). For a confirmation of these principles, see Case C-382/12P, *MasterCard and others* v. *Commission*, EU:C:2014:2201.

[102] Case 26/76, *Metro SB-Großmärkte GmbH & Co. KG* v. *Commission* [1977] ECR 1875, para. 20; and confirmed in Case 75/84, *Metro SB-Großmärkte GmbH & Co. KG* v. *Commission* [1986] ECR 3021, para. 65.

[103] Case 56/65, *Société Technique Minière* v. *Maschinenbau Ulm*, 249.

[104] The exact title of the Notice is: 'Commission Notice on Agreements of Minor Importance which Do Not Appreciably Restrict Competition under Article 101(1) of the Treaty Establishing the European Union (De Minimis)' [2014] OJ C 291/1.

circumstances in which it considers that agreements which may have as their effect the prevention, restriction or distortion of competition within the internal market do not constitute an appreciable restriction of competition under Article 101 of the Treaty'.[105] With the exception of hard-core restrictions,[106] the Commission here considers that a 10 per cent aggregate market share for the parties to horizontal agreements and a 15 per cent aggregate market share for parties to vertical agreements will not appreciably restrict competition within the meaning of Article 101(1).[107] Importantly, the Commission and the Courts thereby investigate an individual agreement's economic context. And where it finds that the agreement forms part of a network of agreements, these cumulative effects will be taken into account and the market share threshold is reduced to 5 per cent both for agreements between competitors and for agreements between non-competitors.[108]

b. Article 101(3): Exemptions through Pro-competitive Effects

Where an agreement has been found to be anticompetitive under Article 101(1), it will be void under Article 101(2) – unless it is justified under Article 101(3).

Article 101(3) is designed to exempt anticompetitive agreements that have – overall – pro-competitive effects. Within the Union legal order, it is meant to be the sole place where pro- and anticompetitive effects are balanced. In its Guidelines on the application of Article 101(3),[109] the Commission has summarised the function of the provision as follows:

> Agreements that restrict competition may at the same time have pro-competitive effects by way of efficiency gains. Efficiencies may create additional value by lowering the cost of producing an output, improving the quality of the product or creating a new product. When the pro-competitive effects of an agreement outweigh its anti-competitive effects the agreement is on balance pro-competitive and compatible with the objectives of the [EU] competition rules. The net effect of such agreements is to promote the very essence of the competitive process, namely to win customers by offering better products or better prices than those offered by rivals. This analytical framework is reflected in Article [101(1)] and Article [101(3)]. *The latter provision expressly acknowledges that restrictive agreements may generate objective economic benefits so as to outweigh the negative effects of the restriction of competition.*[110]

---

[105] *Ibid.*, para. 3.

[106] *Ibid.*, para. 13. In Case C-226/11, *Expedia* v. *Autorité de la concurrence and Others*, EU:C:2012:795, the Court clarified that 'an agreement that may affect trade between Member States and that has an anti-competitive object constitutes, by its nature and independently of any concrete effect that it may have, an appreciable restriction on competition' (*ibid.*, para. 37).

[107] 'Commission Notice on agreements of minor importance' (n. 104 above), para. 8.

[108] *Ibid.*, para. 10. On this contextual examination of a single agreement, see n. 67 above.

[109] Commission, 'Guidelines on Article [101(3)]' (n. 73 above).

[110] *Ibid.*, para. 33 (emphasis added). For an early analysis of the guidelines, see L. Kjolbye, 'The New Guidelines on the Application of Article 81(3): An Economic Approach to Article 81' (2004) 25 ECLR 566.

According to the Commission, Article 101(3) consequently constitutes the exclusive medium for weighing the anticompetitive against the pro-competitive effects of an agreement. This view has been confirmed in *Metropole*:

> It is only in the precise framework of that provision that the pro and anti-competitive aspects of a restriction may be weighed. Article [101(3)] of the Treaty would lose much of its effectiveness if such an examination had to be carried out already under Article [101(1)] of the Treaty.[111]

Importantly, Article 101(3) potentially applies to *all* agreements that violate Article 101(1) – and covers even restrictions per object.[112] It has direct effect and can therefore be invoked as a protective shield by any undertaking (see section (aa)).[113] However, in an effort to enhance legal certainty, the Union has adopted a variety of regulations that provide detailed criteria as to when certain categories of agreements are exempted under Article 101(3) (see section (bb)).

aa. Direct Exemptions under Article 101(3)

Article 101(3) makes an exemption conditional on four cumulative criteria. The first two criteria are positive, the other two negative in nature.[114]

Positively, Article 101(3) stipulates that the agreement must 'contribute … to improving the production or distribution of goods or to promoting technical or economic progress, while allowing consumers a fair share of the resulting benefit'.[115] Where the agreement thus generates *productive* or

---

[111] Case T-112/99, *Métropole Télévision (M6)* v. *Commission*.

[112] See Case T-17/93, *Matra Hachette SA* v. *Commission* [1994] ECR II-595, para. 85: '[T]he Court considers that, in principle, no anti-competitive practice can exist which, whatever the extent of its effects on a given market, cannot be exempted, provided that all the conditions laid down in Article [101(3)] of the Treaty are satisfied and the practice in question has been properly notified to the Commission.'

[113] The direct effect of Art. 101(3) did not always exist. Indeed, it was one of the 'revolutionary' changes brought by Regulation 1/2003 on the implementation of the rules on competition laid down in Arts. [101 and 102] of the Treaty [2003] OJ L 1/1. On this point, see (online) Chapter 17B, section 4(a).

[114] There has been a spirited debate on whether these criteria – all of which are 'economic' in nature – are exhaustive or not. The Commission considers them exhaustive (see Commission, 'Guidelines on Article [101(3)]' (n. 73 above), para. 42): 'The four conditions of Article [101(3)] are also exhaustive. When they are met the exception is applicable and may not be made dependent on any other condition. Goals pursued by other Treaty provisions can be taken into account to the extent that they can be subsumed under the four conditions of Article [101(3)].' Nonetheless, it is important to note that the Treaties' competition rules cannot be completely isolated from other policies; and this is particularly true for those policies – like environmental policy – that contain an express horizontal clause (see Art. 11 TFEU (emphasis added): 'Environmental protection requirements must be integrated *into the definition and implementation of the Union's policies and activities*, in particular with a view to promoting sustainable development').

[115] Art. 101(3) TFEU.

dynamic efficiencies,[116] these efficiency gains might outweigh the economic inefficiencies identified in Article 101(1). The Courts have historically given a broad interpretation to this efficiency defence.[117]

Second, these pro-competitive gains may however only outweigh any anti-competitive effects where consumers get a fair share in the resulting overall benefit. What is a 'fair share'? According to the Commission, '[t]he concept of "*fair share*" implies that the pass-on of benefits must at least compensate consumers for any actual or likely negative impact caused to them by the restriction of competition found under Article [101(1)]'. 'If such consumers are worse off following the agreement, the second condition of Article [101(3)] is not fulfilled.'[118]

Third, in any event, Article 101(3) will not allow anticompetitive restrictions that are 'not indispensable' for the pro-competitive effects of the agreement; nor will it, fourth, allow agreements which 'eliminat[e] competition in respect of a substantial part of the products in question'.[119] A violation of either one of these two negative conditions will mean that an agreement cannot benefit from an exemption.

With regard to the indispensability of a restriction, the Commission has developed a twofold test. 'First, the restrictive agreement as such must be reasonably necessary in order to achieve the efficiencies. Secondly, the individual restrictions of competition that flow from the agreement must also be reasonably necessary for the attainment of the efficiencies.'[120] The first test thereby requires 'that the efficiencies be specific to the agreement in question in the sense that there are no other economically practicable and less restrictive means of achieving the efficiencies'.[121] Once this global test has been passed, the Commission will then analyse the indispensability of each individual restriction of competition. Here, it will assess 'whether individual restrictions are reasonably necessary in order to produce the efficiencies'.[122]

Finally, a specific restriction – even if indispensable for the pro-competitive effects of the agreement – must not substantially eliminate competition. This absolute limit on the exemptability of an agreement will be a function of the structure of the market.[123]

---

[116] For an elaboration of this, see Commission, 'Guidelines on Article [101](3)' (n. 73 above), paras. 48ff. The typical example for an agreement enhancing 'productive efficiency' is a 'specialisation agreement'. A 'research and development' agreement is an example for an agreement that may enhance dynamic efficiency. For a brief analysis of such a horizontal cooperation agreement, see section 2(c) below.

[117] J. Goyder and A. Albors-Llorens, *Goyder's EC Competition Law* (Oxford University Press, 2009), 150.

[118] Commission, 'Guidelines on Article [101](3)' (n. 73 above), para. 85.

[119] Art. 101(3) TFEU.

[120] Commission, 'Guidelines on Article [101](3)' (n. 73 above), para. 73.

[121] *Ibid.*, para. 75.   [122] *Ibid.*, para. 78.

[123] *Ibid.*, para. 107: 'Whether competition is being eliminated within the meaning of the last condition of Article [101(3)] depends on the degree of competition existing prior to the agreement and on the impact of the restrictive agreement on competition, i.e. the reduction in competition that the agreement brings about. The more competition is already weakened in the market concerned, the slighter the further reduction required for competition to be eliminated within the meaning of Article [101(3)].'

bb. *Exemptions by Category: Block Exemption Regulations*

In order to enhance legal certainty, Article 101(3) envisages that an entire 'category of agreements' can be exempted. Article 103 thereby allows the Council to 'lay down detailed rules for the application of Article 101(3)'.[124] This legal base was used early on, and in a way that delegated the power to exempt agreements 'en bloc' to the Commission.[125] The Commission has indeed adopted a variety of so-called 'block exemption regulations'.[126] A selection of these can be found in Table 17.2.

Many block exemption regulations here originally followed a vertical 'category' approach. They would contain a 'white list' of desirable clauses, and a 'blacklist' of hard-core restrictions for each type of agreement. This formal approach towards block exemptions has been overtaken by a more flexible and economic approach. Absent any hard-core restrictions, modern block exemptions will thus generally make the exemption dependent on a market-share threshold. Importantly, even in the presence of a block exemption, the Commission always retains the power to withdraw the benefit of a block exemption from an individual agreement.[127]

Table 17.2 Block Exemption Regulations (Selection)

(Commission) Block Exemptions	
Regulation 330/2010	Categories of Vertical (Distribution) Agreements
Regulation 461/2010	Categories of Vertical Agreements in the Motor Vehicle Sector
Regulation 1217/2010	Categories of Research and Development Agreements
Regulation 1218/2010	Categories of Specialisation Agreements
Regulation 316/2014	Categories of Technology Transfer Agreements

[124] Art. 103(2)(b) TFEU.

[125] Council Regulation 19/65 on application of [ex-]Art. 85(3) of the [EEC] Treaty to certain categories of agreements and concerted practices [1965] OJ L 36/533; and Council Regulation 2821/71 on application of [ex-]Art. 85(3) of the [EEC] Treaty to categories of agreements, decisions and concerted practices [1971] OJ L 285/46. However, the Council may of course also directly adopt block exemptions. See for example: Council Regulation 487/2009 on the application of [ex-]Art. 81(3) of the [EC] Treaty to certain categories of agreements and concerted practices in the air transport sector, [2009] OJ L 148/1.

[126] See Commission Regulation 330/2010 on the application of Art. 101(3) of the Treaty on the Functioning of the European Union to categories of vertical agreements and concerted practices [2010] OJ L 102/1; Commission Regulation 461/2010 on the application of Art. 101(3) of the Treaty on the Functioning of the European Union to categories of vertical agreements and concerted practices in the motor vehicle sector [2010] OJ L 129/52; Commission Regulation 1217/2010 on the application of Art. 101(3) of the Treaty on the Functioning of the European Union to categories of research and development agreements [2010] OJ L 335/36; Commission Regulation 1218/2010 on the application of Art. 101(3) of the Treaty to categories of specialisation agreements [2010] OJ L 335/43; Commission Regulation 316/2014 on the application of Art. 101(3) of the Treaty to categories of technology transfer agreements [2014] OJ L 93/17. For the numerous 'sectoral' block exemption regulations, see http://ec.europa.eu/competition/antitrust/legislation/legislation.html.

[127] See Art. 29 of Regulation 1/2003 (Withdrawal in individual cases) [2003] OJ L 1/1.

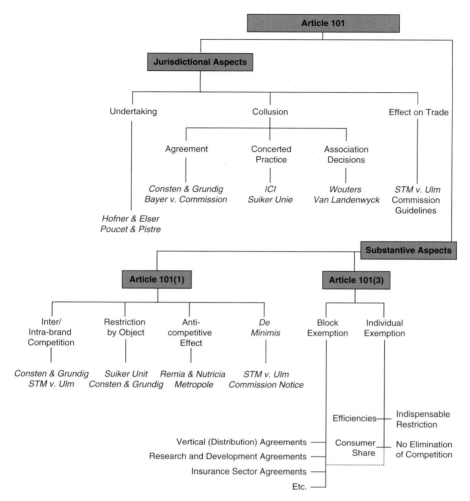

Figure 17.3 Elements of Article 101 Summary (Flowchart)

c. In Particular: (Horizontal) Cooperation Agreements

Agreements between competitors that fix prices or limit production are the most dangerous collusions under Article 101.[128] There are nonetheless situations, where horizontal 'cooperation'– a much nicer word than 'collusion'– is seen as potentially pro-competitive.[129] These 'joint ventures' are subject to

128 For an analysis of these 'cartel agreements', see Goyder and Albors-Llorens, *Goyder's EC Competition Law* (n. 117 above), ch. 9; R. Wish, *Competition Law* (Oxford University Press, 2009), ch. 13. The Commission has also offered its Guidelines on these agreements, see Commission, 'Guidelines on the Applicability of Article 101 of the Treaty on the Functioning of the European Union to Horizontal Co-operation Agreements' ('Horizontal Guidelines') [2011] OJ C 11/1.

129 Horizontal Guidelines, para. 2: 'Horizontal co-operation agreements can lead to substantial economic benefits, in particular if they combine complementary activities, skills or assets. Horizontal co-operation can be a means to share risk, save costs, increase investments, pool know-how, enhance product quality and variety, and launch innovation faster.'

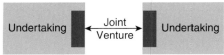

'Article 101' Joint Venture

'Full-function' Joint Venture

Figure 17.4 Forms of Joint Ventures

Article 101,[130] unless the joint venture constitutes a new economic entity. In the latter case, the Merger Regulation (and not Article 101) may apply where a joint venture performs 'on a lasting basis all the functions of an autonomous economic entity'– a so-called 'full-function joint venture' (see Figure 17.4).[131]

The best-known category of cooperation agreements is 'research and development' (R&D) agreements, that is: agreements through which various undertakings join forces to share, say, the investment costs for the development of a new product. Such agreements may or may not restrict competition; yet, where they restrict competition, they can still be justified under Article 101(3) when they 'contribute … to improving the production or distribution of goods or to promoting technical or economic progress'. With regard to R&D agreements, the Commission has adopted a specific block exemption where the market share between competing undertakings does not exceed 25 per cent of the relevant product and technology market.[132]

d. In Particular: (Vertical) Distribution Agreements

The success story of modern economies is a story of specialisation and the division of labour.[133] Specialisation might take place within one undertaking or between various undertakings. An undertaking that has specialised in the *production* of a particular product may indeed prefer not to *distribute* its products

---

[130] See Joined Cases T-374–5/94, T-384/94 and T-388/94, *European Night Services and others* v. *Commission* [1998] ECR II-3141; Joined Cases T-185/00, T-216/00, T-299/00 and T-300/00, *Métropole télévision and others* v. *Commission* [2002] ECR II-3805; Case T-328/03, *O2 (Germany)* v. *Commission* [2006] ECR II-1231.

[131] On this point, see section 4(b/aa) below. For an analysis of the complex overlap between Art. 101 and the Merger Regulation with regard to joint ventures, see N. Tyson, 'Joint Venture Regulation under European Competition Laws: An Update' (2007) 13 ELJ 408.

[132] Regulation 1217/2010, Arts. 2 and 4(2). The Regulation however also includes a list of 'hard-core restrictions' in Art. 5 and 'excluded restrictions' in Art. 6.

[133] For the sociological account of this success story, see E. Durkheim, *The Division of Labour in Society* (Free Press, 1984).

itself. It might rather hire an independent undertaking that is specialised in the – wholesale or retail – distribution business.[134]

Such agreements concluded between producers and distributors are called 'distribution agreements'. They are 'vertical' agreements concluded between non-competitors and, as such, less dangerous to competition than horizontal agreements. This final section will briefly look at the two principal types of distribution agreements and analyse the block exemption for vertical agreements.

aa. *Exclusive and Selective Distribution Agreements*

Exclusive distribution agreements are agreements that guarantee a distributor the exclusive right to distribute a producer's goods within a certain territory. Depending on whether or not that territorial exclusivity is granted only vis-à-vis other distributors, Union law distinguishes between relative and absolute territorial protection. Absolute territorial protection is traditionally regarded as a *per se* hard-core restriction on trade.[135] For the exclusion of parallel trade – that is: trade that is conducted outside the official distribution channels – entails the danger that barriers to trade are reconstructed along national lines and thus interfere with the internal market. By contrast, exclusive distribution agreements with relative territorial protection will not automatically infringe Article 101(1);[136] yet they may still be found to restrict competition – for example, where they contain a direct or indirect export ban imposed on the distributor.[137]

Selective distribution agreements do not grant a distributor territorial exclusivity but limit the distribution channels to 'selected' official distributors. Third parties who are not part of the selective distribution system can thus be prevented from selling goods. The commercial reason for establishing a selective distribution system may lie in the need for complex after-sale services or may stem from the wish to maintain a particular luxury image.

The Court has, in general, been very understanding when it comes to addressing selective distribution agreements. In *Metro* v. *Saba*,[138] it has held that the producer of high-quality and technically complex goods can indeed prevent a low-cost 'cash and carry' wholesaler from distributing its products. The Court nevertheless clarified that certain selective distribution systems would violate Article 101(1):

---

[134] For a path-breaking analysis of these issues from an economic perspective, see R. Coase, 'The Nature of the Firm' (1937) 4 *Economica* 386; and O. E. Williamson, 'The Vertical Integration of Production: Market Failure Considerations' (1971) 61 *American Economic Review* 112.

[135] See Case 56 and 58/64, *Consten and Grundig* v. *Commission*.

[136] Case 56/65, *Société Technique Minière* v. *Maschinenbau Ulm*.

[137] For this point, see also the discussion on the Vertical Block Exemption Regulation in the next section.

[138] Case 26/76, *Metro SB-Großmärkte* v. *Commission* [1977] ECR 1875.

> [R]esellers [must be] chosen on the basis of *objective criteria of a qualitative nature* relating to the technical qualifications of the reseller and his staff and the suitability of his trading premises and that such *conditions are laid down uniformly for all potential resellers and are not applied in a discriminatory fashion.*[139]

Selective distribution agreements consequently do not violate the EU competition rules where the dealers are selected on objective and qualitative criteria. The principle has become known as the 'Metro doctrine'.[140]

bb. 'Vertical' Block Exemption Regulation

The (latest) Block Exemption Regulation for vertical agreements was adopted in 2010.[141] It exempts all vertical agreements, provided that neither the producer nor the distributor enjoys a market share above 30 per cent.[142] The Regulation is based on the liberal principle that all is allowed that is not prohibited. Prohibited contractual clauses are enumerated in two 'blacklists' that distinguish between 'hard-core restrictions' and 'excluded restrictions'. Hard-core restrictions are restrictions that prevent the *entire* agreement from being exempted. They are found in Article 4 of the Regulation and cover, *inter alia*, any 'restriction of the territory into which, or of the customers to whom, the [distributor] may sell the contract goods or services'. However, not all exclusive or selective distribution agreements that fall within the scope of Article 101(1) are blacklisted. The Regulation indeed exempts a number of them, namely:

> i.   the restriction of active sales into the exclusive territory or to an exclusive customer group reserved to the supplier or allocated by the supplier to another buyer, where such a restriction does not limit sales by the customers of the buyer,
> ii.   the restriction of sales to end users by a buyer operating at the wholesale level of trade,

---

[139]   *Ibid.*, para. 20 (emphasis added).

[140]   The Court has confirmed and developed the doctrine in subsequent jurisprudence: see Case 75/84, *Metro v. Commission (II)* [1986] ECR 3021; and much more recently, Case C-230/16, *Coty v. Parfümerie Akzente*, EU:C:2017:941, para. 24: '[T]he organisation of a selective distribution network is not prohibited by Article 101(1) TFEU, to the extent that resellers are chosen on the basis of objective criteria of a qualitative nature, laid down uniformly for all potential resellers and not applied in a discriminatory fashion, that the characteristics of the product in question necessitate such a network in order to preserve its quality and ensure its proper use and, finally, that the criteria laid down do not go beyond what is necessary.'

[141]   See (Commission) Regulation 330/2010 (n. 85 above). For a discussion of this Regulation, see R. Wish and D. Bailey, 'Regulation 330/2010: The Commission's New Block Exemption for Vertical Agreements' (2010) 47 *CML Rev.* 1757; M. Mesch, 'Exclusive Dealing Agreements within the Scope of the Block Exemption Regulation' (2017) 38 ECLR 366.

[142]   Commission Regulation 330/2010 (n. 85 above), Arts. 2 and 3 (1).

iii.   the restriction of sales by the members of a selective distribution system to unauthorised distributors within the territory reserved by the supplier to operate that system,[143] and

iv.   the restriction of the buyer's ability to sell components, supplied for the purposes of incorporation, to customers who would use them to manufacture the same type of goods as those produced by the supplier …[144]

'Excluded restrictions' are restrictions that do not prevent the exemption of the entire agreement but that deny a specific clause from being individually exempted. These specific clauses are listed in Article 5 and concern, in particular, non-compete obligations that are imposed on the distributor.

3. Dominant Undertaking(s): Market Abuse

The second pillar of EU competition law focuses on the – bad – behaviour of a single undertaking. For Article 102 does not require the collusive behaviour of two or more economic actors. It sanctions the *unilateral* behaviour of a dominant undertaking where this behaviour amounts to a 'market abuse'. The provision states:

Any abuse by one or more undertakings of a dominant position within the internal market or in a substantial part of it shall be prohibited as incompatible with the internal market in so far as it may affect trade between Member States.

Such abuse may, in particular, consist in:

(a) directly or indirectly imposing unfair purchase or selling prices or other unfair trading conditions;

(b) limiting production, markets or technical development to the prejudice of consumers;

(c) applying dissimilar conditions to equivalent transactions with other trading parties, thereby placing them at a competitive disadvantage;

(d) making the conclusion of contracts subject to acceptance by the other parties of supplementary obligations which, by their nature or according to commercial usage, have no connection with the subject of such contracts.

Article 102 here encapsulates a number of fundamental choices with regard to the Union's *economic* constitution. First: by concentrating on a '*dominant* position within the internal market' it goes beyond pure monopolies and is thus wider

---

[143]   The provision must be read together with Art. 4(c), which blacklists the following contractual clause: 'the restriction of active or passive sales to end users by members of a selective distribution system operating at the retail level of trade, without prejudice to the possibility of prohibiting a member of the system from operating out of an unauthorised place of establishment'.

[144]   *Ibid.*, Art. 4(b).

than its US counterpart.[145] But by insisting on market *abuse*, it is also narrower than the US prohibition. For unlike the latter, Article 102 will not directly outlaw the creation of market dominance:

> [A] finding that an undertaking has such a dominant position is not in itself a ground of criticism of the undertaking concerned. It is in no way the purpose of Article [102] to prevent an undertaking from acquiring, on its own merits, the dominant position on a market. Nor does that provision seek to ensure that competitors less efficient than the undertaking with the dominant position should remain on the market. Thus, not every exclusionary effect is necessarily detrimental to competition. Competition on the merits may, by definition, lead to the departure from the market or the marginalisation of competitors that are less efficient and so less attractive to consumers from the point of view of, among other things, price, choice, quality or innovation.[146]

Dominance is thus not itself prohibited – only the *abuse* of a dominant position. And, like Article 101, the prohibition of market abuse will only apply where the abusive behaviour 'may affect trade between Member States'.[147] Yet when this abuse is shown to have Union-wide effects it appears to be prohibited as such, for Article 102 has – unlike Article 101 – no 'third paragraph' exempting abusive behaviour on the grounds of its pro-competitive effects.

In sum, a violation of Article 102 therefore requires the fulfilment of three criteria. First, we must establish what the 'market' is in which the undertaking operates. Second, the undertaking must be 'dominant' within that market. And, third, the undertaking must have 'abused' its dominance.[148] All three aspects will be discussed below in sections (a)–(c). A final section (d) will analyse whether the Union legal order has – despite the absence of express exemptions – nonetheless allowed for 'objective justifications' of abusive conduct.

---

[145] Section 2 of the US Sherman Act states: 'Every person who shall monopolize, or attempt to monopolize, or combine or conspire with any other person or persons, to monopolize any part of the trade or commerce among the several States, or with foreign nations, shall be deemed guilty of a felony[.]'

[146] Case C-209/10, *Post Danmark* v. *Konkurrencerådet*, EU:C:2012:172, paras. 21–2.

[147] On this criterion in the context of Art. 101, see section 1(d) above.

[148] Art. 102 TFEU does not mention a 'restriction of competition' as part of this provision. However, the Court has found that this element is an implied requirement; see Case T-203/01, *Michelin* v. *Commission (Michelin II)* [2003] ECR II-4071, para. 237: 'Unlike Article [101(1) TFEU], Article [102 TFEU] contains no reference to the anti-competitive aim or anticompetitive effect of the practice referred to. However, in the light of the context of Article [102 TFEU], conduct will be regarded as abusive only if it restricts competition.' By contrast, the Court has expressly held that a violation of Art. 102 is not subject to a *de minimis* threshold (Case C-23/14, *Post Danmark*, para. 73: 'It follows that fixing an appreciability (*de minimis*) threshold for the purposes of determining whether there is an abuse of a dominant position is not justified').

a. The 'Market': Product and Geographic Dimensions

Dominance is a relational concept: it is the power to master *something*; and under Article 102 this 'something' is the 'market'. However, there is not one market in which all undertakings compete. Undertakings compete in different products and in different areas. The market concept is thus a concept with two dimensions: a *product* dimension and a *geographic* dimension. The first dimension concerns the question as to what goods or services compete with each other. Where two products do not compete, they are not in the same market. Accordingly, there is not one market but many separate 'product' markets. Two competing goods must however also 'physically' meet in the same area. This aspect of the market concept is called its geographic dimension.

How has the Union legal order defined both dimensions? In relation to the product market, it concentrates on the 'interchangeability' of two products. In the words of the European Court in *Hoffmann-La Roche*:

> The concept of the relevant market in fact implies that there can be effective competition between the products which form part of it and this presupposes that there is a *sufficient degree of interchangeability between all the products* forming part of the same market in so far as a specific use of such products is concerned.[149]

The interchangeability or 'substitutability' of a product typically expresses itself in *demand* substitution. Demand substitution analyses whether the consumer regards two products as interchangeable 'by reason of the products' characteristics, their prices and their intended use'.[150] The principal test here is that of cross-price elasticity. Cross-price elasticity analyses whether a 'small but significant non-transitory increase in price' (SSNIP) in one product incentivises consumers to switch to another product.[151] Where this is the case, two goods are – from an econometric point of view – in the same product market.

---

[149]   Case 85/76, *Hoffmann-La Roche & Co. AG v. Commission* [1979] ECR 461, para. 28 (emphasis added). See also Case 6/72, *Europemballage and Continental Can v. Commission*, para. 32: 'The definition of the relevant market is of essential significance, for the possibilities of competition can only be judged in relation to those characteristics of the products in question by virtue of which those products are particularly apt to satisfy an inelastic need and are only to a limited extent interchangeable with other products.'

[150]   Commission, 'Notice on the Definition of Relevant Market for the Purposes of [Union] Competition Law' [1997] OJ C 372/5, para. 7.

[151]   *Ibid.*, para. 15: 'The assessment of demand substitution entails a determination of the range of products which are viewed as substitutes by the consumer. One way of making this determination can be viewed as a speculative experiment, postulating a hypothetical small, lasting change in relative prices and evaluating the likely reactions of customers to that increase. The exercise of market definition focuses on prices for operational and practical purposes, and more precisely on demand substitution arising from small, permanent changes in relative prices. This concept can provide clear indications as to the evidence that is relevant in defining markets.' The problem with this – relational – test is

But apart from purely quantitative criteria, the European Court uses additional *qualitative* criteria.[152] And it may even analyse the degree of potential competition by future market entrants. This aspect is called *supply* substitution; that is: the extent to which an undertaking could switch from a non-competing to a competing product.[153]

If two products are (theoretically) found to be competing, they must still be offered in the same geographic market. In the words of the Court:

> The opportunities for competition under Article [102] of the Treaty must be considered having regard to the particular features of the product in question *and with reference to a clearly defined geographic area in which it is marketed and where the conditions of competition are sufficiently homogeneous* ...[154]

Two competing products might not be offered in the same (national) market for legal reasons;[155] and even if two products are competing in a similar legal context, transportation costs might limit the geographic market considerably. The question thus is this: when are competitive conditions 'sufficiently homogeneous' so as to 'be distinguished from neighbouring areas because the conditions of competition are appreciably different in those areas'?[156] That is a question of fact that the Courts will have to answer.

If they have answered it positively, the geographic market for a product so identified must also represent a 'substantial part' of the internal market. What is a 'substantial part' of the European market? The European Courts have established a presumption that the territory of a Member State constitutes a

---

that it cannot measure whether the price of the examined product is – in absolute terms – already inflated. This fallacy of the SSNIP test has become known as the 'Cellophane Fallacy' after the US Supreme Court's decision in *US* v. *Du Pont*, 351 US 377 (1956).

[152]   See Case 27/76, *United Brands Company and United Brands Continentaal BV* v. *Commission* [1978] ECR 207, where the Court found that in light of its distinct qualities, the 'banana market is a market which is sufficiently distinct from other fresh fruit markets' (*ibid.*, para. 35).

[153]   See Case 322/81, *Michelin* v. *Commission (Michelin I)* [1983] ECR 3461, esp. para. 41.

[154]   Case 27/76, *United Brands* v. *Commission*, para. 11 (emphasis added). See also Case T-229/94, *Deutsche Bahn* v. *Commission* [1997] ECR II-1689, para. 92: 'Inasmuch as the applicant submits that the Commission's definition of the geographical market is undermined by the difference in the competitive situation, it is sufficient to state that the definition of the geographical market does not require the objective conditions of competition between traders to be perfectly homogeneous. It is sufficient if they are "similar" or "sufficiently homogeneous" and, accordingly, only areas in which the objective conditions of competition are "heterogeneous" may not be considered to constitute a uniform market.'

[155]   The primary 'culprit' here is often (national) intellectual property rights. On the nature and effects of these rights, see L. Bently and B. Sherman, *Intellectual Property Law* (Oxford University Press, 2008), ch. 1.

[156]   Commission, 'Notice on the Definition of Relevant Market' (n. 150 above), para. 8.

substantial part of the internal market.[157] However, they have equally found this requirement to be satisfied for a part of a Member State,[158] and even a port within a city.[159]

b. Market Dominance

aa. General Considerations

There exists an inverse relationship between the identified 'market' and the potential 'dominance' of an undertaking within that market. The greater the market the smaller will be the likelihood of dominance; and, alternatively, the smaller the market the greater will be the likelihood of dominance. Put colloquially: a big fish in a big pond is different from a big fish in a small pond. And sometimes the pond might be so small that there is only room for one fish.[160]

What then is market dominance? Dominance is wider than monopoly. Whereas monopoly technically refers to a situation in which *one* single undertaking dominates the market, Article 102 is not confined to that situation. But as to when an undertaking is dominant the provision does not tell. The European Courts have therefore tried to define dominance by distinguishing it from related phenomena such as monopoly. In *Hoffmann-La Roche*,[161] the European Court thus held:

> The dominant position thus referred to relates to a position of economic strength enjoyed by an undertaking which enables it to prevent the effective competition being maintained on the relevant market by affording it the power to behave to an appreciable extent independently of its competitors, its customers and ultimately of the consumers. *Such a position does not preclude some competition, which it does where there is a monopoly or a quasi-monopoly,* but enables the undertaking which profits by it, if not to determine, at least to have an appreciable influence on the conditions under which that competition will develop, and in any case to act largely in disregard of it so long as such conduct does not operate to its detriment. *A dominant position must also be distinguished from parallel courses of conduct which are peculiar to oligopolies* in that in an oligopoly the courses of conduct interact, while in the case of an undertaking occupying a dominant position the conduct of the undertaking which derives profits from that position is to a great extent determined unilaterally.[162]

---

[157] See Case 127/73, *Belgische Radio en Televisie (BRT) and others* v. *SABAM and others* [1974] ECR 313; Case 322/81, *Michelin I*; Case C-241/91 P, *Radio TelefisEireann (RTE) and Independent Television Publications Ltd (TTP)* v. *Commission* [1995] ECR I-743.

[158] See Joined Cases 40–8/73, 50/73, 54–6/73, 111/73, 113–14/73, 'Suiker Unie' v. *Commission*.

[159] See Case C-179/90, *Merci convenzionali porto di Genova* v. *Siderurgica Gabrielli* [1991] ECR I-5889.

[160] In Case 22/78, *Hugin* v. *Commission* [1979] ECR 1869, the Court defined the relevant market in such narrow terms that only one undertaking – the plaintiff – was found to inhabit the 'pond' of spare parts for Hugin's cash registers.

[161] Case 85/76, *Hoffmann-La Roche & Co. AG* v. *Commission*.

[162] *Ibid.*, paras. 38–9 (emphasis added).

A dominant position is thus distinct from a monopolistic position as well as from an oligopolistic position. While the former excludes all competition, oligopolies are market structures in which a 'few' undertakings – and not one – dominate the market.[163]

But what characterises market dominance specifically? The Court admitted that the answer to that question was determined by several factors, yet nonetheless found that 'among these factors a highly important one is the existence of very large market shares'.[164] Thus, the higher the market share, the higher the probability of dominance. The Court has indeed held that a market share above 50 per cent was a clear indication of market dominance.[165] But even below 50 per cent, the Court may find market dominance. However, a finding of dominance here involves a number of determinants, in particular the structure of the relevant market.[166] This second factor compares the market share of the accused undertaking with those of its biggest competitors.[167] Although an undertaking may not have 'absolute' dominance over the market, it might still enjoy a 'relative' dominance over its competitors.[168] The Court has nonetheless found that if an undertaking has a market share below 40 per cent of the relevant market, a finding of dominance is unlikely.[169]

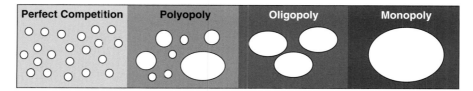

Figure 17.5 Market Structures

---

[163]   *Oligo* means 'few' in Greek.

[164]   *Case 85/76, Hoffmann-La Roche*, para. 39.

[165]   Case C-62/86, *AKZO Chemie BV* v. *Commission* [1991] ECR I-3359, para. 60: 'With regard to market shares the Court has held that very large shares are in themselves, and save in exceptional circumstances, evidence of the existence of a dominant position. That is the situation where there is a market share of 50% such as that found to exist in this case.'

[166]   Case 85/76, *Hoffmann-La Roche*, para. 40: 'A substantial market share as evidence of the existence of a dominant position is not a constant factor and its importance varies from market to market according to the structure of these markets, especially as far as production, supply and demand are concerned.'

[167]   See Case 27/76, *United Brands*, esp. paras. 110ff. The Court is likely to infer dominance where the market share of an undertaking is twice as big as those of all of its competitors combined (Case T-219/99, *British Airways* v. *Commission* [2003] ECR II-5917).

[168]   Other factors that may influence a finding of dominance are entry barriers through the existence of a service network (Case 322/81, *Michelin* v. *Commission*).

[169]   See Commission, 'Guidance on the Commission's Enforcement Priorities in Applying Article [102] of the [FEU] Treaty to Abusive Exclusionary Conduct by Dominant Undertakings' [2009] OJ C 45/7, para. 14.

bb. *Collective Dominance*

A dominant position appears to be fundamentally different from an oligopoly. The latter involves a situation in which a small number of undertakings are – more or less – equally strong within the market, and it would thus seem that none of them could *individually* dominate the market.

But could Article 102 capture these oligopolistic undertakings *collectively*? The concept of collective dominance is suggested by the very wording of the provision. After all, Article 102 refers to an 'abuse of one *or more undertakings of a dominant position*'.[170] And, teleologically, it would be logical to capture situations in which oligopolistic undertakings went beyond 'parallel courses of conduct'.[171] Indeed, a collective *abuse* would have the same consequences as that of a single dominant undertaking.[172]

The European Courts have – belatedly – accepted the idea of collective dominance.[173] In *Vetro et al.* v. *Commission*,[174] three Italian producers of flat glass challenged a Commission decision that had found them guilty of violating Article 102. Their joint market share was 95 per cent, and the Commission claimed that the undertakings would 'present themselves on the market as a single entity and not as individuals'.[175] To cement this argument the Commission pointed to the existence of collusive behaviour under Article 101. Intervening in the proceedings, the United Kingdom objected that it was 'only in very special circumstances that two or more undertakings may jointly hold a dominant position within the meaning of Article [102], namely, when the undertakings concerned fall to be treated as a single economic unit in which the individual undertakings do not enjoy a genuine autonomy in determining their conduct on the market and are not to be treated as economically independent of one another'.[176]

---

[170] Art. 102 TFEU (emphasis added).

[171] Case 85/76, *Hoffmann-La Roche & Co. AG* v. *Commission*, para. 39.

[172] Suffice to say here that once the Union has found collective dominance to exist, the abuse of this dominant position may be collective or individual; see Case T-228/97, *Irish Sugar plc* v. *Commission* [1999] ECR II-2969, para. 66: 'Whilst the existence of a joint dominant position may be deduced from the position which the economic entities concerned together hold on the market in question, the abuse does not necessarily have to be the action of all the undertakings in question. It only has to be capable of being identified as one of the manifestations of such a joint dominant position being held. Therefore, undertakings occupying a joint dominant position may engage in joint or individual abusive conduct. It is enough for that abusive conduct to relate to the exploitation of the joint dominant position which the undertakings hold in the market.'

[173] For an overview of the case law, see R. Wish, 'Collective Dominance', in D. O'Keeffe et al. (eds.), *Judicial Review in European Union Law: Liber amicorum in Honour of Lord Slynn of Hadley* (Kluwer, 2000), 581; R. Nazzini, *The Foundations of European Union Competition Law: The Objectives and Principles of Article 102* (Oxford University Press, 2011), ch. 11.

[174] Joined Cases T-68/89 and T-77–8/89, *Vetro, Pisana and Vernante Pennitalia* v. *Commission* [1992] ECR II-1403. The Commission claimed that this was the first case on collective dominance and for that reason suggested not imposing any fines (*ibid.*, para. 33).

[175] *Ibid.*, para. 31.   [176] *Ibid.*, para. 342.

The General Court – rightly – rejected that argument, since it implied that the notion of 'undertaking' in Article 102 was different from that in Article 101.[177] And moving from text to teleology, the Court continued:

> There is nothing, in principle, to prevent two or more independent economic entities from being, on a specific market, *united by such economic links* that, by virtue of that fact, together they hold a dominant position vis-à-vis the other operators on the same market … However, it should be pointed out that for the purposes of establishing an infringement of Article [102] of the Treaty, it is not sufficient … to 'recycle' the facts constituting an infringement of Article [101], deducing from them the finding that the parties to an agreement or to an unlawful practice jointly hold a substantial share of the market, that by virtue of that fact alone they hold a collective dominant position, and that their unlawful behaviour constitutes an abuse of that collective dominant position.[178]

The simple existence of contractual or collusive relations between the three undertakings was thus not sufficient to establish collective dominance. But what did the requirement that the firms be united by 'economic links' then mean?

Some clarification was given in *CEWAL*,[179] where the European Court confirmed that 'a dominant position may be held by several undertakings'.[180] Collective dominance thereby required that legally independent undertakings 'present themselves or act together on a particular market as a collective entity'.[181] And '[i]n order to establish the existence of a collective entity as defined above, it is necessary to examine the economic links or factors which give rise to a connection between the undertakings concerned'.[182]

The mere existence of collusion within the meaning of Article 101 was inconclusive; yet, such collusion could 'undoubtedly, where it is implemented, result in the undertakings concerned being so linked as to their conduct on a particular market that they present themselves on that market as a collective entity vis-à-vis their competitors, their trading partners and consumers'.[183] All depends on the 'nature and terms of an agreement, from the way in which it is implemented and, consequently, from the links or factors which give rise to a connection between undertakings'.[184]

While an agreement between undertakings may thus indicate collective dominance, the European Courts have found that this is not the only way. And in *Piau*,[185] the General Court provided the following abstract criteria for a finding of collective dominance:

---

[177]   *Ibid.*, para. 358. On the notion of 'undertaking', see section 1(a) above.
[178]   *Ibid.*, paras. 358 and 360 (emphasis added).
[179]   Joined Cases C-395–6/96 P, *Compagnie maritime belge transports SA, Compagnie maritime belge and Dafra-Lines v. Commission* [2000] ECR I-1365.
[180]   *Ibid.*, para. 35.   [181]   *Ibid.*, para. 36.   [182]   *Ibid.*, para. 41.
[183]   *Ibid.*, para. 44.   [184]   *Ibid.*, para. 45.
[185]   Case T-193/02, *Piau v. Commission* [2005] ECR II-209.

Three cumulative conditions must be met for a finding of collective dominance: first, each member of the dominant oligopoly must have the ability to know how the other members are behaving in order to monitor whether or not they are adopting the common policy; second, the situation of tacit coordination must be sustainable over time, that is to say, there must be an incentive not to depart from the common policy on the market; thirdly, the foreseeable reaction of current and future competitors, as well as of consumers, must not jeopardise the results expected from the common policy.[186]

c. Abuse of Market Dominance

If dominance is a relational concept, abuse is a contextual concept. Contextual concepts are like semantic chameleons: their meaning depends on the context in which they are used. What counts as 'abuse' in Article 102 indeed depends not so much on the type of behaviour as such as on its 'context'; namely, that this is the behaviour of a *dominant* undertaking. Thus, where a non-dominant undertaking refuses to supply a distributor, this behaviour is a perfectly legitimate offspring of the freedom of contract. However, were a dominant undertaking to do the same, this might constitute an illegitimate abuse. The abusive character of the behaviour is here added from 'outside'. It is the market structure that 'colours' the behaviour. And since that market structure is – like physical space around big stellar masses – distorted by the very presence of a dominant firm, the latter's action may have an anticompetitive effect, even if the same action of a non-dominant undertaking would not.

The European Court has tried to express this conceptual link between the concept of 'abuse' and market dominance as follows

The concept of abuse is an objective concept relating to the behaviour of an undertaking in a dominant position which is such as to influence the structure of a market where, as a result of the very presence of the undertaking in question, the degree of competition is weakened and which, through recourse to methods different from those which condition normal competition in products or services on the basis of the transactions of commercial operators, has the effect of hindering the maintenance of the degree of competition still existing in the market or the growth of that competition.[187]

What we see as examples of abusive behaviour in Article 102 must be understood in this light. The actions listed in the provision are not illegal as such; they become illegal because of the standing of the actor within the market. For within that market a dominant undertaking has 'a special responsibility'.[188] And because

---

[186] *Ibid.*, paras. 110–11.
[187] Case 85/76, *Hoffmann-La Roche & Co. AG v. Commission*, para. 91.
[188] Case 322/81, *Michelin v. Commission*, para. 57; Case C-209/10, *Post Danmark*, para. 23.

of that special responsibility, there are special duties imposed on a dominant undertaking. However, these special duties will find a limit in its right to self-defence. '[T]he fact that an undertaking is in a dominant position cannot disentitle it from protecting its own commercial interests if they are attacked[.]'[189]

What types of abusive behaviour are covered by Article 102? The provision covers both exploitative as well as exclusionary abuses: it 'is not only aimed at practices which may cause damage to consumers directly, but also at those which are detrimental to them through their impact on an effective competition structure'.[190] The 'maintenance of effective competition on the relevant market' is nonetheless the central aim behind Article 102.[191]

What will 'relevant' market here mean? A restrictive reading would insist that the special duties imposed on a dominant undertaking are confined to the market that it dominates. But the Union legal order has preferred a – slightly – wider reading. It has extended the prohibition of abuse to 'downstream' or 'adjacent' markets in which the undertaking is *not* dominant.[192] The application of Article 102 in 'distinct, but associated' markets is thus possible. However, in *Tetra Pak*,[193] the European Court insisted on 'a link between the dominant position and the alleged abusive conduct, which is normally not present where conduct on a market distinct from the dominated market produces effects on that distinct market'.[194] Article 102 would thus only apply in 'special circumstances' to conduct found in the associated market, in which the undertaking was not dominant.[195]

The following subsections will now look at common forms of abusive behaviour from the (non-exhaustive) list in Article 102.

aa. Article 102[2](a) and 'Predatory Pricing'

The first illustration of abusive behaviour given by Article 102 consists of 'directly or indirectly imposing unfair purchase or selling prices or other unfair trading conditions'.[196]

This wide category includes 'excessive pricing', as well as 'predatory pricing'. The former exploits the consumer, while the latter is designed to exclude a competitor. Excessive pricing is hard to establish.[197] For predatory pricing, on the other hand, the European Courts have developed a detector test that indicates when abusive conduct is, or is likely to be, present.

---

[189]   Case 27/76, *United Brands* v. *Commission*, para. 189.
[190]   Case 6/72, *Europemballage Corporation and Continental Can Company* v. *Commission*, para. 26.
[191]   Case 322/81, *Michelin* v. *Commission*, para. 30.
[192]   See Cases 6–7/73, *Istituto Chemioterapico Italiano and Commercial Solvents Corporation* v. *Commission* [1974] ECR 223.
[193]   Case C-333/94 P, *Tetra Pak International* v. *Commission* [1996] ECR I-5961.
[194]   *Ibid.*, para. 27.
[195]   *Ibid.*
[196]   Art. 102[2](a) TFEU.
[197]   See Case 27/76, *United Brands* v. *Commission*, paras. 235ff. However, see also Case 26/75, *General Motors Continental NV* v. *Commission* [1975] ECR 1367.

In *AKZO*,[198] the European Court had to deal with two undertakings producing organic peroxides. Peroxides are used in the plastics industry, but can equally be used as bleaching agents for flour. AKZO had traditionally been active with regard to both markets, whereas a second company – ECS – had only recently extended its activities from the flour to the plastics market. In order to secure ECS's withdrawal from the plastics market, AKZO attacked its competitor on the flour market by systematically offering 'unreasonably low prices designed to damage ECS's business viability, compelling ECS either to abandon the customer to AKZO or to match a loss-making price in order to retain the customer'.[199] This was a commercially clever strategy, since AKZO used price reductions in a sector which was vital for its competitor but of limited importance to itself.[200] But was this a commercially legitimate strategy? The Court found that AKZO held a dominant position and that therefore 'not all competition by means of price can be regarded as legitimate'.[201]

What then was the distinction between legitimate and illegitimate price competition? In the opinion of the Court it was this:

> Prices below average variable costs (that is to say, those which vary depending on the quantities produced) by means of which a dominant undertaking seeks to eliminate a competitor must be regarded as abusive. A dominant undertaking has no interest in applying such prices except that of eliminating competitors so as to enable it subsequently to raise its prices by taking advantage of its monopolistic position, since each sale generates a loss, namely the total amount of the fixed costs (that is to say, those which remain constant regardless of the quantities produced) and, at least, part of the variable costs relating to the unit produced. Moreover, prices below average total costs, that is to say, fixed costs plus variable costs, but above average variable costs, must be regarded as abusive if they are determined as part of a plan for eliminating a competitor. Such prices can drive from the market undertakings which are perhaps as efficient as the dominant undertaking but which, because of their smaller financial resources, are incapable of withstanding the competition waged against them.[202]

The Court here established a rule and a presumption for illegitimate predatory pricing.[203] Where the price of the product was below average variable costs the pricing policy of an undertaking was abusive *per se*. It thereby would not

---

[198] Case C-62/86, *AKZO Chemie BV* v. *Commission*.

[199] *Ibid.*, para. 9.   [200] *Ibid.*, para. 42.   [201] *Ibid.*, para. 70.   [202] *Ibid.*, paras. 71–2.

[203] The ruling was confirmed in Case C-333/94 P, *Tetra Pak International SA* v. *Commission*, esp. paras. 39ff. According to 'Guidance on Article [102]' (n. 169 above), the Commission will apply a slightly different test (*ibid.*, para. 26): 'The cost benchmarks that the Commission is likely to use are average avoidable cost (AAC) and long-run average incremental cost (LRAIC). Failure to cover AAC indicates that the dominant undertaking is sacrificing profits in the short term and that an equally efficient competitor cannot serve the targeted customers without incurring a loss. LRAIC is usually above AAC because, in contrast to AAC (which only includes fixed costs if incurred during the period under examination), LRAIC includes product specific fixed costs made before the period in which allegedly

matter whether there existed a possibility of recuperating the losses in the long term.[204]

By contrast, where the price was between average variable costs and average total costs, there was still a possibility that this could be an abuse of dominance. However, an abusive behaviour would here only be established where the pricing policy could be shown to be part of a strategic plan to eliminate a competitor. This 'subjective' element within the definition of predatory pricing undermines, to some extent, the Court's idea that the concept of abuse is an 'objective' concept.[205] The General Court has tried to gloss over this development by asserting that an anticompetitive intent and an anticompetitive effect may – occasionally – 'be one and the same thing'.[206]

bb. *Article 102[2](b) and 'Refusal to Supply'*

The Treaties define a second form of abuse as 'limiting production, markets or technical development to the prejudice of consumers'.[207] One can consider the 'refusal to supply' as a generic expression of that category. This potentially abusive type of conduct best illustrates the 'special responsibilities' of a dominant undertaking. For the general principle of freedom of contract would normally allow any contracting party to reject an offer for a contract. But this freedom cannot be granted where the market structure is such that there is no alternative supply.

In *Commercial Solvents*,[208] the Court had to deal with the refusal by the dominant producer of a raw material. The producer had decided to expand its production to the manufacture of the finished product; and in pursuit of this vertical integration strategy, it had decided to cut off the supply of raw materials 'to certain parties in order to facilitate its own access to the market for the derivatives'.[209] In unequivocal terms, the Court found that this was not a legitimate commercial strategy for a dominant undertaking:

> [A]n undertaking being in a dominant position as regards the production of raw material and therefore able to control the supply to manufacturers of derivatives, cannot, just because it decides to start manufacturing these derivatives (in competition with its former customers) act in such a way as to eliminate their competition which in the case in question, would amount to eliminating one of the principal manufacturers of ethambutol in the common market.[210]

abusive conduct took place. Failure to cover LRAIC indicates that the dominant undertaking is not recovering all the (attributable) fixed costs of producing the good or service in question and that an equally efficient competitor could be foreclosed from the market.'

[204] See C-202/07 P, *France Télécom* v. *Commission* [2009] ECR I-2369, esp. para. 110.
[205] See Case 85/76, *Hoffmann-La Roche* v. *Commission*, para. 91.
[206] Case T-340/03, *France Télécom* v. *Commission* [2007] ECR II-107, para. 195.
[207] Art. 102[2](b) TFEU. For a recent overview of exclusionary discrimination under Art. 102 in general, see P. Ibáñez Colomo, 'Exclusionary Discrimination under Article 102 TFEU' (2014) 51 *CML Rev.* 141.
[208] See Cases 6–7/73, *Istituto Chemioterapico Italiano* v. *Commission*.
[209] *Ibid.*, para. 24.   [210] *Ibid.*, para. 25.

The Court consequently considered the refusal to supply an abuse of a dominant position that violated Article 102. This reasoning was confirmed in *Magill*.[211]
In the absence of a comprehensive weekly television guide in Ireland, each television station here published its own guide, while licensing daily newspapers
to produce daily listings free of charge. Magill saw a commercial opportunity
and tried to use it. Yet it was prevented from publishing a comprehensive weekly
guide by the Irish television stations (as well as the BBC). Was this an abuse of a
dominant position? The European Courts thought this was a clear violation of
Article 102[2](b), as the refusal to supply the information 'prevented the appearance of a new product' that the dominant undertakings 'did not offer and for
which there was a potential consumer demand'.[212]

Did *Magill* here endorse a US-inspired 'essential facilities' doctrine?[213] The
question was raised in *Bronner*.[214] The applicant here was a producer of a small
Austrian newspaper, who wished to use the – integrated – home-delivery distribution network of a dominant competitor 'against payment of reasonable remuneration'.[215] Bronner argued that the normal postal delivery service would not
constitute an alternative delivery option, as it would not take place until the late
morning; and the establishment of its own home-delivery service was 'entirely
unprofitable'.[216]

Could he therefore demand to use his competitor's distributional infrastructure? The Court disagreed, and gave an extremely restrictive reading of its prior
jurisprudence. Only when the service was 'indispensable' for carrying on the
business in question, because it was 'impossible' to develop a new product without the service, would the Union – in 'exceptional circumstances' – require
a competitor to make available its facilities.[217] And this was not the case here.
Even if the Court admitted that there was only one nationwide home-delivery
scheme in the Member State,[218] other methods of distribution were available and
it was furthermore not impossible for any publisher of daily newspapers to establish – alone or in cooperation with other publishers – a second home-delivery
scheme.[219] This restrictive stance has been confirmed in later jurisprudence.[220]

cc. Article 102[2](c) and 'Discretionary Pricing'

A third category of abusive behaviour is defined as 'applying dissimilar conditions to equivalent transactions with other trading parties, thereby placing

---

[211] Joined Cases C-241–2/91 P, *Radio Telefis Eireann (RTE) and Independent Television
Publications Ltd (TTP)* v. *Commission*.
[212] *Ibid.*, paras. 54ff.
[213] For critical overviews of the US doctrine, see B. Doherty, 'Just What Are Essential
Facilities?' (2001) 38 *CML Rev.* 397; A. Rodenhausen, 'The Rise and Fall of the Essential
Facilities Doctrine' (2008) 29 ECLR 310.
[214] Case C-7/97, *Bronner* v. *Mediaprint Zeitungs- und Zeitschriftenverlag and others* [1998] ECR
I-7791.
[215] *Ibid.*, para. 8. [216] *Ibid.* [217] *Ibid.*, paras. 38–41. [218] *Ibid.*, para. 42. [219] *Ibid.* para. 44.
[220] See Case C-418/01, *IMS Health* v. *NDC Health* [2004] ECR I-5039; Case T-201/04,
Microsoft v. *Commission* [2007] ECR II-3601.

them at a competitive disadvantage'.[221] The emblematic expression of this type of abuse is discriminatory pricing. Price discrimination may thereby take place directly or indirectly. Direct discrimination might be found where an undertaking charges different prices depending on the nationality or location of its customers.[222] The best-known commercial techniques of indirect price discrimination are discounts or rebates. They have been subject to an extensive European jurisprudence.[223]

In *Hoffmann-La Roche*,[224] the Court was asked to analyse the commercial lure of a loyalty rebate offered by a dominant undertaking. Loyalty or fidelity rebates are discounts that are conditional – regardless of the quantity bought – on the customer's promise to buy exclusively from one undertaking. According to the Commission, this had a discriminatory effect since Roche 'offer[ed] two purchasers two different prices for an identical quantity of the same product depending on whether these two buyers agree or not to forego [*sic*] obtaining their supplies from Roche's competitors'.[225] The Court agreed:

> The *fidelity* rebate, unlike *quantity* rebates exclusively linked with the volume of purchases from the producer concerned, is designed through the grant of a financial advantage to prevent customers from obtaining their supplies from competing producers. Furthermore the effect of fidelity rebates is to apply dissimilar conditions to equivalent transactions with other trading parties in that two purchasers pay a different price for the same quantity of the same product depending on whether they obtain their supplies exclusively from the undertaking in a dominant position or have several sources of supply.[226]

The Court here distinguished between *legitimate* 'quantity rebates' and *illegitimate* 'fidelity rebates'. However, the dividing line between the two has never been easy to draw. This is illustrated by *Michelin I*.[227] Is a 'target discount', that is: a discount that is given once the seller has achieved a given sales target, a quantity or a loyalty discount? The Court found that the discount system operated by Michelin did 'not amount to a mere quantity discount linked solely to the volume of goods purchased', as it 'depended primarily on the dealer's turnover in Michelin tyres without distinction of category and not on the number'.[228] However, neither was the rebate a clear loyalty rebate, as the Commission had not succeeded in demonstrating that the discount system was discriminatory.[229]

---

[221] Art. 102[2](c) TFEU.
[222] Case 27/76, *United Brands* v. *Commission*, paras. 204ff.
[223] For an overview, see A. Jones and B. Sufrin, *EU Competition Law: Text, Cases and Materials* (Oxford University Press, 2014), 454ff.
[224] Case 85/76, *Hoffmann-La Roche* v. *Commission*.
[225] *Ibid.*, para. 80.
[226] *Ibid.*, para. 90 (emphasis added).
[227] Case 322/81, *Michelin* v. *Commission*.
[228] *Ibid.*, paras. 72 and 89.   [229] *Ibid.*, para. 91.

The evolution of the subsequent case law has further blurred the traditional dichotomy between (*per se* legal) quantity discounts and (*per se* illegal) loyalty discounts;[230] and it seemed that the introduction of a more economic approach to Article 102 might ultimately lead the Court to abandon the idea of *per se* rules altogether. Yet this development has recently received a major qualification. For instead of subjecting all rebates to the same economic effects analysis, *Post-Danmark II* has confirmed the older jurisprudence on *per se* rules; and it has now also expressly acknowledged the existence of a middle category in between (pure) quantity and (pure) loyalty rebates. This third category will be subjected to a detailed economic analysis of 'all the circumstances'.[231]

The best view on Article 102 might therefore be that the provision – like Article 101 – distinguishes between practices that are by their very nature anti-competitive and practices that will only violate Article 102 in light of their anticompetitive effects.[232]

dd. Article 102[2](d) and 'Tying or Bundling'

The fourth illustration of an abusive behaviour in Article 102 outlaws the commercial practice of 'making the conclusion of contracts subject to acceptance by the other parties of *supplementary obligations which, by their nature or according to commercial usage, have no connection with the subject of such contracts*'.[233] This mouthful is often simply referred to as 'tying' and 'bundling'. While there is a subtle distinction between both commercial techniques,[234] both express themselves in 'connecting' the sale of one product to the sale of another.[235]

We find a good illustration of this sales technique in *Tetra Pak II*.[236] The case involved a dominant manufacturer of cartons and carton-filling machines. Tetra

---

[230] See Case T-203/01, *Michelin* v. *Commission*; Case C-95/04 P, *British Airways* v. *Commission* [2007] ECR I-2331, paras. 67–8.

[231] Case C-23/14, *Post Danmark A/S* v. *Konkurrenceradet*, EU:C:2015:651, esp. paras. 27–9. For an analysis of the case, see K. Rokita, 'Exclusionary Rebates: Where Are We after *Post Danmark II* and How Did We Get There?' (2016) 41 *EL Rev.* 885.

[232] For this view, see P. Ibáñez Colombo, 'Beyond the "More Economics-Based Approach": A Legal Perspective on Article 102 TFEU Case Law' (2016) 53 *CML Rev.* 709. Whether this is still the case after Case C-413/14 P, *Intel* v. *Commission*, EU:C:2017:632 remains to be seen.

[233] Art. 102[2](d) TFEU (emphasis added).

[234] E. Rousseva, *Rethinking Exclusionary Abuses in EU Competition Law* (Hart, 2010), 219: 'The distinction between bundling and tying is technical. In the case of tying, one of the products, that is the tied product, can be purchased independently. In the case of bundling, no distinction is made between the purchases of the products involved. Either none of the products can be purchased independently of the other (pure bundling) or both products can be purchased independently but their joint sale gives customers a discount (mixed bundling).'

[235] The European Courts appear to use both terms interchangeably; see Case T-201/04, *Microsoft* v. *Commission*, para. 935.

[236] Case T-83/91, *Tetra Pak* v. *Commission* [1994] ECR II-755. But see also Case T-30/89, *Hilti* v. *Commission*.

Pak had tied the sale of the former to the sale of the latter – claiming that the machinery for packaging was indivisible from the cartons. The General Court rejected that claim. Finding that there were independent manufacturers special-ising in cartons for machines from different manufacturers,[237] and that Tetra Pak's own cartons could be used on different machines,[238] carton and carton-filling machines were considered products that could be separately sold. And since their tying was not in line with commercial usage,[239] the dominant undertaking had abused its market power.[240]

This form of analysis was refined in *Microsoft* – one of the longest judgments of European law.[241] The case examined the choice of the software giant to tie a media player to its operating system. The General Court here had recourse to four analytical elements in showing an abuse of dominance. In addition to the existence of two separate products,[242] the Union competition authorities would need to demonstrate that the dominant undertaking 'coerced' customers to buy the tied product by not giving them a choice whether or not to obtain the prod-uct.[243] And even though the Windows Media Player was a media functionality that did not require consumers to pay extra, the Court found

> [I]n consequence of the impugned conduct, consumers are unable to acquire the Windows client PC operating system without simultaneously acquiring Windows Media Player, which means that the condition that the conclusion of contracts is made subject to acceptance of supplementary obligations must be considered to be satisfied.[244]

The third element of the test then examined whether this technique fore-closed competition for the bundled product,[245] while the fourth element ana-lysed the absence of an objective justification for the seemingly abusive conduct.

---

[237] Case T-83/91, *Tetra Pak v. Commission*, para. 82. Much of the argument concentrated on non-aseptic cartons.

[238] *Ibid.*, para. 132.

[239] *Ibid.*, para. 137.

[240] *Ibid.*, para. 140. The judgment was confirmed on appeal; see Case C-333/94 P, *Tetra Pak v. Commission*, where the Court even pointed out that (*ibid.*, para. 37) '[i]t must, moreover, be stressed that the list of abusive practices set out in the second paragraph of Article [102] of the Treaty is not exhaustive … Consequently, even where tied sales of two products are in accordance with commercial usage or there is a natural link between the two products in question, such sales may still constitute abuse within the meaning of Article [102] unless they are objectively justified.'

[241] Case T-201/04, *Microsoft v. Commission*. The judgment contains 1,373 paragraphs of factual and legal arguments.

[242] *Ibid.*, paras. 872ff.   [243] *Ibid.*, paras. 945ff.

[244] *Ibid.*, para. 961. For a criticism of the application of this second criterion in the *Microsoft* decision itself, see Rousseva, *Rethinking Exclusionary Abuses* (n. 234 above), 252: 'the mere fact that consumers did not have to pay an extra price for [the Windows Media Player] and could also freely download an alternative media player meant that consumers had a choice'.

[245] Case T-201/04, *Microsoft v. Commission*, paras. 976ff.

This last element theoretically applies to all types of abuse and will be considered in the final section.

d. Objective Justification: Apparently Abusive Behaviour?

Article 102 contains – unlike Article 101 – no separate paragraph dealing with possible justifications for abuses of a dominant position.[246] Article 102 thus appears to be an 'absolute' prohibition. However, the European Courts do examine whether there exists an 'objective justification' of the apparently abusive behaviour of a market leader.[247] The existence of unwritten grounds of justification is not uncommon and can be seen in other areas of European law. And yet, the idea of objective justifications has remained 'one of the most vague concepts associated with the application of Article [102]'.[248]

In order to explain the European jurisprudence on the concept of objective justification, two jurisprudential lines are traditionally distinguished. According to a first line, the behaviour of a dominant firm is not considered abusive due to a special context. Thus, where a crisis within an industry leads to general supply shortages, the refusal to supply non-traditional customers has not been seen as abusive behaviour.[249] However, the European Courts insist that the special context must be 'beyond the control of the dominant undertaking and which it cannot overcome by any means other than by adopting the conduct which is prima facie abusive'.[250] Moreover, the special context justification has generally not been extended to public policy considerations. Thus, the fact that an undertaking may deal with products that are potentially dangerous for the health of consumers was not deemed an objective justification for the abusive conduct towards a competitor. The undertaking will here need to explain why the special context was not addressed by the relevant public authorities.[251]

---

[246] See Joined Cases T-191/98 and T-212–14/98, *Atlantic Container Line and others* v. *Commission* [2003] ECR II-3275, para. 1109: 'Before considering those grounds for justification, it must be noted at the outset that there is no exception to the principle in [European] competition law prohibiting abuse of a dominant position. Unlike Article [101] of the Treaty, Article [102] of the Treaty does not allow undertakings in a dominant position to seek to obtain exemption for their abusive practices.'

[247] For an analysis of the case law, see Rousseva, *Rethinking Exclusionary Abuses* (n. 234 above), ch. 7.

[248] *Ibid.*, 259. For an overview of the potential defences under Art. 102, see R. Nazzini, *The Foundations of European Union Competition Law: The Objective and Principles of Article 102* (Oxford University Press, 2011), ch. 9.

[249] Case 77/77, *Benzine en Petroleum Handelsmaatschappij and others* v. *Commission* [1978] ECR 1513, esp. paras. 33–4.

[250] Rousseva, *Rethinking Exclusionary Abuses* (n. 234 above), 265.

[251] See Case T-83/91, *Tetra Pak* v. *Commission*, para. 84: 'Moreover, even on the assumption, shared by the applicant, that machinery and cartons from various sources cannot be used together without the characteristics of the system being affected thereby, the remedy must lie in appropriate legislation or regulations, and not in rules adopted unilaterally by manufacturers, which would amount to prohibiting independent manufacturers from conducting the essential part of their business.' See now Commission, 'Guidance on Article

A second jurisprudential line concerns the 'efficiency defence'. In *British Airways*,[252] the European Court indeed appeared to use a relative concept of abuse when examining the legality of a system of discounts and bonuses established by a dominant undertaking. According to the Court, 'the exclusionary effect arising from such a system, which is disadvantageous for competition, may be counterbalanced, or outweighed, by advantages in terms of efficiency which also benefit the consumer'.[253] However, other judgments have expressly pointed in the opposite direction.[254] The most elaborate discussion of the efficiency defence has taken place in *Microsoft*.[255] Here, the General Court appeared to accept the theoretical existence of an objective justification on the grounds of productive or dynamic efficiencies. However, with regard to the practical application of the defence in this case it held that Microsoft had not shown 'that the integration of Windows Media Player in Windows creates technical efficiencies or, in other words, that it "lead[s] to superior technical product performance"'.[256] In sum: while the Commission has shown a positive attitude towards the efficiency defence under Article 102,[257] the legal parameters for this second objective justification have nonetheless remained very vague indeed.

4. EU Merger Control

In order better to compete in the market, a firm may decide to merge with another firm. Mergers are an external form of expansion. They aim to create economies of scale and scope.[258]

Mergers may take place in two directions. They can take place between two previously competing undertakings (horizontal merger); or, they may take place between two firms on different levels of the commercial chain (vertical merger). Either type of merger may raise specific competition concerns under Articles 101 and 102: horizontal mergers restrict competition between competitors, whereas vertical mergers may lead to foreclosure effects on the distribution level.

---

[102]' (n. 169 above), para. 29: 'Exclusionary conduct may, for example, be considered objectively necessary for health or safety reasons related to the nature of the product in question. However, proof of whether conduct of this kind is objectively necessary must take into account that it is normally the task of public authorities to set and enforce public health and safety standards. It is not the task of a dominant undertaking to take steps on its own initiative to exclude products which it regards, rightly or wrongly, as dangerous or inferior to its own product.'

[252] Case C-95/04 P, *British Airways* v. *Commission*.

[253] *Ibid.*, para. 86.

[254] Case T-340/03, *France Télécom* v. *Commission*, esp. para. 217.

[255] Case T-201/04, *Microsoft* v. *Commission*.

[256] *Ibid.*, para. 1159.

[257] For an attempt to provide such guidelines, see now Commission, 'Guidance on Article [102]' (n. 169 above), para. 30. The Commission here suggests four criteria that parallel the four conditions under Art. 101(3).

[258] On the general relation between market structure and economic growth, see F. M. Scherer and D. Ross, *Industrial Market Structure and Economic Performance* (Houghton Mifflin, 1990).

However, merger control pursues a more abstract – higher – goal: it is a policy that aims generally to prevent the creation of market structures whose concentration would *as such* facilitate anticompetitive conduct. Merger control thus fundamentally differs from the prohibitions under Article 101 and 102 TFEU. It does not punish an illegal behaviour that has already taken place; but as a 'structural' policy, it follows an '*ex ante*' approach that aims to *prevent* such illegal behaviour altogether.

Where do we find the EU merger rules? The EU Treaties were surprisingly silent about merger control.[259] The Union however gradually developed it as a third pillar of EU competition law (see section (a)). This development culminated in the adoption of the EU Merger Regulation (EUMR), which constitutes the central legislative tool to control dangerous 'concentrations' within the internal market. The scope of the EUMR is defined by a jurisdictional and a substantive dimension. Jurisdictionally, it is confined to mergers that have a 'European' dimension; and substantively, it only outlaws those mergers that significantly impede effective competition within the internal market. Both dimensions will be discussed in sections (b) and (c). A final section explores the availability of 'merger defences' that can justify anticompetitive market concentrations.

a. Judicial Origins: Merger Control 'by Other Means'

In the absence of an express constitutional base within the EU Treaties, the Union originally based its merger control on Article 102 TFEU.

The expansive use of Article 102 in this context can be seen in *Continental Can*.[260] The Commission had prohibited the acquisition by a US company of the leading Dutch manufacturer of packaging materials on the grounds that the former was already dominant in the German market. This was challenged by the applicant. It argued that the Commission decision was 'based on an erroneous interpretation of Article [102] of the [FEU] Treaty', which was 'trying to introduce a control of mergers'; whereas 'structural measures of undertakings – such as strengthening of a dominant position by way of merger – [did] not amount to abuse of this position within the meaning of Article [102] of the Treaty'.[261] Put differently, Article 102 only outlawed (behavioural) abuses of dominance, and it could not cover (structural) changes in the market following a merger.

The question the Court here had to answer was therefore this: could the acquisition of an undertaking constitute an abuse of a dominant position?[262]

---

[259] This omission appears to have stemmed from a lack of political consensus among the Member States about a general Union merger policy. The ECSC, by contrast, contained a particular merger policy within its scope. For an analysis of the historical origins of Union merger control, see S. Bulmer, 'Institutions and Policy Change: The Case of Merger Control' (1994) 72 *Public Administration* 423.

[260] Case 6/72, *Europemballage Corporation and Continental Can Company Inc.* v. *Commission* [1973] ECR 215.

[261] *Ibid.*, para. 19.

[262] The exact question formulated by the Court was this (*ibid.*, para. 20): 'The question is whether the word "abuse" in Article [102] refers only to practices of undertakings which may directly

Analysing the spirit and general scheme of the EU competition rules, the Court famously found as follows:

> In the absence of explicit provisions one cannot assume that the Treaty, which prohibits in Article [101] certain decisions of ordinary associations of undertakings restricting competition without eliminating it, permits in Article [102] that undertakings, after merging into an organic unity, should reach such a dominant position that any serious chance of competition is practically rendered impossible. *Such a diverse legal treatment would make a breach in the entire competition which could jeopardize the proper functioning of the common market. If, in order to avoid the prohibitions in Article [101], it sufficed to establish such close connections between the undertakings that they escaped the prohibition of Article [101] without coming within the scope of that of Article [102], then, in contradiction to the basic principles of the common market, the partitioning of a substantial part of this market would be allowed* …
>
> *It is in the light of these considerations that the condition imposed by Article [102] is to be interpreted whereby in order to come within the prohibition a dominant position must have been abused.* The provision states a certain number of abusive practices which it prohibits. The list merely gives examples, not an exhaustive enumeration of the sort of abuses of a dominant position prohibited by the Treaty. As may further be seen from letters (c) and (d) of Article [102(2)], the provision is not only aimed at practices which may cause damage to consumers directly, but also at those which are detrimental to them through their impact on an effective competition structure … *Abuse may therefore occur if an undertaking in a dominant position strengthens such position in such a way that the degree of dominance reached substantially fetters competition* …[263]

While honouring the textual insistence of an 'abuse' of market dominance in Article 102, the Court here nonetheless – and ingeniously – found that the mere *strengthening* of a dominant position could amount to such an *abuse*. This exceptionally wide teleological interpretation of Article 102 opened the behavioural provision to a structural phenomenon: mergers that *reinforced* dominance could henceforth be prohibited, where they 'substantially fetter[ed] competition'. Yet due to the scope of Article 102, this indirect form of merger control could not capture mergers by non-dominant undertakings – even if the merger would create a dominant position on the market.[264]

In *British American Tobacco*,[265] the ECJ opened a second indirect route of merger control – this time by means of Article 101. The case concerned an

---

affect the market and are detrimental to production or sales, to purchasers or consumers, or whether this word refers also to changes in the structure of an undertaking, which lead to competition being seriously disturbed in a substantial part of the Common Market.'

[263] *Ibid.*, paras. 25–6 (emphasis added).

[264] See Case T-102/96, *Gencor v. Commission* [1997] ECR II-879, para. 155 (with reference to *Continental Can*): '[O]nly the strengthening of dominant positions and not their creation can be controlled under Article [102] of the Treaty[.]'

[265] Joined Cases 142/84 and 156/84, *British American Tobacco Company Ltd and R. J. Reynolds Industries Inc. v. Commission* [1987] ECR 4487.

agreement between two cigarette manufacturers, Philip Morris and Rothmans, by which the former acquired a 31 per cent shareholding in the latter. While this horizontal agreement contained several safeguards to prevent collusion,[266] two other tobacco companies – in particular, British American Tobacco – challenged the legality of the acquisition agreement. The question thus arose of whether Article 101 could extend to 'merger and acquisition' agreements; and the answer of the Court was as follows:

> It should be recalled that the agreements prohibited by Article [101] are those which have as their object or effect the prevention, restriction or distortion of competition within the common market. *Although the acquisition by one company of an equity interest in a competitor does not in itself constitute conduct restricting competition, such an acquisition may nevertheless serve as an instrument for influencing the commercial conduct of the companies in question so as to restrict or distort competition on the market on which they carry on business.* That may also be the case where the agreement gives the investing company the possibility of reinforcing its position at a later stage and taking effective control of the other company. Account must be taken not only of the immediate effects of the agreement but also of its potential effects and of the possibility that the agreement may be part of a long-term plan. That will be true in particular where, by the acquisition of a shareholding or through subsidiary clauses in the agreement, *the investing company obtains legal or de facto control of the commercial conduct of the other company or where the agreement provides for commercial cooperation between the companies or creates a structure likely to be used for such cooperation.*[267]

The case opened Article 101 as a second – and wider – avenue to pursue a Union merger policy 'by other means'. For unlike Article 102, the use of Article 101 to control mergers and acquisitions would go far beyond mergers of *dominant* undertakings.

Fearful of a merger policy developed exclusively by the European Courts, the Member States suddenly agreed – after 20 years of protracted negotiations – to establish the legislative foundations for a Union merger policy: the EU Merger Regulation.

b. Legislative Foundations: The EU Merger Regulation

The Union's first Merger Regulation was adopted in 1989.[268] Having undergone substantial reform, it was subsequently replaced by a second regime in

---

[266] *Ibid.*, para. 9.

[267] *Ibid.*, paras. 36–9 (emphasis added).

[268] Regulation 4064/89 on the control of concentrations between undertakings [1989] OJ L 395/1. For an early analysis of the (old) Regulation, see J. S. Venit, 'The "Merger" Control Regulation: Europe Comes of Age … or Caliban's Dinner' (1990) 27 *CML Rev.* 7.

Table 17.3 EU Merger Regulation – Structure

EU Merger Regulation 139/2004	
Article 1: Scope	Article 14: Fines
Article 2: Appraisal of concentrations	Article 15: Periodic penalty payments
Article 3: Definition of concentration	Article 16: Review by the Court of Justice
Article 4: Prior notification and prenotification referral	Article 17: Professional secrecy
Article 5: Calculation of turnover	Article 18: Hearing of the parties and of third persons
Article 6: Examination of the notification and initiation of proceedings	Article 19: Liaison with the authorities of the Member States
Article 7: Suspension of concentrations	Article 20: Publication of decisions
Article 8: Powers of decision of the Commission	Article 21: Application of the Regulation and jurisdiction
Article 9: Referral to the competent authorities of the Member States	Article 22: Referral to the Commission
	Article 23: Implementing provisions
Article 10: Time limits for initiating proceedings and for decisions	Article 24: Relations with third countries
Article 11: Requests for information	Article 25: Repeal
Article 12: Inspections by the authorities of the Member States	Article 26: Entry into force and transitional provisions
Article 13: The Commission's powers of inspection	
Implementing Regulation 802/2004	
Informal Commission Notices (Selection)	
(Consolidated) Jurisdictional Notice Guidelines on Horizontal Mergers, Guidelines on Non-horizontal Mergers	

2004. It can today be found in Regulation 139/2004 on the control of concentrations between undertakings (the EUMR, whose structure can be seen in Table 17.3).[269]

The EUMR represents the central control mechanism for mergers within the European Union. It describes its rationale as follows:

---

[269] Regulation 139/2004 on the control of concentrations between undertakings (the EC Merger Regulation) [2004] OJ L 24/1. In the absence of an express EU competence on mergers, the Regulation was primarily based on Art. 352 TFEU.

> Articles [101] and [102], while applicable, according to the case-law of the Court of Justice, to certain concentrations, are not sufficient to control all operations which may prove to be incompatible with the system of undistorted competition envisaged in the Treaty.[270]

The EUMR targets '*significant structural changes*, the impact of which on the market goes *beyond the national borders of any one Member State*'; and it holds that '[s]uch concentrations should, as a general rule, be reviewed exclusively at [Union] level, in application of a "one-stop shop" system and in compliance with the principle of subsidiarity'.[271]

The scope of the EUMR is thereby determined by a jurisdictional and a substantive criterion. Jurisdictionally, only those mergers that have a 'Union' dimension fall within its scope (see section (aa) below). Substantially, the Regulation will only control significant structural changes within the internal market (see section (bb)). A question that the EUMR does not expressly answer is whether there exist 'objective justifications' to a merger (see section (cc)); yet it does recognise the possibility of national public policy justifications (see section (dd)).

Let us explore all four aspects in turn.

aa. Jurisdictional Scope: The 'Union' Dimension

The EUMR is based on a clear jurisdictional division of powers. The Union is exclusively charged to control 'mergers' that have a 'Union dimension', while the Member States remain exclusively competent for mergers falling outside the scope of the Regulation.[272]

The EUMR thereby provides a broad definition of what constitutes a 'merger'. In order to capture legal operations that go beyond a complete fusion of two undertakings, the Regulation adopts the concept of 'concentration'. Article 3 defines such concentrations as follows:

> A concentration shall be deemed to arise where a change of control on a lasting basis results from:
> (a) the *merger* of two or more previously independent undertakings or parts of undertakings, or
> (b) the *acquisition*, by one or more persons already controlling at least one undertaking, or by one or more undertakings, whether by purchase of securities or assets, by contract or by any other means, of direct or indirect control of the whole or parts of one or more other undertakings ...

---

[270] *Ibid.*, recital 7.

[271] *Ibid.*, recital 8 (emphasis added).

[272] *Ibid.*, Art. 21(3), which states: 'No Member State shall apply its national legislation on competition to any concentration that has a [Union] dimension.' However, Art. 21 equally recognises an exception to this rule in Art. 21(4) which will be discussed below.

> The creation of a *joint venture* performing on a lasting basis all the functions of an autonomous economic entity shall constitute a concentration within the meaning of paragraph 1 (b).[273]

The provision here distinguishes between three types of 'mergers' broadly conceived: mergers, acquisitions and (certain) joint ventures (see Figure 17.6).

The EUMR thereby first and foremost captures 'legal' mergers, that is: a fusion of previously independent undertakings into one undertaking.[274] However, it also captures – second – 'takeovers' in the form of 'acquisitions' of control. In this scenario, one undertaking does not formally merge with another but acquires substantive control over it.[275] The idea of 'control' is here broadly defined:

> Control shall be constituted by rights, contracts or any other means which, either *separately or in combination* and having regard to the *considerations of fact or law* involved, confer the *possibility of exercising decisive influence* on an undertaking, in particular by:
> (a) ownership or the right to use all or part of the assets of an undertaking;
> (b) rights or contracts which confer decisive influence on the composition, voting or decisions of the organs of an undertaking.[276]

This definition covers *sole* or *joint* control by another undertaking(s) or persons(s);[277] and the acquisition of such control may result from a change of assets or government of the undertaking. The crucial criterion for a finding of control

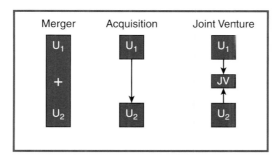

Figure 17.6 EUMR – Three Forms of Concentrations

---

[273] *Ibid.*, Art. 3(1) and (4).

[274] Famous examples of (legal) mergers are the merger of Ernst & Whinney and Young & Co. in 1989 to form Ernst & Young, and the merger between Glaxo Welcome and SmithKline Beecham to from GlaxoSmithKline in 2000.

[275] Famous illustrations here are the acquisition of Mannesmann by Vodaphone (following a hostile takeover bid); and see also the *British American Tobacco* case discussed above.

[276] EUMR, Art. 3(2) (emphasis added).

[277] On the concept of control, see M. Broberg, 'The Concept of Control in the Merger Control Regulation' (2004) 25 ECLR 741.

is the *possibility* of exercising *decisive* influence over an undertaking. Decisive influence means the power to determine the strategic behaviour of the undertaking.[278] Yet by insisting on the mere possibility of such decisive influence, it is 'not necessary to show that the decisive influence is or will be actually exercised'.[279] Decisive influence may stem from *legal* or *factual* power. A minority shareholder, while not legally entitled to control a company, may still be in factual control of its management;[280] yet the General Court has found that the mere acquisition of a minority share within a company will not fall within the EUMR.[281]

Third, and finally, the Merger Regulation also applies to 'joint ventures'. In light of its purpose, the EUMR however here clarifies that it only extends to those joint ventures that perform 'on a lasting basis all the functions of an autonomous economic entity': so-called 'full-function joint ventures'. (All other forms of horizontal cooperation may however be subject to Article 101.)[282]

When will mergers (in a broad sense of the term) have a Union dimension? The Regulation defines this jurisdictional criterion in Article 1 as follows:

> A concentration has a [Union] dimension where:
> (a) the combined aggregate worldwide turnover of all the undertakings concerned is more than EUR 5 000 million; and
> (b) the aggregate [Union]-wide turnover of each of at least two of the undertakings concerned is more than EUR 250 million,
> unless each of the undertakings concerned achieves more than two-thirds of its aggregate [Union]-wide turnover within one and the same Member State.[283]

The application of the EUMR is here made conditional on the aggregate turnover of the undertakings involved. The absolute criterion of turnover was preferred over the relative criterion of market shares, since the former promises a brighter jurisdictional boundary than the latter.[284] The turnover thresholds themselves have been set very high – a legislative decision that limits Union control to the very 'biggest' mergers within Europe. (These high thresholds have however been lowered in the case of a merger that affects at least three Member

---

[278] Commission, 'Consolidated Jurisdictional Notice under Council Regulation 139/2004 on the Control of Concentrations between Undertakings' [2008] OJ C 95/1, para. 18.

[279] *Ibid.*, para. 16.

[280] For an analysis of this point, see V. Rose and D. Bailey, *Bellamy & Child: European Union Law of Competition* (Oxford University Press, 2013), 529ff.

[281] Case T-411/07 *Aer Linhus* v. *Commission*, [2010] ECR II-3691, esp. para. 64.

[282] On the concept of 'joint venture' in general, see section 2(c) above.

[283] EUMR, Art. 1(2).

[284] On the calculation of turnover, see *ibid.*, Art. 5. This calculation may still be devilishly complex – especially in groups; see 'Consolidated Jurisdictional Notice' (n. 278 above), paras. 157–218.

States.)[285] The Member States have nevertheless insisted on retaining their powers where the 'two-thirds rule' applies, that is: where more than two-thirds of the aggregate turnover is effected within one Member State.

bb. Substantive Compatibility: Dominance and SIEC Tests

Once a merger falls within the jurisdictional scope of the EUMR, the Union will need to 'appraise' whether the merger is substantively compatible with the internal market. This appraisal will involve a whole range of factors;[286] yet, the EUMR has generally subjected mergers to a compatibility test. This test has changed over time. While the (old) 1989 Merger Regulation focused on 'dominance', the (new) 2004 Merger Regulation concentrates on whether the merger 'significantly impedes effective competition'.

The *old* Merger Regulation had determined the compatibility of a merger with the internal market as follows:

> A concentration which *creates or strengthens a dominate position* as a result of which effective competition would be significantly impeded in the [internal] market or in a substantial part of it shall be declared incompatible with the [internal] market.[287]

The provision identified two things for a merger to be prohibited. First, the merger would create or strengthen a dominant position (dominance test); and, second, that dominant position would significantly impede effective competition (SIEC test). The 1989 EUMR thus insisted – like the Court in *Continental*

---

[285] EUMR, Art. 1(3) states: 'A concentration that does not meet the thresholds laid down in paragraph 2 has a [Union] dimension where: (a) the combined aggregate worldwide turnover of all the undertakings concerned is more than EUR 2 500 million; (b) in each of at least three Member States, the combined aggregate turnover of all the undertakings concerned is more than EUR 100 million; (c) in each of at least three Member States included for the purpose of point (b), the aggregate turnover of each of at least two of the undertakings concerned is more than EUR 25 million; and (d) the aggregate [Union]-wide turnover of each of at least two of the undertakings concerned is more than EUR 100 million; unless each of the undertakings concerned achieves more than two-thirds of its aggregate [Union]-wide turnover within one and the same Member State.'

[286] EUMR, Art. 2. The provision details the factors that the Commission must take into account: 'In making this appraisal, the Commission shall take into account: (a) the need to maintain and develop effective competition within the common market in view of, among other things, the structure of all the markets concerned and the actual or potential competition from undertakings located either within or out with the [Union]; (b) the market position of the undertakings concerned and their economic and financial power, the alternatives available to suppliers and users, their access to supplies or markets, any legal or other barriers to entry, supply and demand trends for the relevant goods and services, the interests of the intermediate and ultimate consumers, and the development of technical and economic progress provided that it is to consumers' advantage and does not form an obstacle to competition.'

[287] Regulation 4046/89, Art. 2(3).

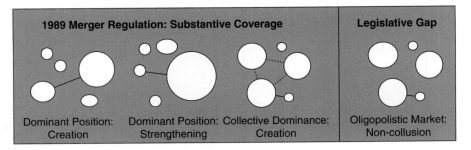

Figure 17.7 Scope of the 1989 Merger Regulation

Can – on the presence of a dominant position; yet unlike *Continental Can*, it not only captured the strengthening of a dominant position but also extended to the *creation* of such a dominant position. And while subsequent jurisprudence clarified that the Regulation also covered situations of collective dominance,[288] the dominance test under the 1989 EUMR nevertheless seemed incapable of applying to oligopolistic situations that could not be classified as collective dominance. For example: if the second and the third biggest undertaking within an oligopolistic market were to merge without gaining dominance, this situation could not – despite a significant impeding effect on the competitive structure of the market – fall within the scope of the old Merger Regulation (see Figure 17.7).

It was this legislative gap that led to a radical reform of the compatibility test in the 2004 Merger Regulation. This new test now states as follows:

> A concentration which would significantly impede effective competition, in the common market or in a substantial part of it, in particular as a result of the creation or strengthening of a dominant position, shall be declared incompatible with the common market.[289]

This new formulation liberates the SIEC test from the dominance test. The existence of a dominant position is here no longer a *precondition* for the prohibition of a merger. The new Merger Regulation thus broadens the compatibility test to the control of mergers that create oligopolistic situations in which no collective dominance can be shown (see Figure 17.8).[290]

---

[288] See Joined Cases C-68/94 and C-30/95, *France and others* v. *Commission* [1998] ECR I-1375, esp. para. 178: '[C]ollective dominant positions do not fall outside the scope of the Regulation[.]' The Court has however subjected a finding of collective dominance to a heavy burden of proof that requires the fulfilment of three conditions; see Case T-342/99, *Airtours* v. *Commission* [2002] ECR II-2585, esp. para. 62.

[289] EUMR, Art. 2(3).

[290] *Ibid.*, recital 25: 'In view of the consequences that concentrations in oligopolistic market structures may have, it is all the more necessary to maintain effective competition in such markets. Many oligopolistic markets exhibit a healthy degree of competition. However, under certain circumstances, concentrations involving the elimination of important competitive constraints that the merging parties had exerted upon each other, as well as a reduction of competitive pressure on the remaining competitors, may, even in the absence of a likelihood of coordination between the members of the oligopoly, result in a significant impediment to effective competition.'

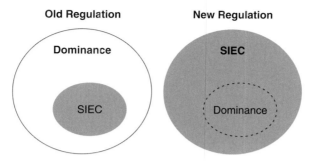

Figure 17.8 Merger Tests: Old and New

The *widened* scope of the 2004 Regulation has made EU merger control more flexible and has also granted the Commission a wider discretion to scrutinise the economic effects of mergers.[291] The Commission's administrative discretion has nonetheless been structured by a number of informal Commission Guidelines. The Commission has indeed extensively explained its appraisal methodology for horizontal and non-horizontal mergers, respectively.[292] Following the lead of the US authorities, it will here start by analysing the market shares of the undertakings concerned and the concentration level of the market.[293] And where an in-depth analysis is required, it will then take a whole range of economic factors into account; but in making its individual assessment, it indeed enjoys a wide margin of discretion.

However, the Court has in the past demonstrated – especially in the *annus terribilus* of 2002 – that it will strike down Commission appraisals where the Union executive did not convincingly prove that the merger violated the EUMR.[294]

cc. Merger Defences: Objective Justifications?

A merger between undertakings will typically be designed to achieve economies of scale and scope. Can these efficiency gains constitute a 'defence' or 'justification' for an otherwise illegal merger?

The EUMR is silent on this point; yet its Article 2 ambivalently requires the Commission, when making its appraisal, to take into account 'the interests of

---

[291] J. Schmidt, 'The New ECMR: "Significant Impediment" or "Significant Improvement"?' (2004) 41 *CML Rev.* 1555 at 1564.

[292] Commission, 'Guidelines on the Assessment of Horizontal Mergers under the Council Regulation on the Control of Concentrations between Undertakings' [2004] OJ C 31/5; Commission, 'Guidelines on the Assessment of Non-horizontal Mergers under the Council Regulation on the Control of Concentrations between Undertakings' [2008] OJ 265/6.

[293] E.g. 'Guidelines on the Assessment of Horizontal Mergers' (n. 292 above), para. 14.

[294] In 2002, the General Court annulled three major Commission decisions on mergers, including T-342/99, *Airtours* v. *Commission*. On the burden of proof in merger cases generally, see R. Bailey, 'Standard of Proof in EC Merger Proceedings: A Common Law Perspective' (2003) 40 *CML Rev.* 84.

the intermediate and ultimate consumers, and the development of technical and economic progress provided that it is to consumers' advantage and does not form an obstacle to competition'.[295] The Horizontal Merger Guidelines are slightly more explicit and expressly refer to an 'Efficiency Defence' in the following way:

> The Commission considers any substantiated efficiency claim *in the overall assessment of the merger*. It may decide that, as a consequence of the efficiencies that the merger brings about, *there are no grounds for declaring the merger incompatible with the common market pursuant to Article 2(3) of the Merger Regulation*. This will be the case when the Commission is in a position to conclude on the basis of sufficient evidence that the efficiencies generated by the merger are likely to enhance the ability and incentive of the merged entity to act pro-competitively for the benefit of consumers, thereby counteracting the adverse effects on competition which the merger might otherwise have.[296]

The Commission here appears to acknowledge efficiency gains as an objective justification. These gains will be taken into account in the overall assessment of the merger. Importantly however, the Commission insists that the consumer benefits must be 'substantial', 'merger specific' and 'verifiable'.[297] The General Court has confirmed these conditions in *Ryanair v. Commission*, in which the Court offered an extensive interpretation of the efficiency defence.[298]

The Guidelines also acknowledge a second defence: the 'failing firm' defence.[299] This situation covers 'rescue mergers'. Rescue mergers are mergers where one undertaking merges with another that is failing in the market. The defence is defined as follows:

> The Commission may decide that an otherwise problematic merger is nevertheless compatible with the common market if one of the merging parties is a failing firm. The basic requirement is that the deterioration of the competitive structure that follows the merger *cannot be said to be caused by the merger*. This will arise where the competitive structure of the market would deteriorate to at least the same extent in

---

[295] EUMR, Art. 2(1)(b).

[296] Horizontal Guidelines (n. 128 above), para. 77 (emphasis added). On the efficiency defence under the EUMR, see D. Gerard, 'Merger Control Policy: How to Give Meaningful Consideration to Efficiency Claims' (2006) 40 *CLM Rev* 1367; H. Iversen, 'The Efficiency Defence in EC Merger Control' (2010) 31 ECLR 370.

[297] Horizontal Guidelines (n. 128 above), paras. 79–86.

[298] Case T-342/07, *Ryanair v. Commission*, [2010] II-3457, paras. 386–443. For a recent analysis of the efficiency defence, see P. Kuoppamäki and S. Torstila, 'Is There a Future for an Efficiency Defence in EU Merger Control?' (2016) 41 *EL Rev.* 687.

[299] For academic discussions, see G. Monti and E. Rousseva, 'Failing Firms in the Framework of the EC Merger Regulation' (1999) 24 *EL Rev.* 38; I. Kokkoris, 'Failing Firm Defence in the European Union: A Panacea for Mergers?' (2006) 27 ECLR 494.

the absence of the merger. *The Commission considers the following three criteria to be especially relevant for the application of a 'failing firm defence'. First, the allegedly failing firm would in the near future be forced out of the market because of financial difficulties if not taken over by another undertaking. Second, there is no less anti-competitive alternative purchase than the notified merger. Third, in the absence of a merger, the assets of the failing firm would inevitably exit the market.*[300]

The Commission, as well as the Court,[301] have thereby approached the 'failing firm' defence through the question of causality. A merger will not fulfil the SIEC test, where the change in the market structure would have come about even in the absence of the merger. Such a 'rescue' merger would consequently be objectively justified under the EUMR.

dd. National Derogations: Public Policy Justifications

Can a merger that has been cleared by the Union still be prohibited by a Member State? While the Member States are generally excluded from assessing mergers with a Union dimension, the EUMR indeed recognises this possibility in Article 21. The fourth paragraph of this provision here states:

Member States may take appropriate measures to protect legitimate interests other than those taken into consideration by this Regulation and compatible with the general principles and other provisions of [Union] law. *Public security, plurality of the media and prudential rules shall be regarded as legitimate interests* … Any other public interest must be communicated to the Commission by the Member State concerned and shall be recognised by the Commission after an assessment of its compatibility

---

[300]   Horizontal Guidelines (n. 128 above), paras. 89–90 (emphasis added).

[301]   Cases C-68/94 and C-30/95, *France and others* v. *Commission*, esp. paras. 112–14: 'It must be observed, first of all, that the fact that the conditions set by the Commission for concluding that there was no causal link between the concentration and the deterioration of the competitive structure do not entirely coincide with the conditions applied in connection with the United States "failing company defence" is not in itself a ground of invalidity of the contested decision. Solely the fact that the conditions set by the Commission were not capable of excluding the possibility that a concentration might be the cause of the deterioration in the competitive structure of the market could constitute a ground of invalidity of the decision. In the present case, the French Government disputes the relevance of the criterion that it must be verified that the acquiring undertaking would in any event obtain the acquired undertaking's share of the market if the latter were to be forced out of the market. However, in the absence of that criterion, a concentration could, provided the other criteria were satisfied, be considered as not being the cause of the deterioration of the competitive structure of the market even though it appeared that, in the event of the concentration not proceeding, the acquiring undertaking would not gain the entire market share of the acquired undertaking. Thus, it would be possible to deny the existence of a causal link between the concentration and the deterioration of the competitive structure of the market even though the competitive structure of the market would deteriorate to a lesser extent if the concentration did not proceed.'

with the general principles and other provisions of [Union] law before the measures referred to above may be taken. The Commission shall inform the Member State concerned of its decision within 25 working days of that communication.[302]

The provision allows Member States to object to a merger within their territory in order to protect legitimate interests not taken into account in the Regulation. These national objections may relate to one of the public policy concerns expressly mentioned in Article 21 or to any other public interest that the Commission considers worthy of protection.[303] However, it goes without saying that the last word rests with the European Court of Justice. It is for the Court to ultimately rule on the proportionality of the national interest invoked.[304]

Conclusion

EU competition law has traditionally been embedded within the Union's internal market. The Union is here entitled to 'regulate' and 'police' the internal market to ensure undistorted competition. The two sections within the EU Treaties' competition chapter thereby correspond to the two principal forms of market interference. Section 1 regulates private undertakings, whereas section 2 establishes a Union regime governing State aid. This chapter looked at the various rules that police private undertakings; and three legal pillars of EU competition law were here identified: Article 101, Article 102 and the EU Merger Regulation.

Article 101 prohibits anticompetitive collusions between undertakings that distort competition within the internal market. We saw above that the Union has given a wide jurisdictional scope to the EU competition rules: any agreement that directly or indirectly, actually or potentially affects the patters of trade between Member States will be caught – although the Court has generally insisted on a *de minimis* threshold. Once an agreement falls within the jurisdictional scope of European Union law, its pro- and anticompetitive elements will be analysed. The Court here splits its analysis into two parts: it will analyse an agreement's anticompetitive effects within Article 101(1), while exploring its pro-competitive effects under Article 101(3). Due to the Union's historic task of creating an internal market, vertical agreements have been of particular importance to the Union; and distribution agreements indeed continue to occupy a prominent place within the case law of the Courts.

Article 102 reviews the unilateral behaviour of dominant undertakings. Importantly, the provision does not outlaw dominance *per se* but only the *abuse*

---

[302] EUMR, Art. 21(4) (emphasis added). For an analysis of the provision, see D. Gerard, 'Protectionist Threats against Cross-border Mergers: Unexplored Avenues to Strengthen the Effectiveness of Article 21 ECMR' (2008) 45 *CML Rev.* 987.

[303] For an application of Art. 21(4) EUMR, see Case M.567, *Lyonnaise des Eaux/Northumbrian Water* [1996] OJ C 11/3.

[304] See Case C-42/01, *Portugal v. Commission* [2004] ECR I-6079.

of market dominance. The idea that a dominant undertaking is subject to special rules and responsibilities results from their dominating the market. Various forms of abuse were analysed in section 3 of this chapter.

By contrast, section 4 explored the Union's legislative response to market structures being 'distorted' by market dominance. The EU Merger Regulation here aims to control 'concentrations' that might 'significantly impede effective competition' within the internal market. Importantly, the Union's merger policy is a 'structural' policy: it aims not to *punish* illegal market behaviour but rather tries to *prevent* the creation of market structures facilitating such illegal behaviour.

What about the EU competition rules applying to the State? With the rise of 'mixed economies', modern States have become major players within their national markets. States may thereby interfere with market forces in a number of ways.[305] The EU Treaties expressly address two types of such state interferences. In Article 106 we find a first – casual – reference to public undertakings (and undertakings endowed with public functions). The entire Section 2 of the

Table 17.4 Chapter 17B: Summary Contents

Introduction
1. Public Undertakings and Public Services
a. Public Undertakings (and Undertakings with Special Rights)
b. Services of General Economic Interest
2. State Aid I: Jurisdictional Aspects
a. The Concept of 'State Aid'
b. Selectivity of the Aid
3. State Aid II: Substantive Aspects
a. Automatic Justifications: Article 107(2)
b. Discretionary Justifications: Article 107(3)
c. In Particular: Regional Aid
4. Enforcing EU Competition Law
a. Enforcement through the States: Articles 101 and 102
b. Enforcement against the States: State Aid
Conclusion
Further Reading

---

[305]   For an excellent general analysis of the various ways in which a State could interfere with the competition rules, see T. Prosser, *The Limits of Competition Law: Markets and Public Services* (Oxford University Press, 2005); E. Szyszczak, *The Regulation of the State in Competitive Markets in the EU* (Hart, 2007); W. Sauter and H. Schepel, *State and Market in European Union Law* (Cambridge University Press, 2009).

competition chapter is however dedicated to a second type of market interference: State aid. State aid is financial assistance paid out of State resources that assist specific undertakings to fight the forces of competition. These 'public' interferences into the internal market are discussed in my (online) Chapter 17B, whose contents can be seen in Table 17.4.

FURTHER READING

Books

P. Akman, *The Concept of Abuse in EU Competition Law* (Hart, 2012)

G. Amato, *Antitrust and the Bounds of Power: The Dilemma of Liberal Democracy in the History of the Market* (Hart, 1997)

J. Cook and C. Kerse, *EC Merger Control* (Sweet & Maxwell, 2009)

A. Ezrachi, *EU Competition Law: An Analytical Guide to the Leading Cases* (Oxford University Press, 2016)

J. Goyder, *EU Distribution Law* (Hart, 2011)

A. Jones and B. Sufrin, *EU Competition Law: Text, Cases and Materials* (Oxford University Press, 2016)

R. Nazzini, *The Foundations of European Union Competition Law: The Objective and Principles of Article 102* (Oxford University Press, 2011)

O. Odudu, *The Boundaries of EC Competition Law: The Scope of Article 81* (Oxford University Press, 2006)

V. Rose and D. Bailey (eds.), *Bellamy & Child: European Union Law of Competition* (Oxford University Press, 2013)

E. Rousseva, *Rethinking Exclusionary Abuses in EU Competition Law* (Hart, 2010)

R. Wish and D. Bailey, *Competition Law* (Oxford University Press, 2015)

Articles (and Chapters)

A. Albors-Llorens, 'The Role of Objective Justification and Efficiencies in the Application of Article 82 EC' (2007) 44 *CML Rev.* 1727

J. Faull, 'Effect on Trade between Member States' (1999) 26 *Fordham Corporate Law Institute* 481

D. Gerard, 'Merger Control Policy: How to Give Meaningful Consideration to Efficiency Claims' (2006) 40 *CML Rev.* 1367

B. Hawk, 'System Failure: Vertical Restraints and EC Competition Law' (1995) 32 *CML Rev.* 973

P. Ibáñez Colomo, 'Exclusionary Discrimination under Article 102 TFEU' (2014) 51 *CML Rev.* 141

A. Jones, 'Woodpulp: Concerted Practice and/or Conscious Parallelism' (1993) 6 ECLR 264

I. Lianos, 'Collusion in Vertical Relations under Article 81 EC' (2008) 45 *CML Rev.* 1027

G. Monti, 'The Scope of Collective Dominance under Article 82 EC' (2001) 38 *CML Rev.* 131

O. Odudu and D. Bailey, 'The Single Economic Entity Doctrine in EU Competition Law' (2014) 51 *CML Rev.* 1721

J. Schmidt, 'The New ECMR: "Significant Impediment" or "Significant Improvement"?' (2004) 41 *CML Rev.* 1555

A. Weitbrecht, 'From Freiburg to Chicago and Beyond: The First 50 Years of European Competition Law' (2008) 29 ECLR 81

R. Wish and D. Bailey, 'Regulation 330/2010: The Commission's New Block Exemption for Vertical Agreements' (2010) 47 *CML Rev.* 1757

R. Wish and B. Sufrin, 'Article 85 and the Rule of Reason' (1987) 7 *YEL* 1

A. Witt, 'From *Airtours* to *Ryanair*: Is the More Economic Approach to EU Merger Law Really about More Economics?' (2012) 49 *CML Rev.* 217

Cases on the Website

Joined Cases 56 and 58/64, *Consten and Grundig*; Case 56/65, *Société Technique Minière*; Case 6/72, *Continental Can*; Joined Cases 6–7/73, *Commercial Solvents*; Case 15/74, *Centrafarm*; Case 26/76, *Metro v. Saba*; Case 85/76, *Hoffman-La Roche*; Case 322/81, *Michelin I*; Joined Cases 25–6/84, *Ford v. Commission*; Case 42/84, *Remia and Nutricia*; Case 161/84, *Pronuptia*; Joined Cases 142 and 156/84, *British American Tobacco*; Case 62/86, *AKZO*; Joined Cases T-68 and 77–8/89, *Vetro v. Commission*; Case 234/89, *Delimitis*; Case C-41/90, *Hofner and Elser*; Case T-83/91, *Tetra Pak II*; Joined Cases C-159–60/91, *Poucet and Pistre*; Joined Cases C-241–2/91P, *Magill*; Case C-333/94P, *Tetra Pak*; Case T-41/96, *Bayer v. Commission*; Joined Cases C-395–6/96P, *CEWAL*; Case C-7/97, *Bronner*; Case T-112/99, *Metropole Television*; Case T-203/01 *Michelin II*; Case T-193/02, *Piau*; Case C-95/04P, *British Airways*; Case T-201/04, *Microsoft*; Case T-342/07, *Ryanair*; Case C-209/10, *Post Danmark*

18

Internal Policies
An Overview

Contents

Introduction

The European Union began its life as a purely *economic* union. When born in 1958, its principle task was to 'establish … a common market and progressively approximate … the *economic* policies of Member States'.[1] The creation of the common market thereby included, in particular, the establishment of 'a system ensuring that competition in the common market is not distorted'.[2] Yet outside the few additional economic areas covered by the 1958 Rome Treaty, the Union seemed powerless.

This picture began to change in 1972, when the Member States decided to expand the spectrum of positive Union policies. This expansion was originally based on the Union's general competences: Articles 115 and 352; and on the bases of both provisions, several 'flanking policies' gradually developed. (These policies were so called because they were said to only 'flank' the establishment of the internal market.) Starting with the Single European Act, the Union was indeed given ever more specific competences in ever-wider fields. These express competences can today be found in Part III of the TFEU entitled 'Internal Policies and Internal Actions' (see Table 18.1).

No textbook can – of course – provide a meaningful overview of all 24 internal Union policies. Yet what a textbook should do is to offer a compass through the substantive law of the Union. For not only are most cases discussed in this book – even the most 'constitutional' ones – embedded in a substantive policy area, the great majority of Union legislation deals with a specific 'policy', and that policy provides the substance with which European citizens – buyers, employees and consumers – primarily come into contact.

Five of the 24 internal Union policies have already been discussed in the previous chapters: the four fundamental freedoms (Titles I–IV) were discussed in Chapters 13–16, while European competition policy (Title VII) was discussed in Chapter 17. This chapter wishes to add a – brief – overview of four policy areas that have come to also significantly affect the lives of European citizens. Section 1 provides an introduction to the Union's Economic and Monetary Policy. This policy is not only responsible for the creation of a common European currency – the euro – which has become a leading world currency; it recently provoked enormous controversy over the powers of the European Union to interfere with national economic choices. Section 2 moves to 'Social Policy'. This is an important internal policy for a continent that prides itself as being the 'social continent'.[3] Section 3 then explores the Treaty Title on 'Consumer Protection', which has had an enormous impact on national contract laws. Section 4 looks – finally – at the Union's regional or cohesion policy.

---

[1] Ex-Art. 2 EEC.

[2] *Ibid.*, Ex-Art. 3(f). From the very beginning, the Union was also charged to build 'a common policy in the sphere of transport' (see ex-Art. 3(e)), and to create a 'European Social Fund in order to improve employment opportunities for workers' (see ex-Art. 3(i)).

[3] A. Giddens et al. (eds.), *Global Europe, Social Europe* (Polity, 2006); F. Scharpf, 'The European Social Model' (2002) 40 *Journal of Common Market Studies* 645.

Table 18.1 Internal Policies – Overview

Part III TFEU – Union Policies and Internal Actions			
Title I	The Internal Market	Title XIII	Culture
Title II	Free Movement of Goods	Title XIV	Public Health
Title III	Agriculture and Fisheries	Title XV	Consumer Protection
Title IV	Free Movement of Persons, Services and Capital	Title XVI	Trans-European Networks
Title V	Area of Freedom, Security and Justice	Title XVII	Industry
Title VI	Transport	Title XVIII	Economic, Social and Territorial Cohesion
Title VII	Competition, Taxation and Approximation of Laws	Title XIX	Research and Technological Development and Space
Title VIII	Economic and Monetary Policy	Title XX	Environment
Title IX	Employment	Title XXI	Energy
Title X	Social Policy	Title XXII	Tourism
Title XI	The European Social Fund	Title XXIII	Civil Protection
Title XII	Education, Vocational Training, Youth and Sport	Title XXIV	Administrative Cooperation

With €325 billion at its disposal, this policy represents one-third of the Union budget and is tremendously important in creating a Europe that recognises its 'regions' as a third level of government below the Member States.

1. Economic and Monetary Policy

The integration of national markets into a 'common' market reaches a new stage in a monetary union. Within a monetary union, the various State currencies are replaced by a single Union currency.[4] Monetary integration here goes well beyond the free movement of capital: for not only can a national currency be freely converted into another currency, the abolition of national currencies removes the very possibility of national governments to influence the strength of their respective currencies. Fluctuations in exchange rates between various currencies are impossible, and the price of a French product can now be directly compared to that of a German product.

---

[4] One of the tasks of the 1787 US Constitution had been to centralise the power to issue legal tender by conferring it to the federal Union. Art. I – Section 8 grants Congress the power 'to coin Money, regulate the Value thereof, and of foreign Coin', while Section 10 adds that '[n]o State shall … coin Money; emit Bills of Credit; make any Thing but gold and silver Coin a Tender in Payment of Debts'.

When the European Union was born. monetary union seemed as utopian as unnecessary. The international stability of the money market was still regulated by the Bretton Woods system and the creation of a European regime seemed superfluous.[5] This situation however dramatically changed with the decline of the Bretton Woods regime in the late 1960s. The demise of that international system indeed triggered a variety of European – intergovernmental – responses. The possibility of economic and monetary union was therefore seriously explored in the 1970 Werner Report.[6] The report called for the realisation of monetary union 'to ensure growth and stability within the [Union] and reinforce the contribution it can make to an economic and monetary equilibrium in the world and make it a pillar of stability'.[7] Disagreement however existed on how to achieve this aim: should economic union precede monetary union; or should monetary union precede and precipitate economic union?[8] The dispute was never resolved; but a compromise would – after years of debate and delay – lead to the establishment of the European Monetary System in 1979.[9]

The decisive move towards a – supranational – monetary union would however only start with the 1992 Maastricht Treaty. The move towards monetary union 'constituted the most important development in European integration since the Treaty of Rome'.[10] The Maastricht TEU envisaged the creation of a single European currency in three stages; and it thereby tied the creation of such a *monetary* union to the *economic* convergence of the Member States. The insistence on a constitutional connection between economic and monetary union represented a (nominal) victory of the 'economist school' over the 'monetarist school'. For the 'economists' had successfully pleaded that a functioning monetary union required a degree of (macro)economic unity. This view made enormous sense; yet, as we shall see below, not only had the need for an economic nexus been severely undervalued, it also meant that for the first time in its history, the Union was forced to adopt a 'differential' approach to European integration. For only those Member States that fulfilled certain economic 'convergence criteria' could become 'euro-States'.

---

[5] The 'Bretton Woods' system is the name given to the financial rules established at the Bretton Woods (New Hampshire, USA) Conference, where the major industrial nations of the world decided to set up a system of fixed exchange rates. The static exchange rates were designed to provide stability to the international financial system. Against this background, a European monetary system seemed superfluous (see H. Ungerer, *A Concise History of European Monetary Integration* (Quorum Books, 1997), 46).

[6] For the 'Werner Report', see A. G. Harryvan and J. van der Harst (eds.), *Documents on European Union* (St Martin's Press, 1997), 169.

[7] *Ibid.*, 170.

[8] The former option was advocated by Germany and is known as the 'coronation theory', and its advocates were referred to as the 'economists'. The second option was argued by France and is known as the 'locomotive theory', and its advocates were known as the 'monetarists'.

[9] For a historical overview of this phase, see H. James, *Making the European Monetary Union* (Harvard University Press, 2012), chs. 3–5.

[10] M. Chang, *Economic and Monetary Union* (Palgrave, 2016), 16.

We find the constitutional regime governing 'Economic and Monetary Policy' today in Title VIII of the Treaty on the Functioning of the European Union (Table 18.2). It is divided into a number of chapters. Chapter 1 deals with economic policy and provides the Union with a – weak – 'coordinating competence' in macroeconomic matters. Chapter 2 deals with monetary policy, and the Union is here granted a – strong – exclusive competence whose exercise lies in general with the European Central Bank (ECB). Chapters 3–5 deal with institutional aspects within this policy area, including those that result from the constitutional choice for differential integration. All chapters are complemented by various Protocols, and much of the primary law has been extensively elaborated and concretised in secondary Union law.

This section cannot do justice to the complexity and technicality of the law within this policy area and will therefore concentrate on four aspects of the EMU regime. Section (a) will start by looking at the general Union powers over economic policy. Section (b) looks at the differential integration approach, and the distinction between 'euro-States' and non-participating States within this area. Sections (c) and (d) will finally explore the two core functions for EU monetary policy strictly speaking. The 'primary' function of the ECB here is to guarantee price stability; a task that is complemented by its 'secondary' function of ensuring the stability of the financial system within the European Union.

a. Economic Policy: Coordinating the Member States

Monetary union cannot survive economic disunion.[11] It is for that reason that the EU Treaties have joined *economic* integration and *monetary* integration together. However, the two branches within EMU are an extremely unequal couple: while the Union enjoys an exclusive competence for monetary policy,[12] it is confined to a 'coordinating competence' for economic policy.[13] Economic policy here means macroeconomic policy, that is: that branch of economics that deals with the 'big' economic factors within the economy as a whole. Macroeconomic choices here include fiscal choices, such as the level of taxation and public spending.

The Union competence(s) with regard to economic policy can be found in Chapter 1 of the EMU Title. The Member States are here asked in Article 120 to 'conduct their economic policies with a view to contributing to the achievement of the objectives of the Union'; and to assist the Member States in this task, the Union is entitled to adopt 'broad guidelines' for the Member

---

[11] A. Hinarejos, 'Fiscal Federalism in the European Union: Evolution and Future Choices for EMU' (2013) 50 *CML Rev.* 1621.

[12] Art. 3(1) TFEU states: 'The Union shall have exclusive competence in monetary policy for the Member States whose currency is the euro'.

[13] *Ibid.*, Art. 5(1) states: 'The Member States shall coordinate their economic policies within the Union. To this end, the Council shall adopt measures, in particular broad guidelines for these policies. Specific provisions shall apply to those Member States whose currency is the euro.'

Table 18.2 Treaty Title on EMU – Overview

Title VIII: Economic & Monetary Policy			
Article 119: EMU – General Aims			
Chapter 1 – Economic Policy		**Chapter 3 – Institutional Provisions**	
Article 120	Member State Duties	Article 134	Economic and Financial Committee
Article 121	Broad Economic Guidelines	Article 135	Commission Proposals
Article 122	Financial Assistance in Emergencies		
Article 123	Prohibition of ECB Credit or Refinancing	**Chapter 4 – Euro Member States**	
Article 124	Prohibition of Privileged Access	Article 136	Legal Basis for Economic Measures
Article 125	Prohibition of Liability Assumption	Article 137	Euro-group (and its Protocol)
Article 126	Excessive Government Deficit	Article 138	Common Positions within IOs
Chapter 2 – Monetary Policy		**Chapter 5 – Transitional Provisions**	
Article 127	Objectives/Powers of the ESCB	Article 139	Member States with a Derogation
Article 128	ECB Power to Issue Euro	Article 140	Admission Procedure and Criteria
Article 129	ESCB Structure	Article 141	ECB General Council
Article 130	E(S)CB Independence	Article 142	Exchange Rate Policies
Article 131	Amendment of National Legislation	Article 143	Balance of Payments Difficulties
Article 132	Normative Instruments	Article 144	National Emergency Measures
Article 133	Legislative Competence		
Protocols:			
Protocol No. 12 on the Excessive Deficit Procedure; Protocol No. 13 on the Convergence Criteria; Protocol No. 14 on the Euro Group; Protocol No. 15 on the United Kingdom; Protocol No. 16 on Denmark			

States under Article 121.[14] Cast in the form of *recommendations*, these guidelines form part of the Union's soft law; yet, with the adoption of and refinement of the Union's 'Stability and Growth' Pact, harder limits on the economic and fiscal powers of the Member States have gradually emerged (see section (aa) below). From the very beginning, Chapter 1 also contained a financial assistance clause in Article 122 '[w]here a Member State is in difficulties or is seriously threatened with severe difficulties'. This assistance seemed however limited to temporary assistance; yet as a result of the financial crisis starting in 2008 – and despite the wording of the Treaties – the Union has developed permanent financial assistance mechanisms for Member States undergoing economic difficulties (see section (bb) below).

aa. The Stability and Growth Pact and Beyond

The Stability and Growth Pact (SGP) is not an international 'pact' but refers to a resolution of the European Council.[15] It was designed to 'safeguard … sound government finances as a means to strengthening the conditions for price stability'. To that effect it envisaged the adoption of two Council Regulations: one on 'the strengthening of the surveillance of budgetary positions' and another on 'the implementation of the excessive deficit procedure'. The two regulations were subsequently adopted and have ever since been known as the 'preventive arm' and the 'corrective arm' of the Stability and Growth Pact.[16]

The 'preventive arm' has set up a legislative regime for a 'multilateral surveillance procedure' set out in Article 121 TFEU.[17] Regulation 1466/97 here establishes detailed rules 'so as to prevent, at an early stage, the occurrence of excessive general government deficits and to promote the surveillance and coordination of economic policies'.[18] The Regulation tries to achieve this by requiring Member States to define a 'medium-term objective' for its budgetary position every three years,[19] and to establish a 'stability programme' (euro-States) or 'convergence programme' (non-euro-States) that 'provides an essential basis for the sustainability of public finances which is conducive to price stability, strong sustainable growth and employment creation'.[20] These programmes are to be evaluated by the Union institutions in order to 'assess whether the economic assumptions on which the programme is based are plausible' and whether the measures being taken or proposed 'are sufficient to achieve the medium-term budgetary objective over the cycle'.[21]

---

[14] *Ibid.*, Art. 121(2).

[15] See Resolution of the European Council on the Stability and Growth Pact [1997] OJ C 236/1.

[16] The two regulations were amended and reformed in 2005 and 2011. For an overview of the 2005 reform, see J. V. Louis, 'The Review of the Stability and Growth Pact' (2006) 43 *CML Rev.* 85. For the 2011 reform, see R. M. Lastra and J.-V. Louis, 'European Economic and Monetary Union: History, Trends, and Prospects?' (2013) 32 YEL 57.

[17] The legal basis for this can be found in Art. 121(6) TFEU.

[18] Regulation 1466/97, Art. 1.   [19] *Ibid.*, Art. 2(a).

[20] *Ibid.*, Arts. 3(1) and 7(1) respectively.   [21] *Ibid.*, Arts. 5 and 9 respectively.

The 'corrective arm' is shaped around Article 126. The provision ominously states: 'Member States shall avoid excessive government deficits.'[22] But how does the Union enforce this prohibition? The Treaties have defined an 'excessive deficit' by reference to two quantitative criteria that are set out in Protocol No. 12 On the Excessive Deficit Procedure. These two criteria are: an annual deficit below 3 per cent of gross domestic product (GDP) and a total debt below 60 per cent of GDP.[23] (To make this a little more concrete: a country with a GDP of 100 billion must not run an annual deficit by borrowing more than 3 billion a year, and it must not have more than 60 billion of total debt.) What happens if a State has been found to go beyond these deficit limits? The text of Article 126 appears to be all about words – and very little about action. Yet it contains in Article 126(14) a legal competence that allows the Union to adopt more specific rules and this has happened in the form of Regulation 1467/97 implementing the excessive deficit procedure. Much of the Regulation however continued to treat the Member States with velvet gloves.[24]

These soft EMU arrangements broke down in the aftermath of the 2008 financial crisis. For, while having started as a crisis within the (private) banking sector, the crisis quickly developed into a 'sovereign' debt crisis as the governments of the Member States 'bailed out' failing banks and thereby transformed their 'private' debts into 'public' debts. And with government deficits and debts rising to shocking heights, a serious rethinking of the EMU arrangements began. Found to be closer to a 'non-governance' than a governance regime,[25] the Union frantically started to reform the 'economic' branch of EMU. With the much-needed constitutional reform blocked by the United Kingdom,[26] the Union and the other Member States had to follow two alternative paths: one in the form of *Union legislation*, the other in the form of *international treaties*.

The pursuit of the first path led to the adoption of two major legislative reform packages called the 'Six-Pack' and the 'Two-Pack'. The former was adopted in 2011 and is a collection of six Union measures that aim to strengthen

---

[22] Art. 126(1) TFEU. The United Kingdom has negotiated a softer version in Protocol No. 15 On Certain Provisions Relating to the United Kingdom of Great Britain and Northern Ireland. Its Art. 5 states (emphasis added): 'The United Kingdom shall *endeavour* to avoid an excessive government deficit.'

[23] Protocol No. 12 On the Excessive Deficit Procedure, Art. 1.

[24] For the constitutional option to impose fines, see however Art. 126(11) TFEU: 'to impose fines of an appropriate size'. The sanction regime is treated in Arts. 7 and 11–16 of Regulation 1467/97. According to Art. 12, the fine will, as a minimum, comprise a component equal to 0.2 per cent of GDP.

[25] D. Adamski, 'National Power Games and Structural Failures in the European Macroeconomic Governance' (2012) 49 *CML Rev.* 1319 at 1361. The 'non-governance' quality is nowhere better illustrated than in the past refusal of the Council to adopt a recommendation against Germany and France for having failed to comply with the SGP. This non-action was challenged by the Commission; yet the Court also applied a light touch towards this 'political question' (Case C-27/04, *Commission* v. *Council* [2004] ECR I-6649).

[26] On the uncompromising economic 'nationalism' or, better, 'City' favouritism of the Cameron Conservative government, see Editorial (2012) 49 *CML Rev.* 1.

the 'preventive' and 'corrective' aspects of the SGP.[27] The latter was adopted in 2013 and consists of two further regulations that complement the Six-Pack procedures.[28] The most important and concrete result of these measures is the formal establishment of the 'European Semester' – an annual cycle of economic and fiscal policy coordination between the Union and the Member States.

These legislative reforms were complemented by a second reform strategy: the conclusion of international agreements between the Member States themselves (so called *inter se* agreements) to further strengthen their economic and fiscal coordination. The best expression of this second path is the conclusion of the Treaty on Stability, Coordination and Governance (the Fiscal Compact).[29] This is an international treaty concluded by 25 Member States 'to strengthen the economic pillar of the economic and monetary union by adopting a set of rules intended to foster budgetary discipline through a fiscal compact'.[30] The core provision within the Fiscal Compact is thereby Article 3. It requires the contracting parties to guarantee or enshrine in their national law – preferably constitutional law – the 'golden rule' of a balanced budget,[31] and it also includes an automatic correction mechanism ('debt brake').[32] To ensure the application

[27] The legislative package that attracted the most public attention is the so-called 'six-pack', see Regulation 1173/2011 on the effective enforcement of budgetary surveillance in the euro area [2011] OJ L 306/1; Regulation 1174/2011 on enforcement measures to correct excessive macroeconomic imbalances in the euro area [2011] OJ L 306/8; Regulation 1175/2011 amending Council Regulation 1466/97 on the strengthening of the surveillance of budgetary positions and the surveillance and coordination of economic policies [2011] OJ L 306/12; Regulation 1176/2011 on the prevention and correction of macroeconomic imbalances [2011] OJ L 306/25; Council Regulation 1177/2011 amending Regulation 1467/97 on speeding up and clarifying the implementation of the excessive deficit procedure [2011] OJ L 306/33; Council Directive 2011/85/EU on requirements for budgetary frameworks of the Member States [2011] OJ L 306/41.

[28] Regulation 472/2013 on the strengthening of economic and budgetary surveillance of member states in the euro area experiencing or threatened with serious difficulties with respect to their financial stability [2013] OJ L 140/1; Regulation No. 473/2013 on common provisions for monitoring and assessing draft budgetary plans and ensuring the correction of excessive deficit of the Member States in the euro area [2013] OJ L 140/11.

[29] The official title is Treaty on Stability, Coordination and Governance in the Economic and Monetary Union. It was concluded by all the Member States apart from the United Kingdom and the Czech Republic. For an extensive analysis of the Treaty, see S. Peers, 'The Stability Treaty: Permanent Austerity or Gesture Politics?' (2012) 8 *ECLR* 404.

[30] Fiscal Compact, Art. 2.

[31] *Ibid.*, Art. 3(1)(a): 'the budgetary position of the general government of a Contracting Party shall be balanced or in surplus'. This rule is defined by reference to the 'Stability and Growth Pact' (*ibid.* Art. 3(1)(b)): 'the rule under point (a) shall be deemed to be respected if the annual structural balance of the general government is at its country-specific medium-term objective, as defined in the revised Stability and Growth Pact, with a lower limit of a structural deficit of 0.5% of the gross domestic product at market prices'.

[32] *Ibid.*, Art. 3(1)(e), which contains the automatic correction mechanism and states: '[I]n the event of significant observed deviations from the medium-term objective or the adjustment path towards it, a correction mechanism shall be triggered automatically. The mechanism shall include the obligation of the Contracting Party concerned to implement measures to correct the deviations over a defined period of time.'

Table 18.3 EU Fiscal Governance Measures

Stability and Growth Pact	Regulation 1466/97 on the strengthening of the surveillance of budgetary positions and the surveillance and coordination of economic policies (Preventive Arm)
	Regulation 1467/97 on speeding up and clarifying the implementation of the excessive deficit procedure (Corrective Arm)
Six-Pack	Regulation 1173/2011 on the effective enforcement of budgetary surveillance in the euro
	Regulation 1174/2011 on enforcement measures to correct excessive macroeconomic imbalances in the euro area
	Regulation 1175/2011 amending Council Regulation 1466/97 on the strengthening of the surveillance of budgetary positions and the surveillance and coordination of economic policies
	Regulation 1176/2011 on the prevention and correction of macroeconomic imbalances
	Regulation 1177/2011 amending Regulation 1467/97 on speeding up and clarifying the implementation of the excessive deficit procedure
	Directive 2011/85 on requirements for budgetary frameworks of the Member States
Two-Pack	Regulation 472/2013 on the strengthening of economic and budgetary surveillance of member states in the euro area experiencing or threatened with serious difficulties with respect to their financial stability
	Regulation No. 473/2013 on common provisions for monitoring and assessing draft budgetary plans and ensuring the correction of excessive deficit of the Member States in the euro area
Fiscal Compact	Treaty on Stability, Coordination and Governance in the Economic and Monetary Union

of these – international law – rules established between the Member States, the Fiscal Compact recruits and borrows some of the Union's supranational institutions – in particular, the European Court of Justice.[33] This peculiar arrangement creates many constitutional problems, and it is hoped that the Union will eventually 'unionise' the Fiscal Compact into Union legislation.

bb. Financial Assistance: Prohibitions and Conditions

Apart from establishing a legal framework for coordinating national fiscal policies, Chapter 1 of Title VIII pursues a second task. It also aims to restrict the power of the Member States to 'trick' market forces by obtaining 'cheap' money from public lenders. This task is to be achieved by four provisions: Articles 122–5 TFEU. They circumscribe the way in which Member States can receive financial assistance from the Union or other States. They have gained a considerable

---

[33] *Ibid.*, Art. 8.

degree of political notoriety in the aftermath of the 2008 Global Financial Crisis; and in particular with regard to the Greek 'bailout'.[34]

The first of these four provisions is Article 122 and concerns emergency situations. It positively allows the Union to grant financial assistance '[w]here a Member State is in difficulties or is seriously threatened with severe difficulties caused by natural disasters or exceptional occurrences beyond its control'.[35] This competence has been used in 2010 to establish the European Financial Stability Mechanism (EFSM) with 'a view to preserving the financial stability of the European Union'.[36] The EFSM is entitled to raise funds up to €60 billion on the financial markets that are guaranteed by the Union budget as collateral. These funds can be distributed as grants or loans to the Member States in need.[37] However, designed as an emergency instrument, the EFSM is intended to only apply to short and exceptional occurrences and its funds are fairly limited.

Second, under Article 123, neither the European Central Bank nor the National Central Banks are allowed to offer any overdraft or credit facilities to any public authorities; nor to 'directly' (!) purchase public debt instruments from the States. In the past, the ECB has however partly evaded this prohibition by buying sovereign bonds not directly from a government but indirectly (!) on the market. In particular: the ECB's decisions to establish a 'Securities Markets Programme',[38] and later an 'Outright Monetary Transactions' (OMT) Programme have undercut much of the substance of Article 123.[39] Especially the second programme has attracted much controversy, particularly in Germany where it was challenged before the German Constitutional Court on the grounds that it was ultra vires and impaired Germany's constitutional identity. Despite its strong prejudices, the German Court nevertheless asked for a preliminary ruling; and in *Gauweiler*,[40] the European Court clarified that the bond-buying programme did not violate Article 123.[41]

---

[34] For an analysis of the (2010) Greek 'bailout' through the (international) loan facility agreement, see H. Hofmeister, 'To Bail Out or Not to Bail Out? Legal Aspects of the Greek Crisis' (2011) 13 CYELS 113.

[35] Art. 122(2) TFEU. This general competence for all Member States is complemented by a special legal competence for Member States with a derogation in Art. 143 TFEU.

[36] See Regulation 407/2010 [2010] OJ L 118/1, Art. 1.   [37] *Ibid.*, Arts. 3–6.

[38] For the 'Securities Markets Programme', see ECB Decision 2010/5 establishing a securities market programme [2010] OJ L 124/8. For a critical review of that decision, see Editorial, 'Debt and Democracy: "United States Then, Europe Now"?' (2012) 49 *CML Rev.* 1833 at 1838: 'The purpose of Article 123 TFEU would therefore be defeated if the ECB unconditionally declared it would buy from investors bonds issued by a heavily indebted Member State for an unlimited amount.'

[39] For an analysis of these 'unconventional' ECB measures, see T. Beukers, 'The New ECB and Its Relationship with the Eurozone: Between Central Bank Independence and Central Bank Intervention' [2013] 50 *CML Rev.* 1579 at 1591ff.

[40] Case C-62/14, *Gauweiler and others*, EU:C:2015:400. For an extensive analysis of the case, see D. Adamski, 'Economic Constitution of the Euro Area after the *Gauweiler* Preliminary Ruling' (2015) 52 *CML Rev.* 1451.

[41] Case C-62/14, *Gauweiler*, paras. 94–5: 'It is clear from its wording that Article 123(1) TFEU prohibits the ECB and the central banks of the Member States from granting overdraft

Third, Article 124 generally prohibits any privileged access to financial institutions offered to the Union or the Member States.[42]

Finally, Article 125 contains the fourth and infamous 'no-bailout' clause. It expressly prohibits the Union and the Member States from assuming the debts of any (other) Member State and provides:

> The Union shall not be liable for or assume the commitments of central governments, regional, local or other public authorities, other bodies governed by public law, or public undertakings of any Member State … A Member State shall not be liable for or assume the commitments of central governments, regional, local or other public authorities, other bodies governed by public law, or public undertakings of another Member State.

The meaning of this prohibition has been highly controversial. Did it mean that every single Member State was, with regard to the financial markets, 'on its own'? Or could the Union or the Member States offer financial assistance to a Member State *without assuming its debts*?

This question was raised in the context of the creation of the European Stability Mechanism (ESM) in 2012. The latter is the permanent mechanism that was set up by the *euro*-Member States as 'an international financial institution'.[43] Based on Article 136(3),[44] the ESM is an international organisation based on an international treaty between the euro-States that aims to mobilise funding up to €700 billion and to provide financial support to ESM members that are 'experiencing, or are threatened by, severe financing problems' and where that financial aid is 'indispensable to safeguard the financial stability of the euro area as a whole and of its Member States'.[45]

Does this (international) arrangement violate the text or spirit of the 'no-bailout' clause in Article 125 TFEU? There are strong textual and teleological

---

facilities or any other type of credit facility to public authorities and bodies of the Union and of Member States and from purchasing directly from them their debt instruments. It follows that that provision prohibits all financial assistance from the ESCB to a Member State, but does not preclude, generally, the possibility of the ESCB purchasing from the creditors of such a State, bonds previously issued by that State.'

[42] Art. 124 TFEU.

[43] ESM Treaty, Art. 1. An e-version of the Treaty can be found at: www.european-council .europa.eu/media/582311/05-tesm2.en12.pdf.

[44] For the text of the provision, see section 1(b) below.

[45] ESM Treaty, Art. 3. One of the fundamental conditions of the ESM Treaty is also that a Member State must have ratified the Fiscal Compact, *ibid.*, preamble 5: 'This Treaty and the TSCG are complementary in fostering fiscal responsibility and solidarity within the economic and monetary union. It is acknowledged and agreed that the granting of financial assistance in the framework of new programmes under the ESM will be conditional, as of 1 March 2013, on the ratification of the TSCG by the ESM Member concerned[.]'

arguments on either side of the fence.[46] And in *Pringle*,[47] a member of the Irish Parliament challenged the legality of the ESM before the Irish Supreme Court, which subsequently referred a number of preliminary question to the European Court of Justice. The Court here squarely confirmed the constitutionality of the ESM. Finding that Article 125 was not intended to prohibit all forms of financial assistance to another Member State,[48] the Court held that the purpose of the provision was solely 'to ensure that the Member States follow a sound budgetary policy' and to 'ensure … that the Member States remain subject to the logic of the market when they enter into debt'.[49] And this logic would not be distorted by financial assistance to a Member State under the ESM:

> [Article 125] prohibits the Union and the Member States from granting financial assistance as a result of which the incentive of the recipient Member State to conduct a sound budgetary policy is diminished … However, Article 125 TFEU does not prohibit the granting of financial assistance by one or more Member States to a Member State which remains responsible for its commitments to its creditors provided that the conditions attached to such assistance are such as to prompt that Member State to implement a sound budgetary policy … The granting of financial assistance to an ESM Member in the form of a credit line … in no way implies that the ESM will assume the debts of the recipient Member State. On the contrary, such assistance amounts to the creation of a new debt, owed to the ESM by that recipient Member State, which remains responsible for its commitments to its creditors in respect of its existing debts.[50]

According to this judicial interpretation, the 'no-bailout' clause only prohibits the *direct* or *joint* assumption of debt by the Union or the Member States of financial responsibilities of an indebted Member State. Under this narrow construction, all aid programmes that financially assist near-bankrupt Member States *indirectly* would seem to be fully constitutional under Article 125.[51] Importantly,

---

[46] For two excellent analyses of this question, see P. Athanassiou, 'Of Past Measures and Future Plans for Europe's Exit from the Sovereign Debt Crisis: What Is Legally Possible (and What Is Not)' (2011) 36 *EL Rev.* 558; M. Ruffert, 'The European Debt Crisis and European Union Law' (2011) 48 *CML Rev.* 1777.

[47] Case C-370/12, *Pringle v. Government of Ireland, Ireland and the Attorney General* EU:C:20:756. For an extensive analysis of this case, see B. de Witte and T. Beukers, '*Pringle* – Case Comment' (2013) 50 *CML Rev.* 805.

[48] Case C-370/12, *Pringle*, para. 130.   [49] *Ibid.*, 135.   [50] *Ibid.*, paras. 136–9.

[51] For this view, see A. de Gregorio Merino, 'Legal Developments in the Economic and Monetary Union during the Debt Crisis: The Mechanisms of Financial Assistance' [2012] 49 *CML Rev.* 1613, at 1627. By contrast, eurobonds would, according to the author, not be constitutional, since here all 'Euro area Member States would be the guarantors of the issuances, and each of the guarantors would be liable indistinctly (jointly and severally) for the whole of the issuances.' A system of 'mutualisation of debt' would, in the author's view, 'clearly breach Article 125 TFEU' (*ibid.*, 1630–1). For the same view, see Athanassiou, 'Of Past Measures' (n. 46 above), 572.

financial assistance given by the ESM will however be subject to 'conditions', and this 'conditionality' of EU assistance is a central principle of the ESM:

> If indispensable to safeguard the financial stability of the euro area as a whole and of its Member States, the ESM may provide stability support to an ESM Member subject to strict conditionality, appropriate to the financial assistance instrument chosen. Such conditionality may range from a macro-economic adjustment programme to continuous respect of pre-established eligibility conditions.[52]

The procedure for granting stability support is thereby set out in Article 13 of the ESM Treaty, which states:

> [T]he [ESM] Board of Governors shall entrust the European Commission – in liaison with the ECB and, wherever possible, together with the IMF – with the task of negotiating, with the ESM Member concerned, a memorandum of understanding (an 'MoU') detailing the conditionality attached to the financial assistance facility. The content of the MoU shall reflect the severity of the weaknesses to be addressed and the financial assistance instrument chosen.[53]

The most notorious illustration here is probably the 'macroeconomic adjustment programme of Greece' and the Greek memorandum of understanding that followed the third European bailout of that eurozone member.[54]

b. Euro-membership: Differential Integration

Economic coordination constitutes a necessary precondition for monetary union. Indeed: monetary union will only work if there exists a strong economic 'convergence' between the Member States. From the very beginning, therefore, only those States that fulfilled certain economic criteria would be entitled to participate in monetary union. These economic 'convergence criteria' are defined in Article 140 TFEU and Protocol No. 13 On the Convergence Criteria. While constitutionally open to all Member States, euro-membership depends on the fulfilment of these convergence criteria.

The EU Treaties establish *four* such convergence criteria. First, a Member State must achieve 'a high degree of price stability'.[55] This is defined as an inflation

---

[52] Art. 12 ESM Treaty.

[53] Art. 13(3) ESM Treaty; see also Art. 7(2) of Regulation 472/2013 (n. 28 above).

[54] Council Implementing Decision 2015/1411 approving the macroeconomic adjustment programme of Greece (2015) OJ L219/12; 'Memorandum of Understanding between the European Commission acting on Behalf of the European Stability Mechanism and the Hellenic Republic and the Bank of Greece' (https://ec.europa.eu/info/files/memorandum-understanding-greece-august-2015_en).

[55] Art. 140(1) TFEU – first indent.

rate that will not exceed 1.5 per cent above that of the three best performing Member States.[56] Second, a Member State must have a sustainable financial
position – that is, it must not have an excessive government deficit.[57] Such an
excessive deficit exists where a government's annual deficit goes over 3 per cent
of the GDP; or where its total debt exceeds 60 per cent GDP.[58] The reason
behind both economic criteria is the idea that monetary inflation is typically a
result of government debt.[59] Third, a Member State must have previously par-
ticipated in the European Monetary System for at least two years without any
devaluation.[60] Finally, the nominal average long-term interest rate of a Member
State must not exceed that of the three best performing Member States by more
than 2 per cent.[61]

Non-fulfilment of any one of these criteria means that a Member State is
deemed to be not economically ready to participate in monetary union. This system of differential integration consequently distinguishes between those States
that can and have adopted the euro (euro-States), and those Member States that
are subject to a (temporary) derogation until they satisfy the convergence criteria. The euro-State 'insiders' would thereby be governed by provisions specific to
them, which are set out in Chapter 4 of Title VIII. The most important provision
here is Article 136, which states:

> 1.   In order to ensure the proper functioning of economic and monetary union, and
>   in accordance with the relevant provisions of the Treaties, the Council shall, in
>   accordance with the relevant procedure from among those referred to in Articles
>   121 and 126, with the exception of the procedure set out in Article 126(14),
>   adopt measures specific to those Member States whose currency is the euro:
>   (a)   to strengthen the coordination and surveillance of their budgetary discipline;

---

[56]   Protocol No. 13 On the Convergence Criteria, Art. 1.

[57]   Art. 140(1) TFEU – second indent, which refers to Art. 126(6) TFEU.

[58]   Protocol No. 12 On the Excessive Deficit Procedure, Art. 1.

[59]   R. E. Baldwin, *The Economics of European Integration* (McGraw-Hill, 2009), 492. The author
       also provides an excellent account on the 'German' origins of the 3 per cent threshold:
       'Germany had long operated a "golden rule", which specifies that budget deficits are only
       acceptable if they correspond to public investment spending (on roads, telecommunica-
       tions and other infrastructure). The idea is that public investment is a source of growth,
       which eventually generates the resources needed to pay for the initial borrowing. The
       German "golden rule" considered that public investment typically amounts to some 3 per
       cent of GDP. Hence the Maastricht Treaty requirement that budget deficits should not
       exceed 3 per cent of GDP.' With regard to the 60 per cent total debt threshold, there was
       an even more mundane origin, for the 60 per cent ceiling was the average debt level when
       the Maastricht Treaty was being negotiated in 1991 (*ibid.*).

[60]   Art. 140(1) TFEU – third indent. Prior to the Maastricht Treaty, the Member States had
       established between themselves a (first) European Monetary System (EMS) that came to an
       end with the adoption of the euro. Today, there exists a (second) EMS for those Member
       States that have not adopted the euro. This EMSII is entirely voluntary, and the countries
       that have joined are: Estonia, Lithuania and Denmark.

[61]   Art. 4 of Protocol No. 13 On the Convergence Criteria.

(b) to set out economic policy guidelines for them, while ensuring that they are compatible with those adopted for the whole of the Union and are kept under surveillance.

2. For those measures set out in paragraph 1, only members of the Council representing Member States whose currency is the euro shall take part in the vote. A qualified majority of the said members shall be defined in accordance with Article 238(3)(a).

3. The Member States whose currency is the euro may establish a stability mechanism to be activated if indispensable to safeguard the stability of the euro area as a whole. The granting of any required financial assistance under the mechanism will be made subject to strict conditionality.

The provision constitutes the legal basis for *reinforced* economic coordination among euro-States, which are here expressly entitled to use the competences in Articles 121 and 126 among themselves. The provision has been used to adopt Union legislation laying down a stricter coordination regime among euro-States, while Article 136(3) TFEU has served as the legitimacy base for the European Stability Mechanism (ESM) – all discussed above.[62]

By contrast, 'Member States with a derogation' are subject to a number of transitional provisions set out in Chapter 5 of Title VIII. The EU Treaties, importantly, conceive membership in the monetary union as a constitutional obligation of *all* (!) Member States. The decision whether to join the 'euro' is thus theoretically not in the hands of each Member State but subject to a *Union* decision. Member States with a derogation are therefore reviewed, at least once every two years, to see whether they have made progress in fulfilling 'their obligations regarding the achievement of economic and monetary union'.[63] After a positive finding that the convergence criteria are fulfilled,[64] the Council can abrogate the derogation by means of a decision by 'the unanimity of the Member States whose currency is the euro and the Member State concerned, on a proposal from the Commission and after consulting the European Central Bank'.[65]

Two States have categorically refused to abide by this constitutional logic and requested a constitutional 'opt-out' from the obligation to partake in monetary union. These two 'outsiders' are the United Kingdom and Denmark. Their constitutional 'opt-outs' are – respectively – given in Protocols 15 and 16. The

---

[62] For a symbolic reason, the Member States felt that this *inter se* agreement between the euro-States would not be constitutional, unless there was an express legal competence in the Treaties. And since Art. 122 TFEU was of no avail, the European Council chose the option of adding a competence by means of the simplified amendment procedure in Art. 48(6) TEU (see Decision 2011/199 amending Art. 136 of the Treaty on the Functioning of the European Union with regard to a stability mechanism for Member States whose currency is the euro [2011] OJ L 91/1). This amendment was however purely symbolic.

[63] Art. 140(1) TFEU.

[64] *Ibid.*, Art. 140(2), which sets out the procedural requirements for such a finding.

[65] Art. 140(3) TFEU.

Table 18.4 Differential Integration within EMU

States within the euro zone		States with a derogation	States with an opt-out
Austria (1999)	Latvia (2014)	Bulgaria	Denmark
Belgium (1999)	Lithuania (2015)	Czech Republic	United Kingdom
Cyprus (2008)	Luxembourg (1999)	Estonia	
Estonia (2011)	Malta (2008)	Hungary	
Finland (1999)	Netherlands (1999)	Poland	
France (1999)	Portugal (1999)	Romania	
Germany (1999)	Slovakia (2009)		
Greece (2001)	Slovenia (2007)		
Ireland (1999)	Spain (1999)		
Italy (1999)		Sweden	

former specifies in clear terms that '[u]nless the United Kingdom notifies to the Council that it intends to adopt the euro, it shall be under no obligation to do so'[66] and, in the meantime, the United Kingdom would 'retain its powers in the fields of monetary policy according to national law'.[67] A similar situation governs Denmark, which was given 'an exemption'.[68] Apart from these two (permanent) outsiders, the legal position of Sweden is slightly ambivalent. The country has not formally obtained a constitutional opt-out, yet it enjoys an informal exemption that *politically* locates it in between a constitutional derogation and a constitutional opt-out.

c. Monetary Policy: Price Stability

The power to influence the supply of money has a long and distinguished history, which is tied to the emergence of national central banks.[69] These central banks were charged to – directly or indirectly – regulate the circulation of money within their respective national economies. The economic rationale behind the regulation of money is (relatively) straightforward. For money is not simply a medium of exchange. Changes in the amount of circulating money

---

[66] Protocol No. 15 On Certain Provisions Relating to the United Kingdom of Great Britain and Northern Ireland, para. 1.

[67] *Ibid.*, para. 3.

[68] Protocol No. 16 On Certain Provisions Relating to Denmark, esp. para. 1: 'In view of the notice given to the Council by the Danish Government on 3 November 1993, Denmark shall have an exemption. The effect of the exemption shall be that all Articles and provisions of the Treaties and the Statute of the ESCB referring to a derogation shall be applicable to Denmark.'

[69] C. Giannini, *The Age of Central Banks* (Edward Elgar, 2011), chs. 1–2.

within a market may lead to *deflation* or *inflation*. Deflation refers to a situation when money 'dries up', a scenario that potentially limits economic growth. By contrast, inflation is said to occur when there is an over-supply of money – a scenario that reduces its 'real' purchasing power.[70] But the quantity of a currency within a national market also determines of course its relationship to other currencies; and the regulation of money has therefore also become an important international task. For example: if a State devalues its currency by printing significantly more money, foreign creditors whose investments are measured in that currency will lose.

For those States that have joined monetary union, it is the European Union that now enjoys an exclusive competence in 'monetary policy'.[71] But who exercises this competence, and according to what objectives? The EU Treaties have charged the European System of Central Banks – in particular: the European Central Bank – with the task of monetary policy. The delegation of monetary policy to a – public – central bank reflects a broad economic consensus built up in the twentieth century. However, when the ECB was born no such consensus existed with regard to the specific objectives of central banks.[72] According to the 'French model', the tasks of a central bank include not only price stability but a number of broader *political* objectives like the stabilisation of the business cycle; and in implementing these political objectives, the central bank would be *dependent* on the executive. By contrast, the 'German model' has traditionally argued that price stability should be the exclusive concern of central banks; and in discharging only '*non*-political' objectives, a central bank should be completely *independent* from the executive branch.

The ECB has closely followed the 'German model'.[73] The European Treaties have thus insisted on the ECB's independence,[74] and they have given absolute primacy to the maintenance of price stability within the eurozone.[75] However, the Treaties also acknowledge the potential task of the E(S)CB to 'support the general economic policies in the Union with a view to contributing to the achievement of the objectives of the Union as laid down in Article 3 of the Treaty on European Union'. And according to Article 127(6) TFEU, the Council could

---

[70] The printing of money by a government has thus been compared to a 'form of taxation' (see J. M. Keynes, *A Tract on Monetary Reform* (Macmillan, 1924), 41: 'A Government can live by this means when it can live by no other. It is the form of taxation which the public finds hardest to evade and even the weakest Government can enforce, when it can enforce nothing else').

[71] Art. 3(1)(c) TFEU.

[72] On the two conceptions of central banks, see P. de Grauwe, *Economics of Monetary Union* (Oxford University Press, 2009), 163.

[73] *Ibid.*, 165: 'The success of the German model of central banking is an intriguing phenomenon. After all, when the EU countries negotiated the Maastricht Treaty the Anglo-French model of central banking prevailed in almost all the EU member states.' The reason why this nonetheless happened is the 'monetarist counter-revolution' that took place in the 1980s.

[74] On the independence of the ECB, see Chapter 6, section 3(a).

[75] Art. 119(2), as well as Art. 127(1) TFEU.

even 'confer specific tasks upon the European Central Bank concerning policies relating to the prudential supervision of credit institutions and other financial institutions'. These additional objectives are however only secondary objectives. For they must always be '[w]ithout prejudice to the objective of price stability'.[76] The control of price inflation is thus a *primus* that has no *pares*.

How does the ECB maintain price stability within the eurozone? The ECB enjoys the exclusive right to authorise the issue of euro banknotes (and coins) within the Union.[77] The ECB thereby determines the desirable quantity of money within the internal market via four principal instruments. The first instrument is known as 'open market operations'[78] – that is, 'the buying or selling of securities with the aim of increasing or reducing money market liquidity'.[79] This instrument is the most direct method of influencing the money market, and has been described as 'the most important instrument of the monetary policy of the ECB'.[80]

The second instrument is 'standing facilities'. These offer (commercial) banks the opportunity to obtain money from the ECB. The latter here operates as a 'bankers' bank',[81] and especially as the 'lender of last resort'.[82] And by setting interest or 'discount' rates at which commercial banks can borrow or deposit money, the ECB indirectly influences the credit market and interest rate for all commercial banks within the internal market.[83] The set 'interest rates' of the ECB over the last two decades can be seen in Figure 18.1.

The third instrument is minimum reserve requirements.[84] It is the most indirect instrument to determine the availability of money within the market. For by requiring certain deposits as a bank reserve with the ECB or a national central bank, the ECB can also regulate liquidity within the European money market.

---

[76] *Ibid.*, Art. 127(1).   [77] *Ibid.*, Art. 128.

[78] Protocol No. 4 On the Statute of the European System of Central Banks and of the European Central Bank, Art. 18.

[79] De Grauwe, *Economics of Monetary Union* (n. 72 above), 215.

[80] *Ibid.*

[81] See R. G. Hawtrey, *The Art of Central Banking* (Routledge, 1970), 116: 'The central bank is a banker's bank. It affords to the other banks of the community, the competitive banks, the same facilities as they afford to their customers. The competitive banks make payments to one another by drawing on balances at the central bank … and they replenish their balances, when low, by borrowing from the central bank.'

[82] The phrase that central banks are 'lenders of last resort' was made famous by W. Bagehot's 'Lombard Street' (see *Lombard Street: A Description of the Money Market* (Cosimo Classics, 2006)).

[83] M. H. de Kock, *Central Banking* (St Martin's Press, 1974), 150: 'The theory underlying the use of the discount rate as a principal instrument of credit control under the gold standard was, briefly, that changes in the discount rate of the central bank would bring about more or less corresponding changes in local money rates generally, and that such changes in money rates would, through their operation on the supply and demand for money and credit and on the institutional flow of capital, have the effect of re-adjusting the domestic levels of prices, costs, production and trade, and correcting any disequilibrium in the balance of payments.'

[84] ESCB Statute, Art. 19.

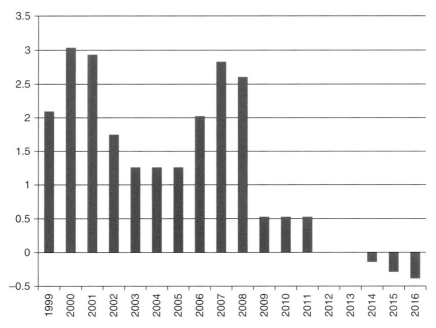

Figure 18.1 ECB Interest Rates

A fourth instrument that the ECB can employ to influence the value of the European currency is one that it cannot employ alone. This fourth instrument consists in the setting of exchange rates with other currencies. Even if the ECB is entitled 'to conduct foreign-exchange operations', its external relations power is subject to the special treaty-making procedure set out in Article 219 TFEU.[85] And here it is not the ECB, but the Council of Ministers – that is: the Member States within one branch of the Union legislature – that exercise primary political responsibility. According to some writers, there is consequently 'a degree of inconsistency, and possibly conflict' between giving the ECB independence from political control in the internal sphere of the eurozone, while leaving the determination of the exchange rates 'in the hands of the political authorities'.[86] However, this constitutional choice has a long historical pedigree and reflects the particularly political nature of foreign affairs.

d. Supervisory Function: Financial Stability

The task of guaranteeing the overall stability of the financial system is a classic objective of all central banks. Indeed, '[b]y the turn of the 1930s it had become evident that supervision constituted a primary function for purposes of banking stability'.[87]

[85] For an analysis of the treaties concluded here, see M. Lopez Escudero, 'La Politique de change de l'euro' (2011) 47 *CDE* 369.
[86] Lastra and Louis, 'European Economic and Monetary Union' (n. 16 above), 123.
[87] Giannini, *Age of Central Banks* (n. 69 above), 108.

Yet despite its overall importance, this objective is not listed among the key objectives of the ECB.[88] Instead, the European Treaties traditionally acknowledged that it was the principal responsibility of national authorities to conduct the prudential supervision of banks.[89] And while the EU Treaties did entitle the Council to 'confer specific tasks upon the European Central Bank' within this field,[90] for a long time, this enabling clause had not been used. The supervision of banks and the financial system was generally thus left to the Member States;[91] and this decentralised solution constituted '[o]ne of the most peculiar features' of the eurozone's legal system.[92] Its inefficient and disorganised nature chiefly contributed to the financial crisis of the last decade.[93]

The critical question after the start of the crisis was thus this: how could financial stability within the Union be reinforced? The Union reform of the banking system attempted – in a first step – to build on the traditional decentralised solution. Financial supervision was still left in the hands of national authorities, whose *coordination* was however reinforced through the establishment of the 'European System of Financial Supervision'. The latter consists of four EU agencies: the European Systemic Risk Board, responsible for macro-prudential oversight,[94] the European Banking Authority,[95] the European Insurance and Occupational Pensions Authority and the European Securities and Markets Authority that are all three charged with micro-supervisory tasks.[96]

This first reform has now been complemented by a second – dramatic – move towards a European 'banking union'.[97] The European banking union is designed

---

[88]   These basic objectives are listed in Art. 127(2) TFEU. It was apparently the opposition by the United Kingdom that led to the exclusion of 'prudential supervision of credit institutions' from the list of basic tasks.

[89]   Art. 127(5) TFEU.   [90]   *Ibid.*, Art. 127(6).

[91]   L. Dragomir, *European Prudential Banking Regulation and Supervision: The Legal Dimension* (Routledge, 2010), esp. 238 and 244.

[92]   De Grauwe, *Economics of Monetary Union* (n. 72 above), 184.

[93]   See N. Moloney, 'EU Financial Market Regulation after the Global Financial Crisis: "More Europe" or More Risks?' (2010) 47 *CML Rev.* 1317, esp. 1324: '[The crisis], by contrast, has not only slowed down the integration process. It has exposed the pathology of the internal market and the destructive consequences which follow where regulatory liberalization is not matched by supervisory co-ordination; the weaknesses of the home Member State control model have been laid bare.'

[94]   See Regulation 1092/2010 on European Union macro-prudential oversight of the financial system and establishing a European Systemic Risk Board [2010] OJ L 331/1; Regulation 1096/2010 conferring specific tasks upon the European Central Bank concerning the functioning of the European Systemic Risk Board [2010] OJ L 331/162.

[95]   Regulation 1093/2010 establishing a European Supervisory Authority [2010] OJ L 331/12.

[96]   Regulation 1094/2010 establishing a European Supervisory Authority (European Insurance and Occupational Pensions Authority) [2010] OJ L 331/48; and Regulation 1095/2010 establishing a European Supervisory Authority (European Securities and Markets Authority) [2010] OJ L 331/84.

[97]   See Commission, 'Communication: A Roadmap towards Banking Union', COM (2012) 510 final. For academic analyses of the banking union, see R. M. Lastra, 'Banking Union and Single Market: Conflict or Companionship?' (2013) 36 *Fordham International Law Journal* 1190; N. Moloney, 'European Banking Union: Assessing Its

to break the unreliable nexus between *national* banks and their *national* supervision. It broadly consists of three pillars: the Single Supervisory Mechanism, the Single Resolution Mechanism and the European Deposit Insurance Scheme. The most important and central pillar here is the Single Supervisory Mechanism (SSM) set out in Regulation 1024/2013.[98] This centralised supervisory mechanism, adopted under Article 127(6), replaces the decentralised supervisory system of the past by charging the ECB to 'contribut[e] to the safety and soundness of credit institutions and the stability of the financial system within the Union'.[99]

The role of the ECB is here however limited in two significant ways. First, the Union's Central Bank will only be competent to supervise credit institutions *within the euro-States*. And, second, rejecting total centralisation, Regulation 1024/2013 has set up a divided power system in which the ECB cooperates with the competent national authorities.[100] The division of supervisory tasks thereby follows a functional criterion: the ECB is only responsible for 'significant' credit institutions,[101] whereas the competent national authorities will supervise the 'less significant' credit institutions. The idea behind this 'champions league' model (*Lastra*) appears to be that the ECB's direct supervisory powers should be confined to institutions whose misconduct could threaten the Union financial system as a whole. At the moment, these are the 130 biggest banks within the eurozone, including BNP Paribas (France), Deutsche Bank (Germany) and the Bank of Ireland (Ireland).

2. Social Policy

The European Treaties contained – from the very start – a Title on 'Social Policy'. It recognised 'the need to promote improved working conditions and an improved standard of living for workers', and thereby admitted that this would not come about 'only from the functioning of the common market'.[102] However, a closer look at the original Social Policy Title revealed a striking

---

Risks and Resilience' (2014) 51 *CML Rev.* 1609; and K. Alexander, 'European Banking Union: A Legal and Institutional Analysis of the Single Supervisory Mechanism and the Single Resolution Mechanism' (2015) 40 *EL Rev.* 154.

[98] Regulation 1024/2013 conferring specific tasks on the European Central Bank concerning policies relating to the prudential supervision of credit institutions [2013] OJ L 287/63; Regulation 468/2014 establishing the framework for cooperation within the Single Supervisory Mechanism [2014] OJ L 141/1.

[99] Regulation 1024/2013, Art. 1.

[100] Art. 6(1): 'The ECB shall carry out its tasks within a single supervisory mechanism composed of the ECB and national competent authorities. The ECB shall be responsible for the effective and consistent functioning of the SSM.' And according to Art. 6(2): '[b]oth the ECB and national competent authorities shall be subject to a duty of cooperation in good faith'.

[101] The criterion of 'significance' is defined in Art. 6(4) of the Regulation. It has been estimated that this roughly translates into the biggest 150 banks (out of the about 6,000 credit institutions within the Union) which will fall under the direct supervision of the ECB.

[102] Ex-Art. 117 EEC.

'[s]ocial minimalism',[103] because the area seemed to be almost exclusively 'reserved' to the Member States.

This social minimalism was challenged in 1972.[104] In an attempt to provide the Union with a 'human face', the European Council here called upon the Union to progressively develop a European social policy. Based on the Union's general competence(s),[105] this Union policy was however depended on the demands of the internal market and the unanimous consent of the Member States. An independent social policy therefore only emerged when the 1986 Single European Act gave the Union a special competence over the health and safety of workers. Thereafter, the Union was given ever wider and stronger social competences. The constitutional framework for social policy can today be found in Title X of the Union's internal policies part and can be seen in Table 18.5.

This section explores four aspects of this policy. We shall start with a closer look at the scope and nature of the Union competence in this field. The legislative competence given in Article 153 has been particularly embattled in the past; and as a result of these battles, it is one of the most complex competences within the EU Treaties. Article 153 is however not the only source of EU social law. It is complemented by a private form of 'legislation', namely collective agreements between the social partners. Having explored these two sources of EU employment law in section (a), sections (b) and (c) briefly analyse two substantive aspects of that law. Finally, we shall look at one of the most important principles of employment law generally: the equal pay principle. It is set out in Article 157 and, as we shall see below, it goes beyond pay to include equal treatment between men and women in the workplace.

a. Social Policy: Competence and Procedure

aa. Union Legislation: Article 153 – Scope and Nature

To what extent can the Union adopt social policy legislation and what degree of decisional autonomy will it enjoy?

---

[103] J. Kenner, *EU Employment Law: From Rome to Amsterdam and Beyond* (Hart, 2002), 2.

[104] On the 1972 Paris Summit, see Bulletin of the European Communities, Bulletin EC 10-1972 at 19: 'Social Policy: The Heads of State and Government emphasized that vigorous action [in] the social sphere is to them just as important as achieving Economic and Monetary Union. They consider it absolutely necessary to secure an increasing share by both sides of industry in the [Union]'s economic and social decisions. They ask the Institutions after consulting both sides of industry to draw up an action programme before 1 January 1974 providing practical measures and the means for them, within the scope of the Social Fund, based on suggestions put forward by the Heads of Government and the Commission during the Conference. The programme must implement a coordinated policy for employment and vocational training, to improve working and living conditions, secure the collaboration of workers in the function of undertakings, facilitate according to the conditions in each country the conclusion of collective European agreements in appropriate areas and strengthen and coordinate action for protecting the consumer.'

[105] These general competences were ex-Art. 100 (now Art. 115) and ex-Art. 235 EEC (now Art. 352 TFEU) – both of which require unanimity.

Table 18.5 Social Policy Provisions – Overview

Title X: Social Policy			
Article 151	Objectives	Article 157	Equal Pay Principle
Article 152	Social Partners	Article 158	Paid Holiday Schemes
Article 153	Legislative Competence	Article 159	Commission Reports (1)
Article 154	Commission Consultation of Social Partners	Article 160	Social Protection Committee
Article 155	'Agreements' between Social Partners	Article 161	Commission Reports (2)
Article 156	Commission Coordination of National Actions		
Union Legislation & Collective Agreements (Selection) Directive 2003/88 on the Organisation of Working Time Directive 2006/54 on Equal Treatment Directive 2001/23 on Transfer of Undertakings Framework Agreement on Part-time Work Framework Agreement on Fixed-term Work			

Past battles over the scope and nature of the Union's social policy competence can only be understood if placed in historical perspective. Absent any legislative competence for social policy in the Rome Treaty, the 1986 Single European Act had granted the Union such a competence for the first time; yet this competence was confined to 'encouraging improvements, *especially in the working environment, as regards the health and safety of workers*'.[106] This seemed not much more than a 'health and safety' competence, but in a famous judicial showdown over whether this competence could carry the EU Working Time Directive, the European Court clarified that it preferred a 'broad interpretation' of that competence. In *United Kingdom* v. *Council*,[107] the Court thus held against the wishes of the United Kingdom that:

> There [was] nothing in the wording of [that competence] to indicate that the concepts of 'working environment', 'safety' and 'health' as used in that provision should, in the absence of other indicators, be interpreted restrictively, and not as embracing all factors, physical or otherwise, capable of affecting the health and safety of the worker in his working environment, including in particular certain aspects of the organization of working time. On the contrary, the words 'especially in the working environment' militate in favour of a broad interpretation of the powers which [the social competence] confers upon the Council for the protection of the health and safety of workers.[108]

---

[106] Ex-Art. 118a(1) EEC (added emphasis).
[107] Case C-84/94, *United Kingdom* v. *Council* [1996] ECR I-5755.   [108] *Ibid.*, para. 15.

This broad understanding of social policy has been codified and is today broken down into 11 (!) aspects that can be found in Article 153 TFEU. The provision states:

> With a view to achieving the objectives of Article 151, the Union shall support and complement the activities of the Member States in the following fields:
> (a) improvement in particular of the working environment to protect workers' health and safety;
> (b) working conditions;
> (c) social security and social protection of workers;
> (d) protection of workers where their employment contract is terminated;
> (e) the information and consultation of workers;
> (f) representation and collective defence of the interests of workers and employers, including co-determination, subject to paragraph 5;
> (g) conditions of employment for third-country nationals legally residing in Union territory;
> (h) the integration of persons excluded from the labour market, without prejudice to Article 166;
> (i) equality between men and women with regard to labour market opportunities and treatment at work;
> (j) the combating of social exclusion;
> (k) the modernisation of social protection systems without prejudice to point (c).[109]

Most of these expressly enumerated policy fields deal with the protection of 'workers', and Article 153 indeed constitutes the primary source of European labour law. Within these 11 fields, the Union is entitled to adopt 'measures designed to encourage cooperation between Member States' that must nonetheless *'exclud[e] any harmonisation of the laws and regulations of the Member States'*.[110] This exclusion of all harmonisation appears to make Article 153 a complementary competence. Yet for the fields referred to in (a)–(i), the Union is entitled to establish and harmonise 'minimum requirements' for all Member States 'by means of directives'. This part of Article 153 therefore qualifies it as a shared competence,[111] albeit a shared competence that will always allow the Member States to go beyond the minimum Union standard. And to make matters even more complex: the general ability of the Union to 'take initiatives to ensure coordination of Member States' social policies' may characterise Article 153 as a coordinating competence.[112] The complex structure of the competence can be seen in Figure 18.2.

Which legislative procedure needs to be followed for social policy measures? Employment legislation under Article 153 is generally adopted following the ordinary legislative procedure and will thus require the co-decision of the European Parliament and the Council by a qualified majority.[113] However, for

---

[109] Art. 153(1) TFEU.
[110] *Ibid.*, Art. 153(2)(a) (emphasis added).   [111] *Ibid.*, Art. 4(2)(b).   [112] *Ibid.*, Art. 5(3).
[113] *Ibid.*, Art. 153(2) – second indent.

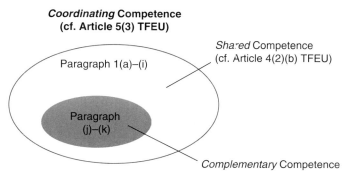

Figure 18.2 Social Policy Competence – Nature(s)

the specific policy fields (c), (d), (f) and (g) the Treaty exceptionally insists on a special legislative procedure in which Parliament is only consulted and the Council must act by unanimity.[114]

Finally, Article 153(4) and (5) contains an external limit to all Union legislation adopted on the basis of Article 153. It states:

> The provisions adopted pursuant to this Article:
> – shall not affect the right of Member States to define the fundamental principles of their social security systems and must not significantly affect the financial equilibrium thereof,
> – shall not prevent any Member State from maintaining or introducing more stringent protective measures compatible with the Treaties.
> The provisions of this Article shall not apply to pay, the right of association, the right to strike or the right to impose lock-outs.

bb. Private 'Legislation': Agreements between Social Partners

The existence of a legislative procedure allowing the Union to adopt 'official' legislation is only the 'public' side of the story. It is complemented by a 'private' or 'corporatist' procedure that leaves the substance of European employment law to an agreement between management and labour as 'social partners'. The Union here recognises the role of social partners in industrial societies,[115] and allows them to engage in private rule-making directly.

---

[114] *Ibid.*, Art. 153(2) – third indent. For fields (d), (f) and (g) the Council may however decide, acting unanimously on a proposal from the Commission and after consulting the European Parliament, to render the ordinary legislative procedure applicable.

[115] For a specific constitutional recognition of the role of social partners in the EU, see Art. 152 TFEU: 'The Union recognises and promotes the role of the social partners at its level, taking into account the diversity of national systems. It shall facilitate dialogue between the social partners, respecting their autonomy.' Art. 154 subsequently tasks the Commission to promote the consultation of management and labour at Union level (para. 1), while equally requiring it to consult both social partners before submitting proposals in the social policy field (para. 2).

Table 18.6 EU Collective Agreements (Selection)

Cross-sector agreements	Sectoral agreements
European Framework Agreement on Part-time Work (1997)	European Agreement on the Organisation of Working Time of Seafarers (1998)
European Framework Agreement on Fixed-term Work (1999)	European Agreement on the Organisation of Working Time of Mobile Staff in Civil Aviation (2000)
European Framework Agreement on Work Related Stress (2004)	European Framework Agreement on the Prevention from Sharp Injuries in the Hospital and Healthcare Sector (2009)
European Framework Agreement on Parental Leave (2009)	European Framework Agreement on the Protection of Occupational Health and Safety in the Hairdressing Sector (2016)
European Framework Agreement on Inclusive Labour Markets (2010)	

The procedure for this private 'legislation' is established in Article 155. The provision allows for the conclusion of (collective) 'agreements' between 'management' and 'labour' within all the areas covered by Article 153. These agreements may be cross-sector agreements and are here negotiated by cross-industry 'representatives'.[116] Sector-specific social agreements, by contrast, will be concluded by the social partners within a specific sector.[117] A selection of such social agreements concluded at Union level is provided in Table 18.6.

Collective agreements are 'private' agreements that the social partners may wish to have implemented 'in accordance with the procedures and practices specific to management and labour and the Member States'.[118] However, where the social partners so desire, they can also request the Union to implement the agreement through a Council decision.[119] The social agreement will here be transformed into Union law.

[116] With regard to cross-industrial social dialogues, the Commission generally recognises three 'representative' organisations: 'BusinessEurope' (see www.businesseurope.eu), the 'European Centre of Employers and Enterprises Providing Public Services' (CEEP, see www.ceep.eu); and the 'European Trade Union Confederation' (ETUC, see www.etuc .org). For a critical analysis of the concept and practice of social 'representativeness', see N. Pérez-Solórzano Borragán and S. Smismans, 'Representativeness: A Tool to Structure Interest Intermediation in the European Union?' (2012) 50 *Journal of Common Market Studies* 403.

[117] For each special economic sector, the Commission entertains a list of representative organisations (see http://ec.europa.eu/social/main.jsp?catId=480).

[118] Art. 155(2) TFEU – first alternative.

[119] Art. 155(2) – second alternative. The Council here acts on a proposal from the Commission, and 'shall act unanimously where the agreement in question contains one or more provisions relating to one of the areas for which unanimity is required pursuant to Article 153(2)'. The Council need not act through a 'decision' in the technical sense of Art. 288[4] TFEU but can also use other instruments, like a 'directive'.

What are the (dis)advantages of private lawmaking in the form of collective agreements? On the one hand, allowing the two sides of industry – that is, the parties that are particularly affected by social legislation – to regulate the problem themselves promises a 'local' solution to a 'local' problem. On the other hand, 'delegating' the legislative function to private parties involves the danger of a democratic deficit.[120] For without the European and national parliaments, who makes sure that all affected social interests are represented? The question of the 'representativeness' of collective agreements has proved to be very controversial indeed.[121] For even if the social partners are seen as functional representatives of the interests involved, '[c]ollective agreements with a normative function signed by employers' organisations and trade unions do not sit easily with traditional democratic theory'.[122] Private 'legislation' simply lacks the public elements that we normally identify with democratic representativity.

b. Employment Legislation I: Protection at Work

aa. General Principles

The text of the original social policy competence focused, as we saw above, on health and safety in the working environment.[123] This traditional aspect of employment protection indeed continues to head the list of enumerated subjects in Article 153(1), and subparagraph (a) has been used to adopt (Framework) Directive 89/391 on the introduction of measures to encourage improvements in the safety and health of workers at work.[124] The directive imposes a general and strict obligation on the employer 'to ensure the safety and health of workers in every aspect related to the work'.[125] Unable to specify every single aspect for every particular working environment, the directive thereby delegates power to the Council to adopt individual directives for a number of specified areas.[126]

---

[120] See L. Betten, 'The Democratic Deficit of Participatory Democracy in Community Social Policy' (1998) 23 *EL Rev.* 20.

[121] For a judicial battle over the exclusion of a 'social partner' from the negotiations of a social agreement. see Case T-135/96, *UEAPME* v. *Council* [1998] ECR II-2335, esp. paras. 88–9. The Court here concluded that where the 'representativeness' of the social partners had not been shown, the Council (and the Commission) would have to refuse to implement the agreement.

[122] S. Smismans, 'The European Social Dialogue between Constitutional and Labour Law' (2007) 32 *EL Rev.* 341.

[123] See text of ex-Art. 118(a) EEC above.

[124] Directive 89/391 on the introduction of measures to encourage improvements in the safety and health of workers at work [1989] OJ L 183/1.

[125] *Ibid.*, Art. 5(1).

[126] A number of such individual directives have been adopted in the past. The relationship between these 'daughter' directives and the 'mother' directive is clarified in Art. 16(3), which states: 'The provisions of this Directive shall apply in full to all the areas covered by the individual Directives, without prejudice to more stringent and/or specific provisions contained in these individual Directives.'

The Pregnant Workers Directive is such a 'daughter' directive.[127] It entitles women to 'a continuous period of maternity leave of a least 14 weeks allocated before and/or after confinement in accordance with national legislation and/or practice'.[128] During this time, a pregnant woman's employment rights must be ensured, except with regard to her usual pay, since the directive only requires 'an adequate allowance' during maternity leave. The directive is complemented by the Parental Leave Directive – that implements the EU collective agreement on the matter.[129] It applies to women and men by offering both parents the right to spend a period of time with their child, especially in the event of a child's sickness.[130]

Maternity and parental leave constitute a relatively uncontroversial expression of 'social Europe'. But what about the other competence heads enumerated in Article 153(1)? Much more controversial has been the use of the competence to regulate 'working conditions' under subparagraph (b), and here in particular the adoption of the Working Time Directive.[131] The latter establishes *minimum* periods of rest for workers and applies, apart from some exceptions, to all employment sectors in the public and private spheres.[132] These rest periods concern 'daily rest',[133] 'weekly rest'[134] and 'annual leave'.[135] The directive also lays down a general limit on working time in Article 6 by stipulating that 'the

[127] Directive 92/85 on the introduction of measures to encourage improvements in the safety and health at work of pregnant workers and workers who have recently given birth or are breastfeeding (tenth individual directive within the meaning of Article 16(1) of Directive 89/391 [1992] OJ L 348/1).

[128] *Ibid.*, Art. 8(1).

[129] Directive 2010/18 implementing the revised Framework Agreement on parental leave [2010] OJ L 68/13. The directive put into effect the revised Framework Agreement on parental leave concluded on 18 June 2009 by the European cross-industry social partner organisations (BUSINESSEUROPE, UEAPME, CEEP and ETUC).

[130] *Ibid.*, clause 7(1): 'Member States and/or social partners shall take the necessary measures to entitle workers to time off from work, in accordance with national legislation, collective agreements and/or practice, on grounds of force majeure for urgent family reasons in cases of sickness or accident making the immediate presence of the worker indispensable.'

[131] Directive 2003/88 concerning certain aspects of the organisation of working time [2003] OJ L 299/9.

[132] *Ibid.*, Art. 1(3). For a list of specific derogations, see Arts. 17–22.

[133] *Ibid.*, Art. 3: 'Member States shall take the measures necessary to ensure that every worker is entitled to a minimum daily rest period of 11 consecutive hours per 24-hour period.'

[134] *Ibid.*, Art. 5: 'Member States shall take the measures necessary to ensure that, per each seven-day period, every worker is entitled to a minimum uninterrupted rest period of 24 hours plus the 11 hours' daily rest referred to in Article 3.'

[135] Art. 7(1): 'Member States shall take the measures necessary to ensure that every worker is entitled to paid annual leave of at least four weeks in accordance with the conditions for entitlement to, and granting of, such leave laid down by national legislation and/or practice.' The Court has held that annual leave was a 'particularly important principle of European Union social law' (see Case C-214/10, *KHS* v. *Schulte* [2011] ECR I-11757, para. 23). Annual leave thereby means paid (!) annual leave; and the Court has clarified that pay and leave are 'two aspects of a single right' (see Case C-131/04 and 257/04, *Robinson-Steele* [2006] ECR I-2531, para. 58).

average *working time* for each seven-day period, including overtime, does not exceed 48 hours'.[136]

A challenging interpretative problem has here been the very definition of 'working time'. The directive defines it as 'any period during which the worker is working, at the employer's disposal *and* carrying out his activity or duties, in accordance with national laws and/or practice'.[137] This wording seemed to suggest that actual work ('carrying out his activities') is required to count as work; yet the Court has given a broader meaning to the concept by essentially focusing on the 'disposal' element. The Court has thus held that 'on-call service' on the premises of the employer constitutes work – even if the employee was not actively working during this time. In light of the 48 hours per week limit, this has had significant consequences for the medical profession. In *Simap*, the Court thus famously held:

> [I]n the scheme of the directive, [working time] is placed in opposition to rest periods, the two being mutually exclusive. In the main proceedings, the characteristic features of working time are present in the case of time spent on call by doctors in primary care teams where their presence at the health centre is required. It is not disputed that during periods of duty on call under those rules, the first two conditions are fulfilled. Moreover, even if the activity actually performed varies according to the circumstances, the fact that such doctors are obliged to be present and available at the workplace with a view to providing their professional services means that they are carrying out their duties in that instance.[138]

This generous interpretation has had an unintended side effect. For the broader the scope of 'working time', the more Member States may decide to opt out of the obligations imposed by the directive.[139]

bb. Atypical Work

Having surveyed the principles governing *full*-time employment, what rules apply to alternative forms of employment, such as part-time work?

The various alternative employment formats are often referred to as 'atypical work',[140] even if they have increasingly become typical in the last decade(s).[141] The steady rise of 'atypical' work in modern economies is Janus-faced. On the

---

[136]   Working Time Directive. Art. 6(b) (emphasis added).
[137]   *Ibid.*, Art. 2(1) (emphasis added).
[138]   See Case C-303/98, *Simap* [2000] ECR I-7963, paras. 47–8.
[139]   The option is offered by Art. 22 of the directive. For an analysis of this point, see C. Barnard, *EU Employment Law* (Oxford University Press, 2012), 550.
[140]   M. Jeffery, 'Not Really Going to Work? Of the Directive on Part-time Work, "Atypical Work" and Attempts to Regulate It' (1998) 27 *Industrial Law Journal* 193.
[141]   Or, to put it even strikingly: 'In the post-modern labour market the "typical" worker had become "atypical"' (Kenner, *EU Employment Law* (n. 103 above), 279).

one hand, it offers greater flexibility for the employer (and the employee), and has thus been promoted as an employment-generating instrument.[142] On the other hand, it entails the danger of placing the employee in a weaker position vis-à-vis the employer; and for that reason, the question has arisen to what extent the 'typical' standard of employee protection should be extended to 'atypical' work.

The Union has – through the social partners – addressed this social question by regulating specific types of 'atypical' employment relationships. The two most important regulatory efforts here relate to part-time work,[143] as well as fixed-term work.[144]

Both forms of atypical work are governed by two protective principles: the principle of non-discrimination and the principle of *pro rata temporis*.[145] Importantly, the prohibition of discrimination between 'typical' and 'atypical' work exclusively relates to the 'employment conditions',[146] and will not cover dismissals.[147] And even for employment conditions, the Member States are, where justified by 'objective reasons', allowed to 'make access to particular conditions of employment subject to a period of service, time worked or earnings qualification'.[148] The principle of *pro rata temporis*, on the other hand, demands – wherever possible – to extend all the benefits enjoyed by full-time workers to part-time workers.

With regard to fixed-term contracts, the Union has added a third protective principle: the no-abuse principle. Union law here does not question the first-time use of a fixed-term contract over a typical employment contract. It indeed leaves this question to the national legislators (and private employers). Yet Member States are required to have protective measures in place so as to prevent abuse arising from the overuse of successive fixed-term contracts. The relevant provision of Union law, incorporating the European Framework Agreement on Fixed-Term Work, here states:

---

[142] K. Riesenhuber, *European Employment Law: A Systematic Exposition* (Intersentia, 2012), 413.

[143] Directive 97/81 concerning the Framework Agreement on part-time work concluded by UNICE, CEEP and the ETUC [1998] OJ L 14/9.

[144] Directive 99/70 concerning the framework agreement on fixed-term work concluded by ETUC, UNICE and CEEP [1999] OJ L 175/43.

[145] See clause 4 of the Framework Agreement on Part-time Work: '(1) In respect of employment conditions, part-time workers shall not be treated in a less favourable manner than comparable full-time workers solely because they work part time unless different treatment is justified on objective grounds. (2) Where appropriate, the principle of *pro rata temporis* shall apply.' For the equivalent provision with regard to fixed-term work, see clause 4 of that agreement.

[146] For a broad definition of this phrase, see Case C-268/06, *IMPACT* [2008] ECR I-2483; Case C-395/08, *INPS* v. *Bruno and others* [2010] ECR I-5119.

[147] Riesenhuber, *European Employment Law* (n. 142 above), 429.

[148] Clause 4(4) of the Agreement on Part-time Work. For an equivalent provision see also clause 4(4) of Agreement on Fixed-term Work.

> Measures to Prevent Abuse (Clause 5)
>
> To prevent abuse arising from the use of successive fixed-term employment contracts or relationships, Member States … shall, where there are no equivalent legal measures to prevent abuse, introduce in a manner which takes account of the needs of specific sectors and/or categories of workers, one or more of the following measures:
>
> (a) objective reasons justifying the renewal of such contracts or relationships;
> (b) the maximum total duration of successive fixed-term employment contracts or relationships;
> (c) the number of renewals of such contracts or relationships.[149]

Member States must choose one of these three options; and in light of option (a)'s flexibility, it is often this option that finds itself adopted. The Court has nevertheless clarified that even with regard to the potentially unlimited 'objective reasons' requirement, there will be European limits. For example: in *Pérez López*,[150] the Court examined the practice within Spanish hospitals of employing about 25 per cent of its workforce on fixed-term contracts. The case had been brought by a nurse, whose contract in the University Hospital of Madrid had been renewed seven (!) times. When offered an eighth successive contract, she had enough and claimed that the Spanish law allowing for such a practice violated the Union rule on the matter. The Court agreed. For even if the relevant Spanish law on hospital staff offered 'objective reasons' for the use of temporary staff, the actual practice pointed to an overly flexible interpretation in which permanent needs were addressed by temporary workers:

> The renewal of fixed-term employment contracts or relationships in order to cover needs which, in fact, are not temporary in nature but, on the contrary, fixed and permanent is not justified for the purposes of clause 5(1)(a) of the framework agreement, in so far as such use of fixed-term employment contracts or relationships conflicts directly with the premise on which the framework agreement is founded, namely that employment contracts of indefinite duration are the general form of employment relationship, even though fixed-term employment contracts are a feature of employment in certain sectors or in respect of certain occupations and activities. In order for clause 5(1)(a) of the framework agreement to be complied with, it must therefore be specifically verified that the renewal of successive fixed-term employment contracts or relationships is intended to cover temporary needs[.][151]

The Court here clarified that the interpretation of clause 5(1)(a) must always be seen in light of the Union framework agreement, 'namely to place limits on successive recourse to fixed-term employment contracts or relationships'

---

[149] Directive 99/70 concerning the framework agreement on fixed-term work concluded by ETUC, UNICE and CEEP, (1999) OJ L 175/43, Annex – Clause 5(1).
[150] Case 16/15, *Pérez López v. Servicio Madrileño de Salud*, EU:C:2016:679.
[151] *Ibid.*, para. 48–9.

because 'the benefit of stable employment is viewed as a major element in the protection of workers'.[152]

c. Employment Legislation II: Protection against Dismissal

The Union is – under Article 153(1)(d) – entitled to adopt legislation for the 'protection of workers where their employment contract is terminated'. This competence has been used to regulate three key moments of industrial restructuring: the *transfer* of an undertaking, the *downsizing* of an undertaking and the *insolvency* of an undertaking.

aa. Substantive Guarantees: The Transfers of Undertakings Directive

What are the rights of employees in the event of a transfer of an undertaking to a new employer? While employees will generally wish to be transferred alongside the undertaking, the new owner of the business might not necessarily want to keep all staff – especially in the event of a 'merger', whose main purpose will normally be the reduction of the combined workforce of the two previously independent companies.

The question thus arises to what extent Union law protects the interests of the workforce against the interests of a new business owner; and the Transfers of Undertakings Directive answers this question principally in favour of the employee:

> The transferor's rights and obligations arising from a contract of employment or from an employment relationship existing on the date of a transfer shall, by reason of such transfer, be transferred to the transferee.[153]

The employment contract should thus – in its entirety – be transferred to the new employer.[154] And in particular: the transfer must not 'in itself constitute grounds for dismissal by the transferor or the transferee'.[155] The sole exception admitted is dismissal relating to 'economic, technical or organizational reasons entailing changes in the workforce'.[156]

---

[152] *Ibid.*, paras. 26–7.

[153] Directive 2001/23 on the approximation of the laws of the Member States relating to the safeguarding of employees' rights in the event of transfers of undertakings, businesses or parts of undertakings or businesses [2001] OJ L 82/16, Art. 3(1). This general rule applies to public and private undertakings engaged in economic activities. However, the exception to this rule relates to the transfer of administrative functions from one public authority to another, see Art. 1(1)(c): 'An administrative reorganisation of public administrative authorities, or the transfer of administrative functions between public administrative authorities, is not a transfer within the meaning of this Directive.'

[154] See Case 324/86, *Daddy's Dance Hall* [1988] ECR 739.

[155] Transfers of Undertakings Directive, Art. 4(1) – first sentence.

[156] *Ibid.*, Art. 4(2) – second sentence.

In light of this – relatively protected – status of employees, the critical question in past jurisprudence has been what counts as a 'transfer' of an 'undertaking' and what does not. The directive itself clarifies that it covers full as well as partial transfers,[157] and the European Courts have given a broad interpretation to the concept. Regardless of whether or not the result of a sales contract,[158] the Court considers 'any legal change in the person of the employer' as a legal transfer.[159] While there must consequently be a change in the identity of the employer, the directive insists, on the other hand, that the *transferred undertaking must 'retain … its identity'*.[160] The idea behind this criterion is to exclude situations in which the new employer did not *receive* an 'old business' from someone else but rather *took* the business on the market.

The dividing line between the two phenomena is nevertheless devilishly difficult. The Court has traditionally preferred an overall assessment of various criteria.[161] The application of these criteria is however often not very clear. For example, if a cleaning lady is dismissed by a bank (her direct employer) but subsequently hired by a cleaning service that also cleans for the bank, is that a transfer of an undertaking – entitling the cleaning lady to claim the same hourly pay? In *Schmidt*,[162] the Court found that this was the case; yet in *Süzen*,[163] it held that 'the mere fact that the service provided by the old and the new awardees of a contract is similar does not therefore support the conclusion that an economic entity has been transferred'.[164] The post-*Süzen* case law has therefore insisted that a transfer of an undertaking only takes place where there is a transfer of

---

[157] *Ibid.*, Art. 1(1)(a).

[158] In addition to a sales contract, the Court has equally accepted as transfers temporary leases, see Case 324/86, *Daddy's Dance Hall*; (temporary) contracting-out arrangements, see Case C-209/91, *Watson Rask and Kirsten Christensen* v. *Iss Kantineservice* [1992] ECR I-5755.

[159] Case C-234/98, *Allen and others* v. *Amalgamated Construction* [1999] ECR I-8643, para. 17.

[160] Transfers of Undertakings Directive, Art. 1(1)(b) (emphasis added).

[161] These criteria are summed up as the '*Spijkers* criteria' – see Case 24/85, *Spijkers* v. *Gebroeders Benedik Abattoir CV and Alfred Benedik en Zonen* [1986] ECR 1119, para. 13: 'In order to determine whether those conditions are met, it is necessary to consider all the facts characterizing the transaction in question, including the type of undertaking or business, whether or not the business's tangible assets, such as buildings and movable property, are transferred, the value of its intangible assets at the time of the transfer, whether or not the majority of its employees are taken over by the new employer, whether or not its customers are transferred and the degree of similarity between the activities carried on before and after the transfer and the period, if any, for which those activities were suspended. It should be noted, however, that all those circumstances are merely single factors in the overall assessment which must be made and cannot therefore be considered in isolation.'

[162] Case C-392/92, *Schmidt* v. *Spar- und Leihkasse* [1994] ECR I-1311.

[163] Case C-13/95, *Süzen* v. *Zehnacker Gebäudereinigung GmbH Krankenhausservice* [1997] ECR I-1259.

[164] *Ibid.*, para. 15. The Court continued (*ibid.*, para. 16): 'The mere loss of a service contract to a competitor cannot therefore by itself indicate the existence of a transfer within the meaning of the directive. In those circumstances, the service undertaking previously entrusted with the contract does not, on losing a customer, thereby cease fully to exist, and a business or part of a business belonging to it cannot be considered to have been transferred to the new awardee of the contract.'

'significant tangible or intangible assets' or where the new employer takes over 'a major part of the workforce'.[165]

bb. Procedural Guarantees: The Collective Redundancies and Insolvency Directives

What happens where an undertaking has decided to reduce its workforce during an industrial crisis, or where – in the worst-case scenario – it has become completely insolvent? In these situations in which the economic conditions for an undertaking have changed for the worse, Union law does not grant any substantive rights to employees; yet it imposes certain *procedural* obligations on the undertaking or the State to protect the rights of workers.

Union law deals with the former situation in its Collective Redundancies Directive.[166] As its name indicates, the directive does not deal with *individual* dismissals but only deals with *collective* dismissals. These 'mass' redundancies are not prohibited, as Union law does not wish to interfere with the entrepreneurial freedom to take necessary business decisions. However, the directive imposes procedural obligations on the employer to consult with the worker representatives in good time,[167] to notify the competent public authority[168] and to wait for 30 days before effecting the planned dismissals.[169] The last obligation is to give time to the public authorities involved to find mutually acceptable alternatives to the redundancies.[170]

When will these procedural obligations apply? The Directive defines its personal scope as follows:

> '[C]ollective redundancies' means dismissals effected by an employer for one or more reasons not related to the individual workers concerned where, according to the choice of the Member States, the number of redundancies is:
> (i)   either, over a period of 30 days:
>   –   at least 10 in establishments normally employing more than 20 and less than 100 workers,
>   –   at least 10% of the number of workers in establishments normally employing at least 100 but less than 300 workers,
>   –   at least 30 in establishments normally employing 300 workers or more,
> (ii) or, over a period of 90 days, at least 20, whatever the number of workers normally employed in the establishments in question.[171]

---

[165] *Ibid.*, para. 21. For an excellent analysis of the case law, see G. Barrett, 'Light Acquired on Acquired Rights: Examining Developments in Employment Rights on Transfers of Undertakings' (2005) 42 *CML Rev.* 1053.

[166] Directive 98/59 on the approximation of the laws of the Member States relating to collective redundancies [1998] OJ L 225/16. For an analysis of the origins of the directive, see A. M. Lofaso, 'Retermination Job Rights of British Workers Affected by Collective Redundancies' (1996) 16 YEL 277; A. P. van der Mei. 'Collective Redundancies: Judicial Fine-tuning of a Classic Concept of EU Labour Law' (2017) 42 *EL Rev.* 82.

[167] *Ibid.*, Art. 2.   [168] *Ibid.*, Art. 3.   [169] *Ibid.*, Art. 4(1).

[170] *Ibid.*, Art. 4(2). See Case C-188/03, *Junk* v. *Kühnel* [2005] ECR I-885.

[171] Collective Redundancies Directive, Art. 1(a).

The provision leaves Member States a choice between (i) and (ii); and where option (ii) is chosen – such as in the United Kingdom – the central problem arises what counts as 'the establishment in question'. The Court gave an answer to this problem in *USDAW*.[172] The Union of Shop, Distributive and Allied Workers (USDAW), a trade union with almost half a million members in the United Kingdom, here brought proceedings against Woolworths' decision to dismiss thousands of employees. The trade union thereby claimed that the scope of option (ii) 'is not limited to a situation in which at least 20 employees in each establishment are made redundant' but equally 'encompasses a situation in which at least 20 employees of the same employer are made redundant over a period of 90 days'.[173] The Court however roundly rejected the idea by pointing to the text and purpose of the directive and clarified that 'establishment in question' indeed referred to each individual Woolworths shop.[174]

Finally, what rights – if any – do employees have in the event of an undertaking's insolvency? This dramatic situation is partly regulated by the Insolvency Protection Directive.[175] The latter is again not designed as a Union instrument against dismissals as such. It rather protects the employee as a (potential) 'creditor' of an undertaking, which may no longer be able to fully pay their salary. The directive requires Member States to establish so-called 'Guarantee Institutions', which are to ensure 'payment of employees' outstanding claims resulting from contracts of employment or employment relationships, including, where provided for by national law, severance pay on termination of employment relationships'.[176] The organisation and financing of these guarantee institutions falls within the discretion of the Member States.[177] The national authorities may thereby limit the *public* guarantee of these private law claims.[178] These discretionary powers have prevented the direct effect of the directive; yet where a Member State completely fails to establish a national guarantee institution, it may be liable to pay compensation under the *Francovich* doctrine.[179]

d. In Particular: The Equal Pay Principle

The equal pay principle has been the classic pillar of the Union's social policy. Prior to the creation of Article 153 TFEU, it indeed constituted its sole legal weapon. The provision can today be found in Article 157, which states:

---

[172] Case C-80/14, *Union of Shop, Distributive and Allied Workers (USDAW) and B. Wilson* v. *WW Realisation 1 Ltd and Others*, EU:C:2015:291.

[173] *Ibid.*, para. 34.   [174] *Ibid.*, para. 68.

[175] Directive 2008/94 on the protection of employees in the event of the insolvency of their employer [2008] OJ L 283/36.

[176] *Ibid.*, Art. 3.   [177] *Ibid.*, Art. 5.   [178] *Ibid.*, Art. 4.

[179] Indeed: Joined Cases C-6/90 and C-9/90, *Francovich and others* v. *Italy* [1991] ECR I-5357 dealt with the Union's insolvency directive. For a discussion of the case, see Chapter 11, section 3(a).

1. Each Member State shall ensure that the principle of equal pay for male and female workers for equal work or work of equal value is applied.
2. For the purpose of this Article, 'pay' means the ordinary basic or minimum wage or salary and any other consideration, whether in cash or in kind, which the worker receives directly or indirectly, in respect of his employment, from his employer.

Equal pay without discrimination based on sex means:

(a) that pay for the same work at piece rates shall be calculated on the basis of the same unit of measurement;
(b) that pay for work at time rates shall be the same for the same job.

The equal pay principle had originally been introduced with a 'double aim'. While it was 'to ensure social progress and seek the constant improvement of living and working conditions', it was equally 'to avoid a situation in which undertakings established in States which have actually implemented the principle of equal pay suffer a competitive disadvantage in intra-[Union] competition as compared with undertakings established in States which have not yet eliminated discrimination against women workers'.[180]

Would Article 157 be sufficiently clear and precise to have direct effect? Its wording gave ambivalent signals, yet the European Court confirmed that the principle of equal pay was directly effective,[181] and that it would – despite being addressed to the Member States – apply to private employers alike. However, the Court has insisted that the scope of Article 157(1) was strictly confined to equal *pay* as defined in Article 157(2). It would not extend to equality in all working conditions.[182]

---

[180] Case 43/75, *Defrenne v. Société anonyme belge de navigation aérienne Sabena* [1976] ECR 455, paras. 8–10. To some, it is however clear that Art. 157 'was not introduced because of a high-minded pursuit of the ideal of general equality', but rather because 'France already had equal pay laws and was concerned that its firms would be disadvantaged in the common market because firms in other countries with no equal pay laws would be able to use women workers as a form of cheap labour' (see A. C. L. Davies, *EU Labour Law* (Edward Elgar, 2013), 109).

[181] Case 43/75, *Defrenne v. Société anonyme belge de navigation aérienne Sabena*, para. 24. The Court originally declared only a part of the prohibition – the prohibition of direct discrimination – to be directly effective by finding that indirect discrimination could 'only be identified by reference to more explicit implementing provisions of a [Union] or national character' (*ibid.*, para. 18). However, the Court subsequently held the prohibition of indirect pay discrimination to be also directly effective, see Case 262/88, *Barber* v. *Guardian Royal Exchange Assurance Group* [1990] ECR I-1889, para. 37: '[Article 157(1)] 'applies directly to all forms of discrimination which may be identified solely with the aid of the criteria of equal work and equal pay referred to by the article in question'.

[182] See Case 149/77, *Defrenne v. Société anonyme belge de navigation aérienne Sabena (3)* [1978] ECR 1365. The Court has however given a broad teleological meaning to 'pay' (see Case 262/88, *Barber*, para. 12: '[T]he concept of pay, within the meaning of the second paragraph of Article [157], comprises any other consideration, whether in cash or in kind, whether immediate or future, provided that the worker receives it, albeit indirectly, in respect of his employment from his employer'.

The constitutional right to equal pay under Article 157(1) is strengthened by a legislative competence that allows the Union, under Article 157(3), to adopt more specific additional rules. It states:

> The European Parliament and the Council, acting in accordance with the ordinary legislative procedure, and after consulting the Economic and Social Committee, shall adopt measures to ensure the application of the principle of equal opportunities and equal treatment of men and women in matters of employment and occupation, including the principle of equal pay for equal work or work of equal value.

This legislative competence constitutes the basis of one of the most adjudicated and successful pieces of Union legislation: Directive 2006/54 – the Equal Treatment Directive.[183] The rights granted under the directive go well beyond the scope of Article 157(1). Its purpose 'is to ensure the implementation of the principle of *equal opportunities and equal treatment* of men and women in matters of employment and occupation'.[184] The directive thus covers not only equal 'pay' but equal 'treatment' generally, and even stretches to regulate equal 'opportunities'.

Let us look at the scope and nature of the equal pay principle in section (aa) below. Thereafter, we shall explore the wider idea of equal treatment and equal opportunities in section (bb).

aa. Pay Discrimination: Direct and Indirect Forms

Discrimination occurs where equal situations are treated unequally. Article 157(1) expressly prohibits sex discrimination by insisting on 'equal pay for male and female workers for equal work or work of equal value'.

'Pay' here means 'the ordinary basic or minimum wage or salary and any other consideration, whether in cash or in kind, which the worker receives directly or indirectly, in respect of his employment, from his employer'.[185]

Discrimination may thereby take place directly or indirectly. According to the Equal Treatment Directive, direct discrimination arises

> where one person is treated *less favourably on grounds of sex* than another is, has been or would be treated *in a comparable situation*.[186]

Indirect discrimination, by contrast, will arise

---

[183] Directive 2006/54 on the implementation of the principle of equal opportunities and equal treatment of men and women in matters of employment and occupation (recast) [2006] OJ L 204/23.

[184] Equal Treatment Directive, Art. 1 (emphasis added).

[185] Art. 157(2) TFEU.

[186] Equal Treatment Directive, Art. 2(1)(a) (emphasis added).

where an apparently neutral provision, criterion or practice [that] would put persons of one sex at a *particular disadvantage compared with persons of the other sex*, unless that provision, criterion or practice is objectively justified by a legitimate aim, and the means of achieving that aim are appropriate and necessary.[187]

The two core elements behind both forms of discrimination are the existence of a *comparable* situation, in which a person is treated less favourably *because of her (or his) sex*.

What is a comparable situation? Can a woman claim that a man doing equal work but working for a different employer earns more? Or, must she find a comparator in her own company? The Court originally tended towards the wider comparator.[188] However, it subsequently opted for the more restrictive comparator. In *Lawrence*,[189] the Court thus found that where the difference in treatment '*cannot be attributed to a single source, there is no body which is responsible for the inequality and which could restore equal treatment*'.[190] Where one employer pays women less than another employer pays men, Article 157(1) would consequently not apply. The Court has, on the other hand, held that a woman need not point to a man who is *presently* employed by the same company. She may refer to past employees, but the comparator must be a real person and not a 'hypothetical male worker'.[191]

With regard to direct discrimination, the prohibition of unequal pay is relatively straightforward. However, this is often not as easy when it comes to indirect forms of discrimination. In *Bilka-Kaufhaus*,[192] a group of German department stores had created an occupational pension scheme as an integral part of their employment contracts. It was open to all employees, but part-time workers would only receive their pension if they had worked full time for at least 15 years. Was this rule indirectly discriminating against women? The European Court found that this would be the case, *if* it were found that a much lower proportion of women worked full time. The existence of a pay–inequality praxis between men and women may thus point to an indirectly discriminatory rule. However, the Court accepted that a discriminatory practice might sometimes not be the result of sex discrimination but could be explained by 'objectively justified factors unrelated to any discrimination on grounds of sex';[193] and this possibility is also expressly referred to in the Equal Treatment Directive. There might indeed exist legitimate economic reasons behind a rule that favours full-time

---

[187] *Ibid.*, Art. 2(1)(b) (emphasis added). See also Case C-322/98, *Kachelmann* v. *Bankhaus Hermann Lampe* [2000] ECR I-7505, esp. para. 23.

[188] See Case 43/75, *Defrenne (2)*.

[189] Case C-320/00, *Lawrence and others* v. *Regent Office Care* [2002] ECR I-7325.

[190] *Ibid.*, para. 18 (emphasis added). For a criticism of the 'single source rule' ruling, see S. Fredman, 'Marginalising Equal Pay Laws' (2004) 33 *Industrial Law Journal* 281.

[191] Case 129/79, *Macarthys* v. *Smith* [1980] ECR 1275, esp. paras. 11–15.

[192] Case 170/84, *Bilka-Kaufhaus GmbH* v. *Karin Weber von Hartz* [1986] ECR 1607.

[193] *Ibid.*, paras. 29–30.

work or that make pay differences dependent on professional seniority or academic qualifications.[194]

bb. Beyond Pay: Equal Treatment and Positive Action

While the material scope of Article 157(1) TFEU is limited to equal pay, the Union's legislative competence under Article 157(3) TFEU is broader. It allows the Union to adopt general measures to give effect to 'the principle of equal *opportunities* and equal *treatment* of men and women in matters of employment and occupation'. The principal legislative act to implement the competence is the 'Equal Treatment Directive'. It goes expressly beyond pay discrimination by covering 'access to employment' as well as all 'working conditions' generally.[195] The central provision can thereby be found in Article 14, which states:

> There shall be no direct or indirect discrimination on grounds of sex in the public or private sectors, including public bodies, in relation to:
> a. conditions for access to employment, to self-employment or to occupation, including selection criteria and recruitment conditions, whatever the branch of activity and at all levels of the professional hierarchy, including promotion;
> b. access to all types and to all levels of vocational guidance, vocational training, advanced vocational training and retraining, including practical work experience;
> c. employment and working conditions, including dismissals, as well as pay as provided for in Article [157] of the [FEU] Treaty;
> d. membership of, and involvement in, an organisation of workers or employers, or any organisation whose members carry on a particular profession, including the benefits provided for by such organisations.[196]

This general prohibition of discrimination between men and women in employment relationships is nonetheless qualified in one respect. With regard to *access* to employment including the training thereto (a/b), direct discrimination on a characteristic relating to sex is not prohibited where such a characteristic 'constitutes a genuine and determining occupational requirement' that

---

[194] Case 109/88, *Handels- og Kontorfunktionærernes Forbund I Danmark v. Dansk Arbejdsgiverforening, acting on behalf of Danfoss* [1989] ECR 3199, esp. para. 25: '[W]here it appears that the application of criteria, such as the employee's mobility, training or length of service, for the award of pay supplements systematically works to the disadvantage of female employees: (i) the employer may justify recourse to the criterion of mobility if it is understood as referring to adaptability to variable hours and varying places of work, by showing that such adaptability is of importance for the performance of the specific tasks which are entrusted to the employee, but not if that criterion is understood as covering the quality of the work done by the employee; (ii) the employer may justify recourse to the criterion of training by showing that such training is of importance for the performance of the specific tasks which are entrusted to the employee; (iii) the employer does not have to provide special justification for recourse to the criterion of length of service.'
[195] Equal Treatment Directive, Art. 1.
[196] *Ibid.*, Art. 14(1).

is proportionate.[197] This exception reflects past jurisprudence, especially in the context of women's involvement in the police and military service.[198]

Does the directive also allow for 'positive action'? The idea of positive action refers to situations in which a public authority actively tries to positively encourage an underrepresented group. The Equal Treatment Directive says nothing about positive action *by the Union*. However, its Article 3 cross-references the permission for positive action *by the Member States* offered in Article 157(4) TFEU. And the latter allows for national measures 'providing for specific advantages in order to make it easier for the underrepresented sex to pursue a vocational activity or to prevent or compensate for disadvantages in professional careers'.

The question in EU jurisprudence has been how far this justification can go, and in particular whether it can justify positive *discrimination*. Positive discrimination refers to situations where a candidate of one sex – normally a woman – is given *preferential* treatment over an equally qualified member of the opposite sex. Should we allow discrimination against *individual* men so as to fight the *structural* discrimination of women?[199] In the past, the Court of Justice has struggled with this idea, especially in the context of 'quotas' reserved for women. In *Abrahamsson*,[200] the Court outlawed a Swedish rule that positively discriminated in favour of female candidates less qualified then their male counterparts where women were underrepresented in public sector employment; whereas in *Kalanke*,[201] it even went further and outlawed a German law that gave preference to female candidates in the event of *equally* qualified men. These cases mean that 'hard quotas' in favour of female workers will violate EU sex-discrimination law. The Court has however come to allow 'soft quotas' that must nevertheless take into account the principle of individual merit.[202]

3. Consumer Protection

Unlike social policy, there was no Treaty Title dedicated to consumer protection in the original Rome Treaty. The reason for this omission was twofold. First,

---

[197] *Ibid.*, Art. 14(2).

[198] Case 222/84, *Johnston v. Chief Constable of the Royal Ulster Constabulary* [1986] ECR 1651; Case C-273/97, *Sirdar v. The Army Board and Secretary of State for Defence* [1999] ECR I-7403; Case C-285/98, *Kreil v. Germany* [2000] ECR I-69. See generally, G. Anagnostaras, 'Sex Equality and Compulsory Military Service: The Limits of National Sovereignty over Matters of Army Organization' (2003) 28 *EL Rev.* 713.

[199] On this question, see S. Fredman, 'Affirmative Action and the European Court of Justice: A Critical Analysis', in J. Shaw (ed.), *Social Law and Policy in an Evolving European Union* (Hart, 2000), 171; D. Schiek, 'Sex Equality Law after *Kalanke* and *Marschall*' (1998) 4 ELJ 148.

[200] Case C-407/98, *Abrahamsson and Anderson v. Fogelqvist*, [2000] ECR I-5539.

[201] Case C-450/93, *Kalanke v. Freie Hansestadt Bremen* [1995] ECR I-3051.

[202] See Case C-476/99, *Lommers v. Minister van Landbouw, Natuurbeheer en Visserij* [2002] ECR I-2891.

an autonomous area within the law of contract dealing specifically with 'consumer protection' had not yet emerged in the 1950s; and, secondly, the simple assumption behind the 1957 Treaty was that the consumer would automatically 'benefit from the process of integration through the enjoyment of a more efficient market, which will yield more competition allowing for wider choice, lower prices and higher-quality products and services'.[203] Consumer welfare was indeed perceived as an automatic 'by-product of the common market'.[204]

With the rise of the 'consumer movement' in the second half of the twentieth century, the European Union gradually developed a more direct form of consumer protection. In the wake of the 1972 Paris Summit, the Union indeed passed a series of resolutions proposing a Union policy on consumer protection.[205] But how could these political ambitions be translated into European law? In the absence of a Treaty Title on consumer protection, the Union (again) used its 'internal market' power(s), namely Articles 114 and 115 TFEU. Ever since the 1992 Maastricht Treaty, these general competences have been complemented by a specific competence on 'Consumer Protection'. Forming by itself Title XV within the Union's internal policies, Article 169 TFEU today states:

1. In order to promote the interests of consumers and to ensure a high level of consumer protection, the Union shall contribute to protecting the health, safety and economic interests of consumers, as well as to promoting their right to information, education and to organise themselves in order to safeguard their interests.
2. The Union shall contribute to the attainment of the objectives referred to in paragraph 1 through:
   (a) measures adopted pursuant to Article 114 in the context of the completion of the internal market;
   (b) measures which support, supplement and monitor the policy pursued by the Member States.
3. The European Parliament and the Council, acting in accordance with the ordinary legislative procedure and after consulting the Economic and Social Committee, shall adopt the measures referred to in paragraph 2(b).
4. Measures adopted pursuant to paragraph 3 shall not prevent any Member State from maintaining or introducing more stringent protective measures. Such measures must be compatible with the Treaties. The Commission shall be notified of them.

---

[203] S. Weatherill, *EU Consumer Law and Policy* (Edward Elgar, 2006), 4.
[204] J. Stuyck, 'European Consumer Law after the Treaty of Amsterdam: Consumer Policy in or beyond the Internal Market?' (2000) 37 *CML Rev.* 367 at 377.
[205] See Council Resolution of 14 April 1975 on a preliminary programme of the European Economic Community for a consumer protection and information policy [1975] OJ C 92/1.

The provision does not define the concept of 'consumer'; this has been left to the Union legislator and the Court.[206] However, it clearly expresses the commitment of the Union to ensure a *high* level of consumer protection.[207]

This commitment is to be pursued in two ways. Paragraph 2(a) expressly acknowledges the continued importance of 'internal market' harmonisation measures under Article 114 for consumer policy. By contrast, paragraph 2(b) contains a legislative competence for specific 'measures which support, supplement and monitor the policy pursued by the Member States'. This special consumer competence is a shared competence;[208] yet, it is a shared competence that – when exercised – cannot 'prevent any Member State from maintaining or introducing more stringent protective measures'. (The nature of these minimum harmonisation competences was discussed in Chapter 7.) Unlike consumer legislation adopted under Article 114 – a competence that allows for total as well as minimum harmonisation,[209] legislation adopted under Article 169 should thus be minimum harmonisation.

In the adoption of EU consumer legislation, Article 169 has however so far been 'of pale significance'.[210] The central consumer law competence today thus continues to be Article 114. In the past, the latter has been used to adopt an impressive – albeit diverse and incoherent – range of Union legislation (see Table 18.7). The Union has thereby followed a dual and complementary approach. It has tried to lay down general – horizontal – ground rules that are complemented by specific – vertical – rules for particular consumer problems. Under both approaches, the Union has traditionally laid down minimum requirements that allow Member States to go beyond the consumer rights established by European law; yet, the Union executive has recently pushed hard for a shift towards maximum harmonisation.[211] This shift has been particularly counterproductive, since the method of maximum harmonisation overemphasises the internal market goal over European consumer law and policy.[212]

---

[206] A statutory definition of 'consumer' can be found, for example, in Art. 2(1) of the Consumer Rights Directive (n. 217 below), which states: '"consumer" means any natural person who, in contracts covered by this Directive, is acting for purposes which are outside his trade, business or profession'.

[207] See also: Art. 12 TFEU: 'Consumer protection requirements shall be taken into account in defining and implementing other Union policies and activities'; Art. 114(3) TFEU, which requires the Union to 'take as a base a high level of [consumer] protection' when adopting Union legislation under this legal base.

[208] Art. 4(2)(f) TFEU.

[209] On Article 114 TFEU and the various harmonisation methods, see Chapter 14, section 3 above.

[210] Weatherill, *EU Consumer Law and Policy* (n. 203 above), 70. One of the few Union measures that was adopted under the specific consumer policy competence was Directive 98/6 on consumer protection in the indication of the prices of products offered to consumers [1998] OJ L 80/31.

[211] The (attempted) move has received much academic criticism (see H. Micklitz and N. Reich, 'Crónica de una muerte annunciada: The Commission Proposal for a "Directive on Consumer Rights"' (2009) 46 *CML Rev.* 471).

[212] G. Howells, C. Twigg-Flesner and T. Wilhelmsson, *Rethinking EU Consumer Law* (Routledge, 2017), ch. 1.

Table 18.7 EU Consumer Measures (Selection)

Horizontal harmonisation	Vertical harmonisation
Product Liability Directive (1985/374)	Distance Marketing of Consumer Financial Services Directive (2002/65)
Unfair Terms in Consumer Contracts Directive (1993/13)	Misleading & Comparative Advertising Directive (2006/114)
Consumer Sales Directive (1999/44)	Consumer Credit Directive (2008/48)
Unfair Commercial Practices Directive (2005/29)	Toy Safety Directive (2009/48)
Misleading and Comparative Advertising Directive (2006/114)	Regulation on the Provision of Food Information to Consumers (1169/2011)
Consumer Rights Directive (2011/83)	Package Travel Directive (2015/2302)

Looking closely at the various measures listed in Table 18.7 shows that the Union traditionally employs the Union instrument of the 'directive' within consumer law. Unlike 'regulations', directives always require transposition into national law; and, as may be recalled from Chapter 3, the Court of Justice has long held that directives cannot be invoked to neutralise national laws in proceedings between private parties. This lack of horizontal direct effect – somewhat ironically – means that a consumer theoretically protected by Union legislation cannot invoke his European rights in judicial proceedings against a private business.[213]

The Union legal order has nevertheless tried to strengthen the judicial enforcement of EU consumer law. In addition to the general obligation on national courts to interpret national law 'as far as possible' in line with Union law (under the doctrine of consistent interpretation),[214] the Union legal order has specifically insisted that European consumer law will have to be applied *ex officio* by a national court.[215] This does not mean that a European consumer directive will have to be directly applied by a national court but rather that a national judge must always, and as an official obligation, evaluate the national law in light of European consumer law – even if the parties did not expressly invoke the latter in the judicial proceedings. And importantly, where a national court fails to (indirectly) apply an EU consumer directive, the consumer may be entitled to claim damages from the State under the *Francovich* doctrine.[216]

---

[213]   See Case C-91/92, *Dori* v. *Recreb* [1994] ECR I-3325.

[214]   On the duty of consistent interpretation, see Chapter 3, section 3(b).

[215]   On this duty within the context of an effective national remedy, see generally Chapter 11, section 2(b); and specifically Case C-240/98, *Océano Grupo Editorial SA* v. *Roció Murciano Quintero* [2000] ECR I-4941; Case C-243/08, *Pannon* v. *Erzsébet Sustikné Győrfi* [2009] ECR I-4713.

[216]   Case C-168/15, *Tomášová* v. *Slovenská republika*, EU:C:2016:602. The case involved a pensioner who had concluded a consumer credit contract, which fixed, *inter alia* a penalty interest rate of 91.25 per cent. Tomášová was ordered to repay the credit by a court but

With these constitutional preliminaries behind us, let us now look at four substantive aspects of EU consumer law. Sections (a) and (b) analyse how the interests of consumers are protected through Union rules governing the formation and content of consumer contracts. Section (c) explores the European rules on commercial practices, which stand somewhere between consumer and competition law. Section (d) looks at the European 'tort' rules governing product liability.

a. Forming Contracts: The Consumer Rights and Sales Directives

In the – imaginary – world of perfectly rational economic actors, the conclusion of contracts operates under conditions of complete information and conscious choice. But what about situations in which the consumer concludes a contract over the phone without ever seeing the purchased product, or where s/he was 'talked into' a good by a zealous salesperson in the middle of a busy train station? In both cases, the consumer is negotiating in an environment that is not a 'business environment' and, with his economic senses temporarily numbed, he may come to regret ill-considered choices. To regulate these situations, many legal orders have adopted consumer protection laws for what is – respectively – called 'distance selling' and 'off-premise' (doorstep) selling. While these sales methods are not prohibited as such, the consumer is permitted to gain additional information – like seeing the goods – or time to regain a cool conscious mind.

For the Union legal order, Directive 2011/83 on consumer rights provides this form of consumer protection.[217] Despite its 'grandiose' title, the directive has been said to be 'trivial'.[218] Its express aim is to 'lay down standard rules for the common aspects of *distance* and *off-premises* contracts';[219] and it is indeed confined to giving special consumer rights for these two modes of contract formation. A 'distance contract' refers to a contract concluded 'without the simultaneous physical presence of the trader and the consumer, with the exclusive use of one or more means of distance communication',[220] such as mail or telephone. An 'off-premises contract', on the other hand, is a contract concluded 'in a place

---

instead of paying, she decided to bring an action for damages against the Slovak Republic – arguing that the relevant district court had not – even though obliged under the principle of effectiveness – applied of its own motion EU consumer law. The Court here held that 'an infringement of EU law is sufficiently serious where it was made in manifest breach of the case-law of the Court in the matter' (*ibid.*, para. 26); and went on to examine whether the line of cases requiring the ex officio application of EU consumer law by national courts had already been 'settled' case law.

[217] Directive 2011/83 on consumer rights [2011] OJ L 304/64.

[218] S. Weatherill, 'The Consumer Rights Directive: How and Why a Quest for "Coherence" Has (Largely) Failed' (2012) 49 *CML Rev.* 1279.

[219] Consumer Rights Directive, preamble 2. According to Art. 3(1), the directive applies to 'any contract concluded between a trader and a consumer'. However, Art. 3(3) lists a number of exceptions, such as financial services contracts (subpara. (d)), and immovable property contracts (subpara. (e)).

[220] Consumer Rights Directive, Art. 2(7).

which is not the business premises of the trader'.[221] As we have seen, this could range from the doorstep of the consumer's home to the middle of a busy train station.

The principal idea in regulating the formation of these two types of contracts is to provide the consumer with more knowledge and a 'cooling-off' period.[222] The first is achieved by imposing extensive information requirements on the seller.[223] The 'cooling-off' period is created by means of a 'right of withdrawal'.

The right of withdrawal is the core right under the Consumer Rights Directive. It provides the consumer with a period of 14 days within which s/he can cancel the contract 'without giving any reason'.[224] From a contract law perspective, this right seems, at least temporarily, to suspend the binding nature of a contract, since it allows the consumer to unilaterally terminate the contract simply because s/he has changed her mind.[225] In the event of a withdrawal, the consumer must return the goods within 14 days after cancellation,[226] while the trader must reimburse all payments (including the standard delivery costs) to the consumer within the same period.[227] The consumer will generally bear the direct costs of returning the goods,[228] and s/he may also have to pay for the diminished value or the use of the goods.[229]

What (mandatory) rights will the consumer also have against the seller? Many legal orders have established standardised implied terms for sales contracts and the Union has done so through Directive 1999/44 on the Sale of Consumer Goods.[230] The central pillar of the directive is the principle of conformity, according to which '[t]he seller must deliver goods to the consumer which are in conformity with the contract of sale'.[231] This means that the goods must comply with the contractual description,[232] be fit for purpose[233] or 'show the quality

---

[221] Ibid., Art. 2(8).

[222] Ibid., recital 37: 'Since in the case of distance sales, the consumer is not able to see the goods before concluding the contract, he should have a right of withdrawal. For the same reason, the consumer should be allowed to test and inspect the goods he has bought to the extent necessary to establish the nature, characteristics and the functioning of the goods. Concerning off-premises contracts, the consumer should have the right of withdrawal because of the potential surprise element and/or psychological pressure. Withdrawal from the contract should terminate the obligation of the contracting parties to perform the contract.'

[223] Ibid., Arts. 6–8.

[224] Ibid., Art. 9. This period is extended to 12 months where the trader has failed to inform the consumer of the right of withdrawal; see Art. 10.

[225] Ibid., Art. 12: 'The exercise of the right of withdrawal shall terminate the obligations of the parties: (a) to perform the distance or off-premises contract; or (b) to conclude the distance or off-premises contract, in cases where an offer was made by the consumer.'

[226] Ibid., Art. 14.   [227] Ibid., Art. 13.   [228] Ibid., Art. 14(1).

[229] Ibid., Art. 14(2)–(5). See also Case C-489/07, Messner v. Krüger [2009] ECR I-7314.

[230] Directive 1999/44 on certain aspects of the sale of consumer goods and associated guarantees [1999] OJ L 171/12.

[231] Ibid., Art. 2(1).   [232] Ibid., Art. 2(2)(a).   [233] Ibid., Art. 2(2)(b) and (c).

and performance which are normal in goods of the same type and which the consumer can reasonably expect'.[234]

If the goods do not conform to the contract, the consumer is entitled to have the goods repaired or replaced.[235] If these primary remedies are impossible or disproportionate,[236] the consumer will be entitled to ask for an appropriate reduction of the price or rescind the contract.[237] These primary and secondary remedies are mandatory. They must be used within two years from the delivery of the goods,[238] and their use must be notified to the seller within two months from the date on which the defect occurred.[239]

b. Policing Contracts: The Unfair Terms Directive

The autonomy of the contracting parties constitutes the intellectual corner-stone behind all contracts. The parties are legally bound because they freely consented to be bound. Should there be limits to this freedom? Should *public* authorities intervene to protect the *private* interests of the – weaker – contract party?

Unfair contractual terms and their public control are a very old phenomenon.[240] However, only in the twentieth century was the classic freedom of contract philosophy subjected to a thorough realist critique.[241] The latter (partly) discredited the myth of legal equality by pointing to the social imbalances in the bargaining power over many contracts. Consumer contracts often constitute one class of such imbalanced contracts – especially where the consumer is faced with so-called 'standard terms'.

The Unfair Terms in Consumer Contracts Directive addresses this problem at the European level.[242] The aim of the directive has been described as follows:

---

[234] *Ibid.*, Art. 2(2)(d). Art. 2(3) additionally states: 'There shall be deemed not to be a lack of conformity for the purposes of this Article if, at the time the contract was concluded, the consumer was aware, or could not reasonably be unaware of, the lack of conformity, or if the lack of conformity has its origin in materials supplied by the consumer.'

[235] *Ibid.*, Art. 3(2). This is, of course, free of charge. For a definition of this concept, see Art. 3(4).

[236] *Ibid.*, Art. 3(3). According to the provision, '[a] remedy shall be deemed to be disproportionate if it imposes costs on the seller which, in comparison with the alternative remedy, are unreasonable' when taking into account a number of factors.

[237] *Ibid.*, Art. 3(5).   [238] *Ibid.*, Art. 5(1).   [239] *Ibid.*, Art. 5(2).

[240] See W. Shakespeare, *The Merchant of Venice*, in S. Wells and G. Taylor (eds.), *The Oxford Shakespeare: The Complete Works* (Oxford University Press, 2005), 453.

[241] This critique was spearheaded by the US 'Realists' and was subsequently continued by the 'Critical Legal Theorists'; see K. Llewellyn, 'What Price Contract? – An Essay in Perspective' (1931) 40 *Yale LJ* 704; D. Kennedy, 'The Political Stakes in "Merely Technical" Issues of Contract Law' (2001) 10 *European Review of Private Law* 7.

[242] Directive 93/13 on unfair terms in consumer contracts [1993] OJ L 95/29.

> [T]he system of protection introduced by the Directive is based in the idea that the consumer is in a weaker position vis-à-vis the seller or supplier, as regards both his bargaining power and his level of knowledge. This leads to the consumer agreeing to terms drawn up in advance by the seller or supplier without being able to influence the content of those terms.[243]

The directive tries to protect consumers – not businesses – by patrolling the commercial fairness of contractual terms that have 'not been individually negotiated'.[244] This will always be the case, where a contractual term 'has been drafted in advance and the consumer has therefore not been able to influence the substance of the term, particularly in the context of a preformulated standard contract'.[245] These standard form contracts essentially place the consumer in a take-it-or-leave-it position in which he either accepts all the terms of the contract or goes somewhere else. These standard form contracts have become ubiquitous today and cover such diverse contracts as classic sales contracts, tenancy agreements,[246] as well as electricity-supply contracts.[247]

Importantly, not all non-negotiated terms will fall within the scope of the directive. For under Article 4, the unfairness review will never relate to 'the definition of the *main subject of the contract* nor to the *adequacy of the price and remuneration*'.[248] This – dramatic – exclusion may be justified by reference to the priority of the parties and the market to define the 'core' terms of the contract. Yet the exclusion of the main subject matter of the contract and the price ratio limits the scope of the directive to the control of 'peripheral' contractual terms.

What standard of unfairness does the directive apply to these non-negotiated terms? While emphasising the specificity of each contractual context,[249] a general definition of unfairness is given in Article 3 of the directive. The provision states:

> A contractual term which has not been individually negotiated shall be regarded as unfair if, contrary to the requirement of *good faith*, it causes a *significant imbalance* in the parties' rights and obligations arising under the contract, to the detriment of the consumer.[250]

---

[243] Case C-137/08, *VB Pénzügyi Lízing Zrt.* v. *Ferenc Schneider* [2010] ECR I-10847, para. 46.

[244] Unfair Terms Directive, Art. 3(1).   [245] *Ibid.*, Art. 3(2).

[246] For a case dealing with this, see: Case C-488/11, *Asbeek Brusse and de Man Garabito*, EU:C:2013:341.

[247] For a case dealing with this, see Case C-92/11, *RWE Vertrieb AG* v. *Verbraucherzentrale Nordrhein-Westfalen*, EU:C:2013:180.

[248] Unfair Terms Directive, Art. 4(2). The condition that the directive attaches to this exclusion is that the contractual terms on these core issues 'are in plain intelligible language' (*ibid.*). This condition is fairly frequently litigated before the European Court.

[249] *Ibid.*, Art. 4(1): '[T]he unfairness of a contractual term shall be assessed, taking into account the nature of the goods or services for which the contract was concluded and by referring, at the time of conclusion of the contract, to all the circumstances attending the conclusion of the contract and to all the other terms of the contract or of another contract on which it is dependent.'

[250] *Ibid.*, Art. 3(1) (emphasis added).

This test defines a contractual term as unfair by reference to two criteria. The first – objective – criterion refers to a 'significant imbalance' between the parties caused by a contractual term. It examines the *content* of the contract, yet only declares those terms unfair that are *significantly* detrimental to the consumer. In order to concretise this abstract threshold, the directive provides 'an indicative and non-exhaustive list' of such unfair terms in an Annex.[251] This Annex is frequently referred to by the European Courts, which have transformed it into 'a judge-made "grey list" of pre-formulated unfair terms'.[252] Importantly, however, it is not a blacklist: a term appearing in the list will not necessarily be considered unfair.

An – objectively – unfair contract is however not the only requirement. A second – subjective – criterion requires that this result must have been contrary to 'good faith'. The vague definition of this idea in the directive has not helped much to clarify what is meant here.[253] Courts and commentators have consequently struggled to come to terms with it.[254]

In one of the most important interpretations of both criteria, the Court of Justice has given the following definitions in *Aziz*:

> Article 3(1) of the directive must be interpreted as meaning that:
> – the concept of 'significant imbalance', to the detriment of the consumer, must be assessed in the light of an analysis of the rules of national law applicable in the absence of any agreement between the parties, in order to determine whether, and if so to what extent, the contract places the consumer in a less favourable legal situation than that provided for by the national law in force. To that end, an assessment of the legal situation of that consumer having regard to the means at his disposal, under national law, to prevent continued use of unfair terms, should also be carried out;

[251] *Ibid.*, Art. 3(3). The Annex contains a 'grey list' of 17 such clauses. These clauses are not automatically unfair but only provide a presumption of such unfairness. It includes, for example, terms which have the object or effect of 'inappropriately excluding or limiting the legal rights of the consumer *vis-à-vis* the seller or supplier or another party in the event of total or partial non-performance or inadequate performance by the seller or supplier of any of the contractual obligations, including the option of offsetting a debt owed to the seller or supplier against any claim which the consumer may have against him' (*ibid.*, (b)); or 'requiring any consumer who fails to fulfil his obligation to pay a disproportionately high sum in compensation' (*ibid.*, (e)).

[252] H. Micklitz and N. Reich, 'The Court and Sleeping Beauty: The Revival of the Unfair Contract Terms Directive (UCTD)' (2014) 51 *CML Rev.* 771 at 789.

[253] Unfair Contract Terms Directive, recital 16: 'whereas, in making an assessment of good faith, particular regard shall be had to the strength of the bargaining positions of the parties, whether the consumer had an inducement to agree to the term and whether the goods or services were sold or supplied to the special order of the consumer; whereas the requirement of good faith may be satisfied by the seller or supplier where he deals fairly and equitably with the other party whose legitimate interests he has to take into account'.

[254] See H. Collins, 'Good Faith in European Contract Law' (1994) 14 *Oxford Journal of Legal Studies* 229. For an analysis of the judicial struggle to give meaning to the term, see P. Nebbia, *Unfair Terms in Europe: A Study in EC and Comparative Law* (Hart, 2006).

> – in order to assess whether the imbalance arises 'contrary to the requirement of good faith', it must be determined whether the seller or supplier, dealing fairly and equitably with the consumer, could reasonably assume that the consumer would have agreed to the term concerned in individual contract negotiations.[255]

If a court finds a term to be 'unfair' it will, under Article 6 of the directive, 'not be binding on the consumer'.[256] For a judicial finding of unfairness will lead a term to be declared void. The contract as such may however continue – albeit under the condition that it is capable of continuing without the unfair term(s). Under the directive, national courts are thus not entitled to rewrite or amend a contractual term. This was expressly clarified in *Banco Español de Crédito*,[257] where the Court of Justice held:

> It thus follows from the wording of Article 6(1) that the national courts are required only to exclude the application of an unfair contractual term in order that it does not produce binding effects with regard to the consumer, without being authorised to revise its content. That contract must continue in existence, in principle, without any amendment other than that resulting from the deletion of the unfair terms, in so far as, in accordance with the rules of domestic law, such continuity of the contract is legally possible.[258]

c. Policing Business: The Unfair Commercial Practices Directive

Unfair terms in a consumer contract may be the *illegal* result of a *legal* exploitation of an unequal bargaining power. However, consumers might equally be tied to a *legal* term that is the result of an *illegal* misrepresentation or duress. National contract law will here typically allow the misled or aggrieved party to rescind the contract. However, if that party is a consumer, many legal orders go even further and prohibit certain commercial misrepresentations or aggressions as unfair commercial practices.

For the Union legal order, this has happened through the Unfair Commercial Practices (UCP) Directive.[259] The declared – dual – aim of this harmonisation measure is to '*directly* protect ... consumer economic interests from unfair business-to-consumer commercial practices',[260] while '*indirectly* protect[ing]

---

[255] Case C-415/11, *Aziz v. Caixa d'Estalvis de Catalunya, Tarragona i Manresa*, EU:C:2013:164, para. 76.

[256] Unfair Contract Terms Directive, Art. 6(1).

[257] Case C-618/10, *Banco Español de Crédito v. Calderón Camino*, EU:C:2012:349.

[258] *Ibid.*, para. 65.

[259] Directive 2005/29 of the European Parliament and of the Council of 11 May 2005 concerning unfair business-to-consumer commercial practices in the internal market [2005] OJ L 149/22.

[260] The scope of the directive is expressly confined to business-to-consumer commercial practices, *ibid.*, Art. 3(1).

legitimate businesses from their competitors who do not play by the rules'.[261] Conceived as a punitive instrument, it will not affect the consumer contract as such but rather requires the Member States to 'lay down penalties for infringements of national provisions adopted in application of th[e] Directive'.[262]

The central aim of the UCP directive is to outlaw 'commercial practices' that are 'unfair'. The Court has thereby given 'a particularly wide definition to the concept of commercial practices' that includes all commercial acts 'which clearly form part of an operator's commercial strategy and relate directly to the promotion thereof and its sales development'.[263] This could potentially include the commercial practice of selling goods at a loss (à la *Keck*), prize draws as part of a sales strategy (à la *Familiapress*); and it can even cover the use of an unfair contract term in a standard-form contract.[264]

When is a commercial practice 'unfair'? The UCP Directive here follows a sophisticated structure of legislative concretisations. It starts with an abstract prohibition in Article 5 that generally outlaws all unfair commercial practices and states:

1. Unfair commercial practices shall be prohibited.
2. A commercial practice shall be unfair if:
   (a) it is contrary to the requirements of professional diligence, and
   (b) it materially distorts or is likely to materially distort the economic behaviour with regard to the product of the average consumer whom it reaches or to whom it is addressed, or of the average member of the group when a commercial practice is directed to a particular group of consumers.

A duty of care is here imposed. It is centred on the relevant and relative professional standard,[265] whose violation is likely to 'materially distort[]' the average consumer's decision to buy.[266] The unfair nature of a commercial practice must

---

[261] *Ibid.*, recital 8 (emphasis added).

[262] *Ibid.*, Art. 13. According to Art. 3(2): 'This Directive is without prejudice to contract law and, in particular, to the rules on the validity, formation or effect of a contract.' On the relationship between the directive and contract law generally, see S. Whittaker, 'The Relationship of the Unfair Commercial Practices Directive to European and National Contract Laws', in S. Weatherill and U. Berlitz (eds.), *The Regulation of Unfair Commercial Practices under EC Directive 2005/29: New Rules and New Techniques* (Hart, 2007), 139.

[263] Joined cases C-261/07 and C-299/07, *VTB-VAB NV* v. *Total Belgium and Galatea BVBA* v. *Sanoma Magazines Belgium* [2009] ECR I-2949, paras. 49–50. On the requirement that the commercial practice must 'directly' relate to the promotion of a business' own goods, see Case C-391/12, *RLvS Verlagsgesellschaft* v. *Stuttgarter Wochenblatt*, EU:C:2013:669.

[264] Case C-453/10, *Pereničová and Perenič*, EU:C:2012:144.

[265] Art. 2(h) UCP Directive defines professional diligence as 'the standard of special skill and care which a trader may reasonably be expected to exercise towards consumers, commensurate with honest market practice and/or the general principle of good faith in the trader's field of activity'.

[266] *Ibid.*, Art. 2(e) defines this as follows: 'to materially distort the economic behaviour of consumers' means using a commercial practice to appreciably impair the consumer's ability to make an informed decision, thereby causing the consumer to take a transactional decision that he would not have taken otherwise'.

consequently be determined by reference to two cumulative criteria. It must deviate from the *internal* standard of a profession, while having a (potentially) distorting *external* effect on the average consumer.

This abstract definition leaves much room for doubt, and for this reason the directive outlaws two specific categories of unfair practices. These specific categories are with regard to '*misleading* commercial practices' and '*aggressive* commercial practices'.[267] Misleading practices cover 'false information' or deceiving presentation (Article 6) but also misleading omissions (Article 7). By contrast, aggressive practices relate to harassment, coercion or undue influence (Articles 8–9) that directly impair the consumer's freedom of choice. These specific prohibitions are still fairly open-ended, and for this reason the UCP Directive finally contains a 'blacklist' of unfair practices in its Annex I – both with regard to misleading and aggressive commercial practices – that 'are in all circumstances considered unfair'.[268] Whenever a commercial practice falls within any one of these 31 black-listed practices or within the scope of the more specific prohibitions in Articles 6–9, there is no further need to explore the respective standard of professional diligence or the effect of the practice on the average consumer.[269]

The best way to analyse the conformity of a commercial practice with the UCP Directive is thus to start from the back – beginning with the Annex and gradually moving, via the broader prohibitions in Articles 6–9, towards the general prohibition in Article 5 (see Figure 18.3). Importantly: due to the maximum or total harmonisation method used for the Directive, Member States cannot go beyond the practices outlawed within the Directive.[270]

d. Sanctioning Business: The Product Liability Directive

The right to safety against defective products is at the core of any Consumer Bill of Rights.[271] It entered public consciousness after one of the biggest pharmaceutical scandals of the twentieth century.[272] The latter catalysed the adoption of national tort legislation regulating the liability of producers.

---

[267] The former are set out in Arts. 6 and 7 and the latter are treated in Arts. 8 and 9 of the UCP Directive.

[268] *Ibid.*, Annex I. The Annex outlaws 23 misleading commercial practices, such as '[c]laiming that the trader is about to cease trading or move premises when he is not' (*ibid.*, para. 15); and it also prohibits eight aggressive commercial practices, such as '[m]aking persistent and unwanted solicitations by phone, fax, e-mail or other remote media except in circumstances and to the extent justified under national law to enforce a contractual obligation' (*ibid.*, para. 26).

[269] Case C-435/11, *CHS Tour Services* v. *Team4 Travel*, EU:C:2013:574, esp. para. 39.

[270] UCP Directive, Art. 4: 'Member States shall neither restrict the freedom to provide services nor restrict the free movement of goods for reasons falling within the field approximated by this Directive.' For a very strict reading of the provision, see Joined cases C-261/07 and C-299/07, *VTB-VAB NV* v. *Total Belgium* and *Galatea BVBA* v. *Sanoma Magazines Belgium*.

[271] For a historical overview of the (US and British) evolution of product liability law, see J. Stapleton, *Product Liability* (Cambridge University Press, 1994), chs. 2–3.

[272] On the 'Thalidomide scandal', see: https://www.theguardian.com/society/2012/sep/01/thalidomide-scandal-timeline.

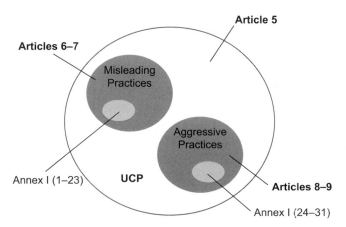

Figure 18.3 Structure of the UCP Directive

The Union addresses the problem of consumer damage caused by defective products in its 1985 Product Liability Directive.[273] The aim of the directive is to – fully – harmonise, within the internal market, the differing levels of liability governing defective products.[274] Defective products are products that do 'not provide the safety which a person is entitled to expect'.[275] In *Boston Scientific*, the Court thereby clarified that, with regard to particularly sensitive products – like pacemakers, an entire class of products may be found defective:

> The safety which the public at large is entitled to expect, in accordance with that provision, must therefore be assessed by taking into account, inter alia, the intended purpose, the objective characteristics and properties of the product in question and the specific requirements of the group of users for whom the product is intended … [T]the potential lack of safety which would give rise to liability on the part of the producer under Directive 85/374 stems, for products such as those at issue in the main proceedings, from the abnormal potential for damage which those products might cause to the person concerned. Accordingly, where it is found that such products belonging to the same group or forming part of the same production series have a potential defect, it is possible to classify as defective all the products in that group or series, without there being any need to show that the product in question is defective.[276]

---

[273] Directive 85/374 on the approximation of the laws, regulations and administrative provisions of the Member States concerning liability for defective products [1985] OJ L 210/29.

[274] On the maximum or total harmonisation methodology of the directive, see Case C‑52/00, *Commission* v. *France* [2002] ECR I‑3827.

[275] *Ibid.*, Art. 6(1). According to Art. 6(2): 'A product shall not be considered defective for the sole reason that a better product is subsequently put into circulation.'

[276] Joined Cases C‑503/13 and C‑504/13, *Boston Scientific Medizintechnik GmbH* v. *AOK Sachsen-Anhalt – Die Gesundheitskasse and Betriebskrankenkasse RWE*, EU:C:2015:148, paras. 38–41.

The EU directive protects against these defective products by means of two core principles. First, liability for the damage caused by a defective good lies generally with the 'producer' and not the supplier. And, second, liability will generally be strict – that is, without the need to show fault.[277]

The concept of the 'producer' has been given a wide meaning within the directive. The producer is not only the manufacturer of the finished product, but also the producer of any raw material or of a component part of it.[278] And fundamentally: any supplier of the product 'shall be treated as its producer' in situations where the real producer of the product cannot be identified.[279] (This secondary liability compensates for the unenforceability of the producer's primary liability; and it follows that where the producer can be identified, the supplier's liability has come to an end.) The rationale behind these legal presumptions is to never leave the consumer without an identifiable defendant.[280] A strict rule of secondary liability is also established for importers of products from outside the Union.[281] The reason behind this is the – legitimate – fear that a Union consumer may not be able or willing to bring a tort action in a jurisdiction outside the European Union. By contrast, no secondary liability applies to 'users' of a product that injures a final consumer.[282]

To what extent is the product liability strict? The directive expressly provides that the injured person is 'required to prove the damage, the defect and the causal relationship between defect and damage'.[283] However, once this is done, there is no requirement to prove the negligence of the producer because his liability is indeed 'strict'. But how strict is it? The directive does contain a number of provisions limiting, or even excluding, producers' liability. Temporarily, liability is limited to a period of ten years from the date on which the producer put the actual product into circulation;[284] and – substantively – Member States may limit

---

[277] *Ibid.*, Art. 1: 'The producer shall be liable for damage caused by a defect in his product.'

[278] *Ibid.*, Art. 3(1). According to Art. 5, where there is more than one producer, they shall be liable 'jointly and severally'.

[279] *Ibid.*, Art. 3(3).

[280] In the words of Weatherill, *EU Consumer Law and Policy* (n. 203 above), 138: 'In the light of this provision, commercial prudence dictates that suppliers of products should maintain careful records of the source of goods which they supply. Without such records, the buck will stop with them.'

[281] Product Liability Directive, Art. 3(2).

[282] See Case C-495/10, *Centre hospitalier universitaire de Besançon* v. *Thomas Dutrueux and Caisse primaire d'assurance maladie du Jura* [2011] ECR I-14155.

[283] Product Liability Directive, Art. 4. A defect is defined in Art. 6 as a situation whereby a product 'does not provide the safety which a person is entitled to expect'. Art. 9 on the other hand defines the notion of 'damage' for the purposes of the directive. It is (a) 'damage caused by death or by personal injuries'; and within certain limits, (b) damage to the personal property of the consumer.

[284] *Ibid.*, Art. 11. Within the period, there is another limitation period for the consumer must bring a claim within three years after 'the plaintiff became aware, or should reasonably have become aware, of the damage, the defect and the identity of the consumer' *ibid.*, (Art. 10).

the damage claim to €70 million.[285] A much greater qualification of the idea of strict producer liability is finally made in Article 7 of the directive. It contains a series of exculpatory factors that absolve the producer from tort liability. The most controversial of these factors is called the 'development risk defence' (or 'state-of-the-art defence'). It states:

> The producer shall not be liable as a result of this Directive if he proves ... *that the state of scientific and technical knowledge at the time when he put the product into circulation was not such as to enable the existence of the defect to be discovered* ...[286]

The legislative rationale behind this defence is to unclog any discouragement that a product liability regime may have on the development of new products. However, there is a danger that this exemption has shifted product liability, in the most important field of application of the directive, to a de facto negligence regime.

It all depends — of course — what the defence is supposed to mean. The European Court of Justice has not yet decisively chosen one interpretation over the other.[287] Two extreme constructions are possible.[288] Under a strict construction, the defence would only work where the available scientific procedures to discover the defect were unknown. A wider construction would exculpate risks that could have been discovered through existing scientific procedures but had not yet been discovered. This second version of the defence comes close to a negligence approach. By allowing the producer to point to an objective lack of knowledge within the scientific community, s/he is effectively measured against a foreseeability standard; and that shifts the risk of any unforeseeable defects back to the consumer.[289]

---

[285] *Ibid.*, Art. 16.

[286] *Ibid.*, Art. 7(e) (emphasis added). The defence is not a mandatory rule of Union law, for Art. 15(1)(b) allows the Member States to remove it in their national implementing legislation.

[287] See Case C-300/95, *Commission* v. *United Kingdom* [1997] ECR I-2649. In that case, the Court simply clarified that the defence did — obviously — 'not contemplate the state of knowledge of which the producer in question actually or subjectively was or could have been apprised' (para. 27). To employ the defence 'the producer of a defective product must prove that the *objective state of scientific and technical knowledge*, including the most advanced level of such knowledge, at the time when the product in question was put into circulation was not such as to enable the existence of the defect to be discovered' (para. 28, emphasis added).

[288] On these two possibilities, see J. Stapleton, 'Product Liability Reform – Real or Illusory?' (1986) 6 *Oxford Journal of Legal Studies* 392 at 417.

[289] C. Newdick, 'The Development Risk Defence of the Consumer Protection Act 1987' (1988) 47 *Cambridge Law Journal* 455, esp. at 460: 'There is no doubt that the development risk defence in this form sits uneasily in a measure designed to introduce strict product liability'.

4. (Regional and) Cohesion Policy

The social and economic conditions within a political community can significantly differ. In England, the 'North' has come to economically differ from the 'South'; and in Germany the 'East' continues to be distinct and 'poorer' when compared to the 'West'. In order to soften excessive socio-economic variations between regions, many modern States have therefore created 'cohesion' policies that aim to foster substantially similar conditions for all their citizens.

A cohesion policy aims to favour 'backward' regions and has an economic and a social rationale. They aim to maximise the economic potential of the State as a whole, while they are equally an expression of social solidarity. The latter demands that all members of a political community should enjoy substantially similar living and working conditions.[290]

Already the original Rome Treaty recognised the need for 'reducing the differences existing between the various regions and the backwardness of the less favoured regions';[291] yet it exclusively entrusted this task to the economic forces of the (internal) market.[292] This blind belief in the invisible hand of the (internal) market changed with the accession of the United Kingdom and Ireland.[293] For the first enlargement 'accentuat[ed] the disparity in wealth between regions' and therefore accelerated 'the passage from a "passive" to a "positive" regional policy'.[294] This positive regional policy was born in 1975 in the shape of the European Regional Development Fund. The Fund was originally designed as an 'accompanying measure', since it had been 'developed to cope with the detrimental effects or negative consequences of the main [Union] policies'.[295] The weakness of the new Union 'policy' soon became apparent. Not only was the first Fund's budget extremely low, the policy appeared to have 'much – if not more – to do with a desire for redistribution *among the States* than with a policy of [Union] distribution to benefit unfavoured *regions*'.[296]

These severe birth defects were gradually cured. The 1986 Single European Act gave the Union a clear constitutional competence to promote 'Economic

---

[290] On the relationship between citizenship and cohesion policy in the EU, see F. Strumia, 'Remedying the Inequalities of Economic Citizenship in Europe: Cohesion Policy and the Negative Right to Move' (2011) 17 ELJ 725.

[291] 1957 EEC Treaty, preamble.

[292] On the origins and structure of the EU Cohesion Policy, see J. Bachtler et al., *EU Cohesion Policy and European Integration* (Ashgate, 2013); R. Leonardi, *Cohesion Policy in the European Union: The Building of Europe* (Palgrave, 2005).

[293] I. Bache, *Europeanization and Multilevel Governance: Cohesion Policy in the European Union and Britain* (Rowman & Littlefield, 2008), 40: 'The British government in particular pushed for the fund, being in need of something tangible to persuade a reluctant public and Parliament of the benefits of EEC membership.'

[294] Y. Meny, 'Should the Community Regional Policy Be Scrapped?' (1982) 19 *CML Rev.* 373.

[295] M. Keating and B. Jones, *Regions in the European Community* (Oxford University Press, 1985), 20.

[296] Meny, 'Should the Community Regional Policy Be Scrapped?' (n. 294 above), 377.

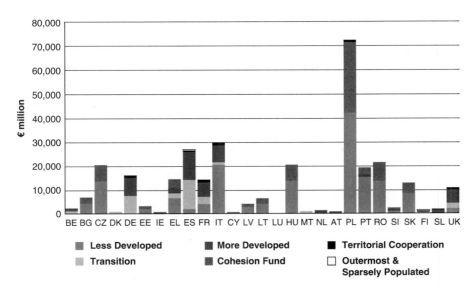

Figure 18.4 Cohesion Policy: National Distribution

and Social Cohesion'; and after a major reform in 1988,[297] this policy became – certainly in financial terms – a core policy of the Union. The 1992 Maastricht Treaty reinforced this status even further, and the Lisbon Treaty has added a new element. Today, the Union's cohesion policy has indeed three distinct cohesion dimensions: *economic* cohesion, *social* cohesion and *territorial* cohesion. It disposes of €325 billion – about one-third of the EU budget, distribution of which is a significant political act. The main beneficiary Member States can be seen in Figure 18.4. Constitutionally, the policy can be found in Title XVIII of the 'Internal Policies' Part of the TFEU, which is complemented by a Protocol and further elaborated by Union legislation (see Table 18.8).

Within Title XVIII, the Union enjoys a shared competence to establish a Union cohesion policy.[298] Its central aim(s), as defined by Article 174 TFEU, are as follows:

[T]he Union shall aim at *reducing disparities between the levels of development of the various regions and the backwardness of the least favoured regions*. Among the regions concerned, particular attention shall be paid to *rural areas, areas affected by industrial transition, and regions which suffer from severe and permanent natural or demographic handicaps* such as the northernmost regions with very low population density and island, cross-border and mountain regions.[299]

The provision commits the Union to reduce regional disparities, and in particular the backwardness of the least-favoured regions. This general constitutional

---

[297] For an analysis of these reforms, see W. Mansell and J. Scott, 'European Regional Development Policy: Confusing Quantity with Quality?' (1993) 18 *EL Rev.* 87 at 91ff.

[298] Art. 4(2)(c) TFEU.   [299] Art. 174 TFEU – second and third indent (emphasis added).

Table 18.8 Cohesion Policy Provisions – Overview

Title XVIII: Economic, Social and Territorial Cohesion	
Article 174	Cohesion Policy Aims
Article 175	Definition of the 'Structural Funds' (paragraph 1); and Legal Competence for 'Specific Actions' outside the Funds (paragraph 3)
Article 176	European Regional Development Fund
Article 177	Legal Competence for the 'Tasks, Priority Objectives and the Organisation of the Structural Funds' (paragraph 1); and Legal Competence for the 'Cohesion Fund' (paragraph 2)
Article 178	Legal Competence for Implementing Regulations Relating to the European Regional Development Fund (paragraph 1); and Cross-reference to Specific Sectoral Competences of the Other Structural Funds
Protocol No. 28 On Economic, Social and Territorial Cohesion	
Regulation 1303/2013 on 'Common Provisions' for all Funds Regulation 1301/2013 on the ERDF Concerning the Growth and Jobs Goal Regulation 1299/2013 on the ERDF concerning the Territorial Cooperation Goal Regulation 1300/2013 on the Cohesion Fund	

aim has been concretised through Union legislation. The legislative package underpinning Title XVIII has changed dramatically over time. The latest package applies for the period between 2014 and 2020 and consists of a range of Regulations dealing with the 'Structural and Investment Funds'. Subject to a Common Provisions Regulation (CPR),[300] these five funds are:

- the European Regional Development Fund[301]
- the European Social Fund[302]

---

[300] Regulation 1303/2013 laying down common provisions on the European Regional Development Fund, the European Social Fund, the Cohesion Fund, the European Agricultural Fund for Rural Development and the European Maritime and Fisheries Fund and laying down general provisions on the European Regional Development Fund, the European Social Fund, the Cohesion Fund and the European Maritime and Fisheries Fund [2013] OJ L 347/320. There do exist a number of other EU funds, such as the European Globalisation Adjustment Fund that shall however not be discussed here.

[301] Regulation 1301/2013 on the European Regional Development Fund and on specific provisions concerning the investment for growth and jobs goal [2013] OJ L 347/289.

[302] This Fund is set up in Regulation 1304/2013 on the European Social Fund [2013] OJ L 347/470. The European Social Fund has its own Treaty Title, see Title XI 'The European Social Fund', whose main provision is Art. 162 TFEU and states: 'In order to improve employment opportunities for workers in the internal market and to contribute thereby to raising the standard of living, a European Social Fund is hereby established in accordance with the provisions set out below; it shall aim to render the employment of workers easier and to increase their geographical and occupational mobility within the Union, and to facilitate their adaptation to industrial changes and to changes in production systems, in particular through vocational training and retraining.'

- the Cohesion Fund[303]
- the European Agricultural Fund for Rural Development[304]
- the European Maritime and Fisheries Fund.

Only the first and the third Funds shall interest us here, since only these have traditionally had specific 'regional' or 'cohesion' objectives. Streamlined to the European Council's 'Europe 2020 Strategy' on smart, sustainable and inclusive growth, their objectives can now be found in Article 89 CPR and state:

> 1. The Funds shall contribute to developing and pursuing the actions of the Union leading to strengthening of its economic, social and territorial cohesion in accordance with Article 174 TFEU. The actions supported by the Funds shall also contribute to the delivery of the Union strategy for smart, sustainable and inclusive growth.
> 2. For the purpose of the mission referred to in paragraph 1, the following goals shall be pursued:
>   (a) Investment for growth and jobs in Member States and regions, to be supported by the Funds; and
>   (b) European territorial cooperation, to be supported by the ERDF.[305]

The two principal objectives of the Union's regional and cohesion policy are therefore 'investment for growth and jobs',[306] and 'territorial cooperation'.[307] They are given a specific 'regional' or 'cohesion' perspective through the European Regional and Development Fund and the Cohesion Fund, respectively.

a. The European Regional Development Fund

aa. Objectives and Regions
The Treaties define the task of the European Regional Development Fund (ERDF) in the following terms:

> The European Regional Development Fund is intended to help to redress the main regional imbalances in the Union though participation in the development and *structural adjustment of regions whose development is lagging behind and in the conversion of declining regions.*[308]

These two express aims have been complemented by a third – additional – aim: European territorial cooperation. All three aims are specified and defined in the Union legislation governing the ERDF, in particular 'ERDF Regulation

---

[303] Regulation 1300/2013 on the Cohesion Fund [2013] OJ L 347/281.
[304] Regulation 1305/2013 on support for rural development by the European Agricultural Fund for Rural Development (EAFRD) [2013] OJ L 347/487.
[305] Art. 89 CPR.   [306] *Ibid.*, Art. 90.   [307] *Ibid.*, Art. 92.
[308] Art. 176 TFEU (emphasis added). See also Art. 2 ('Tasks of the ERDF') of the 2013 ERDF Regulation.

I' with regard to the growth and jobs objective,[309] and 'ERDF Regulation II' dealing with the territorial cooperation objective.[310]

With regard to the 'investment for growth and jobs' objective, the priorities of the ERDF can be found in Article 5 of the first ERDF Regulation. It mirrors the general objectives of all Structural and Investment Funds, which are as follows:

1. strengthening research, technological development and innovation
2. enhancing access to, and use and quality of, ICT
3. enhancing the competitiveness of SMEs
4. supporting the shift towards a low-carbon economy in all sectors
5. promoting climate change adaptation, risk prevention and management
6. preserving and protecting the environment and promoting resource efficiency
7. promoting sustainable transport and removing bottlenecks in key network infrastructures
8. promoting sustainable and quality employment and supporting labour mobility
9. promoting social inclusion, combating poverty and any discrimination
10. investing in education, training and vocational training for skills and lifelong learning by developing education and training infrastructure
11. enhancing institutional capacity of public authorities and stakeholders and efficient public administration.

The ERDF adopts a methodology of thematic concentration – that is, it concentrates its financial allocations on the first four objectives. The support of objectives 1–4 is thereby dependent on the type of region concerned.[311]

---

[309] Regulation 1301/2013 on the European Regional Development Fund and on specific provisions concerning the investment for growth and jobs goal (n. 301 above).

[310] Regulation 1299/2013 on specific provisions for the support from the European Regional Development Fund to the European territorial cooperation goal [2013] OJ L 347/259.

[311] Art. 4(1) ERDF Regulation I: 'The thematic objectives set out in the first paragraph of Article 9 of Regulation (EU) No 1303/2013 and the corresponding investment priorities set out in Article 5 of this Regulation to which the ERDF may contribute under the Investment for growth and jobs goal, shall be concentrated as follows: (a) in more developed regions: (i) at least 80% of the total ERDF resources at national level shall be allocated to two or more of the thematic objectives set out in points 1, 2, 3 and 4 of the first paragraph of Article 9 of Regulation (EU) No 1303/2013; and (ii) at least 20% of the total ERDF resources at national level shall be allocated to the thematic objective set out in point 4 of the first paragraph of Article 9 of Regulation (EU) No 1303/2013; (b) in transition regions: (i) at least 60% of the total ERDF resources at national level shall be allocated to two or more of the thematic objectives set out in points 1, 2, 3 and 4 of the first paragraph of Article 9 of Regulation (EU) No 1303/2013; and (ii) at least 15% of the total ERDF resources at national level shall be allocated to the thematic objective set out in point 4 of the first paragraph of Article 9 of Regulation (EU) No 1303/2013; (c) in less developed regions: (i) at least 50% of the total ERDF resources at national level shall be allocated to two or more of the thematic objectives set in out in points 1, 2, 3 and 4 of the first paragraph of Article 9 of Regulation (EU) No 1303/2013; and (ii) at least 12% of the total ERDF resources at national level shall be allocated to the thematic objective set out in point 4 of the first paragraph of Article 9 of Regulation (EU) No 1303/2013.'

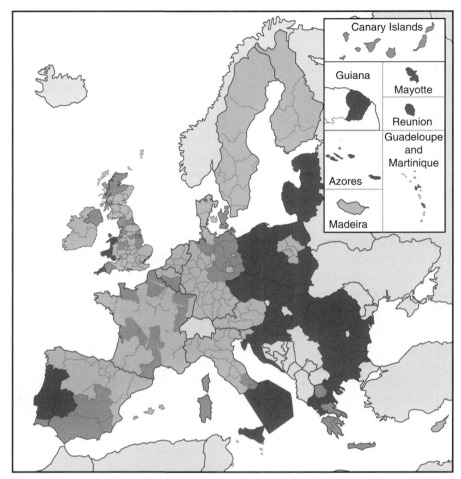

Structural Funds (ERDF and ESF) eligibility 2014–2020

Category

■ Less developed regions   ■ Transition regions   ■ More developed regions

Figure 18.5 Structural Funds – Eligibility (2014–20)

The Union distinguishes between three types of regions. 'Less developed regions' are regions whose GDP per capita is less than 75 per cent of the average Union GDP. 'Transitional regions' are regions whose GDP per capita is between 75 and 90 per cent of the average Union GDP. Finally, 'more developed regions' are regions whose GDP per capita is above 90 per cent of the average Union GDP.

Specific provisions with regard to the 'territorial cooperation' objective are set out in a second ERDF Regulation. The latter states that '[i]n order to support the harmonious development of the Union's territory at different levels, the ERDF should support cross-border, transnational and interregional cooperation under the European territorial cooperation goal'.[312] These three forms

---

[312] Regulation 1299/2013, preamble 4. For definitions of these three forms of cooperation, see Art. 2.

of territorial cooperation however only apply to subregions along 'all internal and certain external land borders' as well as subregions along certain maritime borders of the Union.[313] The investment priorities under the territorial cooperation objective are different from the investment priorities under its 'investment for growth and jobs' objective and depend on the form of cooperation involved.[314]

To provide a legal framework for the various forms of inter-regional cooperation, the Union has created the 'European Grouping for Territorial Cooperation'.[315] This is a Union instrument that is specifically designed 'to facilitate and promote, in particular, territorial cooperation, including one or more of the cross-border, transnational and interregional strands of cooperation, between its members'.[316]

bb. Administrative Principles and Implementation

The Union cohesion policy follows four key principles.[317] According to the principle of 'concentration', the Union will concentrate its financial resources on the poorest regions, and within these regions only on specific aspects. Second, financial assistance offered by the ERDF follows a 'programming' principle. This means that the ERDF does not support autonomous projects, but that individual projects must form part of a multiannual programme that follows specific priorities.[318] Third, according to the principle of 'partnership' the Fund pursues its work in 'close cooperation' with the Member States in accordance with the principle of subsidiarity.[319] Moreover, Member States are asked to conclude 'Partnership Agreements' with the competent regional and local authorities as well as the relevant economic and social partners, which are to be involved in all stages of the programming process.[320] Fourth, and most importantly, there is the principle of 'additionality'. In negative terms, it mandates that '[s]upport from the Funds for the Investment for growth and jobs shall not replace public or equivalent structural expenditure by a Member State'.[321] In positive terms, this means that projects supported by the ERDF must always – in part – be co-financed by the Member States (or the region).[322]

---

[313] Regulation 1299/2013, Art. 3(1).

[314] Regulation 1299/2013, Art. 7.

[315] See Regulation 1082/2006 on a European grouping of territorial cooperation (EGTC), (2006) OJ L 210/19. The Regulation was based on Art. 175 TFEU – third indent, and was significantly amended by Regulation 1302/2013. For an analysis of the regulation, see M. Pechstein and M. Deja, 'Was ist und wie funktioniert ein EVTZ?' (2011) *Europarecht* 357.

[316] Regulation 1082/2006, Art. 1(2).

[317] See http://ec.europa.eu/regional_policy/how/principles/index_en.cfm.

[318] CPR, Art. 4(1).

[319] *Ibid.*, Art. 4(3); and Arts. 5 and 10.

[320] *Ibid.*, Art. 5.

[321] *Ibid.*, Art. 95(2); and Annex X.

[322] *Ibid.*, Art. 27 and Art. 60. The latter provision states in paragraph 1: 'The Commission decision adopting a programme shall fix the co-financing rate or rates and the maximum amount of support from the ESI Funds in accordance with the Fund-specific rules.'

b. The Cohesion Fund

The Union's cohesion policy was significantly reinforced in 1992 when the Maastricht Treaty introduced Economic and Monetary Union (EMU). Its creation originally 'reflect[ed] demands from the less developed Member States for assistance in coping with the disciplines associated with the establishment of monetary union'.[323] The reason for this thematic link between cohesion policy and EMU has been aptly described as follows:

> Cohesion becomes all the more imperative as a necessary corollary of a principal objective of the [EU Treaties], economic and monetary union. First, it will be necessary in order to ensure the high degree of sustainable convergence required for entry into the third stage of EMU; and second, since EMU means a surrender of fiscal and monetary control, it is the price of agreement of the less prosperous and weaker currency Member States which are to be deprived of these tools – what in a federation would be called regional equalization payments.[324]

The 1992 Treaty consequently set up the 'Cohesion Fund'. It is governed by its own Regulation,[325] which is supplemented by the general rules established in the horizontal 'Common Provisions Regulation'.[326] The Cohesion Fund is, as its name indicates, exclusively pursuing a convergence objective. Its sole purpose is 'to strengthen … the economic, social and territorial cohesion of the [Union] in the interests of promoting sustainable development'.[327]

Unlike the 'regional' nature of the ERDF, the Cohesion Fund was conceived as 'an instrument of *national rather than regional* convergence and cohesion'.[328] It thus grants assistance by reference to a national – not a regional – standard. As Protocol No. 28 clarifies, financial assistance is limited to 'Member States with a per capita GNP of less than 90% of the Union average which have a programme leading to the fulfilment of the conditions of economic convergence as set out in Article 126'.[329] (This definition betrays the original link between the Cohesion Fund and EMU, and it also explains why financial support under the Cohesion Fund to Member States that are found to have an excessive government deficit was originally 'conditional' on taking effective actions to correct this deficit.) However, the 2013 Cohesion Fund Regulation appears to have severed this specific link with the EMU. The investment aid under the Cohesion Fund seems no longer 'conditional' on tackling an excessive government deficit, but generally

---

[323] A. Evans, *EU Regional Policy* (Oxford University Press, 2005), 14.

[324] R. Lane, 'New Community Competences under the Maastricht Treaty' (1993) 30 *CML Rev.* 939 at 961.

[325] Cohesion Fund Regulation (n. 303 above).

[326] CPR (n. 300 above).

[327] Art. 1(1) Cohesion Fund Regulation.

[328] J. Scott, 'Regional Policy: An Evolutionary Perspective'. in P. Craig and G. de Búrca (eds.), *The Evolution of EU Law* (Oxford University Press, 2011), 625 at 646 (emphasis added).

[329] Protocol No. 28 On Economic, Social and Territorial Cohesion, eleventh indent.

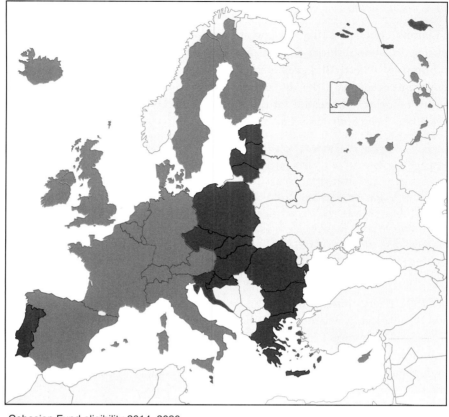

Cohesion Fund eligibility 2014–2020

Category

  GNI/head < 90% of EU27 average   Phasing-out support   Other Member States

Figure 18.6 Cohesion Fund: Eligibility (2014–20)

aims to 'provide a financial contribution to projects in the field of environment and trans-European networks in the area of transport infrastructure'.[330]

The Cohesion Fund will be subject to the same administrative principles that govern the ERDF – that is, concentration, programming, partnership and conditionality. With regard to the principle of concentration, the Cohesion Fund is however much more 'concentrated'. Its scope of assistance is constitutionally confined, in Article 177 TFEU, to only 'provide a financial contribution to projects in the fields of environment and trans-European networks in the area of transport'.[331] The Cohesion Fund will thus only finance projects within two areas – namely, the environment and transport – and within these policy areas the EU Treaties indeed expressly refer to the Fund.[332]

---

[330] Cohesion Fund Regulation, preamble 1.   [331] Art. 177 TFEU – second indent.
[332] The Cohesion Fund is expressly mentioned in Title XVI on 'Trans-European Networks', and here especially in Art. 171 TFEU; as well as in the Treaty's Environmental Title, and here especially Art. 192 TFEU.

The Fund's specific investment priorities are set out in Article 4 of the Cohesion Fund Regulation, which states:

> The Cohesion Fund shall support the following investment priorities within the thematic objectives set out in the first paragraph of Article 9 of Regulation (EU) No 1303/2013, in accordance with the development needs and growth potential referred to in point (a)(i) of Article 15(1) of that Regulation and set out in the Partnership Agreement:
> (a) supporting the shift towards a low-carbon economy in all sectors …
> (b) promoting climate change adaptation, risk prevention and management …
> (c) preserving and protecting the environment and promoting resource efficiency …
> (d) promoting sustainable transport and removing bottlenecks in key network infra-structures …
> (e) enhancing institutional capacity of public authorities and stakeholders and effi-cient public administration through actions to strengthen the institutional capac-ity and the efficiency of public administrations and public services related to the implementation of the Cohesion Fund.

Conclusion

Having started as an economic Union that primarily concentrated on the creation of the internal market and the removal of distortions of competition, the Union has come to regulate almost all areas of social life. The various internal areas in which the Union can legislate are listed in Part III of the TFEU and this chapter explored four of the 24 internal policies in which the Union is entitled to act. Importantly: European legislation on a given matter does of course not mean that the Union replaces the Member States. The degree of Union involvement depends on the category of Union competence; and the Union indeed often adopts the philosophy of cooperative federalism, according to which the Union enacts a 'unitary' frame that allows for national diversity.

This chapter began with an analysis of the – presently – most controversial policy of the Union: Economic and Monetary Union (EMU). We saw above that 'economic and monetary policy' continues to be an imbalanced cou-ple: while the Union has a – weaker – coordination competence for macro-economic matters, it enjoys an exclusive competence for its monetary policy. This imbalance will need to be addressed by future EU Treaty amendments. Even if the Union presently 'solves' this problem by having recourse to inter-national agreements between (some) Member States, this unprincipled prag-matism will simply not do in the long term and a further 'consolidation' of the eurozone and – perhaps – a move towards fiscal union will soon have to be made.[333]

---

[333] For a future analysis here, see A. Hinarejos and R. Schütze (eds.), *Fiscal Federalism and the European Union: Past, Present, Future* (Oxford University Press – in preparation).

Table 18.9 Chapter 18B: Summary Contents

Sections 2 and 3 explored the involvement of the Union in two 'core' areas of 'private' law – namely, employment law and contract law. The adoption of Union legislation here has dramatically reshaped both private law areas in the national legal systems of the Member States. Indeed, it is hard to imagine what British employment and contract law would look like in the absence of Union rules! Section 4 finally provided a – brief – overview of the Union's cohesion policy. This policy is fundamentally important for a 'Europe of the Regions'; and, simply looking at the Union budget, it represents one of the most important internal policies of the Union.

What about the external policies of the European Union? The Union has been historically characterised as a 'civilian' power on the international scene. For a long time, the Union indeed solely exercised economic powers, yet this classification must be (partly) qualified since the establishment of its Common Foreign and Security Policy. Chapter 18B provides an overview of the four most important external policies of the Union. Section 1 starts with the Common Commercial Policy, which represents the 'oldest' and most centralised external policy. Section 2 looks at the – complex – legal foundations of the Union's development policy. Section 3 moves to the Common Foreign and Security Policy; whereas section 4 explores the 'politics' of association and enlargement. The structure of this online chapter can be seen in Table 18.9.

FURTHER READING

Books

J. Bachtler et al., *EU Cohesion Policy in Practice* (Rowman & Littlefield, 2016)

C. Barnard, *EU Employment Law* (Oxford University Press, 2012)

M. Chang, *Economic and Monetary Union* (Palgrave, 2016)

A. Evans, *EU Regional Policy* (Oxford University Press, 2005)

F. Fabbrini, *Economic Governance in Europe* (Oxford University Press, 2016)

P. de Grauwe, *Economics of Monetary Union* (Oxford University Press, 2014)

G. Howells, C. Twigg-Flesner and T. Wilhelmsson, *Rethinking EU Consumer Law* (Routledge, 2017)

J. Kenner, *EU Employment Law: From Rome to Amsterdam and Beyond* (Hart, 2002)

K. Riesenhuber, *European Employment Law: A Systematic Exposition* (Intersentia, 2012)

C. Twigg-Flesner (ed.), *Research Handbook on EU Consumer and Contract Law* (Elgar, 2016)

S. Weatherill, *EU Consumer Law and Policy* (Edward Elgar, 2014)

Articles (and Chapters)

K. Alexander, 'European Banking Union: A Legal and Institutional Analysis of the Single Supervisory Mechanism and the Single Resolution Mechanism', (2015) 40 *EL Rev.* 154

K. Armstrong, 'The New Governance of EU Fiscal Discipline' (2013) 38 *EL Rev.* 601

H. Collins, 'Good Faith in European Contract Law' (1994) 14 *Oxford Journal of Legal Studies* 229

S. Fredman, 'Affirmative Action and the European Court of Justice: A Critical Analysis', in J. Shaw (ed.), *Social Law and Policy in an Evolving European Union* (Hart, 2000), 171

M. Herdegen, 'Price Stability and Budgetary Restraints in the Economic and Monetary Union: The Law as Guardian of Economic Wisdom' (1998) 35 *CML Rev.* 9

N. Kountouris, 'EU Law and the Regulation of "Atypical" Work"', in A. Bogg et al (eds.), *Research Handbook on EU Labour Law* (Elgar, 2016), 246

R. M. Lastra and J.-V. Louis, 'European Economic and Monetary Union: History, Trends, and Prospects?' (2013) 32 YEL 57

Y. Meny, 'Should the Community Regional Policy Be Scrapped' (1982) 19 *CML Rev.* 373

H. Micklitz and N. Reich, 'The Court and Sleeping Beauty: The Revival of the Unfair Contract Terms Directive (UCTD)' (2014) 51 *CML Rev.* 771

S. Sciarra, 'Collective Agreements in the Hierarchy of European Community Sources' in P. Davies et al. (eds.), *European Community Labour Law: Principles and Perspectives* (Oxford University Press, 1996), 189

J. Scott, 'Regional Policy: An Evolutionary Perspective' in P. Craig and G. de Búrca (eds.), *The Evolution of EU Law* (Oxford University Press, 2011), 625

J. Struyck, 'The Court of Justice and the Unfair Commercial Practices Directive' (2015) 52 *CML Rev.* 721

S. Weatherill, 'The Consumer Rights Directive: How and Why a Quest for "Coherence" Has (Largely) Failed' (2012) 49 *CML Rev.* 1279

Cases on the Website

Case 170/84, *Bilka-Kaufhaus*; Case C-392/92, *Schmidt*; Case 450/93, *Kalanke*; Case C-84/94, *United Kingdom* v. *Council*; Case C-13/95, *Süzen*; Case 303/98, *Simap*; Case 407/98, *Abrahamsson*; Case C-320/00, *Lawrence*; Case C-415/11, *Aziz*; Case C-370/12, *Pringle*; Case C-503/13, *Boston Scientific*; Case C-62/14, *Gauweiler*; Case 80/14, *USDAW*; Case C-16/15, *Pérez López*

19

Epilogue
Brexit and the Union: Past, Present, Future

Contents

Introduction

While a distinguished British war hero strongly commended the 'United States of Europe' in 1946,[1] when it came to joining the first supranational project – the 1951 European Coal and Steel Community – the view of the (then) British

---

[1] This had been done by none other than Sir Winston Churchill in 1946, see: www.youtube .com/watch?v=Ln4SRnt4VE0.

government was that 'the Durham miners simply won't wear it'.[2] The reasons for this early rejection of European integration were economic and political in nature. Not only did the British economy produce as much coal as the rest of Europe combined;[3] politically, irritations arose from the French insistence on 'supranationalism' – a 'foreign' idea that ran counter to the British ideal of parliamentary sovereignty.[4]

When it came, a few years later, to choosing between the British Commonwealth and the 1957 European Economic Community (EEC), the British government again unconditionally favoured the former over the latter.[5] Once more, economic reasons come to complement geopolitical ones. For not only would the 'common market' be incompatible with the imperial preference system that guaranteed cheap agricultural goods; British foreign policy still followed its 'three circles' logic in which Europe simply ranked last.[6]

To contain the consequences of its choice against the 'common market', the British government nevertheless quickly proposed an organisation to rival the EEC: the 1960 European Free Trade Association (EFTA). The creation of EFTA thereby followed a dual aim. Positively, it created a free trade area that would allow Britain to trade with six other European States, while at the same time keeping its imperial preference system.[7] Negatively, on the other hand, it was hoped that EFTA would dissolve the (supranational) common market in a (intergovernmental) free trade area 'like a lump of sugar in an English cup of tea'.[8] This second aim however turned out to be wishful thinking, and in an extraordinary act of pragmatic reorientation, membership in the European common market suddenly became a British priority in the early 1960s.[9] Yet Britain's first application to join the Union, made in 1961, was rejected by France. In a famous 1963 press conference General de Gaulle – then President of France – gave the following reasons for France's veto:

[2]   This was the view of the Labour government of the time (see K. Morgan, *Labour in Power: 1945–1951* (Oxford University Press, 1985), 420).

[3]   M. Camps, *Britain and the European Community 1955–1963* (Oxford University Press, 1964), 3.

[4]   S. George, *An Awkward Partner: Britain in the European Community* (Oxford University Press, 1996), 21; Camps, *Britain and the European Community* (n. 3 above), 4: 'Co-operation with Europe was desirable; integration with Europe was not.'

[5]   For the classic analysis here, see G. St. J. Barclay, *Commonwealth or Europe* (University of Queensland Press, 1970).

[6]   In Churchill's famous words (quoted ibid., 16): 'I feel the existence of three great circles … The first circle for us is naturally the British Commonwealth and Empire, with all that that comprises. Then there is also the English-speaking world in which we, Canada and the other British Dominions and the United States play so important a part. And finally there is United Europe.'

[7]   Unlike a 'common market', a 'free trade area' allows each Member State to retain its own commercial policy towards third countries. On this distinction, see below.

[8]   I am grateful to Anne Deighton for having pointed me to this wonderful 'British' treasure. For the historical context of the phrase, see J. Ellison, *Threatening Europe: Britain and the Creation of the European Community, 1955–58* (Palgrave, 2000), 2.

[9]   D. Gowland and A. Turner, *Reluctant Europeans: Britain and European Integration 1945–1998* (Longman, 2000), 115: 'By early 1960, therefore, the options available to British

> Great Britain applied for membership of the Common Market. It did so after refusing earlier to participate in the community that was being built, and after then having created a free trade area with six other states, and finally … after having put some pressure on the Six in order to prevent the [putting into effect] of the Common Market from really getting started. Britain thus in its turn requested membership, but on its own conditions. This undoubtedly raises for each of the six States and for England problems of a very great dimension. England is, in effect, insular, maritime, linked through its trade, markets, and food supply to very diverse and often very distant countries. Its activities are essentially industrial and commercial, and only slightly agricultural. It has, throughout its [history], very marked and original customs and traditions. In short, the nature, structure, and economic context of England differ profoundly from those of the other States of the Continent.[10]

This rejection came as a shock. Britain had seriously overestimated its bargaining power; and it was a shock to be repeated when de Gaulle vetoed a second British application in 1967. Only the third membership application would succeed – and only once the French General had left the political stage. It led to the signing of the Accession Treaty on 22 January 1972; and on 1 January 1973, Britain joined the European Union (together with Ireland and Denmark). Ever since, however, Britain has never been the happiest of Member States. Doubts about European integration persisted; and while British governments subsequently embraced the liberal project of the 'single market', the idea of an accompanying 'political union' continued to be resolutely rejected. This rejection reached its climax in 2016, when a referendum on British EU membership yielded a popular majority for 'Brexit' – the British exit from the European Union.

This – separate – chapter aims to explore the past, present and future of that decision. Section 1 offers a historical overview of British membership in the Union. With its commitment to European integration often selective or minimal, the United Kingdom has come to be seen as an 'awkward partner' within the European Union.[11] Section 2 explores the process of withdrawal in some detail and here in particular the nature and content of Article 50 TEU – the provision that regulates the Brexit process. Section 3 subsequently analyses the future status of 'European Union' law after a repeal of the 1972 European Communities Act. Will all directly applicable European law suddenly disappear? And what, in particular, will happen to all international agreements concluded

policymakers had narrowed down alarmingly. As a matter of fact, Macmillan and his colleagues faced an extremely simply choice: either to enter the [EU] on the same terms as the original founders – something that had so far been regarded as anathema – or to remain outside, with all the attendant economic and political risks … It must be emphasised that the decision to apply for entry was taken not in a fit of Euro-enthusiasm, but out of a reluctant recognition that it represented the lesser of two evils.'

[10]   A. G. Harryvan and J. van der Harst, *Documents on European Union* (Macmillan, 1997), 132 at 134.

[11]   George, *Awkward Partner* (n. 4 above).

by the Union? Section 4 finally tries to look even farther into the future and presents the alternative partnership options that are presently discussed. Will the United Kingdom join the EFTA States (again); or will it join a customs union with the EU; or will it favour a 'Canada plus' deal?

Let us look at all of these questions in turn.

1. Britain in the European Union: An 'Awkward Partner'?

a. 'Second Thoughts': The 1975 Membership Referendum

Having joined the 'common market' in 1973, 'second thoughts' about EU membership soon emerged. For once a Labour government had entered Downing Street in 1974, it instantly tried to renegotiate the 'Tory Terms' of EU membership.[12] Under pressure from its left wing, Harold Wilson – then Prime Minister and leader of the Labour Party – had been forced to promise a 'fundamental renegotiation' of the British membership of the Union.[13] The 1974 Labour Party Manifesto therefore read as follows:

> Britain is a European nation, and a Labour Britain would always seek a wider co-operation between the European peoples. But a profound political mistake made by the [Conservative] Government was to accept the terms of entry to the Common Market, and to take us in without the consent of the British people. This has involved the imposition of food taxes on top of rising world prices, crippling fresh burdens on our balance of payments, and a draconian curtailment of the power of the British Parliament to settle questions affecting vital British interests. This is why a Labour Government will immediately seek a fundamental renegotiation of the terms of entry … In preparing to re-negotiate the entry terms, our main objectives are these:
> – Major changes in the Common Agricultural Policy, so that it ceases to be a threat to world trade in food products, and so that low-cost producers outside Europe can continue to have access to the British food market.
> – New and fairer methods of financing the Community Budget …
> – As stated earlier, we would reject any kind of international agreement which compelled us to accept increased unemployment for the sake of maintaining a fixed parity, as is required by current proposals for a European Economic and Monetary Union …
> – The retention by Parliament of those powers over the British economy needed to pursue effective regional, industrial and fiscal policies[.][14]

---

[12] On this point, see specifically Gowland and Turner, *Reluctant Europeans* (n. 9 above), ch. 13: 'Renegotiating "Tory Terms"'.

[13] *Ibid.*, 213: 'One of Wilson's main reasons for holding the referendum had been to prevent an irreparable split in the Labour ranks.'

[14] 1974 Labour Party Manifesto: 'Let us work together – Labour's way out of the crisis', available at www.labour-party.org.uk/manifestos/1974/Feb/1974-feb-labour-manifesto.shtml.

These four points represent four political cleavages that became fundamental fault lines in all future British–Union relations. Especially the budget issue became an intractable bone of contention. In the view of the British political establishment, the standard formula for membership contributions severely disadvantaged the United Kingdom; and the latter was therefore entitled to a 'rebate' so as to reduce its net contributions to the Union budget.

All these demands for a 'fundamental renegotiation' might have simply been rejected by the other Member States on the grounds that the ink of the 1972 Accession Treaty had barely dried; yet faced with a conflict in the 'honeymoon' period of British membership, the 1975 Dublin European Council found a compromise that offered some minor-yet-not-insignificant changes to please the British. The Labour Prime Minister therefore recommended continued membership in the Union; and the subsequent vote in Parliament supported the government's position – a result that was nevertheless overwhelmingly due to 'conservative' votes.[15] The Labour government had however also promised a referendum on Union membership and the Referendum Act 1975 therefore determined that the people themselves could, on 5 June 1975, decide whether the United Kingdom should remain or leave the European Union.[16] Two-thirds of the votes cast favoured continued Union membership; and this – almost enthusiastic – support provided strong democratic legitimacy to the British decision to join (and remain) in the Union.

b. A Market without a State: The Thatcher Vision

Would the 1975 referendum ease the 'awkward' relationship between Britain and the Union? With the coming into power of the Conservative Party in 1979, high hopes existed.[17] They were soon dashed. The rebate issue quickly returned to the fore and was henceforth pursued with unbending zealousness: Britain wanted its 'own money back'![18] And, in order to achieve this aim, Britain adopted a strategy of (un)civil disobedience by deliberately obstructing the Council in 1982 – a strategy inspired by France's empty chair policy 20 years earlier.[19] This policy

---

[15] The majority of Labour MPs had come to reject, against the wishes of its own government, the renegotiated terms as insufficient (137 votes in favour and 145 against); and without the overwhelming conservative support (249 votes in favour and 8 against), the United Kingdom would have left the European Union in 1975.

[16] The 1975 referendum question was: 'Do you think that the United Kingdom should stay in the European Community (Common Market)?' And again: while the Labour government recommended a positive vote, the official Labour Party line was negative.

[17] During the 1970s and 1980s, the Conservative Party was seen as the 'party of Europe'. This becomes even clearer if it is recalled that during much of the 1980s, the Labour Party's official policy was committed to a withdrawal from the Union (see A. Geddes, *Britain and the European Union* (Palgrave 2013), 224).

[18] For the famous part of the Thatcher speech, see: www.youtube.com/watch?v=pDqZdZ5iZdY.

[19] For a discussion of the empty chair crisis, see Chapter 1, section 2(b). However, unlike France, Britain lost this battle as, surprisingly, the Council called for a majority vote to

of obstructionism irritated France so much that it openly suggested that the UK should search for an alternative status to full Union membership – a suggestion that was instantly rejected. Progress on the British Budgetary Question, colloquially termed the 'Bloody British Question',[20] was finally made in 1984 when the 'Fontainebleau' European Council reached an agreement on a complex mechanism that still applies today (see Figure 19.1).[21]

Did the end of the rebate 'war' inaugurate a period of European 'peace'? A short peace indeed followed; yet short it was. In 1985, an 'ideological' alliance between Thatcher's Britain and the European Union had suddenly emerged in the form of the Commission's White Paper 'Completing the Internal Market'. The paper had a British 'father': Lord Cockfield – a close collaborator of Thatcher – who had become EU Commissioner for the Internal Market in 1985; and the 'British' idea was seized upon by (then) Commission President Jacques Delors. However, whereas for Britain 'the single market was an end in itself that could raise to a European stage the liberalizing and deregulatory elements of the Thatcherite project', for the European Commission and most Continental European States – it was 'a means to an end, that end being deeper economic and political integration'.[22]

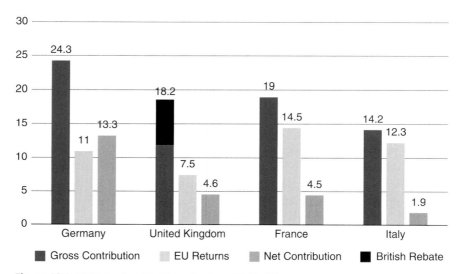

Figure 19.1 EU Membership Contributions (2014–20)

break the deadlock – a move that signalled the beginning of the end of the Luxembourg Compromise. A similar episode of British obstructionism would recur in 1996 in response to the ban on British beef following the BSE crisis. On the British policy of non-cooperation with the EU, see V. Miller, 'The Policy of Non-Cooperation with the EU', House of Commons Research Paper 96/74.

[20] R. Jenkins, *A Life at the Centre* (Pan Books, 1991), ch. 27.
[21] For the original mechanism, see Council Decision 85/257 on the Community's System of own Resources [1985] OJ L 128/15.
[22] Geddes, *Britain and the European Union* (n. 17 above), 70.

To that effect, the 1985 Milan European Council called for a major institutional reform of the Union: the 1986 Single European Act (SEA). The SEA was a decisive yet very small step towards political integration.[23] Yet the very idea that Europe could re-regulate markets and offer social rights to workers was anathema to the (then) British government. Furious to discover that the single market project was more that an exercise in deregulation, Thatcher set out her (Conservative) vision in 1988 in a famous speech at the College of Europe in Bruges:

> We have not successfully rolled back the frontiers of the state in Britain only to see them reimposed at a European level, with a European superstate exercising a new dominance from Brussels … [T]he Treaty of Rome itself was intended as a Charter for Economic Liberty … By getting rid of barriers, by making it possible for companies to operate on a Europe-wide scale, we can best compete with the United States, Japan and the other new economic powers emerging in Asia and elsewhere. It means action to *free* markets, to *widen* choice and to produce greater economic convergence through *reduced* government intervention. Our aim should not be more and more detailed regulation from the centre: it should be to deregulate, to remove the constraints on trade and to open up[.][24]

This speech became the prelude and source of accepted Euroscepticism within the Conservative Party;[25] and henceforth a section within the party would hold the 'Thatcherite' line – especially after the 1992 Treaty on European Union.

c. From Maastricht to Lisbon: 'A Europe of Bits and Pieces'

The 1992 Treaty on European Union represented 'a new stage in the process of European integration'.[26] Not only would it lay the foundations for 'Economic and Monetary Union' (EMU), a significant push towards political union had been made – especially by means of reducing the national veto in the Council.[27] Yet the 1992 TEU was also a constitutional compromise.

---

[23] Far from being a surrender to continental views, British interests had predominantly found their way into the SEA (see George, *Awkward Partner* (n. 4 above) 184: '[T]he British achieved real progress in areas that mattered to them. Majority voting was extended only in limited areas … [and] [s]pecifically excluded from the rules on majority voting were the areas of taxation, free movement of persons, health controls, and employees' rights … The other clear victory for the British view was that no major increase was proposed in the powers of the European Parliament').

[24] Harryvan and van der Harst, *Documents on European Union* (n. 10 above), 244–5 (emphasis added).

[25] Geddes, *Britain and the European Union* (n. 17 above), 229. The Bruges Speech led to the creation of one of the best-known Eurosceptic think tanks: the Bruges Group. For a self-presentation of the group, see: www.brugesgroup.com.

[26] Preamble of the TEU.   [27] For a brief history, see Chapter 1, section 3.

Politically sensitive areas, like foreign and security policy and justice and home affairs, had remained intergovernmental; and even within the supranational parts of the European Union, the Maastricht Treaty had created 'a Europe of bits and pieces'.[28] With regard to EMU, for example, Britain had secured an opt-out;[29] and, having vehemently opposed further integration on social matters, it had received a second 'opt-out' here which meant that the envisaged social chapter within the EU Treaties had to be abandoned in favour of an 'Agreement on Social Policy concluded between the Member States of the European Community *with the exception of the United Kingdom of Great Britain and Northern Ireland*'.[30]

This second opt-out would eventually be dropped when a Labour government returned to power in 1997; yet the British ambivalence towards 'full' membership obligations remained; and when it came to the 1997 Treaty of Amsterdam, Britain (and Ireland) not only decided to opt out of the incorporation of the Schengen Agreement,[31] it also extrapolated itself from the Treaty Title on 'Visas, Asylum, Immigration and other Policies related to the Free Movement of Persons'.[32] The same strategy of 'differential' membership surfaced with the 2007 Lisbon Treaty, where the United Kingdom obtained a partial opt-out from the EU Charter of Fundamental Rights;[33] and even more remarkably, Britain was allowed a complete opt-out of the already existing (!) Union law on police and judicial cooperation in criminal matters.[34] This was cherry-picking at its best or worst – depending on one's point of view.

[28] The famous phrase comes from D. Curtin, 'The Constitutional Structure of the Union: A Europe of Bits and Pieces' (1993) 30 CML Rev. 17.

[29] See Protocol On certain Provisions relating to the United Kingdom of Great Britain and Northern Ireland (1992) OJ C191/87, esp. preamble 1: 'Recognizing that the United Kingdom shall not be obliged or committed to move to the third stage of Economic and Monetary Union without a separate decision to do so by its government and Parliament'. The opt-out can today be found in Protocol No. 15 to the EU Treaties.

[30] The Agreement can be found in the Protocol On Social Policy (1992) OJ C191/90 (emphasis added).

[31] See Protocol On the Application of Certain Aspects of Article 7a of the Treaty Establishing the European Community to the United Kingdom and to Ireland (1997) OJ C340/97. The provisions can today be found in Protocols 19 and 20 to the present EU Treaties.

[32] See Protocol On the Position of the United Kingdom and Ireland (1997) OJ 340/99. The provisions can today be found in Protocol 21 to the present EU Treaties.

[33] See Protocol No. 30 On the Application of the Charter of Fundamental Rights of the European Union to Poland and the United Kingdom. For a discussion of this partial opt-out, see Chapter 12, section 4(b/bb).

[34] See Protocol No. 36 On Transitional Provisions, esp. Art. 10. The possibility of an opt-out of all (!) acts in this area is here made in Art. 10(4), after a transitional period of five years; while Art. 10(5) allows the United Kingdom 'at any time, afterwards, [to] notify the Council of its wish to participate in acts which have ceased to apply pursuant to paragraph 4'. For an overview of the issues here, see House of Lords – EU Committee, 'EU Police and Criminal Justice Measures: The UK's 2014 Opt-Out Decision' (2013) HL Paper 159. The full opt-out was indeed used by David Cameron see below.

d. After Lisbon: The Path to Withdrawal from the Union

aa. From Lisbon to the Referendum: The Rise of Euroscepticism

By 2009, the United Kingdom was two-thirds in and one-third out of the European Union. While remaining a 'full' member in form, its various opt-outs had exempted it from core EU obligations and placed it at the margins of Europe. This strategy of semi-detachedness took a decidedly more Eurosceptic turn with the coming into power of the Conservative Party in 2010. Fearing to lose out to the United Kingdom Independence Party (UKIP) – founded in 1993 as a response to the Maastricht Treaty – the Conservatives had become an essentially Eurosceptic party.[35] And, although forced to work within a coalition, the Coalition Programme already heralded a 'nationalist' move away from closer European integration:

> The Government believes that Britain should play a leading role in an enlarged European Union, but that no further powers should be transferred to Brussels without a referendum. This approach strikes the right balance between constructive engagement with the EU to deal with the issues that affect us all, and protecting our national sovereignty …
> – We will ensure that there is no further transfer of sovereignty or powers over the course of the next Parliament. We will examine the balance of the EU's existing competences and will, in particular, work to limit the application of the Working Time Directive in the United Kingdom.
> – We will amend the 1972 European Communities Act so that any proposed future treaty that transferred areas of power, or competences, would be subject to a referendum on that treaty – a 'referendum lock'. We will amend the 1972 European Communities Act so that the use of any *passerelle* would require primary legislation.
> – We will examine the case for a United Kingdom Sovereignty Bill to make it clear that ultimate authority remains with Parliament.[36]

The external and internal outcomes of these commitments are well known. The most significant external expression is the completely senseless – though highly symbolic – veto of the EU Fiscal Compact by the British government so as to fulfil its first promise.[37] A response to the second and third – internal – commitments was the European Union Act 2011. The Act provided for a 'referendum lock' for future amendment treaties transferring new competences

---

[35] D. Baker et al., 'Sovereign Nations and Global Markets: Modern British Conservatism and Hyperglobalisation' (2002) 4 *British Journal of Politics and International Relations* 399 at 404.

[36] For a copy of the Coalition Programme, see: www.gov.uk/government/publications/the-coalition-documentation. The Programme also contained a commitment to exercise the opt-out in the area of police and judicial cooperation in criminal matters (see n. 34 above).

[37] See *Financial Times* (9 December 2011): 'Britain's Cold Shoulder for Europe'. The 'senselessness' of the decision stemmed from the fact that – in substance – these were reforms favoured by the Conservative government; and all that Cameron achieved was to remove Britain from the negotiating table when the eurozone decided to go ahead anyway.

to the Union,[38] while it also reconfirmed 'national' parliamentary sovereignty as the core constitutional principle of the British Constitution.[39]

But there would be more: in an attempt to win over Eurosceptic voters (and to please its own right wing), the Conservative Party finally promised – just as the Labour Party had done in 1975 – a 'fundamental renegotiation' of the British terms of EU membership and an 'in–out' referendum.[40] Winning the 2015 national elections, the Cameron government almost immediately set out its demands in a letter to the European Council in November of that year,[41] and a European Union Referendum Act 2015 was duly adopted. Following intense negotiations in early 2016, the European Council and the other Member States offered the United Kingdom an olive branch in the form of the – pompously styled – 'New Settlement for the United Kingdom within the European Union'.[42] Based on these not-insignificant concessions, a referendum was called for 23 June 2016; and a (slight) majority of voters within the United Kingdom here expressed their wish to leave the European Union.[43]

---

[38] For an analysis of the Act, see M. Gordon and M. Dougan, 'The United Kingdom's European Union Act 2011: "Who Won the Bloody War Anyway?"' (2012) 37 *EL Rev.* 3.

[39] For the text of s. 18 of the Act, see Chapter 4, section 2.

[40] An informal promise was first made, by David Cameron, on 23 January 2013 in his 'Bloomberg Speech'; and a formal promise was then made in the 2014 Tory Manifesto, which committed the Party to hold a referendum by the end of 2017. For the bellicose language of the manifesto, see (*ibid.*, 18): 'If you want more EU red tape, more interference from Brussels, a bigger EU budget and no referendum – vote Labour. They are the ones who signed away power after power to the EU and refused to give the British people a vote, and they are the ones who opened the door for uncontrolled migration.'

[41] For a copy of the letter, see: www.gov.uk/government/publications/eu-reform-pms-letter-to-president-of-the-european-council-donald-tusk.

[42] European Council, A New Settlement for the United Kingdom within the European Union (2016) OJ C69/1. This cannot be the place to fully analyse the Union concessions in any detail but the most important concession was probably a safeguard mechanism for 'situations of inflow of workers from other Member States of an exceptional magnitude over an extended period of time, *including as a result of past policies following previous enlargements*' (*ibid.*, 9, emphasis added). The 'New Settlement' here allowed a Member State to limit access to non-contributory in-work benefits for a period of up to four years from the commencement of employment. Conveniently, the Commission already declared, in advance, that such a situation presently existed in the United Kingdom and that the latter would consequently be 'justified in triggering the mechanism in the full expectation of obtaining approval' (*ibid.*, 15). The great irony with regard to this concession is, of course, that the entire situation is partly (or fully) the result of the United Kingdom's own choices. For when Eastern Enlargement took place in 2004, the United Kingdom (together with Ireland and Sweden) decided not to insist – as all other Member States did – on transitional limitations on the free movement of workers with the result that instead of the expected 13,000 migrants approximately 600,000 migrants had arrived by 2006 (House of Lords, European Union: Fifty-Third Report, available at: https://publications.parliament.uk/pa/ld200506/ldselect/ldeucom/273/27302.htm, para. 86).

[43] With a turnout of 72 per cent of the electorate, 52 per cent decided to leave, while 48 per cent voted to remain.

While constitutionally not binding, the referendum result was nevertheless accepted by all main parties as politically binding. The 'New Settlement' was called off the table;[44] and the United Kingdom henceforth began to prepare its withdrawal from the European Union.

bb. *Triggering the Withdrawal Process: The* Miller *Judgment*

Under British constitutional law, referenda do not have any binding legal force; and it was therefore clear that the British Parliament would need to 'ratify' the result of the popular vote. What was unclear, however, was whether this parliamentary 'ratification' would need to happen at the beginning or the end of the withdrawal process. Would Parliament need to be involved in 'triggering' the withdrawal process – laid down in Article 50 TEU? Or would it only need to give its consent to the repeal of the 1972 European Communities Act?

In order to exit the European Union, a Member State must notify its intention to the Union 'in accordance with its own constitutional requirements';[45] and within the United Kingdom, the question of which branch of the British State would be entitled to notify the referendum result soon gave rise to a constitutional battle between the British government (executive) and the British Parliament (legislative). Relying on the ancient powers of the royal prerogative, the former claimed that it alone was entitled to trigger Article 50. This view was challenged in *R. (Miller)* v. *Secretary of State for Exiting the European Union* on the grounds that a notification to the European Union required the *prior* consent of the British Parliament.[46]

In its *Miller* judgment, the United Kingdom Supreme Court was faced with two contradictory features of the – unwritten – British Constitution. According to a first principle, 'ministers generally enjoy a power freely to enter into and to terminate treaties without recourse to Parliament'; whereas, in accordance with a second principle, 'ministers are not normally entitled to exercise any power they might otherwise have if it results in a change in UK domestic law' unless authorised by a parliamentary statute.[47] These two principles can only be harmoniously combined in a classic dualist legal order, as any changes introduced by international treaties 'outside' the United Kingdom will – theoretically – have no automatic effects 'inside' the domestic legal order; and the Supreme Court consequently started out as follows:

---

[44] Joint Statement by the Presidents of the European Parliament, the European Council and the Commission (Brussels, 24 June 2016), available at: http://europa.eu/rapid/press-release_STATEMENT-16–2329_en.htm: '[T]he "New Settlement for the United Kingdom within the European Union", reached at the European Council on 18–19 February 2016, will now not take effect and ceases to exist. There will be no renegotiation.'

[45] Art. 50(1) TEU.

[46] *R. (Miller)* v. *Secretary of State for Exiting the European Union* [2017] UKSC 5.

[47] *Ibid.*, para. 5.

> There is little case law on the power to terminate or withdraw from treaties, but, as a matter of both logic and practical necessity, it must be part of the treaty-making prerogative … Subject to any restrictions imposed by primary legislation, the general rule is that the power to make or unmake treaties is exercisable without legislative authority and that the exercise of that power is not reviewable by the courts … This principle rests on the so-called dualist theory, which is based on the proposition that international law and domestic law operate in independent spheres. The prerogative power to make treaties depends on two related propositions. The first is that treaties between sovereign states have effect in international law and are not governed by the domestic law of any state … The second proposition is that, although they are binding on the United Kingdom in international law, treaties are not part of UK law and give rise to no legal rights or obligations in domestic law.[48]

But did this dualist reasoning apply to European Union law? In a judgment full of internal contradictions and intellectual gaps, the Supreme Court struggled to find a convincing answer that cut the Gordian knot created by the traditional–dualist British legal order and the modern–monist Union legal order. When discussing the effect of Union law in the United Kingdom, this is what the Supreme Court had to say:

> In one sense, of course, it can be said that the 1972 Act is the source of EU law, in that, without that Act, EU law would have no domestic status. *But in a more fundamental sense and, we consider, a more realistic sense, where EU law applies in the United Kingdom, it is the EU institutions which are the relevant source of that law. The legislative institutions of the EU can create or abrogate rules of law which will then apply domestically, without the specific sanction of any UK institution* … In our view, then, although the 1972 Act gives effect to EU law, it is not itself the originating source of that law. It is … the 'conduit pipe' by which EU law is introduced into UK domestic law. So long as the 1972 Act remains in force, its effect is to constitute *EU law an independent and overriding source of domestic law* … The 1972 Act effectively operates as a partial transfer of law-making powers, or an assignment of legislative competences, by Parliament to the EU law-making institutions (so long as Parliament wills it)[.][49]

The 1972 Act is here portrayed as a 'conduit pipe' or 'bridge' that allows directly applicable (!) EU law into the British legal order without the need for a *specific* act of transposition into British law. On the basis of this monist position,[50]

---

[48] *Ibid.*, paras. 54–5.   [49] *Ibid.*, paras. 61, 65 and 68 (emphasis added).

[50] To repeat: under a classic dualist doctrine, there cannot be any 'directly applicable' European rights; and a withdrawal from the Union could therefore *never* change any British (!) rights, as all British rights are a result of British law – not European law. That this view was rejected by the Supreme Court for European Union law is confirmed in para. 90 when the Court admitted that '[i]n 1972, for the first time in the history of the United Kingdom, a dynamic, international [!] source of law was grafted onto, and above, the well-established existing sources of domestic law: parliament and the courts'. Alas, the owl of Minerva only spreads its wings with the fall of dusk!

Union law was – for the first time – expressly recognised as an 'independent' source of 'British' law and expressly placed above 'ordinary' parliamentary legislation. And it was this – monist – view that allowed the Court to argue that a withdrawal from the European Union would constitute 'a fundamental change which justifies the conclusion that *prerogative powers cannot be invoked to withdraw from the EU Treaties*'.[51] The Supreme Court consequently held that the British Parliament had to specifically empower the government before a notification to the European Council could take place. Parliament duly passed the European Union (Notification of Withdrawal) Act 2017 in which it authorised the British Prime Minister to trigger Article 50 TEU and to thereby begin the official Brexit process.[52]

2. *Withdrawing from the Union: Article 50 TEU*

The European Union is not a sovereign State but a Union of States; and unlike sovereign States, it allows its Member States to withdraw or 'secede' from the Union. With the 2007 Lisbon Treaty, this right to withdraw has been expressly codified in Article 50 TEU. The provision states:

1. Any Member State may decide to withdraw from the Union in accordance with its own constitutional requirements.
2. A Member State which decides to withdraw shall notify the European Council of its intention. In the light of the guidelines provided by the European Council, the Union shall negotiate and conclude an agreement with that State, setting out the arrangements for its withdrawal, taking account of the framework for its future relationship with the Union. That agreement shall be negotiated in accordance with Article 218(3) of the Treaty on the Functioning of the European Union. It shall be concluded on behalf of the Union by the Council, acting by a qualified majority, after obtaining the consent of the European Parliament.
3. The Treaties shall cease to apply to the State in question from the date of entry into force of the withdrawal agreement or, failing that, two years after the notification referred to in paragraph 2, unless the European Council, in agreement with the Member State concerned, unanimously decides to extend this period.
4. For the purposes of paragraphs 2 and 3, the member of the European Council or of the Council representing the withdrawing Member State shall not participate in the discussions of the European Council or Council or in decisions concerning it. A qualified majority shall be defined in accordance with Article 238(3)(b) of the Treaty on the Functioning of the European Union …

What is the history and nature of the provision? While Article 50(1) TEU declares the sovereign right of each Member State to withdraw from the Union, its intention to do so must be formally notified to the European Council

[51] *Ibid.*, para. 83 (emphasis added).
[52] s. 1(1) of the Act states: 'The Prime Minister may notify, under Article 50(2) of the Treaty on European Union, the United Kingdom's intention to withdraw from the EU.'

according to Article 50(2). For the United Kingdom, this happened on 29 March 2017, when the British Prime Minister May sent a letter to the President of the European Council. This started the two-year negotiation period envisaged in Article 50(3).[53] How will the withdrawal be negotiated? Let us look at this question in this second section.

a. Article 50: Constitutional History and Nature

Most sovereign States categorically prohibit secessions from their territory;[54] while most international organisations implicitly permit withdrawals of their Member States.[55] Within the European Union, a sovereign 'right' to withdraw has always been implicit in the Union legal order.[56] The Lisbon Treaty has made

[53] Can the notification be withdrawn? The question has been hotly debated. For arguments in favour, see A. Sari, 'Reversing a Withdrawal Notification under Article 50 TEU: Can a Member State Change Its Mind?' (2017) 42 *EL Rev.* 451; P. Craig, 'Brexit: A Drama in Six Acts' (2016) 41 *EL Rev.* 447, esp. at 463–5. One important counter-argument here is however the so-called 'Kaufmann Amendment' (J. Dammann, 'Can Member States Rescind Their Declaration of Withdrawal from the European Union?' (2017) 23 *Columbia Journal of European Law* 265 at 302), which had suggested including the following sentence into Art. 50 (2) TEU: 'The notification to withdraw can be revoked at any time by a declaration addressed to the European Council'; and given that the amendment was not (!) included, it could be argued that a right to revoke the notification has been rejected. This however need not necessarily be the case. For in light of the numerous amendment proposals, the drafters of the provision may simply not have had time to specifically consider the issue; or they thought that the inclusion of an express reference to the right to withdraw from the withdrawal was simply unnecessary in light of the background principles offered by the Vienna Convention of the Law of Treaties. Art. 68 of the latter states: 'A notification or instrument provided for in article 65 or 67 [termination or withdrawal from an international treaty], may be revoked at any time before it takes effect.'

[54] Some federal States appear to be more tolerant with regard to secessionist claims by their constituent units. For the Canadian constitutional order, see *Reference Re Secession of Quebec* [1998] 2 SCR 217.

[55] On the 'sovereign' right of withdrawal, see T. Christakis, 'Article 56: Denunciation of or Withdrawal from a Treaty Containing No Provision regarding Termination, Denunciation or Withdrawal', in O. Corten and V. Klein (eds.), *The Vienna Convention on the Law of Treaties: A Commentary – Volume II* (Oxford University Press, 2011), 1251. This is not uncontested: see N. Feinberg, 'Unilateral Withdrawal from an International Organisation' (1963) 39 BYIL 189. Today, the 1969 Vienna Convention on the Law of Treaties has clarified that a right to withdrawal depends on whether the parties to a treaty agreed to it either expressly or implicitly.

[56] For the same view, see J. H. H. Weiler, 'Alternatives to Withdrawal from an International Organisation: The Case of the European Economic Community' (1985) 20 *Israel Law Review* 282. It is however unclear how that conclusion is reached. For while Weiler generally holds 'that orthodox *legal* analysis would confirm, in the context of the EEC, Feinberg's general conclusion against the automatic right of unilateral withdrawal' (*ibid.*, 287 – emphasis added), he nonetheless finds that, *politically*, and in the absence of techniques for avoiding all obligations arising under European law '[i]f a Member State cannot accept these obligations, better it be allowed to withdraw, even unilaterally' (*ibid.*, 298). For the opposite view, see T. Bruha and C. Nowak, 'Recht auf Austritt aus der Europäischen

this implicit right explicit; yet the contours of the right have remained unclear. An overview of the history of Article 50 may here offer some insights.

aa. Drafting History during the European Convention

Article 50 was first conceived during the European Convention leading up to the (failed) 2004 Constitutional Treaty.[57] Whose brainchild Article 50 thereby is has been eagerly contested by two putative 'fathers'.[58] Yet it seems that the idea of a withdrawal clause first emerged from a contribution of the British member of the Convention, whose suggestion drew on the 'Cambridge Draft Treaty' edited by Professor Alan Dashwood.[59] This Cambridge draft advocated a unilateral and automatic right to withdraw for each Member State; and, importantly, in doing so, it did not even envisage a withdrawal agreement. All that was needed was a formal notification from the withdrawing Member State; while the Union was, in its turn, entitled to unilaterally adjust its institutional structure after the withdrawal.[60]

This 'State-centred' version was heavily criticised by the more 'integrationist' Convention members;[61] and it contrasts strikingly with the proposal made by the European Commission. In its 'Penelope Project',[62] the Commission indeed suggested a much more 'Union-centred' withdrawal provision. It read:

> 1. Where a revision to the Constitution has entered into force and a Member State has not been able to adopt it in accordance with its constitutional requirements, such State may, after a period of two years after the entry into force of that revision, apply to withdraw from the Union. In that case the Union shall commence negotiations with the Member State concerned in order to conclude an agreement governing their future relations …

Union? Anmerkungen zu Artikel I-59 des Entwurfs eines Vertrages über eine Verfassung für Europa' (2004) 42 *Archiv des Völkerrechts* 1.

[57] For a brief discussion of the European Convention, see Chapter 1, section 4(a).

[58] The two auto-proclaimed 'fathers' are the Italian Giuliano Amato, then a Vice-President of the European Convention, and the British diplomat, Lord Kerr.

[59] See European Convention, Contribution by Mr P. Hain: Constitutional Treaty of the European Union, CONV 345/1/02 (Brussels, 16 October 2002).

[60] *Ibid.*, Art. 27: '1. Any Member State may withdraw from the European Union. It shall address to the Council its notice of intention to withdraw. 2. The Council, meeting in the composition of the Heads of State or Government and acting by unanimity, shall determine, after consulting the Commission and the European Parliament, the institutional adjustments to this Treaty that such withdrawal entails. 3. For the purpose of this Article, the Council, sitting in the composition of Heads of State or Government, and the Commission shall act without taking into account the vote of the nationals of the withdrawing Member State. The European parliament shall act without taking into account the position of the Members of Parliament elected in that State.'

[61] For an overview of the various amendment proposal here, see European Convention, Scheda di analisi delle proposte di emendamento riguardanti l'appartenenza all'Unione: Progetto di articoli relativi al titolo X della Parte I (articoli da 43 a 46), CONV 672/03 (Brussels, 14 April 2003).

[62] http://ec.europa.eu/archives/emu_history/documents/treaties/Penelope%20pdf_en.pdf.

3. If the agreement governing future relations between the Union and the request-
    ing Member State is not concluded within a period of six months following the
    opening of negotiations, the Member State shall cease to be a member of the
    Union on 1 January of the year following the expiry of that period. In that case,
    the respective rights and obligations of the Union and the Member State leaving
    it shall, for no more than two years, continue to be governed by the law applica-
    ble on the day when the requesting State left the Union ...
4. The Member State leaving the Union may continue to be a contracting party to
    the Agreement on the European Economic Area.[63]

The Commission draft here offered a *conditional* and *limited* right of withdrawal
in one situation: where a Member State had been outvoted in the (newly suggested) qualified majority revision procedure,[64] it would not be forced to stay
within the Union and could consequently leave after two years of unsuccessful
ratification. The provision thereby evoked the idea of a future-relations agreement
to be concluded within a period of six months after the opening of the negotiations; and where no agreement had been reached, the State would (almost)
immediately cease to be a Union Member. However, in this case, the departing
State would still be subject to a transitional arrangement that applied the unrevised
(!) EU Treaties for another two years (maximum); and − mysteriously − the withdrawing State would also remain a party to the Agreement on the EEA.[65]

None of the two − extreme − draft versions would be adopted by the
European Convention. The Presidium indeed offered a compromise. Although
heavily based on the State-centred view and acknowledging a unilateral and
unconditional right to withdrawal, it nevertheless insisted on the obligation that
'the Union shall negotiate and conclude an agreement with that State, setting
out the arrangements for its withdrawal, taking account of the framework for its
future relationship with the Union'.[66] The Presidium however quickly clarified
that 'such an agreement should not constitute a condition for withdrawal so as
not to void the concept of voluntary withdrawal of its substance';[67] and after a
two-year period without reaching a withdrawal agreement, the membership
obligations of the withdrawing State would therefore automatically cease.[68] It is,
with minor amendments, this version that can today be found in Article 50 TEU.

---

[63] *Ibid.*, Art. 103.
[64] According to Art. 101 of the Commission Draft Treaty, future Treaty revisions were no
      longer subject to a unanimous agreement by all the Member States but henceforth allowed
      for a qualified majority of five-sixths or three-quarters of the Member States (depending
      on which part of the Constitutional Treaty would be amended).
[65] That this should − legally − not be possible will be explained below.
[66] European Convention, Presidium − Title X: Union Membership, CONV 648/03 (Brussels,
      2 April 2003), esp. Art. 46(2).
[67] *Ibid.*, p. 9.
[68] *Ibid.*, Art. 46(3) (emphasis added): 'This Constitution shall cease to apply to the State in
      question as from the date of entry into force of the withdrawal agreement *or, failing that,
      two years after the notification* referred to in paragraph 2.'

bb. The Nature and Character of Article 50

What is the nature and character of Article 50? The provision represents a compromise between the 'State-centred' and the 'Union-centred' versions tabled during the European Convention. This compromise solution is however much closer to the former than the latter. For like the Cambridge draft, the right to withdraw from the Union is unconditional and unilateral; however unlike the Cambridge draft, this right is no longer automatic, since Article 50 imposes a procedural obligation to try to reach a mutual understanding in the form of a 'withdrawal agreement'.[69]

Importantly, unlike either the Cambridge and Commission drafts, Article 50 TEU today envisages two (!) separate agreements that a Member State may conclude after it has notified its wish to withdraw. A 'withdrawal agreement', designed to settle past commitments, is here distinguished from a future-relations agreement to be concluded after withdrawal. The withdrawal agreement should however already 'tak[e] account of the framework for [a withdrawing State's] future relationship with the Union', yet it is not to settle this relationship; nor will it deal with the future constitutional adjustments to the Union. For any changes to the EU Treaties require a unanimous Member State agreement, whereas the withdrawal agreement was specifically designed as an ordinary international agreement between the Union (!) and the departing Member State. Unlike an accession treaty, the withdrawal agreement will thus not constitute primary law of the Union and therefore cannot amend the EU Treaties.

Interestingly, the final version of Article 50 makes no mention of a transition period; nor does it refer to a continued EEA 'membership' of the departing state. These matters were rightly dropped, because the former can be dealt with in the withdrawal agreement itself, while the latter must be achieved by a future-relations agreement.

b. Negotiating Brexit: Institutional and Procedural Aspects

There is no obligation to *conclude* a withdrawal agreement under Article 50; yet, as was argued above, there is an obligation to *negotiate* on the Union and the United Kingdom. Who negotiates the withdrawal agreement, and according to which procedure(s)? Figure 19.2 offers a stylised outline of the various elements of the withdrawal process. We shall start with the institutional aspects and subsequently explore some of the procedural and substantive aspects of the negotiations.

---

[69] The wording of Art. 50 TEU only imposes an obligation to negotiate such an agreement on the Union; yet such a duty equally exists with regard to the United Kingdom. This duty, while not directly based on Art. 50 TEU, derives from the UK's (continued) status as a Member State of the Union and the duty of loyal cooperation under Art. 4(3) TEU. For the opposite view, insisting on a purely unilateral obligation on the Union, see C. Hillion, 'Accession and Withdrawal in the Law of the European Union', in A. Arnull and D. Chalmers (eds.), *The Oxford Handbook of European Union Law* (Oxford University Press, 2015), 126; A. Łazowski, 'Inside But Out? The UK and the EU', in A. Jakab and D. Kochenov (eds.), *The Enforcement of EU Law and Values: Ensuring Member States' Compliance* (Oxford University Press, 2017), 493.

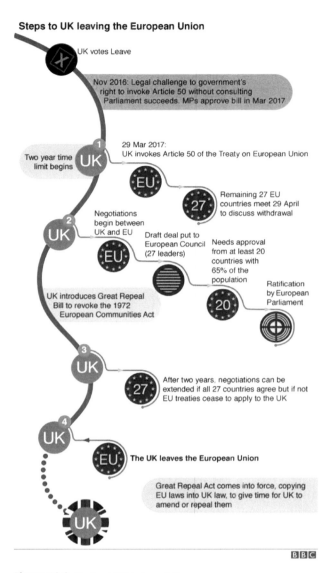

Figure 19.2 Stylised Withdrawal Process

aa. *Institutional Structures and Negotiating Teams*

In the aftermath of the Brexit Referendum, the United Kingdom created a new ministry: the Department for Exiting the European Union (DExEU) that is headed by its Secretary of State, David Davis (Figure 19.3). The Department's task is to ensure an orderly Brexit and to conduct the international negotiations with the European Union.[70] The Secretary of State

---

[70] DExEU's principal aims are set out in the government's 2017 White Paper 'The United Kingdom's Exit from and New Partnership with the European Union'. The paper is available at: www.gov.uk/government/publications/the-united-kingdoms-exit-from-and-new-partnership-with-the-european-union-white-paper.

thereby heads the British negotiation team,[71] whose terms of reference were laid down in June 2017.[72]

In addition, a Joint Ministerial Committee on EU Negotiations has been established so as to allow the heads of the devolved administrations of Northern Ireland, Scotland and Wales direct input into the negotiations. And within the Westminster Parliament itself, the Select Committee on the European Union is tasked with scrutinising the government's negotiating strategy.

On the European Union side, Article 50 directly calls on the European Council to draw up 'guidelines'; and the remaining 27 Member States and the Union also have, inspired by a reference to Article 218(3) TFEU,[73] called on the Commission and the Council to draw up more specific 'negotiating directives' and to nominate the Commission as the Union negotiator.[74] The Commission has thereby set up an independent unit dealing specifically with Brexit: the Article 50 Task

Figure 19.3 DExEU Secretary of State: David Davis

[71] For the biographies of the Civil Service representatives of the British negotiating team, see: www.gov.uk/government/publications/biographies-of-the-civil-service representatives-for-the-negotiations-with-the-eu.

[72] For the terms, see: www.gov.uk/government/publications/terms-of-reference-for-the-article-50-negotiations-between-the-united-kingdom-and-the-european-union.

[73] The provision states: 'The Commission … shall submit recommendations to the Council, which shall adopt a decision authorising the opening of negotiations and, depending on the subject of the agreement envisaged, nominate the Union negotiator or the head of the Union's negotiating team.'

[74] Statement after the Informal Meeting of the 27 Heads of State or Government, 15 December 2016, available at: www.consilium.europa.eu/en/press/press-releases/2016/12/15/statement-informal-meeting-27.

Force.[75] Led by the EU Chief Negotiator, Michel Barnier (Figure 19.4), it consists of a small team of experts on issues ranging from the internal market to international trade. The Commission has thereby been asked to integrate representatives from the Council as well as the European Council; and the Union negotiator is also obliged to 'systematically report' to the European Council, the Council and the Parliament.[76]

bb. Procedural Stages and Substantive Issues

The European Council has insisted on a 'phased approach' to the negotiations that must concentrate exclusively on the 'withdrawal agreement'.[77] A first phase was to deal with issues directly resulting from withdrawal, whereas a second phase would eventually turn to the future 'framework' of cooperation between the United Kingdom and the Union.

During the first phase three main problems were discussed: the situation of citizens (and businesses) that have exercised their free movement rights, the 'Irish question', and a financial settlement for British commitments.[78]

Figure 19.4 EU Chief Negotiator: Michel Barnier

---

[75] For an overview, see https://ec.europa.eu/info/departments/taskforce-article-50-negotiations-united-kingdom_en.

[76] Statement after the Informal Meeting of the 27 Heads of State or Government (n. 74 above), paras. 3 and 7.

[77] For the European Council Brexit Guidelines, see www.consilium.europa.eu/en/press/press-releases/2017/04/29/euco-brexit-guidelines. This approach had not been favoured by the British negotiation team, which had hoped to tie the United Kingdom's exit directly to a new partnership agreement. This was however already impossible from a practical point of view. And from a more theoretical perspective, the argument has even been made that the negotiation procedure for the withdrawal agreement is, in any case, a Union matter (see A. Łazowski, 'Withdrawal from the European Union and Alternatives to Membership' (2012) 37 *EL Rev.* 523 at 527: 'The TEU leaves the decision on withdrawal to the domestic constitutional laws, while at the same time providing an EU procedural framework for departure').

[78] European Council Brexit Guidelines (n. 77 above), paras. 8–11.

The first issue has been relatively uncontroversial: the rights of EU citizens in the UK and the rights of British citizens in the EU-27 'derived from Union law and based on past life choices' will be guaranteed.[79]

The second problem – the Irish border question – has proved to be the hardest problem; and at the time of writing this edition, a diplomatic formula has been chosen to postpone the issue to the second stage of the negotiations.[80]

The third issue turned out to be easier than originally expected. For the Union here followed a 'divorce model' and approached the outstanding financial commitments from the premise that '[a] single financial settlement should be based on the principle that the United Kingdom must honour its share of the financing of all the obligations undertaken while it was a member of the Union'.[81] This view sharply contrasted with a British opinion advocating a 'club model' and according to which 'Article 50 TEU allows the UK to leave the EU without being liable for outstanding financial obligations under the EU budget or other financial instruments'.[82] Yet again a compromise was found that allowed the negotiations to move to the second stage.

What will be discussed during the 'second phase' of the Brexit negotiations? The Guidelines adopted by the European Council here first and foremost concentrate on 'transitional arrangements' and a 'transitional period' of around two years.[83] Proposed by the British government itself, this period is meant to offer

---

[79] See Joint Report from the negotiators of the European Union and the United Kingdom Government on progress during phase 1 of negotiations under Art. 50 TEU on the United Kingdom's orderly withdrawal from the European Union, available at: https://ec.europa .eu/commission/brexit-negotiations/negotiating-documents-article-50-negotiations-united-kingdom_en, para. 6. Despite having found a general solution to the citizen problem, there remain, sadly, a number of unsettled specifics that will need to be worked out in the future!

[80] *Ibid.*, paras. 49–50: 'In the absence of agreed solutions, the United Kingdom will maintain full alignment with those rules of the Internal Market and the Customs Union which, now or in the future, support North–South cooperation, the all-island economy and the protection of the 1998 Agreement. In the absence of agreed solutions, as set out in the previous paragraph, the United Kingdom will ensure that no new regulatory barriers develop between Northern Ireland and the rest of the United Kingdom, unless, consistent with the 1998 Agreement, the Northern Ireland Executive and Assembly agree that distinct arrangements are appropriate for Northern Ireland. In all circumstances, the United Kingdom will continue to ensure the same unfettered access for Northern Ireland's businesses to the whole of the United Kingdom internal market.'

[81] Council, Directives for the negotiation of an agreement with the United Kingdom, available at: https://ec.europa.eu/commission/publications/negotiating-directives-article-50-negotiations_en, para. 25.

[82] House of Lords, European Union Committee, 'Brexit and the EU Budget', available at: https://publications.parliament.uk/pa/ld201617/ldselect/ldeucom/125/125.pdf, para. 133.

[83] European Council Guidelines (Second Phase), available at: www.consilium.europa.eu/media/32236/15-euco-art50-guidelines-en.pdf.

a smooth and orderly withdrawal; and, according to the Union, the United Kingdom would – while formally outside the Union – still need to apply all EU law and it would, in particular, need to 'continue to participate in the Customs Union and the Single Market (with all four freedoms) during the transition'.[84] Importantly: the transitional period would however not extend British 'membership' inside the Union; it would, rather, like a reverse accession process, extend the Union *acquis* to a third State on the basis of an international treaty.[85]

Finally, and most importantly, during the second phase of the negotiations, the 'framework' for the future relationship between the United Kingdom and the Union will need to be discussed. In the words of the European Council:

> While an agreement on a future relationship between the Union and the United Kingdom as such can only be finalised and concluded once the United Kingdom has become a third country, Article 50 TEU requires to take account of the framework for its future relationship with the Union in the arrangements for withdrawal. To this end, an overall understanding on the framework for the future relationship should be identified during a second phase of the negotiations under Article 50 TEU. We stand ready to engage in preliminary and preparatory discussions to this end in the context of negotiations under Article 50 TEU[.][86]

The second phase of the negotiations should thus end with a bridge from membership to partnership; yet again, this bridge is not the future (trade) agreement itself.

c. Conclusion and Ratification I: The United Kingdom

The British process of treaty ratification will be determined by two acts: the Constitutional Reform and Governance Act 2010 and the European Union Act 2011; but it is not yet clear how precisely the two acts will operate in relation to the withdrawal agreement.

According to section 20 of the 2010 Act, international treaties need to be laid before Parliament 21 sitting days prior to ratification and may only be concluded if neither House has opposed the ratification during this period. If a negative

---

[84] *Ibid.*, para. 4. According to the Guidelines this would also imply that 'changes to the acquis adopted by EU institutions, bodies, offices and agencies will have to apply both to the United Kingdom and the EU', '[a]ll existing regulatory, budgetary, supervisory, judiciary and enforcement instruments and structures will also apply', and the United Kingdom 'will have to continue to comply with EU trade policy' (*ibid.*).

[85] In nature, these obligations should therefore be international law obligations; yet if the Union acquis is extended, the doctrines of supremacy and direct effect – these quintessential characteristics of European law – should be part of the withdrawal agreement. At the same time, 'as a third country, [the United Kingdom] will no longer participate in or nominate or elect members of the EU institutions' (*ibid.*, para. 3).

[86] European Council Brexit Guidelines (First Phase), para. 5.

vote however solely comes from the House of Lords, the Statute states that the treaty may still be ratified 'if a Minister of the Crown has laid before Parliament a statement indicating that the Minister is of the opinion that the treaty should nevertheless be ratified and explaining why'.[87] Following the 'ordinary' British treaty-making procedure therefore places Parliament's power between consultation and consent. For British constitutional law does not generally require a parliamentary debate or a positive parliamentary vote but simply relies on the absence in a negative vote in 'the Commons'.

For the European Union, however, a special procedure may apply, as section 23 of the 2010 Act expressly defers to 'a treaty that is subject to a requirement imposed by Part I of the European Union Act 2011'.[88] The latter contains a special ratification procedure in section 2:

Treaties amending or replacing TEU or TFEU

(1) A treaty which amends or replaces TEU or TFEU is not to be ratified unless –
    (a) a statement relating to the treaty was laid before Parliament in accordance with section 5,[89]
    (b) the treaty is approved by Act of Parliament, and
    (c) the referendum condition or the exemption condition is met.

(2) The referendum condition is that –
    (a) the Act providing for the approval of the treaty provides that the provision approving the treaty is not to come into force until a referendum about whether the treaty should be ratified has been held throughout the United Kingdom or, where the treaty also affects Gibraltar, throughout the United Kingdom and Gibraltar,
    (b) the referendum has been held, and
    (c) the majority of those voting in the referendum are in favour of the ratification of the treaty.

(3) The exemption condition is that the Act providing for the approval of the treaty states that the treaty does not fall within section 4.

The provision here replaces, within the context of European Union law, the negative vote of the Commons with a – stronger – positive vote in Parliament; and it even subjects *certain* EU Treaty amendments to a popular referendum.[90]

---

[87] Constitutional Reform and Governance Act 2010, s. 20(7) and (8).

[88] *Ibid.*, s. 23(1)(c).

[89] Section 5(1) of the European Union Act 2011 states: 'If a treaty amending TEU or TFEU is agreed in an inter-governmental conference, a Minister of the Crown must lay the required statement before Parliament before the end of the 2 months beginning with the date on which the treaty is agreed.'

[90] Section 4 here lists the situations in which a referendum is required and identifies these situations with EU treaty amendments where the Union's competences or powers are *extended*. Textually, then, a removal of Union competences (through withdrawal from the Union) would therefore not be subject to a referendum requirement. However, high politics may here once more trump legal analysis.

But would section 2 actually apply to the withdrawal agreement in the first place? The provision covers 'treaties amending or replacing [the] TEU or TFEU'; and while the withdrawal agreement cannot amend the EU Treaties,[91] the question arises whether 'withdrawing' from the EU Treaties can nevertheless be characterised as 'replacing' the EU Treaties. All depends here on the meaning of 'replacing'; and, in a restrictive sense, the withdrawal agreement is of course *not* replacing the EU Treaties, while in a broader sense one could argue that any transitional arrangements within the withdrawal agreement can be seen as having a 'replacing' effect for European Union law within the United Kingdom. If that argument is accepted, the 2011 Act would constitute both the *lex specialis* and *lex posterior* to the 2010 Act; and the withdrawal agreement would therefore require the unconditional and positive consent of the British Parliament. If that argument is not accepted, then the (residual) Constitutional Reform and Governance Act 2010 would apply – unless the British Parliament decided to impose the requirement of a 'meaningful vote' on the withdrawal agreement by other means.[92]

d. Conclusion and Ratification II: The European Union

What about the ratification of the withdrawal agreement by the European Union? For the Union, Article 50 TEU states that the agreement 'shall be concluded on behalf of the Union by the Council, acting by a qualified majority, after obtaining the consent of the European Parliament'; and the provision also clarifies that the member of the Council 'representing the withdrawing Member State shall not participate in the discussions' in the Council, where a super-qualified majority, as defined in Article 238(3)(b) TFEU, is to apply.[93]

Let us unpack these requirements one by one.

First, both branches of the EU legislator need to give their respective consent. For the Council, a special majority applies: 'the qualified majority shall be defined as at least 72% of the members of the Council representing the participating Member States, comprising at least 65% of the population of these States'.[94] This 72 per cent of the 27 Member States equates to 20 Member States; and in a Union without the United Kingdom a blocking minority of 35% of the Union population translates into about 155 million people. Importantly, unlike

---

[91] On this point, see section 2(a/bb) above: the withdrawal agreement cannot amend the EU Treaties because the agreement is, unlike an accession treaty, not primary law.

[92] At the time of writing, this seems to be happening through an amendment added to the EU (Withdrawal) Bill. For an early analysis of this, see M. Elliott's blog, 'Does the Government Defeat on Clause 9 of the EU (Withdrawal) Bill Mean Parliament Has "Taken Back Control?"', at: https://publiclawforeveryone.com/2017/12/14/does-the-government-defeat-on-clause-9-of-the-eu-withdrawal-bill-mean-parliament-has-taken-back-control.

[93] Art. 50(2) and (4) TEU.   [94] Art. 238(3)(b) TFEU.

the general rule in Article 16(4) TEU, a blocking minority of only three – not four – states would seem to be sufficient.[95]

With regard to the European Parliament, Article 50 specifies that it must give its consent; and consent here means the 'majority of the votes cast'.[96] Would these votes include the British Members of the European Parliament? Article 50 does not contain an express exclusion rule here, and the argument has therefore been made that all MEPs – including the British MEPs – should be entitled to vote on the withdrawal agreement.[97] Teleological reasons strengthen this argument: MEPs do not represent their Member State but directly represent the European citizens as a collectivity.[98] The point is however not uncontested; and others have indeed argued that the exclusion rule within Article 50 with regard to the British representative in the (European) Council should also apply, analogously, to the European Parliament.[99]

What about the European Court of Justice? The argument has been made that 'the jurisdiction of the Court over the withdrawal agreement does not seem to be restricted'; and that, in particular, 'the *renvoi* in Article 50 TEU to Article 218 TFEU opens the possibility of the European Court of Justice intervening … by way of an advisory opinion based on Article 218 (11) TFEU'.[100] Textually, this is however not at all clear: for Article 50 TEU refers only to the third paragraph of Article 218 TFEU, which exclusively deals with the negotiation stage. This could, contrariwise, be taken to mean that all the other stages in the life of the withdrawal agreement are exclusively governed by Article 50; and since the provision is silent on the jurisdiction of the Court, it would appear that the *ex ante* jurisdiction of the Court under Article 218(11) is unavailable. This would also make enormous sense in light of the two-year time limit imposed by the provision. Because in the absence of an extension, a judicial objection would be tantamount to a judicial veto of the agreement.

---

[95] Alas, if Germany and France agreed to reject the agreement, they would only need another Member State with a population of 10 million to block the agreement.

[96] Rule 82 of the European Parliament's Rules of Procedure is entitled 'Withdrawal from the Union' and states: 'If a Member State decides, pursuant to Article 50 of the Treaty on European Union, to withdraw from the Union, the matter shall be referred to the committee responsible. Rule 81 shall apply *mutatis mutandis*. Parliament shall decide whether to give its consent to an agreement on the withdrawal by a majority of the votes cast.'

[97] In favour of this view, see D. Harvey, 'What Role for the European Parliament under Article 50 TEU?' (2017) 42 *EL Rev.* 585 at 600: '[U]ntil the day on which the withdrawal agreement enters into force, UK MEPs will continue to particulate in the workings of the European Parliament and, as a consequence, vote on any withdrawal agreement.'

[98] On this point, see Chapter 5, section 2.

[99] Łazowski, 'Withdrawal from the European Union' (n. 77 above), 528: 'It has to be emphasised that a departing country will be treated as a third country during such negotiations, and therefore will not participate in consensus-building in the European Council and the Council or in the voting, should that prove necessary. Although Art. 50 TEU is silent on this, it seems reasonable to expect that the same rule will apply to the elected members of the European Parliament from the departing country.'

[100] Hillion, 'Accession and Withdrawal' (n. 69 above), 141–2.

3. Transitioning Out: European Union Law after Brexit

As long as the United Kingdom remains inside the European Union, its formal membership is a full membership for all matters unrelated to Brexit. This must mean two things: positively, the United Kingdom remains formally entitled to participate in all the ordinary work of the EU institutions as if Article 50 TEU had not been triggered; while it must also, negatively, fulfil all its obligations as a current Member State. It is hard to see how there can be any differentiation of its 'ordinary' membership rights; while it is equally hard to accept that a departing member could already be relieved of some of its obligations. The better view therefore insists that all rights and obligations of a full member are retained; and this, in particular, means that during the withdrawal process the United Kingdom cannot behave as it were already outside the Union.[101]

Yet on 30 March 2019 (unless extended), the United Kingdom will have exited the European Union.[102] From the perspective of the *monist* Union legal order, European Union law will henceforth cease to apply within the United Kingdom. From the perspective of a classic *dualist* legal order, this would however not necessarily have to follow. For, as long as the European Communities Act 1972 was in existence, it could – following a strict dualism – be taken to mean that all European Union law 'created or arising by or under the Treaties' would continue to apply as long as the Act itself was not repealed. From a dualist perspective, European law would thus continue to extend to the United Kingdom until the 1972 Communities Act was itself repealed; and in order to do this, the British government has been preparing a 'Great Repeal Bill' – now more mundanely entitled the 'European Union (Withdrawal) Bill.[103]

a. The European Union (Withdrawal) Bill: Functions and Content

The functions of the Withdrawal Bill are manifold; and in the explanatory notes accompanying the government's original proposal, four such functions are identified. In addition to repealing the European Communities Act 1972, its main function is to 'convert EU law as it stands at the moment of exit into domestic

---

[101]   As long as the UK is thus inside the Union it cannot negotiate, let alone conclude, international trade agreements. This is an exclusive competence of the European Union. On this point, see Chapter 7, section 2(a) and (online) Chapter 18B, section 1(a).

[102]   EU membership only ends after the two-year period (or as extended) has expired. The withdrawing Member State is not allowed to depart earlier unless a mutual agreement has been reached. This follows from the mutual (!) obligation to reach an agreement within two years. The idea that a repeal of the 1972 Act would also end EU membership is based on a fallacy. For even if the repeal of the Act would remove the validity of EU law within the United Kingdom, Art. 50 TEU would still insist – from the EU perspective – on the continued membership of the departing state until the end of the two-year limit.

[103]   The following section is based on the original draft bill, as introduced by the British government on 13 July 2017. Since it was first presented various amendments have been suggested. The original draft as well as the 'Explanatory Notes' and the subsequent amendments, can be found at: https://services.parliament.uk/bills/2017-19/europeanunionwithdrawal/documents.html.

Table 19.1 European Union (Withdrawal) Bill

Clause	Provision
1	Repeal of the European Communities Act 1972
2	Saving for EU-derived Domestic Legislation
3	Incorporation of Direct EU Legislation
4	Saving for Rights under Section 2(1) ECA
5	Exceptions to Savings and Incorporation
6	Interpretation of Retained EU Law
7	Dealing with Deficiencies arising from Withdrawal
8	Complying with International Obligations
9	Implementing the Withdrawal Agreement
10	Corresponding Powers involving Devolved Authorities
11	Retaining EU Restrictions in Devolved Legislation
12–19	Financial, General and Final Provisions

law before the UK leaves the EU'.[104] This second function is especially necessary in light of the Supreme Court's *Miller* judgment – discussed above – according to which 'the ECA is not itself an originating source of EU law, but rather the "conduit pipe" through which EU law flows into UK domestic law' and which implies that all directly effective EU law would cease to apply after Brexit.[105] With regard to non-directly applicable EU law – like EU directives – such a 'conversion' from European into British law was seen as unnecessary as implementation legislation on the basis of section 2(2) of the European Communities Act had already achieved such a conversion into domestic law.

The content of the original European Union (Withdrawal) Bill can be seen in Table 19.1. Clause 1 here unambiguously states: 'The European Communities Act 1972 is repealed on exit day.' The rest of the Bill then tries to mitigate that result by first clarifying, in Clause 2, that 'EU-derived domestic legislation' 'continues to have effect in domestic law on and after exit day'. (This clarification was deemed necessary as, under British constitutional law, secondary legislation normally lapses with the primary legislation on which it is based.) By contrast, 'direct EU legislation', operating before exit day, will henceforth be incorporated as a 'part of domestic law' by means of Clause 3. But since the latter clause primarily covers EU secondary or tertiary law, adopted as EU regulations or decisions, Clause 4 subsequently expands the incorporation to any rights or obligations that have in the past arisen under EU primary law, and especially the

[104] Explanatory Notes, para. 2.   [105] *Ibid.*, para. 19.

EU Treaties. The main exception here is the Charter of Fundamental Rights;[106] and the Union principle of State liability under *Francovich*.[107]

What is the status of 'retained' European Union law after the withdrawal? Clause 5 here offers the following rules:

> (1) The principle of the supremacy of EU law does not apply to any enactment or rule of law passed or made on or after exit day.
>
> (2) Accordingly, the principle of the supremacy of EU law continues to apply on or after exit day so far as relevant to the interpretation, disapplication or quashing of any enactment or rule of law passed or made before exit day.
>
> (3) Subsection (1) does not prevent the principle of the supremacy of EU law from applying to a modification made on or after exit day of any enactment or rule of law passed or made before exit day if the application of the principle is consistent with the intention of the modification.

The provision clarifies that 'retained' Union law will continue to enjoy 'supremacy' over British law adopted *prior* to Brexit; whereas any British legislation adopted *after* Brexit will henceforth be able to amend or repeal 'retained' European Union law. Complex domestic questions are bound to arise under paragraph 3. The question here will inevitably be what constitutes a 'modification' (supremacy retained) as opposed to an 'amendment' or 'repeal' (supremacy not retained), especially if 'modifications' to European Union law are allowed to be made by the executive.[108] Be that as it may, as regards the British courts, Clause 6 underlines the judicial aspect of the supremacy question. It states:

> (1) A court or tribunal –
>   (a) is not bound by any principles laid down, or any decisions made, on or after exit day by the European Court, and
>   (b) cannot refer any matter to the European Court on or after exit day.
>
> (2) A court or tribunal need not have regard to anything done on or after exit day by the European Court, another EU entity or the EU but may do so if it considers it appropriate to do so.
>
> (3) Any question as to the validity, meaning or effect of any retained EU law is to be decided, so far as that law is unmodified on or after exit day and so far as they are relevant to it –
>   (a) in accordance with any retained case law and any retained general principles of EU law, and

---

[106] European Union (Withdrawal) Bill, s. 5(4).   [107] *Ibid.*, sch. 1, s. 4.

[108] Clause 7 here states: 'A Minister of the Crown may by regulations make such provision as the Minister considers appropriate to prevent, remedy or mitigate – (a) any failure of retained EU law to operate effectively, or (b) any other deficiency in retained EU law, arising from the withdrawal of the United Kingdom from the EU.'

> (b) having regard (among other things) to the limits, immediately before exit day, of EU competences.
>
> (4) But –
>
> (a) the Supreme Court is not bound by any retained case law,
>
> (b) the [Scottish] High Court of Justiciary is not bound by any retained EU case law ...

The jurisprudence of the European Court of Justice will consequently cease to be binding on British courts after Brexit; yet as regards retained EU law, the provision also states that its meaning will continue to be determined by 'retained case law', that is: the jurisprudence of the European Court of Justice before Brexit. The only two courts that are not bound by past precedents of the European Court are the British Supreme Court (and the highest Scottish criminal court) – both of whom will be allowed to (re)assert their position at the top of the judicial hierarchy within the United Kingdom.

b. In Particular: International Agreements of the European Union

In what must count as one of the greatest misrepresentations during the referendum campaign, Lord Lawson confidently told his BBC Radio 4 audience the following 'truth':

> First of all our trade relations with the rest of the world remain totally unchanged because the European Union did not negotiate as the European Union ... [It is] not allowed to, [it is] not a member of the World Trade Organization, it negotiated on behalf of the member states. So all our arrangements with the rest of the world remain totally unchanged.[109]

Nothing could of course be further from the truth. For not only is the Union a member of the WTO, it generally concludes its international agreement under its 'own name'; and even if the Member States sometimes join the Union in what is called a 'mixed agreement',[110] the Union enjoys its own legal personality and assumes 'its' international obligations as distinct from those separately assumed by the Member States.

Leaving the European Union therefore – undoubtedly – means leaving behind those international treaties to which the United Kingdom is not an independent party, because with regard to all 'pure' Union agreements, only the Union – and

[109] BBC Radio 4, *The World at One* (29 February 2016). Lawson's words have been variously reported, *inter alia* by the BBC itself, see: www.bbc.co.uk/news/uk-politics-35698856. This was one of 'the' key moments when the lack of knowledge of EU law in the highest political classes of the United Kingdom became painfully obvious.

[110] On mixed agreements, see Chapter 8, section 4(a).

not the Member States – is a party to those agreements. On Brexit day, these Union agreements will simply dissolve for the United Kingdom.[111]

The situation is slightly more complex with regard to mixed agreements, that is: agreements to which both the Union and the Member States are joint parties. Technically, the United Kingdom is here an independent signatory to these treaties; and it could therefore – theoretically – continue to enjoy all the rights and obligations arising under international law after Brexit. Yet this reading has been put into question by EU external relations specialists, who have – rightly – pointed out that this logic will not hold for so-called 'bilateral' mixed agreements.[112] These are international agreements to which a Member State is a party qua membership of the Union.

A good illustration here is the EEA Agreement – discussed below. The Agreement is a mixed agreement, which defines its two 'contracting parties' as, on the one hand, the 'EFTA States' and, on the other hand, the '[Union] and the [EU] Member States'.[113] The United Kingdom, while listed as a Member State of the European Union, is nevertheless not an 'independent' signatory party to that international agreement. While formally listed as a State signatory, it is only a contracting party qua membership of the Union and once its Union membership is revoked, the EEA Agreement will cease to apply to the United Kingdom.[114]

With regard to 'multilateral' mixed agreements, on the other hand, matters are different. whenever the United Kingdom is an 'original' contracting party in its own right, all treaty obligations incurred under a mixed agreement will continue to apply to it after Brexit.[115] This is – with some minor exceptions – the case for the WTO Agreement.[116] The United Kingdom would indeed remain a member of the WTO after its withdrawal; and in the absence of an alternative partnership agreement with the Union, its relationship with the

---

[111]   Under international law a seceding State may, sometimes, continues to be bound by an international treaty concluded by the entity from which it is seceding; yet this applies only to a very limited number of treaties. On this point, see T. Sparks, 'Brexit and the Bravehearted: An Independent Scotland, the European Treaties and the Law of Succession' (forthcoming).

[112]   See especially M. Cremona, 'UK Trade Policy', in M. Dougan (ed.), *The UK After Brexit: Legal and Policy Challenges* (Intersentia, 2017), 247 esp. at 251ff.

[113]   Agreement on the European Economic Area ('EEA Agreement') (1994) OJ L1/3, Art. 2(b) and (c).

[114]   This is why, in my view, Art. 103(4) of the Commission's Penelope Draft was wrong.

[115]   This may however not mean that a third party could not itself terminate the international agreement on the grounds that a fundamental change of circumstance has taken place when the United Kingdom is no longer a Member State of the Union. For the international principles governing a fundamental change of circumstances, see Art. 62 of the Vienna Convention of the Law of Treaties.

[116]   Under Art. XI(1) WTO Agreement, 'original membership' is defined as the contacting parties of the GATT 1947 as well as the European Union; and since the UK – and not the European Union – was an original member of the GATT, it would remain an independent member of the WTO. For a long discussion with regard to Britain's WTO status, see L. Bartels, 'The UK's Status in the WTO Post-Brexit', in R. Schütze and S. Tierney (eds.), *The United Kingdom and the Federal Principle* (Hart, 2018 – forthcoming).

Union would fall back to be governed by WTO terms.[117] This 'hard Brexit' scenario is therefore often referred to as the 'WTO model'.

4. Frameworks for the Future: Alternative Relations with the Union

What will the future relationship between the United Kingdom and the European Union look like? The precise nature of that relationship can only be negotiated *after* the British exit; and the reason for the strict separation between the 'withdrawal agreement' and the 'future-relations' agreement is simply time. The negotiation of a comprehensive trade agreement may take between five and ten years, whereas the withdrawal agreement needs to be concluded within two years following notification; and even if Article 50 allows for an extension of this period,[118] it is unlikely to be extended for a significantly longer period of time.

What types of alternative partnerships are presently available? While the United Kingdom can, and will, of course try to get a 'bespoke' agreement that works best for itself, what models has the EU so far developed for third States wishing to be closely associated with the Union? Three such models shall be presented in this final section: the EEA model ('Norway model'), the Customs Union model ('Turkey model') and the Free Trade Agreement model ('Canada model'). In terms of economic association with the single market, each of these models will offer less than EU membership but more than WTO membership with the 'Norway model' offering the closest association and the 'Canada model' offering the loosest association in this context (see Figure 19.5).

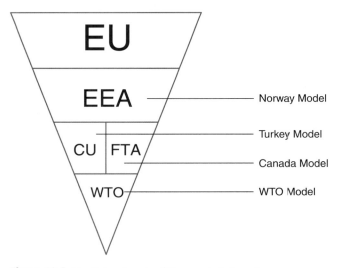

Figure 19.5 Declining Levels of Economic Integration

[117] For a brief overview of the structure of the WTO Agreement, see (online) Chapter 18B, section 1(c/aa).

[118] According to Art. 50(3) TEU, the European Council, acting unanimously, must here agree with the withdrawing Member State.

a. Joining the European Economic Area: The 'Norway Model'

The Agreement on the European Economic Area (EEA) was signed in 1992 and entered into force on 1 January 1994.[119] It brings together the European Union (and its Member States) with the EFTA States except for Switzerland.[120]

The agreement aims to establish a 'homogenous' free trade area;[121] and thereby covers the free movement of goods (Part II), the free movement of persons, services and capital (Part III), competition law (Part IV); while it also regulates flanking policies that are relevant to the four freedoms (Part V).[122] The provisions within Parts I-V are (almost) identical to those in the EU Treaties. However, the EEA is not a customs union but a 'fundamentally improved free trade area';[123] and the EFTA states have consequently retained their freedom to negotiate commercial agreements with third states. The EEA Agreement equally leaves the EFTA states free to autonomously act in other important areas of EU competence (see Table 19.2). They will however have to pay some sums into the Union budget.

Table 19.2 EEA Agreement: Substantive Coverage

EEA: Covered	EEA: Not Covered
Free Movement: Goods	Common Commercial Policy
Free Movement: Persons	Common Agricultural Policy
Free Movement: Services	Common Foreign and Security Policy
Free Movement: Capital	Area of Freedom, Security & Justice
Competition Law (and State Aid)	European Monetary Union

[119] EEA Agreement (n. 113 above).
[120] The EFTA comprises today four States: Iceland, Liechtenstein, Norway and Switzerland. The latter is however not part of the EEA, as the ratification of the EEA Agreement was rejected in a referendum. The EU–Swiss relations are therefore based on a wide range and great number of bilateral agreements (see S. Breitenmoser, 'Sectoral Agreements between the EC and Switzerland: Contents and Context' (2003) 30 CMLR 1137). The 'Swiss model' comes nevertheless substantively very close to the EEA model. The major 'institutional' difference relates to how regulatory homogeneity with Union legislation is achieved. The Union has here been highly critical of the Swiss model, and it may therefore not be a viable option for the future relations between the Union and the United Kingdom. In this sense, see C. Tobler, 'One of Many Challenges after "Brexit": The Institutional Framework of an Alternative Agreement – Lessons from Switzerland and Elsewhere?' (2016) 23 *Maastricht Journal of European and Comparative Law* 575.
[121] EEA Agreement (n. 113 above), Art. 1.
[122] Part V of the EEA Agreement contains rules on 'Social Policy', 'Consumer Protection', 'Environment', 'Statistics' and 'Company Law'.
[123] S. Norberg, 'The Agreement on a European Economic Area' (1992) 29 CMLR 1171 at 1173.

The central aim behind the EEA is 'to provide for the fullest possible realization of the free movement of goods, persons, services and capital within the
whole European Economic Area, *so that the internal market established within
the European Union is extended to the EFTA States*'.[124] And, in order to achieve
that aim, the EEA Agreement does not only duplicate the European Union's
provisions on 'negative integration'; on the contrary, a significant part of the
Agreement deals with 'positive integration' so as to ensure regulatory alignment between the EU Member States and the EFTA Member States. This
idea of a (dynamic) legislative homogeneity indeed 'is the key principle in the
EEA'.[125]

Positive integration or legislative alignment is thereby achieved in a dual
manner. On the one hand, all relevant pre-1992 Union acts – listed in the
Agreement's Annexes – had to be incorporated into the domestic legal orders
of the EFTA States. With regard to post-1992 developments, on the other hand,
the Agreement calls on an 'EEA Joint Committee' to update the Agreement's
Annexes and Protocols in light of new legislative developments within the
Union.[126] The EEA Joint Committee is thereby composed of representatives
of the Union and the EFTA States and will act 'by agreement between the
[Union], on the one hand, and the EFTA States speaking with one voice, on
the other'.[127] In the past, and in (almost) all cases, the EEA Joint Committee
has agreed to simply 'rubber-stamp' the relevant EU acts;[128] and the principle
of legislative homogeneity has therefore – uncharitably – been identified with
European 'hegemony'; or at least with a significant democratic deficit.[129] For the

---

[124] Case C-452/01, *Ospelt and Schlössle Weissenberg Familienstiftung* (2003) ECR I-9743, para.
29 (emphasis added).

[125] G. Baur, 'Decision-making Procedure and Implementation of New Law', in C.
Baudenbacher (ed.), *The Handbook of EEA Law* (Springer, 2016), 45 at 51. The EEA idea
of a 'dynamic' adaptation is often contrasted with the 'static' adaptation under the Swiss
bilateral model.

[126] See Art. 102(1) EEA Agreement: 'In order to guarantee the legal security and the homogeneity of the EEA, the EEA Joint Committee shall take a decision concerning an amendment of an Annex to this Agreement as closely as possible to the adoption by the [Union]
of the corresponding new [Union] legislation with a view to permitting a simultaneous
application of the latter as well as of the amendments of the Annexes to the Agreement.
To this end, the [Union] shall, whenever adopting a legislative act on an issue which is
governed by this Agreement, as soon as possible inform the other Contracting Parties in
the EEA Joint Committee. These committees are listed in Protocol 37. The modalities of
such an association are set out in the relevant sectoral Protocols and Annexes dealing with
the matter concerned.' Union acts that are relevant for the EEA, are labelled as 'Text with
EEA relevance'.

[127] *Ibid.*, Art. 93(2).

[128] Legislative exemptions and adaptions are nevertheless possible, see J. Jonsdottir, *Europeanization
and the European Economic Area* (Routledge, 2012), 50–3. If it were to come to a disagreement between the Union and the EFTA States, the disputed part of the EEA Agreement
would be provisionally suspended (EEA Agreement (n. 113 above), Art. 102(5)).

[129] See H. Haukeland Fredriksen and C. Franklin, 'Of Pragmatism and Principles: The EEA
Agreement 20 Years on' (2015) 52 *CML Rev.* 629 at 633. This has been accepted by the

simple extension of Union legislation to the EFTA States means that it applies to States that have not been represented in the Union legislature.

However, there is nonetheless a degree of normative and substantive 'heterogeneity' between the EU and the EEA. The greatest normative difference here relates to the nature of EEA law: 'EEA law does not entail a transfer of legislative powers' because it lacks supremacy and direct effect.[130] There are moreover also substantive differences. For the commitment towards 'the fullest possible realization' of the single market does not signify its 'full' realisation. The Court of Justice has thus clarified that its fundamental freedoms jurisprudence 'cannot be transposed in its entirety' into the EEA Agreement 'since such movements take place in a different legal context'.[131] With regard to the free movement of persons, for example, the EEA Agreement indeed does not have provisions on 'citizenship' while it positively have – unlike the EU Treaties – a general safeguard clause that allows each contracting party to temporarily derogate from a fundamental freedom if 'serious economic, societal or environmental difficulties' were to arise.[132]

b. Joining a Customs Union: The 'Turkey Model'

The 1963 Association Agreement with Turkey ('Ankara Agreement') constitutes the oldest existing association agreement of the Union.[133] The purpose of the Ankara Agreement was 'to promote the continuous and balanced strength of trade and economic relations between the parties'; and this aim of a closer economic partnership was to be primarily pursued through a customs union.[134] This customs union covers trade in goods and would involve:

Norwegian government itself, which considers EEA membership as a form of 'integration without co-determination' (see EEA Review Committee (Norwegian government), 'Outside and Inside: Norway's Agreement with the European Union'), available at: www.europarl.europa.eu/meetdocs/2009_2014/documents/deea/dv/0226_13_/0226_13_en.pdf.

[130] Case E-04/01, *Karlsson* (2002), esp. para. 28. The EFTA Court has however accepted the doctrines of indirect effect and state liability. For the former, see Case E-1/07, *Criminal proceedings against A* (2007), para. 39: '[N]ational courts are bound to interpret national law, and in particular legislative provisions specifically adopted to transpose EEA rules into national law, as far as possible in conformity with EEA law'. And, with regard to the latter, see Case E-09/97, *Erla María Sveinbjörnsdóttir v. Iceland* (1998), para. 62: '[I]t is a principle of the EEA Agreement that the Contracting Parties are obliged to provide for compensation for loss and damage caused to individuals by breaches of the obligations under the EEA Agreement for which the EFTA States can be held responsible.'

[131] See Case C-540/07, *Commission v. Italy* (2009) ECR I-10983, para. 69.

[132] Art. 112 EEA Agreement (n. 113 above).

[133] Agreement establishing an Association between the European Economic [Union] and Turkey, signed at Ankara on 12 September 1963 by the Republic of Turkey, on the one hand, and by the Member States of the [EU] and the [Union], on the other ((1973) OJ C 113/1). Many provisions within the Ankara Agreement are further clarified by an additional Protocol: Additional Protocol and Financial Protocol ((1972) OJ L 293/4).

[134] Ankara Agreement, Art. 2.

> – the prohibition between Member States of the [Union] and Turkey, of customs duties on imports and exports and of all charges having equivalent effect, quantitative restrictions and all other measures having equivalent effect which are designed to protect national production in a manner contrary to the objectives of this Agreement;
> – the adoption by Turkey of the Common Customs Tariff of the [Union] in its trade with third countries, and an approximation to the other [EU] rules on external trade.[135]

The Ankara Agreement also envisaged the future abolition of restrictions on the free movement of persons,[136] services[137] and capital;[138] yet these provisions were originally of a programmatic nature and therefore seen as non-legally enforceable norms. The implementation of the Ankara Agreement indeed heavily relied on a form of 'positive integration'; and the central decision-making body here was the 'Association Council'.[139] It consists of members of the Union (and its Member States), on the one hand, and Turkish representatives on the other; and it adopts its decisions by unanimous agreement.[140]

With regard to the free movement of goods, the Association Council's most important decision is Decision 1/95.[141] The latter establishes 'the rules for implementing the final phase of the Customs Union' by extending – almost always verbatim – the Union's own free movement of goods provisions to Turkey. In order to achieve this 'enlargement' of the internal market in goods, Turkey thereby promises to harmonise Turkish legislation of direct relevance to the operation of the internal market 'as far as possible with [Union] legislation'.[142]

---

[135] *Ibid.*, Art. 10(2).

[136] *Ibid.*, Art. 12: 'The Contracting Parties agree to be guided by Articles [45–7] the [FEU Treaty] Treaty for the purpose of progressively securing freedom of movement for workers between them.' And Art. 13: 'The Contracting Parties agree to be guided by Articles [49–52] and Article [54] of the [FEU] Treaty for the purpose of abolishing restrictions on freedom of establishment between them.'

[137] *Ibid.*, Art. 14: 'The Contracting Parties agree to be guided by Articles [51, 52 and 54–61] of the [FEU] Treaty for the purpose of abolishing restrictions on freedom to provide services between them.'

[138] *Ibid.*, Art. 20: 'The Contracting Parties shall consult each other with a view to facilitating movements of capital between Member States of the [Union] and Turkey which will further the objectives of this Agreement.'

[139] Ibid., Art. 22(1): 'In order to attain the objectives of this Agreement the Council of Association shall have the power to take decisions in the cases provided for therein. Each of the Parties shall take the measures necessary to implement the decisions taken.'

[140] *Ibid.*, Art. 23 – third indent.

[141] Decision No. 1/95 of the EC–Turkey Association Council of 22 December 1995 on implementing the final phase of the Customs Union (1996) OJ L35/1.

[142] *Ibid.*, Art. 54(1). These areas of direct relevance are defined as follows (*ibid.*, para. 2): 'Areas of direct relevance to the operation of the Customs Union shall be commercial policy and agreements with third countries comprising a commercial dimension for industrial

And were there to exist an – unresolvable – difference of opinion, the Union or Turkey can both 'take the necessary protection measures'.[143]

What is the substantive coverage of the EU–Turkey Customs Union? A customs union, unlike a free trade area, aims to abolish all customs-related barriers with regard to goods produced by the contracting parties but also third country goods 'in free circulation' within the customs Union. In order to achieve this aim and avoid deflections of trade,[144] the customs union will have a common commercial policy towards third states; and in the case of the EU–Turkish customs union, this 'common' policy is almost completely the European Union's commercial policy. Turkey has indeed promised to adopt 'substantially similar' commercial policy measures to those of the Union,[145] and in particular to 'align itself on the Common Customs Tariff'.[146] The customs union also aims to eliminate all non-tariff barriers to trade in goods;[147] and it equally incorporates much of the Union's competition rules.[148]

c. A (Preferential) Free Trade Agreement: The 'Canada Model'

The European Union has established a wide net of bilateral trade agreements with third States. Depending on whether or not they go beyond 'WTO treatment', one distinguishes between preferential and non-preferential trade agreements. An example of the latter could be seen in the 1994 Partnership and Cooperation Agreement between the Union and Russia, where the parties simply agreed to afford each other most-favoured-nation treatment.[149] Preferential trade agreements, by contrast, grant a specific advantage to a third state that goes beyond WTO treatment; and these agreements must – in order to be WTO conform – either create a customs union or a free trade area.[150]

A good illustration of such a preferential trade agreement is CETA: the free trade agreement concluded in 2017 between the European Union and

---

products, legislation on the abolition of technical barriers to trade in industrial products, competition and industrial and intellectual property law and customs legislation. The Association Council may decide to extend the list of areas where harmonization is to be achieved in the light of the Association's progress.'

[143] *Ibid.*, Art. 58(2). These measures will subsequently be examined by the EU–Turkey Customs Union Joint Committee, but ultimately they will be subject to international arbitration (*ibid.*, Art. 61).

[144] Deflections of trade occur when a third State chooses that Member State within a customs union that offers it the easiest entry into the union.

[145] *Ibid.*, Art. 12.   [146] *Ibid.*, Art. 13.

[147] For example: Art. 5 of Decision 1/95 reproduces Art. 34 TFEU and states 'Quantitative restrictions on imports and all measures having equivalent effect shall be prohibited between the parties.'

[148] *Ibid.*, Arts. 32ff.

[149] See 1994 Partnership and Cooperation Agreement between Russia and the European Communities [1997] OJ L 327/3, esp. Art. 10.

[150] See Art. XXIV GATT.

Canada.[151] With CETA, the two contracting parties '[f]urther strengthen their close economic relationship'; and while building on their respective rights and obligations under the WTO, CETA's aim is to create a free trade area in the form of 'an expanded and secure market for their goods and services through the reduction or elimination of barriers to trade and investment'.[152]

Having been negotiated over seven years, and covering over 1,000 pages, CETA has 30 chapters that cover such diverse matters as trade in goods,[153] investment (capital)[154] and services,[155] as well as a wide range of flanking policies.[156] Within the context of the free movement of services, the Agreement also envisages a WTO-like form of the free movement of persons.[157] And while in no way representing anything close to the EEA or Customs Union arrangements, discussed above, CETA also contains a chapter on 'regulatory cooperation';[158] and it has set up a CETA Joint Committee, composed of representatives of the EU and Canada, that may take decisions by mutual consent.[159] The most controversial part of the Agreement originally related to its 'dispute settlement' mechanism;[160] and after severe reservations voiced by civil society, the original ISDS provisions have now been replaced by a court system that will exercise public – not private – powers.[161]

In light of its substantive scope and institutional infrastructure, CETA forms part of the 'new generation' of free trade agreements. Its principal effect will be an (almost) total reduction of tariffs and it also promises to significantly reduce non-tariff barriers in goods. And going beyond the substantive scope of a customs union arrangement, it enhances the legal commitments with regard to the liberalisation of services and investment; while it is also committed to a soft regulatory convergence. But because CETA creates – like EFTA – a free trade area, the Canada model allows each party to conduct its own commercial policy vis-à-vis the rest of the world.

d. Of Hard Choices and Red Lines: European and British Perspectives

Which of the three models comes potentially closest to the future trade relationship between the United Kingdom and the European Union? The three models, discussed above, offer three distinct association formats whose respective characteristics are summarised in Table 19.3.

---

[151] CETA stands for Comprehensive Economic and Trade Agreement. The text of CETA can be found in (2017) OJ L11/23. The agreement provisionally applies but is not yet in force as all the Member States need to ratify it according to their constitutional requirements.

[152] *Ibid.*, preamble 1 and 2. See also Art. 1.4: 'The Parties hereby establish a free trade area in conformity with Article XXIV of GATT 1994 and Article V of the GATS.'

[153] *Ibid.*, Ch. 2.   [154] *Ibid.*, Ch. 8.

[155] *Ibid.*, see esp. Chs. 9, 13 and 14.

[156] For example: competition policy (Chs. 17 and 18) as well as labour law matters (Ch. 23) and environmental policy (Ch. 24) are covered by CETA.

[157] *Ibid.*, Ch. 10 ('Temporary Entry and Stay of Natural Persons for Business Purposes').

[158] *Ibid.*, Ch. 21.   [159] *Ibid.*, Arts 26.1 and 26.3.   [160] *Ibid.*, Ch. 29.

[161] ISDS stands for Investor State Dispute Settlement.

Table 19.3 Future Relationship Models: Comparison

	EEA 'Norway Model'	Customs Union 'Turkey Model'	Preferential FTA 'Canada Model'
Free Movement of Goods	High	High	Medium
... of agricultural Goods	Low	Low	Medium
Free Movement of People	High	Low	Low
Free Movement of Services	High	Low	Medium
Free Movement of Capital	High	Low	Medium
EU Competition Law	High	Medium	Low
EU Commercial Policy	Low	Medium	Low
Shadowing EU Legislation	High	Medium	Low

Importantly, and once again, none of the three models offers full access to the single market.[162] Full 'membership' of the single market can only be achieved through full membership of the Union; and all non-membership arrangements will consequently only offer *partial* access to the single market. The 'golden rule' of Union association is thereby this: the degree to which a third State is willing to accept positive integration via Union legislation will directly determine the degree to which it is entitled to enjoy the benefits of negative integration via access to the single market. This is the first 'constitutional' principle behind all European integration,[163] and if the Union were to give it up, the integrity of the Union would itself be endangered.

With full access to the internal market barred for third States outside the Union, the Union has also established a second 'red line': it insists that the single market, characterised by four fundamental freedoms, is itself indivisible. In the words of the European Council:

> Preserving the integrity of the Single Market excludes participation based on a sector-by-sector approach. A non-member of the Union, that does not live up to the same obligations as a member, cannot have the same rights and enjoy the same benefits

---

[162] In almost all official publications I have seen in the last two years, it is wrongly assumed that the EEA Agreement gives 'full' access (access as if a Member State of the Union) to the single market; yet this is simply not the case. All of the criteria in Table 19.3 must therefore be relative, ranging from a high degree to a low degree of access to the single market.

[163] On the relationship between negative and positive integration, see R. Schütze, *From International to Federal Union* (Oxford University Press, in preparation).

as a member. In this context, the European Council welcomes the recognition by the British Government that the four freedoms of the Single Market are indivisible and that there can be no 'cherry picking'.[164]

This Union 'red line' is not at all meant to 'punish' the United Kingdom;[165] it is simply based on the idea that the four fundamental freedoms are a living compromise between the 'economic' and 'political' aspects of European integration; and to unravel that compromise runs the danger of inviting other States to reduce the European Union to an essentially economic project without a 'human face'.[166]

What about the British wishes and the British 'red lines'? Her Majesty's Government has spelled out a number of principles in its White Paper, 'The United Kingdom's Exit from and New Partnership with the European Union'. The most important principle here are: 'taking [back] control of our own laws', 'maintaining the Common Travel Area' with Ireland, 'controlling immigration', 'ensuring free trade with European markets' and 'securing new trade agreements with other countries'.[167]

When measured against the three existing trade models, outlined above, which model comes closest to the British position? Each of the three models will formally give back full 'sovereignty' to the United Kingdom; yet, from a substantive point of view, participation in the EEA would still amount to following three-quarters of European Union legislation.[168] With regard to the ability to fully control immigration, the EEA option would also not work, as 'the free

---

[164] European Council Negotiating Guidelines (First Phase), para. 1.

[165] K. Nicolaidis, 'Brexit Arithmetics', in J. Armour and H. Eidenmüller, *Negotiating Brexit* (Beck-Hart-Nomos, 2017), 89 at 90: 'To restate the root of all misperceptions: For the EU, this is a truism; it would be absurd for Brussels to offer a deal to a third-country-to-be that is more valuable than the value of membership itself … But the message sent is not the message received: the British side hears this EU statement as a desire to "punish" the UK.'

[166] This is not to say that the four freedoms cannot be legally separated; indeed, the very concept of a customs union is based on the idea that the free movement of goods can be separated from the other three freedoms. Yet the European (!) 'Single Market' as a package 'deal' comprising the four fundamental freedoms is a historical achievement of the Union that offers 'big' businesses as well as 'little' workers a stake in the European project. To reduce or take away the freedom of persons from that 'package deal' would, in my view, fundamentally undermine one of the values most associated with the benefits of European integration and further perilously undermine the popular legitimacy problems of the European Union. *Contra*, C. Barnard, 'Brexit and the Internal Market', in F. Fabbrini (ed.), *The Law & Politics of Brexit* (Oxford University Press, 2017), 201.

[167] White Paper, 'United Kingdom's Exit from and New Partnership with the European Union' (n. 70 above). Among the 12 principles mentioned, these are principles two, four, five, eight and nine.

[168] This is the estimate offered by the Norwegian government (n. 129 above).

movement of persons is a key element of the EEA Agreement'.[169] A customs union or a free trade agreement would thus present better options when it comes to the British principles of 'taking back' control and 'controlling immigration'. This seems to have been accepted by HM Government:

> The Government will prioritise securing the freest and most frictionless trade possible in goods and services between the UK and the EU. We will not be seeking membership of the Single Market, but will pursue instead a new strategic partnership with the EU, including an ambitious and comprehensive Free Trade Agreement and a new customs agreement.[170]

This choice will, however, in all probability, mean a lower degree of access to the single market; and it would also mean that the Irish border question remains, in principle, unresolved. For, as we saw above, the Union generally makes the degree of access to its single market dependent on the willingness of third states to shadow EU law; and the rejection of the free movement of persons should, in theory, mean that the common travel area with Ireland is impossible once the 'internal' border between the Republic of Ireland and Northern Ireland becomes an external border of the European Union.

Can the inherent 'trade-offs' within each model be negotiated away? The United Kingdom government hopes this can be done and has, optimistically, invoked the idea of a 'bespoke' agreement – whatever that means.[171] What relative bargaining power will it have to achieve a tailor-made British deal? Its absolute and relative trading power vis-à-vis the Union can be gleaned from Table 19.4. Constituting the fifth largest national economy in the world, the United Kingdom would certainly be in a stronger negotiating position than either Norway, Turkey or Canada; yet, in relative terms, it still only represents one-fifth of the economic size of the European Union (minus the UK). And the trade relations with the Union reflect that economic imbalance: for whereas the EU is by far the largest trading partner for the United Kingdom with approximately 50 per cent (!) of all total trade; British trade will only represent between 15 and 20 per cent of all trade conducted by the Union. So, even if the United Kingdom will be one of the most important trading partners of the EU after its withdrawal, its relative bargaining power will be significantly smaller than that of the EU.

---

[169] V. Reding, 'Free Movement of People and the European Economic Area', in EFTA Court, *The EEA and the EFTA Court: Decentred Integration* (Hart, 2014), 193. However, this does not (!) mean that there are no control or better safeguard mechanisms to limit the inflow of workers from other EEA States. We should assume that Art. 112 EEA Agreement will give at least – if not more – possibilities to the UK than the mechanism envisaged in the 'New Settlement' treaty negotiated by David Cameron (see n. 42 above).

[170] White Paper, 'United Kingdom's Exit from and New Partnership with the European Union' (n. 70 above), 35.

[171] House of Lords, Brexit: Options for Trade (House of Lords, 2016), para. 248: 'We are not clear what the Government means by this term.' The report can be found at: https://publications.parliament.uk/pa/ld201617/ldselect/ldeucom/72/7202.htm.

Table 19.4 Absolute and Relative Trading Power

Economic Size (GDP, $bn.)	EU Trading Partners (% EU trade)
United States (18.569)	United States (17.5)
European Union (16.398)	China (14.8)
China (11.199)	Switzerland (7.2)
Japan (4939)	Russia (6)
Germany (3467)	Turkey (4)
United Kingdom (2619)	Norway (3.5)
France (2465)	Canada (1.8)

This economic imbalance is joined by a 'legal' imbalance. Legally, the Union is simply not an 'easy' negotiating partner when compared to the unitary United Kingdom. The Union is composed of various and diverse Member States that will need to find a compromise among themselves; and in the best-case scenario, this means a qualified majority in the Council under the Union's Common Commercial Policy.[172] However, as the Canada Agreement shows, the Union may be forced, by its Member States, to choose a mixed agreement and in such a situation, the 'bespoke' British agreement would have to safely pass 27+1 parliamentary veto points. This is likely to make the Union much less flexible in its negotiations; and this degree of 'inflexibility' will be further increased by the very fact that the Union has a written constitution, whereas the United Kingdom has not. The Union negotiator as well as the Union's own legislature will indeed by bound by the fundamental principles of the Union legal order – a legal limitation that has, at times, perplexed a country that has come to reify the supremacy of parliamentary politics over the supremacy of constitutional principles.

Conclusion

From the very start, Britain's feelings towards European integration were complex. An imperial and global power at the end of the Second World War, its economic and ideological commitments often differed fundamentally from those in 'Europe'; and it therefore should have come as no surprise that the kind

---

[172] Art. 207(4) TFEU states: 'For the negotiation and conclusion of the agreements referred to in paragraph 3, the Council shall act by a qualified majority. For the negotiation and conclusion of agreements in the fields of trade in services and the commercial aspects of intellectual property, as well as foreign direct investment, the Council shall act unanimously where such agreements include provisions for which unanimity is required for the adoption of internal rules.' For a discussion of the scope and nature of the EU's Common Commercial Policy, see (online) Chapter 18B, section 1.

invitation to join the Schuman Plan was rejected. Britain's decision to join the 'common market' in the 1970s was predominantly of an economic nature; and its profound doubts towards any 'federal' or 'political' union have been a recurring theme throughout its membership.

Britain's critical attitude towards transfers of legislative powers to the European Union has found numerous expressions in a wide range of 'opt-outs'. They have given the United Kingdom, in the words of the British government, a unique place within the Union: 'No other country has the same special status in the EU.'[173] And yet, even this half-way house 'inside' and 'outside' the European Union could not prevent a British referendum in which the majority of British citizens decided to opt out of Union membership altogether. Triggering the 'withdrawal' procedure of Article 50 TEU, the reasons quoted for leaving, were the wish of the British people to restore 'national self-determination' and to become again a fully sovereign State in the international sphere.[174]

This chapter has tried to explore some of the − innumerable − legal issues created by the Brexit process. Section 2 started by giving a quick overview of the drafting history of Article 50 so as to better understand its nature and content. The provision grants, as we saw above, an unconditional and unlimited right of withdrawal from the Union. The only condition mentioned is the − procedural − obligation to negotiate a withdrawal agreement so as to guarantee a smooth exit. At the time of writing, this British withdrawal agreement is being drafted with the negotiations having moved into the second phase. Many issues however remain intractable, and most importantly of all: the Irish border question. Much here depends on what the 'future-relations' agreement between the United Kingdom and the Union will look like; and it is hoped that the withdrawal agreement or a transitional period will offer a − temporary − solution until a final alternative partnership arrangement is concluded.

Sections 3 and 4 analysed two sides of the future after Brexit. Section 3 looked at the British preparations for repealing the European Communities Act 1972 as well as the future status of (retained) European Union law in the United Kingdom. Section 4 presented the three main partnership models currently 'traded' as candidates for a future EU–UK relationship (see Figure 19.6).

Affiliation with the European Economic Area would undoubtedly represent the 'softest' Brexit. This option would not necessarily imply that the United Kingdom joins EFTA;[175] yet it would mean that it principally accepts the free

---

[173]   HM Government, 'Alternatives to Membership: Possible Models for the United Kingdom Outside the European Union', at: www.gov.uk/government/publications/alternatives-to-membership-possible-models-for-the-united-kingdom-outside-the-european-union, para. 2.10.

[174]   The official Art. 50 letter can be found at: www.gov.uk/government/publications/prime-ministers-letter-to-donald-tusk-triggering-article-50.

[175]   Momentarily, the EEA Agreement is constructed as a bilateral relationship between the Union and EFTA and thus requires membership of either organisation. However, there is no legal reason why a (future) EEA Agreement could not be conceived as a trilateral or multilateral trade agreement, especially in light of the fact that the United Kingdom would, in all likelihood, economically and politically dominate EFTA.

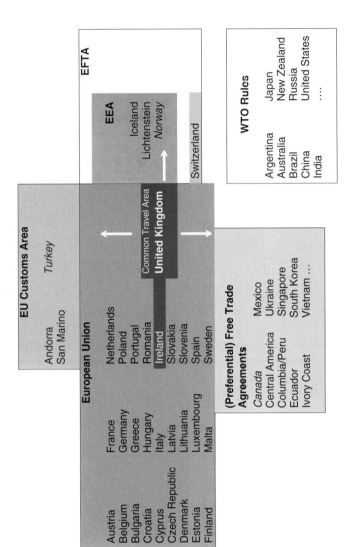

Figure 19.6 *Quo vadis* United Kingdom?

movement of persons while also committing itself to shadowing a significant proportion of EU legislation (and paying a partial membership fee). These consequences could to some extent be avoided if the United Kingdom joined a customs union arrangement. It would here retain control over immigration, yet it would not gain access to the EU internal market in services; and this arrangement would also significantly limit its capacity to conclude future international trade agreements with third States. What about a comprehensive free trade agreement? The latter option seems today the most likely route in light of the European and British negotiating positions; and a 'Canada plus' arrangement appears indeed very probable. However, it must not be forgotten that this option will also have its inherent 'trade-offs' and that other third States – including Canada – may become upset if too good a deal were to be struck.[176]

Be that as it may, no one knows what the future holds; and we must wait and see what the next years hold in stock for Great Britain as well as the European Union. From the European Union's side, the door to membership remains legally open – even once the United Kingdom has exited the Union.[177]

FURTHER READING

Books

J. Armour and H. Eidenmüller (eds.), *Negotiating Brexit* (Beck-Hart-Nomos, 2017)

K. Armstrong, *Brexit Time: Leaving the EU – Why, How and When?* (Cambridge University Press, 2017)

M. Dougan, *The UK After Brexit: Legal and Policy Challenges* (Intersentia, 2017)

EFTA Court, *The EEA and the EFTA Court: Decentred Integration* (Hart, 2014)

F. Fabbrini (ed.), *The Law & Politics of Brexit* (Oxford University Press, 2017)

A. Geddes, *Britain and the European Union* (Palgrave, 2013)

S. George, *An Awkward Partner: Britain in the European Community* (Oxford University Press, 1994)

D. Gowland and A. Turner, *Reluctant Europeans: Britain and European Integration 1945–1998* (Longman, 2000)

Articles (and Chapters)

P. Craig, 'Brexit: A Drama in Six Acts' (2016) 41 *EL Rev.* 447

L. Gormley, 'Brexit – Never Mind the Whys and Wherefores? Fog in the Channel, Continent Cut Off!' (2017) 40 *Fordham International Law Journal* 1175

C. Hillion, 'Accession and Withdrawal in the Law of the European Union', in D. Chalmers and A. Arnull (eds.) *The Oxford Handbook of European Union Law* (Oxford University Press, 2015), 126

A. Łazowski, 'Withdrawal from the European Union and Alternatives to Membership' (2012) 37 *European Law Review* 523

---

[176] European Council Guidelines (Second Phase), para. 7.

[177] Art. 50(5) TEU: 'If a State which has withdrawn from the Union asks to rejoin, its request shall be subject to the procedure referred to in Article 49.' For a brief discussion of the accession process under Art. 49 TEU, see (online) Chapter 18B, section 4(d).

N. Neuwahl, 'CETA as a Potential Model for (Post-Brexit) UK–EU Relations' (2017) 22 *EFA Rev.* 279

S. Peers, 'Living in Sin: Legal Integration Under the EC–Turkey Customs Union' (1996) 7 *EJIL* 411

A. Tatham, '"Don't Mention Divorce at the Wedding, Darling!" EU Accession and Withdrawal after Lisbon', in A. Biondi et al. (eds.), *EU Law After Lisbon* (Oxford University Press, 2012), 128

C. Tobler, 'One of Many Challenges after "Brexit": The Institutional Framework of an Alternative Agreement – Lessons from Switzerland and Elsewhere?' (2016) 23 *Maastricht Journal of European and Comparative Law* 575

A. Young, *R. (Miller)* v. *Secretary of State for Exiting the European Union*: Thriller or Vanilla?' (2017) 42 *EL Rev.* 280

20

Appendix
How to Study European Law

1

How to Find the EU Treaties

The EU Treaties constitute the primary law of the Union.[1] The formula the 'EU Treaties' or simply 'the Treaties' commonly refers to two Treaties: the Treaty on European Union (TEU) and the Treaty on the Functioning of the European Union (TFEU).

The 'Treaties' are the result of a long 'chain novel' of consecutive treaties (see Table 20.1). They started out from three 'Founding Treaties' that created the European Coal and Steel Community (1951), the European Atomic Energy Community (1957) and the European (Economic) Community (1957). A myriad of subsequent 'Amendment Treaties' and 'Accession Treaties' gradually changed the textual basis of the three Communities significantly; and this first treaty base would be complemented by a second treaty base in 1992, when the Maastricht Treaty created the (old) European Union.

To simplify the – very complex – textual foundations of the old European Union and European Communities Treaties, the Member States tried to create a single treaty in the early 2000s. The 2004 Constitutional Treaty was indeed intended to repeal all previous treaties;[2] and it was to merge the European Union with the European Communities. Yet the attempt to 'recreate' *one* Union, with *one* legal personality, on the basis of *one* treaty failed; and the Member States thereafter resorted to yet another 'Amendment Treaty': the 2007 Reform Treaty – also called the Lisbon Treaty.

Despite its modest name, the Lisbon Treaty constitutes a radical new 'chapter' in the Union's constitutional chain novel. For while it formally builds on the original 'Founding Treaties', it has nonetheless 'merged' the old 'Community' legal order with the old 'Union' legal order into a new 'Union' legal order.

---

[1] The European Treaties are the 'primary law' but not primary legislation of the Union. For the concept of legislation refers to a *unilateral* act, whereas the Treaties are *multilateral* treaties – albeit with constitutional effects once they are ratified by all Member States. Alas, how long will it take Nigel Foster to understand this (see his *EU Treaties and Legislation* (Oxford University Press, 2017), 1)? To speak of 'primary legislation' is to assume that the EU Treaties have been adopted by one author, and even if one sees such an author in the collectivity of the Member States acting as 'Masters of the Treaties', it is then impossible to refer to Union (primary) legislation as 'secondary legislation'. For this is not just inelegant but incorrect. One simply cannot consider the same Member States that have concluded the EU Treaties as the secondary authors of Union legislation. The author of Union legislation is the Union, acting today through its Parliament and its Council, and not the Member States.

[2] Art. IV-437 Constitutional Treaty. This would have simplified matters significantly, see J.-C. Piris, *The Lisbon Treaty: A Legal and Political Analysis* (Cambridge University Press, 2010), 20: 'Up until 2004, the original 1957 Treaties had been amended and complemented fifteen times. As a result, there were about 2,800 pages of primary law contained in seventeen Treaties or Acts[.]'

Table 20.1 European Treaties – Chronology

Signed	Name	Published	Entry
1951	Treaty establishing the European Coal and Steel Community	Founding Treaty★	1952
1952	European Defence Community	Founding Treaty	Failed
1957	Treaty establishing the European (Economic) Community	Founding Treaty★★	1958
1957	Treaty establishing the European Atomic Energy Community	Founding Treaty	1958
1962	Protocol on the Netherlands Antilles (1962)	[1964] OJ 150	1964
1965	Protocol on the Privileges and Immunities of the European Communities	[1967] OJ 152	1967
1965	Treaty establishing a Single Council and a Single Commission of the European Communities (Merger Treaty)	[1967] OJ 152	1967
1970	Treaty amending certain Budgetary Provisions	[1971] OJ L 2	1971
1972	Accession Treaty with Denmark, Ireland and the United Kingdom	[1972] OJ L 73	1973
1977	Treaty amending certain financial Provisions	[1977] OJ L 359	1977
1975	Treaty amending certain Provisions of the Protocol on the Statute of the European Investment Bank	[1978] OJ L 91	1978
1979	Accession Treaty with Greece	[1979] OJ L 291	1981
1984	Greenland Treaty	[1985] OJ L 29	1985
1985	Accession Treaty with Spain and Portugal	[1985] OJ L 302	1986
1986	Single European Act	[1987] OJ L 169	1987
1992	Treaty on European Union	[1992] OJ C 191★★★	1993
1994	Accession Treaty with Austria, Finland and Sweden	[1994] OJ C 241	1995
1997	Treaty of Amsterdam	[1997] OJ C 340	1999
2001	Treaty of Nice	[2001] OJ C 80	2003
2003	Accession Treaty with the Czech Republic, Estonia, Cyprus, Latvia, Lithuania, Hungary, Malta, Poland, Slovenia and Slovakia	[2003] OJ L 236	2004

Table 20.1 (cont.)

Signed	Name	Published	Entry
2004	Treaty establishing a Constitution for Europe	[2004] OJ C 310	Failed
2005	Accession Treaty with the Republic of Bulgaria and Romania	[2005] OJ L 157	2007
2007	Treaty of Lisbon amending the Treaty on European Union and the Treaty establishing the European Community	[2007] OJ C 306	2009
2007	Charter of Fundamental Rights of the European Union	[2007] OJ C 303	2009
2012	Accession Treaty with the Republic of Croatia	[2012] OJ L 112	2013

*The Treaty expired in 2002.
** For a consolidated version of the Treaty establishing the European Community, see [2002] OJ C 325.
*** For a consolidated version of the Treaty on European Union, see *ibid*.

Table 20.2 Consolidated Versions of the European Treaties

Consolidated Versions of the European Treaties	
Treaty on European Union and the Treaty on the Functioning of the European Union; as well as the Charter of Fundamental Rights of the European Union	[2016] OJ C 202
Treaty establishing the European Atomic Energy Community	[2016] OJ C 203

Nevertheless, unlike the 2004 Constitutional Treaty, the 2007 Lisbon Treaty has not created a single treaty base for the European Union. Instead, it recognises the existence of two (main) treaties: the Treaty on European Union and the Treaty on the Functioning of the European Union. The division into two EU Treaties thereby follows a functional criterion: the Treaty on European Union (TEU) contains the general provisions defining the Union, while the Treaty on the Functioning of the European Union (TFEU) contains the specific provisions with regard to the Union institutions and policies. One of the new features of the post-Lisbon era is the possibility of minor treaty amendments instigated by European Council Decisions. In addition

Table 20.3 European Council Decisions Amending the Treaties

European Council Decisions Amending the Treaties	
European Council Decision 2011/199 (amending Article 136 of the Treaty on the Functioning of the European Union with regard to a stability mechanism for Member States whose currency is the euro)	[2012] OJ L 91/1

Table 20.4 Structure of the TEU and TFEU

	EU Treaty		FEU Treaty
Title I	Common Provisions	Part I	Principles
Title II	Democratic Principles	Part II	Citizenship (Non-Discrimination)
Title III	Institutions	Part III	Union (Internal) Policies
Title IV	Enhanced Cooperation	Part IV	Overseas Associations
Title V	External Action, and CFSP	Part V	External Action
Title VI	Final Provisions	Part VI	Institutions & Finances
		Part VII	General & Final Provisions
Protocols (37) Charter of Fundamental Rights			

to 'Amendment Treaties' there are now also 'Amendment Decisions' adopted by the European Council (see Table 20.3).

The EU Treaties can today be found on the European Union's EUR-Lex website: http://eur-lex.europa.eu/collection/eu-law/treaties.html, but there are also a number of solid paper copies such as Blackstone's *EU Treaties & Legislation* or my own *EU Treaties and Legislation* collection.

What is the structure of today's EU Treaties? The structure of the TEU and TFEU is shown in Table 20.4. The (longer) TFEU is divided into 'Parts' – 'Titles' – 'Chapters' – 'Sections' – 'Articles', while the (shorter) TEU only starts with a division into 'Titles'. The EU Treaties are joined by numerous Protocols and the 'Charter of Fundamental Rights'. According to Article 51 TEU, Protocols to the Treaties 'shall form an integral part thereof'; and the best way to make sense of them is to see them as legally binding 'footnotes' to a particular article or section of the Treaties. By contrast, the Charter is 'external' to the Treaties; yet it also has 'the same legal value as the Treaties'.[3]

---

[3] Art. 6(1) (new) TEU.

How to Find (and Read) EU Secondary Law

The Union publishes all of its acts in the *Official Journal of the European Union*. Paper versions can be found in every library that houses a 'European Documentation Centre', but electronic versions are also openly available on the Union's EUR-Lex website: http://eur-lex.europa.eu/oj/direct-access .html. The Union distinguishes between two *Official Journal* series: the L-series and the C-series. The former contains all legally binding acts adopted by the Union (including its international agreements), while the latter publishes all other information and notices. Originally, only the paper version of the *Official Journal* was 'authentic';[4] but since 1 July 2013, electronic versions of the Official Journal (e-OJ) are equally authentic and therefore endowed with formal legal force.[5]

Union secondary law will first mention the instrument in which it is adopted. It will typically have the form of a 'Regulation', a 'Directive' or a 'Decision'. This will be followed by two figures. In the past, where the Union act was a regulation, the figure was: number/year; while for directives and decisions this was inversed: year/number. However, since 2015, this has changed and all main Union instruments are now arranged by year/ number.

Where the year and number are known for a given EU act, the easiest way to find it is to use the Union's EU-lex search engine: http://eur-lex.europa .eu/homepage.html. Importantly, there may be two or more acts for a given number combination, especially where a 'legislative' act has been followed by a non-legislative act. For two types of non-legislative acts – namely: 'delegated' and 'implementing' acts – the EU Treaties require that they contain the word 'delegated' or 'implementing' in their title.[6] This is to indicate – at first glance – that these executive acts have been adopted according to a particular decision-making procedure.

[4] Case C-161/06, *Skoma-Lux sro* v. *Celní ředitelství Olomouc*, (2007) ECR I-10841.
[5] See Regulation (EU) No. 216/2013 on the electronic publication of the Official Journal of the European Union, (2013) OJ L 69/1.
[6] See Arts. 290(3) and 291(4) TFEU respectively.

What is the structure of a piece of Union legislation? After its 'Title' there follows a brief summary of the decision-making procedure that led to the adoption of the act – including a reference to the legal competence on which it was based. Thereafter comes the 'Preamble', which sets out the reasons for which the Union act has been adopted. The content of the act is subsequently set out in various 'articles', which may be grouped into 'Sections' and 'Chapters'. For very technical Union legislation, there may also be an Annex – which, like a 'Schedule' in a UK statute, adds detailed provisions 'outside' the core content of the act. To illustrate this legislative structure, let us take a closer look at the Services Directive as it would be published in the *Official Journal*.

Figure 20.1 Services Directive: Analysis

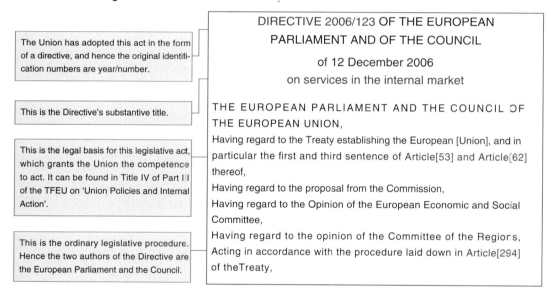

The Union has adopted this act in the form of a directive, and hence the original identification numbers are year/number.

This is the Directive's substantive title.

This is the legal basis for this legislative act, which grants the Union the competence to act. It can be found in Title IV of Part III of the TFEU on 'Union Policies and Internal Action'.

This is the ordinary legislative procedure. Hence the two authors of the Directive are the European Parliament and the Council.

DIRECTIVE 2006/123 OF THE EUROPEAN PARLIAMENT AND OF THE COUNCIL

of 12 December 2006

on services in the internal market

THE EUROPEAN PARLIAMENT AND THE COUNCIL OF THE EUROPEAN UNION,

Having regard to the Treaty establishing the European [Union], and in particular the first and third sentence of Article[53] and Article[62] thereof,

Having regard to the proposal from the Commission,

Having regard to the Opinion of the European Economic and Social Committee,

Having regard to the opinion of the Committee of the Regions,

Acting in accordance with the procedure laid down in Article[294] of the Treaty,

Whereas:

(1) The European [Union] is seeking to forge ever closer links between the States and peoples of Europe and to ensure economic and social progress. . . .

(2) A competitive market in services is essential in order to promote economic growth and create jobs in the European Union. . . .

(118) In accordance with paragraph 34 of the Interinstitutional Agreement on better law-making, Member States are encouraged to draw up, for themselves and in the interest of the [Union], their own tables, which will, as far as possible, illustrate the correlation between the Directive and the transposition measures, and to make them public,

The following numbered paragraphs are the 'preambles' to the Union act. They are meant to 'explain' the intention of the Union legislator.

HAVE ADOPTED THIS DIRECTIVE:

CHAPTER I

GENERAL PROVISIONS

Article 1
Subject matter

1. This Directive establishes general provisions facilitating the exercise of the freedom of establishment for service providers and the free movement of services, while maintaining a high quality of services.
2. This Directive does not deal with the liberalisation of services of general economic interest, reserved to public or private entities, nor with the privatisation of public entities providing services. . . .

Union legislation is typically structured into Chapters; and within Chapters, there may be 'Sections'. If it is a longer piece of secondary law, then there may even be 'Titles' above the Chapter headings. Very specific provisions of the a Union act may be placed within an 'Annex'. These Annexes are like 'Schedules' in UK Statutes.

The first article typically sets out what the Union act is supposed to achieve.

Article 4
Definitions

For the purposes of this Directive, the following definitions shall apply:

1) 'service' means any self-employed economic activity, normally provided for remuneration, as referred to in Article [57] of the Treaty . . .

One of the first articles of the Union act will typically contain a provision that provides 'legislative definitions' of the terms used.

CHAPTER IV

FREE MOVEMENT OF SERVICES

SECTION 1
Freedom to provide services and related derogations

Article 16
Freedom to provide services

1. Member States shall respect the right of providers to provide services in a Member State other than that in which they are established.

The Member State in which the service is provided shall ensure free access to and free exercise of a service activity within its territory.

Member States shall not make access to or exercise of a service activity in their territory subject to compliance with any requirements which do not respect the following principles:

This is the substantive heart of the Services Directive, which was discussed in Chapter 16 of this book.

(a) non-discrimination: the requirement may be neither directly nor indirectly discriminatory with regard to nationality or, in the case of legal persons, with regard to the Member State in which they are established;

(b) necessity: the requirement must be justified for reasons of public policy, public security, public health or the protection of the environment;

(c) proportionality: the requirement must be suitable for attaining the objective pursued, and must not go beyond what is necessary to attain that objective. . . .

CHAPTER VIII

FINAL PROVISIONS

Article 44

Transposition

1. Member States shall bring into force the laws, regulations and administrative provisions necessary to comply with this Directive before 28 December 2009.

They shall forthwith communicate to the Commission the text of those measures.

When Member States adopt these measures, they shall contain a reference to this Directive or shall be accompanied by such a reference on the occasion of their official publication. The methods of making such reference shall be laid down by Member States.

2. Member States shall communicate to the Commission the text of the main provisions of national law which they adopt in the field covered by this Directive. . . .

Done at Strasbourg, 12 December 2006.

For the European Parliament
The President
J. BORRELL FONTELLES
For the Council
The President
M. PEKKARINEN

Due to this being a directive, the Union act will need to be 'implemented' by the Member States (see Chapter 3). A directive will thus contain a deadline for its transposition – here about three years after its adoption.

According to Article 297 TFEU, legislative acts need to be signed by the President of the European Parliament and the President of the Council.

3

How to Find (and Read) EU Court Judgments

All EU cases are identified by a number/year figure. Cases before the Court of Justice are preceded by a C-, while cases decided before the General Court are preceded by a T- (for the French 'Tribunal').[7] The Civil Service Tribunal pre-fixed its cases with an F- (for the French 'Fonction publique'). Following this unique figure come the names of the parties to the case. A full case name would for example be: Case C-144/04, *Werner Mangold* v. *Rüdiger Helm*. However, since no one can remember all the numbers or all the parties, EU cases often get simply abbreviated by the main party; in our case *Mangold*.

In the past, judgments of all EU Courts were published in paper form in the purple-bound *European Court Reports* (ECR). Cases decided by the Court of Justice were published in the ECR-I series; cases decided by the General Court were published in the ECR-II series, while cases decided by the Civil Service Tribunal were published in the ECR-SC series. However, as of 2012, the entire Court of Justice of the European Union decided to go 'paperless' and it now publishes its judgments only electronically.[8] The two principal websites here are the Court's own curia website (http://curia.europa.eu/jcms/jcms/j_6), and the Union's general EUR-Lex website (http://eur-lex.europa.eu/homepage.html). For the purposes of this book, the easiest way is however to go to www.schutze.eu, which contains all the judgments mentioned in the main text – including the 'Lisbon' version of all classic EU Court judgments.

Once upon a time, judgments issued by the European Court were – to paraphrase Hobbes –'nasty, brutish and short'. Their shortness was partly due to a structural division the Court made between the 'Issues of Fact and of Law' (or later: 'Report for the Hearing'), which set out the facts, procedure and the arguments of the parties, on the one hand, and the 'Grounds of Judgment' on the other. Only the latter constituted the judgment *sensu stricto* and was often very short indeed. For the Court originally followed the 'French' ideal of trying to put the entire judgment into a single 'sentence'! A judgment like *Van Gend en Loos* contains about 2,000 words – not more than an undergraduate essay.

---

[7] Importantly: cases decided before the creation of the General Court will have no prefix at all. For there was only one court: the Court of Justice.

[8] In the absence of a 'page number' in a printed book, the Union henceforth has recourse to a 'European Case Law Identifier'. This is composed of EU: C[T/F]:Year: Number.

Figure 20.2 *Mangold* Judgment: Analysis

<table>
<tr><td>

This is a summary of the substantive issues involved.

</td><td>

JUDGMENT OF THE COURT (Grand Chamber)

22 November 2005

(Directive 1999/70/EC – Clauses 2, 5 and 8 of the Framework Agreement on fixed-term work – Directive 2000/78/EC – Article 6 – Equal treatment as regards employment and occupation – Age discrimination)

</td></tr>
<tr><td>

This is a C-case before the European Court of Justice. It is the 144th case registered in 2004.

</td><td>

In Case C-144/04,
REFERENCE for a preliminary ruling under Article [267 TFEU] from the Arbeitsgericht München (Germany), made by decision of 26 February 2004, registered at the Court on 17 March 2004, in the proceedings

</td></tr>
<tr><td>

This is a summary of the procedural issues involved.

</td></tr>
<tr><td></td><td>

Werner Mangold

v

</td></tr>
<tr><td>

These are the names of the parties to the (national) proceedings.

</td><td>

Rüdiger Helm,

THE COURT (GRAND CHAMBER)

</td></tr>
<tr><td>

This indicates the composition of the ECJ in this specific case – here: the Grand Chamber. This is a collegiate judgment: all the judges sign the judgment and thus speak with a single voice for 'the' Court.

</td><td>

Composed of P. Jann, President of the First Chamber, acting as President, C.W.A. Timmermans, A. Rosas and K. Schiemann, Presidents of Chambers, R. Schintgen (Rapporteur), S. von Bahr, J.N. Cunha Rodrigues, R. Silva de Lapuerta, K. Lenaerts, E. Juhász, G. Arestis, A. Borg Barthet and M. Ilešič, Judges,
Advocate General: A. Tizzano

</td></tr>
<tr><td>

This is a reference to the Advocate General in the case. In the modern printed version, the Opinion of the Advocate General preceded the judgment.

</td><td>

. . .

Judgment

1. This reference for a preliminary ruling concerns the interpretation of Clauses 2, 5 and 8 of the Framework Agreement on fixedterm contracts concluded on 18 March 1999 ('the Framework Agreement'), put into effect by Council Directive 1999/70/EC of 28 June 1999 concerning the framework agreement on fixedterm work concluded by ETUC, UNICE and CEEP (OJ 1999 L 175, p. 43), and of Article 6 of Council Directive 2000/78/EC of 27 November 2000 establishing a general framework for equal treatment in employment and occupation (OJ 2000 L 303, p. 16).
2. The reference has been made in the course of proceedings brought by Mr Mangold against Mr Helm concerning a fixed-term contract by which the former was employed by the latter ('the contract').

</td></tr>
<tr><td>

Having given a brief synopsis of the issues involved, the Court starts by presenting the legal context, that is: the relevant norms of European and national law.

</td><td>

Legal context
The relevant provisions of [Union] law
    The Framework Agreement

</td></tr>
</table>

3. According to Clause 1, '[t]he purpose of this Framework Agreement is to:

    (a) improve the quality of fixed-term work by ensuring the application of the principle of non-discrimination;

    (b) establish a framework to prevent abuse arising from the use of successive fixed-term employment contracts or relationships'. . . .

The relevant provisions of national law

14 Paragraph 1 of the Beschäftigungsförderungsgesetz (Law to promote employment), as amended by the law of 25 September 1996 (BGBl. 1996 I, p. 1476) ('the BeschFG 1996'), provided . . .

The main proceedings and the questions referred for a preliminary ruling

20 On 26 June 2003 Mr Mangold, then 56 years old, concluded with Mr Helm, who practises as a lawyer, a contract that took effect on 1 July 2003.

> This is one of the most important sections for the reader of a judgment. The Court here presents the facts and the procedure(s) of the specific case.

21 Article 5 of that contract provided that:

    '1. The employment relationship shall start on 1 July 2003 and last until 28 February 2004.

    2. The duration of the contract shall be based on the statutory provision which is intended to make it easier to conclude fixed-term contracts of employment with older workers (the provisions of the fourth sentence, in conjunction with those of the fourth sentence, of Paragraph 14(3) of the TzBfG . . .), since the employee is more than 52 years old . . .

31 Those were the circumstances in which the Arbeitsgericht München decided to stay proceedings and to refer the following questions to the Court of Justice for a preliminary ruling:

    '1(a) Is Clause 8(3) of the Framework Agreement . . . to be interpreted, when transposed into domestic law, as prohibiting a reduction of protection following from the lowering of the age limit from 60 to 58? . . . '

> The Court quotes the preliminary questions referred to by the national court.

Admissibility of the reference for a preliminary ruling

32 At the hearing the admissibility of the reference for a preliminary ruling was challenged by the Federal Republic of Germany, on the grounds that the dispute in the main proceedings was fictitious or contrived. Indeed, in the past Mr Helm has publicly argued a case identical to Mr Mangold's, to the effect that Paragraph 14(3) of the TzBfG is unlawful. . . .

> We saw in Chapter 10, section 4 that the Court will first check if the national court was entitled to use the preliminary reference procedure under Article 267 TFEU.

Concerning the questions referred for a preliminary ruling

On Question 1(b)

40 In Question 1(b), which it is appropriate to consider first, the national court asks whether, on a proper construction of Clause 5 of the Framework Agreement, it is contrary to that provision for rules of domestic law such as those at issue in the main

> In the main part of the judgment, the Court will answer each of the preliminary questions, one by one. Sometimes, it may change their order – as in this case; or it may decide that one question was not admissible, or that the answer to one question makes its response to another unnecessary. (In many direct actions, the Court has come to clearly separate the 'Arguments of the Parties' from the 'Findings of the Court' for each of the legal points raised.)

proceedings to contain none of the restrictions provided for by that clause in respect of the use of fixed-term contracts of employment. . . .

On those grounds, the Court (Grand Chamber) hereby rules:

> This is the core 'ratio decidendi' of the judgment.

1. On a proper construction of Clause 8(3) of the Framework Agreement on fixed-term contracts concluded on 18 March 1999, put into effect by Council Directive 1999/70/EC of 28 June 1999 concerning the framework agreement on fixed-term work concluded by ETUC, UNICE and CEEP, domestic legislation such as that at issue in the main proceedings, which for reasons connected with the need to encourage employment and irrespective of the implementation of that agreement, has lowered the age above which fixed-term contracts of employment may be concluded without restrictions, is not contrary to that provision. . . .

This world of short judgments is – sadly or not – gone. A typical judgment issued today will, on average, be four to five times as long as *Van Gend*. (And in the worst-case scenario, a judgment, especially in the area of EU competition law, may be as long as 100,000 words – a book of about 300 pages!) This new comprehensiveness is perhaps the product of a more refined textualist methodology, but it also results from a change in the organisation and style of judgments. Modern judgments have come to integrate much of the facts and the parties' arguments into the main body of a 'single' judgment, and this has especially made many direct actions much longer and much more repetitive!

The structure of a modern ECJ judgment given under the preliminary reference procedure may be studied by looking at Figure 20.2.

4

How to Find EU Academic Resources

The literature with regard to European Union law has exploded in the last 30 years. Today, there exists a forest of European law journals and generalist textbooks. Moreover, since the mid 1990s 'European' law has increasingly developed specialised branches that are sometimes even taught separately at university (as is the case at my own university). The three main branches here are: European *constitutional* law, European *internal market* law and European *competition* law. The first was explored in Parts I and II, while the second branch (and elements of the third branch) were covered in Part III. In addition to these three 'bigger' branches, the last two decades have also seen the emergence of many 'smaller' branches, such as European *external relations* law, European *labour* law and European *environmental* law. And there now also exist specialised LLM courses on EU consumer law and EU tax law.

The list of journals (Table 20.5) and textbooks (Table 20.6) is by no means comprehensive. It is meant to point the interested reader to a first gateway for an in-depth study of a particular part of European Union law. My selection focuses primarily on English-language academic sources. But it goes without saying that European Union law is a 'European' subject with journals and textbooks in every language of the Union.

Table 20.5 Main Academic Journals: General and Specific

Generalist Journals	Specialist Journals
Cahiers de droit européen	*EC Tax Law*
Cambridge Yearbook of European Legal Studies	*European Business Law Review*
Common Market Law Review	*European Competition Journal*
Diritto dell' Unione europea	*European Competition Law Review*
European Law Review	*European Constitutional Law Review*
European Law Journal	*European Foreign Affairs Review*
Europarecht	*European Public Law*
Fordham International Law Journal	*European Intellectual Property Review*
Journal of Common Market Studies	*European Review of Private Law*
Maastricht Journal of European and Comparative Law	*European State Aid Law Quarterly*
Yearbook of European Law	*Legal Issues of Economic Integration*

Table 20.6 European Union Law: Specialised Textbooks (in English)

Constitutional/Administrative	Internal Market/Competition	Other Special Areas
A. von Bogdandy and J. Bast (eds.), *Principles of European Constitutional Law* (Hart, 2011)	C. Barnard, *The Substantive Law of the EU* (Oxford University Press, 2016)	P. Eeckhout, *EU External Relations Law* (Oxford University Press, 2011)
S. Douglas-Scott, *Constitutional Law of the European Union* (Pearson, 2002)	G. Davies, *European Union Internal Market Law* (Routledge, 2001)	P. Koutrakos, *EU Law of International Relations* (Hart, 2015)
T. Hartley, *The Foundations of European Union Law* (Oxford University Press, 2014)	J. Pila and P. Torremans, *European Intellectual Property Law* (Oxford University Press, 2016)	B. Van Vooren and R. Wessel, *EU External Relations Law: Text, Cases and Materials* (Cambridge University Press, 2014)
R. Schütze, *European Constitutional Law* (Cambridge University Press, 2015)	J. McMahon, *EU Agricultural Law* (Oxford University Press, 2007)	C. Barnard, *EU Employment Law* (Oxford University Press, 2012)
R. Schütze, *Foreign Affairs and the EU Constitution: Selected Essays* (Cambridge University Press, 2016)	F. Weiss and C. Kaupa, *European Union Internal Market Law* (Cambridge University Press, 2014)	A. C. L. Davies, *EU Labour Law* (Edward Elgar, 2013)
J. Weiler, *The Constitution of Europe* (Cambridge University Press, 1999)	K. Bacon, *European Union Law of State Aid* (Oxford University Press, 2017)	K. Riesenhuber, *European Employment Law* (Intersentia, 2012)
P. Craig, *EU Administrative Law* (Oxford University Press, 2012)	J. Goyder and A. Albors-Llorens, *Goyder's EC Competition Law* (Oxford University Press, 2009)	J. Jans and H. Vedder, *European Environmental Law* (Europa Law Publishing, 2012)
D. Curtin, *Executive Power of the European Union* (Oxford University Press, 2009)	V. Korah, *An Introductory Guide to EC Competition Law* (Hart, 2007)	L. Krämer, *EU Environmental Law* (Sweet & Maxwell, 2016)
H. Hofmann, C. Rowe and A. Türk, *Administrative Law and Policy of the European Union* (Oxford University Press, 2011)	A. Jones and B. Sufrin, *EU Competition Law: Text, Cases, and Materials* (Oxford University Press, 2016)	S. Weatherill, *EU Consumer Law and Policy* (Edward Elgar, 2014)
K. Lenaerts, *EU Procedural Law* (Oxford University Press, 2015)	R. Wish and D. Bailey, *Competition Law* (Oxford University Press, 2015)	B. Terra and P. Wattel, *European Tax Law* (Kluwer, 2012)

5

How to Use the Companion Webpage

The companion webpage for this textbook can be found at: www.schutze.eu. Its principal aim is to allow readers to have all the EU cases, EU legislation as well as some of the recommended readings at their fingertips.

To that effect, each online chapter contains full-text versions of all the cases dealt with specifically in that chapter; and, where these cases were decided prior to the Lisbon Treaty, they have been 'Lisbonised' and renumbered (Figure 20.3). In this way, students will be able to read *Costa* v. *ENEL* or *Cassis de Dijon* as if they were decided under the TEU/TFEU today (Figure 20.4).

With regard to EU legislation, all Union acts and international agreements mentioned in the main text are linked to the *Official Journal of the European Union*, while the 'Further Readings' tab (Figure 20.5) will direct the reader to the publishers' website of a specific book or article; and, if you are on campus and your university has online access to the publisher, you should be able to read and/or download the specific article or chapter directly.

The webpage also contains a range of extra learning materials for each chapter (Figure 20.6); and there are also some general revision materials – including some revision slides and case summaries (Figure 20.7). Finally, for those who cannot get enough of European Union law, there are two additional online chapters: Chapter 17B complements the EU competition law chapter, while Chapter 18B offers an overview of the external policies of the European Union.

Figure 20.3 List of Lisbonised Cases

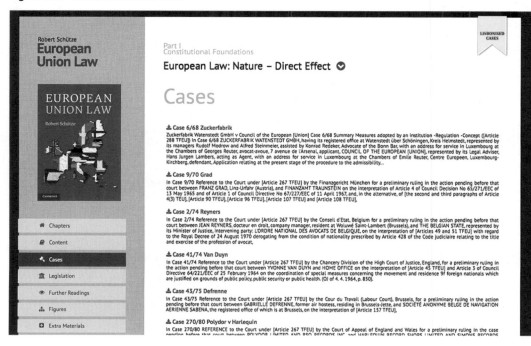

Figure 20.4 *Van Duyn*: Lisbonised

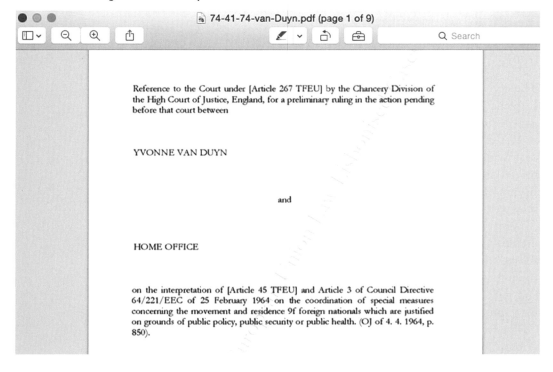

Figure 20.5 Chapters: Further Readings

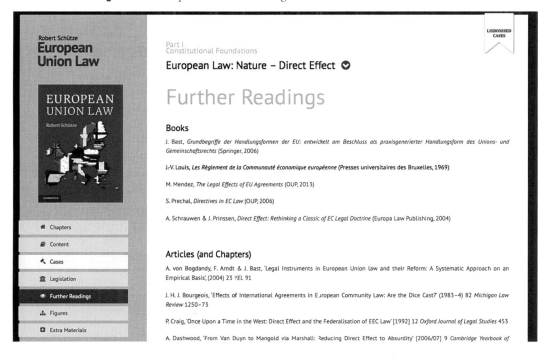

Figure 20.6 Chapters: Extra Materials

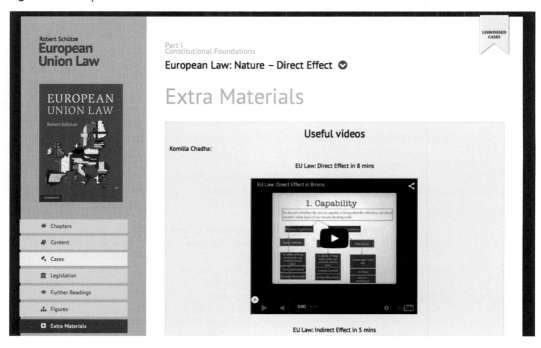

Figure 20.7 Revision Slides: Example

ORDINARY LEGISLATIVE PROCEDURE

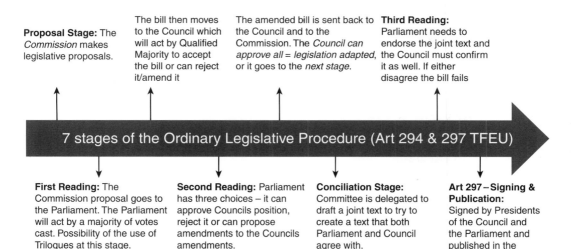

Index